Chinese Maritime Cases Series

Series Editors
Martin Davies, Tulane University Law School, New Orleans, LA, USA
Jiang Lin, Law School, Shanghai Maritime University, Shanghai, China

The primary aim of this series is to, for the first time, provide the academics, practitioners and businessmen worldwide with a crucial source to perceive how the specially designed Chinese maritime courts apply, interpretate and develop the shipping law in practice to strike a balance of interest among the domestic and international market players. Each year, China trades with other states in trillions of USD, and more than 90% of the cargoes are carried by ocean-going ships. In view of the enormous trade volume and maritime activities, foreign trading houses, shipping companies and marine underwriters, as well as their legal advisors, are keen to track down the developments of Chinese maritime law and court practice so as to predicate and avoid the potential problems or resolve the emerging disputes properly. Cases and judgments are regarded as a crucial source of learning. However, so far, no serial Chinese casebooks, which contain full English translation of selected judgments, have been published. The authors try to make an audacious break-through in this field. This series has a secondary aim: to establish a core part of the database, which can be further developed to be an innovative tool for the foreign students, professors and lawyers to have a systematic study of Chinese maritime law.

More information about this series at https://link.springer.com/bookseries/16710

Martin Davies · Jiang Lin
Editors

Chinese Maritime Cases

Selection for Year of 2015

Volume 1

Springer

Editors
Martin Davies
Law School
Tulane University
New Orleans, LA, USA

Jiang Lin
Law School
Shanghai Maritime University
Shanghai, China

ISSN 2730-9851 ISSN 2730-986X (electronic)
Chinese Maritime Cases Series
ISBN 978-3-662-63715-9 ISBN 978-3-662-63716-6 (eBook)
https://doi.org/10.1007/978-3-662-63716-6

© The Editor(s) (if applicable) and The Author(s), under exclusive license to Springer-Verlag GmbH, DE, part of Springer Nature 2021
This work is subject to copyright. All rights are solely and exclusively licensed by the Publisher, whether the whole or part of the material is concerned, specifically the rights of translation, reprinting, reuse of illustrations, recitation, broadcasting, reproduction on microfilms or in any other physical way, and transmission or information storage and retrieval, electronic adaptation, computer software, or by similar or dissimilar methodology now known or hereafter developed.
The use of general descriptive names, registered names, trademarks, service marks, etc. in this publication does not imply, even in the absence of a specific statement, that such names are exempt from the relevant protective laws and regulations and therefore free for general use.
The publisher, the authors and the editors are safe to assume that the advice and information in this book are believed to be true and accurate at the date of publication. Neither the publisher nor the authors or the editors give a warranty, expressed or implied, with respect to the material contained herein or for any errors or omissions that may have been made. The publisher remains neutral with regard to jurisdictional claims in published maps and institutional affiliations.

This Springer imprint is published by the registered company Springer-Verlag GmbH, DE part of Springer Nature.
The registered company address is: Heidelberger Platz 3, 14197 Berlin, Germany

Preface

To provide the legal professions worldwide with a good reference of Chinese maritime adjudication, this book, being the second in the series, delicately selects dozens of influential maritime cases heard by Chinese Maritime Courts and their appeal courts – Provincial High People's Courts and the Supreme People's Court of China. The selection covers a wide scope of disputes including carriage of goods by sea contract, charterparty, shipbuilding, ship sale and purchase, marine insurance, mortgage and collision.

Reading the judgments in this book, which are literally translated from the original Chinese version, readers will gain a better comprehension of the Chinese maritime law and a real sense how Chinese maritime judges apply the law to decide the issues in practice. This book offers excellent case study materials and will benefit the personnel engaged in the shipping, legal, judicial, arbitral and educational sectors. It is expected to promote mutual understanding and exchange of views, on which basis the international maritime justice will be further credited and enhanced.

It is worth noting that with the prosperous developments of international trade and shipping in the past decades, China has experienced steady growth of cross-board disputes arising from maritime transactions and admiral affairs. Those emerging disputes and the underlying causes seem to be distinctive in comparison with their counterparts in foreign countries. That is largely due to the fact that the scale of the shipping and circumferential markets in China is impressive and their operation is unique, which are clearly demonstrated in this book.

The selected cases involve multiple parties, and between them, there exist complicated business and legal relationships. Thus, while trialing the cases, Chinese judges interpret and apply the law in a creative way to resolve the novel questions, the answers to which cannot be found in international conventions or customs or foreign statutes or caselaw. In one sense, Chinese maritime courts are in an unrivaled situation to analyze and assess, in depth and breadth, the evolving disputes in the trade and shipping world and promote Chinese maritime judgments, as well as domestic legislative instruments, to be precedents for reference purpose worldwide.

This book does not only show the fruitful outcomes of Chinese maritime adjudication, but also casts a light on the trend of evolution of Chinese maritime legislation. For every maritime nation, the previous judgments make valuable contributions to present interpretation and application of the law and future legislation.

April, 2021

Dong Nian Yin
Professor in Law
Shanghai Maritime University
Shanghai, China

Acknowledgments

The editors would like to acknowledge the following for their assistance with the Chinese end of this project: from Shanghai Maritime University Law School, Prof. Dong Nian Yin, Prof. Shi Cheng Yu and Prof. Cun Qiang Cai; from Shanghai Maritime Court, Judge Tong Wang, Judge Zhen Kun Jia and Judge Hai Long Lin; Assistants to Editors in particular Hui Zeng, Yu Ming Wang, Yun Fei Han, Rui Ying Chen, Yu Tong Wang and Mu Fan Jia Yang.

The editors would also like to acknowledge the following present and former students of Tulane University Law School, who have served as Assistant Editors for the American part of this project: Richard Beaumont (2014–2015); Scott Ferrier (2015–2016); Guyer Bogen (2017–2018); Lindsey Magee Gordley and Katherine Kaplan (2018–2019); Erica Endlein (2019–2020); Robert Bradley and Mary Katherine Koch (2020–2021).

The editors also acknowledge the efforts of Jocelyn Mahan and Andrea Felice of IQNection for their work in building the companion Web site for this project, www.chinesemaritimecases.com.

About the Editors

Professor Martin Davies is Admiralty Law Institute Professor of Maritime Law at Tulane University Law School in New Orleans and Director of the Tulane Maritime Law Center.

He holds the degrees of M.A. and B.C.L. from Oxford University, England, and an LL.M. from Harvard Law School. Before joining Tulane, he was Harrison Moore Professor of Law at The University of Melbourne in Australia and before that he taught at Monash University, The University of Western Australia and Nottingham University. He has also been a visiting professor at universities in China, Italy, Azerbaijan and Singapore. In 2019, he was elected to be Titulary Member of the Comité Maritime International (CMI).

He is the author (or co-author) of books on maritime law, international trade law, conflict of laws and the law of torts. He has also published many journal articles on these topics. He has extensive practical experience as a consultant for over 30 years on maritime matters and general international litigation and arbitration, in Australia, Hong Kong, Singapore and the USA.

Associate Professor Jiang Lin (John Lin) is Associate Professor of Maritime Law at Shanghai Maritime University and Deputy Director of Shipping Policy and Law Research Center of Shanghai International Shipping Institute. He is also Adjunct Professor at Tulane University Law School.

After graduation with a B.Sc. degree from Shanghai Maritime University in 1996 and an LL.M. degree from Southampton University in 1999, he commenced his legal career at Sinclair Roche & Temperley (SRT) and later jointed Ince & Co. He was dually qualified as English solicitor and Chinese lawyer. In 2008, he came back to his mother college to be a lecturer and researcher. Meanwhile, he keeps practicing English and Chinese laws at Sinopar Law Firm. He is also an arbitrator with China Maritime Arbitration Association, Shanghai Arbitration Commission and Shanghai International Arbitration Center and a supporting member of London Maritime Arbitrators' Association.

He is the author and chief editor of two serial books: *Shanghai Shipping Policy and Law Development White Book* and *Shipping Finance Law Review*. He also writes books and articles on cruise commerce, off-shore trade and insurance.

John Lin is a member of Jiusan Society, one of the eight democratic parties in China.

Table of Contents

Table of Cases by Name of Plaintiff in Judgment of First Instance...... xiii
Table of Cases by Jurisdiction (Which Chinese Court Makes the Effective Judgment).. xxiii
Table of Cases by Cause of Action for Maritime Cases in the People's Republic of China... xxxiii
List of Maritime Courts and Their Appeal and Petition Courts in the People's Republic of China............................. xliii
List of Causes of Action for Maritime Cases in the People's Republic of China (Extracted from the Regulations on Causes of Action for Civil Disputes made by The Supreme People's Court of the People's Republic of China 2020) xlv
Table of References li

Table of Cases by Name of Plaintiff in Judgment of First Instance

AIG Europe Ltd. v. Shanghai Heming Shipping Service Co., Ltd.
Tianjin Branch et al. (2014) Hu Hai Fa Shang Chu Zi No. 116,
judgment of first instance of Shanghai Maritime Court 1

Allianz China General Insurance Co., Ltd. v. Youda (Shanghai)
International Freight Co., Ltd. et al. (2014) Hu Hai Fa Shang Chu Zi
No. 361, *judgment of first instance of Shanghai Maritime Court* 11

A.P. Moller-Maersk A/S v. Shanghai Chanlian Xieyun Logistics Co.,
Ltd. et al. (2012) Guang Hai Fa Chu Zi No. 329, *judgment of first
instance of Guangzhou Maritime Court* 45

A.P. Moller-Maersk A/S v. Shanghai Chanlian Xieyun Logistics Co.,
Ltd. et al. (2013) Yue Gao Fa Min Si Zhong Zi No. 162, *judgment
of second instance of Guangdong High People's Court* 58

A.P. Moller-Maersk A/S v. Shanghai Chanlian Xieyun Logistics Co.,
Ltd. et al. (2015) Min Ti Zi No. 119, *judgment of retrial
of The Supreme People's Court* 76

China Transport Groupage International (Shenzhen)
Limited v. Shenzhen Zhongyi Freight Forwarding Co., Ltd. (2014)
Guang Hai Fa Chu Zi No. 102, *judgment of first instance
of Guangzhou Maritime Court* 83

China Transport Groupage International (Shenzhen)
Limited v. Shenzhen Zhongyi Freight Forwarding Co., Ltd. (2015)
Yue Gao Fa Min Si Zhong Zi No. 138, *judgment of second instance
of Guangdong High People's Court* 93

China Transport Groupage International (Shenzhen)
Limited v. Shenzhen Zhongyi Freight Forwarding Co., Ltd. (2017)
Zui Gao Fa Min Shen Zi No. 104, *judgment of retrial of The Supreme
People's Court* 107

Changhang Phoenix Co., Ltd. v. Wuhan Tairun Marine Service Co., Ltd. et al. (2014) Wu Hai Fa Shang Zi No. 01755, *judgment of first instance of Wuhan Maritime Court* 121

China Geology and Mining Corporation v. Tianjin Kangjie Import and Export Trade Co., Ltd. et al. (2014) Jin Hai Fa Shang Chu Zi No. 153, *judgment of first instance of Tianjin Maritime Court* 131

China Geology and Mining Corporation v. Tianjin Kangjie Import and Export Trade Co., Ltd. et al. (2015) Jin Gao Min Si Zhong Zi No. 77, *judgment of second instance of Tianjin High People's Court* ... 152

China Guangfa Bank Stock Co., Ltd. Nanjing Chengxi Branch v. Nanjing Hengshunda Shipping Co., Ltd. et al. (2015) Wu Hai Fa Shang Zi No. 00205, *judgment of first instance of Wuhan Maritime Court* 171

China Minsheng Bank Co., Ltd. (Xiamen Branch) v. Fujian Guanhai Shipping Co., Ltd. et al. (2015) Xia Hai Fa Shang Chu Zi No. 216, *judgment of first instance of Xiamen Maritime Court* 179

China Ping An Property Insurance Co., Ltd. Guangdong Branch v. Guangzhou Hang Jie Logistics Co., Ltd. (2013) Guang Hai Fa Chu Zi No. 1014, *judgment of first instance of Guangzhou Maritime Court* 199

China Ping An Property Insurance Co., Ltd. Guangdong Branch v. Guangzhou Hang Jie Logistics Co., Ltd. (2014) Yue Gao Fa Min Si Zhong Zi No. 204, *judgment of second instance of Guangdong High People's Court* 207

China Shipping Logistics Co., Ltd. v. Jiangsu Zhongtai Bridge Steel Structure Co., Ltd. (2014) Hu Hai Fa Shang Chu Zi No. 1068, *judgment of first instance of Shanghai Maritime Court* 215

China Shipping Logistics Co., Ltd. v. Jiangsu Zhongtai Bridge Steel Structure Co., Ltd. (2015) Hu Gao Min Si (Hai) Zhong Zi No. 25, *judgment of second instance of Shanghai High People's Court* 240

Chongqing Red Dragonfly Oil Limited Liability Company v. PICC Property and Casualty Company Limited Chongqing Branch (2015) Wu Hai Fa Shang Zi No. 00151, *judgment of first instance of Wuhan Maritime Court* 267

Connexions (Asia) Limited v. J&S Worldwide Logistics Co., Ltd. et al. (2012) Guang Hai Fa Shang Chu Zi No. 704, *judgment of first instance of Guangzhou Maritime Court* 283

Connexions (Asia) Limited v. J&S Worldwide Logistics Co., Ltd. et al. (2015) Yue Gao Fa Min Si Zhong Zi No. 10, *judgment of second instance of Guangdong High People's Court* 293

Connexions (Asia) Limited v. Shenzhen J&S Worldwide Logistics
Ltd. et al. (2015) Min Shen Zi No. 3206, *ruling of retrial of The
Supreme People's Court* 309

COSCO Container Lines Co., Ltd. v. Shenzhen Finigate Integrated
Logistics Co., Ltd. Qingdao Branch et al. (2014) Qing Hai Fa Hai
Shang Chu Zi No. 751, *judgment of first instance of Qingdao Maritime
Court* 313

COSCO Container Lines Co., Ltd. v. Shenzhen Finigate Integrated
Logistics Co., Ltd. Qingdao Branch et al. (2015) Lu Min Si Zhong Zi
No. 152, *judgment of second instance of Shandong High
People's Court*.. 324

COSCO Container Lines Co., Ltd. v. Shenzhen Finigate Integrated
Logistics Co., Ltd. Qingdao Branch et al. (2016) Zui Gao Fa Min
Shen No. 2157, *ruling of retrial of The Supreme People's Court* 334

Daewoo Shipbuilding & Maritime Engineering Co., Ltd. v. Glory
Advance Corporation (2014) Xia Hai Fa Que Zi No. 1, *judgment
of first instance of Xiamen Maritime Court*............................ 339

Export-Import Bank of China et al. v. Nanjing Wujiazui Ship
Building Co., Ltd. et al. (2014) Wu Hai Fa Shang Chu Zi No. 00470,
judgment of first instance of Wuhan Maritime Court 349

Fan Sen (V.S) Shanghai International Freight Forwarding Co., Ltd.
v. Zhongman Petroleum & Natural Gas Group Co., Ltd. (2014) Hu
Hai Fa Shang Chu Zi No. 1112, *judgment of first instance of Shanghai
Maritime Court* 363

Fujian Guanhai Shipping Co., Ltd. v. Shanghai Huaya Ship Fuel
Company (2015) Hu Hai Fa Shang Chu Zi No. 47, *judgment of first
instance of Shanghai Maritime Court* 381

GUO Jiangbao v. Xiamen Chengyi Shipping Co., Ltd. (2014) Xia Hai
Fa Shang Chu Zi No. 452, *judgment of first instance of Xiamen
Maritime Court* 393

Hainan Weilong Shipping Engineering Co., Ltd. v. Hainan Yuehai
Shipping Logistics Co., Ltd. (2014) Qiong Hai Fa Shang Chu Zi No.
87, *judgment of first instance of Haikou Maritime Court* 407

Hainan Weilong Shipping Engineering Co., Ltd. v. Hainan Yuehai
Shipping Logistics Co., Ltd. (2015) Qiong Min San Zhong Zi No. 2,
judgment of second instance of Hainan High People's Court 418

Hong Kong Everglory Shipping Co., Ltd. et al. v. TAN Dingzhao
et al. (2014) Guang Hai Fa Shang Chu Zi No. 340, *judgment of first
instance of Guangzhou Maritime Court* 433

Hongxin (HK) Container Development Limited v. Shanghai Hongsheng Gangtai Shipping Co., Ltd. et al. (2015) Xia Hai Fa Shang Chu Zi No. 378, *judgment of first instance of Xiamen Maritime Court* 453

Huayu Electrical Appliance Group Co., Ltd. v. JC Logistics Service Co., Ltd. Ningbo Branch (2013) Yong Hai Fa Shang Chu Zi No. 579, *judgment of first instance of Ningbo Maritime Court* 469

Huayu Electrical Appliance Group Co., Ltd. v. JC Logistics Service Co., Ltd. Ningbo Branch (2014) Zhe Hai Zhong Zi No. 72, *judgment of second instance of Zhejiang High People's Court* 476

Huayu Electrical Appliance Group Co., Ltd. v. JC Logistics Service Co., Ltd. Ningbo Branch (2015) Min Ti Zi No. 19, *judgment of retrial of The Supreme People's Court* 485

Hunan Zoomlion International Trade Co., Ltd. et al. v. Shanghai GCL International Co., Ltd. et al. (2012) Hu Hai Fa Shang Chu Zi No. 1208, *judgment of first instance of Shanghai Maritime Court* 491

Hunan Zoomlion International Trade Co., Ltd. et al. v. Shanghai GCL International Co., Ltd. et al. (2014) Hu Gao Min Si (Hai) Zhong Zi No. 119, *judgment of second instance of Shanghai High People's Court* 552

Hunan Zoomlion International Trade Co., Ltd. et al. v. Shanghai GCL International Co., Ltd. et al. (2016) Zui Gao Fa Min Shen No. 1602, *ruling of retrial of The Supreme People's Court* 600

JIANG Haiping v. Shanghai New Qiao Insurance Brokers Ltd. (2014) Hu Hai Fa Shang Chu Zi No. 1410, *judgment of first instance of Shanghai Maritime Court* 607

JIANG Haiping v. Shanghai New Qiao Insurance Brokers Ltd. (2015) Hu Gao Min Si (Hai) Zhong Zi No. 57, *judgment of second instance of Shanghai High People's Court* 615

Jiangsu Eastern Heavy Industry Co., Ltd. v. Nanjing Twin Rivers Shipping Co., Ltd. (2012) Jin Hai Fa Shang Chu Zi No. 784, *judgment of first instance of Tianjin Maritime Court* 625

Jianxin Finance Leasing Co., Ltd. v. Wenzhou Changjiang Energy Shipping Co., Ltd. (2015) Jin Hai Fa Shang Chu Zi No. 663, *judgment of first instance of Tianjin Maritime Court* 647

LI Chunjiang et al. v. Tanggu Water Conservancy Project Company et al. (2013) Jin Hai Fa Shang Chu Zi No. 521, *judgment of first instance of Tianjin Maritime Court* 661

LI Xuelan et al. v. Ningbo Jialili Shipping Co., Ltd. (2015) Guang Hai Fa Chu Zi No. 397, *judgment of first instance of Guangzhou Maritime Court* 675

LIN Guihe v. PICC Property and Casualty Company Limited Shunde Branch (2008) Guang Hai Fa Chu Zi No. 259, *judgment of first instance of Guangzhou Maritime Court* 689

LIN Guihe v. PICC Property and Casualty Company Limited Shunde Branch (2014) Yue Gao Min Si Zhong Zi No. 112, *judgment of second instance of Guangdong High People's Court* 701

LIN Guihe v. PICC Property and Casualty Company Limited Shunde Branch (2016) Zui Gao Fa Min Shen No. 1452, *ruling of retrial of The Supreme People's Court* 727

LIU Fengxi v. Ningbo Junsheng Yuanda Shipping Co., Ltd. et al. (2015) Wu Hai Fa Shang Zi No. 00599, *judgment of first instance of Wuhan Maritime Court* 731

MAO Chuanwu v. Fengdu County Fengping Shipping Investment Co., Ltd. (2015) Wu Hai Fa Shang Zi No. 00134, *judgment of first instance of Wuhan Maritime Court* 737

Mitsui O.S.K. Lines, Ltd. v. Guangdong Shunde Local Product Import and Export Co., Ltd. et al. (2014) Guang Hai Fa Chu Zi No. 339, *judgment of first instance of Guangzhou Maritime Court* 747

Mund & Fester GmbH & Co. KG v. Pangang Group World Trade Panzhihua Co., Ltd. et al. (2011) Wu Hai Fa Shang Zi No. 00300, *judgment of first instance of Wuhan Maritime Court* 761

Nanjing Jinan Welding Technology Co., Ltd. v. Nanjing Lansheng Shipbuilding Co., Ltd. (2014) Wu Hai Fa Shang Zi No. 00369, *judgment of first instance of Wuhan Maritime Court* 781

Nanjing Jinan Welding Technology Co., Ltd. v. Nanjing Lansheng Shipbuilding Co., Ltd. (2015) E Min Si Zhong Zi No. 00064, *judgment of second instance of Hubei High People's Court* 788

Operating Department of China Continent Property & Casualty Insurance Co., Ltd. v. China Shipping Logistics Co., Ltd. (2014) Hu Hai Fa Shang Chu Zi No. 1509, *judgment of first instance of Shanghai Maritime Court* 799

People's Insurance Company of China Hangzhou Branch v. Tribute Ship Holding S.A. (2014) Da Hai Shang Chu Zi No. 21, *judgment of first instance of Dalian Maritime Court* 811

Qingdao Huashun Shipping Co., Ltd. v. Marc Loud Schiffahrts
Gesellschaft mbH & Co. KG. et al. (2014) Qing Hai Fa Que Zi
No. 7-1, *judgment of first instance of Qingdao Maritime Court* 823

Qinhuangdao Heshun Shipping Co., Ltd. v. China People's Property
Insurance Co., Ltd. Qinhuangdao City Branch (2015) Jin Hai Fa
Shang Chu Zi No. 287, *judgment of first instance of Tianjin
Maritime Court* 831

Qinhuangdao Heshun Shipping Co., Ltd. v. China People's Property
Insurance Co., Ltd. Qinhuangdao City Branch (2015) Jin Gao Min Si
Zhong Zi No. 93, *judgment of second instance of Tianjin High
People's Court*.. 842

Qinhuangdao Heshun Shipping Co., Ltd. v. China People's Property
Insurance Co., Ltd. Qinhuangdao City Branch (2016) Zui Gao
Fa Min Shen No. 1395, *ruling of retrial of The Supreme
People's Court*.. 854

Shandong Xianglong Industrial Group Co., Ltd. v. NCS Co., Ltd.
et al. (2011) Jin Hai Fa Shang Chu Zi No. 465, *judgment of first
instance of Tianjin Maritime Court* 859

Shanghai Eastern Shipping Material Co., Ltd. v. Beihai Honghai
Shipping Co., Ltd. et al. (2009) Guang Hai Fa Chu Zi No. 97,
judgment of first instance of Guangzhou Maritime Court 877

Shanghai Eastern Shipping Material Co., Ltd. v. Beihai Honghai
Shipping Co., Ltd. et al. (2012) Yue Gao Fa Min Si Zhong Zi No. 148,
judgment of second instance of Guangdong High People's Court 891

Shanghai Wan Feng International Freight Forwarding Co., Ltd.
v. Fujian Hongxing Electronic Technology Co., Ltd. (2014) Hu Hai
Fa Shang Chu Zi No. 1496, *judgment of first instance of Shanghai
Maritime Court* 925

Shanghai Yizhou Waterway Engineering Co., Ltd. v. QIU Guohua
(2013) Hu Hai Fa Hai Chu Zi No. 60, *judgment of first instance
of Shanghai Maritime Court* 943

Shanghai Yizhou Waterway Engineering Co., Ltd. v. QIU Guohua
(2015) Hu Gao Min Si (Hai) Zhong Zi No. 32, *judgment of second
instance of Shanghai High People's Court*....................... 967

Shanghai Jielong Industrial Group Co., Ltd. Yutian Packaging and
Printing Branch v. Norasia Container Lines Limited et al. (2012) Hu
Hai Fa Shang Chu Zi No. 1011, *judgment of first instance of Shanghai
Maritime Court* 987

Shanghai Jielong Industrial Group Co., Ltd. Yutian Packaging and
Printing Branch v. Norasia Container Lines Limited et al. (2013) Hu
Gao Min Si (Hai) Zhong Zi No. 132, *judgment of second instance
of Shanghai High People's Court* 999

Shanghai Jielong Industrial Group Co., Ltd. Yutian Packaging and
Printing Branch v. Norasia Container Lines Limited et al. (2015) Min
Shen Zi No. 573, *ruling of retrial of The Supreme People's Court* 1010

SHAN Yongzhen et al. v. LIANG Mingren (2014) Da Hai Shi Chu Zi
No. 121, *judgment of first instance of Dalian Maritime Court* 1015

SHAN Yongzhen et al. v. LIANG Mingren (2015) Liao Min San
Zhong Zi No. 201, *judgment of second instance of Liaoning High
People's Court* 1022

Shenzhen COSCO Logistics Co., Ltd. v. Guangdong Yanlin Energy
Limited by Share Ltd. (2012) Guang Hai Fa Chu Zi No. 910,
judgment of first instance of Guangzhou Maritime Court 1031

Shenzhen COSCO Logistics Co., Ltd. v. Guangdong Yanlin Energy
Limited by Share Ltd. (2014) Yue Gao Fa Min Si Zhong Zi No. 197,
judgment of second instance of Guangdong High People's Court 1042

Silvery Dragon Prestressed Materials Co., Ltd. (Tianjin) v. Dalian
Pei Hua International Logistics Co., Ltd. (2014) Jin Hai Fa
Shang Chu Zi No. 698, *judgment of first instance of Tianjin
Maritime Court* 1053

Station Ocean Administration Beihai Branch v. Wang Jianlong et al.
(2013) Qing Hai Fa Hai Shang Chu Zi No. 986, *judgment of first
instance of Qingdao Maritime Court* 1067

Suqian Rongxiang Shipping Co., Ltd. v. China United Property
Insurance Co., Ltd. Jiangsu Branch (2014) Wu Hai Fa Shang Zi
No. 01351, *judgment of first instance of Wuhan Maritime Court* 1079

Tai-I Jiangtong (Guangzhou) Co., Ltd. v. American President Lines,
Ltd. (2013) Guang Hai Fa Chu Zi No. 552, *judgment of first instance
of Guangzhou Maritime Court* 1089

Tai-I Jiangtong (Guangzhou) Co., Ltd. v. American President Lines,
Ltd. (2015) Yue Gao Fa Min Si Zhong Zi No. 24, *judgment
of second instance of Guangdong High People's Court* 1107

Tianjin Tianguan Ocean International Freight Forwarding Co., Ltd.
v. Yantai Fuhai International Ship Management Co., Ltd. et al.
(2014) Jin Hai Fa Shang Chu Zi No. 772, *judgment of first instance
of Tianjin Maritime Court* 1117

WANG Hong v. Jiangsu Yuanhai Logistics Co., Ltd. et al. (2014)
Wu Hai Fa Shi Zi No. 00040, *judgment of first instance of Wuhan
Maritime Court* 1127

WANG Jun v. Dalian Tiger Beach Tourism Development Co., Ltd.
(2013) Da Hai Shi Chu Zi No. 78, *judgment of first instance of Dalian
Maritime Court* 1143

WU Guangbao et al. v. Anqing City Yingjiang District Xinzhou
Country Ferry Station (2015) Wu Hai Fa Shang Chu Zi No. 00827,
judgment of first instance of Wuhan Maritime Court 1153

Wuhan Ling Da Compressor Co., Ltd. v. Falcon Insurance Company
(Hong Kong) Limited (2014) Wu Hai Fa Shang Zi No. 01268,
judgment of first instance of Wuhan Maritime Court 1163

WU Jinya v. Nanjing Haijing Shipping Co., Ltd. (2015) Wu Hai Fa
Shang Chu Zi No. 00123, *judgment of first instance of Wuhan
Maritime Court* 1177

Xiamen Yida Sihai Import & Export Co., Ltd. v. A.P. Moller—
Maersk A/S Co., Ltd. (2014) Xia Hai Fa Shang Chu Zi No. 583,
judgment of first instance of Xiamen Maritime Court 1193

XIE Hongjian v. WENG Kaiheng (2015) Qiong Hai Fa Shang Chu Zi
No. 80, *judgment of first instance of Haikou Maritime Court* 1205

XIE Hongjian v. WENG Kaiheng (2015) Qiong Min San Zhong Zi
No. 84, *judgment of second instance of Hainan High People's Court* ... 1214

XUE Haibing et al. v. Sun Shell Shipping Co., Ltd. (2015) Hai Shi
Chu Zi No. 3, *judgment of first instance of Beihai Maritime Court* 1221

Yantai Maritime Safety Administration of the People's Republic
of China v. China People's Property Insurance Co., Ltd. Qingdao
Branch (2011) Qing Hai Fa Shang Chu Zi No. 187, *judgment of first
instance of Qingdao Maritime Court* 1241

Yantai Maritime Safety Administration of the People's Republic
of China v. China People's Property Insurance Co., Ltd. Qingdao
Branch (2014) Lu Min Si Zhong Zi No. 107, *judgment of second
instance of Shandong High People's Court* 1250

Yue Hai (Fan Yu) Petrochemicals Storage Transportation
Development Co., Ltd. v. Shanghai Port Fuxing Shipping Co., Ltd.
(2014) Guang Hai Fa Zhong Zi No. 55, *judgment of first instance of
Guangzhou Maritime Court* 1263

Zhuhai Jiaxun Saite Electronic Co., Ltd. v. Shenzhen Shi Chang
Freight Co., Ltd. et al. (2015) Guang Hai Fa Chu Zi No. 182,
judgment of first instance of Guangzhou Maritime Court 1309

Zhuhai Xiangzhou Haiyun Co., Ltd. v. Sanya Hongrui Engineer Co., Ltd. et al. (2014) Qiong Hai Fa Shang Chu Zi No. 80, *judgment of first instance of Haikou Maritime Court* 1321

Zhuhai Xiangzhou Haiyun Co., Ltd. v. Sanya Hongrui Engineer Co., Ltd. et al. (2015) Qiong Min San Zhong Zi No. 25, *judgment of second instance of Hainan High People's Court* 1337

Zhumadian South China Sea Shipping Co., Ltd. v. People's Insurance Company of China Property and Casualty Co., Ltd. Zhumadian Branch (2014) Wu Hai Fa Shang Chu Zi No. 00795, *judgment of first instance of Wuhan Maritime Court* 1355

Zhumadian South China Sea Shipping Co., Ltd. v. People's Insurance Company of China Property and Casualty Co., Ltd. Zhumadian Branch (2015) E Min Si Zhong Zi No. 00058, *judgment of second instance of Hubei High People's Court* 1377

ZHONG Kangqiu v. Fujian Chengxing Fuel Oil Co., Ltd. (2014) Hai Shang Chu Zi No. 203, *judgment of first instance of Beihai Maritime Court* 1395

Table of Cases by Jurisdiction (Which Chinese Court Makes the Effective Judgment)

Effective Judgments Made by Maritime Courts
Shanghai Maritime Court

AIG Europe Ltd. v. Shanghai Heming Shipping Service Co., Ltd. Tianjin Branch et al. (2014) Hu Hai Fa Shang Chu Zi No. 116, *judgment of first instance of Shanghai Maritime Court* 1

Allianz China General Insurance Co., Ltd. v. Youda (Shanghai) International Freight Co., Ltd. et al. (2014) Hu Hai Fa Shang Chu Zi No. 361, *judgment of first instance of Shanghai Maritime Court* 11

Fan Sen (V.S) Shanghai International Freight Forwarding Co., Ltd. v. Zhongman Petroleum & Natural Gas Group Co., Ltd. (2014) Hu Hai Fa Shang Chu Zi No. 1112, *judgment of first instance of Shanghai Maritime Court* 363

Fujian Guanhai Shipping Co., Ltd. v. Shanghai Huaya Ship Fuel Company (2015) Hu Hai Fa Shang Chu Zi No. 47, *judgment of first instance of Shanghai Maritime Court* 381

Operating Department of China Continent Property & Casualty Insurance Co., Ltd. v. China Shipping Logistics Co., Ltd. (2014) Hu Hai Fa Shang Chu Zi No. 1509, *judgment of first instance of Shanghai Maritime Court* 799

Shanghai Wan Feng International Freight Forwarding Co., Ltd. v. Fujian Hongxing Electronic Technology Co., Ltd. (2014) Hu Hai Fa Shang Chu Zi No. 1496, *judgment of first instance of Shanghai Maritime Court* 925

Tianjin Maritime Court

Jiangsu Eastern Heavy Industry Co., Ltd. v. Nanjing Twin Rivers Shipping Co., Ltd. (2012) Jin Hai Fa Shang Chu Zi No. 784, *judgment of first instance of Tianjin Maritime Court* 625

Jianxin Finance Leasing Co., Ltd. v. Wenzhou Changjiang Energy Shipping Co., Ltd. (2015) Jin Hai Fa Shang Chu Zi No. 663, *judgment of first instance of Tianjin Maritime Court* 647

LI Chunjiang et al. v. Tanggu Water Conservancy Project Company et al.
(2013) Jin Hai Fa Shang Chu Zi No. 521, *judgment of first instance
of Tianjin Maritime Court*.. 661
Shandong Xianglong Industrial Group Co., Ltd. v. NCS Co., Ltd. et al.
(2011) Jin Hai Fa Shang Chu Zi No. 465, *judgment of first instance
of Tianjin Maritime Court*.. 859
Silvery Dragon Prestressed Materials Co., Ltd. (Tianjin) v. Dalian Pei Hua
International Logistics Co., Ltd. (2014) Jin Hai Fa Shang Chu Zi No. 698,
judgment of first instance of Tianjin Maritime Court 1053
Tianjin Tianguan Ocean International Freight Forwarding Co., Ltd. v.
Yantai Fuhai International Ship Management Co., Ltd. et al. (2014)
Jin Hai Fa Shang Chu Zi No. 772, *judgment of first instance of Tianjin
Maritime Court*... 1117

Qingdao Maritime Court

Qingdao Huashun Shipping Co., Ltd. v. Marc Loud Schiffahrts
Gesellschaft mbH & Co. KG et al. (2014) Qing Hai Fa Que Zi No. 7-1,
judgment of first instance of Qingdao Maritime Court 823
Station Ocean Administration Beihai Branch v. WANG Jianlong et al.
(2013) Qing Hai Fa Hai Shang Chu Zi No. 986, *judgment of first instance
of Qingdao Maritime Court* 1067

Dalian Maritime Court

People's Insurance Company of China Hangzhou Branch v. Tribute Ship
Holding S.A. (2014) Da Hai Shang Chu Zi No. 21, *judgment of first
instance of Dalian Maritime Court*................................. 811
WANG Jun v. Dalian Tiger Beach Tourism Development Co., Ltd. (2013)
Da Hai Shi Chu Zi No. 78, *judgment of first instance of Dalian
Maritime Court*... 1143

Guangzhou Maritime Court

Hong Kong Everglory Shipping Co., Ltd. et al. v. TAN Dingzhao et al.
(2014) Guang Hai Fa Shang Chu Zi No. 340, *judgment of first instance
of Guangzhou Maritime Court* 433
LI Xuelan et al. v. Ningbo Jialili Shipping Co., Ltd. (2015) Guang Hai
Fa Chu Zi No. 397, *judgment of first instance of Guangzhou Maritime
Court*.. 675
Mitsui O.S.K. Lines, Ltd. v. Guangdong Shunde Local Product Import
and Export Co., Ltd. et al. (2014) Guang Hai Fa Chu Zi No. 339, *judgment
of first instance of Guangzhou Maritime Court* 747

Yue Hai (Fan Yu) Petrochemicals Storage Transportation Development
Co., Ltd. v. Shanghai Port Fuxing Shipping Co., Ltd. (2014) Guang Hai
Fa Zhong Zi No. 55, *judgment of first instance of Guangzhou Maritime
Court*.. 1263
Zhuhai Jiaxun Saite Electronic Co., Ltd. v. Shenzhen Shi Chang Freight
Co., Ltd. et al. (2015) Guang Hai Fa Chu Zi No. 182, *judgment of first
instance of Guangzhou Maritime Court* 1309

Wuhan Maritime Court

Changhang Phoenix Co., Ltd. v. Wuhan Tairun Marine Service Co., Ltd.
et al. (2014) Wu Hai Fa Shang Zi No. 01755, *judgment of first instance
of Wuhan Maritime Court*.. 121
China Guangfa Bank Stock Co., Ltd. Nanjing Chengxi Branch v. Nanjing
Hengshunda Shipping Co., Ltd. et al. (2015) Wu Hai Fa Shang Zi No.
00205, *judgment of first instance of Wuhan Maritime Court*............. 171
Chongqing Red Dragonfly Oil Limited Liability Company v. PICC Property
and Casualty Company Limited Chongqing Branch (2015) Wu Hai Fa Shang
Zi No. 00151, *judgment of first instance of Wuhan Maritime Court*........ 267
Export-Import Bank of China et al. v. Nanjing Wujiazui Ship Building Co.,
Ltd. et al. (2014) Wu Hai Fa Shang Chu Zi No. 00470, *judgment of first
instance of Wuhan Maritime Court*...................................... 349
LIU Fengxi v. Ningbo Junsheng Yuanda Shipping Co., Ltd. et al. (2015)
Wu Hai Fa Shang Zi No. 00599, *judgment of first instance of Wuhan
Maritime Court*... 731
MAO Chuanwu v. Fengdu County Fengping Shipping Investment Co.,
Ltd. (2015) Wu Hai Fa Shang Zi No. 00134, *judgment of first instance
of Wuhan Maritime Court*.. 737
Mund & Fester GmbH & Co. KG v. Pangang Group World Trade
Panzhihua Co., Ltd. et al. (2011) Wu Hai Fa Shang Zi No. 00300,
judgment of first instance of Wuhan Maritime Court.................... 761
Suqian Rongxiang Shipping Co., Ltd. v. China United Property Insurance
Co., Ltd. Jiangsu Branch (2014) Wu Hai Fa Shang Zi No. 01351, *judgment
of first instance of Wuhan Maritime Court*............................. 1079
WANG Hong v. Jiangsu Yuanhai Logistics Co., Ltd. et al. (2014)
Wu Hai Fa Shi Zi No. 00040, *judgment of first instance of Wuhan
Maritime Court*... 1127
WU Guangbao et al. v. Anqing City Yingjiang District Xinzhou Country
Ferry Station (2015) Wu Hai Fa Shang Chu Zi No. 00827, *judgment of first
instance of Wuhan Maritime Court*..................................... 1153
Wuhan Ling Da Compressor Co., Ltd. v. Falcon Insurance Company
(Hong Kong) Limited (2014) Wu Hai Fa Shang Zi No. 01268, *judgment
of first instance of Wuhan Maritime Court*............................ 1163
WU Jinya v. Nanjing Haijing Shipping Co., Ltd. (2015) Wu Hai Fa Shang
Chu Zi No. 00123, *judgment of first instance of Wuhan Maritime Court*.... 1177

Xiamen Maritime Court

China Minsheng Bank Co., Ltd. (Xiamen Branch) v. Fujian Guanhai Shipping Co., Ltd. et al. (2015) Xia Hai Fa Shang Chu Zi No. 216, *judgment of first instance of Xiamen Maritime Court* 179

Daewoo Shipbuilding & Maritime Engineering Co., Ltd. v. Glory Advance Corporation (2014) Xia Hai Fa Que Zi No. 1, *judgment of first instance of Xiamen Maritime Court* 339

GUO Jiangbao v. Xiamen Chengyi Shipping Co., Ltd. (2014) Xia Hai Fa Shang Chu Zi No. 452, *judgment of first instance of Xiamen Maritime Court*. 393

Hongxin (HK) Container Development Limited v. Shanghai Hongsheng Gangtai Shipping Co., Ltd. et al. (2015) Xia Hai Fa Shang Chu Zi No. 378, *judgment of first instance of Xiamen Maritime Court* 453

Xiamen Yida Sihai Import & Export Co., Ltd. v. A.P. Moller—Maersk A/S Co., Ltd. (2014) Xia Hai Fa Shang Chu Zi No. 583, *judgment of first instance of Xiamen Maritime Court* 1193

Beihai Maritime Court

XUE Haibing et al. v. Sun Shell Shipping Co., Ltd. (2015) Hai Shi Chu Zi No. 3, *judgment of first instance of Beihai Maritime Court*. 1221

ZHONG Kangqiu v. Fujian Chengxing Fuel Oil Co., Ltd. (2014) Hai Shang Chu Zi No. 203, *judgment of first instance of Beihai Maritime Court*. 1395

Effective Judgments Made by Appeal Courts

Shanghai High People's Court

China Shipping Logistics Co., Ltd. v. Jiangsu Zhongtai Bridge Steel Structure Co., Ltd. (2014) Hu Hai Fa Shang Chu Zi No. 1068, *judgment of first instance of Shanghai Maritime Court* 215

China Shipping Logistics Co., Ltd. v. Jiangsu Zhongtai Bridge Steel Structure Co., Ltd. (2015) Hu Gao Min Si (Hai) Zhong Zi No. 25, *judgment of second instance of Shanghai High People's Court* 240

JIANG Haiping v. Shanghai New Qiao Insurance Brokers Ltd. (2014) Hu Hai Fa Shang Chu Zi No. 1410, *judgment of first instance of Shanghai Maritime Court*. 607

JIANG Haiping v. Shanghai New Qiao Insurance Brokers Ltd. (2015) Hu Gao Min Si (Hai) Zhong Zi No. 57, *judgment of second instance of Shanghai High People's Court*. 615

Shanghai Yizhou Waterway Engineering Co., Ltd. v. QIU Guohua (2013) Hu Hai Fa Hai Chu Zi No. 60, *judgment of first instance of Shanghai Maritime Court*. 943

Shanghai Yizhou Waterway Engineering Co., Ltd. v. QIU Guohua (2015) Hu Gao Min Si (Hai) Zhong Zi No. 32, *judgment of second instance of Shanghai High People's Court*. 967

Tianjin High People's Court

China Geology and Mining Corporation v. Tianjin Kangjie Import and
Export Trade Co., Ltd. et al. (2014) Jin Hai Fa Shang Chu Zi No. 153,
judgment of first instance of Tianjin Maritime Court 131
China Geology and Mining Corporation v. Tianjin Kangjie Import and
Export Trade Co., Ltd. et al. (2015) Jin Gao Min Si Zhong Zi No. 77,
judgment of second instance of Tianjin High People's Court 152

Shandong High People's Court

Yantai Maritime Safety Administration of the People's Republic of China
v. China People's Property Insurance Co., Ltd. Qingdao Branch (2011)
Qing Hai Fa Shang Chu Zi No. 187, *judgment of first instance of Qingdao
Maritime Court*. 1241
Yantai Maritime Safety Administration of the People's Republic of China
v. China People's Property Insurance Co., Ltd. Qingdao Branch (2014)
Lu Min Si Zhong Zi No. 107, *judgment of second instance of Shandong
High People's Court*. 1250

Liaoning High People's Court

SHAN Yongzhen et al. v. LIANG Mingren (2014) Da Hai Shi Chu Zi
No. 121, *judgment of first instance of Dalian Maritime Court* 1015
SHAN Yongzhen et al. v. LIANG Mingren (2015) Liao Min San Zhong Zi
No. 201, *judgment of second instance of Liaoning High People's Court* 1022

Guangdong High People's Court

China Ping An Property Insurance Co., Ltd. Guangdong Branch v.
Guangzhou Hang Jie Logistics Co., Ltd. (2013) Guang Hai Fa Chu Zi No.
1014, *judgment of first instance of Guangzhou Maritime Court* 199
China Ping An Property Insurance Co., Ltd. Guangdong Branch v.
Guangzhou Hang Jie Logistics Co., Ltd. (2014) Yue Gao Fa Min Si Zhong
Zi No. 204, *judgment of second instance of Guangdong High
People's Court* 207
Shanghai Eastern Shipping Material Co., Ltd. v. Beihai Honghai Shipping
Co., Ltd. et al. (2009) Guang Hai Fa Chu Zi No. 97, *judgment of first
instance of Guangzhou Maritime Court* 877
Shanghai Eastern Shipping Material Co., Ltd. v. Beihai Honghai Shipping
Co., Ltd. et al. (2012) Yue Gao Fa Min Si Zhong Zi No. 148, *judgment
of second instance of Guangdong High People's Court* 891
Shenzhen COSCO Logistics Co., Ltd. v. Guangdong Yanlin Energy
Limited by Share Ltd. (2012) Guang Hai Fa Chu Zi No. 910, *judgment
of first instance of Guangzhou Maritime Court*. 1031

Shenzhen COSCO Logistics Co., Ltd. v. Guangdong Yanlin Energy
Limited by Share Ltd. (2014) Yue Gao Fa Min Si Zhong Zi No. 197,
judgment of second instance of Guangdong High People's Court 1042
Tai-I Jiangtong (Guangzhou) Co., Ltd. v. American President Lines, Ltd.
(2013) Guang Hai Fa Chu Zi No. 552, *judgment of first instance
of Guangzhou Maritime Court* 1089
Tai-I Jiangtong (Guangzhou) Co., Ltd. v. American President Lines, Ltd.
(2015) Yue Gao Fa Min Si Zhong Zi No. 24, *judgment of second instance
of Guangdong High People's Court* 1107

Hubei High People's Court

Nanjing Jinan Welding Technology Co., Ltd. v. Nanjing Lansheng
Shipbuilding Co., Ltd. (2014) Wu Hai Fa Shang Zi No. 00369, *judgment
of first instance of Wuhan Maritime Court* 781
Nanjing Jinan Welding Technology Co., Ltd. v. Nanjing Lansheng
Shipbuilding Co., Ltd. (2015) E Min Si Zhong Zi No. 00064, *judgment
of second instance of Hubei High People's Court*. 788
Zhumadian South China Sea Shipping Co., Ltd. v. People's Insurance
Company of China Property and Casualty Co., Ltd. Zhumadian Branch
(2014) Wu Hai Fa Shang Chu Zi No. 00795, *judgment of first instance
of Wuhan Maritime Court*. 1355
Zhumadian South China Sea Shipping Co., Ltd. v. People's Insurance
Company of China Property and Casualty Co., Ltd. Zhumadian Branch
(2015) E Min Si Zhong Zi No. 00058, *judgment of second instance
of Hubei High People's Court*. 1377

Hainan High People's Court

Hainan Weilong Shipping Engineering Co., Ltd. v. Hainan Yuehai
Shipping Logistics Co., Ltd. (2014) Qiong Hai Fa Shang Chu Zi No. 87,
judgment of first instance of Haikou Maritime Court 407
Hainan Weilong Shipping Engineering Co., Ltd. v. Hainan Yuehai
Shipping Logistics Co., Ltd. (2015) Qiong Min San Zhong Zi No. 2,
judgment of second instance of Hainan High People's Court. 418
XIE Hongjian v. WENG Kaiheng (2015) Qiong Hai Fa Shang Chu Zi No.
80, *judgment of first instance of Haikou Maritime Court* 1205
XIE Hongjian v. WENG Kaiheng (2015) Qiong Min San Zhong Zi No. 84,
judgment of second instance of Hainan High People's Court. 1214
Zhuhai Xiangzhou Haiyun Co., Ltd. v. Sanya Hongrui Engineer Co., Ltd.
et al. (2014) Qiong Hai Fa Shang Chu Zi No. 80, *judgment of first instance
of Haikou Maritime Court*. 1321
Zhuhai Xiangzhou Haiyun Co., Ltd. v. Sanya Hongrui Engineer Co., Ltd.
et al. (2015) Qiong Min San Zhong Zi No. 25, *judgment of second instance
of Hainan High People's Court* 1337

Effective Judgments Made by Petition Court
The Supreme People's Court

A.P. Moller-Maersk A/S v. Shanghai Chanlian Xieyun Logistics Co., Ltd. et al. (2012) Guang Hai Fa Chu Zi No. 329, *judgment of first instance of Guangzhou Maritime Court* 45

A.P. Moller-Maersk A/S v. Shanghai Chanlian Xieyun Logistics Co., Ltd. et al. (2013) Yue Gao Fa Min Si Zhong Zi No. 162, *judgment of second instance of Guangdong High People's Court* 58

A.P. Moller-Maersk A/S v. Shanghai Chanlian Xieyun Logistics Co., Ltd. et al. (2015) Min Ti Zi No. 119, *judgment of retrial of The Supreme People's Court* 76

China Transport Groupage International (Shenzhen) Limited v. Shenzhen Zhongyi Freight Forwarding Co., Ltd. (2014) Guang Hai Fa Chu Zi No. 102, *judgment of first instance of Guangzhou Maritime Court* 83

China Transport Groupage International (Shenzhen) Limited v. Shenzhen Zhongyi Freight Forwarding Co., Ltd. (2015) Yue Gao Fa Min Si Zhong Zi No. 138, *judgment of second instance of Guangdong High People's Court* 93

China Transport Groupage International (Shenzhen) Limited v. Shenzhen Zhongyi Freight Forwarding Co., Ltd. (2017) Zui Gao Fa Min Shen Zi No. 104, *judgment of retrial of The Supreme People's Court* 107

Connexions (Asia) Limited v. J&S Worldwide Logistics Co., Ltd. et al. (2012) Guang Hai Fa Shang Chu Zi No. 704, *judgment of first instance of Guangzhou Maritime Court* 283

Connexions (Asia) Limited v. J&S Worldwide Logistics Co., Ltd. et al. (2015) Yue Gao Fa Min Si Zhong Zi No. 10, *judgment of second instance of Guangdong High People's Court* 293

Connexions (Asia) Limited v. Shenzhen J&S Worldwide Logistics Ltd. et al. (2015) Min Shen Zi No. 3206, *ruling of retrial of The Supreme People's Court* 309

COSCO Container Lines Co., Ltd. v. Shenzhen Finigate Integrated Logistics Co., Ltd. Qingdao Branch et al. (2014) Qing Hai Fa Hai Shang Chu Zi No. 751, *judgment of first instance of Qingdao Maritime Court* 313

COSCO Container Lines Co., Ltd. v. Shenzhen Finigate Integrated Logistics Co., Ltd. Qingdao Branch et al. (2015) Lu Min Si Zhong Zi No. 152, *judgment of second instance of Shandong High People's Court* 324

COSCO Container Lines Co., Ltd. v. Shenzhen Finigate Integrated Logistics Co., Ltd. Qingdao Branch et al. (2016) Zui Gao Fa Min Shen No. 2157, *ruling of retrial of The Supreme People's Court* 334

Huayu Electrical Appliance Group Co., Ltd. v. JC Logistics Service Co., Ltd. Ningbo Branch (2013) Yong Hai Fa Shang Chu Zi No. 579, *judgment of first instance of Ningbo Maritime Court* 469

Huayu Electrical Appliance Group Co., Ltd. v. JC Logistics Service Co., Ltd. Ningbo Branch (2014) Zhe Hai Zhong Zi No. 72, *judgment of second instance of Zhejiang High People's Court* 476

Huayu Electrical Appliance Group Co., Ltd. v. JC Logistics Service Co., Ltd. Ningbo Branch (2015) Min Ti Zi No. 19, *judgment of retrial of The Supreme People's Court* 485

Hunan Zoomlion International Trade Co., Ltd. et al. v. Shanghai GCL International Co., Ltd. et al. (2012) Hu Hai Fa Shang Chu Zi No. 1208, *judgment of first instance of Shanghai Maritime Court*............... 491

Hunan Zoomlion International Trade Co., Ltd. et al. v. Shanghai GCL International Co., Ltd. et al. (2014) Hu Gao Min Si (Hai) Zhong Zi No. 119, *judgment of second instance of Shanghai High People's Court* 552

Hunan Zoomlion International Trade Co., Ltd. et al. v. Shanghai GCL International Co., Ltd. et al. (2016) Zui Gao Fa Min Shen No. 1602, *ruling of retrial of The Supreme People's Court*.................... 600

LIN Guihe v. PICC Property and Casualty Company Limited Shunde Branch (2008) Guang Hai Fa Chu Zi No. 259, *judgment of first instance of Guangzhou Maritime Court* 689

LIN Guihe v. PICC Property and Casualty Company Limited Shunde Branch (2014) Yue Gao Min Si Zhong Zi No. 112, *judgment of second instance of Guangdong High People's Court* 701

LIN Guihe v. PICC Property and Casualty Company Limited Shunde Branch (2016) Zui Gao Fa Min Shen No. 1452, *ruling of retrial of The Supreme People's Court* 727

Qinhuangdao Heshun Shipping Co., Ltd. v. China People's Property Insurance Co., Ltd. Qinhuangdao City Branch (2015) Jin Hai Fa Shang Chu Zi No. 287, *judgment of first instance of Tianjin Maritime Court* 831

Qinhuangdao Heshun Shipping Co., Ltd. v. China People's Property Insurance Co., Ltd. Qinhuangdao City Branch (2015) Jin Gao Min Si Zhong Zi No. 93, *judgment of second instance of Tianjin High People's Court* 842

Qinhuangdao Heshun Shipping Co., Ltd. v. China People's Property Insurance Co., Ltd. Qinhuangdao City Branch (2016) Zui Gao Fa Min Shen No. 1395, *ruling of retrial of The Supreme People's Court*......... 854

Shanghai Jielong Industrial Group Co., Ltd. Yutian Packaging and Printing Branch v. Norasia Container Lines Limited et al. (2012) Hu Hai Fa Shang Chu Zi No. 1011, *judgment of first instance of Shanghai Maritime Court*.. 987

Shanghai Jielong Industrial Group Co., Ltd. Yutian Packaging and Printing Branch v. Norasia Container Lines Limited et al. (2013) Hu Gao Min Si (Hai) Zhong Zi No. 132, *judgment of second instance of Shanghai High People's Court* 999

Shanghai Jielong Industrial Group Co., Ltd. Yutian Packaging and Printing
Branch v. Norasia Container Lines Limited et al. (2015) Min Shen Zi
No. 573, *ruling of retrial of The Supreme People's Court* 1010

Table of Cases by Cause of Action for Maritime Cases in the People's Republic of China

193. Dispute over liability for ship collision damage
Hong Kong Everglory Shipping Co., Ltd. et al. v. TAN Dingzhao et al. (2014) Guang Hai Fa Shang Chu Zi No. 340, *judgment of first instance of Guangzhou Maritime Court* 433
LI Xuelan et al. v. Ningbo Jialili Shipping Co., Ltd. (2015) Guang Hai Fa Chu Zi No. 397, *judgment of first instance of Guangzhou Maritime Court* 675
Shanghai Eastern Shipping Material Co., Ltd. v. Beihai Honghai Shipping Co., Ltd. et al. (2009) Guang Hai Fa Chu Zi No. 97, *judgment of first instance of Guangzhou Maritime Court*. 877
Shanghai Eastern Shipping Material Co., Ltd. v. Beihai Honghai Shipping Co., Ltd. et al. (2012) Yue Gao Fa Min Si Zhong Zi No. 148, *judgment of second instance of Guangdong High People's Court*. 891
XUE Haibing et al. v. Sun Shell Shipping Co., Ltd. (2015) Hai Shi Chu Zi No. 3, *judgment of first instance of Beihai Maritime Court*. 1221

194. Dispute over liability for contact of vessel
Yue Hai (Fan Yu) Petrochemicals Storage Transportation Development Co., Ltd. v. Shanghai Port Fuxing Shipping Co., Ltd. (2014) Guang Hai Fa Zhong Zi No. 55, *judgment of first instance of Guangzhou Maritime Court* 1263

196. Dispute over liability for damage of ship pollution
WANG Jun v. Dalian Tiger Beach Tourism Development Co., Ltd. (2013) Da Hai Shi Chu Zi No. 78, *judgment of first instance of Dalian Maritime Court* 1143

200. Dispute over liability for personal injury at sea
SHAN Yongzhen et al. v. LIANG Mingren (2014) Da Hai Shi Chu Zi No. 121, *judgment of first instance of Dalian Maritime Court* 1015

SHAN Yongzhen et al. v. LIANG Mingren (2015) Liao Min San Zhong Zi
No. 201, *judgment of second instance of Liaoning High People's Court* ... 1022

201. Dispute over illegal lien on ship, cargoes carried by ship, bunkers and stores of ship

Shandong Xianglong Industrial Group Co., Ltd. v. NCS Co., Ltd. et al. (2011) Jin Hai Fa Shang Chu Zi No. 465, *judgment of first instance of Tianjin Maritime Court*. 859
WANG Hong v. Jiangsu Yuanhai Logistics Co., Ltd. et al. (2014) Wu Hai Fa Shi Zi No. 00040, *judgment of first instance of Wuhan Maritime Court*. 1127
ZHONG Kangqiu v. Fujian Chengxing Fuel Oil Co., Ltd. (2014) Hai Shang Chu Zi No. 203, *judgment of first instance of Beihai Maritime Court*. 1395

202. Dispute over contract of carriage of goods by sea or sea-connected waters

AIG Europe Ltd. v. Shanghai Heming Shipping Service Co., Ltd. Tianjin Branch et al. (2014) Hu Hai Fa Shang Chu Zi No. 116, *judgment of first instance of Shanghai Maritime Court*. 1
Allianz China General Insurance Co., Ltd. v. Youda (Shanghai) International Freight Co. Ltd. et al. (2014) Hu Hai Fa Shang Chu Zi No. 361, *judgment of first instance of Shanghai Maritime Court*. 11
A.P. Moller-Maersk A/S v. Shanghai Chanlian Xieyun Logistics Co., Ltd. et al. (2012) Guang Hai Fa Chu Zi No. 329, *judgment of first instance of Guangzhou Maritime Court* 45
A.P. Moller-Maersk A/S v. Shanghai Chanlian Xieyun Logistics Co., Ltd. et al. (2013) Yue Gao Fa Min Si Zhong Zi No. 162, *judgment of second instance of Guangdong High People's Court* 58
A.P. Moller-Maersk A/S v. Shanghai Chanlian Xieyun Logistics Co., Ltd. et al. (2015) Min Ti Zi No. 119, *judgment of retrial of The Supreme People's Court*. 76
China Shipping Logistics Co., Ltd. v. Jiangsu Zhongtai Bridge Steel Structure Co., Ltd. (2014) Hu Hai Fa Shang Chu Zi No. 1068, *judgment of first instance of Shanghai Maritime Court*. 215
China Shipping Logistics Co., Ltd. v. Jiangsu Zhongtai Bridge Steel Structure Co., Ltd. (2015) Hu Gao Min Si (Hai) Zhong Zi No. 25, *judgment of second instance of Shanghai High People's Court* 240
Connexions (Asia) Limited v. J&S Worldwide Logistics Co., Ltd. et al. (2012) Guang Hai Fa Shang Chu Zi No. 704, *judgment of first instance of Guangzhou Maritime Court*. 283

Connexions (Asia) Limited v. J&S Worldwide Logistics Co., Ltd. et al.
(2015) Yue Gao Fa Min Si Zhong Zi No. 10, *judgment of second instance
of Guangdong High People's Court*...................................... 293
Connexions (Asia) Limited v. J&S Worldwide Logistics Co., Ltd. et al.
(2015) Min Shen Zi No. 3206, *ruling of retrial of The Supreme
People's Court* 309
COSCO Container Lines Co., Ltd. v. Shenzhen Finigate Integrated
Logistics Co., Ltd. Qingdao Branch et al. (2014) Qing Hai Fa Hai Shang
Chu Zi No. 751, *judgment of first instance of Qingdao Maritime Court*.... 313
COSCO Container Lines Co., Ltd. v. Shenzhen Finigate Integrated
Logistics Co., Ltd. Qingdao Branch et al. (2015) Lu Min Si Zhong Zi
No. 152, *judgment of second instance of Shandong High People's Court*.... 324
COSCO Container Lines Co., Ltd. v. Shenzhen Finigate Integrated
Logistics Co., Ltd. Qingdao Branch et al. (2016) Zui Gao Fa Min Shen
No. 2157, *ruling of retrial of The Supreme People's Court* 334
Fan Sen (V.S) Shanghai International Freight Forwarding Co., Ltd. v.
Zhongman Petroleum & Natural Gas Group Co., Ltd. (2014) Hu Hai Fa
Shang Chu Zi No. 1112, *judgment of first instance of Shanghai
Maritime Court*. 363
Hunan Zoomlion International Trade Co., Ltd. et al. v. Shanghai GCL
International Co., Ltd. et al. (2012) Hu Hai Fa Shang Chu Zi No. 1208,
judgment of first instance of Shanghai Maritime Court................. 491
Hunan Zoomlion International Trade Co., Ltd. et al. v. Shanghai GCL
International Co., Ltd. et al. (2014) Hu Gao Min Si (Hai) Zhong Zi No.
119, *judgment of second instance of Shanghai High People's Court* 552
Hunan Zoomlion International Trade Co., Ltd. et al. v. Shanghai GCL
International Co., Ltd. et al. (2016) Zui Gao Fa Min Shen No. 1602,
ruling of retrial of The Supreme People's Court. 600
Mitsui O.S.K. Lines, Ltd. v. Guangdong Shunde Local Product Import
and Export Co., Ltd. et al. (2014) Guang Hai Fa Chu Zi No. 339, *judgment
of first instance of Guangzhou Maritime Court* 747
Mund & Fester GmbH & Co. KG v. Pangang Group World Trade
Panzhihua Co., Ltd. et al. (2011) Wu Hai Fa Shang Zi No. 00300,
judgment of first instance of Wuhan Maritime Court. 761
Operating Department of China Continent Property & Casualty Insurance
Co., Ltd. v. China Shipping Logistics Co., Ltd. (2014) Hu Hai Fa Shang Chu
Zi No. 1509, *judgment of first instance of Shanghai Maritime Court* 799
People's Insurance Company of China Hangzhou Branch v. Tribute Ship
Holding S.A. (2014) Da Hai Shang Chu Zi No. 21, *judgment of first
instance of Dalian Maritime Court*..................................... 811
Shanghai Jielong Industrial Group Co., Ltd. Yutian Packaging and Printing
Branch v. Norasia Container Lines Limited et al. (2012) Hu Hai Fa
Shang Chu Zi No. 1011, *judgment of first instance of Shanghai
Maritime Court*. 987

Shanghai Jielong Industrial Group Co., Ltd. Yutian Packaging and Printing
Branch v. Norasia Container Lines Limited et al. (2013) Hu Gao Min Si
(Hai) Zhong Zi No. 132, *judgment of second instance of Shanghai High
People's Court* 999
Shanghai Jielong Industrial Group Co., Ltd. Yutian Packaging and Printing
Branch v. Norasia Container Lines Limited et al. (2015) Min Shen Zi
No. 573, *ruling of retrial of The Supreme People's Court* 1010
Silvery Dragon Prestressed Materials Co., Ltd. (Tianjin) v. Dalian Pei Hua
International Logistics Co., Ltd. (2014) Jin Hai Fa Shang Chu Zi No. 698,
judgment of first instance of Tianjin Maritime Court 1053
Tai-I Jiangtong (Guangzhou) Co., Ltd. v. American President Lines, Ltd.
(2013) Guang Hai Fa Chu Zi No. 552, *judgment of first instance
of Guangzhou Maritime Court* 1089
Tai-I Jiangtong (Guangzhou) Co., Ltd. v. American President Lines, Ltd.
(2015) Yue Gao Fa Min Si Zhong Zi No. 24, *judgment of second instance
of Guangdong High People's Court* 1107
Tianjin Tianguan Ocean International Freight Forwarding Co., Ltd.
v. Yantai Fuhai International Ship Management Co., Ltd. et al. (2014)
Jin Hai Fa Shang Chu Zi No. 772, *judgment of first instance of Tianjin
Maritime Court*. 1117
Xiamen Yida Sihai Import & Export Co., Ltd. v. A.P. Moller—Maersk
A/S Co., Ltd. (2014) Xia Hai Fa Shang Chu Zi No. 583, *judgment of first
instance of Xiamen Maritime Court* 1193
Zhuhai Jiaxun Saite Electronic Co., Ltd. v. Shenzhen Shi Chang Freight
Co., Ltd. et al. (2015) Guang Hai Fa Chu Zi No. 182, *judgment of first
instance of Guangzhou Maritime Court* 1309

205. Dispute over ship operation contract

WU Guangbao et al. v. Anqing City Yingjiang District Xinzhou Country
Ferry Station (2015) Wu Hai Fa Shang Chu Zi No. 00827, *judgment of first
instance of Wuhan Maritime Court*. 1153

206. Dispute over ship sales and purchases contract

Shanghai Yizhou Waterway Engineering Co., Ltd. v. QIU Guohua (2013)
Hu Hai Fa Hai Chu Zi No. 60, *judgment of first instance of Shanghai
Maritime Court*. 943
Shanghai Yizhou Waterway Engineering Co., Ltd. v. QIU Guohua (2015)
Hu Gao Min Si (Hai) Zhong Zi No. 32, *judgment of second instance
of Shanghai High People's Court*. 967

207. Dispute over shipbuilding contract

Export-Import Bank of China et al. v. Nanjing Wujiazui Ship Building Co., Ltd. et al. (2014) Wu Hai Fa Shang Chu Zi No. 00470, *judgment of first instance of Wuhan Maritime Court* 349
Hainan Weilong Shipping Engineering Co., Ltd. v. Hainan Yuehai Shipping Logistics Co., Ltd. (2014) Qiong Hai Fa Shang Chu Zi No. 87, *judgment of first instance of Haikou Maritime Court*................... 407
Hainan Weilong Shipping Engineering Co., Ltd. v. Hainan Yuehai Shipping Logistics Co., Ltd. (2015) Qiong Min San Zhong Zi No. 2, *judgment of second instance of Hainan High People's Court*............ 418
Jiangsu Eastern Heavy Industry Co., Ltd. v. Nanjing Twin Rivers Shipping Co., Ltd. (2012) Jin Hai Fa Shang Chu Zi No. 784, *judgment of first instance of Tianjin Maritime Court*................................. 625
MAO Chuanwu v. Fengdu County Fengping Shipping Investment Co., Ltd. (2015) Wu Hai Fa Shang Zi No. 00134, *judgment of first instance of Wuhan Maritime Court*.. 737
Nanjing Jinan Welding Technology Co., Ltd. v. Nanjing Lansheng Shipbuilding Co., Ltd. (2014) Wu Hai Fa Shang Zi No. 00369, *judgment of first instance of Wuhan Maritime Court* 781
Nanjing Jinan Welding Technology Co., Ltd. v. Nanjing Lansheng Shipbuilding Co., Ltd. (2015) E Min Si Zhong Zi No. 00064, *judgment of second instance of Hubei High People's Court*.................... 788

210. Dispute over ship dismantling contract

XIE Hongjian v. WENG Kaiheng (2015) Qiong Hai Fa Shang Chu Zi No. 80, *judgment of first instance of Haikou Maritime Court* 1205
XIE Hongjian v. WENG Kaiheng (2015) Qiong Min San Zhong Zi No. 84, *judgment of second instance of Hainan High People's Court*............ 1214

211. Dispute over ship mortgage contract

China Guangfa Bank Stock Co., Ltd. Nanjing Chengxi Branch v. Nanjing Hengshunda Shipping Co., Ltd. et al. (2015) Wu Hai Fa Shang Zi No. 00205, *judgment of first instance of Wuhan Maritime Court*............ 171
China Minsheng Bank Co., Ltd. (Xiamen Branch) v. Fujian Guanhai Shipping Co., Ltd. et al. (2015) Xia Hai Fa Shang Chu Zi No. 216, *judgment of first instance of Xiamen Maritime Court* 179
Daewoo Shipbuilding & Maritime Engineering Co., Ltd. v. Glory Advance Corporation (2014) Xia Hai Fa Que Zi No. 1, *judgment of first instance of Xiamen Maritime Court* 339

212. Dispute over voyage charter party

Shenzhen COSCO Logistics Co., Ltd. v. Guangdong Yanlin Energy
Limited by Share Ltd. (2012) Guang Hai Fa Chu Zi No. 910, *judgment
of first instance of Guangzhou Maritime Court*...................... 1031
Shenzhen COSCO Logistics Co., Ltd. v. Guangdong Yanlin Energy
Limited by Share Ltd. (2014) Yue Gao Fa Min Si Zhong Zi No. 197,
judgment of second instance of Guangdong High People's Court 1042

213(1) Dispute over time charter party

Zhuhai Xiangzhou Haiyun Co., Ltd. v. Sanya Hongrui Engineer Co., Ltd.
et al. (2014) Qiong Hai Fa Shang Chu Zi No. 80, *judgment of first instance
of Haikou Maritime Court*.. 1321
Zhuhai Xiangzhou Haiyun Co., Ltd. v. Sanya Hongrui Engineer Co., Ltd.
et al. (2015) Qiong Min San Zhong Zi No. 25, *judgment of second instance
of Hainan High People's Court*.................................... 1337

213(2) Dispute over bareboat charter party

Changhang Phoenix Co., Ltd. v. Wuhan Tairun Marine Service Co., Ltd.
et al. (2014) Wu Hai Fa Shang Zi No. 01755, *judgment of first instance
of Wuhan Maritime Court*... 121

214. Dispute over ship financial leasing contract

Jianxin Finance Leasing Co., Ltd. v. Wenzhou Changjiang Energy
Shipping Co., Ltd. et al. (2015) Jin Hai Fa Shang Chu Zi No. 663,
judgment of first instance of Tianjin Maritime Court 647

219. Dispute over contract on lease of shipping container

Hongxin (HK) Container Development Limited v. Shanghai Hongsheng
Gangtai Shipping Co., Ltd. et al. (2015) Xia Hai Fa Shang Chu Zi No. 378,
judgment of first instance of Xiamen Maritime Court 453

221. Dispute over contract on custody of cargo in port

China Geology and Mining Corporation v. Tianjin Kangjie Import and
Export Trade Co., Ltd. et al. (2014) Jin Hai Fa Shang Chu Zi No. 153,
judgment of first instance of Tianjin Maritime Court 131
China Geology and Mining Corporation v. Tianjin Kangjie Import and
Export Trade Co., Ltd. et al. (2015) Jin Gao Min Si Zhong Zi No. 77,
judgment of second instance of Tianjin High People's Court 152

223. Dispute over freight forwarding contract on the sea or sea-connected waters

China Transport Groupage international (Shenzhen) Limited v. Shenzhen Zhongyi Freight Forwarding Co., Ltd. (2014) Guang Hai Fa Chu Zi No. 102, *judgment of first instance of Guangzhou Maritime Court*. 83

China Transport Groupage international (Shenzhen) Limited v. Shenzhen Zhongyi Freight Forwarding Co., Ltd. (2015) Yue Gao Fa Min Si Zhong Zi No. 138, *judgment of second instance of Guangdong High People's Court*. 93

China Transport Groupage international (Shenzhen) Limited v. Shenzhen Zhongyi Freight Forwarding Co., Ltd. (2017) Zui Gao Fa Min Shen Zi No. 104, *judgment of retrial of The Supreme People's Court*. 107

China Ping An Property Insurance Co., Ltd. Guangdong Branch v. Guangzhou Hang Jie Logistics Co., Ltd. (2013) Guang Hai Fa Chu Zi No. 1014, *judgment of first instance of Guangzhou Maritime Court*. 199

China Ping An Property Insurance Co., Ltd. Guangdong Branch v. Guangzhou Hang Jie Logistics Co., Ltd. (2014) Yue Gao Fa Min Si Zhong Zi No. 204, *judgment of second instance of Guangdong High People's Court*. 207

Huayu Electrical Appliance Group Co., Ltd. v. JC Logistics Service Co., Ltd. Ningbo Branch (2013) Yong Hai Fa Shang Chu Zi No. 579, *judgment of first instance of Ningbo Maritime Court* 469

Huayu Electrical Appliance Group Co., Ltd. v. JC Logistics Service Co., Ltd. Ningbo Branch (2014) Zhe Hai Zhong Zi No. 72, *judgment of second instance of Zhejiang High People's Court* 476

Huayu Electrical Appliance Group Co., Ltd. v. JC Logistics Service Co., Ltd. Ningbo Branch (2015) Min Ti Zi No. 19, *judgment of retrial of The Supreme People's Court* 485

Shanghai Wan Feng International Freight Forwarding Co., Ltd. v. Fujian Hongxing Electronic Technology Co., Ltd. (2014) Hu Hai Fa Shang Chu Zi No. 1496, *judgment of first instance of Shanghai Maritime Court*. 925

225. Dispute over contract for marine stores and spare parts supply

Fujian Guanhai Shipping Co., Ltd. v. Shanghai Huaya Ship Fuel Company (2015) Hu Hai Fa Shang Chu Zi No. 47, *judgment of first instance of Shanghai Maritime Court*. 381

226. Dispute over contract for employment of seaman

GUO Jiangbao v. Xiamen Chengyi Shipping Co., Ltd. (2014) Xia Hai Fa Shang Chu Zi No. 452, *judgment of first instance of Xiamen Maritime Court*. 393

LIU Fengxi v. Ningbo Junsheng Yuanda Shipping Co., Ltd. et al. (2015) Wu Hai Fa Shang Zi No. 00599, *judgment of first instance of Wuhan Maritime Court*. 731

230. Dispute over marine insurance contract on the sea or sea-connected waters

JIANG Haiping v. Shanghai New Qiao Insurance Brokers Ltd. (2014) Hu Hai Fa Shang Chu Zi No. 1410, *judgment of first instance of Shanghai Maritime Court* 607
JIANG Haiping v. Shanghai New Qiao Insurance Brokers Ltd. (2015) Hu Gao Min Si (Hai) Zhong Zi No. 57, *judgment of second instance of Shanghai High People's Court.* 615
LIN Guihe v. PICC Property and Casualty Company Limited Shunde Branch (2008) Guang Hai Fa Chu Zi No. 259, *judgment of first instance of Guangzhou Maritime Court* 689
LIN Guihe v. PICC Property and Casualty Company Limited Shunde Branch (2014) Yue Gao Min Si Zhong Zi No. 112, *judgment of second instance of Guangdong High People's Court.* 701
LIN Guihe v. PICC Property and Casualty Company Limited Shunde Branch (2016) Zui Gao Fa Min Shen No. 1452, *ruling of retrial of The Supreme People's Court* 727
Qinhuangdao Heshun Shipping Co., Ltd. v. China People's Property Insurance Co., Ltd. Qinhuangdao City Branch (2015) Jin Hai Fa Shang Chu Zi No. 287, *judgment of first instance of Tianjin Maritime Court* 831
Qinhuangdao Heshun Shipping Co., Ltd. v. China People's Property Insurance Co., Ltd. Qinhuangdao City Branch (2015) Jin Gao Min Si Zhong Zi No. 93, *judgment of second instance of Tianjin High People's Court.* 842
Qinhuangdao Heshun Shipping Co., Ltd. v. China People's Property Insurance Co., Ltd. Qinhuangdao City Branch (2016) Zui Gao Fa Min Shen No. 1395, *ruling of retrial of The Supreme People's Court* 854
Suqian Rongxiang Shipping Co., Ltd. v. China United Property Insurance Co., Ltd. Jiangsu Branch (2014) Wu Hai Fa Shang Zi No. 01351, *judgment of first instance of Wuhan Maritime Court* 1079
Wuhan Ling Da Compressor Co., Ltd. v. Falcon Insurance Company (Hong Kong) Limited (2014) Wu Hai Fa Shang Zi No. 01268, *judgment of first instance of Wuhan Maritime Court* 1163
Zhumadian South China Sea Shipping Co., Ltd. v. People's Insurance Company of China Property and Casualty Co., Ltd. Zhumadian Branch (2014) Wu Hai Fa Shang Chu Zi No. 00795, *judgment of first instance of Wuhan Maritime Court.* 1355
Zhumadian South China Sea Shipping Co., Ltd. v. People's Insurance Company of China Property and Casualty Co., Ltd. Zhumadian Branch (2015) E Min Si Zhong Zi No. 00058, *judgment of second instance of Hubei High People's Court.* 1377

231. Dispute over contract for protection and indemnity insurance on the sea or sea-connected waters

Chongqing Red Dragonfly Oil Limited Liability Company v. PICC Property and Casualty Company Limited Chongqing Branch (2015) Wu Hai Fa Shang Zi No. 00151, *judgment of first instance of Wuhan Maritime Court* 267

Yantai Maritime Safety Administration of the People's Republic of China v. China People's Property Insurance Co., Ltd. Qingdao Branch (2011) Qing Hai Fa Shang Chu Zi No. 187, *judgment of first instance of Qingdao Maritime Court* 1241

Yantai Maritime Safety Administration of the People's Republic of China v. China People's Property Insurance Co., Ltd. Qingdao Branch (2014) Lu Min Si Zhong Zi No. 107, *judgment of second instance of Shandong High People's Court* 1250

236. Dispute over contract for construction of dock or harbor

Station Ocean Administration Beihai Branch v. WANG Jianlong et al. (2013) Qing Hai Fa Hai Shang Chu Zi No. 986, *judgment of first instance of Qingdao Maritime Court* 1067

243. Dispute over marine development and utilization of sea

LI Chunjiang v. Tanggu Water Conservancy Project Company et al. (2013) Jin Hai Fa Shang Chu Zi No. 521, *judgment of first instance of Tianjin Maritime Court* 661

245. Dispute over ownership of ship

WU Jinya v. Nanjing Haijing Shipping Co., Ltd. (2015) Wu Hai Fa Shang Chu Zi No. 00123, *judgment of first instance of Wuhan Maritime Court* ... 1177

247. Dispute over confirmation of maritime claim

Qingdao Huashun Shipping Co., Ltd. v. Marc Loud Schiffahrts-Gesellschaft mbH & Co. KG. (2014) Qing Hai Fa Que Zi No. 7-1, *judgment of first instance of Qingdao Maritime Court* 823

List of Maritime Courts and Their Appeal and Petition Courts in the People's Republic of China

Maritime Courts	Appeal Courts	Petition Court
Shanghai Maritime Court http://shhsfy.gov.cn/hsfyytwx/hsfyytwx/	Shanghai High People's Court http://www.hshfy.sh.cn/	The Supreme People's Court of the People's Republic of China http://www.court.gov.cn/
Tianjin Maritime Court http://tjhsfy.chinacourt.gov.cn/index.html	Tianjin High People's Court http://tjfy.chinacourt.gov.cn/index.shtml	
Qingdao Maritime Court http://qdhsfy.sdcourt.gov.cn/qdhsfy/sjb/index.html	Shandong High People's Court http://sdcourt.gov.cn/	
Dalian Maritime Court http://www.dlhsfy.gov.cn/court/	Liaoning High People's Court http://lnfy.chinacourt.gov.cn/index.shtml	
Guangzhou Maritime Court http://www.gzhsfy.gov.cn/	Guangdong High People's Court http://www.gdcourts.gov.cn/	
Wuhan Maritime Court http://whhsfy.hbfy.gov.cn/	Hubei High People's Court http://www.hbfy.gov.cn/	
Haikou Maritime Court http://www.hkhsfy.gov.cn/	Hainan High People's Court http://www.hicourt.gov.cn/	
Xiamen Maritime Court http://www.xmhsfy.gov.cn/	Fujian High People's Court http://www.fjcourt.gov.cn/	
Ningbo Maritime Court https://www.nbhsfy.cn/court/index.html	Zhejiang High People's Court http://www.zjsfgkw.cn/	
Beihai Maritime Court http://www.bhhsfy.gov.cn/platformData/infoplat/pub/bhhs_32/shouye_1003/index.html	Guangxi Zhuang Autonomous Region High People's Court http://www.gxcourt.gov.cn/	
Nanjing Maritime Court www.njhsfy.gov.cn/	Jiangsu High People's Court http://www.jsfy.gov.cn/	

List of Causes of Action for Maritime Cases in the People's Republic of China (Extracted from the Regulations on Causes of Action for Civil Disputes made by The Supreme People's Court of the People's Republic of China 2020)

Part 6 Ownership Dispute	
49. Dispute over return of property buried underground	
Part 7 Usufruct Dispute	
55. Dispute over exploration right	
Part 8 Mortgage Dispute	
67. Dispute over mortgage	
(8) Dispute over mortgage of movables	
(9) Dispute over mortgage of vessels and aircrafts under manufacture	
(10) Dispute over floating charge of movables	
(11) Dispute over right of mortgage of ceiling amount	
68. Dispute over right of pledge	
(1) Dispute over right of pledge of movables	
(2) Dispute over right of re-pledge	
(3) Dispute over right of pledge of ceiling amount	
(7) Dispute over right of pledge of warehouse receipts	
(8) Dispute over right of pledge of bills of lading	
(9) Dispute over right of pledge of equity interest	
(12) Dispute over right of pledge of receivables	
69. Dispute over right of lien	
Part 10 Contract Dispute	
74. Dispute over liability for fault in contracting	
76. Dispute over confirming the validity of contract	
(1) Dispute over confirming the validity of contract	
(2) Dispute over confirming the invalidity of contract	
77. Dispute over contract for assignment of creditor's rights	
103. Dispute over contract of loan	
(1) Dispute over contract of financial loan	
104. Dispute over contract of suretyship	
106. Dispute over pledge contract	
114. Dispute over contract for contracting work	
(1) Dispute over contract for processing	

(continued)

(continued)

(2) Dispute over contract for manufacturing
(5) Dispute over contract for testing
(6) Dispute over contract for inspecting
116. Dispute over contract for carriage
(3) Dispute over contract for carriage of passengers by waterway
(4) Dispute over contract for carriage of goods by waterway
(10) Dispute over contract for combined transport
(11) Dispute over contract for combined transport by multiple way
118. Dispute over contract of warehouse
119. Dispute over agency contract
(1) Dispute over contract for agency contract for import/ export
121. Dispute over commission contract
123. Dispute over intermediary contract
143. Dispute over right of recourse
Part 19 Maritime Dispute
193. Dispute over liability for ship collision damage
194. Dispute over liability for contact of vessel
195. Dispute over liability for damage to facility in the air or under water
196. Dispute over liability for damage of ship pollution
197. Dispute over liability for marine pollution damage on the sea or sea-connected waters
198. Dispute over liability for damage to breeding on the sea or sea-connected waters
199. Dispute over liability for damage to property on the sea or sea-connected waters
200. Dispute over liability for personal injury at sea
201. Dispute over illegal lien on ship, cargoes carried by ship, bunkers and stores of ship
202. Dispute over contract of carriage of goods by sea or sea-connected waters
203. Dispute over contract of carriage of passenger by sea or sea-connected waters
204. Dispute over contract of carriage of luggage by sea or sea-connected waters
205. Dispute over ship operation contract
206. Dispute over ship sales and purchases contract
207. Dispute over shipbuilding contract
208. Dispute over ship repairing contract
209. Dispute over ship rebuilding contract
210. Dispute over ship dismantling contract
211. Dispute over ship mortgage contract
212. Dispute over voyage charter party
213. Dispute over charter party
(1) Dispute over time charter party
(2) Dispute over bareboat charter party
214. Dispute over ship financial leasing contract
215. Dispute over undertaking contract of transporting ship on the sea or sea-connected waters
216. Dispute over undertaking contract of fishing ships
217. Dispute over contract for lease of utensils affixed to ship
218. Dispute over contract for custody of utensils affixed to ship
219. Dispute over contract on lease of shipping container
220. Dispute over contract on custody of shipping container

(continued)

(continued)

221.	Dispute over contract on custody of cargo in port
222.	Dispute over shipping agency contract
223.	Dispute over freight forwarding contract on the sea or sea-connected waters
224.	Dispute over tally contract
225.	Dispute over contract for marine stores and spare parts supply
226.	Dispute over contract for employment of seaman
227.	Dispute over salvage contract
228.	Dispute over contract on refloatation on the sea or sea-connected waters
229.	Dispute over towage contract on the sea or sea-connected waters
230.	Dispute over marine insurance contract on the sea or sea-connected waters
231.	Dispute over contract for protection and indemnity insurance on the sea or sea-connected waters
232.	Dispute over contract for joint transport on the sea or sea-connected waters
233.	Dispute over ship operation loan contract
234.	Dispute over maritime security contract
235.	Dispute over channel and port dredging contract
236.	Dispute over contract for construction of dock or harbor
237.	Dispute over contract for inspection of ship
238.	Dispute over maritime security
239.	Dispute over liability for major transport accident on the sea or sea-connected waters
240.	Dispute over liability for major accident of port operation
241.	Dispute over port operation
242.	Dispute over general average
243.	Dispute over marine development and utilization of sea
244.	Dispute over joint ownership of ship
245.	Dispute over ownership of ship
246.	Dispute over maritime fraud
247.	Dispute over confirmation of maritime claim
Part 20 Business-related Dispute	
256.	Dispute over contract for affiliated operation
258.	Dispute over contract for joint operation
Part 27 Insurance Dispute	
333.	Dispute over contract for property insurance
(4)	Dispute over contract for guarantee insurance
(5)	Dispute over insurer's right of subrogation
335.	Dispute over contract for reinsurance
336.	Dispute over contract for insurance brokerage
337.	Dispute over contract for insurance agency
Part 31 Tort Liability Dispute	
390.	Dispute over liability for damage caused by water transport
(1)	Dispute over liability for personal injury caused by water transport
(2)	Dispute over liability for property damage caused by water transport
392.	Dispute over damage caused by application for pre-litigation property preservation
393.	Dispute over damage caused by application for pre-litigation evidence preservation
395.	Dispute over damage caused by application for advance execution
Part 32 Cases of Declaration of Missing and Declaration of Death	

(continued)

(continued)

400. Application for adjudication of death of citizen	
401. Application for revocation of adjudication of death of citizen	
Part 36 Cases of Holding Properties Unclaimed	
407. Application for determining certain property as ownerless	
408. Application for revocation of determination of certain property as ownerless	
Part 40 Cases of Procedure for Hastening	
418. Application for payment orders	
Part 41 Cases of Procedure of Public Summons for Exhortation	
419. Application for public summons for exhortation	
Part 45 Cases of Application for Preservation	
431. Application for pre-litigation property preservation	
432. Application for pre-litigation behaviors preservation	
433. Application for pre-litigation evidence preservation	
434. Application for pre-arbitration property preservation	
435. Application for pre-arbitration behaviors preservation	
436. Application for pre-arbitration evidence preservation	
437. Property preservation in arbitration proceedings	
438. Evidence preservation in arbitration proceedings	
439. Application for suspending payment of the amount under a letter of credit	
441. Application for suspending payment of the amount under a letter of guarantee	
Part 48 Arbitration Cases	
444. Application for confirmation of effectiveness of arbitration agreements	
445. Application for revocation in arbitral award	
Part 49 Special Maritime Procedure Cases	
446. Application for reservation of maritime claims	
(1) Application for detention of vessels	
(2) Application for auction of detained vessels	
(3) Application for seizure of vessel cargoes	
(4) Application for auction of seizure vessel cargoes	
(5) Application for seizure of bunker oil and ship's stores	
(6) Application for auction of seizure bunker oil and ship's stores	
447. Application for maritime payment orders	
448. Application for maritime injunctions	
449. Application for maritime evidence preservation	
450. Application for establishment of a fund for limitation liability for maritime claims	
451. Application for publicizing notices for assertion of maritime priority rights	
452. Application for registration and repayment of maritime claims	
Part 50 Application for Recognition and Enforcement of Judgments and Awards Cases	
453. Application for enforcement of maritime arbitral award	
454. Application for enforcement of intellectual property arbitral award	
455. Application for enforcement of foreign affairs arbitral award	
456. Application for recognition and enforcement of civil judgment rendered by court of the Hong Kong Special Administrative Region	
457. Application for recognition and enforcement of arbitration award rendered by court of the Hong Kong Special Administrative Region	

(continued)

(continued)

458. Application for recognition and enforcement of civil judgment rendered by court of the Macao Special Administrative Region
459. Application for recognition and enforcement of arbitration award rendered by court of the Macao Special Administrative Region
460. Application for recognition and enforcement of civil judgment rendered by court of Taiwan Special Administrative Region
461. Application for recognition and enforcement of arbitration award rendered by court of Taiwan Special Administrative Region
462. Application for recognition and enforcement of civil judgment rendered by foreign court
463. Application for recognition and enforcement of foreign arbitration award
Part 54 Action of Opposition to Enforcement Cases
471. Offense against enforcement
(1) Offense against enforcement by an outsider
(1) Application for enforcement of objection
472. Objection over the implementation of the distribution plan

Table of References

Chinese Legislation

(2015) Min Si Ta Zi Reply of the Supreme People's Court
Item 2...... People's Insurance (p. 818, p. 819)

Administrative Measures of the Customs of the People's Republic of China for Manifests of Inward and Outward Means of Transport
Art. 9 Para. 3......Tai-I Jiangtong (p. 1110)
Art. 13......Tai-I Jiangtong (p. 1105)

Administrative Measures of the Customs of the People's Republic of China for the Inspection of Imported and Exported Goods
Art. 2......Tai-I Jiangtong (p. 1105)
Art. 17 Para. 2......Tai-I Jiangtong (p. 1105)

Civil Procedure Law of the People's Republic of China
Art. 13 Para. 1......LIN Guihe (p. 721)
Art. 21 Para. 1.......WU Jinya (p. 1178)
Art. 23......China Transport Groupage (p. 90, p. 98, p. 111) China Guangfa (p. 173) Export-Import (p. 350) Nanjing Jinan (p. 782)
Art. 24......Chongqing Red (p. 268) Suqian Rongxiang (p. 1080)
Art. 27......A.P. Moller-Maersk (p. 53, p. 66) Connexions (Asia) (p. 290, p. 300, p. 306) Tai-I Jiangtong (p. 1103) Xiamen Yida (p. 1200)
Art. 28......Mund & Fester (p. 762)
Art. 30......Hong Kong (p. 447) Qingdao Huashun (p. 828)
Art. 56 Para. 2......Jiangsu Eastern (p. 645)
Art. 64......Connexions (Asia) (p. 292, p. 302) MAO Chuanwu (p. 745)
Art. 64 Para. 1......AIG Europe (p. 8) Allianz China (p. 39) China Transport Groupage (p. 91, p. 99, p. 100, p. 103, p. 104, p. 112, p. 113, p. 115, p.116) China Geology (p. 151, p. 160) China Shipping (p. 237, p. 262) Daewoo Shipbuilding (p. 346) Fan Sen (p. 377) Fujian Guanhai (p. 390) GUO Jiangbao (p. 402) Hong Kong (p. 450) Hongxin (HK) (p. 465) Hunan Zoomlion (p. 548, p. 586) JIANG Haiping (p. 614, p. 619) Jianxin Finance (p. 658) LI Chunjiang (p. 672) LI Xuelan (p. 686) LIN Guihe (p. 699, p. 720, p. 722) Mund & Fester (p. 779) Operating Department (p. 808) Qinhuangdao Heshun (p. 841, p. 848) Shandong Xianglong (p. 875) Shanghai Wan (p. 940) Shanghai Yizhou (p. 965, p. 979) Shanghai Jielong (p. 997, p. 1005) Shenzhen COSCO (p. 1047) Silvery Dragon

(continued)

(continued)

(p. 1064) Tai-I Jiangtong (p. 1106) Tianjin Tianguan (p. 1124) WANG Hong (p. 1141) WU Guangbao (p. 1161) Xiamen Yida (p. 1203) XUE Haibing (p. 1238) Yue Hai (p. 1306) Zhumadian South (p. 1373, p. 1385)
Art. 65 Para. 2 Zhumadian South (p. 1362)
Art. 67 Para. 1......LIN Guihe (p. 708)
Art. 70 Sub-Para. 1......Hongxin (HK) (p. 458)
Art. 78......LIN Guihe (p. 712)
Art. 124......WANG Hong (p. 1141)
Art. 137......China Ping (p. 213)
Art. 142......Changhang Phoenix (p. 129) China Guangfa (p. 177) Chongqing Red (p. 281) Export-Import (p. 361) MAO Chuanwu (p. 745) Mund & Fester (p. 779) Nanjing Jinan (p. 787, p. 792) Suqian Rongxiang (p. 1086) WU Guangbao (p. 1161) Wuhan Ling (p. 1175) WU Jinya (p. 1191) Zhumadian South (p. 1375, p. 1387)
Art. 144......China Minsheng (p. 195) COSCO Container (p. 333) Daewoo Shipbuilding (p. 346) Export-Import (p. 361) Hongxin (HK) (p. 465) Jianxin Finance (p. 658) LIU Fengxi (p. 735) Mitsui O.S.K. (p. 758) Tianjin Tianguan (p. 1124)
Art. 152......Export-Import (p. 361)
Art. 153......Qingdao Huashun (p. 829)
Art. 170 Para. 1......JIANG Haiping (p. 623) Yantai Maritime (p. 1261)
Art. 170 Para. 1 Sub-Para. 1......AP. Moller-Maersk (p. 75) China Geology (p. 170) China Shipping Logistics (p. 264) COSCO Container (p. 333) Hainan Weilong (p. 430) Huayu Electrical (p. 484) Hunan Zoomlion (p. 598) Nanjing Jinan (p. 797) Qinhuangdao Heshun (p. 853) Shanghai Eastern (p. 918) Shanghai Yizhou (p. 985) Shanghai Jielong (p. 1009) SHAN Yongzhen (p. 1030) Shenzhen COSCO (p. 1048) Tai-I Jiangtong (p. 1115) Zhuhai Xiangzhou (p. 1352) Zhumadian South (p. 1393)
Art. 170 Para. 1 Sub-Para. 2......China Transport Groupage (p. 104, p. 116, p. 120) Huayu Electrical (p. 490) LIN Guihe (p. 722) Shanghai Eastern (p. 918) Shenzhen COSCO (p. 1048) XIE Hongjian (p. 1219)
Art. 171 Para. 1......Connexions (Asia) (p. 308)
Art. 175......China Shipping (p. 264) Hunan Zoomlion (p. 598) JIANG Haiping (p. 623) Shanghai Yizhou (p. 985) Shanghai Jielong (p. 1009)
Art. 200......COSCO Lines (p. 336) Hunan Zoomlion (p. 605) LIN Guihe (p. 730) Qinhuangdao Heshun (p. 858)
Art. 200 Para. 1......Connexions (Asia) (p. 311) Shanghai Jielong (p. 1012, p. 1013, p. 1014)
Art. 200 Para. 2......Connexions (Asia) (p. 311) Shanghai Jielong (p. 1012, p. 1014)
Art. 200 Para. 6......Connexions (Asia) (p. 311) Shanghai Jielong (p. 1012, p. 1014)
Art. 204 Para. 1......Connexions (Asia) (p. 312) COSCO Lines (p. 336) Hunan Zoomlion (p. 605) LIN Guihe (p. 730) Qinhuangdao Heshun (p. 858) Shanghai Jielong (p. 1014)
Art. 207 Para. 1......A.P. Moller-Maersk (p. 81) China Transport Groupage (p. 120)
Art. 227......ZHONG Kangqiu (p. 1402, p. 1403)
Art. 229......China Transport Groupage (p. 92, p. 100, p. 113) Shanghai Eastern (p. 890) Tianjin Tianguan (p. 1125)
Art. 241......Shanghai Eastern (p. 885, p.899)
Art. 253......AIG Europe (p. 9) Allianz China (p. 40) A.P. Moller-Maersk (p. 57) Changhang Phoenix (p. 130) China Guangfa (p. 178) China Minsheng (p. 196) China Ping (p. 206) China Shipping (p. 238) Chongqing Red (p. 282) Fujian Guanhai (p. 390) GUO Jiangbao (p. 402) Hainan Weilong(p. 416) Hong Kong (p. 451) Huayu Electrical (p. 474, p. 480) Hunan Zoomlion (p. 549) Jianxin Finance (p. 659) LI Chunjiang (p. 672) LIN Guihe (p. 700) LIU Fengxi (p. 735) Mitsui O.S.K. (p. 759) Nanjing Jinan (p. 787, p. 793) Operating Department (p. 808) Shandong Xianglong (p. 876) Shanghai Eastern (p. 919) Shanghai Wan (p. 940) Shanghai Jielong (p. 997) Shenzhen COSCO (p. 1041, p. 1049) Silvery Dragon (p. 1065) Station Ocean (p. 1077) Suqian Rongxiang (p. 1086) WANG Jun (p. 1151) XIE Hongjian (p. 1213, p. 1216, p, 1219) Yantai Maritime (p. 1249) Zhuhai Jiaxun (p. 1319) Zhuhai Xiangzhou (p. 1336) Zhumadian South (p. 1376)

Contract Law of the People's Republic of China
General......Operating Department (p. 808) Shanghai Yizhou (p. 982)
Art. 6 ......Jiangsu Eastern (p. 645) Shanghai Yizhou (p. 965, p. 979)
Art. 8......China Shipping (p. 237, p. 262)

(continued)

(continued)

Art. 8 Para. 1	......Shanghai Yizhou (p. 965, p. 979)
Art. 41	......LIN Guihe (p. 703) Zhuhai Xiangzhou (p. 1346)
Art. 44	......Zhuhai Xiangzhou (p. 1336)
Art. 49	......China Transport Groupage (p. 90, p. 98, p. 102, p. 112, p. 114)
Art. 52	......China Ping (p. 204)
Art. 56	......LIN Guihe (p. 721, p. 722)
Art. 60	......MAO Chuanwu (p. 745) Nanjing Jinan (p. 795) Zhuhai Xiangzhou (p. 1743)
Art. 60 Para. 1	......China Shipping (p. 237, p. 262) Zhuhai Xiangzhou (p. 1335, p. 1336)
Art. 61	......Fujian Guanhai (p. 387, p. 388, p. 390)
Art. 62 Para. 1	......Fujian Guanhai (p. 387)
Art. 65	......A.P. Moller-Maersk (p. 57, p. 70)
Art. 73	......Yantai Maritime (p. 1261)
Art. 77	......Zhuhai Xiangzhou (p. 1342, p. 1344)
Art. 79	......Export-Import (p. 360, p. 361)
Art. 80	......Export-Import (p. 360, p. 361)
Art. 93	......Hongxin (HK) (p. 465) Jianxin Finance (p. 658)
Art. 93 Para. 2	......Hongxin (HK) (p. 463) Jiangsu Eastern (p. 645) Zhuhai Xiangzhou (p. 1349)
Art. 94	......Zhuhai Xiangzhou (p. 1349, p. 1350)
Art. 94 Para. 4	......Changhang Phoenix (p. 127, p. 129) XIE Hongjian (p. 1212, p. 1216, p.1218)
Art. 96	......Changhang Phoenix (p. 127) Zhuhai Xiangzhou (p. 1349)
Art. 96 Para. 1	......XIE Hongjian (p. 1212, p. 1216)
Art. 97	......Changhang Phoenix (p. 127, p. 129) China Geology (p. 148, p. 157) Hongxin (HK) (p. 463, p. 465) Jianxin Finance (p. 658) XIE Hongjian (p. 1212, p. 1216)
Art. 97 Para. 2	......Hongxin (HK) (p. 465)
Art. 107	......A.P. Moller-Maersk (p. 57, p. 70) China Guangfa (p. 177) China Minsheng (p. 194) China Shipping (p. 237, p. 262) Export-Import (p. 361) Hainan Weilong (p. 430) Jianxin Finance (p. 658) LI Chunjiang (p. 672) Nanjing Jinan (p. 787, p. 792, p. 795) Shanghai Wan (p. 940) Zhuhai Xiangzhou (p. 1351)
Art. 108	......Zhuhai Xiangzhou (p. 1351)
Art. 109	......Hainan Weilong (p. 416, p. 423)
Art. 111	......Fujian Guanhai (p. 388, p. 389, p. 390)
Art. 113	......A.P. Moller-Maersk (p. 56, p, 57 p. 69, p. 70) China Shipping (p. 232, p. 235, p. 257, p.260) Fan Sen (p. 377) Hunan Zoomlion (p. 541, p. 579) Nanjing Jinan (p. 796) Silvery Dragon (p. 1063)
Art. 113 Para. 1	......Allianz China (p. 39) China Shipping (p. 237, p. 262) Fan Sen (p. 377) Shenzhen COSCO (p. 1039) Silvery Dragon (p. 1064)
Art. 114 Para. 1	......Hainan Weilong (p. 416,p.423) Hongxin (HK) (p. 464, p. 465)
Art. 119	......Nanjing Jinan (p. 787, p. 792) Shanghai Eastern (p. 906)
Art. 119 Para. 1	......A.P. Moller-Maersk (p. 57, p. 70)
Art. 120	......Zhuhai Xiangzhou (p. 1335)
Art. 121	......A.P. Moller-Maersk (p. 55, p. 68)
Art. 125 Para. 1	......Silvery Dragon (p. 1062, p. 1064) Zhuhai Xiangzhou (p. 1342)
Art. 126 Para. 1	......China Transport Groupage (p. 90, p. 98, p. 111)
Art. 132	......ZHONG Kangqiu (p. 1401, p. 1403)
Art. 133	......ZHONG Kangqiu (p. 1401, p. 1403)
Art. 174	......Fan Sen (p. 377)
Art. 205	......China Guangfa (p. 177) China Minsheng (p. 194)
Art. 206	......China Guangfa (p. 177) China Minsheng (p. 194)
Art. 207	......China Guangfa (p. 177) China Minsheng (p. 194)
Art. 215	......SHAN Yongzhen (p. 1028)
Art. 226	......Hongxin (HK) (p. 465)
Art. 227	......Hongxin (HK) (p. 463, p. 465)
Art. 248	......Jianxin Finance (p. 658)

(continued)

(continued)

Art. 251......Jiangsu Eastern (p. 645) SHAN Yongzhen (p. 1018, p. 1025)
Art. 253......Jiangsu Eastern (p. 645) SHAN Yongzhen (p. 1018, p. 1025)
Art. 260......Jiangsu Eastern (p. 645)
Art. 263......Hainan Weilong (p. 416, p. 423)
Art. 264......Jiangsu Eastern (p. 642, p. 645)
Art. 292......China Shipping (p. 234, p. 237, p. 259, p. 262)
Art. 304......Shanghai Jielong (p. 997, p. 1005)
Art. 311......China Ping (p. 204, p. 205) Hunan Zoomlion (p. 538, p. 576) Operating Department (p. 805, p. 808)
Art. 398......China Transport Groupage (p. 91, p. 99, p. 100, p. 104, p. 112, p. 113, p. 115, p. 116, p. 120) Shanghai Wan (p. 940)
Art. 402......JIANG Haiping (p. 614, p. 619)
Art. 403 Para. 1......Zhuhai Jiaxun (p. 1317)
Art. 403 Para. 2......China Transport Groupage (p. 119)
Art. 405......Shanghai Wan (p. 940)
Art. 406 Para. 1......Huayu Electrical (p. 474, p. 480)

Customs Law of the People's Republic of China
General...... Shandong Xianglong (p. 870)
Art. 14......Tai-I Jiangtong (p. 1105)
Art. 24 Para. 1......Tai-I Jiangtong (p. 1104)
Art. 24 Para. 2......Tai-I Jiangtong (p. 1105)
Art. 24 Para. 3......Tai-I Jiangtong (p. 1105)
Art. 86 Para. 3......Tai-I Jiangtong (p. 1104)

Domestic Waterway Cargo Carriage Insurance Clauses (2009 Edition)
Art. 6......Chongqing Red (p. 280)
Art. 20......Chongqing Red (p. 281)

Fishery Law of the People's Republic of China
Art. 11 Para. 1......WANG Jun (p. 1149, p. 1151)

General Principles of the Civil Law of the People's Republic of China
Art. 63......Mund & Fester (p. 776, p. 779)
Art. 63 Para. 2......LI Chunjiang (p. 672)
Art. 87......Hongxin (HK) (p. 461, p. 465)
Art. 106......Station Ocean (p. 1077)
Art. 106 Para. 1......Nanjing Jinan (p. 787, p. 792)
Art. 134 Para. 1 Sub-Para. 4......Nanjing Jinan (p. 787, p. 792)
Art. 135......China Ping (p. 212)
Art. 137......China Ping (p. 212)
Art. 140......China Ping (p. 205) Hainan Weilong (p.424) Operating Department (p. 808)
Art. 170 Para. 1 Sub-Para. 2......China Ping (p. 213)
Art. 170 Para. 1 Sub-Para. 3......China Ping (p. 213)

General Rules of Judicial Appraisal Procedure of the Ministry of Justice
General......LIN Guihe (p. 718)
Art. 22......LIN Guihe (p. 718, p. 729)

Guaranty Law of the People's Republic of China
General......Changhang Phoenix (p. 126)
Art. 18......China Guangfa (p. 177) China Minsheng (p. 193, p. 194) Jianxin Finance (p. 658)

(continued)

(continued)

Art. 21 Para. 1......China Guangfa (p. 177)
Art. 31......China Minsheng (p. 193, p. 194) Jianxin Finance (p. 658)
Art. 41......LIN Guihe (p. 697)
Art. 42......LIN Guihe (p. 697)

Hong Kong Arbitration Ordinance
General......Shenzhen COSCO (p. 1036)

Hong Kong Companies Ordinance
Part XI......Shanghai Eastern (p. 909)

Implementation Measures of the Regulations on Management of Ocean Dumping of the People's Republic of China
General......Station Ocean (p. 1076)

Insurance Law of the People's Republic of China *[Nb. This statute was enacted in 1995, and revised in 2002, 2009, 2014 and 2015.]*
General......Qinhuangdao Heshun (p. 840, p. 848) LIN Guihe (p. 698) Yantai Maritime (p. 1246, p. 1247, p. 1254, p. 1256, p. 1257, p. 1258)
Art. 10......Shanghai Eastern (p. 915) Wuhan Ling (p. 1175)
Art. 12......LIN Guihe (p. 719, p. 729)
Art. 12 Para. 1......LIN Guihe (p. 720, p. 722)
Art. 12 Para. 2......Chongqing Red (p. 279) Lin Guihe (p. 722)
Art. 12 Para. 6......Chongqing Red (p. 281)
Art. 13......Chongqing Red (p. 278) Suqian Rongxiang (p. 1086)
Art. 13 Para. 1......Chongqing Red (p. 281)
Art. 13 Para. 3......Chongqing Red (p. 281)
Art. 17......Zhumadian South (p. 1370, p. 1375, p. 1383, p. 1387)
Art. 17 Para. 2......Zhumadian South (p. 1375, p. 1387, p. 1391)
Art. 23......Chongqing Red (p. 281) Suqian Rongxiang (p. 1086)
Art. 23 Para. 1......Chongqing Red (p. 281) Zhumadian South (p. 1373, p. 1375, p. 1385, p. 1387)
Art. 23 Para. 2......Zhumadian South (p. 1375, p. 1387)
Art. 23 Para. 3......Chongqing Red (p. 281)
Art. 24 Para. 1......LIN Guihe (p. 699)
Art. 25......Shanghai Eastern (p. 906) Zhumadian South (p. 1373, p. 1375, p. 1385, p. 1387, p. 1389, p. 1392)
Art. 26......Shanghai Eastern (p. 916)
Art. 30......Suqian Rongxiang (p. 1086)
Art. 31......LIN Guihe (p. 703, p. 704)
Art. 40......LIN Guihe (p. 699)
Art. 44......Yantai Maritime (p. 1261)
Art. 50......Yantai Maritime (p. 1248, p. 1255, p. 1256)
Art. 52......Zhumadian South (p. 1388)
Art. 52 Para. 1......Zhumadian South (p. 1390)
Art. 52 Para. 3......Zhumadian South (p. 1390)
Art. 57......Zhumadian South (p. 1392)
Art. 60......Shanghai Eastern (p. 909) Yantai Maritime (p. 1261)
Art. 60 Para. 1......Allianz China (p. 39) Yue Hai (p. 1293)
Art. 60 Para. 3......Yue Hai (p. 1293)

(continued)

(continued)

Art. 65......Yantai Maritime (p. 1246, p. 1247, p. 1248, p. 1249, p. 1254, p. 1255, p. 1256, p. 1259)
Art. 65 Para. 2......Yantai Maritime (p. 1247, p. 1260, p. 1261)
Art. 128......JIANG Haiping (p. 614, p. 618, p. 619)
Art. 184......Yantai Maritime (p. 1260)

Interpretation of the Supreme People's Court on Certain Issues concerning the Application of Law in the Trial of Cases Involving Compensation for Personal Injury
General......LI Xuelan (p. 677) SHAN Yongzhen (p. 1020, p. 1027)
Art. 10......SHAN Yongzhen (p. 1018, p. 1021, p. 1025, p. 1028, p. 1029)
Art. 11......SHAN Yongzhen (p. 1018, p. 1025)
Art. 11 Para. 3......GUO Jiangbao (p. 400)
Art. 17 Para. 1......LI Xuelan (p. 685)
Art. 17 Para. 3......LI Xuelan (p. 685)
Art. 18......LI Xuelan (p. 683) SHAN Yongzhen (p. 1021, p. 1028)
Art. 22......SHAN Yongzhen (p. 1021, p. 1028)
Art. 27......LI Xuelan (p. 681)
Art. 28......LI Xuelan (p. 682) SHAN Yongzhen (p. 1021, p. 1028)
Art. 29......LI Xuelan (p. 681) SHAN Yongzhen (p. 1020, p. 1021, p. 1027 p. 1028)

Interpretation of the Supreme People's Court on Certain Issues concerning the Application of the Guaranty Law of the People's Republic of China
Art. 42......China Minsheng (p. 194)
Art. 80......Shandong Xianglong (p. 875)
Art. 85......Changhang Phoenix (p. 127, p. 129)
Art. 88......China Geology (p. 150, p. 159, p. 168)
Art. 114......Shandong Xianglong (p. 875)

Interpretation of the Supreme People's Court on Issues concerning the Application of Law for the Trial of Cases of Disputes over Sales Contracts
Art 2......Shanghai Fan Sen (p. 377)

Interpretation of the Supreme People's Court on Several Issues concerning the Application of the Contract Law of the People's Republic of China (II)
Art. 19......China Geology (p. 169)
Art. 29 Para. 1......Hongxin (HK) (p. 464)
Art. 29......A.P. Moller-Maersk (p. 74) Hainan Weilong (p. 425)

Interpretation of the Supreme People's Court on Several Issues concerning the Application of the Insurance Law of the People's Republic of China (I)
Art. 1......Yantai Maritime (p. 1246, p. 1254, p. 1260)
Art. 3......Yantai Maritime (p. 1247, p. 1254)

Interpretation of the Supreme People's Court on Several Issues concerning the Application of the Insurance Law of the People's Republic of China (II)
Art. 9......Zhumadian South (p. 1391)
Art. 16......Operating Department (p. 808)
Art. 16 Para. 2......China Ping (p. 205)

(continued)

(continued)

Interpretation of the Supreme People's Court on Several Issues concerning the Application of the Law of the Application of Law for Foreign-related Civil Relations of the People's Republic of China (I)
Art. 8 Para. 2......Xiamen Yida (p. 1201)
Art. 19......Hongxin (HK) (p. 460) Wuhan Ling (p. 1171)

Interpretation of the Supreme People's Court on the Application of the Civil Procedure Law of the People's Republic of China
Article 25 Zhumadian South China (p. 1356)
Art. 90......China Transport Groupage (p. 103, p. 104, P. 115, P. 116) China Minsheng (p. 195) LIN Guihe (p. 720, p. 722) Shenzhen COSCO (p. 1047, p. 1048)
Art. 90 Para 2......Huayu Electrical (p. 490)
Art. 91 Para 1......Hongxin (HK) (p. 458)
Art. 92......China Minsheng (p. 193)
Art. 92 Para 2......WU Guangbao (p. 1161)
Art. 93......China Geology (p. 166)
Art. 93 Para 1......Hongxin (HK) (p. 462)
Art. 93 Para 1 Sub Para 5......Shanghai Eastern (p. 914)
Art. 99 Para 3......XIE Hongjian (p. 1228)
Art. 102......XIE Hongjian (p. 1217)
Art. 105......Hongxin (HK) (p. 342)
Art. 115......Zhuhai Xiangzhou (p. 1347)
Art 121 Para 1......LIN Guihe (p. 716, p. 717)
Art. 196......Shanghai Eastern (p.919)
Art. 202 Para 1......Shanghai Eastern (p.919)
Art. 304......ZHONG Kangqiu (p. 1403)
Art. 307......ZHONG Kangqiu (p. 1403)
Art. 312......ZHONG Kangqiu (p. 1403)
Art. 395 Para 2......COSCO Container (p. 336) Hunan Zoomlion (p. 605)
Art. 407 Para 2......A.P. Moller-Maersk (p. 81)

Interpretation of the Supreme People's Court on the Application of the Special Maritime Procedure Law of the People's Republic of China
Art. 1......Connexions (Asia) (p. 290, p. 300) WANG Hong (p. 1128)

Interpretation on Certain Issues concerning the Determination of Compensation Liability for Mental Damage in Civil Torts of the Supreme People's Court
General......LI Xuelan (p. 677)
Art. 8 Para. 2......LI Xuelan (p. 684)
Art. 10......LI Xuelan (p. 684)
Art. 11......SHAN Yongzhen (p. 1020, p. 1027)

Labor Contract Law of the People's Republic of China
Art. 30 Para. 1......LIU Fengxi (p. 735)
Art. 36......Guo Jiangbao (p. 399, p. 402)
Art. 66......LIU Fengxi (p. 734)
Art. 92......LIU Fengxi (p. 735)

Law of the Application of Law for Foreign-related Civil Relations of the People's Republic of China
Art. 3......Tianjin Tianguan (p. 1121)
Art. 4......Daewoo Shipbuilding (p. 346)

(continued)

(continued)

Art. 41......Daewoo Shipbuilding (p. 346) Hongxin (HK) (p. 460) Shandong Xianglong (p. 871, p. 875) Wuhan Ling (p. 1171) Xiamen Yida (p. 1201)
Art. 44......Mund & Fester (p. 773) Shandong Xianglong (p. 872, p. 875) XUE Haibing (p. 1232)

Law of the People's Republic of China on the Administration of the Use of Sea Areas
Art. 2 Para. 1......WANG Jun (p. 1149, p. 1151)
Art. 3 Para. 2......WANG Jun (p. 1149, p. 1151)

Maritime Code of the People's Republic of China
General...... China Geology (p. 149, p. 158) Shandong Xianglong (p. 873) Shanghai Eastern (p. 912) XUE Haibing (p. 1232)
Art. 3......LIN Guihe (p. 697)
Art. 7......WU Jinya (p. 1190, p. 1191)
Art. 9......WU Jinya (p. 1190, p. 1191) ZHONG Kangqiu(p. 1401, p. 1403)
Art. 11......China Minsheng (p. 194)
Art. 13......Operating Department (p. 807, p. 808)
Art. 21......LIU Fengxi (p. 735)
Art. 22 Para. 1......LIU Fengxi (p. 735)
Chapter 4......Operating Department (p. 808)
Art. 41......AIG Europe (p. 8) Hunan Zoomlion (p. 548, p. 586) Shanghai Jielong (p. 997, p. 1005)
Art. 42......Hunan Zoomlion (p. 544, p. 582)
Art. 42 Sub-Para. 1......Hunan Zoomlion (p. 548, p. 586)
Art. 42 Para. 4......COSCO Container (p. 333)
Art. 46......Allianz China (p. 39) Xiamen Yida (p. 1202)
Art. 46 Para. 1......AIG Europe (p. 8) Hunan Zoomlion (p. 548, p. 586) Zhuhai Jiaxun (p. 1318, p. 1319)
Art. 47......Hunan Zoomlion (p. 539, p. 577) Qinhuangdao Heshun (p. 839, p. 847, p. 857)
Art. 48......Hunan Zoomlion (p. 544, p. 582) Shanghai Jielong (p. 997, p. 1005) Xiamen Yida (p. 1202)
Art. 49 Para. 1......Silvery Dragon (p. 1062, p. 1064)
Art. 51......Hunan Zoomlion (p. 538, p. 576) Xiamen Yida (p. 1202) Zhuhai Jiaxun (p. 1318)
Art. 51 Para. 1 Sub-Para. 1......Hunan Zoomlion (p. 538, p. 539, p. 548, p. 576, p. 577, p. 586, p. 604)
Art. 51 Para. 1 Sub-Para. 3......Hunan Zoomlion (p. 538, p. 548, p. 576, p. 586)
Art. 51 Para. 1 Sub-Para. 8......People's Insurance (p. 821)
Art. 51 Para. 1 Sub-Para. 9......People's Insurance (p. 819, p. 821)
Art. 51 Para. 1 Sub-Para. 12......People's Insurance (p. 821)
Art. 51 Para. 2......People's Insurance (p. 820)
Art. 51 Para. 5......Xiamen Yida (p. 1202)
Art. 54......Hunan Zoomlion (p. 548, p. 586)
Art. 55......Allianz China (p. 39) Zhuhai Jiaxun (p. 1318)
Art. 55 Para. 1......Connexions (Asia) (p. 291, p. 301, p. 307) Hunan Zoomlion (p. 548, p. 586) Zhuhai Jiaxun (p. 1318, p. 1319)
Art. 55 Para. 2......Connexions (Asia) (p. 291, p. 301, p. 307) Hunan Zoomlion (p. 548, p. 586) Zhuhai Jiaxun (p. 1318, p. 1319)
Art. 56......AIG Europe (p. 8) Allianz China (p. 34, p. 36, p. 39)
Art. 57......Allianz China (p. 34)
Art. 58......Mund & Fester (p. 778, p. 779)
Art. 59......Allianz China (p. 34) Hunan Zoomlion (p. 547, p. 585)
Art. 59 Para. 1......AIG Europe (p. 8)
Art. 60 Para. 1......Allianz China (p. 39)
Art. 61......Hunan Zoomlion (p. 603, p. 604)
Art. 64......Allianz China (p. 39)
Art. 69 Para. 1......China Shipping (p. 234, p. 237, p. 259, p. 262)

(continued)

(continued)

Art. 71......Allianz China (p. 39) Connexions (Asia) (p. 291, p. 301) People's Insurance (p. 817, p. 820)	
Art. 72......Connexions (Asia) (p. 306) Mund & Fester (p. 775)	
Art. 72 Para. 2......Shandong Xianglong (p. 872)	
Art. 75......Mund & Fester (p. 774, p. 775, p. 779)	
Art. 76......Mund & Fester (p. 774, p. 775, p. 779)	
Art. 78......COSCO Container (p. 333) People's Insurance (p. 817) Shandong Xianglong (p. 872, p. 875)	
Art. 83......Allianz China (p. 39)	
Art. 86......COSCO Container (p. 322, p. 328, p. 330, p. 336) Mitsui O.S.K. (p. 757, p. 758)	
Art. 87......A.P. Moller-Maersk (p. 56, p. 69) COSCO Container (p. 322, p. 328) Shandong Xianglong (p. 874)	
Art. 88......A.P. Moller-Maersk (p. 56, p. 69)	
Art. 92......Tianjin Tianguan (p. 1124)	
Art. 98......Shandong Xianglong (p. 875)	
Art. 100 Para. 2......Shenzhen COSCO (p. 1038, p. 1041, p. 1048)	
Art. 102......Allianz China (p. 28,p.39)	
Art. 103......Allianz China (p. 39)	
Art. 104......Allianz China (p. 39)	
Art. 105......Allianz China (p. 36,p.39)	
Art. 106......Allianz China (p. 39)	
Art. 166......LI Xuelan (p. 686)	
Art. 169......LI Xuelan (p. 678, p. 686) Qingdao Hua (p. 828, p. 829)	
Art. 169 Para. 1......Hong Kong (p. 448, p. 450) Shanghai Eastern (p.886, p.889, p. 899, p. 903, p. 918) XUE Haibing (p. 1237, p. 1238)	
Art. 169 Para. 2......Shanghai Eastern (p. 886, p,889, p. 899, p. 903, p. 918) XUE Haibing (p. 1237, p. 1238)	
Art. 204......Shanghai Eastern (p. 886, p.889, p. 899, p. 900, p. 903, p. 918)	
Art. 207......Shanghai Eastern (p. 886, p. 887, p. 900)	
Art. 207 Para. 1 Sub-Para. 1...... Shanghai Eastern (p. 889, p. 903, p. 918)	
Art. 209......Hunan Zoomlion (p. 547, p. 585) Shanghai Eastern (p. 887, p. 900, p. 904, p. 905, p. 914)	
Art. 210......Hunan Zoomlion (p. 547, p. 586)	
Art. 216......Shanghai Eastern (p. 915)	
Art. 224......Operating Department (p. 806)	
Art. 229......Wuhan Ling (p. 1175)	
Art. 231......Operating Department (p. 806)	
Art. 232......Hunan Zoomlion (p. 542, p. 580)	
Art. 237......Yantai Maritime (p. 1249, p. 1256)	
Art. 238......Yantai Maritime (p. 1249, p. 1256)	
Art. 244 Para. 1 Sub-Para. 1......Qinhuangdao Heshun (p. 841, p. 848)	
Art. 246......LIN Guihe (p. 703)	
Art. 249......LIN Guihe (p. 703)	
Art. 252......AIG Europe (p. 8) China Ping (p. 205) Shanghai Eastern (p. 887, p. 901, p. 906, p. 908) Yantai Maritime (p. 1260, p. 1261)	
Art. 252 Para. 1......China Ping (p. 203, p.205, p. 208) Hong Kong (p. 449, p. 450) Hunan Zoomlion (p. 548, p. 586) People's Insurance (p. 817) Shanghai Eastern (p. 916)	
Art. 255......LIN Guihe (p. 704)	
Art. 257......China Ping (p. 205) Mund & Fester (p. 777, p. 778)	
Art. 257 Para. 1......A.P. Moller-Maersk (p. 54, p. 67, p. 74) China Ping (p. 205) Mund & Fester (p. 779) Tai-I Jiangtong (p. 1104)	
Art. 264......Yantai Maritime (p. 1248, p. 1255, p. 1261)	
Art. 267......A.P. Moller-Maersk (p. 80) China Ping (p. 209, p. 213)	
Art. 269......Allianz China (p. 39) A.P. Moller-Maersk (p. 53, p. 66) Connexions (Asia) (p. 290, p. 300, p. 306) Hong Kong (p. 447) Mitsui O.S.K. (p. 757) People's Insurance (p. 817, p. 821) Shenzhen COSCO (p. 1038) Tai-I Jiangtong (p. 1103, p.1113) Zhuhai Jia (p. 1316)	

(continued)

(continued)

Art. 271 Para. 1......China Minsheng (p. 194)
Art. 273......Qingdao Hua (p. 828) Shanghai Eastern (p. 886, p. 899)
Art. 277......Allianz China (p. 39))
Maritime Traffic Safety Management Regulations of Fuzhou City
Art. 15......XUE Haibing (p. 1232)
Measures for the Implementation of the Regulations on Work-Related Injury Insurance in Fujian Province
Art. 26......GUO Jiangbao (p. 401)
Art. 27......GUO Jiangbao (p. 401)
Measures on the Payment of Litigation Costs
Art. 6......LIN Guihe (p. 721) WANG Hong (p. 1141)
Art. 10......Shenzhen COSCO (p. 1048)
Art. 10 Sub-Para. 2......Shenzhen COSCO (p. 1048)
Art. 12......LIN Guihe (p. 721)
Art. 13 Para. 1......Changhang Phoenix (p. 130) China Guangfa (p. 178) Chongqing Red (p. 282) Export-Import (p. 361) LIU Fengxi (p. 736) MAO Chuanwu (p. 745) Mund & Fester (p. 780) Nanjing Jinan (p. 787) Suqian Rongxiang (p. 1086) WANG Hong (p. 1141) WU Guangbao (p. 1161) Wuhan Ling (p. 1175) WU Jinya (p. 1191) Zhumadian South (p. 1376)
Art. 14......WANG Hong (p. 1141)
Art. 29 Para. 1......LIN Guihe (p. 721)
Art. 29 Para. 2......Shanghai Eastern (p. 919) Shenzhen COSCO (p. 1048)
Art. 38 Para. 3......Shenzhen COSCO (p. 1040, p. 1048)
No.256 Response to Claim Limitation and Related Questions made by China Insurance Regulatory Commission (CIRC) (1999)
General......Yantai Maritime (p. 1248, p. 1256)
Notice of Liaoning High People's Court on Issuing the Minutes of Meeting for Civil Trial of the Courts in the Province [Liao Gao Fa (2009) No. 120]
General......SHAN Yongzhen (p. 1020, p. 1027)
Notice of the Supreme People's Court on Adjustment of the Jurisdiction and the Scope of Cases Entertained by Dalian, Wuhan and Beihai Maritime Courts
General...... WANG Hong (p. 1128)
Art. 2......Chongqing Red (p. 268) Zhumadian South (p. 1356)
Official Reply of the Supreme People's Court on the Limitation of Action of the Carrier's Claim for Compensation against the Consignor, Consignee, or Holder of the Bill of Lading under Carriage of Goods by Sea
General......A.P. Moller-Maersk (p. 54, p. 67, p. 71, p. 79)
Opinions of Xiamen Labor and Social Security Bureau on Several Issues concerning Coverage of Work-Related Injury Insurance
Art. 3......GUO Jiangbao (p. 401)
Property Law of the People's Republic of China
General......LIN Guihe (p. 697)
Art. 5......China Geology (p. 149, p. 159)

(continued)

(continued)

Art. 23......Shandong Xianglong (p. 874)	
Art. 24......WU Jinya (p. 1190, p. 1191)	
Art. 26......China Geology (p. 150, p. 159, p. 162, p. 168) Shandong Xianglong (p. 874)	
Art. 28......China Geology (p. 166)	
Art. 35......China Geology (p. 151, p. 160, p. 170)	
Art. 39......WU Jinya (p. 1191)	
Art. 106......China Geology (p. 167)	
Art. 106 Para. 1......China Geology (p. 148, p. 158)	
Art. 173......China Guangfa (p. 177)	
Art. 176......China Guangfa (p. 177)	
Art. 179......China Guangfa (p. 177)	
Art. 179 Para. 2......China Minsheng (p. 194)	
Art. 187......Changhang Phoenix (p. 128, p. 129)	
Art. 195......China Guangfa (p. 177)	

Provisions of the National Bureau of Statistics on the Composition of Wages
Art. 4......GUO Jiangbao (p. 400)

Provisions of the Supreme People's Court on Several Issues about the Trial of Cases concerning Marine Insurance Disputes
Art. 1......Yantai Maritime (p. 1260)
Art. 14......AIG Europe (p. 8) China Ping (p. 204) Hunan Zoomlion (p. 542, p.581)
Art. 15......Hunan Zoomlion (p. 542, p. 581)

Provisions of the Supreme People's Court on Several Issues concerning the Application of Law in the Trial of Cases of Disputes arising from Delivery of Goods without Original Bill of Lading
Art. 2......Connexions (Asia) (p. 291, p. 301, p. 307)
Art. 14......Mund & Fester (p. 778)

Provisions of the Supreme People's Court on Several Issues Concerning the Trial of Cases of Disputes over Marine Freight Forwarding
Art. 9......Shanghai Wan (p. 940)
Art. 8......Huayu Electrical (p. 474, p. 480, p. 486)
Art. 10......Huayu Electrical (p. 474, p. 480)
Art. 13......China Transport Groupage (p. 89, p. 98, p. 111)

Provisions of the Supreme People's Court on Several Issues concerning the Trial of Injury Insurance Administrative Cases
Art. 3 Para. 1 Sub-Para. 4......MAO Chuanwu (p. 744)
Art. 3 Para. 2......MAO Chuanwu (p. 744)

Provisions of the Supreme People's Court on Some Issues Concerning the Trial of Cases of Disputes over Letter of Credit
Art. 8......Mund & Fester (p. 774)

Provisions of the Supreme People's Court on the Sealing, Seizure and Freezing of Property in the Civil Enforcement of the People's Court
General......China Geology (p. 162)
Art. 8......China Geology (p. 166)
Art. 26......China Geology (p. 162)
Art. 26 Para. 3......China Geology (p. 167)

(continued)

(continued)

Provisions of the Supreme People's Court on the Trial of Certain Issues in Cases of Disputes over Collision of Ships
Art. 4......Hong Kong (p. 448, p. 449, p. 450) Qingdao Huashun (p. 828) XUE Haibing (p. 1238)
Art. 6..,....Shanghai Eastern (p. 912)
Art. 11......Shanghai Eastern (p. 910)

Provisions of the Supreme People's Court on the Trial of Compensation for Property Damage in Cases of Collision and Contact of Ships
Art. 3 Para. 2......XUE Haibing (p. 1234, p. 1235, p. 1236)
Art. 7......XUE Haibing (p. 1237)
Art. 9 Para. 1......Shanghai Eastern (p. 917)
Art. 12......Yue Hai (p. 1304)
Art. 13......XUE Haibing (p. 1237)
Art. 16 Para. 6......XUE Haibing (p. 1236)
Art. 16 Para. 7......XUE Haibing (p. 1237)

Regulations for Safe Navigation in the Waters of the Pearl River Estuary
Art. 8......Hong Kong (p. 441, p. 448)

Regulations Made by the Supreme People's Court for the Application of Laws relating to Hearing the Taiwan-related Civil and Commercial Cases
Art. 1......XUE Haibing (p. 1231)

Regulations of the People's Republic of China Governing the Registration of Ships
General......LIN Guihe (p. 697, p. 720)

Regulations on the Handling of Medical Accidents
Art. 50 Sub-Para. 11......SHAN Yongzhen (p. 1020, p. 1027)

Regulations on the Management of Shipboard Electronic Chart System and Automatic Identification System Equipment for Domestic Sailing Ship
General......Qinhuangdao Heshun (p. 856)
Art. 19......Qinhuangdao Heshun (p. 839, p. 847, p. 851, p. 857)
Art. 21......Qinhuangdao Heshun (p. 849, p. 852, p. 855, p. 857)

Regulations on Work-Related Injury Insurance
General......GUO Jiangbao (p. 399, p. 400)
Art. 33 Para. 1......GUO Jiangbao (p. 400, p.402)
Art. 37 Para. 1 Sub-Para. 2......GUO Jiangbao (p. 402)
Art. 37 Para. 2......GUO Jiangbao (p. 400)

Reply of the China Insurance Regulatory Commission on the Definition of Illegal Acts as Excluded Liabilities in Insurance Clauses
Art. 3......LIN Guihe (p. 698)

Reply of the Supreme People's Court on How to Determine the Statute of Limitation of Right of Demanding Compensation for Coastal and Inland Waterway Goods Transport
General......Operating Department (p. 807, p. 808)

(continued)

(continued)

Safety Production Act of the People's Republic of China
[Nb. This statute is enacted in 2002, and revised in 2009, 2014 and 2015.]
Art. 23......SHAN Yongzhen (p. 1019, p. 1025)

Several Provisions of the Supreme People's Court concerning the Trial of Dispute Cases in relation to Maritime Compensation Liability Limitation
Art. 7......Shanghai Eastern (p. 903)
Art. 11......Qingdao Huashun (p. 829)
Art. 19......Shanghai Eastern (p. 914)

Some Provisions of the Supreme People's Court on Evidence in Civil Procedures
Art. 2......Allianz China (p. 39) Fan Sen (p. 377) Hunan Zoomlion (p. 548, p. 586) Tai-I Jiangtong (p. 1106) Xiamen Yida (p. 1203)
Art. 27 Para. 1......LIN Guihe (p. 715, p. 716, p. 717, p. 730)
Art. 29......LIN Guihe (p.712)
Art. 71......LIN Guihe (p. 718, p. 729)
Art. 41......Hainan Weilong (p. 427)
Art. 74......Allianz China (p. 39)
Art. 76......Hunan Zoomlion (p. 548, p. 586)
Art. 77......Zhuhai Xiangzhou (p. 1341)

Some Provisions of the Supreme People's Court on the Scope of Cases to be Entertained by Maritime Courts
Art. 1......Hong Kong (p. 447) Shanghai Eastern (p. 885, p. 898)
Art. 2 Para. 11......Tai-I Jiangtong (p. 1103)
Art. 11......A.P. Moller-Maersk (p. 53, p. 66) Connexions (Asia) (p. 290, p. 300)
Art. 16......Shenzhen COSCO (p. 1038)

Special Maritime Procedure Law of the People's Republic of China
Art. 2 Para. 3......Shenzhen COSCO (p. 1038)
Art. 6 Para. 1......Tai-I Jiangtong (p. 1103)
Art. 6 Para. 2 Sub-Para. 2......Xiamen Yida (p. 1200)
Art. 6 Para. 2 Sub-Para. 5 ......LIU Fengxi (p. 732)
Art. 19......Daewoo Shipbuilding (p. 346)
Art. 93......China Ping (p. 204, p. 205) Hong Kong (p. 449, p. 450) People's Insurance (p. 817) Shanghai Eastern (p. 916)
Art. 95......Hunan Zoomlion (p. 541, p. 580)
Art. 116......Daewoo Shipbuilding (p. 346, p. 347) Yue Hai (p. 1306)

Special Operation Directory of the Provisions on the Examination and Management of Safety Technical Training for Special Operation Personnel (No.30 Decree of the State Production Safety Supervision and Administration)
Art. 2.1......SHAN Yongzhen (p. 1019, p. 1026)

The People's Republic of China GB/T11253-2007
General...... Mund & Fester (p. 766, p. 767, p. 776)

The People's Republic of China GB/T5526
General......People's Insurance (p. 814)

(continued)

(continued)

The People's Republic of China GB/T17411:2012
General......Fujian Guanhai (p. 386, p. 387)

Tort Liability Law of the People's Republic of China
General......LI Xuelan (p. 677) Operating Department (p. 808)
Art. 2......WANG Hong (p. 1140)
Art. 6......COSCO Container (p. 330)
Art. 6 Para. 1......Yue Hai (p. 1294, p. 1306)
Art. 16......LI Xuelan (p. 685)
Art. 18 Para. 2......LI Xuelan (p. 685)
Art. 26......WANG Jun (p. 1151)
Art. 34......Hong Kong Everglory (p. 437)
Art. 65......WANG Jun (p. 1148, p. 1151)
Art. 66......WANG Jun (p. 1148, p. 1151)

Vessel's Minimum Safety Manning Regulation
General......LIN Guihe (p. 695)
Art. 5......Qingdao Huashun (p. 827)
Art. 7......Qingdao Huashun (p. 827)
Art. 15......Qingdao Huashun (p. 827)

International Conventions and Customs

International Convention for the Unification of Certain Rules of Law Relating to Bills of Lading 1924 (Hague Rules)
Art. 4 Sub-Para. 5......Allianz China (p. 37)

International Convention on Standards of Training, Certification, and Watchkeeping for Seafarers (the STWC Convention)
Chapter 8......Qingdao Huashun (p. 827)

International Hydrographic Organization S-57
General......Qinhuangdao Heshun (p. 839, p. 847, p. 851, p. 857)

International Regulations for Preventing Collisions at Sea, 1972 (COLREG)
General......Qingdao Huashun (p. 828) Shanghai Eastern (p. 903, p. 904) XUE Haibing (p. 1232, p. 1234)
Art. 2 Para. 1......Hong Kong (p. 441, p. 448)
Art. 5......Hong Kong (p. 441, p. 442, p. 448) Qingdao Huashun (p. 827)
Art. 6......Hong Kong (p. 441, p. 442, p. 448) Qingdao Huashun (p. 827) Shanghai Eastern (p. 904, p. 913)
Art. 7......Qingdao Huashun (p. 827)
Art. 8......Shanghai Eastern (p. 904)
Art. 8 Para. 1......Hong Kong (p. 441, p. 448) Shanghai Eastern (p. 907, p. 913)
Art. 9......Qingdao Huashun (p. 828)
Art. 10......Shanghai Eastern (p. 903)

(continued)

(continued)

Art. 10 Para. 1......Shanghai Eastern (p. 907, p. 913)
Art. 13......Qingdao Huashun (p. 827)
Art. 15......Qingdao Huashun (p.827) Shanghai Eastern (p. 907, p. 913)
Art. 16......Shanghai Eastern (p. 904, p. 913)
Art. 17......Shanghai Eastern (p. 913)
Art. 17 Para. 1 Sub Para 2......Shanghai Eastern (p. 907)
Art. 19......Qingdao Huashun (p.827, p. 828)
Art. 34......Shanghai Eastern (p. 904, p. 913)
Art. 35......Qingdao Huashun (p.827)
Art. 35 Para. 1......Hong Kong (p. 441, p. 442, p. 448)

ISO8217:2012
General......Fujian Guanhai (p. 383, p. 386)

Protocol to Amend the International Convention for the Unification of Certain Rules of Law Relating to Bills of Lading 1968 (Hague-Visby Rules)
General......Mund & Fester (p. 778, p. 779)
Art. 2......Allianz China (p. 37)
Chapter IV......Mund & Fester (p. 778)

United Nations Convention on the Carriage of Goods by Sea 1978 (Hamburg Rules)
Art. 6 Sub-Para. 1(a)......Allianz China (p. 37)

Chinese Judgments

(2007) Guang Hai Fa Chu Zi No. 332-3 Civil Ruling......LIN Guihe (p.696)
(2008) Guang Hai Fa Chu Zi No. 234-3 Civil Judgment......LIN Guihe (p. 710, p. 712, p. 713)
(2008) Qing Hai Fa Hai Yan Shang Chu Zi No. 46 Civil Judgment......Yantai Maritime (p. 1246, p. 1253, p. 1260)
(2009) Guang Hai Fa Chu Zi No. 4......Shanghai Eastern (p. 884, p. 897, p. 909, p. 910)
(2009) Guang Hai Fa Chu Zi No. 116......Shanghai Eastern (p. 884, p. 897)
(2009) Guang Hai Fa Chu Zi No. 292......Shanghai Eastern (p. 884, p. 897, p. 909, p. 910)
(2009) Yue Gao Fa Min Si Zhong Zi No. 267 Civil Ruling......Shanghai Eastern (p. 884. P. 897)
(2010) Hai Xing Chu Zi No. 661......LIN Guihe (p. 696)
(2010) Yue Gao Fa Min Si Zhong Zi No. 86 Civil Judgement......Shanghai Eastern (p. 884, p. 886, p. 889, p. 897, p.899, p. 902, p. 906, p. 909, p. 910, p. 911)
(2010) Yue Gao Fa Min Si Zhong Zi No. 87 Civil Judgement......Shanghai Eastern (p. 884, p. 886, p. 889, p. 897,p. 899, p. 902, p. 906, p. 909, p. 910, p. 911)
(2012) Hui Zhong Fa Xing Yi Zhong Zi No. 111 Criminal Ruling......LIN Guihe (p. 692, p. 696)
(2012) Jin Hai Fa Shang Chu Zi No. 836......Shandong Xianglong (p. 871)
(2012) Min Ti Zi No. 142 Civil Judgment......Shanghai Eastern (p. 907, p. 909, p. 910, p. 911, p. 914)
(2013) Jin Hai Fa Shang Chu Zi No. 310 Civil Judgment......Shanghai Yizhou (p. 984)

(continued)

(continued)

(2013) Wu Hai Fa Shang Zi No. 00264 Civil Judgment......MAO Chuanwu (p. 741, p. 743)	
(2013) Xia Hai Fa Shang Chu Zi No. 333 Civil Judgment......ZHONG Kangqiu (p. 1396, p. 1398, p. 1402)	
(2013) Zhe Hai Zhong Zi No. 72 Civil Judgment......Huayu Electrical (p. 486)	
(2014) Guang Hai Fa Chu Zi No. 704 Civil Judgment......Connexions (Asia) (p. 294)	
(2014) Hai Fa Zhi Zi No. 1 of Civil Ruling...... ZHONG Kangqiu (p. 1398, p. 1402)	
(2014) Hai Fa Zhi Zi No. 1-2 of Civil Ruling......ZHONG Kangqiu (p. 1398)	
(2014) Hai Fa Zhi Zi No. 3 Executive Ruling......ZHONG Kangqiu (p. 1402)	
(2014) Hong Min Wu (Shang) Chu Zi No. 554 Civil Judgmen......Operating Department (p. 800)	
(2014) Min Shen Zi No. 2229 Civil Ruling...... Connexions (Asia) (p. 310) Huayu Electrical (p. 485)	
(2014) Qing Hai Fa Deng Zi No. 168 Civil Ruling......Qingdao Huashun (p. 824, p. 825)	
(2014) Wu Hai Fa Shi Zi No. 00040 Civil Ruling......WANG Hong (p. 1128)	
(2014) Xia Hai Fa Ren Zi No. 13 Civil Ruling......Daewoo Shipbuilding (p. 340, p. 345)	
(2014) Xia Hai Fa Ren Zi No. 14 Civil Ruling......Daewoo Shipbuilding (p. 340, p. 345)	
(2014) Yue Gao Fa Min Si Zhong Zi No. 122 Civil Judgment......LIN Guihe (p. 728)	
(2015) Min Min Zhong Zi No. 319 Civil Ruling......Xiamen Yida (p. 1194)	
(2015) Min Shen Zi No. 559 Civil Ruling......A.P. Moller-Maersk (p. 77)	
(2015) Wu Hai Fa Bao Zi No. 00149 Civil Ruling......Changhang Phoenix (p. 123)	
(2016) Zui Gao Fa Min Shen No. 1885 Civil Ruling......China Transport Groupage (p. 108)	

Foreign Legislation and Judgments

Arbitration Act 1996 of the United Kingdom
General......Daewoo Shipbuilding (p. 343, p.344, p. 345)

Britain Law of Property Act 1925
Art. 136......Shandong Xianglong (p. 871, p. 875)

Maritime Law of the Republic of Panama (the 5th Version of 2008)
Art. 244......Daewoo Shipbuilding (p. 346)
Art. 260......Daewoo Shipbuilding (p. 346)

United States Carriage of Goods by Sea Act 1936 (COGSA)
General......Connexions (Asia) (p. 286, p. 288, p. 291, p. 296, p. 298, p. 301, p. 311)

Shanghai Maritime Court
Civil Judgment

AIG Europe Ltd.
v.
Shanghai Heming Shipping Service Co., Ltd. Tianjin Branch et al.

(2014) Hu Hai Fa Shang Chu Zi No.116

Related Case(s) None.

Cause(s) of Action 202. Dispute over contract of carriage of goods by sea or sea-connected waters.

Headnote Carrier held entitled to limit its liability for damage to valuable cargoes because there was insufficient evidence of an act or omission of the carrier with the intent to cause such loss, damage or delay recklessly and with knowledge that such loss or damage would probably be resulted.

Summary The Plaintiff, AIG Europe Ltd., filed this action against the Defendants, Shanghai Heming Shipping Service Co., Ltd. Tianjin Branch and Shanghai Heming Shipping Service Co., Ltd., after invoking its right of subrogation after fulfilling its insurance obligations to IBA Beijing. IBA Beijing contracted with the Defendants to transport a set of cyclotron from Tianjin to Montreal. During transit to the vessel, the main engine fell from the truck and was severely damaged. The court found that the Defendants had born responsibility of IBA Beijing's goods and that a contract of carriage of goods existed. Consequently, the court ordered the Defendants to remunerate the Plaintiff. However, the court found that the Defendants were entitled to a limitation of liability in the amount of 81,212.82 USD because the Plaintiff did not submit any evidence to prove that the damage to the goods involved was caused by an act or omission of the carrier with the intent to cause such loss, damage or delay recklessly and with knowledge that such loss or damage would probably be resulted, so the Defendant Heming Tianjin was entitled to the limitation of liability that the carrier enjoyed.

Judgment

The Plaintiff: AIG Europe Ltd.
Domicile: London, UK.
Legal representative: Jos Stockbroekx, claim settlement manager of marine transportation insurance.
Agent *ad litem*: ZHANG Qin, lawyer of Shanghai Sloma & Co.
Agent *ad litem*: ZHOU Zhiwen, lawyer of Shanghai Sloma & Co.

The Defendant: Shanghai Heming Shipping Service Co., Ltd. Tianjin Branch
Domicile: Tianjin, the People's Republic of China.
Person in charge: WEI Wei, manager.

The Defendant: Shanghai Heming Shipping Service Co., Ltd.
Domicile: Hongkou District, Shanghai City, the People's Republic of China.
Legal representative: ZHU Guoyou, general manager.
Agent *ad litem*: XIA Xiaoping, lawyer of Shanghai Boss & Young Law Firm.
Agent *ad litem*: YIN Yue, lawyer of Shanghai Boss & Young Law Firm.

With respect to the case arising from dispute over contract of carriage of goods by sea, the Plaintiff AIG Europe Ltd. filed an action against the Defendants Shanghai Heming Shipping Service Co., Ltd. Tianjin Branch (hereinafter referred to as Heming Tianjin) and Shanghai Heming Shipping Service Co., Ltd. (hereinafter referred to as Heming Company) before the court on February 13, 2014. The court accepted the case on the same day, organized the collegiate panel according to the law, and held a hearing in public on September 19. Lawyer ZHANG Qin, agent *ad litem* of the Plaintiff, Lawyers XIA Xiaoping and YIN Yue, joint agents *ad litem* of the two Defendants, Heming Tianjin and Heming Company, appeared in court to attend the hearing. Now the case has been concluded.

The Plaintiff alleged that in May 2012, Ion Beam Applications (Beijing) Co., Ltd. (hereinafter referred to as IBA Beijing), person not involved, entrusted the Defendant Heming Tianjin to carry a set of cyclotron (7 packages in total) from Tianjin port in China to Montreal in Canada by sea. Heming Tianjin was to arrange for the carriage of goods involved by sea and relevant inland transport. On June 24, 2012, Heming Tianjin arranged for the transport of the flat rack container (No. HLXU3683746) which loaded the main engine of this set of equipment to the designated transit container station for shipment. During that transport, the goods fell from the carrier's vehicle. On June 26 and July 4 in the same year, all the parties including IBA Beijing, person not involved, Shenzhen Wanyi Mclarens Insurance Assessment Co., Ltd. Shanghai Branch (hereinafter referred to as Mclarens) and the Defendant Heming Tianjin carried out a joint survey on the damaged main engine of the equipment. According to the monitoring report issued by IBA Beijing and the assessment report issued by Mclarens, the main engine of the equipment was seriously damaged and could not be repaired, thus identified as a total loss, which was assessed as EUR332,656.96. Since the Plaintiff underwrote the goods transportation insurance for the aforementioned equipment, the Plaintiff got the insurer's right of subrogation according to the law after payment according to the insurance contract. The Plaintiff claimed that the damage to the goods happened in the period of responsibility of the Defendant Heming Tianjin, and in view of the fact that Heming Tianjin was a non-independent accounting branch of Heming, the Defendants Heming Tianjin and Heming Company should undertake joint and several liability, thus the Plaintiff requested the court to sentence the two Defendants to pay its loss in sum of EUR332,656.96 and the litigation costs.

The Defendant Heming Tianjin argued as follows: 1. the goods involved were actually carried by the transport company entrusted by the shipping company, which had nothing to do with the Defendant; 2. according to the agreement of the insurance contract, the Plaintiff did not have the capacity to recourse; 3. evidence submitted by the Plaintiff could not fully prove the actual value of the goods; 4. although the Defendant needed to indemnify the loss, it should be entitled to the limitation of liability for maritime claims; 5. the expense of re-shipment of the goods involved should be offset from the amount of compensation the Plaintiff claimed.

The Defendant Heming Company argued that although it was the parent company of Heming Tianjin, it did not conclude any shipping contract with the Plaintiff, nor did it know the aforesaid incident, so it should not bear joint and several liability.

The evidence adduced by the Plaintiff, cross-examination of the two Defendants and confirmation of the court are as follows:

1. A sample of bill of lading and the container loading table of the goods involved, to prove the relationship of contract of carriage of goods by sea between the insured IBA Beijing and the Defendant Heming Tianjin. The two Defendants recognized the authenticity and legality of the evidence. Heming Tianjin admitted that it took charge of the carriage of goods and recognized the relationship of contract of carriage of goods with IBA Beijing. Heming Company held that the evidence could not prove it established a contract of carriage with IBA Beijing. The court holds that in this group of evidence, the sample of bill of lading and the container loading table were not officially issued, whose contents cannot prove all the claims held by the Plaintiff in the contract of carriage of goods by sea. Since Heming Tianjin recognized the relationship of contract of carriage of goods by sea with IBA Beijing, so the authenticity and legality shall be confirmed, and the probative force of the contents recognized by Heming Tianjin shall be confirmed.
2. The statement of the accident involved issued by the Defendant Heming Tianjin, to prove that the damage to the goods involved happened during the period of responsibility of the Defendant. The two Defendants held that since the Plaintiff did not provide any original, they did not recognize the authenticity, legality or relevancy of the evidence, but recognized that the goods involved fell off at Tianjin Port when being carried from Beijing to Tianjin. The court holds that although the Plaintiff did not provide the original of evidence 2, the statement of

the accident complied with the admission of the Defendant Heming Tianjin that the goods fell off during the carriage, and there was a signature and seal of Heming Tianjin on the copy without stating the cause of the accident, so the court confirms the authenticity, legality and relevancy of the evidence.

3. The packing list and proforma invoice of the goods involved issued by IBA Beijing, to prove the value of goods involved. The two Defendants cross-examined and held that the packing list and proforma invoice were edited and printed by the insured of the Plaintiff itself and did not recognize the authenticity, legality and relevancy. The court holds that the aforesaid evidence can mutually corroborate evidence 4 of notice of claim, evidence 5 of assessment report and evidence 6 of e-mail, and the probative force of this group of evidence shall be confirmed.

4. Notice of claim that IBA Beijing sent to the Plaintiff, to prove that the insured applied for claim to the Plaintiff. The two Defendants recognized the authenticity, legality and relevancy of the evidence. The court holds that notice of claim is the original and the two Defendants raised no objection to the authenticity, legality and relevancy thereof, so the court confirms the probative force of the evidence.

5. Insurance business license of Mclarens, qualification license of assessor and 2 assessment reports, to prove the value and loss of the goods involved. The two Defendants raised no objection to the authenticity of the evidence, but argued that the Plaintiff submitted the qualification license of one assessor only, therefore the qualification was objected. In addition, the two Defendants alleged they did not participate in the survey, so they were contentious about the probative force of the assessment report. The court holds that since this group of evidence are original documents and the evidence the Plaintiff provided could be prima facie evidence to prove the qualification of Mclarens. Despite the objection raised by the Defendants, they did not provide evidence to the contrary, so the court confirms the authenticity and legality of this group of evidence, and as for the content, it shall be subject to the evidence.

6. Emails with regard to the insurance claim between the Plaintiff and the two Defendants, to prove that the agent of the two Defendants agreed to undertake the responsibility and compensate within the limitation of liability. The two Defendants raised no objection to the authenticity or legality of the evidence, but did not recognize its relevancy. The two Defendants held that the evidence was formed before the Plaintiff filed the suit before the court, and it was the declaration of will of the two Defendants on basis of friendly commercial relationship regardless of the damages and the amount of loss of goods, which did not mean that the two Defendants recognized the damages and the amount of loss of goods. The court confirms the authenticity and legality of this evidence. As for the content, it shall be subject to the evidence.

7. Insurance contract and translation of part of the insurance contract, to prove that the goods involved were underwritten by the Plaintiff, and IBA Beijing was the insured. The two Defendants raised no objection to the authenticity and legality of the evidence, but held the Plaintiff was a co-insurer under the insurance

contract, covering 50% share, so the compensation should be recovered in proportion to the percentage which the Plaintiff insured. The court confirms the authenticity and legality of this evidence. The content shall be subject to the evidence.

8. Statement issued by IBA Beijing, the letter of subrogation that IBA Beijing issued to the Plaintiff and insurance compensation payment voucher of the Plaintiff, to prove that the Plaintiff compensated EUR316,830.39 to the insured according to the insurance contract and, thus entitled to the right of subrogation of the goods involved according to law. The two Defendants raised no objection to the authenticity, legality or relevancy of the evidence except the scope of subrogation. They held that according to the insurance contract, the Plaintiff as a co-insurer only underwrote 50% of the insurance involved, who could only have right of recourse against the Defendant Heming Tianjin within its insurance coverage. The court holds that since the statement and letter of subrogation issued by IBA Beijing are original, and the insurance compensation payment voucher provided by the Plaintiff can be verified, the court confirms the authenticity, legality and relevancy of this evidence.

9. Statement concerning the situation that IBA Beijing sent another piece of equipment to the buyer after the damage happened, and corresponding bill of lading, customs declaration, packing list and invoices, to prove the value of the goods involved. The two Defendants raised no objection to the authenticity of the statement, but held that it was a self-stated material, and they did not recognized the authenticity of other evidence since that was duplicate and irrelevant to this case. The court holds that the aforesaid evidence was provided by the insured of the Plaintiff, which mutually corroborates other evidence, so the probative force shall be confirmed.

The evidence adduced by the two Defendants, cross-examination of the Plaintiff and confirmation of the court are as follows:

A statement of claim and 5 invoices, to prove the disbursement in sum of RMB31,520 paid by the Defendant Heming Tianjin incurred by re-transport of relevant goods. The Plaintiff raised no objection to the authenticity or legality of the evidence, but held that the expenses arising from the return transport to the factory after the accident happened did not fall into the amount of loss of goods as well as the scope of compensation by the Plaintiff, there was no deduction, so the Defendant Heming Tianjin should claim in another action. The court confirms the authenticity and legality of this group of evidence but not the relevancy.

In conclusion of the analysis of the effective evidence aforesaid, combined with the investigation in court, the court finds the facts as follows:

In June 2012, IBA Beijing entrusted the Defendant Heming Tianjin to carry a set of particle accelerator from Tianjin port in China to Montreal in Canada, and to handle the international carriage by sea and relevant inland transport of the goods involved. On June 12, 2012, Heming Tianjin loaded 7 wooden cases into a 20' flat rack container No.HLXU3683746 and a 20' standard container No.FCIU4714006 from IBA Beijing and carried the containers to the container station of Jinri

Container Service Co., Ltd. (hereinafter referred to as Jinri) for shipment. On June 24, 2012, after loading the container in which the main engine laid, due to the trailer's turning, the flat rack container loading the main engine of the equipment overturned from the trailer, giving rise to the damage to assembly of accelerator (main part of the particle accelerator). On June 26 and July 4 in the same year, the shipper IBA Beijing, Mclarens, Jinri and Heming Tianjin sent staff to carry out a joint survey on the damaged main engine of the equipment. According to the assessment report issued by Mclarens, the overturned main engine was seriously damaged and could not be repaired in light of the technical report from the experts from the headquarter in Belgium of IBA Beijing. In analysis of various factors including value of the main part, added-value tax and additional expenses of the damaged goods, the loss reserve was advised to beEUR332,656.96.

On October 24, 2006, the Plaintiff AIG Europe Ltd. concluded the marine insurance policies No.110, No.120 with IBA Beijing, which took effect on January 1, 2007. On August 10, 2007, upon agreement of the parties to the original insurance policy, IBA Beijing was identified as one of the co-insurers. The insurance policy was concluded in Brussels, and took effect at 0000 on July 25, 2007. It was agreed in article 7.7 of the insurance policy that "the duration of the insurance policy is one year, if no registered mail is sent to MARSH S.A within 60 days before the expiration of each year to terminate the contract, it is presumed as a renewal for one year more annually". The insurers under the insurance policy were the Plaintiff and other three insurance companies. The insurance share of the Plaintiff was 50%, and that of other three insurance companies was 50% in total. According to article 7.1.1 of the principal insurer terms, "co-insurance companies promise to keep the decisions made by the principal insurer and agree that 'the principal insurer' shall apply to this company or the principal insurer and the agent or representatives as well. Any decisions made by the principal insurer shall be deemed as decisions made by co-insurance companies and cannot be revoked by them. No objection in any way can be raised thereto". Article 8.6 of the insurance policy agreed that the maximum insurance amount of every transport article was EUR7,500,000. Article 8.10 of the insurance policy agreed the percent of deductible was 5% of the loss, no more than EUR12,500.

After the accident happened, the Plaintiff paid EUR316,830.39 as the actual compensation for the insurance accident to IBA Beijing on November 30, 2012 as recommended in the insurance assessment report after deducting the deductible and insurance brokerage fee. IBA Beijing recognized that it agreed and instructed the Plaintiff to pay the insurance compensation to its parent company, namely IBA S.A. On October 29, 2012, IBA Beijing sent the letter of subrogation to the Plaintiff, recognizing that the insurer had compensated the loss of the circular accelerator C18-9 involved in sum of EUR332,656.96. IBA Beijing agreed the Plaintiff to subrogate it to exercise its rights and remedy methods.

On July 8, 2012, IBA Beijing exported another set of particle circular accelerator C18-9, whose customs declaration value was EUR415,847.07 through Heming

Company. The destination in the bill of lading was Montreal. Due to the damage of the goods involved, IBA Beijing re-sent a set of particle circular accelerator in the same type.

On May 10, 2013 and May 13, 2013, according to the emails between the agents of the Plaintiff and the Defendants, the two Defendants held that the weight of the goods involved was 26,860 kg, and the compensation was USD81,212.82 subject to limitation of liability. The agent of the Plaintiff held that the limitation of liability should be calculated on the basis of the total weight of 29,500 kg according to the bill of lading. In the trial, the Plaintiff recognized that the limitation of liability could be calculated at USD81,212.82 (26,860 kg*2 SDR* USD1.51178/SDR) per container of weight raised by the Defendant.

The court holds that this case is dispute over contract of carriage of goods by sea and the Plaintiff was a business entity registered abroad. In addition, the discharging port and destination of the carriage were in foreign countries, so this case involves foreign elements. The parties may choose the applicable law. Since the Plaintiff and Defendant in the trial agreed to adopt the law of the People's Republic of China as the applicable law to resolve the dispute of this case. The court confirms the governing law shall be the law of the People's Republic of China.

Upon investigation, the Defendant Heming Tianjin recognized the fact that IBA Beijing, the insured of the Plaintiff IBA, entrusted the Defendant to carry the goods involved. So, a relationship of contract of carriage of goods by sea was established between IBA Beijing and the Defendant Heming Tianjin. After being delivered and loaded by the Defendant Heming Tianjin, the goods were damaged due to overturn of the trailer in the container station. According to the law, the Defendant Heming Tianjin, as the carrier, should be liable for damages happening during the period of responsibility.

The Plaintiff was the cargo underwriter of the carriage of the goods by sea. After the insurance accident happened, the Plaintiff compensated the loss of goods as recognized by the assessment company. According to the insurance policy, the insurance share underwritten by the Plaintiff in the insurance contract was 50%, therefore it was the principal insurer. In the meantime, it was agreed in the insurance policy that any decisions made by the principal insurer could not be revoked by co-insurance companies, and should be deemed as decisions made by themselves, they were not permitted to raise any objection in any way. Therefore, it conformed to the contract as well as the law that the Plaintiff had actually paid the loss of goods involved and acquired the right of subrogation in terms of all the loss of goods involved after getting the letter of subrogation from the insured IBA Beijing. It was lack of factual and legal basis that the two Defendants held that the Plaintiff had no right of subrogation or the right of subrogation should be limited to the share of 50%, and the court does not support it.

As for the value of the goods involved, since the carrier did not declare at the customs after taking over the goods, there was no value of the goods involved stated in the customs declaration. However, the Plaintiff submitted the packing list of goods involved, the name and value of goods on the proforma invoices were totally formed according to those on the bill of lading and the customs declaration that IBA Beijing reissued to the consignee due to the damage to goods. In addition, the report of the assessment company also recognized the actual value of the goods involved, so the court confirms the value of goods the Plaintiff claimed. The two Defendants doubted the value of goods claimed by the Plaintiff, but they did not submit any evidence to the contrary, so the court does not adopt the pleas of the two Defendants.

As for the limitation of liability in the case, the Plaintiff recognized the limitation of liability could be calculated at USD81,212.82 per container of weight of the goods in the trial. Upon investigation, the basis to calculate the limitation of liability adopted by the two Defendants conformed to the objective fact. The court confirms that the limitation of liability is USD81,212.82. The Plaintiff claimed the compensation for the total value of goods, but did not submit any evidence to prove the damage to the goods involved was caused by an act or omission of the carrier with the intent to cause such loss, damage or delay or recklessly and with knowledge that such loss or damage would be probably resulted, so the Defendant Heming Tianjin was entitled to the limitation of liability that the carrier enjoyed. The Defendant Heming Tianjin shall compensate the Plaintiff USD81,212.82 according to the limitation of liability. Since the Defendant Heming Tianjin was a branch of the Defendant Heming Company, according to the law, the Defendant Heming Company shall bear supplementary liability to pay such compensation.

In addition, the Defendants claimed the expenses incurred in the transportation of returning to the factory after the damage to be offset in this case. The court holds that as the Plaintiff did not recognize the allegation, and the two Defendants failed to provide any effective evidence to prove such allegation had factual and legal basis, the court does not support it.

In conclusion, according to the Maritime Code of the People's Republic of China Article 41, Article 46 Paragraph 1, Article 56, Article 59 Paragraph1 and Article 252, the Company Law of the People's Republic of China Article 14 Paragraph 1, the Provisions of the Supreme People's Court on Several Issues about the Trial of Cases concerning Marine Insurance Disputes Article 14, and the Civil Procedure Law of the People's Republic of China Article 64 Paragraph 1, the judgment is as follows:

1. The Defendant Shanghai Heming Shipping Service Co., Ltd. Tianjin Branch shall compensate the Plaintiff AIG Europe Ltd. for the loss of goods in sum of USD81,212.82 within ten days after the judgment comes into effect;
2. The Defendant Shanghai Heming Shipping Service Co., Ltd. shall bear supplementary liability for the obligation of compensation which the Defendant Heming Tianjin shall bear as determined in the aforementioned item;
3. Other Claims of the Plaintiff AIG Europe Ltd. shall not Be Supported.

If the Defendants Shanghai Heming Shipping Service Co., Ltd. Tianjin Branch and Shanghai Heming Shipping Service Co., Ltd. fail to fulfill the obligation for payment within the period designated in the judgment, the interest of debt over the delayed period shall be doubled according to the Civil Procedure Law of the People's Republic of China Article 253.

Court acceptance fee in amount of RMB29,021, the Plaintiff AIG Europe Limited shall bear RMB23,806.18, the Defendant Shanghai Heming Shipping Service Co., Ltd. Tianjin Branch shall bear RMB5,214.82, and the Defendant Shanghai Heming Shipping Service Co., Ltd. shall bear supplementary liability to pay the sum that the Defendant Shanghai Heming Shipping Service Co., Ltd. needs to bear.

In case of dissatisfaction with this judgment, the Plaintiff AIG Europe Ltd. may within 30 days upon the service of this judgment, the Defendants Shanghai Heming Shipping Service Co., Ltd. Tianjin Branch and Shanghai Heming Shipping Service Co., Ltd. may within 15 days upon the service of this judgment, submit a statement of appeal to the court, together with copies according to the number of the other parties, and appeal to the Shanghai High People's Court.

Presiding Judge: ZHANG Liang
Acting Judge: YANG Fan
Acting Judge: CHEN Lei

January15, 2015

Clerk: JI Xiaoqing

Appendix: Relevant Law

1. **Maritime Code of the People's Republic of China**
   Article 41 A contract of carriage of goods by sea is a contract under which the carrier, against payment of freight, undertakes to carry by sea the goods contracted for shipment by the shipper from one port to another.
   Article 46 The responsibilities of the carrier with regard to the goods carried in containers covers the entire period during which the carrier is in charge of the goods, starting from the time the carrier has taken over the goods at the port of loading, until the goods have been delivered at the port of discharge. The responsibility of the carrier with respect to non-containerized goods covers the period during which the carrier is in charge of the goods, starting from the time of loading of the goods onto the ship until the time the goods are discharged therefrom. During the period the carrier is in charge of the goods, the carrier shall be liable for the loss of or damage to the goods, except as otherwise provided for in this Section.
   Article 56 The carrier's liability for the loss of or damage to the goods shall be limited to an amount equivalent to 666.67 Units of Account per package or other shipping unit, or 2 Units of Account per kilogramme of the gross weight of the

goods lost or damaged, whichever is the higher, except where the nature and value of the goods had been declared by the shipper before shipment and inserted in the bill of lading, or where a higher amount than the amount of limitation of liability set out in this Article had been agreed upon between the carrier and the shipper.

Where a container, pallet or similar article of transport is used to consolidate goods, the number of packages or other shipping units enumerated in the bill of lading as packed in such article of transport shall be deemed to be the number of packages or shipping units. If not so enumerated, the goods in such article of transport shall be deemed to be one package or one shipping unit.

Where the article of transport is not owned or furnished by the carrier, such article of transport shall be deemed to be one package or one shipping unit.

Article 59 The carrier shall not be entitled to the benefit of the limitation of liability provided for in Article 56 or 57 of this Code if it is proved that the loss, damage or delay in delivery of the goods resulted from an act or omission of the carrier done with the intent to cause such loss, damage or delay or recklessly and with knowledge that such loss, damage or delay would probably result.

......

Article 252 Where the loss of or damage to the subject matter insured within the insurance coverage is caused by a third person, the right of the insured to demand compensation from the third person shall be subrogated to the insurer from the time the indemnity is paid.

The insured shall furnish the insurer with necessary documents and information that should come to his knowledge and shall endeavour to assist the insurer in pursuing recovery from the third person.

2. **Company Law of the People's Republic of China**

    Article 14 A company may set up branches. To set up a branch, the company shall file a registration application with the company registration authority and shall obtain a business license. A branch shall not enjoy the status of an enterprise legal person and its civil liabilities shall be born by its parent company.

    ......

3. **Provisions of the Supreme People's Court on Several Issues About the Trial of Cases Concerning Marine Insurance Disputes**

    Article 14

    The people's court that entertains a case involving any dispute over the insurer's exercise of the right of subrogation to claim for compensations shall only try the legal relationship between the third party causing the insurance accident and the insured.

4. **Civil Procedure Law of the People's Republic of China**

    Article 64 A party shall have the responsibility to provide evidence in support of its own propositions.

    ......

Shanghai Maritime Court
Civil Judgment

Allianz China General Insurance Co., Ltd.
v.
Youda (Shanghai) International Freight Co., Ltd. et al.

(2014) Hu Hai Fa Shang Chu Zi No.361

Related Case(s) None.

Cause(s) of Action 202. Dispute over contract of carriage of goods by sea or sea-connected waters.

Headnote Subrogated goods insurer held entitled to recover for damage to goods that had been improperly stowed by multimodal carrier Defendants, but the Defendants held entitled to limit their liability.

Summary The Plaintiff, Allianz China General Insurance Co., Ltd., through subrogation, filed an action against the Defendants, Youda International Freight Co., Ltd. and others, for damage to three radiators and three drivepipes that were received damaged at the port of destination. The Plaintiff argued that improper stacking of the containers resulted in the damage to the goods, but the Defendants argued that improper internal packaging and a storm caused the damage to the goods.

The court held that the goods were packed properly and that the cause of the damage was the stacking of the goods by the Defendants, despite warnings on the boxes not to do so. Further, the court found that although the storm was strong, it was not fierce enough to have been the cause of the ultimate damage to the goods. The court additionally found that the Defendants at fault were entitled to maritime limitation because the improper packing was done without intent or reckless negligence. The court ordered the Defendants to compensate the loss of the damaged goods in the amount of USD16,449.20 and interest to the Plaintiff Allianz China General Insurance Co., Ltd. together within ten days since the judgment came into effect.

Judgment

The Plaintiff: Allianz China General Insurance Co., Ltd.
Domicile: Tianhe District, Guangzhou, Guangdong, the People's Republic of China.
Legal representative: DU Hanshi (HEINZWALTERDOLLBERG), chairman.
Agent *ad litem*: SUN Jingliang, lawyer of Shanghai TZ & CO.
Agent *ad litem*: HUANG Yu, lawyer of Shanghai TZ & CO.

The Defendant: Youda (Shanghai) International Freight Co., Ltd.
Domicile: Huangpu District, Shanghai, the People's Republic of China.
Legal representative: MIRKOKNEZEVIC, chairman.
Agent *ad litem*: LI Yingchun, lawyer of Beijing Dentons (Shanghai) Law Firm.
Agent *ad litem*: WANG Junqun, lawyer of Beijing Dentons (Shanghai) Law Firm.

The Defendant: UTC PROJECTS, INC.
Domicile: Texas, the United States of America.
Legal representative: MIRKOKNEZEVIC, chairman.
Agent *ad litem*: LI Yingchun, lawyer of Beijing Dentons (Shanghai) Law Firm.
Agent *ad litem*: WANG Junqun, lawyer of Beijing Dentons (Shanghai) Law Firm.

The Defendant: AIRPORT CLEARANCE SERVICE, INC.
Domicile: New York State, the United States of America.
Legal representative: EDWARDVAZ, chairman.
Agent *ad litem*: LI Yingchun, lawyer of Beijing Dentons (Shanghai) Law Firm.
Agent *ad litem*: WANG Junqun, lawyer of Beijing Dentons (Shanghai) Law Firm.

The Defendant: CHIPOLBROK COSMOS MARITIME COMPANY LIMITED.
Domicile: Hong Kong Special Administrative Region of the People's Republic of China.
Legal representative: LI Guiying, company secretary.
Agent *ad litem*: YAN Liping, lawyer of Shanghai HighRoyle Law Firm.
Agent *ad litem*: XIE Xianlin, lawyer of Shanghai HighRoyle Law Firm.

With respect to the case arising from dispute over contract of carriage of goods by sea between the Plaintiff Allianz China General Insurance Co., Ltd. and the Defendants Youda (Shanghai) International Freight Co., Ltd. (hereinafter referred to as Youda Co., Ltd.), UTC PROJECTS, INC. (hereinafter referred to as UTC, INC.), AIRPORT CLEARANCE SERVICE, INC. (hereinafter referred to as AIRPORT, INC.), CHIPOLBROK COSMOS MARITIME COMPANY LIMITED (hereinafter referred to as CHIPOLBROK COSMOS), the Plaintiff filed an action before the court on March 4, 2014. The court accepted the case on March 20, 2014 after the Plaintiff finished collecting all materials and organized the collegiate panel to try the case according to the law. The Defendant CHIPOLBROKCOSMOS challenged the jurisdiction during the period of legal pleas, but the court made (2014) Hu Hai Fa Shang Chu Zi No.361 Civil Ruling to reject it on August 7, 2014. Later the

Defendant CHIPOLBROKCOSMOS lodged an appeal, and the Shanghai High People's Court made a Ruling (2014) Hu Gao Min Si (Hai) Zhong Zi No 142 on November 24, 2014 to dismiss the appeal from the Defendant CHIPOLBROKCOSMOS and affirm the original ruling. The court held hearings in public respectively on December 26, 2014 and January 8, 2015. Lawyers SUN Jingliang and HUANG Yu, agents *ad litem* of the Plaintiff, Lawyer LI Yingchun, joint agent *ad litem* of the Defendants Youda Co., Ltd., UTC, INC, and Lawyer YAN Liping, agent *ad litem* of the Defendant CHIPOLBROKCOSMOS appeared in court to attend the hearings. Now the case has been concluded.

The Plaintiff alleged that on December 20, 2012, the insured of the Plaintiff, Shanghai Electric ALSTOM Baoshan Transformer Co., Ltd. (hereinafter referred to as Shanghai ALSTOM Co., Ltd) entered into the contract with the Defendants Youda Co., Ltd. and UTC, INC. and made an agreement that the Defendants Youda Co., Ltd. and UTC, INC. would provide the logistics service of the transformer and related equipment under PH314-01rev00 project. After the equipment being transported, the insured paid the agency fee and freight, and the Defendant Youda Co., Ltd. offered the invoice to the Plaintiff according to the contract. On January 25, 2013, the Defendant UTC, INC. issued the whole set of clean bills of lading No.121-00258 on behalf of AIRPORT, INC. The Defendant CHIPOL BROKCOSMOS was the owner of the ship involved which loaded the goods. After the goods arrived at the port of destination, on March 5, 2013, the insured got the news from the Defendant UTC, INC. that the surface of five wooden containers loading the replacement parts got severely damaged. On March 11, 2013, the insured sent a letter of claim to the Defendant AIRPORT, INC. On September 17, 2013, Shenzhen Wanyi Insurance Adjustors & Surveyors Co., Ltd. (hereinafter referred to as Wanyi Co., Ltd.) issued the initial report. The report described the process of the goods transportation and the inspection of the damaged goods in detail, and then confirmed that there were 3 drivepipes and 5 radiators damaged. Therefore, the insured claimed against the Plaintiff for the compensation of the substitution of goods valued USD76,820, the packing cost of the substitution of goods RMB17,438.90, the expense of the repackaging, the forklift cancellation and the check of the freight forwarding at the port of destination, USD30,000, the inspection fee of the goods USD73,415.90 and the transportation fee of the substitution of goods RMB306,448.60. After the negotiation between the Plaintiff and the insured, the loss of goods was confirmed as follows: the value of the substitution of the goods USD76,820, the packing cost of the substitution of the goods RMB17,438.90, the expense of the repackaging, the forklift cancellation and the check of the freight forwarding of the port of destination USD5,000. The inspection fee of the goods USD50,000 and the transportation fee of the substitution of the goods RMB306,448.60. The report also confirmed that the deductible excess in the insurance contract, RMB83,859, was deducted, and the Plaintiff was suggested to indemnify the insured USD171,038,08. The Plaintiff, as the insurer of the goods involved, was entitled the right of subrogation according to the law after the Plaintiff paid the insurance compensation RMB1,046,547.79 to the insured. The Plaintiff thought that the damage to the goods involved was caused by the four

Defendants' failure to fulfill their obligation properly. Therefore, the four Defendants should assume the responsibility of joint and several compensation. The Plaintiff claimed to the court to adjudge that the four Defendants should compensate the Plaintiff USD171,038.08 and the interests (calculated from March 4, 2014, and based on the interest rate for liquid capital load in RMB over the corresponding period as promulgated by the People's Bank of China, to the date of payment set by this judgment) jointly and severally, and bear the litigation fee for this case together.

The Defendant Youda Co., Ltd. argued that as the agent of the Defendant UTC, INC. during the transportation of the goods, there was not any negligent act of the agent, therefore it should not bear the responsibility.

The Defendants UTC, INC. and AIRPORT, INC. argued that, 1. the Plaintiff's evidence was not enough to prove the asserted loss; 2. even if the goods damage which the Plaintiff asserted really existed, it arose from special risk during the carriage of goods by sea and insufficient internal packaging strength of goods. Taking the reason of the goods damage into consideration, the two Defendants should not bear the responsibility; 3. even if the evidence provided by the Plaintiff could prove the loss, and the two Defendants should bear the responsibility of the loss, the two Defendants should be entitled the package limitation of liability of maritime claims according to the law; 4. the damage to the goods involved happened during the goods transportation by the Defendant CHIPOLBROKCOSMOS. If the two Defendants bore the responsibility, it should be the Defendant CHIPOL BROKCOSMOS who bore the ultimate responsibility.

The Defendant CHIPOLBROKCOSMOS argued that, 1. bad weather, improper internal packaging of the goods and inappropriate custody of goods together led to the damage to the goods. The unsound packaging of the goods was caused by the insured and the inappropriate custody of goods was caused by the Defendant Youda Co., Ltd, UTC, INC. and AIRPORT, INC. Therefore, the Defendant CHIPOL BROKCOSMOS should not bear the responsibility of compensation; 2. the Plaintiff's claim for the items of the damage to goods and the sum lacked the corresponding evidence to support, therefore, the Plaintiff should bear the consequence of failure to prove; 3. even if the Defendant CHIPOLBROKCOSMOS should bear the corresponding responsibility, the Defendant CHIPOL BROKCOSMOS should be entitled the package limitation of liability of maritime claims according to the law.

The Plaintiff submitted evidence to support the claims, the cross-examination of the four Defendants and the confirmation opinions of the evidence of the court are as follows:

1. Contract, appendix and invoice to prove that the insured Shanghai ALSTOM Co., Ltd. entered into the contract with the Defendant Youda Co., Ltd. and UTC, INC. and agreed that the two Defendants would provide the logistics service of the goods involved. After the goods being transported, the insured paid the agency fee and freight and the Defendant Youda Co., Ltd. provided the invoice to the insured. The four Defendants agreed the effect of this set of the evidence, and recognized the facts of the signing of contract, payment of the

freight and the supply of the invoice and thought that Youda Co., Ltd. was the agent of UTC, INC. in China. The court holds that the corresponding facts of the effect of the evidence, the conclusion of the contract, the payment of the freight and supplement of the invoice shall be confirmed because of the four Defendants' recognition. The legal status of each party during the involved transportation will be stated in the reasoning part of judgment in combination with other evidence and the investigation of the facts in trial.
2. Bill of lading, to prove that the Defendant UTC, INC. had issued the involved bill of lading on behalf of the Defendant AIRPORT, INC. The four Defendants recognized the effect of this evidence, but they thought that the signing agent showed in this bill of lading was UTC OVERSEAS, INC., not the Defendant UTC, INC. in the case. Therefore, it did not recognize the purpose of this evidence. The court holds that the effect of the evidence shall be confirmed because of the four Defendants' recognition. The Defendants Youda Co., Ltd., UTC, INC., AIRPORT, INC. (hereinafter especially referred to as three Defendants), recognized in the hearing that the Defendant Youda Co., Ltd. was authorized by UTC OVERSEAS, INC. to take its seal to issue the involved bill of lading. Besides, the Defendant AIRPORT, INC. had subsequently recognize the act of issue. Therefore, the fact that the Defendant Youda Co., Ltd. replaced the Defendant AIRPORT, INC. to issue the involved bill of lading, therefore the fact that the Defendant Youda Co., Ltd. issued the bill of lading involved on behalf of the Defendant AIRPORT, INC. shall be confirmed.
3. Information of vessel registration, to prove that the Defendant CHIPOL BROKCOSMOS was the owner of the vessel of carriage. The four Defendants accepted the effect and the purpose of the evidence. The court holds that the effect and the purpose of the evidence shall be confirmed because of the four Defendants' recognition.
4. Emails between the UTC, INC. and the insured, to prove that the Defendant UTC, INC. had informed the insured of the information that the surface of 5 wooden containers loading equipment got damaged during the transportation of the goods involved. The three Defendants all recognized the effect and the purpose of this set of evidence. The Defendant CHIPOL BROKCOSMOS also recognized the effect of this set of evidence, but argued that according to the provided unloading report, the condition of the damaged goods was inconsistent with the content of this set of evidence. Therefore, it did not recognize the purpose of the evidence. The court holds that the effect of the evidence shall be confirmed because of the four Defendants' recognition, and the purpose of the evidence will be stated in the reasoning part of judgment in combination with other evidence and identification of the facts in trial.
5. Letter of claim, to prove the fact that the insured had sent the letter of claim to the Defendant AIRPORT, INC. The four Defendants all recognized the effect and the purpose of this evidence. The court holds that the effect and the purpose of this evidence shall be confirmed because of the four Defendants' recognition.

6. Wanyi Co., Ltd.'s qualification certificate, the adjustment report and appendixes, to prove that Wanyi Co., Ltd. had the corresponding qualification of adjusting and adjustment report was legal and effective; damage to the goods involved and the process of the inspection; the negotiated sum of the damaged goods was USD171,038.08; the reason of the damage to goods was caused by the four Defendants' failure to fulfill their obligation properly. The three Defendants recognized the effect of the evidence but did not recognize the fact of the goods damage, the assessment of the loss and confirmation, which the evidence is relied on. The Defendant CHIPOLBROKCOSMOS recognized the effect and the purpose of the evidence of qualification certificate, but thought that the adjustment report confirmed incorrectly on the fact of goods damaged, the conclusion of the loss assessment and the each fee of the substitution of goods handling. Therefore, it did not recognize the effect and the purpose of the evidence of adjusting. The court holds that this adjustment report was presented by the subject that had the qualification of adjusting, so the effect of this evidence shall be confirmed. But the purpose of the evidence will be stated in the reasoning part of judgment with combining with other evidence and identification of the facts in trial.
7. Insurance policy, payment voucher and subrogation assignment, to prove that the Plaintiff obtained the corresponding right of subrogation after the Plaintiff indemnified the insured for the loss of RMB1,046,547,79. The four Defendants all recognized the effect and purpose of this evidence. The court holds that the effect and purpose of these evidence shall be confirmed because of the four Defendants' recognition.
8. Customs declaration, to prove that the insured exported goods involved, whose total value was USD5,568, 415.63, in January 2013. The four Defendants all recognized the effect and purpose of this evidence. The court holds that the effect and purpose of this evidence shall be confirmed because of the four Defendants' recognition.
9. E-mail for jointly testing the damaged goods, to prove that the inspector of HENDRICK Shipping Company employed by Wanyi Co., Ltd. had invited the Defendants UTC, INC. and CHIPOLBROKCOSMOS to take a joint inspection on the damaged goods in America. The four Defendants all recognized the effect and purpose of this evidence. The court holds that the effect and purpose of this evidence shall be confirmed because of the four Defendants' recognition.
10. Air invoice of the substitution, confirmation letter of the substitution by air and two of the air consignment notes, to prove that on February 25, 2014, DHL International Air Express Co., Ltd. Shanghai Branch made a phone call to the insured for confirming the fact that the substitution was shipped, it finished sending and the air freight of the substitution was RMB306,448,60. The three Defendants all recognized the authenticity and legality of the evidence but not its relevancy. The number and the weight of the substitution were inconsistent with the contents written in the adjustment report provided by the Plaintiff. The Defendant CHIPOLBROKCOSMOS did not recognize the effect of the evidence because of lack of the air waybill original, but recognized the authenticity

and legality of the invoice and confirmation letter. But this could only prove that the insured had goods sent, failing to prove the relevancy between the sent goods and this case. The court holds that the numbers 7827490484, 8,677,831,444 noted in the invoice was consistent with the number of air consignment and the content remarked in confirmation letter. The goods marked in the consignment note was "H314 drivepipe" and "H314 radiator" and they were corroborated with the project code H314TK020 marked in the detail of transportation contract whose effect was confirmed by each party. The shipper recorded in the waybill was the insured and the consignee was FIRSTSOLAR, which were identical with that recorded in the transportation contract. The aggregate price of the insured goods recorded in the waybill was identical with the sum of the invoice of substitution provided by the Plaintiff. Under the condition of the four Defendants' recognition of the authenticity and the legality of the invoice and confirmation letter, its relevancy with this case shall be confirmed according to its corroboration with other evidence in this case and then the effect of this evidence could be confirmed. According to the content of this evidence, the fact that the insured had sent 3 radiators and 3 drivepipes of H314 project to the final client FIRSTSOLAR by air on July 4, 2013 and August 12, 2013 separately, the air freight was RMB234, 592.80 and RMB71, 855. 80 separately and the total was RMB306, 448. 60 shall be confirmed.

11. Inspection report presented by American HENDRICK Shipping Company, to prove that the Plaintiff had entrusted adjustment report presenter Wanyi Co., Ltd. to employ the HENDRICK Shipping Company to go to the unloading site to inspect and the adjustment inspector Gary Farris of this company went to the site to inspect. According to the result of the inspection at spot during the time from March 15, 2013 to March 21, 2013, it was confirmed that there were 13 wooden containers got damaged; up to June 6, 2013, HENDRICK Shipping Company confirmed that there were 3 high pressure drivepipe and 3 radiators got damaged in total. The four Defendants all recognized the effect of this evidence, but argued that this report was inconsistent with the content of the adjustment report provided by the Plaintiff. So, they did not recognize with the purpose of the evidence. The court holds that the effect of the evidence shall be confirmed because of the four Defendants' recognition, while the purpose of the evidence will be stated in the reasoning part of judgment in combination with other evidence and identification of the facts in trial.

The three Defendants submitted the evidence to support the pleas, the cross-examination of the Plaintiff and the Defendant CHIPOLBROKCOSMOS and the confirmation of the evidence opinion of the court are as follows:

1. Standard bill of lading that the Defendant AIRPORT, INC. had registered in Ministry of Transport of the People's Republic of China, prove that the Defendant AIRPORT, INC. was the legal non-vessel operating common carrier registered in the Ministry of Transport. The Plaintiff and the Defendant CHIPOL

BROKCOSMOS recognized the effect and the purpose of the evidence. The court holds that this evidence shall be confirmed because of each party's recognition.

2. E-mails among the Defendant Youda Co., Ltd., the Defendant UTC, INC. and ALSTOMGRID INC., to prove that ALSTOMGRID INC. had planned to entrust the Defendant UTC, INC. to transport the goods involved on December 18, 2012. Because ALSTOMGRID INC. had paid part of the freight in China on January 7, 2013, Shanghai ALSTOM Co., Ltd. demanded that Youda Co., Ltd. as the Chinese Branch of the Defendant UTC, INC. should be entered into the contract as a party and that the information of the Defendant Youda Co., Ltd. should be filled in the transportation contract. Therefore, the Defendant Youda Co., Ltd. entered into the involved transportation contract was because of the need of payment arrangement and the Defendant Youda Co., Ltd. was actually the agent of the Defendant UTC, INC. The Plaintiff and the Defendant CHIPOL BROKCOSMOS accepted the effect of the evidence. The Plaintiff thought that the content of the e-mails failed to prove that the Defendant Youda Co., Ltd. was the agent of the Defendant UTC, INC. They both were the same side of signing of the contract, therefore, the Plaintiff did not recognize the purpose of the evidence. The Defendant CHIPOLBROKCOSMOS thought that the booking contract was signed by the Defendant Youda Co., Ltd. and Chinese-Polish Joint Stock Shipping Co., Ltd. (hereinafter referred to as Chinese-Polish Shipping). The Defendant Youda Co., Ltd., as the agent, lacked legal basis, therefore, the purpose of this evidence was not recognized. The court holds that the effect of the evidence shall be confirmed because of the Plaintiff's and the Defendant CHIPOLBROKCOSMOS's recognition, while the purpose of the evidence will be stated in the reasoning part of judgment in combination with other evidence and identification of the facts in trial.

3. E-mails between the Defendant Youda Co., Ltd. and the Defendant UTC, INC., to prove that before shipment of the goods involved, Shanghai ALSTOM Co., Ltd. confirmed orally that the parts of the goods involved could be stacked with two layers. The Plaintiff recognized the effect of this evidence, but thought that these emails were nothing more than the emails between the Defendant Youda Co., Ltd. and the Defendant UTC, INC. without the confirmation of Shanghai ALSTOM Co., Ltd., so the Plaintiff thought that the three Defendants had obligation to take care of the goods in an appropriate way as required in the goods packing. Therefore, the Plaintiff did not recognize the purpose of the evidence. The Defendant recognized the effect and purpose of the evidence. The court holds that the effect of the evidence shall be confirmed because of the Plaintiff's and the Defendant CHIPOLBROKCOSMOS's recognition, while the purpose of the evidence will be stated in the reasoning part of judgment in combination with other evidence and identification of the facts in trial.

4. E-mails between the Defendant UTC, INC. and ALSTOMGRID INC., to prove that after the shipment of the goods involved, the Defendant UTC, INC. had sent ALSTOMGRID INC. the shipment report presented by Shanghai Intertek Inspection Service Co., Ltd. (hereinafter referred to as Tianxiang Company) by

email on January 28, 2013. After knowing the condition of the stacking of the goods, ALSTOMGRID INC. did not raise any objection. The Plaintiff recognized the effect of the evidence, but thought that the insured Shanghai ALSTOM Co., Ltd. had no idea about the stacking condition of the goods and the e-mail was sent after the ship sailed. Therefore, the Plaintiff did not recognize the purpose of the evidence. The Defendant CHIPOLBROKCOSMOS recognized both the effect and purpose of the evidence. The court holds that the effect of the evidence shall be confirmed because of the Plaintiff's and the Defendant CHIPOLBROKCOSMOS's recognition, while the purpose of the evidence will be stated in the reasoning part of judgment in combination with other evidence and identification of the facts in trial.

5. Bill of lading, packing list and the e-mails about another carriage of the transformer and parts carried by the three Defendants for ALSTOMGRID INC. and Shanghai ALSTOM Co., Ltd. presented in April, 2013, to prove that ALSTOMGRID INC. was surprised about that the containers which were loaded with parts could not be piled up, while the stacking was normal. Aiming at this carriage, Shanghai ALSTOM Co., Ltd or ALSTOMGRID INC. clearly confirmed that the parts could be stacked with three layers. These parts had also been stacked in the actual transportation. Though the wooden containers that contained the parts were also marked with the sign "No Stacking", it was allowed to be stacked with three layers in fact and they always did so in practice. The Plaintiff recognized the authenticity and legality of this evidence, but thought that this batch of goods was not the one related with this case. The way of packing, tying and fastening was different. Therefore, the Plaintiff did not recognize its relevancy with the case. The Defendant CHIPOLBROKCOSMOS recognized the effect and purpose of the evidence. The court holds that the authenticity and legality shall be confirmed because of the Plaintiff's and the Defendant CHIPOLBROKCOSMOS's recognition. Because the shipping condition of this batch of goods was similar to the one in this case, it had considerable relevancy with this case. The purpose of these evidence will be stated in the reasoning part of judgment in combination with other evidence and confirmation of the facts in trial.

The Defendant CHIPOLBROKCOSMOS presented the evidence to support the pleas, and the cross-examination of other parties and confirmation of the evidence opinion of the court are as follows:

1. Unloading report signed by SSA Port Terminals and the master of M.V. "CHIPOLBROK GALAXY" involved, to prove that when unloading the goods, the goods whose surface were damaged were the containers No.1, 8, 20 of the unit 1, the containers No.19, 22 of the unit 2, and the container No.20 of the unit 3. The Plaintiff recognized the effect of the evidence, but thought that as for the damaged goods involved, apart from what had been confirmed in the unloading report, the damaged parts from the Plaintiff's adjustment report should also be included. The three Defendants all recognized the effect and purpose of the

evidence. The court holds that this evidence was formed abroad, and did not go through the corresponding notarial certification procedures, and the evidence showed that the damaged wooden containers were different from the adjusting report submitted by the Defendant CHIPOLBROKCOSMOS and the fact confirmed in trial. Therefore, the effect of the evidence shall not be confirmed.
2. Booking contract, prove that when the Defendant Youda Co., Ltd. booked the space and chartered the vessel from the Defendant CHIPOLBROKCOSMOS, it was clearly stated that apart from no stacking of the three subject transformers of 159 tons, other goods were all allowed to be stacked and overlain, meanwhile, the Defendant Youda Co., Ltd. declared and recognized that the size of the goods and stacking condition were described correctly in this booking note, or it would be regarded as a false declaration, and the Defendant Youda Co., Ltd. would bear the costs and loss incurred thereof, and the corresponding consequence of the goods stacked with two layers' custody should be assumed by the three Defendants. The Plaintiff recognized both the effect and the purpose of the evidence. And the three Defendants all recognized the effect of the evidence, but not with the purpose of the evidence, because the booking contract was signed by the Defendant Youda Co., Ltd. and Chinese-Polish Shipping, party not involved in the case. The court holds that the effect of the evidence shall be confirmed because of the recognition by the Plaintiff and the three Defendants, and according to the content of this contract, the charter party and the content of the agreements about the goods involved signed by the Defendant Youda Co., Ltd. and Chinese-Polish Shipping shall be confirmed, while other purpose of the evidence will be stated in the reasoning part of judgment in combination with other evidence and confirmation of the facts in trial.
3. Ship management contract between the Defendant CHIPOLBROKCOSMOS and Chinese-Polish Shipping, to prove that the Defendant CHIPOL BROKCOSMOS was the owner of the ship and Chinese-Polish Shipping was the manager of the ship; the authenticity, legality of the booking contract and the relevancy with this case. The Plaintiff and the three Defendants all recognized the effect of this evidence. The Plaintiff recognized the identity of the owner of the ship, and the effectiveness and authenticity of the booking contract, and thought that the Defendant CHIPOLBROKCOSMOS rather than Chinese-Polish Shipping should be the real carrier of the sea transportation section involved. The three Defendants thought that the contract did not stipulate that Chinese-Polish Shipping could sign the charter party on behalf of the Defendant CHIPOLBROKCOSMOS and this contract stated clearly that Chinese-Polish Shipping rent the ship of the Defendant CHIPOL BROKCOSMOS in the way of the time charter and carried on the actual operation, while the booking contract was signed by the Defendant Youda Co., Ltd. and Chinese-Polish Shipping on its own. Therefore, the purpose of the evidence was not recognized. The court holds that the effect of the evidence shall be confirmed for the agreement of the Plaintiff and the three Defendants, while the purpose of the evidence will be stated in the reasoning part of judgment in combination with other evidence and confirmation of the facts in trial.

4. Joint inspection report and appendixes, to prove that SSA America Dock Service Company was the unloading performing party, the situation of the investigation about the reason for the damaged goods, what was showed in general average statement was that the ship suffered bad weather on the way and the bad weather was the main reason for the damage to the goods. The Plaintiff thought that maritime declaration in the appendixes was irrelevant to this case and just accepted the effect of this report. The three Defendants thought that the offshore wind 7-8 level could not form the bad weather, therefore, they did not recognize the purpose of the evidence. The three Defendants recognized the effect of the evidence, but not the purpose of the evidence because the report could not indicate that the unloading performer was the SSA America Dock Service Company. But they recognized other purposes of proof. The court holds that the effect of the evidence shall be confirmed because of the Plaintiff's and the three Defendants' recognition, while the purpose of the evidence will be stated in the reasoning part of judgment in combination with other evidence and confirmation of the facts in trial.
5. Loading list and the custody picture, to prove that the condition of the custody of the goods was consistent with the shipment plan in the shipment report presented by Tianxiang Company and the photo of the shipment custody in the Plaintiff's evidence. Both the Plaintiff and the three Defendants recognized the effect and purpose of the evidence. The court holds that the effect and purpose of the evidence shall be confirmed because of the Plaintiff and the three Defendants' recognition.

According to the analysis and confirmation of the above evidence and materials with the combination of the investigation in the trial, the court finds the facts as follows:

On December 20, 2012, the insured Shanghai ALSTOM Co., Ltd. entered into the contract with the Defendants Youda Co., Ltd. and UTC, INC. The contract stipulated that Defendants Youda Co., Ltd. and UTC, INC should provide the transportation service which was transporting the goods involved from the factory of the insured in Shanghai Baoshan District to the place agreed in the contract (the final client was FIRSTSOLAR and the address was the Desert Center Street 44,810 in California) according to the transportation plan agreed by both sides (including the transportation by land, sea, and rail) and the corresponding price; the service fee and the sea freight at the place of delivery should be paid to Youda Co., Ltd., the fee in destination should be paid to the American account of the Defendant UTC, INC.; the exchange rate of the payment was USD1 = RMB6.33; the specification, weight and quantity of all the goods involved were stated in the appendix, the gross weight of body of the container No.8 loaded with drivepipes in an unit among them was 2,780 kg, the gross weight of the wooden containers loaded with the radiators of each unit was 2,380 kg and the Defendant Youda Co., Ltd. and the Defendant UTC, INC entered into the contract as the joint counterparts in the contract. The insured paid the service fee of the place of delivery USD36,966 and the sea freight USD270,000 to the Defendant Youda Co., Ltd. The Defendant

Youda Co., Ltd. issued the specified VAT invoice with the corresponding content that was "agency fees" as the price. After the hearing, the Plaintiff confirmed in written that the insured Shanghai ALSTOM Co., Ltd. was the supplier of the whole involved equipment and the goods and service they supplied including equipment production, manufacture, transportation, installation and debugging. Meanwhile, the equipment receiver would not been charged for the fee separately for its installation and debugging.

On December 24, 2012, the Defendant Youda Co., Ltd. sent an e-mail to the Defendant UTC, INC. to inform it to confirm with the principle of Shanghai ALSTOM Co., Ltd. about the stacking of the goods as early as possible. On December 26, the Defendant Youda Co., Ltd. informed the Defendant UTC, INC by e-mail that Shanghai ALSTOM Co., Ltd. orally confirmed that the goods could be stacked with two layers. On December 26, the Defendant Youda Co., Ltd. booked from Chinese-Polish Shipping in the form of e-mail, sent it the weight, quantity, specification of the goods and so on, and signed the charter party with Chinese-Polish Shipping. Also, it confirmed that the goods involved could be piled up or stacked except for the three subjects of 159 tons. The Defendant Youda Co., Ltd. made a declaration to confirm the size and stackable situation of the goods, and it would bear the costs and loss resulted thereof. The charter party confirmed that the sea freight was USD250,000.

Afterwards, the Defendant Youda Co., Ltd. issued the bill of lading involved No.121-00,258 whose letterhead was the Defendant AIRPORT, INC. with the signing seal of UTC OVERSEAS, INC. It was stated clearly in the bill of lading that the consignor was the insured Shanghai ALSTOM Co., Ltd., the consignee was the ALSTOMGRID, INC., the notify party was EXACTAINTERNATIONAL, INC., the freight forwarder of the port of the destination was UTC OVERSEAS, INC., the loading port was Shanghai China, the unloading port was LONGBEACH of America, the name of the ship was M.V. "CHIPOLBROK GALAXYV" and the voyage number of the voyage was 11, the quantity was 77, the name of the goods was transformer, the gross weight of the goods was 647,880 kg, the volume of the goods was 1,456.91 CBM, the freight was prepaid, the issuing place was Shanghai and the issuing date was January 25, 2013.

The open marine transportation insurance contract signed by the Plaintiff and the insured stipulated that the period of responsibility was from April 1, 2012 to March 31, 2013. On March 4, 2014, the Plaintiff indemnified the insured Shanghai ALSTOM Co., Ltd. for the insurance claim of RMB1,046,547.79 (namely USD171,038.08) and obtained the right of subrogation.

The information of the involved ship revealed that vessel flag nation was Hong Kong China, the manager of the ship was Chinese-Polish Shipping and the owner of the ship was the Defendant CHIPOLBROKCOSMOS. The Defendant CHIPOL BROKCOSMOS had signed the management agreement with Chinese-Polish Shipping. The management agreement stipulated that all bill Chinese-Polish Shipping should receive according to the management agreement (except the bill that the Defendant CHIPOLBROKCOSMOS should pay to Chinese-Polish Shipping) and interests were all held as the form of independent bank account and the owner should be the Defendant CHIPOLBROKCOSMOS, All the fee of Chinese-Polish Shipping (on behalf of the Defendant CHIPOLBROKCOSMOS) which was according to this agreement should be paid by the Defendant CHIPOL BROKCOSMOS when Chinese-Polish Shipping required.

The Defendant Youda Co., Ltd. confirmed its responsibility for shipment in the trial and the Defendant CHIPOLBROKCOSMOS was responsible for fixing the position and colligation of the goods after the shipment. The Defendant CHIPOL BROKCOSMOS had no objection to this. And the inspection and supervision work of the goods involved before loading, on loading and about fixing was done by Tianxiang Company assigned by the Defendant Youda Co., Ltd. According to the loading inspection report presented by Tianxiang Company on January 27, 2013, it revealed that before loading, the goods had been stacked on the dock with two layers. When shipping, the goods were stacked with two or three layers. The goods were in good condition when shipment, and did not get clearly damaged caused by operation, shipping and colligation in the operation of shipping and reinforcing. The goods were piled up in the container No.3, 4 and 5 listed in the loading plan and colligated by the polyester packing belt, the steel chain and the steel wire rope and was linked with welded D-ring or slot. After the goods were colligated, the chief mate checked the condition of the colligation of the goods and concluded that the goods had been stacked properly and could compete the planned voyage.

On February 13, 2013, when on the sailing, the ship suffered the 8th level of Beaufort wind scale and the 7th level of Beaufort Sea situation for 6 h and this climate made the ship shake and tilt at that time.

On March 11, 2013, Wanyi Co., Ltd. (this company had qualification for survey, inspection, assessing loss and adjustment after suffering a loss of the subject matter insured) accepted the appointment by the Plaintiff to employ the inspector Gary Farris of HENDRICK Shipping Company in America LONGBEACH Harbor to go to the site to inspect the damaged goods. This inspector presented the inspection report on June 6, 2013. Later, according to this inspection report and related materials about changing the damaged parts presented by the insured, the adjustment officer MAO Peijun who held the qualification certificate conferred by China Insurance Regulatory Commission made the adjustment report about the involved damaged goods.

On March 14, 2013, the inspector Gary arrived at the Dock F of the LONGBEACH Harbor SSA and had a first survey. It was clearly stated in the inspection report of HENDRICK Shipping Company that they had received the photos taken before, during and after the unloading provided by the inspector assigned by UTC, INC. The photos revealed that before the unloading, the wooden containers were stacked with two layers and there was a group of wooden containers stacked with three layers. This inspection confirmed that there were 13 wooden containers got damaged physically at various degree. The size, packing design and material of the 77 wooden containers were similar. The marks outside the packing container were similar and taken the unified form. The project goods of various size were fixed to the solid wood base, platform and pallet with the sliding rail. The vertical plane and roof of the packing containers were made up of single panel which were used as the protective cover fixed on the base when assembling. These covers were made up of the timber frame of 2*4, and on the surface of the side or roof panel, there were the single batten were fixed to its top, middle and bottom part with the nail. The inner container packing and its fixing were different according to the goods of various size and collocation. The exterior of many containers loading the goods suffered fierce wallop. Parts of the packing containers loading the radiators were skew and skewed toward one side seriously, even sometimes skewed to two different sides. Though the radiators inside the wood containers were in the condition of serious inclination, they did not move. So it was clearly that the goods were fixed on the base plate or pallet and in a good condition so that the goods could resist the external force suffered in the sailing course.

On March 15, 2013, Gary of HENDRICK Shipping Company was with the inspector James Ackerman on behalf of the SSA Dock of the unloading side, the captain Robert Harris on behalf of the UTC OVERSEAS, INC., the captain CharlesDeeney on behalf of the Shipowner Protection and Indemnity Club and on-site technicians Mark Fry and Mike Vanderoer of ALSTOM, INC. to take a joint inspection on the 13 wood containers whose surfaces were damaged and 6 suspected damaged packing containers on the dock. And after joint inspection, they confirmed that because the goods in the containers needed to be inspected by the special electronic instrument and special technician and needed to be carried to the appointed place safely to repacking, the 19 containers of the goods needed to be transported to the Ancon Marine. The transportation, opening, inspection and repacking of all wood containers had been finished from March 15 to March 20. On March 17, Hampton-Tedder, as the professional company of the high-voltage electric inspection, was invited to inspect as the independent inspection company.

The inspection report of HENDRICK Shipping Company revealed that the wooden containers of the radiators were all stacked with two layers, on the top of them were put a similar wooded container. When suffering the bad weather, the crusts or frames of the lower layer shifted and tilted to the longitudinal side, which caused the crusts of the wooded containers were crushed, deformed and damaged with different degrees. The inspector Gary, in the communication with the technician Mark Fry of ALSTOMINC., knew that the radiators were usually placed in two different designed wooden containers. One was the cover packaging used in the involved transportation, and structure was obvious that the roof and side panels were used as crusts to provide a physical protection for the goods. These boxes did not possess any physical character of enabling to support the goods of any size on the roof. The warning signs could also prove this. The another was the wooden crate of 4*4. This wooden crate was specially designed and produced and could be used to stack the goods with two layers. When loading the goods of similar size or weight, the damage would not happen.

About the container No.8 of the unit 1, each party in the court trial confirmed that it was the complete collapsed when unloading. The inspection report about the condition related to this container of HENDRICK Shipping Company revealed:

On March 15, when each party took the joint inspection at the dock, it was found that the crust of the wooden container was clearly squashed, drop out and deformed, the side panel or wood material was broken, lost and loose and the inner packs was exposed. Multiple wooden crate containers in the container were also squashed and broken at different degree. The goods in containers (high pressure drivepipe) were exposed. The external bodies of the containers were seriously squashed, which made three high pressure drivepipes in the containers squashed at different degree. There was another wooden container laying on the container No.8 and in the second layer. By the conversation with technician Mark Fry of the ALSTOM, it was known that the fin of high-pressure drivepipe was easy to get damaged when suffering serious external forces. If the fin got damaged at any degree, the whole drivepipe should be changed.

On March 17, when Ancon Marine carried on inspection of the site, it was found that this wooden container, as a whole, was transported from the dock to Ancon Marine and the physical shape was the same as the one seen in the port. When the outer panel of the main box was removed, it was found that: 1. a low-pressure drivepipe and a middle pressure drivepipe were placed side by side into two separate smaller containers and the appearances of the two smaller containers were in good condition without apparent damage from striking. Because the nails securing each side and roof of the wooden containers were partly pulled up, it was obvious that the wooden containers had been moved. When the roofs of the two wooden containers were uncovered, it was found the ends of the drivepipes were placed on the wood bases whose shapes were similar as the ends of the drivepipes, and the polyester foam was used as the stuffing. The fixing of the inside was kept in good condition and the break, crack and other physical defects were not seen. 2. There were three high pressure drivepipes placed in the small wooden containers of the same standard respectively. When the loosen panel of the upper container loading the high pressure drivepipes was removed, it was found that the drivepipes and the accessory containers were wrapped by the big polyester fiber chips; the two ends of the drivepipes were sustained by the pedestal made of the wood, the slice cutting was according to different flexibility and the polyfoam was used as the stuffing; wooden frames were used to prevent the drivepipes from moving, the wooden frame was placed inside the wooden box that was on the top, which was flushed with each solid part of the subject of the casing pipe and was between the space of two pedestals; the longitudinal side panels were supported and secured by the lateral wooden frames, this frame was matched with the prefabricated metal suspension pipe which were fixed on the side panel with the nails; the lateral frame were pulled down because of the external force in the accident, and touched the radiator chips of the drivepipes in many places. In the multiple places, the radiator got physically damaged. Besides, the mobile fin assemblies were cut, tore, pierced or deformed. By the photo taken about the lower part of the hinge pin of the drivepipes, it could be confirmed that the number of the high-pressure drivepipes stacked on the top was No.1301246 and the other were respectively No.130244 and No.130245.

It was stated clearly in the analysis and suggestion of the technical service report presented by the Hampton-Tender Company that according to the inspection of statistics, it was found that the insulating layer and high pressure tap of the spare drivepipes No.1301244 were damaged and the main blade was bent; the insulating layer and high pressure tap of the spare drivepipes No.1301245 got damaged; the head of the insulator of the spare drivepipes No.1301246 and the radiator No.15 and No.18 got damaged; the water vapour could enter into the drivepipes when the insulating layer got damaged. Therefore, the Hampton-Tender Company suggested not applying these drivepipes into use.

Each party recognized in the trial that the radiator in the container No.23 of the unit 2 and the container No.19 of the unit 3 respectively got damaged.

Regarding to the container No.23 of the unit 2, HENDRICK Shipping Company had stated in their presented inspection report that the roof of this container fell on the top radiator, the slat of the longitudinal side panels tilted to the same end, the outer radiator chip of the top radiator inside the container got damaged and the radiator of the outside corner had got curved, deformed and was pushed inward. The part of the damaged radiator chip welded to the horizontal bar of the steel bar was tore or cut down from the joint. Because of the contact with the damaged roof and the friction during the sailing, the grey paint of the surface of the horizontal bar of the top radiator had a lot of wear.

Regarding to the container No.19 of unit 3, the inspection report presented by HENDRICK Shipping Company stated: this container was found damaged. The edge of the longitudinal side panels and the roof of the wooden container suffered considerable strike, which led to physical damages to the upper radiator and the damages to the radiator chip. In respect of the inspection of the damaged area, it was confirmed that the 4 radiator chips of the upper corner of one end were depressed severely, bent, twisted, cut or perforated, and 3 of the radiator chips were cut off or torn up.

Regarding to the container No.20 of unit 3, the inspection report presented by HENDRICK Shipping Company stated: the slats of the longitudinal vertical side panel had been inclined to the same end, so it was obvious that the wooden container was loaded underpart. This container was equipped with 3 painted steel radiators. The top wood board dropped on the radiator on the top layer. The slats of the roof and the side panel were inclined in the same direction.

The adjustment report of Wanyi Co., Ltd. provided by the Plaintiff recorded that all inspections had been completed until April 16, 2013. 5 radiators were found suffering the apparent physical damage that could not be repaired. Combined with technical service report presented by Hampton-Tedder Company, it was finally concluded that 3 drivepipes and 5 radiators were damaged and needed to be replaced.

Combined with the inspection report which listed the damaged items needed to replace by the confirmation of the representative of the ALSTOM, in the report of the general statement of the goods damaged of the first solar power desert sun program of the ALSTOM on May 10,2013, HENDRICK Shipping Company eventually confirmed that the damaged goods needed to replace included 3 high pressure drivepipes of the container No.8 in unit one, the each radiator of the container No.23 in unit two and the container No.19 and No.20 in unit three..

The insured transported 3 radiators and 3 drivepipes of H314 project to the final client FIRSTSOLAR by air respectively on July 4th, 2013 and August 12th, 2013.

The causes of the damage written in the inspection report of HENDRICK Shipping Company were that: the loading form of goods (especially stacked in double layers, or three layers) should be part of the root cause of the loss. The radiator containers and other larger wooden containers were not designed and manufactured according to double stacked standard. All the other wooden containers had red warning signs indicating "no other containers can be stacked on the top" except for 5 small wooden accessory containers original piled up in the 206 berth warehouse. The goods which suffered the physical damage were the goods piled up underpart apparently. These goods were damaged because there were other goods stacked on the top of them. The ship suffered from bad weather in voyage. The damaged containers were irrelevancy with the bad weather, but it was unable to determine the damage to the goods was caused by bad weather completely. Considering the gravity and physical strength and combined with monolayer packing of goods, the roof of the bottom container would also be damaged and lead to similar results in the normal/slightly better weather conditions. In the conversation with the inspector of the Shipowner Protection and Indemnity Club, it was told that according to the survey the ship fixing measures might be insufficient, and might form a destructive force. But the inspector who presented the report was not on board, consequently, the details of the ship could not be confirmed.

The inspection report provided by the Defendant CHIPOLBROKCOSMOS which was presented by captain CharlesDeeney, the inspector of the Shipowner Protection and Indemnity Club showed that: ALSTOM often used the container similar to the involved containers to transport goods and everything went well. As for the involved transportation, the containers lacked internal fixation and internal strength especially at the top of the container. Many containers had the sign marked "do not pile up the goods on the top of it", but people ignored these signs in actual transportation. The ship suffered bad weather of the 8th level of Beaufort wind scale and the 7th level of Beaufort Sea situation. Finally, they reached a conclusion that the climate was the main reason for the collapse of the containers, and the reluctant packaging and the internal fixation that was unstable had increased the degree of the damage.

Each party confirmed in court that most of the involved wooden containers were marked with red warning operation signs "do not put other containers on the top of it".

It is also found that Ancon Marine provided the inspection site and the related inspection and test of the involved damaged goods, the transportation from the dock to the inspection site and the repackaging of the goods for the safe transportation to the destination. According to the inspection report of HENDRICK Shipping Company, UTC, INC. received the invoice of the service fee of Ancon Marine and had paid it. The Defendant Youda Co., Ltd. had a written confirmation that ALSTOM received the fee of USD30,000 from UTC OVERSEAS, INC after the hearing.

The court also finds that Alstom Grid Company confirmed that under the condition that UTC, INC. and the carrier ensured that the wooden containers were stacked safely (the heavy containers were at the bottom and the light were on the top, the maximum limit was three layers and ensured proper colligation and support). On April 26, 2013, when the Defendant UTC, INC. provided the similar transportation service to ALSTOM in April 2013.

The court holds that the case is the dispute over contract of carriage of goods by sea. Because the Defendants UTC, INC. and AIRPORT, INC. were the enterprise legal persons registered in the United States of America, the Defendant CHIPOL BROKCOSMOS was the enterprise legal person registered in the Hong Kong Special Administrative Region of the People's Republic of China, and the destination of the goods involved was the LONGBEACH of America, the case was concerned with foreign affairs. According to law, when the parties of the contract reached an agreement, they could choose the applicable law to settle the dispute concerned with foreign contracts. Each party in the trial accepted to adopt the mainland Chinese law, therefore, the court decides to adopt the mainland Chinese law as the applicable law to deal with the dispute in this case.

1. Regarding to the four defendants' legal status in the involved transportation.

Each party recognized that the Defendant UTC, INC. was the multimodal transport operator of the involved transportation, the Defendant AIRPORT, INC. was the carrier of the sea transportation section, and the Defendant CHIPOL BROKCOSMOS was the actual carrier of the sea transportation section. The court confirms this fact. The legal status of the Defendant Youda Co., Ltd. in this involved transportation has become the issue in this case. The three Defendants argued that the Defendant Youda Co., Ltd. was the agent of the Defendant UTC, INC., the multimodal transport operator, while the Plaintiff and the Defendant CHIPOLBROKCOSMOS thought that the Defendants Youda Co., Ltd. and UTC, INC. were both multimodal transport operators. The court holds that it shall be judged comprehensively from the following two aspects.

a. In respect of the nature of the contract, according to the Maritime Code of the People's Republic of China Article 102: "a multimodal transport contract as referred to in this Code means a contract under which the multimodal transport operator undertakes to transport the goods, against the payment of freight for the entire transport, from the place where the goods were received in his charge to the destination and to deliver them to the consignee by two or more different modes of transport, one of which being sea carriage. The multimodal transport operator as referred to in the preceding paragraph means the person who has entered into a multimodal transport contract with the shipper either by himself or by another person acting on his behalf.", the contract signed by the Defendant UTC, INC., the Defendant Youda Co., Ltd. and the insured Shanghai ALSTOM Co., Ltd. made a consensus that the Defendant UTC, INC. and the Defendant Youda Co., Ltd. transported the goods involved from the factory which located in Baoshan District in Shanghai to destination on the contract by providing land, sea and rail transportation services to the insured. They made an agreement on the fright of each section and charged to the insured. Therefore, the contract shall be confirmed as the multimodal transport contract according to the law. As the part of the multimodal transport contract, the Defendant Youda Co., Ltd. and the Defendant UTC, INC signed the contract together. And there was no evidence showing that the Defendant Youda Co., Ltd. expressed that it was the agent of UTC, INC. to the joint counterpart. Therefore, the Defendants Youda Co., Ltd. and the Defendant UTC, INC. should be identified as the multimodal transport operators.

b In respect of the situation of actual performance of the multimodal transport contract, the Defendant Youda Co., Ltd. had received the sea freight of the sea transportation section and the fee of the land transportation happened in Shanghai according to the contract. The Defendant Youda Co., Ltd. also booked to the manager of the involved ship Chinese-Polish Shipping in its own name, and signed the charter party as the joint counterpart of the contract. Consequently, the Defendant Youda Co., Ltd. shall be confirmed as the manager of multimodal transport contract by its action to arrange and fulfill the multimodal transport contract instead of the agent of the Defendant UTC, INC.

2. Regarding to the reason for the damage to the goods involved.

The Plaintiff argued that it was the custody and stowage of the goods and being stacked with two layers that violated the limited warning on the package of the goods in wooden containers that the goods could not be stacked. Apart from this, the improper fixing and colligation, improper carries' management of the goods in the sea transportation section and the actual carrier was another reason. The three Defendants argued that the unfixed internal packaging of the goods, the improper way of fixing and colligation and the bad weather altogether that caused the damage to the goods did not have an inevitable causal relationship with the way of the custody of the goods. The Defendant CHIPOLBROKCOSMOS argued that the improper internal fixing of the wooden containers and bad weather led to the damage to the goods jointly.

a. Regarding to the issue of colligation and fixation.

According to the inspection report presented by HENDRICK Shipping Company provided that provided by the Plaintiff that: the inspectors did not get on board, he or she could not confirm the details of the fixation of the goods. It might be inappropriate to get the conclusion of improper measures, of colligation and the conclusion of destructive force was derived from the conversation with the inspector of the Shipowner Insurance and Indemnity Club. and the inspection report provided by the Defendant CHIPOLBROKCOSMOS was presented by inspectors of the Shipowner Protection and Indemnity Club and the report did not mention any colligation measures on the ship. According to the Loading inspection report presented by Tianxiang Company who was the outsider of the case of the adjustment report appendix provided by the Plaintiff. We can know that when the goods were loaded on board, the goods were in good condition, and there was not obvious damage in operation loading and fixation and colligation in the process of loading and reinforcing. After loading the goods, they were colligated with polyester packing belts / steel chains / wire ropes so as to link with welded D-ring or slot. And the colligation and fixation of the goods were inspected widely and the conclusion was that the goods were suitable for stacking to complete the planned voyage, and Tianxiang Company did not raise any objection in the process of monitoring the loading. The court holds that, firstly, the Plaintiff could not regard the evidence in the form of "possible" probable conclusion as the basis of the reason for the damage to the goods under the condition that the Plaintiff did not provide valid evidence or professional conclusion that the improper fixation and colligation was the exact reason for the damage to the goods. Secondly, under the condition of no opposite evidence, we should treat the objective condition of proper fixation and colligation during loading confirmed by the loading inspection report as the factual basis of the case which could be confirmed. Therefore, the court does not adopt that the improper colligation and fixation was the reason for the damage to the goods which was provided by the Plaintiff and the three Defendants.

b. Regarding to the problems of bad weather, reluctant packing and internal fixation of wooden containers.

The court holds that in respect of the fact that the ship had suffered the 8th level of Beaufort wind scale and the 7th level Beaufort Sea situation for 6 h when the ship was sailing on the sea. According to the shipping practice, it could be regarded as bad weather, but it was not enough to achieve the degree of terrible weather. The Defendant CHIPOLBROKCOSMOS provided an adjustment report presented by the Shipowner Protection and Indemnity Club showed a conclusion: "the climate was a major factor for the collapse of containers, but the unstable packaging and internal fixation increased the degree of damage." (The report, which was provided to the court, had been interpreted into Chinese by the Defendant CHIPOLBROKCOSMOS). In respect of the conclusion, the court holds that, firstly, each party had confirmed in the trial that one "completely collapsed" was the wooden container No.8 in unit 1, the other 12 wooden containers were damaged on the surface in different degrees. Combining with the inspection report presented by the Plaintiff HENDRICK Shipping Company, we could get the fact that another container was placed on the top of the container No.8 in unit 1, and the cover of the container was terribly squashed, deformed and fallen. Moreover, even several wooden crates were crushed and torn in different degrees. Therefore, the court holds that it was more appropriate to translate the word "collapse" into sloughing instead of falling down. Secondly, according to the inspection report presented by the Plaintiff HENDRICK Shipping Company: "in addition to the 5 small parts of wooden containers which were stacked in 206 berth warehouses, all the other wooden containers were marked with red warning signs: do not put other containers loading goods on the top of it". In respect of the adjustment report provided by the Defendant CHIPOLBROKCOSMOS showed that "A lot of containers were marked with the sign: do not pile up other containers on the top of it", which proved that the involved wooden containers had showed to the carrier with its objective state that it could not and should not be piled up or stacked due to the structure of the container or the internal loading of goods in all aspects of the reason. After the inspection, the involved collapsed container No.8 was confirmed that the nails used to fix each side and the top of the container had been partially pulled out and the container had moved. That was to say, if the top of the wooden container was not stacked with other container but flatted on hold, it would probably move because of the weather but it could not collapse due to the weather. Therefore, we could infer that the weather was not the main reason for the collapse of the containers, but being stacked. Thirdly, the adjustment report provided by the Defendant CHIPOLBROKCOSMOS showed that the inspector thought that the container lacked internal fixation and internal strength especially in the top of the container". The court partly confirmed about this, because both the top and the side panel of the involved wooden container were used as "cover" to provide physical protection for the goods. But it did not have the physical characteristics to the support the goods on the top of it. And it was because of this the identification on the container required that the packing containers could not be stacked with goods in case that the container and goods in it were damaged, so the physical characteristics of the packaging of the roof of the container was not the reason for the aggravation of the damage but the objective status of the container. If the container was not stacked, it would not cause the consequence of goods damage. Finally, the damage to the container No.8 in unit 1 was the most serious, but the low-pressure drivepipes and medium-pressure drivepipes were intact as a result of the internal fixation measures. The radiator on the top of the container No.19 in unit 3 suffered physical damage, and the appearance of the rest radiators was intact. There was a total of 77 pieces of goods involved, on top of 3 unstacked main hosts of transformers, there were still 74 pieces. The damaged goods were only from the containers No.8 in unit 1, No.23 in unit 2 and No.19, 20 in unit 3 among the 13 wooden containers whose surfaces were damaged when unloading the goods. That was to say, only 13 wooden containers were damaged in surface in the involved transportation of the 74 wooden containers, and only four goods were damaged among the 13 containers damaged in surface, the goods in the rest 9 containers were not damaged. As a result, they could not necessarily come to a conclusion that: "the reluctant packing and unstable internal fixation of wooden containers increased the degree of the damage." based on the facts above. Therefore, the court does not adopt the reason for the damage to the goods provided by the four Defendants. However, the Plaintiff's adjustment report showed that the damaged goods containers were associated with the weather, the four Defendants also stressed that the climate was an important reason for the damage to the goods. The court adopts that climate was also a reason for the damage to the goods under the condition that each party defined that climate was the cause of the damage to the goods.

c. Regarding to the issue of the custody and stowage.

Firstly, each party recognized in the hearing that the packing bodies of the involved containers marked "Do not pile up other goods on the top of it", but the goods were stacked with two layers or multi-layers when the goods were stacked in the yard and loaded on the ship. Secondly, according to the previous analysis, the important reason for the collapse of the container No.8 of unit 1 was the stacking. The radiator on the top layer of the container No.23 in unit 2 was damaged, and its roof had fallen on the radiator. The edge of the longitudinal side and roof of the container No.19 in unit 3 suffered considerable strike, which led to the physical damage to radiator on the top layer but the other radiators were well in appearance. Obviously, the wooden container No.20 in unit 3 was loaded at the bottom of the wooden containers. Based on the above facts, the court confirms the fact stated in the adjustment report provided by the Plaintiff that the damaged goods were obviously stacked in the containers at the bottom and, these goods were damaged because other goods were piled up on the top of them. Pulling the threads together, the factors of the weather, the custody and the stowage of the containers and fixation and colligation mentioned above, the court holds that the fundamental factor of the damage to the goods during the sailing was that the carrier did not stack the goods with two layers as the warning sign said. And the bad weather made the ship shook and tilted, which intensified the damage.

3. Regarding to the Issue of the Subject of Responsibility for Goods Damage.

Regarding to the relation between CHIPOLBROKCOSMOS and Chinese-Polish Shipping, the court holds that Chinese-Polish Shipping was the manager of the involved ship, the Defendant CHIPOLBROKCOSMOS was the owner according to the ship registration information. According to the ship management agreement between two parties, all the money and interest received by Chinese-Polish Shipping belonged to the Defendant CHIPOLBROKCOSMOS and all cost should be paid by Chinese-Polish Shipping, except for the expense of management which should be paid by the Defendant CHIPOLBROKCOSMOS. According to the external publicity and the internal agreement, it could be confirmed that Chinese-Polish Shipping was the agent of the Defendant CHIPOLBROKCOSMOS. Therefore, no matter Chinese-Polish Shipping operated the ship in the name of the Defendant CHIPOLBROKCOSMOS or itself, all the consequences shall be borne by the Defendant CHIPOLBROKCOSMOS. Therefore, the corresponding rights and obligations arising from the charter party between Chinese-Polish Shipping and the Defendant Youda Co., Ltd. shall be entitled and taken by the Defendant CHIPOLBROKCOSMOS.

The actual carrier, the Defendant CHIPOLBROKCOSMOS, had no fault in the actual custody and the stowage of the goods which were stacked or piled up the goods according the plan because the stowage plan of goods was operated by Chinese-Polish Shipping, who completed the work according to the charter party confirmed by the Defendant Youda Co., Ltd. And the charter party stipulated that except for three 159 tons of the transformer subjects, all of the other could be piled up or stacked. The Defendant Youda Co., Ltd. shall take the responsibility for the loss resulted from the stacking of goods according to the charter party.

The Defendant Youda Co., Ltd. argued that regarding to the custody and stowage of the goods, the insured Shanghai ALSTOM Co., Ltd. had given an oral confirmation to it that the goods involved could be stacked in transportation. In April 2013, it was given a written confirmation that the same kind of the goods involved could be stacked by the insured in other transport voyage. Therefore, even if the goods were damaged mainly because of being stacked, the three Defendants operated under the direction of the insured and they had no fault. The corresponding responsibility shall be borne by the insured. Regarding to this, the court holds that firstly, according to the emails provided by the three Defendants, it is shown that the Defendant Youda Co., Ltd. replied in the mail and claimed to the Defendant UTC, INC. that Shanghai ALSTOM Co., Ltd. confirmed orally that the goods could be stacked with two layers. However, the e-mail was the internal communication of the multimodal transport operators so it should not have an effect of others. Under the condition that the three Defendants could not provide the other evidence that the insured confirmed the goods could be stacked, they shall take consequences for the lack of the evidence. Secondly, as the professional multimodal transport operators, they should not take the custody plan confirmed by the insured (unless the confirmation stipulated that once damage to the goods caused by the stacking and custody happened, the responsibility should be taken by the insured) as the standard of custody of the goods, but judge the basic condition of the custody of the goods according to the type, weight and packing of goods comprehensively. In this case, the land transportation from the factory to the dock was organized by the Defendant Youda Co., Ltd. and the Defendant UTC, INC., so they should make it clear that how to conduct the custody and shipment according to the packing of goods initially in the factory. Although the original multimodal transport contract was negotiating the sea freight based on the stacking of the goods, considering the voyage safety, the custody plan should be remade according to the packaging requirements. So, the two Defendants had the corresponding fault in the custody and stowage of goods in shipping.

Pulling the threads together, as the multimodal transport operators, the Defendants Youda Co., Ltd. and UTC, INC. were responsible for the entire transportation and they should take the corresponding responsibility of the loss of goods for their fault in the fulfillment of the contract. The Defendant AIRPORT, INC., as the carrier recorded in the bill of lading of the sea transportation section, was responsible for the transportation in the sea transportation section according to the law. The Defendant CHIPOLBROKCOSMOS, as the actual carrier of the carriage of goods by sea, was exempted for having no carriage fault of the loss of the goods since the charter party stipulated that the Defendant Youda Co., Ltd. took the responsibility for the corresponding loss of the goods caused by stacking.

4. Regarding to the issue of determination of amount of compensation of the goods loss.

The issues of this part mainly concentrated on the following respects: (1) the determination of the range of the damage; (2) whether the subject of responsibility could enjoy the package limitation of liability of maritime claims or not; (3) how to calculate the package limitation of liability; (4) the rationality of the Plaintiff to claim for the amount of compensation.

a. Regarding to the issue of determining the range of the damage.

The court holds that firstly, the inspection report provided by the Plaintiff and presented by HENDRICK Shipping Company stated clearly that the damaged goods which needed to change included 3 radiators and 3 high-pressure drivepipes, up to the date of the presentation of the inspection report on June 6, 2013. The adjustment report of Wanyi Co., Ltd. provided by the Plaintiff recorded that all inspections had been completed until April 16, 2013. 5 radiators were found suffering the apparent physical damage that could not be repaired. Combined with technical service report presented by Hampton-Tedder Company, it was finally concluded that 3 drivepipes and 5 radiators were damaged and needed to be replaced. Under the condition that the fact of the damaged goods stated in two reports provided by the Plaintiff were different, considering that the Plaintiff confirmed in the trial that the inspector, presenting the adjustment report, of Wanyi Co., Ltd. did not go to the site to inspect, but Wanyi Co., Ltd. employed HENDRICK Shipping Company which had the corresponding inspection qualification in destination port to replace it to carry out the inspection, and wrote the adjustment report of Wanyi Co., Ltd. according to the inspection report provided by HENDRICK Shipping Company. Therefore, the court holds that the damaged goods to be replaced were 3 high-pressure drivepipes and 3 radiators which was confirmed in the inspection report presented by HENDRICK Shipping Company. Secondly, the insured transported 3 radiators and 3 drivepipes of H314 project as the substitute of the goods to the final client FIRSTSOLAR on July 4, 2013 and August 12, 2013 respectively. This fact could also prove the fact that the 3 damaged radiators needed to change. Pulling the threads together, under the condition that the Plaintiff did not provide further evidence to prove that there were 5 radiators got damaged, the scope of the goods loss shall be subject to 3 high-pressure drive pipes and 3 radiators.

b. Regarding to the issue of whether the subject of responsibility could enjoy the package limitation of liability of maritime claims or not.

The court holds that according to the Maritime Code of the People's Republic of China Article 59, the carrier shall not be entitled to the benefit of the limitation of liability provided for in Article 56 or 57 of this Code if it is proved that the loss, damage or delay in delivery of the goods resulted from an act or omission of the carrier done with the intent to cause such loss, damage or delay or recklessly and with knowledge that such loss, damage or delay would probably result.

In this case, the surfaces of the wooden containers marked clearly that "do not pile up other goods on the top of it", but the goods were stacked with two layers or multilayers no matter when the goods were piled on the dock or in the process of transportation by sea. Regarding to this, the dispute focused on whether the carrier, the actual carrier and multimodal transport operator of carriage of goods by sea had the intentional or gross negligence of the stacking and custody of the goods.

The Defendant CHIPOLBROKCOSMOS, as the actual carrier of the carriage of goods by sea, was exempted because the charter party stipulated that the Defendant Youda Co., Ltd. took the responsibility for the corresponding loss of the goods caused by the stacking, which is confirmed above. There was no evidence to prove that the involved goods damage was caused by the carrier recorded in the bill of lading, the Defendant AIRPORT, INC., whose act or omission done with the intent to cause such loss, damage or delay or recklessly and with knowledge that such loss, damage or delay would probably result. Therefore, the Defendant AIRPORT, INC. enjoyed the package limitation of liability of maritime claims in respect of responsibility for compensation of the loss of the goods. Whether the Defendant Youda Co., Ltd. and the Defendant UTC, INC., as the multimodal transport operators, had the intentional or gross negligence of the stacking and custody of the goods becomes the key of the case.

Firstly, in respect of the actual performance of multimodal transport contract of the Defendants Youda Co., Ltd. and UTC, INC., the Defendants Youda Co., Ltd., UTC, INC. entered into a multimodal transport contract of the whole transportation of the involved goods with the insured Shanghai ALSTOM Co., Ltd. on December 20, 2012. The contract stipulated that the sea freight was USD270,000, but it did not make the packing pattern and matters need attention of goods clearly. Afterwards the Defendant Youda Co., Ltd. e-mailed to the Defendant UTC, INC. on December 24, 2012 that they would confirm the stacking of goods with the manager of Shanghai ALSTOM Co., Ltd. as soon as possible. The Defendant Youda Co., Ltd. e-mailed to the Defendant UTC, INC. to confirm that Shanghai ALSTOM Co., Ltd. made an oral confirmation that the goods could be stacked with two layers on December 26, 2012. On the same day the Defendant Youda Co., Ltd. booked to Chinese-Polish Shipping by e-mail, and sent the weight, quantity and size of the goods to Chinese-Polish Shipping. Then they signed the charter party with Chinese-Polish Shipping to confirm that the goods could be stacked and the sea freight was USD250,000. From the process of signing each contract we could find whether the goods were stacked had an influence on the amount of reserved space of the ship and the corresponding freight. When the Defendant Youda Co., Ltd. signed the charter party with Chinese-Polish Shipping, they confirmed that all goods could be stacked except for three subjects of 159 tons, which indicated that the signing of the charter party and the way of calculating the freight was based on that the goods could be stacked. Under the condition that the sea freight in multimodal transport contract was USD270,000, it could be inferred that the Defendant Youda Co., Ltd. and the Defendant UTC, INC. calculated the sea freight based on that the goods could be stacked. At that time, they did not know the packing of the goods and related warning signs on them. Secondly, from the long-term transportation cooperation practice among the Defendant Youda Co., Ltd., UTC, INC. and the insured, the adjustment report provided by the involved Defendant CHIPOLBROKCOSMOS showed: "according to what we knew, ALSTOM often used similar containers on the picture to transport goods and nothing happened before that." Regarding to the inspection report provided by the Plaintiff that presented by HENDRICK Shipping Co., Ltd., the senior on-site technician Mark Fry of ALSTOM said that the radiator were usually placed in two different designed wooden containers, one was the "cover" packaging of the involved transportation. The external wooden containers only played a protective role whose top area could not bear any excess weight. The other kind wooden containers were of 4*4, and the manufacturing process was more complex. According to the experience, the container could be stacked with two layers and would not be damaged when loading the goods of the similar size and weight of the goods involved in the case. When transporting the similar goods in April 2013, on April 26, ALSTOM confirmed by email that under the condition that the UTC, INC. and the carrier ensured that the wooden containers were stacked safely (the heavy containers were at the bottom and the light containers were on the top, the maximum limit was 3 layers and the containers were bound and support properly), the ALSTOM confirmed that they took the risk of the stacking of the goods. Based on the facts mentioned above, Shanghai ALSTOM Co., Ltd. and the Defendants Youda Co., Ltd., UTC, INC. usually stacked goods with two layers in their cooperation, and some previous packing of the containers could ensure the security of goods when they were stacked.

Pulling the threads together, based on the fact that the Defendants Youda Co., Ltd. and UTC, INC. were not very clear about the packing of goods and warning signs when they entered into the involved multimodal transport contract, and the practice that goods could be stacked in transportation with the long-term cooperation with the insured indicated that the Defendant Youda Co., Ltd. did not have intent or gross negligence of the custody and stacking of the goods when dealing the affairs of multimodal transportation. Therefore, the Defendant Youda Co., Ltd. and the Defendant UTC, INC., as the multimodal transport operators of the involved transportation, had the right to enjoy the package limitation of liability of maritime claims according to the Maritime Code of the People's Republic of China Article 105.

Thirdly, how to calculate the package limitation of liability.

According to the Maritime Code of the People's Republic of China Article 56, the carrier's liability for the loss of or damage to the goods shall be limited to an amount equivalent to 666.67 Units of Account per package or other shipping unit, or 2 Units of Account per kilogram of the gross weight of the goods lost or damaged, whichever is the higher, except where the nature and value of the goods had been declared by the shipper before shipment and inserted in the bill of lading, or where a higher amount than the amount of limitation of liability set out in this Article had been agreed upon between the carrier and the shipper. Where a container, pallet or similar article of transport is used to consolidate goods, the number of packages or other shipping units enumerated in the bill of lading as packed in such article of transport shall be deemed to be the number of packages or shipping units. If not so enumerated, the goods in such article of transport shall be deemed to be one package or one shipping unit.

In regard of this, the Plaintiff claimed that the number of the goods here should be the number recorded on the bill of lading while the gross weight of the goods referred to the total weight of the whole batch of the goods, including the weight of packaging. According to this standard, the claim amount was far from reaching the limitation of the compensation of maritime per package liability. Regarding to this, the court holds that, firstly, the object of the compensation limit was the damaged goods in respect of the literal interpretation of the article, and the goods would not be compensated if they were not damaged, not to mention the limitation. Secondly, referring to the relevant regulation of the relevant international convention, the Protocol to Amend the International Convention for the Unification of Certain Rules of Law Relating to Bills of Lading (namely the "Hague-Visby Rules" promulgated on February 23, 1968), whose Article 2 is the revision of Article 4 Sub-paragraph 5 of the International Convention for the Unification of Certain Rules of Law Relating to Bills of Lading (namely, the "Hague Rules" promulgated on August 25, 1924), stipulates in its (1) that "Unless the nature and value of such goods have been declared by the shipper before shipment and inserted in the bill of lading, neither the carrier nor the ship shall in any event be or become liable for any loss or damage to or in connection with the goods in an amount exceeding the equivalent of 10,000 francs per package or unit or 30 francs per kilo of gross weight of the goods lost or damaged, whichever is the higher."; the United Nations Convention on the Carriage of Goods by Sea, 1978 (namely the "Hamburg Rules") Article 6 Sub-paragraph 1 (a) is that: the liability of the carrier for loss resulting from loss of or damage to goods according to the provisions of Article 5 is limited to an amount equivalent to 835 units of account per package or other shipping unit or 2.5 units of account per kilogram of gross weight of the goods lost or damaged, whichever is the higher. The relevant international conventions all calculate the corresponding compensation limit based on the loss or damage to the goods, so the calculation of the compensation limit on the basis of the loss or damage to the goods can be considered as an international practice. So, pulling the threads together, the case shall calculate the compensation limit on the basis of the loss of goods.

According to the effective evidence in the case, the six damaged and replaced items were loaded in four wooden containers separately. The compensation limit calculated by the freight unit for the damaged goods by the law was 2,666.68 special drawing rights (hereinafter referred to as "SDR"). Calculating by the gross weight of the three damaged drivepipes provided by the Plaintiff, regarding to the 3 damaged drivepipes, because the Plaintiff did not provide the concrete weight of damaged high pressure drivepipes, the weight of the three drivepipes was calculated by using the 2,780 gross weight of the wooden container (the container was loaded with 3 high-pressure drivepipes, 1 medium-pressure drivepipe and 1 low-pressure drivepipe) which had the pressure drivepipes as the standard to do the equal calculation 2,780 * 3/5 = 1,668 kg. Regarding to the 3 damaged radiators, the weight of the 3 damaged radiators was calculated by using the 2380 kg gross weight of the wooden container (3 radiators per wooden containers) which had the radiators as the standard to do the equal calculation 2,380 / 3 * 3 = 2380 kg. And the total gross weight of the damaged goods was 4,048 kg, according to the laws and regulations limit for 4,048 * 2 = 8,096SDR, comparing the two statics and taking the higher limitation of per package liability for the damaged goods 8,096 SDR. (each party on the trial confirmed that the SDR and the dollar exchange rate on the date that the court made the judgment was the standard, that was, 1SDR = USD1.414180 on February 26, 2015), therefore, the package limitation of liability for the damaged goods shall be about USD11,449.20.

Fourthly, the rationality of the Plaintiff to claim for the amount of compensation.

The court no longer repeats the facts on the actual value of the substitute of the goods, packaging costs, air freight because the subject of responsibility enjoys the package limitation of liability of maritime claims according to law.

Regarding to the Plaintiff's appeal of the fee of additional repackaging, forklift cancellation and inspection of 5000 dollars because of the damage to the goods, the court holds that when each party carried out the jointly inspection on the dock, they confirmed that the involved equipment in the containers should be inspected by specialized electronic instrument and the professional technician, and the containers should be repackaged for transporting to appointed location. Therefore, the corresponding fee of the inspection and the repackaging in the equipment site of Ancon Marine that 19 containers were transported to was finally confirmed as the range of the damage to the goods and necessary expenses of the safe transportation to the final client under the condition that each party all accepted. The court supports this fact. The three Defendants had a written confirmation that ALSTOM had the related fee of USD30,000 paid in advance by UTC OVERSEAS, INC. Since the Plaintiff compensated USD5,000 only regarding to this item, the court supports the appeal for USD5,000.

Regarding to the on-site inspection fee of USD50,000 of the final client, the court holds that firstly, the relevant evidence of the inspection costs formed overseas and the Plaintiff did not handle the notarial authenticated procedure, so the court does not confirm the effect of the evidence. Secondly, even if it was true, combined with the written confirmation of the Plaintiff after the trial that the insured was the provider of the whole equipment and provided the corresponding after-sales installation, debugging and other after-sales service, and the after-sales service did not charge separately to the receiver. The service was that the goods should be transported to the final client FIRSTSOLAR Company and ALSTOM sent technicians to install the equipment, inspect and debug, conduct on-site and introduce how to use the equipment. To the equipment provider, this was the service when the goods first installed. To the client who was the receiver, this service was the inspection of the received goods to ensure that the goods received were in good condition. Therefore, there was no inevitable relation to whether the goods were damaged or not. Thirdly, the Plaintiff confirmed in the trial that this inspection contraposed all inspection to 77 pieces of goods involved. The effective evidence showed that when the goods were unloaded on the dock, the joint inspection done by each party confirmed that only 13 wooden containers were found damaged and 6 containers were suspected damaged. The 19 containers loading the goods all shipped to Ancon Marine site to open, unpack and carry on the corresponding technology inspection, and the related service provided by Ancon Marine had been appealed separately by the Plaintiff. Consequently, even if the final inspection of the final client was the inspection of the damaged goods. This inspection was a repeated inspection and the extended inspection of out of the range of damage. So, the corresponding appeal of the Plaintiff was also the repeated appeal for the fee of the inspection. For the reasons given above, the court does not support the appeal.

Regarding to the appeal of interest claimed by the Plaintiff, since it had no corresponding loan basis, it was proper to calculate from March 4, 2014, and base on the interest rate for liquid capital load in RMB over the corresponding period as promulgated by the People's Bank of China, to the date of payment set by this judgment.

In conclusion, the multimodal transport operator of the involved transportation, the Defendants Youda Co., Ltd. and UTC, INC. shall bear the compensation of liability, namely, the amount of goods loss of USD11,449.20 and the necessary repackaging and testing fee of USD5000 for the Plaintiff who had the subrogation right according to the law, when enjoying the package limitation of liability of maritime claims on account of the corresponding wrong custody and stowage of the sea transportation section of the goods. The carrier of the carriage of the goods by sea, the Defendant AIRPORT, INC. shall bear the joint and several liability for the above fee with the Defendants Youda Co., Ltd. and UTC, INC. according to the law. The actual carrier of the sea transportation section involved, the Defendant CHIPOLBROKCOSMOS had no corresponding fault in the accident of the damage of the goods. Therefore, it shall be exempted. According to the Contract Law of the People's Republic of China Article 113 Paragraph 1, the Insurance Law of the People's Republic of China Article 60 Paragraph 1, the Maritime Code of the People's Republic of China Article 46, Article 55, Article 56, Article 60 Paragraph 1, Article 64, Article 71, Article 83, Article 102, Article 103, Article 104, Article 105, Article 106, Article 269 and Article 277, the Civil Procedure Law of the People's Republic of China Article 64 Paragraph 1, and Some Provisions of the Supreme People's Court on Evidence in Civil Procedures Article 2 and Article 74, the judgment is as follows:

1. The Defendant Youda (Shanghai) International Freight Co., Ltd. and the Defendant UTC PROJECTS, INC. shall compensate the loss of the damaged goods of USD16,449.20 and interest(calculated from March 4, 2014, and base on the interest rate for liquid capital load in RMB over the corresponding period as promulgated by the People's Bank of China, to the date of payment set by this judgment) to the Plaintiff Allianz China General Insurance Company Ltd. together within ten days since the judgment comes into effect.
2. The Defendant AIRPORT CLEARANCE SERVICE, INC. shall bear joint and several liability of the first item.

3. Not support other claims of the Plaintiff, Allianz China General Insurance Co., Ltd.

If the Defendants subjected to execution fail to fulfill the obligation with respect to pecuniary payment within the period specified by the judgment, according to the Civil Procedure Law of the People's Republic of China Article 253, the v pay double interest on the debt for the belated payment.

Court acceptance fee in amount of RMB14,219, the Plaintiff Allianz China General Insurance Company Ltd. shall bear RMB12,851 and the Defendants Youda (Shanghai) International Freight Co., Ltd., UTC PROJECTS, INC. and AIRPORT CLEARANCE SERVICE, INC. shall jointly bear RMB1,368.

In case of dissatisfaction with this judgment, the Plaintiff Allianz China General Insurance Co., Ltd., the Defendant Youda (Shanghai) International Freight Co., Ltd. may within 15 days upon the service of this judgment, the Defendant UTC PROJECTS, INC., the Defendant AIRPORT CLEARANCE SERVICE, INC. and the Defendant CHIPOLBROK COSMOS MARITIME COMPANY LIMITED may within 30 days upon the service of this judgment, submit a statement of appeal to the court, together with copies according to the number of the other parties, and appeal to the Shanghai High People's Court.

Presiding Judge: JI Gang
Judge: ZHANG Jianchen
Acting Judge: WANG Huanjin
February 26, 2015
Clerk: GU Chanyan

Appendix: Relevant Law

1. Contract Law of the People's Republic of China

Article 113 Calculation of Damages; Damages to Consumer Where a party failed to perform or rendered non-conforming performance, thereby causing loss to the other party, the amount of damages payable shall be equivalent to the other party's loss resulting from the breach, including any benefit that may be accrued from performance of the contract, provided that the amount shall not exceed the likely loss resulting from the breach which was foreseen or should have been foreseen by the breaching party at the time of conclusion of the contract.

......

2. Insurance Law of the People's Republic of China

Article 60 Where an insured incident occurs for any loss caused by a third party to the subject matter insured, the insurer shall, from the day when it pays insurance money to the insured, subrogate the insured's claim for indemnity against the third party within the extent of the indemnity amount.

......

3. Maritime Code of the People's Republic of China

Article 46 The responsibilities of the carrier with regard to the goods carried in containers covers the entire period during which the carrier is in charge of the goods, starting from the time the carrier has taken over the goods at the port of loading, until the goods have been delivered at the port of discharge. The responsibility of the carrier with respect to non-containerized goods covers the period during which the carrier is in charge of the goods, starting from the time of loading of the goods onto the ship until the time the goods are discharged therefrom. During the period the carrier is in charge of the goods, the carrier shall be liable for the loss of or damage to the goods, except as otherwise provided for in this Section.

The provisions of the preceding paragraph shall not prevent the carrier from entering into any agreement concerning carrier's responsibilities with regard to non-containerized goods prior to loading onto and after discharging from the ship.

Article 55 The amount of indemnity for the loss of the goods shall be calculated on the basis of the actual value of the goods so lost, while that for the damage to the goods shall be calculated on the basis of the difference between the values of the goods before and after the damage, or on the basis of the expenses for the repair. The actual value shall be the value of the goods at the time of shipment plus insurance and freight.

From the actual value referred to in the preceding paragraph, deduction shall be made, at the time of compensation, of the expenses that had been reduced or avoided as a result of the loss or damage happened.

Article 56 The carrier's liability for the loss of or damage to the goods shall be limited to an amount equivalent to 666.67 Units of Account per package or other shipping unit, or 2 Units of Account per kilogramme of the gross weight of the goods lost or damaged, whichever is the higher, except where the nature and value of the goods had been declared by the shipper before shipment and inserted in the bill of lading, or where a higher amount than the amount of limitation of liability set out in this Article had been agreed upon between the carrier and the shipper. Where a container, pallet or similar article of transport is used to consolidate goods, the number of packages or other shipping units enumerated in the bill of lading as packed in such article of transport shall be deemed to be the number of packages or shipping units. If not so enumerated, the goods in such article of transport shall be deemed to be one package or one shipping unit. Where the article of transport is not owned or furnished by the carrier, such article of transport shall be deemed to be one package or one shipping unit.

Article 59 The carrier shall not be entitled to the benefit of the limitation of liability provided for in Article 56 or 57 of this Code if it is proved that the loss, damage or delay in delivery of the goods resulted from an act or omission of the carrier done with the intent to cause such loss, damage or delay or recklessly and with knowledge that such loss, damage or delay would probably result.
......

Article 60 Where the performance of the carriage or part thereof has been entrusted to an actual carrier, the carrier shall nevertheless remain responsible for the entire carriage according to the provisions of this Chapter. The carrier shall be responsible, in relation to the carriage performed by the actual carrier, for the act or omission of the actual carrier and of his servant or agent acting within the scope of his employment or agency.
......

Article 64 If claims for compensation have been separately made against the carrier, the actual carrier and their servants or agents with regard to the loss of or damage to the goods, the aggregate amount of compensation shall not be in excess of the limitation provided for in Article 56 of this Code.

Article 71 A bill of lading is a document which serves as an evidence of the contract of carriage of goods by sea and the taking over or loading of the goods by the carrier, and based on which the carrier undertakes to deliver the goods against surrendering the same. A provision in the document stating that the goods are to be delivered to the order of a named person, or to order, or to bearer, constitutes such an undertaking.

Article 83 The consignee may, before taking delivery of the goods at the port of destination, and the carrier may, before delivering the goods at the port of destination, request the cargo inspection agency to have the goods inspected. The party requesting such inspection shall bear the cost thereof but is entitled to recover the same from the party causing the damage.

Article 102 A multimodal transport contract as referred to in this Code means a contract under which the multimodal transport operator undertakes to transport the goods, against the payment of freight for the entire transport, from the place where the goods were received in his charge to the destination and to deliver them to the consignee by two or more different modes of transport, one of which being sea carriage. The multimodal transport operator as referred to in the preceding paragraph means the person who has entered into a multimodal transport contract with the shipper either by himself or by another person acting on his behalf.

Article 103 The responsibility of the multimodal transport operator with respect to the goods under multimodal transport contract covers the period from the time he takes the goods in his charge to the time of their delivery.

Article 269 The parties to a contract may choose the law applicable to such contract, unless the law provides otherwise. Where the parties to a contract have not made a choice, the law of the country having the closest connection with the contract shall apply.

Article 277 The Unit of Account referred to in this Code is the Special Drawing Right as defined by the International Monetary Fund; the amount of the Chinese currency (RMB) in terms of the Special Drawing Right shall be that computed on the basis of the method of conversion established by the authorities in charge of foreign exchange control of this country on the date of the judgment by the court or the date of the award by the arbitration organization or the date mutually agreed upon by the parties.

4. **Civil Procedure Law of the People's Republic of China**

Article 64 It is the duty of a party to an action to provide evidence in support of his allegations.

......

Article 253 If the person subjected to execution fails to fulfill his obligations with respect to pecuniary payment within the period specified by a judgment or written order or any other legal document, he shall pay double interest on the debt for the belated payment. If the person subjected to execution fails to fulfill his other obligations within the period specified in the judgment or written order or any other legal document, he shall pay a charge for the dilatory fulfillment.

5. **Several Provisions of the Supreme People's Courton Evidencein Civil Procedures**

Article 2 The parties concerned shall be responsible for producing evidence to prove the facts on which their own allegations are based or the facts on which the allegations of the other party are refuted.

Article 74 In the process of litigation, the facts that are recognized as unfavorable to a party itself and the evidence that have been recognized by the parties concerned in the bill of complaint, bill of defense, statements of the parties concerned or the statement of the procurator shall be recognized by the people's court, unless the party concerned goes back on its own words and has adequate evidence to overthrow the evidence.

Guangzhou Maritime Court
Civil Judgment

A.P. Moller-Maersk A/S
v.
Shanghai Chanlian Xieyun Logistics Co., Ltd. et al.

(2012) Guang Hai Fa Chu Zi No.329

Related Case(s) This is the judgment of first instance, and the judgment of second instance and the judgment of retrial are on page 58 and page 76 respectively.

Cause(s) of Action 202. Dispute over contract of carriage of goods by sea or sea-connected waters.

Headnote The Plaintiff ocean carrier held to be entitled to recover cost of five containers by way of container detention fees, as the Defendant freight forwarder's liability for container detention could not exceed the value of the containers; claim was not time-barred because one-year limitation period ran from moment when it became obvious that it was impossible for the consignee to take delivery of the goods because they had been auctioned by customs authorities.

Summary The Plaintiff-Carrier filed an action against the Defendant-Freight Forwarder in a dispute over a contract for the carriage of goods for container detention fee. The Defendant contracted with the shipper to deliver five containers from Shenzhen, China to Nhava Sheva, India. The Defendant confirmed that the consignee would take delivery of the goods and pay the customs clearance in Nhava Sheva. The consignee did not take possession of the goods in Nhava Sheva, and the local Customs authorities auctioned off the goods inside the containers after nearly a year. The court found for the Plaintiff, confirming that it damaged totaling the cost of five new containers, as the detention fee could not be more than the cost of mitigation by purchasing containers to replace the ones detained in Nhava Sheva. The court rejected the Defendants' argument that the Plaintiff's loss had been compensated by proceeds from the auction, holding that there was no evidence that the Plaintiff was entitled to the procedures from the auction of the goods inside the containers. The court also held that Plaintiff's claim was not time-barred by the statute of limitations, as the one-year limitation period only began to run when the customs authorities auctioned the goods, as only then was it clear that it was impossible for the consignee to take delivery.

Judgment

The Plaintiff: A. P. Moller - Maersk A/S
Domicile: 1098 Copenhagen, Denmark.
Legal representative: Morten Engelstoft and Peter Ronnest Andersen.
Agent *ad litem*: CAO Fang, lawyer of Shanghai All Bright Law Office.
Agent *ad litem*: MA Yixing, lawyer of Shanghai All Bright Law Office.

The Defendant: Shanghai Chanlian Xieyun Logistics Co., Ltd. Shenzhen Branch
Domicile: Luohu District, Shenzhen, Guangdong, the People's Republic of China.
Person in charge: CAI Guoliang, general manager.

The Defendant: Shanghai Chanlian Xieyun Logistics Co., Ltd.
Domicile: Shanyang Town, Jinshan District, Shanghai, the People's Republic of China.
Legal representative: WU Liang, general manager.
Agent *ad litem* of the two Defendants: HUANG Sufang, lawyer of Guangdong Shengtang Law Firm.

With respect to the case arising from the dispute over contract of carriage of goods by sea filed by the Plaintiff A. P. Moller-Maersk A/S against the Defendants Shanghai Chanlian Xieyun Logistics Co., Ltd. Shenzhen Branch (hereinafter referred to as "Chanlian Shenzhen") and Shanghai Chanlian Xieyun Logistics Co., Ltd. (hereinafter referred to as "Chanlian"), the Plaintiff mailed the statement of claim to the court on February 27, 2012, which was received by the court on March 1. On April 17, the Plaintiff finished the supplement and amendment of the materials about the sue as required by the court. On April 18, the court accepted the case. Later, a collegiate panel composed of Presiding Judge NI Xuewei, Acting Judge YANG Yaxiao and People's Juror CHEN Xiuling was formed by the court according to the law to try the case, with Clerk LU Shiying being appointed to record the case. The Plaintiff applied for extending the period of adducing proof three times successively and the court permitted them. On March 26, 2013, the court summoned the two parties concerned to exchange evidence before the hearing and held hearings in public for the trial of the case on the same day and on September 11, respectively. CAO Fang, agent *ad litem* of the Plaintiff, HUANG Sufang, agent *ad litem* of the two Defendants, appeared in court to attend the hearings. Now the case has been concluded.

The Plaintiff alleged that: in 2010, Chanlian Shenzhen entrusted the Plaintiff with the carriage of the goods in 5 containers under the bill of ladingNo.859498700 from Yantian Port, Shenzhen to New Delhi, India and the Plaintiff accepted the entrustment of carrying the goods involved. Before and after the goods' arrival at the transshipment port Nhava Sheva, Chanlian Shenzhen requested to change the destination port for many times but then canceled the change. Finally, Chanlian Shenzhen recognized that the shipper would bear the fees arising from the detention in Nhava Sheva and the consignee would undertake customs clearance and take delivery of the goods in Nhava Sheva. On April 29, Chanlian Shenzhen requested to change the shipper into "SHENZHENTRADEANDEXPORTCOLTD" and the consignee into "SATYAOVERSEAS". On June 2, Chanlian Shenzhen requested to change the consignee into "LIMRATRADERSA-3" again. The goods were confiscated by the Nhava Sheva Customs due to non-taking delivery of the goods involved. On February 28, 2011, the Nhava Sheva Customs informed the Plaintiff that the goods had been auctioned and should be delivered by the Plaintiff to the buyers. During the period of detention of the goods involved in Nhava Sheva, the fees arising from the overtime use of containers were totally Rp8,026,425, equaling to RMB1,029,554.51 (according to the exchange rate on the date of the filing of the suit). Chanlian Shenzhen as the shipper who changed the consignor and consignee repeatedly should bear the liability for the loss incurred by the carrier as a result of non-taking delivery of the goods. Considering Chanlian Shenzhen was a branch of Chanlian, Chanlian should bear joint and several liabilities for the loss caused to the carrier by the act of Chanlian Shenzhen. The Plaintiff hence requested the court to order the two Defendants to bear the fee arose from the overtime use of containers in the amount of Rp8,026,425 (RMB1,029,554.51 after exchange according to the rate on the date of filing of the suit) and the litigation cost of this case jointly.

The Plaintiff submitted the following evidence during the period of adducing evidence:

1. Booking confirmation (No.859498700), to prove that Chanlian Shenzhen booked space from the Plaintiff;
2. Bill of lading (No.859498700) which was not issued, to prove that the contractual relationship about carriage of goods by sea between the Plaintiff and Chanlian Shenzhen;
3. E-mails between the Plaintiff and Chanlian Shenzhen from February 26, 2010 to April 16, 2010, to prove that before the arrival of the goods involved in Nhava Sheva, Chanlian Shenzhen had requested to change the destination port for many times and recognized that the shipper would bear the fee arising from the detention of the goods involved in Nhava Sheva and the consignee would undertake customs clearance and take delivery of the goods;
4. E-mails sent by Chanlian Shenzhen to the Plaintiff from April 29, 2010 to June 2, 2010, to prove that Chanlian Shenzhen had requested to change the shipper and consignee twice;
5. Two copies of customs documents, to prove that the goods involved had been auctioned by the customs at the destination port and the customs asked the Plaintiff to deliver the goods to the buyers;
6. The charging standard of the container detention fee, to prove the charging standard that the Plaintiff adopted as a basis for container detention fee.

After the expiration of the period of adducing evidence, the Plaintiff supplemented the following evidence:

7. E-mails between the Plaintiff and the Defendant, export invoices and bank's receipt (payment) vouchers under the bill of lading (No.860320322), to prove

the Chinese name, English name and customer's invoice number of Chanlian Shenzhen and the long-term use of the same E-mail address by Chanlian Shenzhen to have business correspondences with the Plaintiff;
8. Shipping instructions under the bill of lading involved, to prove the shipping instructions towards the carriage involved were made by Chanlian Shenzhen;
9. Statement of Maersk (China) Shipping Shenzhen Branch (hereinafter referred to as "Maersk Shenzhen"),to prove Maersk Shenzhen was the agent of the Plaintiff at the loading port and the e-mails submitted by the Plaintiff was authentic, but because the e-mail box "PRSCSEINS@MAERSK.COM" had been abolished, there was no way to notarize the e-mails downloaded;
10. Business license of Maersk Shenzhen, to prove Maersk Shenzhen was the agent of the Plaintiff at the loading port; and
11. E-mails between the Plaintiff and the Defendant, to prove the e-mail address of the Defendant and that the two parties had negotiated about the carriage involved for many times.

The two Defendants jointly defended that: they had no contractual relationship of carriage of goods by sea with the Plaintiff and there was no basis in law for the Plaintiff to request the Defendants to bear the liability for the container detention fee as they were neither the shipper nor the consignee. The Plaintiff failed to prove the container detention fee had accrued and existed actually. According to the provision of law, the carrier should apply to the court for a ruling of auctioning the goods after 60 days from the date of non-taking delivery of the goods involved, and the fee payable by the shipper or consignee to the Plaintiff should be paid off from the proceeds of auction, rather than being auctioned by the customs when the goods had not taken delivery of for almost one year, hence, the Plaintiff should bear the expanded loss caused by its failure to timely dealing with the goods. The container detention fee that the Plaintiff claimed for had far exceeded the value of the containers and in the case where the container detention fee was higher than the value of a new container, the carrier could reduce the loss by buying a new container. The container detention fee should only be calculated for a period within 60 days from the date of non-taking delivery of the goods and could not be over the price of buying new containers, whichever the amount was lower. The proceeds of the auction of the goods involved dealt by the Nhava Sheva Customs were enough to pay off the container detention fee, hence, the Plaintiff not only had no right to claim for that fee against the shipper, but also should return the rest of the proceeds of auction to the shipper according to the law. The lawsuit filed by the Plaintiff had exceeded the statute of limitations and thus should be rejected by the court.

The two Defendants submitted one group of evidence during the period of adducing evidence: two copies of documents of Nhava Sheva Customs, to prove the proceeds from the auction of the goods involved were enough to pay off the container detention fee, so the Plaintiff had no right to claim such fee from the shipper and the rest of the proceeds from auction in the amount of Rp24,585,175 should be returned to the shipper.

The two Defendants did not recognize the authenticity, legality and relevancy of evidence 1 to evidence 4, evidence 8 and evidence 11 submitted by the Plaintiff, and held that the booking confirmation and bill of lading had no original to be verified, e-mails, as digital data, had not been proved through legal procedure, and the Defendants only had used the e-mail box with the suffix of "COM" instead of "ORG", a party not involved in this case, Maersk Shenzhen, was the agent of the Plaintiff and had interests with the Plaintiff, those explanations in the evidence fell into self-evidence of party not involved in this case and were isolated evidence. The Defendants recognized evidence 5, recognized the authenticity of evidence 6 but did not recognize the legality and relevancy thereof, holding that the standard of the container detention fee was the unilateral assertion made by the Plaintiff which could not be binding upon the two Defendants. The Defendants did not recognize the authenticity of the e-mails in evidence 7, but recognized the e-mail box was used by the Defendants, recognized the authenticity of the bank's receipt (payment) vouchers but not the content the evidence to prove. The Defendants recognized the authenticity of evidence 9 but not the content the evidence to prove. The Defendants had no objection to evidence 10. The Plaintiff recognized the evidence submitted by the Defendants but objected to the contents the evidence to prove.

After the cross-examination in the hearings, the court ascertains the evidence as follows: evidence 5 submitted by the Plaintiff is the same as evidence 1 submitted by the Defendants which was formed out of China, the parties had no objection to its legality, thus the court confirms the probative force of that evidence. The Defendants recognized the authenticity of evidence 6, evidence 7, evidence 9, evidence 10 and the bank's receipt (payment) vouchers in evidence 8 submitted by the Plaintiff, thus the court confirms the probative force of those evidence. The invoices under evidence 7 submitted by the Plaintiff and the bank's receipt (payment) vouchers whose probative force confirmed by the court can support each other, thus the probative force of such invoices can be confirmed by the court. The Defendants did not affirm the rest of evidence submitted by the Plaintiff but failed to submit any evidence to refute them, the Defendants' denying the fact of booking shipping space from the Plaintiff obviously contradicted with their acknowledging the goods involved were carried by the Defendants, and the Defendants failed to make any reasonable explains, therefore, the court confirms evidence 1, evidence 2 and evidence 8 which were submitted by the Plaintiff to prove that Chanlian Shenzhen has booked space from the Plaintiff. The e-mails under the Plaintiff's evidence 3, evidence 4, evidence 11 and evidence 7 were all typescripts without notarization, but the failure of notarization was due to objective reasons, in view of the Defendants' affirming the authenticity of the e-mail box used for correspondence, the court will comprehensively ascertain the content of the e-mails combining with other evidence.

According to the evidence with the probative force ascertained by the court and the circumstances of the hearings, the court finds the following facts:

1. The undisputed facts between the parties

   Both the Plaintiff and the Defendants had submitted the documents of Nhava Sheva Customs' processing department to prove the fact that the goods involved were auctioned by the local customs after arrival at the destination port, and the court ascertains the fact of that section as follow:

   On February 28, 2011, the delivery order No.67 was issued by customs specialist from the processing department, Nhava Sheva Customs, which stated that, on February 21, Nhava Sheva Customs through the auction No.56 sold the goods in the five containers (hereinafter referred to as "the five containers involved") which numbered respectively MSKU9591614, TCNU9520396, AMFU8702814, MSKU9053162, MSKU0824459 located at Maersk (old) Container Freight Station and the goods must be delivered in five days after the issuance of delivery order. Those goods were described as various types of tax-evading Chinese goods. The proceeds from such auction were Rp26,526,500 which had been paid by the buyer M/S Bhavi Impex on February 28, with 12.5% of value-added tax Rp1,025,000 and 5% of value-added tax Rp916,325 being gone into the government's finance department. On the same day, the delivery order No.67 regarding "the delivery of the goods being auctioned" was issued by the processing department of Nhava Sheva Customs to the manager of Maersk (old) Container Freight Station, which stated that, "the customs office instructs your company to deliver the goods under the electronic auction No.56 to the bidder M/S Bhavi Impex who succeeds in auction".

   The Plaintiff alleged that the goods involved were auctioned at the destination port due to non-taking delivery of the goods. According to the documents of Nhava Sheva Customs, such goods, which were still at the container freight station of Maersk during auction, were auctioned due to being identified as tax-evading goods. The time of loading the goods involved at the loading port was on February 13, 2010 and the time of auction was on February 21, 2011. The Plaintiff's statement and the documents of local customs can support each other, therefore, the court ascertains the fact that the goods involved had been taken delivery of by nobody at the destination port for a long time and that they were auctioned by the local customs.

   The charging standard of the fee about the overtime use of 40' containers imported from Nhava Sheva as published by the Plaintiff on its website can be seen as follows: free from the first to the fifth day, Rp940 per container per day from the sixth to the twelfth day, Rp1,598 per container per day from the thirteenth to the nineteenth day, Rp1,786 per container per day from the twentieth to the twenty-sixth day, and Rp4,653 per container per day for those days after.

2. The disputed facts between the parties

1) The English name of Chanlian Shenzhen. The Plaintiff submitted undisputed export invoices about past transactions, e-mails and bank's receipt (payment)

vouchers to prove the English name of Chanlian Shenzhen, which was denied by the Defendants who, however, failed to submitted its correct English name to repute it. The bank's receipt (payment) vouchers submitted by the Plaintiff were originals stating that the payer was Chanlian Shenzhen; the time of payment and the amount could be verified with the rest evidence. The Defendants had the advantage of providing evidence to prove their English name but failed to do so, which was enough to infer that the English name proved by the Plaintiff's evidence was true. The export invoices numbered CN11174552-860,320,322, stamped with Chanlian Shenzhen's confirming chapter about issuing invoice, stated that the English name of the payer was "XENFREIGHTAGENCY LTDSHENZHENOFF", therefore, the court ascertains that the English name of Chanlian Shenzhen is "XENFREIGHTAGENCYLTDSHENZHENOFF" according to it.

2) The status of the Plaintiff. The Defendants alleged that, as the booking confirmation submitted by the Plaintiff showed that the party who accepted the booking was Maersk Shenzhen, a party not involved in this case, the Plaintiff was not the carrier. After investigation, it is found that Maersk Shenzhen with registration number 440301506645877 under the business license, is a branch of MAERSK (China) Shipping Co., Ltd., whose scope of business is to undertake canvassion, booking, issuing the bill of lading, settlement of freight, international shipping agency services and signing contract about relevant business for the ships owned or operated by the Plaintiff. The statement of Maersk Shenzhen specified that Maersk Shenzhen actually undertook the carriage of goods under the bill of ladinginvolved as the Plaintiff's agent in China. The court holds that the above evidence is according to what is written in the booking confirmation and bill of lading, Maersk Shenzhen, the party not involved in this case, whose status as an agent has been made public, actually undertook the booking space of the goods involved as the Plaintiff's agent, and thus the Plaintiff was the carrier of the goods involved.

3) The issue about the booking and performance of the carriage involved. In the hearing, the two Defendants recognized the authenticity of their e-mail box, bank's receipt (payment) vouchers, which specified that the payer was Chanlian Shenzhen, the payee was Maersk Shenzhen and the remark was freight under the undisputed bill of lading, and business license of Maersk Shenzhen. The above evidence proved that Chanlian Shenzhen had business transactions with the Plaintiff. Combined with the fact recognized by the both parties that the goods involved carried by the Plaintiff were auctioned by the local customs at the destination port, even though the booking confirmation, shipping instructions and so on submitted by the Plaintiff were typescripts downloaded from the computer without corresponding originals to be checked with, they corresponded with the shipping operation custom of confirming the booking through shipping company's electronic information transmission platform, the customers code was the same as that under the undisputed bill of lading, the number of service contract, booking number ascertained, time and container number in the evidence could be verified with each other. The Defendants denied in these respects but without any rebutting evidence, while the Plaintiff's statement and

evidence were more persuasive, therefore, the court ascertains the fact about the carriage involved as follows:

In January 2010, Chanlian Shenzhen booked space from the Plaintiff's agent at loading port Maersk Shenzhen, entrusted the Plaintiff with the carriage of goods in seven 40' containers from Huangpu, Guangdong to New Delhi, India. After accepting the booking, the Plaintiff made booking confirmation No.859498700, specifying that the booking party was Chanlian Shenzhen (XENFREIGHTAGE NCYLTDSHENZHENOFF), number of service contract was 409,149, contract customers was SINOLINKSASIALTD, means of transportation was yard to yard, loading port was Huangpu, Guangdong Province, China, destination port was New Delhi, India, department of transportation was Maersk Shenzhen, booking was seven 40' dry cargo containers, date of executing shipment was January 29, estimated time of loading was February 7, the carrying vessel was M.V. "DUMMY", the vessel was estimated to arrive at pier one in Dachan Bay, India on February 10, then the goods would be transshipped by M.V. "NEDLLOYDOCEANIA" through two separate consignments to Madrid Port, New Delhi, India with estimated time of arrival to be respectively February 20 and February 26. Meanwhile, the booking confirmation indicated that please contact our company when changing the content of this booking and the e-mail box for contacting was PRSCSEINS@Maersk.com.

On February 10, 2012, Chanlian Shenzhen sent shipping instructions to the Plaintiff, affirming that the goods had been packed into the five containers which were to be carried from Yantian Port to New Delhi, India, and Chanlian Shenzhen would pay the freight and accept the bill of lading. The shipping instruction whose data was exchanged on February 10 and booking number with 859,498,700 recorded that: customers code was 40,600,306,066, name of the customers was Chanlian Shenzhen, customers code under the contract was 40,900,206,657, name of the company was SINOLINKSASIALTD, company name of the shipper was Chanlian Shenzhen, consignee was SINOLI NKSASIALTD, payer and drawer was Chanlian Shenzhen, the vessel's name was M.V. "MAERSKSTOCKHOLM", port of loading was Yantian Port, China, destination port was New Delhi, India, container number was the number of five containers involved, every container had marked the description of goods, the kind and number of package, weight, measurement and carrier's seal number, the bill of lading was shipped bill of lading, fee and terminal handling charges at loading port, and ocean freight would be prepaid by drawer, fee and terminal handling charges at destination port would be paid by consignee at destination port, and the transport documents were ordered to be given to the drawer.

On February 13, 2010, the five containers involved were loaded by the Plaintiff onto M.V. "MAERSKSTOCKHOLM" and shipped from Yantian Port to Nhava Sheva. The unissued bill of lading No.859498700 whose title was MAERSK recorded that: number of booking confirmation was 859,498,700, shipper was Shenzhen Trade Export Co. Ltd., number of service contract was 409,149, consignee was LIMRATRADERSA-3, the name of vessel was M.V.

"MAERSKSTOCKHOLM", port of loading was Yantian Port, port of discharge was JAWAHARLALNEHRU, the five containers involved were packed with 9,063 rolls of electric resistance wire, freight prepaid, yard to yard, date of loading on board was February 13. During the hearing, the Plaintiff stated that since the Defendant failed to pay the freight, the bill of lading was left in the system remaining unissued and the original had not been delivered to the Defendant yet.

4) The arrival time of the goods at Nhava Sheva. According to the transport plan recorded on the booking confirmation, the shipment took eight to fifteen days from Guangdong, China to New Delhi, India. On February 10, 2010, the shipping instructions of the goods involved were sent out, on February 13, the goods were loaded on board as specified in the bill of lading, during the period from February 26 to June 2, Chanlian Shenzhen, due to the customers' problem about customs clearance, contacted with the Plaintiff's agent at loading port for many times by e-mail to change the destination port, shipper and consignee, and on April 16 recognized that the shipper would go to Nhava Sheva to clear and take delivery of the goods which thus did not need to be transshipped to New Delhi. Therefore, the Plaintiff inferred that the goods had arrived at the port on April 16. Because the Plaintiff had no other evidence to prove the time when the goods involved arrived at the destination port, the arrival time alleged by the Plaintiff was not earlier than the actual arrival time according to the inference from common sense, which did not harm the Defendants' right and interest, therefore, the court ascertains that the arrival time of the goods involved at Nhava Sheva was on April 16, 2010.

Both of the parties chose to apply the laws of the People's Republic of China to try the disputes in this case in the hearing.

The court holds that this case is arising from dispute over contract of carriage of goods by sea. The carriage involved is from Yantian Port, Shenzhen, China to Nhava Sheva, India and the Plaintiff is an enterprise legal person set up out of the People's Republic of China, thus this case involves with foreign elements. The place of dispatch of the carriage involved is in Guangdong and the court is the maritime court of such place of dispatch, according to Article 11 of the Some Provisions of the Supreme People's Court on the Scope of Cases to be Entertained by Maritime Courts and Article 27 of the Civil Procedure Law of the People's Republic of China, the court has jurisdiction over this case. Both of the parties chose to apply the laws of the People's Republic of China at the hearing, according to the Article 269 of the Maritime Code of the People's Republic of China, the parties to a contract may choose the law applicable to such contract, the substantive dispute in this case shall be handled by applying the laws of the People's Republic of China.

The issues of this case lie in: whether the Plaintiff was the competent subject or not, whether the lawsuit filed by the Plaintiff had exceeded the statute of limitation, whether the contractual relationship on carriage of goods by sea had been established between the Plaintiff and the Defendant, whether the proceeds from the auction of the goods' exceeding the container detention fee had deprived the Plaintiff from the right to claim for the container detention fee, and whether the claim amount was rational or not.

Maersk Shenzhen undertook the business of accepting booking and so on as the Plaintiff's agent, who also stated to the court that it acted as the Plaintiff's agent to carry out the operation of bill of lading involved. Combined with the fact that the goods involved were carried by the Plaintiff actually, the Plaintiff shall be identified as the carrier of the transportation involved and is the competent subject as the carrier to lodge the action arising from the dispute over the contract of carriage of goods by sea.

Both the Plaintiff and the Defendants agreed that the case was arising from dispute over contract of carriage of goods by sea with prescribed limitation period of one year, but they had disagreement on the time which such limitation period should be counted from. The Plaintiff alleged that the limitation period for the continuing damages should be calculated from the final date of damage, so the limitation period for this case should be calculated from February 28, 2011, after India Customs had dealt with the goods. The Defendants alleged that the Plaintiff's right was infringed from the date of non-taking delivery of the goods involved, so the limitation period of litigation should be calculated from the date when nobody took delivery of the goods involved after the goods' arrival at the destination port, namely from February 24 as the Plaintiff recognized that the goods involved arrived at the destination port on February 23, 2010. Since there was no cause for suspension or interruption of limitation period existing in this case, the lawsuit filed by the Plaintiff had been time-barred.

According to the Official Reply of the Supreme People's Court on the Limitation of Action of the Carrier's Claim for Compensation against the Consignor, Consignee, or Holder of the Bill of Lading under Carriage of Goods by Sea, the provision of Article 257 Paragraph 1 of the Maritime Code of the People's Republic of China shall apply mutatis mutandis to the limitation period for the carrier's claims against the shipper regarding the carriage of goods by sea, which is one year, counting from the date on which the obligee knew or should have known that his right had been infringed. The key point in this case is how to determine the date on which the Plaintiff "knew or should have known that his right had been infringed". After the goods' arrival at the destination port, the two Defendants had not given up the goods expressly all the way, but told the Plaintiff that the consignee would go to the destination port to clear and take delivery of the goods, so the Plaintiff had reason to wait for the consignee's taking delivery of the goods. Both of the parties had no evidence to prove the deadline of clearance ruled by the authority at the destination port, and Chanlian Shenzhen had promised that the shipper would bear the container detention fee by e-mails on March 30, 2010. The reason why the Plaintiff's right had been infringed was that the containers provided by the Plaintiff for finishing the contract of carriage of goods by sea were occupied overtime. The fact of damage because of overtime occupation was continuing and not until the goods were auctioned by the Nhava Sheva Customs as tax-evading goods, did the Plaintiff know the consignee was impossible to take delivery of the goods and was the damage due to overtime use of containers stopped when the containers' situation of being occupied was ended due to the successful bidder's taking delivery of the goods. The said damage constituted a complete contract debt, therefore, the court ascertains that the limitation period prescribed for the Plaintiff to exercise the right of claim shall be calculated from February 28, 2011, the date when the customs in Nhava Sheva, India sent document regarding "the delivery of the goods being auctioned" to the Plaintiff and thus the date when Plaintiff filed this lawsuit with the court on February 27, 2011 has not exceed the one year prescribed limitation period of action.

The Plaintiff accepted Chanlian Shenzhen's entrustment to arrange the carriage of the goods from Yantian Port, Shenzhen to Nhava Sheva, India. The fact that Chanlian Shenzhen booked space from the Plaintiff, sent out shipping instructions, changed the destination port, shipper and consignee by e-mails and that the goods had been actually carried indicated that Chanlian Shenzhen concluded the contract of carriage of goods by sea with the Plaintiff in his own name and actually performed the contract under which Chanlian Shenzhen was the shipper, while the Plaintiff was the carrier. Accordingly, the contractual relationship about carriage of goods by sea between Chanlian Shenzhen and the Plaintiff had been established according to the law. That contract was both parties' true declaration of intension on the basis of equality and voluntary and did not violate the compulsory provisions of laws and administrative regulations, and thus was legal and effective. Therefore, both of the parties should exercise their right and fulfill their obligation according to the contract and relevant laws. After entrusting the carriage of goods to the Plaintiff, the Defendant neither paid the freight according to the contract, nor obtained the original of bill of lading. Both of the parties' agreeing that the goods were to be taken delivery of by LIMRATRADERSA-3 at destination belonged to the situation that the parties agreed the third party to fulfill obligations, so it shall be deemed that the third party failed to fulfill the obligation when nobody took delivery of the goods at destination the port. According to Article 121 of the Contract Law of the People's Republic of China which stipulates that where a party's breach was attributable to a third party, it shall nevertheless be liable to the other party for breach, the legal consequence due to the failure of the third party to fulfill the obligation of taking delivery of the goods shall be born by Chanlian Shenzhen. Chanlian Shenzhen as the branch established by Chanlian does not possess the status of a legal person and has no independent capacity for civil liability, so the Defendant Chanlian as the legal entity who established Chanlian Shenzhen shall be held liable as the shipper to the Plaintiff jointly with Chanlian Shenzhen.

The precondition of deciding whether the two Defendants' arguments that the proceeds from auction is enough for paying the container detention fee and the Plaintiff has no right to claim from the shipper could be well-grounded or not, is that it exists the fact that the Plaintiff's loss had been compensated by the proceeds from auction. The proceeds from the auction of the goods arranged by the local customs at the destination port was disposed according to the local administrative law. The two Defendants had no evidence to prove that the proceeds from auction could be collected by the Plaintiff and the Plaintiff's loss had been compensated by the proceeds from auction, no clue of compensating the Plaintiff's loss by the proceeds from auction could be found in the customs' documents involved, and the carrier had no right to collect the proceeds from auction concerning the goods disposed by the customs from ordinary ways of every countries' customs on disposing import cargo, therefore, under the circumstance that the two Defendants failed to prove the Plaintiff had been compensated by the proceeds from auction, whether the proceeds from auction had exceed the Plaintiff's loss or not has nothing to do with the Plaintiff's right of claim for compensation according to contract of carriage of goods by sea, and the Plaintiff has the right to claim for the container detention fee from the liable party.

The containers are the tools provided by the Plaintiff for performing the contract of carriage of goods by sea, and under such contract it is the collateral obligation of the shipper or consignee to return containers on time after timely taking delivery of the goods. The loss incurred by the Plaintiff from the long-time occupation of the five containers which prevented such containers involved from being put into transportation timely due to nobody's taking delivery of the goods therein is obvious. The fee about overtime use of containers is the compensation for the Plaintiff's loss caused by the Defendant's delay in performing the obligation under the contract of carriage, according to Article 113 of the Contract Law of the People's Republic of China that where a party failed to perform or rendered non-conforming performance, thereby causing loss to the other party, the amount of damages payable shall be equivalent to the other party's loss resulting from the breach, including any benefit that may be accrued from performance of the contract. The period during which the five containers involved were occupied shall start from April 22, 2010, the sixth day (free period were five days) after the goods involved arrived at the destination port, to February 28, 2011, the date when the goods were appointed to be delivered to the successful bidder. The Plaintiff's charging standard of the container detention fee was published through the internet, though the two Defendants denied that both of the parties had reached agreement on that standard in advance, it is the common practice for domestic and international shipping industry to publish charging standard of the container detention fee through the internet, that charging standard was within reasonable range after examination, and the carrier's purpose of collecting the container detention fee was urging the user to perform actively and return containers timely instead of supporting the user to occupy containers. Therefore, the court adopts the charging standard published by the Plaintiff on the website, and accordingly calculates the fee about the overtime use of five containers involved to be Rp6,921,455 which has been over several times of the total value of the five containers involved. According to common sense, the highest amount towards container detention fee which can be anticipated by the shipper shall be the price of container itself. Where a party breached the contract, the other party shall take the appropriate measures to prevent further loss; where the other party sustained further loss due to its failure to take the appropriate measures, it may not claim damages for such further loss. Article 87 and Article 88 of the Maritime Code of the People's Republic of China stipulate that if the charges to be paid to the carrier have not been paid in full, nor has appropriate security been given, the goods have not been taken delivery of within 60 days from the next day of the ship's arrival at the port of discharge, the carrier may apply to the court for an order on selling the goods by auction, the proceeds from the auction sale shall be used to pay off the charges to be paid to the carrier, if the proceeds fall short of such expenses, the carrier is entitled to claim the difference from the shipper. According to the said stipulations, the Plaintiff is entitled to take measurements according to law to dispose of the goods for preventing the further loss due to the overtime use of containers. The Plaintiff failed to prove that it had taken corresponding measurements to prevent further loss but failed because of the provisions of the local law, therefore, the two Defendants' argument that the Plaintiff had not taken appropriate measurement to prevent further shall be well-grounded. When the loss of container detention fee has accumulated up to the price of a new container, the carrier can buy a new container to prevent further loss. After examination, the market price of a 40' container is about RMB30,000 in recent two years. Taking comprehensive account of the Plaintiff's obligation of preventing further loss, the loss for the breach of contract when signing the contract which can be foreseen by the two Defendants and other relevant elements, the court, at its discretion, decides that the two Defendants shall compensate the Plaintiff jointly for the loss of container detention fee in the amount of RMB150,000.

In conclusion, according to Article 65, Article 107, Article 113 and Article 119 Paragraph 1 of the Contract Law of the People's Republic of China, the judgment is as follows:

1. The Defendants Shanghai Chanlian Xieyun Logistics Co., Ltd. Shenzhen Branch and Shanghai Chanlian Xieyun Logistics Co., Ltd. shall jointly compensate the Plaintiff A. P. Moller - Maersk A/S. for the container detention fee in the amount RMB150,000;
2. Reject other claims of the Plaintiff A.P.Moller- MaerskA/S.

The above obligation with respect to pecuniary payment shall be fulfilled within 10 days after this judgment comes into effect.

For failure to fulfill the obligation with respect to pecuniary payment within the period specified by this judgment, interest on the debt for the delayed period shall be doubled, pursuant to the provisions of Article 253 of the Civil Procedure Law of the People's Republic of China.

Court acceptance fee in amount ofRMB14,066, the Plaintiff shall bear RMB12,017, the Defendants shall bear RMB2,049. The Defendants shall directly pay the part of litigation cost payable by them to the Plaintiff, and the court will not return back separately the litigation cost which be refunded to the Plaintiff.

In the event of dissatisfaction with this judgment, the Plaintiff may within 30 days upon the service of this judgment, and the Defendants may within 15 days upon the service of this judgment submit a statement of appeal to the court, together with copies in the number of the opposite party, to lodge an appeal with the Guangdong High People's Court.

Presiding Judge: NI Xuewei
Acting Judge: YANG Yaxiao
People's Juror: CHEN Xiuling

October16, 2013

Clerk: LU Shiying

Guangdong High People's Court
Civil Judgment

A.P. Moller-Maersk A/S
v.
Shanghai Chanlian Xieyun Logistics Co., Ltd. et al.

(2013) Yue Gao Fa Min Si Zhong Zi No.162

Related Case(s) This is the judgment of second instance, and the judgment of first instance and the judgment of retrial are on page 45 and page 76 respectively.

Cause(s) of Action 202. Dispute over contract of carriage of goods by sea or sea-connected waters.

Headnote Affirm lower court judgment that the Plaintiff carrier was entitled to recover cost of five containers by way of container detention fees, as the Defendant freight forwarder's liability for container detention could not exceed the value of the containers; claim was not time-barred because one-year limitation period ran from moment when it became obvious that it was impossible for the consignee to take delivery of the goods because they had been auctioned by customs authorities.

Summary The Plaintiff-Respondent carrier sued the Defendant-Appellant freight forwarder for damages arising out of the Defendant-Appellant's failure to pay container detention fees for containers in which the Plaintiff-Respondent carried goods from Shenzhen to Nhava Sheva, India. The consignee did not take possession of the goods in Nhava Sheva, and the local customs authorities auctioned off the goods inside the containers after nearly a year. The court of first instance held that a contract of carriage existed between the Plaintiff-Respondent and the Defendant-Appellant; that there was no evidence that the Plaintiff-Respondent was entitled to the proceeds from the auction of the goods inside the containers; and that the Plaintiff-Respondent had brought its action within the statute of limitations because the one-year limitation period did not begin to run until the goods had been auctioned, as only then was it clear that it was impossible for the consignee to appear and take delivery. The appeal court recognized, holding that the facts were correctly found in the original judgment and that the law was correctly applied.

Judgment

The Appellant (the Defendant of first instance): Shanghai Chanlian Xieyun Logistics Co., Ltd. Shenzhen Branch
Domicile: Ocean Building, No.66, Dongmen North Road, Luohu District, Shenzhen, Guangdong, the People's Republic of China.
Person in charge: CAI Guoliang, general manager.
Agent *ad litem*: HUANG Sufang, lawyer of Guangdong Shengtang Law Firm.

The Appellant (the Defendant of first instance): Shanghai Chanlian Xieyun Logistics Co., Ltd.
Domicile: Room 6647, Building 2, No.293, Weichang Road, Jinshan District, Shanghai, the People's Republic of China.
Legal representative: WU Liang, general manager.
Agent *ad litem*: HUANG Sufang, lawyer of Guangdong Shengtang Law Firm.

The Respondent (the Plaintiff of first instance): A.P. Moller-Maersk A/S
Domicile 1098 Copenhagen, Denmark.
Legal representative: Morten Engelstoft and Peter Ronister Anderson.
Agent *ad litem*: CAO Fang, lawyer of Shanghai All Bright Law Office.
Agent *ad litem*: MA Yixing, lawyer of Shanghai All Bright Law Office.

Dissatisfied with (2012) Guang Hai Fa Chu Zi No.329 Civil Judgment rendered by the Guangzhou Maritime Court with respect to the case arising from dispute over contract of carriage of goods by sea, the Appellants Shanghai Chanlian Xieyun Logistics Co., Ltd. Shenzhen Branch (hereinafter referred to as Chanlian Shenzhen) and Shanghai Chanlian Xieyun Logistics Co., Ltd. (hereinafter referred to as Chanlian) filed appeals against the Respondent, A.P. Moller-Maersk A/S (hereinafter referred to as Maersk),to the court. After accepting this case, the court constituted a collegiate panel to try this case. Now the case has been concluded.

Maersk alleged in the court of first instance that: in 2010, Chanlian Shenzhen entrusted Maersk with the carriage of the goods in 5 containers under the bill of ladingNo.859498700 from Yantian Port, Shenzhen to New Delhi, India and Maersk accepted the entrustment of carrying the goods involved. Before and after the goods' arrival at the transshipment port Nhava Sheva, Chanlian Shenzhen requested to change the destination port for many times but then canceled the change. Finally, Chanlian Shenzhen recognized that the shipper would bear the fees arising from the detention in Nhava Sheva and the consignee would undertake customs clearance and take delivery of the goods in Nhava Sheva on April 29, Chanlian Shenzhen requested to change the shipper into "SHENZHENTRADEANDEXPORTCOLTD" and the consignee into "SATYAOVERSEAS". On June 2, Chanlian Shenzhen requested to change the consignee into "LIMRATRADERSA-3" again. The goods were confiscated by the Nhava Sheva Customs due to non-taking delivery of the goods involved. On February 28, 2011, the Nhava Sheva Customs informed Maersk that the goods had been auctioned and should be delivered by Maersk to the buyers. During the period of detention of the goods involved in Nhava Sheva, the fee arising from the overtime use of containers were totally Rp8,026,425, equaling to RMB1,029,554.51 (according to the exchange rate on the date of the filing of the action). Chanlian Shenzhen as the shipper who changed the consignor and consignee repeatedly should bear the liability for the loss incurred by the carrier as a result of non-taking delivery of the goods. Considering Chanlian Shenzhen was a branch of Chanlian, Chanlian should bear joint and several liabilities for the loss caused to the carrier by the act of Chanlian Shenzhen. Maersk hence requested the court of first instance to order Chanlian Shenzhen and Shenzhen to bear the fee arising from the overtime use of containers in the amount of Rp8,026,425 (RMB1,029,554.51 after exchange according to the rate on the date of filing of the action) and the litigation fee of this case jointly.

Maersk submitted the following evidence during the period of adducing evidence in the court of first instance:

1. Booking confirmation (No.859498700), to prove that Chanlian Shenzhen booked space from Maersk;
2. Bill of lading (No.859498700) which was not issued, to prove that the contractual relationship about carriage of goods by sea between Maersk and Chanlian Shenzhen;
3. E-mails between Maersk and Chanlian Shenzhen from February 26, 2010 to April16, 2010, to prove that before the arrival of the goods involved in Nhava Sheva, Chanlian Shenzhen had requested to change the destination port for many times and recognized that the shipper would bear the fee arising from the detention of the goods involved in Nhava Sheva and the consignee would undertake customs clearance and take delivery of the goods;
4. E-mails sent by Chanlian Shenzhen to Maersk from April29, 2010 to June2,2010, to prove that Chanlian Shenzhen had requested to change the shipper and consignee twice;
5. Two copies of customs documents, to prove that the goods involved had been auctioned by the customs at the destination port and the customs asked Maersk to deliver the goods to the buyers;
6. Charging standard of the container detention fee, to prove the charging standard that Maersk adopted as a basis for container detention fee.

   After the expiration of the period of adducing evidence, Maersk supplemented the following evidence:
7. E-mails between Maersk and Chanlian Shenzhen, export invoices and bank's receipt (payment) vouchers under the bill of lading (No.860320322), to prove the Chinese name, English name and customer's invoice number of Chanlian Shenzhen and the long-term use of the same E-mail address by Chanlian Shenzhen to have business correspondences with Maersk;
8. Shipping instructions under the bill of lading involved, to prove the shipping instructions towards the carriage involved were made by Chanlian Shenzhen;
9. Statement of Maersk (China) Shipping Shenzhen Branch (hereinafter referred to as "Maersk Shenzhen"), to prove Maersk Shenzhen was the agent of Maersk

at the loading port and the e-mails submitted by Maersk was authentic, because the e-mail box "PRSCSEINS@MAERSK.COM" had been abolished, there was no way to notarize the e-mails downloaded;
10. Business license of Maersk Shenzhen, to prove Maersk Shenzhen was the agent of Maersk at the loading port;
11. E-mails between both parties, to prove the e-mail address of Chanlian Shenzhen and that the two parties had negotiated about the carriage involved for many times.

Chanlian Shenzhen and Chanlian jointly defended in the court of first instance that: they had no contractual relationship of carriage of goods by sea with Maersk and there was no basis in law for Maersk to request Chanlian Shenzhen and Chanlian to bear the liability for the container detention fee as they were neither the shipper nor the consignee. Maersk failed to prove the container detention fee had accrued and existed actually. According to the provision of law, the carrier should apply to the court for a ruling of auctioning the goods after 60 days from the date of non-taking delivery of the goods involved, and the fee payable by the shipper or consignee to Maersk should be paid off from the proceeds of auction, rather than being auctioned by the customs when the goods had not taken delivery of for almost one year, hence, Maersk should bear the expanded loss caused by its failure to timely dealing with the goods. The container detention fee that Maersk claimed for had far exceeded the value of the containers and in the case where the container detention fee was higher than the value of a new container, the carrier could reduce the loss by buying a new container. The container detention fee should only be calculated for a period within 60 days from the date of non-taking delivery of the goods and could not be over the price of buying new containers, whichever the amount was lower. The proceeds of the auction of the goods involved dealt by the Nhava Sheva Customs were enough to pay off the container detention fee, hence, Maersk not only had no right to claim for that fee against the shipper, but also should return the rest of the proceeds of auction to the shipper according to the law. The action filed by Maersk had exceeded the statute of limitation and thus should be rejected by the court.

Chanlian Shenzhen and Chanlian submitted one group of evidence during the period of adducing evidence in the court of first instance: two copies of documents of Nhava Sheva Customs, to prove the proceeds from the auction of the goods involved were enough to pay off the container detention fee, so Maersk had no right to claim such fee from the shipper and the rest of the proceeds from auction in the amount of Rp24,585,175 should be returned to the shipper.

Chanlian Shenzhen and Chanlian did not recognize the authenticity, legality and relevancy of evidence 1 to evidence 4, evidence 8 and evidence 11 submitted by Maersk, and held that the booking confirmation and bill of lading had no original to be verified, e-mails, as digital data, had not been proved through legal proceeds, and Chanlian Shenzhen and Chanlian only had used the e-mail box with the suffix of "COM" instead of "ORG", Maersk Shenzhen, a party not involved, was the agent of Maersk and had interests with Maersk, those explanations in the evidence fell into self-evidence of party not involved in this case and were isolated evidence. Chanlian Shenzhen and Chanlian recognized evidence 5, recognized the authenticity of evidence 6 but did not recognize the legality and relevancy, holding that the standard of the container detention fee was the unilateral assertion made by Maersk which could not be binding upon Chanlian Shenzhen and Chanlian. Chanlian Shenzhen and Chanlian did not recognize the authenticity of the e-mails in evidence 7, but recognized the e-mail box was used by Chanlian Shenzhen and Chanlian, recognized the authenticity of the bank's receipt (payment) vouchers but not the content the evidence to prove. Chanlian Shenzhen and Chanlian recognized the authenticity of evidence 9 but not the content the evidence to prove. Chanlian Shenzhen and Chanlian had no objection to evidence 10. Maersk recognized the evidence submitted by Chanlian Shenzhen and Chanlian but objected to the contents the evidence to prove.

After the cross-examination in the hearing, the court of first instance ascertained the evidence as follows: evidence 5 submitted by Maersk was the same as evidence 1 submitted by Chanlian Shenzhen and Chanlian which was formed out of China, the parties had no objection to its legality, thus the court of first instance confirmed the probative force of that evidence. Chanlian Shenzhen and Chanlian recognized the authenticity of evidence 6, evidence 7, evidence 9, evidence 10 and the bank's receipt (payment) vouchers in evidence 8 submitted by Maersk, thus the court of first instance confirmed the probative force of those evidence. The invoices under evidence 7 submitted by Maersk and the bank's receipt (payment) vouchers whose probative force confirmed by the court of first instance could support each other, thus the probative force of such invoices could be confirmed by the court of first instance. Chanlian Shenzhen and Chanlian did not affirm the rest of evidence submitted by Maersk but failed to submit any evidence to refute them, Chanlian Shenzhen and Chanlian's denying the fact of booking shipping space from Maersk obviously contradicted with their acknowledging the goods involved were carried by Chanlian Shenzhen and Chanlian, and Chanlian Shenzhen and Chanlian failed to make any reasonable explains, therefore, the court of first instance confirmed evidence 1, evidence 2 and evidence 8 which were submitted by Maersk to prove that Chanlian Shenzhen had booked space from Maersk. The e-mails under Maersk's evidence 3, evidence 4, evidence11 and evidence 7 were all typescripts without the notarization, but the failure of notarization was due to objective reasons, in view of Chanlian Shenzhen and Chanlian' affirming the authenticity of the e-mail box used for correspondence, the court of first instance would comprehensively ascertain the content of the e-mails combining with other evidence.

According to the evidence with the probative force ascertained by the court of first instance and the circumstances of the hearings, the court of first instance found out the following facts:

1. The undisputed facts between the parties

    On February 28, 2011, the delivery order No.67 was issued by customs specialist from the processing department, Nhava Sheva Customs, which stated that, on February 21, Nhava Sheva Customs through the auction No.56 sold the goods in the five containers (hereinafter referred to as "the five containers involved") which respectively numbered with MSKU9591614, TCNU9520396, AMFU8702814, MSKU9053162, MSKU0824459 located at Maersk (old) Container Freight Station and the goods must be delivered in five days after the issuance of delivery order. Those goods were described as various types of tax-evading Chinese goods. The proceeds from such auction were Rp26,526,500 which had been paid by the buyer M/S Bhavi Impex on February 28, with 12.5% of value-added tax Rp1,025,000 and 5% of value-added tax Rp916,325 being gone into the government's finance department. On the same day, the delivery order No.67 regarding "the delivery of the goods being auctioned" was issued by the processing department of Nhava Sheva Customs to the manager of Maersk (old) Container Freight Station, which stated that, the customs office instructed your company to deliver the goods under the electronic auction No.56 to the bidder M/S Bhavi Impex who succeeded in auction.

Maersk alleged that the goods involved were auctioned at the destination port due to non-taking delivery of the goods. According to the documents of Nhava Sheva Customs, such goods, which were still at the container freight station of Maersk during auction, were auctioned due to being identified as tax-evading goods. The time of loading the goods involved at the loading port was on February 23, 2010 and the time of auction was on February 21, 2011. Maersk's statement and the documents of local customs could support each other, therefore, the court of first instance ascertained the fact that the goods involved had been taken delivery of by nobody at the destination port for a long time and that they were auctioned by the local customs.

Charging standard of the fee about the overtime use of 40' containers imported from Nhava Sheva as published by Maersk on its website could be seen as follows: free from the first to the 5th day, Rp940 per container per day from the 6th to the 12th day, Rp1, 598 per container per day from the 13th to the 19th day, Rp1,786 per container per day from the 20th to the 26th day, and Rp4, 653 per container per day for those days after.

2. The disputed facts between the parties
1) The English name of Chanlian Shenzhen. Maersk submitted undisputed export invoices about past transactions, e-mails and bank's receipt (payment) vouchers to prove the English name of Chanlian Shenzhen, which was denied by Chanlian Shenzhen and Chanlian who, however, failed to submitted its correct English name to repute it. The bank's receipt (payment) vouchers submitted by Maersk were originals stating that the payer was Chanlian Shenzhen; the time of payment and the amount could be verified with the rest evidence. Chanlian Shenzhen and Chanlian had the advantage of providing evidence to prove their English name but failed to do so, which was enough to infer that the English name proved by Maersk's evidence was true. The export invoices No. CN11174552-860,320,322, stamped with Chanlian Shenzhen's confirmed chapter about issuing invoice, stated that the English name of the payer was "XENFREIGHTAGENCYLTDSHENZHENOFF", therefore, the court of first

instance ascertained that the English name of Chanlian Shenzhen was "XENFREIGHTAGENCYLTDSHENZHENOFF" according to it.
2) The status of Maersk. Chanlian Shenzhen and Chanlian alleged that, as the booking confirmation submitted by Maersk showed that the party who accepted the booking was Maersk Shenzhen, a party not involved, Maersk was not the carrier. After investigation, it was found that Maersk Shenzhen with registration number 440301506645877 under the business license, was a branch of MAERSK (China) Shipping Co., Ltd., whose scope of business was to undertake canvassion, booking, issuing the bill of lading, settlement of freight, international shipping agency services and signing contract about relevant business for the ships owned or operated by Maersk. The statement of Maersk Shenzhen specified that Maersk Shenzhen actually undertook the carriage of goods under the bill of lading involved as Maersk's agent in China. The court of first instance held that the above evidence were according to what was written in the booking confirmation and bill of lading, Maersk Shenzhen, the party not involved, whose status as an agent had been made public, actually undertook the booking space of the goods involved as Maersk's agent, and thus Maersk was the carrier of the goods involved.
3) The issue about the booking and performance of the carriage involved. In the hearing, Chanlian Shenzhen and Chanlian recognized the authenticity of their e-mail box, bank's receipt (payment) vouchers, which specified that the payer was Chanlian Shenzhen, the payee was Maersk Shenzhen and the remark was freight under the undisputed bill of lading, and business license of Maersk Shenzhen. The above evidence proves that Chanlian Shenzhen had business transactions with Maersk. Combined with the fact recognized by the both parties that the goods involved carried by Maersk were auctioned by the local customs at the destination port, even though the booking confirmation, shipping instructions and so on submitted by Maersk were typescripts downloaded from the computer without corresponding originals to be checked with, they corresponded with the shipping operation custom of confirming the booking through shipping company's electronic information transmission platform, the customers code was the same as that under the undisputed bill of lading, the number of service contract, booking number ascertained, time and container number in the evidence could be verified with each other. Chanlian Shenzhen and Chanlian denied in these respects but without any rebutting evidence, while Maersk's statement and evidence were more persuasive, therefore, the court of first instance ascertained the fact about the carriage involved as follows:
In January 2010, Chanlian Shenzhen booked space from Maersk's agent at loading port Maersk Shenzhen, entrusted Maersk with the carriage of goods in seven 40' containers from Huangpu, Guangdong to New Delhi, India. After accepting the booking, Maersk made the booking confirmation No.859498700, specifying that the booking party was Chanlian Shenzhen (XENFREIGH TAGENCYLTDSHENZHENOFF), number of service contract was 409,149, contract customers was SINOLINKSASIALTD, means of transportation was

yard to yard, loading port was Huangpu, Guangdong, China, destination port was New Delhi, India, department of transportation was Maersk Shenzhen, booking was seven 40' dry cargo containers, date of executing shipment was January29, estimated time of loading was on February 7, the carrying vessel was M.V. "DUMMY", the vessel was estimated to arrive at pier one in Dachan Bay, India on February 10, then the goods would be transshipped by M.V. "NEDLLOYDOCEANIA" through two separate consignments to Madrid Port, New Delhi, India with estimated time of arrival to be respectively February 20 and February 26. Meanwhile, the booking confirmation indicated that please contact our company when changing the content of this booking and the e-mail box for contacting was PRSCSEINS@Maersk.com.

On February 10, 2012, Chanlian Shenzhen sent shipping instructions to Maersk, affirming that the goods had been packed into the five containers which were to be carried from Yantian Port to New Delhi, India, and Chanlian Shenzhen would pay the freight and accept the bill of lading. The shipping instruction whose data was exchanged on February 10 and booking number with 859,498,700 recorded that: customers code was 40,600,306,066, name of the customers was Chanlian Shenzhen, customers code under the contract was 40,900,206,657, name of the company was SINOLINKSASIALTD, company name of the shipper was Chanlian Shenzhen, consignee was SINOLINKSASIALTD, payer and drawer was Chanlian Shenzhen, the vessel's name was M.V. "MAERSKSTOCKHOLM", port of loading was Yantian Port, China, destination port was New Delhi, India, container number was the number of five containers involved, every container had marked the description of goods, the kind and number of package, weight, measurement and carrier's seal number, the bill of lading was shipped bill of lading, fee and terminal handling charges at loading port, and ocean freight would be prepaid by drawer, fee and terminal handling charges at destination port would be paid by consignee at destination port, and the transport documents were ordered to be given to the drawer.

On February 13, 2010, the five containers involved were loaded by Maersk onto M.V. "MAERSKSTOCKHOLM" and shipped from Yantian Port to Nhava Sheva. The unissued bill of lading No.859498700 whose title was MAERSK recorded that: number of booking confirmation was 859,498,700, shipper was Shenzhen Trade Export Co. Ltd., number of service contract was 409,149, consignee was LIMRATRADERSA-3, the name of vessel was M.V. "MAERSKSTOCKHOLM", port of loading was Yantian Port, port of discharge was JAWAHARLALNEHRU, the five containers involved were packed with 9,063 rolls of electric resistance wire, freight prepaid, yard to yard, date of loading on board was February 13. During the hearing, Maersk stated that since Chanlian Shenzhen failed to pay the freight, the bill of lading was left in the system remaining not issued and the original had not been delivered to Chanlian Shenzhen yet.

4) The arrival time of the goods at Nhava Sheva. According to the transport plan recorded on the booking confirmation, the shipment took eight to fifteen days from Guangdong, China to New Delhi, India. On February 10, 2010, the shipping instructions of the goods involved were sent out, on February 13, the goods were loaded on board as specified in the bill of lading, during the period from February 26 to June 2, Chanlian Shenzhen, due to the customers' problem about customs clearance, contacted with Maersk's agent at loading port for many times by e-mail to change the destination port, shipper and consignee, and on April16recognized that the shipper would go to Nhava Sheva to clear and take delivery of the goods which thus did not need to be transshipped to New Delhi. Therefore, Maersk inferred that the goods had arrived at the port on April16. Because Maersk had no other evidence to prove the time when the goods involved arrived at the destination port, the arrival time alleged by Maersk was not earlier than the actual arrival time according to the inference from common sense, which did not harm Chanlian Shenzhen and Chanlian' right and interest, therefore, the court of first instance ascertained that the arrival time of the goods involved at Nhava Sheva was on April 16, 2010.

Both of the parties chose to apply the laws of the People's Republic of China to handle the disputes in this case in the court of first instance.

The court of first instance held that this case was arising from dispute over contract of carriage of goods by sea. The carriage involved was from Yantian Port, Shenzhen, China to Nhava Sheva, India, and Maersk was an enterprise legal person set up out of the People's Republic of China, thus this case involved with foreign elements. The place of dispatch of the carriage involved was in Guangdong and the court of first instance was the maritime court of such place of dispatch, according to the Some Provisions of the Supreme People's Court on the Scope of Cases to be Entertained by Maritime Courts Article 11 and the Civil Procedure Law of the People's Republic of China Article 27, the court of first instance had jurisdiction over this case. Both of the parties chose to apply the laws of the People's Republic of China at the hearing, according to the Maritime Code of the People's Republic of China Article 269, the parties to a contract may choose the law applicable to such contract, the substantive dispute in this case should be handled by applying the laws of the People's Republic of China.

The court of first instance concluded the issues of this case in: whether Maersk was the competent subject or not, whether the lawsuit filed by Maersk had exceeded the statute of limitation, whether the contractual relationship on carriage of goods by sea had been established between both parties, whether the proceeds from the auction of the goods' exceeding the container detention fee had deprived Maersk from the right to claim for the container detention fee, and whether the claim amount was rational or not.

Maersk Shenzhen undertook the business of accepting booking and so on as Maersk's agent, who also stated to the court of first instance that it acted as Maersk's agent to carry out the operation of bill of lading involved. Combined with the fact that the goods involved were carried by Maersk actually, Maersk should be identified as the carrier of the transportation involved and was the competent subject as the carrier to lodge the action arising from the dispute over the contract of carriage of goods by sea.

Both Maersk and Chanlian Shenzhen and Chanlian agreed that the case was arising from dispute over contract of carriage of goods by sea with prescribed limitation period of one year, but they had disagreement on the time which such limitation period should be counted from. Maersk alleged that the limitation period for the continuing damages should be calculated from the final date of damage, so the limitation period for this case should be calculated from February 28, 2011, after India customs had dealt with the goods. Chanlian Shenzhen and Chanlian alleged that Maersk's right was infringed from the date of non-taking delivery of the goods involved, so the limitation period of litigation should be calculated from the date when nobody took delivery of the goods involved after the goods' arrival at the destination port, namely from February 24 as Maersk recognized that the goods involved were arrived at the destination port on February 23, 2010. Since there was no cause for suspension or interruption of limitation period existing in this case, the action filed by Maersk had been time-barred.

The court of first instance held that, according to the Official Reply of the Supreme People's Court on the Limitation of Action of the Carrier's Claim for Compensation against the Consignor, Consignee, or Holder of the Bill of Lading under Carriage of Goods by Sea, the Maritime Code of the People's Republic of China Article 257 Paragraph 1 should apply mutatis mutandis to the limitation period for the carrier's claims against the shipper regarding the carriage of goods by sea, which was one year, counting from the date on which the obligee knew or should have known that his right had been infringed. The key point in this case was how to determine the date on which Maersk "knew or should have known that his right had been infringed". After the goods' arrival at the destination port, Chanlian Shenzhen and Shenzhen had not given up the goods expressly all the way, but told Maersk that the consignee would go to the destination port to clear and take delivery of the goods, so Maersk had reason to wait for the consignee's taking delivery of the goods. Both of the parties had no evidence to prove the deadline of clearance ruled by the authority at the destination port, and Chanlian Shenzhen had promised that the shipper would bear the container detention fee by e-mails on March 30, 2010. The reason why Maersk's right had been infringed was that the containers provided by Maersk for finishing the contract of carriage of goods by sea were occupied overtime. The fact of damage because of overtime occupation was continuing and not until the goods were auctioned by the Nhava Sheva Customs as tax-evading goods, did Maersk know the consignee was impossible to take delivery of the goods and was the damage due to overtime use of containers stopped when the containers' situation of being occupied was ended due to the successful bidder's taking delivery of the goods. The said damage constituted a complete contract debt, therefore, the court of first instance ascertained that the limitation period prescribed for Maersk to exercise the right of claim should be calculated from February 28, 2011, the date when the customs in Nhava Sheva, India sent document regarding "the delivery of the goods being auctioned" to Maersk and thus the date when

Plaintiff filed this action with the court of first instance on February 27, 2011 had not over the one year prescribed statute of limitations.

Maersk accepted Chanlian Shenzhen's entrustment to arrange the carriage of the goods from Yantian Port, Shenzhen to Nhava Sheva, India. The fact that Chanlian Shenzhen booked space from Maersk, sent out shipping instructions, changed the destination port, shipper and consignee by e-mails and that the goods had been actually carried indicated that Chanlian Shenzhen concluded the contract of carriage of goods by sea with Maersk in its own name and actually performed the contract under which Chanlian Shenzhen was the shipper, while Maersk was the carrier. Accordingly, the contractual relationship about carriage of goods by sea between Chanlian Shenzhen and Maersk had been established according to the law. That contract was both parties' true declaration of intension on the basis of equality and voluntary and did not violate the compulsory provisions of laws and administrative regulations, and thus was legal and effective. Therefore, both of the parties should exercise their right and fulfill their obligation according to the contract and relevant laws. After entrusting the carriage of goods to Maersk, Chanlian Shenzhen neither paid the freight according to the contract, nor did it obtain the original of bill of lading. Both of the parties' agreeing that the goods were to be taken delivery of by LIMRATRADERSA-3 at destination belonged to the situation that the parties agreed the third party to fulfill obligations, so it should be deemed that the third party failed to fulfill the obligation when nobody took delivery of the goods at destination port. According to the Contract Law of the People's Republic of China Article 121 which stipulates that where a party's breach was attributable to a third party, it should nevertheless be liable to the other party for breach, the legal consequence due to the failure of the third party to fulfill the obligation of taking delivery of the goods should be born by Chanlian Shenzhen. Chanlian Shenzhen as the branch established by Chanlian did not possess the status of a legal person and had no independent capacity for civil liability, so Chanlian as the legal entity who established Chanlian Shenzhen should be held liable as the shipper to Maersk jointly with Chanlian Shenzhen.

The precondition of deciding whether Chanlian Shenzhen and Shenzhen' arguments that the proceeds from auction were enough for paying the container detention fee and Maersk had no right to claim against the shipper could be well-grounded or not, was that the fact that Maersk's loss had been compensated by the proceeds from auction existed. The proceeds from the auction of the goods arranged by the local customs at the destination port was disposed according to the local administrative law. Chanlian Shenzhen and Shenzhen had no evidence to prove that the proceeds from auction could be collected by Maersk and Maersk's loss had been compensated by the proceeds from auction, no clue of compensating Maersk's loss by the proceeds from auction could be found in the customs' documents involved, and the carrier had no right to collect the proceeds from auction concerning the goods disposed by the customs from ordinary ways of every countries' customs on disposing import cargo, therefore, under the circumstance that Chanlian Shenzhen and Chanlian failed to prove Maersk had been compensated by the proceedings from auction, whether the proceeds from auction had exceed Maersk's loss or not had nothing to do with Maersk's right of claim for compensation according to contract of carriage of goods by sea, and Maersk had the right to claim for the container detention fee from the liable party.

The containers were the tools provided by Maersk for performing the contract of carriage of goods by sea, and under such contract it was the collateral obligation of the shipper or consignee to return containers on time after timely taking delivery of the goods. The loss incurred by Maersk from the long-time occupation of the five containers which prevented such containers involved from being put into transportation timely due to nobody's taking delivery of the goods therein was obvious. The fee about overtime use of containers was the compensation for Maersk's loss caused by the Chanlian Shenzhen's delay in performing the obligation under the contract of carriage, according to the Contract Law of the People's Republic of China Article 113, where a party failed to perform or rendered non-conforming performance, thereby causing loss to the other party, the amount of damages payable should be equivalent to the other party's loss resulting from the breach, including any benefit that may be accrued from performance of the contract. The period during which the five containers involved were occupied should start from April 22, 2010, the 6th day (free period were five days) after the goods involved arrived at the destination port, to February 28, 2011, the date when the goods were appointed to be delivered to the successful bidder. Maersk's charging standard of the container detention fee was published through the internet, though Chanlian Shenzhen and Shenzhen denied that both of the parties had reached agreement on that standard in advance, it was the common practice for domestic and international shipping industry to publish charging standard of the container detention fee through the internet, that charging standard was within reasonable range after examination, and the carrier's purpose of collecting the container detention fee was urging the user to perform actively and return containers timely instead of supporting the user to occupy containers. Therefore, the court of first instance adopted the charging standard published by Maersk on the website, and accordingly calculated the fee about the overtime use of five containers involved to be Rp6,921,455 which had been over several times of the total value of the five containers involved. According to common sense, the highest amount towards container detention fee which could be anticipated by the shipper should be the price of container itself. Where a party breached the contract, the other party should take the appropriate measures to prevent further loss; where the other party sustained further loss due to its failure to take the appropriate measures, it might not claim damages for such further loss. The Maritime Code of the People's Republic of China Article 87 and Article 88 stipulated that "if the charges to be paid to the carrier have not been paid in full, nor had appropriate security been given, the goods have not been taken delivery of within 60 days from the next day of the ship's arrival at the port of discharge, the carrier may apply to the court of first instance for an order on selling the goods by auction, the proceeds from the auction sale should be used to pay off the charges to be paid to the carrier, if the proceeds fall short of such expenses, the carrier is entitled to claim the difference from the shipper". According to the said stipulations, Maersk was entitled to take measurements according to law to dispose of the goods for preventing the further loss due to the overtime use of containers. Maersk failed to prove that it had taken corresponding measurements to prevent further loss but failed because of the provisions of the local law, therefore, Chanlian Shenzhen's and Chanlian's argument that Maersk had not taken appropriate measurement to prevent further should be well-grounded. When the loss of container detention fee had accumulated up to the price of a new container, the carrier could buy a new container to prevent further loss. After examination, the market price of a 40' container was about RMB30,000 in recent two years. Taking comprehensive account of Maersk's obligation of preventing further loss, the loss for the breach of contract when signing the contract which could be foreseen by Chanlian Shenzhen and Shenzhen and other relevant elements, the court of first instance, at its discretion, decided that Chanlian Shenzhen and Shenzhen should compensate Maersk jointly for the loss of container detention fee in the amount of RMB150,000.

In conclusion, according to the Contract Law of the People's Republic of China Article 65, Article 107, Article 113 and Article 119 Paragraph 1, judgment of first instance was as follows: 1. Shanghai Chanlian Xieyun Logistics Co., Ltd. Shenzhen Branch and Shanghai Chanlian Xieyun Logistics Co., Ltd. should jointly compensate A.P.Moller-Maersk A/S for the container detention fee in the amount RMB150,000; 2. reject other claims of A.P.Moller-Maersk A/S. The above obligation with respect to pecuniary payment should be fulfilled within 10 days after this judgment came into effect. Court acceptance fee of first instance of the casein amount of RMB14,066, A.P. Moller-Maersk A/S. should bear RMB12,017, Shanghai Chanlian Xieyun Logistics Co., Ltd. Shenzhen Branch and Shanghai Chanlian Xieyun Logistics Co., Ltd. should bear RMB2,049.

Chanlian Shenzhen and Chanlian dissatisfied with the original judgment, and filed an appeal before the court, requested that: revoke the first item of the original judgment; and order Maersk to bear the litigation fees. The reasons were as follows:

1. It was inconsistent with the fact that the original court ascertained the goods involved arrived at Newport, Mumbai on April16, 2010. The time of arrival of the goods involved should be prior to March24, 2010, the court of second instance should clearly find that. In evidence 3 submitted by Maersk, the translation in Chinese of the email sent by Maersk on March30, 2010 was "Please inform who should bear the container detention fee, please confirm, thanks". Therefore, container detention fee had generated since from March30, 2010. While in light of evidence 6 of Maersk, the free-charge period in Newport, Mumbai was 5 days, detention fee would be charged from the 6th day. Accordingly, in the case where container detention fee had generated from March30, 2010, the goods had arrived in Newport, Mumbai at least on March 24, 2010.
2. The statute of limitations of the claim for container detention fee in this case should be calculated from the time Maersk knew or should have known the day the container detention generated. It was wrong that the original court held the statute of limitations of this case should start from the time when Newport Customs sent the document concerning delivery of auctioned goods to Maersk. When the containers of Maersk were occupied overdue, the detention fee had

already generated. While neither the shipper nor the consignee paid the sum, Maersk ought to know its rights had been infringed, the statute of limitations should commence. To say the least, if the original court confirmed the fact that Chanlian Shenzhen contacted with the agent of Maersk at the port of shipment to change port of destination, shipper, consignee and etc. because of customs clearance and confirmed on April16 that the consignee would clear the customs and take delivery of the goods in Mumbai, then since from June 2, 2010, the shipper or the consignee neither took delivery of the goods, nor did they pay Maersk the container detention fee, Maersk should know its rights had been impaired at that time, and the statute of limitations of this case should commence. However, Maersk only filed a suit until February 27, 2012, it had exceeded the one-year statute of limitations. According to the Official Reply of the Supreme People's Court on the Limitation of Action of the Carrier's Claim for Compensation against the Consignor, Consignee or Holder of the Bill of Lading under Carriage of Goods by Sea (hereinafter referred to as the Official Reply), the statute of limitations of this case should be one year, calculated from the day when the aggrieved party knew or should have known his rights have been infringed rather than the day when the aggrieved party knew or should have known that the impairment of his rights had terminated. Maersk knew or should have known that its rights had been infringed on the day when the free-charge period of the containers involved expired and the detention fee commenced, but not until the occupation of container ended up (namely after the infringement was completely terminated). In addition, Maersk, as the carrier of the goods involved, should know the time when the goods were confiscated and auctioned by the customs, but not the case where it only knew the goods were auctioned until the Mumbai Newport customs informed it to deliver the goods to a new buyer by the customs. According to shipping practice, if the goods were confiscated by the local customs, the local customs would notify the carrier the first time. There would be a long period from the time of confiscation, auction of the goods to the time when the carrier was instructed to deliver the goods to the new buyer by the customs. According to the customs documents and the translation thereof in evidence 5 submitted by Maersk in the original instance, the goods involved were auctioned on February 21, 2011 by the disposal department of the customs, the goods involved were confiscated by the local customs on February 21, 2011, Maersk should at least be aware of the day when the goods were confiscated by local customs, the shipper or the consignee could not take delivery of the goods. Thus, granted that the calculation commenced from the day when the goods were confiscated by the customs, it had exceeded one-year statute of limitations.

3. The proceeds of the auction of the goods by the customs in Newport Mumbai were enough to pay for the container detention fee generating from the containers, Maersk failed to adduce evidence to prove it had applied to the local customs for paying off the sum of the subject case, as well as the trace of the auction. In the meantime, Maersk did not provide evidence to prove the carrier was not entitled to recovery from the proceeds of auction according to the local

law. Thus, the liability for failure of fulfilling burden of proof should be undertaken by Maersk.
4. As for the booking space and performance of the transport of the goods involved, since the evidence submitted by Maersk was insufficient to prove the goods were entrusted for transport by Chanlian Shenzhen and Chanlian, the original court determined Chanlian Shenzhen and Chanlian were the shippers only based on the copy of the booking confirmation and printed copy of emails, it did not conform to the facts.

Maersk made oral defense in the second instance as follows:

1. As for the time of arrival of the goods involved, the original court inferred it was April16, 2010, Chanlian Shenzhen and Chanlian alleged it was prior to March 24, 2010, it was meaningless to argue about this issue in the second instance. No matter it was April 16, 2010 or prior to March 24, 2010, the ascertainment would not be affected.
2. As for the commencement of the statute of limitations, it was correctly identified by the original court, Maersk did not know the damage to its rights arising from the containers' being continuously occupied until the customs sent the declaration and notice due to non-taking delivery of the goods at the port of destination, Maersk could not be recovered from the proceeds of auction, as a result, the actual loss happened to the carrier. That time of point should be the time that Maersk knew or should have known its rights had been damaged.
3. As for whether the carrier was entitled to proceeds from the auction by the customs, Maersk did not get the proceeds from the auction of the goods, it could not prove one thing that did not happen, if Chanlian Shenzhen and Chanlian alleged that Maersk obtained the auction proceeds, then they should adduce evidence.
4. As for the ascertainment of the evidence, most of the evidence was provided by Maersk Shenzhen Branch, a party not involved with this case, but not Maersk itself, and the relationship between Maersk Shenzhen Branch and Maersk could not be the basis to deny the effectiveness of the evidence.

In summary, Maersk requested the court of second instance to affirm the original judgment.

Upon hearing, the court finds out that: the facts found by the original court except the time of arrival of the goods involved were verified, the court hereby confirms. It is also found out that:

1. Maersk claimed for container detention fee in sum of Rp8,026,425 against Chanlian Shenzhen and Chanlian in the original instance, and submitted a container detention tariff as evidence, of which the contents are as follows: February 23 to 27, 2010 (5 days) - Pp0.00; February 28, 2010 to March 6, 2010 (7 days) - Pp6,580; March 7 to 13, 2010 (7 days) - Pp11,186; March 14 to 20, 2010 (7 days) - Pp12,502; March 21, 2010 to February 28, 2011 (345 days) - Pp1,605,285. Maersk upon examination by the first instance confirmed the

goods involved arrived in Newport, Mumbai on February 23, 2010. There is a mistake in the ascertainment of the original court on the time of arrival.
2. Chanlian Shenzhen and Chanlian confirmed in the second instance the authenticity of the email Maersk sent to Chanlian Shenzhen on March 30, 2010 in the evidence submitted by Maersk, of which the contents read as Maersk inquired Chanlian Shenzhen whether it knew about the consignee, and requested it to inform who would bear the container detention fee.
3. The carrier as shown in the title of the B/L involved is Maersk, while the carrying party in the booking confirmation is Maersk Shenzhen, the booking party is Chanlian Shenzhen, of which the number is 859498700, the same as the number of the B/L, but the destination (discharge) port stated in the booking confirmation has been changed from New Delhi, India to Newport, Mumbai.

The court holds this case is arising from dispute over contract of carriage of goods by sea. Newport, Mumbai, India is the destination port and the place where the detention of the containers of the carrier happened, therefore this case was concerning foreign-related maritime dispute. The parties concerned have no objection to the jurisdiction of the original court or the application of law, the court hereby confirms.

Based on the grounds of appeal of Chanlian Shenzhen and Chanlian, the court concludes the issues in this case as follows: (1) whether Maersk Shenzhen and Chanlian Shenzhen established a relationship of contract of carriage of goods by sea; (2) how to calculate the container detention fee claimed by Maersk and whether such sum should be deducted from the proceeds of auction by Mumbai Customs; (3) whether the action filed by Maersk has exceeded the statute of limitations.

In respect of the first issue, Chanlian Shenzhen alleged that the evidence adduced by Maersk was insufficient to prove the transport of the goods was entrusted by Chanlian Shenzhen, because the evidence Maersk adduced to prove they established a relationship of contract of carriage of goods by sea is a copy of booking confirmation and emails issued by itself. Upon verification, the customs' documents submitted by Chanlian Shenzhen in the original instance are the same with those documents of the Newport Customs submitted by Maersk in the original instance, it suggests the two parties have no question about the fact of the disposal of the goods by the customs, in the meantime, Chanlian Shenzhen admitted the authenticity of the email box, and confirmed the bank payment voucher which was adopted as a fixed mode in the business provided by Maersk as well as the authenticity of the email Maersk sent to it on March 30,2010 and made defense based thereon. Therefore, in terms of the goods involved, Chanlian Shenzhen and Maersk established a relationship of contract of carriage of goods by sea. The appeal claim of Chanlian Shenzhen that it did not entrust Maersk with the transport of the goods involved lacks factual basis, the court does not support.

In respect of the second issue, whether a relationship of contract of carriage of goods by sea between Chanlian Shenzhen and Maersk, Maersk has performed the obligation under the carriage contract, it has carried the goods involved to the destination port, but no body took delivery of the goods, resulting in the shipper's failure to return the containers to Maersk, therefore, Maersk's claiming for container detention fee against Chanlian Shenzhen and its parent company Chanlian has factual basis. The container detention fee Maersk claimed is calculated on the basis of the rate published on its website, Chanlian Shenzhen has never raised any objection, it should be deemed as consent of the two parties on the calculation standard of container detention fee. In addition, the description of the goods in the letter issued by the handing department of the Newport customs is "tax-evaded Chinese articles", it shows the goods involved violated the law concerning tax of India, and were confiscated and disposed by the customs. Since neither the parties submitted any evidence about relevant law of India to prove whether the detention fee should be collected by the carrier and whether the sum should be deducted from the proceeds of auction by the customs. According to the rules of distribution of the burden of proof, Chanlian Shenzhen and Chanlian alleged Maersk should collect the proceeds of auction and deduct the container detention fee, then they should provide the local law of India to prove, but they failed to do so, they should bear the legal consequence for failure of fulfilling burden of proof. Maersk calculated the container detention fee of the five containers on the basis of the standard published on the website in sum of INR6,921,455. Chanlian Shenzhen and Chanlian argued the sum was much too high, and it should be limited to the re-purchase price of containers. The court holds that the container belongs to transport method, the use of container is a supplementary issue, it is a contractual obligation that the shipper should return the container in time. The calculation standard of container detention fee should be deemed as liquidated damages agreed by the parties in terms of the shipper's detention of containers. According to the Interpretation of the Supreme People's Court on Several Issues concerning the Application of the Contract Law of the People's Republic of China (II) Article 29, "where the a party claims that the agreed amount of liquidated damages is too high and shall be appropriately reduced, the people's court shall, on the basis of the actual losses, take into account the performance of the contract, the degree of fault of the parties and the expected benefits, etc., make a ruling measured according to the principle of fairness and good faith", combined with the factor that the loss caused by shipper's breach of contractual obligation to return the container can be foreseen when they parties concluded the contract of carriage of goods by sea, the container detention fee should be limited within the re-purchase price complies with actual situation of this case, it is basically reasonable that decided at discretion that the container detention fee of the five containers should be RMB150,000 yuan on basis of the market price of a 40' GP container was about RMB3,000 yuan, which may be maintained.

In respect of the third issue, according to the provision of the Official Reply that "the carrier's title to compensation in terms of carriage of goods by sea against the shipper, the consignee or the holder of the bill of lading, without being provided in other laws, in the Maritime Code of the People's Republic of China Article 257 Paragraph 1, the statute of limitations should be one year, commencing from the day when the obligee knew or should have known his rights was been infringed", the statute of limitations of the claim of Maersk for container detention fee against Chanlian Shenzhen and Chanlian should be calculated from the day when Maersk knew or should have known its rights was been infringed. The facts of this case suggest after the goods arrived at the destination port, the containers could not be returned because of non-taking delivery of goods loaded therein, such infringement lasted until the auction of the goods by the Newport customs, that was to say, the containers were returned after Maersk delivered the goods to the new buyer according to the instruction of the customs, at that time, the infringement terminated, and the amount of the container detention fee was fixed. Therefore, the limitation for Maersk to exercise the right of claim should be calculated from the time when the Newport customs sent the document on delivery of the auctioned goods, namely February 28, 2011, to the time when Maersk filed this action, namely February 27, 2012, which has not exceeded the statutory limitations. The ascertainment of the original court should be correct, the court will affirm. The allegation of Chanlian Shenzhen and Chanlian that the claim of Maersk exceeded the statute of limitations lacks evidence, the court does not support.

In summary, the facts are clearly found, the law is correctly applied, and the decision is properly made in the original judgment, which shall be affirmed according to law. The appeals of Chanlian Shenzhen and Chanlian lack basis, which shall be dismissed, according to the Civil Procedure Law of the People's Republic of China Article 170 Paragraph 1 Sub-paragraph 1, the judgment is as follows:

Dismiss the appeal, and affirm the original judgment.

Court acceptance fee of second instance in amount of RMB3,300 yuan shall be jointly born by the Appellants Shanghai Chanlian Xieyun Logistics Co., Ltd. Shenzhen Branch and Shanghai Chanlian Xieyun Logistics Co., Ltd.

The judgment is final.

Presiding Judge: DU Yixing
Acting Judge: WU Siying
Acting Judge: YE Dan
June19, 2014
Clerk: PAN Wanqin

The Supreme People's Court of the People's Republic of China Civil Judgment

A.P. Moller-Maersk A/S
v.
Shanghai Chanlian Xieyun Logistics Co., Ltd. et al.

(2015) Min Ti Zi No.119

Related Case(s) This is the judgment of retrial, and the judgment of first instance and the judgment of second instance are on page 45 and page 58 respectively.

Cause(s) of Action 202. Dispute over contract of carriage of goods by sea or sea-connected waters.

Headnote The Plaintiff carrier's claim for container detention was time-barred by statute of limitations because one-year limitation period began to run when the Defendant freight forwarder acknowledged its responsibility to pay container detention fee, and not from the (later) moment when it became obvious that it was impossible for the consignee to take delivery of the goods, as lower courts had held; lower court decisions reversed.

Summary The Plaintiff carrier sued the Defendant freight forwarder for damages arising out of the Defendants' failure to pay container detention fees for containers in which the Plaintiff carried goods from Shenzhen to Nhava Sheva, India. The consignee did not take possession of the goods in Nhava Sheva, and the local Customs authorities auctioned off the goods inside the containers after nearly a year. The courts of first and second instance held that: (1) a contract of carriage existed between the Plaintiff and the Defendant; (2) there was no evidence that the Plaintiff was entitled to the proceeds from the auction of the goods inside the containers; and (3) the Plaintiff had brought its action within the period allowed by the statute of limitations because the one-year limitation period did not begin to run until the goods had been auctioned, as only then was it clear that it was impossible for the consignee to appear to take delivery. The Supreme People's Court reversed, holding that the statute of limitations for the Plaintiff's claim for compensation ran from the day the Plaintiff knew or should have known of the infringement of its rights, which happened when the Defendant made a commitment to the Plaintiff by e-mail that it would bear the container detention fees, months before the goods were auctioned by the customs authorities.

Judgment

The Claimant of Retrial (the Defendant of first instance, the Appellant of second instance): Shanghai Chanlian Xieyun Logistics Co., Ltd. Shenzhen Branch.
Domicile: Luohu District, Shenzhen, Guangdong, the People's Republic of China.
Person in charge: CAI Guoliang, manager.
Agent *ad litem*: HUANG Sufang, lawyer of Guangdong Shengtang Law Firm.
Agent *ad litem*: ZHENG Xia, trainee lawyer of Guangdong Shengtang Law Firm.

The Claimant of Retrial (the Defendant of first instance, the Appellant of second instance): Shanghai Chanlian Xieyun Logistics Co., Ltd.
Domicile: shanyang town, Jinshan District, Shanghai, the People's Republic of China.
Legal representative: WU Liang, general manager.
Agent *ad litem*: HUANG Sufang, lawyer of Guangdong Shengtang Law Firm.
Agent *ad litem*: ZHENG Xia, trainee lawyer of Guangdong Shengtang Law Firm.

The Respondent of Retrial (the Plaintiff of first instance, the Respondent of second instance): A.P. Moller-Maersk A/S.
Domicile: 1098 Copenhagen, Denmark.
Legal representatives: Morten Engelstoft and Peter Ronister Andersen.
Agent *ad litem*: CAO Fang, lawyer of Shanghai All Bright Law Office.
Agent *ad litem*: MA Yixing, lawyer of Shanghai All Bright Law Office.

Dissatisfied with (2013) Yue Gao Fa Min Si Zhong Zi No.162 Civil Judgment rendered by the Guangdong High People's Court with respect to the case arising from dispute over carriage of goods by sea with the Respondent of Retrial, A. P. Moeller-Maersk A/S (hereinafter referred to as Maersk), the Claimants of Retrial Shanghai Chanlian Xieyun Logistics Co., Ltd. Shenzhen Branch (hereinafter referred to as Chanlian Shenzhen) and Shanghai Chanlian Xieyun Logistics Co., Ltd. (hereinafter referred to as Chanlian), applied for a retrial before the court. On April 14, 2015, the court made a Civil Ruling (2015) Min Shen Zi No.559 to bring up the case. The court formed a collegiate panel and held a hearing in pubic on October13, 2015 to try the case. HUANG Sufang, agent *ad litem* of the Claimants of Retrial Chanlian Shenzhen and Chanlian, and CAO Fang, agent *ad litem* of Maersk, appeared in court to attend the hearing. Now the case has been concluded.

Chanlian Shenzhen and Chanlian dissatisfied with the judgment of second instance, and applied for retrial with the court, and alleged that:

1. The ascertainment of the courts of first instance and second instance in respect of the starting point of the statute of limitations was wrong, "statute of limitations shall begin when the entitled person knows or should know that his rights have been infringed upon" being interpreted as "the day of termination of the infringement" and "loss of the amount of the date of determination" constituted wrong application of law, which should be corrected.

2. Container detention fee happened after the containers involved were occupied overdue. In the case where neither the shipper nor the shipper paid Maersk, Maersk ought to know that its right had been infringed and the limitation of action should commence. According to the evidence submitted by Maersk, Maersk had already been aware of the occurrence of container detention fee on March 30, 2010, Maersk's statute of limitations should commence calculation thereby. Even if the shippers had been changed for several times, the case had already exceeded the statute of limitations from the day the shipper was finally confirmed, namely June 2, 2010.
3. Maersk, as the carrier, should know that the goods had been confiscated and auctioned by the customs, rather than wait for the customs to inform it of the delivery of the goods before it knew that the goods had been auctioned. The goods involved were auctioned by the customs on February 21, 2011, even if calculated from that day, the statute of limitations had expired.
4. It was held in (2002) Min Si Ti Zi No.7 Civil Judgment rendered by the Supreme People's Court of the People's Republic of China that the starting point of the statute of limitations of the container detention fee should start from the second day after the expiration of the rent-free period.

To sum up, it expired the statute of limitation for one year when Maersk filed an action to the court on February 27, 2012. Chanlian Shenzhen and Chanlian requested the court to revoke the judgments of first instance and second instance, and to amend the judgment to reject the claims of Maersk and order Maersk to bear all the litigation fees.

Maersk defended as follows:

1. Since the shipper did not abandon the goods, but instead it changed the shipper constantly, Maersk had been waiting for the shipper to take delivery of the goods, it knew it could not be recovered from the proceeds of auction until it received the notice of delivery of goods from the customs, only at that time did Maersk knew it suffered loss, therefore, the statute of limitations was correct if calculated from the receipt of the notice from the customs.
2. Maersk's loss was container detention fee, a loss in continuing increase. There was no deadline of performance of taking delivery of the goods, the shipper did not refuse to take delivery of the goods or pay the freight, on the contrary it indicated it would bear the container detention fee. As a result, Maersk could not recognize Chanlian Shenzhen was unable to fulfill its obligations until the customs informed it of the auction, the statute of limitations could only be commenced at that time. The day on which the infringing act ended was February 28, 2011, when Maersk received the notice of customs and the day when the empty containers were returned after the goods therein were delivered.
3. Even if the statute of limitations was calculated according to the allegation of Chanlian, the claim for container detention fee from April 16, 2011 to February 28, 2012 did not exceed the statute of limitations.

4. In shipping practice, the carrier would not be informed of the auction of the customs, Chanlian and others claimed Maersk should know the auction on February 21, 2011, it lacked basis. Maersk's action did not exceed the statute of limitations, the decision of the judgment of second instance was correct and should be affirmed. Maersk requested the court to dismiss the application for retrial of Chanlian.

After hearing, the court finds that both parties have no objection to the basic facts found in the judgment of second instance. Maersk upon inquiry confirmed in the retrial that the containerized goods involved arrived in Newport Mumbai on February 23, 2010, the period for free of charge of the containers involved was five days after arrival in the port, namely, February 24 to 28, 2010. Container detention fee was collected from the next day after such period expired, namelyMarch1, 2010. Chanlian Shenzhen and Chanlian had no objection. The court should confirm the fact to which the parties have no objection.

The court holds that the case is arising from dispute over container detention fee under contract of carriage of goods by sea. The parties raised no objection to the jurisdiction of the original courts or the application of the law of the People's Republic of China, the court hereby confirms. According to the application for retrial of Chanlian Shenzhen and Chanlian, and the defense of Maersk, the court holds that the issues in this case are that, whether the lawsuit Maersk brought to the court of first instance on February 27, 2012 exceeded the statute of limitations.

Maersk accepted the commission of Chanlian Shenzhen to transport the goods involved from Yantian in Shenzhen to Newport in Mumbai, India. Chanlian Shenzhen and Maersk established a relationship of contract of carriage of goods by sea, Maersk is the carrier, and Chanlian Shenzhen is the shipper. Both parties should exercise their rights and perform their obligations as stipulated in the contract and according to the law. Maersk provided containers to load the goods and delivered the goods safely to the port of destination, it has fulfilled the carrier's obligations. The shipper has the obligation to promptly take delivery of the goods and return the containers to the carrier. But after the goods arrived at the port of destination, the shipper designated by Chanlian Shenzhen did not take delivery of the goods, resulting in that the containers involved cannot be put into normal use for occupation overdue, which constituted a breach of contract. Maersk claimed for loss of container detention fee resulting from delay in performance of the obligation to return the container based on the contract of carriage of goods by sea against Chanlian Shenzhen, it has factual and legal basis. According to the Official Reply of the Supreme People's Court on the Limitation of Action of the Carrier's Claim for Compensation against the Consignor, Consignee or Holder of the Bill of Lading under Carriage of Goods by Sea, the statute of limitations of this case should be one year, calculated from the day when the aggrieved party knew or should have known his rights have been infringed. Therefore, Maersk's entitlement to claim for compensation for container detention fee should be subject to the statute of limitations from the day Maersk knew or should have known of the infringement on it.

The carrier Maersk and the shipper Chanlian Shenzhen did not separately agree upon the rate of container detention fee, Maersk alleged it should subject to the rate published on its website from March 1, 2010, Chanlian Shenzhen and Chanlian did not raise objection. The goods involved arrived in Newport, Mumbai on February 23, 2010, the free of charge period of the containers involved expired on February, 28. Since no one took delivery of the goods in the port of destination, the containers had not returned to the carrier Maersk in time after the expiry of the free-use period, it should pay Maersk the container detention fee from March 1, Maersk's right to claim for the container detention fee has generated, namely, Maersk knew or should know that its rights had been infringed from March 1, 2010. Maersk also confirmed in the fax on March 30, 2010 that container detention fee had generated. Although Chanlian Shenzhen still continually instructed to change the port of destination after the goods involved arrived in Newport, Mumbai, but ultimately it did not actually change. It does not affect the right of claiming for the container detention fee of the carrier Maersk. The right of Maersk to claim compensation for breach of contract due to delay in performance of the obligation to return the containers does not arise from the day of termination of the infringement, and the determination of the amount of compensation does not affect the exercise of Maersk's title to sue. It lacked basis for Maersk to claim that the statute of limitation should be calculated from when the infringing act ended on the ground that its right was continuously infringed upon. The judgment of second instance ordered to auction the goods involved, the damage with regard to the container detention fee was terminated and the amount of the container detention fee was fixed. It apparently does not comply with the provision "from the day when the aggrieved party knew or should have known his rights were infringed". In this case, Maersk knew or ought to know that the date of infringement was March 1, 2010, Chanlian Shenzhen made a commitment to the shipper that it would bear the container detention fee on March 30, 2010 by e-mail. The declaration of will of Chanlian Shenzhen constituted the circumstance where statute of limitations is interrupted due to the person against whom the claim was brought up agreeing to fulfill the obligations, as prescribed in the Maritime Code of the People's Republic of China Article 267. Therefore, the statute of limitations of the subject case should commence from March 30, 2010, the action filed by Maersk on February 27, 2012 exceeded the one-year statute of limitations.

According to the charging standard of container detention fee published on Maersk's website, the 1st day to the 5th day after the container was unloaded at the destination (or inland container yard) was free of charge, container detention fee would be charged from the next day after such period expires. Thus it could be seen that container detention fee was not calculated from the time when the shipper took delivery of the goods, it generated whether the shipper actually took delivery of the goods. The carrier was entitled to container detention fee against the obligor, whether it could afford or not, the entitlement to such fee would not be affected. Chanlian Shenzhen did not object allegation of Maersk that the container detention fee should be collected from March 1, 2010, the faxes between the two parties on March 30, 2010 also suggested that both sides knew that container detention fee had generated. Maersk held the statute of limitations should be commenced at the time when the customs informed it of the auction of the good on the ground that the time of taking delivery of the goods and the uncertainty to confirm whether Chanlian Shenzhen would fulfill its obligation to pay could not be decided, the court does not support. The purpose of the carrier to collect container detention fee was to push the user's timely return of the container and speed up the circulation of the container. The carrier should bring a lawsuit with regard to loss resulting from the failure of the container user to return the container in time within the time limit stipulated by law. Otherwise, the carrier would lose the entitlement to claim. Maersk alleged that the calculation of the statute of limitations should be calculated on the basis of different the time of occurrence of the container detention fee, such allegation lacks of factual and legal basis, the court does not support.

In summary, the judgments of first instance and second instance held that Maersk's filing the case did not exceed the one-year statute of limitations, incorrectly applied the law and shall be corrected. The application of retrial of Chanlian and Chanlian Shenzhen shall be established, and the court supports it. According to the Civil Procedure Law of the People's Republic of China Article 207 Paragraph 1, the Interpretation of the Supreme People's Court on the Application of the Civil Procedure Law of the People's Republic of China Article 407 Paragraph 2, the judgment is as follows:

1. Revoke (2013) Yue Gao Fa Min Si Zhong Zi No.162 Civil Judgment of the Guangdong High People's Court;
2. Revoke (2012) Guang Hai Fa Chu Zi No.329 Civil Judgment of the Guangzhou Maritime Court;
3. Reject the claims of A.P. Muller-Maersk A/S.

Court acceptance fee of first instance in amount of RMB14,066 yuan and that of second instance in amount of RMB3,300 yuan, shall be born by A. P. Muller-Maersk A/S.

The judgment is final.

Presiding Judge: HU Fang
Judge: GUO Zhonghong
Judge: YU Xiaohan

November 26,2015

Clerk: LI Na

Guangzhou Maritime Court
Civil Judgment

China Transport Groupage International (Shenzhen) Limited
v.
Shenzhen Zhongyi Freight Forwarding Co., Ltd.

(2014) Guang Hai Fa Chu Zi No.102

Related Case(s) This is the judgment of first instance, and the judgment of second instance and the judgment of retrial are on page 93 and page 107 respectively.

Cause(s) of Action 223. Dispute over freight forwarding contract on the sea or sea-connected waters.

Headnote Goods agent held to be entitled to be repaid by a freight forwarder for container demurrage that agent had paid to an ocean carrier but court, exercising its discretion, ordered less than full repayment.

Summary The Defendant freight forwarder arranged for two containers of goods to be carried from China to Algeria. The containers remained at the port in Algeria for an extended period of time because no-one appeared to take delivery of them. The Plaintiff was the Defendant's cargo agent in dealing with the ocean carrier. The Plaintiff paid the container demurrage to the ocean carrier, and sued the Defendant after it refused to repay the amount paid to the ocean carrier. The court found for the Plaintiff but, exercising its discretion, awarded a less amount than that claimed by the Plaintiff.

Judgment

The Plaintiff: China Transport Groupage International (Shenzhen) Limited
Domicile: Room 01–07, Floor 37, Pengnian Square, Jiabing Road, Nanhu Street, Luohu District, Shenzhen, Guangdong.
Legal representative: SUN Peilun, general manager.
Agent *ad litem*: ZHENG Xia, employee.
Agent *ad litem*: HUANG Sufang, lawyer of Guangdong Shengtang Law Firm.

The Defendant: Shenzhen Zhongyi Freight Forwarding Co., Ltd.
Domicile: Unit 14L, Sun Island Building, South Dongmen Road, Luohu District, Shenzhen, Guangdong.
Legal representative: XU Zhigang, general manager.
Agent *ad litem*: CAO Wending, lawyer of Guangdong Chenggong Law Firm.

With respect to the case arising from dispute over freight forwarding contract, the Plaintiff, China Transport Groupage International (Shenzhen) Limited, filed an action against the Defendant, Shenzhen Zhongyi Freight Forwarding Co., Ltd., before the court on October 18, 2013. After accepting this case, the court formed the collegiatepanel consisting of Presiding Judge CHANG Weiping, Judge PINGYANG Danke and Acting Judge JIANG He, subsequently, Judge ZHAI Xin and Acting Judge XU Chunlong replaced the trial members PINGYANG Danke and JIANG He according to the law. Clerk ZHUANG Zhilong acted as the case recorder. On April1, 2014, the Plaintiff filed an application to add ZHANG Jing as the co-Defendant, the court rejected the application according to the law. On March 27, 2014, the court summoned both parties concerned to exchange evidence before the court hearing and held hearings on September 4 and October 16 respectively. ZHANG Jing, the employee of the Defendant also as the former agent *ad litem* of the Defendant was replaced by CAO Wending, agent *ad litem* of Guangdong Chenggong Law Firm on August 31, 2014. HUANG Sufang, agent *ad litem* of the Plaintiff China Transport Groupage International (Shenzhen) Limited and CAO Wending, agent *ad litem* of the Defendant participated in the two hearings. ZHENG Xia, the agent *ad litem* of the Plaintiff, participated in the hearing on September 4. Now the case has been concluded.

The Plaintiff alleged that: on December 2012, the Plaintiff was entrusted by the Defendant to carry a consignment of goods by sea from Chi Hai Bay, Shenzhen, China to the destination of Alger, Algeria. The Plaintiff entrusted Mediterranean Shipping Co., Ltd. (hereinafter referred to as "Mediterranean") to carry the goods involved, the number of the bill of lading was MSCUDI791056, the number of containers were CAXU9726132 and MSCU9235002 respectively. No one took delivery of the goods involved after the goods arrived at the port of destination, the containers were used extendedly. By the end of September 30, 2013, the container detention fee raised up to USD25,536 and USD1,051 of container unloading charge, totally up to USD26,587 (equivalent to RMB163,510.05 yuan, currency hereafter referred to RMB without particular refer). The Plaintiff as the Defendant's goods agent disbursed above charges to Mediterranean, but the Defendant refused to pay the charges to the Plaintiff. The Plaintiff requested the court to order the Defendant to pay the container detention fees and container unloading charge at the port of destination in an amount of RMB163,510.05 yuan and burden the court acceptance fee.

The Plaintiff submitted the following documents within the time limit for adducing evidence:

1. Book note the Defendant issued to the Plaintiff;
2. E-mails between the Plaintiff and the Defendant;
3. Notice on the correlative charges resulted from non-taking delivery of the goods involved issued by the Defendant to the Plaintiff, express sheet and online express query result, to prove that the principal-agent relation between the Plaintiff and the Defendant was tenable, and the Plaintiff had notified the Defendant of the situation of the correlative charges resulted from non-taking delivery of the goods involved;
4. 4.Letter of guarantee issued by the Defendant to the Plaintiff, to prove that the Defendant guaranteed to undertake all the economic loss resulted from non-taking delivery of the goods involved, and should bear joint and several liability together with the shipper and consignee under the bill of lading;
5. Mediterranean's booking order conformation;
6. Bill of lading issued by Mediterranean, to prove that Mediterranean was the carrier of the goods involved and the rate of the charges of the involved containers at the port of destination;
7. E-mails between Li Sheng Mediterranean Shipping (Shanghai) Co., Ltd., Shenzhen Branch (hereinafter referred to as Mediterranean Shenzhen) and the Plaintiff, to prove the charges arising from non-taking delivery of the goods involved at the port of destination;
8. Dynamic inquiry records of the goods involved from Mediterranean's website, to prove that involved containers arrived at the Alger Port on December 28, 2012 and were retained at the port;
9. Proof issued by Mediterranean Shenzhen;
10. Check receipt and acknowledgement of receipt issued by Hang Seng Bank;
11. Letter of authorization for payment the Plaintiff issued to CASA China Ltd. (hereinafter referred to as CASA China), to prove that no one took delivery of the goods involved after goods arrived at the port of destination, and the Plaintiff had paid the container detention fees in amount of USD25,536 and the container unloading charge in amount of USD1,051 resulted from non-taking delivery of the goods involved at the port of destination;
12. Information of business registration of Li Sheng Mediterranean Shipping (Shanghai) Co., Ltd, (hereinafter referred to as Mediterranean Shanghai) and Mediterranean Shenzhen, to prove that Mediterranean Shenzhen had the right to provide services including canvassing cargo, issuing bill of lading, settling freight and concluding contracts for self-owned or operated ships of Mediterranean;
13. Phone-call record between the Plaintiff's employee and LAI Zicong;
14. Bank transfer record of the amendment fee that ZHANG Jing paid to the Plaintiff for the goods involved;

15. Bank transfer record of the goods involved that ZHANG Jing paid to the Plaintiff, to prove that the goods involved were managed by the Defendant's employee ZHANG Jing who entrusted the Plaintiff in the name of the Defendant, and ZHANG Jing delivered the booking note of the goods involved to the Plaintiff and paid correlative fees.

The Defendant argued that: 1. the Defendant had never sent booking note of the goods involved in the form of email or fax to the Plaintiff. According to the evidence provided by the Plaintiff, the shipper of the goods involved should be Hong Kong Shijin Changqing International Group Co., Ltd. (hereinafter referred to as Shijin) and the Defendant was not the shipper of the goods involved; 2. in the written materials submitted by the Defendant to the court, the proof that ZHANG Jing was the Defendant's employee could not suggest that ZHANG Jing was the Defendant's employee. ZHANG Jing wrote and signed the proof in the form of the Defendant's authority, ZHANG Jing was the legal representative of the Shijin; 3. in this case, email address, kelly@chinawinline.com used by ZHANG Jing was actually the Defendant's. After ZHANG Jing's original Yahoo email was out of service, ZHANG Jing used the Defendant's email as business connection tool; 4. the seal on the booking note submitted by the Plaintiff was inconsistent with that the Defendant actually used. The goods involved were not included in the letter of guarantee issued by the Defendant to the Plaintiff, and this letter of guarantee was irrelevant to this case; 5. the Defendant had not paid any charges of the goods involved to the Plaintiff, and the Defendant did not constitute a freight forwarding contract relationship with the Plaintiff; and 6. no one took delivery of the goods involved after the goods arrived at the port of destination more than 60 days, the carrier Mediterranean should have the obligation to promptly loss. The Plaintiff had not provided computation basis of the container detention fee and the container unloading charges should be born by the carrier on its own account and should not charge the Defendant. In conclusion, the Defendant requested the court to reject the Plaintiff's claims.

The Defendant submitted the following documents within the time limit for adducing evidence:

1. Testimony of the witness LAI Zicong, to prove that the booking note submitted by the Plaintiff was not issued by the Defendant, the seal affixed on bill of lading was fake and had no effect to the Defendant;
2. Previous booking note and payment voucher between the Plaintiff and the Defendant, to prove that in the previous transactions both parties had already agreed in the booking note in terms of consignee, the consignor, the goods, the carrier and the freight;
3. E-mails in terms of previous transactions between the Plaintiff and the Defendant, and the Defendant's official seal, to prove the previous transaction practices between the Plaintiff and the Defendant and the true official seal of the Defendant;

4. Record of QQ between the Plaintiff and the Defendant;
5. E-mails between the Plaintiff and the Defendant, to prove the transaction practice and business communication ways between the Plaintiff and the Defendant;
6. Booking notes of Shijin, the bill of lading of the previous transportation and a statement issued by Shijin, to prove that Shijin as the shipper entrusted the Plaintiff to transport the goods involved.

The Defendant had no objection to the authenticity of evidence 4–6 and evidence 8, 14, 15 provided by the Plaintiff, the court ascertains the authenticity of three pieces of evidence. The Plaintiff did not admit the authenticity, legality or relevancy of the evidence provided by the Defendant. The Plaintiff's evidence 1 and 2 was ascertained by LAI Zicong during the court trial and had confirmed one another with the ascertained evidence. It was recorded that the Defendant's email was kelly@chinawinline.com, and the Plaintiff had always communicated with the user of above email about the transportation of the relevant goods and issues that fee happened at the port of destination. The Defendant ascertained that the suffix techstar of the email was the Defendant, and ascertained that the email belonged to the Defendant. The court ascertains the probative force of the Plaintiff's evidence 1 and 2; the Plaintiff's evidence 9–12 has original documents to verify or can be checked in the website of Shenzhen Market Supervision and Administration Bureau and had confirmed one another with the ascertained evidence. The Defendant was not sure but did not submit counter evidence, the court ascertains the probative force of the evidence. The Plaintiff's evidence 13 was ascertained by the Defendant's witness LAI Zicong, and the court ascertains the probative force of this evidence. The Plaintiff's evidence 7 had confirmed one another with the ascertained evidence, the court ascertains the probative force of this evidence. For other evidence disputed by both parties should be ascertained comprehensively with the court trial and the evidence having been admitted.

Based on the evidence having been admitted, and combined with the trial in court, the court ascertains the following facts:

On September 29, 2012, ZHANG Jing sent the booking note to the Plaintiff through QQ to entrust the Plaintiff to transport two 40-foot containers' cargo from Huangpu, China to Alger, Algeria. The booking note recorded that the shipper was the Defendant, the prepared carrying ship and the voyage was MSC Bettina 1241R, the closing date was October 17, and it was affixed with the Defendant's official seal. The Plaintiff in the name of its own booked shipping space with Mediterranean after accepting the entrustment, the booking number issued by Mediterranean was 181MGG2TC01A83619. On October 11, 2012, No.MSCU9235002 container under No.181MGG2TC01A83619 booking note was taken delivery. After the goods were loaded in the container, they could not be loaded on the carrying ship for shipment. On October 19, ZHANG Jing contacted with the Plaintiff in terms of the transportation of No.CAXU9726132 container under No.181MGG2TC01A83902 booking note, but the goods could not be loaded in M.V. "MSC Livorno" on October 31. On October 30, 2012, ZHANG Jing suggested to combine the forwarding matters of No.MSCU9235002 and No.CAXU9726132 containers into one, and continued to use the Defendant's email box kelly@chinawinline.com to contact with the Plaintiff (alexlai@sczs.casalogistics.com) to communicate issues of the goods involved.

On November 10, No.MSCU9235002 and No.CAXU9726132 containers were loaded on M.V. "MSC TARANTO" at the Port of Chiwan. On November 13, Shenzhen Sinotrans Shipping Agency Co., Ltd., as the agent of Mediterranean, issued No.MSCUDI791056 bill of lading. This bill of lading recorded that the shipper was Million Trading Limited; the consignee should be ordered by BANQUE AL BARAKA D'ALGERIE; the cargo were 2,311 boxes of shampoo and loaded in two 40-foot containers of which the number were No.MSCU9235002 and No.CAXU9726132; the place of delivery was Old Huangpu Port and the port of loading was Port of Chiwan, China; the port of discharge was Alger, Algeria; the freight was prepaid; the carrying ship and voyage was M.V. "MSC TARANTO" and 1244R respectively; the rent-free period of the 40-foot container was seven days and the container detention fee was USD24 each day from the 8th to 15th day, the container detention fee was USD48 each day after the 16th day. On November2 and November13, 2012, ZHANG Jing had respectively paid the freight of the goods involved in sum of USD3,950 and USD3,300 and the amendment charge in sum of RMB200 yuan to the Plaintiff.

On December 11, 2012, the goods involved were transported to the Barcelona, Spain and were discharged at the dock. On December 26, the goods were loaded on M.V. "HANSE FORTUNE" and arrived at Port of Alger on December 28. On September 25, 2013, the dynamic result queried from Mediterranean's website showed that container was retained in Alger.

The goods involved were retained at the port of destination after arrival, Mediterranean Shenzhen notified the Plaintiff that the correlative charges resulted from non-taking delivery of the goods involved through email. The Plaintiff sent emails to the kelly@chinawinline.com notifying that the correlative charges resulted from non-taking delivery of the goods involved at the port of destination and asked for the information of the shipper. On September 11, 2013, Mediterranean Shenzhen sent the email notifying the Plaintiff that by September 30, container detention fees were USD25,536 and container unloading charge was USD1,051. The Plaintiff sent an email in terms of the above-mentioned situation to kelly@chinawinline.com on September 16.

In October 2013, the Plaintiff issued a letter of authorization for payment to CASA China, to entrust CASA China to pay Mediterranean Shipping (Hong Kong) Co., Ltd. (hereinafter referred to as Mediterranean Hong Kong), the agent of Mediterranean, a total amount of USD26,587, the container detention fees of No. CAXU9726132 and No.MSCU9235002 containers that resulted from the non-taking delivery of the goods involved at the port of destination. On October 8, CASA China issued a check of Hang Seng Bank No.143489 of which the amount was USD26,587 to Mediterranean Hong Kong, and Mediterranean Hong Kong signed the said check. On October 11, Mediterranean Shenzhen issued two pieces of evidence for the two containers involved, which recorded that the goods involved arrived at the port of the destination on December 28, 2012 and was retained at the port of destination because of non-taking delivery of the goods; by September 30, 2013, the two containers had incurred container detention fees in amount of USD25,536 and container unloading charge in amount of USD1,051 (the calculation method of each 40-foot container was: from January4 to January11, 2013, 8 days in total, USD24 per day per container, from January12 to September 30, 2013, 262 days in total, USD48 per day per container. The Plaintiff entrusted CASA China to pay Mediterranean Hong Kong appointed by Mediterranean Shenzhen the above-mentioned charges in Hong Kong.

On June 8, 2013, the Defendant issued a letter of guarantee to the Plaintiff, agreeing as follows: the Defendant should make an accurate declaration of all the goods that the Defendant entrusted the Plaintiff to transport; the Defendant should be liable for all losses or responsibilities of the Plaintiff, the Plaintiff's employees or agents arising from inaccurate description of the goods, shortage of goods, jetsam or non-taking delivery of the goods; where the Plaintiff, the Plaintiff's employees or Plaintiff's agents were sued because of inaccurate description of the goods, shortage of goods, jetsam or non-taking delivery of the goods, the Defendant should pay the legal fees, attorney's fee and notary fee; owing to the inaccurate description of the goods, shortage of goods, jetsam or non-taking delivery of the goods, the Plaintiff's ship, other ships or the Plaintiff's possession suffered detention or retention, the Defendant should compensate the economic losses caused to the Plaintiff. The Defendant should pay the cash deposit or bail to avoid detention or retention; the Defendant should unconditionally bear joint and several liability with the shipper, consignee or other irrelevant persons under the bill of lading, and jointly undertake obligations of the letter of guarantee; the effect of the letter of guarantee should not affect the Plaintiff's advocating rights to the shipper, consignee or other irrelevant persons under the bill of lading; the period of the letter of guarantee was two years after the primary liability period was expired, it should be subject to and be interpreted by Chinese laws, the parties concerned under the letter of guarantee had rights to bring a lawsuit before Chinese courts.

It is found out that Mediterranean Shanghai was an exclusively foreign-owned company set up by Mediterranean in China. Mediterranean Shenzhen was subordinated to Mediterranean Shanghai and its scope of business was to provide services of canvassing cargo, issuing bills of lading, settling freights and signing service contracts for the ships owned or operated by Mediterranean.

During the trial, both parties chose the laws of the People's Republic of China to solve the substantive dispute of this case.

The court holds that this case is arising from dispute over freight forwarding contract. The goods in this case were transported from Huangpu, China through Port of Chiwan, Shenzhen to Alger port, Algeria by sea. The Plaintiff and the Defendant had disputes out of the correlative charges resulted from non-taking delivery of the goods involved at the port of destination, and this case involves with foreign-related factors. According to the Provisions of the Supreme People's Court on Several Issues concerning the Trial of Cases of Disputes over Marine Freight Forwarding Article 13, this case should be under the jurisdiction of the maritime court. The Defendant's domicile and the place where the contract was performed are within the jurisdiction of the court, according to the Civil Procedure Law of People's Republic of China Article 23, an action instituted for a contract dispute should be under the jurisdiction of the people's court at the place of domicile of the Defendant or at the place where the contract is performed. According to the Contract Law of People's Republic of China Article 126 Paragraph 1, parties to a foreign-related contract may select the applicable law for resolution of a contractual dispute. The Plaintiff and the Defendant chose the laws of the People's Republic of China to solve the substantive dispute of this case, this case should be subjected to the laws of the People's Republic of China.

ZHANG Jing in the name of the Defendant issued the booking note to the Plaintiff, the shipper and seal of the shipper on the booking note were the Defendant. ZHANG Jing used the Defendant's email box to contact with the Plaintiff about the shipping of the relevant goods and paid the freight and amendment charge of the goods involved. Based on the record in the booking note, the email address used by ZHANG Jing and the contents of the emails, the Plaintiff had reason to believe the agency power of ZHANG Jing who was the Defendant's employee and the authenticity of the booking note. The Defendant denied the authenticity of the Defendant's seal on the booking note and argued that booking note issued by ZHANG Jing was only her individual act and had no relation to the Defendant, but the Defendant had no effective evidence to support, thus this argument is untenable. According to the Contract Law of People's Republic of China Article 49, "if an actor has no power of agency, oversteps the power of agency, or the power of agency has expired and yet concludes a contract in the principal's name, and the counterpart has reasons to trust that the actor has the power of agency, the act of agency shall be effective", the Plaintiff and the Defendant established a freight forwarding relationship according to the law in which the Defendant was the principal and the Plaintiff was the agent. The letter of guarantee issued by the Defendant to the Plaintiff ensured that the Defendant should undertake all economic losses or liabilities resulted from the inaccurate description of the goods, shortage of goods, jetsam or non-taking delivery of the goods and should unconditionally bear joint and several liability together with the shipper, consignee or other irrelevant persons. The letter of guarantee was voluntarily issued by the Defendant and the Defendant failed to prove there were exemptions, nor did it prove that the letter of guarantee was issued for the purpose of transportation of specified goods, and should be contained in the maritime freight forwarding contract in this case. The maritime freight forwarding contract is the declaration of real intention of the both parties, and does not violate legal and administrative provisions, which should be legal and valid. The parties should exercise rights and perform obligations according to the contract and relevant laws and regulations.

With respect to the claim about the container unloading charge in amount of USD1,051, the Plaintiff failed to prove that the container unloading charge should be charged by the carrier or the port part, it neither proved that the authorized subject actually had charged that sum, nor did it prove whether the container unloading charge was the necessary fee resulted from non-taking delivery of the goods involved at the port of destination. According to the Civil Procedure Law of People's Republic of China Article 64 Paragraph 1, a party should have the burden to provide evidence for its claims, the claim of the Plaintiff was lack of factual evidence and shall not be supported.

With respect to the claim about the container detention fees in amount of USD25,536, based on the emails between the Plaintiff and the Defendant about the non-taking delivery of the goods involved at the port of destination and request of adding the shipper's information, and the dynamic inquiry result of the goods involved from Mediterranean's website, it could be ascertained that the containers involved were retained at the port of destination because of non-taking delivery of on the condition that the Defendant did not provide contrary evidence. Mediterranean as the carrier that provided the containers involved suffered losses out of extended use of containers and should have the rights to claim. Mediterranean could claim against the Plaintiff for the transportation of the goods involved or enforce the claim through retaining and auctioning the goods involved according to the law, the above option was Mediterranean's right but not its obligation. It was proper that the Plaintiff advanced the container detention fees of the goods involved at the port of destination for Mediterranean. The Plaintiff had paid the carrier the losses of container detention fees resulted from non-taking delivery of the goods at the port of destination. According to the Contract Law of People's Republic of China Article 398, "the principal shall prepay the expenses for handling the commissioned affair. Any expense necessary for handling the commissioned affair advanced by the agent shall be repaid with interest by the principal", the Plaintiff paid the container detention fees in order to deal with the Defendant's agent matters, the Defendant as the principal should repay the sum. But the reasonable sum of the container detention fees should be determined on the basis of the losses caused to the container provider during the period when the containers are occupied. The container provider could prevent further loss by buying new container on condition of the long-term occupation of the container. The accumulative upper limit of the actual loss caused by the extended use of container should not exceed new container price at the same period and same specification in the market. Combined with the shipping practices, the court ascertains at discretion that the losses suffered by the carrier Mediterranean resulted from long-term occupation of the involved container should be RMB30,000 yuan of each 40-foot container in an amount of RMB60,000 yuan of two containers' detention fee. The sum exceeding this amount claimed by the Plaintiff shall not be supported.

Pulling the threads together, according to the Contract Law of People's Republic of China Article 398, and the Civil Procedure Law of the People's Republic of China Article 64 Paragraph 1, the judgment is as follows:

1. The Defendant, Shenzhen Zhongyi Freight Forwarding Co., Ltd., shall pay the Plaintiff, China Transport Groupage International (Shenzhen) Limited, the container detention fees in amount of RMB60,000 yuan;
2. Reject other claims of the Plaintiff.

The above obligation of payment shall be fulfilled within 10 days after this judgment comes into effect.

If the Defendant fails to perform the obligation to pay money according to the period specified in this judgment, it shall double the payment of interest on the debt during the period of delay according to the Civil Procedure Law of the People's Republic of China Article 229..

Court acceptance fee in amount of RMB3,570.2 yuan, the Plaintiff China Transport Groupage International (Shenzhen) Limited shall bear RMB2,260.12 yuan, the Defendant Shenzhen Zhongyi Freight Forwarding Co., Ltd. shall bear RMB1,310.08 yuan.

If not satisfy with the judgment, the Plaintiff China Transport Groupage International (Shenzhen) Limited and the Defendant Shenzhen Zhongyi Freight Forwarding Co., Ltd. may submit a statement of appeal within 15 days upon the service of this judgment, with duplicates in the number of the other parties, to lodge an appeal with the Guangdong High People's Court.

Presiding Judge: CHANG Weiping

Judge: ZHAI Xin

Acting Judge: XU Chunlong

March 12, 2015

Clerk: ZHUANG Zhifa

Guangdong High People's Court
Civil Judgment

China Transport Groupage International (Shenzhen) Limited
v.
Shenzhen Zhongyi Freight Forwarding Co., Ltd.

(2015) Yue Gao Fa Min Si Zhong Zi No.138

Related Case(s) This is the judgment of second instance, and the judgment of first instance and the judgment of retrial are on page 83 and page 107 respectively.

Cause(s) of Action 223. Dispute over freight forwarding contract on the sea or sea-connected waters.

Headnote Goods agent exceeded its authority to act on behalf of freight forwarder by paying container demurrage to ocean carrier, so it was not entitled to reimbursement by freight forwarder; reversing lower court decision.

Summary The initial dispute arose out of the Plaintiff's payment of container demurrage charges on behalf of the Defendant. In the court of first instance, the Defendant was required to pay the Plaintiff 60,000 RMB for demurrage charges that the Plaintiff had paid to an ocean carrier for detention of two containers at a port in Algeria. The Defendant appealed. The appeal court reversed, holding that payment of the container demurrage charges involved did not fall within the scope of the Plaintiff's authority as the Defendant's goods agent.

Judgment

The Appellant (the Defendant of first instance): Shenzhen Zhongyi Freight Forwarding Co., Ltd.
Domicile: Unit 14L, Sun Island Building, South Dongmen Road, Luohu District, Shenzhen, Guangdong.
Legal representative: XU Zhigang, general manager.
Agent *ad litem*: CAO Wending, lawyer of Guangdong Chenggong Law Firm.
Agent *ad litem*: CHEN Jianji, trainee lawyer of Guangdong Chenggong Law Firm.

The Respondent (the Plaintiff of first instance): China Transport Groupage International (Shenzhen) Limited.
Domicile: Rm 01–07, Floor 37, Pengnian Square, Jiabing Road, Nanhu Street, Luohu District, Shenzhen, Guangdong.
Legal representative: SUN Peilun, general manager.
Agent *ad litem*: HUANG Sufang, lawyer of Guangdong Shengtang Law Firm.
Agent *ad litem*: ZHENG Xia, trainee lawyer of Guangdong Shengtang Law Firm.

Dissatisfied with (2014) Guang Hai Fa Chu Zi No.102 Civil Judgment rendered by Guangzhou Maritime Court concerning the case arising from dispute over maritime freight forwarding contract, the Appellant Shenzhen Zhongyi Freight Forwarding Co., Ltd. (hereinafter referred to as Zhongyi) lodged an appeal against the Respondent China Transport Groupage International (Shenzhen) Limited (hereinafter referred to as Transport Groupage) before the court. After accepting this appeal, the court legally constituted the collegiate panel to try the case. CAO Wending and CHEN Jianji, agents *ad litem* of Zhongyi, and HUANG Sufang, agent *ad litem* of Transport Groupage, appeared in court to attend the hearings. Now the case has been concluded.

Transport Groupage alleged in first instance that: in December 2012, Transport Groupage was entrusted by Zhongyi to carry a consignment of goods by sea from Chi Hai Bay, Shenzhen, China to the destination of Alger, Algeria. Transport Groupage entrusted Mediterranean Shipping Co., Ltd. (hereinafter referred to as "Mediterranean") to carry the goods involved, the number of the bill of lading was MSCUDI791056, the number of containers were CAXU9726132 and MSCU9235002 respectively. No one took delivery of the goods involved after the goods arrived at the port of destination, the containers were used extendedly. By the end of September 30, 2013, the container detention fees raised up to USD25,536 and USD1,051 of container unloading charge, totally up to USD26,587 (equivalent to RMB163,510.05 yuan, currency hereafter referred to RMB without particular refer). Transport Groupage as Zhongyi's cargo agent disbursed above charges to Mediterranean, but Zhongyi refused to pay the charges to Transport Groupage. Transport Groupage requested the court of first instance to order Zhongyi to pay the container detention fees and container unloading charge at the port of destination in an amount of RMB163,510.05 yuan and burden the court acceptance fee.

Transport Groupage submitted the following documents within the time limit for adducing evidence in the first instance: 1. book note the Zhongyi issued to Transport Groupage;2. e-mails between Transport Groupage and Zhongyi; 3. notice on the correlative charges resulted from non-taking delivery of the goods involved issued by Zhongyi to Transport Groupage, express sheet and online express query result; 4.letter of guarantee issued by Zhongyi to Transport Groupage;5. Mediterranean's booking order conformation; 6. bill of lading issued by Mediterranean;7. e-mails between Li Sheng Mediterranean Shipping (Shanghai) Co., Ltd., Shenzhen Branch (hereinafter referred to as Mediterranean Shenzhen) and Transport Groupage; 8. dynamic inquiry records of the goods involved from Mediterranean's website; 9. proof issued by Mediterranean Shenzhen; 10. check receipt and acknowledgement of receipt issued by Hang Seng Bank;11.letter of authorization for payment Transport Groupage issued to CASA China Ltd. (hereinafter referred to as CASA China), to prove that no one took delivery of the goods involved after goods arrived at the port of destination, and Transport Groupage had paid the container detention fees in amount of USD25,536 and the container unloading charge in amount of USD1,051 resulted from non-taking delivery of the goods involved at the port of destination; 12.information of business registration of Li Sheng Mediterranean Shipping (Shanghai) Co., Ltd, (hereinafter referred to as Mediterranean Shanghai) and Mediterranean Shenzhen, to prove that Mediterranean Shenzhen had the right to provide services including canvassing cargo, issuing bill of lading, settling freight and concluding contracts for self-owned or operated ships of Mediterranean; 13.phone-call record between Transport Groupage's employee and LAI Zicong; 14.bank transfer record of the amendment fee that ZHANG Jing paid to Transport Groupage for the goods involved; 15. bank transfer record of the goods involved that ZHANG Jing paid to Transport Groupage.

Zhongyi argued in first instance that: 1. Zhongyi had never sent booking note of the goods involved in the form of email or fax to Transport Groupage. According to the evidence provided by Transport Groupage, the shipper of the goods involved should be Hong Kong Shijin Changqing International Group Co., Ltd. (herein after referred to as Shijin) and Zhongyi was not the shipper of the goods involved; 2. in the written materials submitted by Zhongyi to the court of first instance. The proof that ZHANG Jing was Zhongyi's employee, but it did suggest that ZHANG Jing was Zhongyi's employee. ZHANG Jing wrote and signed the proof in the form of Zhongyi's authority, ZHANG Jing was the legal representative of the Shijin; 3. in this case, email address, kelly@chinawinline.com used by ZHANG Jing was actually Zhongyi's. After ZHANG Jing's original Yahoo email was out of service, ZHANG Jing used Zhongyi's email as business connection tool; 4. the seal on the booking note submitted by Transport Groupage was inconsistent with that Zhongyi actually used. The goods involved were not included in the letter of guarantee issued by Zhongyi to Transport Groupage, and this letter of guarantee was irrelevant to this case; 5. Zhongyi had not paid any charges of the goods involved to Transport Groupage, and Zhongyi did not constitute a freight forwarding contract relationship with Transport Groupage; and 6. no one took delivery of the goods involved after the goods arrived at the port of destination more than 60 days, the carrier Mediterranean should have the obligation to prompt loss. Transport Groupage had not provided computation basis of the container detention fees and the container unloading charges should be born by the carrier on its own account and should not charge Zhongyi. In conclusion, Zhongyi requested the court to reject Transport Groupage's claims.

Based on the evidence having been admitted, and combined with the trial in court, the court of first instance ascertained the following facts:

On September 29, 2012, ZHANG Jing sent the booking note to Transport Groupage through QQ to entrust Transport Groupage to transport two 40-foot containers' goods from Huangpu, China to Alger, Algeria. The booking note recorded that the shipper was Zhongyi, the prepared carrying ship and the voyage was MSC Bettina 1241R, the closing date was October 17, and it was affixed with Zhongyi's official seal. Transport Groupage in the name of its own booked shipping space with Mediterranean after accepting the entrustment, the booking number issued by Mediterranean was 181MGG2TC01A83619. On October 11, 2012, No. MSCU9235002 container under No.181MGG2TC01A83619 booking note was taken delivery of. After the goods were loaded in the container, they could not be loaded on the carrying ship for shipment. On October 19, ZHANG Jing contacted with Transport Groupage in terms of the transportation of No.CAXU9726132 container under No.181MGG2TC01A83902 booking note, but the cargo could not be loaded in M.V. "MSC Livorno" on October 31. On October 30, 2012, ZHANG Jing suggested to combine the forwarding matters of No.MSCU9235002 and No. CAXU9726132 containers into one, and continued6 to use Zhongyi's email box kelly@chinawinline.com to contact with Transport Groupage (alexlai@sczs.casal-ogistics.com) to communicate issues of the goods involved.

On November10, No.MSCU9235002 and No.CAXU9726132 containers were loaded on M.V. "MSC TARANTO" at the Port of Chiwan. On November13, Shenzhen Sinotrans Shipping Agency Co., Ltd., as the agent of Mediterranean, issued No.MSCUDI791056 bill of lading. This bill of lading recorded that the shipper was Million Trading Limited; the consignee should be ordered by BANQUE AL BARAKA D'ALGERIE; the cargo were 2,311 boxes of shampoo and loaded in two 40-foot containers of which the number were No.MSCU9235002 and No.CAXU9726132; the place of delivery was the Old Huangpu Port and the port of loading was Port of Chiwan, China; the port of discharge was Alger, Algeria; the freight was prepaid; the carrying ship and voyage was M.V. "MSC TARANTO" and 1244R respectively; the rent-free period of the 40-foot container was seven days and the container detention fee was USD24 each day from the 8th to 15th day, the container detention fee was USD48 each day after the 16th day. On November, 2 and November 13, 2012, ZHANG Jing had respectively paid the freight of the goods involved in amount of USD3,950 and USD3,300 and the amendment charge in amount of RMB200 yuan to Transport Groupage.

On December 11, 2012, the goods involved were transported to the Barcelona, Spain and were discharged at the dock. On December 26, the goods were loaded on M.V. "HANSE FORTUNE" and arrived at Port of Alger on December 28. On September 25, 2013, the dynamic result queried from Mediterranean's website showed that container was retained in Alger.

The goods involved were retained at the port of destination after arrival, Mediterranean Shenzhen notified Transport Groupage that the correlative charges resulted from non-taking delivery of the goods involved through email. Transport Groupage sent emails to the kelly@chinawinline.com notifying that the correlative charges resulted from non-taking delivery of the goods involved at the port of destination and asked for the information of the shipper. On September 11, 2013, Mediterranean Shenzhen sent the email notifying Transport Groupage that by September 30, container detention fees were USD25,536 and container unloading charge was USD1,051. Transport Groupage sent an email in terms of the above-mentioned situation to kelly@chinawinline.com on September 16.

In October 2013, Transport Groupage issued a letter of authorization for payment to CASA China, to entrust CASA China to pay Mediterranean Shipping (Hong Kong) Co., Ltd. (hereinafter referred to as Mediterranean Hong Kong), the agent of Mediterranean, a total amount of USD26,587, the container detention fees of No.CAXU9726132 and No.MSCU9235002 containers that resulted from the non-taking delivery of the goods involved at the port of destination. On October 8, CASA China issued a check of Hang Seng Bank number with No.143489 of which the amount was USD26,587 to Mediterranean Hong Kong, and Mediterranean Hong Kong signed the said check. On October 11, Mediterranean Shenzhen issued two pieces of evidence for the two containers involved, and it recorded that the goods involved arrived at the port of the destination on December 28, 2012 and was retained at the port of destination because of non-taking delivery of the goods; by September 30, 2013, the two containers had incurred container detention fees in amount of USD25,536 and container unloading charge in amount of USD1,051 (the calculation method of each 40-foot container was: from January 4 to January 11, 2013, 8 days in total, USD24 per day per container, from January 12 to September 30, 2013, 262 days in total, USD48 per day per container. Transport Groupage entrusted CASA China to pay Mediterranean Hong Kong appointed by Mediterranean Shenzhen the above-mentioned charges in Hong Kong.

On June 8, 2013, Zhongyi issued a letter of guarantee to Transport Groupage, agreeing as follows: Zhongyi should make an accurate declaration of all the goods that Zhongyi entrusted Transport Groupage to transport; Zhongyi should be liable for all loss or responsibilities of Transport Groupage, Transport Groupage's employees or agents arising from inaccurate description of the goods, shortage of goods, jetsam or non-taking delivery of the goods; where Transport Groupage, Transport Groupage's employees or Transport Groupage's agents were sued because of inaccurate description of the goods, shortage of goods, jetsam or non-taking delivery of the goods, Zhongyi should pay the legal fees, lawyer's fee and notary fee; owing to the inaccurate description of the goods, shortage of goods, jetsam or non-taking delivery of the goods, Transport Groupage's ship, other ships or Transport Groupage's possession suffered detention or retention, Zhongyi should compensate the economic losses caused to Transport Groupage. Zhongyi should pay the cash deposit or bail to avoid detention or retention; Zhongyi should unconditionally bear joint and several liability with the shipper, consignee or other irrelevant persons under the bill of lading, and jointly undertake obligations of the letter of guarantee; the effect of the letter of guarantee should not affect Transport Groupage's advocating rights to the shipper, consignee or other irrelevant persons under the bill of lading; the period of the letter of guarantee was two years after the primary liability period was expired, it should be subject to and be interpreted by Chinese laws, the parties concerned under the letter of guarantee had rights to bring a lawsuit before Chinese courts.

It was found out that Mediterranean Shanghai was an exclusively foreign-owned company set up by Mediterranean in China. Mediterranean Shenzhen was subordinated to Mediterranean Shanghai and its scope of business was to provide services of canvassing goods, issuing bills of lading, settling freights and signing service contracts for the ships owned or operated by Mediterranean.

During the trial of first instance, both parties chose the laws of the People's Republic of China to solve the substantive dispute of this case.

The court of first instance held that this case was arising from dispute over freight forwarding contract. The goods in this case were transported from Huangpu, China through Port of Chiwan, Shenzhen to Alger port, Algeria by sea. Transport Groupage and Zhongyi had disputes out of the correlative charges resulted from non-taking delivery of the goods involved at the port of destination, and this case involved with foreign-related factors. According to the Provisions of the Supreme People's Court on Several Issues concerning the Trial of Cases of Disputes over Marine Freight Forwarding Article 13, this case should be under the jurisdiction of the maritime court. Zhongyi's domicile and where the contract was performed were within the jurisdiction of the court of first instance, according to the Civil Procedure Law of People's Republic of China Article 23, an action instituted for a contract dispute should be under the jurisdiction of the people's court at the place of domicile of Zhongyi or at the place where the contract was performed. According to the Contract Law of People's Republic of China Article 126 Paragraph 1, parties to a foreign-related contract would select the applicable law for resolution of a contractual dispute. Transport Groupage and Zhongyi chose the laws of the People's Republic of China to solve the substantive dispute of this case, this case should be subjected to the laws of the People's Republic of China.

ZHANG Jing in the name of Zhongyi issued the booking note to Transport Groupage, the shipper and seal of the shipper on the booking note were Zhongyi. ZHANG Jing used Zhongyi's email box to contact with Transport Groupage about the shipping of the relevant goods and paid the freight and amendment charge of the goods involved. Based on the record in the booking note, the email address used by ZHANG Jing and the contents of the emails, Transport Groupage had reason to believe the agency power of ZHANG Jing who was Zhongyi's employee and the authenticity of the booking note. Zhongyi denied the authenticity of Zhongyi's seal on the booking note and argued that booking note issued by ZHANG Jing was only her individual act and had no relation to Zhongyi, but Zhongyi had no effective evidence to support, thus this argument was untenable. According to the Contract Law of People's Republic of China Article 49, "if an actor has no power of agency, oversteps the power of agency, or the power of agency has expired and yet concludes a contract in the principal's name, and the counterpart has reasons to trust that the actor has the power of agency, the act of agency shall be effective", Transport Groupage and Zhongyi established a freight forwarding contract relationship according to the law, under which Zhongyi was the principal and Transport Groupage was the agent. The letter of guarantee issued by Zhongyi to Transport Groupage ensured that Zhongyi should undertake all economic losses or liabilities resulted from the inaccurate description of the goods, shortage of goods, jetsam or non-taking delivery of the goods and should unconditionally bear joint and several liability together with the shipper, consignee or other irrelevant persons. The letter of guarantee was voluntarily issued by Zhongyi and Zhongyi failed to prove there were exemptions, nor did it prove that the letter of guarantee was issued for the purpose of transportation of specified goods, and should be contained in the maritime freight forwarding contract in this case. The maritime freight forwarding contract was the declaration of real intention of the both parties, and did not violate legal and administrative provisions, which should be legal and valid. The parties should exercise rights and perform obligations according to the contract and relevant laws and regulations.

With respect to the claim about the container unloading charge in amount of USD1,051, Transport Groupage failed to prove that the container unloading charge should be charged by the carrier or the port part, it neither proved that the authorized subject actually had charged that sum, nor did it prove whether the container unloading charge was the necessary fee resulted from non-taking delivery of the goods involved at the port of destination. According to the Civil Procedure Law of People's Republic of China Article 64 Paragraph 1, a party should have the burden to provide evidence for its claims, the claim of Transport Groupage was lack of factual evidence and should not be sustained.

With respect to the claim about the container detention fees in amount of USD25,536, based on the emails between Transport Groupage and Zhongyi about the non-taking delivery of the goods involved at the port of destination and request of adding the shipper's information, and the dynamic inquiry result of the goods involved from Mediterranean's website, it could be ascertained that the containers involved were retained at the port of destination because of non-taking delivery of on the condition that Zhongyi did not provide contrary evidence. Mediterranean as the carrier that provided the containers involved suffered losses out of extended use of containers and should have the rights to claim. Mediterranean could claim against Transport Groupage for the transportation of the goods involved or enforce the claim through retaining and auctioning the goods involved according to the law, the above option was Mediterranean's right but not its obligation. It was proper that Transport Groupage advanced the container detention fees of the goods involved at the port of destination for Mediterranean. Transport Groupage had paid the carrier the loss of container detention fees resulted from non-taking delivery of the goods at the port of destination. According to the Contract Law of People's Republic of China Article 398, "the principal shall prepay the expenses for handling the commissioned affair. Any expense necessary for handling the commissioned affair advanced by the agent should be repaid with interest by the principal", Transport Groupage paid the container detention fees in order to deal with Zhongyi's agent matters, Zhongyi as the principal should repay the sum. But the reasonable sum of the container detention fees should be determined on the basis of the losses caused to the container provider during the period when the containers are occupied. The container provider could prevent further loss by buying new container on condition of the long-term occupation of the container. The accumulative upper limit of the actual loss caused by the extended use of container should not exceed new container price at the same period and same specification in the market. Combined with the shipping practices, the court of first instance ascertained at discretion that the losses suffered by the carrier Mediterranean resulted from long-term occupation of the container involved should be RMB30,000 yuan of each 40-foot container and in an amount of RMB60,000 yuan of two container. The sum exceeding this amount claimed by Transport Groupage should not be supported.

Pulling the threads together, according to the Contract Law of People's Republic of China Article 398 and the Civil Procedure Law of the People's Republic of China Article 64 Paragraph 1, judgment of first instance was as follows: 1. Shenzhen Zhongyi Freight Forwarding Co., Ltd. should pay Transport Groupage International (Shenzhen) Limited the container detention fees in amount of RMB60,000 yuan; 2. reject other claims of Transport Groupage International (Shenzhen) Limited. The above obligation of payment should be fulfilled within 10 days after the judgment came into effect. If Shenzhen Zhongyi Freight Forwarding Co., Ltd. failed to perform the obligation to pay money according to the period specified in this judgment, it should double the payment of interest on the debt during the period of delay according to the Civil Procedure Law of the People's Republic of China Article 229. Court acceptance fee of this case in amount of RMB3,570.2 yuan, Transport Groupage International (Shenzhen) Limited should bear RMB2,260.12 yuan, Shenzhen Zhongyi Freight Forwarding Co., Ltd. should bear RMB1,310.08 yuan.

By virtue of dissatisfaction with the civil judgment rendered by the court of first instance, Zhongyi lodged an appeal before the court, requesting that: revoke the first item of judgment of first instance and change to reject all claims filed by Transport Groupage and to adjudge that the court fees of the first and second instances should be born by Transport Groupage, based on the following reasons:

Firstly, Zhongyi and Transport Groupage did not exist commission contract relationship in terms of the goods involved, Transport Groupage's claim for compensation liability against Zhongyi lacked factual and legal basis. The matters of export agent of the goods involved were all conducted between the third party ZHANG Jing and Transport Groupage, and were irrelevant to Zhongyi. 1. ZHANG Jing was not the clerk of Zhongyi, she had told LAI Zicong (the clerk of Transport Groupage) when she sent the booking note to him that the email box of Zhongyi her used was bought from Zhongyi. 2. The booking note that ZHANG Jing sent to the Transport Groupage was fake. 3. The export freight and amendment charge of the goods involved were all directly paid to Transport Groupage by ZHANG Jing through bank transfer by her own individual account in Hong Kong; and 4. Zhongyi and Transport Groupage had long-term business cooperation, and it was common and reasonable to issue a letter of guarantee in standard form. The letter of guarantee involved was a general guarantee to the performance of the long-term business cooperation but not the commitment of responsibility in terms of the transportation of the goods involved, and it could not be decided that Zhongyi and Transport Groupage had commission contract relationship based thereon.

Secondly, the action of ZHANG Jing did not constitute apparent agency. ZHANG Jing was not the clerk of Zhongyi, the action that she issued the forged booking note with the seal of Zhongyi to Transport Groupage was unauthorized agency. Zhongyi completely opposed it and ZHANG Jing should be solely responsible for subsequent consequences. During the investigation of the second instance, Zhongyi opposed the allegation of Transport Groupage that Zhongyi had paid the container detention fee of the goods involved and argued that the evidence of Transport Groupage could not prove that Zhongyi had actually paid the charge.

Transport Groupage argued in second instance that:

1. ZHANG Jing issued the booking note to Transport Groupage, affixed with the official seal of Zhongyi and contacted with Transport Groupage about the freight forwarding matters of the goods involved by the email box of Zhongyi. Zhongyi did not raise any objection to Transport Groupage in the case where that Zhongyi well-knew the above situation. Transport Groupage had every reason to believe that ZHANG Jing was the clerk of Zhongyi and ZHANG Jing's action was on behalf of Zhongyi.
2. ZHANG Jing entrusted Transport Groupage to arrange the shipping of the goods involved on behalf of Zhongyi and paid Transport Groupage the relevant charges happening therefrom. Transport Groupage arranged the transportation of the goods involved to the port of destination as agreed and timely told Zhongyi the situation of the correlative charges resulting from non-taking delivery of the goods involved at the port of destination and had completely fulfilled the legal obligation as a freight forwarder. Zhongyi and Transport Groupage established a freight forwarding contract relationship, Zhongyi was the principal and Transport Groupage was the agent.
3. Based on the freight forwarding contract relationship with Zhongyi, Transport Groupage paid the carrier container detention fee resulting from non-taking delivery of the goods involved at the port of destination, Zhongyi as the principal should repay this sum to Transport Groupage. Transport Groupage requested the court to dismiss the appeal and affirm the original judgment.

Transport Groupage submitted the following additional evidence to the court in the second instance:

1. Other booking notes that ZHANG Jing issued to Transport Groupage in the name of Zhongyi to book shipping space, the confirmation of costs issued by Transport Groupage, and relevant email records, to prove the transaction practice that Zhongyi booked space from Transport Groupage through ZHANG Jing and ZHANG Jing arranged another company in Hong Kong paid the booking charges to Transport Groupage was consistent with this case;
2. Online tracking records of the containers by August13, 2015, to prove that the containers involved had been hollowed out by the customs;
3. Notarial certificate of the check receipt of Hang Seng Bank, to prove that Transport Groupage actually paid the charges involved.

With the exception of the fact that whether Transport Groupage had paid the charges involved, relevant evidence could prove other facts having been ascertained in the first instance, the court hereby ascertains.

Zhongyi did not admit the authenticity, legality or relevancy of the above supplementary evidence provided by Transport Groupage, and considered that the evidence 1 had no relation to this case and could not prove the existent principal-agent relationship between Zhongyi and Transport Groupage; the printout of the online tracking records of the containers could not prove that the relevancy between container and the transportation involved; the payable item on Hang Seng Bank's check was not clear, even this check was issued, it could not prove that Transport Groupage had actually paid the charges. the court ascertains that evidence 1 and 2 had no relation to this case and should not be admitted. The check receipt of Hang Seng Bank was notarized by entrusted notary and handled transmission formality, the court ascertains the authenticity of the check. As to the probative force of this evidence to the pact to prove, the court will analyze in combination with other evidence.

The court holds that this case is concerning dispute over freight forwarding contract. The container detention fees involved resulted from port of Alger, the port of destination, thus this case involves foreign-related factors. The both parties had no objection to the applicable law in the second instance and the court hereby ascertains. Based on the claims and pleas of the both parties and combined with the investigation in trial, the court ascertains the issues to be determined in the second instance as follows: whether Transport Groupage and Zhongyi established freight forwarding relationship in terms of the transportation of the goods involved; whether Transport Groupage actually paid the container detention fees of the goods involved; whether the container detention fees paid by Transport Groupage is the reasonable and necessary in order to finish the commission matters.

With respect to issue that whether Transport Groupage and Zhongyi established freight forwarding contract relationship in terms of the transportation of the goods involved. The principal reason that Zhongyi claimed it had no freight forwarding contract relationship with Transport Groupage lied in that ZHANG Jing's action did not constitute apparent agency and ZHANG Jing's unauthorized agency had no binding force to Zhongyi. Upon investigation, ZHANG Jing entrusted Transport Groupage to transport the goods involved in the name of Zhongyi, the booking note recorded that Zhongyi was the shipper, and it was affixed with the official seal of Zhongyi. Zhongyi ascertained that the email box used by ZHANG Jing during the transportation of the goods involved was the company's, and Transport Groupage had the reason to believe that ZHANG Jing had the right to sign the freight forwarding contract of the goods involved on behalf of Zhongyi. Zhongyi claimed that the seal on the booking note was fake but failed to provide relevant evidence to prove, the court denies this claim and ascertains that ZHANG Jing's action in this case constitutes apparent agency. The Contract Law of People's Republic of China Article 49 prescribes that if an actor has no power of agency, oversteps the power of agency, or the power of agency has expired and yet concludes a contract in the principal's name, and the counterpart has reasons to trust that the actor has the power of agency, the act of agency should be effective, Zhongyi should bear all the consequences that ZHANG Jing entrusted Transport Groupage to transport the goods involved in the name of Zhongyi. Zhongyi and Transport Groupage established freight forwarding contract relationship in terms of the shipping of the goods involved, under which Zhongyi was the principal and Transport Groupage was the agent.

With respect to issue that whether Transport Groupage actually paid the container detention fees of the goods involved. The goods involved were carried by Mediterranean and the containers involved were owned by Mediterranean, if the containers were extendedly used, Mediterranean would charge relevant container detention fees. The evidence that CASA China used to prove the payment it advanced includes payment order, check receipt of Hang Seng Bank and the acknowledgement of receipt thereof. Generally, the actual expenditure and income under a bill should be checked out through bank. In this case, the check receipt has the seal of Mediterranean Hong Kong thereon, but it just can prove that Mediterranean Hong Kong had received the check issued by CASA China, but cannot prove payment situation under this check. What's more, the payment order made unilaterally by Transport Groupage recorded that Mediterranean Hong Kong was the agent of Mediterranean, but this fact lacked valid evidence to prove that Mediterranean had relation to Mediterranean Hong Kong in terms of shipping of the goods involved and Mediterranean Hong Kong was the agent of Mediterranean to handle relevant issues, thus Transport Groupage's paying the charges to Mediterranean Hong Kong should be deemed as payment of the containers detention fees involved to Mediterranean. The business scope of Mediterranean and Mediterranean Shenzhen concerning charges is only limited to settlement freights for vessels owned or operated by Mediterranean, but does not include collection of other charges except freights on behalf of Mediterranean. Mediterranean, Mediterranean Hong Kong and Mediterranean were enterprises established and registered in different countries or different areas and should independent in law. In this case, no evidence can prove that Mediterranean entrusted Mediterranean Hong Kong or Mediterranean Shenzhen to collect the containers detention fees involved, or can prove that Mediterranean had received the containers detention fees involved, thus the above evidence is insufficient to prove that Transport Groupage had paid Mediterranean the containers detention fees involved through other parties. According to the Civil Procedure Law of People's Republic of China Article 64 Paragraph 1, "a party shall have the burden to provide evidence for its claims" and the Interpretation of the Supreme People's Court on the Application of the Civil Procedure Law of the People's Republic of China Article 90, "a party shall provide evidence to prove the facts on which his claims are based or to repudiate the facts on which the claims of the opposing party are based, unless it is otherwise prescribed by any law. Where a party fails to provide evidence or the evidence provided is insufficient to support his claims before a judgment is entered, the party bearing the burden of proof shall take the adverse consequences", Transport Groupage should bear the adverse consequences for failure of proof. The ascertainment that Transport Groupage had paid the containers detention fees involved in the first instance are inappropriate and the court corrects it.

With respect to issue that whether the container detention fees paid by Transport Groupage are the reasonable and necessary in order to finish the commission matters, the container detention fees claimed by Transport Groupage was not the charge as agreed in the freight forwarding contract between Zhongyi and Transport Groupage, and Transport Groupage had also ascertained that charges were advanced payment. According to the Contract Law of People's Republic of China Article 398, "the principal shall prepay the expenses for handling the commissioned affair. Any expense necessary for handling the commissioned affair advanced by the agent shall be repaid with interest by the principal". Under a freight forwarding contract, the agent should pay in advance the fee in order to deal with the commission matters, in the case where that the agent does not make payment in advance, the agent should only pay the fees for principal's benefit and such payment should be necessary to finish the commission matters.

The payment advanced by freight forwarder should be limited to reasonable fees arising from the import and export of goods. As to the abnormal and extra charges, the freight forwarder should ask for principal's permission before advancement, otherwise the principal was entitled to reject it. In terms of this case, the goods involved under the arrangement of Transport Groupage have been transported and arrived in the port of destination, the relevant freight forwarding matters in this case had been completed. The container detention fee resulted from non-taking delivery of the goods involved at the port of destination naturally belong to penalty under the contract of maritime transportation and not necessary charge that should be advanced in order to finish the freight forwarding matters. The freight forwarder should first ask for the principal's permission before payment. Transport Groupage without the permission of the principal paid the containers detention fees involved and claimed against Zhongyi, it lacks basis and should be rejected. The ascertainment in judgment of first instance that Zhongyi should pay the advancement to Transport Groupage constitutes incorrect application of law, the court hereby corrects it.

The container detention fees involved do not fall into the scope of expenses or losses Transport Groupage is entitled to, and Transport Groupage did not raise any claims based on the contents of the letter of guarantee issued by Zhongyi, thus the effectiveness of the letter of guarantee does not affect the determination of responsibility in this case. the court will not review and decide the effectiveness of the letter of guarantee.

Pulling the threads together, the facts are incorrectly ascertained, the law is wrongly applied and the result is improperly handled in the judgment of first instance, the court hereby corrects it. Zhongyi's appeal is well-grounded, and the court hereby supports it. Pursuant to the Contract Law of People's Republic of China Article 398, the Civil Procedure Law of People's Republic of China Article 64 Paragraph 1, Article 170 Paragraph 1 Sub-paragraph 2 and the Interpretation of the Supreme People's Court on the Application of the Civil Procedure Law of the People's Republic of China Article 90, the judgment is as follows:

1. Revoke (2014) Guang Hai Fa Chu Zi No.102 Civil Judgment made by Guangzhou Maritime Court of the People's Republic of China;

2. Reject the claims of China Transport Groupage International (Shenzhen) Limited against Shenzhen Zhongyi Freight Forwarding Co., Ltd.

Court acceptance fee of first instance in amount of RMB3,570.2 yuan shall be born by China Transport Groupage International (Shenzhen) Limited.

Court acceptance fee of second instance in amount of RMB1,310.8 yuan, shall be born by China Transport Groupage International (Shenzhen) Limited. Shenzhen Zhongyi Freight Forwarding Co., Ltd. has prepaid the court acceptance fee of second instance in amount of RMB1,310.8 yuan, it will be refunded by the court, China Transport Groupage International (Shenzhen) Limited shall pay the court RMB1,310.8 within 10 days after this judgment comes into effect.

The judgment is final.

Presiding Judge: DU Yixing
Acting Judge: MO Fei
Acting Judge: GU Enzhen
December 17, 2015
Clerk: PAN Wanqin

Appendix: Relevant Law

1. **Contract Law of People's Republic of China**
   Article 398 The principal shall prepay the expenses for handling the commissioned affair. Any expense necessary for handling the commissioned affair advanced by the agent shall be repaid with interest by the principal.
2. **Civil Procedure Law of People's Republic of China**
   Article 64 A party shall have the burden to provide evidence for its claims.
   A people's court shall investigate and collect evidence which a party and its litigation representative are unable to collect for some objective reasons and evidence which the people's court deems necessary for trying a case.
   A people's court shall, under statutory procedures, verify evidence comprehensively and objectively.
   Article 170 After hearing an appellate case, the people's court of second instance shall handle the case respectively according to the following circumstances:
(1) If the facts were clearly found and the law was correctly applied in the original adjudication, the appeal shall be rejected by a adjudication and the original adjudication shall be sustained.
(2) If in the original adjudication the facts were incorrectly found and the law was incorrectly applied, the people's court of second instance may amend, revoke or change the original judgment by a adjudication.

(3) If in the original judgment the facts were not clearly found, the judgment shall be rescinded and the case remanded by an order to the original people's court for a retrial, or the people's court of second instance may amend the judgment after investigating and clarifying the facts.

(4) If the in the original judgment a violation of the prescribed procedure which include omission of relevant parties or illegal default judgment, the judgment shall be rescinded and the case remanded by an order to the original people's court for a retrial.

After the original people's court rendered the judgment in a retrial of their case, the people's court of second instance shall not retry the case and reject the appeal of the parties.

3. **Interpretation of the Supreme People's Court on the Application of the Civil Procedure Law of the People's Republic of China**

Article 90 A party shall provide evidence to prove the facts on which his claims are based or to repudiate the facts on which the claims of the opposing party are based, unless it is otherwise prescribed by any law.

Where a party fails to provide evidence or the evidence provided is insufficient to support his claims before a judgment is entered, the party bearing the burden of proof shall take the adverse consequences.

The Supreme People's Court of the People's Republic of China Civil Judgment

China Transport Groupage International (Shenzhen) Limited

v.

Shenzhen Zhongyi Freight Forwarding Co., Ltd.

(2017) Zui Gao Fa Min Shen Zi No.104.

Related Case(s) This is the judgment of retrial, and the judgment of first instance and the judgment of second instance are on page 83 and page 93 respectively.

Cause(s) of Action 223. Dispute over freight forwarding contract on the sea or sea-connected waters.

Headnote On retrial by the Supreme People's Court, reversing lower court decisions that freight forwarder (the Plaintiff at first instance, the Respondent on SCC retrial) was entitled to recover container demurrage from the Defendant goods shipper (the Defendant at first instance, the Appellant on SCC retrial) on the basis that goods shipper had produced new evidence that it had already paid the charges.

Summary The Plaintiff (freight forwarder) sued the Defendant (shipper) for container demurrage and landing charges incurred at the port of destination. The Defendant claimed that the Plaintiff failed to prove that the goods were not accepted after their arrival at the discharging port. The court of first instance found in favor of the Plaintiff, holding that the Defendant was obliged to pay the fees. However, the court of first instance also held the Plaintiff as a shipper should have estimated the maximum container demurrage based on the value of a container when entering into the contract. Thus, the amount of fees was adjusted according to the market value of a container. The Defendant appealed, alleging that the Plaintiff-Respondent did not have standing and failed to prove that it gave reasonable notice to the consignee when the goods arrived at the destination port. The Plaintiff-Respondent alleged that the notice obligation was unenforceable since the contact information provided by the Defendant-Shipper on the bill of lading was invalid. The appeal court found in favor of the Plaintiff-Respondent and held there was no breach of the notice obligation. Therefore, the appeal court dismissed the appeal and sustained the first-instance judgment.

The Supreme People's Court granted the Defendant-Shipper's application for a retrial, and held that the Appellant (the Defendant-Shipper at first instance) was not liable to pay the overdue charges, as it had produced new evidence to show that it had already paid.

Judgment

The Claimant of Retrial (the Plaintiff of first instance, the Respondent of second instance): China Transport Groupage International (Shenzhen) Limited.
Domicile: Rm 01–07, Floor 37, Pengnian Square, Jiabing Road, Nanhu Street, Luohu District, Shenzhen, Guangdong.
Legal representative: SUN Peilun, general manager.
Agent *ad litem*: HUANG Sufang, lawyer of Beijing Dentons (Shenzhen) Law Firm.

The Respondent of Retrial (the Defendant of first instance, the Appellant of second instance): Shenzhen Zhongyi Freight Forwarding Co., Ltd.
Domicile: Unit 14L, Sun Island Building, South Dongmen Road, Luohu District, Shenzhen, Guangdong.
Legal representative: XU Zhigang, general manager of the company.
Agent *ad litem*: CAO Wending, lawyer of Guangdong Chenggong Law Firm.

With respect to the case arising from dispute over maritime freight forwarding contract between the Claimant of Retrial, China Transport Groupage International (Shenzhen) Limited (hereinafter referred to as Transport Groupage), and the Respondent of Retrial, Shenzhen Zhongyi Freight Forwarding Co., Ltd. (hereinafter referred to as Zhongyi), the Claimant of Retrial disagreed with the Guangdong High People's Court (hereinafter referred to as the court of second instance) (2015) Yue Gao Fa Min Si Zhong Zi No.138 Civil Judgment, and appealed to the court for retrial. The court made (2016) Zui Gao Fa Min Shen No.1885 Civil Ruling to retry the case. The court formed a collegiate panel according to law, and held a hearing in public on April 12, 2017. Agent *ad litem* of Transport Groupage, HUANG Sufang, agent *ad litem* of Zhongyi, CAO Wending, appeared in court to attend the hearing. Now the case has been concluded.

Transport Groupage claimed to the Guangzhou Maritime Court (hereinafter referred to as the court of first instance) that: in December 2012, Transport Groupage was entrusted by Zhongyi to carry a consignment of goods by sea from Chi Hai Bay, Shenzhen, China to the destination of Alger, Algeria. Transport Groupage entrusted Mediterranean Shipping Co., Ltd. (hereinafter referred to as "Mediterranean") to carry the goods involved, the number of the bill of lading was MSCUDI791056, the number of containers were CAXU9726132 and MSCU9235002 respectively. No one took delivery of the goods involved after the goods arrived at the port of destination, the containers were used extendedly. By the end of September 30, 2013, the container detention fees raised up to USD25,536 and USD1,051 of container unloading charge, totally up to USD26,587 (equivalent to RMB163,510.05 yuan, currency hereafter refers to RMB without particular refer). Transport Groupage as Zhongyi's cargo agent disbursed above charges to Mediterranean, but Zhongyi refused to pay the charges to Transport Groupage. Transport Groupage requested the court of first instance to order Zhongyi to pay the container detention fees and container unloading charge at the port of destination in an amount of RMB163,510.05 yuan and burden the court acceptance fee.

The court of first instance found out that:

On September 29, 2012, ZHANG Jing sent the booking note to Transport Groupage through QQ to entrust Transport Groupage to transport two 40-foot containers' cargo from Huangpu, China to Alger, Algeria. The booking note recorded that the shipper was Zhongyi, the prepared carrying ship and the voyage was MSC Bettina 1241R, the closing date was October 17, and it was affixed with Zhongyi's official seal. Transport Groupage in the name of its own booked shipping space with Mediterranean after accepting the entrustment, the booking number issued by Mediterranean was 181MGG2TC01A83619. On October 11, 2012, No. MSCU9235002 container under No.181MGG2TC01A83619 booking note was taken delivery. After the goods was loaded in the container, they could not be loaded on the carrying ship for shipment. On October 19, ZHANG Jing contacted with Transport Groupage in terms of the transportation of No.CAXU9726132 container under No.181MGG2TC01A83902 booking note, but the cargo could not be loaded in M.V. "MSC Livorno" on October 31. On October 30, 2012, ZHANG Jing suggested to combine the forwarding matters of No.MSCU9235002 and No. CAXU9726132 containers into one, and continued to use Zhongyi's email box kelly@chinawinline.com to contact with Transport Groupage (alexlai@sczs.casal-ogistics.com) to communicate issues of the goods involved.

On November 10, No.MSCU9235002 and No.CAXU9726132 containers were loaded on M.V. "MSC TARANTO" at the port of Chiwan. On November13, Shenzhen Sinotrans Shipping Agency Co., Ltd., as the agent of Mediterranean, issued No.MSCUDI791056 bill of lading. This bill of lading recorded that the shipper was Million Trading Limited; the consignee should be ordered by BANQUE AL BARAKA D'ALGERIE; the goods was 2,311 boxes of shampoo and loaded in two 40-foot containers of which the number were No.MSCU9235002 and No.CAXU9726132; the place of delivery was the Old Huangpu Port and the port of loading was port of Chiwan, China; the port of discharge was Alger, Algeria; the freight was prepaid; the carrying ship and voyage was M.V. "MSC TARANTO" and 1244R respectively; the rent-free period of the 40-foot container was seven days and the container detention fee was USD24 each day from the 8th to 15th day, the container detention fee was USD48 each day after the 16th day. On November 2 and November 13, 2012, ZHANG Jing had respectively paid the freight of the goods involved in amount of USD3,950 and USD3,300 and the amendment charge in amount of RMB200 yuan to Transport Groupage.

On December 11, 2012, the goods involved was transported to the Barcelona, Spain and were discharged at the dock. On December 26, the goods was loaded on M.V. "HANSE FORTUNE" and arrived at port of Alger on December 28. On

September 25, 2013, the dynamic result queried from Mediterranean's website showed that container was retained in Alger.

Since the goods involved were retained at the port of destination after arrival, Mediterranean Shenzhen notified Transport Groupage that the correlative charges resulted from non-taking delivery of the goods involved through email. Transport Groupage sent emails to the kelly@chinawinline.com notifying that the correlative charges resulted from non-taking delivery of the goods involved at the port of destination and asked for the information of the shipper. On September 11, 2013, Mediterranean Shenzhen sent the email notifying Transport Groupage that by September 30, container detention fees were USD25,536 and container unloading charge was USD1,051. Transport Groupage sent an email in terms of the above-mentioned situation to kelly@chinawinline.com on September 16.

In October 2013, Transport Groupage issued a letter of authorization for payment to CASA China Limited (hereinafter referred to as CASA China), to entrust CASA China to pay Mediterranean Shipping (Hong Kong) Co., Ltd. (hereinafter referred to as Mediterranean Hong Kong), the agent of Mediterranean, a total amount of USD26,587, the container detention fees of No.CAXU9726132 and No. MSCU9235002 containers that resulted from the non-taking delivery of the goods involved at the port of destination. On October 8, CASA China issued a check of Hang Seng Bank number with No.143489 of which the amount was USD26,587 to Mediterranean Hong Kong, and Mediterranean Hong Kong signed the said check. On October 11, Mediterranean Shenzhen issued two pieces of evidence for the two containers involved, and it recorded that the goods involved arrived at the port of the destination on December 28, 2012 and was retained at the port of destination because of non-taking delivery of the goods; by September 30, 2013, the two containers had incurred container detention fees in amount of USD25,536 and container unloading charge in amount of USD1,051 (the calculation method of each 40-foot container was: from January 4 to January 11, 2013 (8 days), USD24 per day per container, from January 12 to September 30, 2013 (262 days), USD48 per day per container). Transport Groupage entrusted CASA China to pay Mediterranean Hong Kong appointed by Mediterranean Shenzhen the above-mentioned charges in Hong Kong.

On June 8, 2013, Zhongyi issued a letter of guarantee to Transport Groupage, agreeing as follows: Zhongyi should make an accurate declaration of all the goods that Zhongyi entrusted Transport Groupage to transport; Zhongyi should be liable for all losses or responsibilities of Transport Groupage, Transport Groupage's employees or agents arising from inaccurate description of the goods, shortage of goods, jetsam or non-taking delivery of the goods; where Transport Groupage, Transport Groupage's employees or Transport Groupage's agents were sued because of inaccurate description of the goods, shortage of goods, jetsam or non-taking delivery of the goods, Zhongyi should pay the legal fees, lawyer's fee and notary fee; owing to the inaccurate description of the goods, shortage of goods, jetsam or non-taking delivery of the goods, Transport Groupage's ship, other ships or Transport Groupage's possession suffered detention or retention, Zhongyi should compensate the economic losses caused to Transport Groupage. Zhongyi should pay the cash deposit or bail to avoid detention or retention; Zhongyi should unconditionally bear joint and several liability with the shipper, consignee or other irrelevant persons under the bill of lading, and jointly undertake obligations of the letter of guarantee; the effect of the letter of guarantee should not affect Transport Groupage's advocating rights to the shipper, consignee or other irrelevant persons under the bill of lading; the period of the letter of guarantee was two years after the primary liability period was expired, it should subject to and be interpreted by Chinese laws, the parties concerned under the letter of guarantee had rights to bring a lawsuit before Chinese courts.

It was found out that Mediterranean Shanghai was an exclusively foreign-owned company set up by Mediterranean in China. Mediterranean Shenzhen was subordinated to Mediterranean Shanghai and its scope of business was to provide services of canvassing goods, issuing bills of lading, settling freights and signing service contracts for the ships owned or operated by Mediterranean.

During the trial, both parties chose the laws of the People's Republic of China to solve the substantive dispute of this case.

The court of first instance held that this case was arising from dispute over freight forwarding contract. The goods in this case were transported from Huangpu, China through Port of Chiwan, Shenzhen to Alger port, Algeria by sea. Transport Groupage and Zhongyi had disputes out of the correlative charges resulted from non-taking delivery of the goods involved at the port of destination, and this case involved with foreign-related factors. According to the Provisions of the Supreme People's Court on Several Issues concerning the Trial of Cases of Disputes over Marine Freight Forwarding Article 13, this case should be under the jurisdiction of the maritimecourt. Zhongyi's domicile and where the contract was performed are within the jurisdiction of the court of first instance, according to the Civil Procedure Law of People's Republic of China Article 23, an action instituted for a contract dispute should be under the jurisdiction of the people's court at the place of domicile of Zhongyi or at the place where the contract was performed. According to the Contract Law of People's Republic of China Article 126 Paragraph 1, parties to a foreign-related contract may select the applicable law for resolution of a contractual dispute. Transport Groupage and Zhongyi chose the laws of the People's Republic of China to solve the substantive dispute of this case, this case should be subjected to the laws of the People's Republic of China.

ZHANG Jing in the name of Zhongyi issued the booking note to Transport Groupage, the shipper and seal of the shipper on the booking note were Zhongyi. ZHANG Jing used Zhongyi's email box to contact with Transport Groupage about the shipping of the relevant goods and paid the freight and amendment charge of the goods involved. Based on the record in the booking note, the email address used by ZHANG Jing and the contents of the emails, Transport Groupage had reason to believe the agency power of ZHANG Jing who was Zhongyi's employee and the authenticity of the booking note. Zhongyi denied the authenticity of Zhongyi's seal on the booking note and argued that Booking Note issued by ZHANG Jing was only its individual action and had no relation to Zhongyi, but Zhongyi had no effective evidence to support, thus this argument was untenable. According to the

Contract Law of People's Republic of China Article 49, "if an actor has no power of agency, oversteps the power of agency, or the power of agency had expired and yet concludes a contract in the principal's name, and the counterpart had reasons to trust that the actor has the power of agency, the act of agency should be effective", Transport Groupage and Zhongyi established a freight forwarding contract relationship according to the law, under which Zhongyi was the principal and Transport Groupage was the agent. The letter of guarantee issued by Zhongyi to Transport Groupage ensured that Zhongyi should undertake all economic losses or liabilities resulted from the inaccurate description of the goods, shortage of goods, jetsam or non-taking delivery of the goods and should unconditionally bear joint and several liability together with the shipper, consignee or other irrelevant persons. The letter of guarantee was voluntarily issued by Zhongyi and Zhongyi failed to prove there were exemptions, nor did it prove that the letter of guarantee was issued for the purpose of transportation of specified goods, and should be contained in the maritime freight forwarding contract in this case. The maritime freight forwarding contract was the declaration of real intention of the both parties, and did not violate legal and administrative provisions, which should be legal and valid. The parties should exercise rights and perform obligations according to the contract and relevant laws and regulations.

With respect to the claim about the container unloading charge in amount of USD1,051, Transport Groupage failed to prove that the container unloading charge should be charged by the carrier or the port part, it neither proved that the authorized subject actually had charged that sum, nor did it prove whether the container unloading charge was the necessary fee resulted from non-taking delivery of the goods involved at the port of destination. According to the Civil Procedure Law of People's Republic of China Article 64 Paragraph 1, a party should have the burden to provide evidence for its claims, the claim of Transport Groupage was lack of factual evidence and should not be sustained.

With respect to the claim about the container detention fees in amount of USD25,536, based on the emails between Transport Groupage and Zhongyi about the non-taking delivery of the goods involved at the port of destination and request of adding the shipper's information, and the dynamic inquiry result of the goods involved from Mediterranean's website, it could be ascertained that the containers involved were retained at the port of destination because of non-taking delivery of on the condition that Zhongyi did not provide contrary evidence. Mediterranean as the carrier that provided the containers involved suffered losses out of extended use of containers and should have the rights to claim. Mediterranean could claim against Transport Groupage for the transportation of the goods involved or enforce the claim through retaining and auctioning the goods involved according to the law, the above option was Mediterranean's right but not its obligation. It was proper that Transport Groupage advanced the container detention fees of the goods involved at the port of destination for Mediterranean. Transport Groupage had paid the carrier the losses of container detention fees resulted from non-taking delivery of the goods at the port of destination. According to the Contract Law of People's Republic of China Article 398, "the principal shall prepay the expenses for handling the commissioned affair. Any expense necessary for handling the commissioned affair advanced by the agent shall be repaid with interest by the principal", Transport Groupage paid the container detention fees in order to deal with Zhongyi's agent matters, Zhongyi as the principal should repay the sum. But the reasonable sum of the container detention fees should be determined on the basis of the losses caused to the container provider during the period when the containers were occupied. The container provider could prevent further loss by buying new container on condition of the long-term occupation of the container. The accumulative upper limit of the actual loss caused by the extended use of container should not exceed new container price at the same period and same specification in the market. Combined with the shipping practices, the court of first instance ascertained at discretion that the losses suffered by the carrier Mediterranean resulted from long-term occupation of the container involved should be RMB30,000 yuan of each 40-foot container and in an amount of RMB60,000 yuan of two container. The sum exceeding this amount claimed by Transport Groupage should not be supported.

Pulling the threads together, according to the Contract Law of People's Republic of China Article 398 and the Civil Procedure Law of the People's Republic of China Article 64 Paragraph 1, judgment of first instance was as follows: 1. Shenzhen Zhongyi Freight Forwarding Co., Ltd. should pay Transport Groupage International (Shenzhen) Limited the container detention fees in amount of RMB60,000 yuan; 2. reject other claims of Transport Groupage International (Shenzhen) Limited. The above obligation of payment should be fulfilled within 10 days after the judgment came into effect. If Shenzhen Zhongyi Freight Forwarding Co., Ltd. failed to perform the obligation to pay money according to the period specified in this judgment, it should double the payment of interest on the debt during the period of delay according to the Civil Procedure Law of the People's Republic of China Article 229. Court acceptance fee of this case in amount of RMB3,570.2 yuan, Transport Groupage International (Shenzhen) Limited should bear RMB2,260.12 yuan, Shenzhen Zhongyi Freight Forwarding Co., Ltd. should bear RMB1,310.08 yuan.

Zhongyi disagreed with judgment of first instance and appealed to revoke judgment of first instance, change to reject the claims of Transport Groupage.

The court of second instance found out that: the facts confirmed by the court of first instance had evidence to prove except whether Transport Groupage actually paid the freight involved, so the court of second instance confirmed them.

The court of second instance held that:

This case was concerning dispute over freight forwarding contract. The container detention fees involved resulted from port of Alger, the port of destination, thus this case involved foreign-related factors. The both parties had no objection to the applicable law in the second instance and the court hereby ascertained. Based on the claims and pleas of the both parties and combined with the investigation in trial, the court ascertained the issues to be determined in the second instance as follows: whether Transport Groupage and Zhongyi established freight forwarding contract relationship in terms of the transportation of the goods involved; whether Transport Groupage actually paid the container detention fees of the goods involved; whether the container detention fees paid by Transport Groupage was the reasonable and necessary in order to finish the commission matters.

With respect to issue that whether Transport Groupage and Zhongyi established freight forwarding contract relationship in terms of the transportation of the goods involved. The principal reason that Zhongyi claimed it had no freight forwarding contract relationship with Transport Groupage lied in that ZHANG Jing's action did not constitute apparent agency and ZHANG Jing's unauthorized agency had no binding force to Zhongyi. Upon investigation, ZHANG Jing entrusted Transport Groupage to transport the goods involved in the name of Zhongyi, the booking note recorded that Zhongyi was the shipper, and it was affixed with the official seal of Zhongyi. Zhongyi ascertained that the email box used by ZHANG Jing during the transportation of the goods involved was the company's, and Transport Groupage had the reason to believe that ZHANG Jing had the right to sign the freight forwarding contract of the goods involved on behalf of Zhongyi. Zhongyi claimed that the seal on the booking note was fake but failed to provide relevant evidence to prove, the court of second instance denied this claim and ascertains that ZHANG Jing's action in this case constituted apparent agency. The Contract Law of People's Republic of China Article 49 prescribed that if an actor had no power of agency, overstepped the power of agency, or the power of agency had expired and yet concluded a contract in the principal's name, and the counterpart had reasons to trust that the actor had the power of agency, the act of agency should be effective, Zhongyi should bear all the consequences that ZHANG Jing entrusted Transport Groupage to transport the goods involved in the name of Zhongyi. Zhongyi and Transport Groupage established freight forwarding contract relationship in terms of the shipping of the goods involved, under which Zhongyi was the principal and Transport Groupage was the agent.

With respect to issue that whether Transport Groupage actually paid the container detention fees of the goods involved. The goods involved were carried by Mediterranean and the containers involved were owned by Mediterranean, if the containers were extendedly used, Mediterranean would charge relevant container detention fees. The evidence that Transport Groupage used to prove the payment it advanced includes payment order, check receipt of Hang Seng Bank and the acknowledgement of receipt thereof. Generally, the actual expenditure and income under a bill should be checked out through bank. In this case, the check receipt had the seal of Mediterranean Hong Kong thereon, but it just could prove that Mediterranean Hong Kong had received the check issued by CASA China, but could not prove payment situation under this check. What's more, the payment order made unilaterally by Transport Groupage recorded that Mediterranean Hong Kong was the agent of Mediterranean, but this fact lacked valid evidence to prove that Mediterranean had relation to Mediterranean Hong Kong in terms of shipping of the goods involved and Mediterranean Hong Kong was the agent of Mediterranean to handle relevant issues, thus Transport Groupage's paying the charges to Mediterranean Hong Kong should be deemed as payment of the containers detention fees involved to Mediterranean. The business scope of Mediterranean and Mediterranean Shenzhen concerning charges was only limited to settlement freights for vessels owned or operated by Mediterranean, but did not include collection of other charges except freights on behalf of Mediterranean. Mediterranean, Mediterranean Hong Kong and Mediterranean were enterprises established and registered in different countries or different areas and should independent in law. In this case, no evidence could prove that Mediterranean entrusted Mediterranean Hong Kong or Mediterranean Shenzhen to collect the containers detention fees involved, or could prove that Mediterranean had received the containers detention fees involved, thus the above evidence was insufficient to prove that Transport Groupage had paid Mediterranean the containers detention fees involved through other parties. According to the Civil Procedure Law of People's Republic of China Article 64 Paragraph 1, "a party shall have the burden to provide evidence for its claims" and Article 90 of the Interpretation of the Supreme People's Court on the Application of the Civil Procedure Law of the People's Republic of China, "a party shall provide evidence to prove the facts on which its claims are based or to repudiate the facts on which the claims of the opposing party are based, unless it is otherwise prescribed by any law. Where a party fails to provide evidence or the evidence provided is insufficient to support its claims before a judgment is entered, the party bearing the burden of proof shall take the adverse consequences", Transport Groupage should bear the adverse consequences for failure of proof. The ascertainment that Transport Groupage had paid the containers detention fees involved in the first instance are inappropriate and the court of second instance corrected it.

With respect to issue that whether the container detention fees paid by Transport Groupage were the reasonable and necessary in order to finish the commission matters, the container detention fees claimed by Transport Groupage was not the charge as agreed in the freight forwarding contract between Zhongyi and Transport Groupage, and Transport Groupage had also ascertained that charges were advanced payment. According to the Contract Law of People's Republic of China Article 398, "the principal shall prepay the expenses for handling the commissioned affair. Any expense necessary for handling the commissioned affair advanced by the agent shall be repaid with interest by the principal". Under a freight forwarding contract, the agent should pay in advance the fee in order to deal with the commission matters, in the case where that the agent did not make payment in advance, the agent should only pay the fees for principal's benefit and such payment should be necessary to finish the commission matters.

The payment advanced by freight forwarder should be limited to reasonable fees arising from the import and export of goods. As to the abnormal and extra charges, the freight forwarder should ask for principal's permission before advancement, otherwise the principal was entitled to reject it. In terms of this case, the goods involved under the arrangement of Transport Groupage had been transported and arrived in the port of destination, the relevant freight forwarder matters in this case had been completed. The container detention fee resulted from non-taking delivery of the goods involved at the port of destination naturally belonged to penalty under the contract of maritime transportation and not necessary charge that should be advanced in order to finish the freight forwarder matters. The freight forwarder should first ask for the principal's permission before payment. Transport Groupage without the permission of the principal paid the containers detention fees involved and claimed against Zhongyi, it lacked basis and should be rejected. The ascertainment in judgment of first instance that Zhongyi should pay the advancement to Transport Groupage constitutes incorrect application of law, the court of second instance hereby corrected it.

The container detention fees involved did not fall into the scope of expenses or losses Transport Groupage was entitled to, and Transport Groupage did not raise any claims based on the contents of the letter of guarantee issued by Zhongyi, thus the effectiveness of the letter of guarantee did not affect the determination of responsibility in this case. the court of second instance would not review and decide the effectiveness of the letter of guarantee.

Pulling the threads together, the facts were incorrectly ascertained, the law was wrongly applied and the result was improperly handled in the judgment of first instance, the court of second instance hereby corrected it. Zhongyi's appeal was well-grounded, and the court of second instance hereby supported it. Pursuant to the Contract Law of People's Republic of China Article 398, the Civil Procedure Law of People's Republic of China Article 64 Paragraph 1, Article 170 Paragraph 1 Sub-paragraph 2 and the Interpretation of the Supreme People's Court on the Application of the Civil Procedure Law of the People's Republic of China Article 90, the judgment was as follows: 1. Revoke (2014) Guang Hai Fa Chu Zi No.102 Civil Judgment made by Guangzhou Maritime Court of the People's Republic of China; 2. reject the claims of Transport Groupage against Zhongyi. Court acceptance fee of first instance in amount of RMB3,570.2 yuan and court acceptance fee of second instance in amount of RMB1,310.8 yuan shall be born by Transport Groupage.

Transport Groupage disagreed with the judgment of second instance and applied for retrial that: firstly, Transport Groupage had actually paid the container overuse fee. In the first instance, Transport Groupage provided the power of attorney issued to CASA China, the cheque receipt and cheque receipt of Hang Seng Bank, the certificate issued by Mediterranean Shenzhen, the industrial and commercial registration information of Mediterranean and Mediterranean Shenzhen, *Confirmation Letter* issued by CASA China, which was enough to prove that it had paid USD26,587 under the Hang Seng Bank cheque to Mediterranean Hong Kong. In the retrial, Transport Groupage supplemented the certificate issued by the Chinese entrusted notary and Hong Kong Lawyer YANG Mou, and the certificate of authorization of the Mediterranean notarized and certified in Switzerland, which respectively confirmed that the above cheque had been actually cashed and that Mediterranean had entrusted the Mediterranean Hong Kong to collect it the container detention fee. The evidence provided by Transport Groupage was sufficient to prove that it had actually paid the carrier Mediterranean the detention fee for the container involved. Secondly, Zhongyi should repay the container detention fee to Transport Groupage. In the case where the freight forwarding contract was not rescinded in advance, the entrustment should continue until the goods were delivered at the destination port. The costs incurred before the goods were delivered at the destination port belonged to the necessary costs incurred under the freight forwarding contract involved. When Zhongyi entrusted Transport Groupage to handle the freight forwarder affairs of the goods involved, it did not specifically indicate which freight forwarder matters and fees were entrusted to Transport Groupage, and did not specify that Transport Groupage needed the prior consent of Zhongyi before making payment. According to the operating conventions of the sea freight forwarder industry, it should be determined that Zhongyi's entrusted matters included entrusting Transport Groupage to handle all necessary matters concerning the export and transportation of the goods involved and pay all expenses incurred during the export transportation of the goods involved. Transport Groupage's advance payment of the container detention fee in this case belonged to the trustee's necessary advance payment for handling the entrusted affairs. Transport Groupage entered into a transportation contract with Mediterranean in its own name. Mediterranean could choose Transport Groupage as a relative to claim its rights. In the case where Mediterranean claimed the rights of Transport Groupage as its counterpart, it was in compliance with the law for Transport Groupage to pay the costs involved to Mediterranean. Thirdly, the court of second instance did not hear the validity of the guarantee letter issued by Zhongyi, omitting Transport Groupage's claim. In conclusion, Transport Groupage required to revoke the judgment of second instance and affirm judgment of first instance.

Zhongyi argued that: firstly, the evidence provided by Transport Groupage was insufficient to prove that it had actually paid the carrier the container detention fee. The notarized documents of Hang Seng Bank cheque receipt issued by Transport Groupage could only prove that the copy of the cheque was consistent with the original, but could not prove the redemption of the cheque. *Confirmation Letter* submitted during the retrial also failed to reflect the redemption of the disputed money in the case. Mediterranean and Mediterranean Shenzhen were limited to "settlement of freight" for ships owned or operated by Mediterranean, and did not include other fees other than the collection of freight. Secondly, Transport Groupage's payment of container detention fees without the consent of the client was not a reasonable and necessary fee for the completion of the entrusted matters. The goods involved had been booked and shipped by Transport Groupage, and had arrived at the destination. The freight forwarder matters had been fulfilled. The container detention fee due to unattended delivery at the destination port was a liquidated damage under the contract for the carriage of goods by sea, and it was not a necessary fee to be paid for the completion of freight forwarding. Thirdly, the guarantee issued by Zhongyi did not include the goods involved, and the container detention fee involved was not a fee or loss that Transport Groupage could claim. The facts confirmed by the court of second instance were clear, and the application of law was correct, which should be recognized.

In retrial, Transport Groupage supplemented the notarized and certified text of the identity certificate and authorization certificate of the representative of the Mediterranean, *Confirmation Letter* and *Declaration* issued by the Chinese entrusted notary and Hong Kong region lawyer YANG Mou, to prove that the fact that it had actually paid USD26,587. After cross-examination, Zhongyi did not recognize the authenticity and relevancy of the certificate of identification of the representative of Mediterranean and the power of authorization, but had no objection to the authenticity of other evidence, and held that the authenticity of contents could not be recognized, the evidence could not prove whether the check was cashed. After review, the evidence submitted by Transport Groupage in the re-examination was the original evidence, which has gone through the notarization certification or notarization procedures outside the domain with company's seal, Zhongyi has no reason to object to the above evidence. As to the evidence submitted by Transport Groupage in retrial, the court accepts the evidence.

After trial, the court finds out that, except that the facts that Mediterranean entrusted Mediterranean Hong Kong to collect transportation fees and Transport Groupage actually paid USD26,587 were not confirmed by the court of second instance, which were proved by the evidence of Transport Groupage in retrial, other facts confirmed by the courts of first and second instances can be proved by relevant evidence, so the court confirmed them.

In addition, the court finds out that: Mediterranean stated in writing on September 13, 2012 that Mediterranean Hong Kong was its designated agent in Mainland China, Taiwan region and Hong Kong region. From April 1, 1998, it had the right to accept orders, booking cabins, freight charges, port miscellaneous fees, container detention fee and other related fees on behalf of Mediterranean in Mainland China and Hong Kong region. Hang Seng Bank paid USD26,587 under the cheque (number xxx) involved on October 10, 2013.

The court holds that:

The case is the dispute over maritime freight forwarding contract with foreign-related factors, the courts of first and second instances chose to apply the laws of the People's Republic of China to deal with the case according to the unanimous agreement of both parties, which is correct. According to Transport Groupage's retrial application and Zhongyi's defense, the issue of the retrial in this case is the authenticity, necessity and rationality of Transport Groupage's payment of the container detention fee.

Transport Groupage accepted the commission of Zhongyi to arrange the transportation of container goods involved. Transport Groupage claimed that it had paid the container detention fee, but said that it did not directly pay the carrier Mediterranean, but entrusted CASA China to pay the agent, Mediterranean Hong Kong. Regarding this fact, Transport Groupage provided evidence such as the power of attorney issued to CASA China, the Hang Seng Bank's cheque receipt and cheque receipt in the first instance, to respectively prove that: in October 2013, Transport Groupage entrusted CASA China to pay Mediterranean Hong Kong container detention use fee of involved, in aggregate amount of USD26,587; on October 8, 2013, CASA China issued a check of Hang Seng Bank with the amount of USD26,587 and the number xxx, which was signed by Mediterranean Hong Kong. In the re-examination, Transport Groupage supplemented the notarized and certified texts of the identity certificate and authorization certificate of the representative of the Mediterranean, to prove that the Mediterranean entrusted Mediterranean Hong Kong to collect the transportation charges such as container detention fee. Meanwhile, Transport Groupage provided additional evidence such as *Confirmation Letter* and *Declaration* issued by a Chinese notary public and Hong Kong region lawyer Yang Mou, to prove that Hang Seng Bank paid the amount of USD26,587 under the cheque involved on October 10, 2013, namely excluding the possibility that the money under the check was not actually paid. By supplementing the above-mentioned evidence, Transport Groupage made the payment facts it proved to be indeed sufficient and sufficient. The facts that Transport Groupage entrusted CASA China to pay the container detention use fee and container unloading fee of USD26,587 to Mediterranean Hong Kong should be confirmed. Whereas the fact that Mediterranean Hong Kong could be charged by Mediterranean on its behalf, it should be determined that Transport Groupage completed the payment to Mediterranean.

Although the shipper stated on the bill of lading of the case involved was Milin Company, the bill of lading was issued based on Transport Groupage's booking requirements for shipping, which was proved the carrier contractual relationship was established by the transfer of the bill of lading between the carrier and the third party holding the bill of lading, the carrier claimed the rights to the shipper of the booking based on the transportation contract relationship formed by the booking and was not affected by the issuance of the bill of lading. There was also no evidence in this case that Milin Company really existed and its accurate contact information; Transport Groupage had right to book a consignment with the carrier Mediterranean in its own name, the reasons are sufficient. When Mediterranean chose Transport Groupage as the counterparty of the transportation contract to claim the rights, Transport Groupage should pay Mediterranean the container detention fee directly according to the Contract Law of the People's Republic of China Article 403 Paragraph 2. Transport Groupage notified Zhongyi in time and found that the container goods arrived at the destination port without being taken, before and after the container detention fee happened and paid, and fulfilled the notification obligation. The bill of lading issued by Mediterranean for the goods involved already stated the standard for the carrier to charge the container for overdue use. Zhongyi claimed that the container detention fee involved was an additional abnormal fee incurred in dealing with the unexpected situation, which was not consistent with the facts. Transport Groupage promptly notified Zhongyi to pay the container detention fee, and Zhongyi neglected to pay, and Transport Groupage really needed to pay a reasonable fee to Mediterranean. Zhongyi claimed that Transport Groupage had no right to make advance payment without authorization, so there is no factual or legal basis for container detention fee. Zhongyi issued a guarantee letter to Transport Groupage on June 8, 2013, promising to bear all the losses and liabilities caused to Transport Groupage due to unmanned pickup and other reasons for all the goods entrusted to Transport Groupage for booking and consignment. The company did not pay Transport Groupage the container detention fee involved in violation of its promise, and there was no factual or legal basis. Transport Groupage requested Zhongyi to pay its reasonable advance payment for container detention, which should be supported.

The court of first instance held that, container providers could avoid the expansion of losses by resetting new containers. The cumulative upper limit of losses caused by the overdue use of containers should not exceed the replacement price of new containers of the same specification in the same period of the market. Combined with shipping practice, the container detention fee of involved was determined to be 60,000 yuan as appropriate, and Transport Groupage's claim exceeding this amount was not supported. Transport Groupage had no objection and required to affirm the original judgment in retrial, so the court will follow it.

Pulling the threads together, Transport Groupage provided new evidence to prove that it had actually paid the container detention fee, which was wrongly confirmed by the court of second instance, which shall be corrected. The court of first instance held that Zhongyi should be liable, which is correct and shall be confirmed. According to the Contract Law of the People's Republic of China Article 398, the Civil Procedure Law of the People's Republic of China Article 170 Paragraph 1 Sub-paragraph 2, Article 207 Paragraph 1, the judgment of this court is as follows:

1. Revoke the Guangdong High People's Court (2015) Yue Gao Fa Min Si Zhong Zi No.138 Civil Judgment;
2. Affirm the Guangzhou Maritime Court (2014) Guang Hai Fa Chu Zi No.102 Civil Judgment.

Court acceptance fee of first instance in amount of RMB3,570.2 yuan, China Transport Groupage International (Shenzhen) Limited shall bear 2,260.12 yuan, and Shenzhen Zhongyi Freight Forwarding Co., Ltd. shall bear 1,310.08 yuan; court acceptance fee of second instance in amount of RMB1310.08 yuan, shall be born by China Transport Groupage International (Shenzhen) Limited.

The judgment is final.

Presiding Judge: YU Xiaohan

Acting Judge: HUANG Xiwu

Acting Judge: ZHANG Kexin

June 23, 2017

Clerk: CHEN Hui

Wuhan Maritime Court
Civil Judgment

Changhang Phoenix Co., Ltd.
v.
Wuhan Tairun Marine Service Co., Ltd. et al.

(2014) Wu Hai Fa Shang Zi No.01755

Related Case(s) None.

Cause(s) of Action 213(2). Dispute over bareboat charter party.

Headnote Bareboat charterer ordered to redeliver chartered vessels and to pay damages for failure to deliver at the end of a 12-month charter, rejecting charterer's argument that there was an oral agreement for a three-year term; owner held not entitled to recover under guarantee contracts, because guarantor' obligation terminated at the end of the 12-month period, and charterer's default happened after the end of that period.

Summary The Plaintiff, Changhang Phoenix Co., Ltd. sued the Defendants Wuhan Tairun Marine Service Co., Ltd., HUANG Qinbao, and MEI Yifan for breach of contract. Phoenix entered into a Combined Transport charter party for two vessels with Tairun offered Phoenix two guarantees for the hire: (1) RMB150,000 guarantee deposit per ship; and (2) two properties belonging to HUANG Qinbao and MEI Yifan, respectively, whose scope of liability covered the entire debt and liability for breach under the charter party. Phoenix argued that Tairun, through its failure to pay Phoenix in June 2014, had defaulted on the charter party agreement. Tairun argued that, though the contract was for 12 months, the parties verbally agreed to three years, so it was not obliged to redeliver the two ships. Qinbao and Yi Fan argued that the contract term extended only for 12 months, and since default happened after that time, they were no longer liable. The court ordered Tairun to redeliver the ships and pay appropriate damages according to the charter party; further, the court found Phoenix did not have to return the RMB150,000 deposit of Tairun. Finally the court dismissed the case between Phoenix and the aforementioned properties of Qinbao and Yi Fan, ruling that the extent of their liability, according to the original 12 month agreement.

Judgment

The Plaintiff: Changhang Phoenix Co., Ltd.
Domicile: Huijiang Building, No.39 Minquan Road, Jianghan District, Wuhan, Hubei.
Organization code: 17,767,908-X.
Legal representative: WANG Tao, chairman of the board.
Agent *ad litem*: WAN Zaoyuan, male, Han, born on January 3, 1958, legal counsel. Domicile: No.75 Daxing Road, Shuishangdi District, Wuhan, Hubei, ID:42010019580103171X.
Agent *ad litem*: CHEN Xiqing, male, Han, born on December 24, 1964, employee. Domicile: 01-01, No.35 Binjiang Road, Jiangan District, Wuhan, Hubei, ID:420100196412241750.

The Defendant: Wuhan Tairun Marine Service Co., Ltd.
Domicile: 1-601, No.18 Taihe Garden Cuiyuan, Economic-Technological Development Area, Wuhan, Hubei.
Legal representative: QIN Baoshuang, general manager.

The Defendant: HUANG Qinbao, female, Han, born on January 20, 1941
Domicile: 02-02, No.51-3 Jianyi Road, Qiaokou District, Wuhan, Hubei, ID:420105194501201649.
Agent *ad litem*: MEI Xue, male, Han, born on April 21, 1941, HUANG Qinbao's husband.
Domicile: 02-02, No.51-3 Jianyi Road, Qiaokou District, Wuhan, Hubei, ID:420105194104211632.

The Defendant: MEI Yifan, former name Mei Fulong, male, Han, born on July 12, 1977
Domicile: 02-02, No.51-3 Jianyi Road, Qiaokou District, Wuhan, Hubei, ID:420105197707121613.
Agent *ad litem*: MEI Xue, male, Han, born on April 21, 1941, MEI Yifan's father.
Domicile: 02-02, No.51-3 Jianyi Road, Qiaokou District, Wuhan, Hubei, ID:420105194104211632.

With respect to the case arising from dispute over bareboat charter party filed by the Plaintiff Changhang Phoenix Co., Ltd. (hereinafter referred to as "Phoenix") against the Defendants Wuhan Tairun Marine Service Co., Ltd. (hereinafter referred to as "Tairun"), HUANG Qinbao and MEI Yifan on December 18, 2014, the court accepted this case on the same day and tried the case under summary procedure. Because the trial of this case had lasted for almost 3 months, on March 20, 2015, with the agreement of all the parties concerned, the court continued to try this case under summary procedure according to law. On April 13, 2015, Phoenix applied for litigation preservation to seal up and freeze the property valued RMB20,012,578.47 (currency hereinafter referred to is RMB) of Tairun, at the same time, to seal up the ownership which was provided as a guarantee for Tairun by HUANG Qinbao and

MEI Yifan. On April 20, 2015, the court made (2015) Wu Hai Fa Bao Zi No.00149 Civil Ruling, permitting the Phoenix's application and sealed up the ownership of HUANG Qinbao's and MEI Yifan's property respectively according to the law. (The numbers of the certificate of ownership of their houses were Wu Fang Quan Zheng Shi Zi No.2008020697 and Wu Fang Quan Zheng Jing Zi No.2011005732). On May 14, 2015, the court heard the case in public, WAN Zaoyuan and CHEN Xiqing, Phoenix's agents *ad litem*, as well as QINBaoshuang, Tairun's legal representative and MEI Xue, agent *ad litem* jointly entrusted by HUANG Qinbao and MEI Yifan, appeared in court and participated in the action. After the hearing, the parties concerned failed to reach a consensus with mediation carried by the court. Now the case has been concluded.

The Plaintiff Phoenix alleged that: on June 19, 2013, Phoenix and Tairun concluded *Combined Transport Charter Party* (hereinafter referred to as the "charter party").The contract agreed to charter M.V. "RONG JIANG 2002" and M.V. "RONG JIANG 2003" to Tairun by bareboat with a term from June 19, 2013 to June 18, 2014, the hire thereof was RMB25,000 per month per ship. The hire should be paid and ended according to the delivery and the redelivery of ships and it should be paid monthly. Once Tairun was default, Phoenix could terminate the contract and recover ships. HUANG Qinbao and MEI Yifan used their own property to provide collateral. After signing the contract, Phoenix performed the obligation of delivery, but the Defendant owed to pay the hire since June 30, 2014, the demand for that failed many times. Therefore, Phoenix filed an action before the court and requested the court to rule:

1. *Combined Transport Charter Party* signed between Phoenix and Tairun should be terminated;
2. Tairun should redeliver M.V. "RONG JIANG 2002" and M.V. "RONG JIANG 2003" to the ship basement at the port where Phoenix located;
3. Tairun should pay the loss of hire in amount of RMB300,000 and ship insurance premium in amount of RMB31,328.47 by the end of December 31, 2014;
4. According to the contract, Tairun should pay the loss of hire (including ship hire and overdue penalty) and insurance premium from December 31, 2014 to the actual date of redelivery. The default deposit in amount of RMB300,000 paid by Tairun should be reserved by Phoenix;
5. HUANG Qinbao and MEI Yifan should undertake several and joint liability for claim 2, 3 and 4 within the value of guarantee property;
6. The litigation fee should be born by the three Defendants.

The Defendant Tairun contended that: 1. the deposit in amount of 300,000RMB was charter deposit, when buying a ship, deposited was necessary; 2. despite the written charter party stated that charter duration was 12 months, when signing the contract, the two parties agreed to renew 3 years verbally. Tairun had invested a lot on the two vessels in the earlier stage, if they terminated the contract by now, Tairun would suffer lots of loss, therefore they did not agree to terminate the contract.

The Defendant HUANG Qinbao and the Defendant MEI Yifan contended that: the contract period was one year, the property of HUANG Qinbao's and MEI Yifan's only mortgaged the hire in the contract period. Tairun had fully paid the hire of the contract period, so both of them should not undertake the liability for mortgage.

The Plaintiff Phoenix submitted the following evidence to the court during the period of producing evidence:

1. Details and documents about the hire paid by Tairun, to prove the fact that Tairun owed the hire.
2. Insurance document that Phoenix paid for the two involved ships, to prove Phoenix paid the two ships' insurance premium according to agreement.
3. Ownership certificates and bareboat charter registration certificates of M.V. "RONG JIANG 2002" and M.V. "RONG JIANG 2003", to prove Phoenix has the rights of use and possession of the ships involved.
4. Copy of Tairun's business license and identity certificate of legal representative, to prove Tairun's right as principal.
5. Charter party of the ships involved, to prove Tairun's contractual basis of its rights and obligations.
6. Documents of ships' delivery and acceptance, to prove Phoenix had performed the obligation of delivery according to the contract.
7. HUANG Qinbao's and MEI Yifan's guarantee letters of commitment, copies of ID cards and house ownership certificates, to prove HUANG Qinbao and MEI Yifan should undertake several and joint liability to Tairun's obligation to pay the hire.
8. HUANG Qinbao's and MEI Yifan's residence booklets' copies, to prove the owner "MEI Fulong" on the houses ownership certificate of mortgaged property was MEI Yifan's former name.
9. Notice on redelivery of Ship of Phoenix, to prove Phoenix demanded Tairun to redeliver the ships, but Tairun failed to do so.

The Defendants Tairun, HUANG Qinbao and MEI Yifan had no disagreements about the above evidence, the court admits.

The Defendants Tairun, HUANG Qinbao and MEI Yifan did not submit any evidence materials to the court.

After the trial, the court finds out the following facts: on June 19, 2013, Phoenix and Tairun signed the charter party, in which Phoenix agreed to charter M.V. "RONG JIANG 2002" and M.V. "RONG JIANG 2003" by bareboat to Tairun. It was provided therein that the charter duration was 12 months, from June 19, 2013 to June 18, 2014 (specific date subject to each ship's redelivery time). After the charter duration expired, if both parties had no disagreements, Tairun would renew hire for another 1-2 years and they would make a written agreement on charter duration and other business terms by that time. The hire was RMB25,000 per month per ship and should be paid once a month. The first instalment of hire should be remitted to Phoenix's designated bank account within one week before delivery of ship, the following hire should be paid within 15 working days in advance, daily overdue charge of 10% of the hire would be applied, 10 days late would be regarded as default and Phoenix could terminate the contract at any time, take back the ships as well as withhold the deposit. The hire would be counted pursuant to the days when the formalities of delivery and redelivery of ships were completed and Phoenix should cover the ships' insurance premium, Tairun should pay RMB13,850 per ship per year one-time to Phoenix before delivery. The total insurance premiums of the two ships were RMB27,700. During charter duration, ships' necessary maintenance, repair and inspection should be covered by Tairun.

The contract also stated: Tairun offered Phoenix two types of guarantees for the hire. The first one was RMB150,000 guarantee deposit per ship and had been remitted to Phoenix's account before delivery. The second one was two real estates of which the certificate number were Wu Fang Quan Zheng Jing Zi No.2011005732 (the owner on house ownership certificate was MEI Yifan, whose former name was MEI Fulong) and Wu Fang Quan Zheng Shi Zi No.2008020697 (the owner on house ownership certificate was HUANG Qinbao). The scope of guarantee was Tairun's whole debt and breach liability under the charter party. Tairun should provide a written letter of commitment to Phoenix and hand property ownership certificates to Phoenix before delivery. Delivery and redelivery place agreed in the contract was in the berth base in Wuhan Port designated by Phoenix.

On the day of signing contract, HUANG Qinbao and MEI Yifan provided letters of commitment respectively and confirmed that they had offered their own properties to Phoenix as mortgage. During the contract period, the above properties should not be transferred, nor should they be used as other mortgage. The original property ownership certificates should be handed over to Phoenix, when the cooperation expired they would terminate contract and discharge the mortgages. After that, HUANG Qinbao and MEI Yifan gave Phoenix their original property ownership certificates, but the two parties did not go to the property administration department to conduct mortgage registration formalities.

On June 22, 2013, Phoenix delivered and Tairun took over M.V. "RONG JIANG 2002" and M.V. "RONG JIANG 2003". The two parties confirmed to calculate the hire of the two ships from August 12, 2013 due to repair of the two ships.

On June 28, 2013, Tairun paid guarantee deposit for the ships in amount of RMB300,000, insurance premium in amount of RMB27,000 and down payment in amount of RMB50,000 to Phoenix, and also paid the due hire within the duration of the charter party. On January 16, 2014, Phoenix informed Tairun and demanded redelivery of the ships, handling formalities for throwing the charter and refunding the guarantee deposit. On January 26, Tairun replied that they had spent a lot of money in repairing and maintaining the ships involved to perform the charter party. If Phoenix took back the ships, it would cause heavy losses to Tairun and Tairun was willing to buy these two ships. After that Tairun continued to pay Phoenix hire till June 2014. Tairun defaulted hire and continued to occupy and use the ships till now since from July 2014. On October 20, 2014, Phoenix informed Tairun that the contract had expired and Tairun should redeliver the two ships to the appointed place within a month after they received the letter. Tairun's legal representative, QINBaoshuang signed on the letter.

At the same time the court finds out that: 1. during the charter of the ships involved, Phoenix bought insurance for them twice and the total insurance premium was RMB31,328.47. There into, the first insurance premium was RMB11,839 per ship, the total amount was RMB23,678, which was paid by Tairun to Phoenix and Phoenix then paid to the insurer. The period of insurance was valid from 0000 on July 4, 2013 to 2400 on December 31, 2013. The second insurance premium was RMB3,060.19 for M.V. "RONG JIANG 2002" and RMB4,590.28 for M.V. "RONG JIANG 2003", and RMB7650.47 in total, they were paid by Phoenix, the period of insurance was valid from 0000 on January 1, 2014 to 0000 on December 31, 2014. 2. The relationship between HUANG Qinbao and MEI Yifan was mother and son, MEI Yifan's former name was MEI Fulong, which was the ownership of house of Wu Fang Quan Zheng Jing Zi No.2011005732. Two sets of real estates had bank mortgage. 3. On June 23, 2015,Tairun's legal representative, QIN Baoshuang remitted RMB100,000 to the court as charter hire which was paid by Tairun to Phoenix.

The court holds that this case is arising from dispute over bareboat charter party. Both parties established bareboat charter party and mortgage security contract relationship, their rights and obligations should subject to the Contract Law of the People's Republic of China, the Guaranty Law of the People's Republic of China, the Property Law of the People's Republic of China and other laws. Therefore, above-mentioned laws and relevant judicial interpretations should be the applicable law to deal with disputes in this case.

Based on allegations, defenses, statements as well as evidence provided by each party. The court holds that there are four issues in this case: 1. whether charter party involved should be terminated or not; 2. the nature of the guarantee deposit in amount of RMB300,000 Tairun paid to Phoenix and whether Phoenix is entitled to that sum or not; 3. whether HUANG Qinbao and MEI Yifan should undertake mortgage guarantee responsibility or not; and 4. the amount of insurance premium Tairun should pay to Phoenix.

1. Whether the charter party involved should be terminated or not.

The charter party involved was Phoenix's and Tairun's true declaration of intention, it was established according to law, and should be legal and effective, both parties should abide by it. As the owner, Phoenix delivered two ships M.V. "RONG JIANG 2002" and M.V. "RONG JIANG 2003" to Tairun. As a charterer, Tairun should pay the hire during the possession and use of the ships to Phoenix strictly adhered to contract. During the period mentioned in charter party, namely from June 19, 2013 to June 18, 2014, Tairun paid off the hire as agreed in the contract. When the charter duration was expired, the two parties did not sign a written charter party, Tairun should redeliver the ships to Phoenix. However, since July 2014, Tairun continued to occupy and use the ships involved till today, actually the two parties should have formed bareboat charter party relationship. In the case of no written contract, the rights and obligations between the two parties should be judged by original charter party, Tairun should pay the hire to Phoenix on time according to the standard of original contract. Since July 2014 till now, Tairun did not pay the hire to Phoenix, its delay performance in debt constituted default and made Phoenix frustrate the purpose of contract. According to the Contract Law of the People's Republic of China Article 94 Paragraph 4, Phoenix, had the right to terminate the contract. According to the Contract Law of the People's Republic of China Article 96: "according to Article 93 Paragraph 2 and Article 94 in the contract, a party demanding termination of a contract should notify the other party. The contract should be terminated upon the receipt of the notice by the other party. If the other party objects to such termination, it may petition the People's Court or an arbitration institution to adjudicate the validity of the termination of the contract." Phoenix notified Tairun to redeliver the two ships on October 20, 2014, actually it was a contract termination notice. QIN Baoshuang, the legal representative of Tairun signed on the letter and showed no disagreements about it. Therefore, the court confirms the charter party signed by Phoenix and Tairun has terminated since October 20, 2014.

According to the Contract Law of the People's Republic of China Article 97, after the termination of a contract, performance should cease if the contract has not been performed; if the contract has been performed, a party may, according to the circumstances of performance or the nature of the contract, demand the other party to restore such party to its original state or adopt other remedial measures, and such party should have the right to demand compensation for damages. Therefore, Phoenix had the right to demand Tairun to redeliver the ships and pay Phoenix's loss of hire caused by Tairun's failure of redelivery of the ships. During the period in which Tairun refused to redeliver the ships, it still continued to possess and use the ships involved, according to the charter party signed by Tairun and Phoenix, Tairun should pay Phoenix the loss of hire in amount of RMB25,000 per month per ship and overdue penalty as per 10% of the hire per day since July 2014 till the actual date Tairun redelivered the ships. Phoenix alleged that Tairun should pay the loss of hire from July 2014 to December 2014 in amount of RMB300,00, as well as the hire and overdue penalty from December 31,2014 to the ships' actual redelivery date, it complies with legal provisions, the court support.

2. The nature of the guarantee deposit in amount of RMB300,000 Tairun paid to Phoenix and whether Phoenix is entitled to that or not.

The RMB300,000 guarantee deposit stated in the charter party was stipulated in the guarantee for charter clause. This showed that both Phoenix and Tairun held this sum was creditor's right guarantee under the charter party, actually it belonged to pledge over cash. After signing the contract, Tairun paid RMB300,000 to Phoenix, the money should be deemed to be handed over to creditor and be specified. Therefore, according to the Interpretations of the Supreme People's Court on Several Issues concerning the Application of the Guaranty Law of the People's Republic of China Article 85: "where the debtor or a third party transfers the possession of its special account, sealed money, deposit or other forms of money to the creditor as pledge for the creditor's rights after specifying the above money, the creditor should be entitled to have priority in receiving payment with such money if the debtor does not perform obligation." Phoenix was entitled to the deposit to offset the debt of Tairun.

3. Whether HUANG Qinbao and MEI Yifan should undertake mortgage guarantee responsibility or not.

Although the charter party involved had mortgage terms, HUANG Qinbao and MEI Yifan did not sign on the contract and the letter of commitment did not have signature confirmation either. Therefore, there was no written mortgage guarantee contract between Phoenix and HUANG Qinbao and MEIYifan. However, through investigation in court, HUANG Qinbao and MEI Yifan did not deny the fact that they provided Phoenix with their own properties as mortgage for Tairun's liability under the charter party involved. In fact, Phoenix and HUANG Qinbao and MEI Yifan did have the intention to establish mortgage guarantee contract. Therefore, the court determines that Phoenix and HUANG Qinbao and MEI Yifan have established a mortgage contract in fact and had legal effect. Because HUANG Qinbao and MEI Yifan did not conduct mortgage registration at property registration authority, according to the Property Law of the People's Republic of China Article 187, "as for the mortgage of a property as prescribed in Item (1), (2) or (3) of Paragraph 1 of Article 180 of this Law or a building under construction as prescribed in Item (5), mortgage registration should be made. The right to mortgage should be established as of the date of registration.", Phoenix did not establish mortgage right, therefore it is not entitled to preferred right in properties as priority right for claim.

In spite of this, given that the mortgage contract between Phoenix and HUANG Qinbao, MEI Yifan took effect, HUANG Qinbao and MEI Yifan promised to undertake the mortgage guarantee liabilities for the creditor's rights of Phoenix against Tairun. Therefore, although the right of mortgage enjoyed by Phoenix did not establish, HUANG Qinbao's and MEI Yifan's responsibilities and obligations under the specific scope of mortgage contract could not be exempted. Given that both parties did not sign a written mortgage contract, the court will determine the scope and the responsibility of mortgage of HUANG Qinbao and MEIYilong in light of the terms of the charter party and letter of commitment as well as daily experience.

HUANG Qinbao and MEIYifan stated in the letter of commitment that, "during the contract period with Changhang Company, we undertake that the above properties should not be transferred, nor used as other mortgage, the original house ownership certificates will be given to Changhang Company and no loss registration can be undergone. When the cooperation expires and the contract terminates, the mortgage can be discharged". According to daily experience, when a third party decides to provide the debtor with its own property as mortgage, it should know clearly about the contents in the master contract signed between debtor and creditor.

According to the charter party of Phoenix and Tairun, after the expiry of the charter for 12 months, if two parties have no disagreements, they can reflect for another 1 to 2 years and they can determine charter duration through written document and other business clause by that time. The court holds that the contract performance period of Phoenix and Tairun stated in the letter of commitment provided by HUANG Qinbao and MEI Yifan, should be 12 months provided in the charter party, the clause that "when the cooperation expires and the contract terminates, the mortgage shall be discharged" meant that the mortgage would be discharged by the end of the 12-month charter duration. In the factual mortgage contract between Phoenix and HUANG Qinbao, MEI Yifan, both parties limited the scope of mortgage guarantee liability, it only includes the liabilities due to Tairun's performance of the charter party occurring in the 12-month charter. However, Tairun fully paid all the hire in above-mentioned charter duration, the hire and overdue penalty it owed happened after the 12-month charter duration expired exceeded HUANG Qinbao and MEI Yifan's guarantee scope, therefore, HUANG Qinbao and MEI Yifan should not undertake guarantee responsibilities for the debt that Tairun owed to Phoenix in this case. Phoenix required that should undertake several and joint liability for Tairun's debt within the value of properties provided by them, it has no factual or legal basis, the court does not support.

4. The amount of insurance premium Tairun should pay to Phoenix.

According to the charter party, Tairun should undertake ships' insurance premium during the charter duration. The two ships' insurance premiums totaled RMB313,28.47, Tairun paid RMB27,000, and Phoenix advanced RMB4,328.47 which should be paid by Tairun. The claim of Phoenix's demanding Tairun to pay full amount of the insurance premiums does not tally with the fact, the court does not support.

In conclusion, according to the Contract Law of the People's Republic of China Article 94 Paragraph 4 and Article 97, the Property Law of the People's Republic of China Article 187, the Interpretations of the Supreme People's Court on Several Issues concerning the Application of Guaranty Law of the People's Republic of China Article 85and the Civil Procedure Law of the People's Republic of China Article 142, the judgment is as follows:

1. Confirm the charter party signed between the Plaintiff Changhang Phoenix Co., Ltd. and the Defendant Wuhan Tairun Marine Service Co., Ltd. terminated as of October 20, 2014;
2. The Defendant Wuhan Tairun Marine Service Co., Ltd. shall redeliver M.V. "RONG JIANG 2002" and M.V. "RONG JIANG 2003" to the anchorage base of Wuhan port designated by the Plaintiff Changhang Phoenix Co., Ltd. within 10 days since this judgment comes into effect;
3. The Defendant Wuhan Tairun Marine Service Co., Ltd. shall compensate the Plaintiff Changhang Phoenix Co., Ltd. RMB300,000 and insurance premium RMB4,328.47 from July 2014 to December 2014, in aggregate amount of

RMB304,328.47, which shall be paid within 10 days on the day of judgment comes into effect;
4. The Defendant Wuhan Tairun Marine Service Co., Ltd. shall compensate the Plaintiff Changhang Phoenix Co., Ltd. for the loss of hire from December 31, 2014 to the actual redelivery day of the ships (RMB25,000 per ship per month), and shall pay overdue penalty according to the standard of 10% of the hire per ship per day;
5. The guarantee deposit in amount of RMB300,000 paid by the Defendant Wuhan Tairun Marine Service Co., Ltd. shall not be returned, the Plaintiff Changhang Phoenix Co., Ltd. shall take priority in compensation to cover the loss of hire which shall be paid by the Defendant Wuhan Tairun Marine Service Co., Ltd.;
6. Reject the claim of the Plaintiff Changhang Phoenix Co., Ltd. against the Defendants HUANG Qinbao and MEI Yifan;
7. Reject the other claims of the Plaintiff Changhang Phoenix Co., Ltd.

Court acceptance fee in amount of RMB9,300, charged a half RMB4,650 due to applying summary procedure, the Plaintiff Changhang Phoenix Co., Ltd. shall bear RMB651 and the Defendant Wuhan Tairun Marine Service Co., Ltd. shall bear RMB3,999. The Defendant Wuhan Tairun Marine Service Co., Ltd. shall bear the legal fare together with item 3 of this judgment to the Plaintiff Changhang Phoenix Co., Ltd.

If the Defendant Wuhan Tairun Marine Service Co., Ltd. fails to fulfill the obligation to pay the money within the specified period by this judgment, according to the Civil Procedure Law of the People's Republic of China Article 253, it shall pay the debt interest in double during the delay period.

If not satisfy with the judgment, a party shall submit statement of appeal to the court within 15 days upon service of this judgment, and shall submit copies according to the people number of opposite party, and appeal to the Hubei High People's Court.

When submitting appellate petition, according to the amount of appeal of dissatisfaction with the judgment and the Measures on the Payment of Litigation Costs Article 13 Paragraph1, the Appellant shall pay appeal costs in advance, the sum shall be remitted to Hubei High People's Court (Payee: non-tax revenue of Hubei Fiscal Department; account number: 052101040000369-1, opening bank: Agricultural Bank of China Wuhan Donghu Branch. If the payer uses bank transfer and bank remittance and other ways to pay, he/she shall mark Hubei High People's Court or Hubei High People's Court's institution code "103001" in the bank credential application column.) If the Appellant fails to pay litigation fee in advance within 7 days after the period of appeal expires, the appeal shall be deemed to be withdrawn automatically.

Judge: ZHANG Yu

June 17, 2015

Clerk: WANG Peilin

**Tianjin Maritime Court
Civil Judgment**

China Geology and Mining Corporation
v.
Tianjin Kangjie Import and Export Trade Co., Ltd. et al.

(2014) Jin Hai Fa Shang Chu Zi No.153

Related Case(s) This is the judgment of first instance and the judgment of second instance is on page 152.

Cause(s) of Action 221. Dispute over contract on custody of cargo in port. (Editor's Note: This cause of action is chosen as it appears to be closest to the underlying dispute between the parties.)

Headnote Dispute between importer, port agent and freight forwarders over ownership of goods held to be resolved by who had paid for the goods, and not who held the customs release sheets enabling them to be delivered from the container yard to which they had been imported.

Summary The Plaintiff was the Defendant Kangjie's agent. The two parties concluded an import agency agreement. According to the agreement, if the Plaintiff paid the Defendant Kangjie for the goods, ownership of the goods was transferred to the Plaintiff.

The Plaintiff and the Defendants Kangjie and Tanghe concluded a port agency agreement. According to that agreement, the Plaintiff was agent and importer for the Defendant Kangjie, and the Defendant Tanghe were freight forwarders charged with facilitating delivery to the Defendant Kangjie.

The Plaintiff delivered the goods' bills of lading to the Defendant Kangjie, and the Defendant Kangjie stored the goods at Pengfa Yard. The Defendant Kangjie did not pay the Plaintiff for the goods. Consequently, the Plaintiff sold the goods to a Third Party. The Third Party paid the Plaintiff, but the Plaintiff could not deliver the goods to Third Party because the Defendants had possession of the goods' customs release sheets. Because the Plaintiff could not deliver the goods to the Third Party, the Third Party filed an action against the Plaintiff in another court.

The Defendants' actions regarding the goods' customs release sheets were as follows. The Defendant Tanghe borrowed capital from the Defendant Kangjie. As collateral, the Defendant Tanghe gave the Defendant Kangjie the goods' customs release sheets. The Defendant Kangjie then sold the goods to the Defendant Zhongse Logistics. The Defendant Zhongse Logistics then sold the goods to Zhongse International Trade. Then, the Defendants Zhongse Logistics and Zhongse International Trade and Pengfa Yard (where the goods were stored) signed a transfer of ownership of goods certificate.

The issues before the court were as follows:

1. Whether the Defendant Kangjie owned the goods;
2. What were the legal relationships between the Defendants Zhongse Logistics and Zhongse International Trade and the Defendants Kangjie and Zhongse Logistics;
3. Whether the Defendant Zhongse International Trade owned the goods; and
4. Whether the Defendant Zhongse International Trade acquired the goods via bona fide acquisition.

The court held the Defendant Kangjie did not own the goods because they never paid for them; rather, the Plaintiff owned the goods because the Plaintiff paid for them. Further, the true legal relationships between the Defendants Zhongse Logistics and Zhongse International Trade and the Defendants Kangjie and Zhongse Logistics reflected loan agreements, not sales contracts. As such, those agreements were invalid.

The court also held the Defendant Zhongse International Trade did not own the goods because the Defendant Kangjie's transfer to the Defendant Zhongse Logistics was an unauthorized disposition.

Additionally, the Defendant Zhongse International Trade did not acquire the goods via bone fide acquisition. The goods were seized by another court, and that court notified the Defendant Tanghe and Pengfa Yard to assist with the enforcement of the court order. After the court's notice, the Defendant Kangjie sold the goods to the Defendant Zhongse Logistics, which sold the goods to the Defendant Zhongse International Trade. Here, the Defendant Kangjie transferred customs release sheets to the Defendant Zhongse Logistics, which transferred the customs release sheets to the Defendant Zhongse International Trade. Transferring customs release sheets does not constitute delivery of goods. Moreover, the Defendant Zhongse Logistics never proved the Defendant Kangjie informed Pengfa Yard (the actual possessor of the goods) of the transfer. Because the actual possessor of the goods was never informed, the Defendant Kangjie failed to complete delivery of the goods to the Defendant Zhongse Logistics. Because the Defendant Zhongse Logistics never had possession of the goods, the Defendants Zhongse International Trade could not have acquired the goods via bone fide acquisition.

The court held that the Plaintiff's right to take delivery of the goods from Pengfa Yard was obstructed by Defendants' wrongful possession of the customs release sheets, and the Defendants were ordered to return the customs release sheets to the Plaintiff.

Judgment

The Plaintiff: China Geology and Mining Corporation
Domicile: 7/F, Zhejiang Building, 26/F, Anzhen Xili No.3 Area, Chaoyang District, Beijing.
Legal representative: SONG Yongqi, general manager.
Agent *ad litem*: YUAN Weiming, lawyer of Tianjin Shi Yang Law Firm.
Agent *ad litem*: SHI Jian, company employee.

The Defendant: Tianjin Kangjie Import and Export Trade Co., Ltd.
Domicile: Room 502-1, A Building, No.6 Haitai Green Industrial Base, Haitai Development No.6, Huayuan Industrial Zone, Tianjin.
Legal representative: HAN Kun, chairman.
Agent *ad litem*: ZHANG Wenda, lawyer of Tianjin Winners Law Firm.
Agent *ad litem*: SHI Puhai, lawyer of Tianjin Winners Law Firm.

The Defendant: Tianjin Tanghe Logistics Co., Ltd.
Domicile: 645B19, Aviation Industry Support Center, No.1 Baohang Road, Airport Economic Zone, Binhai New District, Tianjin.
Legal representative: QIN Yongshuai, chairman.
Agent *ad litem*: ZHANG Wenda, lawyer of Tianjin Winners Law Firm.
Agent *ad litem*: SHI Puhai, lawyer of Tianjin Winners Law Firm.

The Defendant: Zhongse Logistics (Tianjin) Co., Ltd.
Domicile: No.0117, No.1 Building, No.188 New Road, Binhai High-tech District, Binhai Science and Technology Park, No.13888 Jinhan Highway, Tianjin.
Legal representative: SONG Jun, chairman.
Agent *ad litem*: LIU Jinyi, lawyer of Beijing Dentons Law Firm,
Agent *ad litem*: Tan Zhenghua, lawyer of Beijing Dentons Law Firm,

The Defendant: Zhongse International Trade Co., Ltd.
Domicile: Room 909, No.1 Building, Beijing Office, West Railway Station South Square, Fengtai District, Beijing.
Legal representative: LI Xiaoying, chairman.
Agent *ad litem*: LIU Jinyi, lawyer of Beijing Dentons Law Firm,
Agent *ad litem*: LIU Ruiqi, lawyer of Beijing Dentons Law Firm,

With respect to the case arising from dispute over return of customs release sheets, the Plaintiff China Geology and Mining Corporation filed an action against the Defendants Tianjin Kangjie Import and Export Trade Co., Ltd. (hereinafter referred to as "Kangjie") and Tianjin Tanghe Logistics Co., Ltd. (hereinafter referred to as "Tanghe") before the court. The court accepted this case on March 5 and applied summary procedures according to the law. In the trial, Tanghe put forward the application to the court to suspend the proceeding, the court granted according to the law that the case was suspended. The Plaintiff applied to resume the hearing, and the court granted and restored the action according to the law. On June 10,

2014, due to the complexity of the case, it was not appropriate to apply summary procedures for trial, the court ruled according to the law to transfer the case into the ordinary process and constituted a collegiate panel for trial. On September 24, 2014, the Plaintiff applied for adding Zhongse Logistics (Tianjin) Co., Ltd. (hereinafter referred to as "Zhongse Logistics") and Zhongse International Trade Co., Ltd. (hereinafter referred to as "Zhongse International Trade") as the joint Defendants, the court granted according to the law and informed them to participate in the proceeding. In the trial, the Plaintiff filed an application for action preservation, requesting the court to order the four Defendants that the transfer, mortgage and pledge of goods under the bills of lading of PSI-111023 and PSI-111024 and the customs release sheet of the goods on M.V. "JIN FENG" 04 voyage were forbidden, and the court granted according to the law. The case held hearings in public on June 23, 2014 and January 4, 2015. In the first time of hearing, WANG Wei and WU Ximei, the agents *ad litem* of the Plaintiff, and SHI Puhai, the joint agent *ad litem* of the Defendants Kangjie and Tanghe attended the court. In the second time of hearing, YUAN Weiming and SHI Jian, the agents *ad litem* of the Plaintiff, and ZHANG Wenda, the joint agent *ad litem* of the Defendants Kangjie and Tanghe and LIU Jinyi, the agent *ad litem* of the Defendant Zhongse Logistics, and LIU Jinyi and LIU Ruiqi, the agents *ad litem* of the Defendant Zhongse International Trade attended the hearings. Now the case has been concluded.

The Plaintiff alleged that the Plaintiff made a nickel ore import agency agreement with Kangjie on October 17, 2011, and the Plaintiff was as the trustee. On November 4, 2011, the Plaintiff and Kangjie made a nickel ore import agency agreement and agreed that: title to goods was owned by the Plaintiff, and Tanghe Company was commissioned to be responsible for the port agency business of goods under the agreement; Kangjie should bear the port agency fees of goods. Afterwards the Plaintiff and Kangjie terminated the nickel ore import agency agreement, the Plaintiff resold the nickel ore to Beijing Datang Fuel Co., Ltd. (hereinafter referred to as Datang). Because Tanghe was the port agent for the goods involved, holding the original copies of bills of lading of PSI-111023 and PSI-111024 and the customs release sheet of the goods of M.V. "JIN FENG" 04 voyage (a copy of the bill of lading stamped with the carrier and the ship agency's specific picking goods seal, inspection and quarantine seal, the customs release seal). Tanghe without permission of the Plaintiff, privately delivered the customs release sheet to Kangjie. Kangjie made a contract for purchasing goods (hereinafter referred to as sales contract No.1) with Zhongse Logistics, delivering the customs release sheet involved to Zhongse Logistics, then Zhongse Logistics made a contract for the sale of goods (hereinafter referred to as sales Contract No.2) with Zhongse International Trade, delivering the customs release sheet involved to Zhongse International Trade. The Plaintiff considered that it was the owner of the goods involved, the four Defendants violated the ownership, the customs release sheets should be returned to the Plaintiff. Therefore, it requested the court to judge that: 1. confirm that the Plaintiff should enjoy the ownership of the goods involved; 2. the four Defendants should return the two customs release sheets corresponding to the bills of lading No.PSI-111023 and No.PSI-111024 to the Plaintiff; 3. the court fees in this case should be born by the four Defendants.

The Defendants Kangjie and Tanghe argued that: 1. the goods in M.V. "JIN FENG" involved had been filed a litigation by Datang to Tianjin Second Intermediate People's Court (hereinafter referred to as the Tianjin Second Intermediate Court) before the action of this case. The judgment had already come into force, confirming that the ownership of the goods was enjoyed by Datang, but did not belong to the Plaintiff. 2. The goods involved had been ruled to be preserved in the Tianjin Second Intermediate Court, Tanghe received the preservation ruling and the implementation order of assistance, and should not return the customs release sheets to the Plaintiff, and the customs release sheets were not possessed by Kangjie and Tanghe. In summary, the claim of the Plaintiff did not set up, it requested the court to reject the claims.

Zhongse Logistics argued that: 1. the Plaintiff was not the real owner of the goods involved, and Kangjie was the owner of the goods. According to the nickel ore import agency contract between the Plaintiff and Kangjie, Kangjie was the Plaintiff's bailor, the Plaintiff had no right to make a sales contract. According to the import goods declaration, the Plaintiff was only the operating agency, Kangjie was the consignee, and actually paid for the goods tax. Therefore, Zhongse Logistics had gained the ownership of goods, and was transferred, and the ownership of goods was now handed in Zhongse International Trade. 2. Even if the Plaintiff was the owner of the goods, Zhongse Logistics also accorded with the conditions of bona fide acquisition, and had paid for a reasonable price to Kangjie. To sum up, Zhongse International Trade was the owner of the goods, it requested the court to reject the Plaintiff's claims.

Zhongse International Trade argued that: 1. it agreed with Zhongse Logistics Company's defense. 2. Zhongse International Trade and Zhongse Logistics made a purchases and sales contract and paid a reasonable price and gained the customs release sheets which was the symbol of the ownership of goods, which meant that, Zhongse International Trade was the real and final owner of the goods involved. 3. The Plaintiff and Kangjie was the debt relationship. 4. According to the provisions of Article 10 of the Supreme People's Court's Certain Rules on the Trial of Non-original Bill of Lading Delivery of Goods, the original bill of lading involved was handed in Zhongse International Trade, so Zhongse International Trade was the real owner of the goods, it requested the court to reject the Plaintiff's claims.

According to the Plaintiff's claims and the pleas of the four Defendants, the court summarizes the issues in this case: 1. whether Zhongse International Trade was the owner of goods involved; and 2. whether the four Defendants had the obligation to return the two customs release sheets.

The Plaintiff provided the following evidence to prove its claims: evidence 1, imported nickel ore port agency agreement (agreement No.CGM-KJ-TH-DL001), to prove that Tanghe dealt with the declaration, inspection, custody and other business for the Plaintiff, the goods were owned by the Plaintiff and without the written notice of the Plaintiff, Tanghe was strictly prohibited releasing the goods; evidence 2, nickel ore import agency contract (agreement No.CGM-KJ-KLNI001), to prove that the Plaintiff and Kangjie agreed that Kangjie should pay the full amount of payment in installment after the Plaintiff's acceptance day within 80 days, and after Kangjie paid each payment, the Plaintiff transferred the cargo ownership to Kangjie; evidence 3, declaration of imported goods, to prove that the goods had been declared; evidence 4, purchases and sales contract, to prove that the Plaintiff and foreign sellers concluded a goods sales contract; evidence 5, B/L No. PSI-111023 and PSI-111024, to prove that the Plaintiff was the consignee of the goods; evidence 6, temporary invoice, to prove that the seller of goods issued a temporary invoice, the total invoice amount was USD49,373,334.58; evidence 7, the notice of acceptance of outward payments, to prove that the Plaintiff paid USD493,733,458 according to the temporary invoice to the foreign sellers; evidence 8, final invoice, to prove that the foreign sellers issued the final invoice to the Plaintiff, the final price of goods was USD4,886,181; evidence 9, (2013) Jing Hai Cheng Nei Min Zheng Zi No.04106 *Notarization* provided by Beijing Haicheng Notary Office, to prove that the Plaintiff informed Tanghe of stopping the release of the goods, compensating the losses and terminating the contract; evidence 10, (2013) Jing Hai Cheng Nei Min Zheng Zi No.04109 *Notarization* provided by Beijing Haicheng Notary Office, to prove that the Plaintiff informed Pengfa Freight Forwarding Co., Ltd. in Tianjin Development Zone (hereinafter referred to as Pengfa) that Tanghe had terminated the contract with the Plaintiff, in the absence of the direction of the Plaintiff to release the goods, Pengfa should not release the goods; evidence 11, (2013) Jing Hai Cheng Nei Min Zheng Zi No.04107 *Notarization* provided by Beijing Haicheng Notary Office, to prove that the Plaintiff informed Fifth Harbor of Tianjin Port (hereinafter referred to as Fifth Port) that the Plaintiff had terminated the contract with Tanghe, in the absence of the direction of the Plaintiff to release the goods, Fifth Port should not release the goods; evidence 12, (2013) Jing Hai Cheng Nei Min Zheng Zi No.04110 *Notarization* provided by Beijing Haicheng Notary Office, to prove that the Plaintiff informed Fourth Harbor of Tianjin Port (hereinafter referred to as Fourth Port) and Northern Fertilizer Logistics Distribution Co., Ltd. (hereinafter referred to as Northern Fertilizer) that the Plaintiff had terminated the contract with Tanghe, in the absence of the direction of the Plaintiff to release the goods, Fourth Port and Northern Fertilizer should not release the goods; evidence 13, nickel ore price summary, to prove that on April 21, 2014, Ferroalloy Online Network published that the nickel ore price of the nickel content of 1.8%–1.85% was RMB600–RMB620 (70% was RMB420 yuan–RMB434 yuan). The price of nickel ore sold by Kangjie to Zhongse Logistics was RMB3,573,343 yuan which was lower than the market price mentioned above; evidence 14, Tianjin Second Intermediate Court civil ruling, to prove that on June 6, 2013, Tianjin Second Intermediate Court ruled that the goods involved should be sealed; evidence 15, price of nickel ore published by Asian Metal Network and website introduction, to prove that on April 21, 2014, Asian Metal Network published that the nickel ore price of the nickel content of 1.8%–1.9% was RMB580 yuan–RMB620 yuan (70% was RMB406 yuan–RMB434 yuan). The price of nickel ore sold by Kangjie to Zhongse Logistics was lower than the market price mentioned above; evidence 16, ferronickel and nickel ore market review and news published by Asian Metal Network, to prove that nickel market prices rose sharply in 2014 as a result of the ban on raw ore exports from Indonesia-the world's main nickel supplier, and between March and May 2014, nickel ore prices continued to rise; evidence 17, (2014) Jing Hai Cheng Nei Min Zheng Zi No.10709 *Notarization* provided by Beijing Haicheng Notary Office, to prove that on April 21, 2014, Ferroalloy Online Network published that the nickel ore price of the nickel content of 1.8%–1.85% was RMB580 yuan–RMB610 yuan (70% was RMB406 yuan–RMB427 yuan). The price of nickel ore sold by Kangjie to Zhongse Logistics was RMB3,573,343 yuan which was lower than the market price mentioned above; evidence 18, (2014) Jing Hai Cheng Nei Min Zheng Zi No.10709 *Notarization* provided by Beijing Haicheng Notary Office, to prove that on April 21, 2014, Ferroalloy Online Network published that the nickel ore price of the nickel content of 1.8%–1.85% was RMB590 yuan–RMB620 yuan (70% was RMB413 yuan–RMB434 yuan). The price of nickel ore sold by Kangjie to Zhongse Logistics was RMB3,573,343 yuan which was lower than the market price mentioned above; evidence 19, China Judgments Online Court accepted the legal precedent that Ferroalloy Online Network and Asian Metal Network were the references to goods prices; evidence 20, the call recording and text records of the employee of Plaintiff's company FENG Yan and employee in Zhongse Logistics WU Yan, to prove that Zhongse International Trade and Kangjie used "Low-sell and High-buy" for financing loans, which was in violation of the mandatory provisions of Chinese financial regulations, and the contract was invalid; evidence 21, survey record of Pengfa and the invalid statement of M.V. "JIN FENG" of nickel ore transferring certification of title of goods, to prove that on April 19, 2013, Pengfa received the assistance in enforcement of Tianjin Second Intermediate Court on goods involved. Pengfa issued the relevant stamped materials to Zhongse Logistics was June 2, 2014, but on June 25, 2016, it issued an invalid statement. Pengfa did not know the existence of Zhongse International Trade. Zhongse Logistics in April 2014 did not ask Pengfa about the title of goods involved. Evidence 1-12, 14, 17, 18, 20, 21 were original copies.

The joint cross-examination opinions for the Plaintiff's evidence of the Defendants Kangjie and Tanghe were that: the authenticity and legality of evidence 1 was recognized, the contract had been partially fulfilled, the agreement between the Plaintiff and Kangjie in Beijing Chaoyang District People's Court had a pending litigation, and the agreement had nothing to do with the case. After the storage of goods of M.V. "JIN FENG", Kangjie consulted with Datang to accept the agreement. Datang and the Plaintiff concluded a separate agreement for sales of goods. Datang had fulfilled payment obligations in the agreement between the Plaintiff, so the owner of goods was Datang; no objection to evidence 2-4. The authenticity, legality and relevancy of evidence 5 was recognized, but the purpose of proof was not recognized. The bill of lading was a bearer bill of lading, the actual holder was the consignee; no objection to evidence 6-8. The authenticity, legality and relevancy of evidence 9 was recognized, but the purpose of proof was not recognized, Kangjie really received the notarization attached to the letter behind, but Kangjie did not recognize the performance of the contract the letter described and the compensation the Plaintiff claimed; the authenticity, legality and relevancy of evidence 10-12 was recognized, but the purposes of proof were not recognized. Kangjie did not clearly know whether Pengfa, Fifth Port, Fourth Port and North Fertilizer received or not. The authenticity of evidence 13 was recognized, but the legality and relevancy was not recognized. Kangjie and Zhongse Logistics concluded a nickel ore sales and purchases agreement, the goods price was studied out by both parties based on the experience and market prices of the goods, and did not refer to the published price of Ferroalloy Online Network; no objection to evidence 14. The authenticity of evidence 15, 16 was recognized, but the legality and relevancy was not recognized, the price of goods did not refer to Asian Metal Network, and its authority had no confirmation of third party; The authenticity and legality of evidence 17, 18 was recognized, but the relevancy was not recognized, and the two parties did not refer to Ferroalloy Online Network published price. The authenticity and relevancy of evidence 19 was not recognized, the two cases in this case should not be referred; the authenticity, legality and relevancy of evidence 20 was not recognized, the identity of the two parties of communication could not be recognized, and it also cannot reflect the relevancy of the case; the authenticity, legality and relevancy of evidence 21 was recognized, the transcript proved that Zhongse Logistics submitted the confirmation of cargo rights stamped by Pengfa was not legally acquired, and it also showed that Zhongse Logistics and Zhongse International Trade did not due obligations to verify the actual source, transferring the customs release sheets at a price lower one-third than the market price and the corresponding nickel ore did not exist in good faith situation.

The joint cross-examination opinions of the Defendants Zhongse Logistics and Zhongse International Trade were that: they had no objection to authenticity of evidence 1 and evidence 2, but part of agreement of the contract was illegal, and they did not recognize the contents of evidence. The Plaintiff, under the guise of the sale of nickel ore, concealed the true purpose of financing and guaranty, the Plaintiff and Kangjie were agency relationship, not property rights relationship, and Kangjie was the real owner. They had no objection to authenticity and legality of evidence 3, but they did not recognize the purpose of proof, and Kangjie was the real owner; they did not recognize the authenticity, legality and relevancy of evidence 4, the Plaintiff failed to provide a Chinese translation document of qualified translation company; they had no objection to authenticity and legality of evidence 5, but they did not recognize the proof contents. The Plaintiff was not the consignee of goods, Zhongse International Trade had already held customs release sheets the bill of lading corresponding to, and was the owner of the goods under the bill of lading; they did not recognize the authenticity, legality and relevancy of evidence 6, the evidence was formed beyond the border, and it should be used as evidence after notary certification procedures; they recognized the authenticity and legality of evidence 7, but did not recognize the relevancy, to prove that the Plaintiff as Kangjie's assignee, issuing and accepting on behalf of him; they did not recognize the authenticity, legality and relevancy of evidence 8, the evidence was formed beyond the border, and it should be used as evidence after notary certification procedures; they recognized the authenticity and legality of evidence 9, but did not recognize the relevancy, to prove that Tanghe did not recognize that the Plaintiff was goods owner, and had delivered goods to Kangjie; they recognized the authenticity and legality of evidence 10-12, but did not recognize the relevancy and purposes of proof; they did not recognize the authenticity of evidence 13; they had no objection to authenticity and legality of evidence 14, but they did not recognize the relevancy, and it could not explain goods seized by Tianjin Second Intermediate Court was the disputed goods in this case; they did not recognize the authenticity, legality and relevancy of evidence 15 and 16, the evidence submitted by the Plaintiff was displayed on its own equipment and did not exclude the possibility of technical treatment. Asian Metal Network only referred to nickel content, did not involve iron and water content, even if it was real, but it also had nothing to do with the case of goods. Asian Metal Network emphasized not to take responsibility for information flaws, which illustrated that they were lack of confidence to the information provided by their own. There were a lot of sites to provide market prices of metal, only a very small number of authorities, and the Plaintiff could not prove that authority of the Asian Metal Network; they recognized the authenticity and legality of evidence 17, 18, but did not recognize the relevancy and the purposes of proof. Zhongse Logistics referred to My Steel Net as the price of goods transactions, it subjectively was good, and based on the contract with Shanghai Steel and trade practices, so the Plaintiff submitted Ferroalloy Information Network, which was not relevancy with the case, and goods prices in this case should be based on My Steel Network; they recognized the authenticity and legality of evidence 19, but did not recognize the relevancy and purposes of proof, China Judgments Online quoted both Ferroalloy Online Network and Asian Metal Network had only one judgment, quoted My Steel Network was far more than that, so it could be seen that My Steel Network in the judicial practice was widely cited; they did not recognize the authenticity, legality and relevancy of evidence 20, recording evidence was audio-visual information, easy to forge and could not prove its objective reality. Mr. Wu in the recording could not been known, and the recording cannot prove the identity of the other caller. It could not be seen the relation with Zhongse Logistics and goods involved from the recording contents; they had no objection to the authenticity of evidence 21, but the respondents' statements were untrue.

The court confirms the Plaintiff's evidence as follows: the four Defendants had no objection to the authenticity of evidence 1-3, 5, the court confirms it; evidence 1, 2 can prove that the Plaintiff as Kangjie's agent, imported the goods involved, and the two parties concluded a nickel ore import agency contract. To handle the freight forwarding business of the goods involved in the Tianjin Port, The Plaintiff, Kangjie and Tanghe concluded a nickel ore port agency agreement. The two contracts agreed that: the ownership of the goods belonged to the Plaintiff. If Kangjie paid the goods prices, the Plaintiff should transfer the ownership to Kangjie; evidence 3 can prove that the goods involved had finished customs clearance; the Plaintiff provided the original copy of evidence 4, and it can be confirmed with evidence 2, so the court confirms the authenticity; the Plaintiff provided original copies of evidence 6-8, and Kangjie had no objection to authenticity of the three evidence, so the court confirms the authenticity of the three evidence; evidence 4-8 can prove that the Plaintiff concluded a purchases and sales goods involved contract with the foreign seller. The Plaintiff paid the prices, and through the L/C bank obtained two sets of the original bill of lading; the Plaintiff submitted notarizations of evidence 9-12, and Tanghe recognized receiving evidence 9, Pengfa recognized receiving evidence 10, so the court confirms the authenticity of the four evidence, but whether the import nickel ore port agency agreement between the Plaintiff, Tanghe and Kangjie was canceled and whether Tanghe breached the contract involved another action, so it was not within the scope of this case; evidence 13, 15-18, public information on the webpage, so the court confirms the authenticity; the court confirms the authenticity of evidence 14, and it can prove that goods involved were sealed by Tianjin Second Intermediate Court on June 6, 2013; evidence 20, the Plaintiff could not prove the identities of the both communicating parties, but Zhongse Logistics did not recognize it, so the court cannot confirm the effect of evidence; evidence 21, witness testimony, the content of it must be confirmed when combined with other evidence.

The Defendants Kangjie and Tanghe jointly provided the following evidence in order to prove their pleas: evidence 1, sales contract concluded between Zhongse Logistics and Tianjin Purple Mine International Co., Ltd. (hereinafter referred to as "Purple Mine"); evidence 2, contract for the sales of goods concluded between Zhongse International Trade and Purple Mine, two evidence together proved that the sales contract between Kangjie and Zhongse Logistics was a part of chain sale and final repurchases, essentially a financing loan contract, rather than an ordinary sales contract, so customs release sheet which was assigned by Zhongse Logistics should have been repurchased.

The cross-examination opinions of the Plaintiff to the Defendants Kangjie and Tanghe's evidence: it had no objection to the apparent authenticity of the two contracts.

The cross-examination opinions of the Defendants Zhongse Logistics and Zhongse International Trade to the Defendants Kangjie and Tanghe's evidence: they had no objection to the apparent authenticity of the two contracts. But Zhongse Logistics and Purple Mine signed an agreement to terminate the contract after signing the sales contract. After that, Zhongse Logistics concluded a sales contract with Purple Mine. These two contracts were sales contracts, not the financing and loan contracts claimed by Kangjie.

The court confirms the authenticity of the two evidence provided by the Defendants Kangjie and Tanghe, however, in the absence of other evidence to corroborate, it cannot prove that Purple Mine, Zhongse Logistics and Zhongse International Trade concluded a sales contract in order to repurchase the goods involved, so the court does not confirm the effect of evidence in the two contracts.

The Defendant Zhongse Logistics provided the following evidence in order to prove its pleas: evidence 1, sales contract No.1; evidence 2, agreement on transfer of goods, evidence 1, 2, to prove that Kangjie and Zhongse Logistics concluded a contract for sales of goods. Kangjie in the contract and other transaction documents committed that it had full and uncontested ownership of goods, and it was willing to bear heavier liability for breach of contract. Zhongse Logistics had reason to believe that Kangjie was the owner of the goods; evidence 3, proof of transfer of goods, to prove that Kangjie and Tanghe jointly recognized the transfer of goods to Zhongse Logistics, and to enhance Zhongse Logistics made sure Kangjie was the real owner of goods; evidence 4, Zhongse Logistics inventory confirmation, to prove that Zhongse Logistics did duty of care of checking goods to the storage party Pengfa; evidence 5, goods purchase contract, cargo transfer, bill of lading, transfer receipt and invoice referred to M.V. "JIN FENG", to prove that Kangjie sold nickel in a similar manner (including the terms of contract, the flow of goods, etc.) to Zhongse Logistics, but also with Zhongse Logistics engaged in freight forwarding business and other related cooperation. The two parties were long-term trading partners, so Zhongse Logistics had a reliable foundation to Kangjie; evidence 6, certificate and invoice of the goods payment paid by Zhongse Logistics to Kangjie, to prove that Zhongse Logistics according to the goods purchase contract paid the goods payment; evidence 7, (2014) Jing Tai Da Zheng Jing Zi No.5471 *Notarization* provided by Tianjin Taida Notary Office; evidence 8, (2014) Jing Chang An Nei Jing Zheng Zi No.23651 *Notarization* provided by Beijing Changan Notary Office; evidence 9, the translation document of (2014) Jing Chang An Nei Jing Zheng Zi No.23651 *Notarization* provided by Beijing Yibangda Translation Co., Ltd, evidence 7-9, to prove that the transaction price of goods involved was 70% higher than the plate price My Steel Network published, combined trading practices, customer relationships, price structures, origins of goods, the number of purchase and other factors, the price Zhongse Logistics paid to Kangjie company was reasonable; evidence 10, two information service contract Zhongse Logistics and Shanghai Steel Alliance concluded, information service costs and invoices Zhongse Logistics paid to Shanghai Steel Alliance, to prove that Shanghai Steel Alliance as My Steel Network's business unit for two consecutive years provided paid information services to Zhongse Logistics, the mineral market price My Steel Network published was the important reference Zhongse Logistics engaged in sales of goods outside; evidence 11, legal precedent on the China Judgments Online Court where the court recognized My Steel Network as a reference for the sale price of goods, to prove that the market price of mineral resources My Steel Network published in the judicial practice was widely recognized throughout the courts and was authoritative; evidence 12, customs release sheet with No.PSI-111023; evidence 13, customs release sheet with No.PSI-111024; evidence 14, translation of customs release sheets of Beijing Yibanda Translation Co., Ltd, evidence 12-14, to prove that Kangjie had delivered two customs release sheets to Zhongse Logistics, Zhongse Logistics had occupied the goods under the bill of lading; evidence 15, (2014) Jing Chang An Nei Jing Zheng Zi No.25331 *Notarization* provided by Beijing Changan Notary Office; evidence 16, (2014) Jing Chang An Nei Jing Zheng Zi No.25905 *Notarization* provided by Beijing Changan Notary Office, evidence 15 and evidence 16, to prove that in 9 aspects of site location, market breadth, product type, business unit, registered capital, listing, number of employees, and citation of Chinese Judgment Online, etc., My Steel Network was far beyond China Ferroalloy Online Network the Plaintiff put forward, the authority of My Steel Network status was no doubt; evidence 17, statistical table of prices of My Steel Network, to prove that in 42 cases where the parties freely agreed price, totally 24 parities, 5 price cuts and 13 fare increases, to prove that most of the trading subjects directly referred to prices My Steel Network published as the transaction price, and even took the initiative to reduce prices. The Plaintiff said that the price My Steel Network published was less than the general market price, whose view could not be established. Evidence had original copies.

The cross-examination opinions of the Plaintiff on the Defendant Zhongse Logistics's evidence: the authenticity of evidence 1 retained objection, Kangjie in the contract committed that its ownership of the goods itself was the basic condition of the contract, which should be not constituted a good reason Zhongse Logistics held that Kangjie was the owner of the goods, and the contract price agreed in the contract was much lower than the market price; the authenticity of evidence 2 retained objection; the authenticity of evidence 3 retained objection. Tanghe was the freight forwarder, not the custodian, and its confirmation should not be the basis of strengthening Zhongse Logistics determining the ownership; the authenticity of evidence 4 retained objection. The confirmation did not involve the ownership of the goods, which referred to the "our company stored in" was only Zhongse Logistics's statement, not Tanghe's confirmation; the authenticity of evidence 5 retained objection, which cannot prove that the two parties were long-term trading partners, there was a basis for trust, and the existence of trust base cannot be the legal reasons Zhongse Logistics judged the ownership; they had no objection to authenticity of evidence 6, where the existence of long-term business relationship between the two sides, the bank vouchers cannot determine the relevancy with the sale in the case, and the payment time did not match the payment after the receipt of invoices and goods the contract agreed; they had no objection to authenticity of evidence 7, the nickel ore price My Steel Network published and which quality was the same with goods involved had a long gap with the price another authoritative website China Ferroalloy Online Network published, and there was doubt that whether the site price was accurate; they had no objection to authenticity of evidence 8, 9; they had no objection to authenticity of evidence 10, and search the price information on My Steel Network did not require registration; they had no objection to authenticity of evidence 11, but price My Steel Network published was generally lower than the market price; they had no objection to authenticity of evidence 12-14, but transfer of customs release sheet did not mean the transfer of ownership of goods. Customs release sheet did not have any records about Kangjie, which cannot demonstrate that Kangjie was the owner; they had no objection to authenticity of evidence 15, 16, but cannot be based on the size of site creation unit to determine the accuracy of its data provided, data China Ferroalloy Online Network provided was the same with the data several other sites, but the data of My Steel Network and the data of other sites had a long gap, therefore, comprehensive comparison of the data that each site referred to each other had more advantages; they had no objection to authenticity of evidence 17.

The joint cross-examination opinions of the Defendants Kangjie and Tanghe against the Defendant Zhongse Logistics was: they had no objection to the authenticity of evidence 1, but had objection to the legality. The contract was not a sales contract, but the financing loan contract, the goods involved was actually a loan guaranty, Kangjie would lastly repurchased at a higher price; they had no objection to authenticity of evidence 2, 3, but had objection to the purpose of proof; authenticity of evidence 4 could not be recognized, they did not know how Pengfa sealed and confirmed; evidence 5 had nothing to do with the case, and it could not prove that Kangjie and Zhongse Logistics had a long-term relationship and trust base; they had no objection to evidence 6; they recognized the authenticity and legality of evidence 7, but not the relevancy. The price the parties agreed in purchase contract did not refer to the website standard, but the parties agreed on it by themselves; they recognized the authenticity and legality of evidence 8, 9, but not relevancy, and the two notarizations were only for the copy and safe of the contents on websites, which had no relevancy with the case; they did not recognize the authenticity of evidence 10, and it had nothing to do with price standard; they recognized the authenticity, legality of evidence 11, but not the relevancy. The case was not the case of the Supreme Court Gazette, so the court did not need to refer or cite; they recognized the authenticity of evidence 12-14, but not the proof of purpose. Zhongse Logistics received customs release sheet, but the goods were still in the warehouse and were not changed, and the delivery was the mortgage in financing loan contract; they recognized the authenticity and legality of evidence 15-17, but not relevancy, the two parties did not agree that regarding any site price as the contract price standard.

The Defendant Zhongse International Trade had no objection to all 17 evidence of the Defendant Zhongse Logistics.

The court confirms the Defendant Zhongse Logistics's evidence as follows: Kangjie and Tanghe had no objection to the authenticity of evidence 1-3 had no objection, and the court confirms the evidence. Three evidence can prove that Kangjie and Zhongse Logistics had the legal relationship of the sales contract; Zhongse Logistics provided the original copies of evidence 4, 5, the court confirms the authenticity, but evidence 5 had no relevancy with the case, so the court does not confirm the effect of evidence; evidence 7-9 was the information on public website, and the court confirms the authenticity; authenticity of evidence 10-11 is confirmed by the court, but it had no relevancy with the case. So the court does not confirm its effect of evidence. The Plaintiff and the other three Defendants had no objection to the authenticity of evidence 12-14, and the court confirms the authenticity. But the nature of the customs release sheets was the creditor's rights certificate, not the document of title; the court confirms the authenticity of evidence 15-17, but it was not associated with the case, so the effect of evidence is not confirmed.

The Defendant Zhongse International Trade provided the following evidence to prove its pleas: evidence 1, sales contract No.2; evidence 2, confirmation of delivery concluded by Zhongse Logistics and Zhongse International Trade on May 8, 2014, evidence 1, 2, to prove that Zhongse Logistics and Zhongse International Trade concluded a contract for the sale of goods, so Zhongse Logistics had reason to believe that Zhongse Logistics was the owner of the goods; evidence 3, proof of the transfer of goods; evidence 4, warehousing agreement and inventory accounting change statement, evidence 3, 4, to prove that Zhongse Logistics and Pengfa jointly recognized the transfer of goods to Zhongse International Trade, which enhanced that Zhongse International Trade believed that Zhongse Logistics was the real owner of the goods; evidence 5, information in Zhongse Logistics Charter and in the national enterprise credit information network; evidence 6, goods sales contract, delivery confirmation, cargo transfer certificate, bill of lading and invoices referred to M.V. "JIN YUE", evidence 5, 6, to prove that Zhongse Logistics sold nickel to Zhongse International Trade in a similar manner, and the parties had close business contacts, so Zhongse International Trade had no reason not to believe its own wholly owned subsidiary of Zhongse Logistics; evidence 7, settlement agreement; evidence 8, three loan contracts and fund payment vouchers Zhongse Logistics and Zhongse International Trade concluded; evidence 9, nine goods sales contracts in addition to M.V. "JIN FENG" and M.V. "JIN YUE" Zhongse Logistics and Zhongse International Trade concluded and evidence to prove that Zhongse Logistics delivered the goods; evidence 10, invoices Zhongse Logistics issued to Zhongse International Trade, evidence 7-10, to prove that under the three loan contracts, the creditor's rights Zhongse International Trade had against Zhongse Logistics partly offset the creditor's rights Zhongse Logistics had against Zhongse International Trade under the 11 contracts for the sale of goods. Zhongse International Trade by way of set-off, had paid reasonable consideration of good involved to Zhongse Logistics; evidence 11, the customs release sheet No. PSI-111023; evidence 12, the customs release sheet No.PSI-111024; evidence 13, the translation of the customs release sheets Beijing Yibangda Co., Ltd. provided, to prove that the two customs release sheets were delivered to Zhongse International Trade, and International Trade had been in possession of goods under the bill of lading. All the evidence had original pieces.

The cross-examination opinions of the Plaintiff to the Defendant Zhongse International Trade were as follows: evidence 1, the contractual agreement itself could not be a reason that Zhongse International Trade believed that Zhongse Logistics had ownership of the goods. The contract for the sale of goods was only a document signed for the financing arrangement; evidence 2, Zhongse Logistics had no ownership of goods, bill of lading was neither a document of title; evidence 3, 4, Pengfa was not the consignee, it could not determine the ownership of the goods; the company had no objection to the authenticity of evidence 5; evidence 6, except order to release the goods, the company had no objection to the authenticity, precisely because Zhongse Logistics had the special relationship with Zhongse International Trade, Zhongse International Trade did not review in fact whether Zhongse Logistics had the ownership of goods, the mutual trust could not confront the third party; evidence 7-10, where relationship of Zhongse Logistics and Zhongse International Trade, there was a doubt whether they had lending behavior and payment and others, and according to our law, the company's lending was not allowed; the company had no objection to authenticity of evidence 11-13, but the transfer of bills of lading did not mean that the transfer of goods, therefore goods involved had not yet completed delivery.

The joint cross-examination of the Defendants Kangjie and Tanghe to the Defendant Zhongse International Trade's evidence was as follows: they recognized the authenticity of evidence 1, but the contract was indeed a part of a chain loan contract, and the purpose of proof was not established; they recognized the authenticity, legality and relevancy of evidence 2, but purpose of proof not, which cannot prove that Zhongse International Trade was kind for a lower price before receiving the customs release sheets; they recognized the authenticity of evidence 3, but not legality. The ownership of goods before was not legal, and the ownership of goods afterwards was not legal naturally; they recognized the authenticity of evidence 4, and the evidence had no effect to prove that the goods was owned by Zhongse International Trade; they did not recognize the authenticity of evidence 5 of articles of association but had no objection to the information of company information website; they recognized the authenticity of evidence 6, but it had nothing to do with the case; they recognized the authenticity of evidence 7-10, which were the internal files between Zhongse Logistics and Zhongse International Trade and could not prove that Zhongse International Trade paid a reasonable consideration; they recognized the authenticity of evidence 11-13, but it was not the transfer of goods, was the circulation of collateral in the loan contract.

The Defendant Zhongse Logistics had no objection to Zhongse International Trade's 17 evidence.

The court confirms the Defendant Zhongse International Trade's evidence as follows: Zhongse Logistics had no objection to the authenticity of evidence 1, 2, the court confirms it, which could prove that Zhongse Logistics and Zhongse International Trade concluded a sales contract No.2. But the time evidence 2 recorded that Zhongse Logistics delivered the customs release sheets to Zhongse International Trade was on May 8, 2014, which was not according to the time Zhongse Logistics issued the demonstration to the court on July 24, 2014; so the court confirms the fact that the customs release sheets were delivered to Zhongse International Trade, but does not confirm the time delivering on May 8, 2014; combined with the Plaintiff's evidence 21, the court recognized the authenticity of Zhongse Logistic's evidence 4, 5. But Pengfa as warehouse person involved, the confirmation of the real right of goods cannot produce the legal effect of the transfer of property rights. Pengfa though claimed to make the seal of evidence 4 transfer of goods invalidate, but whether the storage agreement Pengfa and Zhongse International Trade concluded and Pengfa's contractual obligations to Zhongse Logistics in transfer of goods can be canceled, which needs to be resolved separately, and is not in the trial of the case; the court confirms the authenticity of evidence 5, 6, but it is not associated with the case, so the court does not confirm the effect of evidence; Zhongse Logistics had no objection to evidence 7-10, without objection, the Plaintiff and Kangjie, Tanghe had objection to the authenticity of the four evidence, but failed to provide evidence to prove, so the court confirms the authenticity, which can prove that Zhongse Logistics paid the fees; the Plaintiff and the other three Defendants had no objection to the authenticity of evidence 11-13, so the court confirms the authenticity, but the nature of the customs release sheets is the certificate of the creditor's rights, not the document of title.

The court finds out that: on October 17, 2011, the Plaintiff and Kangjie concluded an import agency agreement with the contract number CGM-KJ-DLNI002. The Plaintiff was Kangjie's agent and imported laterite nickel ore. The agreement stipulated that the unit price was RMB628.28 yuan/ton; Kangjie should pay fully in batches with 80 days after the Plaintiff accepted. After Kangjie paid each payment, the Plaintiff should transfer corresponding ownership of goods to Kangjie on the payment day. If Kangjie failed to pay out the payment in time, the Plaintiff had right to deal with goods and forfeiture deposit; the Plaintiff agreed to use freight forwarding company recommended by Kangjie, the two parties and the recommended freight forwarding company concluded three-party freight forwarding agreement, and Kangjie paid to the corresponding fees stimulated in the freight forwarding agreement. On the same day, the Plaintiff and DH KINGSTONE HOLDING Co., Ltd. (hereinafter referred to as DH) concluded No.11DHWM-NIHG purchases and sales contract, and the Plaintiff purchased 50,000 ± 10% tons of laterite nickel ore. The contract agreed: "price is CIF China Newport 84.3$/T; the total price of goods was USD5,215,000 (±10%); the Plaintiff should issue an 90 days insurance, irrevocable and untransferable letter of credit to DH with 5 days after signing the contract, the amount of the issuance of the L/C is 100% CIF total contract amount of goods". On October 27, 2011, DH issued two temporary invoices to the Plaintiff, the Plaintiff according to the amount of temporary invoices through the issuing bank paid the payment of goods involved to DH. On November 24, 2011, DH issued the final invoice to the Plaintiff. In order to handle the freight forwarding business of the involved laterite nickel ore in Tianjin Port, the Plaintiff, Kangjie and Tanghe concluded a port agency agreement on import nickel ore with the contract number of ZK-KL-DL02, which stipulated that the Plaintiff imports nickel ore to Kangjie, they assigned Tanghe as the freight forwarding company of the goods; the ownership of goods was owned by the Plaintiff; after Tanghe received the written delivery instruction that the consignee was Kangjie issued by the Plaintiff, the company should strictly according to the Plaintiff's instruction delivered the goods to Kangjie.

55,970 tons of laterite nickel ore were loaded on M.V. "JIN FENG" on October 6, 2011 from the Philippines Surrey to China Tianjin Port. The ship agency of M.V. "JIN FENG" issued two set of original bills of lading with the number of PSI-111023 and PSI-111024 on behalf of the captain. After the goods arrived at Tianjin Port, the Plaintiff handed over the original bills of lading and other documents to Tanghe for the customs declaration, inspection, storage and other related business of the goods in Tianjin Port according to the import port nickel agent agreement signed with Tanghe. Tanghe took the goods from the carrier on behalf of the Plaintiff, and handled the relevant port import procedures, and held two original involved customs release sheets. Goods involved were stored in Pengfa's yard.

As Kangjie failed to pay the payment according to the import port nickel agent contract with the Plaintiff, on May 8, 2012, the Plaintiff concluded a purchases and sales contract with Datang, and the two parties agreed that Datang purchased the goods involved from the Plaintiff and the unit price (including loading fees) was RMB550 yuan/ton. After the contract was concluded, Datang paid the payment to the Plaintiff in batches, but the Plaintiff failed to deliver the goods to Datang. Tianjin Second Intermediate Court accepted (2013) Er Zhong Min Er Chu Zi No.139 that Datang sued the Plaintiff on June 4, 2013. Tianjin Second Intermediate Court ruled to allow Datang's property preservation application, sealed up 55,903.6 tons of nickel the Plaintiff deposited in Pengfa's cargo yard, and issued the notice of assisting the enforcement to Tanghe and Pengfa on June 6, 2013. Tianjin Second Intermediate Court made the decision on December 16, 2013 that Datang had received 12,389 tons of goods according to the sales contract and should not return to the Plaintiff again. The Plaintiff should return RMB23,064,000 yuan to Datang and losses from June 1, 2012 to payment day designed by the judgment (the interest should be calculated on the basis of the benchmark interest rate of the People's Bank of China). Tianjin High People's Court recognized the judgment, and it had come into effect. Datang had applied for the implementation to Tianjin Second Intermediate Court based on the judgment which had come into effect. The case was carrying out now, the goods involved had not been relieved sealing up.

Tanghe said that because it needed to lend money from Kangjie, and it would deliver the two customs release sheets to Kangjie as collateral. Kangjie concluded a goods purchases contract with Zhongse Logistics on April 21, 2014, and Kangjie sold the goods involved to Zhongse Logistics. The contract agreed that the unit price of the goods was RMB357.3343 yuan/ton, the total amount of payment was RMB20,000,000 yuan. In addition, the contract also agreed the acceptance standards of goods; delivery time, place, manner; payment terms such as the settlement. On the same day, Zhongse Logistics paid RMB15,000,000 yuan to Kangjie, and the two parties concluded a cargo transfer agreement, and Kangjie delivered two customs release sheets to Zhongse Logistics. While the two parties concluded the transfer certificate of ownership of goods with Tanghe. On April 30, 2014, Zhongse Logistics paid RMB5,000,000 yuan to Kangjie, thus, all payment was paid out.

Zhongse Logistics concluded a goods sales contract with Zhongse International Trade on April 23, 2014, and the unit price of goods in the contract was RMB371 yuan/ton, and the total amount of payment was RMB20,764,870 yuan. Zhongse Logistics, Zhongse International Trade and Pengfa concluded a transfer certificate of ownership of goods on April 25, 2014. Zhongse International Trade and Pengfa also concluded the warehousing agreement and statement of changes in inventory on the same day. The two parties concluded a settlement agreement on May 23, 2014, and agreed that they settled the payment in the way of offset. Pengfa issued the invalid statement of the transfer certificate of the ownership of nickel ore of M. V. "JIN FENG" on June 25, 2014. The company said that it was the staff's error that on June 2, 2014 it sealed the transfer certificate of the ownership of goods on April 25, 2014 and now claimed it was void. Two involved customs release sheets had been delivered to Zhongse International Trade by Zhongse Logistics, which was held by Zhongse International Trade. The Plaintiff held that the four Defendants violated their ownership, they should return the involved customs release sheets to the Plaintiff, and then sued.

The court holds that the case is the dispute over return of customs release sheets.

1. Whether Kangjie had ownership over the goods involved.

   The court holds that the Plaintiff concluded the purchases and sales contract with the foreign seller in its own name and paid the full payment through the letter of credit according to the purchases and sales contract, and obtained the two sets of original bills of lading. Tanghe, as the agent of the Plaintiff, took the goods from the carrier by the original bills of lading, at this time, the Plaintiff had ownership over the goods involved. The import agency contract concluded between the Plaintiff and Kangjie was legally established and came into effect, which was binding on the both parties. According to the contract, if Kangjie paid the payment, it could obtain the corresponding ownership of the goods. Kangjie did not pay for the goods involved, therefore, it could not obtain the ownership of the goods. In the hearing of the case, Kangjie recognized that it agreed to withdraw the import agency contract with the Plaintiff, and the court did not hear the case because the Plaintiff claimed that confirming the validity of the rescission of the contract had another case to sue. Even if the import agency contract was canceled, according to the Contract Law of the People's Republic of China Article 97, the Plaintiff had not yet transferred the ownership of the goods to Kangjie, and terminated the performance, so the Plaintiff was still the owner of the goods involved. In the first hearing of this case, Kangjie also recognized that the owner of the goods involved was the Plaintiff. To sum up, Kangjie did not enjoy the ownership of the goods involved.

2. Legal relationship between Kangjie and Zhongse Logistics, and the legal relationship between Zhongse Logistics and Zhongse International Trade.

   Kangjie claimed that the contract with Zhongse Logistics and the contract between Zhongse Logistics and Zhongse International Trade were in the name of sales contracts, in fact, they were loan contracts, so the contracts were invalid. The court holds that the contents of contract concluded by Kangjie and Zhongse Logistics and the transfer agreement of the ownership of goods issued by Kangjie to Zhongse Logistics, and the transfer certificate of ownership of goods can initially prove that they were sales contracts. Although Kangjie advocated that the contracts were loan contracts, but it failed to provide sufficient and effective evidence to prove that Purple Mine was its related company. Zhongse International Trade and Purple Mine concluded a sales contract in order to repurchase the goods involved. Therefore, the court does not support Kangjie's claim. So Kangjie had legal relationships of the sales contract with the other two companies.

3. Whether Zhongse International Trade had the ownership of the goods involved.

Kangjie did not have the ownership of the goods involved; the behavior of selling the goods involved to Zhongse Logistics was unauthorized disposition. Zhongse Logistics and Zhongse International Trade claimed that they obtained the ownership of goods involved in good faith. The court holds that according to the Property Law of the People's Republic of China Article 106 Paragraph 1, where a person untitled to dispose a real property or movable property transfers the real property or movable property to an assignee, the owner has the right to recover the real property or movable property. Except it is otherwise prescribed by law, once it is under any of the following circumstances, the assignee should obtain the ownership of the real property or movable property: (1) the assignee accepted the real property or movable property in good faith; (2) the real property or movable property was transferred at a reasonable price; or (3) the transferred real property or movable property should have been registered in case registration is required by law, and should have been delivered to the assignee in case registration is not required. Whether the claims of Zhongse Logistics and Zhongse International Trade were established, the court according to the elements of bona fide acquisition analyzes as follows:

1. The goods involved had been sealed up by the court, whether it is applicable to bona fide acquisition.
   On November 7, 1999, the Reply of the Supreme People's Court to the Hebei High People's Court on whether the Property Sealed by the People's Court is Resold to Protect People's Interests Obtained in Good Faith clearly showed that: the property seized by the people's court legally is resold, the buyer does not apply the bona fide acquisition in principle. In regard of this case, on June 6, 2013, Tianjin Second Intermediate Court ruled that the goods involved were seized legally, and on June 19, 2013, the court sent Tanghe and Pengfa a notice of assisting enforcement, and the ruling had come into effect and was published legally. The time of signing the sales contract between Kangjie and Zhongse Logistics was on April 21, 2014, and the time of signing sales contract between Zhongse Logistics and Zhongse International Trade was on April 23, 2014. Which were all after the seizure of goods involved of Tianjin Second Intermediate Court, therefore, Zhongse Logistics and Zhongse International Trade should not apply bona fide acquisition system in principle.

2. Whether Zhongse Logistics was in possession of the goods involved.
   According to the provisions of the Maritime Code of the People's Republic of China, the bill of lading is the document of title when the goods was during the carriage of goods by sea. Before the issuing of the bill of lading or the holder of the bill of lading takes the delivery note by the original bill of lading, the bill of lading no longer has the effect of document of title. Customs release sheets are taken by the holder of the original bill of lading from the carrier or his agent through the original bill of lading. Seal the release chapter of the shipping agency and the customs in a copy of the bill of lading (or D/O), it can apply the vouchers from the port department of the stored goods, it is not a bill of lading, and then after exchanging the customs release sheets, the bill of lading has lost its effect of the certificate of title. According to the Property Law of the People's Republic of China Article 5, the type and content of property is determined by law. Therefore, under the circumstances that Chinese relevant laws do not regulate the legal nature of the customs release sheets, the customs release sheets cannot be identified as documents of title. The court does not support Zhongse Logistics and Zhongse International Trade's claim that transfer of the customs release sheets was finishing the delivery of the goods.

As mentioned above, the occupier of the customs release sheet should have the right of taking goods to the port storage company, which should be the certificate of creditor's right. The goods involved in the storage of Pengfa, was the situation that it was occupied by the third party. The transfer of customs release sheets was the transfer of the right to take delivery of goods, which applied the indication delivery regulated in Article 26 of the Property Law of the People's Republic of China. The Interpretation of the Supreme People's Court on Several Issues concerning the Application of the Guaranty Law of the People's Republic of China Article 88 stipulates that: "where the pledgor takes possession of the property which is indirectly possessed, it shall be deemed to be the handover when the owner of the pledge contract is notified in writing", according to the spirit of the provisions of this article, the assignor should not only deliver the customs release sheet to the assignee, but should also inform the third person in actual possession of the goods of the fact of requesting transfer of goods. When meeting these two conditions, it could complete the delivery of goods. In this case, when Kangjie transferred the customs release sheets to Zhongse Logistics, the goods involved were in the state of seizure. Zhongse Logistics failed to provide evidence to prove that Kangjie had informed Pengfa of the fact that it transferred the delivery request to Zhongse Logistics, and the company did not meet the two conditions of indication delivery, therefore, Kangjie failed to complete the delivery of goods involved to Zhongse Logistics involved. According to the Property Law of the People's Republic of China, to transfer the possession, except that there is an agreement of the transfer of possession between the parties, there must be the delivery of the chose in possession, thus which can be called a completion of the transfer. Whether Kangjie was the owner of the goods involved, it failed to complete the delivery to Zhongse Logistics, therefore, Zhongse Logistics failed to obtain possession of the goods involved. Because Zhongse Logistics was not the occupier of the involved good, the transfer to Zhongse International Trade could not apply bona fide acquisition, and Zhongse Logistics could not obtain the ownership of goods involved. In summary, when the goods involved were sold to Zhongse International Trade, it has been seized by Tianjin Second Intermediate Court, so Zhongse International Trade did not apply bona fide acquisition in principle. Even if bona fide acquisition is applicable, Zhongse International Trade cannot get the ownership of the goods involved because Zhongse Logistics was not the occupier of goods involved. Whether Zhongse International Company was in good faith when assigning the goods involved or whether the price was reasonable was of no effect to the case, the court will not identify these two elements any more.
3. Whether the four Defendants should return the two custom release sheets to the Plaintiff.
As mentioned above, Zhongse International Trade failed to obtain the ownership of the goods involved, but because of the dispute over the sales of goods involved between the Plaintiff and Datang, according to Tianjin Second Intermediate Court's effective ruling, ownership of the 12,389 tons of goods had

been transferred to Datang, the Plaintiff enjoyed the ownership of 43,681 tons of remained goods.

The Plaintiff and Tanghe were in the freight forwarding contractual relation. The customs release sheets obtained by Tanghe when it was as a trustee in the handling business should be returned to the Plaintiff, but Tanghe handed over the customs release sheets to Kangjie, Kangjie transferred it to Zhongse Logistics, and Zhongse Logistics transferred it to the Zhongse International Trade. Zhongse International Trade failed to obtain the ownership of the goods involved, the possession of the customs release sheet obstructed the Plaintiff's right to take the delivery of goods against Pengfa. According to the Property Law of the People's Republic of China Article 35, the Defendant should exclude nuisance, and return the customs release sheet to the Plaintiff directly. Tanghe, Kangjie and Zhongse Logistics were not in actual possession of customs release sheet, therefore, the three did not have the obligation to return. As for how to deal with goods involved between the Plaintiff and Datang, it can be resolved in other way.

Pulling the threads together, according to the Property Law of the People's Republic of China Article 35 and the Civil Procedure Law of the People's Republic of China Article 64 Paragraph 1, the judgment is as follows:

1. The Plaintiff China Geology and Mineral Corporation shall enjoy the ownership of the 43,681 tons of nickel ore under No.PSI-111023 and No.PSI-111024 bills of lading of M.V. "JIN FENG" 04 voyage.
2. The Defendant Zhongse International Trade Co., Ltd. shall return two original customs release sheets of goods under No.PSI-111023 and No.PSI-111024 bills of lading of M.V. "JIN FENG" 04 voyage to the Plaintiff China Geological and Mineral Corporation.
3. Reject other claims of the Plaintiff.

Court acceptance fee in amount of RMB100 yuan, and preservation fee in amount of RMB30 yuan, shall been born by the four Defendants jointly and severally.

If not satisfy with this judgment, any parties shall within fifteen days as of the service of this judgment, submit a statement of appeal to the court, with eight duplicates, so as to make an appeal before Tianjin High People's Court. If the fee is not paid within seven days after the period of appeal expires, the appeal will be automatically withdrawn. (Deposit bank: Agricultural Bank of China Tian Tiancheng Branch02200501040006269; name of account: Tianjin High People's Court Financial Section).

Presiding Judge: ZHANG Lina
Acting Judge: CAO Ke
Acting Judge: WANG Huiran

March 18, 2015

Clerk: MA Jihai

Tianjin High People's Court
Civil Judgment

China Geology and Mining Corporation
v.
Tianjin Kangjie Import and Export Trade Co., Ltd. et al.

(2015) Jin Gao Min Si Zhong Zi No.77

Related Case(s) This is the judgment of second instance, and the judgment of first instance is on page 131.

Cause(s) of Action 221. Dispute over contract on custody of cargo in port. (Editor's Note: This cause of action is chosen as it appears to be closest to the underlying dispute between the parties.)

Headnote Affirm lower court decision that dispute between importer, port agent and freight forwarders over ownership of goods was resolved by who had paid for the goods, and not who held the customs release sheets enabling them to be delivered from the container yard to which they had been imported.

Summary China Geology and Mining Co. (hereinafter referred to as "G&M") filed an action against Tianjin Kangjie Import and Export Trade Co., Zhongse Logistics Co., Zhongse International Trade Co., and Tianjin Tanghe Logistics (collectively "the Defendants") alleging ownership of a shipment of laterite nickel ore. G&M was the agent of Kangjie entrusted with having the goods delivered to China. G&M enlisted the assistance of Tianjin Tanghe Logistics Co., a Chinese freight forwarder, to handle all of the proper procedures for importing the material. G&M provided the freight forwarder with the bills of lading and other documents necessary to claim the cargo. Due to Kangjie's failure to pay for the goods, G&M, according to their contract, gained ownership and responsibility of disposal of the goods. Tianjin Tanghe Logistics Co., Kangjie, and the other Defendants, however, established collateral contracts for these goods, transferring ownership between select Defendants. The court of first-instance found that these contracts were largely illegal and that transfer of these goods was impermissible since G&M was the rightful owner of the goods involved. On appeal, the court of second-instance ruled against any "good-faith" ownership defense and recognized the determination of the court of first-instance.

Judgment

The Appellant (the Defendant of first instance): Tianjin Kangjie Import and Export Trade Co., Ltd.
Domicile: Room 502-1, A Building, No. 6 Haitai Green Industrial Base, Haitai Development No. 6, Huayuan Industrial Zone, Tianjin.
Legal representative: HAN Kun, chairman of the company.
Agent *ad litem*: HAN Ming, lawyer of Tianjin Yungong Law Firm.
Agent *ad litem*: MA Jing, lawyer of Tianjin Yungong Law Firm.

The Appellant (the Defendant of first instance): Zhongse Logistics (Tianjin) Co., Ltd.
Domicile: No. 0117, No. 1 Building No. 188 New Road, Binhai High-tech District, Binhai Science and Technology Park, No. 13888 Jinhan Highway, Tianjin.
Legal representative: SONG Jun, chairman of the company.
Agent *ad litem*: LIU Jinyi, lawyer of Beijing Dentons Law Firm.
Agent *ad litem*: TAN Zhenghua, lawyer of Beijing Dentons Law Firm.

The Appellant (the Defendant of first instance): Zhongse International Trade Co., Ltd.
Domicile: Room 909, No. 1 Building, Beijing office, West Railway Station south square, Fengtai District, Beijing.
Legal representative: LI Xiaoying, chairman of the company.
Agent *ad litem*: LIU Jinyi, lawyer of Beijing Dentons Law Firm.
Agent *ad litem*: LIU Ruiqi, lawyer of Beijing Dentons Law Firm.

The Respondent (the Plaintiff of first instance): China Geology and Mining Corporation
Domicile: 7/F, Zhenjiang Building, 26/F, Anzhen Xili No. 3 Area, Chaoyang District, Beijing
Legal representative: SONG Yongqi, general manager of the company.
Agent *ad litem*: ZHANG Yutian, lawyer of Shandong Minyang Law Firm.
Agent *ad litem*: YUAN Jie, lawyer of Tianjin Wisely Law Firm.

The Defendant of first instance: Tianjin Tanghe Logistics Co., Ltd.
Domicile: 645B19 Aviation Industry support Center, No. 1 Baohang Road Airport Economic Zone Binhai New District, Tianjin.
Legal representative: QIN Yongshuai, chairman.

With respect to the case arising from dispute over return of customs release sheets between the Appellants, Tianjin Kangjie Import and Export Trade Co., Ltd. (hereinafter referred to as Kangjie), Zhongse Logistics (Tianjin) Co., Ltd. (hereinafter referred to as Zhongse Logistics), Zhongse International Trade Co., Ltd. (hereinafter referred to as Zhongse Trade), and the Respondent, China Geology and Mining Corporation (hereinafter referred to as G&M General), and the Defendant of first instance, Tianjin Tanghe Logistics Co., Ltd. (hereinafter referred to as

Tanghe), the Appellants disagreed with the Tianjin Maritime Court (hereinafter referred to as the court of first instance) (2014) Jin Hai Fa Shang Chu Zi No.153 Civil Judgment (hereinafter referred to as judgment of first instance) and appealed to the court. After accepting it, the court formed a collegiate panel, and held a hearing in public on June 9, 2015. Agents *ad litem* of the Appellant Kangjie, HAN Ming and MA Jing, agents *ad litem* of the Appellant Zhongse Logistics, LIU Jinyi and TAN Zhenghua, agents *ad litem* of the Appellant Zhongse Trade, LIU Jinyi and LIU Ruiqi, agents *ad litem* of the Respondent G&M General, ZHANG Yutian and YUAN Jie, appeared in court to attend the hearing. After a legal summons, the Defendant of first instance Tanghe did not appear in court without any justified reasons, the court judged the case by default. Now the case has been concluded.

G&M General claimed that: G&M General concluded *Import Agency Agreement* of nickel ore with Kangjie on October 17, 2011, and G&M General was trustee according to that agreement. On November 4, 2011, G&M General and Kangjie concluded *Nickel Ore Import Agency Agreement* with Tanghe that G&M General enjoyed the ownership of the goods, and it entrusted Tanghe to assist the port agency operation of the goods under the contract; Kangjie was responsible for the goods' port agency fee. After that, G&M General and Kangjie terminated *Import Agency Agreement* of nickel ore, and G&M General resold the nickel ore to Beijing Datang Fuel Co., Ltd. (hereinafter referred to as Datang). Because Tanghe was the port agent for the goods involved, and it held the original copies of the bills of lading and the customs release sheets (the copy of the bill of lading was stamped with the special delivery stamp of the carrier's agent, the special stamp for inspection and quarantine, and the customs clearance stamp) for the goods under No.PSI-111023 and No.PSI-111024 bills of lading carried by M.V. "JIN FENG" 04 voyage. Tanghe, without G&M General's permission, delivered the customs release sheets to Kangjie. Kangjie concluded *Goods Purchases Contract* with Zhongse Logistics and delivered the customs release sheets to Zhongse Logistics. Then, Zhongse Logistics concluded *Goods Sales Contract* with Zhongse Trade and delivered the customs release sheets to Zhongse Trade. G&M General held it was the goods' owners, and Kangjie, Tanghe, Zhongse Logistics and Zhongse Trade wrongfully infringed upon G&M General's ownership and the customs release sheets should be returned to G&M General. Therefore, G&M General required the court of first instance that: 1. confirm that G&M General enjoyed the right of ownership of the goods involved; 2. Kangjie, Tanghe, Zhongse Logistics and Zhongse Trade should return the two customs release sheets corresponding to No. PSI-111023 and No.PSI-111024 bills of lading; 3. Kangjie, Tanghe, Zhongse Logistics and Zhongse Trade should bear litigation fees of the case.

Kangjie and Tanghe jointly argued that: 1. before the action of the case, Datang filed a civil action before the Tianjin Second Intermediate People's Court (hereinafter referred to as Tianjin Second Court). The judgment of that court confirmed that Datang owned the goods, the goods were not owned by G&M General; 2. the goods were preserved by the Tianjin Second Court, and Tanghe received the preservation ruling and the notice of assistance of enforcement, so Tanghe should not return the customs release sheets to G&M General. The customs release sheets were not held by Kangjie and Tanghe. In conclusion, the claims of G&M General could not be established, so they required the court to reject the claims.

Zhongse Logistics argued that: 1. G&M General was not the goods' real owner, and Kangjie was the actual owner of the goods. According to *Import Agency Contract* of nickel ore between G&M General and Kangjie, Kangjie was G&M General's client, and G&M General had no right to form a sales and purchases contract with others. According to the import goods declaration, G&M General was only the operating agency, and Kangjie was the consignee that paid the tax on the goods. Therefore, Zhongse Logistics obtained the right of ownership of the goods, and ownership was transferred to Zhongse Trade by circulation. 2. Even if G&M General was the owner of the goods, Zhongse Logistics, according with the bona fide acquisition's conditions, paid Kangjie a reasonable price for the goods. In conclusion, Zhongse Trade was the owner of the goods, so it required the court to reject G&M General's claims.

Zhongse Trade argued that:

1. It agreed with Zhongse Logistics's arguments;
2. Zhongse Trade and Zhongse Logistics concluded the sales and purchases contract, and paid a reasonable price and obtained the customs release sheets, namely Zhongse Trade was the real and final owner of the goods involved;
3. G&M General and Kangjie had a debt relationship;
4. According to the Provisions of the Supreme People's Court on Several Issues concerning the Application of Law in the Trial of Goods Delivery Cases without Original Bills of Lading Article 10, the original bills of lading were held by Zhongse Trade, so Zhongse Trade was the real owner of the goods. So, it required the court to reject G&M General's claims.

The court of first instance found out that: on October 17, 2011, G&M General and Kangjie concluded No.CGM-KJ-DLNI002 *Import Agency Agreement*. G&M General was Kangjie's agent and imported laterite nickel ore. The agreement stipulated that the unit price was RMB628.28 yuan/wet ton; Kangjie should fully pay the payment of goods within 80 days after G&M General accepted. After Kangjie made each payment, G&M General should transfer ownership of goods to Kangjie on the payment day. If Kangjie failed to pay on time, G&M General had the right to deal with the goods and forfeiture deposit; G&M General agreed to use a freight forwarding company recommended by Kangjie. The two parties and the recommended freight forwarding company concluded a tripartite freight forwarding agreement, and Kangjie paid the corresponding fees stipulated in the freight forwarding agreement. On the same day, tripartite and DH KINGSTONE HOLDING Co., Ltd. (hereinafter referred to as DH) concluded a purchases and sales contract, G&M General purchased 50,000 ± 10% tons of laterite nickel ore. The contract stated that the price was CIF China Xingang 84.3 USD/ton; the total price of the goods was 4,215,000 USD (±10%); L/C; G&M General should issue a 90-day irrevocable and non-transferrable letter of credit to DH within 5 days of concluding the contract. The amount of the issuance of the L/C was 100% of the CIF total contract amount of goods. On October 27, 2011, DH issued two temporary invoices to G&M General. According to the amount of temporary invoices through the issuing bank, G&M General paid DH for the goods. On November 24, 2011, DH issued the final invoices to G&M General. In order to handle the freight forwarding business involving nickel ore in Tianjin Port, G&M General, Kangjie and Tanghe concluded No.ZK-KL-DL02 *Nickel Ore Import Port Agency Agreement*. It stipulated that G&M General should import nickel ore to Kangjie, they appointed Tanghe as the freight forwarder; the right of ownership of the goods was enjoyed by G&M General; after Tanghe received written delivery order from G&M General that Kangjie was the consignee, Tanghe should strictly follow G&M General's order to deliver the goods to Kangjie.

On October 6, 2011, 55,970 tons of laterite nickel ore were loaded onto M.V. "JIN FENG" from Surrey Philippines to Tianjin China. M.V. "JIN FENG"s broker issued two sets of original bills of lading, No.PSI-111023 and No.PSI-111024, on behalf of the captain. After the goods arrived at Tianjin Port, G&M General handed over the original bills of lading and other documents to Tanghe for customs declaration, inspection, storage and other related business of the goods in Tianjin Port according to *Nickel Ore Import Port Agency Agreement* concluded by Tanghe. Tanghe took the goods from the carrier on behalf of G&M General and handled the relevant port import procedures. Tanghe held two original customs release sheets. The goods were stored in the yard of Tianjin Development Zone Pengfa Freight Forwarder Co., Ltd. (hereinafter referred to as Pengfa).

Because Kangjie failed to pay the payment of goods according to *Import Agency Agreement* with G&M General. On May 8, 2012, G&M General concluded the purchases and sales contract with Datang, and the two parties agreed that Datang would purchase the goods from G&M General at a unit price (including loading fee) of RMB550 yuan/wet ton. After the contract was concluded, Datang paid G&M General in batches, but G&M General failed to deliver the goods to Datang. On June 4, 2013, Datang filed an action before the Tianjin Second Court.

Tanghe said that it needed to borrow money from Kangjie, and Tanghe delivered the two customs release sheets to Kangjie as mortgage. Kangjie concluded *Goods Purchases Contract* with Zhongse Logistics on April 21, 2014 that Kangjie sold the goods involved to Zhongse Logistics. The contract agreed that the unit price of the goods was RMB357.3343 yuan/ton, and the total amount was RMB20,000,000 yuan. In addition, the contract also stipulated the acceptance standards of goods, the delivery time, place, manner and payment terms. On the same day, Zhongse Logistics paid RMB15,000,000 yuan to Kangjie, and the two parties concluded *Transfer Agreement of Ownership of Goods* that Kangjie delivered two customs release sheets to Zhongse Logistics. Meanwhile, the two parties concluded *Transfer Certificate of Ownership of Goods* with Tanghe. On April 30, 2014, Zhongse Logistics paid RMB5,000,000 yuan to Kangjie. Up to now, all payments of goods were paid.

On April 23, 2014, Zhongse Logistics concluded *Goods Sales Contract* with Zhongse Trade, and the unit price for the goods was RMB371.00 yuan/ton. The total amount of the payment was RMB20,764,870 yuan. Zhongse Logistics,

Zhongse Trade and Pengfa concluded *Transfer Certificate of Ownership of Goods* on April 25, 2014. Zhongse Trade and Pengfa also concluded *Warehousing Agreement* and *Statement of Changes in Inventory Account* on the same day. Zhongse Logistics and Zhongse Trade concluded a settlement agreement on May 23, 2014 to off-set the payment of goods. Pengfa issued *Statement of Transfer Certificate Being Invalid regarding the Ownership of Nickel Ore on M.V. "JIN FENG"* on June 25, 2014, stating that it was the result of a staff's error that Pengfa sealed *Transfer Certificate of Ownership of Goods* on April 25, 2014, and now stated that it was void. The two customs release sheets involved had been delivered to Zhongse Trade by Zhongse Logistics, which were held by Zhongse Trade.

The court of first instance held that, the case was the dispute over return of customs release sheet.

Firstly, whether Kangjie enjoyed the right of ownership of goods involved.

The court of first instance held that, G&M General concluded a purchases and sales contract with a foreign seller and paid in full via a letter of credit according to the purchases and sales contract. G&M General thereafter obtained two original bills of lading. Tanghe, G&M General's agent, took the goods from the carrier by the original bills of lading. At this time, G&M General enjoyed the right of ownership of the goods involved. *Import Agency Agreement* concluded by G&M General and Kangjie was established according to law and came into effect, binding to both parties. According to the contract, after Kangjie paid the payment of goods, it could obtain the corresponding ownership of goods. Kangjie did not pay for the goods involved. Therefore, it could not obtain the right of ownership of the goods involved. During the trial of the case, Kangjie recognized that it agreed to cancel the *Import Agency Agreement* with G&M General. The court of first instance did not try it because G&M General claimed that confirming the validity of the cancellation of the contract was involved in a separate case. Even if the import agency agreement was canceled, according to the Contract Law of the People's Republic of China Article 97, G&M General had not yet transferred the ownership of the goods to Kangjie. G&M General was still the owner of the good involved. In the first time of hearing of this case, Kangjie also recognized that G&M General was the owner of the goods. In conclusion, Kangjie did not enjoy the right of ownership of the goods involved.

Secondly, legal relationship between Kangjie and Zhongse Logistics, Zhongse Logistics and Zhongse Trade.

Kangjie held that the contract with Zhongse Logistics and the contract between Zhongse Logistics and Zhongse Trade were sales contracts, but in fact, they were loan contracts, so the contracts should be invalid. The court of first instance held that, the contents of the contract between Kangjie and Zhongse Logistics, *Transfer Agreement of Ownership of Goods* issued by Kangjie to Zhongse Logistics and *Transfer Certificate of Ownership of Goods* could initially prove that they were in relation of purchases and sales contract. However, Kangjie advocated that the contracts were loan contracts but failed to provide sufficient and effective evidence to prove that Tianjin Purple Mine International Trade Co., Ltd. (hereinafter referred to as Purple Mine) was its related company. Zhongse Trade and Purple Mine concluded a sales contract in order to repurchase the goods involved. Therefore, the court of first instance did not support the argument of Kangjie. Legal relationship between Kangjie and Zhongse Logistics, Zhongse Logistics and Zhongse Trade was purchases and sales contract legal relationship.

Thirdly, whether Zhongse Trade enjoyed the right of ownership of goods involved.

Kangjie did not have the right of ownership of the goods. Selling those goods to Zhongse Logistics was an unauthorized disposition. Zhongse Logistics and Zhongse Trade claimed that they obtained the ownership of the goods in good faith. The court of first instance held that, according to the Property Law of the People's Republic of China Article 106 Paragraph 1, where a person not entitled to dispose of real property or movable property transferred the real property or movable property to an assignee, the owner had the right to recover the real property or movable property. Except as was otherwise prescribed by law, once it was under any of the following circumstances, the assignee should obtain the ownership of the real property or movable property: (1) the assignee accepted the real property or movable property in good faith; (2) the real property or movable property was transferred at a reasonable price; (3) the transferred real property or movable property should have been registered in case registration was required by law, and should have been delivered to the assignee in case registration was not required. As to whether the claims of Zhongse Logistics and Zhongse Trade were established, the court of first instance, according to the elements of bona fide acquisition, analyzed as follows:

1. The goods involved were sealed up by the court, whether or not it was applicable to the bona fide acquisition principle.
   On November 7, 1999, the Reply of the Supreme People's Court to the Hebei High People's Court on whether the Property Sealed by the People's Court is Resold to Protect People's Interests Obtained in Good Faith (hereinafter referred to as the Reply) clearly showed that the property seized by the people's court was legally resold, and the buyer could not count for the bona fide acquisition principle. In this case, on June 6, 2013, Tianjin Second Court ruled that the goods involved were seized legally. On June 19, 2013, the court sent Tanghe and Pengfa the notice of assistance of enforcement. The ruling came into effect and was published legally. On April 21, 2014, purchases and sales contract between Kangjie and Zhongse Logistics was concluded, and the conclusion of the purchases and sales contract between Zhongse Logistics and Zhongse Trade was on April 23, 2014. All of this happened after the seizure of goods by Tianjin Second Court. Therefore, Zhongse Logistics and Zhongse Trade could not apply regarding the bona fide acquisition principle.
2. Whether Zhongse Logistics was in possession of the goods involved.
   According to the provisions of the Maritime Code of the People's Republic of China, the bill of lading was a document of title for the goods during a carriage of goods by sea. Before issuing the bill of lading or when the holder of the bill of lading took the delivery note by the original bill of lading, the bill of lading

no longer had the effect of document of title. The holder of the original bill of lading took a customs release sheet from the carrier or his agent through the original bills of lading. Seal the release chapter of the shipping agency and the customs in a copy of the bill of lading (or D/O), it could apply for vouchers from the port department where the goods were stored. It was not a bill of lading, and then after exchanging the customs release sheets, the bill of lading lost its effect of the certificate of title. According to the Property Law of the People's Republic of China Article 5, law determined the type and content of property. Therefore, Chinese relevant laws did not regulate the legal nature of the customs release sheets. The customs release sheets could not be identified as a document of title. The court of first instance did not support Zhongse Logistics and Zhongse Trade's argument that the transfer of a customs release sheets counted as the delivery of the goods.

As mentioned above, the occupier of the customs release sheets should have the right to take the goods to the port warehousing company. This right should be the certificate of creditor's rights. The goods involved in Pengfa's storage were occupied by a third person. The transfer of the customs release sheets was a transfer of the right of request to take delivery of goods, which triggered indication delivery regulated by the Property Law of the People's Republic of China Article 26. The Interpretation of the Supreme People's Court on Several Issues concerning the Application of the Guaranty Law of the People's Republic of China Article 88 (hereinafter referred to as the Guaranty Law Interpretation) stipulated that: "where the pledgor takes possession of the property which is indirectly possessed, it shall be deemed to be the handover when the owner of the pledge contract is notified in writing." According to the spirit of this Article, the assignor should not only deliver the customs release sheet to the assignee, but it should also inform the third person in actual possession of the goods of transferring the request for delivering the goods. After meeting these two conditions, it could complete the delivery of goods. In this case, when Kangjie transferred the customs release sheets to Zhongse Logistics, the goods involved were in a state of seizure. Zhongse Logistics failed to provide evidence to prove that Kangjie informed Pengfa of the fact that it transferred the delivery request to Zhongse Logistics, and Kangjie did not meet the two conditions of indication delivery. Therefore, Kangjie failed to complete the delivery of the goods to Zhongse Logistics. According to the provisions of the Property Law of the People's Republic of China, the possession of the transfer, except when there was an agreement of the transfer of possession between the parties, the delivery of possession could complete the delivery. Whatever Kangjie owned the goods involved, it failed to complete the delivery to Zhongse Logistics. Therefore, Zhongse Logistics failed to obtain possession of the goods involved. Because Zhongse Logistics was not the occupier of the goods, the transfer to Zhongse Trade could not to apply bona fide acquisition principle. Zhongse Logistics could not obtain the ownership of goods involved.

In conclusion, when the goods were sold to Zhongse Trade, they had been seized by Tianjin Second Court, so Zhongse Trade could not take advantage of the bona fide acquisition principle. Even if the bona fide acquisition principle applied, Zhongse Trade could not own the goods because Zhongse Logistics was not the occupier of the goods. Whether Zhongse Trade was in good faith when assigning the goods involved or whether the price was reasonable did not affect the case, and the court of first instance would not speak to those two conditions further.

Fourthly, whether Kangjie, Tanghe, Zhongse Logistics and Zhongse Trade should return G&M General the two customs release sheets.

As mentioned above, Zhongse Trade failed to obtain the ownership of the goods involved. Due to the dispute over the sales of goods involved between G&M General and Datang and the Tianjin Second Court's ruling, the ownership of the 12,389 tons of goods had been transferred to Datang. G&M General owned 43,681 tons of remaining goods.

G&M General and Tanghe had a freight forwarding relationship. The customs release sheets obtained by Tanghe when it was trustee in the handling business should be returned to G&M General, but Tanghe handed over the customs release sheets to Kangjie. Then, Kangjie transferred them to Zhongse Logistics, and Zhongse Logistics transferred them to Zhongse Trade. Zhongse Trade failed to obtain ownership of the goods. Following, the possession of the customs release sheets obstructed G&M General's right to take the delivery of goods from Pengfa. According to the Property Law of the Peoples Republic of China Article 35, Tanghe, Kangjie and Zhongse Logistics should avoid nuisance and return the customs release sheets to G&M General directly. Tanghe, Kangjie and Zhongse Logistics were not in actual possession of the customs release sheets. Therefore, they did not have the obligation to return them. As for how to deal with goods involved between G&M General and Datang, it should be settled in other way.

Accordingly, according to the Property Law of the People's Republic of China Article 35, the Civil Procedure Law of the People's Republic of China Article 64 Paragraph 1, the court of first instance judged as follows: 1. G&M General should enjoy the right of ownership of the 43,581 tons of nickel ore under No.PSI-111023 and No.PSI-111024 bills of lading carried by M.V. "JIN FENG" 04 voyage. 2. Zhongse Logistics should return G&M General the two customs release sheets of the goods under No.PSI-111023 and No.PSI-111024 bills of lading carried by M.V. "JIN FENG" 04 voyage. 3. Reject other claims of G&M General. Court acceptance fee in amount of RMB100 yuan, preservation fee in amount of RMB30 yuan, should be jointly and severally born by Kangjie, Tanghe, Zhongse Logistics and Zhongse Trade.

Kangjie disagreed with judgment of first instance, and appealed to the court to revoke judgment of first instance, send back to retry or change the judgment, litigation fees of the two cases should be born by G&M General. Facts and reasons: firstly, the facts confirmed by the court of first instance were unclear. G&M General accepted the commission of Kangjie and imported the goods involved from abroad in its own name. Therefore, the relationship between Kangjie and G&M General was a contract of brokerage. The court of first instance did not confirm this legal relationship, which was wrong confirmation of fact. Secondly, application of law of the court of first instance was wrong. The goods purchased by G&M General from abroad should be delivered to the client Kangjie in time. After the goods involved arrived in Tianjin Port, through the tripartite port agency agreement, G&M General handed it over to Tanghe that was designated by Kangjie. Tanghe took the goods from the carrier and went through the relevant import procedures, and stored the goods in Pengfa's goods yard. After G&M General completed the entrusted affairs and Kangjie received the goods, G&M General only had the right to request remuneration and advance fees, not ownership of the goods. Therefore, the court of first instance applied the Property Law of the People's Republic of China to judge the case, which was wrong application of law.

As to opinions of the appeal of Kangjie, G&M General argued that: firstly, judgment of first instance held that Kangjie and G&M General were in the foreign freight forwarding contract relationship, which was correct, and the parties had no objection. The content of the foreign freight forwarding contract reflected the characteristics of multiple contract relationships, and should not simply be classified as an entrustment contract, brokerage contract or a certain type of well-known contract. Secondly, *Import Agency Agreement* and *Nickel Ore Import Agency Agreement* had clear agreement on the right of ownership of the goods involved. Kangjie did not pay the purchase price to G&M General, nor did G&M General transfer the goods rights to Kangjie. Thirdly, according to *Nickel Ore Import Agency*, Tanghe was the freight forwarder of G&M General, not an agent of Kangjie. Tanghe had no right to receive the goods involved on behalf of Kangjie. According to the agreement, after Kangjie paid the corresponding payment to G&M General, G&M General issued a valid release order to Tanghe, and the corresponding cargo rights belonged to Kangjie. However, in this case, Kangjie did not pay the payment to G&M General, nor did G&M General issue a release order to Tanghe. Therefore, Kangjie alleged that it had received the goods, and accordingly claimed that it enjoyed right of ownership, which lacked basis. Fourthly, Kangjie had admitted that the ownership of the goods involved was enjoyed by G&M General in the hearing of first instance, so it had no right to object to this. So it required the court to dismiss the appeal of Kangjie.

Zhongse Logistics and Zhongse Trade stated that, they agreed with the appeal opinions of Kangjie. G&M General was only the trustee of Kangjie and had no right to dispose of the goods involved. Kangjie was the owner of the goods involved.

Tanghe did not appear in court, and did not submit opinions in written.

Zhongse Logistics and Zhongse Trade disagreed with judgment of first instance, and appealed to the court to revoke judgment of first instance, send back to retry or change the judgment, litigation fees of the two cases should be born by G&M General. Facts and reasons: firstly, the court of first instance did not confirm that Kangjie enjoyed the right of ownership of goods involved, which was wrong confirmation of fact. 1. G&M General and Kangjie had a foreign freight forwarding contract legal relationship. Kangjie was the principal of G&M General. G&M General was only the trustee of Kangjie. 2. Under the pretext of nickel ore sales, G&M General provided Kangjie with financing, and used the goods involved as a guaranty to provide financing. 3. According to relevant regulations, enterprises must not violate the national regulations to handle lending or disguised loan financing business. Enterprise loan contracts violated relevant financial regulations and were invalid contracts. Therefore, the agreement that G&M General provided Kangjie with financing and paid off the goods before it was owned by G&M General was invalid. G&M General was only the import agent of Kangjie, and Kangjie was the real cargo owner. In addition, the customs declaration form for imported goods submitted by G&M General also clearly stated that the receiving unit was Kangjie. Secondly, the court of first instance had wrong application of law on "the goods involved have been seized by the court, whether it should be obtained in good faith", and the basic confirmation of the facts whether Tianjin Second Court conducted public announcement about the property seized. 1. According to the principle that the new law is superior to the old law, the question of whether the goods involved had been sealed up by the court should be obtained in good faith should apply the Provisions of the Supreme People's Court on the Sealing, Seizure and Freezing of Property in the Civil Enforcement of the People's Court (hereinafter referred to as the Sealing, Seizure and Freezing Regulation) but not the Reply. According to the Provisions of the Supreme People's Court on the Sealing, Seizure and Freezing of Property in the Civil Enforcement of the People's Court, for goods that had been sealed up, whether the system of good faith acquisition could be applied depended on whether the court's sealing up had been announced publicly. If the court did not directly control the property and was handed over to others, the court should affix a seal or take other measures sufficient to publicize the seal. 2. A number of employees of Zhongse Logistics had checked the site where Pengfa deposited the goods involved, but did not see the court affixing seals or other publicity measures in the warehouse or other relevant locations, G&M General also did not provide evidence to prove that the Tianjin Second Court adopted a seal or other appropriate method to publicize the seal while making the preservation decision. Unaware of the existence of the seizure, Zhongse Logistics concluded a purchases and sales contract with Kangjie, and then concluded a purchases and sales contract with Zhongse Trade. Thirdly, the court of first instance had wrong application of law on "whether Zhongse Logistics occupied the goods involved". 1. The customs release sheets had nothing to do with the setting of the guaranty, nor should the Guaranty Law Interpretation apply to its delivery. Meanwhile, the court of first instance applied analogy to the Guaranty Law Interpretation in violation of the rule of law and legal provisions. 2. The court of first instance should strictly apply the provisions of the Property Law of the People's Republic of China on the delivery of orders. Article 26 stipulated that in case a third party had legally possessed the chattel prior to the establishment or alienation of a chattel's real right, the person assuming the obligation of delivery might, instead of delivery, alien the right to request the third party to return the original object. Therefore, in this case, the key to measuring whether the goods were delivered was whether Kangjie transferred the right to request Pengfa to deliver the goods to Zhongse Logistics. Since the customs release sheets themselves represented the right to request the goods from the warehousing party, when Kangjie delivered the customs release sheets to Zhongse Logistics, it had already transferred the right to request Pengfa to deliver the goods to Zhongse Logistics. In addition, according to *Inventory Confirmation of Zhongse Logistics (Tianjin) Co., Ltd.*, it could be proved that Kangjie notified Pengfa of the fact that the right to request for delivery was transferred to Zhongse Logistics.

As to the appeal opinions of Zhongse Logistics and Zhongse Trade, G&M General argued that: firstly, the confirmation of facts of the court of first instance that G&M General was the right holder of ownership of goods involved was clear. 1. There was a foreign freight forwarding relationship between G&M General and Kangjie, and there was no financing loan relationship. The agreement on ownership between the two parties did not violate the legal provisions, and G&M General concluded a contract in its own name, and must independently bear risks and responsibilities, it was agreed that Kangjie retained ownership before payment, which was according to common sense and customary practice in foreign freight forwarding business. 2. The declaration form for imported goods could not prove that the receiving unit, Kangjie, was the owner of the goods, but could only prove that there was a foreign freight forwarding relationship between G&M General and Kangjie. 3. During the trial of first instance, Kangjie also recognized in court that the ownership of the goods involved was owned by G&M General. Secondly, the court of first instance confirmed that Zhongse Logistics and Zhongse Trade did not apply the system of good faith acquisition, which was correct. Because the bona fide acquisition of the movable property right must be a condition where a person of unauthorized disposal occupies the property and completes the delivery, because Zhongse Logistics had never occupied the goods involved, it did not meet the legal requirements for bona fide acquisition, so it was correct that the court of first instance comprehensively judged that Zhongse Trade could not obtain ownership of the goods involved from Zhongse Logistics based on the system of good faith acquisition. Thirdly, the legal nature of customs release sheets of the court of first instance was correct. 1. The bill of lading was the proof of the ownership of the goods only when the goods represented by the bill of lading were in transit by sea. The consignee exchanged the bill of lading for the customs release sheet. The carrier's recovery of the bill of lading meant the end of the transportation and there were no longer any goods transported on the way. Therefore, the legal facts and conditions of the customs bill of lading as a proof of property had disappeared. 2. The customs release sheet as a proof of property right lacked a legal basis. 3. The customs release sheet was only the procedure and certificate issued by the carrier to the consignee to take the goods at the port, and it was just a general certificate of creditor's rights. Fourthly, the contract consideration paid by Zhongse Logistics to Kangjie and the contract price paid by Zhongse Trade to Zhongse Logistics were unreasonable, so acquisition in good faith should not apply. Fifthly, Zhongse Trade, Zhongse Logistics, Kangjie, and Purple Mine constituted a financing loan relationship, which violated the prohibitive provisions of Chinese financial regulations, and the contract concluded by them should be invalid. Therefore, Zhongse Logistics and Zhongse Trade could not obtain the right of ownership of goods involved and the corresponding customs release sheets.

Kangjie stated that, it agreed with the appeal opinions of Zhongse Logistics and Zhongse Trade.

Tanghe did not appear in court, and did not submit opinions in written.

During second instance, Zhongse Logistics submitted an additional seal notice from other court, to prove that the court should take appropriate measures sufficient to publicize the seizure when carrying out the preservation.

G&M General cross-examined that, this piece of evidence was the content of the online query, which could not confirm the authenticity, and the court had many forms of publicity, not limited to the announcement.

Kangjie and Zhongse Trade recognized the authenticity, legality and relevancy of the above evidence.

G&M General submitted the following evidence: evidence 1, nickel ore price on April 23, 2014 published on websites, to prove that the price of Zhongse Logistics' sale of the goods involved to Zhongse Trade was lower than 70% of the market price. Zhongse Trade did not constitute a good faith acquisition; evidence 2, nickel ore price on May 9, 2014 published on websites, to prove that the price of Zhongse Trade's sale of the goods involved to Purple Mine was lower than 50% of the market price, which indicated that Kangjie, Zhongse Logistics, Zhongse Trade and Purple Mine had a financing relationship called trading, which was actually a loan, not a normal trading relationship.

Kangjie cross-examined that: the above evidence was from the Internet, and was not notarized, so it did not recognize the authenticity, legality and relevancy.

Tanghe did not appear in court, and did not submit cross-examination opinion in written.

Kangjie, Zhongse Trade and Tanghe did not submit new evidence.

After comprehensive analysis of the parties' evidence and cross-examination opinions, the court holds that, the evidence submitted by Zhongse Logistics can be checked on website, so the court confirms the authenticity, but the evidence had no relevancy to the case, so the court does not confirm the purpose of proof. The two groups of evidence submitted by G&M General can be checked on website, so the court confirms the authenticity, the purpose of proof shall be confirmed combined with other evidence.

The facts found out by the court of first instance could be proved by evidence, so the court confirms them.

The court also finds out that, on October 17, 2011, G&M General and Kangjie concluded in *Import Agency Agreement* that "G&M General is responsible for issuing a 90-day forward letter of credit according to the foreign trade contract after receiving the RMB4.028 million guaranty deposit paid by Kangjie. If Kangjie fails to pay the deposit to G&M General in a timely manner, and G&M General cannot issue the certificate on time, the relevant responsibility shall be born by the Kangjie. The ratio of the margin for the issuance of the issuance is 15% of the total value of the foreign trade contract. After Kangjie pays each payment, G&M General should transfer the corresponding cargo rights to Kangjie on the day of payment; if Kangjie fails to pay off the goods in time, G&M General has the right to process the goods and confiscate the deposit".

On May 8, 2012, the outsider Datang as the buyer and G&M General as the seller signed *Purchases and Sales Contract* with the number xxx-GFNK003-015,701 that Datang purchased the laterite nickel mine from G&M General. G&M General issued a special invoice for value-added tax of RMB31,623,050 yuan to Datang in batches on May 15 and May 25, 2012. On May 22, May 23, and May 24, 2012, Kangjie paid RMB23,064,000 yuan in batches to G&M General through transfers and remittances. The payment was recorded as collection and payment for Datang. G&M General recorded this payment as the payment for Kangjie in the company's accounting vouchers. On May 25, 2012, Kangjie issued a receipt to Datang, stating that it received RMB23.064 million yuan from Datang. On May 29, 2012, Datang paid two forward acceptance bills totaling RMB7 million yuan to G&M General. On June 25, 2012, G&M General issued the *Official Letter of Transfer of Cargo Rights* to Datang and instructed the freight forwarder to release the goods, and delivered 12,389 tons of goods to Datang.

Zhongse Trade was the sole shareholder of Zhongse Logistics.

The tax-included prices of the laterite nickel mines published in the same interval as the goods involved grade specifications at the Tianjin Port on April 23, 2014 were 590–620 yuan/ton, 600–640 yuan/ton, 650–670 yuan/ton, 580–610 yuan/ton.

The court holds that: the case is the dispute over return of customs release sheets. Issues are that: firstly, how to confirm the right of ownership of goods involved; secondly, whether Zhongse Logistics and Zhongse Trade obtained the goods involved in good faith.

Firstly, how to confirm the right of ownership of goods involved.

Import Agency Agreement concluded by G&M General and Kangjie, *Nickel Ore Import Agency Agreement* concluded by G&M General, Kangjie and Tanghe were the true intention of the parties, the contents did not violate the laws and regulations, so they are legal and valid. According to *Import Agency Agreement*, entrusted by Kangjie, G&M General was responsible for importing nickel ore, and finally should take *Purchases and Sales Contract* concluded by G&M General and the foreign seller DH as the foreign trade import contract determined by the agreement. Meanwhile, *Import Agency Agreement* also clearly stipulated the conditions and timing of the transfer of ownership of the goods involved, namely after Kangjie paid each batch of payment, G&M General transferred the corresponding right of goods on the payment day. Afterwards, *Nickel Ore Import Agency Agreement* concluded by G&M General, Kangjie and Tanghe further clarified that the ownership of the goods involved belonged to G&M General and detailed the process of transferring the ownership of the goods, namely after receiving the delivery order from G&M General, the ownership of the corresponding goods belonged to Kangjie. At the same time, Tanghe should strictly follow the delivery order of G&M General. In this case, after fulfilling the payment obligations under *Purchases and Sales Contract*, G&M General obtained the ownership of the goods under the above bill of lading after obtaining the two original bills of lading PSI-111023 and PSI-111024 by way of letter of credit, then it obtained the right of ownership. When Kangjie did not pay the goods, the ownership of the goods did not transfer.

Regarding Zhongse Logistics and Zhongse Trade, Kangjie paid the total amount of RMB23,064,000 yuan in batches, the two forward acceptance drafts of RMB7,000,000 yuan, and the guaranty deposit of RMB4,028,000 yuan, which fulfilled payment obligation under *Import Agency Agreement* and obtained the ownership of the goods according to law. The court holds that, RMB4.028 million yuan guaranty deposit is a performance guaranty set by G&M General and Kangjie in *Import Agency Agreement*, and the applicable conditions are agreed. When Kangjie failed to fulfill the obligation to pay for the goods under *Import Agency Agreement*, the liability of the deposit and the offset of the money belonged to the rights claims between specific parties under the agreement. Kangjie did not raise this defense. Zhongse Logistics and Zhongse Trade also did not provide evidence to prove the actual payment of the money, so the court does not confirm it. In case of disputes, G&M General and Kangjie may settle separately. Meanwhile, according to the judgment in effect in another case, it was determined that the payment of Kangjie on behalf of Datang was RMB23,064,000 yuan and the forward acceptance bill paid by Datang was RMB7 million yuan, which was the behavior under the purchase and sale contract but not the performance of Kangjie's obligation to pay for the goods under *Import Agency Agreement*. Because Zhongse Logistics and Zhongse Trade failed to provide the opposite evidence sufficient to overturn the fact, according to the Interpretation of the Supreme People's Court on the application of the Civil Procedure Law of the People's Republic of China Article 93 that the facts that have been confirmed by the legally effective judgment of the people's court need not be proved by the parties, unless the parties have the contrary evidence sufficient to overturn, the court does not support the claim of it.

Meanwhile, after obtaining the ownership of the goods involved through the payment of redemption of letter of credit, G&M General sold it to Datang, according to the determination of the effective judgment in another case, Datang obtained the ownership of 12,389 tons of goods involved according to law. According to the Property Law of the People's Republic of China Article 28, if the legal documents of the people's court or arbitration committy or the expropriation decision of the people's government lead to the establishment, alteration, transfer or extinction of property rights, the legal document or the expropriation decision of the people's government shall take legal effect, from the date when the judgment in the other case came into effect, Datang had ownership of 12,389 tons of the 55,970 tons of goods involved, and G&M General had ownership of the remaining 43,581 tons of goods.

Secondly, whether Zhongse Logistics and Zhongse Trade obtained the goods involved in good faith.

As to whether the property sealed up by the people's court according to law applied to the acquisition in good faith. According to the Provisions of the Supreme People's Court on the Sealing, Seizure and Freezing of Property in the Civil Enforcement of the People's Court, Article 8, if the movable property is sealed up or seized, the people's court may directly control the property. If the people's court delivers the sealed and seized movable property to the control of another person, it shall affix a seal to the movable property or adopt other appropriate means sufficient to publicize the sealed and seized property. During the seizure of the goods involved, Tianjin Second Court, though it was not suitable for direct control of possession due to the bulk of the goods, was then handed over to the warehousing party Pengfa for continued control, and Tanghe and Pengfa were served to assist the implementation book, the action only took effect against Tanghe and Pengfa, and did not produce sufficient publicity effects. Meanwhile, according to Article 26 Paragraph 3, if the people's court's sealing, seizure or freezing is not publicly announced, its effectiveness should not be against a bona fide third party, in the absence of evidence that Tianjin Second Court adopted seals, announcements, or other actions sufficient to publicize that the goods involved have been sealed, the effectiveness of the sealing of the goods involved cannot be against a bona fide third party. According to the Property Law of the People's Republic of China, the third party can obtain the ownership of the goods involved in good faith.

As to whether Zhongse Logistics and Zhongse Trade obtained the goods involved in good faith. The court holds that, the basis of the system of obtaining in good faith is the principle of publicity of the property rights, and the property rights have the credibility after publicity, even if the content of the announcement and the ownership are inconsistent, the transferee who reasonably trusts the announcement as a bona fide third party should also protect its trading interests. According to the Property Law of the People's Republic of China Article 106, the assignee should obtain the ownership of the real property or movable property: (1) the assignee accepted the real property or movable property in good faith; (2) the real property or movable property was transferred at a reasonable price; (3) the transferred real property or movable property should have been registered in case registration was required by law, and should have been delivered to the assignee in case registration was not required. The court analyzes them as follows:

1. As to the problem about good faith. The two customs release sheets involved were not proof of property rights, but a kind of claim voucher requesting the withdrawal of the goods involved. It cannot be assumed that the holder of the customs release sheets was the owner of the goods, and thus the holder held the goods indirectly. Although there were other similar trade transactions between Kangjie and Zhongse Logistics, this background was only a reference factor for judging whether the trust was reasonable or not, and it cannot reduce its duty of care. Especially when the customs released sheets involved were converted from copies of the bill of lading, the consignee's notify party recorded on it was G&M General not Kangjie. As a trading company, Zhongse Logistics should possess professional judgment ability and corresponding legal knowledge, and had a relatively high duty of care. In the case where Zhongse Logistics did not provide evidence to prove that it took active measures to verify the ownership of the goods with the relevant units and finally reached reasonable trust, its misunderstanding of the nature of the customs release sheets cannot be a reason for good faith.
2. As to the problem about delivery of movable property. The goods involved were deposited in Pengfa, belonging to the situation of third party's possession. In the

case of no direct delivery in this case, only the method of instructional delivery could be used. Though the Property Law of the People's Republic of China Article 26 has relevant provision about instructional delivery, namely in case a third party has legally possessed the chattel prior to the establishment or alienation of a chattel's real right, the person assuming the obligation of delivery may, instead of delivery, alien the right to request the third party to return the original object, the conditions for the establishment of the right to request the third party to return the reduced object are not specified. In this regard, the court holds that instructional delivery, as a conceptual delivery, only occurs with the transfer of the right of return and indirect possession, and the lack of direct possession changes results in the lack of publicity in the change of property rights, according to the Guaranty Law Interpretation Article 88, where the pledgor takes possession of the property which is indirectly possessed, it shall be deemed to be the handover when the owner of the pledge contract is notified in writing, the notification of the direct occupier should be regarded as a condition for the completion of delivery. In this case, Kangjie failed to fulfill the obligation to deliver the goods involved when Zhongse Logistics did not provide evidence to prove that Kangjie had notified Pengfa of the fact that it had transferred its right to request for delivery.

In conclusion, Zhongse Logistics failed to fulfill its due diligence obligations when accepting the goods involved, which cannot be deemed as in good faith, and failure to meet the notification conditions for delivery instructions in the case of third party's possession, so regardless of whether the transaction price was reasonable, Zhongse Logistics failed to meet the conditions for obtaining in good faith and did not have ownership of the goods involved.

As to the problem about whether Zhongse Trade obtained the goods involved in good faith. The court holds that, without obtaining ownership, Zhongse Logistics sold the goods involved to Zhongse Trade, which was an act of no right to dispose. In the course of this transaction, as mentioned above, the duty to pay attention to the contents of the customs release sheets was not fulfilled, and the wrong understanding of the nature of the customs release sheets cannot be a reason for Zhongse Trade to have good faith. Meanwhile, under the system of good faith acquisition, when Zhongse Logistics has no right to dispose of the goods involved, Zhongse Trade, as the sole shareholder of Zhongse Logistics, should have an investment holding relationship and the difference between the transaction price and the mainstream transaction price between the two companies as reference factors for whether Zhongse Trade had good faith. sealed up the goods involved and served Pengfa with a notice of assistance of enforcement, Pengfa, as the warehousing party, always actually occupied the goods, if Pengfa maliciously disposed or cooperated with others in maliciously disposing of the goods involved, it would expose it to the risk of corresponding civil and even criminal liability, as a rational market subject, Pengfa's seal confirmation of the transfer of ownership of the goods was inconsistent with common sense without the interest in the ownership of the goods involved. Combined with *Statement of Transfer Certificate being Invalid regarding the Ownership of Nickel Ore on M.V. "JIN FENG"*, there are reasons to suspect that during the transaction between Zhongse Logistics and Zhongse Trade, the date of formation of the relevant documents does not match the time of payment, and this further shook the foundation of the integrity of the transaction between Zhongse Logistics and Zhongse Trade. Taking all of the above into consideration, the court holds that Zhongse Trade Corporation does not have good faith in the transaction of the goods involved.

As to the problem about the rationality of the transfer price between Zhongse Logistics and Zhongse Trade. Neither Zhongse Logistics nor Zhongse Trade provided the price reference basis on the transaction day, nor submitted evidence to prove the reasonableness of their transaction prices. According to the evidence submitted in second instance of G&M General, a comprehensive comparison of the transaction prices published on the four websites showed that on April 23, 2014, the transaction price range of laterite nickel mines in the same range as the goods involved in Tianjin Port was 580–670 yuan/ton. According to the Interpretation of the Supreme People's Court on Several Issues concerning the Application of the Contract Law of the People's Republic of China (II) Article 19, if the transfer price does not reach the guide price of the trading place at the time of the transaction or the market transaction price is 70%, it can generally be regarded as a clearly unreasonable low price. Even if the lowest value of the above price range was 580 yuan/ton as the reference price, the transaction price of 371 yuan/ton between Zhongse Logistics and Zhongse Trade had not reached 70% of the reference price, so the transaction price should not be regarded as a reasonable price. Zhongse Logistics and Zhongse Trade proposed that the two companies had a controlling relationship, so they could determine the internal transaction price by themselves, and the price determination was also related to the borrowing background between shareholders. The court holds that, subject to the right to punish and do not harm the interests of third parties, market subjects may follow the principle of equality and fairness, determine the transaction price autonomously according to their will, and be protected by law. Specifically, in the case of the system of good faith acquisition in this case, the determination of price is of course the market subject's independent negotiation, but the reasonable price is the prerequisite for the legal protection of the bona fide third party, but not the parties can dispose of their own rights, so the court does not support the claim of Zhongse Logistics and Zhongse Trade.

In conclusion, in the process of trading, Zhongse Trade cannot be regarded as good faith, and the transaction price was not a reasonable price. Therefore, regardless of whether Zhongse Logistics delivered the goods, Zhongse Trade did not meet the conditions for obtaining in good faith and did not have any ownership.

As mentioned above, Kangjie was not the owner of the goods involved, nor had Zhongse Logistics and Zhongse Trade constituted acquisition in good faith. After the two customs clearance sheets involved were transferred to Zhongse Trade, as for whether G&M General had the right to claim the return. The court holds that, G&M General entrusted Tanghe to handle port operations for the goods involved, and the two parties established a freight forwarding contract relationship. The customs release sheets were the trustee's property acquired in the process of handling the entrusted matters, and the entrusting G&M General was entitled to the ownership. However, Tanghe handed over the customs release sheets to Kangjie, and finally transferred to Zhongse Trade through Zhongse Logistics. The possession behavior of Zhongse Trade hindered the exercise of the rights of G&M General. According to the Property Law of the People's Republic of China Article 35, in case a real right is under obstruction or may be obstructed, the right holder may require the removing of the impediment or the termination of the danger, G&M General had the right to claim the return of the customs release sheets to Zhongse Trade.

Pulling the thread together, the facts confirmed by the court of first instance were clear, and the application of law was correct. The appeal of Kangjie, Zhongse Logistics, Zhongse Trade lacks basis, so the court does not support it. According to the Civil Procedure Law of the People's Republic of China Article 170 Paragraph 1 Sub-paragraph 1, the judgment is as follows:

Dismiss the appeal, and affirm the original judgment.

Court acceptance fee of first instance in amount of RMB100 yuan, preservation fee in amount of RMB30 yuan, shall be born according to judgment of first instance, court acceptance fee of second instance in amount of RMB300 yuan, the Appellants, Tianjin Kangjie Import and Export Trade Co., Ltd., Zhongse Logistics (Tianjin) Co., Ltd. and Zhongse International Trade Co., Ltd. shall bear RMB100 yuan respectively.

The judgment is final.

Presiding Judge: GENG Xiaoning
Acting Judge: LI Shanchuan
Acting Judge: TANG Na

August 5, 2015

Clerk: SUN Chao

Wuhan Maritime Court
Civil Judgment

China Guangfa Bank Stock Co., Ltd. Nanjing Chengxi Branch
v.
Nanjing Hengshunda Shipping Co., Ltd. et al.

(2015) Wu Hai Fa Shang Zi No.00205

Related Case(s) None.

Cause(s) of Action 211. Dispute over ship mortgage contract.

Headnote Mortgagee bank held to be entitled to recover in full from mortgagor shipowner and guarantors for failure to repay loan, mortgagee to be entitled to priority payment from sale of vessels provided as security for the loan.

Summary The Plaintiff China Guangfa Bank claimed that the Defendant Nanjing Hengshunda Shipping Co., Ltd. had repaid neither the principal nor the interest on a RMB30 million loan it had received from the bank and that it was liable for repayment of the full amount including interest. Furthermore, the Plaintiff claimed that the Defendants Jiangsu Huahai Shipping Group, Gao Sheng, and Gao Liying were jointly and severally liable as guarantors for repayment of the debt and that the bank was entitled to priority payment of the debt from the sale of vessels posted as security by the Defendants Nanjing Hengshunda Shipping Co., Ltd., Wuhu Chenguang Shipping Co., Ltd. and Nanjing Haijin Shipping Co., Ltd. The court found fully in favor of Plaintiff China Guangfa Bank regarding its claims against all the Defendants.

Judgment

The Plaintiff: China Guangfa Bank Stock Co., Ltd. Nanjing Chengxi Branch
Domicile: No.73 Beijing West Road, Gulou District, Nanjing, Jiangsu.
Organization code: 77,397,130–0.
Legal representative: WANG Gang, president.
Agent *ad litem*: TAO Yongxiang, lawyer of Jiangsu Tongda Law Firm.

The Defendant: Nanjing Hengshunda Shipping Co., Ltd.
Domicile: Room505, No.300 Emei Road, Xiongzhou Street, Liuhe District, Nanjing, Jiangsu.
Organization code: 71,624,845–8.
Legal representative: GAO Sheng, chairman of the board.
Agent *ad litem*: WANG Liang, male, Han, born on February5, 1979, employee.
Domicile: Room107, No.59 Changjinglou West Street, Xuanwu District, Nanjing, Jiangsu.

The Defendant: Jiangsu Huahai Shipping Group
Domicile: Room 309, No.105 Heng Shun Yuan Building, No.399 Xiongzhou South Road, Longchi Street, Liuhe District, Nanjing, Jiangsu.
Organization code: 24,990,122–6.
Legal representative: GAO Cunhao, general manager.
Agent *ad litem*: ZHU Xiaolong, lawyer of Beijing Zhongyin(Nanjing) Law Firm.

The Defendant: GAO Sheng, male, Han, born on January 1, 1970
Domicile: No.165 Kanwo, Kan'ao Village, Suao Town, Pingtan County, Fujian.
Agent *ad litem*: WANG Liang, male, Han, born onFebruary5, 1979.
Domicile: Room107, No.59 Changjinglou West Street, Xuanwu District, Nanjing, Jiangsu.

The Defendant: GAO Liying,female, Han, born onSeptember11, 1971
Domicile: No.165 Kanwo, Kan'ao Village, Suao Town, Pingtan County, Fujian.
Agent *ad litem*: WANG Liang, male, Han, born on February 5,1979.
Domicile: Room107, No.59 Changjinglou West Street, Xuanwu District, Nanjing, Jiangsu.

The Defendant: Wuhu Chenguang Shipping Co., Ltd.
Domicile: No.16 Jiusan Road, Huaqiao Industrial Park, Wuhu County, Anhui.
Organization code: 14,957,024–7.
Legal representative: GAO Sheng, chairman of the board.
Agent *ad litem*: WANG Liang, male, Han, born on February5, 1979.
Domicile: Room107, No.59 Changjinglou West Street, Xuanwu District, Nanjing, Jiangsu.

The Defendant: Nanjing Haijin Shipping Co., Ltd.
Domicile: Room 542, No.300 Emei Road, Xiongzhou Street, Liuhe District, Nanjing, Jiangsu.
Organization code: 57,156,012–4.
Legal representative: ZHANG Xingguo, chairman of the board.
Agent *ad litem*: WANG Liang, male, Han, born on February5,1979.
Domicile: Room107, No.59 Changjinglou West Street, Xuanwu District, Nanjing, Jiangsu.

With respect to the case arising from dispute over ship mortgage contract filed by the Plaintiff China Guangfa Bank Stock Co., Ltd. Nanjing Chengxi Branch (hereinafter referred to as "Guangfa Bank")against the Defendants, Nanjing Hengshunda Shipping Co., Ltd. (hereinafter referred to as "HSD"),Jiangsu Huahai Shipping Group.(hereinafter referred to as "Huahai"), Wuhu Chenguang Shipping Co., Ltd. (hereinafter referred to as "Chenguang"), Nanjing Haijin Shipping Co., Ltd. (hereinafter referred to as "Haijin"), GAO Sheng and GAO Liying, the Plaintiff Guangfa Bank applied for property preservation before litigation and requested the court to freeze the above Defendants' bank deposits of RMB 30 million yuan or seal up, freeze other properties at equal value on January15, 2015, the court made a ruling permitting the application. On January21, 2015, the Plaintiff Guangfa Bank filed an action to the court. This case is concerning dispute over maritime contract which is under the exclusive jurisdiction of maritime court, and the domiciles of the Defendants HSD, Huahai, Chenguang and Haijin are all under the jurisdiction of the court, the court has jurisdiction over the case according to the Civil Procedure Law of the People's Republic of China Article 23. After entertaining the case, the court appointed Judge YAN Hong to solely hear the case. The court held the hearing in public on April 8, 2015, TAO Yongxiang, the agent *ad litem* of the Plaintiff Guangfa Bank, WANG Liang, the agent *ad litem* of the Defendants HSD, Chenguang, Haijin, GAO Sheng and GAO Liying, and ZHU Xiaolong, the agent *ad litem* of the Defendant Huahai appeared in court and participated in the litigious action. During the hearing, the parties, upon mediation under the direction of the court, failed to reach an agreement for great divergence. After trial, now the case has been concluded.

The Plaintiff Guangfa Bank alleged that, on September 17, 2012, the Plaintiff loaned RMB30 million yuan to the Defendant HSD and the loan period was one year. On September 25, 2013, the Plaintiff Guangfa Bank extended the loan period of the principal in amount of RMB30 million yuan owed by the Defendant HSD for one year, the Defendant HSD took its ship M.V. "HENG SHUN DA 88", the Defendant Chenguang took its ship M.V. "XIN CHEN MIN" and the Defendant Haijin took its ship M.V. "HAI JIN 58" as mortgage for the Defendant HSD's above RMB30 million rollover loan. The Defendant Huahai, GAO Sheng and GAO Li Ying provided surety for the loan. After the expiration of the loan, the Defendant HSD failed to pay any principal and interest. Therefore, the Plaintiff Guangfa Bank requested the court to order that: 1.the Defendant HSD should repay the principal in amount of RMB30million yuan to the Plaintiff and pay the interest thereon (the interest should be calculated at the rate of 7.8% per annum of the loan principal RMB30million over the period from December 21, 2013, the next day the Defendant HSD paid the interest for the last time to the date confirmed by the court); 2. the Defendants Huahai, GAO Sheng and GAO Li Ying should bear the joint and several liability to cover above debt; 3. the Plaintiff Guangfa Bank the collaterals provided by the Defendants HSD, Chenguang and Haijin for the above loan and be entitled to be paid in priority by the proceeds of auction or sale; 4. the litigation costs should be born by the Defendants.

The Defendants HSD, Chenguang, Haijin, GAO Sheng and GAO Liying acknowledged the fact of loan and had no objection to the Plaintiff Guangfa Bank's claims.

The Defendant Huahai defended: 1. the other Defendants had provided guarantee in full amount for the debt involved and the Defendant Huahai only provided surety, the obligee should realize the mortgage right in priority; 2. it did not know the matter the Plaintiff Guangfa Bank underwent the rollover, its liability for guarantee should be exempted.

The Plaintiff Guangfa Bank summited the following evidence to support its claims:

1. *RMB Short-term Loan Contract* and receipt for a loan, to prove that the Plaintiff Guangfa Bank granted RMB30million yuan loan to the Defendant HSD.
2. *Surety Contract* concluded by the Defendant Huahai and the Plaintiff Guangfa Bank, *Surety Contract* signed by the Defendants GAO Sheng, GAO Li Ying and the Plaintiff Guangfa Bank, *Mortgage Contract* concluded by the Defendants HSD, Chenguang, Haijin and the Plaintiff Guangfa Bank, to prove that the Defendant HSD borrowed RMB30million yuan from the Plaintiff Guangfa Bank, the Defendants Huahai, GAO Sheng and GAO Li Ying provided guarantee of surety liability for the Defendant HSD, the Defendants HSD, Chenguang and Haijin provided mortgage guarantee.
3. *Contract of RMBLoan Rollover* and *Mortgage Contract* concluded by the Defendants HSD, Chenguang and Haijin respectively with the Plaintiff Guangfa Bank about the loan rollover, to prove the Defendants Huahai, GAO Sheng and GAO Li Ying provided guarantee and the Defendants HSD, Chenguang and Haijin provided mortgage guarantee for the loan rollover.
4. Certificates of mortgage registration of three ships M.V. "HENG SHUN DA 88", M.V. "XIN CHENMIN" and M.V. "HAI JIN 58", to prove above ships had been undertook mortgage registration for the loan rollover and the Plaintiff Guangfa Bank was the mortgagee.
5. Payment voucher of litigation fees and preservation fees, to prove the Plaintiff Guangfa Bank paid litigation fee and preservation fee of this case.

All the Defendants did not summit any evidence to the court.

All the Defendants had no objection to the authenticity of the evidence summitted by the Plaintiff Guangfa Bank, the court ascertains the evidence that summitted by the Plaintiff Guangfa Bank.

After trial, the court finds that on September 17,2012, the Defendant HSD and the Plaintiff Guangfa Bank signed *RMB Short-term Loan Contract* numbered with (136,131)12 Yin Ren Duan Dai Zi No.011, agreed that the amount of loan was RMB30million yuan and the loan period was one year, from September 17, 2012 to September 16, 2013, the interest should be settled per season and paid regularly, the principal should be repaid at maturity. On the same day, the Defendants GAO Sheng and GAO Li Ying signed *Surety Contract* with the Plaintiff Guangfa Bank, agreeing that the master contract of the guarantee contract was *RMB Short-term*

Loan Contract concluded by the Defendant HSD and the Plaintiff Guangfa Bank on September 17, 2012 and its amendments or supplements(including but not limited to contract of rollover); the method of guarantee was joint and several liability for guarantee, if there were several guarantors, every guarantor was joint guarantor and should bear joint and several liability for guarantee; the scope of guarantee liability included the principal, interest, penalty interest, compound interest, liquidate damages and damages under the master contract, fees arising from realizing the rights of creditor and mortgage (including but not limited to litigation fees, arbitration fees and attorney's fees) and the other accrued expense; the period of guarantee was two years, starting from the expiry date of the obligor's performance of obligation under the master contract. On that day, the Defendant Huahai also signed *Surety Contract* with the Plaintiff Guangfa Bank for the Defendant HSD's loan, of which the contents were basically the same as those of the above-mentioned *Surety Contract*.

For the loan under *RMB Short-term Loan Contract* numbered with (136,131)12 Yin Ren Duan Dai Zi No.011 and concluded by the Defendant HSD and the Plaintiff Guangfa Bank, the Defendants HSD, Chenguang and Haijin signed *Mortgage Contract* respectively with the Plaintiff Guangfa Bank on September 17,2012, the Defendant HSD took its ship M.V. "HENG SHUN DA 88", the Defendant Chenguang took its ship M.V. "XIN CHEN MIN" and the Defendant Haijin took its ship M.V. "HAI JIN 58" as mortgage to the Plaintiff Guangfa Bank, the scope of mortgage was the same as the scope of guarantee of the above-mentioned *Surety Contract*. Thereafter, the ship mortgage registration certificates of M.V."HENG SHUN DA 88", M.V. "XIN CHEN MIN" and M.V. "HAI JIN 58" whose mortgagee was the Plaintiff Guangfa Bank were undertook at the ship registration authority, the registered amount of guarantee of M.V. "HENG SHUN DA 88" was RMB9,181,800 yuan, the registered amount of guarantee of M.V."XIN CHEN MIN" was RMB9,385,500 yuan, and that of M.V."HAI JIN 58" was RMB11,432,700 yuan.

On September 26, 2012, the Plaintiff Guangfa Bank granted the loan in amount of RMB 30 million yuan to the Defendant HSD. Due to failure for repaying the loan after the expiry date, the Defendant HSD and the Plaintiff Guangfa Bank signed *Contract of RMB Loan Rollover* on September 25,2013, the guarantors expressed therein, the Defendants Huahai, GAO Sheng and GAO Li Ying also signed the contract. It was agreed that the rollover period was one year, from September 25, 2013 to September24, 2014, the fixed rate of the rollover was 7.8%, the interest should be settled per season, 20th of the first month of every quarter was the interest settlement day and 21st was the interest payment day. The principal and interest should be paid off at the expiry date of the loan. On the same day, the Defendants HSD, Chenguang and Haijin respectively signed *Mortgage Contract* with the Plaintiff Guangfa Bank again, the master contract was *Contract of RMB Loan Rollover* signed by the Defendant HSD and the Plaintiff Guangfa Bank on September 25, 2013, the scope of mortgage was the same as those of the previously signed *Mortgage Contract*.

During the period of loan, the Defendant HSD paid the interest until December 20, 2013, and stopped paying the interest from December 21, 2013 and had not paid the principal.

The court holds that the case is arising from dispute over a bottomry bond. *RMB Short-term Loan Contract, Contract of RMB Loan Rollover, Mortgage Contract of Maximum Amount* and *Surety Contract* signed by the Plaintiff Guangfa Bank respectively with the Defendants HSD, Huahai, GAO Sheng, GAO Li Ying, Chenguang and Haijin, are declarations of true intent of the parties concerned, established according to the law and should be legal and effective, every party should exercise civil rights according to the contract and law and perform the contract obligation fully and honestly.

According to the agreement of *RMB Short-term Loan Contract*, the Plaintiff Guangfa Bank provided RMB 30 million yuan loan to the Defendant HSD, the Defendant HSD failed to repay the principal and the interest at the expiry date and after the period of rollover as agreed, which constitutes default, the Plaintiff Guangfa Bank was entitled to the principal and the interest by the Defendant HSD according to the agreement of contract. The Plaintiff Guangfa Bank's claim that the Defendant HSD should repay the principal in amount of RMB 30 million yuan and the interest thereon (the interest should be calculated at the rate of 7.8% per annum on base of the loan principal RMB30million yuan over the period from December 21, 2013, the next day the Defendant HSD paid interest for the last time to the date designated by the court when the principal and interest would be paid off) had contractual basis and did not violate the prohibitive provisions of law and regulations, the court supports the Plaintiff's claims.

The Defendants Huahai, GAO Sheng, GAO Li Ying signed *Surety Contract* with the Plaintiff Guangfa Bank, should as agreed bear the joint and several liability for the principal, interest, penalty interest, compound interest of the loan that owed by the Defendant HSD, fees arising from realizing the creditor's right and so on. The Defendant Huahai defended that it did not know the rollover of loan owed by the Defendant HSD, its liability for guarantee should be exempted. However, *Surety Contract* signed by the Plaintiff Guangfa Bank and the Defendant Huahai expressed that the master contract was *RMB Short-term Loan Contract* which was signed by the Defendant HSD and the Plaintiff Guangfa Bank on September 17, 2012 and its amendments or supplements (including but not limited to the contract of rollover), and *Contract of RMB Loan Rollover* signed by the Defendant HSD and the Plaintiff Guangfa Bank on September 25, 2013 ranked the Defendant Huahai as guarantor, the Defendant Huahai also signed on *Contract of RMB Loan Rollover*, so the Defendants Huahai's above defenses cannot be supported by the court.

The Defendants HSD, Chenguang and Haijin respectively took their own ships M.V. "HENG SHUN DA 88", M.V. "XIN CHEN MIN" and M.V. "HAI JIN 58" as mortgage for the Defendant HSD's loan, when the Defendant HSD defaulted the obligation, the Plaintiff Guangfa Bank should be entitled to be paid in priority from the payment from converting the collateral into money, or the proceeds of the auction or sale of the ships according to the contract and law.

The Property Law of the People's Republic of China Article 176 provides, where a secured credit involves both physical and personal security, if the obligor fails to pay its due debts or any circumstance for realizing the property for security as stipulated by the parties concerned occurs, the obligee shall realize the obligee's rights according to the stipulations; where there is no such stipulation or the stipulations are not explicit, and the obligor provides his/its own property for the security, the obligee shall realize the obligee's rights firstly by the security by property; and where a third party provides the security by property, the obligee may realize the obligee's rights with the physical security or may require the guarantor to assume the guaranty liability. The third party for providing the security may, after assuming the security liability, is entitled to recourse payments against the obligor. According to this article, the Plaintiff Guangfa Bank should realize the creditor's right from the collateral M.V. "HENG SHUN DA 88" provided by the Defendants HSD in priority.

Pulling the thread together, the Plaintiff Guangfa Bank's claims are legal and based on fact, the court supports its claims according to law.

According to the Contract Law of the People's Republic of China Article 107, Article 205, Article 206 and Article 207, the Property Law of the People's Republic of China Article 173, Article 176, Article 179 and Article 195, the Guaranty Law of the People's Republic of China Article 18 and Article 21 Paragraph 1, the Civil Procedure Law of the People's Republic of China Article 142, the judgment is as follows:

1. The Defendant Nanjing Hengshunda Shipping Co., Ltd. shall payback loan principal in amount of RMB30million and the interest thereon to the Plaintiff China Guangfa Bank Co., Ltd. Nanjing Chengxi Branch (the interest shall be calculated at the rate of 7.8% per annum ascertained by the contract over the period from 21 December 2013 to the date of payment ascertained by the judgment);
2. The Plaintiff China Guangfa Bank Co., Ltd. Nanjing Chengxi Branch enjoys the right of mortgage over M.V. "HENG SHUN DA 88" which is owned by the Defendant Nanjing Hengshunda Shipping Co., Ltd., it is entitled to be paid in priority from the proceeds of auction, sale of M.V. "HENG SHUN DA 88" or converting M.V. "HENG SHUN DA 88" into money within RMB9,181,800 according to the creditor's right ascertained by the first term of judgment, and realize the creditor's right from the collateral M.V. "HENG SHUN DA 88" owned by the Defendant Nanjing Hengshunda Shipping Co., Ltd. in priority;
3. The Plaintiff China Guangfa Bank Co., Ltd. Nanjing Chengxi Branch enjoys the right of mortgage over M.V. "XIN CHEN MIN" owned by the Defendant Wuhu Chenguang Shipping Co., Ltd., it is entitled to be paid in priority from the proceeds of auction or sale of M.V. "XIN CHEN MIN" or converting M.V. "XIN CHEN MIN" into money within RMB9,385,500 according to the creditor's right ascertained by the first term of judgment;

4. The Plaintiff China Guangfa Bank Co., Ltd. Nanjing Chengxi Branch enjoys the right of mortgage over M.V. "HAI JIN 58" owned by the Defendant Nanjing Haijin Shipping Co., Ltd., it is entitled to be paid in priority from the proceeds of auction or sale of M.V. "HAI JIN 58" or converting M.V. "HAI JIN 58" into money within RMB11,432,700 according to the creditor's right ascertained by the first term of judgment;
5. The Defendants Jiangsu Huahai Shipping Group, GAO Sheng and GAO Li Ying shall bear the joint and several liabilities for the Defendant Nanjing Hengshunda Shipping Co., Ltd.'s debt ascertained by the first term of judgment.

If the obligors fail to fulfill obligations with respect to pecuniary payment within the period specified by the judgment, they shall pay double interest on the debt for the delayed period according to the Civil Procedure Law of the People's Republic of China Article 253.

Court acceptance fee in amount of RMB225,769, which shall be charged in half due to the application of summary procedure, and the application fee for property preservation before litigation of RMB5,000, total amount of RMB117,884.50, shall be jointly born by the Defendants Nanjing Hengshunda Shipping Co., Ltd., Jiangsu Huahai Shipping Group, GAO Sheng, GAO Li Ying, Wuhu Chenguang Shipping Co., Ltd. and Nanjing Haijin Shipping Co., Ltd.

In the event of dissatisfaction with this judgment, any party may within 15 days upon the service of this judgment submit a statement of appeal to the court, together with copies according to the number of the opposite parties and appeal to Hubei High People's Court. When submitting the statement of appeal, in terms of the claim amount in the appeal that dissatisfies this judgment, the appellant shall prepay the appeal costs according to the Measures on the Payment of Litigation Costs Paragraph 1 of Article 13. Payee of the remittance: Non-tax Revenue Special Account of Hubei Finance Department. Account Number: 052101040000369–1, opening bank: Agricultural Bank of China Wuhan Donghu Branch. When paying the cost in bank transfer, bank remittance and so on, the payer shall note "Hubei High People's Court" or Hubei High People's Court's unit number "103,001" on the blank of purpose of the voucher. If the appellant fails to prepay the litigation costs within 7 days after the expiration of appeal, the appeal will be deemed to be withdrawn automatically.

Judge: YAN Hong

June 11, 2015

Clerk: MO Junchao

Xiamen Maritime Court
Civil Judgment

China Minsheng Bank Co., Ltd. (Xiamen Branch)

v.

Fujian Guanhai Shipping Co., Ltd. et al.

(2015) Xia Hai Fa Shang Chu Zi No.216

Related Case(s) None.

Cause(s) of Action 211. Dispute over ship mortgage contract.

Headnote Mortgagee bank held entitled to recover from borrower's guarantor, with priority over other possible claims.

Summary The Plaintiff lender entered into a loan agreement with the Defendant borrower. The Defendant guarantors entered into mortgage contracts with the Plaintiff lender. The mortgage contracts guaranteed the Defendant guarantors' repayment of its loan by providing the Plaintiff lender with mortgages over two vessels and rights to use various sea areas in the event of the Defendant borrower's default. The Defendant borrower defaulted, and the Plaintiff lender called in the loan pursuant to the parties' underlying loan agreement. The court held the Defendant guarantors were liable to the Plaintiff lender for the Defendant borrower's default. The Plaintiff lender was entitled to priority compensation from the vessel proceeds and rights to use various sea areas (should these be auctioned by the court). The court further held the Defendant guarantors were entitled to compensation from the Defendant borrower.

Judgment

The Plaintiff: China Minsheng Bank Co., Ltd. (Xiamen Branch).
Domicile: Floor 7–8, Lixin Plaza, 90 Hubin South Road, Xiamen, Fujian.
Representative: QIU Yiheng, president.
Agent *ad litem*: GUO Zheng, lawyer of Fujian Trend Law Firm.
Agent *ad litem*: GUO Fan, lawyer of Fujian Trend Law Firm.

The Defendant: Fujian Guanhai Shipping Co., Ltd.
Domicile: No.1 Lianjiang Road, Guantou Town, Lianjiang County, Fuzhou Fujian.
Legal representative: LIN Cailong.
Agent *ad litem*: LI Ling, lawyer of Beijing Yingke (Fuzhou) Law Firm.
Agent *ad litem*: ZHUANG Juanjuan, lawyer of Beijing Yingke (Fuzhou) Law Firm.

The Defendant: Shengyang Holding Co., Ltd.
Domicile: No.18 Xia Que Road, Hong Kong SAR.
Legal representative: WU Zhongxiao.

The Defendant: Fujian Guanhai Shipyard Industry Co., Ltd.
Domicile: Guanqi Village, Guantou Town, Lianjiang County, Fuzhou, Fujian.
Legal representative: LIN Cailong.
Agent *ad litem*: LI Ling, lawyer of Beijing Yingke (Fuzhou) Law Firm.
Agent *ad litem*: ZHUANG Juanjuan, lawyer of Beijing Yingke (Fuzhou) Law Firm.

The Defendant: LIN Cailong, male, born on September 11, 1944, Han, living in Lijiang County, Fujian.
Agent *ad litem*: LI Ling, lawyer of Beijing Yingke Law Firm Fuzhou Office.
Agent *ad litem*: ZHUANG Juanjuan, lawyer of Beijing Yingke Law Firm Fuzhou Office.

The Defendant: Fujian Guanhai Kemen Industry Co., Ltd.
Domicile: 19-2B Yuquan residential district, Fengcheng Town, Lijiang County, Fuzhou, Fujian.
Legal representative: LIN Cailong.
Agent *ad litem*: LI Ling, lawyer of Beijing Yingke (Fuzhou) Law Firm.
Agent *ad litem*: ZHUANG Juanjuan, lawyer of Beijing Yingke (Fuzhou) Law Firm.

The Defendant: Fujian Lianjiang County Baolong Real Estate Development Co., Ltd.
Domicile: Floor 1, Red Star Garden, Guantou Town, Lijiang County, Fuzhou, Fujian.
Legal representative: LIN Cailong.
Agent *ad litem*: LI Ling, lawyer of Beijing Yingke (Fuzhou) Law Firm.
Agent *ad litem*: ZHUANG Juanjuan, lawyer of Beijing Yingke (Fuzhou) Law Firm.

With respect to the case arising from dispute over ship mortgage contract filed by the Plaintiff, China Minsheng Bank Co., Ltd. (Xiamen Branch) (hereinafter referred to as Minsheng Xiamen), against the Defendants, Fujian Guanhai Shipping Co., Ltd.(hereinafter referred to as Guanhai Shipping), Shengyang Holding Co., Ltd. (hereinafter referred to as Shengyang), Jincheng Shipping Service Co., Ltd. (hereinafter referred to as Jincheng), Fujian Guanhai Shipyard Industry Co., Ltd. (hereinafter referred to as Guanhai Shipyard), LIN Cailong, Fujian Guanhai Kemen Industry Co., Ltd. (hereinafter referred to as Kemen), and Fujian Lianjiang County Baolong Real Estate Development Co., Ltd. (hereinafter referred to as Baolong) on February 10, 2015 before Fujian High People's Court, this case was transferred to the court on March 6, 2015. The court, after entertaining the case organized the collegiate panel according to the law. The Plaintiff applied for property preservation on March 10, 2015, and provided corresponding guaranty. The court rendered a ruling to grant that application. The corresponding properties of Guanhai Shipping, Guanhai Shipyard, LIN Cailong, Baolong, and Kemen were preserved accordingly. The court held a hearing in public on May 14, 2015. GUO Zheng and GUO Fan, agents *ad litem* of the Plaintiff, LI Ling and ZHUANG Juanjuan, agents *ad litem* jointly entrusted by the Defendants, Guanhai Shipping, Guanhai Shipyard, LIN Cailong and Kemen, appeared in the hearing and participated in the litigious action. The Defendants Shengyang and Jincheng, upon summon by the court, failed to appear in court without justified reasons and refused to participate in the litigation, the court proceeded the trial by default. After the hearing, the Plaintiff applied to withdraw the action against Jincheng, the court made a ruling to permit the same. Now the case has been concluded.

The Plaintiff alleged that on June 9, 2010, the Defendant Guanhai Shipping signed *Fixed Asset LoanContract* (hereinafter referred to as *Loan Contract*) with the Plaintiff. It was agreed in *Loan Contract* that the Defendant Guanhai Shipping borrowed RMB35,000,000 from the Plaintiff. The life of the loan was 8 years, from June 9, 2010 to June 9, 2018. The annual interest rate was 6.534% and the interest was calculated quarterly. The Defendant Guanhai Shipping amortized the principal by 24 stages. On June 8, the same year, Guanhai Shipyard and LIN Cailong signed *Contract of Guarantee* and *Personal Guarantee Contract* respectively as guarantors jointly and severally liable, who should bear joint and several liability for the all debts involved in *Loan Contract*. On January 17, 2013, Shengyang signed *Mortgage Contract* with the Plaintiff, in which it was agreed that M.V. "GUANHAI 228" owned by Shengyang would be mortgaged to the Plaintiff. On May 7, 2013, Guanhai Shipyard signed *Mortgage Contract* with the Plaintiff, agreeing that M.V. "GUANHAI 228" owned by Guanhai Shipyard was mortgaged to the Plaintiff. On August 5, 2014, Guanhai Shipyard signed two *Mortgage Contracts of the Right to Use Sea Areas* with the Plaintiff. It was agreed that the right to use sea areas of the factory grounds of Fujian Shipyard Inc. owned by Guanhai Shipyard would be mortgaged to the Plaintiff. On February13, 2014 and on August 5, 2014, Kemen signed sequentially two *Mortgage Contracts of the Right to Use Sea Areas* with the Plaintiff. It was agreed that the right to use the two sea areas where one was in Kemen South Coast in Luoyuan Bay and the other was in Kemen operation area,

Luoyuan Bay Harbor District, Fuzhou Port enjoyed by Kemen would be mortgaged to the Plaintiff. The mortgages created on the above-mentioned ship and the right to use sea areas had been registered, and the scope of guarantee was the debts under *Loan Contract* involved. On June 17, 2014, the Plaintiff signed *Supplementary Agreement* with Baolong, Guanhai Shipping, Guanhai Shipyard, Kemen and LIN Cailong. It agreed that Baolong, Guanhai Shipyard, Kemen and LIN Cailong jointly guaranteed for Guanhai Shipping. After *Loan Contract* was signed, the Plaintiff lent RMB35,000,000 to Guanhai Shipping as agreed. However, Guanhai Shipping only repaid RMB47,000,000, the still remained in arrears. As of January12, 2015, the overdue interest by Guanhai Shipping was RMB6,947,095.5. Therefore, on January 21, 2015, the Plaintiff made the acceleration of maturity declaration that all Guanhai Shipping loans fell due and payable. But the company failed to perform repayment obligations or guarantor either failed to perform the joint and several liabilities. Therefore, the Plaintiff requested the court: 1. the Defendant Guanhai Shipping should pay the loan principal in amount of RMB303,000,000 and the interest thereon due until the date of paying off the loan (including normal loan interest, overdue interest and compound interest, as of January12, 2015, due interest was RMB6,947,095.5); 2. the Defendant Guanhai Shipping should bear the lawyer's fee in amount of RMB1,500,000 incurred by the Plaintiff's realizing the creditor's rights; 3.the Defendant Shengyang should bear guarantee obligation for the loan principal and interest thereon aforementioned, as well as lawyer's fee against the mortgage created over M.V. "GUANHAI 228", the ship owned by it; the Plaintiff was entitled to take priority in compensation from the proceeds of converting into money, auction, selling off M.V. "GUANHAI"; 4. the Defendant Guanhai Shipyard should bear guarantee obligation for the aforementioned loan principal, the interest thereon, and the lawyer's fee against the mortgage created over M.V. "GUANHAI 238"; the Plaintiff to have the right of priority of compensation from the price of converting into money, auction, selling off M.V. "GUANHAI"; 5. the Defendant Guanhai Shipyard should bear the mortgage guarantee obligation with the right to use sea areas (Ownership certificate number: Guo Hai Zheng 2013B35012205155, Guo Hai Zheng 2012B35012204292) where located on the factory grounds of Fujian Shipyard Inc. had by Guanhai Shipyard for the Plaintiff engaged in aforementioned loan principal and interest thereof, as well as lawyer's fee; in while the Plaintiff to have the right of priority of compensation from the price of converting into money, auction, selling off the right to use sea areas; 6. the Defendant Kemen to bear the mortgage guarantee obligation with the right to use the two sea areas (Ownership certificate number: Guo Hai Zheng: 103,570,094, Guo Hai Zheng: 103,570,095) where one was located on Kemen South Coast in Luoyuan Bay and the other was located on Fuzhou Port Luoyuan Bay harbor district Kemen operation area had by Kemen for the Plaintiff engaged in aforementioned loan principal and interest thereof, as well as lawyer's fee; the Plaintiff to have the right of priority of compensation from the price of converting into money, auction, selling off the right to use sea areas; 7. the Defendant Guanhai Shipyard, LIN Cailong, Baolong to bear the joint and several liability for the aforementioned loan principal, interest and penalties thereof, as well as lawyer's fee and liquidated damages; 8. the Defendants mentioned above should jointly bear all the litigation fee of the case. After the trial, the Plaintiff proposed a written application to the court, requesting that the partial loan interest should be deducted from the interest portion of the above-mentioned first claim, which in amount of RMB201,389.9 from the fourth quarter in 2014 under the IOU No.9929201029161996 that had been accepted on December20, 2014 and December21, 2014.

The Plaintiff submitted the following evidence to support its claims:

Evidence 1, loan certification, to prove that the Plaintiff had paid all loans in amount of RMB35,000,000 as agreed to the Defendant Guanhai;

Evidence 2, *Loan Contract* (Number: Gong Jie Dai Zi Di 2010 Xia No.0191), which was to prove the Defendant Guanhai Shipping lent RMB35,000,000 and life of loan as well as lending rate herewith;

Evidence 3, *Contract of Guarantee*(Number: Gong Dan Bao Zi Di 2010 Xia No.0007);

Evidence 4, *Personal Guarantee Contract* (Number: Ge Dan Bao Zi Di 2010 Xia No.0032),to prove the Defendants Guanhai Shipping and LIN Cailong should undertake guarantee liability jointly and severally under *Loan Contract*;

Evidence 5, *Mortgage Contract* (Number: Gong Dan Di Zi Di 2012 Xia No.0002);

Evidence 6, *Ship Mortgage Registration Certification*, to prove jointly that the Defendant Jincheng mortgaged M.V. "BAO CHANG HAI" owned by itself to the Plaintiff for the purpose of standing a guarantee for the Defendant Guanhai Shipping's fulfilling the debts under *Loan Contract* in amount of RMB40,000,000 and other debts;

Evidence 7, *Mortgage Contract* (Number: Gong Dan Di Zi Di 2013 Xia No.0001);

Evidence 8, *Ship Mortgage Registration Certification*, to prove jointly that the Defendant Shengyang mortgaged M.V."GUANHAI 228" owned by himself to the Plaintiff for the purpose of standing a guarantee for the Defendant Guanhai Shipping abiding by the all debts here under *Loan Contract*;

Evidence 9, *Mortgage Contract* (Number: Gong Dan Di Zi Di 2013 Xia No.0002);

Evidence 10, *Ship Mortgage Registration Certification*, to prove jointly that the Defendant Guanhai Shipyard mortgaged M.V. "GUANHAI238" owned by himself to the Plaintiff for the purpose of standing a guarantee for the Defendant Guanhai Shipping abiding by the all debts here under *Loan Contract*;

Evidence 11, two *Mortgage Contracts of the Right to Use Sea Areas* [Number: Gong Dan Di Zi Di 2014 Xia No.0004 (1), Gong Dan Di Zi Di 2014 Xia No.0004 (2)];

Evidence 12, two *Mortgage Registration Certifications of the Right to Use Sea Areas* (Number: Min Hai Yu Di 2014 No.013, Min Hai Yu Di 2014 No.014), to jointly prove that the Defendant Guanhai Shipyard mortgaged the right to use the two sea areas to the Plaintiff for the purpose of standing a guarantee for the Defendant Guanhai Shipping abiding by the all debts here under *Loan Contract*;

Evidence 13, two *Mortgage Contracts of the Right to Use Sea Areas* (Number: Gong Dan Di Zi Di 2014 Xia No.0001, Gong Dan Di Zi Di 2014 Xia No.0005);

Evidence 14, two *Mortgage Registration Certifications of the Right to Use Sea Areas* (Number: Min Hai Yu Di 2014 No.002, Min Hai Yu Di 2014 No.011), to prove that the Defendant Kemen mortgaged the right to use the two sea areas to the Plaintiff for the purpose of standing a guarantee for the Defendant Guanhai Shipping abiding by the all debts here under *Loan Contract*;

Evidence 15, *Supplementary Agreement* [Number: Gong Jie Dai Zi Di 2010 Xia No.0191 Bu (007)], to prove pursuant to the agreement the Defendants Bao Long Co., Guanhai Shipyard, Kemen and LIN Cailong should undertake guarantee liabilities for the debts here under *Loan Contract*;

Evidence 16, *Notice regarding Paying All Loan Back in Advance*, to prove the Plaintiff made the acceleration of maturity declaration about all loans of Guanhai Shipping, LIN Cailong etc. here under *Loan Contract*, and the Defendant Guanhai Shipping were asked to repay loan principal as well as interest within 5 days after accept of the notice;

Evidence 17, interest settlement lists, to prove as of January12, 2015, the overdue interest by Guanhai Shipping was 6,947,095.5;

Evidence 18, *Loan Rollover Agreement* (Number: Gong Dai Zhan Zi Di ZH1300000014585), to prove the Plaintiff agreed one-year extension for RMB4,000,000 with the Defendant in January 2013 on debt rollover;

Evidence 19, *Loan Rollover Agreement* (Number: Gong Dai Zhan Zi Di ZH1400000010975), to prove the Plaintiff agreed one-year extension for RMB38,200,000 with the Defendant on January 1, 2014 about debt rollover;

Evidence 20, Chinese version of *Ship Mortgage Registration Certification* on M. V."Bao Chang Hai", and evidence 21, the Chinese version of *Ship Mortgage Registration Certification* on M.V."GUANHAI 228", to prove the situation of the two aforesaid ships mortgage registration;

Evidence 22, *Agency Agreement Entrusted in Litigation and Arbitration Cases* and invoice of early lawyer fees, to prove the Defendant should undertake fees in the case as agreed;

Evidence 23, the certificate, and evidence 24, the ship registration record of the manuscript, to jointly prove the Defendant Shengyang mortgaged M.V. "GUANHAI 228" owned by itself to the Plaintiff for the purpose of standing a guarantee for the Defendant Guanhai Shipping abiding by the all debts here under *Loan Contract*.

The Defendants Guanhai Shipping, Guanhai Shipyard, LIN Cailong, Kemen and Baolong defended that they requested the court to reject the claims of the Plaintiff regarding lawyer fees in amount of RMB1,500,000. It did not recognized the claim of the Plaintiff regarding lawyer fees in amount of RMB300,000 for lack of relevant remittance record. With regard to counting interest, according to the records on the interest settlement lists of evidence 17, the total overdue interest should be paid by Guanhai Shipping was RMB6, 688, 462.03, rather than RMB6,947,095.5 claimed by the Plaintiff.

The Defendants Guanhai Shipping, Guanhai Shipyard, LIN Cailong, Kemen and Baolong did not submit any evidence on the disputed facts in the case.

The Defendant Shengyang did not defend and submit any evidence or documents to the court.

After the trial of proof and cross-examination, in respect of evidence in this case, the ascertainment opinions and analysis of the court are as follows:

As for the evidence 1, 2, 3, 4, 7, 8, 9, 10, 11, 12, 13, 14, 15, 16, 17, 18, 19, 22, 23 and 24, these all copies conforming original copies after being checked and are relevant with suit facts of this case. Therefore, the court ascertains the probative force thereof. Evidence 5, 6, 20 submitted by Plaintiff could be verified with originals, since the Plaintiff has withdrawn the suit to Jincheng, the above evidence is not relevant with the suit facts in this case, so the court does not ascertain the probative force thereof. Evidence 21 is translation of evidence 8, the Defendant had no objection to the translation contents, so the court ascertains the probative force thereof.

According to the above ascertained evidence and the investigations in the hearing, the court ascertains the following facts:

On June 8, 2010, the Plaintiff signed *Contract of Guarantee* numbered Ge Dan Bao Zi Di 2010 Xia No.0032 with the Defendant LIN Cailong, wherein it agreed that to ensure the performance of *Loan Contract* numbered Gong Jie Dai Zi Di 2010 Xia No.0191, LIN Cailong agreed to offer guarantee for all or part of the debts under the main contract as agreed pursuant to this contract; The guarantee master obligation under this contract was in amount of RMB35,000,000; it was of the mode of joint liability guarantee; The guarantee included principal in amount of RMB35,000,000 and interest, default interest, compound interest, penalty, damage awards, expense of credit realization and guarantee (including but not limit in legal cost, fee, travel charge and etc.) hereof, as well as other reasonable costs; the guarantee period was a contractual period of two years after the day when the primary liability was expired; The expiration of debts fulfilled by the main debtor included each debt due under the condition of the main debtor amortizing the debts, also the date of maturity announced by the creditors of the debt in advance as agreed in the main contract.

On June 9, 2010, the Plaintiff signed *Contract of Guarantee* numbered Gong Dan Bao Zi Di 2010 Xia No.0007 with the Defendant Guanhai Shipyard, wherein it agreed that to ensure the performance of *Loan Contract* numbered Gong Jie Dai Zi Di 2010 Xia No.0191, the Defendant agreed to offer guarantee for all or part of the debts under the main contract as agreed pursuant to this contract; the guarantee master obligation under this contract was in amount of RMB35,000,000; it was of the mode of joint liability guarantee; the guarantee included principal in amount of RMB35,000,000 and interest, default interest, compound interest, penalty, damage awards, expense of credit realization and guarantee (including but not limit in legal cost, fee, travel charge and etc.) hereof, as well as other reasonable costs; the guarantee period was a contractual period of two years after the day when the primary liability was expired; the expiration of debts fulfilled by the main debtor included each debt due under the condition of the main debtor amortizing the debts, also the date of maturity announced by the creditors of the debt in advance as agreed in the main contract.

On June 9, 2010, the Plaintiff, as a lender, signed *Loan Contract* numbered Gong Jie Dai Zi Di 2010 Xia No.0191 with Guanhai Shipping, as a borrower. According to Chapter 2 The Purpose of the Loan and Chapter 3 Loan Amount and Period" of the contract: the lender provided the loan in amount of RMB35,000,000 to the borrower for the purpose of building two 80300DWT goods ship, the loan period hereby since June9, 2010 to June 9, 2018 in total of 8 years. According to Chapter 4 Contract Interest Calculation, the loan interest rate under the contract was 6.534% (namely, the 8 year loan benchmark interest rate suitable for that of the day signing this contract announced by of the signing of this contract up to 10%); the daily interest loan under this contract was calculated interest quarterly, and the expiry date for interest was the 20th day of the end of each quarter; as for the principal loan due and payable but unpaid, the lender calculated overdue penalty interest, since the overdue date (including the day) according to the loan contract interest rate up to 50% (called "overdue interest rates"); for the overdue penalty interest the borrower could not pay on time, according to the overdue interest monthly, on the expiry date for interest or the date same as it, the lender calculated compound interest, according to the overdue days, monthly accrued; after signing this contract, in case of the people's Bank of China to adjust the benchmark interest rate, the contract loan interest rate automatically floats based on the new benchmark interest rate according to the 10% floating ratio of this contract; for loans that had been issued, the adjusted loan interest rate of the contract after the first interest rate adjustment date from the beginning of the next day on the loan began to apply; if loan contract interest rate changed, the overdue interest and punitive interest rate under this contract, automatically changed in proportion, and contractual loan interest rates also began to apply with sectional calculation. According to Chapter 6 Loan Repayment, the borrower to repay the principal loan according to Annex 2 agreed date and amount of the installment repayment, and the borrower should ensure funding in the repayment account so adequate that the lender could collect at the date of redemption and expiration interest; due to the borrower's repayment account lack of funds for lenders to fully deduct, it constituted the borrower overdue, the borrower hereto should pay overdue penalty interest and compound interest pursuant to overdue interest. According to Annex 2 of the contract, the date and amount of repayment were as follows: on June 20, 2012, RMB14,000,000; on September 20, 2012, RMB14,000,000; on December 20, 2012, RMB14,000,000; on March 20, 2013, RMB14,000,000; on June 20, 2013, RMB14,000,000; on September 20, 2013, RMB14,000,000; on December 20, 2013, RMB14,000,000; on March 20, 2014, RMB14,000,000; on June 20, 2014, RMB14,000,000; on September 20, 2014, RMB14,000,000; on December 20, 2014, RMB14,000,000; on March 20, 2015, RMB14,000,000; on June 20, 2015, RMB14,000,000; on September 20, 2015, RMB14,000,000; on December 20, 2015, RMB14,000,000; on March 20, 2016, RMB14,000,000; on June 20, 2016, RMB14,000,000; on September 20, 2016, RMB14,000,000; on December 20, 2016, RMB14,000,000; onMarch 20, 2017, RMB14,000,000; on June 20, 2017, RMB14,000,000; on

September 20, 2017, RMB14,000,000; on December 20, 2017, RMB14,000,000; on March 20, 2018, RMB28,000,000; in total RMB35,000,00. According to Chapter 7 Guarantee, to ensure the loan could be repaid under the contract, the parties agreed to take the following one or several guarantees: guarantee, see *Contract of Guarantee* numbered Gong Dan Bao Zi Di 2010 Xia No.0007; guarantee, see *Contract of Guarantee* numbered Ge Dan Bao Zi Di 2010 Xia No.0032; mortgage procedures under this contract of the two built vessels (480,300DWT bulk carrier, 5 80300DWT bulk cargo ship) after the ship delivered at the same time. According to Article 13 in Chapter 10 of the contract Responsibility for Breach of the Contract, the occurrence of any of the following circumstances were regarded as the borrower's default... 13.2 the borrower failed to repay the maturity of the repayment within the repayment period as agreed. According to Article 14, in the event of aforesaid default by the borrower, the lender, in addition to the corresponding rights agreed in the contract, also had the right to declare that the all or part loans under this contract was due immediately, to call the loan and stop lending. According to Article 15, should realize creditor's rights, thereby the lender sued for breach of the contract by the borrower, the borrower should undertake the expenses of litigation, fees, travel and others for the realization of creditor and mortgage.

On January 17, 2013, Shengyang signed *Mortgage Contract* numbered Gong Dan Bao Zi 2013 Xia No.0001 with the Plaintiff, wherein it agreed that to ensure the performance of *Loan Contract* numbered Gong Jie Dai Zi Di 2010 Xia No.0191, Shengyang agreed to offer mortgage guarantee for all or part of the debt under the main contract as agreed pursuant to this contract; the guarantee principal of master obligation under this contract was in amount of RMB35,000,000, the duration of the primary liability was since June 9, 2010 to June 9, 2018 in total of 8 years; the mortgage guarantee included principal in amount of RMB35,000,000 and interest, default interest, compound interest, penalty, damage awards, expense of credit realization and guarantee (including but not limit in the disposal of the mortgaged property fees, fee, travel charge and etc.) hereof, as well as other reasonable costs; the mortgaged property was M.V. "GUANHAI 228"; if the debt expiration agreed in the main contract (including the maturity declaration by the Plaintiff according to the main contract or this contract), while the debtor of the main contract failed to pay off the debts as agreed, the Plaintiff had the mortgage right at any time to dispose of the mortgaged property under this contract. After signing the above contract, the parties, on January 17, 2013, managed the first priority to the mortgage registration at the location of M.V. "GUANHAI228" in Hong Kong Marine Department.

In January 2013, the Plaintiff signed *Loan Rollover Agreement* numbered Gong Dai Zhan Zi Di ZH1300000014585 with Guanhai Shipping as a borrower, Guanhai Shipyard, LIN Cailong and Shengyang, as a guarantors, on debt rollover matters and *Loan Contract* numbered with Gong Jie Dai Zi Di 2010 Xia No.0191, agreed that: the principal amount of the debt rollover was RMB40,000,000 from January 18, 2013 to January 18, 2013, wherein the contractual loan interest rate was 10%, and the overdue penalty interest rate suitable during and after the extension period was aforesaid contractual loan interest rate up to 50%, thereupon the guarantors Guanhai Shipyard, LIN Cailong and Shengyang agreed to continue to fulfill the agreement with the Plaintiff in *Contract of Guarantee* and *Mortgage Contract*, and to bear responsibility for security of all debt obligations of the borrower under *Loan Contract* and loan extension agreement; if the aforesaid guarantor was a warrantor, then the guarantor agreed the warranty period was two years since the expiration of the loan under this agreement; except otherwise agreed upon in the agreement, the terms in *Loan Contract* and above mortgage contract continue to be valid.

On May 7, 2013, Guanhai Shipyard signed *Mortgage Contract* numbered Gong Dan Di Zi Di 2013 Xia No.0002, wherein agreed that to ensure the performance of *Loan Contract* numbered Gong Jie Dai Zi Di 2010 Xia No.0191, Guanhai Shipyard agreed to offer mortgage guarantee for all or part of the debts under the main contract as agreed pursuant to this contract; the guarantee principal of master obligation under this contract was in amount of RMB35,000,000, the duration of the primary liability since June 9, 2010 to June9, 2018 in total of 8 years; the mortgage guarantee included principal in amount of RMB35,000,000 and interest, default interest, compound interest, penalty, damage awards, expense of credit realization and guaranty (including but not limit in the disposal of the mortgaged property fees, fee, travel charge and etc.) hereof, as well as other reasonable costs; the mortgaged property was the ship (M.V. "GUANHAI 238") under construction with the assessed value was RMB75,990,000; if the debt expiration agreed in the main contract (including the maturity declaration by the Plaintiff according to the main contract or this contract), while the debtor of the main contract failed to pay off the debts as agreed, the Plaintiff had the mortgage right at any time to dispose of the mortgaged property under this contract. After signing the above contract, the parties, on May 30, 2013, managed *Ship Mortgage Registration Certification* numbered DY0800130010 at the location of M.V. "GUANHAI 238" in Fujian Marine Department.

On January17, 2014, the Plaintiff signed *Loan Rollover Agreement* No. ZH1400000010975 with Guanhai Shipping as a borrower, Guanhai Shipyard, LIN Cailong, Shengyang, Kemen and Baolong, as guarantors, on debt rollover matters under *Loan Contract* numbered Gong Jie Dai Zi Di 2010 Xia No.0191. Article 1 of the contract agreed that according to *Loan Contract*, the principal was in amount of RMB35,000,000 and the principal amount of the debt rollover was RMB40,000,000. Article 2 of the contract agreed that according to *Loan Contract*, the loan period was 8 years from June 9, 2010 thereto June 9, 2018, issuing by five sums in total of RMB35,000,000, in which IOU number was 9,929,201,229,881,299, the project loan in amount of RMB38,200,000 from January 18, 2012 to January 18, 2013, hereinafter 1 year debt rollover, on January 18, 2014 expired, the one year debt rollover duration from January 18, 2014 to January 18, 2015, during which the contractual interest rate was 12%, the overdue penalty rate during and after the debt rollover up to 50% of aforesaid contractual interest rate. Article 3 of the contract agreed that, the borrower Guanhai Shipping, the guarantor Guanhai Shipyard, LIN Cailong, Shengyang, Kemen and Baolong agreed to continue to fulfill the agreement with the Plaintiff in *Contract of*

Guarantee and *Mortgage Contract*, and to bear responsibility for security of all debt obligations of the borrower under *Loan Contract* and this agreement; if the aforesaid guarantor was a warrantor, then the guarantor agreed the warranty period was two years since the expiration of the loan under this agreement. Article 3 of the contract agreed that except otherwise agreed upon in the agreement, the terms in *Loan Contract* and above mortgage contract continue to be valid, herewith the parties should bear their obligations.

On February 13, 2014, the Plaintiff signed*Mortgage Contracts of the Right to Use Sea Areas* numbered Gong Dan Di Zi Di 2014 Xia No.0001 with the Kemen Industry Co., wherein it agreed that to ensure the performance of *Loan Contract* numbered Gong Jie Dai Zi Di 2010 Xia No.0191, Kemen Industry Co. agreed to offer guaranty for all or part of the debts under the main contract as agreed pursuant to this contract; the guarantee master obligation under this contract was in amount of RMB35,000,000; the mortgage guarantee included principal in amount of RMB35,000,000 and interest, default interest, compound interest, penalty, damage awards, expense of credit realization and guarantee (including but not limit in the disposal of the mortgaged property fees, fee, travel charge and etc.) hereof, as well as other reasonable costs; the mortgaged property was the right to use sea area located in the southern area of Luoyuan Bay Kemen port (Ownership certificate number: Guo Hai Zheng 103,570,094); if the debt expiration agreed in the main contract (including the maturity declaration by the Plaintiff according to the main contract or this contract), while the debtor of the main contract failed to pay off the debts as agreed, the Plaintiff had the mortgage right at any time to dispose the mortgaged property under this contract. After signing the above contract, the parties, on February 20, 2014, handled the mortgage registration of the right to use sea area to Fujian Marine Fisheries Office, which stated: the loan contract numbered Gong Jie Dai Zi Di 2010 Xia No.0191.

On June 17, 2014, the Plaintiff as a lender signed *Supplementary Agreement* numbered Gong Jie Dai Zi Di 2010 Xia No.0191 Bu (007) with Guanhai Shipping as a borrower, Guanhai Shipyard, LIN Cailong, Baolong and Kemen as guarantors, agreed that Guanhai Shipping signed *Loan Contract* numbered Gong Jie Dai Zi Di 2010 Xia No.0191 with the Plaintiff on June 9, 2010, Guanhai Shipyard signed *Contract of Guarantee* numbered Gong Dan Bao Zi Di 2010 Xia No.0007 with the Plaintiff, Guanhai Shipyard signed *Mortgage Contract* numbered Gong Dan Di Zi Di 2013 Xia No.0001 (clerical error, the contract actually between Shengyang and the Plaintiff) and *Mortgage Contract* numbered Gong Dan Di Zi Di 2013 Xia No.0002 with the Plaintiff, LIN Cailong signed *Contract of Guarantee* numbered Ge Dan Bao Zi Di 2010 Xia No.0032 with the Plaintiff, Baolong signed *Mortgage Contract* numbered Gong Dan Di Zi Di 2013 Xia No.0005 with the Plaintiff, Kemen signed *Mortgage Contract* numbered Gong Dan Di Zi Di 2014 Xia No.0001 with the Plaintiff; by the parties, and reported to the examination and approval by the bank credit process, agreed on adding following mortgaged properties on *Loan Contract* numbered Gong Jie Dai Zi Di 2010 Xia No.0191: 1. the right to use sea area owned by Guanhai Shipyard (Ownership certificate number: Guo Hai Zheng 2013B35012205155, Guo Hai Zheng

2012B35012204292), 2. the right to use sea area owned by Kemen (Ownership certificate number: Guo Hai Zheng 103,570,094); according to the reply, at this time, *Mortgage Contracts of the Right to Use Sea Areas* with the number of Gong Dan Di Zi Di 2014 Xia No.0004 [1] [2] signed with Guanhai Shipyard, *Mortgage Contracts of the Right to Use Sea Areas* with the number of Gong Dan Di Zi Di 2014 Xia No.0005 signed with Kemen; in respect of changes above, in witness whereof the parties hereto have caused this agreement to be executed; the original repayment period and amortization period stay unchangeable, and the repayment amount at each period as follows: on June 20, 2012, RMB12,400,000; on September 20, 2012, RMB12,400,000; on December 20, 2012, RMB12,400,000; on March 20, 2013, RMB2,000,000; on June 20, 2013, RMB2,000,000; on July 18, 2013, RMB1,800,000; on September 20, 2013, RMB2,000,000; on December 20, 2013, RMB2,000,000; on March 20, 2014, RMB5,000,000; on June 20, 2014, RMB5,000,000; on September 20, 2014, RMB5,000,000; on December 20, 2014, RMB5,000,000; on January 18, 2015, RMB38,200,000; on March 20, 2015, RMB16,000,000; on June 20, 2015, RMB16,000,000; on September 20, 2015, RMB16,000,000; on December 20, 2015, RMB16,000,000; on March 20, 2016, RMB18,000,000; on June 20, 2016, RMB18,000,000; on September 20, 2016, RMB18,000,000; on December 20, 2016, RMB18,000,000; on March 20, 2017, RMB20,000,000; on June 20, 2017, RMB20,000,000; on September 20, 2017, RMB20,000,000; on December 20, 2017, RMB20,000,000; on March 20, 2018, RMB19,000,000; on June 9, 2018, RMB9,800,000; in total RMB35,000,00; Guanhai Shipyard, LIN Cailong, Baolong and Kemen agreed to continue bearing the guarantee obligation as agreed of the guarantee contract; Guanhai Shipyard agreed to provide the maximum amount of guarantee to the obligation under the mortgage contracts of the right to use sea areas numbered Gong Dan Di Zi Di 2014 Xia No.0004 [1],[2]; Kemen agreed to provide the maximum amount of guarantee to the obligation under *Mortgage Contracts of the Right to Use Sea Areas* numbered Gong Dan Di Zi Di 2014 Xia No.0005; other terms of *Loan Contract* unchangeable, this agreement was the supplementary agreement of *Loan Contract* numbered Gong Jie Dai Zi Di 2010 Xia No.0191, it had the same effect as the contract.

On August 5, 2014, the Plaintiff signed *Mortgage Contracts of the Right to Use Sea Areas* numbered Gong Dan Di Zi Di 2014 Xia No.0004 [1] with Guanhai Shipping, wherein it agreed that to ensure the performance of *Loan Contract* numbered Gong Jie Dai Zi Di 2010 Xia No.0191, Guanhai Shipyard agreed to offer guarantee for all or part of the debts under the main contract as agreed pursuant to this contract; the guarantee master obligation under this contract was in amount of RMB35,000,000; the period of the loan was 8 years on which from June 9, 2010 to June 9, 2018; the mortgage guarantee included principal in amount of RMB35,000,000 and interest, default interest, compound interest, penalty, damage awards, expense of credit realization and guarantee (including but not limit in the disposal of the mortgaged property fees, fee, travel charge and etc.) hereof, as well as other reasonable costs; the mortgaged property was the right to use sea area located on the factory grounds of Fujian Shipyard Inc. (ownership certificate number: Guo Hai Zheng 2013B35012205155); if the debt expiration agreed in the main contract (including the maturity declaration by the Plaintiff according to the main contract or this contract), while the debtor of the main contract failed to pay off the debts as agreed, the Plaintiff had the mortgage right at any time to dispose of the mortgaged property under this contract. On the same day, the Plaintiff signed another *Mortgage Contracts of the Right to Use Sea Areas* numbered Gong Dan Di Zi Di 2014 Xia No.0004 [2] with Guanhai Shipyard, wherein agreed mortgage property was the right to use sea area located on the factory grounds of Fujian Shipyard Inc. (ownership certificate number: Guo Hai Zheng 2013B35012205155), and the other contents same as *Mortgage Contracts of the Right to Use Sea Areas* numbered Gong Dan Di Zi Di 2014 Xia No.0004 [1]. On the same day, the Plaintiff signed *Mortgage Contracts of the Right to Use Sea Areas* numbered Gong Dan Di Zi Di 2014 Xia No.0005 with Kemen, wherein agreed mortgage property was the right to use sea area located on Fuzhou Port Luoyuan Bay harbor district Kemen operation area (ownership certificate number: Guo Hai Zheng 103,570,095), and the other contents same as *Mortgage Contracts of the Right to Use Sea Areas* numbered Gong Dan Di Zi Di 2014 Xia No.0004 [1]. After signing the above three contracts, the parties, on August 22, 2014, separately handledthe mortgage registration of the right to use sea area to Fujian Marine Fisheries Office, which stated: the loan contract numbered Gong Jie Dai Zi Di 2010 Xia No.0191.

On January 21, 2015, the Plaintiff served *Notice regarding Paying All Loan Back in Advance*, which stated: hereinafter signing *Loan Contract* numbered Gong Jie Dai Zi Di 2010 Xia No.0191, the Plaintiff issued the loan of RMB35,000,000 to Guanhai Shipping as agreed; *Supplementary Agreement* agreed that Baolong, Guanhai Shipyard, Kemen and LIN Cailong offered guarantee for Guanhai Shipping; Guanhai Shipping only repaid the principal of RMB47,000,000, the other loan failure of payment within the period as agreed, until January 12, 2015 Guanhai Shipping failure to pay overdue principal of RMB20,000,000 (RMB5,000,000 on March 20, 2014, RMB5,000,000 on June 20, 2014, RMB5,000,000 on September 20, 2014, RMB5,000,000 on December 20, 2014), and interest of RMB6,947,095.5, hereby the guarantors Guanhai Shipyard and LIN Cailong etc. also failed to perform the joint and several liabilities as agreed; Guanhai Shipping had been in breach of the contract, according to Article 13(2) and Article 14 of *Loan Contract*, the Plaintiff declared to Guanhai Shipping, Shengyang, Guanhai Shipyard, Kemen, Baolong and LIN Cailong etc. that the loan of RMB303,000,000 under *Loan Contract* and *Supplementary Agreement* was due immediately, Guanhai Shipping should within 5 days upon the service of this notice, repay the principal of RMB303,000,000 and the interest of RMB6,947,095.5 to the Plaintiff. Guanhai Shipping, Guanhai Shipyard, Kemen, Baolong and LIN Cailong signed for the notice on the same day, but Guanhai Shipping until now did not repay the loan above to the Plaintiff, or the other Defendants either performed the relevant guarantee liabilities. The Defendant Baolong ascertained that at the stage of trial, the act of signature for *Notice regarding Paying All Loan Back in Advance* indicated the ascertainment of the joint and several guarantee liabilities for the debts under *Loan Contract*.

In April 2015, the Plaintiff (as Party A) signed *Agency Agreement Entrusted in Litigation and Arbitration Cases* with Fujian Trend Law Firm (as Party B), wherein agreed that: Party A engaged Party B for the agency of the action, and Party B accepted the commission forthwith the assignment of lawyer GUO Zheng as entrusted agent on the action and implement stages of the first, second instance and retrial; in the way of lawyer's risk agency, the fee payment of upper limit of the total was RMB2,100,000 on different collect ways: (1) cash collection part, the rate of 0.7%, with the maximum amount not exceeding RMB2,100,000, (2) repossessed assets way, obtained court bonded ruling and completed the formalities for transfer of ownership of assets, to pay the debt amount as the base, calculated according to the cash collection mode of different clearance time and the corresponding rate of 50%, the subsequent contract period the cash collection, cash clearance rate was calculated according to the compensating payment, (3) nol-pros or reconciliation, fees of RMB200,000, (4) complete payment of the fee after seizure formalities, such as according to the requirements of Party A, Party B would pay after complement seizure formalities early startup cost, fully the seizure of cash or cash equivalents assets, paid activation fees of RMB300,000, (5) the early Article 1 and 2, the legal fees paid to deduct early activation fee. (6) The fees above included lawyers engaged in related to the case mentioned all the expenses incurred (valuation fee court except legal fees and the security fee and other fee. After signature of the commission agreement, Fujian Chuangyuan Law Firm on May 12, 2015 issued 3 VAT invoices of fees total in RMB300, 000, but the Plaintiff still failed to payment of above expenses.

Another identification showed that from June 9, 2010 to April 17, 2012, the Plaintiff issued 5 loans to Guanhai Shipping as agreed, IOU numbers separately were: 9,929,201,029,161,996, 9,929,201,029,161,997, 9,929,201,029,161,998, 9,929,201,029,161,999 and 9,929,201,229,881,299, in total of RMB35,000,000. Guanhai Shipping failed to pay full loan interest as agreed from September 21, 2014. Up to January 12, 2015, according to the enterprise loans accounting system data of China Minsheng Bank, Guanhai Shipping still owed the loan principal of RMB303,000,000, of which IOU 9,929,201,229,881,299 owed RMB38,200,000.

The court holds that the case arising from dispute over ship mortgage contract. *Loan Contract* between the Plaintiff and Guanhai Shipping, thereto *Contract of Guarantee, Mortgage Contract, Mortgage Contracts of the Right to Use Sea Areas* and *Supplementary Agreement* involved among the Plaintiff and Guanhai Shipyard, Shengyang, LIN Cailong, Baolong, herewith Kemen Inc. etc., are all the presentation of the parties' true meaning without violation of the mandatory provisions of laws and regulations, which is deemed to be legal and effective, so the parties should perform pursuant to the agreement. Hereinafter signing *Loan Contract*, the Plaintiff fulfilled the obligation of issuing the loan principal in amount of RMB350,000,000 to Guanhai Shipping, although Guanhai Shipping repaid the loan principal in amount of RMB47,000,000, it failed to perform interest in full since September 21, 2014 as agreed or the failure of the loan principal in amount of RMB38,200,000 expired on January18, 2015 under IOU 9,929,201,229,881,299, hereby in breach of the contract. According to Article 13 Paragraph 2 and Article 14 in *Loan Contract*, after the occurrence of default events by Guanhai Shipping repaid maturing payable debt as agreed, the Plaintiff had the right to declare that the loan was due immediately and called the loan. Whereas the Plaintiff made the acceleration of maturity declaration to Guanhai Shipping by the way of service of *Notice regarding Paying All Loan Back in Advance* on January 21, 2015, so the court ascertains that except the loan in amount of RMB38,200,000 under IOU 9,929,201,229,881,299 as agreed expired on January 18, 2015, the other debts should expire on January 21, 2015. Guanhai Shipping should after the loan expired repay all last loan principal to the Plaintiff, and since September 21, 2014 to the date actual paid off, according to *Loan Contract* and *Loan Rollover Agreement* No. ZH1400000010975, pay interest outstanding, overdue penalty, compound interest. The Plaintiff confessed the acceptance of partial loan interest in amount of RMB201,389.9 of the fourth quarter under IOU 9,929,201,029,161,996, according to the Interpretation of the Supreme People's Court on Certain Issues Concerning the Application of the "Civil Procedure Law of the People's Republic of China" Article 92, "if one party in the hearing, or in the complaint, the respondent, the agent and other written materials, for the fact that has been detrimental to clear recognition, the other party shall have no need to submit evidence", the court ascertains thereof.

In respect of the liabilities for warrantee and guarantee. Firstly, Guanhai Shipyard signed with the Plaintiff *Contract of Guarantee* (Gong Dan Bao Zi Di 2010 Xia No.0007) agreed that Guanhai Shipyard undertook guaranty liabilities jointly and severally for the loan by Guanhai Shipping under *Loan Contract*; LIN Cailong signed with the Plaintiff *Contract of Guarantee* (Ge Dan Bao Zi Di 2010 Xia No.0032) agreed that LIN Cailong undertook guaranty liabilities jointly and severally for the loan by Guanhai Shipping under *Loan Contract*; according to Article 18 of the Guaranty Law of the People's Republic of China, that the Plaintiff asked Guanhai Shipyard, LIN Cailong to separately undertake guarantee liabilities jointly and severally for the above loan by Guanhai Shipping that could be observed according to law, so the court supports it. Secondly, in respect of Baolong whether to undertake guaranty liabilities jointly and severally. The Defendant Baolong confessed in hearing that the signature act on *Notice regarding Paying All Loan Back in Advance* indicated that it surely undertook guarantee liabilities jointly and severally for Guanhai Shipping loan under *Loan Contract*. According to the Interpretation of the Supreme People's Court on the Application of the Civil Procedure Law of the People's Republic of China Article 92, the court ascertains the fact the correspond guarantee relationship was established. Whereas, claim that the Plaintiff requested Baolong should undertake guarantee liabilities jointly and severally, which can be observed in law, so the court supports. according to the Guaranty Law of the People's Republic of China Article 31, the guarantors Guanhai Shipyard, LIN Cailong and Baolong should be entitled to compensation from Guanhai Shipping, after the guarantee liabilities.

In respect of mortgage guarantee liabilities, first, Shengyang signed with the Plaintiff *Mortgage Contract* (Gong Dan Di Zi Di 2013 Xia No.0001), agreed that Shengyang offered guarantee mortgage for Guanhai Shipping debts under *Loan*

Contract by M.V."GUANHAI 228", and according to the relevant laws of the home port located in Hong Kong Special Administration Region, had handled the first priority to the mortgage registration, so the Plaintiff had the right to priory to compensate by the ship. Secondly, Guanhai Shipyard signed *Mortgage Contract* (Gong Dan Di Zi Di 2013 Xia No.0002) with the Plaintiff, where of agreed that Guanhai Shipyard offered guarantee mortgage for Guanhai Shipping debts under *Loan Contract* by M.V."GUANHAI 238", and had handled *Ship Mortgage Registration Certification* at the location of M.V. "GUANHAI 238" in Fujian Marine Department, so the Plaintiff had the right to prior to compensate by the ship. Finally, Kemen signed two *Mortgage Contracts of the Right to Use Sea Areas* with the Plaintiff, whereof separately agreed Kemen offered guarantee mortgage for Guanhai Shipping debts under *Loan Contract* by the right to use sea area located in the southern area of Luoyuan Bay Kemen port (Ownership certificate number: Guo Hai Zheng 103,570,094) and the right to use sea area located on Fuzhou Port Luoyuan Bay harbor district Kemen operation area (Ownership certificate number: Guo Hai Zheng 103,570,095); Guanhai Shipyard signed two *Mortgage Contracts of the Right to Use Sea Areas* with the Plaintiff, whereof separately agreed Guanhai Shipyard offer guarantee mortgage for Guanhai Shipping debts under *Loan Contract* by the right to use sea areas (Ownership certificate number: Guo Hai Zheng 2013B35012205155,Guo Hai Zheng 2012B35012204292) where located on the factory grounds of Fujian Shipyard Inc.; above which had handled the mortgage registration to Fujian Ocean and Fishery Hall, so the Plaintiff had the right to prior to compensate by above mortgage properties.

In respect of the lawyer fees. The Plaintiff claimed that the Defendant should under the lawyer fees for the creditor's right in this case according to *Agency Agreement Entrusted in Litigation and Arbitration Cases* as agreed. The Defendant defended that the Plaintiff only submitted the invoice of the lawyer fees in amount of RMB300,000 but not the record of remittance, so the Defendant requested the court to dismiss part the claims of the Plaintiff's fees. The court holds that although the borrower Guanhai Shipping according to *Loan Contract* should undertake the fees of the Plaintiff for the creditor's right in this case, according to *Agency Agreement Entrusted in Litigation and Arbitration Cases*, venture agent relation agreed between the Plaintiff and its agent, thereof the Plaintiff should pay different standards of agent expenses regarding different agent effects and litigation results concerning repossession, nol-pros or reconciliation. Whereas in the case of trial stage, the effects or results above was still uncertain, as well as the amount of the fees, besides, the Plaintiff did not pay the fees above, so the situation of the claim for fees is not established. The court does not support.

To sum up, according to the Contract Law of the People's Republic of China Article 107, Article 205, Article 206, Article 207, the Property Law of the People's Republic of China Article 179 Paragraph 2, the Maritime Code of the People's Republic of China Article 11 and Article 271 Paragraph 1, the Guaranty Law of People's Republic of China Article 18 and Article 31, the Interpretation of the Supreme People's Court on Certain Issues Concerning the Application of the Guaranty Law of the People's Republic of China Article 42, the Civil Procedure

Law of the People's Republic of China Article 144, the Interpretation of the Supreme People's Court on the Application of the Civil Procedure Law of the People's Republic of China Article 90, the judgment is as follows:

1. The Defendant, Fujian Guanhai Shipping Co., Ltd. shall pay RMB30, 300,000 to the Plaintiff, China Minsheng Bank Co., Ltd. (Xiamen Branch) within ten days after this judgment takes into effect, and hereof interest, overdue penalty interest, and compound interest (with the principal base of RMB26, 480,000, the interest by Article 5 of *Loan Contract* counted at the eight-year loan benchmark interest rate risen by 10%, the overdue interest by Article 5 of *Loan Contract* counted at the eight-year loan benchmark interest rate risen by 50%, and interest from September 21, 2015 to the day of full settlement counted; with the principal base of RMB38,200,000, the interest by Article 2 of *Loan Rollover Agreement* (Gong Dai Zhan Zi Di No.ZH1400000010975) counted at the annual interest rate by 12%, the penalty interest by Article 2 of *Loan Rollover Agreement* (Gong Dai Zhan Zi Di No.ZH1400000010975) counted at the annual interest rate by 12% risen by 50%, and interest from September 21, 2015 to the day of full settlement counted; compound interest: the above failure interest of payment with the period specified by Article 5 of *Loan Contract* counted at the eight-year loan benchmark interest rate risen by 50%; the above interest, shall deduct the part of accepted interest by the Plaintiff of RMB201,389.9);
2. The Plaintiff, China Minsheng Bank Co., Ltd. (Xiamen Branch) shall have the right of M.V."GUANHAI 228", M.V."GUANHAI 228", the right to use the sea area locating on Kemen South Coast in Luoyuan Bay (Ownership certificate number: Guo Hai Zheng: 103,570,094), the right to use the sea area locating on Fuzhou Port Luoyuan Bay harbor district Kemen operation area (Ownership certificate number: Guo Hai Zheng: 103,570,095),the right to use sea areas locating on the factory grounds of Fujian Shipyard Inc. (Ownership certificate number: Guo Hai Zheng 2013B35012205155,Guo Hai Zheng 2012B35012204292), and the priority of compensation from the price of converting into money, auction, selling off the above properties within the scope by fist items of the judgment;
3. The Defendants, Fujian Guanhai Shipyard Industry Co., Ltd., Fujian Lianjiang County Baolong Real Estate Development Co., Ltd. and LIN Cailong shall undertake the joint and several liabilities for the debt by Fujian Guanhai Shipping of the first items of the judgment;
4. The Defendants, Fujian Guanhai Shipyard Industry Co., Ltd., Fujian Lianjiang County Baolong Real Estate Development Co., Ltd. and LIN Cailong shall have the right to claim compensation to the Defendant Fujian Guanhai Shipping, after they undertake the guarantee liabilities; and
5. Reject the other claims of the Plaintiff, China Minsheng Bank Co., Ltd. Xiamen Branch.

If the Defendants fail to perform the obligation to pay money according to the period specified in this judgment, it shall double the payment of interest on the debt during the period of delay according to the Civil Procedure Law of the People's Republic of China Article 253.

Court acceptance fee in amount of RMB1,599,035, the property preservation fee of RMB5,000, in amount of RMB1,604,035, the Plaintiff, China Minsheng Bank Co., Ltd. (Xiamen Branch) shall bear RMB7,725 and the Defendants, Fujian Guanhai Shipping Co., Ltd., Fujian Guanhai Shipyard Industry Co., Ltd., Fujian Lianjiang County Baolong Real Estate Development Co., Ltd., and LIN Cailong shall jointly bear RMB1,596,310.

If not satisfy with the judgment, the Plaintiff, China Minsheng Bank Co., Ltd. (Xiamen Branch) and the Defendants, Fujian Guanhai Shipping Co., Ltd., Fujian Guanhai Shipyard Industry Co., Ltd., Fujian Guanhai Kemen Industry Co., Ltd., Fujian Lianjiang County Baolong Real Estate Development Co., Ltd., and LIN Cailong may within 15 days as of the service of this judgment, while the Defendant, Shengyang Holding Co., Ltd. may within 30 days, submit a statement of appeal to the court, together with duplicates in the number of the counterparties, so as to make an appeal before Fujian High People's Court.

Presiding Judge: CAI Fujun

Judge: HUANG Yi

Judge: YU Jianlin

December 22, 2015

Acting Clerk: LI Yue

Attachment: Main Legal Provisions of this Case and the Implementation of the Application Tips

Firstly, Appendix: Relevant Law

1. **Contract Law of the People's Republic of China**
   Article 107 Types of Liabilities for Breach If a party fails to perform its obligations under a contract, or rendered non-conforming performance, it shall bear the liabilities for breach of contract by specific performance, cure of non-conforming performance or payment of damages, etc.
   Article 205 Time of Interest Payment The borrower shall pay the interest at the prescribed time. Where the time of interest payment was not prescribed or clearly prescribed, and cannot be determined according to Article 61 hereof, if the loan term is less than one year, the interest shall be paid together with the principal at the time of repayment; if the loan term is one year or longer, the interest shall be paid at the end of each annual period, and where the remaining period is less than one year, the interest shall be paid together with the principal at the time of repayment.

Article 206 Time of Principal Repayment The borrower shall repay the principal at the prescribed time. Where the time of repayment was not prescribed or clearly prescribed, and cannot be determined according to Article 61 hereof, the borrower may repay at any time; and the lender may demand repayment from the borrower within a reasonable time.

Article 207 Delayed Repayment Interest Where the borrower failed to repay the loan at the prescribed time, it shall pay delayed repayment interest according to the contract or the relevant stipulations of the state.

2. **Property law of the People's Republic of China**

   Article 179 In order to ensure the payment of debts, an obligor or a third party mortgages his/its properties to the oblige without transferring the possession of such properties, and when the obligor fails to pay due debts or any circumstance as stipulated by the parties concerned for realizing the mortgage right happens, the oblige has the right to seek preferred payments from such properties.

3. **Maritime Code of the People's Republic of China**

   Article 11 The right of mortgage with respect to a ship is the right of preferred compensation enjoyed by the mortgagee of that ship from the proceeds of the auction sale made according to law where and when the mortgagor fails to pay his debt to the mortgagee secured by the mortgage of that ship.

   Article 271 The law of the flag State of the ship shall apply to the mortgage of the ship.

4. **Guaranty law of the People's Republic of China**

   Article 18 A suretyship of joint and several liability refers to a suretyship contract wherein the parties agree that the surety and the debtor shall be jointly and severally liable.

   Where the debtor of a suretyship of joint and several liability defaults when the time limit for his performance of the obligation provided in the principal contract expires, the creditor may demand that the debtor perform his obligation, or demand that the surety undertake the suretyship liability within the scope of the suretyship agreement.

   Article 31 The surety, after his assumption of the suretyship liability, shall be entitled to recourse against the debtor.

5. **Civil Procedure Law of the People's Republic of China**

   Article 144 of the Defendant by summons, refuses to appear in court without proper reason, or without the permission of the court withdraws during the period, may make a judgment by default.

6. **Interpretation of the Supreme People's Court on the application of the Civil Procedure Law of the People's Republic of China**

   Article 99 The fact that the parties are based on the fact that the claim made by themselves or the basis of the claim against the other party shall provide evidence to prove it, except otherwise provided by law.

   Before making a decision, the parties fail to provide evidence or evidence is not sufficient to prove the facts of the claim, the parties bear the burden of proof to bear the adverse consequences of the parties.

7. **Interpretation of the Supreme People's Court on Certain Issues concerning the Application of the Guaranty Law of the People's Republic of China**
   Article 42 the decision of a people's court to ensure people undertake suretyship liability or liability should be in the text of the judgment explicitly guarantee people to enjoy the rights prescribed in Article 31 of the Guaranty law. The verdict is not clear right of recourse, the guarantor can only bear liability according to the facts, be sued.
   Ensure the limitation of recourse debtor; the guarantor assumes liability to the creditor date.
8. **Civil Procedure Law of the People's Republic of China**
   Article 239 The period of application execution is two years. Application execution of the suspension of the prescription, the interruption of the application of the law of the suspension, interruption of the provisions of the suspension. During the provisions of the preceding paragraph, of the period of performance specified by the legal document of the last day of calculated; specified by the legal document for the phased implementation of, from the specified for each performance of the period of the last day of calculated; legal documents not specified performance period, calculated from the legal instruments in force on the date of.
   Article 253 Who fails to perform the obligation of paying money during the period specified by the judgment, ruling or other legal documents, and shall double pay interest on the debt during the period of delay in performance. Who fails to perform other duties as specified by the judgment, ruling and other legal instruments, the person in charge shall pay the deferred payment.

Guangzhou Maritime Court
Civil Judgment

China Ping An Property Insurance Co., Ltd. Guangdong Branch
v.
Guangzhou Hang Jie Logistics Co., Ltd.

(2013) Guang Hai Fa Chu Zi No.1014

Related Case(s) This is the judgment of first instance and the judgment of second instance is on page 207.

Cause(s) of Action 223. Dispute over freight forwarding contract on the sea or sea-connected waters.

Headnote Subrogated goods insurer's claim to recover damages from freight forwarder for water damage to goods held not to be time-barred because under Chinese law, one-year limitation period runs from the time when the insurer pays the cargo-owner's claim.

Summary The Plaintiff, a goods insurer, was subrogated to the rights of its assured, the owner of a goods of wooden products that the Defendant freight forwarder agreed to transport from Huangpu to Shanghai. The goods were damaged by water after the carrying ship was involved in a collision with another ship. The court held that the Plaintiff was entitled to recover damages from the Defendant. The Plaintiff's claim was not time-barred because under Chinese law, the one-year limitation period for subrogated goods claims runs from the time when the insurer pays the claim.

Judgment

The Plaintiff: China Ping An Property Insurance Co., Ltd. Guangdong Branch.
Domicile: Building 16, 17, 27, 28 No.160 Tiyu Eastern Road, Tianhe District, Guangzhou, Guangdong.
Principal: LYU Chengdao, general manager.
Agent *ad litem*: YANG Yike, lawyer of Guangdong Sheng Dian Law Firm.
Agent *ad litem*: WANG Jiang Feng, lawyer of Guangdong Sheng Dian Law Firm.

The Defendant: Guangzhou Hang Jie Logistics Co., Ltd.
Domicile: Room 802, No.479 Qing Nian Road, Guangzhou Economic and Technological Development Zone, Guangzhou, Guangdong.
Legal representative: LIAO Daobing, general manager.
Agent *ad litem*: DUAN Weiwu, lawyer of Geenen Foreign Legal Service Center.
Agent *ad litem*: LIN Dahuan, employee.

With respect to the case arising from dispute over multimodal transport contract filed by the Plaintiff, China Ping An Property Insurance Co., Ltd. Guangdong Branch against the Defendant, Guangzhou Hang Jie Logistics Co., Ltd. on October 12, 2013, the court accepted the case and organized the collegiate panel consisting of Presiding Judge SONG Ruiqiu, Judge LI Zhengping and Acting Judge HU Shi according to the law, The court organized the parties concerned to exchange evidence before trial and held a hearing in public on January 3, 2014. YANG Yike, Lawyer of the Plaintiff, DUAN Weiwu, Lawyer of the Defendant appeared in court and participated in the action. After trial, now the case has been concluded.

The Plaintiff alleged that in 2011, the Plaintiff issued a domestic water and land goods transportation insurance policy and underwrote the transportation risk from Gaobu Town, Dongguan to Jiading District, Shanghai of the wooden products of the insured Dongguan Mu Lin Sen Packaging Sci-Tech Co., Ltd. (hereinafter referred to as "MLS"). MLS entrusted the Defendant to transport the wooden products and the Defendant entrusted the Xiamen Yuan Peng Container Logistics Co., Ltd. (hereinafter referred to as "Yuanpeng") to arrange for the shipment from Huangpu Port in Guangzhou to Shanghai. During the period of carriage of Yuanpeng, the carrying ship came across a collision accident, as a result, the goods was soaked in water and partially damaged. After that, the insured MLS reported the accident to the Plaintiff, and filed a claim application. After the occurrence of the accident, the survey company recognized the loss of the cargo caused by the collision was RMB81,000. The Plaintiff paid the insurance compensation in amount of RMB80,769.23 and MLS transferred all rights and interests of the subject matter insured to the Plaintiff. Due to the noncompliance of the Defendant as a carrier, the Defendant should bear the liability for the loss of the shipper MLS caused by its breach of contract. The Plaintiff requested the court to judge the Defendant to compensate the Plaintiff RMB80,769.23 and the interests thereon (from the day when the case was filed to the date of payment designated by the judgment on the basis of the loan interest rate over the same period promulgated by the Bank of China) and bear the court acceptance fee.

The Plaintiff presented the following evidential materials within the time limit for adducing evidence:

1. Letter of Indemnity and Subrogation, bank transfer voucher, accounting certificate, to prove the Plaintiff paid the insurance compensation and gained the right of subrogation;
2. A policy and clause of domestic water and land cargo transportation insurance, to prove relationship of insurance contract between the Plaintiff and the insured;

3. Claim application and damaged property list, to prove that the insured's claim and the losses it reported;
4. Insurance assessment report, to prove the accident and loss adjusters survey conclusion;
5. Power of attorney and delivery note, to prove that the Defendant carried the goods in fact;
6. (2012) Sui Luo Fa Li Min Chu Zi No.12 Civil Ruling; and 7. (2012) Sui Zhong Fa Li Min Zhong Zi No.60 Civil Ruling, to prove the fact that the Plaintiff sued the Defendant;
7. (2013) Guang Hai Fa Chu Zi No.119 Civil Judgment, to prove a judgment in terms of the same accident.

The Defendant defended that: firstly, the Defendant was the applicant of the insurance involved, but not the involved third party causing the accident, the Plaintiff was not entitled to claim against the Defendant; secondly, the Defendant was irresponsible for the damage to the goods, such damage was caused by the collision of the carrying ship, the Plaintiff had no right to claim; thirdly, the insurance subrogation was insurer exercising the right to claim the object should be limited to those responsible for the insurer caused the accident, which is mainly based on the principle of fairness, because the damage caused by the accident should ultimately by the liability to pay compensation. In this case, the Defendant was not the agent of the accident insurer, nor received any compensation in the accident. Therefore, the Plaintiff requested the Defendant compensation was unfair and unreasonable; fourthly, according to the law, the statute of limitations that the Defendant exercised right of subrogation was one year. And the statute of limitation was not interrupted by the Plaintiff withdrawing the appeal or dismissing the appeal. The date when the Plaintiff began to exercise the right of subrogation should be calculated from the day the Plaintiff fulfilled the insurance, namely calculated from November 23, 2011. However, the Plaintiff instituted the appeal on October 12, 2013, beyond the statute of limitation. In summary, the Defendant demanded the court to reject all the claims presented by the Plaintiff.

The Defendant proved the domestic cargo transportation insurance agreement during the limit for adducing evidence to prove that the Defendant was the insured and the Plaintiff had no right to claim against the Defendant.

After the court trial cross-examination, the Defendant confirmed all the evidence proved by the Plaintiff of its authenticity, legality and relevancy. In allusion to the domestic cargo transportation insurance agreement which the Defendant proved, the Plaintiff did not confirm it because the period of validity of the agreement was from April 15, 2012 to April 14, 2013 when had no relevancy with the case. The court believes that the evidence submitted by the Plaintiff are mutual corroborated, and the Defendant had no objection, so the court confirms the probative force; the evidence submitted by the Plaintiff showed that the insurance accident happened in 2011, and the domestic cargo transportation insurance agreement submitted by the Defendant was from April 15, 2012 to April 14, 2013, which had no relevancy with the case, so the court does not admit the probative force.

Based on the above evidence, combined with the trial, the court ascertains the following facts:

1. Facts concerning the carriage of goods

   On August 14, 2011, MLS issued domestic goods shipping instructions to the Defendant, the Defendant sealed and accepted the commission. The orders form prescribed that the MLS was the shipper, and the delivery address was Hu'an Wei Industrial Second Village of Gaopu town, Dongguan. The delivery person was Shanghai Jia Bei Packaging Materials Co. Ltd. (hereinafter referred to as Jiabei). The address was Shuang Zhu Road, Hua Ting Town of Jiading District, Shanghai. The goods was European standard card boards in a 40ft container, the way of transportation was door to door. On behalf of the transportation insurance, the value of the goods was RMB150,000 and the freight was RMB4,300. Loading port was Huangpu port, port of destination was Shanghai port. Transport vessel was M.V. "LI PENG No.1". The client promised to observe the right, obligation, liability of commissioned party, entrusting party, and consignee limit in waterway container goods transport rules, Domestic waterway goods transport rules, freight and relevant rules of miscellaneous charges.

   After that, the Defendant in its own name to entrust Yuanpeng involved in the shipment of goods from Huangpu port to Shanghai port of coastal transport. Then, the Defendant picked up the container from the appointed place and transported the container from Huangpu Port and delivered to Yuanpeng. After received the goods, Yuanpeng concluded the bill of lading No. LP1122NHPSH005 to the Defendant. The date of leaving the port was August 21, 2011. Transport clause was CY to CY for a 40ft container. Vessel's name was M.V. "LI PENGNo.1". Loading port was Huangpu Port and destination port was Shanghai Port. Consignor was the Defendant. Consignee was Shanghai Kun Shi Logistics Co., Ltd. (hereinafter referred to as "Kunshi") the number of the container was TGHU6558213, the seal number was 090,104, container type was 40 HQ. Goods were woods weighting 29.8 tons. Relevant rights and obligations of carrier, actual carrier, consignor and consignee were applicable to the rules of domestic waterway transport of goods.

   M.V. "LI PENGNo.1" left the port after loading the goods. On August 26, 2011, when the vessel traveled to the Wu Song Kou anchorage, another vessel collided M.V. "LI PENGNo.1", caused flooding water of M.V. "LI PENGNo.1"'s cabin and damaged the goods. After M.V. "LI PENGNo.1" arrived at the destination port Shanghai Port, Kunshi took delivery of the goods and transported the goods to MLS Shanghai branch's warehouse. Finally, MLS Shanghai branch transported the goods to the consignee Shanghai Jiabei Company.

2. Facts about insurance of cargo transportation

   On August 15, 2011, Ping An Insurance issued a domestic water and land goods transportation insurance policy. The insurance recorded: the insured was MLS Company, the number of the commercial voucher or the bill of lading was LP1122NHPSH005, transport tool was M.V. "LI PENGNo.1", voyage number was 1122 N, the shipment date was August 15, 2011, from Gaobu Town,

Dongguan to Jiading District, Shanghai. The insurance premiums was RMB150,000. Insured goods were woods. The number of the container was TGHU6558213/090104, underwriting conditions were all risks. Application of Inland Waterway and Land Cargo Transportation Insurance Clauses (revised on September 21, 2009). The deductible amount for each accident should be 10% of the amount of the loss for each cabinet, or 3,000 of the amount of each cabinet, whichever was higher.

After accepting the Plaintiff's commission on September 1, 2011, Shanghai Fan Hua Tian Heng Insurance Survey Co., Ltd. (hereinafter referred to as Survey) appointed a surveyor immediately to the container yard of Sinotrans Shanghai Zhang Hua Bang Logistics Co., Ltd. with Mr. Chen on behalf of the carrier to site survey. On September 7, surveyor of Fan Hua Tian Heng Adjuster, Shanghai Yue Zhi Insurance Surveys Co. Ltd. on behalf of the offending M.V. "BI HUA SHAN", on behalf of the collided vessel M.V. "LI PENGNo.1" Shanghai Hai Shen Insurance Surveys Co., Ltd. and the consignee's presenter LIU Jian Hua in consignees' warehouse located in No.1751 Wai Gang Wai Qian Highway Jiading District, Shanghai began a four-way joint survey, inventory of goods involved in the container. On November 7, they issued an insurance assessment report, recognized that: according to the collection of relevant materials, the goods in the container values about RMB150,000; the goods has seriously been immersed in water, the woods was peeling and out of shape, they could only be relegated for use with the general building scrap materials. According to estimates, the residual value of the goods was about 40%, the loss of the goods was about RMB90,000. According to the policy agreed, the deductible for each container was RMB300 or 10% the value of the loss. The accident adjusted loss was RMB81,000.

On November 11, 2011, the Plaintiff paid the insurance reparations RMB80,769.23 to MLS appoint account. On November 17, 2011, MLS provided the letter of intent about payment intention and equity transfer, to transfer the right of claim in the amount of insurance compensation to the Plaintiff.

Besides, on October 29, 2012, the Plaintiff sued to Guangzhou Luogang District People's Court in Guangdong of the same claims in this case. And on November 2, 2012, Guangzhou Luogang District People's Court made the decision to make the case off the docket. The Plaintiff was not satisfied with the adjudication and sued to Guangzhou Intermediate People's Court in Guangdong. On January 7, 2013, the Guangzhou Intermediate People's Court dismissed the appeal and recognized the original judgment.

The court holds that the Plaintiff subrogated the MLS Company instituted the appeal. The Plaintiff claimed that the cargo entrusted the Defendant to transport were damaged and demanded the Defendant to compensate liquidated damage liability the cargo involved in transport, including two different transport sector of land and coastal and two different modes of transport. Therefore, this case is a multimodal transport contract dispute.

After the damage happened, the Plaintiff paid the insurance compensation to the MLS Company. According to the Article 252 paragraph 1 of the Maritime Code of the People's Republic of China, where the loss of or damage to the subject matter insured within the insurance coverage is caused by a third person, the right of the insured to demand compensation from the third person shall be subrogated to the insurer from the time the indemnity is paid. Article 93 of the Maritime Procedure Law of the People's Republic of China, where an accident covered is caused by a third party, the insurer after having indemnified the insured, in entitled to claim compensation against the third party by exercising the right of subrogation in so far as the assured has been indemnified." The Plaintiff gained the insured MLS Company's right to claim the compensation of the third person in the scope of insurance compensation. According to the Provisions of the Supreme People's Court on Several Issues about the Trial of Cases concerning Marine Insurance Disputes Article 14 accepted the insurer exercises the right of subrogation to request compensation disputes over the right of the people's court shall only resulted in the legal relationship between the third person accident insurance and the insured a hearing. The court will only hearing on the legal relationship between the Defendant and the insured MLS Company.

MLS Company send to the Defendant and the Defendant sealed the power of attorney is the true consensus of the multimodal transport contract between MLS Company and the Defendant. The two sides set up multimodal transport contract according to the law. Without the invalid circumstances condition stipulated in the Article 52 of the Contract Law of People's Republic of China, the contract is legal and effective, and it is binding on both the Plaintiff and the Defendant MLS Company is the consignor, the Defendant is the multimodal transport operator.

After the Defendant accepted the cargo involved in the transport of the commission, the Defendant submandated other companies to transport the cargo from the factory of MLS Company to Huangpu Port by land, Huangpu Port to Shanghai Port by sea, and Shanghai Port to the warehouse of Shanghai Jiabei Company by land.When the vessel traveled to the Wu Song Kou anchorage during the period of coastal transportation, another vessel collided the Li Peng No.1, caused flooding water of Li Peng No.1's cabin and damaged the cargo. The Article 311 of the Contract Law of People's Republic of China stipulated that the carrier is liable for damages in case of damage to or loss of the cargoes in the course of carriage, provided that it is not liable for damages if it proves that such damage to or loss of the cargoes is caused by force majeure, the intrinsic characteristics of the cargoes, reasonable depletion, or the fault of the consignor or consignee." Where there is no evidence to prove that the damage was caused by the exemption from liability, the Defendant shall be liable for damages. The argument that the Defendant reckoned that the Plaintiff has no right to claim against the Defendant have no legal and factual reason. So the court will not support the claim.

The Defendant argued that the Plaintiff requested the Defendant to claim the right to claim has been over the limitation of action. The court reckons that this case shall be appropriate for the law which adjust the transportation of the coastal transportation. On the provisions of the statute of limitations shall apply to the Supreme People's Court on how to determine the coastal, inland waterway transport compensation for the period of time during the period of limitation of action, according to the subordinate, according to what stipulated in the first paragraph of Article 257 of the Maritime Code of the People's Republic of China, combined with trial practice, the right of shipper and the consignee claim for compensation to the carrier from the contract of carriage of cargo by sea or inland waterway, or the right of carrier to claim for compensation to the shipper and the consignee from the contract of carriage of cargo by sea or inland waterway; the period of limitation shall be one year, calculated from the date of delivery or the delivery of the cargo shall be delivered from the carrier. The Plaintiff gained the insured MLS Company's right to claim the compensation of the third person in the scope of insurance compensation and the period of limitation shall be one year. According to the provisions paragraph 2 of Article 16 of the Interpretation of the Supreme People's Court on Several Issues Concerning Application of the Insurance Law of the People's Republic of China (II) and paragraph 1 of Article 60 of the Insurance Law, the right of subrogation of the insurer of the period of limitation of action should be obtained from the starting point of the right of subrogation, and Article 252 of the Maritime Code of the People's Republic of China, where the loss of or damage to the subject matter insured within the insurance coverage is caused by a third person, the right of the insured to demand compensation from the third person shall be subrogated to the insurer from the time the indemnity is paid." The period of limitation of action of the right of subrogation of the insurer shall be calculated from the insured compensate insurance payment date. The Plaintiff compensate the insurance payment to MLS Company on November 11, 2011, so the period of limitation of action of the right of subrogation of the Plaintiff shall be calculated from that day. On October 29, 2012, the Plaintiff sued to Guangzhou Luogang District People's Court in Guangdong province. According to Article 140 of the General Principles of the Civil Law of the People's Republic of China, "a limitation of action shall be discontinued if suit is brought or if one party makes a claim for or agrees to fulfillment of obligations. A new limitation shall be counted from the time of the discontinuance." The period of limitation of action shall be recalculated on October 29, 2012. On October 12, 2013, the Plaintiff sued to the court, when it is in the limitation of the period of limitation.

In respect of the amount of compensation and the interest thereon, the economic loss in amount of RMB80,769.23 claimed by the Plaintiff against the Defendant was less than the loss of cargo RMB8,100, so the claim shall be supported. About the interest, the court supports the interest shall be calculated from October 29, 2012 to the payment day prescribed herein at the loan interest rate of working capital of enterprises for the same period provided by the People's Bank of China.

To sum up, according to paragraph 1 of Article 252 of the Maritime Code of the People's Republic of China, Article 311 of the Contract Law of the People's Republic of China and Article 93 of the Special Maritime Procedure Law of the People's Republic of China, the judgment is hereby rendered as follows:

The Defendant Guangzhou Hang Jie Logistics Co., Ltd. shall indemnify the Plaintiff China Ping An Property Insurance Co., Ltd. Guangdong Branch for the losses of RMB80,769.23 and the interest thereon (the interest shall be calculated from October 29, 2012 to the payment day prescribed herein on the basis of the interest rate of loan of the same kind over the same period promulgated by the People's Bank of China).

The obligations of paying the above-mentioned amounts shall be fulfilled within ten days as of the effectiveness of this judgment.

Where any party fails to perform the obligation of paying above-mentioned amounts within the period prescribed herein, such party shall, according to Article 253 of the Civil Procedure Law of the People's Republic of China, double pay the interest for the period of delayed performance.

The case entertainment fee in amount of RMB1,819 advanced by China Ping An Property Insurance Co., Ltd. Guangdong Branch, shall be directly returned thereto by the Defendant Guangzhou Hang Jie Logistics Co., Ltd., the court will not return and charge.

In event of dissatisfaction with this judgment, the Plaintiff may, within 15 days upon service of this judgment, and the Defendant may, within 15 days upon service of this judgment, with duplicates being submitted in terms of the number of the other parties, to lodge an appeal with the Guangdong High People's Court.

Presiding Judge: SONG Ruiqiu
Judge: LI Zhengping
Acting Judge: HU Shi

August 22, 2014

Clerk: ZHANG Xiujie

Guangdong High People's Court
Civil Judgment

China Ping An Property Insurance Co., Ltd.
Guangdong Branch
v.
Guangzhou Hang Jie Logistics Co., Ltd.

(2014) Yue Gao Fa Min Si Zhong Zi No.204

Related Case(s) This is the judgment of second instance, and the judgment of first instance is on page 199.

Cause(s) of Action 223. Dispute over freight forwarding contract on the sea or sea-connected waters.

Headnote Reversing lower court decision that subrogated cargo insurer could recover damages from freight forwarder for water damage to cargo, because freight forwarder had not acted as multimodal carrier but merely as forwarding agent arranging carriage by others and so could not be held liable as carrier.

Summary The Plaintiff, a cargo insurer, was subrogated to the rights of its assured, the owner of a cargo of wooden products that the Defendant freight forwarder agreed to transport from Huangpu to Shanghai. The cargo was damaged by water after the carrying ship was involved in a collision with another ship. The court of first instance held that the Plaintiff was entitled to recover damages from the Defendant and that the Plaintiff's claim was not time-barred because under Chinese law, the one-year limitation period for subrogated cargo claims runs from the time when the insurer pays the claim. On appeal by the Defendant, the appeal court reversed the lower court's decision, holding that the Defendant had not acted as multimodal carrier, but merely as a forwarding agent arranging carriage by others.

Judgment

The Appellant (the Defendant of first instance): Guangzhou Hang Jie Logistics Co., Ltd.
Domicile: Room 802, 479 Qingnian Road, Economic and Technical Development Zones, Guangzhou, Guangdong Province.
Legal representative: LIAO Daobing, general manager.
Agent *ad litem*: DUAN Weiwu, lawyer of Guangdong Jinglun Law Firm.
Agent *ad litem*: SHAN Qingwei, trainee lawyer of Guangdong Jinglun Law Firm.

The Respondent (the Plaintiff of first instance): China Ping An Property Insurance Co., Ltd. Guangdong Branch.
Domicile: Building 16–28, 160 Tiyu East Road, Tianhe District, Guangzhou City, Guangdong Province.
Person in charge: LYU Chengdao, general manager.
Agent *ad litem*: YANG Yike, lawyer of Guangdong Shengdian Law Firm.
Agent *ad litem*: LI Xuequn, lawyer of Guangdong Shengdian Law Firm.

The Appellant, Guangzhou Hang Jie Logistics Co., Ltd. (hereinafter referred to as "Hangjie Logistics"), dissatisfied with (2013) Guang Hai Fa Chu Zi No.1014 Civil Judgment rendered by Guangzhou Maritime Court in respect of the case of dispute over maritime freight forwarding contract filed by the Respondent, China Ping An Property Insurance Co., Ltd. Guangdong Branch (hereinafter referred to as "PAIC Guangdong") against it, lodged an appeal before the court,. The court, after entertaining this case, organized the collegiate panel according to the law and tried this case. DUAN Weiwu and SHAN Qingwei, agents *ad litem* of Hangjie Logistics, and YANG Yike, agent *ad litem* of PAIC Guangdong participated in the pre-trial investigation organized by the court. Now the case has been concluded.

Hangjie Logistics dissatisfied the first-instance judgment, and filed an appeal to the court, requested that: 1. the judgment of first instance should be withdrawn and amended to dismiss all the claims of PAIC Guangdong according to the law; and 2. PAIC Guangdong should bear all the litigation fees. The main reasons were as follows:

1. The facts were incorrectly ascertained in the judgment of first instance.
   Hangjie Logistics, as the freight forwarder, instead of the multimodal transport operator or the carrier, handled the relevant transport procedures, and should not bear the compensation responsibility. First, Hangjie Logistics signed the freight forwarding contract with Dongguan Mulinsen, which was the framework agreement and the fundamental basis of the legal relationship between Hangjie Logistics and Dongguan Mulinsen. The contract stated that Dongguan Mulinsen entrusted Hangjie Logistics to arrange the transport of the cargo from the designated warehouse to the designated place of delivery in domestic coastal harbor cities and harbor cities along rivers by water or truck, and to handle the transport procedures. Second, the letter of entrustment, one of the evidence in the subject case, only stated the specific transport mode, expenses, rules and the like of the subject transport under the framework agreement. It was also expressed in the statement of the letter of entrustment that the principal only entrusted the agent to issue the waybill and arrange the transport as well as the settlement on his behalf. Third, Dongguan Mulinsen issued the container claim handling statement after the occurrence of the subject accident, it contained the statement of the agent from Hangjie Logistics therein.
2. The laws were incorrectly applied in the judgment of first instance.

First, according to paragraph 1 of Article 252 of the Maritime Code of the People's Republic of China, the losses suffered by Dongguan Mulinsen were caused by the carrier, namely Xiamen Yuanpeng, instead of Hangjie Logistics. Hangjie Logistics neither constituted a breach of contract, nor did it violate anyone's right, therefore it should not bear any responsibility. Second, even if PAIC Guangdong was entitled to exercise the subrogation right against Hangjie Logistics, such claim had exceeded the limitation of action. According to the relevant provision of Article 267 of the Maritime Code of the People's Republic of China, "the limitation of action shall not be discontinued if the Appellant withdraws his action or his submission for arbitration, or his action has been rejected by a decision of the court", the action filed by PAIC Guangdong in respect of the same claim before Guangdong Luogang People's Court was dismissed, it did not discontinue the limitation of action. PAIC Guangdong paid the insurance proceed and obtained the right of subrogation on November 23, 2011, then filed the action on October 12, 2013. This claim exceeded the one-year statutory limitation of action.

To sum up, Hangjie Logistics requested the court to support its claims according to the law.

In the second instance, PAIC Guangdong contended as follows:

1. Hangjie Logistics was the carrier rather than the agent under the multimodal transport contract, it should bear the compensation responsibility. Subject to the evidence materials of the first instance, Hangjie Logistics signed the relevant agreement with Dongguan Mulinsen in respect of the damaged cargo involved. This agreement stated that Hangjie Logistics arranged the transport by means of DO to DO. Meanwhile, Hangjie Logistics concluded the contract with Xiamen Yuanpeng and booked space in its own name, and it was Hangjie Logistics who issued the Delivery Note. If Hangjie Logistics was the agent, it should conclude the contract in the principal's name. Thus, the claim that Hangjie Logistics was the agent lacked factual basis.
2. The claim of Hangjie Logistics that PAIC Guangdong was not entitled to exercise the right of subrogation was wrong. Both the Maritime Code of the People's Republic of China and the Contract Law of the People's Republic of China expressly provided that the insurer was entitled to recover against the third party, and the third party was not definitely the actual infringer. Thus, PAIC Guangdong's recovering against Hangjie Logistics according to the multimodal transport contract had legal basis, and Hangjie Logistics, as the carrier, had the obligation to safely transport the shipper's cargo.
3. In respect to the limitation of action, PAIC Guangdong agreed with conclusion ascertained by the court of the first instance.

To sum up, PAIC Guangdong requested the court to affirm the original judgment according to the law.

Hangjie Logistics submitted the following evidence in the second instance: evidence 1, the original copy of the freight forwarding contract, to prove the entrustment contract relationship between Hangjie Logistics and Dongguan Mulinsen; evidence 2, the original copy of the container claim statement issued by Dongguan Mulinsen, to prove that Dongguan Mulinsen recognized it entrusted

Hangjie Logistics to arrange the transport and handle the insurance procedures after the occurrence of the accident involved. PAIC Guangdong did not examine the aforementioned evidence. The court holds that the two pieces of evidence submitted by Hangjie Logistics in the second instance were both original copies, and were relevant to the basic fact of the subject case, thus they shall be admitted as the evidence to determine the facts of this case.

After trial, the court finds that the facts ascertained by the court of the first instance were true, and it is also found:

1. Hangjie Logistics signed a freight forwarding contract with Dongguan Mulinsen. This contract stated that the two parties reached the following agreement in terms of the matter that Dongguan Mulinsen entrusted Hangjie Logistics to handle the domestic container transport procedures on its behalf: (1) arrangement of transport and confirmation procedures: a. Dongguan Mulinsen entrusted Hangjie Logistics in writing to arrange the transport of the cargo from the designated warehouse to the designated place of delivery in domestic coastal harbor cities and harbor cities along rivers by water or truck, and to handle the transport procedures; b. Hangjie Logistics should confirm the transport mode by written form and handle the transport procedures of the cargo of Dongguan Mulinsen and follow up the delivery of the cargo to the Doors, storage yard, CFS designated by Hangjie Logistics (providing agent service such as DO-DO, CY-DO, CY-CY, DO-CY, etc.); etc. (2) Obligations of Dongguan Mulinsen: a. the forwarder note filled in by Dongguan Mulinsen should state the following facts at least: the name of the shipper and the consignee, transport clauses, transport expenses, settlement modes, etc.; b. Dongguan Mulinsen should confirm the payment of freight and service charges in time as required by Hangjie Logistics, and should pay the freight and miscellaneous charges to Hangjie Logistics timely and fully under agreed payment terms; etc. (3) Hangjie Logistics should: a. confirm the freight forwarding letter from Dongguan Mulinsen timely; b. reply the situation of the subject cargo of Dongguan Mulinsen in the process of transport; c. submit the freight confirmation sheet to Dongguan Mulinsen timely after dispatching a vehicle; d. is obliged to arrange the cargo insurance on Dongguan Mulinsen's behalf, and assist Dongguan Mulinsen to claim against the insurer and the carrier in the event of the occurrence of damage to cargo; e. ensure the carrier deliver the cargo consigned for shipment by Dongguan Mulinsen to the designated place of delivery safely and readily and deliver the cargo to the consignee within the agreed period. Where the loss of cargo was caused by force majeure, government act, or other nature disaster, Hangjie Logistics should not be liable for compensation. (4) Dual responsibility: a. where the direct carrier (lorry, vessel) failed to start shipment or arrive in time as required by Dongguan Mulinsen due to nature disaster such as flood, typhoon, strong cold air, etc., or other force majeure, or government act, Hangjie Logistics should inform Dongguan Mulinsen in time, and provide the cargo current condition of in port and en route at any time as required, and endeavor to protect the cargo free from damage; etc. (5) Both

parties agreed that: a. the payment to Dongguan Mulinsen by Hangjie Logistics of expenses for the service of Dongguan Mulinsen's handling the DO-DO transport procedures should maintain stability; and b. Dongguan Mulinsen should maintain steady cargo volume. (6) Expenses and Settlement: Dongguan Mulinsen should pay the advanced fees and service charge according to written payment voucher, Hangjie Logistics' written notice when the cargo delivered to the doors of Dongguan Mulinsen. (7) others: the contract period was from June 1, 2011 to May 31, 2012; etc.
2. Dongguan Mulinsen issued letter of instruction to Hangjie Logistics on August 14, 2011. Item 2 of the letter of instruction indicated: the principal had treated the entrustee as the agent when he signed the entrustment, and had entrusted the agent to issue the waybill and arrange the coastal transport, road transport, terminal operation and expenses settlement on his behalf.
3. Container claim statement issued by Dongguan Mulinsen on November 26, 2011 stated that it entrusted Hangjie Logistics to handle the transport procedures from Dongguan to Shanghai and arrange insurance, the container was damaged due to the collision happened to the carrying vessel owned by Xiamen Yuanpeng during the shipment from Guangzhou Huangpu Port to Shanghai Port. Hangjie Logistics purchased insurance against F.P.A (Free from Particular Average) for the subject cargo. PAIC compensated RMB80,769.23 in terms of the cargo involved with Hangjie Logistics' assistance. Hangjie Logistics agented to handle the transport procedures, follow up the cargo and arrange the insurance, and assisted in the insurance claim, it had fulfilled its due obligations.

The court holds that PAIC Guangdong, after compensating the insured, Dongguan Mulinsen in terms of the cargo loss, obtained the right of subrogation, then filed the action, alleging that Hangjie Logistics should bear the responsibility as the carrier against its breach of contract. Hangjie Logistics contented that it was the agent instead of the carrier. After the hearing, the court ascertains that Hangjie Logistics is the agent, thus this case is arising from dispute over freight forwarding contract. It is improper that the court of first instance ascertained the cause of the action as dispute over multimodal transport contract, the court hereby corrects.

The two parties had no objection to the transport, cause of cargo damage, PAIC Guangdong's obtaining the right of subrogation and the amount of compensation, the court ascertains the same. According to the grounds of appeal held by Hangjie Logistics, the court concludes the main outstanding issues of this case as follows: 1. the legal position of Hangjie Logistics; and 2. whether the claim of PAIC Guangdong exceeded the statutory limitation of action.

In respect of the first issue, the facts of this case indicated that Dongguan Mulinsen signed the freight forwarding contract with Hangjie Logistics, of which the duration was from June 1, 2011 to May 31, 2012. The container claim statement issued by Dongguan Mulinsen on November 26, 2011 proved the authenticity of this freight forwarding contract. Consequently, this contract was out of the true intention of Dongguan Mulinsen and Hangjie Logistics. And the contents thereof do not violate the prohibitive provisions of the laws of the People's Republic of

China, so this contract shall be legal and effective. The incident involved happened within the contract's effective duration. The rights and obligations of the two parties shall be bounded by this contract. This freight forwarding contract stated the rights and obligations of Dongguan Mulinsen as the principal and Hangjie Logistics as the agent, including that Dongguan Mulinsen should fill in and deliver the freight forwarding letter to Hangjie Logistics, confirm the payment of advanced freight and service charge in time and fully pay the freight to Hangjie Logistics; Hangjie Logistics should confirm the letter of entrustment, follow up and reply the situation of the cargo in transport, purchase the cargo insurance and pay the charges in advance on Dongguan Mulinsen's behalf, etc. In this case, the contents of the freight forwarding letter issued by Dongguan Mulinsen to Hangjie Logistics on August 14, 2011 are corresponded to those of the freight forwarding contract. Subject to the dual responsibilities agreed in the freight forwarding contract, there was no presentation about responsibilities of the carrier, and the settlement mode of freight was agreed to be paid by Dongguan Mulinsen in advance and finally undertaken by Hangjie Logistics, whilst Dongguan Mulinsen should pay Hangjie Logistics the service charges. Furthermore, although the freight forwarding letter issued by Dongguan Mulinsen stated the rights, obligations and liability undertaken to comply with by the principal shall be applied to the Regulations on Carriage of Containers by Water, the Regulations on Carriage of Goods by Water and the relevant regulations on freight and miscellaneous charges between the agent and principal, consignee, it is insufficient to presume Hangjie Logistics as the carrier. Paragraph 2 of the statement of the freight forwarding letter indicates that Dongguan Mulinsen treated Hangjie Logistics as the agent when signing the letter of entrustment. Consequently, the available evidence of this case cannot determine Hangjie Logistics to be the carrier, the company is the freight forwarder of Dongguan Mulinsen. This fact was wrongly ascertained by first instance and shall be corrected. The allegation of PAIC Guangdong that Hangjie Logistics was the carrier lacks factual basis and the allegation that Hangjie Logistics should bear the transport responsibilities of carrier lacks evidence, whilst PAIC Guangdong failed to prove the losses were caused by Hangjie Logistics' breach of agent's obligations, thus the court will not support such claim.

In respect to the second issue, this cause is arising from dispute over maritime freight forwarding contract rather than a multimodal transport contract. According to Article 135 of the General Principles of the Civil Law of the People's Republic of China, "except as otherwise stipulated by law, the limitation of action regarding applications to a people's court for protection of civil rights shall be two years, the limitation of action of this case is two years but not one year." According to Article 137 of the General Principles of the Civil Law of the People's Republic of China, that limitation of action shall begin when the entitled person knows or should know that his rights have been infringed upon, PAIC Guangdong, as the obligee of subrogation right, had the same legal position as Dongguan Mulinsen to file this action. Thus, the limitation of action shall commerce from the time when Dongguan Mulinsen knew or should know that its rights was infringed. It is found that the cargo was damaged due to the carrying vessel happened a collision on August 26,

2011, and PAIC Guangdong entrusted insurance surveyors to survey the damage to the subject cargo on September 1, 2011. Thus Dongguan Mulinsen knew or should know that its rights was infringed on September 1, 2011 at the latest, the limitation of action shall be calculated from that date. PAIC Guangdong filed an action before Guangdong Luogang District People's Court in respect of the same claim, the court made a ruling which rejected to entertain the claim on November 2, 2012, PAIC Guangdong dissatisfied with the ruling and instituted an appeal to Guangdong Intermediate People's Court, and the court rejected the appeal and sustained the original ruling on January 7, 2013. Hangjie Logistics alleged that the limitation of action of this case should not be discontinued due to the act of PAIC Guangdong filing an action, as prescribed in Article 267 of the Maritime Code of the People's Republic of China that the limitation of time shall not be discontinued if the Appellant withdraws his action or his submission for arbitration, or his action has been rejected by a decision of the court. The court holds that the limitation of action shall apply to the provisions of the Civil Procedure Law of the People's Republic of China due to this case is arising from dispute over freight forwarding contract. It is incorrect that Hangjie Logistics alleged that the provisions of Article 267 of the Maritime Code of the People's Republic of China should apply, and the court will not support. After PAIC Guangdong filed an action Guangdong Luogang People's Court, Guangdong Luogang District People's Court and Guangdong Intermediate People's Court made a ruling rejecting the entertainment but did not transfer the case to Guangzhou Maritime Court, it did not affect the constitution of discontinuance of limitation of action due to lawsuit being brought. PAIC Guangdong filed the action before the court of first instance on October 20, 2013, it did not exceed two-year statutory limitation of action. The court will not support the allegation of Hangjie Logistics that the claim of PAIC Guangdong exceeded the limitation of action.

In conclusion, the facts were not clearly ascertained and the laws were not correctly applied in the original judgment, the decision was improper and shall be corrected in light of law. The appeal filed by Hangjie Logistics is well grounded and shall be supported. According to Article 137 of Civil Procedure Law of the People's Republic of China, and sub-paragraph 2 and 3 of paragraph 1 of Article 170 of the General Principles of the Civil Law of the People's Republic of China, the judgment is as follows:

1. Revoke (2013) Guang Hai Fa Chu Zi No.1014 Civil Judgment rendered by Guangzhou Maritime Court; and
2. Reject the claims of China Ping An Property Insurance Co., Ltd. Guangdong Branch.

Court acceptance fees of first instance and second instance in amount of RMB3,638, shall fully be born by China Ping An Property Insurance Co., Ltd. Guangdong Branch. China Ping An Property Insurance Co., Ltd. Guangdong Branch shall pay the sum of the second instance in amount of RMB1,819 within ten days as of the effectiveness of this judgment and the same sum having been advanced by Guangzhou Hang Jie Logistics Co., Ltd. will be refunded by the court.

This judgment is final.

Presiding Judge: DU Yixing
Acting Judge: GU Enzhen
March 27, 2015
Clerk: PAN Wanqin

Appendix: Relevant Law

1. **Civil Procedure Law of the People's Republic of China**
   Article 170 After trying a case on appeal, the people's court of second instance shall, in the light of the following situations, dispose of it accordingly:

   (1) if the facts were clearly ascertained and the law was correctly applied in the original judgment, the appeal shall be rejected in the form of a judgment and the original judgment shall be recognized;
   (2) if the application of the law was incorrect in the original judgment, the said judgment shall be amended according to the law;
   (3) if in the original judgment the facts were incorrectly or not clearly ascertained and the evidence was insufficient, the people's court of second instance shall make a written order to set aside the judgment and remand to case to the original people's court for retrial, or the people's court of second instance may amend the judgment after investigating and clarifying the facts; or
   (4) if there was violation of legal procedure in making the original judgment, which may have affected correct adjudication, the judgment shall be set aside by a written order and the case remanded to the original people's court for retrial.

   The parties concerned may appeal against the judgment or written order rendered in a retrial of their case.

2. **General Principles of the Civil Law of the People's Republic of China**
   Article 135 Except as otherwise stipulated by law, the limitation of action regarding applications to a people's court for protection of civil rights shall be two years.
   Article 137 A limitation of action shall begin when the entitled person knows or should know that his rights have been infringed upon. However, the people's court shall not protect his rights if 20 years have passed since the infringement. Under special circumstances, the people's court may extend the limitation of action.

Shanghai Maritime Court
Civil Judgment

China Shipping Logistics Co., Ltd.
v.
Jiangsu Zhongtai Bridge Steel Structure Co., Ltd.

(2014) Hu Hai Fa Shang Chu Zi No.1068

Related Case(s) This is the judgment of first instance and the judgment of second instance is on page 240.

Cause(s) of Action 202. Dispute over contract of carriage of goods by sea or sea-connected waters.

Headnote Freight forwarder held to be entitled to recover damages for unpaid freight and interest on late payments of freight for two large projects.

Summary The Plaintiff freight forwarding contracted with the Defendant to provide shipping services in relation to two large projects. The Plaintiff sued after the Defendant delayed payment of freight and refused to return the bid bond that the Plaintiff had prepaid. The court found for the Plaintiff, awarding it damages for unpaid freight and for interest on the late payments of freight.

Judgment

The Plaintiff: China Shipping Logistics Co., Ltd.
Legal representative: HUANG Xiaowen.
Agent *ad litem*: LI Chenbiao, lawyer of Shanghai Office of Beijing Zhong Lun Law Firm.
Agent *ad litem*: CHEN Liang, lawyer of Shanghai Office of Beijing Zhong Lun Law Firm.

The Defendant: Jiangsu Zhongtai Bridge Steel Structure Co., Ltd.
Legal representative: CHEN Yu.
Agent *ad litem*: ZHANG Xiaobin, lawyer of Jiangsu Jijiang Law firm.

With respect to the case arising from dispute over contract of carriage of goods by sea and contract of sea freight forwarding with the Defendant, Jiangsu Zhongtai Bridge Steel Structure Co., Ltd., the Plaintiff, China Shipping Logistics Co., Ltd. filed an action and applied for property preservation on August 26, 2014. The court, after accepting this case on the same day, formed a collegiate panel according to the law, and gave a ruling to permit the Plaintiff's application for property preservation according to the law. The court froze the Defendant's bank deposit RMB (hereinafter all the following currencies are RMB if not specified) 13,500,000 yuan, and attached and detained the other equivalent property of the Defendant. The court held two hearings in public for this case respectively on November 25, 2014 and on December 15, 2014. Agent *ad litem*, CHEN Liang, entrusted by the Plaintiff, and agent *ad litem*, ZHANG Xiaobin, entrusted by the Defendant, appeared in court to attend the lawsuits of the two hearings. This case has been concluded.

The Plaintiff alleged that the Plaintiff and the Defendant entered into a contract of shipping services regarding the "Indian Bridge" and the "Danish Bridge" from 2013 to 2014. According to the contract, the Plaintiff should provide the relevant transport service and performed the transport contract by stages; the Defendant should pay various freight and miscellaneous fees in time within 30 days after receiving the Plaintiff's invoice with the payment method being draft or bank transfer. Up to August 22, 2014, the Plaintiff had kept the contract, however the Defendant delayed the payment of the freight and miscellaneous fees, RMB11,947,278.12, and various empty fees, demurrage fees, storage fees and overdue fees, totaling RMB256,765.34, recognized by itself. Additionally, the Defendant did not return the bid bond, RMB400,000, prepaid by the Plaintiff. Moreover, the Defendant also violated the contract agreements to pay the partial freight by means of acceptance draft, thereby causing the loss of the Plaintiff. Therefore, the Plaintiff requested the decree as the following:

1. The Defendant should pay the Plaintiff various freight and miscellaneous fees, RMB10,254,589.47 in total, delayed in the Indian Bridge Project, as well as the corresponding interests (the rates of interests, calculated according to the bank loan interests in the coterminous rate, were respectively: 1. the freight of the third batch in the Indian Bridge Project, RMB3,355,390.49, should be calculated starting on January 21, 2014 and terminating on the day when the judgment took effect; 2. the freight of the fourth batch in the Indian Bridge Project, RMB6,642,433.64, should be calculated starting on July 19, 2014 and terminating on the day when the judgment took effect; 3. other overdue fees, empty fees and demurrage fees, RMB256,765.34, should be calculated starting on August 18, 2014 and terminating on the day when the judgment took effect.)
2. The Defendant should pay the Plaintiff delayed interest loss, RMB687,979.96, due to delivering the long-term acceptance of the draft.
3. The Defendant should restitute the bid bond of the Indian Bridge Project, RMB200,000, to the Plaintiff.
4. The Defendant should pay the Plaintiff various freight and miscellaneous fees, RMB1,949,453.99, and the corresponding interests delayed in the Danish

Bridge Project (the rate, according to the bank loan interests in the coterminous rate, should be calculated starting on March 30, 2014 and terminating on the day when the judgment took effect.).
5. The Defendant should restitute the bid bond of the Danish Bridge Project, RMB200,000, to the Plaintiff.
6. The "India Bridge Shipping Service Contract" should be terminated.
7. The Defendant should undertake all of the court acceptance fees and preservation application fee, RMB5,000.

The Defendant argued as follows:

1. It recognized the amount in arrears of the freight, put forward by the Plaintiff, which references that up to November 5, 2014, the Defendant still defaulted in its payment for the Plaintiff of the third batch of the freight, RMB3,355,390.49 and the fourth batch of the freight RMB6,642,433.64 in the "Indian Bridge Project", and the freight, RMB1,949,453.99 in the "Danish Bridge Project", the total freight in arrears being RMB11,947,278.12.
2. It did not recognize the discount loss of acceptance of the draft. According to the second stipulation of Article 4 of *Shipping Service Contract* concerning the "Indian Bridge" signed by both of the parties: "party A shall pay the freight by means of bank transfer or the draft issued by the bank accepted by Party B." The acceptance draft is the payment method stipulated by both the Plaintiff and the Defendant, and during the process of the actual performance of the contract, the Defendant, from December 2013, paid the freight of RMB15,500,000 by means of acceptance draft, to which the Plaintiff did not raise any objection; the Plaintiff's requiring the Defendant for undertaking the discount losses had no factual evidence and legal basis, nor did its advocating of the late payment interests.
3. As for the demurrage charge and the empty charge, since both of the Plaintiff and the Defendant had already reached an agreement about those losses, and the Plaintiff recognized it in the court; and the Defendant agreed to undertake the demurrage charge and the empty charge, this totaled RMB90,000, according to the agreement. On the grounds that the Defendant had not performed the agreement yet, the Plaintiff requested the Defendant to undertake the demurrage charge and the empty charge, RMB256,765.24, which had no factual evidence and legal basis. The Defendant thought that since this portion of the losses was recognized by both parties and it represented both parties' actual meaning, both parties should perform according to the agreement, even though not performing would not affect the legal force. Besides, this agreement was reached during the process of proceeding with this case, and it did not stipulate the time limit for performance.
4. The Defendant did not affirm the evidence, offered by the Plaintiff, concerning losses of the demurrage charge and the empty charge calculated by the actual carrier. According to the third stipulation of Article III of *Shipping Service Contract* concerning the "Indian Bridge" signed by both parties: the price of this

contract shall include the barging freight and all of the related fees for the transportation project", other terms of the contract did not stipulate the demurrage charge and the empty charge, which had already been included in the freight. There was no contractual relationship between the actual carrier and the Defendant, and according to the principle of relativity of contract, the Defendant should not undertake the related demurrage charge and the empty charge. Since the actual carrier had a stake with the Defendant, the evidence it put forth could not be regarded as the basis of the verdict.
5. Because the Plaintiff caused damage to the goods during the transporting process, the Danish customer had already lodged a claim to the Defendant for 140,000 Euros. Since the Plaintiff did not provide the ships with a hoisting appliance as acquired, the cargoes could not be loaded at the Indian port, and the Indian customer had already lodged a claim to the Defendant for 978,000 dollars.
6. According to the first stipulation of Article IV of *Shipping Service Contract* concerning the "Indian Bridge" signed by both of the parties, the Plaintiff must submit the tax rebate for the declaration and the cancellation procedures for export earnings and the related materials within 30 days after the Plaintiff completed cargo declaration and shipping of every batch. However up to November 5, 2014, the Plaintiff had not submitted the report of the related materials for the fourth batch of the cargo.
7. As for the Plaintiff's claim to terminating the *Shipping Service Contract* signed by both parties, the Defendant thought that there was no legal basis for this claim and did not affirm it. Actually, the Defendant had already paid more than RMB19,700,000 as the freight; that there still existed residual money not paid was because the Plaintiff also violated the contract during the carriage process and it rejected to accept the bank acceptance given by the Defendant; and it unexpectedly lodged a lawsuit to the court, but even so, the Defendant had already made a commitment to pay in early November of 2014, therefore the Defendant's act did not constitute a fundamental breach of the contract and currently there merely existed a dispute over the interest of the late payment, and obviously the Plaintiff's request to terminate the contract did not have any legal basis.

In order to prove its claim and the Defendant's cross-examination, the opinions of the Plaintiff are as follows:

Evidence 1: the carriage contract of the Indian Bridge. It proved the contractual carriage relationship between the Plaintiff and the Defendant and the time for Defendant's paying the freight. The Defendant had no objection to the "three attributes" of this evidence.

Evidence 2: the confirmation of the freight related to the Indian Bridge Project and the email. Those proved that the Defendant recognized to pay the freight and miscellaneous fees, RMB9,997,824.13 for the Indian Bridge Project. The Defendant had no objection to the authenticity of the evidence and recognized in the pleading that it was still in arrears of the third batch of freight, RMB3,355,390.49, and the fourth batch of freight, RMB6,642,433.64.

Evidence 3: the carriage contract of the Danish Bridge. It proved the contractual carriage relationship between the Plaintiff and the Defendant and the time for Defendant's paying the freight. The Defendant had no objection to the "three attributes" of this evidence.

Evidence 4: the confirmation of the freight related to the Danish Bridge Project and the email. Those proved that the Defendant recognized to pay the freight and miscellaneous fees for the Danish Bridge Project and to return the margin, a total of RMB2,149,453.99. The Defendant had no objection to the "three attributes" of this evidence, but it stated that it had already been put forward on the sixth page of the freight affirmation that as for the paint damage of the goods caused during the period of barging and unloading on Shanghai waterfront, if the Danish side claimed for the compensation, it would be deducted from the freight related, and the Danish side has already made the claim.

Evidence 5: the confirmation of the second batch of the transport planning in the Indian Bridge, mails, explanation of demurrage emptying, cost confirmation and time statistics confirmation of barging and loading. Those proved that there existed barging demurrage and emptying in the second batch of the transportation of the Indian Bridge, and the Defendant confirmed to pay the demurrage charge, RMB67,500 and emptying charge, RMB130,000. The Defendant could not confirm the authenticity of the partial copies, and thought that evidence five mainly focused on the demurrage charge and emptying charge of the second batch of barge and both of the parties had already reached an agreement on those charges, which should be performed according to the agreement reached on September 17, 2014.

Evidence 6: the confirmation of the third batch of transportation planning in the Indian Bridge, the time statistics of barging and loading, and the statement of charge. Those proved the third batch of transportation in the Indian Bridge incurred the charge of barge and demurrage, RMB20,000. The Defendant's cross-examining opinion on evidence six is the same as evidence five, and at the same time it thought that the agreement, reached on September 17, 2014, was focused on the costs of the second, the third, and the fourth batches of the Indian Bridge Project, therefore it should be performed together according to this agreement.

Evidence 7: the situation statement of Tianjin Hua Jie Logistics Co., Ltd. and China Shipping Logistics Co., Ltd. It proved that Tianjin Hua Jie Logistics Co., Ltd. and China Shipping Logistics Co., Ltd., as the agent of the Plaintiff, arranged the second and third batch of transportation in the Indian Bridge. The Defendant had no objection to evidence seven, and indicated that the second, the third, and the fourth batch of the transportation business in the Indian Bridge Project had already been performed specifically and the Defendant had no objection.

Evidence 8: the confirmation mail of the fourth batch of the transporting calculation in the Indian Bridge, the final statement of the charge, the confirmation of the time statistics of the barging and loading and the cost confirmation of the Shanghai Guangyu International Freight Agency Co., Ltd. ("Shanghai Guangyu"). Those proved that the fourth batch of the transportation incurred barging demurrage charge, RMB35,000, and the storage charge, RMB4,265. The Defendant's cross-examining opinion on this evidence was the same as evidence five and six.

Evidence 9: the receipt of the bid bond for the Indian Bridge. It proved that the Plaintiff paid the Defendant RMB200,000 as margin for the Indian Bridge Project. The Defendant had no objection to the "three attributes" of this evidence.

Evidence 10: acceptance draft. It proved that the Defendant paid the partial charge of the second and the third batch for the Indian Bridge by means of acceptance draft, which caused the delay in payment and incurred the loss of interest. The Defendant had no objection to the authenticity of evidence ten, but it thought that the Defendant should not pay the discount loss or delay the interest on payment.

Evidence 11: contract for loan of the working capital and the tax list of transferring. Those proved that, due to the Defendant's delay of payment, the Plaintiff got a loan from the bank. The Defendant had no objection to the authenticity of this evidence, but it thought that this evidence had no relevancy with this case, because the Plaintiff borrowed RMB200,000,000, and the Defendant was only in the arrears of RMB10,000,000, which could not be taken as evidence to prove that the Defendant's delay of payment caused the Plaintiff's borrowing money.

Evidence 12: the tender document. It proved that the Plaintiff bid on the Defendant for the Indian Bridge Project. The Defendant had no objection to the "three attributes" of this evidence.

Evidence 13: the receipt and the collection certificate of the acceptance draft. Those proved that the acceptance draft with the tail number 7533-7535 (RMB3,000,000) was accepted on June 27, 2014 after the maturity, and the Plaintiff did not have the endorsement transfer. The Defendant did not object to the authenticity of this evidence but thought that it could not prove that the Defendant should pay the Plaintiff the discount interest of the acceptance draft, and at the same time as for the freight, RMB15,500,000, paid for the Plaintiff by the Defendant in that way, the Plaintiff only provided the certificate of the acceptance at maturity of RMB3,000,000, and the Defendant had reason to believe that other acceptance drafts had already been transferred by the Plaintiff.

Evidence 14: the bill and invoice issued by Shanghai Guangyu for the third batch of barging fees and demurrage fees in the Indian Bridge. Those proved that the third batch of the Indian Bridge incurred extra fees, RMB481,696, including unpaid RMB20,000 which should have been paid by the Defendant. The Defendant thought that the Plaintiff could not present the original evidence, so the Defendant could not confirm the authenticity and the evidence could not prove the specific amount of the demurrage fees actually paid for the Defendant by the Plaintiff or the causes of paying the demurrage fees. There was no contractual relationship between the Defendant and Shanghai Guangyu, and the contract between the Plaintiff and the Defendant had already been explicitly stipulated in terms of the contract price, so the Defendant should not pay the demurrage fees.

Evidence 15: the bill and invoice issued by Shanghai Guangyu for the fourth batch of barging fees and demurrage fees in the Indian Bridge. Those proved that the Plaintiff paid Shanghai Guangyu barging fees and demurrage fees,

RMB976,680 in the fourth batch of the Indian Bridge, including the unpaid RMB35,000 for the Defendant and the storage fees of RMB4265.64. The cross-examining opinion on this evidence of the Defendant was the same as that of the fourteenth evidence.

Evidence 16: the certification issued by Shanghai Dongdaming Branch of China Merchants Bank Co., Ltd. ("CMB Dongdaming Branch"), the original bank acceptance draft with the tail number 0115, and the collection certificate of the bank acceptance draft with the tail number 3286. Those proved that the bank acceptance draft (RMB3,000,000) with the tail number 7533-7573 was accepted on June 27, 2014, No.9745 and No.9747-9749 bank acceptance drafts (RMB5,500,000) on July 28, 2014, and No.9746 (RMB1,000,000) on September 1, 2014, but the deadline of the corresponding interest advocated by the Defendant was July 28, that was acceptance draft maturity; No.2780 bank acceptance draft (RMB2,000,000) was accepted on October 28, 2014, No.3286 bank acceptance draft (RMB2,000,000) matured on November 30, 2014, and the Plaintiff entrusted the bank to collect on December 8, 2014. The maturity date of No.0115 bank acceptance draft (RMB2,000,000) was January 9, 2015, and this draft had not been endorsed and transferred up to now, and the Plaintiff ensured that it would not endorse and transfer this draft before the maturity date, and the deadline of corresponding interest advocated by the Plaintiff was the court day, that was December 15, 2014. The Defendant thought that a tearing and sticking mark existed in the bank certificate, so the Defendant had objection to the authenticity of the evidence, and the Plaintiff should provide the corresponding collection certificate rather than the certificate issued by the bank. There was no objection to the original copies of the collection certificate of No.0115 and No.3286 acceptance drafts.

Evidence 17: the detailed information about the invoice issuing and the situation of the outgoing mails and the express circulation. Those proved that the following invoice, sent by the Plaintiff in terms of express, were signed by the Defendant: (1) the invoice of RMB9,657,812.33 in the second batch of the Indian Bridge was signed by the Defendant on September 17, 2013; (2) the invoice of RMB988,292.66 of the second batch of the Indian Bridge was signed by the Defendant on October 17, 2013; (3) the invoice of RMB9,209,296.49 of the third batch of the Indian Bridge was signed by the Defendant on December 22, 2013; (4) the invoice of RMB642,433.64 of the fourth batch of the Indian Bridge was signed by the Defendant on June 19, 2014; (5) the invoice of RMB1,949,453.99 of the Danish Bridge was signed by the Defendant on February 28, 2014. The Defendant had no objection to the authenticity of STO courier receipt, and it confirmed that it had received the invoice for SFExpress but could not remember the concrete time, and it could not confirm the fax of SFExpress courier receipt.

In order to support its defensing opinions, the Defendant submitted the following rebuttal evidence and the Plaintiff's cross-examining opinions:

Evidence 1: the confirmations of the fees and the time for demurrage on September 17, 2014. Those proved that after the Plaintiff prosecuted, both of the parties, the Plaintiff and the Defendant, had entered into a negotiation on the demurrage fees and the empty fees and finally reached an agreement that the

Defendant should undertake the total fee, RMB90,000, and that fee was confirmed as the total related fee for the second, the third, and the fourth batch of the Indian Bridge. Because the content of the negotiation not only included the empty fees and the demurrage fees but also the interest and so on, the Defendant planned to pay all the fees after finishing all the negotiation. The Plaintiff had no objection to the authenticity of the two sets of evidence, but it thought that the two sets of evidence could only prove the result of the negotiation of the second batch in the Indian Bridge, which the Defendant did not actually performed, so the Plaintiff still advocated the fees according to the actual expenses.

Evidence 2: a copy of an e-mail. It proved that the Indian customer lodged a claim for 978,000 dollars. The Plaintiff did not confirm the "three attributes" of this e-mail and thought that it could not prove that the Defendant suffered the related losses.

Evidence 3: a copy of an e-mail. It proved that the Danish customer lodged a claim for 140,000 Euros. The Plaintiff stated that it had transferred this e-mail to the Defendant and confirmed the authenticity of this e-mail, but it did not confirm the purpose of the evidence; and according to the acquaintance from the Danish agency, there was not a huge claim at all and even if there was, it had no relationship with this case and there was not any causality between the compensation for the cargo damage and the payment of the freight.

Evidence 4: a collection of photos. They proved that the Plaintiff caused the cargo damage during the process of transporting. The Plaintiff did not confirm the authenticity, relevancy and validity, and the relevancy between those photos and the transporting of the Danish Bridge could not be verified and it could not help to achieve the purpose of proof of the Defendant.

The court's certificating opinions of the evidence from both of the parties, the Plaintiff and the Defendant, are as follows.

As for the evidence 1, 2, 3, 9, and 12 of the Plaintiff, the Defendant had no objection to their "three attributes" and the proving matters, and the court recognizes the evidentiary effect and probative force. The Defendant also had no objection to the "three attributes" of the Plaintiff's evidence 4 and the court recognizes that. Regarding the Defendant put it that its business manager had made a note on the confirmation slip of the freight, the court thought that the note was just made unilaterally from the Defendant, the Defendant needed to present other evidence to prove whether the content of the note was verified, and it lacked evidence to advocate to deduct the freight in back pay only by resorting to the note. Besides, taking into consideration that in the written pleading and trial of this case, the Defendant recognized that it was still in arrears for the Plaintiff of the third batch of freight, RMB3,355,390.49 and the fourth, RMB6,642,433.64 for the Indian Bridge Project, and the freight, RMB1,949,453.99 for the Danish Bridge Project and owed the Indian Bridge Project and the Danish Bridge Project the bid bond, each RMB200,000, and the Defendant was willing to pay and return those above freight and bid bond, and it expected to solve those problems under the condition of consensus of the interests with the Plaintiff, the Defendant's opinions had already constituted the legal self-admission, so the court recognized and as for this the

Defendant did not need to prove it. The fifth group of the Plaintiff's evidence was mainly used to prove that during the cargo transporting process of the second batch in the Indian Bridge Project, there incurred barging demurrage charge and empty charge and the their specific amount, even though the Defendant thought that the partial evidence was just copies and therefore could not be confirmed, the Defendant also indicated and illustrated that on September 17, 2014, after communication, the Plaintiff, the Defendant, and the third party, Zhangjiagang City Huaji Logistics Co., Ltd. (the actual barging carrier), confirmed that the second batch of the barging empty charge was RMB50,000 and the second batch of barging factory wharf demurrage charge was RMB40,000, and after the signed confirmation of those three parties, the Plaintiff had no objection to this, therefore the court recognizes this fact. As for the point put forward by the Plaintiff that despite reaching an agreement from the three parties, the Defendant did not actually perform, the court will make a statement below about whether the Plaintiff's opinion of advocating the original amount was valid. At the same time, the Defendant indicated that the three parties' confirmation referred to the negotiation and confirmation of the second, third, and fourth batch of the related demurrage charge, empty charge, and storage charge in the Indian Bridge; the court holds that seeing from the content of the three parties' confirmation, it showed clearly to aim at the second batch of barging empty charge and demurrage charge not concern the third and the fourth batch, and the Defendant had no evidence to prove that Zhangjiagang City Huaji Logistics Co., Ltd. was the barging party of the third and fourth batch of cargo transporting, therefore the Defendant's related opinions lacked evidence and the court does not affirm. The Defendant had no objection to evidence 7 of the Plaintiff, adduced by the third party, and the court recognized its probative force. Regarding evidence 6, 8, 14, and 15 of the Plaintiff, the Plaintiff attempted to prove that there incurred demurrage charges and storage charges during the short barging transporting process of the third and fourth batch of the Indian Bridge Project, the Defendant did not affirm those evidence and indicated that there did not occur barging demurrage and extra storage showed by the Plaintiff, and even if there happened, it was caused by the Plaintiff. The court holds that even though the Plaintiff could prove that it paid the actual barging carrier and the wharf the corresponding charges, with only the available information submitted by the Plaintiff it could not prove directly that the barging demurrage and extra storage, etc. claimed by the Plaintiff were caused by the aspect of the Defendant, therefore the court cannot affirm the evidentiary effect and the probative force of those evidential materials. With respect to evidence Ten of the Plaintiff, the acceptance draft, the Defendant had no objection to its authenticity and the court recognizes its probative force; combining opinions of both sides, it could prove that the Defendant paid the Plaintiff the freight of the second batch and partial freight of the third batch for the Indian Bridge Project, RMB15,500,000, by means of long-term bank acceptance, but it needed to combine with other evidence for comprehensive recognition to judge whether that was delayed payment, and the specific recognition would be shown below. The Defendant had no objection to the authenticity of evidence 11 of the Plaintiff, contract for loan and the tax list of transferring, but it thought that it was irrelevant to this case and could not prove that it was because of the Defendant's delayed payment that caused the Plaintiff to borrow a loan from the bank, and the court holds that the defense of the Defendant was valid; one of the proof aims of the Plaintiff's providing the evidence was to prove the standard of interest losses of the delayed payment, and the Defendant had already recognized in the court trial that the calculating standard for the default losses should be adopted when it formed the default in delayed payment, which the Plaintiff also recognized, therefore the court recognizes the calculating standard for the interest losses of the delayed payment, confirmed by both sides. As for evidence 13 of the Plaintiff, the court holds that the Plaintiff provided the receipt and the collection certificate from the entrust bank of three acceptance drafts, the numbers all being the same, which could prove that those three drafts were all used to entrust the bank to collect and enter into the account after maturity; evidence 16 of the Plaintiff were the certificates issued by the entrusted bank for collection, and the Defendant pointed out that there were marks of tearing and sticking in this certificate and objected to its authenticity; the court holds that even though there existed sticking marks, analyzing those marks, they were torn from the middle part of the documents and the two torn parts were completely anastomotic from their content, and it was impossible for the Plaintiff to fake; the Defendant was the applying drawer of those acceptance drafts, and it also could investigate the accepting of those drafts from the accepting bank, Agricultural Bank of China Jingjiang Branch, therefore the court recognizes the evidentiary effect and probative force of the bank certification. As for the draft with the tail number, 9746 and the maturity, July 28, 2014, the actual accepting date was September 1, 2014, but the Plaintiff also recognized the advocated deadline of the overdue interest, July 28, 2014, and the court recognizes that. The collection certificate of the draft with the tail number, 0115 and that with 3826 were both original copies, and the Defendant had no objection to those, and the court recognizes its evidentiary effect and probative force. The Defendant had objection to the tracer through seal confirmation by the third party, the express company in evidence Seventeen, and the court recognizes its evidentiary effect and probative force; as for the fax of SF-Express, the Defendant had objection to the authenticity of its form but recognized that the corresponding invoice had been received, and the Defendant did not provide the contrary evidence to deny the authenticity of the fax of the courier receipt within the time regulated by the court, therefore the court recognizes the evidentiary effect of this material, which would prove the time, advocated by the Plaintiff, when the Defendant received the related invoice of the freight.

Evidence 1 of the Defendant: it agreed with two copies of materials of evidence 5 of the Plaintiff, the Plaintiff had no objection to its authenticity, and the court recognizes its probative force; as for whether the certification and the purpose of this evidence submitted by the Defendant could be achieved, the court will make certification comprehensively according to the content recorded in this evidence and combining other evidence. Evidence 2 of the Defendant: it was a printed copy, and the Defendant argued that it was the e-mail sent by the Indian customer, the third party, but it could not provide the original mail through notarial certification and conforming to the important document of evidential form; besides the Plaintiff denied receiving this e-mail, therefore the court does not affirm the probative force of this material. Evidence 3 and 4 of the Defendant: the Plaintiff recognized that it had received this mail forwarded by the Defendant, that was evidence 3, but it did not affirm the evidential purpose; as for evidence 4, the Plaintiff did not affirm its "three attributes", and the court holds that the Defendant, through providing this evidence, aimed at proving that during the process of performing the Danish Bridge Contract, the cargo damage was caused by the Plaintiff's actions, further bringing about the claim from the Danish customer; however, this evidential purpose could not be achieved merely from this e-mail and photos, therefore the court does not affirm the probative forces of those two groups of materials.

According to the above verdict evidence and combining the investigation of the trial, the facts of this case ascertained by the court are as follows.

1. The signing of the Indian Bridge Contract. The Plaintiff and the Defendant signed *Maritime Service Contract of Indian Driva Gila Bud Bridge Steel Tower and Steel Beams* (hereinafter referred to as "Indian Bridge Contract") in Jingjiang Jiangsu on March 29, 2013. In Article 1 of the contract, the Plaintiff should be responsible for the following work according to the batch of goods: barge, providing the materials of the transporting project of the steel beam and steel tower for the Indian Bridge received by the Defendant's own factory area of the domestic dispatch place, Jingjiang Industrial Park, and the ship of the wharf barging (the charge related with shipment would be undertaken by the Defendant), barging binding, strengthening, gasket, transporting to the ship on Shanghai Port/berthing and congregating, customs declaration & commodity inspection, shipment, binding, strengthening, gasket, ship transporting to Indian Kandla Port and unloading and delivering. It was further made clear in Annex II. The rate/price list and shipping service condition made further definitude, that the Defendant shall be in charge of floating shipment in the Defendant's own factory area of the dispatch place, Jingjiang Industrial Park, and the Plaintiff shall provide the suitable barging and cooperate with the shipment and shall be in charge of barging binding, strengthening and gasket and so on. In Annex V, barging service terms, before shipping the Plaintiff and the Defendant shall sign for transition on the goods delivery order of this voyage, and after the goods arrived at the designated spot, the Plaintiff shall be in charge of submitting the goods delivery order to the department of the shipping port for transition and inspection. After the Plaintiff and the Defendant determined the shipping date, the Defendant issued the shipping notice accordingly, and the Plaintiff must confirm that within 24 h after receiving the Defendant's shipping notice and berth ships on the Defendant's port two days before shipping. Under the conditions stated, the Plaintiff did not receive the Defendant's shipping notice, the Plaintiff berthed its ship on the Defendant's port by its own, the Defendant did not undertake any responsibility, and the Plaintiff itself undertook the risk and responsibility and all of the resulting charges. During the process of performing the contract, the Plaintiff should designate one specialized manager to take

charge of transporting coordination, and the Plaintiff should be in full charge of transportation. In the first paragraph of Article 3, contract price, this contract is a price-fixed contract, and it shall take the final settlement as the standard as for the specific chargeable tonnage. The amount of the contact should be divided into two parts, and the price should be temporarily determined like the following, the sea freight being 4,377,004 dollars and the domestic barge and the local charge on seaport being RMB2,988,920. The cargo should be divided into five batches to ship: the first batch includes 9,117.43 revenue tons and 2,955 weight tons; the second 15,486.19 revenue tons and 2,891 weight tons; the third 23,037.18 revenue tons and 3,527 weight tons; the fourth 13,391.81 revenue tons and 2,814 weight tons; the fifth 4,091.68 revenue tons and 2,381 weight tons; the total five batches include 65,124.29 revenue tons and 14,568 weight tons. The specific rates and price are as follows: from the Defendant's own wharf to Shanghai Port, the charge of short barge should be RMB80/weight ton, including packing charge, dunnage charge and two days' demurrage charge free; the ground local charge of Shanghai port should be RMB28/revenue ton; the short barging charge is determined temporarily as RMB1,165,440 and the ground local charge of Shanghai port is determined temporarily as RMB1,823,480. As for the sea freight (heavy lift vessel) from Shanghai Port to Kandla Port, the unit price of the first batch is 90 dollars/revenue tons and the unit prices of the second, third, fourth, and fifth batch are all 63.5 dollars/revenue tons, and the sea freights of the five batches are respectively 820,569 dollars, 983,373 dollars, 1,462,861 dollars, 850,380 dollars, and 259,822 dollars, temporarily determined as 4,377,004 dollars. According the third paragraph of Article 3, Contract Price, of the contract, the contract price shall include the lighterage of the transporting project (including unloading not loading), the sea freight (including loading not unloading), the local lump sum charge of Shanghai Port, customs inspection fee, the charge for binding, stowing, packing and ship insuring of ship and the steel structure on the barge, profits, taxes and charges of the maritime coordination and accreditation, managing charges, and all the other charges related to transporting (except the stipulated charges in the contract). The charging standards in Annex IV are as follows: (1) the lump sum form of contract billing shall be implemented in port charges (as for the port revenue ton, it should take the weight on the bill of lading as the standard and the port local charge should include harbor charge, the agency fees of the space booking, port constructing fee, tallying and list taking fee and costume and inspection fee.); (2) all of the port charges related to shipping port are already included in the contract price, so there is no need to calculate separately. It was stipulated in the first paragraph of Article IV, manner of paying, that the Plaintiff shall provide the special invoice for the transporting business, clean bills of lading, customs declaration and the related customs documentation of every batch of maritime cargo, and the documentation should meet the requirement of credit; after the Defendant confirms the amount, it should arrange for the freight payment within 30 days after receiving the invoice. The Plaintiff must submit the tax refund of custom declaration, the verification procedures of export and the related documentation within 30 days after finishing the customs clearance and shipment of every batch. The Defendant should pay the freight by means of bank transfer or the draft issued by the Plaintiff's accepted bank. According to the 20th term of Article 7, Paragraph 2 of the contract, the Plaintiff should send the full set of clean bills of lading, meeting the requirement of the Defendant's credit within seven working days after sailing, and the tax refund documents of export, the foreign exchange procedures of verification, shipping order, the original copies of the certificates regulated by other credits within 2 weeks to the Defendant by express (providing the scanning copies by mail before sending out). According to the 2nd term of Article 8, Paragraph 1 of the contract, when the Defendant breaks the contractual regulation and does not pay the Plaintiff freight costs on time, it should undertake the responsibility of breach. In Term 1, Paragraph 2, of Article 11, the contract's operation and termination, of the contract, when the party is in the contractual period, if the other party breaks the contractual regulation and no remedy is reached or has already failed to remedy its breach of contract within ten days after receiving the written notice from the party, then the party can terminate the agreement immediately by means of written notice.

2. The performance of the Indian Bridge Contract. Both the Plaintiff and the Defendant recognized, and there was no objection to the fact that the payment of the freight and the transportation of the first batch in the Indian Bridge Project had already been completed.

After sending off the second batch of the cargo in the contract of Indian Bridge Project, the Plaintiff issued an invoice with total amount of RMB9,657,812.33 for the Defendant on September 25, 2013 and sent it to the Defendant by means of express, and the Defendant signed and accepted on September 27. The Plaintiff again issued an invoice with total amount of RMB988,292.66 for the Defendant on October 15, 2013 and sent it to the Defendant by means of express, and the Defendant signed and accepted on October 17. After that, the Defendant paid the Plaintiff the second batch of the cargo freight in the Indian Bridge Contract by means of cash or bank acceptance, and the specific situations of the payment were as follows. 1. The Defendant delivered three bank acceptance drafts with the same amount being respectively RMB1,000,000 to the Plaintiff (the numbers were respectively XXXXXXXXXXXXXXXX, XXXXXXXXXXXXXXXX, XXXXXXXXXXXXXXXX), the issuing dates were all December 26, 2013, and the maturity dates were all June 26, 2014. The Plaintiff delivered those three acceptance drafts to CMB Dongdaming Branch for consignment collection on June 27, 2014, and all the money entered into the account of the Plaintiff on July 3; 2. The Defendant paid the Plaintiff the cash of RMB1,000,000 on January 3, 2014; 3. The Defendant delivered five bank acceptance drafts with the same amount being respectively RMB1,000,000 and one with the amount being RMB1,500,000 to the Plaintiff (the numbers was XXXX-XXXX), the issuing dates were all January 28, 2014, and the maturity dates were all July 28, 2014. On July 28, 2014, the Plaintiff entrusted CMB

Dongdaming Branch to make collections with 5 pieces of drafts and received all funds into its account by collection. On September 1, 2014, the Plaintiff entrusted CMB Dongdaming Branch to make collections with the draft No. XXXX and received all funds into its account by collection; 4. On April 29, 2014, the Defendant delivered a piece of bank acceptance bill with the sum of RMB2 million to the Plaintiff; the date of its bill was on April 28, 2014 and the due date was on October 28, 2014. On October 28, 2014, the Plaintiff entrusted CMB Dongdaming Branch to make collections with the draft and received all funds into its account by collection. The Plaintiff had recognized that the sum of RMB146,094 served as the remaining freight of the second batch of cargo; thus, the freight principal of the second batch of cargo had been all paid and the remaining sum of RMB1,853,906 had been served as the freight of third batch of cargo. Moreover, the Defendant once received the Plaintiff's charge confirmation sheet which recorded the second lighterage of Indian bridge with the sum of RMB130,000 and the second demurrage of factory wharf with the sum of RMB67,500. On September 17, 2014, through the three parties' exchanges by the Plaintiff, the Defendant and Zhangjiagang City Huaji Logistics Co., Ltd. as the person not involved in this case (the actual carrier of barge), recognized that the second empty charge of barge was in sum of RMB50,000 and the second demurrage barge factory wharf was in sum of RMB40,000; it was also recognized that the charge confirmation sheet should be signed or sealed by the representatives from the three sides.

When the third batch of cargo subordinate to the Indian Bridge Contract was shipped, the Plaintiff, on December 20, 2013, issued a piece of invoice to the Defendant with the total sum of RMB9,209,296.49 and sent it to the Defendant by express; the Defendant signed for the invoice on December 22, 2013. Afterwards, the Defendant paid several parts of freight by bank acceptance bill and its specific circumstances were as follows: 1. the amount of RMB1,853,906 in the bank acceptance bill whose date was on April 28, 2014 with the sum of RMB2 million; 2. on May 30, 2014, the Defendant delivered a piece of bank acceptance bill with the sum of 2 million yuan to the Plaintiff; the date of its bill was on May 30, 2014 and the due date was on November 30, 2014; on December 2, 2014, the Plaintiff entrusted CMB Dongdaming Branch to make collections with the draft and, on December 8, 2014, received all funds into its account by collection; 3. on July 9, 2014, the Defendant delivered a piece of bank acceptance bill with the sum of 2 million yuan to the Plaintiff; the date of its bill was on July 9, 2014 and the due date was on January 9, 2015; on December 15, 2014, the Plaintiff submitted the original bank acceptance bill in the court of first instance hearing and did not make any endorsement; the Plaintiff ensured that the bank acceptance bill should not be endorsed by the due date of the bill and claimed that the delayed payment interest of the fund should be calculated until the date of December 15, 2014 (the date of the court of first instance). From the outset of hearing the case, the Defendant recognized to owe the Plaintiff the freight of the third batch of cargo with the amount of RMB3,355,390.49.

When the fourth batch of cargo subordinate to the Indian Bridge Contract was shipped, on May 7, 2014, the Defendant recognized the freight of the fourth batch of cargo with the sum of RMB968,292.45 and verified the expenses of domestic trade barge and Shanghai Harbor Ground Operation with the sum of RMB685,401.66 on the Plaintiff's charge confirmation sheet. The Plaintiff issued the above mentioned freight invoice to the Defendant on June 18, 2014 and sent it by express to the Defendant who signed for it the next day. From the outset of hearing the case, the Defendant recognized to owe the Plaintiff the freight of the fourth batch of cargo with the amount of RMB6,642,433.64.

Both of the Plaintiff and the Defendant recognized that the fifth batch of cargo subordinate to the Indian Bridge Contract had not been carried out.

3. Conclusion and performance of Denmark Bridge Contract. On January 27, 2014, both parties of the Plaintiff and the Defendant signed *Steel Structural Parts of Denmark Bridge Transport Service Contract* (hereinafter referred to as Denmark Bridge Contract). Pursuant to Article 1 of the contract, according to the requirement of cargo batches the Plaintiff should provide the barge of the second batch of cargo for the steel structural parts of Denmark bridge at the domestic departure place where the Defendant factory wharf in Jingjiang Industrial Zone was located, cargo receipt on board (the Defendant in charge of its shipment), colligation, consolidation as well as cargo pad; and then the Plaintiff should provide the barge at Shanghai Harbor hook or rail/mooring congregation, custom and inspection, shipment, colligation, consolidation, cargo pad, cargo insurance as well as the transportation by sea in ships to Copenhagen Harbor (the Plaintiff's responsibility excluding the unloading at the destination port). Pursuant to Paragraph 1 of Article 6 "On the Price" of the Contract, this contract should be the fixed unit price agreement. The sum in the contract should be divided into two parts and the price should be arranged for the time being as follows: ocean freight containing taxes totaling RMB281,913.3; domestic barge expenses and harbor handling expenses totaling RMB32,849.03. Pursuant to Paragraph 2, the price in the contract should contain the same transportation items with the above mentioned Indian Bridge Contract except the item "ocean freight (loading but with no discharging)". Pursuant to Paragraph 3 on Payment Condition, the Plaintiff should issue a VAT invoice with 6% deduction after the ship bears off; if any temporary change in policy meant that the Plaintiff could not provide the deductible VAT invoice of the ocean freight, the Defendant should accept the ocean freight which was balanced by the plain VAT invoice and the Plaintiff should deduct the relevant taxation in expense confirmation. The Defendant should pay the full amount in cash within 30 days by the date of receiving the invoice and declaration form. Pursuant to Article 9 of the Contract "On Indemnity", if one party in this contract did not fulfill its responsibilities by convention or made any fault so as to cause the financial loss of the other side, it should claim for indemnity to the

default party in written form according to the relevant articles of this contract. When the subject cargo was shipped, the Plaintiff sent the Defendant the expense confirmation totaling USD319,399.36 (6.1 as the current exchange rate); on February 21, 2014, the Defendant signed and sealed on the expense confirmation sheet and noted that the above mentioned data was checked correctly. Since the paint was damaged in the period of barging and unloading at Shanghai Wharf, the relevant liability should be undertaken by transport unit if Denmark client claims for indemnity. The subject indemnity should be deducted from transportation expenses. On February 27, 2014, the Plaintiff issued the freight invoice totaling USD319,399.36 to the Defendant and sent it by express to the Defendant who signed for it the next day. In the court hearing, the Plaintiff recognized to have received the Defendant's forwarded e-mail in regard to Denmark client's claim to the Defendant for the indemnity of EUR140,000.

4. Information on Correspondence Negotiation by the Plaintiff and the Defendant
On July 14, 2014, the Plaintiff sent several documents concerning the payment of project freight and its operation by mail or express; the Plaintiff claimed that the Defendant's overdue time for the projection freight, which was supposed to be paid to the Plaintiff, seriously departed from the articles of the contract and effected the Plaintiff's capital turnover and production scheduling; the Plaintiff wanted the Defendant to make arrangement for payment as soon as possible and finish the confirmation of expense incurred as fast as he could, which included: 1. freight. Uncleared Freight of the Third Batch of Indian Bridge in sum of RMB3,355,390.49; uncleared freight of the Fourth Batch of Indian Bridge in aggregate amount of RMB6,642,433.64; freight of Denmark Bridge in sum of RMB1,949,454.24. 2. Bid Bond. tendering for the Defendant's American Bridge Project (noting: it was recognized to be unconcerned with this case by the Plaintiff and the Defendant) and the Denmark Bridge Project, the Plaintiff respectively submitted the cash deposit in sum of RMB200,000 (totaling RMB400,000) for each project; the projects above mentioned had finished all tendering while the Defendant had not sent back the cash deposit to the Plaintiff on time according to the return date of tender documents; the Defendant should send them back as soon as possible. 3. Without Expense Confirmation. The Second Batch of Barge Empty Charge in aggregate amount of RMB130,000; Demurrage Charge for Domestic Trade Barge in aggregate amount of RMB67,500; Demurrage Charge for Domestic Trade Barge Concerning the Third Batch of Indian Bridge in sum of RMB20,000; terminal Storage Charge for the Fourth Batch of Indian Bridge in sum of RMB4,265.34; Barge Overdue Fee in sum of RMB35,000; totaling RMB256,765.34; as for the foregoing expenses incurred, the Defendant should submit confirmation before the date of July 18. 4. Interest Subsidy of Acceptance Bill & Penalty for Overdue Payment. As for the Plaintiff's partial discount interest damages arising from the Defendant's payment for acceptance bill, the interest subsidy totaled RMB546,097.23 and should be confirmed before the date of 18 July. Meanwhile, combined with the two parties' agreement on the term of freight

payment, the Plaintiff's overdue capital cost had been added on account of the Defendant's overdue payment for the freight; pursuant to relevant legal legislation, as for those contracting parties who had not made any convention on the penalty standard for overdue payment, it should be calculated based on the interest rate standard for the loan over the corresponding period with the same kind as promulgated by the People's Bank of China. On July 17, 2014, as for the correspondence of the project freight and relevant operation, the Defendant replied the Plaintiff as follows: (1) pursuant to the freight confirmation sheet signed & sealed by the Defendant and the invoice issued by the Plaintiff concerning the third batch of cargo of Indian bridge, the remaining freight, in sum of RMB3,355,390.49, should be paid according to the monthly freight payment sheet; (2) pursuant to the freight confirmation sheet signed & sealed by the Defendant and the invoice issued by the Plaintiff concerning the fourth batch cargo of Indian bridge, the freight, in sum of RMB6,642,433.64, should be paid according to the monthly freight payment sheet; (3) pursuant to the freight confirmation sheet signed & sealed by the Defendant and the invoice issued by the Plaintiff concerning the cargo freight of Denmark bridge, the freight, in sum of RMB1,949,453.99, should be paid according to the monthly freight payment sheet; (4) with regard to the cash deposit submitted by the Plaintiff for tendering the Defendant's American Bridge Project and the Denmark Bridge Project (totaling 2* RMB200,000), it should be returned in the schedule of monthly freight payment; (5) in term of the unconfirmed expenses mentioned by the Plaintiff, we have raised doubts several times to you; the so-called expenses were not only caused by us but at a large extent created by the Plaintiff; what's more, it also brings us some losses so we reserve the claim rights. The Defendant suggested that these disputes should be solved by negotiation after the whole project. Later on, since the Defendant still had not paid, the Plaintiff sued the Defendant in the court.

The court also finds out that when tendering for the American Bridge Project and the Denmark Bridge Project, the Plaintiff respectively submitted the cash deposit in aggregate amount of RMB200,000 (totaling in RMB400,000) for each project. The Defendant recognized the sum of the subject cash deposit and recognized it should be returned. In the hearing, the Defendant recognized that it did not compensate the foreign side in regard to the relevant issues regarding the Indian bridge and Denmark bridge. Both the Plaintiff and the Defendant recognized that the interest standard to the overdue payment should be calculated based on the one-year loan interest rate as promulgated by the People's Bank of China.

The court holds that the Plaintiff and the Defendant involved had no objection to the contractual relation established by signing the transportation service contract. Although the contract was named as the transportation service contract, it was in fact subordinate to the comprehensive contract containing cargo transportation and freight forwarder from the analysis of the content. In the hearing, the two parties recognized that the cause of this case should be determined as the contract of carriage of goods by sea and the dispute of carriage agency by sea; which is also confirmed by the court according to the law. The contract involved was set up by law and came into legal force which should legally bind the two parties, who should strictly obey the contract and bear the liability of the contract; once violated the contract, one should bear the relevant default liabilities. If there was no specific agreement on default liability, it shall be settled according to the relevant legal regulations and rules.

According to verified facts and the Defendant's confession, the Defendant recognized it owed the Plaintiff the third batch of freight subordinate to the Indian bridge contract in sum of RMB3,355,390.49, the fourth batch of freight in sum of RMB6,642,433.64, the freight subordinate to the Denmark bridge in sum of RMB1,949,453.99 including ocean freight, drayage, ground operation expense at Shanghai Wharf (harbor expense), etc. Moreover, as to the cash deposit in sum of RMB400,000 for tendering the Indian bridge and Denmark bridge projects, the Defendant should pay for it, which is confirmed by the court. Pursuant to Paragraph 1 of Article 4 in the Indian Bridge Contract signed by both parties concerning "the Defendant should plan to pay the freight within 30 days when receiving the invoice and affirming the sum" and Paragraph 6 of Article 3 in the Denmark Bridge Contract concerning "the Defendant should plan to pay all the money by cash within 30 days when receiving the invoice and customs declaration", the Defendant's payment exceeded the time limit and did not pay in full, which evidently violates the agreement and thus the Defendant should bear the relevant liability for breach of contract.

In regard to the liability for breach of contract concerning delayed payment, the Defendant owed the above mentioned freight, which violated the agreement, and should bear the relevant liability for breach of contract. Although the contract involved made an agreement regarding the liability for breach of contract, there was no agreement on its specific calculation standard. Thus, in accordance to the principle of "following the legal rules once without any agreement", pursuant to the provision of Article 113 of the Contract Law of People's Republic of China "Where a party fails to perform its obligations under the contract or its performance fails to conform to the agreement and cause losses to the other party, the amount of compensation for losses shall be equal to the losses caused by the breach of contract, including the interests receivable after the performance of the contract, provided not exceeding the probable losses caused by the breach of contract which has been foreseen or ought to be foreseen when the party in breach concludes the contract", it is in conformity with the law that the Plaintiff claimed for the Defendant to pay the interest of the delayed payment. It is confirmed by court that, with both parties' agreement, the standard on the interest of the delayed payment should be calculated based on a one-year loan interest rate as promulgated by the People's Bank of China. The Defendant entered a plea that it was due to the Plaintiff who damaged the shipped cargo and caused the foreign party's claim for compensation, thus, the Plaintiff should also bear the liability for breach of contract; therefore, it should not be authorized that the Plaintiff claimed the Defendant to bear the delayed payment interest for breach of contract. The court holds that though the Defendant argued that there was the claim for compensation from a person who was not involved, the Defendant did not provide the relevant evidence in conformity with law and could not prove the fact and the compensation for the cargo damage; in addition, there was no agreement in the contract involved to support that the Defendant should dishonor or delay the freight. Therefore, since the Defendant lacks sufficient evidence and it should be confirmed not to institute a countersuit in terms of the cargo damage; the cargo damage is not subordinate to the scope of the trial so the court should not adopt the Defendant's claim; the Defendant should make other claims if it has new evidence. The court once again warmed both parties, if there indeed was the claim for compensation from a foreign party, the Plaintiff and the Defendant should be required to cooperate with each other and negotiate with the foreign side; when involved in the lawsuit, the party not involved should also provide convenience and actively cooperate so as to avoid losing the suit for lack of evidence; and where after the expending damage served as the basis to claim for compensation; the court requires both parties to discard past grievances in order to internationally maintain the legitimate rights and interests as well as the good image of China's trade and shipping enterprises.

Regarding to the timeframe of the delayed interest payment, there are two circumstances as follows: one is that it was unpaid until the deadline; the other is that payment was carried out beyond the agreed time though it was paid before the lawsuit. It should be separated hereto to calculate the beginning and ending time for the interest.

Specifically, regarding to the freight in sum of RMB1,949,453.99 subordinate to the Denmark Contract, pursuant to the agreement, the Defendant should pay off all the money within 30 days after receiving the invoice. It is now found out that the Defendant received the invoice on February 28, 2014 and did not pay according to the agreement. Therefore, depending on the evidence and law, the court supports the Plaintiff's claim for calculating the relevant delayed payment interest starting from the date of March 30, 2014. The interest damage of the sum of RMB1,949,453.99 subordinate to the Denmark Contract should be calculated based on the one-year loan interest rate as promulgated by the People's Bank of China from the date on March 30, 2014 to the time when the judgment takes effect.

As for the argument for not paying the third and fourth batch of freight subject to the Indian Bridge, the Defendant argued as follows: 1. there was a claim for compensation coming from the foreign side; 2. the Plaintiff did not deliver the relevant document of the fourth batch freight so the Defendant did not pay it off. As for the first argument, according to the court, since the above mentioned opinion had clarified that it was untenable, there is no need to give unnecessary details. As for the second argument, the Plaintiff recognized that the relevant document had not been delivered and been temporarily seized as the carrier since the Defendant did not pay off the freight. The court holds that regardless of whether the Plaintiff had the right to exercise the seizure right as a carrier, only based on the agreement of the parties, delivering the document is not the premise of the Defendant's payment. Moreover, the Defendant also recognized that not receiving the document influenced its right of export rebates; the Defendant did not file any counterclaim so the Plaintiff's not delivering the document cannot be the cause for the Defendant's refusing or delaying the payment. In addition, for lack of just cause and not paying the freight by agreement, the Defendant should be supposed to bear the liability for breach of contract. Based on the fact-finding, the Defendant received the invoice of the fourth batch of freight in sum of RMB6,642,433.64 on June 19, 2014 and should plan to pay off the freight within 30 days after receiving the invoice by agreement; however, since the Defendant had not paid until now, the court confirms the Plaintiff's claim by law that the interest damage of the delayed payment should be calculated from July 19, 2014 to the date when the judgment takes effect. The Defendant received the invoice of the third batch of freight in sum of RMB9,209,296.49 on December 22,2013 and should plan to pay off the freight within 30 days after receiving the invoice by agreement. However, the Defendant did not pay within the 30 days by agreement and chose to pay partial freight by bank's acceptance bill on April 29, May 30, and July 9, 2014. The Defendant recognized that there was still the unpaid freight in sum of RMB3,355,390.49. The court hereto holds that the interest damage of the delayed payment corresponding to the arrears in sum of RMB3,355,390.49 should be calculated from the date of January 21, 2014 to the time when the judgment takes effect. As for the partial overdue freight, it should be calculated separately by facts: 1. the beginning and ending time for the interest damage of the delayed payment in sum of RMB1,853,906 should start from January 21, 2014 to October 28, 2014; 2. the beginning and ending time for the interest damage of the delayed payment in sum of RMB2,000,000 should start from January 21, 2014 to November 30, 2014; 3. the beginning and ending time for the interest damage of the delayed payment in sum of RMB2,000,000 should start from January 21, 2014 to December 15, 2014. All the interest should be calculated based on one-year loan interest rate as promulgated by the People's Bank of China.

Particularly, in regard to the 6 months' time limit from the date of bank's acceptance bill to the due date, the Plaintiff also claimed that the Defendant was supposed to pay the interest damage of the relevant delayed payment. Pursuant to Article 69 Paragraph 1 of the Maritime Code of the People's Republic of China, the court holds that "the shipper should pay the freight to the carrier as agreed". Pursuant to Article 292 of the Contract Law of People's Republic of China that "a passenger, a shipper or consignee should pay the ticket-fare or freight." It can be seen that the shipper should bear the legal liability of paying the freight. Although the contract involved subordinated to the comprehensive contract, its main content still belonged to the transport contract; as the carrier, the Plaintiff enjoyed the principal right to obtain the freight; as the shipper, the Defendant has the main liability of paying the freight. Pursuant to the agreement in the Indian bridge "the Defendant should plan to pay off the freight within 30 days after receiving the invoice" and "the Defendant should pay the freight by bank transfer or the bank bill of exchange under the Plaintiff's recognition", the Defendant should bear the liability of paying off all the freight before the date of payment as agreed; the bill of exchange can be divided into presentation bill, fixed date bill, use acceptance bill, etc. However, according to provisions of law and contract agreement, even if the Defendant chose to pay by the bill of exchange, it should still be limited by the due date, which meant the due date and pay date of draft should be within the last payment date rather than the day of delivery. At present, the Defendant not only paid the freight later than the payment day but most sum already paid was by means of use acceptance bill; and the time for delivery for the bill was always later than the payment day by either 2 months or 6 months. In consideration of the characters of bill acceptance, unless the Plaintiff transfers the acceptance bill by endorsement when receiving it, or else, to the Plaintiff, it will get loss and cannot obtain the full amount within the date as agreed in the contract whether the Plaintiff accepts by discount ahead of time or waits for its collection after the expiration of the bill acceptance period. according to the fact-findings, the Plaintiff chose to accept collection by waiting for the expiration of use bill acceptance period. Therefore, in terms of this case, use bill acceptance used by the Defendant to pay the freight violated the agreement and also damaged the Plaintiff's right to obtain the full amount of freight by law, which caused the loss to the Plaintiff; so, the court supports the Plaintiff's claim for the compensation of the delayed payment interest. Pursuant to Article 113 of the Contract Law of People's Republic of China, "Where a party fails to perform its obligations under the contract or its performance fails to conform to the agreement and cause losses to the other party, the amount of compensation for losses shall be equal to the losses caused by the breach of contract, including the interests receivable after the performance of the contract, provided not exceeding the probable losses caused by the breach of contract which has been foreseen or ought to be foreseen when the party in breach concludes the contract". Obviously, the Defendant should know that the use bill acceptance would cause damage to the Plaintiff as the means of paying freight; the loss should be foreseen by the Defendant when entering into a contract with the Plaintiff.

Similarly, as for the second batch of cargo subordinate to the Indian contract, both parties had no contest on that the freight capital had been paid off but they had a dispute on the interest of the delayed payment; according to the above mentioned statements, the Plaintiff's relevant claim should be supported. Combined with the facts of the overdue freight payment subordinate to the second batch of cargo, the corresponding results should be as follows: 1. the beginning and ending time for the interest damage of the delayed payment in sum of RMB2,000,000 should start from October 27, 2013 to June 26, 2014; 2. the beginning and ending time for the interest damage of the delayed payment in sum of RMB5,657,801.34 should start from October 27, 2013 to July 28, 2014; 3. the beginning and ending time for the interest damage of the delayed payment in sum of RMB842,198.66 should start from November 16, 2013 to July 28, 2014; 4. the beginning and ending time for the interest damage of the delayed payment in sum of RMB146,094 should start from November 16, 2013 to October 28, 2014. All the interest above mentioned should be calculated based on one-year loan interest rate as promulgated by the People's Bank of China.

As for the Plaintiff's claim for the demurrage charge, empty charge, and storage charge in aggregate amount of RMB256,765.34 subordinate to the second, third, and fourth batch of cargo concerning Indian bridge, the Defendant did not recognize it and argued that both parties had come to an agreement on it; the Defendant agreed with the contract to bear the demurrage charge and empty charge totally in sum of RMB90,000; though by agreement it aimed at the second batch of the freight, orally it covered the whole sum of the second, third, and fourth batch of freight; what's more, the contract made by both parties was subordinate to the fixed price contract and the demurrage charge, empty charge and storage charge had covered in the transportation expenses. Therefore, there is no need to calculate the charges separately. The Plaintiff claimed that as for the second batch of demurrage charge and empty charge in sum of RMB90,000 made by three-party (including the two parties) agreement, the Defendant did not pay it off yet. Therefore, the Plaintiff had a right to claim the payment according to the actual expenses; in addition, the sum of RMB90,000 as agreed only pertained to the second batch of demurrage charge and empty charge and did not include the third and the fourth expenses; what's more, in the fixed price as agreed, the unit price of drayage was RMB80 per ton including colligation charges and demurrage charges and there was no demurrage charge within 2 days. Thus, when beyond 2 days, demurrage charge should be born by a party. The court holds that since the price in the contract pertained to a fixed price and there is no demurrage charge within 2 days in terms of the drayage as agreed, according to the semantic interpretation of the contract, the demurrage charge should be born when demurrage days of the ships were beyond 2 days; however, there is not a clear agreement in the contract with respect to the specific standard of the demurrage charge; the Plaintiff, as the party of through transportation, also failed to submit the written agreement with the party of barge concerning demurrage charge; from the Plaintiff's statement, it showed that the payment was determined by the party of barge without any evidence to prove whether the demurrage charge standard claimed by the barge party suited the current market condition; what's more, the payment to the barge party could not be distinguished whether it had connection with this case and the Defendant. The Defendant disagreed with these facts concerning the demurrage charge for the barge. Therefore, the court does not support the Plaintiff's claim for the so-called demurrage charge for the third and fourth batch of cargo. With respect to the storage charge, each party stuck to the argument and the Plaintiff did not submit any evidence to show it was the Defendant's fault that caused that charges. The Plaintiff as the opposite party of the transportation service contract signed with the Defendant, pursuant to the contract agreement, both parties should conduct the delivery list as for the shipment; the list not only had to contain the record of shipment but also the arrival time of the ship, the departure time of the ship; in addition, the list should be recognized by the Plaintiff and the Defendant's signature; the Plaintiff at least should submit the living delivery record signed by the Defendant; however, the Defendant denied the facts claimed by the Plaintiff; also, the Plaintiff, as the party who put forward the claim, could not submit any sufficient evidence. Therefore, since the relevant claims lacks evidence, the court refuses to support it. In respect to the demurrage charge and empty charge caused by transporting the second batch of cargo concerning the Indian bridge, since the Plaintiff and the Defendant together with the actual carrier had confirmed the expenses, according to the relativity of contract, the Defendant should pay the relevant demurrage charge and empty charge in sum of RMB90,000 to the Plaintiff who is the whole course carrier; the sum of RMB90,000 aimed at the second batch of cargo transportation. Whereas the three parties recognized the actual sum by negotiation after the Plaintiff brought the lawsuit and there is no actual payment time in the agreement, the court refuses to support the Plaintiff's claim for the compensation of the delayed payment interest towards the Defendant.

In respect to the Plaintiff's claim for relieving the Indian Bridge Contract, the Plaintiff asserted that, according to the contract agreement, the Defendant caused the overdue payment so the Plaintiff had the rescission right of the contract; however, the Defendant held that overdue payment did not pertain to a fundamental breach of contract and disagreed to relieve it; the court holds that the Plaintiff's claim was according to Section 1 of the Paragraph 2 "the two parties should, throughout the contract period, conduct the termination of this agreement by written notice once the following situations occur" of Article 11 "the enforcement and termination of the contract"; the main content is as follows: "once one party violates the provision of this contract and still or already could not remedy the nonperformance within 10 days from the day of receiving the other side's written notice". First, in the process of fulfilling the contract, the Plaintiff did not issue the written notice concerning the termination of the agreement according to the provision of that Article to exercise the rescission right of the contract; therefore, there should be no argument whether the Defendant had remedied the performance within 10 days from the day of receiving the other party's written notice; in addition, since the Plaintiff had brought the lawsuit, it obviously did not suit that agreement. However, the Plaintiff claimed that the action of filing the lawsuit can be seen as the written notice concerning the termination of the agreement, which lacks legal justification. Since the overdue payment of the Defendant did not pertain to the fundamental breach, which led to the failure of contract purpose by one party's violation pursuant to the provision of the contract law, the court refuses to support the Plaintiff's claim for rescinding the contract for lack of contractual and legal justification.

In conclusion, according to the Contract Law of the People's Republic of China Article 8, Article 60 Paragraph 1, Article 107, Article 113 Paragraph 1, Article 292, the Maritime Code of the People's Republic of China Article 69 Paragraph 1, the Civil Procedure Law of the People's Republic of China Article 64 Paragraph 1, the judgment is as follows:

1. The Defendant, Jiangsu Zhongtai Bridge Steel Structure Co., Ltd., shall pay the Plaintiff, China Shipping Logistics Co., Ltd., the freight subordinate to the Indian Bridge Contract in aggregate of RMB9,997,824.13 and the interest loss thereof (the interest shall be calculated based on the one-year loan interest rate as promulgated by the People's Bank of China as follows: the capital RMB3,355,390.49 as the cardinal value from January 21, 2014 to the date of payment set by this judgment; the capital RMB6,642,433.64 as the cardinal value from July 19, 2014 to the date of payment set by this judgment) within 10 days after the judgment comes into effect;

2. The Defendant, Jiangsu Zhongtai Bridge Steel Structure Co., Ltd., shall pay the Plaintiff, China Shipping Logistics Co., Ltd., the delayed interest loss caused by the Defendant, Jiangsu Zhongtai Bridge Steel Structure Co., Ltd.'s overdue payment of the use bill acceptance within 10 days after the judgment comes into effect (the interest shall be calculated based on the one-year loan interest rate as promulgated by the People's Bank of China as follows: the capital RMB3,000,000 as the cardinal value from October 27, 2013 to June 26, 2014; the capital RMB5,657,801.34 as the cardinal value from October 27, 2013 to July 28, 2014; the capital RMB842,198.66 as the cardinal value from November 16, 2013 to July 28, 2014; the capital RMB146,094 as the cardinal value from November 16, 2013 to October 28, 2014; the capital RMB1,853,906 as the cardinal value from January 21, 2014 to October 28, 2014; the capital RMB2,000,000 as the cardinal value from January 21, 2014 to November 30, 2014; the capital RMB2,000,000 as the cardinal value from January 21, 2014 to December 15, 2014);
3. The Defendant, Jiangsu Zhongtai Bridge Steel Structure Co., Ltd., shall return to the Plaintiff, China Shipping Logistics Co., Ltd., the tender bond subordinate to the Indian Bridge Project in aggregate amount of RMB200,000 within 10 days after the judgment comes into effect;
4. The Defendant, Jiangsu Zhongtai Bridge Steel Structure Co., Ltd., shall pay the Plaintiff, China Shipping Logistics Co., Ltd., the freight subordinate to the Denmark Bridge Contract in aggregate amount of RMB1,949,453.99 and the interest loss thereof within 10 days after the judgment comes into effect (the interest shall be calculated based on the one-year loan interest rate as promulgated by the People's Bank of China as follows: the capital RMB1,949,453.99 as the cardinal value from March 30, 2014 to the date of payment set by this judgment);
5. The Defendant, Jiangsu Zhongtai Bridge Steel Structure Co., Ltd., shall return to the Plaintiff, China Shipping Logistics Co., Ltd., the tender bond subordinate to the Denmark Bridge Project in aggregate amount of RMB200,000 within 10 days after the judgment comes into effect;
6. The Defendant, Jiangsu Zhongtai Bridge Steel Structure Co., Ltd., shall pay the Plaintiff, China Shipping Logistics Co., Ltd., the demurrage charge for short-time barge and empty charge in sum of RMB90,000 within 10 days after the judgment comes into effect;
7. Reject other claims of the Plaintiff, China Shipping Logistics Co., Ltd.

If the obligation of paying money is not performed within the time limit as prescribed in this judgment, interests of the debt of the delayed performance period shall be double paid by the Defendant, Jiangsu Zhongtai Bridge Steel Structure Co., Ltd., according to the Civil Procedure Law of the People's Republic of China Article 253.

Court acceptance fee in amount of RMB87,804 and the litigation preservation fee in amount of RMB5,000, the Plaintiff, China Shipping Logistics Co., Ltd., shall bear RMB804, and the Defendant, Jiangsu Zhongtai Bridge Steel Structure Co., Ltd., shall bear RMB92,000.

If not satisfy with this judgment, the parties concerned can submit copies of the original petitions to the court within 15 days of the date of service of the judgment and appeal to the Shanghai High People's Court.

Presiding Judge: KE Yonghong
Acting Judge: PAN Yan
People's Juror: LI Youwen

December 19, 2014

Clerk: CHEN Mengqi

Appendix: Relevant Law

1. **Contract Law of the People's Republic of China**
   Article 8 A lawfully established contract shall be legally binding on the parties thereto, each of whom shall perform its own obligations according to the terms of the contract, and no party shall unilaterally modify or terminate the contract. The contract established according to law is protected by law.
   Article 60 Each party shall fully perform its own obligations as agreed upon.
   Article 107 If a party fails to perform its obligations under a contract, or its performance fails to satisfy the terms of the contract, it shall bear the liabilities for breach of contract such as to continue to perform its obligations to take remedial measures, or to compensate for losses.
   Article 113: Where a party fails to perform its obligation under the contract or its performance fails to conform to the agreement and cause losses to the other party, the amount of compensation for losses shall be equal to the losses caused by the breach of contract, including the interests received after the performance of the contract, provided not exceeding the probable losses caused by the breach of contract which has been foreseen or ought to be foreseen when the party in breach concludes the contract.
   Article 292 A passenger, a consignor or a consignee shall pay the ticket-fare or freight.
2. **Maritime Code of the People's Republic of China**
   Article 69 The shipper shall pay the freight to the carrier as agreed.
3. **Civil Procedure Law of the People's Republic of China**

   Article 64 The party is responsible for providing evidence for the claims.

Shanghai High People's Court
Civil Judgment

China Shipping Logistics Co., Ltd.
v.
Jiangsu Zhongtai Bridge Steel Structure Co., Ltd.

(2015) Hu Gao Min Si (Hai) Zhong Zi No.25

Related Case(s) This is the judgment of second instance, and the judgment of first instance is on page 215.

Cause(s) of Action 202. Dispute over contract of carriage of goods by sea or sea-connected waters.

Headnote Affirming lower court decision holding freight forwarder entitled to recover damages for unpaid freight and interest on late payments of freight for two large projects.

Summary The Plaintiff freight forwarding contracted with the Defendant to provide shipping services in relation to two large projects. The Plaintiff sued after the Defendant delayed payment of freight and refused to return the bid bond that the Plaintiff had prepaid. The court of first instance found for the Plaintiff, awarding it damages for unpaid freight and for interest on the late payments of freight. The Defendant appealed. The appeal court recognized, holding that the facts were clearly found in the original judgment, and the law was correctly applied.

Judgment

The Appellant (the Defendant of first instance): Jiangsu Zhongtai Bridge Steel Structure Co., Ltd.
Legal representative: CHEN Mou.
Agent *ad litem*: ZHANG Xiaobin, lawyer of Jiangsu Jijiang Law Firm.

The Respondent (the Plaintiff of first instance): China Shipping Logistics Co., Ltd.
Legal representative: HUANG Moumou.
Agent *ad litem*: LI Chenbiao, lawyer of Beijing Zhonglun (Shanghai) Law Firm.
Agent *ad litem*: CHEN Liang, lawyer of Beijing Zhonglun (Shanghai) Law Firm.

Dissatisfied with the Civil Judgment (2014) Hu Hai Fa Shang Chu Zi No.1068 rendered by Shanghai Maritime Court with respect to the case arising from dispute over contract of carriage of goods by sea and maritime freight forwarding contract, the Appellant Jiangsu Zhongtai Bridge Steel Structure Co., Ltd. (hereinafter referred to as ZTSS) instituted an appeal with the court against China Shipping Logistics Co., Ltd. (hereinafter referred to as China Shipping). The court, after docketing and entertaining this case on February 5, 2015, constituted a collegiate panel according to the law, and held a hearing in public on April 1, 2015. ZHANG Xiaobin, agent *ad litem* of ZTSS, and LI Chenbiao, agent *ad litem* of China Shipping, appeared in court to attend the hearing. Now the case has been concluded.

China Shipping alleged that China Shipping and ZTSS entered into a contract of shipping service about the "Indian Bridge" and the "Danish Bridge" from 2013 to 2014. By the contract, China Shipping should provide the relevant transport service and performed the transport contract by stages; ZTSS should pay various freight and miscellaneous fees in time within 30 days after receiving China Shipping's invoice with the payment method being draft or bank transfer. Up to August 22, 2014, China Shipping had kept the contract, however ZTSS delayed the payment of the freight and miscellaneous fees in sum of RMB11,947,278.12, and various empty fees, demurrage fees, storage fees and overdue fees, totally RMB256,765.34, recognized by itself, and besides ZTSS did not return the bid bond, RMB400,000, prepaid by China Shipping. What's more, ZTSS also violated the contract agreements to pay the partial freight by means of acceptance draft, thereby causing the loss of China Shipping. Therefore, China Shipping requested the court of first instance to order as follows: 1. ZTSS paid China Shipping freights and miscellaneous fees in sum of RMB10,254,589.47 in total, delayed in the Indian Bridge Project, as well as the corresponding interests. (the rates of interests, calculated according to the bank loan interests in the coterminous rate, were respectively as follows: (1) the freight of the third batch in the Indian Bridge Project, RMB3,355,390.49, should be calculated starting on January 21, 2014 and terminating on the day when the judgment was taken into effect; (2) the freight of the fourth batch in the Indian Bridge Project, RMB6,642,433.64, should be calculated starting on July 19, 2014 and terminating on the day when the judgment was taken into effect; (3) other overdue fees, empty fees and demurrage fees, RMB256,765.34, should be calculated starting on August 18, 2014 and terminating on the day when the judgment was taken into effect); 2. ZTSS should pay China Shipping delayed interest loss, RMB687,979.96, due to delivering the long-term acceptance of draft; 3. ZTSS should restitute the bid bond of the Indian Bridge Project, RMB200,000, to China Shipping; 4. ZTSS should pay China Shipping various freight and miscellaneous fees, RMB1,949,453.99, and the corresponding interests delayed in the Danish Bridge Project (the rate, according to the bank loan interests in the coterminous rate, should be calculate starting on March 30, 2014 and terminating on the day when the judgment was taken into effect); 5. ZTSS should restitute the bid bond of the Danish Bridge Project, RMB200,000, to China Shipping; 6. the "India Bridge Shipping Service Contract" should be terminated;

7. ZTSS should undertake all of the court of first instance acceptance fee and preservation application fee, RMB5,000.

ZTSS argued as follows:

1. It recognized the amount in arrears of the freight, put forward by China Shipping, which was referred that up to November 5, 2014, ZTSS still defaulted in its payment for China Shipping of the third batch of the freight, RMB3,355,390.49 and the fourth batch of the freight RMB6,642,433.64 in the "Indian Bridge Project", and the freight, RMB1,949,453.99 in the "Danish Bridge Project", the total freight in arrears being RMB11,947,278.12.
2. It did not confirm the discount losses of the acceptance draft advocated by China Shipping. According to the second stipulation of Article 4 of *Shipping Service Contract* concerning the "Indian Bridge" signed by both parties: "Party A should pay the freight by means of bank transfer or the draft issued by the bank accepted by Party B", the acceptance draft was the payment method stipulated by both of China Shipping and ZTSS, and during the process of the actual performance of the contract, ZTSS, from December 2013, paid the freight of RMB15,500,000 by means of acceptance draft, to which China Shipping did not raise any objection; China Shipping's requiring ZTSS for undertaking the discount losses had no any factual evidence and legal basis, and so did its advocating of the late payment interests.
3. As for the demurrage charge and the empty charge, since both of China Shipping and ZTSS had already reached an agreement about those losses, and China Shipping recognized at court; and ZTSS agreed to undertake the demurrage charge and the empty charge, totally RMB90,000, according to the agreement. On the grounds that ZTSS had not performed the agreement yet, China Shipping requested ZTSS to undertake the demurrage charge and the empty charge, RMB256,765.24, which had no factual evidence and legal basis. ZTSS thought that since this part of losses was recognized by both parties and it represented both actual meaning, so both parties should perform this according the agreement, even though not performing would not affect the legal force. Besides, this agreement was reached during the process of proceeding for this case, and it did not stipulate the time limit for performance.
4. ZTSS did not recognized the evidence, offered by China Shipping, concerning losses of the demurrage charge and the empty charge calculated by the actual carrier. According to Article 3 Paragraph 3 of the *Shipping Service Contract* concerning the "Indian Bridge" signed by both parties: "the price of this contract should include the barging freight and all of the related fees for the transportation project", other terms of the contract did not stipulate the demurrage charge and the empty charge, which had already been included in the freight. There was no contractual relationship between the actual carrier and ZTSS, and according to the principle of relativity of contract, ZTSS should not undertake the related demurrage charge and the empty charge. Since the actual carrier had a stake with ZTSS, the evidence it put forward could not be regarded as the basis of settling the case.

5. Because China Shipping brought damage to the goods during the transporting process, the Danish customer had already lodged a claim to ZTSS for 140,000 Euros. Since China Shipping did not provide the ships with hoisting appliance as acquired, these cargoes could not be loaded at the Indian port, and the Indian customer had already lodged a claim to ZTSS for 978,000 dollars.
6. According to Article 4 Paragraph 1 of *Shipping Service Contract* concerning the "Indian Bridge" signed by both parties, China Shipping must submit the tax rebate for the declaration and the cancellation procedures for export earnings and the related materials within 30 days after China Shipping completed cargo declaration and shipping of every batch, however up to November 5, 2014, China Shipping had not still submit the related a report of the related materials for the fourth batch of the cargoes.
7. As for China Shipping's claim to terminating the *Shipping Service Contract* signed by both parties, ZTSS thought that there was not any legal basis for this claim and did not affirm it. Actually, ZTSS had already paid more than RMB19,700,000 as the freight; that there still existed residual money not paid was because China Shipping also violated the contract during the carriage process and it rejected to accept the bank acceptance given by ZTSS; and it unexpectedly lodged a lawsuit to the court of first instance, but even so, ZTSS had already made a commitment to pay in early November of 2014, therefore ZTSS's act did not constitute a fundamental breach of the contract and currently there merely existed dispute over the interest of the late payment, and obviously China Shipping's request to terminate the contract did not have any legal basis.

In order to prove its claim and ZTSS's cross-examination, the opinions of China Shipping were as follows:

1. Carriage contract of the Indian Bridge, to prove the contractual carriage relationship between China Shipping and ZTSS and the time for Defendant's paying the freight. ZTSS had no objection to the "three attributes" of this evidence.
2. Confirmation of the freight related to the Indian Bridge Project and the email, to prove that ZTSS recognized to pay the freight and miscellaneous fees, RMB9,997,824.13 for the Indian Bridge Project. ZTSS had no objection to the authenticity of the evidence and recognized in the pleading that it was still in arrears of the third batch of freight, RMB3,355,390.49, and the fourth batch of freight, RMB6,642,433.64.
3. Carriage contract of the Danish Bridge, to prove the contractual carriage relationship between China Shipping and ZTSS and the time for Defendant's paying the freight. ZTSS had no objection to the "three attributes" of this evidence.
4. Confirmation of the freight related to the Danish Bridge Project and the email, to prove that ZTSS recognized to pay the freight and miscellaneous fees for the Danish Bridge Project and to return the margin, totally RMB2,149,453.99. ZTSS had no objection to the "three attributes" of this evidence, but it put that it had already been put forward on the sixth page of the freight affirmation that as

for the paint damage of the goods caused during the period of barging and unloading on Shanghai waterfront, if the Danish side claimed for the compensation, it would be deducted from the freight related, and the Danish side had already made the claim.
5. Confirmation of the second batch of the transport planning in the Indian Bridge, mails, explanation of demurrage emptying, cost confirmation and time statistics confirmation of barging and loading, to prove that there existed barging demurrage and emptying in the second batch of the transportation of the Indian Bridge, and ZTSS confirmed to pay the demurrage charge, RMB67,500 and emptying charge, RMB130,000. ZTSS did not confirm the authenticity of the partial copies, and thought that evidence five mainly focused on the demurrage charge and emptying charge of the second batch of barge and both parties had already reached an agreement on those charges, which should be performed according to the agreement reached on September 17, 2014.
6. Confirmation of the third batch of transportation planning in the Indian Bridge, the time statistics of barging and loading, the statement of charge, to prove the third batch of transportation in the Indian Bridge incurred the charge of barge and demurrage, RMB20,000. ZTSS held a cross-examining opinion on evidence six was the same as evidence five, and at the same time it thought that the agreement, reached on September 17, 2014, was focused on the costs of the second, the third and the fourth batches of the Indian Bridge Project, therefore it should be performed together according to this agreement.
7. Statement of Tianjin Hua Jie Logistics Co., Ltd. and China Shipping Logistics Co., Ltd., to prove that Tianjin Hua Jie Logistics Co., Ltd. and China Shipping Logistics Co., Ltd., as the agent of China Shipping, arranged the second and third batch of transportation in the Indian Bridge. ZTSS had no objection to evidence seven, and indicated that the second, the third and the fourth batch of the transportation business in the Indian Bridge Project had already been performed specifically and ZTSS had no objection.
8. The confirmation mail of the fourth batch of the transporting calculation in the Indian Bridge, the final statement of the charge, the confirmation of the time statistics of the barging and loading and the cost confirmation of the Shanghai Guangyu International Freight Agency Co., Ltd.(hereinafter referred to as Shanghai Guangyu), to prove that the fourth batch of the transportation incurred barging demurrage charge, RMB35,000, and the storage charge, RMB4,265. ZTSS held a cross-examining opinion on this evidence was the same as evidence five and six.
9. Receipt of the bid bond for the Indian Bridge, to prove that China Shipping paid ZTSS RMB200,000 as margin as for the Indian Bridge Project. ZTSS had no objection to the "three attributes" of this evidence.
10. Acceptance draft, to prove that ZTSS paid the partial charge of the second and the third batch for the Indian Bridge by means of acceptance draft, which caused the delay in payment and incurred the loss of interest. ZTSS had no objection to the authenticity of evidence ten, but it thought that ZTSS should not pay the discount loss or delay the interest on payment.

11. Contract for loan of the working capital and the tax list of transferring, to prove that, due to ZTSS's delay of payment, China Shipping got a loan from the bank. ZTSS had no objection to the authenticity of this evidence, but it thought that this evidence had no relevancy with this case, because China Shipping borrowed RMB200,000,000, and ZTSS was only in the arrears of RMB10,000,000, which could not be taken as an evidence to prove that ZTSS's delay of payment caused China Shipping's borrowing money.
12. Tender document, to prove that China Shipping bid on ZTSS as for the Indian Bridge Project. ZTSS had no objection to the "three attributes" of this evidence.
13. Receipt and the collection certificate of the acceptance draft, to prove that the acceptance draft with the tail number 7533-7535 (totally RMB3,000,000) was accepted on June 27,2014 after the maturity, and China Shipping did not have the endorsement transfer. ZTSS did not have objection to the authenticity of this evidence but thought that it could not prove that ZTSS should pay China Shipping the discount interest of the acceptance draft, and at the same time as for the freight, totally RMB15,500,000, paid for China Shipping by ZTSS in that way, China Shipping only provided the certificate of the acceptance at maturity of RMB3,000,000, and ZTSS had reason to believe that other acceptance drafts had already been transferred by China Shipping.
14. Bill and invoice issued by Shanghai Guangyu as for the third batch of barging fees and demurrage fees in the Indian Bridge, to prove that the third batch of the Indian Bridge incurred extra fees, RMB481,696, including unpaid RMB20,000 which should have been paid by ZTSS. ZTSS thought that China Shipping could not present the original evidence, so ZTSS could not confirm the authenticity and the evidence could not prove the specific amount of the demurrage fees actually paid for ZTSS by China Shipping or the causes of paying the demurrage fees. There was not contractual relationship between ZTSS and Shanghai Guangyu, and the contract between China Shipping and ZTSS had already been explicitly stipulated in terms of the contract price, so ZTSS should not pay the demurrage fees.
15. Bill and invoice issued by Shanghai Guangyu as for the fourth batch of barging fees and demurrage fees in the Indian Bridge, to prove that China Shipping paid Shanghai Guangyu barging fees and demurrage fees, RMB976,680 in the fourth batch of the Indian Bridge, including the unpaid RMB35,000 for ZTSS and the storage fees RMB4265.64. The cross-examining opinion on this evidence of ZTSS was the same as that of the fourteenth evidence.
16. Certification issued by China Merchants Bank Co., Ltd. Shanghai Dongdaming Branch (hereafter referred to as CMB Dongdaming Branch), the original bank acceptance draft with the tail number 0115, and the collection certificate of the bank acceptance draft with the tail number 3286, to prove that the bank acceptance draft (totally RMB3,000,000) with the tail number 7533-7573 was accepted on June 27, 2014, No.9745 and No.9747-9749 bank acceptance drafts (totally RMB5,500,000) on July 28, 2014, and No.9746 (totally RMB1,000,000) on September 1, 2014, but the deadline of the corresponding interest advocated by ZTSS was July 28, that was acceptance draft maturity;

No.2780 bank acceptance draft (totally RMB2,000,000) was accepted on October 28, 2014, No.3286 bank acceptance draft (totally RMB2,000,000) matured on November 30, 2014, and China Shipping entrusted the bank to collect on December 8, 2014. The maturity date of No.0115 bank acceptance draft (totally RMB2,000,000) was January 9, 2015, and this draft had not been endorsed and transferred up to now, and China Shipping ensured that it would not endorse and transfer this draft before the maturity date, and the deadline of corresponding interest advocated by China Shipping was the court of first instance day, that was December 15, 2014. ZTSS thought that there existed tearing and sticking mark in the bank certificate, so ZTSS had objection to the authenticity of the evidence, and China Shipping should provide the corresponding collection certificate rather than the certificate issued by the bank. There was no objection to the original copies of the collection certificate of No.0115 and No.3286 acceptance drafts.

17. Detailed information about the invoice issuing and the situation of the outgoing mails and the express circulation, to prove that the following invoice, sent by China Shipping in terms of express, were signed by ZTSS: (1) the invoice of RMB9,657,812.33 in the second batch of the Indian Bridge was signed by ZTSS on September 27, 2013; (2) the invoice of RMB988,292.66 of the second batch of the Indian Bridge was signed by ZTSS on October 17, 2013; (3) the invoice of RMB9,209,296.49 of the third batch of the Indian Bridge was signed by ZTSS on December 22, 2013; (4) the invoice of RMB642,433.64 of the fourth batch of the Indian Bridge was signed by ZTSS on June 19, 2014; (5) the invoice of RMB1,949,453.99 of the Danish Bridge were signed by ZTSS on February 28, 2014. ZTSS had no objection to the authenticity of STO courier receipt, and it confirmed that it had received the invoice for SF-Express but could not remember the concrete time, and it could not confirm the fax of SF-Express courier receipt.

In order to support its defensing opinions, ZTSS submitted the following rebuttal evidence and China Shipping's cross-examining opinions:

1. Confirmations of the fees and the time for demurrage on September 17, 2014, to prove that after China Shipping prosecuted, both parties, China Shipping and ZTSS, had entered into a negotiation on the demurrage fees and the empty fees and finally reached an agreement that ZTSS should undertake the total fee, RMB90,000 and that fee was confirmed as the total related fee for the second, the third and the fourth batch of the Indian Bridge. Because the content of the negotiation not only included the empty fees and the demurrage fees but also the interest and so on, ZTSS planned to pay all the fees after finishing all the negotiation. China Shipping had no objection to the authenticity of the two sets of evidence, but it thought that the two sets of evidence could only prove the result of the negotiation of the second batch in the Indian Bridge, and ZTSS actually did not performed that actually, so China Shipping still advocated the fees according to the actual expenses.

2. A copy of e-mail, to prove that the Indian customer lodged a claim for 978,000 dollars. China Shipping did not confirm the "three attributes" of this e-mail and thought that it could not prove that ZTSS suffered the related losses.
3. A copy of e-mail, to prove that the Danish customer lodged a claim for 140,000 Euros. China Shipping put it that it had transferred this e-mail to ZTSS and confirmed the authenticity of this e-mail, but it did not confirm the purpose of the evidence; and according to the acquaintance from the Danish agency, there was not huge claim at all and even if there was, it had no relationship with this case and there was not any causality between the compensation for the cargo damage and the payment of the freight.
4. A collection of photos, to prove that China Shipping caused the cargo damage during the process of transporting. China Shipping did not confirm the authenticity, relevancy and legality, and the relevancy between those photos and the transporting of the Danish Bridge could not been verified and it could not help to achieve the purpose of proof of ZTSS.

The court of first instance's certificating opinions of the evidence from both of the parties, China Shipping and ZTSS, were as follows.

As for the evidence 1, 2, 3, 9, and 12 of China Shipping, ZTSS had no objection to their "three attributes" and the proving matters, and the court of first instance recognized the evidentiary effect and probative force. ZTSS also had no objection to the "three attributes" of China Shipping's evidence 4 and the court of first instance recognized that. Regarding ZTSS put it that its business manager had made a note on the confirmation slip of the freight, the court of first instance thought that the note was just made unilaterally from ZTSS, ZTSS needed to present other evidence to prove whether the content of the note was verified, and it lacked evidence to advocate to deduct the freight in back pay only by resorting to the note. Besides, taking into consideration that in the written pleading and trial of this case, ZTSS recognized that it was still in arrears for China Shipping of the third batch of freight, RMB3,355,390.49 and the fourth, RMB6,642,433.64 for the Indian Bridge Project, and the freight, RMB1,949,453.99 for the Danish Bridge Project and owed the Indian Bridge Project and the Danish Bridge Project the bid bond, each RMB200,000, and ZTSS was willing to pay and return those above freight and bid bond, and it expected to solve those problems under the condition of consensus of the interests with China Shipping, ZTSS's opinions had already constituted the legal self-admission, so the court of first instance recognized and as for this ZTSS did not need to prove it. The fifth group of China Shipping's evidence was mainly used to prove that during the cargo transporting process of the second batch in the Indian Bridge Project, there incurred barging demurrage charge and empty charge and the their specific amount, even though ZTSS thought that the partial evidence was just copies and therefore could not be confirmed, ZTSS also indicated and illustrated that on September 17, 2014, after communication, China Shipping, ZTSS, and the third party, Zhangjiagang City Huaji Logistics Co., Ltd. (the actual barging carrier), confirmed that the second batch of the barging empty charge was RMB50,000 and the second batch of barging factory wharf demurrage charge was

RMB40,000, and after the signed confirmation of those three parties, China Shipping had no objection to this, therefore the court of first instance recognized this fact. As for the point put forward by China Shipping that despite reaching an agreement from the three parties, ZTSS did not actually perform, the court of first instance would make a statement below about whether China Shipping's opinion of advocating the original amount was valid. At the same time, ZTSS indicated that the three parties' confirmation referred to the negotiation and confirmation of the second, third, and fourth batch of the related demurrage charge, empty charge, and storage charge in the Indian Bridge; the court of first instance held that seeing from the content of the three parties' confirmation, it showed clearly to aim at the second batch of barging empty charge and demurrage charge not concern the third and the fourth batch, and ZTSS had no evidence to prove that Zhangjiagang City Huaji Logistics Co., Ltd. was the barging party of the third and fourth batch of cargo transporting, therefore ZTSS's related opinions lacked evidence and the court of first instance did not affirm. ZTSS had no objection to evidence 7 of China Shipping, adduced by the third party, and the court of first instance recognized its probative force. Regarding evidence 6, 8, 14, and 15 of China Shipping, China Shipping attempted to prove that there incurred demurrage charges and storage charges during the short barging transporting process of the third and fourth batch of the Indian Bridge Project, ZTSS did not affirm those evidence and indicated that there did not occur barging demurrage and extra storage showed by China Shipping, and even if there happened, it was caused by China Shipping. The court of first instance held that even though China Shipping could prove that it paid the actual barging carrier and the wharf the corresponding charges, with only the available information submitted by China Shipping it could not prove directly that the barging demurrage and extra storage, etc. claimed by China Shipping were caused by the aspect of ZTSS, therefore the court of first instance did not affirm the evidentiary effect and the probative force of those evidential materials. With respect to evidence Ten of China Shipping, the acceptance draft, ZTSS had no objection to its authenticity and the court of first instance recognized its probative force; combining opinions of both sides, it could prove that ZTSS paid China Shipping the freight of the second batch and partial freight of the third batch for the Indian Bridge Project, RMB15,500,000, by means of long-term bank acceptance, but it needed to combine with other evidence for comprehensive recognition to judge whether that was delayed payment, and the specific recognition would be shown below. ZTSS had no objection to the authenticity of evidence 11 of China Shipping, contract for loan and the tax list of transferring, but it thought that it was irrelevant to this case and could not prove that it was because of ZTSS's delayed payment that caused China Shipping to borrow a loan from the bank, and the court of first instance held that the defense of ZTSS was valid; one of the proof aims of China Shipping's providing the evidence was to prove the standard of interest losses of the delayed payment, and ZTSS had already recognized in the court of first instance trial that the calculating standard for the default losses should be adopted when it formed the default in delayed payment, which China Shipping also recognized, therefore the court of first instance recognized the calculating standard for the interest losses of the delayed payment, confirmed by both sides. As for evidence 13 of China Shipping, the court of first instance held that China Shipping provided the receipt and the collection certificate from the entrust bank of three acceptance drafts, the numbers all being the same, which could prove that those three drafts were all used to entrust the bank to collect and enter into the account after maturity; evidence 16 of China Shipping were the certificates issued by the entrusted bank for collection, and ZTSS pointed out that there were marks of tearing and sticking in this certificate and objected to its authenticity; the court of first instance held that even though there existed sticking marks, analyzing those marks, they were torn from the middle part of the documents and the two torn parts were completely anastomotic from their content, and it was impossible for China Shipping to fake; ZTSS was the applying drawer of those acceptance drafts, and it also could investigate the accepting of those drafts from the accepting bank, Agricultural Bank of China Jingjiang Branch, therefore the court of first instance recognized the evidentiary effect and probative force of the bank certification. As for the draft with the tail number, 9746 and the maturity, July 28, 2014, the actual accepting date was September 1, 2014, but China Shipping also recognized the advocated deadline of the overdue interest, July 28, 2014, and the court of first instance recognized that. The collection certificate of the draft with the tail number, 0115 and that with 3826 were both original copies, and ZTSS had no objection to those, and the court of first instance recognized its evidentiary effect and probative force. ZTSS had objection to the tracer through seal confirmation by the third party, the express company in evidence Seventeen, and the court of first instance recognized its evidentiary effect and probative force; as for the fax of SF-Express, ZTSS had objection to the authenticity of its form but recognized that the corresponding invoice had been received, and ZTSS did not provide the contrary evidence to deny the authenticity of the fax of the courier receipt within the time regulated by the court of first instance, therefore the court of first instance recognized the evidentiary effect of this material, which would prove the time, advocated by China Shipping, when ZTSS received the related invoice of the freight.

  Evidence 1 of ZTSS: it agreed with two copies of materials of evidence 5 of China Shipping, China Shipping had no objection to its authenticity, and the court of first instance recognized its probative force; as for whether the certification and the purpose of this evidence submitted by ZTSS could be achieved, the court of first instance would make certification comprehensively according to the content recorded in this evidence and combining other evidence. Evidence 2 of ZTSS: it was a printed copy, and ZTSS argued that it was the e-mail sent by the Indian customer, the third party, but it could not provide the original mail through notarial certification and conforming to the important document of evidential form; besides China Shipping denied receiving this e-mail, therefore the court of first instance did not affirm the probative force of this material. Evidence 3 and 4 of ZTSS: China Shipping recognized that it had received this mail forwarded by ZTSS, that was evidence 3, but it did not affirm the evidential purpose; as for evidence 4, China Shipping did not affirm its "three attributes", and the court of first instance held that ZTSS, through providing this evidence, aimed at proving that during the process of performing the Danish Bridge Contract, the cargo damage was caused by China Shipping's actions, further bringing about the claim from the Danish customer; however, this evidential purpose could not be achieved merely from this e-mail and photos, therefore the court of first instance did not affirm the probative forces of those two groups of materials.

According to the above verdict evidence and combining the investigation of the trial, the facts of this case ascertained by the court of first instance were as follows.

1. The signing of the Indian Bridge Contract. China Shipping and ZTSS signed *Maritime Service Contract of Indian Driva Gila Bud Bridge Steel Tower and Steel Beams* (hereinafter referred to as "Indian Bridge Contract") in Jingjiang Jiangsu on March 29, 2013. In Article 1 of the contract, China Shipping should be responsible for the following work according to the batch of goods: barge, providing the materials of the transporting project of the steel beam and steel tower for the Indian Bridge received by ZTSS's own factory area of the domestic dispatch place, Jingjiang Industrial Park, and the ship of the wharf barging (the charge related with shipment would be undertaken by ZTSS), barging binding, strengthening, gasket, transporting to the ship on Shanghai Port/berthing and congregating, customs declaration & commodity inspection, shipment, binding, strengthening, gasket, ship transporting to Indian Kandla Port and unloading and delivering. It was further made clear in Annex II. The rate/price list and shipping service condition made further definitude, that ZTSS should be in charge of floating shipment in ZTSS's own factory area of the dispatch place, Jingjiang Industrial Park, and China Shipping should provide the suitable barging and cooperate with the shipment and should be in charge of barging binding, strengthening and gasket and so on. In Annex V, barging service terms, before shipping China Shipping and ZTSS should sign for transition on the goods delivery order of this voyage, and after the goods arrived at the designated spot, China Shipping should be in charge of submitting the goods delivery order to the department of the shipping port for transition and inspection. After China Shipping and ZTSS determined the shipping date, ZTSS issued the shipping notice accordingly, and China Shipping must confirm that within 24 h after receiving ZTSS's shipping notice and berth ships on ZTSS's port two days before shipping. Under the conditions stated, China Shipping did not receive ZTSS's shipping notice, China Shipping berthed its ship on ZTSS's port by its own, ZTSS did not undertake any responsibility, and China Shipping itself undertook the risk and responsibility and all of the resulting charges. During the process of performing the contract, China Shipping should designate one specialized manager to take charge of transporting coordination, and China Shipping should be in full charge of transportation. In the first paragraph of Article 3, contract price, this contract is a price-fixed contract, and it should take the final settlement as the standard as for the specific chargeable tonnage. The amount of the contact should be divided into two parts, and the price should be temporarily determined like the following, the sea freight being 4,377,004 dollars and the domestic barge and the local charge on seaport being

RMB2,988,920. The cargo should be divided into five batches to ship: the first batch includes 9,117.43 revenue tons and 2,955 weight tons; the second 15,486.19 revenue tons and 2,891 weight tons; the third 23,037.18 revenue tons and 3,527 weight tons; the fourth 13,391.81 revenue tons and 2,814 weight tons; the fifth 4,091.68 revenue tons and 2,381 weight tons; the total five batches include 65,124.29 revenue tons and 14,568 weight tons. The specific rates and price are as follows: from ZTSS's own wharf to Shanghai Port, the charge of short barge should be RMB80/weight ton, including packing charge, dunnage charge and two days' demurrage charge free; the ground local charge of Shanghai port should be RMB28/revenue ton; the short barging charge is determined temporarily as RMB1,165,440 and the ground local charge of Shanghai port is determined temporarily as RMB1,823,480. As for the sea freight (heavy lift vessel) from Shanghai Port to Kandla Port, the unit price of the first batch is 90 dollars/revenue tons and the unit prices of the second, third, fourth, and fifth batch are all 63.5 dollars/revenue tons, and the sea freights of the five batches are respectively 820,569 dollars, 983,373 dollars, 1,462,861 dollars, 850,380 dollars, and 259,822 dollars, temporarily determined as 4,377,004 dollars. According the third paragraph of Article 3, Contract Price, of the contract, the contract price should include the lighterage of the transporting project (including unloading not loading), the sea freight (including loading not unloading), the local lump sum charge of Shanghai Port, customs inspection fee, the charge for binding, stowing, packing and ship insuring of ship and the steel structure on the barge, profits, taxes and charges of the maritime coordination and accreditation, managing charges, and all the other charges related to transporting (except the stipulated charges in the contract). The charging standards in Annex IV are as follows: (1) The lump sum form of contract billing should be implemented in port charges (as for the port revenue ton, it should take the weight on the bill of lading as the standard and the port local charge should include harbor charge, the agency fees of the space booking, port constructing fee, tallying and list taking fee and costume and inspection fee.); (2) All of the port charges related to shipping port are already included in the contract price, so there is no need to calculate separately. It was stipulated in the first paragraph of Article IV, manner of paying, that China Shipping should provide the special invoice for the transporting business, clean bills of lading, customs declaration and the related customs documentation of every batch of maritime cargo, and the documentation should meet the requirement of credit; after ZTSS confirms the amount, it should arrange for the freight payment within 30 days after receiving the invoice. China Shipping must submit the tax refund of custom declaration, the verification procedures of export and the related documentation within 30 days after finishing the customs clearance and shipment of every batch. ZTSS should pay the freight by means of bank transfer or the draft issued by China Shipping's accepted bank. According to the 20th term of Article 7, Paragraph 2 of the contract, China Shipping should send the full set of clean bills of lading, meeting the requirement of ZTSS's credit within seven working days after sailing, and the tax refund documents of export, the

foreign exchange procedures of verification, shipping order, the original copies of the certificates regulated by other credits within 2 weeks to ZTSS by express (providing the scanning copies by mail before sending out). According to the 2nd term of Article 8, Paragraph 1 of the contract, when ZTSS breaks the contractual regulation and does not pay China Shipping freight costs on time, it should undertake the responsibility of breach. In Term 1, Paragraph 2, of Article 11, the contract's operation and termination, of the contract, when the party is in the contractual period, if the other party breaks the contractual regulation and no remedy is reached or has already failed to remedy its breach of contract within ten days after receiving the written notice from the party, then the party can terminate the agreement immediately by means of written notice.
2. The performance of the Indian Bridge Contract. Both China Shipping and ZTSS recognized, and there was no objection to the fact that the payment of the freight and the transportation of the first batch in the Indian Bridge Project had already been completed.

After sending off the second batch of the cargo in the contract of Indian Bridge Project, China Shipping issued an invoice with total amount of RMB9,657,812.33 for ZTSS on September 25, 2013 and sent it to ZTSS by means of express, and ZTSS signed and accepted on September 27. China Shipping again issued an invoice with total amount of RMB988,292.66 for ZTSS on October 15, 2013 and sent it to ZTSS by means of express, and ZTSS signed and accepted on October 17. After that, ZTSS paid China Shipping the second batch of the cargo freight in the Indian Bridge Contract by means of cash or bank acceptance, and the specific situations of the payment were as follows.

1 ZTSS delivered three bank acceptance drafts with the same amount being respectively RMB1,000,000 to China Shipping (the numbers were respectively XXXXXXXXXXXXXXXX, XXXXXXXXXXXXXXXX, XXXXXXX XXXXXXXXX), the issuing dates were all December 26, 2013, and the maturity dates were all June 26, 2014. China Shipping delivered those three acceptance drafts to CMB Dongdaming Branch for consignment collection on June 27, 2014, and all the money entered into the account of China Shipping on July 3; 2. ZTSS paid China Shipping the cash of RMB1,000,000 on January 3, 2014; 3. ZTSS delivered five bank acceptance drafts with the same amount being respectively RMB1,000,000 and one with the amount being RMB1,500,000 to China Shipping (the numbers was XXXX-XXXX), the issuing dates were all January 28, 2014, and the maturity dates were all July 28, 2014. On July 28, 2014, China Shipping entrusted CMB Dongdaming Branch to make collections with 5 pieces of drafts and received all funds into its account by collection. On September 1, 2014, China Shipping entrusted CMB Dongdaming Branch to make collections with the draft No.XXXX and received all funds into its account by collection; 4. On April 29, 2014, ZTSS delivered a piece of bank acceptance bill with the sum of RMB2 million to China Shipping; the date of its bill was on April 28, 2014 and the due date was on October 28,

2014. On October 28, 2014, China Shipping entrusted CMB Dongdaming Branch to make collections with the draft and received all funds into its account by collection. China Shipping had recognized that the sum of RMB146,094 served as the remaining freight of the second batch of cargo; thus, the freight principal of the second batch of cargo had been all paid and the remaining sum of RMB1,853,906 had been served as the freight of third batch of cargo. Moreover, ZTSS once received China Shipping's charge confirmation sheet which recorded the second lighterage of Indian bridge with the sum of RMB130,000 and the second demurrage of factory wharf with the sum of RMB67,500. On September 17, 2014, through the three parties' exchanges by China Shipping, ZTSS and Zhangjiagang City Huaji Logistics Co., Ltd. as the person not involved in this case (the actual carrier of barge), recognized that the second empty charge of barge was in sum of RMB50,000 and the second demurrage barge factory wharf was in sum of RMB40,000; it was also recognized that the charge confirmation sheet should be signed or sealed by the representatives from the three sides.

When the third batch of cargo subordinate to the Indian Bridge Contract was shipped, China Shipping, on December 20, 2013, issued a piece of invoice to ZTSS with the total sum of RMB9,209,296.49 and sent it to ZTSS by express; ZTSS signed for the invoice on December 22, 2013. Afterwards, ZTSS paid several parts of freight by bank acceptance bill and its specific circumstances were as follows: 1. the amount of RMB1,853,906 in the bank acceptance bill whose date was on April 28, 2014 with the sum of RMB2 million; 2. on May 30, 2014, ZTSS delivered a piece of bank acceptance bill with the sum of 2 million yuan to China Shipping; the date of its bill was on May 30, 2014 and the due date was on November 30, 2014; on December 2, 2014, China Shipping entrusted CMB Dongdaming Branch to make collections with the draft and, on December 8, 2014, received all funds into its account by collection; 3. on 9 July 2014, ZTSS delivered a piece of bank acceptance bill with the sum of 2 million yuan to China Shipping; the date of its bill was on July 9, 2014 and the due date was on January 9, 2015; on December 15, 2014, China Shipping submitted the original bank acceptance bill in the court of first instance of first instance hearing and did not make any endorsement; China Shipping ensured that the bank acceptance bill should not be endorsed by the due date of the bill and claimed that the delayed payment interest of the fund should be calculated until the date of December 15, 2014 (the date of the court of first instance of first instance). From the outset of hearing the case, ZTSS recognized to owe China Shipping the freight of the third batch of cargo with the amount of RMB3,355,390.49.

When the fourth batch of cargo subordinate to the Indian Bridge Contract was shipped, on May 7, 2014, ZTSS recognized the freight of the fourth batch of cargo with the sum of RMB968,292.45 and verified the expenses of domestic trade barge and Shanghai Harbor Ground Operation with the sum of RMB685,401.66 on China Shipping's charge confirmation sheet. China Shipping issued the above mentioned freight invoice to ZTSS on June 18, 2014 and sent it by express to ZTSS who signed for it the next day. From the outset of hearing the case, ZTSS recognized to owe China Shipping the freight of the fourth batch of cargo with the amount of RMB6,642,433.64.

Both of China Shipping and ZTSS recognized that the fifth batch of cargo subordinate to the Indian Bridge Contract had not been carried out.

3. Conclusion and performance of Denmark Bridge Contract. On January 27, 2014, both parties of China Shipping and ZTSS signed *Steel Structural Parts of Denmark Bridge Transport Service Contract* (hereinafter referred to as Denmark Bridge Contract). Pursuant to Article 1 of the contract, according to the requirement of cargo batches China Shipping should provide the barge of the second batch of cargo for the steel structural parts of Denmark bridge at the domestic departure place where ZTSS factory wharf in Jingjiang Industrial Zone was located, cargo receipt on board (ZTSS in charge of its shipment), colligation, consolidation as well as cargo pad; and then China Shipping should provide the barge at Shanghai Harbor hook or rail/mooring congregation, custom and inspection, shipment, colligation, consolidation, cargo pad, cargo insurance as well as the transportation by sea in ships to Copenhagen Harbor (China Shipping's responsibility excluding the unloading at the destination port). Pursuant to Paragraph 1 of Article 6 "On the Price" of the Contract, this contract should be the fixed unit price agreement. The sum in the contract should be divided into two parts and the price should be arranged for the time being as follows: ocean freight containing taxes totaling RMB281,913.3; domestic barge expenses and harbor handling expenses totaling RMB32,849.03. Pursuant to Paragraph 2, the price in the contract should contain the same transportation items with the above mentioned Indian Bridge Contract except the item "ocean freight (loading but with no discharging)". Pursuant to Paragraph 3 on Payment Condition, China Shipping should issue a VAT invoice with 6% deduction after the ship bears off; if any temporary change in policy meant that China Shipping could not provide the deductible VAT invoice of the ocean freight, ZTSS should accept the ocean freight which was balanced by the plain VAT invoice and China Shipping should deduct the relevant taxation in expense confirmation. ZTSS should pay the full amount in cash within 30 days by the date of receiving the invoice and declaration form. Pursuant to Article 9 of the Contract "On Indemnity", if one party in this contract did not fulfill its responsibilities by convention or made any fault so as to cause the financial loss of the other side, it should claim for indemnity to the default party in written form according to the relevant articles of this contract. When the subject cargo was shipped, China Shipping sent ZTSS the expense confirmation totaling USD319,399.36 (6.1 as the current exchange rate); on February 21, 2014, ZTSS signed and sealed on the expense confirmation sheet and noted that the above mentioned data was checked correctly. Since the paint was damaged in the period of barging and unloading at Shanghai Wharf, the relevant liability should be undertaken by transport unit if Denmark client claims for indemnity. The subject indemnity should be deducted from transportation expenses. On February 27, 2014, China

Shipping issued the freight invoice totaling USD319,399.36 to ZTSS and sent it by express to ZTSS who signed for it the next day. In the court of first instance hearing, China Shipping recognized to have received ZTSS's forwarded e-mail in regard to Denmark client's claim to ZTSS for the indemnity of EUR140,000.

4. Information on Correspondence Negotiation by China Shipping and ZTSS

On July 14, 2014, China Shipping sent several documents concerning the payment of project freight and its operation by mail or express; China Shipping claimed that ZTSS's overdue time for the projection freight, which was supposed to be paid to China Shipping, seriously departed from the articles of the contract and effected China Shipping's capital turnover and production scheduling; China Shipping wanted ZTSS to make arrangement for payment as soon as possible and finish the confirmation of expense incurred as fast as he could, which included: 1. freight. Uncleared Freight of the Third Batch of Indian Bridge in sum of RMB3,355,390.49; uncleared freight of the Fourth Batch of Indian Bridge in aggregate amount of RMB6,642,433.64; freight of Denmark Bridge in sum of RMB1,949,454.24. 2. Bid Bond. tendering for ZTSS's American Bridge Project (noting: it was recognized to be unconcerned with this case by China Shipping and ZTSS) and the Denmark Bridge Project, China Shipping respectively submitted the cash deposit in sum of RMB200,000 (totaling RMB400,000) for each project; the projects above mentioned had finished all tendering while ZTSS had not sent back the cash deposit to China Shipping on time according to the return date of tender documents; ZTSS should send them back as soon as possible. 3. Without Expense Confirmation. The Second Batch of Barge Empty Charge in aggregate amount of RMB130,000; Demurrage Charge for Domestic Trade Barge in aggregate amount of RMB67,500; Demurrage Charge for Domestic Trade Barge Concerning the Third Batch of Indian Bridge in sum of RMB20,000; terminal Storage Charge for the Fourth Batch of Indian Bridge in sum of RMB4,265.34; Barge Overdue Fee in sum of RMB35,000; totaling RMB256,765.34; as for the foregoing expenses incurred, ZTSS should submit confirmation before the date of July 18. 4. Interest Subsidy of Acceptance Bill & Penalty for Overdue Payment. As for China Shipping's partial discount interest damages arising from ZTSS's payment for acceptance bill, the interest subsidy totaled RMB546,097.23 and should be confirmed before the date of 18 July. Meanwhile, combined with the two parties' agreement on the term of freight payment, China Shipping's overdue capital cost had been added on account of ZTSS's overdue payment for the freight; pursuant to relevant legal legislation, as for those contracting parties who had not made any convention on the penalty standard for overdue payment, it should be calculated based on the interest rate standard for the loan over the corresponding period with the same kind as promulgated by the People's Bank of China. On July 17, 2014, as for the correspondence of the project freight and relevant operation, ZTSS replied China Shipping as follows: (1) pursuant to the freight confirmation sheet signed & sealed by ZTSS and the invoice issued by China Shipping concerning the third batch of cargo of Indian bridge, the remaining freight, in sum of RMB3,355,390.49, should be paid according to the monthly freight payment sheet; (2) pursuant to the freight confirmation sheet signed & sealed by ZTSS and the invoice issued by China Shipping concerning the fourth batch cargo of Indian bridge, the freight, in sum of RMB6,642,433.64, should be paid according to the monthly freight payment sheet; (3) pursuant to the freight confirmation sheet signed & sealed by ZTSS and the invoice issued by China Shipping concerning the cargo freight of Denmark bridge, the freight, in sum of RMB1,949,453.99, should be paid according to the monthly freight payment sheet; (4) with regard to the cash deposit submitted by China Shipping for tendering ZTSS's American Bridge Project and the Denmark Bridge Project (totaling 2* RMB200,000), it should be returned in the schedule of monthly freight payment; (5) in term of the unconfirmed expenses mentioned by China Shipping, we have raised doubts several times to you; the so-called expenses were not only caused by us but at a large extent created by China Shipping; what's more, it also brings us some losses so we reserve the claim rights. ZTSS suggested that these disputes should be solved by negotiation after the whole project. Later on, since ZTSS still had not paid, China Shipping sued ZTSS in the court of first instance.

The court of first instance also found out that when tendering for the American Bridge Project and the Denmark Bridge Project, China Shipping respectively submitted the cash deposit in aggregate amount of RMB200,000 (totaling in RMB400,000) for each project. ZTSS recognized the sum of the subject cash deposit and recognized it should be returned. In the hearing, ZTSS recognized that it did not compensate the foreign side in regard to the relevant issues regarding the Indian bridge and Denmark bridge. Both China Shipping and ZTSS recognized that the interest standard to the overdue payment should be calculated based on the one-year loan interest rate as promulgated by the People's Bank of China.

The court of first instance held that China Shipping and ZTSS involved had no objection to the contractual relation established by signing the transportation service contract. Although the contract was named as the transportation service contract, it was in fact subordinate to the comprehensive contract containing cargo transportation and freight forwarder from the analysis of the content. In the hearing, the two parties recognized that the cause of this case should be determined as the contract of carriage of goods by sea and the dispute of carriage agency by sea; which was also confirmed by the court of first instance according to the law. The contract involved was set up by law and came into legal force which should legally bind the two parties, who should strictly obey the contract and bear the liability of the contract; once violated the contract, one should bear the relevant default liabilities. If there was no specific agreement on default liability, it should be settled according to the relevant legal regulations and rules.

According to verified facts and ZTSS's confession, ZTSS recognized it owed China Shipping the third batch of freight subordinate to the Indian bridge contract in sum of RMB3,355,390.49, the fourth batch of freight in sum of RMB6,642,433.64, the freight subordinate to the Denmark bridge in sum of RMB1,949,453.99 including ocean freight, drayage, ground operation expense at Shanghai Wharf (harbor expense), etc. Moreover, as to the cash deposit in sum of RMB400,000 for tendering the Indian bridge and Denmark bridge projects, ZTSS should pay for it, which was confirmed by the court of first instance. Pursuant to Paragraph 1 of Article 4 in the Indian Bridge Contract signed by both parties concerning "ZTSS should plan to pay the freight within 30 days when receiving the invoice and affirming the sum" and Paragraph 6 of Article 3 in the Denmark Bridge Contract concerning "ZTSS should plan to pay all the money by cash within 30 days when receiving the invoice and customs declaration", ZTSS's payment exceeded the time limit and did not pay in full, which evidently violates the agreement and thus ZTSS should bear the relevant liability for breach of contract.

In regard to the liability for breach of contract concerning delayed payment, ZTSS owed the above mentioned freight, which violated the agreement, and should bear the relevant liability for breach of contract. Although the contract involved made an agreement regarding the liability for breach of contract, there was no agreement on its specific calculation standard. Thus, in accordance to the principle of "following the legal rules once without any agreement", pursuant to the provision of Article 113 of the Contract Law of People's Republic of China "Where a party fails to perform its obligations under the contract or its performance fails to conform to the agreement and cause losses to the other party, the amount of compensation for losses should be equal to the losses caused by the breach of contract, including the interests receivable after the performance of the contract, provided not exceeding the probable losses caused by the breach of contract which has been foreseen or ought to be foreseen when the party in breach concludes the contract", it is in conformity with the law that China Shipping claimed for ZTSS to pay the interest of the delayed payment. It is confirmed by court that, with both parties' agreement, the standard on the interest of the delayed payment should be calculated based on a one-year loan interest rate as promulgated by the People's Bank of China. ZTSS entered a plea that it was due to China Shipping who damaged the shipped cargo and caused the foreign party's claim for compensation, thus, China Shipping should also bear the liability for breach of contract; therefore, it should not be authorized that China Shipping claimed ZTSS to bear the delayed payment interest for breach of contract. The court of first instance held that though ZTSS argued that there was the claim for compensation from a person who was not involved, ZTSS did not provide the relevant evidence in conformity with law and could not prove the fact and the compensation for the cargo damage; in addition, there was no agreement in the contract involved to support that ZTSS should dishonor or delay the freight. Therefore, since ZTSS lacks sufficient evidence and it should be confirmed not to institute a countersuit in terms of the cargo damage; the cargo damage is not subordinate to the scope of the trial so the court of first instance should not adopt ZTSS's claim; ZTSS should make other claims if it has new evidence. The court of first instance once again warmed both parties, if there indeed was the claim for compensation from a foreign party, China Shipping and ZTSS should be required to cooperate with each other and negotiate with the foreign side; when involved in the lawsuit, the party not involved should also provide convenience and actively cooperate so as to avoid losing the suit for lack of evidence; and where after the expending damage served as the basis to claim for compensation; the court of first instance required both parties to discard past grievances in order to internationally maintain the legitimate rights and interests as well as the good image of China's trade and shipping enterprises.

Regarding to the timeframe of the delayed interest payment, there are two circumstances as follows: one is that it was unpaid until the deadline; the other is that payment was carried out beyond the agreed time though it was paid before the lawsuit. It should be separated hereto to calculate the beginning and ending time for the interest.

Specifically, regarding to the freight in sum of RMB1,949,453.99 subordinate to the Denmark Contract, pursuant to the agreement, ZTSS should pay off all the money within 30 days after receiving the invoice. It is now found out that ZTSS received the invoice on February 28, 2014 and did not pay according to the agreement. Therefore, depending on the evidence and law, the court of first instance supported China Shipping's claim for calculating the relevant delayed payment interest starting from the date of March 30, 2014. The interest damage of the sum of RMB1,949,453.99 subordinate to the Denmark Contract should be calculated based on the one-year loan interest rate as promulgated by the People's Bank of China from the date on March 30, 2014 to the time when the judgment takes effect.

As for the argument for not paying the third and fourth batch of freight subject to the Indian Bridge, ZTSS argued as follows: 1. there was a claim for compensation coming from the foreign side; 2. China Shipping did not deliver the relevant document of the fourth batch freight so ZTSS did not pay it off. As for the first argument, according to the court of first instance, since the above mentioned opinion had clarified that it was untenable, there is no need to give unnecessary details. As for the second argument, China Shipping recognized that the relevant document had not been delivered and been temporarily seized as the carrier since ZTSS did not pay off the freight. The court of first instance held that regardless of whether China Shipping had the right to exercise the seizure right as a carrier, only based on the agreement of the parties, delivering the document is not the premise of ZTSS's payment. Moreover, ZTSS also recognized that not receiving the document influenced its right of export rebates; ZTSS did not file any counterclaim so China Shipping's not delivering the document cannot be the cause for ZTSS's refusing or delaying the payment. In addition, for lack of just cause and not paying the freight by agreement, ZTSS should be supposed to bear the liability for breach of contract. Based on the fact-finding, ZTSS received the invoice of the fourth batch of freight in sum of RMB6,642,433.64 on June 19, 2014 and should plan to pay off the freight within 30 days after receiving the invoice by agreement; however, since ZTSS had not paid until now, the court of first instance confirmed China Shipping's claim by law that the interest damage of the delayed payment should be calculated from July 19, 2014 to the date when the judgment takes effect. ZTSS received the invoice of the third batch of freight in sum of RMB9,209,296.49 on December 22, 2013 and should plan to pay off the freight within 30 days after receiving the invoice by agreement. However, ZTSS did not pay within the 30 days by agreement and chose to pay partial freight by bank's acceptance bill on April 29, May 30, and July 9, 2014. ZTSS recognized that there was still the unpaid freight in sum of RMB3,355,390.49. The court of first instance hereto held that the interest damage of the delayed payment corresponding to the arrears in sum of RMB3,355,390.49 should be calculated from the date of January 21, 2014 to the time when the judgment takes effect. As for the partial overdue freight, it should be calculated separately by facts: 1. the beginning and ending time for the interest damage of the delayed payment in sum of RMB1,853,906 should start from January 21, 2014 to October 28, 2014; 2. the beginning and ending time for the interest damage of the delayed payment in sum of RMB2,000,000 should start from January 21, 2014 to November 30, 2014; 3. the beginning and ending time for the interest damage of the delayed payment in sum of RMB2,000,000 should start from January 21, 2014 to December 15, 2014. All the interest should be calculated based on one-year loan interest rate as promulgated by the People's Bank of China.

Particularly, in regard to the 6 months' time limit from the date of bank's acceptance bill to the due date, China Shipping also claimed that ZTSS was supposed to pay the interest damage of the relevant delayed payment. Pursuant to Article 69 Paragraph 1 of the Maritime Code of the People's Republic of China, the court of first instance held that "the shipper should pay the freight to the carrier as agreed". Pursuant to Article 292 of the Contract Law of People's Republic of China that "a passenger, a shipper or consignee should pay the ticket-fare or freight." It can be seen that the shipper should bear the legal liability of paying the freight. Although the contract involved subordinated to the comprehensive contract, its main content still belonged to the transport contract; as the carrier, China Shipping enjoyed the principal right to obtain the freight; as the shipper, ZTSS has the main liability of paying the freight. Pursuant to the agreement in the Indian bridge "ZTSS should plan to pay off the freight within 30 days after receiving the invoice" and "ZTSS should pay the freight by bank transfer or the bank bill of exchange under China Shipping's recognition", ZTSS should bear the liability of paying off all the freight before the date of payment as agreed; the bill of exchange can be divided into presentation bill, fixed date bill, use acceptance bill, etc. However, according to provisions of law and contract agreement, even if ZTSS chose to pay by the bill of exchange, it should still be limited by the due date, which meant the due date and pay date of draft should be within the last payment date rather than the day of delivery. At present, ZTSS not only paid the freight later than the payment day but most sum already paid was by means of use acceptance bill; and the time for delivery for the bill was always later than the payment day by either 2 months or 6 months. In consideration of the characters of bill acceptance, unless China Shipping transfers the acceptance bill by endorsement when receiving it, or else, to China Shipping, it will get loss and cannot obtain the full amount within the date as agreed in the contract whether China Shipping accepts by discount ahead of time or waits for its collection after the expiration of the bill acceptance period. according to the fact-findings, China Shipping chose to accept collection by waiting for the expiration of use bill acceptance period. Therefore, in terms of this case, use bill acceptance used by ZTSS to pay the freight violated the agreement and also damaged China Shipping's right to obtain the full amount of freight by law, which caused the loss to China Shipping; so, the court of first instance supported China Shipping's claim for the compensation of the delayed payment interest. Pursuant to

Article 113 of the Contract Law of People's Republic of China, "Where a party fails to perform its obligations under the contract or its performance fails to conform to the agreement and cause losses to the other party, the amount of compensation for losses should be equal to the losses caused by the breach of contract, including the interests receivable after the performance of the contract, provided not exceeding the probable losses caused by the breach of contract which has been foreseen or ought to be foreseen when the party in breach concludes the contract". Obviously, ZTSS should know that the use bill acceptance would cause damage to China Shipping as the means of paying freight; the loss should be foreseen by ZTSS when entering into a contract with China Shipping.

Similarly, as for the second batch of cargo subordinate to the Indian contract, both parties had no contest on that the freight capital had been paid off but they had a dispute on the interest of the delayed payment; according to the above mentioned statements, China Shipping's relevant claim should be supported. Combined with the facts of the overdue freight payment subordinate to the second batch of cargo, the corresponding results should be as follows: 1. the beginning and ending time for the interest damage of the delayed payment in sum of RMB2,000,000 should start from October 27, 2013 to June 26, 2014; 2. the beginning and ending time for the interest damage of the delayed payment in sum of RMB5,657,801.34 should start from October 27, 2013 to July 28, 2014; 3. the beginning and ending time for the interest damage of the delayed payment in sum of RMB842,198.66 should start from November 16, 2013 to July 28, 2014; 4. the beginning and ending time for the interest damage of the delayed payment in sum of RMB146,094 should start from November 16, 2013 to October 28, 2014. All the interest above mentioned should be calculated based on one-year loan interest rate as promulgated by the People's Bank of China.

As for China Shipping's claim for the demurrage charge, empty charge, and storage charge in aggregate amount of RMB256,765.34 subordinate to the second, third, and fourth batch of cargo concerning Indian bridge, ZTSS did not recognize it and argued that both parties had come to an agreement on it; ZTSS agreed with the contract to bear the demurrage charge and empty charge totally in sum of RMB90,000; though by agreement it aimed at the second batch of the freight, orally it covered the whole sum of the second, third, and fourth batch of freight; what's more, the contract made by both parties was subordinate to the fixed price contract and the demurrage charge, empty charge and storage charge had covered in the transportation expenses. Therefore, there is no need to calculate the charges separately. China Shipping claimed that as for the second batch of demurrage charge and empty charge in sum of RMB90,000 made by three-party (including the two parties) agreement, ZTSS did not pay it off yet. Therefore, China Shipping had a right to claim the payment according to the actual expenses; in addition, the sum of RMB90,000 as agreed only pertained to the second batch of demurrage charge and empty charge and did not include the third and the fourth expenses; what's more, in the fixed price as agreed, the unit price of drayage was RMB80 per ton including colligation charges and demurrage charges and there was no demurrage charge within 2 days. Thus, when beyond 2 days, demurrage charge should be born by a party. The court of first instance held that since the price in the contract pertained to a fixed price and there is no demurrage charge within 2 days in terms of the drayage as agreed, according to the semantic interpretation of the contract, the demurrage charge should be born when demurrage days of the ships were beyond 2 days; however, there is not a clear agreement in the contract with respect to the specific standard of the demurrage charge; China Shipping, as the party of through transportation, also failed to submit the written agreement with the party of barge concerning demurrage charge; from China Shipping's statement, it showed that the payment was determined by the party of barge without any evidence to prove whether the demurrage charge standard claimed by the barge party suited the current market condition; what's more, the payment to the barge party could not be distinguished whether it had connection with this case and ZTSS. ZTSS disagreed with these facts concerning the demurrage charge for the barge. Therefore, the court of first instance did not support China Shipping's claim for the so-called demurrage charge for the third and fourth batch of cargo. With respect to the storage charge, each party stuck to the argument and China Shipping did not submit any evidence to show it was ZTSS's fault that caused that charges. China Shipping as the opposite party of the transportation service contract signed with ZTSS, pursuant to the contract agreement, both parties should conduct the delivery list as for the shipment; the list not only had to contain the record of shipment but also the arrival time of the ship, the departure time of the ship; in addition, the list should be recognized by China Shipping and ZTSS's signature; China Shipping at least should submit the living delivery record signed by ZTSS; however, ZTSS denied the facts claimed by China Shipping; also, China Shipping, as the party who put forward the claim, could not submit any sufficient evidence. Therefore, since the relevant claims lacks evidence, the court of first instance refused to support it. In respect to the demurrage charge and empty charge caused by transporting the second batch of cargo concerning the Indian bridge, since China Shipping and ZTSS together with the actual carrier had confirmed the expenses, according to the relativity of contract, ZTSS should pay the relevant demurrage charge and empty charge in sum of RMB90,000 to China Shipping who is the whole course carrier; the sum of RMB90,000 aimed at the second batch of cargo transportation. Whereas the three parties recognized the actual sum by negotiation after China Shipping brought the lawsuit and there is no actual payment time in the agreement, the court of first instance refused to support China Shipping's claim for the compensation of the delayed payment interest towards ZTSS.

In respect to China Shipping's claim for relieving the Indian Bridge Contract, China Shipping asserted that, according to the contract agreement, ZTSS caused the overdue payment so China Shipping had the rescission right of the contract; however, ZTSS held that overdue payment did not pertain to a fundamental breach of contract and disagreed to relieve it; the court of first instance held that China Shipping's claim was according to Section 1 of the Paragraph 2 "the two parties should, throughout the contract period, conduct the termination of this agreement by written notice once the following situations occur" of Article 11 "the enforcement and termination of the contract"; the main content is as follows: "once one party violates the provision of this contract and still or already could not remedy the nonperformance within 10 days from the day of receiving the other side's written notice". First, in the process of fulfilling the contract, China Shipping did not issue the written notice concerning the termination of the agreement according to the provision of that Article to exercise the rescission right of the contract; therefore, there should be no argument whether ZTSS had remedied the performance within 10 days from the day of receiving the other party's written notice; in addition, since China Shipping had brought the lawsuit, it obviously did not suit that agreement. However, China Shipping claimed that the action of filing the lawsuit can be seen as the written notice concerning the termination of the agreement, which lacks legal justification. Since the overdue payment of ZTSS did not pertain to the fundamental breach, which led to the failure of contract purpose by one party's violation pursuant to the provision of the contract law, the court of first instance refused to support China Shipping's claim for rescinding the contract for lack of contractual and legal justification.

In conclusion, according to the Contract Law of the People's Republic of China Article 8, Article 60 Paragraph 1, Article 107, Article 113 Paragraph 1, Article 292, the Maritime Code of the People's Republic of China Article 69 Paragraph 1, the Civil Procedure Law of the People's Republic of China Article 64 Paragraph 1, the judgment is as follows: 1. Jiangsu Zhongtai Bridge Steel Structure Co., Ltd., should pay China Shipping Logistics Co., Ltd., the freight subordinate to the Indian Bridge Contract in aggregate of RMB9,997,824.13 and the interest loss thereof (the interest should be calculated based on the one-year loan interest rate as promulgated by the People's Bank of China as follows: the capital RMB3,355,390.49 as the cardinal value from January 21, 2014 to the date of payment set by this judgment; the capital RMB6,642,433.64 as the cardinal value from July 19, 2014 to the date of payment set by this judgment) within 10 days after the judgment comes into effect; 2. Jiangsu Zhongtai Bridge Steel Structure Co., Ltd., should pay China Shipping Logistics Co., Ltd., the delayed interest loss caused by Jiangsu Zhongtai Bridge Steel Structure Co., Ltd.'s overdue payment of the use bill acceptance within 10 days after the judgment comes into effect (the interest should be calculated based on the one-year loan interest rate as promulgated by the People's Bank of China as follows: the capital RMB3,000,000 as the cardinal value from October 27, 2013 to June 26, 2014; the capital RMB5,657,801.34 as the cardinal value from October 27, 2013 to July 28, 2014; the capital RMB842,198.66 as the cardinal value from November 16, 2013 to July 28, 2014; the capital RMB146,094 as the cardinal value from November 16, 2013 to October 28, 2014; the capital RMB1,853,906 as the cardinal value from January 21, 2014 to October 28, 2014; the capital RMB2,000,000 as the cardinal value from January 21, 2014 to November 30, 2014; the capital RMB2,000,000 as the cardinal value from January 21, 2014 to December 15, 2014);3. Jiangsu Zhongtai Bridge Steel Structure Co., Ltd., should return to China Shipping Logistics Co., Ltd., the tender bond subordinate to the Indian Bridge Project in aggregate amount of RMB200,000 within 10 days after the judgment comes into effect; 4. Jiangsu Zhongtai Bridge Steel Structure Co., Ltd., should pay China Shipping Logistics Co., Ltd., the freight subordinate to the

Denmark Bridge Contract in aggregate amount of RMB1,949,453.99 and the interest loss thereof within 10 days after the judgment comes into effect (the interest should be calculated based on the one-year loan interest rate as promulgated by the People's Bank of China as follows: the capital RMB1,949,453.99 as the cardinal value from March 30, 2014 to the date of payment set by this judgment);5. Jiangsu Zhongtai Bridge Steel Structure Co., Ltd., should return to China Shipping Logistics Co., Ltd., the tender bond subordinate to the Denmark Bridge Project in aggregate amount of RMB200,000 within 10 days after the judgment comes into effect; 6. Jiangsu Zhongtai Bridge Steel Structure Co., Ltd., should pay, China Shipping Logistics Co., Ltd., the demurrage charge for short-time barge and empty charge in sum of RMB90,000 within 10 days after the judgment comes into effect; 7. Reject other claims of China Shipping Logistics Co., Ltd. Court acceptance fee in amount of RMB87,804 and the litigation preservation fee in amount of RMB5,000, China Shipping Logistics Co., Ltd., should bear RMB804, and Jiangsu Zhongtai Bridge Steel Structure Co., Ltd., should bear RMB92,000.

ZTSS dissatisfied with the original judgment, filed an appeal, alleging that: ZTSS had paid the freights as agreed in the contract, and the method of payment provided in the contract contained bank's acceptance bills. China Shipping did not raise any objection when ZTSS paid the acceptance bill. At the same time, in view of the characteristics of bank's acceptance bill, it can be transferred upon endorsement, ZTSS's paying the acceptance bill did not necessarily lead to the loss of discounting or collection. Accordingly, ZTSS requested the court to rescind the second item of the original judgment, and amend the judgment according to the law.

China Shipping responded that: firstly, according to the contract, there was no agreement that ZTSS could pay the freights by means of bank's acceptance bill, what was agreed in the contact was bank's bill of exchange. During the performance of the contract, ZTSS submitted six-month forward acceptance bills. The honoring time under the forward acceptance bills had far exceeded that designated in the contract, namely the payment period within 30 days upon receipt of invoice. Therefore, ZTSS's payment of the freights did not comply with the contract, it constituted improper performance of contract, resulting in the loss to China Shipping, ZTSS should bear the liability therefor. China Shipping requested the court to reject the appeal and affirm the original judgment.

During the second instance, both parties did not submit new evidence.

The court finds out that:

The facts found in the first instance can be proved by relevant evidence, the parties neither raised objection nor submitted new evidence. The court ascertains the facts found in the first instance.

The court holds that:

This case is arising from dispute over contract of carriage of goods by sea and maritime freight forwarding contract. According to the Contract Law of PRC, the parties shall fully perform its own obligations as agreed upon, otherwise, the breaching party shall bear the corresponding liability for breach of contract. In the subject case, the contractual relationship between the two parties has been established according to law. Therefore, the parties shall fully perform their respective obligations according to the contract. ZTSS and China Shipping shall fulfill their obligations in light of the contract. Subject to the facts having been ascertained, ZTSS was obliged to arrange payment within 30 days after the receipt of invoice, but ZTSS failed to do so, instead, it paid part of the freights through bank's acceptance bills. Therefore, ZTSS constituted a breach of contract. At the same time, even if ZTSS chose to payment method of bill of exchange, it should be subject to the last payment period, that is to say, the due day or payment day of the bill of exchange should be within the last payment due date. ZTSS paid the freights later than the last payment due date, and the freights having been paid was six-month forward acceptance bills, of which the honoring days were all later than the last payment due date. Such act of ZTSS led to China Shipping's failure of obtaining full freight within the contract period, resulting in the loss of China Shipping. It is proper that the court of first instance supported China Shipping's claim for loss of interest on the delayed payment.

In summary, the facts were clearly found in the original judgment, and the law was correctly applied. ZTSS's appeal grounds cannot be established, the court does not support its appeal. according to Article 170 paragraph 1 Sub-paragraph 1 and Article 175 of the Civil Procedure Law of the People's Republic of China, the judgment is as follows:

Dismiss the appeal and affirm the original judgment.

Court acceptance fee in amount of RMB7,244.85 yuan, shall be born by the Appellant Jiangsu Zhongtai Bridge Steel Structure Co., Ltd.

The judgment is final.

Presiding Judge: SUN Chenmin

Acting Judge: ZHANG Wen

Acting Judge: FENG Guanghe

May 4, 2015

Clerk: LUO Gang

Appendix: Relevant Law

1. Civil Procedure Law of the People's Republic of China

Article 172 After hearing an appellate case, the people's court of second instance shall handle the case respectively according to the following circumstances:

(1) If the facts were clearly found and the law was correctly applied in the original judgment, the appeal shall be rejected by a judgment and the original judgment shall be sustained;
(2) If the law was incorrectly applied in the original judgment, the judgment shall be amended according to law;

(3) If in the original judgment the facts were incorrectly found or were not clearly found and the evidence was inconclusive, the judgment shall be rescinded and the case remanded by an order to the original people's court for a retrial, or the people's court of second instance may amend the judgment after investigating and clarifying the facts; or
(4) If in the original judgment a violation of the prescribed procedure may have affected the correctness of the judgment, the judgment shall be rescinded and the case remanded by an order to the original people's court for a retrial.

The parties may appeal against the judgment or ruling rendered in a retrial of their case.

Article 175 The judgments and rulings of a people's court of second instance shall be final.

Wuhan Maritime Court
Civil Judgment

Chongqing Red Dragonfly Oil Limited Liability Company
v.
PICC Property and Casualty Company Limited Chongqing Branch

(2015) Wu Hai Fa Shang Zi No.00151

Related Case(s) None.

Cause(s) of Action 231. Dispute over contract for protection and indemnity insurance on the sea or sea-connected waters.

Headnote The Plaintiff cargo owner was entitled to recover under cargo insurance policy with the Defendant insurer; the Plaintiff's insurable interest was established by the manner in which it had conducted itself after the cargo was damaged; insurer's argument that Plaintiff had waived rights of subrogation was rejected, because insurer was still entitled to proceed against the third party who had caused the damage.

Summary The Plaintiff Chongqing Red Dragonfly Oil Limited Liability Company brought an action against PICC Property Co., Ltd. Chongqing Branch, after an accident at sea caused damage to the cargo of soybean meal shipped by the Plaintiff's wholly-owned subsidiary. The Plaintiff alleged that it contracted with the Defendant to cover the Plaintiff's cargo against all risks. The Defendant contended that the Plaintiff gave up right to recovery against a third party. The court held that the Plaintiff had an insurance interest in the soybean meal involved, that the Defendant was not entitled to exercise subrogation rights against a third party. The Defendant was ordered to compensate the Plaintiff for damage to the cargo and salvage costs.

Judgment

The Plaintiff: Chongqing Red Dragonfly Oil Limited Liability Company.
Domicile: No.66 Jiuchikan, Yuzhong District, Chongqing City.
Institution code: 20,284,344-4.
Legal representative: WANG Yinfeng, president.
Agent *ad litem*: HUANG Xuejun, lawyer of Chongqing Wancheng Law Firm.

The Defendant: PICC Property and Casualty Company Limited Chongqing Branch.
Domicile: No.40 Cangbai Road, Yuzhong District, Chongqing City.
Institutioncode: 90,288,369-0.
Legal representative: LONG Baoyong, general manager.
Agent *ad litem*: WEI Qingsong, lawyer of Huiye (Nanjing) Law Firm.
Agent *ad litem*: LIU Zhuan, lawyer of Huiye (Nanjing) Law Firm.

The Third Party: Anqing City Hengfeng Shipping Co., Ltd.
Domicile: Layer 2, Building1-2, Service Center, Council of Agriculture, Changfeng Town, Anqing City, Fujian Province.
Institution code: 75,681,613-0.
Legal representative: XU Huan, general manager.
Agent *ad litem*: XIAO Dongsheng, lawyer of Beijing Yingke (Wuhan) Law Firm.
Agent *ad litem*: CHEN Fei, lawyer of Beijing Yingke (Wuhan) Law Firm.

With respect to the case arising from dispute over insurance contract of carriage of goods by sea-connected areas filed litigation by the Plaintiff, Chongqing Red Dragonfly Oil Limited Liability Company (hereinafter referred to as "Grease Company") against the Defendant, PICC Property and Casualty Company Limited Chongqing Branch (hereinafter referred to as "Insurance Company") and the Third Party, Anqing City Hengfeng Shipping Co., Ltd. (hereinafter referred to as "Shipping Company") before the court on January 15, 2015. Because this case was the maritime dispute, which was under exclusive jurisdiction of maritime court and the domicile of the Defendant was within the jurisdiction region of the court, pursuant to the provisions of Article 2 of Notice of the Supreme People's Court on Adjustment of the Jurisdiction and the Scope of Cases Entertained by Dalian, Wuhan and Beihai Maritime Courts [Fa Fa (2002) No.274] and Article 24 of Civil Procedure Law of the People's Republic of China, the court has the jurisdiction over this case. After the court registered and accepted the case, this case applied the ordinary procedure, and the court constituted the collegiate panel with YI Lu, as Presiding Judge, and Judge CAI Sian, and Acting Judge CHEN Lin, to try the case according to the law. In the trial, the court allowed the claim that the Defendant Insurance Company applied to add the Shipping Company as the third party to take part in the trial according to the law. And the court held the hearing in public to try this case on April 27, 2015. HUANG Xuejun, agent *ad litem* entrusted by the Plaintiff, WEI Qingsong, LIU Zhuan, agents *ad litem* entrusted by the Defendant, and CHEN Fei,agent *ad litem* entrusted by the Third Party, participated in the trial. Now the case has been concluded.

The Plaintiff, Grease Company, alleged that it signed domestic cargo carriage open cover agreement with the Defendant on January 23, 2014, which stated that the Defendant covered the soybean meal produced and sold by the Plaintiff in line with domestic waterway carriage upon cargo against all risks. On September 28 of the same year, the Plaintiff entrusted its wholly-owned subsidiary, Kaixin Grain and Oil Co., Ltd. (hereinafter referred to as Kaixin Company), to sign No.HQTSL-0897 contract of carriage of goods by waterway with the Third Party. The Third Party arranged M.V. "YU JIANG HAI 666" to carry the soybean meal involved. On October 30, 2014, M.V. "YU JIANG HAI 666" committed collision with M.V. "CHUAN MA 66" and M.V. "ZHONG TAI 66" in Linjiang Ping, Yichang City, Hubei Province, which caused cargo damage of the soybean meal involved. After the occurrence of the insurance incident, the Defendant and Renxiang (Beijing) Insurance Assessment Co., Ltd. (hereinafter referred to as Assessment Company), under their loss assessment and residual treatment, ascertained that the cargo loss of the Plaintiff, due to the aforementioned insurance incident, valued RMB5,254,558.78 and the salvage fee valued RMB46,435.05. The Defendant refused to indemnity in the reason of the Plaintiff's giving up the recovery right against the Third Party. Therefore, the Plaintiff filed litigation before the court, requested that: the Defendant should pay the insurance indemnity RMB5,254,558.78, and the salvage fee RMB46,435.05, and the interest thereon (the interest should be calculated at the loan interest rate of the People's Bank of China bank for the contemporary period of time from November 25, 2014 to the actual payday of the Defendant), and bear the litigation fees.

The Defendant Insurance Company contended that the Plaintiff had no insurable interest against the cargo involved, and the Plaintiff had given up the recovery right against the third party, which caused the loss of Defendant's insurance subrogation rights; the Plaintiff was not the party of the contract of carriage of goods by waterway involved, even if the Defendant had obtained the subrogation right, it should not recover from the Third Party. Meanwhile, the Plaintiff and the Defendant had not reached the compensation agreement against the insurance incident involved. Therefore, the Defendant requested the court to reject the claims of the Plaintiff.

The Third Party Shipping Company contended that: 1. the Third Party was the freight forwarding agent instead of the carrier in the carriage involved; 2. the Plaintiff and the Defendant failed to notify the Third Party during the residual treatment, it could not recognize the amount of cargo loss and salvage fee alleged by the Plaintiff; 3. the contract of carriage of goods by sea signed by Kaixin Company and the Third Party had expressly agreed that the Third Party should bear only the liability of compensation against the loss outside the insurance contract. In conclusion, it requested the court to judge according to the law.

The Plaintiff submitted the following evidence to support its claims within the time limit:

1. The Plaintiff's business license, institution code certificate and tax registration certificate, to prove that the Plaintiff was proper Plaintiff. The Defendant cross-examined that it had no objection to the authenticity of this evidence and had objection to its proving object. The Third Party cross-examined that it had no objection to this evidence. The court recognizes the evidence because the Defendant and the Third Party had no objection to the authenticity of this evidence.

2. Domestic cargo carriage open cover agreement signed by the Plaintiff, waterway cargo carriage insurance clauses (2009 Edition), payment receipt over the premium in amount of RMB25,780.76 the Plaintiff paid to the Defendant on October 31, 2014 (hereinafter referred to as payment receipt), No.01234032 premium invoice issued by the Defendant (hereinafter referred to as the premium invoice), premium list issued by the Defendant in October 2014, to prove that the Plaintiff had the cargo involved covered for domestic waterway carriage upon cargo against all risks through the Defendant.

The Defendant cross-examined that it had no objection to the authenticity and the relevancy of the open cover agreement, insurance clauses, payment receipt and premium invoice, and had no objection to the authenticity to the premium list, but held that the premium list could not prove the price and the quantity of the cargo involved.

The Third Party cross-examined that it had no objection to the authenticity and the relevancy of the open cover agreement, insurance clauses, payment receipt and premium invoice, and had no objection to the authenticity to the premium list, but held that it could not prove the price and the quantity of the cargo involved only through the premium list.

3. The power of attorney issued by the Plaintiff on September 26, 2014, articles of association of Kaixin Company, the HQTSL-0897 contract of carriage of goods by water signed by Kaixin Company and the Third Party on September 28, 2014, to prove that the Plaintiff entrusted Kaixin Company to sign a contract of carriage with the Third Party against the cargo involved.

The Defendant did not affirm the authenticity of the power of attorney for it was the copy instead of the original. The Defendant had no objection to the articles of association of Kaixin Company, but it could only prove the fact that Kaixin Company was a wholly owned subsidiary company of the Plaintiff. The Defendant had no objection to the contract of carriage of goods by water.

The Third Party cross-examined that the power of attorney and the articles of association of Kaixin Company should be verified by the court, and it recognized the evidence validity of the contract of carriage of goods by water.

The court recognizes the probative force of the power of attorney because the Plaintiff had submitted the original after the trial and the Defendant did not submit rebuttal evidence to overthrow the content of the power of attorney. The court recognizes the probative force of the articles of association of Kaixin Company, which proved that Kaixin Company was a wholly owned subsidiary company of the Plaintiff, because the Defendant had no objection to it. The court affirms the contract of carriage of goods by water because the Defendant and the Third Party had no objection to it.

4. Incident statement jointly signed, confirmed and issued by the Third Party, Assessment Company and the Plaintiff's representative on November 14, 2014 (hereinafter referred to as incident statement), field survey records issued by Assessment Company, the inland waterway traffic incident investigation report

issued by Yichang Maritime Safety Administration on December 29, 2014, to prove the damaged facts of the cargo involved.

The Defendant cross-examined that it had no objection to the incident statement and the field survey records. The Defendant did not recognize the authenticity of inland waterway traffic incident investigation report because it was the copy instead of the original.

The Third Party cross-examined that it had no objection to the authenticity of the incident statement and did not recognized the authenticity of the field survey records, it requested the court to verify the authenticity of inland waterway traffic incident investigation report.

The court recognizes the incident statement because both the Defendant and the Third Party had no objection to it. The court recognizes the probative force of the field survey records for the witness LI Songlin, surveyor of Assessment Company, recognized the authenticity of it before the court. The court affirms the probative force of inland waterway traffic incident investigation report for the sailor of M.V. "YU JIANG HAI 666" XU Zhipeng, attending trial, recognized its authenticity before the court.

5. Operation contract over soybean meal signed by the Plaintiff and Yichang City Xianglong Gangfu Co., Ltd. (hereinafter referred to as Gangfu Company) on November 1, 2014, warehousing listing and billing details issued by Gangfu Company on November 15, 2014, bank payment receipt, in amount of RMB46,435.05, which the Plaintiff respectively paid to Gangfu Company on November 4 and 18,2014, through China Merchants Bank, invoices issued by Gangfu Company to Kaixin Company on November 19, 2014, to prove that the Plaintiff had paid extra salvage fee, RMB46,435.05 due to the cargo damage.
The Defendant cross-examined that there was no objection to this group of evidence.

The Third Party cross-examined that there was no objection to the authenticity of this group of evidence but it had objection to details against the constitution of the salvage fee.

The court recognizes the authenticity of this group because the Defendant and the Third Party had no objection to that.

The court affirms the probative force of salvage fee proved by this group of evidence, despite the Third Party had objection to it, whereas failing to submit rebuttal evidence to overthrow it.

6. Insurance incident compensation agreement signed by the Plaintiff and the Defendant on November 14, 2014 (hereinafter referred to as compensation agreement), letters issued by the Defendant to the Plaintiff at 1228 of October 31, 2014 (hereinafter referred to as the letters), to prove that the Defendant had agreed to pay cargo loss involved and the loss in the process of transship.
The Defendant did not recognize the authenticity of the compensation agreement for it had neither set up nor came into effect. The Defendant had not given cross-examination opinion against the letters.

The Third Party had not given cross-examination opinion for this group of evidence, saying it was irrelevant to it.

The court recognizes the authenticity of the contents of compensation agreement, combining the representations during the trial of the Plaintiff's staff LONG Jinrong, notarization submitted by the Defendant and the testimony of witness LANG Jianzhong, but the Plaintiff's signatures and closing time in compensation agreement was retroactive afterwards. The court does not confirm the letter for it was a copy rather than the original.

7. Sales contract signed by the Plaintiff, the Defendant, Assessment Company, and the outsider, Kangfu Agriculture and Livestock Cultivation Cooperatives of Duodao District, Jingmen City (hereinafter referred to as Cultivation Cooperatives) on November 14, 2014, to prove that the residual value of the damaged cargo involved was RMB2,961,128.

The Defendant had no objection to the authenticity of the sales contract.

The Third Party had objection to the sales contract due to its not being informed by the Plaintiff and the Defendant for present during cargo loss treatment.

The court affirms the sales contract because the Defendant had no objection to its authenticity.

8. Notice of refusal issued by the Defendant on December 2, 2014, to prove that the Defendant refused to pay the indemnity.

The Defendant had no objection to the authenticity of the evidence.

The Third Party had not given cross-examination opinion for the evidence, saying it was irrelevant to it.

The court affirms the evidence because the Defendant had no objection to it.

9. Similar indemnity materials, to prove that the Defendant should bear the insurance compensation responsibility against the cargo damage involved. The Defendant and the Third Party did not recognize the evidence because it was irrelevant to the case.

The court does not confirm the evidence because it was irrelevant to the case.

The Defendant Insurance Company submitted the following evidence to rebut the claims of the Plaintiff during the trial:

1. Industrial and commercial registration information of Kaixin Company which was searched by the Defendant from the national enterprise credit information publicity system (Chongqing), contract of carriage of goods by water signed by Kaixin Company and the Third Party on September 28, 2014, to prove that Kaixin Company was independent legal person which differed from the Plaintiff, and the Plaintiff had no insurable interest over the cargo involved.

The Plaintiff had no objection to the authenticity of the evidence, but it could not prove that the Plaintiff had no insurable interest over the cargo involved.

The Third Party had no objection to the evidence.

The court affirms the evidence because the Plaintiff and the Third Party had no objection to it, but the evidence could not prove that the Plaintiff had no insurable interest over the cargo involved.

2. Material transfer list signed by the Defendant's staff LANG Jianzhong on November 17, 2014, to prove that the Plaintiff had not performed disclosure obligation, and provided relevant evidence materials of carriage against cargo involved to the Defendant until November 17, 2014.

The Plaintiff had no objection to the authenticity of the evidence, but had objection to its object of proof, and alleged that this evidence could prove the authenticity of the compensation agreement issued by the Plaintiff and the Defendant on November 14, 2014.

The Third Party had not given cross-examination opinion for the evidence was irrelevant to it.

The court affirms the evidence because the Plaintiff had no objection to it.

3. (2015) Yu Zheng Zi No.13479 notarization issued by Chongqing Notary Office on April 7, 2015, to prove that the Defendant had withdrawn its offer to the Plaintiff of bearing the insurance liability on November 14, 2014.

The Plaintiff did not recognize the authenticity, legality and the relevancy of the notarization.

The Third Party had not given cross-examination opinion for the evidence was irrelevant to it.

The court affirms the evidence because it was original and the Plaintiff failed to submit rebuttal evidence to overthrow it.

4. FAIRICC/WH/14004 assessment report issued by Assessment Company, to prove that the Plaintiff failed to perform the derogation obligation after the occurrence of the incident, which caused further loss, the Defendant should not bear insurance responsibility against the further loss.

The Plaintiff had no objection to the authenticity of the assessment report, but had objection to state loss of expanding part, and had no objection to determined amount of cargo loss.

The Third Party did not recognize the assessment report because it was unilaterally provided without the permission of the third party.

The court affirms the authenticity and the determined amount of cargo loss of the assessment report, because the Plaintiff had no objection to these, despite the Third Party had objection to the assessment report, whereas failing to submit rebuttal evidence to overthrow it. As to the loss of expanding part stated in the assessment report, which lacked evidence to support it, thus it shall not be recognized by the court.

5. *Domestic Waterway Cargo Carriage Insurance Clauses* (2009 Edition), to prove that the Defendant should not bear insurance responsibility against the cargo loss of expanding part involved.

The Plaintiff had no objection to the authenticity of the evidence, but had objection to its object of proof, and alleged that the Defendant was responsible for the treatment of damaged soybean meal involved after the incident and the further loss did not exist.

The Third Party had no objection to the authenticity of the evidence, but held that it could not prove that the third party failed to perform the derogation obligation after the occurrence of the incident.

The court affirms the evidence because the Plaintiff and the Third Party had no objection to it.

To rebut the Plaintiff's claims, the Defendant Insurance Company applied for the witness LANG Jianzhong and LI Songlin to testify before trial. The witness LANG Jianzhong, male, Han, born on January 15, 1972, whose domicile was 7–7, No.5 Pipa Shan Zheng Street Yuzhong District Chongqing, whose citizen identity number was 51222319720115003X, was deputy general manager of the Insurance Company. The witness LI Songlin, male, Han, born on July 16, 1983, whose domicile was 125 Qunyi Avenue, Wang Jia He town, Huangpi District, Wuhan City, Hubei Province, whose citizen identity number was 420,116,198,307,167,659, was the assessor of the Assessment Company.

The witness LANG Jianzhong stated that: I am deputy general manager of the Defendant Insurance Company. On November 13, 2014, I arrived at the scene of the insurance incident. After the field survey, we, the Insurance Company, confirmed the amount of the cargo loss involved, and arranged the auction bid against damaged cargo with the Plaintiff and Assessment Company. I drafted the compensation agreement and signed it, but the Plaintiff did not sign immediately. The Plaintiff failed to submit the compensation agreement to the Defendant after they had taken it away. The Plaintiff submitted the insurance claim materials, including the contract of carriage of goods by waterway, to the Defendant on November 17, 2014.

The witness LI Songlin stated that: the Defendant entrusted the Assessment Company for cargo damage assessment involved on October 30, 2014. I, as appointed assessor of the Assessment Company, arrived at the scene of the incident the next day, found that the cargo involved was partly into the river because of the ship collision M.V. "YU JIANG HAI 666"happening in Linjiang Ping, Yichang City, Hubei Province with the outsider vessel and damaged. Although local Maritime Safety Administration sent floating crane ship for rescue operations, the damaged cargo was finally shipped to the dock warehouses for storage after the day of November 4, due to salvage fees. On November 8, I started the treatment of the residual value and arranged the auction with the Plaintiff and the Defendant. I informed the Third Party via email and failed to receive the response. After the bidding, in witness and participation of the Assessment Company, the damaged cargo was sold to the Cultivation Cooperatives. After the inspection of Assessment

Company, the amount of cargo loss was determined as over RMB526,000,000, including expanding loss. This loss happened before the damaged cargo had transferred to the dock warehouse. The amount could not be determined despite its existence.

With respect to the testimony of the witness LANG Jianzhong, the court holds that the Plaintiff staff LONG Jinrong did not signed compensation agreement on November 14, 2014, combined with the representation of the Plaintiff's staff LONG Jinrong before the court. With respect to the testimony of the witness LI Songlin, the court affirms the testimony because the contents reached mutual corroboration with the evidence submitted by the Plaintiff and the Defendant.

To refute the Plaintiff's claims, the Third Party Shipping Company, submitted HQTSL-0897 contract of carriage of goods by water signed by Kaixin Company and the Third Party on September 28, 2014, the inland waterway traffic incident investigation report issued by Yichang Maritime Safety Administration on December 29, 2014, to prove that the Third Party was the freight forwarding agent of Kaixin Company instead of the carrier in the carriage of cargo legal relationship involved.

The Plaintiff and the Defendant had no objection to the authenticity of this group of evidence.

The court affirms this group of evidence because the Plaintiff and the Defendant had no objection to it, but this group of evidence by itself could not prove that the Third Party was the freight forwarding agent of Kaixin Company.

It is found that after the trial:

The Plaintiff Grease Company, the Defendant Insurance Company signed domestic cargo carriage open cover agreement in January 2014, in which stated that Article 1: "the Defendant covered the soybean meal under the Plaintiff's production and sales against all risks according to *Domestic Waterway Cargo Carriage Insurance Clauses* (2009 Edition)"; Article 3: "the Plaintiff shall send ship name list of concluded voyage contracts this day to the Defendant, the Defendant shall input information in the system and conduct pre-insurance according to the ship name provided by the Plaintiff (policy has came into force), the Defendant shall official input information and cover the Plaintiff after the Plaintiff has provided relevant information such as shipment time, absolute quantity of the subject matter of insurance, and quoted price of the shipment date, etc."; Article 4, the "insured amount" clause: "the value of insurance shall be determined according to the actual value of the cargo"; Article 6: "the insurance value shall be the actual value plus freight and miscellaneous charges"; Article 8: "duration of insurance begin from the cargo across the ship's rail to picked up by the destination port vehicle"; Article 10: "once the Plaintiff suffered the loss within insurance coverage, the Plaintiff shall immediately notify the Defendant or the Defendant's insurance agency, and immediately take effective measures to rescue, protection, consolidation, in order to reduce the expanding loss of the subject matter of insurance. Once the Defendant has reached an agreement on the compensation with the Plaintiff, the Defendant shall pay compensation within ten working days"; Article 11: "the absolute deductible excess for each incident is RMB5,000; during the effective period of this agreement, if the Plaintiff failed to submit the insurance list to the Defendant timely for information input, the Defendant shall still be liable for the insurance liability over this indemnity case. Direct, reasonable expenses of rescuing or protecting the cargo caused by the occurrence of insurance incident of the Plaintiff, the Defendant shall pay the salvage fees under mutual agreement; After the occurrence of insurance incident of the Plaintiff, the Defendant shall take the price of soybean meal at the date of buying the insurance as the indemnity"; Article 16: "the term of the agreement begin from 0000 of January 25, 2014 to 2400 of January 24, 2015".

Domestic Waterway Cargo Carriage Insurance Clauses (2009 Edition) stipulated in Article 5: "this insurance is classified into the basic risks and all risks, the insurer shall respectively bear insurance responsibility according to the risk stated in the insurance policy"; Article 6:"under basic risks, the insurer shall compensate the following insurance cargo loss and expense caused by insurance incident according to the terms of these clauses: the vessel commit collision, stranding, bridges and terminal collapsed; the loss caused by incidents happened during loading and unloading or transshipment; the cargo missing caused by the disorder and direct reasonable expenses paid for salvage or cargo protection when the aforementioned disasters and incidents happened"; Article 7: "under all risks, the insurer shall compensate the following loss beyond the basic risks: the loss of cargo missing due to breakage of packing; the loss caused by rain when transported comply with the safety regulations and transport"; Article 20: "where loss within the insurance coverage occurs on the insured goods and the insurance amount is equal to or higher than the insured value, the insurer shall calculate the compensation according to the actual loss, but the maximum amount of indemnification shall be within the limit of the insured value; Where the insurance amount is less than the insured value, the insurer shall calculate the compensation based on the proportion of the insurance amount and the insured value for its loss amount and the sue and labor charges paid. The insurer shall calculate separately the amount of indemnification for the damaged goods and the direct and reasonable costs paid for the rescue or protecting the goods and not exceed the limit of the insurance amount respectively".

The Plaintiff Grease Company entrusted Kaixin Company to sign the contract of carriage of goods by waterway with the Third Party for its soybean meal shipment from Yide Port, Nantong City, Jiangsu Province, to Chongqing Port. Kaixin Company signed HQTSL-0897 contract of carriage of goods by waterway with the Third Party on September 28, 2014, agreed that the Third Party arranged M.V. "YU JIANG HAI 666" to carry 2,600 tons of soybean meal (70 kg per bag) from Yide Port, Nantong City, Jiangsu Province, to Chongqing Port; the unit freight was RMB116 per ton (including invoices and port construction fee); the Third Party should take full responsibility for the cargo safety, and ensure the cargo without shortage, damage, mildew, and pollution. The Third Party should bear the compensation responsibility according to soybean meal sales price when the aforementioned problems appeared. The cargo should be covered by the shipper. The loss out of the insurance liability shall be born by the Third Party when it happened. The Third Party has the duty to provide related claim proving documents. During the carriage, the Third Party shall immediately fulfill its notify obligation and actively arrange rescue operation when the incident appeared; the Third Party should bear the rejected part or insufficient part instead of the insurance company if the cargo damage and the expanding loss for rescue not timely was caused by the Third Party. After signing the aforementioned contract, the Third Party arranged M. V. "YU JIANG HAI 666" to load soybean meal of 2,351.37 tonnes (33,591 pieces) of the Plaintiff in Yide Port, Nantong City, Jiangsu Province, and started shipment to Chongqing Port on October 9, 2014.

The Plaintiff Grease Company paid premium RMB3,288.05 to the Defendant for covering the soybean meal. The Defendant then issued No.PYDS201 450010000000846 policy to the Plaintiff (hereinafter referred to as the No.46 policy). This policy stated that the applicant and the insured was the Plaintiff Grease Company; Port of shipment was Yide Port, Nantong City, Jiangsu Province, the port of destination was Chongqing Port; the subject matter of the insurance was 33,591 pieces of 43% soybean meal; carrying vessel was M.V. "YU JIANG HAI 666"; insured amount was RMB8,220,124.16; the absolute deductible excess for each incident is RMB3,000.

On October 30, 2014, M.V. "YU JIANG HAI 666" committed collision with M. V. "CHUAN MA 66" and M.V. "ZHONG TAI 66" and caused port side damaged and water ingress of the cabin, when anchoring and waited for passing water gate and water supply in anchorage of Linjiang Ping, Yichang City, Hubei Province. On November 1, the Plaintiff signed soybean meal operation contract with Gangfu Company, to rent the company warehouse for storage of rescued 1,185 tons of the damaged soybean meal. Therefore, the Plaintiff paid all expenses, including handling charge, in amount of RMB46,435.05, respectively on November 4 and 18, 2014 to Gangfu Company.

After the occurrence of the insurance incident, the Defendant appointed Assessment Company to the scene of the incident immediately to assess the damage condition of the soybean meal involved. Assessment Company confirmed that the quantity of the cargo stated on the Plaintiff's cargo receipt was 2,352.64 tons; damaged soybean meal stored in Gangfu Company warehouse was 1,185 tons; damaged soybean meal kept on M.V. "YU JIANG HAI 666" was 9,456 pieces and 65.2 tons of bulk soybean meal, which for a total of 727.12 tons. Thus, Assessment Company deduced that there was 440.48 tons of soybean meal lost in the river. Assessment Company also confirmed that No.46 policy stated that the soybean meal price involved was RMB3,495.89 per ton. The soybean meal involved was 70 kg per bag, the policy stated that total soybean meal were 33,591 pieces, the quantity of soybean meal involved was 2,351.37 tons (33,591*70/1000). The premiums list of October submitted by the Plaintiff stated that the unit price was RMB3,494 per ton, the value of 2,351.37 tons soybean meal involved was RMB8,215,686.78 (3,494*2,351.37) in good condition though the assessment.

On November 14, 2014, in order to reduce loss, and through the bid arranged by the Assessment Company, the Plaintiff and the Defendant signed the sales contract of the damaged soybean meal with an outsider Cultivation Cooperatives in witness and participation of the Assessment Company, Cultivation Cooperatives bought

1,912.12 tons of the damaged soybean meal with the price of RMB2,961,128, and to pay full payment to the Plaintiff. Considering the actual value of the soybean meal involved was RMB8,215,686.78, it is determined that the cargo loss against damaged soybean meal the Plaintiff suffered was RMB5,254,558.78. According to Article 6 of domestic cargo carriage open cover agreement involved, the insured value of soybean meal involved was RMB8,488,445.7 (8,215,686.78 + 116 * 2,351.37).

The Plaintiff Grease Company and the Defendant the Insurance Company reached preliminary compensation intention over soybean meal damaged issues involved on November 14, 2014, the Defendant agreed to fully compensate the real value of the damaged soybean meal, bear salvage fees against the damaged soybean meal, and should be entitled to deal with the damaged soybean meal. The Plaintiff should transfer claim materials, such as the original insurance policy, certificate material of cargo value, claims application, subrogation form, maritime incident report, related material of the vessel, carriage agreement signed with the Third Party, carriage agreement between the Third Party and the actual carrier, etc. to the Defendant. The Defendant'sstaff LANG Jianzhong delivered the compensation agreement the Plaintiff's staff LONG Jinrong after signing. OnNovember 17, the Plaintiff submitted the relevant claim materials to the Defendant, but failed to submit compensation agreement with the Plaintiff's signature and confirmation to the Defendant. Under this condition, the Defendant's staff LANG Jianzhong withdrew the declaration, which agreed to compensate the cargo loss and the salvage fee stated in the compensation agreement due to the damage amount involved citing its claim rights via emails sending to the Plaintiff's staff YANG Chengfan on November 20, 2014.

It is also found that Kaixin Company is a wholly owned subsidiary of the Plaintiff, these two companies have both same legal representative and domicile.

The court holds that:

This case is dispute over an insurance contract of carriage ofgoods by sea-connected areas. Taking the found fact and allegation of each party into consideration, the case has the following issues: first, whether the Plaintiff has insurable interest over the soybean meal involved. Second, whether the Defendant should be entitled to exercise the subrogation rights against the Third Party. Third, what insurance coverage the Defendant should bear for the insurance incident involved.

1. Whether the Plaintiff has insurable interest over the soybean meal involved.

   Pursuant to the provisions of Article 13 of the Insurance Law of People's Republic of China, an insurance contract is formed when a policy holder applies for insurance and the insurer accepts the application. The Plaintiff paid premium of soybean meal involved to the Defendant, the Defendant issued No.46 policy to the Plaintiff, which shall prove that the insurance contract of carriage of cargo by sea-connected areas had been established based on this policy and domestic cargo carriage open cover agreement between two parties.

Pursuant to the provisions of Paragraph 2 of Article 12 of the Insurance Law of the People's Republic of China, the insured in property insurance shall have an insurable interest in the object insured at the time an incident covered by the insurance occurs. The Defendant contended that the Plaintiff had no insurable interest over soybean meal involved, and thus the insurance contract of carriage of cargo by sea-connected areas based on No.46 policy involved was void. The court holds that this Defendant's claim shall not be supported. The reasons are as follows: first, the Plaintiff actively performed the derogation obligation, took various rescue measures and was damaged soybean meal involved, after derogation duty actively, saved soybean meal involved to the best extent possible after the occurrence of the cargo damage. The Plaintiff's rescue behavior means that it had economic relationship over the soybean meal involved, judged by the daily life common sense. Second, the Defendant immediately arranged staff and appointed Assessment Company to the scene for incident facts investigation and loss after knowing the occurrence of the insurance incident over soybean meal involved. The Defendant initiatively negotiated with the Plaintiff, and promised to compensate all the cargo loss and salvage fees in written under the condition of actual loss undetermined. The Defendant did not mention the insured interests even if it rejected to compensate the Plaintiff's loss in written, and declined for the reason of losing the subrogation right. Thus it is found that the Defendant had not thought the Plaintiff did not have insurable interest over soybean meal involved during the processing of soybean meal insurance incident involved. Third, although the contract of carriage of goods by waterway involved was signed by Kaixin Company and the third party, taking the power of attorney issued by the Plaintiff into consideration, the court holds that the Plaintiff appointed, instead of entrusted, its subsidiary Kaixin Company to sign the contract of carriage involved with the third party. Because the power of attorney confirmed the substantial clause of the contract of carriage, such as the carrying vessel name, cargo name, contract number, port of shipment and port of destination, etc., it means that the Plaintiff had been confirmed the content of the contract with the third party, and only appointed Kaixin Company to sign the contract of carriage with the third party. Therefore, the rights and obligations under the contract of carriage of goods by waterway involved shall be born by the Plaintiff rather than Kaixin Company. In conclusion, the Plaintiff has the legally recognized interest on soybean meal involved, the Defendant's claim that the Plaintiff did not have insurable interest shall not be supported.

Based on the fact that the Plaintiff had the insurable interest of soybean meal involved, and the Defendant had issued insurance policy of the soybean meal, as a result, insurance contract of carriage of cargo by sea-connected areas had been established according to law and effective between the Plaintiff and the Defendant based on No.46 policy. Insurance contract based on No.46 policy between the Plaintiff Grease Company and the Defendant Insurance Company, which did not violate the compulsory provisions of laws and administrative rules and regulations, became effective when it was established. A lawfully established contract legally binds both parties of the Plaintiff and the Defendant, both the parties shall perform their obligations respectively according to the law. The Plaintiff, as the applicant and the insured, had fulfilled the obligation of paying insurance premium. The Defendant, as the insurer, shall perform insurance liability of paying indemnity after the occurrence of insurance incident.

2. Whether the Defendant should be entitled to exercise the subrogation rights against the Third Party.

   The Defendant contended that it should not bear insurance liability to pay indemnity of the cargo involved for the Plaintiff's unilaterally giving up subrogation right against the Third Party, according to Article 9 of the contract of carriage of goods by waterway "loss, outside the scope of insurance liability, shall be born by the Third Party if happened". The court holds that the Defendant's claim shall not be supported. The reasons are as follows: first, Article 8 of the contract of carriage of goods by waterway involved was the premise of Article 9. Article 8 of this contract stated that the Third Party shall take full responsibility for the safety of the consigned cargo, otherwise should bear compensation obligation based on sales price. This statement means that the Third Party shall take full responsibility for soybean meal involved under the contract of carriage, which would not reduce by other responsibility mechanism. Under this premise, the supplementary statement of Article 9, which states that loss, outside the scope of insurance liability, shall be born by the Third Party if happening, shall be interpreted as the Third Party shall bear supplementary liability in case the Defendant's compensation was not enough to cover the Plaintiff's actual loss. But the supplementary compensation liability of the Third Party shall not exempt from its bearing all liability according to Article 8 of the carriage contract against soybean meal involved. In other words, the Defendant still can exercise the subrogation right after bearing insurance compensation liability based on No.46 policy, and recover from the third party according to Article 8 of the contract of carriage, and the Third Party shall not invoke the provisions of Article 10 of the contract of carriage for defense that the Defendant had lost the subrogation right. The provision of Paragraph 4, Article 14 of carriage contract supports this explanation. The clause expressly states that the Third Party shall bear the rejected part or insufficient part instead of the Defendant Insurance Company if the cargo damage was caused by the Third Party.

3. What insurance coverage the Defendant should bear for the insurance incident involved.

   The soybean meal involved suffered wet damage due to vessel collision during the period of the insurance liability, which belongs to "the insurance cargo loss and expenses caused by vessel collision" stipulated in Article 6 of *Domestic Waterway Cargo Carriage Insurance Clauses* (2009 Edition) the two sides agreed to apply. Extra damage cargo handling charge paid by the Plaintiff of the soybean meal involved, meets the stipulation Article 6 of this clause that the cargo missing caused by the disorder and direct and reasonable expenses paid for salvage or cargo protection when the aforementioned disasters and incidents happened. Thus, the Defendant shall bear the insurance liability of paying compensation to the Plaintiff. The cargo loss the Plaintiff suffered due to the cargo damages was RMB5,254,558.78, salvage fee was RMB46,435.05, the insured amount was RMB8,220,124.16, the insurance value was RMB8,488,445.7, and the absolute deductible excess was RMB3,000. According to the provisions of Article 20 of *Domestic Waterway Cargo Carriage Insurance Clauses* (2009 Edition), the Defendant shall compensate RMB5,085,461.07 for the cargo loss and RMB44,967.23 for salvage fee, totally RMB5,130,428.3, to the Plaintiff.

According to the provisions of Article 23 of the Insurance Law of People's Republic of China, "the insurer shall, after receiving a claim for indemnity or payment of insurance benefits from the insured or the beneficiary, determine the matter without delay. If the circumstances are complex, the insurer shall determine the matter within 30 days, unless the insurance contract provides otherwise. The insurer shall inform the insured or the beneficiary of the outcome. If responsibility lies with the insurer, the insurer shall fulfill its obligation for such indemnity or payment within 10 days after an agreement is reached with the insured or the beneficiary. If there are stipulations in the insurance contract on the period within which indemnification or payment should be made, then the insurer shall fulfill its obligation accordingly". The Defendant rejected to compensate and to bear the insurance liability in written on December 2, 2014, the Plaintiff was entitled to request the Defendant Insurance Company to pay the interest over the cargo loss and handling charge. Because there was no formal agreement on compensation against the cargo damage involved between the Plaintiff and the Defendant, the interest shall not be calculated from November 25, 2014 the Plaintiff alleged, and shall be calculated from the next day after the Defendant's rejection. Therefore, the Plaintiff is entitled to calculate the interest on a principal of RMB5,130,428.3, calculate at the loan interest rate of the People's Bank of China bank for the contemporary period of time from December 3, 2014 to the date of payment set by this judgment.

To sum up, according to Article 12 Paragraph 6, Article 13 Paragraph 1 and Paragraph 3, Article 23 Paragraph 1 and Paragraph 3 of the Insurance Law of the People's Republic of China, and Article 142 of the Civil Procedure Law of the People's Republic of China, judgment is as follows:

1. The Defendant PICC Property and Casualty Company Limited Chongqing Branch shall pay the Plaintiff Chongqing Red Dragonfly Oil Limited Liability Company indemnity of RMB5,130,428.3 and interest thereof within 10 days after this judgment enters into effect (the interest shall be calculated at the loan interest rate of the People's Bank of China bank for the contemporary period of time from December 3, 2014 to the date of payment set by this judgment);

2. Reject other claims of Chongqing Red Dragonfly Oil Limited Liability Company.

For failure to fulfill the obligation of payment within the period designated by this judgment, interest on the debt for the delayed period shall be doubled, pursuant to the provisions of Article 253 of the Civil Procedure Law of the People's Republic of China.

Court acceptance fee in amount of RMB48,906,the Plaintiff Chongqing Red Dragonfly Oil Limited Liability Company shall bear RMB1,574, and the Defendant PICC Property and Casualty Company Limited Chongqing Branch shall bear RMB47,332. Court acceptance fee of this case, which shall be born by the Defendant PICC Property and Casualty Company Limited Chongqing Branch, shall be paid to the Plaintiff together with the insurance indemnity.

In case of dissatisfaction with this judgment, each party may within 15 days as of the service of this judgment, submit a statement of appeal to the court, together with 5 copies and appeal to the Hubei High People's Court.

The appellant shall prepay the acceptance fee of the appeal when submitting the appeal petition, according to the amount of the appeal request of dissatisfaction with this judgment, and pursuant to the provisions of paragraph 1, Article 13 of the Measures on the Payment of Litigation Costs to Hubei High People's Court (deposit bank: Agricultural Bank of China, Wuhan City Donghu Branch; account: Non-taxable Income Financial Account of Finance Department, Hubei Province; account number: 052101040000369-1. Usage column of bank receipts shall indicate the "Hubei High People's Court" or Hubei High People's Court's unit code "103,001"). If the appellant fails to prepay the acceptance fee within 7 days after the expiration of time limit, the appeal shall be withdrawn automatically.

Presiding Judge: YI Lu
Judge: CAI Sian
Acting Judge: CHEN Lin

May 18, 2015

Clerk: ZHANG Xuemin

Guangzhou Maritime Court
Civil Judgment

Connexions (Asia) Limited
v.
J&S Worldwide Logistics Co., Ltd. et al.

(2012) Guang Hai Fa Shang Chu Zi No.704

Related Case(s) This is the judgment of first instance, and the judgment of second instance and the ruling of retrial are on page 293 and page 309 respectively.

Cause(s) of Action 202. Dispute over contract of carriage of goods by sea or sea-connected waters.

Headnote The Plaintiff shipper succeeded in claim for delivery without presentation of original bill of lading against carrier in whose name bill of lading was issued; damages were calculated at the export value of the goods in the customs declaration, and not the invoice price charged by the shipper to its foreign buyer.

Summary The Plaintiff arranged with Taiwan J&S to ship belts from China to New York. Taiwan J&S issued a bill of lading naming Shenzhen J&S (the first Defendant) as the carrier, the Plaintiff as shipper and the Plaintiff's buyer in New York as consignee. Through the medium of an NVOCC named Ocean Bridge, Taiwan J&S then contracted with the second Defendant, Hanjin Shipping, to be the actual carrier of the goods. The second Defendant issued a bill of lading naming Ocean Bridge as shipper and consignee. The second Defendant delivered the goods to Ocean Bridge in New York in return for the original bill of lading that it had issued. At that time, the Plaintiff was still holding the original bills of lading issued in the name of the first Defendant. The Plaintiff did receive some payment from its buyer, but it allocated that payment to other debts due to it from the buyer. The Plaintiff sued both of the Defendants, claiming that it had suffered loss as a result of delivery of the goods without presentation of the original bills of lading, that loss being the balance of the purchase price owing from its buyer. The court held that the first Defendant was the carrier in relation to the Plaintiff because it appeared to be so from the bill of lading, and so the first Defendant was liable to the Plaintiff for delivery of the goods without presentation of the original bills of lading. Damages were calculated as being the export value of the goods in the customs declaration made on shipment, not the balance of the invoice value to be paid by the buyer. The second Defendant was not liable to the Plaintiff as it had delivered the goods in return for the full set of original bills of lading issued by itself.

Judgment

The Plaintiff: Connexions (Asia) Limited.
Domicile: Room 1310-1312, 13 Floor, Lu Plaza, No.2, Wing Yip Street, Kwun Tong, Kowloon, the Hong Kong Special Administrative Region of the People's Republic of China.
Legal representative: YUAN Caiqiong, director.
Agent *ad litem*: HUANG Fulong, lawyer of Guangdong Shengtang Law Firm.
Agent *ad litem*: HUANG Xiaoli, lawyer of Guangdong Shengtang Law Firm.

The Defendant: J&S Worldwide Logistics Co., Ltd.
Domicile: H-I, 22 Floor, Building 5, Wei Peng Garden, Zhenzhong Road, Futian District, Shenzhen City, Guangdong, the People's Republic of China.
Legal representative: LIU Ruiqin, executive director.
Agent *ad litem*: CHEN Longjie, lawyer of Shanghai Wintell & Co. (Guangzhou) Law Firm.
Agent *ad litem*: ZHENG Cairong, lawyer of Shanghai Wintell & Co. (Guangzhou) Law Firm.

The Defendant: Hanjin Shipping Co., Ltd.
Domicile: Hanjin Shipping Building, Yeouido Dong 25-11, Yeongdeungpo District, Seoul, the Republic of Korea.
Legal representative: JIN Yongmin, representative director.
Agent *ad litem*: ZHANG Xinwei, lawyer of Shanghai GL & Co. (Guangzhou) Law Firm.
Agent *ad litem*: WANG Pei, lawyer of Shanghai GL & Co. (Guangzhou) Law Firm.

With respect of the case arising from dispute over contract of carriage of goods by sea by the Plaintiff Connexions (Asia) Limited against the Defendants J&S Worldwide Logistics Co., Ltd. (hereinafter referred to as "Shenzhen J&S") and Hanjin Shipping Co., Ltd. (hereinafter referred to as "Hanjin") before the court on June 16, 2012. After entertaining this case, the court formed a collegiate panel composed of Presiding Judge FU Junyang, Judge LI Lifei and Judge PINGYANG Danke according to law. Then because of the working arrangements, the collegiate panel was changed to compose of Presiding Judge CHANG Weiping, Judge LI Lifei and Judge PINGYANG Danke, and ZENG Huifen was appointed as Clerk. The court held hearings in public on April 23 and July 18, 2013. YUAN Caiqiong, the Plaintiff's legal representative, and HUANG Fulong and HUANG Xiaoli, its agents *ad litem*, CHEN Longjie and ZHENG Cairong, agents *ad litem* of the Defendant Shenzhen J&S, ZHANG Xinwei and WANG Pei, agents *ad litem* of the Defendant Hanjin appeared in court to attend the trial. Now the case has been concluded.

The Plaintiff alleged: In July 2011, a batch of belts of the Plaintiff was carried by Shenzhen J&S from Ningbo, China to New York, USA, and Shenzhen J&S issued No.JSNYC110706 B/L to it. Hanjin was the actual carrier, the Plaintiff was the shipper under the B/L involved, and also the holder of the original B/L. But, after the arrival of the goods at the port of destination, the two Defendants delivered the goods on August 15, 2011 without the original B/L, which caused the Plaintiff's failure for receipt of the balance payment of goods under B/Lin sum of USD227,291.04 except the 20% advance payment. Shenzhen J&S as contracting carrier and Hanjin as the actual carrier of the goods involved, should deliver the goods against surrendering the original B/L. The two Defendants should assume joint and several liability for the huge loss sustained by the Plaintiff for delivery of goods without the original B/L. The Plaintiff requested the court to order both of the Defendants to compensate the Plaintiff the loss under No.JSNYC110706 B/L in sum of USD227,291.04 (the dollars currency translated into RMB according to reference rate of dollar against RMB at 1:6.395 prevailing on August 15, 2011 published by China Foreign Exchange Trade System which was authorized by the People's Bank of China was RMB1,453,526.2) and interest thereon (the interest should be calculated from August 15, 2011 according to the working capital loan interest rate promulgated by the People's Bank of China over the same period); and the Defendants should assume the court fees and the notarization and authentication fee of this case.

The Plaintiff submitted the following evidence within the time limit for adducing evidence:

1. Notarization and authentication documents of proforma invoice, commercial invoice, packing list, bank remittance notice and mail of advice of drawing;
2. Witness testimony of Michael Shun Forrest and attachment thereto;
3. B/L;
4. Records of delivery of goods;
5. Web page information and record information of chineseshipping.com.cn, a secondary website of the Ministry of Transport;
6. Reply letter of LUO Linguang;
7. Homepage information of Shenzhen J&S Express (H.K.) Limited, commercial registration and record information tracer of Shenzhen J&S, page information and annual report of online search center of Hong Kong Companies Registry;
8. Business license of the translation company. The supplementary evidence submitted by the Plaintiff after the hearing on April 23, 2013 is as follow:
9. Lawyer's letter issued by Wang Jing & Co. (Shenzhen) Law Firm;
10. Reply letter and the attachment thereto of LUO Linguang; and
11. Email in reply of Shenzhen J&S.

The Defendant Shenzhen J&S defended:

1. Shenzhen J&S did not issue the B/L involved, and it was not the proper Defendant;
2. Where the United States Carriage of Goods by Sea Act (COGSA) applied according to the paramount clause on the back of the B/L involved, Shenzhen J&S should not undertake the liability for delivery of goods without an original B/L;
3. The Plaintiff did not suffer any loss because of delivery of goods without the original B/L; and
4. The value of goods involved claimed by the Plaintiff was the value of re-sale by the middleman, but the amount of loss of the goods caused by delivery of goods without the original B/L should be the value of the goods at the time of loading, namely the export declaration price.

The Defendant Shenzhen J&S submitted the following evidence within the time limit for adducing evidence:

1. No.JSNYC110706 B/L;
2. The Defendant's sample of B/L;
3. Notarial certificate of mails concerning booking space and booking note between the Plaintiff and Taiwan J&S Air Freight Forwarding Co., Ltd. Ningbo Office (hereinafter referred to as Taiwan J&S Ningbo Office);
4. Employment Certificate of Helen;
5. Labor contract between Helen and Ningbo Zhongji Foreign Enterprise Services Cooperation (Zhongji Cooperation);
6. Labor dispatching agreement between Zhongji Cooperation and Taiwan J&S Ningbo Office;
7. Certificate of registration of resident office of foreign (regional) enterprise of Taiwan J&S Ningbo Office;
8. No.OBIGNBNY10127500 B/L;
9. Lawyer's letter of the Plaintiff;
10. The reply of Taiwan J&S to lawyer's letter;
11. The United States Carriage of Goods by Sea Act 1936;
12. Federal Bills of Lading Act;
13. No.2011032 commercial invoice;
14. Packing List;
15. No.310420110549415324 customs declaration;
16. Transfer voucher.

The supplementary evidence submitted by Shenzhen J&S after the hearing on April 23, 2013 is as follow:

17. Labor contract between Helen and Zhongji Cooperation (of which the contract period was from May 1, 2010 to April 30, 2012).

The Defendant Hanjin defended:

1. The Plaintiff was neither the shipper or the consignee under the B/L issued by Hanjin, nor the holder of the B/L, and it was not the proper Plaintiff; and
2. Hanjin had delivered the goods to straight consignee according to the B/L issued by itself, while the B/L on which the Plaintiff's action based was not issued by Hanjin, and the fact alleged by the Plaintiff that Hanjin delivered the goods without the original B/L did not exist. The Plaintiff was not entitled to claim Hanjin to undertake joint and several liability for delivery of goods without the original B/L.

The Defendant Hanjin submitted the following evidence within the time limit for adducing evidence:

1. No.HJSCNJBA10127500 B/L issued by Hanjin; and
2. No.OBIGNBNY10127500 Telex Release B/L of Oceanic Bridge International, Inc. (hereinafter referred to as "Oceanic Bridge").

After examining the evidence in the hearing, Shenzhen J&S confirmed the authenticity of the Plaintiff's evidence 3 to 6 and evidence 8 to 10, Hanjin had no objection to the Plaintiff's evidence 3 to 6 and evidence 8 to 11; the Plaintiff confirmed the authenticity of evidence 1 to 3, evidence 9 to 12 and evidence 15 to 17 of Shenzhen J&S, and Hanjin raised no objection to the evidence of Shenzhen J&S; the Plaintiff confirmed the authenticity of evidence 1 of Hanjin, and Shenzhen J&S confirmed the evidence of Hanjin. The court confirms the probative force of the evidence that the parties raised no objection to. The bank remittance notice of Hengsheng Bank Limited of the Plaintiff's evidence 1 is the original, and the court confirms probative force of this notice. Other evidence of the Plaintiff's evidence 1 and evidence 11, evidence 4 to 8 of Shenzhen J&S and evidence 2 of Hanjin can corroborate other evidence having been confirmed, the court hereby admits.

According to evidence having been verified and admitted above, combining with the trial investigation, the court identifies the facts of this case as follows:

On May 12, 2011, the Plaintiff signed a sales contract with Silver Goose Accessories Co., Ltd. (Silver Goose) based on No.PI109778 order. In the contract they agreed that the Plaintiff would supply 231,780 pairs of belts to Silver Goose, under FOB Shanghai, the total price of the goods was USD284,113.80, the delivery day was June 25, the consignee was Mike. S. Forrest, 20% of the price was prepaid, and the remaining 80% would be paid by telegraphic transfer against the copy of B/L. On July 6, the Plaintiff issued No.AU004811 commercial invoice to Silver Goose which recorded that the goods involved would be shipped from Ningbo to New York on July 10 or around, and the packing list which recorded the container number was HJCU1611199 on the same day. On May 12, 2011, the Plaintiff also signed a sales contract with Silver Goose based on No.PI109779 order in which they agreed that the Plaintiff supplied 80,040 pairs of belt to Silver Goose, the total price of the goods was USD98,440.56, July 15 was the delivery day, and the rest part would be paid in the same method as that agreed in the No.PI109778 order. On

July 21, the Plaintiff issued No.AU004855-1 commercial invoice and the packing list which recorded the container number was HJCU4157665 on the same day.

On May 21, 2011, Hengsheng Bank Limited sent a remittance notice to the Plaintiff, which recorded the Plaintiff's account received a remittance in sum of USD76,510.87 from Silver Goose from America. On the same day, the Plaintiff received an email from Silver Goose, in which said Silver Goose had paid USD76,510.87 as advance deposit under No.PI109778 and No.PI109779 orders.

In June, the Plaintiff's employee contacted with Helen an employee of Taiwan J&S Ningbo Office about booking space of goods under No.PI109778 order involved. Taiwan J&S Ningbo Office booked space with Ocean Bridge in the name of J&S Express Ningbo Ltd. (J&S Ningbo).The sample of No. OBIGNBNY10127500 B/L of Ocean Bridge given out on July 9, (not issued) recorded that: booking number was No.HJSCNJBA10127500, J&S Ningbo was the shipper, Date International Co., Ltd. was the consignee and the notify party, the goods were 19,315 packs PU belts loaded in two 40 ft containers numbered with HJCU1611199 and HJCU1293164. That sample of B/L also sealed on "Telex Release, Date July 11, 2011". On July 10, 2011, Hanjin issued No. HJSCNJBA10127500 B/L, recording Dalian International Freight Co., Ltd. (Dalian Ocean Bridge) was the shipper, Ocean Bridge was the consignee and the notify party, Ningbo was the port of loading, New York was port of discharge, 19,315 packs of PU belts loaded in two 40 ft containers numbered with HJCU1611199 and HJCU1293164 on M.V."Hanjin Shanghai" Voyage 0117E, CY to CY, freight prepaid.

On July 10, 2011, Helen, an employee of Taiwan J&S Ningbo Office on behalf of the carrier Shenzhen J&S issued No.JSNYC110706 original B/L to the Plaintiff, which recorded: the title was Shenzhen J&S, the Plaintiff was the shipper, Silver Goose was the consignee and the notify party, Ningbo was port of loading, New York was the port of discharge, the goods involved were 19,315 packs PU belts loaded in two 40 ft containers numbered with HJCU1611199 and HJCU1293164 on M.V."Hanjin Shanghai" Voyage 0117E, CY to CY, the shipper was in charge of loading, counting and packing, freight was to be collect. It was recorded on the front of the B/L that "unless otherwise provided, the goods should be carried in good condition according to quantity and packages recorded below from the place of receipt to the place of delivery according to the clauses of the B/L. The holder of B/L or the agent thereof should take delivery of the goods with an original B/L. The carrier and the holder of B/L should be bound by rights and obligations provided in clauses of B/L (without prejudice to application of the common law bonding the acts of trading party), the contract has been concluded as hereby proved". Article 7.3 of the "Paramount Clause" on the back of B/L records that "if COGSA shall compulsorily apply to the present B/L, it shall be binding upon the carriage of goods by sea, goods carried on deck and inboard included, or only applies to the goods carried on deck according to the representation in B/L above mentioned".

Upon investigation, on July 6, 2011, the containers numbered with HJCU1611199 and HJCU1293164 were delivered to the shipper in Ningbo. On July 7, the containers after loading the goods involved were sent to the export wharf later than entering into the yard. On July 9, the containers involved were loaded onto M.V."Hanjin Shanghai" Voyage 0117E in Ningbo. On July 10, M.V."Hanjin Shanghai" set sail. The vessel arrived in New York on August 9. On August 10, the loading was completed. On August 12, Hanjin received No.HJSCNJBA10127500 original B/L issued by itself. On August 15, the containers involved were delivered to the consignee in New York. On August 19, the consignee returned the empty containers. The Plaintiff had been holding full set of original No.JSNYC110706 B/L until the time that this action was filed. This B/L was though slightly different from the B/L of Shenzhen J&S docketed in the Ministry of Transport, it conforms to the sample of B/L that Shenzhen J&S showed in court.

On March 30, PAN Lidong, a lawyer of Guangdong Wang Jing & Co. (Shenzhen), sent a lawyer's letter to Shenzhen J&S on behalf of the Plaintiff and carbon copied Taiwan J&S Ningbo Office, in which it claimed against Shenzhen J&S for loss of USD306,043.49 caused by delivery of the goods under No. JSNYC110706 and No.JSNYC110715 B/Ls without the original B/Ls, legal fee in sum of USD4,000, and requested a confirm receipt of the lawyer's letter within 5 days after the sending of the same. On April 6, LUO Linguang replied to the lawyer's letter of the Plaintiff by email (larryeagle@gmail.com) and carbon copied LIU Ruiqin (jsszxmarketing@jsexpress.com.hk), the legal representative of Shenzhen J&S. The reply said Silver Goose had paid 20% of the price under No. PI109778 and No.PI109779 orders in sum of USD76,510.87 as deposit to the Plaintiff on May 20, 2011. The balance payment in sum of USD227,290.24 under No.PI109778 order was paid on August 3, 2011, and the balance payment in sum of USD78,752.45 under No.PI109779 order was unpaid because the products failed the quality inspection of buyer. The signature of this email was LUO Linguang, Shenzhen J&S Express Ningbo Co., Ltd. On April 16, 2012, Shenzhen J&S sent emails to the Plaintiff's attorney RAO Zhenhua, a lawyer of Wang Jing & Co. (Shenzhen) by jsszxmarketing@jsexpress.com.hk, saying in terms of the subject dispute involved "please refer to our reply and related documents, and contact with Mr.Luo if you have any questions", and carbon copied LUO Linguang.

As for the facts of this case the parties disputed, the court identifies as follows:

To prove the Plaintiff's loss in sum of USD227,291.04 caused by delivery of goods without the original B/L by the Defendants, the Plaintiff submitted evidence 1 proforma invoice, commercial invoice, packing list, bank remittance notice, mail of advice of drawing and evidence 2 Michael Shun Forrest's witness testimony. The Plaintiff's evidence 1 recorded that the value of goods involved was USD284,113.80 and the Plaintiff received 20% of the price under No.PI109778 and No.PI109779 orders in sum of USD76,510.87 as deposit remitted by Silver Goose on May 21, 2011. Michael Shun Forrest the former sales president of Silver Goose testified in court, to prove that the Plaintiff had received 20% of the price under No. PI109778 and No.PI109779 orders as deposit (the deposit in sum of USD56,822.76 under No.PI109778 order, the deposit in sum of USD19,688.11 under No.PI109779 order, USD76,510.87 in total) on May 21, 2011. On around August 4, Silver Goose paid USD227,290.24 to the Plaintiff as the balance payment under No.PI109778 order. On August 16, the Plaintiff asked for permission of Silver Goose to use the payment of No.PI109778 order which had been received for other trade via e-mail, and reported to Silver Goose on August 25 when Silver Goose confirmed by e-mail on the same day. So the Plaintiff claimed for loss in sum of USD227,291.04. The Defendants Shenzhen J&S and Hanjin held that the Plaintiff had received the payment in full amount and suffered no loss. Shenzhen J&S held that USD284,113.80 was the value of re-sale by middleman while the amount of loss caused by delivery of goods without the original B/L should be the value of the goods at the time of shipment plus insurance and freight. Shenzhen J&S submitted evidence 13 invoice of Qingdao Fortune Arts & Crafts Co., Ltd. (hereinafter referred to as "Fortune"), evidence 14 packing list of Fortune, evidence 15 customs declaration and evidence 16 transfer voucher. It was recorded in No.310420110549415324 export customs declaration of which the declaration day was July 7, 2011 that the export port was Beilun customs, the operating and shipping unit was Fortune, the transport means was M.V."Hanjin Shanghai" Voyage 0117E, the number of delivery order was NJBA10127500, the goods were loaded in two 40 ft containers numbered with HJCU1611199 and HJCU1293164, the goods were 19,315 packs of belts made of PU, and the total price was USD132,114.6. Evidence 13 and evidence 14 can prove that value of the goods at the time of loading was USD132,114.6. Evidence 16 records that the Plaintiff has separately received USD76,510.87 namely 20% of the price as deposit under No. PI109778 and No.PI109779 orders and the balance payment in sum of USD227,290.24 under No.PI109778 B/L. The Plaintiff had no objection to the authenticity of evidence 15 and 16. To sum up, the court confirms the facts that customs declaration value of the goods involved was USD132,114.6 on FOB basis, the Plaintiff received USD76,510.87 namely 20% of the price as deposit under No. PI109778 and No.PI109779 orders and the balance payment in sum of USD227,290.24 of No.PI109778 order, as well as the fact that the Plaintiff used USD227,290.24 for other trades.

In the trial, the parties agreed to apply the law of the People's Republic of China to resolve the dispute of this case.

The court holds that: this case is concerning dispute over a contract of carriage of goods by sea. This case involves foreign-related factor because the goods involved were shipped from Ningbo China to New York. According to Article 1 of Interpretation of the Supreme People's Court on the Application of the Special Maritime Procedure Law of the People's Republic of China and Article 11 of the Some Provisions of the Supreme People's Court on the Scope of Cases to be Entertained by Maritime Courts, this case should be under special jurisdiction of maritime court. The place of the departure of the goods involved is under the jurisdiction of the court, according to Article 27 of the Civil Procedure Law of the People's Republic of China, an action instituted for a dispute arising from transport contract shall be under the jurisdiction of the people's court located in the place of the departure, so the court has jurisdiction over this case. The parties agreed that law of the People's Republic of China should apply, so according to Article 269 of the Maritime Code of the People's Republic of China, law of the People's Republic of China shall apply to deal with substantial dispute of this case.

According to the facts having been ascertained, the Plaintiff booked space with Taiwan J&S Ningbo Office in the name of shipper, Taiwan J&S Ningbo Office issued a full set of original B/Ls as agent of the carrier Shenzhen J&S. Though this B/L was not a NVOCC B/L of Shenzhen J&S having docketed with the Ministry of Transport, it was according to the sample of B/L that Shenzhen J&S showed in court. Shenzhen J&S did not prove the resource of the B/Ls involved issued by Taiwan J&S Ningbo Office was illegal. So the court confirms the Plaintiff's proposition that Shenzhen J&S was the carrier involved. The contract of carriage of goods by sea signed by the Plaintiff and Shenzhen J&S was formed, under which the Plaintiff was the shipper and Shenzhen J&S was the carrier. This contract which is real intentions of both parties shall be lawful and effective, and be binding upon both parties. Shenzhen J&S arranged Hanjin for the carriage of the goods involved after the Plaintiff's entrustment. Hanjin was the actual carrier in the legal relationship of carriage of goods by sea.

Shenzhen J&S claimed the law of the USA should apply to determine the assumption of liability according to the clause on the back of No.JSNYC110706 B/L. The court holds that there is a express clause recorded on the front of the B/L "the holder of B/L or the agent thereof must take delivery of the goods with an original B/L. The carrier and the holder of B/Ls will be bound by the rights and obligations as provided in clauses of B/Ls (without prejudice to application of the common law bonding the acts of trading party), the contract has been concluded as hereby proved", this contract is real intentions of the shipper and the carrier, and shall be binding upon the Plaintiff and Shenzhen J&S, both parties should fulfill obligations according to the contract. In this case, Shenzhen J&S who issued the B/Ls did not prove the B/Ls involved fell into the circumstance of compulsory application of COGSA. This claim is lack of factual and legal basis, and shall be rejected. Article 71 of the Maritime Code of the People's Republic of China provides: "a bill of lading is a document which serves as an evidence of the contract of carriage of goods by sea and the taking over or loading of the goods by the carrier, and based on which the carrier undertakes to deliver the goods against surrendering the same. A provision in the document stating that the goods are to be delivered to the order of a named person, or to order, or to bearer, constitutes such an undertaking". The Plaintiff held the full set of original bill. Shenzhen J&S's delivery of the goods without original B/L violated the provision above, infringed the rights of the Plaintiff as the shipper who held the original B/Ls. According to Article 2 of the Provisions of the Supreme People's Court on Several Issues concerning the Application of Law in the Trial of Cases of Disputes arising from Delivery of Goods without Original Bill of Lading: "where a carrier delivers goods without an original bill of lading in violation of law, damaging the rights of the holder of the original bill of lading under the bill of lading, the holder of the original bill of lading may require the carrier to bear the civil liability for the losses resulting therefrom", the Plaintiff shall be entitled to compensation against the Defendant. According to Article 55 Paragraph 1 and Paragraph 2 of the Maritime Code of the People's Republic of China, the amount of compensation for the loss of the goods involved shall be calculated on the basis of the actual value of the goods, the actual value shall be the value of the goods at the time of shipment plus insurance and freight. The claim of Shenzhen J&S that the value of the goods involved should be USD132,114.6 as recorded in customs declaration before shipment, shall be supported according to the law. The Plaintiff requested USD284,113.80, namely the balance payment according to 80% of the value of goods agreed on sales contract at the time of re-sale, such claim has no legal basis and shall be rejected. According to the facts ascertained in trial, the Plaintiff had received all the price and used that for other trades, Shenzhen J&S's delivery of goods without an original B/L did not cause loss to the Plaintiff, the claim of the Plaintiff that Shenzhen J&S should pay for loss of the goods involved and the interest thereon has no factual basis, and shall be rejected. The notarization and authentication fee is cost of the party for fulfilling litigation responsibility or undertaking burden of proof to protect procedural or substantial interests, the court will not support the claim of the Plaintiff that the notary and authentication fee should be undertaken by the Defendants, which lacks factual and legal basis. Hanjin as the actual carrier, had received the full set of original B/L issued by itself, the claim of the Plaintiff that Hanjin shall undertake joint and several liability for delivery of goods without the original B/L lacks factual and legal basis shall be rejected.

In summary, according to Article 64 of the Civil Procedure Law of the People's Republic of China, the judgment is as follows:

Reject the claims of the Plaintiff Connexions (Asia) Limited.

Court acceptance fee in amount of RMB18,601.27, shall be born by the Plaintiff Connexions (Asia) Limited.

In case of dissatisfaction with this judgment, the Plaintiff Connexions (Asia) Limited and the Defendant Hanjin Shipping Co., Ltd. may within 30 days upon the service of this judgment, the Defendant Shenzhen J&S Worldwide Logistics Co., Ltd. may within 15 days upon the service of this judgment, submit a statement of appeal to the court, together with copies according to the number of the opposite parties, and appeal to the Guangdong High People's Court.

Presiding Judge: CHANG Weiping
Judge: LI Lifei
Judge: PINGYANG Danke

August 20, 2014

Clerk: ZENG Huifen

Guangdong High People's Court
Civil Judgment

Connexions (Asia) Limited
v.
J&S Worldwide Logistics Co., Ltd. et al.

(2015) Yue Gao Fa Min Si Zhong Zi No.10

Related Case(s) This is the judgment of second instance, and the judgment of first instance and the ruling of retrial are on page 283 and page 309 respectively.

Cause(s) of Action 202. Dispute over contract of carriage of goods by sea or sea-connected waters.

Headnote Affirming lower court decision awarding the Plaintiff shipper damages for delivery without presentation of original bill of lading against carrier in whose name bill of lading was issued; damages were calculated at the export value of the goods in the customs declaration, and not the invoice price charged by the shipper to its foreign buyer.

Summary The Plaintiff arranged with Taiwan J&S to ship belts from China to New York. Taiwan J&S issued a bill of lading naming Shenzhen J&S (the first Defendant) as the carrier, the Plaintiff as shipper and the Plaintiff's buyer in New York as consignee. Through the medium of an NVOCC named Ocean Bridge, Taiwan J&S then contracted with the second Defendant, Hanjin Shipping, to be the actual carrier of the goods. The second Defendant issued a bill of lading naming Ocean Bridge as shipper and consignee. The second Defendant delivered the goods to Ocean Bridge in New York in return for the original bill of lading that it had issued. At that time, the Plaintiff was still holding the original bills of lading issued in the name of the first Defendant. The Plaintiff did receive some payment from its buyer, but it allocated that payment to other debts due to it from the buyer. The Plaintiff sued both of the Defendants, claiming that it had suffered loss as a result of delivery of the goods without presentation of the original bills of lading, that loss being the balance of the purchase price owing from its buyer. The court of first instance held that the first Defendant was the carrier in relation to the Plaintiff, and so the first Defendant was liable to the Plaintiff for delivery of the goods without presentation of the original bills of lading, but the second Defendant was not liable to the Plaintiff as it had delivered the goods in return for the original bill of lading issued by itself. Damages were assessed as the export value of the goods in the customs declaration made on shipment. The Plaintiff and the first Defendant both appealed. The appeal court recognized the lower court's decision that the first

Defendant was liable to the Plaintiff, and that the Plaintiff's loss was to be assessed at the export value of the cargo, not the invoice value charged to the Plaintiff's American buyer. The (non-)liability of the second Defendant was not contested on appeal.

Judgment

The Appellant (the Plaintiff of first instance): Connexions (Asia) Limited.
Domicile: Room 1310-1312, 13 Floor, Lu Plaza, No.2, Wing Yip Street, Kwun Tong, Kowloon, the Hong Kong Special Administrative Region of the People's Republic of China.
Legal representative: YUAN Caiqiong, director.
Agent *ad litem*: HUANG Fulong, lawyer of Guangdong Shengtang Law Firm.
Agent *ad litem*: HUANG Xiaoli, lawyer of Guangdong Shengtang Law Firm.

The Appellant (the Defendant of First Instance): J&S Worldwide Logistics Co., Ltd.
Domicile: H-I, 22 Floor, Building 5, Wei Peng Garden, Zhenzhong Road, Futian District, Shenzhen City, Guangdong Province, the People's Republic of China.
Legal representative: LIU Ruiqin, executive director.
Agent *ad litem*: CHEN Longjie, lawyer of Shanghai Wintell & Co. (Guangzhou) Law Firm.
Agent *ad litem*: ZHENG Cairong, lawyer of Shanghai Wintell & Co. (Guangzhou) Law Firm.

The Defendant of First Instance: Hanjin Shipping Co., Ltd.
Domicile: Hanjin Shipping Building, Yeouido Dong 25-11, Yeongdeungpo District, Seoul, the Republic of Korea.
Legal representative: JIN Yongmin, representative director.
Agent *ad litem*: ZHANG Xinwei, lawyer of Shanghai GL & Co. (Guangzhou) Law Firm.
Agent *ad litem*: WANG Pei, lawyer of Shanghai GL & Co. (Guangzhou) Law Firm.

Unsatisfied with the Civil Judgment (2014) Guang Hai Fa Shang Chu Zi No.704 the case arising from dispute over contract of carriage of goods by sea, the Appellants Connexions (Asia) Limited (hereinafter referred to as Connexions) and J&S Worldwide Logistics Co., Ltd. (hereinafter referred to as Shenzhen J&S) with the Defendant of first instance, Hanjin Shipping Co., Ltd. (hereinafter referred to as Hanjin) involved, filed an appeal with the court. After entertaining this case, the court formed a collegiate panel according to law. HUANG Fulong and HUANG Xiaoli, agents *ad litem* of Connexions, ZHENG Cairong, agent *ad litem* of Shenzhen J&S, and ZHANG Xinwei, agent *ad litem* of Hanjin appeared in court to attend the trial. Now the case has been concluded.

Connexions alleged in the first instance: in July 2011, Connexions' a batch of belts were carried by Shenzhen J&S from Ningbo, China to New York, USA, and Shenzhen J&S issued No.JSNYC110706 B/L to it. Hanjin was the actual carrier, Connexions was the shipper under the B/L involved, and also the holder of the original B/L. But, after the arrival of the goods at the port of destination, Shenzhen J&S and Hanjin delivered the goods on August 15, 2011 without the original B/L, which caused Connexions' failure for receipt of the balance payment of goods under B/L in sum of USD227,291.04 except the 20% advance payment. Shenzhen J&S as contracting carrier and Hanjin as the actual carrier of the goods involved, should deliver the goods against surrendering the original B/L. Shenzhen J&S and Hanjin should assume joint and several liability for the huge loss sustained by Connexions for delivery of goods without the original B/L. Connexions requested the court to order both Shenzhen J&S and Hanjin to compensate Connexions the loss under No.JSNYC110706 B/L in sum of USD227,291.04 (the dollars currency translated in to RMB according to reference rate of dollar against RMB at 1:6.395 prevailing on August 15, 2011 published by China Foreign Exchange Trade System which was authorized by the People's Bank of China was RMB1,453,526.2) and interest thereon (the interest should be calculated from August 15, 2011 according to the working capital loan interest rate promulgated by the People's Bank of China over the same period); and Shenzhen J&S and Hanjin should assume the court fees and the notarization and authentication fee of this case.

Connexions submitted the following evidence within the time limit for adducing evidence in the first instance:

1. Notarization and authentication documents of proforma invoice, commercial invoice, packing list, bank remittance notice and mail of advice of drawing;
2. Witness testimony of Michael Shun Forrest and attachment thereto;
3. B/L;
4. Records of delivery of goods;
5. Web page information and record information of chineseshipping.com.cn, a secondary website of the Ministry of Transport;
6. Reply letter of LUO Linguang;
7. Homepage information of Shenzhen J&S Express (H.K.) Limited, commercial registration and record information tracer of Shenzhen J&S, page information and annual report of online search center of Hong Kong Companies Registry; and
8. Business license of the translation company.

The supplementary evidence submitted by Connexions after the hearing on April 23, 2013 is as follow:

9. Lawyer's letter issued by Wang Jing & Co. (Shenzhen) Law Firm;
10. Reply letter and the attachment thereto of LUO Linguang; and
11. Email in reply of Shenzhen J&S.

Shenzhen J&S defended in the first instance:

1. Shenzhen J&S did not issue the B/L involved, and it was not the proper Defendant;
2. Where the United States Carriage of Goods by Sea Act 1936 (COGSA) applied according to the paramount clause on the back of the B/L involved, Shenzhen J&S should not undertake the liability for delivery of goods without an original B/L;
3. Connexions did not suffer any loss because of delivery of goods without the original B/L; and
4. The value of goods involved claimed by Connexions was the value of re-sale by the middleman, but the amount of loss of the goods caused by delivery of goods without the original B/L should be the value of the goods at the time of loading, namely the export declaration price.

Shenzhen J&S submitted the following evidence within the time limit for adducing evidence:

1. No.JSNYC110706 B/L;
2. The Defendant's sample of B/L;
3. Notarial certificate of mails concerning booking space and booking note between Connexions and Taiwan J&S Air Freight Forwarding Co., Ltd. Ningbo Office (hereinafter referred to as Taiwan J&S Ningbo Office);
4. Employment Certificate of Helen;
5. Labor contract between Helen and Ningbo Zhongji Foreign Enterprise Services Cooperation (Zhongji Cooperation);
6. Labor dispatching agreement between Zhongji Cooperation and Taiwan J&S Ningbo Office;
7. Certificate of registration of resident office of foreign (regional) enterprise of Taiwan J&S Ningbo Office;
8. No.OBIGNBNY10127500 B/L;
9. Lawyer's letter of Connexions;
10. The reply of Taiwan J&S to lawyer's letter;
11. The United States Carriage of Goods by Sea Act 1936;
12. Federal Bills of Lading Act;
13. No.2011032 commercial invoice;
14. Packing List; and
15. No.310420110549415324 customs declaration;
16. Transfer voucher.
    The supplementary evidence submitted by Shenzhen J&S after the hearing on April 23, 2013 was as follow:
17. Labor contract between Helen and Zhongji Cooperation (of which the contract period was from May 1, 2010 to April 30, 2012).

Hanjin defended in the first instance:

1. Connexions was neither the shipper or the consignee under the B/L issued by Hanjin, nor the holder of the B/L, and it was not the proper Plaintiff; and
2. Hanjin had delivered the goods to straight consignee according to the B/L issued by itself, while the B/L on which Connexions's action based was not issued by Hanjin, and the fact alleged by Connexions that Hanjin delivered the goods without the original B/L did not exist. Connexions was not entitled to claim Hanjin to undertake joint and several liability for delivery of goods without the original B/L.

Hanjin submitted the following evidence within the time limit for adducing evidence in the first instance:

1. No.HJSCNJBA10127500 B/L issued by Hanjin; and
2. No.OBIGNBNY10127500 Telex Release B/L of Oceanic Bridge International Inc. (hereinafter referred to as "Oceanic Bridge").

After examining the evidence in the hearing, Shenzhen J&S confirmed the authenticity of Connexions's evidence 3 to 6 and evidence 8 to 10, Hanjin had no objection to Connexions's evidence 3 to 6 and evidence 8 to 11; Connexions confirmed the authenticity of evidence 1 to 3, evidence 9 to 12 and evidence 15 to 17 of Shenzhen J&S, and Hanjin raised no objection to the evidence of Shenzhen J&S; Connexions confirmed the authenticity of evidence 1 of Hanjin, and Shenzhen J&S confirmed the evidence of Hanjin. The court of first instance confirmed the probative force of the evidence that the parties raised no objection to. The Bank remittance notice of Hengsheng Bank Limited of Connexions's evidence 1 was the original, and the court of first instance confirmed probative force of this notice. Other evidence of Connexions' evidence 1 and evidence 11, evidence 4 to 8 of Shenzhen J&S and evidence 2 of Hanjin could corroborate other evidence having been confirmed, the court of first instance hereby admitted.

The court of first instance found the following facts: on May 12, 2011, Connexions signed a sales contract with Silver Goose Accessories Co., Ltd. (Silver Goose) based on No.PI109778 order. In the contract they agreed that Connexions would supply 231,780 pairs of belts to Silver Goose, under FOB Shanghai, the total price of the goods was USD284,113.80, the delivery day was June 25, the consignee was Mike. S. Forrest, 20% of the price was prepaid, and the remaining 80% would be paid by telegraphic transfer against the copy of B/L. On July 6, Connexions issued No.AU004811 commercial invoice to Silver Goose which recorded that the goods involved would be shipped from Ningbo to New York on July 10 or around, and the packing list which recorded the container number was HJCU1611199 on the same day. On 12 May 2011, Connexions also signed a sales contract with Silver Goose based on No.PI109779 order in which they agreed that Connexions supplied 80,040 pairs of belt to Silver Goose, the total price of the goods was USD98,440.56, July 15 was the delivery day, and the rest part would be paid in the same method as that agreed in the No.PI109778 order. On July 21,

Connexions issued No.AU004855-1 commercial invoice and the packing list which recorded the container number was HJCU4157665 on the same day.

On May 12, 2011, Hengsheng Bank Limited sent a remittance notice to Connexions, which recorded Connexions' account received a remittance in sum of USD76,510.87 from Silver Goose from America. On the same day, Connexions received an email from Silver Goose, in which said Silver Goose had paid USD76,510.87 as advance deposit under No.PI109778 and No.PI109779 orders.

In June, Connexions' employee contacted with Helen an employee of Taiwan J&S Ningbo Office about booking space of goods under No.PI109778 order involved. Taiwan J&S Ningbo Office booked space with Ocean Bridge in the name of J&S Express Ningbo Ltd. (J&S Ningbo).The sample of No. OBIGNBNY10127500 B/L of Ocean Bridge given out on July 9,(not issued) recorded that: booking number was No.HJSCNJBA10127500, J&S Ningbo was the shipper, Date International Co., Ltd. was the consignee and the notify party, the goods were 19,315 packs PU belts loaded in two 40 ft containers numbered with HJCU1611199 and HJCU1293164. That sample of B/L also sealed on "Telex Release, Date July 11, 2011". On July 10, 2011, Hanjin issued No. HJSCNJBA10127500 B/L, recording Dalian International Freight Co., Ltd. (Dalian Ocean Bridge) was the shipper, Ocean Bridge was the consignee and the notify party, Ningbo was the port of loading, New York was port of discharge, 19,315 packs of PU belts loaded in two 40 ft containers numbered with HJCU1611199 and HJCU1293164 on M.V."Hanjin Shanghai" Voyage 0117E, CY to CY, freight prepaid.

On July 10, 2011, Helen, an employee of Taiwan J&S Ningbo Office on behalf of the carrier Shenzhen J&S issued No.JSNYC110706 original B/L to Connexions, which recorded: the title was Shenzhen J&S, Connexions was the shipper, Silver Goose was the consignee and the notify party, Ningbo was port of loading, New York was the port of discharge, the goods involved were 19,315 packs PU belts loaded in two 40 ft containers numbered with HJCU1611199 and HJCU1293164 on M.V."Hanjin Shanghai" Voyage 0117E, CY to CY, the shipper was in charge of loading, counting and packing, freight was to be collect. It was recorded on the front of the B/L that "unless otherwise provided, the goods should be carried in good condition according to quantity and packages recorded below from the place of receipt to the place of delivery according to the clauses of the B/L. The holder of B/L or the agent thereof should take delivery of the goods with an original B/L. The carrier and the holder of B/L should be bound by rights and obligations provided in clauses of B/L (without prejudice to application of the common law bonding the acts of trading party), the contract has been concluded as hereby proved". Article 7.3 of "Paramount Clause" on the back of B/L recorded that "if COGSA should compulsorily apply to the present B/L, it should be binding upon the carriage of goods by sea, goods carried on deck and inboard included, or only applies to the goods carried on deck according to the representation in B/L above mentioned".

Upon investigation, on July 6, 2011, the containers numbered with HJCU1611199 and HJCU1293164 were delivered to the shipper in Ningbo. On July 7, the containers after loading the goods involved were sent to the export wharf later than entering into the yard. On July 9, the containers involved were loaded onto M.V."Hanjin Shanghai" Voyage 0117E in Ningbo. On July 10, M.V."Hanjin Shanghai" set sail. The vessel arrived in New York on August 9. On August 10, the loading was completed. On August 12, Hanjin received No.HJSCNJBA10127500 original B/L issued by itself. On August 15, the containers involved were delivered to the consignee in New York. On August 19, the consignee returned the empty containers. Connexions had been holding full set of original No.JSNYC110706 B/L until the time that this action was filed. This B/L was though slightly different from the B/L of Shenzhen J&S having docketed in the Ministry of Transport, it conformed to the sample of B/L that Shenzhen J&S showed in court.

On March 30, PAN Lidong, lawyer of Guangdong Wang Jing & Co. (Shenzhen), sent a lawyer's letter to Shenzhen J&S on behalf of Connexions and carbon copied Taiwan J&S Ningbo Office, in which it claimed against Shenzhen J&S for loss of USD306,043.49 caused by delivery of the goods under No. JSNYC110706 and No.JSNYC110715 B/Ls without the original B/Ls, legal fee in sum of USD4,000, and requested a confirm receipt of the letter's letter within 5 days after the sending of the same. On April 6, LUO Linguang replied to the lawyer's letter of Connexions by email (larryeagle@gmail.com) and carbon copied LIU Ruiqin (jsszxmarketing@jsexpress.com.hk), the legal representative of Shenzhen J&S. The reply said Silver Goose had paid 20% of the price under No. PI109778 and No.PI109779 orders in sum of USD76,510.87 as deposit to Connexions on May 20, 2011. The balance payment in sum of USD227,290.24 under No.PI109778 order was paid on August 3, 2011, and the balance payment in sum of USD78,752.45 under No.PI109779 order was unpaid because the products failed the quality inspection of buyer. The signature of this email was LUO Linguang, Shenzhen J&S Express Ningbo Co., Ltd. On April 16, 2012, Shenzhen J&S sent emails to Connexions's attorney RAO Zhenhua, a lawyer of Wang Jing & Co. (Shenzhen) by jsszxmarketing@jsexpress.com.hk, saying in terms of the subject dispute involved "please refer to our reply and related documents, and contact with Mr.Luo if you have any questions", and carbon copied LUO Linguang.

The court of first instance held that to prove Connexions' loss in sum of USD227,291.04 caused by delivery of goods without the original B/L by Shenzhen S&J and Hanjin, Connexions submitted evidence 1 proforma invoice, commercial invoice, packing list, bank remittance notice, mail of advice of drawing and evidence 2 Michael Shun Forrest's witness testimony. Connexions' evidence 1 recorded that the value of goods involved was USD284,113.80 and Connexions received 20% of the price under No.PI109778 and No.PI109779 orders in sum of USD76,510.87 as deposit remitted by Silver Goose on May 21, 2011. Michael Shun Forrest the former sales president of Silver Goose testified in court, to prove that Connexions had received 20% of the price under No.PI109778 and No. PI109779 orders as deposit (the deposit in sum of USD56,822.76 under No. PI109778 order, the deposit in sum of USD19,688.11 under No.PI109779 order, USD76,510.87 in total) on May 21, 2011. On around August 4, Silver Goose paid USD227,290.24 to Connexions as the balance payment under No.PI109778 order. On August 16, Connexions asked for permission of Silver Goose to use the payment of No.PI109778 order which had been received for other trade via e-mail, and reported to Silver Goose on August 25 when Silver Goose confirmed by e-mail on the same day. So Connexions claimed for loss in sum of USD227,291.04. Shenzhen J&S and Hanjin held that Connexions had received the payment in full amount and suffered no loss. Shenzhen J&S held that USD284,113.80 was the value of re-sale by middleman while the amount of loss caused by delivery of goods without the original B/L should be the value of the goods at the time of shipment plus insurance and freight. Shenzhen J&S submitted evidence 13 invoice of Qingdao Fortune Arts & Crafts Co., Ltd. (hereinafter referred to as "Fortune"), evidence 14 packing list of Fortune, evidence 15 customs declaration and evidence 16 transfer voucher. It was recorded in No.3104201105494153248 export customs declaration of which the declaration day was July 7, 2011 that the export port was Beilun customs, the operating and shipping unit was Fortune, the transport means was M.V."Hanjin Shanghai" Voyage 0117E, the number of delivery order was NJBA10127500, the goods were loaded in two 40 ft containers numbered with HJCU1611199 and HJCU1293164, the goods were 19,315 packs of belts made of PU, and the total price was USD132,114.6. Evidence 13 and evidence 14 can prove that value of the goods at the time of loading was USD132,114.6. Evidence 16 records that Connexions has separately received USD76,510.87 namely 20% of the price as deposit under No.PI109778 and No.PI109779 orders and the balance payment in sum of USD227,290.24 under No.PI109778 B/L. Connexions had no objection to the authenticity of evidence 15 and 16. To sum up, the court of first instance confirmed the facts that customs declaration value of the goods involved was USD132,114.6 on FOB basis, Connexions received USD76,510.87 namely 20% of the price as deposit under No.PI109778 and No.PI109779 orders and the balance payment in sum of USD227,290.24 of No.PI109778 order, as well as the fact that Connexions used USD227,290.24 for other trades.

In the trial, the parties agreed to apply the law of the People's Republic of China to resolve the dispute of this case.

The court of first instance held that: this case was concerning dispute over a contract of carriage of goods by sea. This case involved foreign-related factor because the goods involved were shipped from Ningbo China to New York. According to Article 1 of Interpretation of the Supreme People's Court on the Application of the Special Maritime Procedure Law of the People's Republic of China and Article 11 of the Some Provisions of the Supreme People's Court on the Scope of Cases to be Entertained by Maritime Courts, this case should be under special jurisdiction of maritime court. The place of the departure of the goods involved was under the jurisdiction of the court of first instance, according to Article 27 of the Civil Procedure Law of the People's Republic of China, an action instituted for a dispute arising from transport contract should be under the jurisdiction of the people's court located in the place of the departure, so the court of first instance has jurisdiction over this case. The parties agreed that law of the People's Republic of China should apply, so according to Article 269 of the Maritime Code of the People's Republic of China, law of the People's Republic of China should apply to deal with substantial dispute of this case.

According to the facts having been ascertained, Connexions booked space with Taiwan J&S Ningbo Office in the name of shipper, Taiwan J&S Ningbo Office issued a full set of original B/Ls as agent of the carrier Shenzhen J&S. Though this B/L was not a NVOCC B/L of Shenzhen J&S having docketed with the Ministry of Transport, it was according to the sample of B/L that Shenzhen J&S showed in court. Shenzhen J&S did not prove the resource of the B/Ls involved issued by Taiwan J&S Ningbo Office was illegal. So the court of first instance confirmed Connexions' proposition that Shenzhen J&S was the carrier involved. The contract of carriage of goods by sea signed by Connexions and Shenzhen J&S was formed, under which Connexions was the shipper and Shenzhen J&S was the carrier. This contract which was real intentions of both parties should be lawful and effective, and be binding upon both parties. Shenzhen J&S arranged Hanjin for the carriage of the goods involved after Connexions' entrustment. Hanjin was the actual carrier in the legal relationship of carriage of goods by sea.

Shenzhen J&S claimed the law of the USA should apply to determine the assumption of liability according to the clause on the back of No.JSNYC110706 B/L. The court of first instance held that there was a express clause recorded on the front of the B/L "the holder of B/L or the agent thereof must take delivery of the goods with an original B/L. The carrier and the holder of B/Ls will be bound by the rights and obligations as provided in clauses of B/Ls (without prejudice to application of the common law bonding the acts of trading party), the contract has been concluded as hereby proved", this contract was real intentions of the shipper and the carrier, and should be binding upon Connexions and Shenzhen J&S, both parties should fulfill obligations according to the contract. In this case, Shenzhen J&S who issued the B/Ls did not prove the B/Ls involved fell into the circumstance of compulsory application of COGSA. This claim was lack of factual and legal basis, and should be rejected. Article 71 of the Maritime Code of the People's Republic of China provides: "a bill of lading was a document which serves as an evidence of the contract of carriage of goods by sea and the taking over or loading of the goods by the carrier, and based on which the carrier undertakes to deliver the goods against surrendering the same. A provision in the document stating that the goods were to be delivered to the order of a named person, or to order, or to bearer, constitutes such an undertaking". Connexions held the full set of original bill. Shenzhen J&S's delivery of the goods without original B/L violated the provision above, infringed the rights of Connexions as the shipper who held the original B/Ls. According to Article 2 of the Provisions of the Supreme People's Court on Several Issues concerning the Application of Law in the Trial of Cases of Dispute arising from Delivery of Goods without an Original Bill of Lading: "where a carrier delivers goods without an original bill of lading in violation of law, damaging the rights of the holder of the original bill of lading under the bill of lading, the holder of the original bill of lading may require the carrier to bear the civil liability for the losses resulting therefrom", Connexions should be entitled to compensation against the Defendant. According to Article 55 Paragraph 1 and Paragraph 2 of the Maritime Code of the People's Republic of China, the amount of compensation for the loss of the goods involved should be calculated on the basis of the actual value of the goods, the actual value should be the value of the goods at the time of shipment plus insurance and freight. The claim of Shenzhen J&S that the value of the goods involved should be USD132,114.6 as recorded in customs declaration before shipment, should be supported according to the law. Connexions requested USD284,113.80, namely the balance payment according to 80% of the value of goods agreed on sales contract at the time of re-sale, such claim has no legal basis and should be rejected. According to the facts ascertained in trial, Connexions had received all the price and used that for other trades, Shenzhen J&S's delivery of goods without an original B/L did not cause loss to Connexions, the claim of Connexions that Shenzhen J&S should pay for losses of the goods involved and the interest thereon had no factual basis, and should be rejected. The notarization and authentication fee was cost of the party for fulfilling litigation responsibility or undertaking burden of proof to protect procedural or substantial interests, the court of first instance did not support the claim of Connexions that the notary and authentication fee should be undertaken by the Defendants, which lacked factual and legal basis. Hanjin as the actual carrier, had received the full set of original B/L issued by itself, the claim of Connexions that Hanjin should undertake joint and several liability for delivery of goods without the original B/L lacked factual and legal basis should be rejected.

In summary, according to Article 64 of the Civil Procedure Law of the People's Republic of China, the court of first instance referred judgment of first instance as follows: reject the claims of Connexions. Court acceptance fee in amount of RMB18,601.27 should be born by Connexions.

Connexions dissatisfied with the original instance, and filed an appeal, requested the court to amend the judgment. The main reasons are as follows:

1. The value of the goods involved was wrongly identified by the original court. Firstly, judging from the entities, Connexions was the shipper under the B/L, the loss Connexions claimed against the carrier were on its own account, they were not sustained by other parties for example producer, and any party involved in international trade chain. Obviously, the loss Connexions suffered was expectable loss of payment of goods under the sales contract with the American buyer. Secondly, in terms of the trade relationship and the transport relationship, the transport relationship established along with the sales contract between Connexions and the American buyer at the same time, the trade relationship corresponding to the transport relationship was the sales contractual relationship between Connexions and the American buyer, thus the loss of the consignee (Connexions) in the subject transport should be decided on the basis of the sales contract. The B/L, as the evidence for the claim, corresponded to the documents of the sales contract between Connexions and the American buyer, theses documents having gone through notarization and authentication handled by Connexions and Shenzhen J&S could prove Connexions as the consignee sold the goods involved at a price of USD284,113.8, thus the loss of Connexions under the transport contract should be USD284,113.8 rather than USD132,114.6 as shown in customs declaration. Thirdly, it was not rare that the customs

declaration price was higher than the actual price of goods in practice, in the case where the customs declaration was in conformity with the documents which could prove the value of the goods, the actual trade price might be adopted as the actual value of the goods. Let alone neither the operator or consignee in the customs declaration was Connexions, it was irrelevant thereto. Finally, "the price at the time of shipment" as provided in law did not refer to the price in the first sale after the goods were produced, it was "the price when the goods are loaded on board" in the transport contractual relationship. No matter whether the goods were involved with re-sale, it was not the key to determine the loss of the consignee or the holder of the B/L. The original court neglected the fact that the transport contractual relationship established on the basis of the realization of the sales contract concluded by Connexions and the American buyer, and failed to identify the price of goods in sum of USD132,114.6 fixed in the sales contract as the value of the goods involved, it was wrong application of law.
2. The analysis of the original court on the causation relationship between delivery of goods and the loss. Firstly, using the payment of the American buyer for other trades did not affect the obligation of the carrier to deliver the goods against the surrendering of B/L, or the fact that the delivery of goods by carrier resulted in the loss of Connexions, the change of use of the payment was an agreement upon negotiation between Connexions and the American buyer; secondly, since the B/L was still held by Connexions, Connexions could control the flow of the goods, then it was willing to use the payment of the American buyer for other trades; thirdly, when the B/L had not surrendered to the American buyer, Connexions and the American buyer made another arrangement for the payment having been collected after negotiation. In this case, Connexions did not collect payment from the American buyer. The delivery of goods without an original B/L by the carrier directly caused Connexions' loss of control of the goods, and finally Connexions could not collect payment as the consideration of goods from the buyer, neither the American buyer nor any other potential buyer. To sum up, Connexions requested the court to support its appeal.

As to the appeal of Connexions, Shenzhen J&S defended as follows:

1 The original court correctly identified the price of the goods, the value of the goods should be subject to the customs declaration price of the export goods. The provisions of the maritime law concerning the loss of goods under a contract of carriage of goods by sea, without consideration of profits of cargo owner, loss of goods should be subject to the value of the goods at the time of shipment plus insurance and freight. The value of the goods had been fixed at the time of shipment, no matter who was the Appellant, the carrier should bear same liability. Connexions unilaterally stressed the sales contract it concluded with the American buyer, and evaded the sales contract it signed with the actual consignee Fortune and confounded the concept of the value of the goods at the time of shipment, it had no basis.

2 Connexions should prove the following three facts to support it suffered loss due to the carrier's delivery of goods without an original B/L: it still held the original B/L, it suffered loss and there was a causation relationship between the surrendering of B/L and payment of the goods involved. None of the three conditions could be dispensable, its claim for the loss only on the basis of holding of B/L could not stand. Firstly, the American buyer had paid Connexions the full price of the goods, Connexions suffered no loss. Secondly, there was no causation relationship between the surrendering of B/L and payment of goods. In international trades, surrendering of B/L was not the condition of payment of goods, especially in the case of a straight B/L in this case. Thirdly, Connexions could track the goods through the website of the actual carrier, the empty container loading the goods involved had been returned to the actual carrier before August 22, 2011. On the morning of August 25, 2011, Connexions neither mentioned the taking delivery of the goods in the email it sent to the overseas buyer, nor did it issue statement of claim against the carrier in time, it only raised a claim in 7 months after the incident. It showed Connexions did not take the B/L as the evidence to take delivery of goods. In the event that Connexions found difficult to solve the problem under the sales contract, it transferred the risk to the carrier, it was unfair to the carrier.

3 Shenzhen J&S was not the proper Defendant. During the process of conclusion and performance of the transport contract, Shenzhen J&S never participated in. The signature of the employee of Taiwan J&S Ningbo Office, the party not involved in this case, was "Helen, J&S Express Ningbo Ltd.", and the address was expressed "B.1506 DA-SHI-DAI BUILDING, No.105 RENMIN ROAD NINGBO, CHINA". It could be seen from the letter sent by the attorney of Connexions to Shenzhen J&S and Taiwan J&S Ningbo Office on March 30, 2012, Connexions was clear about that Taiwan J&S Ningbo Office and agent of Shenzhen J&S were one and the same entity, there was no signature or seal in the lower right corner, only the time of shipment and the employee Helen showed up thereon. Connexions knew Helen was an employee of Taiwan J&S Ningbo Office through booking space, there was no reason for it to hold the B/L was issued by it.

Shenzhen J&S also dissatisfied with the original instance, and filed an appeal, requested the court to correct the facts unclearly found in the original judgment. The main reasons are as follows: Shenzhen J&S was not proper Defendant of this case. Taiwan J&S Ningbo Office never expressed it was the agent of Shenzhen J&S or mentioned Shenzhen J&S to Connexions during the whole process of conclusion of the transport contract. Based on the actual booking space, the original judgments ascertained Connexions contacted with ZHUANG Subo, an employee of Taiwan J&S Ningbo Office. In the exchange of emails, he never expressed he was the employee or agent of Shenzhen J&S. Although Taiwan J&S Ningbo Office used the standard B/L, it did not sign or seal on the signature blank. "J&S WORLDWIDE LOGISTICS LTD AS AGENT FOR THE CARRIER" in the lower right corner were fonts printed in advance. Only the day of shipment and an employee Helen showed up. While during the process of booking space, Connexions was well knew Helen was an employee of Taiwan J&S Ningbo Office, it had no reason to hold the B/L was issued by Taiwan J&S Ningbo Office, or to make it believe the doer had obtained authorization of Shenzhen J&S. Unless when Taiwan J&S Ningbo Office issued the B/L, was affixed with the seal of S&J or its own seal with the declaration that it acted as the agent of Shenzhen J&S, namely "AS AGENT FOR J&S WORLDWIDE LOGISTICS LTD.", could the B/L be identified to be issued by Taiwan J&S Ningbo Office as the agent of Shenzhen J&S. In view of the non-existence of the assumption above, Shenzhen J&S should not bear any legal consequence for the act of Taiwan J&S Ningbo Office. In summary, Shenzhen J&S requested the court of second instance to support its appeal.

As to the appeal of Shenzhen J&S, Connexions defended as follows:

1 No matter what identification Shenzhen J&S or Taiwan J&S Ningbo Office took to negotiate with Connexions in the process of conclusion of the contract, the identification of carrier should subject to the B/L.
2 The consignee and consignor under the B/L involved, the time and place of issue as well as issuer were clear, they were not printed thereon as alleged by Shenzhen J&S, the B/L was legal and effective.
3 The time when Connexions got the B/L did not affect the obligation of the carrier under a contract of goods by sea to deliver goods against surrendering of B/L. Connexions could not collect the payment of goods, it was entitled to compensation in the event that it had obtained the B/L and held the same.

Hanjin defended in the second instance that the ascertainment on the position of Shenzhen J&S of the original court and it agreed with the defense of Connexions.

Upon examination, the court holds the facts found by the original court are verified, and hereby ascertains. It is also found that:

1 The parties concerned confirmed Connexions held the straight B/L numbered with JSNYC110706 which recorded Shenzhen J&S as the carrier, but the goods under that bill of lading have been delivered before the carrier took back the original B/L.
2 The words on the face of the original B/L held by Connexions are blue, and the specific contents are printed black fonts, "July 10, 2011/NINGBO, HELEN" in the lower right corner are black fonts printed thereon, and the English name of Shenzhen J&S "J&S WORLDWIDE LOGISTICS LTD" below these words are blue fonts, which is the content of the standard B/L, which below this line "AS AGENT FOR THE CARRIER", it is blank. The English name of Taiwan J&S also contains Shenzhen J&S.
3 Connexions cannot submit the sales contract between it and Fortune to prove the procurement cost of the goods involved.

The court holds that this case is arising from dispute over contract of carriage of goods by sea. Since the destination of the goods involved is New York, America, this case involves foreign element. The parties concerned raised no objection to jurisdiction exercised by the original court according to Article 27 of the Civil Procedure Law of the PRC as well as the application of law according to Article 269 of the Maritime Code of the PRC, therefore the court hereby confirms.

In view of no objection raised by the parties to the ascertainment of the original court that Hanjin should not bear legal liability in terms of the dispute in the subject case, the identification of liability of Hanjin will not be examined in the second instance. In light of the grounds of appeal held by Connexions and Shenzhen J&S, the court holds the issues in this case are as follows: 1. the legal position of Shenzhen J&S and the determination of assumption of legal liability; 2. the actual value of the goods involved; and 3. whether Connexions suffered loss due to the release of goods without original B/L by Shenzhen J&S.

In respect of the first issue, Connexions sued Shenzhen J&S requested the latter to bear the liability for delivery of goods without an original B/L. According to Article 72 of the Maritime Code of the PRC, "a bill of lading is a document which serves as an evidence of the contract of carriage of goods by sea", and Article 1 of the Provisions of the Supreme People's Court on Several Issues concerning the Application of Law during the Trial of Cases about Delivery of Goods without an Original Bill of Lading (hereinafter referred to as the Provisions on Delivery of Goods without an bill of lading), "the term "original bill of lading" as mentioned in these provisions shall refer to a straight bill of lading, an order bill of lading or a bearer bill of lading", the premise of delivery of goods by the carrier is surrendering of an original bill of lading (including straight bill of lading), in this case, the parties concerned confirmed Connexions held the straight B/L numbered with JSNYC110706 which recorded Shenzhen J&S as the carrier, but the goods under that bill of lading have been delivered before the carrier took back the original B/L. Connexions, as the proposer, has fulfilled its burden of proof preliminarily, it can prove the carrier Shenzhen J&S as recorded in the B/L delivered the goods involved without an original B/L. Shenzhen J&S refuted it was not the carrier in the subject case, and it had no knowledge of the issue of the B/L involved; the B/L was issued by Taiwan J&S Ningbo Office, it should assume relevant liability. Shenzhen J&S submitted mail exchanges concerning booking space between Taiwan J&S Ningbo Office and Connexions, booking order, incumbency certification of ZHUANG Subo, the handler in Taiwan J&S Ningbo Office, the reply to the lawyer's letter and other evidence materials. Upon verification, the B/L involved is basically same with the standard B/L submitted by Shenzhen J&S in the original instance, the words on the face of the B/L are blue, and the specific contents are printed black fonts, "July 10, 2011/NINGBO, HELEN" in the lower right corner are black fonts printed thereon, and the English name of Shenzhen J&S "J&S WORLDWIDE LOGISTICS LTD" below these words are blue fonts, which is the content of the standard B/L, which below this line "AS AGENT FOR THE CARRIER", it is blank. The facts above suggest Taiwan J&S Ningbo Office used the blank B/L of Shenzhen J&S to accept the transport of the goods involved. Shenzhen J&S is a NVOCC put on file at the Ministry of Transport, the names of it and Taiwan J&S have "Yu Da" (in Chinese), and "J&S" in English, Shenzhen J&S cannot prove Taiwan J&S or Taiwan J&S Ningbo Office illegally used the blank B/L, the blank B/L mentioned above is sufficient to make a third party in good faith have no reason to doubt that Taiwan J&S Ningbo Office has obtained the authority of Shenzhen J&S and issued the B/L. Therefore, although the evidence produced by Shenzhen J&S can prove the transport involved was carried out by Taiwan J&S, but the fact that Shenzhen J&S is the carrier under the B/L involved cannot be overturned, Shenzhen J&S shall bear the legal liability for failure of fulfilling burden of proof. The court ascertains Shenzhen J&S is the carrier, and does not support the allegation of Shenzhen J&S that it was not the carrier. Connexions and Shenzhen J&S established relationship of contract of carriage of goods by sea, the contractual relationship is legitimate and effective, the two parties shall perform their obligations as agreed. According to Article 2 of the Provisions of the Supreme People's Court on Several Issues concerning the Application of Law in the Trial of Cases of Disputes arising from Delivery of Goods without Original Bill of Lading, "Where a carrier delivers goods without an original bill of lading in violation of law, damaging the rights of the holder of the original bill of lading under the bill of lading, the holder of the original bill of lading may require the carrier to bear the civil liability for the loss resulting therefrom", Shenzhen J&S as the carrier shall undertake the legal liability for delivery of goods without an original B/L.

In respect of the second issue, in this case, Connexions failed to submit evidence to prove it concluded a sales contract with Fortune and the price of the goods involved, but the invoice, packing list, customs declaration and other evidence submitted by Shenzhen J&S can prove the goods were declared at a price of USD132,114.6 at the time of shipment, in the case of lack of evidence to prove the sales contract between Shenzhen J&S and Fortune, the price of customs declaration shall be referred to when deciding the procurement cost of the goods involved, that is to say, the procurement cost of the goods of Connexions is USD132,114.6. In the meantime, the transport terms is freight to be collected, Connexions suffered no loss of freight or insurance, therefore, according to Article 55 Paragraph 1 and 2 of the Maritime Code of the PRC, "The amount of indemnity for the loss of the goods shall be calculated on the basis of the actual value of the goods so lost" and "The actual value shall be the value of the goods at the time of shipment plus insurance and freight", USD132,114.6 shall be decided as the actual value of the goods involved. The appellant claim of Connexions that the actual value of the goods involved shall be the price as agreed in the sales contract between it and Silver Goose Accessories Co., Ltd. (hereinafter referred to as Silver Goose), since the contract price is not the procurement cost of the goods paid by Connexions, thus such claim lacks legal basis, the court does not support.

In respect of the third issue, in this case, Connexions confirmed it had the balance payment of the goods involved from Silver Goose, but Connexions and Silver Goose negotiated other arrangement of the balance payment, namely, to pay other trades between the two companies. The court holds the agreement mentioned above between Connexions and Silver Goose is negotiation in trade segment.

In summary, the original judgment, of which the facts were clearly found and the law was correctly applied, the decision was proper, shall be maintained. The appeals of Connexions and Shenzhen J&S lack basis, and shall be dismissed.

According to Article 171 Paragraph 1 of the Civil Procedure Law of the People's Republic of China, the judgment is as follows:

Dismiss the appeals and affirm the original judgment.

Court acceptance fee of the second instance in amount of RMB18,651.27 yuan, Connexions (Asia) Limited shall bear RMB18,601.27 yuan, and J&S Worldwide Logistics Co., Ltd. shall bear RMB50 yuan.

Presiding Judge: DU Yixing
Acting Judge: LI Minyao
Acting Judge: YE Dan
March 31, 2015
Court clerk: Pan Wanqin

Appendix: Relevant Law

1 Civil Procedure Law of the People's Republic of China

Article 170 After hearing an appellate case, the people's court of second instance shall handle the case respectively according to the following circumstances:

(1) If the facts were clearly found and the law was correctly applied in the original judgment, the appeal shall be rejected by a judgment and the original judgment shall be sustained;
(2) If the law was incorrectly applied in the original judgment, the judgment shall be amended according to law;
(3) If in the original judgment the facts were incorrectly found or were not clearly found and the evidence was inconclusive, the judgment shall be rescinded and the case remanded by an order to the original people's court for a retrial, or the people's court of second instance may amend the judgment after investigating and clarifying the facts; or
(4) If in the original judgment a violation of the prescribed procedure may have affected the correctness of the judgment, the judgment shall be rescinded and the case remanded by an order to the original people's court for a retrial.

The parties may appeal against the judgment or ruling rendered in a retrial of their case.

The Supreme People's Court of the People's Republic of China
Civil Ruling

Connexions (Asia) Limited
v.
Shenzhen J&S Worldwide Logistics Ltd. et al.

(2015) Min Shen Zi No.3206

Related Case(s) This is the ruling of retrial, and the judgment of first instance and the judgment of second instance are on page 283 and page 293 respectively.

Cause(s) of Action 202. Dispute over contract of carriage of goods by sea or sea-connected waters.

Headnote Refusing shipper's application for retrial to hear new evidence about value of goods misdelivered by Defendant without presentation of original bill of lading; lower court decisions recognized.

Summary The courts of first and second instance held the first Defendant liable for misdelivery of the Plaintiff shipper's goods without presentation of the original bill of lading, but awarded only the export value of the goods appearing on the Customs declaration at the time of shipment, rather than the invoice value charged to the Plaintiff's American buyer. The Plaintiff petitioned the Supreme People's Court to order a retrial, arguing that it had new evidence showing the value of the goods at the time of the shipment. The court held that the rulings of the first and second instance were correct and that there was no basis for a retrial.

Ruling

The Claimant of Retrial (the Plaintiff of first instance and the Appellant of second instance): Connexions (Asia) Limited.
Domicile: Room 1310-1312, 13 Floor, Lu Plaza, No.2 Wing Yip Street, Kwun Tong, Kowloon, the Hong Kong Special Administrative Region of the People's Republic of China.
Legal representative: YUAN Caiqiong, director.
Agent *ad litem*: HUANG Fulong, lawyer of Guangdong Shengtang Law Firm.
Agent *ad litem*: FANG Jibin, lawyer of Guangdong Shengtang Law Firm.

The Respondent of Retrial (the Defendant of first instance and the Appellant of second instance): J&S Worldwide Logistics Co., Ltd.
Domicile: H-I, 22 Floor, Building 5, Wei Peng Garden, Zhenzhong Road, Futian District, Shenzhen City, Guangdong Province, the People's Republic of China.
Legal representative: LIU Ruiqin, executive director.
Agent *ad litem*: CHEN Longjie, Shanghai Wintell & Co. (Guangzhou) Law Firm.
Agent *ad litem*: ZHENG Cairong, Shanghai Wintell & Co. (Guangzhou) Law Firm.

The Defendant of first instance: Hanjin Shipping Co., Ltd.
Domicile: Hanjin Shipping Building, Yeouido Dong 25-11, Yeongdeungpo District, Seoul, Republic of Korea.
Legal representative: JIN Yongmin, representative director.
Agent ad litem: ZHANG Xinwei, lawyer of Shanghai Gl Co. (Guangzhou) Law Firm.
Agent ad litem: WANG Pei, lawyer of Shanghai GL Co. (Guangzhou) Law Firm.

Dissatisfied with (2015) Yue Gao Fa Min Si Zhong Zi No.10 Civil Judgment rendered by the Guangdong High People's Court with respect to the case arising from dispute over contract of carriage of goods by sea, Connexions (Asia) Limited (hereinafter referred to as Connexions), petitioned for a retrial before the court against the Respondent J&S Worldwide Logistics Ltd. (hereinafter referred to as Shenzhen J&S) with the Defendant of first instance, Hanjin Shipping Co., Ltd. (hereinafter referred to as Hanjin) involved. The court made a Civil Ruling (2014) Min Shen Zi No.2229, and decided to try this case. The court formed a collegiate panel to review this case. After review, the case has been concluded.

Connexions claimed in the retrial as follows:

1. The total price of the goods identified in the judgment of second instance was incorrect. The judgments of first and second instance identified the trade price (FOB) between Silver Goose Accessories Co., Ltd. (hereinafter referred to as Silver Goose) as USD284,113.8, but did not ascertain the trade price as the value of the goods in the time of shipment, but admitted the price USD132,114.6 stated in the customs declaration of Qingdao Fortune Arts& Crafts Co., Ltd. (hereinafter referred to as Fortune), a party not involved in this case. In fact, Connexions paid the procurement cost in sum of USD245,992.08 to Fortune, the latter made a mistake in the price of goods when declared with the customs. For this purpose, Fortune issued *Presentation of Condition* on October 8, 2015 and provided relevant evidential documents to clarify. The evidence as new evidence is sufficient to overturn the ascertainment of the judgments of first and second instance. 2. It was wrong that the judgment of second instance attributed the loss of payment of goods to ordinary trading negotiation. Connexions negotiated with Silver Goose to change the use of the payment of goods for other trades, Connexions did not receive the balance payment of the goods involved, it did suffer certain loss. Connexions did not hand over the original B/L to the buyer when it did not receive the balance payment of the goods. The carrier Shenzhen J&S did not deliver the goods

against the original B/L, resulting in Connexions' loss of control of the goods, and suffered loss of payment of goods. The judgment of second instance neglected the illegality of the carrier's delivering the goods without an original B/L and the causation relationship between such action and the loss of payment of goods.

In summary, the judgment of second instance affirmed the judgment of first instance, rejecting the claims of Connexions, such decision constituted wrong ascertainment of facts and application of law. Connexions, in accordance of Article 200 Paragraph 1, 2 and 6 of the Civil Procedure Law of the People's Republic of China, so it petitioned for a retrial.

The Respondent Shenzhen J&S submitted defense as follows:

1 The total price of the goods identified in the judgment of second instance was correct. The goods involved was purchased by Connexions from Fortune, and then sold to an America buyer, both the procurement cost and declaration price were USD132,114.6, which should be taken as the value in the time of shipment. According to Article 55 of the Maritime Code of the PRC, the profit of cargo owner should not be taken into account.
2 It was correct that the judgment of second instance ascertained there was no causation relationship between delivery of goods without an original B/L and the loss of goods. The buyer had paid the price of goods in full amount to Connexions, the surrendering of B/L was irrelevant with the payment of goods, the B/L did not serve as the document of title to take delivery of the goods involved; at least, when the buyer took delivery of the goods, Connexions sustained no loss; according to the laws of the destination port America, including the Carriage of Goods by Sea Act 1936 and the Federal Bills of Lading Act, a straight B/L is not evidence of taking delivery of the goods, the carrier had reason to deliver the goods to the consignee as recorded in the straight in the B/L. Connexions raised no objection to the delivery of goods against the consignee or the carrier, it suggested Connexions had admitted the carrier's delivery of goods without an original B/L.

In summary, the ascertainment of facts and the application of law of second instance are correct, Shenzhen J&S requested the court to dismiss the application for retrial filed by Connexions.

The court holds that this case is arising from dispute over contract of goods by sea. The courts of first and second instance applied the law of the PRC to resolve this case according to the choice of the parties concerned. Connexions was the consignee under the B/L involved and held the B/L all the time. It is proper that the courts of first and second instance identified Shenzhen J&S as the carrier and Hanjin as the actual carrier. None of the parties raised any objection to the delivery of goods in the port of destination, New York, America. According to the application for retrial, the key of review of this case lies in the determination of price of the goods involved and the assumption of such loss.

According to the facts found in the first and second instance, Connexions (the seller of export goods) and Silver Goose (the buyer of export goods) agreed in their sales contract that the offshore price (FOB Shanghai) of the 231,780 sets of belts was USD284,113.80; the buyer prepaid 20%, the remaining 80% of the price would be paid by telegraphic transfer against surrendering a copy of B/L. In light of the notice of remittance of China Hengsheng Bank Limited issued on May 21, 2011 and Michael Shun Forrest, the former vice-sales president, stated in court of first instance that Connexions had received 20% of the deposit under the order PI109778 in sum of USD56,822.72 (USD284,113.8 * 20%). On August 4, 2011, Silver Goose paid the balance payment in sum of USD227,290.24 under the order PI109778. On August 15, the containerized goods were delivered to the consignor Silver Goose in New York. On August 16, Connexions requested Silver Goose for consent to pay other trades with the price of goods it had received in an e-mail, and Silver Goose confirmed by e-mail on the same day. Therefore, it is proper that the judgments of first and second instance confirmed Connexions used USD227,290.24 for other trades.

Connexions has received the agreed price before the delivery of goods involved, it suggests the delivery of goods does not affect the collection of Connexions, the carrier Shenzhen J&S negotiated with the buyer to change the use of the sum, the 80% balance payment would not be treated as the price of the goods involved, Connexions could not collect the such sum, it is a risk arising from Connexions's changing the use of the sum. Actually, it transferred the risk of collection of other payments in a same amount to the transport involved in this case. Such risk does not arise from delivery of goods without an original B/L, it is irrelevant with Shenzhen J&S. The ascertainment of the courts of first and second instance that Connexions should not bear the risk or loss arising therefrom has factual and legal basis.

Shenzhen J&S submitted the invoice, packing list and customs declaration of Fortune to prove the declaration price of the goods was USD132,114.6. Connexions submitted the Statement issued by Fortune and other documents like the orders, invoices and vouchers of payment in the retrial as a supplement, to prove the procurement cost of the goods involved paid by Connexions to Shenzhen J&S is USD245,992.08, the evidence was irrelevant with the risk of collection of payment, and cannot overturn the decisions of judgments of the first and second instance.

In summary, it is proper of the judgments of first and second instance to reject the claims of Connexions. The court, according to Article 204 Paragraph 1 of the Civil Procedure Law of the People's Republic of China, renders the ruling as follows:

Dismiss the application for retrial of Connexions (Asia) Limited.

Presiding Judge: HU Fang
Judge: GUO Zhonghong
Judge: YU Xiaohan

December 29, 2015

Clerk: LI Na

Qingdao Maritime Court
Civil Judgment

COSCO Container Lines Co., Ltd.
v.
Shenzhen Finigate Integrated Logistics Co., Ltd. Qingdao Branch et al.

(2014) Qing Hai Fa Hai Shang Chu Zi No.751

Related Case(s) This is the judgment of first instance, and the judgment of second instance and the ruling of retrial are on page 324 and page 334 respectively.

Cause(s) of Action 202. Dispute over contract of carriage of goods by sea or sea-connected waters.

Headnote Ocean carrier held not entitled to recover container detention fees from NVOCC and import agents after containers containing solid waste refused entry to China at port of discharge, as no contractual relationship between ocean carrier and the Defendants.

Summary The Plaintiff COSCO Container Lines, Ltd. was engaged as a carrier of fifteen containers of goods from Egypt to Qingdao. The containers were revealed to contain solid waste, which is prohibited by the state from being imported. The goods were not taken for delivery. The Plaintiff asserted that the four Defendants were jointly and severally liable for the container detention fee of RMB561,015, together with interest and court fees, claiming the Finigate Companies were the consignee of the bill of lading, and were thus obliged to pay the charge. The Plaintiff further contended that Henan C&T was obligated by the customs authority to return ship the goods, and thus, should be jointly and severally liable for the Plaintiff's losses arising from the Defendants' non performance. The Defendants Finigate Companies answered that they were not liable for the Plaintiff's expenses, because they were the assigned agent of the NVOCC, and they delivered the goods to Henan C&T, who was the actual consignee of the goods. The Defendants Finigate Companies alleged that the Plaintiff had separately established a new contractual relationship with the Yatai Company for the return shipment of the goods. The Defendant Henan C&T contended that they were not liable for the Plaintiff's expenses, because they were an import agent, and thus had no contractual relationship with the Plaintiff, as they neither held the bill of lading, nor were they the specified consignee.

The court held Finigate Integrated Logistics Co., Ltd. to be the consignee. The Defendant Finigate Qingdao, as an agent of Shanghai Finigate, handled the delivery order (D/O) with the Plaintiff against a bill of lading affixed with the seal of Shanghai Finigate. However, because the goods were solid waste that could not be imported legally, Shanghai Finigate was unable to deliver the goods. The court held that to recover an unpaid carrier detention fee, the Plaintiff can seek recourse against the shipper, but the Plaintiff has no legal claim against Shanghai Finigate for the expense. Further, the Plaintiff did not have a contractual relationship with Henan C&T, nor did the Plaintiff establish a relationship of contract of carriage of goods by sea with Finigate Qingdao or Shenzhen Finigate. Thus, the court rejected all of the Plaintiff's claims, with court fees assigned to the Plaintiff.

Judgment

The Plaintiff: COSCO Container Lines Co., Ltd.
Domicile: No.378 Dongdaming Road, Shanghai.
Legal representative: YE Weilong, chairman.
Agent *ad litem*: LI Shengzhou, lawyer of Shandong Hailin & Co Law Firm.
Agent *ad litem*: LIU Guogang, lawyer of Shandong Hailin & Co Law Firm.

The Defendant: Shenzhen Finigate Integrated Logistics Co., Ltd. Qingdao Branch.
Domicile: Room 1007, Building No.1, No.19 Zhangzhouer Road, Qingdao City, Shandong.
Person in charge: BI Yongping, manager.

The Defendant: Shenzhen Finigate Integrated Logistics Co., Ltd.
Domicile: Room 003, Floor 8, Block D, Jingjiyibai Mansion (Jinlong Mansion, Caiwuwei), Guiyuan Street, Luohu District, Shenzhen City, Guangdong.
Legal representative: KUANG Xiaoqing, director.

The Defendant: Shanghai Finigate Integrated Logistics Co., Ltd.
Domicile: 18G, Pudong Avenue No.2000, Pudong New Area, Shanghai.
Legal representative: KUANG Xiaoqing, general manager.
Agent *ad litem* jointly entrusted by the three Defendants: HUANG Sufang, lawyer of Guangdong Shengtang Law Firm.

The Defendant: Henan Commerce & Trade Co., Ltd.
Domicile: Floor 12, Block B, Jinmao Mansion, No.115 Wenhua Road, Zhengzhou City, Henan.
Legal representative: SUN Zhe, chairman.
Agent *ad litem*: CHEN Gang, lawyer of Shandong Bolun Law Offices.
Agent *ad litem*: LI Yufeng, lawyer of Shandong Bolun Law Offices.

With respect to the case arising from dispute over contract of carriage of goods by sea, the Plaintiff COSCO Container Lines Co., Ltd. filed an action against the Defendants Shenzhen Finigate Integrated Logistics Co., Ltd. Qingdao Branch (hereinafter referred to as Finigate Qingdao), Shenzhen Finigate Integrated Logistics Co., Ltd. (hereinafter referred to as Shenzhen Finigate), Shanghai Finigate Integrated Logistics Co., Ltd. (hereinafter referred to as Shanghai Finigate), and Henan Commerce & Trade Co., Ltd. (hereinafter referred to as Henan C&T) before the court. After entertaining this case, the court constituted a collegiate panel and held a hearing in public to try the case. LI Shengzhou and LIU Guogang, agents *ad litem* of the Plaintiff, HUANG Sufang, agent *ad litem* of the Defendants Finigate Qingdao, Shenzhen Finigate and Shanghai Finigate (hereinafter the three Defendants referred to as Finigate Companies), and LI Yufeng, agent *ad litem* of the Defendant Henan C&T appeared in court and participated in the proceeding. Now the case has been concluded.

The Plaintiff alleged that as the carrier, it carried goods in 15 containers from Sokhna Port in Egypt to Qingdao Port in May 2013. The number of the bill of lading (B/L) was COSU4503033050. The B/L specified that the shipper was T.E.A. M TRADE and the consignee was Finigate Integrated Logistics Co., Ltd. The above mentioned goods in 15 containers arrived at Qingdao Port on July 10, 2013, but were not taken delivery of. Afterwards, upon inspection by the Qingdao Inspection and Quarantine Technology Center, the goods involved were solid waste, and Huangdao Customs ordered to return the goods. During this period, the Plaintiff suffered a huge loss of the container detention fee in sum of RMB561,015. Finigate Qingdao and Shanghai Finigate as the consignee, Shenzhen Finigate as the parent company of Finigate Qingdao, and Henan C&T as the subject of duty for the return shipment of the goods as ordered by Huangdao Customs, should jointly and severally undertake the obligation for payment of the container detention fee mentioned above. For this purpose, the Plaintiff instituted an action before the court, requesting the court to order that the four Defendants jointly and severally pay the Plaintiff the container detention fee in sum of RMB561,015 and the interest thereon, together with the court fees of this case.

The Plaintiff submitted the following evidential documents to the court in order to support its claims:

1. No.COSU4503033050 B/L, to prove that in May 2013, the Plaintiff, as the carrier, carried the goods in 15 containers involved. Thereinto, the consignee specified in the B/L that the consignee was Finigate Integrated Logistics Co., Ltd.; the port of loading was Sokhna Port in Egypt; the port of discharge was Qingdao Port. The Defendant Finigate Qingdao handled delivery order (D/O) with the Plaintiff against the B/L affixed with the seal of Shanghai Finigate.
2. The business registration information of Finigate Qingdao published by the national enterprise credit information system, to prove that the registered place of Finigate Qingdao was Room 1007, No.1 Building, No.19 Zhangzhouer Road, Qingdao City. This address was the consignee's domicile as specified in the B/L.

3. The return shipment decision of Huangdao Customs, to prove that the goods involved were solid waste prohibited by the state from being imported, Huangdao Customs ordered Henan C&T to return the goods.
4. Application for return shipment, to prove that, the Defendant Henan C&T applied to Huangdao Customs for return shipment of the goods in this case on March 31, 2014.
5. Invoice of document exchange fee and pay-in slip, to prove that Finigate Qingdao paid the Plaintiff document exchange fee in sum of RMB15,585 on July 26, 2013.
6. The information of B/L published on the Plaintiff's website, to prove that, the goods in 15 containers involved were discharged from the vessel on July 10, 2013. The containers were taken delivery of and returned on April 12, 2014.
7. The detention fee rate published on the Plaintiff's website, to prove that the detention fee rate of the containers involved was as follows: free from 1st to 7th day, RMB60 per day from the 8th to 15th day, RMB120 per day from the 16th to 30th day and RMB180 per day from the 31st to 9999th day.
8. The standard rate of the main shipping companies in the market, to prove that the detention fee rate published on the Plaintiff's website was roughly equivalent to the market price over the same period.
9. The contact information in Chinese and English published on the website of Finigate Integrated Logistics Co., Ltd., to prove that in the page of English contact information on the website of Finigate Integrated Logistics Co., Ltd., Finigate Qingdao was the same as the English name of the consignee as specified in the B/L involved. The email box of Finigate Qingdao published on the website info@finigate.net was the email of Finigate Qingdao so as admitted by it. Therefore, Finigate Qingdao was the consignee specified in the B/L.

The Defendants Finigate Companies confirmed the authenticity of evidence 1 to 6 and evidence 9. As for evidence 7, the Defendants Finigate Companies argued that the rate was published by the Plaintiff at its discretion. The Plaintiff did not inform Finigate Companies in advance and get the authorization of them. It should not be binding on them. As for evidence 8, Finigate Companies held it was a unilateral statement,which could not stand for the general rate in the market.

Henan C&T confirmed the authenticity of evidence 1 to 7 and evidence 9, but did not admit the authenticity or the legality of evidence 8, which could not prove the calculating standard of customary detention fee.

The Defendants Finigate Companies jointly rebutted as follows:

1. Finigate Companies, just as the assigned agent of the NVOCC, delivered the goods involved to Henan C&T. Henan C&T was the actual consignee of the goods involved. The expenses involved should be taken by Henan C&T.
2. After the goods arrived at the port on July 10, 2013, Finigate Companies exchanged the D/O with the Plaintiff on July 25, 2013 and surrendered the D/O to Henan C&T on the same day. After surrendering the D/O to Henan C&T, all the rights and obligations in terms of the goods had been exchanged to Henan

C&T. Therefore, the expenses of the goods involved should be taken by Henan C&T.
3. Finigate Companies were not the subject of obligation and liability for return shipment of the goods involved. The reason why the goods involved could not declare import and was ordered by Huangdao Customs to return was that the goods involved were solid wastes prohibited by the state from being imported. Finigate Companies had no fault and should not take any consequence arising therefrom.
4. The Plaintiff accepted the commission of Yatai Energy Co., Ltd. (hereinafter referred to as Yatai Company) and returned the goods involved from Qingdao Port to Gaoxiong in Taiwan region. The Plaintiff issued a return B/L. The Plaintiff established a new relationship of contract of carriage of goods by sea with Yatai Company. The relevant expenses generated in the departure port of the return shipment should not be born by the Defendants.
5. The Plaintiff neither provided evidence to prove the start-stop time of the expenses involved nor evidence to prove the basis of calculation. The amount it claimed far exceeded the actual losses it suffered.

To sum up, the Defendant required the court to reject the claims filed by the Plaintiff.

To support their defense, the Defendants Finigate Companies submitted the following evidence:

1. The query of transportation dynamics of the goods involved published on the Plaintiff's website, to prove that goods involved arrived at Qingdao Port on July 10, 2013.
2. House B/L with official seal issued by Henan C&T to Finigate Companies when taking delivery of the goods involved and the invoice of exchanging document fee issued by Finigate Companies according to the instruction of Henan C&T, to prove that: (1) Henan C&T, as the consignee taking delivery of the goods involved from Finigate Companies and Henan C&T, was the actual consignee of the goods involved. (2) Finigate Companies had delivered the goods involved to Henan C&T. All the expenses incurred by the goods at Qingdao Port should be bore by Henan C&T.
3. The handling notification to Finigate Companies issued by Shandong Hailin & Co. Law Firm consigned by the Plaintiff.
4. The decision of return shipment of Huangdao Customs of the People's Republic of China.
5. The online declaration query of Huangdao Customs.

Evidence 3 to 5 is to prove that: (1) Henan C&T was the actual consignee and the subject liable to return the goods involved; (2) Henan C&T as the consignee declared import of the goods involved with Huangdao Customs on August 2, 2013; (3) Henan C&T as the consignee submitted a return shipment application to Huangdao Customs; (4) the expenses incurred by return shipment because of the incapable of regular customs clearance should be born by Henan C&T. It was irrelevant to Finigate Companies.

6. The email issued by the Plaintiff's agent COSCO Container Lines Shipping Agent Co., Ltd. to Finigate Companies on April 3, 2014, to prove that the Plaintiff accepted the commission of Yatai Company and dealt with the return shipment of the goods involved.
7. The B/L and translation version of the return shipment B/L, to prove that:

(1) The Plaintiff arranged return shipment for the goods and issued return shipment B/L. The shipper on the B/L was Yatai Company;
(2) The Plaintiff established a new relationship of contract of carriage of goods by sea with Yatai Company in terms of the return shipment;
(3) The expenses involved were incurred by the new established relationship of contract of carriage of goods by sea with Yatai Company and were not expenses arising from the contract of carriage of goods by sea between the Plaintiff and Finigate Companies. The expenses involved were irrelevant to Finigate Companies; and
(4) Finigate Companies was not a party to the return transportation contract, Finigate Companies need not pay the Plaintiff the relevant expenses generated before the return shipment.

8 The query of transportation dynamics of the goods involved published on the Plaintiff's website, to prove that the goods involved have been returned from Qingdao Port to Gaoxiong Port in Taiwan region on April 15, 2014.

The Plaintiff had no objection to the authenticity of evidence 1 to 5, but objected to the content the evidence 2 tended to prove. The Plaintiff considered that whether Finigate Companies were the actual consignee of the goods involved had no effect on the determination of rights and obligations of Finigate Companies and the Plaintiff as stipulated in the B/L. The authenticity of evidence 6, 7 and 8 need to be verified, but the Plaintiff did not reply within the time specified by the court.

The Defendant Henan C&T had no objection to the authenticity of evidence 1 to 8, but objected to the legality of evidence 2. The Defendant Henan C&T held that the consignee of this B/L was not the Defendant. Changle Huarong Industry & Trade Co., Ltd. (hereinafter referred to as Changle Company), the actual consignee, established a relationship of contract of carriage of goods by sea with the Defendant Finigate Qingdao, the consignee of the B/L.

The Defendant Henan C&T rebutted that:

1. Henan C&T had no contractual relationship with the Plaintiff. The Plaintiff as the carrier only established right and obligation relationship with the consignee and the holder of B/L;
2. The goods involved had been returned, according to practice, the container usage charge should be settled; and
3. The position of Henan C&T was import agent, and it properly performed the obligations of the agency contract. The reason why the goods could not be

imported was that Changle Company broke the import agent agreement and imported solid waste prohibited by the state, which led to the return of the goods. Henan C&T therefore sustained a great loss. Its credit rating in the customs descended from level AA to level B. Even though there happened liability, such liability should be born by Changle Company, which was irrelevant to Henan C&T. To sum up, the Defendant Henan C&T required the court to reject claims of the Plaintiff.

To support its defense, Henan C&T submitted the following evidence:

1. Import agent agreement, to prove the position of Henan C&T was an import agent. This batch of bunker was an import agent business after signing the import agent agreement with Changle Company. The agreement clearly prescribed that all the liabilities arising from the import of this batch of goods should be born by Changle Company.
2. A copy of automatic import license (there was no original, which was withdrawn by the customs in the process of import agency), to prove that this licenses clearly stipulated that Changle Company was the actual import customer and Henan C&T was just the import agent.
3. Purchase and sales contract signed by Henan C&T and Yatai Company, this contract combined with evidence 1 was to prove that Henan C&T had fully performed the obligations specified in the import agent agreement and Henan C&T had no faults.

The Plaintiff had no objection to the authenticity of evidence 1, but questioned the authenticity of evidence 2 and 3. The Defendants Finigate Companies questioned the authenticity of all the evidence submitted by the Defendant Henan C&T.

For the evidence submitted by the Plaintiff and the Defendants, the court ascertains as follows:

As for the evidence of the Plaintiff, the two Defendants had no objection to the authenticity of evidence 1 to 6 and evidence 9; evidence 7 and 8 was printed from the Plaintiff's website, therefore the court admits the pro forma authenticity of the evidence submitted by the Plaintiff. As for the evidence submitted by the Defendants Finigate Companies, the Defendant Henan C&T had no objection to the authenticity thereof; the Plaintiff had no objection to the authenticity of evidence 1 to 5 submitted by Finigate Companies. Though the authenticity of evidence 6 to 8 is not confirmed, the three pieces of evidence are held by the Plaintiff. Under the circumstance that the Plaintiff did not submit evidence to the contrary, the court admits the authenticity thereof. As for the evidence submitted by Henan C&T, the Plaintiff and the Defendants Finigate Companies had objection to the authenticity of evidence 2 and 3. The court holds that evidence 3 is the original, though evidence 2 is a copy, it can corroborate the evidence submitted by the Plaintiff and the Defendants and the facts they stated. Therefore, the court admits the pro forma authenticity of the evidence submitted by Henan C&T.

Combined with the evidence submitted by the Plaintiff and the Defendants and the statements in court, the court ascertains the following facts:

In January 2013, the Defendant Henan C&T signed the No.FO 11-18/2012 fuel oil purchase and sales contract with Yatai Company (Sino Brighten Energy Limited), which arranged that Henan C&T bought 300 tons of fuel oil of which the place of origin was Egypt, from Yatai Company and the price was CIF USD580 per ton. It required payment by L/C and container transportation.

On May 15, 2013, MTS LOGISTIC issued No.MTSQING22513 full set of original B/Ls in terms of the goods. The B/Ls record that the shipper is T.E.A.M TRADE Company (hereinafter referred to as T Company) in Egypt; the consignee or order is Yatai Company; the notify party is Henan C&T; the port of loading is Sokhna Port in Egypt; the port of discharge is Qingdao Port; the goods are fuel oil used for refining and processing; the net weight is 300.535 tons; and the freight is prepaid.

In terms of the above-mentioned goods, MTS LOGISTICS commissioned the Plaintiff for shipment. The Plaintiff did not issue original B/L. The duplicate of No. COSU4503033050 B/L issued by the Plaintiff states that the shipper is the T Company. The consignee is Finigate Integrated Logistics Co., Ltd. (domicile: Room 1007, Building No.1, No.19 Zhangzhouer Road, Qingdao City). Other contents are the same as those stipulated in No.MTSQING22513 B/L.

On July 10, 2013, the goods were discharged from the vessel after arriving at Qingdao Port. On July 26, the Defendant Finigate Qingdao exchanged the D/O of the goods with the Plaintiff against the duplicate of the B/L with Shanghai Finigate's seal affixed thereon and paid the document exchange fee in sum of RMB15,585.

The Defendant Henan C&T alleged that it accepted the commission of Changle Company and took over No.MTSQING22513 original B/L issued by MTS LOGISTICS through negotiation payment, but there was no endorsement of T Company, Yatai Company or relevant bank. Henan C&T delivered the B/L to Finigate Qingdao after endorsing on the back of the original B/L, exchanged the D/O issued by the Plaintiff and applied for handling import customs clearance procedure to Huangdao Customs.

The goods involved were used lubricating oil which were solid waste prohibited by the state from being imported. Huangdao Customs issued (2013) Huang Guan Ji Ze Tui Zi No.30 notification of order of return shipment on December 27, 2013, ordering Henan C&T to return the above-mentioned goods before March 28, 2014.

On March 31, 2014, Henan C&T submitted the written application for return shipment to Huangdao Customs. The matters concerned with return shipment were actually handled by Qingdao Hangmei International Logistic Co., Ltd. under the commission of Yatai Company. On April 12, Hangmei International Logistic Co., Ltd. handled the procedure of taking delivery of containers and return shipment. On April 15, the goods in 15 containers were loaded on board and returned. According to the declaration of the Plaintiff, Yatai Company only paid the return freight and CFS charge, but not the container detention fee.

The Plaintiff claimed that according to the stipulation of the front of B/L "demurrage and detention fee shall be calculated at the rate published on the website of COSCO Container Lines Co., Ltd. (www.coscon.com). If there is any ambiguity or doubt, please query according to the demurrage rate query." According to the rate published on the Plaintiff's website that the detention fee rate of container involved was free from the 1st to 7th day, RMB60 per day from the 8th to 15th day, RMB120 per day from the 16th to 30th day, RMB180 per day from the 31st to 9999th day. In this case, the 15 containers were discharged from the vessel on July 10, 2013 and delivered and returned on April 12, 2014. The corresponding container detention fee was: (1) July 10, 2013 to July 16, 2013, 7 days in total, RMB0; (2) July 17, 2013 to July 24, 2013, 8 days in total, RMB15*8*60 = 7,200; (3)July 25, 2013 to August 8, 2013, 15 days in total, RMB15*15*120 = 27,000; (4) August 9, 2013 to April 12, 2014, 247 days in total, RMB15*247*180 = 666,900, in aggregate amount ofRMB701,100. The Plaintiff only claimed for RMB561,015.

The court also finds out that the actual import customer is Changle Company, a party not involved in this case. Henan C&T is the foreign trade agent of Changle Company. The two parties signed an import agency agreement in terms of goods involved on July 23, 2013.

Finigate Companies alleged, Shanghai Finigate cooperated with the NVOCC MTS LOGISTICS, and it handled domestic relevant procedures of goods on behalf of MTS LOGISTICS. As the destination port was Qingdao, Shanghai Finigate commissioned Finigate Qingdao to handle document exchange procedure. The consignee Finigate Integrated Logistics Co., Ltd. stated in the B/L of the Plaintiff did not register in China.

The Plaintiff claimed that Finigate Companies were the consignee of the B/L involved. According to the provisions of the Maritime Code of People's Republic of China (hereinafter referred to as the CMC), they were obliged to pay the container detention fee. The Defendant Henan C&T was the subject of obligation for the return shipment as ordered by Huangdao Customs and they should bear the joint and several liability for the losses of the Plaintiff due to the non-performance of statutory obligation.

All of the above facts can be ascertained on the basis of the evidence.

The court holds that this case is arising from dispute over container detention fee during the process the Plaintiff performing a contract of carriage of goods by sea. For the goods in 15 containers involved, there are two relatively independent relationships of contract of carriage of goods by sea: a relationship of contract of carriage of goods by sea in which the Plaintiff is the actual carrier and a relationship of contract of carriage of goods by sea in which MTS LOGISTICS is a NVOCC.

In the relationship of contract of carriage of goods by sea in which the Plaintiff is the actual carrier, MTS LOGISTICS is the shipper booking space and T Company is the shipper taking over the goods. After the goods involved arrived at Qingdao Port, the act that Shanghai Finigate signed the duplicate of B/L and exchanged the D/O from the Plaintiff indicates that Shanghai Finigate is the consignee and Finigate Qingdao is the agent of Shanghai Finigate. After the Plaintiff exchanged the D/O with Shanghai Finigate, it should deliver the goods. Since the goods are solid wastes prohibited by the state from being imported. The goods failed the customs. Therefore, Shanghai Finigate could not actually deliver the goods and finally returned the goods. The container detention fee is expenses incurred by the non-performance of actually delivery of goods due to administrative management rather than expenses generated under the circumstance where that "if the goods were not taken delivery of at the port of discharge or if the consignee has delayed or refused the taking delivery of the goods" as provided in Article 86 of the CMC. According to Article 87 of the CMC, if the freight, demurrage to be paid to the carrier has not been paid in full, nor has appropriate security been given, the carrier may have a lien, to a reasonable extent, on the goods. For the goods under lien, the shipper may apply for auction. The proceeds from the auction sale shall be used to pay off the correlative charge paid to the carrier. If the proceeds fall short of such expenses, the carrier is entitled to claim the difference from the shipper. In this case, the Plaintiff as the carrier, in terms of the unpaid container detention fee, is entitled to compensation through exercising the title to the goods and recourse the insufficient amount against the shipper. Therefore, the claim that the Plaintiff required Shanghai Finigate to bear the expense involved has no factual or legal basis. It shall not be supported.

In respect of the claim that the Plaintiff required Henan C&T and Finigate Companies to jointly and severally undertake the liability on ground that Henan C&T was the subject of obligation for the return shipment of the goods ordered by Huangdao Custom, the court holds that Henan C&T is the holder of the original B/L issued MTS LOGISITCS and the foreign trade agent of the actual consignee Changle Company. The container detention fee claimed by the Plaintiff was incurred under the relationship of contract of carriage of goods by sea, but the Plaintiff did not establish a relationship of contract of carriage of goods by sea with Henan C&T, besides, they are not parties concerned in the same legal relationship of B/L. Therefore, the claim that the Plaintiff required Henan C&T to bear joint and several liability cannot stand.

Finigate Qingdao and Shenzhen Finigate did not establish a relationship of contract of carriage of goods by sea. Therefore, the claim that the Plaintiff required the two companies to undertake the liability shall not be supported by the court. Accordingly, the judgment is as follows:

1. Reject the claims filed by the Plaintiff COSCO Container Lines Co., Ltd. against the Defendant Shenzhen Finigate Integrated Logistics Co., Ltd. Qingdao Branch.
2. Reject the claims filed by the Plaintiff COSCO Container Lines Co., Ltd. against the Defendant Shenzhen Finigate Integrated Logistics Co., Ltd.
3. Reject the claims filed by the Plaintiff COSCO Container Lines Co., Ltd. against the Defendant Shanghai Finigate Integrated Logistics Co., Ltd.; and
4. Reject the claims filed by the Plaintiff COSCO Container Lines Co., Ltd. against the Defendant Henan Commerce & Trade Co., Ltd.

Court acceptance fee in amount of RMB9,410, shall be born by the Plaintiff COSCO Container Lines Co., Ltd.

In event of dissatisfaction with this judgment, any party may submit six statements of appeal to the court within 15 days upon service of this judgment, so as to file an appeal before the Shandong High People's Court.

Presiding Judge: ZHANG Xianli
Judge: WANG Yane
Judge: WANG Keke

January 4, 2015

Acting Clerk: XU Wenwen

Shandong High People's Court
Civil Judgment

COSCO Container Lines Co., Ltd.
v.
Shenzhen Finigate Integrated Logistics Co., Ltd. Qingdao Branch et al.

(2015) Lu Min Si Zhong Zi No.152

Related Case(s) This is the judgment of second instance, and the judgment of first instance and the ruling of retrial are on page 313 and page 334 respectively.

Cause(s) of Action 202. Dispute over contract of carriage of goods by sea or sea-connected waters.

Headnote Affirming lower court decision that ocean carrier was not entitled to recover container detention fees from NVOCC and import agents after containers containing solid waste were refused entry to China at port of discharge, as there was no contractual relationship between ocean carrier and Defendants.

Summary The Plaintiff COSCO appealed the lower court judgment, which dismissed all of the Plaintiff-carrier's claims of liability against the Defendants regarding the container detention fee Plaintiff incurred due to the fact that no one took delivery of the goods. The lower court found that the Plaintiff could seek recourse against the shipper for shipping illicit goods, but that the other named Defendants bore no liability regarding the container detention fee. The court recognized the lower court's judgment of the Defendants' liability, and rejected Plaintiff's arguments that Qingdao Finigate and Shanghai Finigate were liable for the charge because they breached their contract as consignees by failing to take delivery of the goods.

Judgment

The Appellant (the Plaintiff of first instance): COSCO Container Lines Co., Ltd.
Domicile: No.378 Dongdaming Road, Shanghai.
Legal representative: YE Weilong, chairman.
Agent *ad litem*: LI Shengzhou, lawyer of Shandong Hailin & Co Law Firm.
Agent *ad litem*: LIU Guogang, lawyer of Shandong Hailin & Co Law Firm.

The Respondent (the Defendant of first instance): Shenzhen Finigate Integrated Logistics Co., Ltd. Qingdao Branch.
Domicile: Room 1007, Building No.1, No.19 Zhangzhouer Road, Qingdao City, Shandong Province.
Representative: LIU Ziqi, manager.
Agent *ad litem*: HUANG Sufang, lawyer of Guangdong Shengtang Law Firm.

The Respondent (the Defendant of first instance): Shenzhen Finigate Integrated Logistics Co., Ltd.
Domicile: Room 003, Floor 8, Block D, Jingjiyibai Mansion (Jinlong Mansion, Caiwuwei), Guiyuan Street, Luohu District, Shenzhen City, Guangdong Province.
Legal representative: KUANG Xiaoqian, director.
Agent *ad litem*: HUANG Sufang, lawyer of Guangdong Shengtang Law Firm.

The Respondent (the Defendant of first instance): Shanghai Finigate Integrated Logistics Co., Ltd.
Domicile: 18G, Pudong Avenue No.2000, Pudong New Area, Shanghai.
Legal representative: KUANG Xiaoqian, general manager.
Agent *ad litem*: HUANG Sufang, lawyer of Guangdong Shengtang Law Firm.

The Respondent (the Defendant of first instance): Henan Commerce & Trade Co., Ltd.
Domicile: Floor 12, Block B, Jinmao Mansion, No.115 Wenhua Road, Zhengzhou City, Henan Province.
Legal representative: SUN Zhe, chairman.
Agent *ad litem*: CHEN Gang, Shandong Bolun Law Offices.
Agent *ad litem*: LI Yufeng, Shandong Bolun Law Offices.

Dissatisfied with (2014) Qing Hai Fa Hai Shang Chu Zi No.751 Civil Judgment rendered by Qingdao Maritime Court with respect of the case arising from dispute over contract of carriage of good by sea, the Appellant COSCO Container Lines Co., Ltd. (hereinafter referred to as COSCO), filed an appeal against the Respondents, Shenzhen Finigate Integrated Logistics Co., Ltd. Qingdao Branch (hereinafter referred to as Finigate Qingdao), Shenzhen Finigate Integrated Logistics Co., Ltd. (hereinafter referred to as Shenzhen Finigate), Shanghai Finigate International Logistics Co., Ltd. (hereinafter referred to as Shanghai Finigate), Henan Commerce& Trade Co., Ltd. (hereinafter referred to as Henan C&T) before the court. After entertaining this case, the court formed a collegiate panel according to the law to and held a hearing in public. LI Shengzhou and LIU Guogang, agents *ad litem* entrusted by the Appellant COSCO, and HUANG Sufang, agent *ad litem* jointly entrusted by the Respondents Finigate Qingdao, Shenzhen Finigate and Shanghai Finigate (hereinafter referred to as Finigate Companies) appeared in court to attend the trial. The Appellant Henan C&T, upon summons by the court, refused to appear in court without proper reason. Now the case has been concluded.

  COSCO alleged in the court of first instance that as the carrier, it carried goods in 15 containers from Sokhna Port in Egypt to Qingdao Port in May 2013.

The number of the bill of lading (B/L) was COSU4503033050. The B/L specified that the shipper was T.E.A.M TRADE and the consignee was Finigate Integrated Logistics Co., Ltd. The above mentioned goods in 15 containers arrived at Qingdao Port on July 10, 2013, but were not taken delivery of. Afterwards, upon inspection by the Qingdao Inspection and Quarantine Technology Center, the goods involved were solid waste, and Huangdao Customs ordered to return the goods. During this period, COSCO suffered a huge loss of the container detention fee in sum of RMB561,015. Finigate Qingdao and Shanghai Finigate as the consignee, Shenzhen Finigate as the parent company of Finigate Qingdao, and Henan C&T as the subject of duty for the return shipment of the goods as ordered by Huangdao Customs, should jointly and severally undertake the obligation for payment of the container detention fee mentioned above. For this purpose, COSCO instituted an action before the court of first instance, requesting the court to order that Finigate Companies and Henan C&T jointly and severally pay COSCO the container detention fee in sum of RMB561,015 and the interest thereon, together with the court fees of this case.

The court of first instance found the following facts:

In January 2013, Henan C&T signed the No.FO 11–18/2012 fuel oil purchase and sales contract with Yatai Company (Sino Brighten Energy Limited), which arranged that Henan C&T bought 300 tons of fuel oil of which the place of origin was Egypt, from Yatai Company and the price was CIF USD580 per ton. It required payment by L/C and container transportation.

On May 15, 2013, MTS LOGISTIC issued No.MTSQING22513 full set of original B/Ls in terms of the goods. The B/Ls recorded that the shipper was T.E.A.M TRADE Company (hereinafter referred to as T Company) in Egypt; the consignee or order was Yatai Company; the notify party was Henan C&T; the port of loading was Sokhna Port in Egypt; the port of discharge was Qingdao Port; the goods are fuel oil used for refining and processing; the net weight was 300.535 ton; and the freight was prepaid.

In terms of the above-mentioned goods, MTS LOGISTICS commissioned COSCO for shipment. COSCO did not issue original B/L. The duplicate of No. COSU4503033050 B/L issued by COSCO stated that the shipper was the Egyptian T Company. The consignee was Finigate Integrated Logistics Co., Ltd (domicile: Room 1007, Building No.1, No.19 Zhangzhouer Road, Qingdao City). Other contents were the same as those stipulated in No.MTSQING22513 B/L.

On July 10, 2013, the goods were discharged from the vessel after arriving at Qingdao Port. On July 26, Finigate Qingdao exchanged the D/O of the goods with COSCO against the duplicate of the B/L with Shanghai Finigate's seal affixed thereon and paid the document exchange fee in sum of RMB15,585.

Henan C&T alleged that it accepted the commission of Changle Company and took over No.MTSQING22513 original B/L issued by MTS LOGISTICS through negotiation payment, but there was no endorsement of Egyptian T Company, Yatai Company or relevant bank. Henan C&T delivered the B/L to Finigate Qingdao after endorsing on the back of the original B/L, exchanged the D/O issued by COSCO and applied for handling import customs clearance procedure to Huangdao Customs.

The goods involved were used lubricating oil which belonged to solid waste prohibited by the state from being imported. Huangdao Customs issued (2013) Huang Guan Ji Ze Tui Zi No.30 notification of order of return shipment on December 27, 2013, ordering Henan C&T to return the above-mentioned goods before March 28, 2014.

On March 31, 2014, Henan C&T submitted the written application for return shipment to Huangdao Customs. The matters concerned with return shipment were actually handled by Qingdao Hangmei International Logistic Co., Ltd. under the commission of Yatai Company. On April 12, Hangmei International Logistic Co., Ltd. handled the procedure of taking delivery of containers and return shipment. On April 15, the goods in 15 containers were loaded on board and returned. According to the declaration of COSCO, Yatai Company only paid the return freight and CFS charge, but not the container detention fee.

COSCO claimed that according to the stipulation of the front of B/L "demurrage and detention fee should be calculated at the rate published on the website of COSCO Container Lines Co., Ltd. (www.coscon.com). If there was any ambiguity or doubt, please query according to the demurrage rate query." According to the demurrage rate published on COSCO's website that the detention fee rate of container involved was free from the 1st to 7th day, RMB60 per day from the 8th to 15th day, RMB120 per day from the 16th to 30th day, RMB180 per day from the 31st to 9999th day. In this case, the 15 containers were discharged from the vessel on July 10, 2013 and delivered and returned on April 12, 2014. The corresponding container detention fee was: (1) July 10, 2013 to July 16, 2013, 7 days in total, RMB0; (2) July 17, 2013 to July 24, 2013, 8 days in total, RMB15*8*60 = 7,200; (3) July 25, 2013 to August 8, 2013, 15 days in total, RMB15*15*120 = 27,000; (4) August 9, 2013 to April 12, 2014, 247 days in total, RMB15*247*180 = 666,900, in aggregate amount of RMB701,100. COSCO only claimed for RMB561,015.

The court of first instance also found out that the actual import customer was Changle Company, a party not involved in this case. Henan C&T was the foreign trade agent of Changle Company. The two parties signed an import agency agreement in terms of goods involved on July 23, 2013.

Finigate Companies alleged Shanghai Finigate cooperated with the NVOCC MTS LOGISTICS, and it handled domestic relevant procedures of goods on behalf of MTS LOGISTICS. As the destination port was Qingdao, Shanghai Finigate commissioned Finigate Qingdao to handle document exchange procedure. The consignee Finigate Integrated Logistics Co., Ltd. stated in the B/L of COSCO did not register in China.

COSCO claimed that Finigate Companies were the consignee of the B/L involved. According to the provisions of the Maritime Code of People's Republic of China (hereinafter referred to as the CMC), they were obliged to pay the container detention fee. Henan C&T was the subject of obligation for the return shipment as ordered by Huangdao Customs and they should bear the joint and several liability for the losses of COSCO due to the non performance of statutory obligation.

The court of first instance held that this case was arising from dispute over container detention fee during the process COSCO performing a contract of carriage of goods by sea. For the goods in 15 containers involved, there were two relatively independent relationships of contract of carriage of goods by sea: a relationship of contract of carriage of goods by sea in which COSCO was the actual carrier and a relationship of contract of carriage of goods by sea in which MTS LOGISTICS was a NVOCC.

In the relationship of contract of carriage of goods by sea in which COSCO was the actual carrier, MTS LOGISTICS was the shipper booking space and the T Company was the shipper taking over the goods. After the goods involved arrived at Qingdao Port, the act that Shanghai Finigate signed the duplicate of B/L and exchanged the D/O from COSCO indicates that Shanghai Finigate was the consignee and Finigate Qingdao was the agent of Shanghai Finigate. After COSCO exchanged the D/O with Shanghai Finigate, it should deliver the goods. Since the goods were solid wastes prohibited by the state from being imported. The goods failed the customs. Therefore, Shanghai Finigate could not actually deliver the goods and finally returned the goods. The container detention fee was expense incurred by the non-performance of actually delivery of goods due to administrative management rather than expenses generated under the circumstance where that "if the goods were not taken delivery of at the port of discharge or if the consignee has delayed or refused the taking delivery of the goods" as provided in Article 86 of the CMC. According to Article 87 of the CMC, if the freight, demurrage to be paid to the carrier had not been paid in full, nor had appropriate security been given, the carrier might have a lien, to a reasonable extent, on the goods. For the goods under lien, the shipper might apply for auction. The proceeds from the auction sale should be used to pay off the correlative charge paid to the carrier. If the proceeds fell short of such expenses, the carrier was entitled to claim the difference from the shipper. In this case, COSCO as the carrier, in terms of the unpaid container detention fee, was entitled to compensation through exercising the title to the goods and recourse the insufficient amount against the shipper. Therefore, the claim that COSCO required Shanghai Finigate to bear the expense involved had no factual or legal basis. It should not be supported.

In respect of the claim that COSCO required Henan C&T and Finigate Companies to jointly and severally undertake the liability on ground that Henan C&T was the subject of obligation for the return shipment of the goods ordered by Huangdao Custom, the court of first instance held that Henan C&T was the holder of the original B/L issued MTS LOGISITCS and the foreign trade agent of the actual consignee Changle Company. The container detention fee claimed by COSCO was incurred under the relationship of contract of carriage of goods by sea, but COSCO did not establish a relationship of contract of carriage of goods by sea with Henan C&T, besides they were not parties concerned in the same legal relationship of B/L. Therefore, the claim that COSCO required Henan C&T to bear joint and several liability could not stand.

Finigate Qingdao and Shenzhen Finigate did not establish a relationship of contract of carriage of goods by sea. Therefore, the claim that COSCO required the two companies to undertake the liability should not be supported by the court of first instance.

Accordingly, the court of first instance rendered the judgment as follows: Reject the claims filed by COSCO against Finigate Qingdao; Reject the claims filed by COSCO against Shenzhen Finigate; Reject the claims filed by COSCO against Shanghai Finigate; and Reject the claims filed by COSCO against Henan C&T. Court acceptance fee in amount of RMB9,410 should be born by COSCO.

COSCO dissatisfied with the judgment of first instance, and filed an appeal, alleging as follows:

1. The legal position of Qingdao Finigate was wrongly found in judgment of first instance. Qingdao Finigate was the consignee under the B/L involved. Firstly, according to the invoice of document transfer fee and the pay-in slip submitted by COSCO, Qingdao Finigate paid the document transfer fee in sum of RMB15,585 yuan to COSCO on July 25, 2013, and exchanged for the B/L; Qingdao Finigate admitted its identity of the consignee in the first instance, it clearly stated the consignee name as Qingdao Finigate on the back of the B/L when handling D/O with COSCO. Secondly, the name of the consignee recorded in the B/L Finigate Integrated Logistics Co., Ltd. was nearly the same with that published on the website of Finigate Qingdao, Finigate Integrated Logistics Co., Ltd.; the address of Qingdao Finigate published on its website was identically same with the address of the consignee recorded in the B/L; info@finigate.net, the email box of Qingdao Finigate published on the website was the one Qingdao Finigate admitted in the hearing as its own email box. Thirdly, Qingdao Finigate contacted with the so-called actual consignee in terms of exchange of D/O and taking delivery of goods through the mailbox angela. liu@finigate.net Qingdao Finigate admitted in the first hearing of the first instance, the inscription name Finigate Integrated Logistics was the same as the name of the consignee Finigate Integrated Logistics Co., Ltd. in the B/L. Fourthly, no evidence could prove that Qingdao Finigate was Shanghai Finigate's agent. Therefore, Qingdao Finigate and Shanghai Finigate which signed and sealed the B/L are the consignees under the B/L involved.

2. Judgment of first instance wrongly determined that Finigate Companies should not bear any liability. Firstly, the circumstance where COSCO could not actually deliver the goods did not exist. After the goods were ordered to be shipped back, Yatai Company took delivery of the goods against the D/O issued by COSCO to Qingdao Finigate at the container yard on April 12 2014, and commissioned COSCO to ship the goods back. The above acts suggested the consignee had actually taken delivery of the goods from the carrier. The fact that the goods could not clear customs did not mean incapability of taking delivery. Even if the customs ordered return shipment, the consignee could still take delivery of the goods, and handled return shipment according to the order of the customs. Secondly, if the consignee handled return shipment in a timely manner, then the

container detention fee would not occur, so the cause of generation of the container detention fee lied in that the consignee did not timely take delivery of the goods and handled return shipment. The determination of judgment of first instance that it was the shipper wrongly consigned goods prohibited from being imported by the state that the container detention fee generated was incorrect. Thirdly, judgment of first instance found that Shanghai Finigate had no subjective fault in the goods as being solid waste, it did not implement breach of contract objectively, the law did not impose responsibility, so it was not obliged to pay the container detention fee, such determination was wrong. Whether the consignee breached the contract does not take the subjective fault of the consignee as the prerequisite. According to the provisions of Article 86 of the Maritime Code of the People's Republic of China (hereinafter referred to as the CMC), the consignee should promptly take delivery of the goods after receiving the B/L from the carrier; otherwise, it shall bear and any expenses or risks arising therefrom. The delay and refusal of Qingdao Finigate and Shanghai Finigate to take delivery of the goods involved under the contract of carriage of goods by sea constituted a breach of contract to COSCO, they should bear the liability to pay the container detention fee.

3. The determination of judgment of first instance that ordered Henan C&T was not liable was wrong. Henan C&T was the subject of obligation for return shipment of the goods involved ordered by Huangdao Customs, according to Article 7 of the Administrative Punishment Law of the PRC and Article 6 of the Tort Liability Law of the PRC, Henan C&T failed to arrange return shipment, obviously, it had fault in the container detention fee, it should bear obligation for the container detention fee. In summary, COSCO requested the court to set aside the judgment of first instance and order Finigate Companies and Henan C&T pay COSCO container detention fee in sum of RMB561,015 yuan and the corresponding interest.

The Respondent Finigate Companies jointly defended as follows:

1. The determination on the legal position of the parties concerned in the judgment of first instance was correct. In this case, COSCO did not issue original B/L, but issued a duplicate B/L. The consignee described in duplicate B/L, Finigate Integrated Logistics Co., Ltd. did not register in China, its English name did not comply with that registered by Finigate Companies. Finigate Companies were not the consignee recorded in the duplicate B/L of COSCO. Shanghai Finigate accepted the commission of the NVOCC MTS LOGISTICS to handle transport of the goods involved. Shanghai Finigate affixed its official seal on the duplicate B/L, and commissioned Qingdao Finigate to pay for exchanging documents. So, Shanghai Finigate as the actual carrier of COSCO under the contract of the carriage of goods by sea, was the consignee at the port of destination designated by MTS LOGISTICS and the shipper T Company, the consignee stated in the duplicate B/L. Qingdao Finigate was the agent for exchanging documents of Shanghai Finigate, but not the consignee under the carriage contract. Shenzhen

Finigate did not participate in the transport of goods involved, it was not a party in this case. Finigate Companies were not parties to the carriage contract concluded by COSCO and the shipper T Company, according to the principle of privity of contract, the carriage contract should not bind upon Finigate Companies. Shanghai Finigate was only a third party to perform the obligation for taking delivery of goods which was agreed by the NVOCC MTS LOGISTICS, the shipper T Company and COSCO. Even if Shanghai Finigate did not perform the obligation for taking delivery of the goods or its performance did not satisfy the agreement, then the NVOCC MTS LOGISTICS, the shipper T Company should assume liability for breach of contract to COSCO.

2. The determination on the liability of Finigate Companies in judgment of first instance was correct. Firstly, in this case, Article 64 Paragraph 1 of the CMC, Article 304 of the Contract Law of the People's Republic of China rather than Article 86 of the CMC should apply. According to the shipping practice, the consignee, after exchange for D/O from the carrier, should declare import goods with the customs of the destination port, upon approval by the customs, it could take delivery of the goods from the carrier against the customs clearance permit. The reason why the goods could not be actually imported and the container detention fee generated was the unconformity between the goods actually loaded by the shipper and the name and information of the goods it provided to the carrier, resulting in the carrier's failure to actually deliver the goods to the consignee. COSCO should recover its losses against the shipper which entrusted it to transport the goods involved and established a contractual relationship of the contract of the carriage of goods by sea instead of Finigate Companies with it. Secondly, Finigate Companies had no fault in the container detention fee, and should not undertake liability therefor, the decision of the judgment of first instance was correct. Thirdly, When COSCO handled the return shipment waived to collect the container detention fee from the client, it should bear the consequence, it was not entitled to compensation. In respect of the return shipment, COSCO and Yatai Company set up an independent contract of the carriage of goods by sea. When Yatai Company handled the return shipment, it only paid the return freight and yard charge but not the container detention fee. According to the shipping practice, COSCO has not collected the container detention fee from Yatai Company, it does not conform to the daily operation and logic. COSCO should be liable for the non-collection. Fourthly, the container detention fee COSCO claimed has far exceeded the value of a newly re-purchased container, its claim had no factual or legal basis. Container detention fee is liquidated damages in nature for delay in the performance of under a contract of the carriage of goods by sea. The carrier charges such fee for the purpose of recovering the loss arising from container's being occupied and non-circulated. For long-term detained containers, COSCO could have maintained normal operation by re-purchasing containers of the same type, and should not negatively wait until the loss expanded. According to the market prices in the second half of 2013 and the first half of 2014, the price of replacing a container were much lower than the amount requested by COSCO. Pursuant to

the provisions of Article 114 Paragraph 2 and Article 119 of the Contract Law of the People's Republic of China, where COSCO did not take positive measures to reduce loss, it is not entitled to compensation. In summary, judgment of first instance, of which the facts were clearly found and the law was correctly applied, should be maintained.

The Respondent Henan C&T did not submit defense.

The court finds that on July 25, 2013, Qingdao Finigate paid the document exchange fee to COSCO, and exchanged for the D/O. In addition to Henan C&T, the other parties of this case raised no objection to the facts found in judgment of first instance.

The other facts found by the court are consistent with the facts found in the judgment of first instance.

The court holds: this case is concerning dispute over a claim for container detention fee raised by the actual carrier due to carriage of goods by sea. The issues in this case are as follows: 1. whether Qingdao Finigate, Shanghai Finigate and Shenzhen Finigate should bear the container detention fee; and 2. whether Henan C&T should bear the container detention fee.

In respect of the issue whether Finigate Companies shall be liable, COSCO actually carried the goods involved, and issued a duplicate of No.3050 B/L but not original B/L. The consignee stated in the duplicate of No.3050 B/L Finigate Integrated Logistics Co., Ltd. was not registered in China, COSCO did not produce evidence to prove the legal relationship between the consignee and Finigate Companies. The address of the consignee recorded in the duplicate of No.3050 B/L is the same with that of Qingdao Finigate, and the email box published on the website of Finigate Integrated Logistics Co., Ltd. is the same with that admitted by Qingdao Finigate in the hearing. It cannot prove that Qingdao Finigate is the consignee who is entitled and obliged to timely take delivery of the goods from COSCO. Shanghai Finigate affixed its seal on the duplicate of No.3050 B/L, Qingdao Finigate exchanged for D/O against surrendering the duplicate to COSCO, there is no legal sense, the surrendering of the D/O by COSCO to Qingdao Finigate does not mean that Shanghai Finigate and Qingdao Finigate have the obligation for taking delivery of goods to COSCO. Shanghai Finigate and Qingdao Finigate are not the consignee who has the obligation for timely taking delivery of goods from the carrier as prescribed in the CMC, Huangdao Customs ordered to ship the goods back, their failure of taking delivery of the goods does not violate the law. In this case, the container detention fee generated as the shipper consigned solid waste prohibited from being imported by the state, and the goods could not clear the customs smoothly and timely, the claim of COSCO against Finigate Companies has no legal basis.

In respect of whether Henan C&T should undertake the container detention fee, as mentioned above, the shipper consigned improper goods, making the goods unable to clear the customs smoothly and timely, and resulting in the container detention fee. Henan C&T intended to buy qualified fuel oil, the goods could not clear the customs, it has no subjective fault in the container detention fee. Since

Henan C&T is the import declarer of the goods involved, Huangdao Customs issued a notice of return shipment order to Henan C&T, Henan C&T is the subject of administrative responsibility for return shipment of the goods involved. The allegation of COSCO that Henan C&T should bear the civil liability for the container detention fee on ground that it is the subject of administrative responsibility has no legal basis. Henan C&T did not constitute a civil infringement to COSCO.

In summary, the grounds of appeal of COSCO have no factual or legal basis, the court shall not support. The judgment of first instance found the facts clearly and the judgment shall be affirmed. According to Article 42 Paragraph 4 and Article 78 of the Maritime Code of the People's Republic of China, Article 144 and Article 170 Paragraph 1 Sub-paragraph 1 of the Civil Procedure Law of the People's Republic of China, the judgment is as follows:

Dismiss the appeal and affirm the original judgment.

Court acceptance fee of second instance in amount of RMB9,410 yuan, shall be born by COSCO Container Lines Co., Ltd.

The judgment is final.

Presiding Judge: ZHAO Tong
Acting Judge: WANG Lei
Acting Judge: FENG Yuhan

December 22, 2015

Clerk: ZHAO Fei

The Supreme People's Court of the People's Republic of China Civil Ruling

COSCO Container Lines Co., Ltd.
v.
Shenzhen Finigate Integrated Logistics Co., Ltd. Qingdao Branch et al.

(2016) Zui Gao Fa Min Shen No.2157

Related Case(s) This is the ruling of retrial, and the judgment of first instance and the judgment of second instance are on page 313 and page 324 respectively.

Cause(s) of Action 202. Dispute over contract of carriage of goods by sea or sea-connected waters.

Headnote The Supreme People's Court rejected ocean carrier's application for retrial and recognized lower courts' decisions that ocean carrier was not entitled to recover container detention fees from NVOCC and import agents after containers containing solid waste were refused entry to China at port of discharge.

Summary The Plaintiff carrier claimed container detention fees from the Defendants, freight forwarders, incurred as a result of the fact no one took delivery of the goods at the port of destination. The court of first instance held that the Plaintiff's claim failed. The court found that the Plaintiff could seek recourse against the shipper for shipping illicit goods, but that the other named the Defendants bore no liability regarding the container detention fee. On appeal, the appeal court recognized the lower court's judgment, and rejected the Plaintiff's arguments that Qingdao Finigate and Shanghai Finigate were liable for the charge because they breached their contract as consignees by failing to take delivery of the goods.

The Plaintiff applied to the Supreme People's Court for a retrial. The court recognized the lower courts' judgment and rejected the application for retrial.

Ruling

The Claimant of Retrial (the Defendant of first instance, the Appellant of second instance): COSCO Container Lines Co., Ltd.
Domicile: No. 378 Dongdaming Road, Shanghai.
Legal representative: YE Weilong, chairman.

Agent *ad litem*: ZHU Hailin, lawyer of Shandong Hailin & Co Law Firm.
Agent *ad litem*: LIUGuogang, lawyer of Shandong Hailin & Co Law Firm.

The Respondent (the Defendant of first instance, the Respondent of second instance): Shanghai Finigate Integrated Logistics Co., Ltd.
Domicile: 18G, No.2000, Pudong Avenue, Pudong New Area, Shanghai.
Legal representative: KUANG Xiaoqing, general manager.

The Defendant of first instance, the Respondent of second instance: Shenzhen Finigate Integrated Logistics Co., Ltd. Qingdao Branch.
Domicile: Room 1007, Building No.1, No.19 Zhangzhou Er Road, Shinan District, Qingdao, Shandong.
Person in charge: LIU Ziqi, manager.

The Defendant of first instance, the Respondent of second instance: Shenzhen Finigate Integrated Logistics Co., Ltd.
Domicile: Room 03, Floor 8, Guiyuan Street, Luohu District, Shenzhen, Guangdong.
Legal representative: KUANG Xiaoqing, director.

The Defendant of first instance, the Respondent of second instance: Henan Commerce & Trade Co., Ltd.
Domicile: Floor 12, Block B, Jinmao Building, No.115, Wenhua Road, Zhengzhou, Henan.
Legal representative: SUN Zhe, chairman.

With respect to the case arising from contract of carriage of goods by sea between the Claimant of Retrial, COSCO Container Lines Co., Ltd. (hereinafter referred to as COSCO), and the Respondent of Retrial, Shanghai Finigate Integrated Logistics Co., Ltd. (hereinafter referred to as Shanghai Finigate), the Defendants of first instance and the Respondents of second instance, Shenzhen Finigate Integrated Logistics Co., Ltd. Qingdao Branch, Shenzhen Finigate International Logistics Co., Ltd., Henan Commerce &Trade Co., Ltd., the Claimant of Retrial disagreed with the Shandong High People's Court (2015) Lu Min Si Zhong Zi No.152 Civil Judgment, and applied for retrial. The court formed a collegiate panel to investigate the case, now the case has been concluded.

COSCO claimed that: firstly, the court of second instance confirmed that Shanghai Finigate was not the consignee, which lacked evidence to prove. Shanghai Finigate clearly recognized it as the consignee designated by the shipper during the second-pleading defense and the court hearing. Secondly, the court of second instance confirmed that Shanghai Finigate should not be liable, which obviously violated laws. The fact that the goods involved could not be imported did not mean that they could not be taken delivery of. The consignee should take delivery of the goods in time for return shipment and avoid long-term occupation of the container. Shanghai Finigate failed to withdraw the goods in time after exchanging the bill of lading, so it should be liable for demurrage of container. It required the court to retry the case.

The court holds that, the case is the dispute over contract of carriage of goods by sea container overdue fee, the issue of review is whether Shanghai Finigate should be liable for container overdue fee involved.

Firstly, the facts of the transportation involved and the COPY of the bill of lading can prove the existence of the transportation contract between the shipper and COSCO under the COPY of the bill of lading. The fact that Shanghai Finigate exchanged the bill of lading with COSCO can also prove that it was the consignee who withdrew the goods under the transportation contract. However, according to the facts found in the original instance, there were two transportation contract relationships for the transportation of the goods involved: the contractual relationship of ocean freight transportation with COSCO as the actual carrier and the contract of lading transportation agreement with MTSLOGISTICS as NVOCC. MTSLOGISTICS issued original bill of lading for the transportation of the goods involved for trade circulation. In the contract of ocean freight transportation where COSCO was the actual carrier, COSCO did not issue the original bill of lading, but only issued a COPY bill of lading, recording that the shipper was T.E.A.MTRADE, consignee was Finigate Integrated Logistics Co., Ltd. Although Shanghai Finigate went through the procedures for exchanging the bill of lading, there is no evidence to prove that it has a contract of transportation relationship with COSCO, nor is it obligated to accept the contract of the consignee under the original bill of lading relationship in exchange for the bill of lading. In this case, Shanghai Finigate is only the person appointed by the shipper to take the goods at the port of destination in the transportation contract relationship certified by the COPY bill of lading. With regard to the breach of contract caused by the failure to return the containers in time under the transportation contract, the carrier COSCO should claim the rights of the opposite shipper according to the contract of the transportation contract. Shanghai Finigate should not be liable for paying COSCO the container overdue fee.

Secondly, the fee in the Maritime Code of the People's Republic of China Article 86 is fee caused when no one takes the goods at the port of discharge or the consignee delays or refuses to take delivery of the goods, the captain unloads the goods in the warehouse or other appropriate places. This provision cannot be the legal basis for Shanghai Finigate to bear the container overdue fee. So, the court of second instance judged that Shanghai Finigate should not be liable for the container overdue fee, which is not obviously inappropriate.

Pulling the threads together, the application for retrial of COSCO is not consistent with the situation provided by the Civil Procedure Law of the People's Republic of China Article 200. According to the Civil Procedure Law of the People's Republic of China Article 204 Paragraph 1, the Interpretation of the Supreme People's Court on the Application of the Civil Procedure Law of the People's Republic of China Article 395 Paragraph 2, the ruling is as follows:

Dismiss the application for retrial of COSCO Container Lines Co., Ltd.

Presiding Judge: HU Fang
Judge: LI Guishun
Acting Judge: ZHANG Kexin

December 26, 2016

Clerk: LI Na

Presiding Judge: HU Fang
Judge: LI Guixuan
Acting Judge: ZHANG Kuan

December 20, 2016

Clerk: LI Na

Xiamen Maritime Court
Civil Judgment

Daewoo Shipbuilding & Maritime Engineering Co., Ltd.
v.
Glory Advance Corporation

(2014) Xia Hai Fa Que Zi No.1

Related Case(s) None.

Cause(s) of Action 211. Dispute over ship mortgage contract.

Headnote Mortgagee recovers default judgment for unpaid mortgage payments, with first priority on proceeds of sale of ship at judicial auction.

Summary The Plaintiff sued the Defendant for breach of a ship mortgage contract on the ship M.V. "Glory Advance". The mortgage contract contained an arbitration clause providing that any disputes would be arbitrated in London. Because of the Defendant's default in making mortgage payments, the Plaintiff successfully made a claim in arbitration in London. The arbitrators' award in the Plaintiff's favor was ratified by the court at (2014) Xia Hai Fa Ren Zi No.13 and No.14, in order to establish its enforceability within the People's Republic of China. The Defendant did not appear in court in the present proceedings, which resulted in default judgment. M.V. "Glory Advance" was detained and auctioned by the court. The court held the Plaintiff to be entitled to the proceeds of the auction of M.V. "Glory Advance" with first priority.

Judgment

The Plaintiff: Daewoo Shipbuilding & Maritime Engineering Co., Ltd.
Domicile: No.125 Nandamen Road, Mid District, Seoul, Korea.
Legal representative: GAO Zaihao, representative director/president.
Agent *ad litem*: LI Rongcun, lawyer of Guangdong Jinghai Law Firm.
Agent *ad litem*: YANG Dongyang, lawyer of Guangdong Jinghai Law Firm.

The Defendant: Glory Advance Corporation.
Domicile: Salduba Building, Top Floor, 53rd East Street, Urbanization Obarrio, PO Box 7284, Panama 5, Republic of Panama.

With respect to the case arising from dispute over ship mortgage contract between the Plaintiff, Daewoo Shipbuilding & Maritime Engineering Co., Ltd. (hereinafter referred to as Daewoo Company), after registering its creditor's right in the court, and the Defendant, Glory Advance Corporation, the Plaintiff filed an action to confirm creditor's right before the court on December 23, 2013. After entertaining the case, the court organized the collegiate panel to hear this case. Since the relative facts of the case should be subject to the decision of London arbitration, the court ruled the suspension of the hearing. Later, the court recognized the subject London arbitral awards in (2014) Xia Hai Fa Ren Zi No.13 Civil Ruling and (2014) Xia Hai Fa Ren Zi No.14 Civil Ruling. On January 26, 2015, the court ruled to resume the hearing of the case, and held a hearing in public on March 10, 2015. LI Rongcun and YANG Dongyang, agents *ad litem* entrusted by the Plaintiff Daewoo Company appeared in court and participated in the proceedings; the Defendant, Glory Advance Corporation, after being summoned, refused to appear in court without justified reason, the court heard the case by default. Now the case has been concluded.

The Plaintiff Daewoo Company alleged that on December 1, 2006, H Elephant Corporation as the buyer, a party not involved in the case, signed the shipbuilding contract of M.V. "B Elephant" with it and whereafter signed the addendum No.1, addendum No.2 and addendum No.3 thereto, amending added price and payment period. The buyer under the shipbuilding contract was novated for twice and finally turned out to be Beta Elephant Inc. (hereinafter referred to as Beta Elephant), a party not involved in the case. On July 5, 2010, Beta Elephant as buyer, the Plaintiff as builder, and Noel Venture Limited (hereinafter referred to as Noel Company), a party not involved in the case, signed the addendum No.4, reaching an agreement on obligation and period of payment, afterwards the addendum No.5, agreeing M.V. "Glory Advance" owned by the Defendant as the object of mortgage for Noel Company's debt to guarantee the obligation of payment thereof.

On May 8, 2007, a party not involved in the case, K Elephant Corporation, as the buyer, signed the ship building contract of M.V. "A Elephant" with the Plaintiff, and signed the addendum No.1, addendum No.2 and addendum No.3 on revising the part of added cost and due date for payment. The buyer of shipbuilding contract changed twice and became a party not involved in the case, ALPHA Elephant Inc. (hereinafter referred to as Alpha Elephant Company). On July 5, 2010, Alpha Elephant Company as buyer, the Plaintiff as builder, and Noel Company, signed the addendum No.4, agreed on the payment obligation and due date for payment, then the three parties signed the addendum No.5, agreeing on the decision of considering the Defendant owned M.V. "Glory Advance" as the collateral of Noel Company's debt, to guarantee the fulfillment of the payment.

On July 29, 2011, the Defendant Glory Advance Corporation, as the owner of M.V. "Glory Advance", signed the mortgage contract with the Plaintiff, agreeing on the decision that, according to the shipbuilding contracts of M.V. "A Elephant" and M.V. "B Elephant", the debt of USD41,770,000 along with interests, which should be paid by Noel Company, enjoyed preferential compensation mortgage, and also conducted enrollment of initial hypotheca. The beneficiary of hypotheca was

Daewoo Company, which made the official and permanent enrollment of the preferential compensation mortgage afterwards.

As for the unliquidated fund of the shipbuilding contract of M.V. "B Elephant" and the shipbuilding contract of M.V. "A Elephant", the Plaintiff instituted the arbitration in London in pursuance of the agreement. Your honorable court ratified the validity of the two arbitrations. Due to the fact that M.V. "Glory Advance" was auctioned off, the requests of judgment were as below: 1. the Defendant should compensate for a loss of the Plaintiff with RMB58,700,000; 2. affirm that the Plaintiff enjoyed the priority of preferential compensation hypotheca of third party counterwork; 3. affirm that the Plaintiff had the right of receiving the preferential payments considered the auction fund of M.V. "Glory Advance"; 4. the Defendant should afford debt registration fee of RMB1,000, court acceptance fee, and all the expenses for the case.

In order to prove its claims, the Plaintiff Daewoo Company submitted the following evidential documents to the court:

Evidence 1, notarized shipbuilding contract of M.V. "B Elephant", addendum I, II and III, to prove that the Plaintiff signed the shipbuilding contract with H Elephant Corporation, agreeing on the relevant matters;

Evidence 2, notarized novation agreement and its Chinese translation version on January 18, 2010, to prove that the subject of buyer's building contract was changed from H Elephant Corporation to B Elephant Inc.;

Evidence 3, notarized contract subject change agreement dated February 3, 2010 and its Chinese translation version, to prove that the subject of contract was changed from B Elephant Inc. to Beta Elephant;

Evidence 4, notarized addendum No.4 to the shipbuilding contract of M.V. "B Elephant" and its translation, to prove that the three parties, Beta Elephant as buyer, the Plaintiff as builder, and Noel Company signed the addendums to the shipbuilding contract, agreeing on the decision that Noel Company should fulfill the obligation of payment by affording the second amount of deferred money of USD30,000,000 by 11 instalments, since one month from the delivery date of contract (June 30, 2010);

Evidence 5, Noel's cashier's cheque and its Chinese translation version, to prove that Noel Company provided 11 cashier's cheque to the Plaintiff to guarantee the punctual payment of each period, according to the obligation listed in the addendum No.4 to the shipbuilding contract of M.V. "B Elephant";

Evidence 6, notarized addendum No.5 to the shipbuilding contract of M.V. "B Elephant" and the Chinese translation version thereof, to prove that the three parties, Beta Elephant as buyer, the Plaintiff as builder, and Noel Company signed the addendum No.5 to the shipbuilding contract, and Noel Company guaranteed the fulfillment of debt and validity of the collateral provided;

Evidence 7, notarized shipbuilding contract of M.V. "A Elephant" and the addendum No.1,addendum No.2 and addendum No.3 thereto and the Chinese translation version thereof, to prove that the Plaintiff and K Elephant Corporation signed the shipbuilding contract and agreed on the its relative matters;

Evidence 8, notarized novation agreement dated January 18, 2010 and the Chinese translation version thereof, to prove that the subject of contract was changed from K Elephant Corporation to A Elephant Inc.;

Evidence 9, notarized novation agreement of M.V. "A Elephant" dated February 3, 2010 and the Chinese translated version thereof, to prove that the subject of contract is changed from A Elephant Inc. to Alpha Elephant Company;

Evidence 10, notarized addendum No.4 to the shipbuilding contract of M.V. "B Elephant" and the Chinese translation version thereof, to prove that A Elephant Company as buyer, the Plaintiff as builder, and Noel Company signed the addendum No.4 of shipbuilding contract, agreed on the decision that Noel Company should afford the second amount of deferred payment of USD30,000,000, by 11-period instalment since one month from the delivery date of contract (June 30, 2010);

Evidence 11, Noel's cashier's cheque and its Chinese translation version, to prove that Noel Company provided 11 cashier's cheque to the Plaintiff, to guarantee the punctual payment of each period, according to the obligation listed in the addendum No.4 of the shipbuilding contract of M.V. "A Elephant";

Evidence 12, notarized addendum No.5 to the shipbuilding contract of M.V. "A Elephant" and the Chinese translation version thereof, to prove that Alpha Elephant Company as buyer, the Plaintiff as builder, and Noel Company signed the addendum No.5 to the shipbuilding contract. Alpha Elephant Company and Noel Company guaranteed the fulfillment of the payment and validity of the collateral provided;

Evidence 13, notarized mortgage preliminary registration certificate and the Chinese translation version thereof, to prove the Defendant (the owner of M.V. "Glory Advance") signed the mortgage contract, agreed on the second amount of deferred payment of USD41,770,000, along with interest, budget and fees enjoying preferential compensation mortgage and payment of M.V. "Glory Advance", and attended to the registration of preliminary mortgage at the flag country of M.V. "Glory Advance", Panama Mortgage Registration Authority, according to the shipbuilding contract of "B Elephant" and M.V. "A Elephant";

Evidence 14, notarized permanent registration certificate of preferential compensation mortgage and its Chinese translation version, to prove that General Administration of Public Registration of Ship Selling and Property of the Republic of Panama, made formal registration of the preferential compensation mortgage of M.V. "Glory Advance";

Evidence 15, notarization of M.V. "Glory Advance" and certificate of property, and their Chinese translation version, to prove that the owner of M.V. "Glory Advance" was the Defendant, and the preferential compensation mortgage enjoyed by the Plaintiff registered in detailed list;

Evidence 16, the email reminder from the Plaintiff and unqualified specifications and its Chinese translation version, to prove that the eighth and eleventh amount of money since January 1, 2012, was liquidate at the expiration of tenure though reminded by the Plaintiff repeatedly. As November 22, 2013, the second deferred instalment of M.V. "B Elephant" and M.V. "A Elephant"; the indebtedness of capital and interest each reached USD22,102,719, in total of USD44,205,438;

Evidence 17, the civil ruling paper of (2013) Xia Hai Fa Deng Zi No.34, to prove that the Plaintiff, as the person who enjoyed the preferential compensation mortgage of the ship, already applied for the credit registration to the court, and was authorized by the court on December 23, 2013;

Evidence 18, notarized arbitral award of dispute over shipbuilding contract and its Chinese translation version, to prove that on May 13, 2014, the arbitrator John Colin Sheppard decided that Noel Company should pay the Plaintiff capital and interest of USD20,885,000;

Evidence 19, notarized arbitral award of dispute over shipbuilding contract and its Chinese translation version, to prove that on May 13, 2014, the arbitration John Colin Sheppard decided that Noel Company should pay the Plaintiff capital and interest of USD20,885,000;

Evidence 20, the civil ruling paper of (2014) Xia Hai Fa Ren Zi No.13, to prove that the arbitration award was ratified by the court; and.

Evidence 21, the civil ruling paper of (2014) Xia Hai Fa Ren Zi No.14, to prove that the arbitration award was ratified by the court.

The Defendant, Glory Advance Company, did not plead or submit evidential documents. Though the Defendant was summoned to the court, it failed to appear in court without justified reasons.

After the trial's investigation, the court made following analysis and recognition of the Defendant's evidence:

Evidence 1-6, 8-10, 12-15 and 18-19 are all verified and notarized copies of the originals, and the court recognizes its probative force;

Evidence 5,11 and 16 are copies though, they can mutually confirmed each other and form the evidence chain, and the court recognizes their probative force;

Evidence 17, 20-21, are effective judging documents made by the court according to law, and the court recognizes its probative force.

According to the analysis and recognition of the evidence, and combined with the trial record of this case, the facts found out by the court are as follows:

On December 1, 2006, a party not involved in the case, H Elephant Corporation as buyer, signed the shipbuilding contract of M.V. "B Elephant" (hull number: 5327, oil tanker, with carrying capacity of 317,000t) with the Plaintiff, the cost of shipbuilding was USD132,300,000. Later, the two parties signed the addendum I, II and III on December 1, 2006, March 2, 2007 and November 28, 2008, agreeing on revising the part of added cost and due date of payment. On January 18, 2010, the buyer under the shipbuilding contract was novated from H Elephant Corporation to B Elephant Inc., a party not involved in the case, and on February 3, 2010, from H Elephant Corporation to B Elephant Inc., a party not involved in the case. On July 5 of the same year, Beta Elephant as buyer, the Plaintiff as builder, and a party not involved in the case, Noel Company, signed the addendum No.4, agreeing on the decision that Noel Company should afford the second amount of deferred payment of USD30,000,000, and fulfill the obligation of payment by 11-period instalment, since one month after the delivery date (June 20, 2010) of the contract. On July 5 of the same year, Noel Company provided 11 cashier's cheque to the Plaintiff, to guarantee the punctual payment of each period. On July 29, 2011, Beta Elephant as buyer, the Plaintiff as builder, and Noel Company, signed the addendum No.5, Beta Elephant and Noel Company guaranteed the fulfillment of debt and the validity of the collateral provided, and agreed that the Defendant set preferential compensation mortgage right for the Plaintiff on M.V. "Glory Advance", to guarantee Noel Company's fulfillment of payment obligation of the second amount of money. According to Article 13 of the shipbuilding contract, the relative Article of conflict and arbitration and addendum; the dispute over shipbuilding contract should be submitted to London arbitration. Arbitration Act 1996 of the United Kingdom or its effective revised version, and the rule of London Maritime Arbitrator Association were applicable for arbitration.

On May 8, 2007, K Elephant Corporation as buyer, signed the shipbuilding contract of M.V. "Glory Advance" (hull number: 5330, an oil tanker with carrying capacity of 317,000t) with the Plaintiff, the shipbuilding cost was USD132,300,000. On the same day, the two parties signed the addendum I and II, and on November 28, 2008, the signed addendum III, revised the part of added cost and due date of payment. On January 18, 2010, the buyer under the shipbuilding contract was novated from K Elephant Corporation to A Elephant Inc.. On February 3, the buyer under shipbuilding contract was novated from A Elephant Inc. to Beta Elephant. On July 5 in the same year, Alpha Elephant Company as buyer, the Plaintiff as builder, and Noel Company, signed the addendum No.4, agreed on the decision that Noel Company should afford the second amount of deferred payment of USD30,000,000 to fulfill the obligation of payment, by 11-period instalment, from one month after the delivery date (June 30, 2010) of the contract. On July 5 in the same year, Noel Company provided 11 cashier's cheque to the Plaintiff, to guarantee the punctual payment of each period.

On July 29, 2011, Alpha Elephant Company as buyer, the Plaintiff as builder, and Noel company signed the addendum No.5, Alpha Elephant Company and Noel Company guaranteed the payment of debt and the validity of collateral provided, and all parties agreed on the decision that the Defendant should set the right of preferential compensation mortgage of M.V. "Glory Advance" for the Plaintiff, to guarantee Noel Company's fulfillment of payment obligation of the second amount of money. according to Article 13 of the shipbuilding contract, relative Articles of conflict and arbitration and addendum, the dispute over shipbuilding contract should be submitted to London arbitration. The Arbitration Act 1996 of the United Kingdom or its effective revised version, and the rule of London Maritime Arbitrators Association are applicable for arbitration.

On July 29, 2011, the Plaintiff and the Defendant signed the mortgage contract, agreeing on the second amount of deferred payment of USD41,770,000, along with interest, budget and fees enjoyed preferential compensation mortgage and payment of M.V. "Glory Advance", and attended to the registration of preliminary mortgage at the flag country of M.V. "Glory Advance", Panama Mortgage Registration Authority, according to the shipbuilding contracts of M.V. "B Elephant" and M.V. "A Elephant". According to the Article 19's law and administration of Article of mortgage contract, this mortgage contract, along with its derived or relative non-contractual liability, should be subject to and interpreted by law of the Republic of Panama.

On August 24, 2011, General Administration of Public Registration of Ship Selling and Property of the Republic of Panama, made formal registration of preferential compensation mortgage of M.V. "Glory Advance".

After Noel Company's payment of 7 amount of money engaged in two contracts, it did not defray any period payment. In allusion of Beta Elephant, Alpha Elephant Company and Noel Company's non-payment of debt, the Plaintiff submitted the arbitration in London, according to the Article listed in the shipbuilding contract and its addendum, aiming at the delinquent account of Noel Company. On May 13, 2014, sole arbitrator John Colin Sheppard provided the award with regards to the delinquent account, judged that:

The Plaintiff should claim an indemnity of USD20,885,000 to Noel Company, and win the case by claiming the indemnity of four amount of interest, accumulated from the 8th to 11th period of the second amount of deferred account (the total amount were USD617,500, USD520,000, USD422,500 and USD325,000), in proportion and annual interest rate 10%. The four amount of compound interest's accounting should start from the due date of each period of instalment, of the second amount of deferred account, till the actual interest was defrayed.

On October 13, 2014, the Plaintiff submitted an application, referring to the two London arbitrations to the court to ratify their validity. Through the investigation, the court, by issuing Civil Rulings (2014) Xia Hai Fa Ren Zi No.13 and No.14, ratified the two London arbitrations to be legislative validity within the territory of the People's Republic of China.

In addition, the court ascertains that: M.V. "Glory Advance' was detained by the court, due to the case (2013) Xia Hai Fa Shang Chu Zi No.201 with respect to the dispute over service assignment, among Xiamen Hailong Labor Export Corporation, Glory Advance Corporation and Nuosi Ship Administration Private Co., Ltd.. On December 6, 2013, the court auctioned off the detained M.V. "Glory Advance" of RMB58,700,000. During the duration of the auction's publication, the Plaintiff applied for the claim registration of RMB256,384,260 (USD41,770,000 with exchange rate of 6.1380:1), and was authorized by the court in December 13, 2013.

The court holds that, the Plaintiff Daewoo Company and the Defendant Glory Advance Corporation are both overseas legal person of the People's Republic of China, the flag state of M.V. "Glory Advance" is the Republic of Panama, therefore, this case is a dispute over ship mortgage with overseas affairs. M.V. "Glory Advance" was detained and auctioned by the court according to law, according to the Special Maritime Procedure Law of the People's Republic of China Article 19, the court has jurisdiction to the case. The Plaintiff instituted legal proceeding to the court after the registration of the claims, according to Article 116 of the Special Maritime Procedure Law of the People's Republic of China, this case is an action of affirming rights. As for the applicable laws to the case, the law of the Republic of Panama is applicable for the mortgage contract between the Plaintiff and the Defendant. According to Article 4 and Article 41 of the Law of the People's Republic of China the Applicaiton of Law for Foreign-related Civil Relations of, the law of the Republic of Panama is applicable for investigation of two parties' mortgage contract.

As for the ascertainment of law of the Republic of Panama, the Plaintiff provided notarized Maritime Law of the Republic of Panama (the 5th Version of 2008), and the latest revised Articles. According to Article 260, the mortgage contract of shipbuilding is permitted to be notarized and signed outside Panama's territory, and it should contain mortgagee's name, domicile, collateral account, capital, deadline for performance of security interest, and contract interest, etc., and Article 244 stipulates that the ship mortgage is the priority of compensation. According to the legislation of Panama above, the ship mortgage enjoys the priority since the registration date, the registered mortgage enjoys priority of mortgaged ship within the account of unliquidated ship collateral (interest included).

The initial and permanent certification of mortgage registration, the ship ownership and encumbrance certification submitted by the Plaintiff, proved that the Plaintiff's mortgage proposition was registered according to law of the Republic of Panama. According to its law, the mortgage is effective, and owns the validity of preferential compensation for mortgaged ship. Due to the fact that mortgage guaranteed claims of Plaintiff's proposition is expired, and with the support of the validity ratified by London arbitration and the court's arbitration within the territory of China, the request of preferential compensation of action funds of M.V. "Glory Advance" made by the Plaintiff, shall be supported.

With regard to the mortgage account requested to be realized, the Plaintiff's claim was the proceeds of auction of RMB58,700,000, below the registered creditor amount. The court holds that the Plaintiff's positive decrease of the proceeds of auction was self-disposition, which shall be permitted. The registration creditor fee of RMB1,000 advocated by the Plaintiff is indispensable for claims' realizing the rights of creditor, which shall be supported. As the proposition of legal fee is out of the range, and the mortgage realizing fee could not be proved, the court does not support it.

Pulling the threads together, according to Articles 4 and 41 of the Law of the Application of Law for Foreign-related Civil Relations of the People's Republic of China, Paragraph 1 of Article 64 and Article 144 of the Civil Procedure Law of the

People's Republic of China, and Article 116 of the Special Maritime Procedure Law of the People's Republic of China, the judgment is as follows:

1. The Defendant Glory Advance Corporation shall compensate the Plaintiff Daewoo Shipbuilding & Marine Engineering Co.,Ltd. RMB58,700,000, the Plaintiff shall enjoy the right to be recovered from the mortgage charged on M. V. "Glory Advance" in first priority within the sum of RMB58,700,000, the Plaintiff is entitled to the proceeds of the action of M.V. "Glory Advance";
2. The Defendant Glory Advance Corporation shall pay the claim registration fee in sum of RMB1,000 to the Plaintiff Daewoo Shipbuilding & Marine Engineering Co., Ltd; and
3. Reject the other claims of the Plaintiff.

Court acceptance fee in amount of RMB335,305, shall be born by the Defendant Glory Advance Corporation.

The judgment is final.

Presiding Judge: LI Hong
Acting Judge: WANG Yan
Acting Judge: ZHANG Wei

May 12, 2015

Clerk: LI Hui

Appendix: Relevant Law

1. **Law of the People's Republic of China on Choice of Law for Foreign-related Civil Relationships**

Article 4 If there are mandatory provisions on foreign-related civil relations in the laws of the People's Republic of China, these mandatory provisions shall directly apply.

Article 41 The parties concerned may choose the laws applicable to contracts by agreement. If the parties do not choose, the law at the habitual residence of the party whose fulfillment of obligations can best reflect the characteristics of this contract or other laws which have the closest relation with this contract shall apply.

2. **Civil Procedure Law of the People's Republic of China**

Article 64 It is the duty of a party to an action to provide evidence in support of his allegations.

Article 41 If the Defendant, having been served with a summons, refuses to appear in court without justified reasons, or if he withdraws during a court session without the permission of the court, the court may make a judgment by default.

3. Special Maritime Procedure Law of the People's Republic of China

Article 116 Where any other evidence for maritime claims is provided, the creditors shall, after registering the creditors' rights, bring an action for affirming rights in the maritime court entertaining the registration of creditors' rights. Where the parities conclude an arbitration agreement, that shall promptly apply for arbitration.

The judgment and order made by the maritime court on an action for affirming rights shall be legally effective, the parties shall not file an appeal.

Wuhan Maritime Court
Civil Judgment

Export–Import Bank of China et al.
v.
Nanjing Wujiazui Ship Building Co., Ltd. et al.

(2014) Wu Hai Fa Shang Chu Zi No.00470

Related Case(s) None.

Cause(s) of Action 207. Dispute over shipbuilding contract.

Headnote The Plaintiff banks held entitled to recover on loan to purchaser of a newly-built ship; Defendant shipbuilder held not entitled to withhold delivery of completed ship from purchaser by reason only of purchaser's transfer of its rights under shipbuilding contract to banks in order to obtain the loan.

Summary After entering into a shipbuilding contract, Defendant shipbuilder was to deliver the completed vessel to Defendant purchaser. Defendant purchaser then applied for a loan from the two Plaintiffs. Plaintiff bank filed suit after nondelivery of the vessel to Defendant purchaser. Defendant shipbuilder argued that Defendant purchaser did not have its permission to transfer its rights under the shipbuilding contract to Plaintiff banks, making the transaction between Defendant purchaser and the two Plaintiffs invalid. The court found that the shipbuilding contract stipulated that Defendant purchaser had the right to transfer its rights under the contract to a bank in order to obtain funding, unless Defendant shipbuilder had a valid reason for refusal. Accordingly, the loan contract was valid and enforceable between the Defendants and the Plaintiffs. Defendant shipbuilder was obligated to deliver the vessel to Defendant purchaser.

Judgment

The Plaintiff: Export–Import Bank of China.
Domicile: No.30 at Fu Xing Men Nei Street, Xicheng District, Beijing.
Legal representative: LI Ruogu, president of the bank.
Agent *ad litem*: WANG Pei, lawyer of Hubei Hua Jun& Co. Law Firm.
Agent *ad litem*: ZHANG Jianhao, lawyer of Hubei Hua Jun & Co. Law Firm.

The Plaintiff: China Construction Bank Co., Ltd.Guangzhou Liwan Branch.
Domicile: No.304, Zhongshan Seven Road, Liwan District, Guangzhou, Guangdong Province.
Legal representative: ZHANG Yiping, president of the bank.
Agent *ad litem*: LI Malin, lawyer of Shanghai All Bright (Nanjing) Law Offices.
Agent *ad litem*: CHEN Liang, lawyer of Shanghai All Bright (Nanjing) Law Offices.

The Defendant: Nanjing Wujiazui Ship Building Co., Ltd.
Domicile: Dongjiang, Baguazhou Town, Qixia District, Nanjing, Jiangsu Province.
Legal representative: HANG Heshui, general manager.
Agent *ad litem*: HE Haijun, lawyer of Jiangsu Suyuan Law Firm.

The Defendant: Guangdong Lanhai Shipping Co., Ltd.
Domicile: Room 19B, No.128, Lujing Road, Yuexiu District, Guangzhou, Guangdong Province.
Legal representative: LAN Wenbin, general manager.
Agent *ad litem*: ZHANG Ling, company's employee.

With respect to the case arising from dispute over shipbuilding contract, the Plaintiff, Export–Import Bank of China (hereinafter referred to as "EIBC") filed an action against the Defendants, Nanjing Wujiazui Ship Building Co., Ltd. (hereinafter referred to as "Wujiazui Company") and Guangdong Lanhai Shipping Co., Ltd. (hereinafter referred to as "Lanhai Company"), with China Construction Bank Co., Ltd. Guangzhou Liwan Branch (hereinafter referred to as "CCB Liwan") being the third party, before the court on February 24, 2014. CCB Liwan applied for participating in the case as the co-Plaintiff on April 11, 2014. The court permitted its application according to law. The case was arising from disputes over shipbuilding contract, which was under the special jurisdiction of maritime court. The domicile of the Defendant and Nanjing, Jiangsu Province where the contract was performed was within the jurisdiction of the court. As was provided for in Article 23 of the Civil Procedure Law of the People's Republic of China, the court had the jurisdiction over the case. The court, after entertaining the case, organized the collegiate panel consisting of Judge HOU Wei as Presiding Judge, Judge ZHOU Yanhua and Acting Judge DENG Yi, and held two hearings in public respectively on August 27, 2014 and on January 7, 2015. WANG Pei, agent *ad litem* of the Plaintiff EIBC, LI Malin, agent *ad litem* of the Plaintiff CCB Liwan together with HE Haijun, agent *ad litem* of the Defendant Wujiazui Company appeared in court to attend to trial. In the first hearing, ZHANG Ling, agent *ad litem* of the Defendant Lanhai Company, appeared in court and participated in the action. In the second hearing, the Defendant Lanhai Company refused to appear in court without proper reason after being legally summoned by the court. The court tried this case by default according to the law. Now the case has been concluded. The court, according to the application for pre-litigation preservation of property by the Plaintiff EIBC, arrested M.V. "LANHAI KUAYUE" (hull No: YC012) in the factory of the Defendant Wujiazui Company on January 7, 2014.

The Plaintiff EIBC and CCB Liwan jointly alleged that on November 16, 2006, the Defendants Wujiazui Company and Lanhai Company signed *79600t Bulk Shipbuilding Contract* numbered with WJZ2006-YC012 (hereinafter referred to as "shipbuilding contract"). The contract stipulated that the Defendant Wujiazui Company should build, sell and deliver a bulk carrier (hull No: YC012) to the Defendant Lanhai Company. On June 21, 2011, the Defendant Lanhai Company applied for syndicated loan from the Plaintiff EIBC and CCB Liwan so as to build the above mentioned ship and signed (2011) Li Ji Jian Dai No.003 *Syndicated Loan Contract*. On November 27, 2012, the Defendant Wujiazui Company and the Defendant Lanhai Company signed the delivery documents and confirmed that the Defendant Wujiazui Company had officially transferred all rights and interests related to M.V. "LANHAI KUAYUE" (the above mentioned bulk carrier, (hull No: YC012) to the Defendant Lanhai Company. Thereafter, in order to guarantee the rights of the two Plaintiffs in the above mentioned loan contract, the Defendant Lanhai Company signed *Transfer Agreement of the Ship under Construction* with the two Plaintiffs on December 31, 2012. The contract stipulated that the Defendant Lanhai Company should transfer its rights related to the above mentioned shipbuilding contract and relative documents (including but not limiting to the rights that the two Plaintiffs could, in their own name, require the Defendant Wujiazui Company to deliver the ship) to the two Plaintiffs and inform the Defendant Wujiazui Company of the relative facts of transfer in written. The Defendant Wujiazui Company and the Defendant Lanhai Company signed the relative delivery documents. Therefore, the condition for the delivery of M.V. "LANHAI KUAYUE" had been satisfied. The Plaintiff Lanhai Company should transfer the rights of *Bulk Shipbuilding Contract* and relative documents to the two Plaintiffs and was also responsible for delivering the ship. The two Plaintiffs now filed an action before the court and requested a judgment to sentence: 1. confirm that *Transfer Agreement of the Ship under Construction* numbered with (2012) Li Zhuan Xie No.001 and addendum No.1 thereto, *Notification on Transfer of the Shipbuilding Contract* signed by the two Defendants were legal and valid; 2. the two Defendants should deliver M.V. "LANHAI KUAYUE" to the Plaintiff EIBC immediately; 3. the Defendant should compensate the two Plaintiffs for damages of delay in delivery in amount of RMB5.4 million (hereinafter referred to as RMB) and the interests thereon; and 4. the two Defendants were liable to pay all litigation costs in this case. Afterwards, the Plaintiffs applied for withdrawn of the third claim, the court permitted that in light of law.

The Defendant Wujiazui Company contended that the Defendant Wujiazui Company did receive *Notification on Transfer of the Shipbuilding Contract*, but they did not confirm the content of *Transfer Agreement of the Ship under Construction*. The Defendant Wujiazui Company would without prejudice deliver the ship involved according to the judgment made by court; on the premise of having signed the delivery documents between the two Defendants, the two Plaintiffs informed the Defendant Wujiazui Company in written that the ship should not be delivered to Lanhai Company. As a result, the dispute arose from such failure of actual delivery. Therefore, the two Plaintiffs and the Defendant Lanhai Company should bear the litigation fee.

The Defendant Lanhai Company contended that *Transfer Agreement of the Ship under Construction* did not transfer the ownership of the ship involved, so the two Plaintiffs had no right to require the Defendant Wujiazui Company to deliver the ship.

In order to support its litigation, the Plaintiff EIBC submitted the following evidence to the court within the evidence producing term:

1. The original document of *79600t Bulk Shipbuilding Contract* No. WJ2006-YC012. It proved that there existed contractual relationship between the two Defendants about the ship building. The Plaintiff CCB Liwan and the two Defendants had no objection to authenticity, relevancy and legality of the evidence.
2. The original document of (2011) Li Ji Jian Dai No.003 *Syndicated Loan Contract*. It proved that there existed contractual relationship among the Defendant Lanhai Company and the two Plaintiffs about financial loan. The Plaintiff CCB Liwan and the two Defendants had no objection to authenticity, relevancy and legality of the evidence.
3. The original documents of *Transfer Agreement of the Ship under Construction* and its attachment. It proved that the Defendant Lanhai Company transferred rights and interests covered by ship building contract and relative documents to the two Plaintiffs and informed the Defendant Wujiazui Company in written form. The Plaintiff CCB Liwan had no objection to authenticity of the evidence. The Defendant Wujiazui Company had no objection to authenticity of the evidence and confirmed that Wujiazui Company did receive the agreement, but did not confirm the contents of the agreement. The Defendant Lanhai Company challenged authenticity of the evidence and did not recognize the signature and seal on the agreement and its attachment. Lanhai Company also pointed out that the date was not filled in the addendum No.1.
4. The original certificates of telegraphic transfer (four phases in total). It proved that the Defendant Lanhai Company had performed the contract to pay the Defendant Wujiazui Company money for four phases of ship building. The Plaintiff CCB Liwan and the two Defendants had no objection to authenticity, relevancy and legality of the evidence.
5. The original advice of No.201106-3 and No.2011 06-4 drawing by agent and the original notifications of adding account. It proved that the Plaintiff EIBC had transferred RMB26.5 million to the Plaintiff CCB Liwan's account respectively on December 21, 2011 and on March 8, 2012, after receiving the notification from the Plaintiff CCB Liwan. The Plaintiff CCB Liwan and the two Defendants had no objection to authenticity, relevancy and legality of the evidence.
6. The original agent standing book. It proved that the Plaintiff EIBC made the payment with two loans received on December 21, 2011 and on March 8, 2012 for the third and fourth phases of ship building fee involved. The Plaintiff CCB Liwan and the two Defendants had no objection to authenticity, relevancy and legality of the evidence.

7. The original documents of information inquiry for ship identification number. It proved that the ship involved was called M.V. "LANHAI KUAYUE"(hull No: YC012). The Plaintiff CCB Liwan and the two Defendants had no objection to authenticity, relevancy and legality of the evidence.
8. The original *Complementary Agreement on Syndicated Loan*. It proved that the Plaintiff EIBC took the loan of RMB159 million under *Syndicated Loan Contract*. The Plaintiff CCB Liwan and the two Defendants had no objection to authenticity, relevancy and legality of the evidence.
9. The original document for delivery. it proved that the Defendant Wujiazui Company had transferred all rights related to the ship involved. The Plaintiff CCB Liwan and the two Defendants had no objection to authenticity, relevancy and legality of the evidence.

According to the evidence having been ascertained, the court considers that the evidence presented by the Plaintiff EIBC are original documents, though the Defendant Lanhai Company challenged the authenticity of the evidence, Lanhai Company was unable to submit evidence to the contrary. Besides, the Defendant Wujiazui Company confirmed that the evidence was actually received. Therefore, the court recognizes the evidence. The Plaintiff CCB Liwan and the two Defendants had no objection to authenticity of other evidence submitted by the Plaintiff EIBC, so the court admits all the evidence submitted by the Plaintiff EIBC.

In order to support its claim, the Plaintiff CCB Liwan submitted the following evidence to the court within the evidence producing term:

1. No.2010 Li Ji Jian Dai No.001 *Fixed Assets Loan Contract* and its attachment, (2010) Yue Sui Guang Zheng Nei Jing Zi notarial certificate No.39098. On July 26, 2012, the third party Guangdong Lanyue Energy Development Co., Ltd. (hereinafter referred to as "Lanyue Company") presented original documents including *Specification* and *Modification Agreement on RMB Loan*. It proved that there existed debtor-creditor relationship between the Plaintiff CCB Liwan and the Defendant Lanhai Company. The Plaintiff EIBC had no objection to authenticity, legality and relevancy of the evidence. The two Defendants had no objection to authenticity of the evidence, but challenged the relevancy of the evidence.
2. Notification of loan indexes evaluation and certificates of loan transferring deposit. The number of these documents is 11 respectively. All these documents are original. The fact that the Plaintiff CCB Liwan lent RMB483.7876 million loan was proved here. The Plaintiff EIBC and the two Defendants had no objection to authenticity, relevancy and legality of the evidence.
3. *Notification of Collection for Overdue Loan (Advances)* and notarization. It proved the fact that the Plaintiff CCB Liwan collected debts from the Defendant Lanhai Company. The Plaintiff EIBC and the two Defendants had no objection to authenticity, relevancy and legality of the evidence.

According to the evidence having been ascertained, the court considers that the Plaintiff EIBC and the two Defendants have no objection to authenticity of the above mentioned evidence. Therefore, the court recognizes the evidence. The evidence can be regarded as basis for the settlement of this case.

In order to support its defense, the Defendant Wujiazui Company submitted the following evidence to the court:

1. The original *M.V. "LANHAI KUAYUE" 79600t Bulk Carrier Delivery Document*. It proved that the Defendant Wujiazui Company had performed the obligation of the contract signed with the Defendant Lanhai Company. The Plaintiff EIBC had no objection to authenticity of the evidence, but challenged the contents that evidence proved. The Plaintiff CCB Liwan could not confirm authenticity of the evidence. The Defendant Lanhai Company had objection to authenticity of the evidence.
2. The original *Letter of Advice for not Delivering the Ship YC012 and YC013*. It proved that the Plaintiff CCB Liwan had negotiated with Wujiazui Company and required that Wujiazui Company should not deliver the ship to the Defendant Lanhai Company. After several failures of registration for mortgage of ships under construction, the Plaintiff CCB Liwan signed the right transfer agreement with the Defendant Lanhai Company. When the Defendant Lanhai Company requested for taking over the ship for several times, the Plaintiff CCB Liwan sent the notification of no delivery. Besides, the Defendant Lanhai Company did not pay the final payment for the fifth phase, which caused the failure of round-off work. Therefore, the Defendant Wujiazui Company was not responsible for the delay of the delivery. The two Plaintiffs had no objection to authenticity of the evidence. The Defendant Lanhai Company had no objection to authenticity of the evidence, but challenged the purpose of evidence and considered that the Defendant Wujiazui Company was responsible for breach of the contract.
3. *79600t Bulk Shipbuilding Contract* No.WJZ2006-YC012. It proved that the Plaintiff had no right to require the Defendant Wujiazui Company to bear the responsibility for breach of the contract. The Plaintiff EIBC, CCB Liwan and the Defendant Lanhai Company had no objection to authenticity, relevancy and legality of the evidence.

According to the evidence having been ascertained, the court considers that above mentioned evidence submitted by the Defendant Wujiazui Company can be regarded as basis for the settlement of this case, since the two Plaintiffs and the Defendant Lanhai Company had no objection to authenticity of evidence No.2 and No.3. Although the Plaintiff CCB Liwan cannot confirm the authenticity of the evidence No.1, it cannot provide the evidence to the contrary. Besides, the Plaintiff EIBC and the Defendant Lanhai Company had no objection to evidence. Therefore, the court recognizes the probative evidence and the evidence can be regarded as basis for the settlement of this case.

In order to support its defense, the Defendant Lanhai Company submitted the following evidence to the court:

1. The original (2011) Sui Zhong Fa Min Chu Zi No.22 Civil Judgment. It proved that the third party Lanyue Company, as creditor, had its debt rights on the Defendant Wujiazui Company, which was true and valid. The two Plaintiffs and the Defendant Wujiazui Company had no objection to the authenticity, relevancy and legality of the evidence.
2. The original *Letter of Notification*. It proved that Lanyue Company had transferred partly the creditor's right in the evidence 1 to the Defendant Lanhai Company. The two Plaintiffs and the Defendant Wujiazui Company had no objection to the authenticity, relevancy and legality of the evidence.
3. The original *M.V. "LANHAI KUAYUE" Delivery Memorandum*. It proved that signing the document of M.V. "LANHAI KUAYUE" delivery could not be regarded as the completion of actual delivery. The two Plaintiffs and the Defendant Wujiazui Company had no objection to the authenticity, relevancy and legality of the evidence.
4. *Delivery, Payment and Repayment Memorandum of Understanding*. It proved that two Defendants had reached complementary agreement on payment for the fifth phase of M.V. "LANHAI KAUYUE" building. The two Plaintiffs and the Defendant Wujiazui Company had no objection to the authenticity, relevancy and legality of the evidence.

According to the evidence having been ascertained, the court considers that above mentioned evidence submitted by the Defendant Lanhai Company can be regarded as basis for the settlement of this case, since the two Plaintiffs and the Defendant Wujiazui Company had no objection to authenticity of above mentioned evidence.

According to the evidence submitted by the Plaintiff and the Defendant, cross-examination and the confirming opinions of the court, combined with the investigation by the court, the court finds out the following facts:

On November 16, 2006, the Defendant Lanhai Company signed *79600t Bulk Shipbuilding Contract* (No.WJZ2006-YC012) with the Defendant Wujiazui Company.

The contract stipulates that:

1. The Defendant Wujiazui Company should build, sell and deliver 79600t bulk carrier (hull No.YC012). The payment for ship-building is RMB223 million at the beginning stage. The Defendant Lanhai Company shall pay money to the Defendant Wujiazui Company in five installments. And the currency should be RMB. For the first stage payment, the Defendant Lanhai Company should pay RMB44.6 million within 90 days after the two companies sign the contract and the Defendant Lanhai Company receives the valid receipt voucher, payment notification and the refund guarantee that covers the first stage payment and its interests sent by the Defendant Wujiazui Company. For the second stage payment, the Defendant Lanhai Company should pay RMB44.6 million after the Defendant Wujiazui Company starts to build the ship involved and within 10 days after the Defendant Lanhai Company receives start-building certificate

issued by Classification Society as well as the valid receipt voucher, payment notification and the refund guarantee that covers the second stage payment and its interests sent by the Defendant Wujiazui Company. For the third payment stage, the Defendant Lanhai Company should pay RMB44.6 million after the ship involved is on the slipway in its first section and within 10 days after the Defendant Lanhai Company received the certificate of being on the slipway issued by Classification Society as well as the valid receipt voucher, payment notification from buyer and the refund guarantee that covers the third stage payment and its interests sent by the Defendant Wujiazui Company. For the fourth payment stage, the Defendant Lanhai Company should pay RMB44.6 million after the ship involved is launched into water and within 10 days after the Defendant Lanhai Company receives the certificate of being launched into water issued by Classification Society as well as the valid receipt voucher, payment notification and the refund guarantee that covers the fourth stage payment and its interests sent by the Defendant Wujiazui Company. For the fifth stage payment, the Defendant Lanhai Company should pay RMB44.6 million and other add and subtraction account related to relative clauses of the contract at the delivery of the ship involved. It is due payment.
2. The Defendant Wujiazui Company should deliver the safely afloat ship involved to the Defendant Lanhai Company before or on August 30, 2011 on the condition that the ship should meet all the requirements of technical specification, obtain all the certifications of the Classification Society and the jurisdictional agency, succeed in trial trip or the second trial trip and get the confirmation of taking over the ship from the Defendant Lanhai Company. The exchange of the delivery protocol between the two parties shows completion of the delivery and the delivery thus comes into force. Meanwhile, the ownership of the ship and risk is also transferred to the Defendant Lanhai Company from the Defendant Wujiazui Company. 30 days before the delivery, the Defendant Wujiazui Company shall inform the Defendant Lanhai Company of the delivery time and inform the Defendant Lanhai Company in written form the determined time of delivery 7 days or 3 days before the delivery.
3. No party shall transfer the contract to any individuals, groups, companies and associations without permission of the other parties. The Defendant Lanhai Company has the right to transfer the contract to its financial bank for the sake of fund and the Defendant Wujiazui Company should not refuse without good reasons. The Defendant Lanhai Company has the right to change the name of ship-owner at the moment of delivery and the Defendant Wujiazui Company should then transfer the relative rights to the new ship-owner such as quality assurance of the ship, but the Defendant Lanhai Company should inform Wujiazui Company of preparing relative delivery documents 45 days before the delivery. During the process of performing ship building contract, the Defendant Wujiazui Company applies ship identification for No.CN20116426173, M.V. "LANHAI KUAYUE" which is under construction from Nanjing Maritime Safety Administration. On June 21, 2011, the Defendant Lanhai Company applied for loan from the Plaintiff CCB Liwan so as to solve the problem of fund

shortage related to the program of No.YC012 and No.YC013 ship building. Therefore, the Plaintiff CCB Liwan together with the Plaintiff EIBC made loan to the Defendant Lanhai Company in form of syndication. Those three parties signed the (2011) Li Ji Jian Dai No.003 *Syndicated Loan Contract* and *Complementary Agreement on Syndicated Loan*. The contract stipulates that:

1. The syndication composed of the two Plaintiffs should provide a loan of RMB267.6 million to the Defendant Lanhai Company so as to meet the fund demand for No.YC012 and No.YC013 ship building program. The Plaintiff EIBC provided a loan of RMB159 million and the Plaintiff CCB Liwan provided a loan of RMB108.6 million. The loan period lasts 93 months, starting from the date of first drawing to the deadline.
2. The loan rate should be determined according to each loan. The loan rate would be executed according to the benchmark lending rate stipulated by the People's Bank of China at the same rate as the date of drawing. And the loan rate should be adjusted according to benchmark interest rate on the day of interest adjustment every 12 months starting from the first drawing day to the day that all principal and interest are paid off under this contract. The loan interest would be calculated according to the number of days and be settled or paid according to the number of months.
3. The Defendant Lanhai Company should pay money back to the two Plaintiffs with ten phases, which should start from March 25, 2014 to March 21, 2019. By the time of March 21, 2019, all loans should be paid off. The specific amount of payment should be determined by the actual loan made by the syndication. During the performance of loan contract, the Defendant Lanhai Company actually applied for RMB206,617,600 from the syndication, in which the Plaintiff EIBC offered RMB106 million and the Plaintiff CCB Liwan offered RMB100,617,600.

In order to guarantee the rights of the two Plaintiffs under this loan contract, the Defendant Lanhai Company signed No.2012 Li Zhuan Xie No.001 *Transfer Agreement on the Rights* with the two Plaintiffs on December 31, 2012 so as to transfer the rights and benefits under this ship building contract. The agreement stipulates that:

1. The transferee should be given all funds, rights, benefits and interests that are covered by ship building contract, repayment guarantee, building quality and warranty guarantee, when the transferor transfers all those documents to the transferee.
2. In order to make sure that the transfer agreement has legal effect on the shipyard, the transferor should immediately send *Right Transfer Notification of Ship Building Contract* to the shipyard, after signing the agreement. The transferor should inform the shipyard that all funds, rights, benefits and interests covered by ship building contract mentioned above should be transferred to the transferee. The confirmation of shipyard should also be contained.

3. When all transferors repay the whole debts to the transferee in a satisfactory way, the transferee should transfer the funds, rights, benefits and interests back to the transferor in an acceptable way according to the requirements of transferor. The transferor should compensate full fees, expenditures and lost arising from retransfer.
4. After signing the contract, the transferor should immediately inform the bank of shipyard that all funds, rights, benefits and interests that are covered by repayment guarantee, building quality and warranty guarantee have been transferred to the transferee and the confirmation of shipyard has also been contained. The contract has specifically stipulated that whether the fund obtained by the transferee according to agreement can cover the loan principal and interest fee in full sum or not, the two transferees should accept the compensation according to the proportion of the actual loan balance under the loan contract clauses, while they get the relative fund. If the fund that the transferee has gotten through dealing with the ship under construction or under this agreement exceeds the sum of loan principal and the interest fee, this part of fund that exceeds is allowed by transferor to be compensated by the transferee according to the actual loan balance or to be used as repayment for the debt (including but not limited to trade finance) of transferor and/or connected enterprises Guangdong Lanyue Energy Development Co., Ltd.. After the contract has been signed, the Defendant Lanhai Company sends *Notification on Transfer of the Shipbuilding Contract Rights* according to the contract. The contents of notification are as follows: as the buyer of two 79600t Bulk Carriers (hull No.YC012 and YC013), our company signs the transfer agreement of the ship under construction with Export–Import Bank of China and China Construction Bank Co., Ltd.Guangzhou Liwan Branch. Our company hereby informs you that we have transferred all these funds, rights, benefits and interests under No.WJZ2006-YC012 and No.WJZ2006-YC013 *79600t Bulk Shipbuilding Contracts*, which you may or should pay us, including but not limited to default interest, economic compensation for late delivery and progress payment before delivery under the repayment guarantee, quality cash deposit and interests under the warranty guarantee, since the date of issuing this notification. The above mentioned banks have right to practice all rights that our company has under No.WJZ2006-YC012 and No.WJZ2006-YC013 *79600t Bulk Shipbuilding Contracts*.

At the same time, the following facts are ascertained: During the performance of ship building contract, the Defendant Lanhai Company paid ship price in amount of RMB178,400,000 in total for the first four periods respectively on April 23 and April 9, 2010, on June 27 and November 1, 2011. On November 20, 2012, in order to register for newly-built ship, the two Defendants, the Lanhai Company and the Wujiazui Company, signed a series of documents including *79600t Bulk Carrier "LANHAI KUAYUE" Redelivery Protocol*. The Defendant Lanhai Company (Party A) signed *M.V. "LANHAI KUAYUE" Delivery Memorandum* with Wujiazui Company (Party B) on November 27, 2012. The main clauses of memorandum are as follows:

1. The two parties should immediately sign the relative delivery documents after completing the trial so as to register for the ship.
2. Before the ship is delivered to Party A for real, the above mentioned delivery documents can neither be regarded as the confirmation for documents of building technique or any other attachments or whether the process of ship-building abides by *Ship Building Contract* or not, nor the transfer of ship's risks, nor the change or expiration of right and duty under *Ship Building Contract*.
3. After the two parties has confirmed that the ship which has been built completely abides by *Ship Building Contract* and has agreed on the documents of relative ship building technique, the two parties should conduct the necessary documents for all kinds of trial-start as soon as possible. Party A should then accept the ship entity and departure from the point where Party B delivers the ship. The above mentioned delivery documents would officially be taken into effect between the two parties from the point when Party A accepts the ship entity.
4. Party A does not pay for the fifth payment, when two parties sign this agreement. The two parties should decide another payment plan through friendly negotiation.
5. The right and duty of the two parties under the original contract clauses should keep invariant, apart from the above mentioned contract clauses. In case that this memorandum is inconsistent with the original contract, the former should prevail.

In order to settle the debt and creditor's right among three parties, the Defendant Lanhai Company and Wujiazui Company signed *Delivery, Payment and Repayment Memorandum of Understanding* with the third party Lanyue Company on November 27, 2012. Lanyue Company was connected to the Defendant Lanhai Company. The Defendant Wujiazui Company owed debt to Lanyue Company in other case and the Defendant Lanhai Company did not pay for the fifth stage of ship building fund, so these three parties reached an agreement. According to the agreement, the Defendant Lanhai Company could countervail part of debt that the Defendant Wujiazui Company owed to Lanyue Company with the fifth stage of ship building fund.

The notification was sent to the Defendant Wujiazui Company in written by the Plaintiff CCB Liwan on October 24. The Plaintiff CCB Liwan required that the Defendant Wujiazui Company should not deliver the ship hull No.YC012 and No. YC013 to the Defendant Lanhai Company. At present, although M.V. "LANHAI KUANYUE" has registered for trial, it has not registered for ownership of ship, not delivered for real and still berthing in factory of the Defendant Wujiazui Company.

The court holds that this case is dispute over ship building contract. *79600t Bulk Shipbuilding Contract, Syndication Loan Contract of Guangdong Lanhai Shipping Co., Ltd.* and relative complementary agreement involved are all parties' true declaration of intention. The contractual relationship of financial loan is lawfully established among the two Plaintiffs and the Defendant Lanhai Company. The relationship is legal and valid. All parties should strictly apply with the contract and law, when parties practice their civil rights as well as perform their duties comprehensively.

As to the effectiveness of *Transfer Agreement of the Ship under Construction*. According to the stipulation of Article 79 of the Contract Law of the People's Republic of China, creditor could transfer all of or part of contractual rights to the third party. However, this part of rights that was connected to the nature of contract or had been stipulated by parties or law should not be transferred. The ship building contract involved did not belong to contract that could not be transferred because of the nature of the contract. The first article in chapter 15 of *79600t Bulk Shipbuilding Contract* has stipulated that no party shall transfer this contract to any individuals, groups, companies or associations without written agreement from the other party. Whereas the second article in that chapter supplements that buyer has right to transfer the contract to its financial bank for sake of fund, seller should not refuse without good reasons. The above mentioned clauses showed that the Defendant Wujiazui Company agreed the Defendant Lanhai Company to transfer contract to its financial bank for sake of fund. Therefore, *Transfer Agreement of the Ship under Construction* involved did not violate the relative stipulations of Article 79 of the Contract Law of the People's Republic of China. The transfer agreement shall be valid and legal. After signing *Transfer Agreement of the Ship under Construction*, the Defendant Lanhai Company sent *Notification on Transfer of the Shipbuilding Contract Rights* to the Defendant Wujiazui Company and informed the relative fact of right transfer, thus the Defendant Lanhai Company had performed its duty connected to notification of relative debt transfer. according to Article 80 of the Contract Law of the People's Republic of China, the debt transfer was binding on the Defendant Wujiazui Company.

As to whether the two Plaintiffs could require the Defendant Wujiazui Company to deliver the ship or not. From the perspective of contract purpose, the two Plaintiffs signed *Transfer Agreement of the Ship under Construction* with the Defendant Lanhai Company so as to guarantee that the Defendant Lanhai Company would perform duty of periodical payment for financial loan in the contract. According to *Transfer Agreement of the Ship under Construction* among three parties, the Defendant Lanhai Company should transfer all funds, rights, benefits and interests that were covered by repayment guarantee, building quality, warranty guarantee and ship building contract to the two Plaintiffs. Whereas the problem whether the transfer agreement contained ownership of the ship and issues related to delivery is the issue of the case. *Transfer Agreement of the Ship under Construction* though did not clarify that ownership of the ship and ship delivery were permitted to be transferred through the right transfer, the Defendant Lanhai Company has transferred all funds, rights, benefits and interests under the ship building contract paid by the Defendant Wujiazui Company to the Plaintiff according to *Notification on Transfer of the Shipbuilding Contract Rights*, which is part of *Transfer Agreement of the Ship under Construction*. Therefore, the two Plaintiffs should be able to practice all rights under the ship building contract. According to above mentioned evidence, the court affirms that the Defendant Lanhai Company transferred all rights under the ship building contract including relative ship delivery rights to the two Plaintiffs. The Defendant Lanhai Company signed ship delivery agreement with the Defendant Wujiazui Company on

November 20, 2012. However, the two parties signed the agreement so as to register for ship. The ship has not been delivered for real. The two Plaintiffs are able to claim the rights under the ship building contract from the Defendant Wujiazui Company according to *Transfer Agreement of the Ship under Construction*, in order to guarantee its right under the syndicated loan contract but the two Plaintiffs should not violate the legal benefits of the Defendant Lanhai Company. As the fact that M. V. "LANHIA KUAYUE" is qualified to be delivered, the Defendant Wujiazui Company should immediately deliver M.V. "LANHAI KUAYUE" to the two Plaintiffs according to ship building contract and transfer agreement. With respect to other disputes over the ship building contract, parties shall file separate litigations.

In conclusion, according to Article 79, Article 80 and Article 107 of the Contract Law of the People's Republic of China and Article 142, Article 144 and Article 152 of the Civil Procedure Law of the People's Republic of China, the judgment is as follows:

1. (2012) Li Zhuan Xie No.001 *Transfer Agreement of Ship Building under Construction* (including the addendum, *Notification on Transfer of the Shipbuilding Contract*) that the Plaintiffs Export–Import Bank of China and China Construction Bank Co., Ltd. Guangzhou Liwan Branch signed with the Defendant Guangdong Lanhai Shipping Co., Ltd. shall be legal and valid, and be binding on the Defendant Nanjing Wujiazui Ship Building Co., Ltd.;
2. The Defendant Nanjing Wujiazui Ship Building Co., Ltd. shall immediately deliver M.V. "LANHAI KUAYUE" (hull No.YC012) to the Plaintiffs Export–Import Bank of China and China Construction Bank Co., Ltd. Guangzhou Liwan Branch within 10 days after the effectiveness of this judgment.

Court acceptance fee of RMB49,734, RMB24,817 charged after the two Plaintiffs withdrew part of the claims, and the property preservation fee of RMB5,000, in aggregate amount of RMB29,917 shall be jointly born by the two Defendants.

In the event of dissatisfaction with this judgment, a statement of appeal shall be filed to the court within 15 days upon the service of this judgment, together with copies in the number of the opposite party's amount and an appeal shall be lodged to Hubei High People's Court. The Appellant shall pay litigation fee for appeal in advance according to Article 13 (1) of the Measures on Payment of Litigation Costs, when it submits an appeal. Remittance should be sent to non-tax revenue settlement account of Hubei Finance Department. Bank of deposit: Agricultural Bank of China Wuhan Donghu Branch, account name: non-tax revenue financial special account of Hubei Finance Department, number of account: 05xxx69. Payer should give clear indication of "Hubei High People's Court" in purpose column of bank proof or unit code of Hubei High People's Court, which is "103001", in the event that payment is made through the way of bank transfer or bank remittance. The Appellant shall pay the litigation fee for appeal in advance within 7 days after expiration of appeal period, otherwise, the appeal will be deemed to be withdrawn automatically.

Presiding Judge: HOU Wei
Judge: ZHOU Yanhua
Acting judge: DENG Yi
January 21, 2015
Clerk: CHEN Nan

Shanghai Maritime Court
Civil Judgment

Fan Sen (V.S) Shanghai International Freight Forwarding Co., Ltd.
v.
Zhongman Petroleum & Natural Gas Group Co., Ltd.

(2014) Hu Hai Fa Shang Chu Zi No.1112

Related Case(s) None.

Cause(s) of Action 202. Dispute over contract of carriage of goods by sea or sea-connected waters.

Headnote The Plaintiff freight forwarder held not to be entitled to recover fee caused by customer's decision to change discharge ports, there being no contractual agreement in relation to the reimbursement of the fee.

Summary The Plaintiff, Fan Sen, brought suit against the Defendant, Zhongman Petroleum & Natural Gas Group Co., Ltd. for breach of contract related to shipping drilling rigs from China to Iran. The Plaintiff alleged that the Defendant requested a port change, and advanced $50,000 USD to the Defendant to do so, and was never reimbursed, and that it suffered loss of profits from the Defendant later changing carriers. The court held that the Plaintiff could not recover the $50,000 port-changing fee because it did not meet its evidentiary burden of proving the loss. Regarding the loss of profits, the court held that the agreement that the Plaintiff relied on for calculating damages was merely pre-contractual and thus the court found that these damages were not within the scope of the actual agreement of the parties. Accordingly, the court decided in favour of Zhongman Petroleum & Natural Gas Group Co., Ltd.

Judgment

The Plaintiff: Fan Sen (V.S) Shanhai International Freight Forwarding Co., Ltd.
Domicile: Jiading District, Shanghai city.
Legal representative: YUN Jie, general manager of the company.

Agent *ad litem*: ZHANG Jiasheng, lawyer of Shanghai SLOMA &Co. Law Firm.
Agent *ad litem*: LIU Xianmin, lawyer of Shanghai SLOMA &Co. Law Firm.

Defendant: Zhongman Petroleum & Natural Gas Group Co., Ltd.
Domicile: Pudong New Area, Shanghai.
Legal representative: LI Chundi, chairman of this company.
Agent *ad litem*: LIU Tonghai, lawyer of Beijing Liu Tong Hai Law Firm.
Agent *ad litem*: ZHU Yongzhen, female, Han, the company's employee.

With respect to the case arising from dispute over contract of carriage of goods by sea by the Plaintiff, Fan Sen (V.S) Shanghai International Freight Forwarding Co., Ltd. against the Defendant, Zhongman Petroleum & Natural Gas Group Co., Ltd., the Plaintiff filed an action to the court on September 2, 2014. The court entertained the case on the next day, applied the general procedures to try the case according to law, and held a hearing in public on January 12, 2015, Lawyer ZHANG Jiasheng and Lawyer Liu Xianmin, agents *ad litem* of the Plaintiff, Lawyer LIU Tonghai and ZHU Yongzhen, agents *ad litem* of the Defendant appeared in the court to attend the trial. Now the case has been concluded.

The Plaintiff alleged that on March 3, 2011, the Plaintiff and the Defendant entered into an "export transport agency contract", which noted that the Defendant entrusted the Plaintiff to carry the oil drilling rig from China Shanghai Port, Tianjin Port to Bandar Abbas, Iran. After the shipment of the drilling rig on the way, the Defendant put forward to change the port of discharge to Iran Khomeini Port. Due to changing the port, it generated the minimum amount of additional costs was USD200,000 including cargo stowage on board, cabin and so on. The Defendant issued a letter of guarantee about changing the port to the Plaintiff after mutual negotiation, which appointed that the Defendant firstly paid USD150,000 and permitted that the other ten sets of drilling rigs would be carried by the Plaintiff, wherein when the first five drilling rigs (11,000 cubic meters, plus or minus 5%) were shipped, the Plaintiff would return shipping costs USD10,000 to the Defendant every time. On April 19, 2011, the Defendant entered into a second set of drilling rig shipment charter with the Plaintiff, the Plaintiff delivered the goods to the port of discharge timely according to the requirements in the agreement. Due to the shortage of the drilling rigs during unloading, and it was not the responsibility of the Plaintiff, but the Defendant refused to pay ocean freight, port lump sum charges and land freight, which were approximately RMB2,300,000. In respect of the shortage matters, the two parties reached a memorandum of understanding in July 2011 by negotiation. It clearly indicated that the Plaintiff had no corresponding responsibility of the shortage of goods, but in view of their long-term business contracts and the post shipment of drilling rig, the Plaintiff agreed to indemnify the Defendant RMB34,000 and issued the corresponding files to assist customs clearance of the goods at the port of destination. The two parties signed the "agreement" on August 9, 2011, the Defendant committed to pay off the balance on September 30, 2011, and clearly agreed that the goods volume, port of destination and freight charges, and the following three drilling rigs would be carried by the

Plaintiff. After the above-mentioned "agreement" was signed, the Defendant failed to pay the freight nor entrusted the Plaintiff to transport goods. By the end of December 2011, the two parties entered into an "implementation agreement", in view of the consideration of the Defendant that there were still 10 sets of drilling rigs that commissioned the Plaintiff to carry and withdraw the freight and miscellaneous charges of the second drilling rig as soon as possible, with regard to the second drilling rig of Shanghai Port generated the extra overland freight RMB108,604 due to the volume increases that should not be born by the Plaintiff and the shortage of goods of port of destination losses RMB34,000, the Plaintiff allowed the Defendant to deduct in dealing with the freight and miscellaneous charges and allowed to mitigate the ocean freight of the second set of drilling rig RMB63,000, a total deduction of RMB250,604. With regard to the balance of the freight and miscellaneous charges RMB2,140,862, the Defendant agreed to paid off before the date of January 22, 2012. The agreement made a clear regulation on the transportation issues and breach of contract of the follow-up drilling rigs. After the above-mentioned "implementation agreement" was signed, the Defendant breached the contract again, which neither paid the freight and miscellaneous charges within the agreed date nor commissioned the Plaintiff to carry the follow-up drilling rigs according to the agreement. Because the Defendant breached the contract, the Plaintiff suffered the considerable economic loss and the loss of profits, the Defendant should bear the corresponding liability. Therefore, the Plaintiff requested the judgment to the court: 1. the Defendant should compensate the fees of changing port USD50,000 to the Plaintiff; 2. the Defendant should compensate the loss of profits USD132,000; 3. court acceptance fee should be born by the Defendant.

The Defendant argued that:

1. The claims of the Plaintiff had been settled by the China Maritime Arbitration Commission Shanghai Branch (hereinafter referred to as "Maritime Arbitration Shanghai Branch") arbitral decision for a package settlement, the Plaintiff had not mentioned a letter of guarantee of changing port in the arbitration, and it belonged to repeated prosecution to mention this letter;
2. The letter of guarantee of changing port only agreed that the Defendant needed to pay USD150,000, not confirming advance payment of USD50,000 of changing port to the Plaintiff, and the Plaintiff did not provide evidence related to advancing the corresponding fees to a third party due to changing port, so the Plaintiff's claim of the fees of changing port had no corresponding basis; and
3. Because the Plaintiff did not provide its separate charter cost expense and other cost expense because of transportation, which cannot calculate the profits obtained of the Plaintiff, and the agreement on August 9 involved was an non-complete contract, it was only a reservation clause, which had not any loss in acquirable interests available.

The Plaintiff presented evidence in order to support its claims, the cross-examining opinions of the Defendant and the certified opinion of the court are as follows:

1. Export transportation agency contract was to prove that the relations of contract about carriage of goods by sea of the first set of drilling rig transportation existed, the Defendant recognized the effect of evidence and the purpose of the proof. The court holds that the effect of evidence and the purpose of the proof shall be given identification because of the confirmation of the Defendant.
2. QQ chat records and a letter of guarantees of changing port were to prove that due to the fact that the Defendant changed the port, the Plaintiff and the Defendant confirmed the minimum charges of changing port USD200,000, the Defendant only paid USD150,000, in respect of the fees of changing port USD50,000 advanced by the Plaintiff, the Defendant agreed to compensate in the latter period. The Defendant held that chat records did not handle the corresponding notarization procedures and chat subject was unrecognized, so the Defendant did not confirm the effect of evidence but recognized the effect of evidence of the letter of guarantee of changing port; due to the formation of scheme of chat was not authorized by the Defendant's legal representative, it was not the final will of the Defendant, therefore the purpose of evidence was not recognized. The court holds that the effect of evidence of the letter of guarantee of changing port shall be recognized due to the confirmation of the Defendant, regarding to the effect of evidence of chat and the purpose of proof will be stated in the reasoning part of the judgment with other evidence and the facts of the case through the court.
3. The "agreement" signed by two parties on August 9, 2011 was to prove that the Defendant again committed to pay money in due course and a penalty because of overdue, and committed to entrust the Plaintiff to carry the follow-up consignment, but the Defendant actually failed to fulfill the agreement. The Defendant confirmed the effect of evidence, but did not confirm the purpose of proof, at the latter period, due to the quotation of the Plaintiff was higher than the agreed freight USD41.5 / cubic meters, it was breach of contract by the Plaintiff. The court holds that the effect of evidence should be recognized due to the confirmation of the Defendant, regarding to the purpose of evidence, it will be stated in the reasoning part of the judgment with other evidence and the facts of the case through the court.
4. The letters of the Plaintiff, a note and a reminder from the Defendant were to prove that the Plaintiff had urged the Defendant to paid money, the Defendant seriously breached the contract because of payment delay. The Defendant had no objection to the authenticity and legality of evidence, but the Defendant held that the evidence had not connection to this case, because the corresponding compensation caused by payment delay of the Defendant had already been arbitrated. The court holds that the authenticity and legality of the set of evidence should be recognized because of the confirmation of the Defendant. Regarding to the responsibility of breaching of the contract that the Defendant should bear, because the overdue payment had been cleared and settled in the judgment No.MASH2014016 issued by Maritime Arbitration Shanghai Branch, the court shall not repeat the trial.

5. The implementation agreement was to prove that the Defendant committed to entrust the Plaintiff to carry the corresponding goods according to the agreed freight standard, but the Defendant did not keep an appointment. The Defendant did not entrust the Plaintiff to carry the corresponding goods. The Defendant had no objection to the effect of evidence, but the payment content of the implementation agreement had been arbitrated, so the purpose of evidence of the Plaintiff should not be confirmed. The court holds that the effect of evidence shall be confirmed because of the confirmation of the Defendant. Although the implementation agreement had the protocol of fee exemptions for the second drilling rig transportation-related fee, it also had refinement and continuation to the letter of guarantee of changing port and the "agreement" signed on August 9, 2011. Regarding to the second drilling rig freight matters dispute, because of the arbitration clause of "charter party", the court did not have the appropriate jurisdiction to this dispute, but in respect of the letter of guarantee of changing port formed in the first set of drilling rig cargo transportation, the agreement of August 9, and the content of the implementation agreement and the facts of the case through the court could be agreed by the parties: the Defendant promised that the subsequent three drilling rigs (each of 11,000 cubic meters, plus or minus 5%) would be carried by the Plaintiff, port of destination was Iran Abba Sri Lanka Port or Port Khomeini, freight was USD41.5 / cubic meters, other terms of the contract of carriage referred to the original contract and kept constant, the payment period was extended to 60 days of shipping, the fact that the agreed interest of the deferred payment would be settled at the daily two over one thousand according to the debt was compensate for the Plaintiff's loss shall be recognized. The purpose of proof of evidence will be stated in the reasoning part of the judgment combined with other evidence and the facts of the case through the court.
6. One quoted comparison table, two maritime agency contract were to prove that the Defendant maliciously entrusted a third party to carry the goods, the Defendant maliciously breached the contract. The Defendant confirmed the effect of evidence to the quotes comparison table of the shipped drilling rig of MAPNA project and maritime agency contract, but the effect of evidence of the Plaintiff's quoted comparison table of page 45 should not be confirmed because it had no source and signature of the issuer, because quote comparison table showed that the Plaintiff quoted shipping unit price USD41.5 was higher than USD44 of a mutually agreed price, and the contents of maritime agency contract could prove that the Plaintiff had no intention to carry the corresponding goods, which was breach of the contract by the Plaintiff, therefore the purpose of evidence was not recognized. The court holds that two quoted comparison table had no signature of the issuer and they were not the original copies, the contents of quoted comparative table provided by the MAPNA project was different from the notarized email contents, the Plaintiff also confirmed that under the contradiction of quoted comparative table and the email content provided by the Defendant in the trial, which would be subject to the quotation of the email of the Defendant, so the effect of evidence of quoted comparison table shall not be

recognized; the effect of evidence of maritime agency contract shall be recognized because of the Defendant's confirmation. Regarding to the purpose of the set of evidence, that will be stated in the reasoning part of the judgment combined with other evidence and the facts of the case through the court.

7. The letter was to prove that the Defendant still agreed to fulfill the contract signed by both parties on December 9, 2013, but the Defendant did not fulfill it. The Defendant recognized the effect of evidence, but believed that due to the Plaintiff's quotation of carriage was higher than the Plaintiff's agreed freight unit price of USD41.5, which was the unfulfillment the Plaintiff. The court holds that the effect of evidence should be recognized because of the confirmation of the Defendant, and the purpose of evidence will be stated in the reasoning part of the judgment combined with other evidence and the facts of the case through the court.

The Defendant presented evidence in order to support of its defenses, the cross-examining opinion of the Plaintiff and the confirm opinion of the court are as follows:

1. The email that the Plaintiff quoted that the goods were carried to the Iranian port of Bandar Abbas was to prove that the Plaintiff quoted USD46.5 / cubic meters, which violated the two parties agreed price USD41.5 / cubic meters, the claims for loss of profit of the Plaintiff had no basis; the Defendant complied with the agreement of two parties and let the Plaintiff make an offer, but the Plaintiff ignored. The Plaintiff had no objection to the validity of evidence, but held that the cargo quantity of the Defendant was partial shipment, which failed to meet the agreed requirement of two sides that a single transport volume of 11,000 cubic meters and the e-mail sent by the Defendant to the Plaintiff of June 19, 2012, which required the Plaintiff to reply before 12 at noon of the next day, the Defendant was not giving the Plaintiff a reasonable time to arrange the vessel for the carriage of the goods and the corresponding offer, so the purpose of proof of the Plaintiff should not be recognized. The court holds that the effect of the set of evidence shall be recognized because of the confirmation of the Defendant. Regarding to the purpose of evidence, that will be stated in the reasoning part of the judgment combined with other evidence and the facts of the case through the court.

2. The email asking the Plaintiff to quote the price of the goods carried to Iran Imam Khomeini port was to prove that the Defendant fulfilled its commitments, but the Plaintiff had no sincerity and breached the contract obviously due to over quoted. The Plaintiff had no objection to the effect of evidence, but the Plaintiff considered that the drilling rig quantity exported by the Defendant did not meet the agreed volume of the two parties of 11,000 cubic meters, so the prices quoted should not be subject to the agreement of USD41.5 / cubic meters constraints, therefore the purpose of proof should not be recognized. The court hold that the effect of evidence shall be recognized because of the confirmation

of the Defendant. The purpose of evidence will be stated in the reasoning part of the judgment combined with other evidence and the facts of the case through the court.

3. The maritime agency contract signed by the Defendant with the Tianjin International Hangtong Freight Forwarding Co., Ltd. (hereinafter referred to as "Hangtong Co.") on June 12, 2012 to demonstrate the market price of freight drilling rig transported at that time was USD37.5 / cubic meters, the quoted price of the Plaintiff had no corresponding market competitiveness. The Plaintiff had no objection to the effect of evidence, but considered that the contract proved that the Defendant viciously collaborated with the outsider Hangtong Co. to damage the legitimate interests of the Plaintiff, the Defendant and the Plaintiff should be compensated for the loss of profits of the Plaintiff according to the difference between the agreed price of the agreement of USD41.5 /cubic meters and the contract price of USD37.5 / cubic meters. The court holds that the effect of evidence should be recognized because of the confirmation of the Defendant. The purpose of evidence will be stated in the reasoning part of the judgment combined with other evidence and the facts of the case through the court.

4. The attendance sheet of shipping bidding was to prove the Plaintiff had fulfilled its commitment to the Plaintiff, let the Plaintiff make an offer in the bidding site, however, the Plaintiff went to the scene but did not make an offer. The Plaintiff had no objection to the effect of evidence, but believed that because the Defendant had not given clear and specific shipment volume, the Plaintiff cannot make an offer. The court holds that the effect of evidence shall be recognized because of the confirmation of the Defendant. The purpose of the set of evidence will be stated in the reasoning part of the judgment combined with other evidence and the facts of the case through the court.

5. The email asking the Plaintiff to quote the price of the goods carried to Iraq Port was to prove that the freight quoted to carry goods were much higher, the Defendant had to signed a contract of cargo transportation with other companies because of no market competitiveness. The Plaintiff had no objection to the effect of evidence, but held that whether the quotation of cargo transportation had market competitiveness or not needed to consider sea freight, port charges and other factors. The court holds that the effect of evidence shall be recognized because of the confirmation of the Defendant. The purpose of the set of evidence will be stated in the reasoning part of the judgment combined with other evidence and the facts of the case through the court.

To find out the facts, the court requested the Plaintiff and the Defendant to express the corresponding cross-examination views on the following evidence:

1. The "charter party" signed by the two parties on April 29, 2011, the Plaintiff recognized its authenticity and legality, but held that the agreement was signed for the shipment of the second drilling rig, which had no connection with the case. The Defendant recognized the effect of evidence. The court holds that the authenticity and legality of evidence shall be recognized because of the

confirmation of the Plaintiff and the Defendant, because the claims for the loss of profit of the Plaintiff according to the terms in the "agreement" and "implementation agreement", but the "implementation agreement" was signed for all kinds of fees relief of the second drilling rig and payment of the balance of the freight, so this group of evidence is of considerable relevancy to find out the related facts of the case, and the court confirms the evidence.
2. The cargo shipment customs declarations of MAPNA project, the Plaintiff had no objection to the authenticity and legality of the evidence, but considered that the number of goods showed on declarations and the agreed number of the contract were not the same, and the Plaintiff did not recognize its relevancy to the case. The Defendant recognized the effect of evidence. The court holds that the authenticity and legality of evidence shall be recognized because of the confirmation of the Plaintiff and the Defendant, the declaration showed that the export goods were "delete a single restated and customs clearance again" could prove mutually with the e-mail provided by the Defendant and the fact that the goods carried deferred stated by the Defendant, whose relevancy can be recognized.

According to the analysis of the above evidence and the material combined with investigation of court adjudication, the court find out the facts as follows:

On March 3, 2011, the Plaintiff and the Defendant signed the contract appointed that the Defendant entrusted the Plaintiff to handle one set of 70DZ oil drilling rig and spare parts of some oil wells and other shipping matters from Shanghai / Tianjin Port to Bandar Abbas, Iran, the two parties appointed the transport calculation standards in terms of corresponding sea freight, port handling charges, land transportation handling charges and storage charges of cargo; The mode of payment was 30 days after the ship left the port and released the bill of lading that the Defendant pay all the money to the Plaintiff, the two parties also appointed the mutual rights and obligations and the involved disputes would be under the local maritime court jurisdiction of the Defendant, besides, it attached to agreement that "the Defendant referred to the relevant provisions of this contract and increased a set of drilling rig to the Plaintiff for carriage, the time of carriage was prior to June 1, 2011", both parties confirmed in written after the court that the carriage of the second drilling rig was the fulfillment of the terms. On April 29, 2011, the Defendant entrusted the Plaintiff to carry the second drilling rig equipment and signed a "charter party", the mode of the freight payment of the agreement was that before the goods were shipped to the port of destination, or the Defendant was entitled to lien the goods until freight was settled, which the generated cost and responsibility was assumed by the Plaintiff; the resolution to dispute was arbitration.

On April 12, 2011, due to the change of the port of destination of the first set of drilling rig equipment (change from the Iranian port of Bandar Abbas to Iran Khomeini), the two parties signed the letter of guarantee of changing port, which appointed that the Defendant paid USD150,000 to the Plaintiff and agreed that the follow-up 10 sets of drilling rigs (completed within three years) would be carried by the Plaintiff, the freight would be the most competitive market price of that time and both parties agreed; wherein after the shipment of the first five drilling rigs (11,000 cubic meters, plus or minus 5%), returned USD10,000 to the Defendant each time.

The "agreement" signed on August 9, 2011 and "implementation agreement" signed at the end of the year by two parties clearly appointed that the Defendant committed the subsequent three drilling rigs shipped to Bandar Abbas Port or Khomeini Iranian Port (11,000 cubic meters per set, plus or minus 5%) would be carried by the Plaintiff carrier, shipping freight was USD41.5 / cubic meters, other terms of the contract of carriage referred to the original contract would be kept constant, the payment period was extended to 60 days of shipping, the agreed interest of the deferred payment would be settled at the daily two over one thousand according to the debt was compensate for the Plaintiff's loss.

In terms of the drilling rig equipment of MAPNA project shipped to Iran's Bandar Abbas on September 11, 2012, the total volume of the set of equipment was about 11,000 cubic meters (plus or minus 10%), the Defendant inquired price to the Plaintiff on March 20, 2012 for the first time, required to ship in two batches and the Plaintiff provided the appropriate shipping prices, port sur-charges and land transportation lump sum charges. The Plaintiff promptly replied after half an hour on the same day, "due to the increases of oil price and ship price, shipping freight is USD46.5 / cubic meters, and all payments would be settled within a month". Later, due to Iranian consignee put forward new technical requirements to the drilling rig so that the shipment of drilling rig equipment was delayed, and therefore the Defendant inquired the price of the drilling rig again at 12:52 on June 19, 2012, the inquiry content showed that the drilling rig equipment was shipped for once, the volume was about 12,000 cubic meters, Tianjin export barrack was about 7,500 cubic meters, Shanghai export was about 5,000 cubic meters, the port of destination was the Iranian Port of Bandar Abbas, the timetable for the scheduled was before June 30, 2012, and the name of the ship, age of the ship, shipping time and the mode of payment were required to fill in, and the mode of payment was cash against documents and within 60 days after the departure of the ship, and based on different the mode of payment to fill the corresponding sea freight, port sur-charges, land transportation lump sum charges respectively. The e-mail required the Plaintiff to reply before the noon of June 20, but the Plaintiff did not reply. Later, the drilling rig was carried by the Hangtong Co., the "maritime agency contract" signed with the Defendant had no appointment of land transportation lump sum charges.

Regarding to drilling rig equipment of NIDC project carried to Iran Imam Khomeini port on December 20, 2014, the total volume of the sets of equipment was about 4,500 cubic meters (plus or minus 10%), the Defendant inquired the price to the Plaintiff on November 21, 2013, the Plaintiff replied on November 25 of the same year, but did not give a specific offer. Since the Defendant had not received the offer of the Plaintiff, the Defendant sent an e-mail on November 27 of the same year to the Plaintiff, which invited the Plaintiff to come to the bidding spot on the 28th to discuss the maritime agreement matters, the Plaintiff sent people to there on the 28th, but still made no offer, the Plaintiff sent an email to ask the Defendant whether the shipment volume was 4,000 cubic meters, instead of 11,000 cubic meters (plus or minus 5%), which would have a corresponding quotation according to the reduction of the quantity.

In addition, it also found that on August 26, 2013, the Plaintiff requested the Defendant to continue to fulfill the "agreement" signed by the two parties on August 9, 2011 to pay the loss of interest for overdue payment and pay sea freight, transport fees, cargo damage fees, and filed an action to the court by virtue of the above causes. The Defendant submitted a letter to the court on December 9, 2013 and claimed that the Defendant requested the Plaintiff to continue to fulfill the contract signed by both parties, the specific content were "1. by the end of April 12, 2014, the drilling rigs that were shipped to Iran and the volume of 11,000 cubic meters (plus/minus 5%) would be carried by the Plaintiff at USD41.5 / cubic meters; 2. the drilling equipment of other ports, according to the contract of the parties, at the most competitive in the market and the parties recognized freight, the Plaintiff had priority right of carriage under this condition", the Plaintiff withdrew prosecution against the Defendant on December 25, 2013 for the Defendant agreed to continue to implement the agreement signed by both parties. Later, the Plaintiff submitted arbitration application to the Shanghai Branch of Maritime Arbitration on December 31, 2013, which required the Defendant to pay the unpaid freight and delay of payment penalty, the loss of interest of the contract agreement and lawyers' fees and other losses, after the arbitral tribunal ruled on the Plaintiff's related request, the Defendant should fulfill the adjudication.

The court holds that this case is dispute over maritime transportation contract of goods. Due to the port of destination of transportation was Bandar Abbas Port or Iranian Khomeini Port, so this case involved with the foreign elements. According to law, the contracting parties by consensus could choose the applicable law to solve foreign-related contractual dispute. In court trial, the parties agreed to apply the law of the People's Republic of China, so the court determines to regard the law of the People's Republic of China as the applicable law to judge the disputes of the case.

Firstly, regarding to the claims of the Plaintiff requesting the Defendant to compensate the cost of their changing port.

QQ chat records provided by the Plaintiff was to prove the minimum fee of changing port was USD200,000, and USD50,000 advanced by the Plaintiff negotiated with the Defendant, the Defendant was to pay USD150,000 as compensation for the Defendant agreed to 10 drilling rigs would be shipped by the Plaintiff. Later, the drilling rigs shipped by the Defendant was not entrusted to be carried by the Plaintiff, thus accordingly the Plaintiff requested the Defendant to compensate the advanced fees USD50,000. The court holds that, 1. QQ chat records provided by the Plaintiff did not apply for the corresponding legalization, the proof did not have the corresponding effect of evidence; 2. according to the content on the upper right-hand corner and the content at the bottom of the document, the fact could be known that chat records " V.S and jack1221 (20967690)" were in total 22 pages, but the Plaintiff only submitted the page two and page four to the court and did not provide a complete chat records, so the court does not confirm the chat records as a basis for final decision; 3. from the view of the part of chat records provided by the

Plaintiff, the contents were only the negotiation about the payment of related costs on issues of changing port of the parties, after several negotiation between the two parties, the program was changed several times, it had not finalized; 4. the Plaintiff confirmed in the hearing that the final signed letter of guarantee of changing port were not sent to other parties through chat software, but the written confirmation was settled by the agreed content of the chat records; 5. The written letter of guarantee of changing port confirmed and signed by the Defendant showed that the final confirmed solution of the payment on changing port by mutual agreement was that the Defendant should pay USD150,000, and agreed that the follow-up 10 drilling rigs would be carried (completed within three years) by the Plaintiff, of which the first five drilling rigs (11,000 cubic meters, plus or minus 5%) were shipped, and the Plaintiff returned shipping freight USD10,000 to the Defendant and particularly noted "freight was the market's most competitive of that time and mutually agreed", namely, the ultimately formed solution of the cost of changing port had not been confirmed that the Plaintiff advanced USD50,000 for the Defendant actually because of changing port matters and had not agreed that if there was breach of contract, the Plaintiff had the corresponding rights to request the Defendant to pay USD50,000; 6. in the trial, the Plaintiff confirmed that it was not the actual carrier, and thus under the condition that the Plaintiff did not provide evidence to prove that the Plaintiff actually paid to the actual carrier the fees advanced for the Defendant and the corresponding amount because of changing port of the Defendant, the Plaintiff bore the consequences of inability of providing evidence. Pulling the threads together, the court does not confirm the fact that the Plaintiff actually advanced USD50,000 for the Defendant because of changing port, because that the Plaintiff requested the Defendant to compensate the advanced fees had no corresponding factual basis, so the court does not support it.

Secondly, regarding to the claims of the Plaintiff that the Plaintiff requested the Defendant to pay USD132,000 for loss of profits. The issue mainly involved the following two main issues: 1. the "agreement" and the subsequent "implementation agreement" signed by the two parties on August 9, 2011, in terms of the legal nature of the agreement on the drilling equipment shipment clauses was "pre-contract" or "fundamental contract"; 2. Whether the loss of profits of the Plaintiff's claims was within the range of the loss of reliance interest or not.

(1) With respect to the matters of the "agreement" and the subsequent "implementation agreement" signed by the two parties on August 9, 2011, in terms of the legal nature of the agreement on the drilling equipment shipment clauses was "pre-contract" or "fundamental contract".

Pre-contract referred to an appointment that would make a certain contract in the future. Thus, from the essence of view, the pre-contract should be the complete forms of contract. In other words, compared with other documents which were not constituted a contractual relationship, the fundamental difference was that the pre-contract had the elements of the establishment of contract, namely it had specific two parties or different contracting parties, the contracting parties reached consensus on the main provisions, which the establishment also included the offer and acceptance phase. In other words, per-contract, as a form of contract, which also included the parties, the subjects, the meaning expression and so on. From forms to contents, these elements were clear. Some pre-contract terms were very detailed, which almost all of the content of the future contract was stipulated expressly in the pre-contract. Therefore, as to pre-contract and fundamental contract, they were very difficult to distinguish because both had the deterministic characteristics of the main provisions of the contract, and were applicable to supply the gaps in contract. Therefore, the court holds that the fundamental standard of judging the provision was pre-contract or fundamental contract is the declaration of will of the parties, namely whether the parties had intention to enter into a new contract in the future, in order to explicit specific content of the legal relationship formed in the two parties. If the parties had the intention to enter the contract in the future, then, even if the contents of pre-contract had been very close to the contract, even by the interpretation of contract, which could deduce the entire contents from the pre-contract, however, the declaration of will of the parties should be respected, the possibility of such objective interpretation should be excluded. Therefore, regarding to the nature of the agreed terms of the case shall be judged from the following aspects:

1. According to the "agreement" and the relevant conventions of "implementation agreement", which showed that the nature of terms of the agreement should be considered as pre-contract. The terms of the agreement of the case identified that the Defendant promised that three drilling equipment would be shipped to Bandar Abbas, Iran Khomeini port (11,000 cubic meters each, plus or minus 5%) by the Plaintiff, shipping freight was 41.5 USD / cubic meters; the payment period was extended to 60 days of shipping, the agreed interest of the deferred payment would be settled at the daily two over one thousand according to the debt was compensate for the Plaintiff's loss. The terms of the agreement clearly identified that the shipments and volumes of goods prepared for shipping, the port of destination, the corresponding sea freight amount, payment conditions and the corresponding penalty of overdue payment, which had the main content of a formal contract of carriage. However, while the parties agreed in the "agreement" that the other provisions of contract of carriage were kept contrast according to the "original contract" clause, and before signing the "agreement", the Plaintiff had shipped two drilling equipment to Iran, the shipping parties signed the "export transportation agency contract" on March 3, 2011 for the first set of drilling equipment, the shipping parties signed a "charter party" on April 29, 2011 for the second set of drilling equipment, the rights and obligations of two contracts varied greatly, and the jurisdictions of the agreement were different, the "original contract" specifically referred to which contract should remain to be further clarified in the new contract entered into in the future, in order to finally define the specific details of the legal relationship of the transport of goods between the parties and the appropriate resolution to disputes.

2. The court comprehensively analyzes the fact that the consultations of the parties to reach a contract of carriage of shipping device-specific and the specific performance of subsequent acts, and asked the true intention of the parties, then accordingly hold that the nature of "agreement" was pre-contract.

Firstly, in terms of the level of necessity of contract negotiations, the Defendant inquired the price to the Plaintiff before shipping the drilling equipment, which included not only the freight but also port charges and land transportation lump sum charges, namely even if the two parties had agreed on the amount of sea freight in the agreement, that did not mean that the price of the contract was complete, even for the same volumes and the port of destination, it also formed the corresponding land transportation lump sum charges based on the specific drilling equipment because of the different structure of drilling equipment of the Defendant, therefore the presence or absence and the more or less of land transportation lump sum charges cannot be determined by the reference to the "original contract", which would be adjusted according to costs of the relevant circumstances by the shipment of goods. According to effective evidence in the trial and court investigation, the drilling rig equipment in the MAPNA project, the volume about 11,000 cubic meters, which were shipped to Bandar Abbas on September 11, 2012, was the same as the shipping amount and the port of destination of the shipped drilling equipment by the two parties, but the land freight of Shanghai Port had not been settled with the opposite party of ocean contract. It could be seen that although according to the agreed terms, the parties should be subject to the binding of the agreed terms in the per-contract, the pending articles must be determined by the declaration of will of both parties, and therefore it was not enough to enter into the terms by virtue of agreed terms merely.

Secondly, in terms of the level of fulfillment to achieve this agreement, both parties in the trial were confirmed that the drilling rig equipment under MAPNA project had reached the standard of "agreement" and "implementation agreement", the Defendant first inquiry price for shipment of the equipment, the total volume of about 12 thousand levels of the drilling rig exported to Iran Abbas in two batches, requested the Plaintiff to provide the appropriate shipping prices, port charges and land transportation lump sum charges. The Plaintiff replied as follows: "as the ship price and oil price were rising, sea freight price of 12 thousand levels was USD46.5 / cubic meters, paid off in one month". The Plaintiff in the trial emphasized the reason that quoting higher price than USD41.5 / cubic meters of the agreement was because USD41.5 / cubic meters was sea freight prices for a shipment volume of 11,000 cubic meters of cargo, while the volume of equipment was divided into two batches when the Plaintiff first inquired the price, the cost of the charter of the Defendant would be a corresponding increase, so the higher offer was not in violation of the "Agreement".

The court holds that:

(1) Based on the literal understanding of the Plaintiff's replies involving occurrence of the case, the Plaintiff was unwilling to accept constraints of USD41.5 / cubic meters because of the rising of ship price and oil price, which was considered to be more appropriate to be carried at USD46.5 / cubic meters, it was also apparent that the agreement of USD41.5 / cubic meters was only pre-contract from the declaration of will, and could be adjusted and consulted with objective changes in ship price and oil price and did not have the effect of a formal agreement; and

(2) Taking a step back, even if the explanation of the Plaintiff in the trial was reasonable, it merely proved the pre-contract nature of the "agreement", because the agreement of shipped price of the goods needed both parties to make the appropriate consultations and adjustment according to the specific solutions of the shipped goods (if the clause of the "agreement" was a single persistent explanation, namely as long as a drilling rig met the volume of 11,000 cubic meters, regardless of whether were shipped in batches, the sea freight was always USD41.5 / cubic meters, so the quotation of the Plaintiff USD46.5 / cubic meters was the bench of contract by the Plaintiff).

Due to Iran's consignee made the adjustment of the device technology enabled the device to delay for carriage, and therefore the Defendant made a second inquiry to the shipment of the equipment, at that time, the device complies with the requirement of the "agreement" and shipped in once, but the Plaintiff were not quoted, the Plaintiff claimed that the Defendant was not given enough time to contact the ship and the corresponding quotes. The court holds that if the content of the "agreement" was the determined declaration of will of the Plaintiff, which could constitute the agreement, then the Plaintiff could directly quote at USD41.5 / cubic meters without more consideration when the Defendant made an inquiry, but the Plaintiff did not reply to the inquiry from the Defendant, which indicated that their promised price of the "agreement" USD41.5 / cubic meters was still not sure to carry.

Finally, from the point of view of the Defendant normal business operating practices, the effective evidence in the trial showed that each shipment of drilling rigs of the Defendant had signed the corresponding formal contract. In terms of the two drilling rigs between the Defendant and the Plaintiff, the first set of the drilling rig contract had the pre-contract provisions of the second drilling rig, namely "the Defendant with reference to the relevant provisions of this contract to increase a set of drilling rig delivered to the Plaintiff for carriage, the carriage time was before June 1, 2011". Later, the Defendant actually shipped the second set of drilling rig on April 29, 2011, at that time, the Defendant signed a formal shipment contract "charter party" with the Plaintiff.

Pulling the threads together, taking a step back, even if the "original contract" of the agreement was "export transport agency contract" signed by the two parties on March 3, 2011 as the Plaintiff said, after the consultation, the facts of performance and normal business operating practices, which could see the true declaration of will of the parties at the time. The two parties had the willing to negotiate and adjust for the particular shipment of drilling rigs whether in terms of determined provisions or pending provisions, therefore it could be determined that the nature of "agreement" and "implementation agreement" was pre-contract.

(2) Regarding to whether the loss of profits claimed by the Plaintiff was within the scope of the loss of fiduciary interests.

The Plaintiff confirmed its claim in the trial for loss of profits was possible benefits lost, based on the "Contract Law" Article 113, its claim for loss of profits was calculated as: the freight agreed on "agreement" USD41.5 / cubic meters deducted the sea freight USD37.5 / cubic meters of the Defendant with the third party Hangtong company for MAPNA project drilling rig, multiplied by a transport volume of 11,000 cubic meters, and then multiplied by three drilling rigs the Defendant committed, namely (41.5–37.5) * 11, 000 * 3 = 132,000 (USD). This kind of calculation, which was based on the full implementation of the fundamental contract, to calculate property rights of the Plaintiff that might be realized or obtained, whereas in this case, the "agreement" signed by two parties was only a pre-contract, even if the Defendant had the contracting fault, which only assumed the loss of fiduciary interests to the Plaintiff, namely the actual loss for the signing of contract of the Plaintiff with the Defendant, and the available benefits was not in the scope of the loss of fiduciary interests because of the full implementation of the fundamental contract, which should not be listed in the compensation for breach of pre-contract. Therefore, the Plaintiff's claims shall not be supported.

Pulling the threads together, the court does not support the compensation claims of the Plaintiff for advanced payment for lack of corresponding factual basis; in the condition of the terms of the two parties signed the "agreement" and "implementation agreement" were only pre-contracts, the available profit loss claimed by the Plaintiff was not in the scope of the loss of fiduciary interests because of full implementation of the contract, which is not supported by the court either, so according to the Contract Law of the People's Republic of China Article 113 Paragraph 1, Article 174, Article 2 of The Interpretation of the Supreme People's Court on Issues Concerning the Application of Law for the Trial of Cases of Disputes over Sales Contracts, Article 64 Paragraph 1 of the Civil Procedure Law of the People's Republic of China and Article 2 of the Some Provisions of the Supreme People's Court on Evidence in Civil Procedures, the judgment is as follows:

Not support the claims of the Plaintiff Fan Sen (V.S) Shanghai International Freight Forwarding Co., Ltd.

Court acceptance fee in amount of RMB14,791.80, shall be born by the Plaintiff Fan Sen (V.S) Shanghai International Freight Forwarding Co., Ltd.

If not satisfy with this judgment, the Plaintiff Fan Sen (V.S) Shanghai International Freight Forwarding Co., Ltd. and the Defendant Zhongman Petroleum & Natural Gas Group Co., Ltd. may forward petition for appeal to the court within fifteen days as of the service of judgment, submit a statement of appeal to the court, together with copies in accordance with the number of the opposite parties, and appeal to the Shanghai High People's Court.

Presiding Judge: JI Gang
Acting Judge: WANG Huanijn
People's Juror: ZHANG Yi

January 20, 2015

Clerk: GU Chanyan

Appendix: Relevant Law

1. **Contract Law of the People's Republic of China**
    Article 113 Calculation of Damages; Damages to Consumer Where a party failed to perform or rendered non-conforming performance, thereby causing loss to the other party, the amount of damages payable shall be equivalent to the other party's loss resulting from the breach, including any benefit that may be accrued from performance of the contract, provided that the amount shall not exceed the likely loss resulting from the breach which was foreseen or should have been foreseen by the breaching party at the time of conclusion of the contract.
    Article 174 General Applicability to Contracts for Value For any other contract for value, if the law provides for such contract, such provisions apply; absent any such provision, reference shall be made to the relevant provisions governing sales contracts.
2. **Interpretation of the Supreme People's Court on Issues Concerning the Application of Law for the Trial of Cases of Disputes Over Sales Contracts**
    Article 2 Where both parties have signed preliminary agreements such as purchase offers, purchase orders, subscription books, letters of intent, and memorandums, and have agreed that a sales contract is to be concluded within a certain period of time, if one party does not perform the obligation of concluding a sales contract and the other party requests that it assume liability for breach of the preliminary agreements or demands the rescission of the preliminary agreements and claims compensation for damages, the people's court shall support such claims.

3. **Civil Procedure Law of the People's Republic of China**
   Article 64 It is the duty of a party to an action to provide evidence in support of his allegations.
   ......
4. **Several Provisions of the Supreme People's Court on Evidence In Civil Procedures**
   Article 2 The parties concerned shall be responsible for producing evidence to prove the facts on which their own allegations are based or the facts on which the allegations of the other party are refuted.

   Where any party cannot produce evidence or the evidence produced cannot support the facts on which the allegations are based, the party concerned that bears the burden of proof shall undertake unfavorable consequences.

Shanghai Maritime Court
Civil Judgment

Fujian Guanhai Shipping Co., Ltd.
v.
Shanghai Huaya Ship Fuel Company

(2015) Hu Hai Fa Shang Chu Zi No.47

Related Case(s) None.

Cause(s) of Action 225. Dispute over contract for marine stores and spare parts supply.

Headnote Bunker supplier held liable for supply of defective bunkers; although no specific quality was set out in the supply contract, the oil did not comply with generally applicable national or industry standards.

Summary The Plaintiff, Fujian Guanhai Shipping Co., Ltd. brought suit against the Defendant, Shanghai Huaya Ship Fuel Company, for supplying oil of poor quality that resulted in damage to the Plaintiff's vessel. The oil that was supplied was tested by forensic experts and it was discovered that the oil was below industry standards. The contract between both parties did not stipulate as to the quality of the oil to be provided, but the court determined that when quality terms of oil are unclear, national or industry standards are to be used. The court ordered Shanghai Huaya Ship Fuel Company to retrieve 24.24 tons of oil from the Plaintiff's vessel and refund RMB117,564 for oil and interest fees to the Plaintiff Fujian Guan Hai Co., Ltd.

Judgment

The Plaintiff: Fujian Guanhai Shipping Co., Ltd.
Domicile: Lianjiang County, Fuzhou City, Fujian Province.
Legal representative: LIN Cailong, general manager.
Agent *ad litem*: JIANG Yan, lawyer of Fujian Wuhai Law Firm.

The Defendant: Shanghai Huaya Ship Fuel Company
Domicile: Baoshan District, Shanghai.
Legal representative: YANG Feng, general manager.
Agent *ad litem*: YIN Jiao, lawyer of Shanghai Zhengguan Changhong Law Firm.

With respect to the case arising from dispute over contract for marine stores and spare parts supply filed by the Plaintiff Fujian Guanhai Shipping Co., Ltd. against the Defendant Shanghai Huaya Ship Fuel Company before the court on January 8, 2015, after entertainment on the same day, the court legally tried this case under summary procedure. On February 3, 2015, the court organized both parties to conduct evidence exchange. On March 6, 2015, the court held the hearing in public to try the case. Lawyer JIANG Yan, agent *ad litem* of the Plaintiff and Lawyer YIN Jiao, agent *ad litem* of the Defendant appeared in court to attend the trial. This case has now been concluded.

The Plaintiff alleged that there was a contractual relationship between the Plaintiff and the Defendant, which required that the Defendant should provide 58.568 tons of oil to the Plaintiff. However, the fuel oil provided by the Defendant had quality problems, resulting in damage to the engine of the ship owned by the Plaintiff. Now the Plaintiff had used up 21.768 tons of fuel oil having quality problems and 36.8 tons of fuel oil has not been used yet. The Plaintiff requested the court to rule the Defendant: 1. accept the unused 36.8 tons of fuel oil to be returned and refund RMB178,480 according to the contract price; 2. in terms of the used 21.768 tons of fuel oil, refund RMB105,574.80 according to the contract price; 3. compensate the loss of interest on sum mentioned in the two preceding items, which should be calculated according to the same period of the deposit interest rate of the People's Bank of China from the date of September 20, 2013 until the effective date of the judgment; and 4. bear the court acceptance fee of this case.

The Defendant contended that: 1. the fuel oil had no quality problems, the Defendant did not breach the contract, so the Defendant should not be liable for return and refund; 2. the Plaintiff mixed the fuel oil provided by the Defendant with other fuel oils and had used up them, so the fuel oil cannot be returned; 3. the claim that used fuel oil to be refunded according to the original contract lacked legal basis; 4. even if the Defendant should bear the refund responsibility, the Plaintiff claimed a refund according to the contract price after dragging over a year when fuel prices had dropped sharply, so the Plaintiff should be responsible for the part of the expanded loss; 5. the starting point of the loss of interest claimed by the Plaintiff had no basis. Request the court to reject the claims of the Plaintiff.

As for the facts of the case, evidence submitted by the Plaintiff, the Defendant's cross-examination and the court's authentication are as follows:

1. A copy of the oil supply contract, to prove that there was a contractual relationship between the Plaintiff and the Defendant, which specified the ship received the oil, unit price of the fuel oil and "the supplier must ensure the quality of oil".
2. A copy of the certificate of adding oil, to prove that the Defendant provided 58.568 tons of oil to the Plaintiff on September 13, 2013.
3. A copy of the oil detection and analysis order, to prove that the Plaintiff and the Defendant jointly commissioned Shanghai Run Kai Oil Monitoring Ltd. (hereinafter referred to as Runkai Company) to detect the oil involved.

4. A copy of the test report, to prove the oil involved had quality problems.
5. A copy of (2014) Hu Hai Fa Shanghai Chu Zi No.114 Civil Judgment, to prove the oil involved had quality problems and the Defendant failed to guarantee the quality of oil according to the contract.
6. A copy of the engine logbook, to prove the fuel oil involved remained 36.8 tons.
7. The original oil record book, to prove that the oil record book did not record the fuel oil forwarding situation.

The Defendant confirmed the authenticity, legality, relevancy and probative force of evidence 1; the Defendant confirmed the authenticity, legality, relevancy and probative force of evidence 2, but the Defendant held that the certificate of adding oil had recorded the oil parameter index and the oil price was lower than the market price, which indicated that the Plaintiff was aware of the oil parameter index; the Defendant confirmed the authenticity of evidence 3 and evidence 4, but the Defendant held that both parties had not reached an agreement of test standard when commissioning analysis, so it was not reasonable for Runkai Company to test the oil according to the ISO 8217: 2012 standard and the ISO2005 testing standard was more reasonable; the Defendant confirmed the authenticity, legality and relevancy of evidence 5, but the Defendant held that the oil involved could not been proved to have quality problems for this civil judgment had not come into force; the Defendant confirmed the authenticity of evidence 6, but the Defendant held that it could not prove that the fuel oil involved remained 36.8 tons; the Defendant confirmed the authenticity and legality of evidence 7, but the Defendant held that the oil record book should record but actually did not record the fuel oil forwarding situation.

The court recognizes the authenticity, legality and relevancy of the seven evidence provided by the Plaintiff. As for the establishment of a contractual relationship between the Plaintiff and the Defendant and the fact of adding oil, the court recognizes the probative force of evidence 1-2; as for the oil quality, the court recognizes the probative force of evidence 3-4, but the strength of the probative force of these evidence shall be certified after being combined with the evidence submitted by the Defendant. Since evidence 5 was a civil judgment that had not come into force, the court does not affirm the its probative force; as for the remaining oil amount, the court recognizes the probative force of evidence 6 regarding the daily oil usage, but the remaining oil amount and the concrete figures shall be certified after being combined with other evidence of this case and court investigations; as for whether the situation of mixed oil existed, the court recognizes the probative force of the evidence 7 regarding the situation of every oil adding, but the strength of the probative force of this evidence shall be certified after being combined with other evidence of this case and court investigations.

Evidence submitted by the Defendant, the Plaintiff's cross-examination and the court's authentication are as follows:

1. A copy of opinion of judicial expertise issued by Shanghai Maritime Forensic Center, to prove that the Plaintiff had mixed fuel oil involved in this case with other batches of fuel oil and had used them up.

2. A copy of the engine logbook, to prove the Plaintiff had used up the fuel oil provided by the Defendant from September 23, 2013 to October 12, 2013.
3. The page print of the webpage of Fuel Oil Market Weekly of 20141226, to prove that the unit price of the same kind fuel oil priced at RMB3,500 per ton in December 2014 and the fuel oil price fell sharply.
4. A copy of the assessment report issued by Shanghai Haiheng Marine Services Co., Ltd. (hereinafter referred to as Haiheng Company),to prove that oil fuel provided by the Defendant had no quality problems and the Defendant did not breach the contract.
5. A copy of the damage report of main engine, auxiliary engine and boiler parts and a copy excerpt of the public assessment report issued by Fujian New Foreign Insurance Adjuster Co., Ltd., to prove the Plaintiff started to use the batch of fuel oil involved in this case since September 23, 2013.
6. The print copy of the email that the Plaintiff's agent *ad litem*, JIANG Yan, sent to the Defendant, to prove that the Plaintiff once claimed that the remaining fuel oil was about 26 tons and was stored in the oil compartment.

The Plaintiff confirmed the authenticity, legality and relevancy of evidence 1, but the Plaintiff did not confirm the records regarding fuel oil mixing of the opinion of judicial expertise for the appraiser did not survey the scene; the Plaintiff confirmed the authenticity, legality and relevancy of evidence 2, but the Plaintiff held this evidence could not prove that the Plaintiff used up the fuel oil provided by the Defendant; the Plaintiff did not confirm the authenticity and relevancy of evidence 3 and held that the returns and refunds should be conducted according to the agreed price specified in the contract; the Plaintiff did not confirm the authenticity, legality and relevancy of evidence 4, for the Plaintiff held that this report was made as unilaterally commissioned by the Defendant and did not confirm its probative force; the Plaintiff confirmed the authenticity of evidence 5 and confirmed that the batch of fuel oil involved in this case started to barge into the settling tank form September 23, 2013; the Plaintiff confirmed the authenticity, legality and relevancy of evidence 6, but the Plaintiff held that the claimed 36.8 tons of remaining oil was a figure of 26 tons of oil plus the oil amount of the oil bottom in 3 cabin left.

The court recognizes the authenticity, legality and relevancy of the evidence 1-2, evidence 5-6 provided by the Defendant. Evidence 3 was a page print, which could not prove the price of the fuel oil involved in this case when supplying oil or under current situation and had no relation with the factum probandum, so the court does not affirm its probative force. Since the Defendant did not prove that Haiheng Company and its surveyors had relevant professional qualifications, the court does not affirm the probative force of evidence 4; in addition, this evidence was unilaterally commissioned to be made by the Defendant, so the neutrality cannot be protected. And as for the authentication of oil quality, its probative force could not equal the test report issued by Runkai Company jointly entrusted by both parties and the expertise opinion issued by the forensic center commissioned by the court. As for the remaining oil amount, the court recognizes the probative force of evidence 2, 5-6, but the calculation of remaining oil amount and the concrete figures shall be certified after being combined with other evidence of this case and court investigations; as for whether the situation of mixed oil existed, the court recognizes the probative force of the evidence 1, but the strength of the probative force of this evidence shall be determined after being combined with other evidence of this case and court investigations.

To identify the remaining oil fuel usage and fuel involved, on March 27, 2015, the Plaintiff and the Defendant and the court together surveyed the starboard fuel tank layer of M.V. "GUAN HAI 308" engine room. The court inquired the chief engineer about the involved situations of fuel oil adding, oil usage and storage and made conversation transcripts. The Plaintiff and Defendant confirmed the authenticity, legality and relevancy of the chief engineer conversation transcripts and the content of the notes.

According to the effective evidence and the court investigation, the court ascertains the following facts:

On September 11, 2013, the Plaintiff and the Defendant signed an oil supply contract, agreeing that the Defendant shall provide 80 tons of 180CST fuel oil to M.V. "GUAN HAI 308" belonged to the Plaintiff and the unit price of fuel oil was RMB4,850 per ton. At the same time, Article 4 of the contract agreed that the Defendant must ensure that the oil quality.

On September 13, M.V. "GUAN HAI 308" stored 42.70 tons of fuel oil. From 2350 (September 13) to 0020 (September 14), the Defendant assigned M.V. "CHONGYUAN RAN GONG 02" to supply 58.568 tons of 180CST fuel oil to M.V. "GUAN HAI 308". The involved fuel oil was added into the 3 cabins left. According to the records of the oil record book, 3 cabin left stored 58.61 ton oil after adding oil, indicating that the 3 cabin left only stored 0.042 tons of oil before being added oil, which was equivalent to the empty state. According to records of the oil supply certificate, the density of the added fuel oil was 987.60, the viscosity was 156.70, the sulfur content was 0.92% and the water content was 0.10%.

At 2340 on September 23, the involved fuel oil started to be used. The process of the fuel usage was: being barged to No.2 settling tank after being heated at 3 cabin left, and then being barged to No.2 daily tank after being separated by heating. Among them, the volume of the No.2 settling tank were 20.10 cubic meters and the volume of the No.2 daily tank were 18.20 cubic meters.

From September 26, the engine logbook began to be used to record the situations of ship parts damage, repair and replace.

On October 3, M.V. "GUAN HAI 308" stored 36.80 tons of fuel oil and added new oil at Wusong anchorage. According to the statement of the chief engineer, before adding new oil, the remaining involved fuel oil stored in 3 cabin left was barged to No.2 settling tank and No.2 daily tank to be stored. The oil storage was 25 cubic meters, or about 24.70 tons. The 3 cabin left only kept the oil pan. The new oil weighed 42.38 tons and was added into the 3 cabin left. According to the records of the oil record book, the 3 cabin left stored 43.17 tons of oil after being added oil, indicating that the 3 cabin left stored 0.79 tons of involved oil before being added oil.

On October 4, M.V. "GUAN HAI 308" started using the new added fuel oil. The process of the fuel usage was: being barged to No.1 settling tank after being heated at 3 cabin left, and then being barged to No.1 daily tank after being separated by heating.

On October 19, the Plaintiff and the Defendant jointly commissioned Runkai Company to test the involved fuel oil. On October 22, Runkai Company issued the test report. According to the report records, according to the ISO8217: 2012-180 # quality indicators and the The People's Republic of China GB/T17411: 2012-180 # quality indicators, the water content of oil shall not exceed 0.50% and the total acid value shall not be more than 2.50 mgKOH/g. The actual test results were that the water content of the involved fuel oil is 1.10% and the total acid value was 3.14 mgKOH/g. The test conclusion was that the water content and the acid value of this oil were too high. And the infrared spectrum showed that the oil containing non-petroleum hydrocarbons, so there was a risk of corrosion and mechanical sediments occur when in use.

On November 26, the Defendant of this case petitioned to the court, requesting to order the Plaintiff of this case to pay oil fee and the penalty of late payment. The court entertained the case on the same day, case number (2013) Hu Hai Fa Shang Chu Zi No.1649. On February 24, 2014, the court made a judgment that the Plaintiff of this case shall pay RMB1,388,015.55 oil fee and loss of interest to the Defendant of this case (calculating according to the same period of the deposit interest rate of People's Bank of China from the date of September 20, 2013 until the effective date of the judgment). The Plaintiff and the Defendant of this case confirmed that the oil fee contained the oil fee of the involved batch of fuel oil. The judgment has come into force. The Plaintiff of this case had fulfilled part of the money paying obligation under this judgment. The Plaintiff paid the oil arrears of RMB800,000 to the Defendant of this case, but the remaining part of the oil fee and interest losses were unpaid.

On February 12, 2014, the Plaintiff of this case petitioned to the court, requesting to order the Defendant of this case to compensate losses such as repair costs of damaged parts and schedule losses caused by the fuel oil quality problems. the court entertained the case on the same day, case number (2014) Hu Hai Fa Shang Chu Zi No.114.

On June 10, the Plaintiff and the Defendant jointly confirmed that the court commissioned forensic center to identify the turbine damage accident of M.V. "GUAN HAI 308" and the identified items were the cost of spare parts caused by machinery equipment damage accidents of the fuel oil system after the ship being added the involved fuel oil, expanded self-repair labor costs and ship suspended losses. On July 23, the forensic center issued the expertise opinion, which identified that the involved fuel oil started being used since September 24, 2013. The period of engine damage accident was from September 24, 2013 to October 3, 2014. And the damage extent and the maintenance costs of machinery equipment caused by fuel quality problems were totally RMB188,898. The expertise opinion also identified that the 42.38 tons of fuel oil added on October 3, 2013 mixed with the involved fuel oil in 3 cabin left.

On October 21, 2014, the court ruled that the fuel oil provided by the Defendant of this case had quality problems, the Defendant of this case should compensate the Plaintiff of this case RMB191,548 for breach of contract. And the Defendant of this case was ordered to compensate the Plaintiff of this case RMB111,548 losses and corresponding interest losses. The Plaintiff of this case refused to accept the judgment and has appealed to the Shanghai High People's Court. The case is now under the hearing of appeal.

On March 27, 2015, the court accompanied the Plaintiff and the Defendant to survey the starboard fuel tank layer of M.V. "GUAN HAI 308" engine room, finding that No.1 settling tank and No.1 daily tank were in use, No.2 settling tank and No.2 daily tank stored oil. The Plaintiff and the Defendant both confirmed that No.2 settling tank and No.2 daily tank stored 24.54 cubic meters of oil, altogether 24.24 tons after being conversed according to the 0.9876 density recorded by the oil vouchers.

The court ascertains that the contractual relationship between the Plaintiff and the Defendant was real and effective. The Plaintiff was the oil accepting party and the Defendant was the oil supplying party. According to the contract, the Defendant should ensure the oil quality. If the oil has quality problems, the Defendant should bear the liability for the breach of contract according to the law. The controversy focus of this case: 1. whether the Defendant breached the contract; 2. the form and scope of assuming liability for breach of the contract; 3. and whether the Plaintiff fulfill the obligations of reasonable derogation.

1. Whether the Defendant breached the contract

Although the involved oil receive and supply contract agreed that the Defendant must ensure the oil quality, it did not specifically agree upon the quality standards. According to Article 61 and Paragraph 1 of Article 62 of the Contract Law of the People's Republic of China (hereinafter referred to as the Contract Law), when the quality requirements are unclear, they shall fulfill according to national standards or industry standards. The Plaintiff and the Defendant did not reach a supplementary agreement on the oil quality standards and did not provide evidence to prove the transaction practices, so the involved oil quality shall fulfill according to the national standards. The People' Republic of China GB/T17411: 2012-180 # quality index is the national standard used to measure the quality of domestic marine fuel oil. According to this standard, the water content of oil shall not exceed 0.50% and the total acid value shall not exceed 2.50 mgKOH/g, but according to the test report of Runkai Company, the water content of the involved fuel oil was 1.10% and the total acid value was 3.14 mgKOH/g, so the oil quality did not meet the national standard. In addition, although the Defendant claimed that oil adding certificate recorded the oil index parameters that the Plaintiff should be aware of and it was more reasonable to test oil with the ISO2005 quality indicators, the index of the involved batches of fuel oil did not reach the parameter index recorded on the oil adding certificate, nor according to the ISO2005 standards. Accordingly, the court ascertains that the involved fuel oil provided by the Defendant had quality problems and the Defendant breached the contract.

2. The form and scope of assuming liability for breach of contract

In respect of whether the Defendant should bear the liability for breach of the contract and return the unused fuel oil, the Plaintiff claimed that 36.8 tons of the involved fuel oil remain unused and requested them to be returned to the Defendant. The Defendant argued that the involved fuel oil and the newly added fuel oil were mixed, so the oil cannot be returned. the court ascertains that according to stipulations of Article 61 and Article 111 of the Contract Law, if there is no agreement in the contract on the liability for breach of contract or corresponding transaction practices, the Plaintiff as the damaged party may, in light of the character of the object and the degree of losses, reasonably choose the form to request the Defendant to bear the liabilities for the breach of contract. The judicial expertise opinion has confirmed that using involved fuel oil would cause engine damage of the ship owned by the Plaintiff. In this case, requiring the Plaintiff to continue to use the batch of fuel oil was contrary to common sense. Therefore, the Plaintiff can choose to return the unused fuel oil legally. As for the remaining oil, the Plaintiff and the Defendant both confirmed the period of using the involved fuel oil was from 2340 on September 23, 2013 to October 3, 2013. According to engine logbook records, the oil consumption form September 23 to October 3 was 34.98 tons, and the oil consumption on September 23 was 1.7 tons. Accordingly, the usage of the involved fuel oil was 33.28–34.98 tons, so the involved residual fuel oil was 23.588–25.288 tons. Before adding new oil on October 3, the involved fuel oil was barged to the No.2 settling tank and the No.2 daily tank and 0.79 tons of oil bottom were not split out and remained in the 3 cabin left. So, the remaining oil shall be between 22.798–24.498 tons. The Plaintiff and Defendant both confirmed that the oil storage of the No.2 settling tank and the daily tank of M.V. "GUAN HAI" were 24.24 tons, which was consistent with the remaining oil amount calculated by the engine logbook and the oil record book. The Defendant did not confirm the stored oil in the No.2 settling tank and the daily tank was the involved fuel oil, and the involved fuel oil has been mixed and used up according to the claims of the judicial expertise opinion. The judicial expertise opinion gave a statement about oil mixing on October 3, 2013 adding 42.38 tons of oil into 3 cabin left at Wusong anchorage, which was mixed with the batch of oil with problems in the same tank. The court ascertains that: firstly, the judicial expertise opinion did not conclude that the involved fuel oil had been used up; secondly, the case-related oil adding, oil usage and oil storage were not the items of the judicial expertise opinion. The appraiser did not survey the situations of settling tank and daily tank on board and the oil record book was not included in the identification of the appraisal materials. Therefore, the probative force of the oil mixing statements of the judicial expertise opinion is less than that of the engine logbook and the oil record book of this case, and inconsistent with the court investigations. According to the engine logbook, the records of the oil record book and the statements of the chief engineer of M.V. "GUAN HAI 308", in fact 0.79 tons of fuel oil were not barged out of 3 cabin left and the 0.79 tons of fuel oil mixed with the newly added fuel oil, but this residual was not the situation the Defendant claimed that all the remaining fuel oil mixed with the newly added oil. In sum, the court ascertains that the Plaintiff had completed the initial burden of proof to prove that the remaining 24.24 tons of involved fuel oil sealed in the No.2 settling tank and daily tank were unused and the Defendant failed to prove involved fuel oil had been used up, so the Plaintiff's claim that the Defendant should accept the return of the 24.24 tons of unused fuel oil and refund according to the original contract price for breach of contract is legal and shall be supported. But the court does not support the claim that the part which is beyond 24.24 tons should be returned.

Regarding whether the Defendant should be liable for breach of the contract and refund the used fuel oil. The Plaintiff requested the Defendant to be liable for breach of the contract and fully refund the used fuel oil according to Article 111 of the Contract Law. The Defendant held that the claim lacked legal basis. During the trial, the Plaintiff and Defendant both confirmed that fuel oil was mainly used for ship navigation, power generation, in and out of the port, waterways and small boiler operation, the involved fuel oil achieved these effects during use, but causing the machine damage of the ship owned by the Plaintiff. The court ascertains that, the provisions regarding the liability for breach of the contract in the Contract Law are intended to compensate the damaged party and filled and leveled up to the expected benefits when the damaged party signed the contract. In the case, when the Plaintiff signed the oil receive and supply contract, it is intended to obtain fuel oil with the unit price of RMB4,850 for ship navigation, power generation, in and out of the port, waterways and small boiler operation. The usage effects had been achieved, if without the engine damage accident, the Plaintiff and the Defendant both finished their rights and obligations under the oil supply contract. And due to the engine damage accident, the Plaintiff suffered additional losses. But the Plaintiff had claimed the losses in another case, so it would not comply with the law to claim a full refund in this case. In addition, the provisions regarding the price reducing liability for breach of the contract in the Contract Law are intended to set price according to quality and to achieve the equilibrium of the contract. The Defendant argued that when adding oil, the unit price of RMB4,850 had been lower than the market price, the Plaintiff did not fulfill the burden of proof to prove that fuel oil of such quality can be bought at lower market prices, so the court does not support the Plaintiff's claim to request the Defendant to fully refund the used fuel oil for breach of contract.

Regarding whether the starting point of calculating the interest losses is reasonable. The effective (2013) Hu Hai Fa Shang Hai Chu Zi No.1649 Civil Judgment ruled that the Plaintiff of this case should compensate the Defendant for this case interest losses caused by arrears of oil fees, including the involved fuel oil fee, which should be calculated according to the same period of the deposit interest rate of the People's Bank of China from the date of September 20, 2013. Accordingly, the Plaintiff claimed the interest losses should be calculated from September 20, 2013, but the Defendant considered the starting point unreasonable. The court ascertains that as the Defendant supplied oil with quality problems, the Defendant shall not obtain interest losses of the returned fuel oil fees, so the court does not support the claim that the calculating starting point of the interest loss unreasonable of the Defendant.

3. Whether the Plaintiff fulfill the obligations of reasonable derogation

The Defendant held that the Plaintiff claimed the return and refund after dragging over a year, the fuel prices had dropped sharply, so the Plaintiff should be responsible for the part of the expanded loss. The court ascertains that: firstly, the Plaintiff and the Defendant both negotiated the return and refund before this case was entertained. They turned to resolve disputes through litigation because they could not reach an agreement. The Defendant failed to provide valid evidence to prove that the Plaintiff delayed in returning the oil back; secondly, the decline of fuel oil prices was caused by market factors, which had nothing to do with the Plaintiff dragging; thirdly, the Plaintiff stopped to use and sealed the fuel oil after finding that they had quality problems that could cause engine damage accidents to avoid expanding the extent of engine damage. The Plaintiff has fulfilled its obligations of reasonable derogation, so the court does support the Defendant's claims accordingly.

In conclusion, according to Article 61, Article 111 of the Contract Law of the People's Republic of China and Paragraph 1 of Article 64 of the Civil Procedure Law of the People's Republic of China, the judgment is as follows:

1. The Defendant Shanghai Huaya Ship Fuel Company shall accept the return of the 24.24 tons of fuel oil sealed in No.2 settling tank and No.2 daily tank of M. V. "GUAN HAI 308" and refund RMB117,564 and interests thereon to the Plaintiff Fujian Guan Hai Co., Ltd. within ten days after the judgment came into force (calculated from the date of September 20, 2013 to the day of effectiveness of this judgment on the basis of the deposit interest rate of the People's Bank of China over the same period); and
2. Not support other claims of the Plaintiff Fujian Guan Hai Co., Ltd.

If the Defendant Shanghai Huaya Ship Fuel Company fails to fulfill the payment obligations during the period specified in the judgment, the Defendant shall double the interest during the delay in performance according to the provisions of Article 253 of the Civil Procedure Law of the People's Republic of China.

Court acceptance fee in amount of RMB5,560.82, half charging RMB2,780.41 for being applicable to the summary procedure, the Plaintiff, Fujian Guanhai Shipping Co., Ltd. shall bear RMB1,629.66 and the Defendant, Shanghai Huaya Ship Fuel Company shall bear RMB1,150.75.

In case of dissatisfaction with this judgment, the Plaintiff and the Defendant may within 15 days upon the service of this judgment submit a statement of appeal to the court, together with copies according to the number of the opposite parties, and appeal to the Shanghai High People's Court.

Acting Judge: XU Wei

April 2, 2015

Clerk: GU Chanyan

Appendix: Relevant Law

1. Contract Law of the People's Republic of China

Article 61 Where, after the contract becomes effective, there is no agreement in the contract between the parties on the terms regarding quality, price or remuneration and place of performance, etc. or such agreement is unclear, the parties may agree upon supplementary terms through consultation. In case of a failure in doing so, the terms shall be determined from the context of relevant clauses of the contract or by transaction practices.

Article 62 If the relevant terms of a contract are unclear, nor can it be determined according to the provisions of Article 61 of this Law, the provisions below shall be applied:

(1) If quality requirements are unclear, the State standards or trade standards shall be applied; if there are no State standards or trade standards, generally held standards or specific standards in conformity with the purpose of the contract shall be applied.

...

Article 111 If the quality fails to satisfy the terms of the contract, the breach of contract damages shall be born according to the terms of the contract agreed upon by the parties. If there is no agreement in the contract on the liability for breach of contract or such agreement is unclear, nor can it be determined according to the provisions of Article 61 of this Law, the damaged party may, in light of the character of the object and the degree of losses, reasonably choose to request the other party to bear the liabilities for the breach of contract such as repairing, substituting, reworking, returning the goods, or reducing the price or remuneration.

2. Civil Procedure Law of the People's Republic of China

Article 64 It is the duty of a party to an action to provide evidence in support of his allegations.

...

Xiamen Maritime Court
Civil Judgment

GUO Jiangbao
v.
Xiamen Chengyi Shipping Co., Ltd.

(2014) Xia Hai Fa Shang Chu Zi No.452

Related Case(s) None.

Cause(s) of Action 226. Dispute over contract for employment of seaman.

Headnote Employer held liable to pay injured worker's compensation claim and to pay medical and other injury-related expenses, as well as assisting the injured worker make application for future government pension benefits.

Summary The Plaintiff GUO Jiangbao filed an action against the Defendant Xiamen Chengyi Shipping Co., Ltd. for damages arising from a work-related injury. The Plaintiff was hit by a grab while working on the Defendant's vessel, after which he was hospitalized for 25 days. The Plaintiff was assessed as Level 9 Disability, but the Defendant failed to pay the Plaintiff on his worker's compensation claim. The Plaintiff requested that the court: (1) terminate his employment contract with the Defendant, (2) pay various damages pursuant to his injury, including medical expenses, and (3) order the Defendant to assist the Plaintiff with his work-related injury claim. The court held that the Plaintiff had a valid worker's compensation claim. The court dissolved the employment contract between the Plaintiff and the Defendant and ordered the Defendant to pay the Plaintiff's expenses and cooperate with the Plaintiff's work-related injury insurance claim procedure.

Judgment

The Plaintiff: GUO Jiangbao, male, born on June 2, 1982, Han
Domicile: No.119 Houzeng, Guocuo Village, Fengwei Town, Quangang District, Quanzhou City, Fujian.
Agent *ad litem*: CHANG Fuqin, lawyer of Fujian Dongfang Gezhi Law Firm.

The Defendant: Xiamen Chengyi Shipping Co., Ltd.
Domicile: Floor 7, Jinxing Block, Qixing Road, Siming District, Xiamen, Fujian.
Legal representative: FAN Zhixian, general manager.
Agent *ad litem*: ZHANG Dongshan, lawyer of Fujian Xiayang Law Firm.
Agent *ad litem*: YU Caixing, trainee lawyer of Fujian Xiayang Law Firm.

With respect to the case arising from dispute over contract for employment of seaman, the Plaintiff, GUO Jiangbao filed an action against the Defendant Xiamen Chengyi Shipping Co., Ltd. (hereinafter referred to as "Chengyi Company") on September 9, 2014, the court entertained the case and organized the collegiate panel according to the law. The court organized the pre-trial evidence interchange on October 31, 2014. On February 6, 2015, the court held a hearing in public. GUO Jiangbao and CHANG Fuqin, agent *ad litem* of the Plaintiff, and ZHANG Dongshan, agent *ad litem* of the Defendant appeared in court to attend the trial. During trial, the Plaintiff applied for adding claims, upon agreement by the Defendant, the court permitted the joint trial of separate cases in the hearing. On March 2, 2015, the Defendant submitted supplementary evidence and the court timely organized written cross-examination. Now the case has been concluded.

The Plaintiff alleged that on January 10, 2013, the Plaintiff concluded a contract of labor with the Defendant. On the next day, the Plaintiff was dispatched as an FTR on M.V. "GROWNING" owned by Global Growing Maritime Corporation Limited in Taiwan Area. According to the contract, the Plaintiff's monthly wage included basic wage in sum of USD850, remuneration in sum of USD250 to USD300. On October 28, 2013, the Plaintiff was hit by a grab when working on the vessel and stayed in hospital for 25 days. Xiamen Human Resources and Social Security Bureau recognized that he suffered a work-related injury. Xiamen Work Capacity Assessment Committee affirmed that the injury constituted level 9 permanent disability. However, the Defendant did not pay the Plaintiff for the compensation, so the Plaintiff requested the court to order: (1) terminate the contract of labor between the Plaintiff and the Defendant since the day when the Plaintiff filed the subject suit, namely September 9, 2014; (2) the Defendant should pay the wages during the suspension-of-work-with-pay period in sum of RMB89,177.66, medical expenses in sum of RMB38,166, nursing care fee in sum of RMB5,541.67, hospital food allowance in sum of RMB500, lump-sum disability allowance in sum of RMB61,738.38, lump-sum medical treatment allowance in sum of RMB41,150.2, lump-sum disability employment allowance in sum of RMB41,150.2, assessment fee in sum of RMB320, transportation costs in sum of RMB6,441.6, board and lodging allowance in sum of RMB6,986, communication fee in sum of RMB1,500, copying fee in sum of RMB213.6, medical equipment cost in sum of RMB90, printing fee of Bank of China in sum of RMB20, nutrition fees in sum of RMB30,000, mental injury solatium in sum of RMB3,000, following-up treatment fee in sum of RMB50,000; (3) the Defendant should assist the Plaintiff to handle the work-related injury claim procedure.

The Plaintiff submitted the following evidential materials within the time limit for adducing evidence:

1. Letter of verification of work-related injury and occupational disease of worker in Xiamen, to prove that the Plaintiff suffered work-related injury;
2. Xiamen work capacity assessment certificate, to prove the suspension-of-work-with-pay period should be calculated to the day of work capacity assessment, namely May 23, 2014;
3. Contract of seafarer on board, to prove that the Plaintiff and the Defendant established a labor contract relationship. The Defendant sent the Plaintiff to the vessel belonging to Global Growing Maritime Corporation Limited in Taiwan region for work;
4. The medical record and translation of Islamic Yu Jia Er Ma Si Hospital, to prove the fact that the Plaintiff was treated in the hospital after the injury;
5. The medical record, diagnosis certificate and diagnosis report of Zhongshan Hospital affiliated to Xiamen University, to prove the fact that the Plaintiff was treated in Zhongshan Hospital affiliated to Xiamen University after leaving Islamic Yu Jia Er Ma Si Hospital;
6. The medical record of the First Hospital affiliated to Fujian Medical University, to prove the fact that due to an incorrect diagnosis report of Zhongshan Hospital affiliated to Xiamen University, the Plaintiff was sent to the First Hospital affiliated to Fujian Medical University for treatment;
7. Treatment record, certificate, diagnostic report of the First Hospital affiliated to Xiamen University, to prove that during the examination period, the Defendant designated the Plaintiff to go to the First Hospital affiliated to Xiamen University for medical treatment;
8. Treatment record of Zhongshan Hospital affiliated to Fudan University, to prove that the First Hospital affiliated to Xiamen University advised the Plaintiff to have treatment in the department of chest and orthopedics of a higher-level hospital. Upon the agreement of the Defendant about the further treatment, the Plaintiff went to Zhongshan Hospital affiliated to Fudan University for a further treatment;
9. Invoices of medical expenses, to prove that the Plaintiff paid the medical expenses in advance for the injury he suffered;
10. Invoices of transportation costs, to prove the Plaintiff paid the transportation expenses in advance for the injury he suffered;
11. Board and lodging expense invoice, to prove that the Plaintiff paid the board and lodging expense in advance for the injury he suffered;
12. Transfer details of Bank of China, to prove that the Plaintiff's monthly wage is USD850;
13. Remittance bill, to prove the fact that the Plaintiff's monthly wage is USD850;
14. The receipt issued by the Defendant, to prove that the Defendant took back part of the originals of medical records and receipts of medical expenses, transportation expenses and board and lodging expenses, and agreed to pay the Plaintiff RMB20,054.12, but the Defendant has not paid yet;
15. The invoice of assessment fee, to prove that the Plaintiff paid the assessment fee in sum of RMB320 in advance;

16. Invoice of copying costs, to prove that the Defendant made the Plaintiff copy the medical records for it;
17. Invoice of medical nursing belt, to prove that the Plaintiff paid for the medical nursing belt which the doctor advised him to buy;
18. Invoice of printing cost for transfer details of Bank of China, to prove the printing cost advanced by the Plaintiff for the purpose of proving his wages; and
19. A certificate of the First Hospital affiliated to Xiamen University, to prove that the Plaintiff should continue minimally invasive surgery because of the condition of injury.

The Defendant Chengyi Company agreed to dissolve the labor contract between him and the Plaintiff since September 9, 2014 and coordinate to handle the work-related injury claim procedures, but it argued that: firstly, according to *Seafarer's Labor Contract*, the Plaintiff's wage included the post-performance-wage in amount of USD510/month and the fixed overtime pay in amount of USD170/month. In addition, the annual leave pay had been paid to the Plaintiff according to the standard of USD85/month in advance. The bonus of completion of the contract was ascertained in the light of circumstance of the completion of contract by the Plaintiff within a standard no more than USD85/month. Secondly, the Defendant purchased work-related injury insurance for the Plaintiff, the Plaintiff could apply to the social security institution for work-related injury treatment, rather than claim the full compensation against the Defendant. Thirdly, the period of wages during the suspension-of-work-with-pay was 6 months, the Plaintiff had repeated examination and treatment, the expanded loss arising therefrom should be born by himself. Finally, the Defendant had prepaid the Plaintiff RMB39,700 and lent RMB10,000 later to him, and paid social insurance fees of RMB2,000.48 more, one employee of the Defendant lent RMB2,600 to the Plaintiff, the sums should all be deducted.

To support its defense, the Defendant submitted the following evidence materials:

1. Loan detail list, IOUs, voucher of bank, to prove the Plaintiff borrowed RMB39,700 from the Defendant due to the work-related injury;
2. Electronic receipt of Bank of Jiyou, to prove the wages the Defendant paid to the Plaintiff;
3. Situation statement, to prove that the Plaintiff borrowed RMB6,000 from the Defendant's employee CHEN Zhangxuan on March 3, 2014 and March 17, 2014;
4. Confirmation letter of wages during the suspension-of-work-with-pay period provided by Xiamen Work Capacity Assessment Committee, to prove the suspension-of-work-with-pay period is 6 months, from April 28, 2013 to October 28, 2013;
5. Guide to the seafarer, to prove the procedure of a seafarer to borrow money;
6. IOU, receipt of payment, to prove the Plaintiff borrowed RMB1,000 from the Defendant on February 10, 2015; and

7. Payment certificate of social insurance, to prove after the labor relationship between the Plaintiff and the Defendant, the Defendant paid social insurance in sum of RMB2,000.48 from October 2014 to January 2015 for the Plaintiff.

Upon cross-examination by the Plaintiff and the Defendant, the court authenticates the evidence as follows:

The Defendant raised no objection to the authenticity of evidence 1-15, 18 and 19 submitted by the Plaintiff, and they are related to the basic facts of this case, so the court admits the above-mentioned evidence. The evidence numbered with 9, 10, 11 and 17, of which the object of proof is respectively transportation costs, medical expenses, medical equipment fee. These fees fall into the scope of work-related injury claims, which shall be recognized by the work-related injury insurance agency, the court shall not affirm. Aa for evidence 16, although it is not a formal invoice, but the Plaintiff raised that this sum was expended according to the Defendant's instruction and the receipt was affixed with the seal of the copy shop, the Defendant only defended on ground that the receipt was not a standard invoice, but it did not deny the fact that it ordered the Plaintiff to copy the relevant materials; the court admits this evidence and presumes the fact that the Defendant instructed the Plaintiff to copy the materials.

As for evidence 1 submitted by the Defendant, the IOUs made on March 3, 2014 and March 17, 2014 set forth the purposes as "advance medical expenses for GUO Jiangbao", but the Plaintiff denied the fact, and he did not sign the IOU, so the authenticity cannot be determined, the court does admit the evidence. The rest IOUs and bank transfer voucher were signed by the Plaintiff or his wife, or its authenticity thereof has been confirmed by the Plaintiff, so the court admits this evidence. The Plaintiff had no objection to evidence 2, and the evidence submitted by the Plaintiff can corroborate each other, the court admits the evidence. Evidence 3 is only a unilateral statement by the issuer, and the issuer did not appear in court to be examined, the court does not admit this evidence. Evidence 4 is an authentication opinions issued by a competent authority, and the Plaintiff did not file an administrative reconsideration or lawsuit within the statutory time limit after he received the authentication opinions, so the court admits the evidence. Evidence 5 belongs to the Defendant's internal regulations, the Plaintiff denied he knew the regulations, no evidence can prove that the Defendant has informed the Plaintiff of the regulations, so the court does not admit the evidence. As for evidence 6, the Plaintiff acknowledged the receipt of the corresponding amount, so the court admits the evidence. The object of proof of evidence 7 does not belong to the scope of the trial of this case, the Defendant shall bring another lawsuit in terms of the social insurance it extra paid for the Plaintiff after an effective judgment determines the labor relationship between it and the Plaintiff shall be terminated, so the court does not admit this evidence.

The court collected the long-term doctor's advice order, temperature card and other medical records of GUO Jiangbao from Zhongshan Hospital affiliated to Xiamen University, both of the Plaintiff and the Defendant raised no objection to the authenticity or legality of the evidence, and the evidence is relevant to this case, so the court admits this group of evidence.

Based on the above evidence and the court hearing, the court finds the following facts:

On January 10, 2013, the Plaintiff and the Defendant signed *Seafarer Labor Contract* in terms of matter that the Defendant (Party A) sent the Plaintiff (Party B) to M.V. "Growing", which is owned by Global Growing Maritime Corporation Limited, as an FTR (copper smith) in Taiwan region. It is agreed as follows: during the work on board, the pre-tax wage and remuneration are as follows: 1. post-performance wage: USD510.00 (paid on a fixed date designated by the shipowner per month on board); 2. fixed overtime pay: USD170.00 (fixed overtime pay refers to pay for overtime work on Saturday, Sunday and the official holidays, paid on a fixed date designated by the shipowner per month); 3. annual leave pay USD85.00 (annual leave pay refers to the pay for the annual leave calculated on basis of 5 days bi-monthly, paid in advance on a fixed date designated by the shipowner per month on board); 4. bonus for completion of contract: USD85.00 (a floating mechanism is adopted in determining the bonus for completion of contract, it will be paid by Party A according to the situation of completion of contract by Party B). In addition to the above wage, all the remunerations the shipowner or the charterer pays all belong to Party B and shall be directly given to Party B on board. During the period of this contract, Party A shall, according to the regulations, handle and pay for the endowment insurance, work-related injury insurance, medical insurance, unemployment and maternity insurance. After the Plaintiff got on board, the Defendant respectively transferred USD518.23, USD765, USD765, USD765 and USD430.23 respectively on February 8, 2013, March 8, 2013, April 16, 2013, May 14, 2013, and June 9, 2013. On March 18, 2013, the Defendant purchased work-related injury insurance for the Plaintiff, and paid premiums every month till January of 2015.

On April 28, 2013, the Plaintiff was injured due to the hit of grab on board, then he was sent to the Islamic YuJiaEr Ma Si Hospital for 8 days' treatment and hospitalization. After coming back to the mainland, he was examined and hospitalized in Zhongshan Hospital affiliated to Xiamen University for 17 days from June 25, 2013 to July 12, 2013. It is said in the long-term doctor's advice of the medical record that the nursing grade of the Plaintiff is grade two. The temperature card states that the Plaintiff stayed in the hospital for 17 days from June 25, 2013 to July 12, 2013, but during which he was not in the hospital from July 1 to July 4, and from July 6 to July 10, 9 days in total. After that, the Plaintiff went to the First Hospital affiliated to Fujian Medical University, Zhongshan Hospital affiliated to Fudan University, the First Hospital affiliated to Xiamen University, and other hospitals for treatment.

According to the instructions of the Defendant, the Plaintiff applied for identification of work-related injury and authentication of labor capacity. The printing, copying, scanning, and faxing costs are as follows: copying cost on August 8, 2013: RMB26; copying and faxing costs on December 28, 2013: RMB52; scanning cost on February 11, 2014: RMB15; copying cost on September 4, 2014: RMB12; copying cost on February 13, 2014: RMB23.1; copying fee on September 5, 2014: RMB85.5; the amount in total is RMB213.6. On February 25, 2014, Xiamen

Human Resource and Social Security Bureau made the Plaintiff to authenticate work-related injury. On May 23, 2014, Xiamen Work Capacity Assessment Committee issued the *Xiamen Work Capacity Assessment Conclusion*, which identified the Plaintiff as Grade Nine disability, but it has not specified the nursing grade. On November 20, 2014, the Plaintiff confirmed the suspension-of-word-with-pay period was 6 months as assessed by Xiamen Work Capacity Assessment Committee, the Plaintiff did not apply to the Work Assessment Committee for another assessment after receiving the assessment conclusion within the statutory time limit. In addition, the Plaintiff in order to prove the amount of his wages, expended the printing fee in sum of RMB20 to print the transfer details of the Bank of China. During the trial, the Plaintiff and the Defendant confirmed the labor contract relationship between them, the Defendant was the obligor to pay the wages of the Plaintiff, and the Defendant was willing to cooperate with the Plaintiff in a timely manner to handle the claims procedure.

It is also found that since the Plaintiff was injured on April 20, 2015, the Plaintiff repeatedly told the Defendant to prepay the injury treatment costs. The sums that can be ascertained according to the evidence of the Defendant are as follows: RMB2,000 on June 18, 2013; RMB3,000 on June 25, 2013; RMB2,000 on July 3, 2013; RMB2,000 on July 22, 2013; RMB3,000 on November 4, 2013; RMB8,000 on December 23, 2013; RMB4,000 on January 23, 2014; RMB500 February 26, 2014; RMB500 on March 7, 2014, RMB2,100 on March 10, 2014; RMB10,000 on August 2, 2014; and RMB10,000 on February 10, 2015; the total sum is RMB47,100.

It is also found that when the authentication opinions on the work capacity of the Plaintiff, the average life expectancy announced for the last time in Xiamen is 76.89 years old, the Plaintiff GUO Jiangbaowas at the age of 32.27 on September 9, 2014, the average monthly wage in 2013 in Xiamen was RMB4,655.

The court holds that the case is arising from dispute over contract for seafarer employment, the issue of this case lies in which way shall the Plaintiff protect his legitimate rights and interests after suffering work-related injury. In view that the Plaintiff and the Defendant confirmed the labor contract relationship between them, the Defendant handles the work-related injury insurance procedures for the Plaintiff according to the law, and after the Plaintiff was injured, the work-related injury insurance agency made identification for work-related injury, therefore, *Seafarer Labor Contract* signed by the Plaintiff and the Defendant reflects the true intention of both parties, there established a labor contract relationship between them. The labor contract was established according to law and shall be effective. The Plaintiff requested termination of the labor contract on September 9, 2014, and the Defendant agreed, the termination of contract complies with Article 36 of the Labor Contract Law of the People's Republic of China, the court supports it. According to the provisions of the Regulations on the Work-Related Injury Insurance, the employer, the worker suffering a work-related injury and his close relatives may handle work-related injury insurance claim procedures, and the Plaintiff required the Defendant to handle the procedures and cooperate and the Defendant had no objection, so the court supports it. However, according to the Plaintiff's claims, the

Plaintiff requested to be covered by work-related injury insurance and claimed for compensation for personal injury against the Defendant at the same time. Obviously, the claims of the Plaintiff have conflicts in the application of the law, and since the labor contract relationship was established between the Plaintiff and the Defendant, the Plaintiff after suffering the work-related injury should claim for his legitimate rights according to the Regulations on the Work-Related Injury Insurance. In this regard, the Defendant's defense is established, so the court admits it. The work-related injury insurance allowances shall be determined by the work-related injury insurance institution within their authority. Thus, the medical expenses, labor identification fee, lump-sum disability allowance, lump-sum injury medical allowance, hospital food allowance, further medical treatment expenses, transportation costs and accommodation costs all fall into the coverage work-related injury insurance, the Plaintiff shall apply to the work-related injury insurance agencies for identification and disposal according to the law, so the court will not review. As for the nutrition allowance, mental injury solatium, follow-up treatment costs, transportation and accommodation costs and other compensation for personal injury under labor relationship in this case shall be governed by the Regulations on Work-Related Injury Insurance, according to Article 11 Paragraph 3 of the Interpretation of the Supreme People's Court on Certain Issues concerning the Application of Law in the Trial of Cases Involving Compensation for Personal Injury, the court rejects the claim.

The wages during the suspension-of-work-with-pay period, lump-sum disability employment allowance, hospital nursing expenses claimed by the Plaintiff, according to Article 33 Paragraph 1 and Article 37 Paragraph 2 of the Regulations on Work-Related Injury Insurance, fall into the coverage of work-related injury insurance, the court ascertains them respectively as follows:

1. As for the wages during the suspension-of-work-with-pay period, the Plaintiff shall enjoy a suspension-of-work-with-pay period of six months due to his work-related injury as identified by Xiamen Work Capacity Assessment Committee, the conclusion was delivered to the Plaintiff on December 17, 2014, but he did not apply to the provincial work capacity assessment committee for re-assessment within the statutory limit time, the court hereby confirms the assessment. The Plaintiff failed to prove his wage included service fee in sum of USD250-300, and the labor contract does not specify this service fee shall be born by the Defendant either, so the service fee shall not be incorporated into the wage, let alone the work-related injury insurance. The *Seafarer's Labor Contract* provides an annual leave pay of USD85 and a bonus for completion of contract in sum of USD85, the Defendant reckoned that they were not a part of the monthly wage, but according to Article 4 of the Provisions of the National Bureau of Statistics on the Composition of Wages, bonus belong to wages. Moreover, the Defendant paid wages including the annual leave pay and bonus for completion of contract in full to the Plaintiff. Therefore, the Plaintiff's monthly wage according to the contract shall be USD850. In summary, the Defendant shall pay the Plaintiff wages of suspension-of-work-with-pay period

in sum of USD5,100 (USD850 per month multiplied by 6 months, equivalent to RMB31,499.64 after translating USD currency to RMB at the USD-RMB exchange rate (1:6.1764) prevailing on the day when the assessment conclusion in terms of the suspension-of-work-with-pay period was made, namely December 10, 2014).

2. As for the lump-sum disability employment allowance, according to Articles 26 and 27 of the Measures for the Implementation of the Regulations on Work-Related Injury Insurance in Fujian Province, the Defendant shall pay the Plaintiff a lump-sum disability employment allowance: (76.89 years old which is the average life expectancy announced for the last time in Xiamen- 32.27 years old when the labor relationship was terminated) * RMB4,655 / month which is the average wage of workers in Xiamen one year before the labor relationship was terminated * coefficient 0.2 of disability Grade Nine = RMB41,541.22.

3. As for the hospital nursing expenses, according to Article 3 of the Opinions of Xiamen Labor and Social Security Bureau on Several Issues concerning Coverage of Work-Related Injury Insurance, where medical institutions did not confirm the number of nursing workers or nursing period, if the long-term doctor's advice in the hospital record of the worker who suffers a work-related injury nursing states Grade II, the number of nursing workers and nursing period shall not be calculated. The work capacity assessment of the Plaintiff did not confirm the nursing grade. Therefore, the claim of the Plaintiff for the nursing expenses has no basis in law, the court dismisses it.

The communication costs in sum of RMB1,500, the copying costs (including costs of copying, printing, faxing and scanning) in sum of RMB213.6, and the printing cost for bank transfer details in sum of RMB20 claimed by Plaintiff do not fall into the category of work-related injury insurance. Because the Plaintiff failed to provide evidence to prove the communication cost in sum of RMB1,500, the court does not support it. The copying costs in sum of RMB213.6 happening during the period when the Plaintiff and the Defendant applied for identification of work-related injury and labor capacity, the copying was indeed needed for the identification. In view that the employer shall bear the responsibility to handle work-related injury claim procedures for its workers, and the Plaintiff paid that money according to the Defendant's instruction, so the court supports the claim for copying cost raised by the Plaintiff. As to the printing cost for bank transfer details in sum of RMB20, the Plaintiff spent that sum to prove his claim for the wages, and since this claim stands, the court supports the printing cost.

In summary, the Defendant Chengyi Company shall pay the Plaintiff GUO Jiangbao wages during the suspension-of-work-with-pay period in sum of RMB31,499.64, lump-sum disability employment allowance in sum of RMB41,541.22, the copying costs in sum of RMB213.6 (including the costs of copying, printing, faxing and scanning), and the printing cost for the transfer details in sum of RMB20, and the total sum is RMB73,274.46 (after deducting treatment costs in sum of RMB47,100 the Defendant lent to the Plaintiff), the Defendant shall actually pay the Plaintiff RMB26,174.46.

According to Article 36 of the Labor Contract Law of the People's Republic of China, Article 33 Paragraph 1 and Article 37 Paragraph 1 Sub-paragraph 2 of the Regulations on Work-related Injury Insurance, Article 64 Paragraph 1 of the Civil Procedure Law of the People's Republic of China, the judgment is as follows:

1. Confirm the labor contractual relationship between the Plaintiff GUO Jiangbao and the Defendant, Xiamen Chengyi Shipping Co., Ltd. has been terminated since September 9, 2014;
2. The Defendant Xiamen Chengyi Shipping Co., Ltd. shall pay the Plaintiff GUO Jiangbao the wages during the suspension-of-work-with-pay period, lump-sum disability employment allowance, copying costs, printing cost for transfer details in sum of RMB26,174.46 (after deducting the treatment costs in sum of RMB47,100 which the Defendant lent to the Plaintiff) within ten days after the judgment comes into force;
3. The Defendant Xiamen Chengyi Shipping Co., Ltd. shall cooperate with the Plaintiff GUO Jiangbao to handle the work-related injury insurance claim procedures in time; and
4. Reject other claims of the Plaintiff GUO Jiangbao.

If the Defendant fails to perform the obligation to pay the above-mentioned amounts within the period prescribed herein, the Defendant shall, according to Article 253 of the Civil Procedure Law of the People's Republic of China, double pay the interest for the period of delayed performance.

Court acceptance fee in amount of RMB10, the Plaintiff shall bear RMB9 and the Defendant shall pay RMB1.

In event of dissatisfaction with this judgment, the Plaintiff may, within 15 days upon service of this judgment, and the Defendant may, within 15 days upon service of this judgment, submit a statement of appeal to the court, with duplicates being submitted in terms of the number of the other parties, to lodge an appeal with the Fujian High People's Court.

Presiding Judge: CAI Fujun
Judge: YU Jianlin
Acting Judge: LI Yue

May 12, 2015

Acting clerk: OUYANG Ming

Appendix: Relevant Law

1. **Labor Contract Law of the People's Republic of China**
   Article 36 An employer and an employee may terminate their contract of labor if they so agree after consultations.
2. **Regulations on Work-Related Injury Insurance**
   Article 33 Paragraph 1 A disability allowance shall be paid from the work-related injury insurance funds according to the disability grade in a lump sum, and the standards are: for grade one disability, the employee's wages for 24 months; for grade two disability, the employee's wages for 22 months; for grade three disability, the employee's wages for 20 months; and for grade four disability, the employee's wages for 18 months.
   Article 37 Paragraph 1 In the case of a work-related death of an employee, the directly-related family members of the Employee shall receive a funeral allowance, bereavement payments for dependent family members and a lump sum work-related death allowance from work-related injury insurance funds according to the following provisions:
   (1) Bereavement payments for dependent family members shall be made at a certain percentage of the employee's wage to each of the family members of the employee that before the employee's death was dependent on the employee for primary source of income and that has no work capability. The standards are: 40% per month for the spouse, 30% per person per month for other family members, with an additional 10% on the basis of the afore-mentioned standards per person per month in the case of an elderly living alone or an orphan. The sum of the bereavement payments to all dependent family members so determined shall not be higher than the wage of the employee before his work-related death. the specific scope of dependent family members shall be specified by the administrative department of labour security of the state council.
3. **Civil Procedure Law of the People's Republic of China**
   Article 64 Paragraph1A party shall have the responsibility to provide evidence in support of his own propositions.
4. **Interpretation of the Supreme People's Court on Certain Issues concerning the Application of Law in Trial of Cases involving Compensation for Personal Injury**
   Article13 Paragraph 3 The provision of the article shall not be applicable to labor relationships or work-related injury insurance that are governed by the Regulations on Work-Related Injury Insurance.
5. **Regulations on the Composition of Gross Wages**
   Article 4 The total amount of wages is composed of the following six parts:
   (1) hourly wage;
   (2) piecework;
   (3) bonus;

(4) allowances and allowance;
(5) overtime pay;
(6) wages paid under special circumstances.

6. **Measures for the Implementation of the Regulations on Work-Related Injury Insurance in Fujian Province**

   Article 26 A worker who is disabled due to work, in any one of the following circumstances, the work-related injury insurance fund shall pay a lump-sum medical allowance for work-related injury, and the employer shall pay a lump-sum disability employment:

   (2) Where a worker is identified as seven to ten degree of disability, the employer does not renew the labor (employment) and thus terminates the labor (employment) relationship after the labor (employment) contract expires, or the worder suffers a work-related injury proposes to terminate the labor (employment) contract in writing;

   Article 27 Where a worker who suffers a work-related injury is identified as five to ten level of disability, the lump-sum work-related injury medical allowance and disability allowance shall be respectively calculated. The standards shall be according to difference between the average expected lifetime latterly published in the very coordinating area and the age of the worker when the labour relationship was discharged or terminated as well as the average wage of previous year:

   (2) Lump-sum disability employment allowance: ...... Grade Nine, add 0.2 month each year; ......

7. **Opinions of Xiamen Labor and Social Security Bureau on Several Issues concerning Coverage of Work-Related Injury Insurance**

   The issue of the number of nursing care and the period of nursing during the period of leave pay period.

   According to the provisions of the regulations of the regulations, the worker suffers work-related injury needs nursing care during the suspension-of-work-with-pay period, the number of nursing workers and the nursing period shall be confirmed by the medical institution. Where the medical institution has confirmed the number of nursing workers and nursing period, such confirmation shall be followed, while the medical institution does not or refuse to confirm, the number of nursing workers and nursing period can be handled according to the following provisions:

   (1) The number of nursing workers and nursing period shall be determined according to the nursing grade as prescribed in the long-term doctor's advice in the medical records.
   (2) Long term prescribed on the order of nursing grade two or three, as well as the medical institution has not issued a proof of relevant nursing, the number of nursing workers and nursing period is not determined.

   Workers shall provide a copy of the medical records of long-term medical records, and stamped with the seal of medical institutions, as the treatment of work-related injury in the case of the certificate documents.

(3) According to the result of the identification of labor capacity, nursing grade, the number of nursing workers and nursing period of a worker who suffers work-related injury.

Haikou Maritime Court
Civil Judgment

Hainan Weilong Shipping Engineering Co., Ltd.
v.
Hainan Yuehai Shipping Logistics Co., Ltd.

(2014) Qiong Hai Fa Shang Chu Zi No.87

Related Case(s) This is the judgment of first instance and the judgment of second instance is on page 418.

Cause(s) of Action 207. Dispute over shipbuilding contract.

Headnote The Plaintiff shipbuilder held entitled to recover unpaid balance for completion of construction of ship; two-year limitation period had not expired because the running of the limitation period was interrupted by the Defendant's response to the Plaintiff's claim for payment.

Summary The Plaintiff and the Defendant entered into a shipbuilding contract. The Plaintiff delivered the ship to the Defendant who still owed the Plaintiff a portion of the shipbuilding price. The Plaintiff sent a letter to the Defendant to request the unpaid amount to which the Defendant replied that the Plaintiff's work was unacceptable. The Plaintiff filed an action to recover the payment. The court held that the shipbuilding contract was binding on both parties. The agreement included the balance amount remaining after the ship had been delivered to the Defendant. The Defendant was obliged to fulfill the payment as agreed in the settlement agreement. The court held that Plaintiff's claims did not exceed the two-year statute of limitations, because the running of the limitation period was interrupted by an acknowledgment of the Plaintiff's claim by an authorized officer of the Defendant. Thus, the Defendant has to pay the balance payment of the ship price and the liquidated damages.

Judgment

The Plaintiff: Hainan Weilong Shipping Engineering Co., Ltd.
Domicile: Jinpaigang Development District, Lingao County, Hainan Province, China.
Legal representative: ZHENG Ligang, chairman.
Agent *ad litem*: LU Huimin, lawyer of Hainan Weidun Law Firm.

Agent *ad litem*: CHEN Shumei, lawyer of Hainan Weidun Law Firm.

The Defendant: Hainan Yuehai Shipping Logistics Co., Ltd.
Domicile: Rm.604, B Sanyou Department, No.35, Wuzhishan Road, Haikou City, Hainan Province, China.
Legal representative: TAN Xiaodan, general manager.
Agent *ad litem*: LI Ling, lawyer of Beijing Yingke Law Firm Fuzhou Office.

With respect to the case arising from dispute over shipbuilding contract, the Plaintiff Hainan Weilong Shipping Engineering Co., Ltd., filed an action against the Defendant Hainan Yuehai Shipping Logistics Co., Ltd. before the court on August 11, 2014, the court after entertaining this case on August 12 of the same year, constituted the collegiate panel consisting of Judge CHEN Yinghong as Presiding Judge, Acting Judge BAI Wenying and People's Juror HUANG Xiaobo according to the law. In the course of the time limitation for adducing evidence, the Defendant applied to extend the time limitation. The court allowed the application after examination, the time limitation for adducing evidence was accordingly extended till October 14, 2014. On October 20, the court held a hearing in public. LU Huimin, agent *ad litem* of the Plaintiff and LI Ling, agent *ad litem* of the Defendant, appeared in court to attend the trial. Now the case has been concluded.

The Plaintiff alleged in the statement of claim that on June 2, 2009, *Shipbuilding Contract for the Construction of a 13,800wt Bulk Carrier* was concluded between the Plaintiff and the Defendant, in which the name, amount, specifications, construction basis, cost and payment etc. of the vessel had been agreed, the predetermined ship price was RMB45 million. After signing the contract, the Plaintiff built a 13800t bulk carrier (namely M.V. "HONG XIN 6") for the Defendant as agreed, which was qualified after being inspected. On May 16, 2011, both parties signed *Ship Delivery Agreement* and the Plaintiff delivered the ship to the Defendant. On the same day, both parties signed *Written Agreement*, which confirmed the ship price and the terms of payment. Up to this point the Defendant still owed a balance of payment amounting to RMB1,240,000. On August 25, 2012, the Plaintiff sent a letter to the Defendant claiming the outstanding payment and liquidating damages, but the Defendant refused to pay due to quality problems. The Plaintiff requested the court to rule the Defendant: 1. to pay the outstanding sum of the ship price namely RMB1,240,000; and 2. to pay liquidated damages in sum of RMB818,400; and 3. to bear the court fees.

The Defendant failed to defend within the time limit for adducing, but it defended in the oral hearing:

1. The Defendant had fully paid the ship price involved. The ship concerned was constructed through the finance by International Far Eastern Leasing Co., Ltd., to achieve the financing loans, both parties signed several agreements in the course of performing the contract. The last supplementary agreement was signed on June 16, 2011. According to this supplementary agreement, both parties agreed a total price of RMB44,056,185.28 yuan. The Defendant fully paid this amount on September 23, 2011, there was no payment in arrears.

2. By that date, the time limit for the Plaintiff to initiate procedures had already expired. Even if the Defendant defaulted the payment, there would have been no reasonable grounds for suspending or discontinuing the statute of limitation, (the time limit of July 30, 2014 for the Plaintiff to file a litigation had already passed), whether based on the Plaintiff's claim that the last payment was made on September 22, 2011, or according to the allegation of the Defendant that the last payment date was September 23, 2011. The Plaintiff's claim that the prescription of the Defendant's reminder was interrupted on August 25, 2012 could not be established, and the Plaintiff should bear the corresponding legal consequences of the burden of proof.
3. The liquidated damages in this case agreed upon by both parties were too high, and the Plaintiff did not prove liquidated damages. Therefore, the Defendant requested the courts to reject the Plaintiff's claims.

In the course of the time limitation for adducing evidence, the Plaintiff submitted the following ten sets of evidence to support its claim:

1. *Shipbuilding Contract for the Construction of a 13,800wt Bulk Carrier* and *Supplemental Agreement* thereto, to prove the contractual basis that the Plaintiff constructed the 13,800wt bulk ship (namely M.V. "HONG XIN 6").
2. *Maritime Ship Inspection Certificates*, to prove that M.V. "HONG XIN 6" was qualified after being inspected by China Classification Society Hainan Branch (hereinafter referred to as CCS Hainan).
3. *Protocol of Delivery*, to prove that both parties confirmed the specifications of the ship conformed to ship construction contract and agreed to that the final completion data of the ship inspection department should prevail.
4. *Written Agreement*, to prove that both parties confirmed the amount, terms of payment and the liability for breach of contract in terms of overdue payment of the balance of payment.
5. A letter demanding the balance payment of construction of M.V. "HONG XIN 6", to prove the Plaintiff sent a letter to the Defendant demanding the balance payment on August 25, 2012.
6. *Notification Letter* from the Defendant, to prove that the Defendant received the letter of demand from the Plaintiff, but it established grounds for refusal of payment because of inferior quality and demanding the Plaintiff to pay for the repair fee.
7. *Letter of Reply* from the Plaintiff, to prove that this ship had no inferior quality problem.
8. *Letter of Reply* from the Defendant, to prove that the Defendant required the certification document.
9. Seven sets of *Inspection Notice*, to prove the installation of ship equipment was confirmed upon the signature of the representative on the site of the Defendant.
10. *The Notice on the Establishment of Project Department for the 13,800wt Bulk Carrier and 41 Car/999 Passenger Ship*, to prove that the Defendant's representative WAN Yongzhi is the project manager of M.V. "HONG XIN 6".

In order to counter the Defendant's claim in the oral hearing that it had paid off the total ship price, and furthermore to prove the fact that the ship price was in arrears by the Defendant, the Plaintiff produced in addition the following four sets of evidence:

11. *Statement of Current Accounts of 13,800wt Bulk Carrier* and *Yue Hai Hang Statement of Account*, to prove that the Defendant's legal representative confirmed the Defendant paid RMB13,556,185.28 from June 18 to September 9 in 2009. The Plaintiff transferred RMB8 million yuan to the Defendant in 7 times to assist the Defendant to solve the financing loan capital flow.
12. Voucher of bank transfer and online banking remittance, to prove that the Plaintiff transferred RMB8 million yuan to the Defendant, through the methods including ICBC online banking transfer.
13. *Written Agreement* signed by Far Eastern Leasing Co., Ltd. (hereinafter Far Eastern) with the Defendant, to prove that the purpose of *Supplementary Agreement of 13,800wt of bulk carrier M.V. "HONG XIN 6"* submitted by the Defendant was only signed by the Plaintiff to cooperate with the Defendant, so that it could fulfill this agreement. Thus, this is not the basis for the settlement. In addition, the reason that the Plaintiff's transferring payment to the Defendant is to fulfill the condition and requirement as agreed in the agreement.
14. Detailed statement of settlement of the balance payment, receipt and bank statement, to prove the Defendant only paid RMB4,200,000 yuan for the ship price since May 16, 2011 when both parties confirmed the balance payment.

The Defendant did not object to the authenticity or relevancy of evidence No.1, but it regarded that the contract was only for the filing review, in particular, the ship price is not the actual price. The Defendant did not object to the authenticity or relevancy of evidence No.2, but it did not agree that the construction did reach the agreement. The Defendant did not object to the authenticity or relevancy of evidence No.3, but it argued that the ship price has been paid. The Defendant did not object to the authenticity or relevancy of evidence No.4, but it argued that there was a difference between *Protocol of Delivery* and this evidence. The evidence shows that the Defendant owed RMB5,440,000 yuan for the ship price; however, Article 3 of *Protocol of Delivery* provides "Party A has paid the full amount ship price for M. V. "HONG XIN 6"". It had objection to the authenticity and object of proof of evidence No.5 and argued that this fax was not the one the Defendant received on the date but evidence No.3 of the Defendant (letter). It had no objection to the authenticity and relevancy of evidence No.6 but not its object of proof, arguing that this evidence did not mention the ship construction payment delayed by the Defendant of 1.24 million, nor could it prove that the Defendant had received the letter of call. It had objection to the authenticity and object of proof of evidence No.7, arguing that it was merely the statement of the parties. It had no objection to the authenticity and object of proof of evidence No.8. It had no objection to the authenticity of the inspection notification numbered as 068, 114, 085, 113 and 009 in evidence No.9 but not the ones numbered as 157 and 148 for the lack of confirmation of signature of the representative of the shipowner. It had objection to the authenticity, relevancy and object of proof of evidence No.10, arguing that this evidence was unilaterally made by the Plaintiff, which could not be used as an evidence. It had objection to the authenticity and relevancy of *Statement of Current Accounts of 13,800wt Bulk Carrier* in evidence No.11, arguing that it was a statistical statement unilaterally made by the Plaintiff but merely recognized the facts of the Defendant's payment reflected by No. 1, 2, 3, 4, 5, 7, 9, 10, 12, 16, 18, 20, 21, 22, 26 but did not recognize the relevancy of the other current accounts. As for *Yue Hai Hang Statement of Account*, it only recognized its pro forma authenticity but not its relevancy and object of proof, arguing that it could not be proved to be the statement of account about shipbuilding contract between the Plaintiff and the Defendant. But it recognized the fact that the Defendant actually paid for the ship construction stated in the column of "payment amount on paper". It had no objection to the authenticity of evidence No.12 but not its relevancy and object of proof, arguing that the bank transfer and e-bank voucher simply reflected the money transaction between the personals or individuals. The columns of "Usage" on certain remittance vouchers were not filled or filled in with "cash" or "repayment", which could not prove the relation between it and the shipbuilding project of the Plaintiff and the Defendant. It recognized the authenticity of evidence No.13 but held that this agreement had no direct relation with the dispute of shipbuilding payment in this case. Although this agreement stipulated the pre-condition which should be met by the Defendant to collect the payment but it could not explain that the agreement signed by the Plaintiff and the Defendant on June 16, 2009 was only for coordination with the payment. The Plaintiff had no direct evidence to prove that the agreement signed by both parties on June 16, 2009 was not the basis for settlement. It had no objection to the pro forma authenticity of the bank statement in evidence 14 but not the authenticity of the cash voucher. It had objection to the relevancy and object of proof of this evidence. It held that the statement of bank was only the current account of personal account, which could not suggest that the money transaction had relation to the dispute of shipbuilding payment of the case.

The court ascertains the Plaintiff's evidence as below: the Defendant had no objection to the evidence No.1, 2, 3 and 4 submitted by the Plaintiff from the perspective of authenticity and relevancy; the court confirms the authenticity, relevancy and legality of these four pieces of evidence. The above evidence can prove the Plaintiff had a contractual relationship with the Defendant for the shipbuilding project, this ship has been inspected, and based on the inspection, both parties confirmed the outstanding ship price, the term of payment and payment method on May 16, 2011. The Defendant questioned evidence No.5, it held the facsimile it received from the Plaintiff on August 25,2012 was evidence No.3 but not that one. However, evidence No.3 provided by the Defendant was neither facsimile nor the original, and there was no signature of the Defendant on it, so it is lack of authenticity. The Defendant confirmed the authenticity of evidence No.6 of the Plaintiff, namely, the Defendant agreed the facsimile issued on August 30 of the same year. The content thereof is "the facsimile sent from your company on August 25, 2012, it is not only unreasonable but also unprofessional that your company raised the existing requirements", this evidence shows that the Defendant had received a facsimile. This facsimile was issued by the Plaintiff and the dateline is August 25 m 2012. Since the Defendant cannot prove that the other letters of the Plaintiff have been received on the same day, the court confirmed the authenticity, legality and relevancy and power of the evidence No.5 and 6. These two pieces of evidence can confirm that the Plaintiff demanded the payment of outstanding ship price to the Defendant on August 25, 2012. The Defendant objected the authenticity of evidence No.7, but it had no objection to the authenticity of evidence No.6 and 8. As the contents of the three letters correspond to each other, the court confirmed the authenticity, legality, relevancy and probative force of evidence No.7 and 8, it can prove that the two sides had made representations on the ship's technology and quality. The Plaintiff claimed that WANG Yongzhi was the project representative of the Defendant based on evidence No.10. evidence No.9 consists a signature of WANG Yongzhi, and the ship inspection department issued a certificate for the subject ship. In the absence of any contrary evidence, the court confirmed the authenticity, legality, relevancy and probative value of evidence of three pieces of evidence. The Defendant had no objection to the authenticity of *Yue Hai Hang Statement of Account* consisted in evidence No.11 and only confirms the fact and amount of the payment by the Defendant under *Statement of Current Accounts of 13,800wt Bulk Carrier*. The court holds that *Yue Hai Hang Statement of Account* consists two sections, one is the sum paid by the Defendant to the Plaintiff, the other one is the amount the Defendant received from the Plaintiff. The confirmation signed by the Defendant's legal representative which shows the actual payment is RMB5,556,185.28 yuan, it also means the Defendant received RMB8 million yuan from the Plaintiff. *Statement of Current Accounts of 13,800wt Bulk Carrier* was made by the Plaintiff, but each sum in and out can be corroborated by other evidence. Therefore, the authenticity, legality, relevancy and probative force of evidence thereof could be confirmed. Although the remitter and the receiver in evidence No.12 are not in the name of the Plaintiff and the Defendant, they are clerk or designated person of both parties. The Defendant only made an oral defense without adducing evidence to prove that there are other debtor-creditor relationship; in the light of evidence No.11, 13 and 14 submitted by the Plaintiff, as all of these three pieces of evidence could support the claim, the court confirmed the authenticity, legality, relevancy and probative force thereof. The Defendant had no objection of the authenticity of evidence No.13, combined with other evidence, the court confirms the authenticity, legality, relevancy and probative force thereof. Although the Defendant only admitted the authenticity of the sheets of bank in evidence No.14, the court confirms the authenticity, legality, relevancy and probative force of evidence thereof. This evidence can prove that the Defendant has paid RMB4,200,000 yuan after May 26, 2011, the Defendant has to pay the Plaintiff the ship price, but it still owed RMB1,240,000 yuan.

In order to justify its demurrer, the Defendant submitted three pieces of evidence within the time period for producing evidence:

1. *Supplemental Agreement of the Construction for 13,800wt Bulk Carrier "HONG XIN 6"*, to prove that both parties signed the supplemental agreement on June 16, 2016, it changed the previous contract agreed on May 16 of the same year, in which the ship price was adjusted to RMB44,056,185.28 yuan.
2. The details of payments and electronic transfer vouchers, to prove that from June 18, 2009 to September 23, 2011, the Defendant actually paid the ship price of RMB47,056,185.25 yuan, after deducting deposit for finance in sum of RMB3 million yuan advanced by the Plaintiff, the Defendant had paid the full amount of the ship price.
3. A letter, to prove that the facsimile received by the Defendant on August 25, 2012 was not evidence No.5 submitted by the Plaintiff. In this facsimile, the Plaintiff merely mentioned the problem of defect and quality of the shipbuilding, but not the payment of the ship price; therefore, the statute of limitation had expired, in this case.

The Plaintiff's cross-examination on evidence No.1 adduced by the Defendant presented that the requirements of authenticity and legality were not met. The Plaintiff claimed that there was no original of evidence No.1, that there were no reasonable grounds for the agreement, that the agreed price under this agreement was RMB3 million yuan higher than that determined on May 16, 2011. This is because the purpose of this agreement was merely to meet the lender's and the guarantor's need so as to support the Defendant in achieving loans from them. Therefore, this agreement should not be the basis for settlement. The Defendant claimed that the ship price was paid on the spot, but there was no corresponding evidence. The Plaintiff pointed out the reason why both parties did not have the original copy of that agreement was that there was only one original copy, which had been passed to the financing guarantor Far Eastern. The Plaintiff had no objection to the authenticity or legality of evidence No.2, but dissented with the purpose of proof and considered that it had transferred money to the Defendant for many times in order to assist the Defendant to finance for shipbuilding and meet the financing conditions raised by the lender and the guarantor. The Plaintiff objected to the authenticity and legality of evidence No.3 because there was no original or facsimile to verify.

As for the three pieces of evidence adduced by the Defendant, the court holds that evidence No.1 has no original to verify, so the Plaintiff did not admit or submit valid evidence to refute, in the meantime, the Plaintiff gave a reasonable explanation for the actual purpose of this agreement. Therefore, the Plaintiff's counter-argument is rational. The court objects to the authenticity and legality of this evidence, and holds it cannot be used as the basis of a settlement for both sides. The Plaintiff had no objection to the authenticity of evidence No.2, and the court ascertains its authenticity, but the Plaintiff had submitted evidence to prove that the Defendant owed the balance payment of the ship price. Therefore, the court does not admit the Defendant's allegation that the total cost of the ship had been paid. Evidence No.3 consisted of no original copy or original facsimile to verify, there was no signature of the Plaintiff on it. Therefore, the court does not confirm the authenticity or probative force thereof, and does not accept this defense.

On the basis of the above certification and the court hearing, the court ascertains the facts of the subject case as follows:

On June 2, 2009, *Shipbuilding Contract for the Construction of a 13,800wt Bulk Carrier* was concluded between the Plaintiff and the Defendant, in which the name, amount, specifications, construction basis, cost and payment etc. of the vessel had been agreed, the predetermined ship price was RMB45 million. On May 10, 2011, both parties sign *Supplementary Agreement*. After signing the contract, the Plaintiff built a 13,800wt bulk carrier, of which the name was M.V. "HONG XIN 6" for the Defendant as agreed. The domestic ship inspection center of CCS Hainan after inspection issued an inspection certificate for the ship involved. On May 16, 2011, the two parties signed *Protocol of Delivery*, the Plaintiff delivered the ship in port of Haikou. On the same day, both parties signed *Written Agreement*, which confirmed: 1. the ship price was RMB41 million yuan, the Defendant still owed RMB5,440,000; 2. the loan of RMB3 million the Defendant from Far Eastern should be paid to the account opened in of the Plaintiff; 3. the Defendant should pay RMB4 million to the Plaintiff, if the sum was not paid as agreed, the Plaintiff should pay an interest of 2% thereon. On August 25, 2012, the Plaintiff sent a letter, referring "M.V. "HONG XIN 6" has been delivered to your company on May 16, 2011, so far it has passed 15 months, but your company still owes our company the construction payment in sum of RMB1,240,000 (without interest), we hereby request your company to pay off the sum in arrears. On August 30, 2012, the Defendant replied as: "in view of the contents of the fax on August 25, 2012, the requirements of your company are unreasonable and unprofessional". On August 11, 2014, the Plaintiff filed an action before the court.

In September 2009, the Defendant signed No.IFELC09D011219-C-02 *Agreement* with Far Eastern. The main contents thereof are as follows: the Defendant, Far Eastern and Bank of Shanghai Co., Ltd. Pudong Branch signed *Bank of Shanghai RMB Unit Entrustment Loan Contract*, and the Defendant and the Far Eastern hereby agree as supplement that: 1. the Defendant shall pay RMB3 million yuan, as security for performance of the loan contract and the agreement by the Defendant, to the designated account of Far Eastern by telegraphic transfer within three banking days prior to the date of drawdown as stipulated in the loan contract. 2. Under the loan contract, in addition to conform to all the provisions concerned, the following conditions shall be satisfied so that the Defendant can withdraw RMB33 million yuan: ...... Far Eastern has received a copy of the payment voucher which shows the sum paid by the Defendant to the Plaintiff shall be no less than RMB15 million yuan This bulk carrier shall be insured against all risks and additional oil pollution risk upon confirmation of Far Eastern. The insurance amount under ship all risks shall be no less than RMB45 million yuan. The Plaintiff issued a confirmation to Far Eastern, clarifying that after the Defendant paid the relevant sum to the Plaintiff, there was no debtor-creditor relationship between the Plaintiff and the Defendant. Therefore, *Protocol of Delivery* signed by the Plaintiff and the Defendant emphasized as the following statement: "the Plaintiff has paid the full amount of the ship price of the M.V "HONG XIN 6". After delivery, the Defendant obtained the ownership of M.V. "HONG XIN 6". The debt before the delivery of M.V. "HONG XIN 6" has nothing to do with the Defendant, and after being delivered, the loan thereon has nothing to do with the Plaintiff".

From July 10 to September 8 in 2009, in order to assist the Defendant to finance and loan from Far Eastern and Bank of Shanghai Pudong Branch, and satisfy the Plaintiff transferred RMB8 million yuan to the Defendant in 7 times through online banking. The Defendant remitted RMB1 million yuan to the Plaintiff on July 10, RMB500,000 yuan on July 29, RMB1 million yuan on July 31, RMB500,000 yuan on August 4, RMB15,00,000 yuan on the next day, RMB1 million yuan on August 11, and RMB2,500,000 yuan on September 8. From June 18 to September 9, the Defendant remitted RMB13,556,185.28 yuan to the Plaintiff in total. After deduction, the Defendant has virtually remitted RMB555,618.28 to the Plaintiff. TAN Xiaodan, the legal representative of the Defendant signed on *Yue Hai Hang Statement of Account* on May 9, 2010 to confirm the statement of "the above account reconciliation is accurate". The Plaintiff paid finance deposit in sum of RMB3 million yuan again to the Defendant on September 22, 2011. From June 3, 2011 to March 22, 2012, the Defendant paid RMB37,200,000 yuan to the Plaintiff in 9 times. From the day the two sides signed the contract to the day the subject action, the Defendant paid RMB50,756,185.28 yuan to the Plaintiff, and the last payment was made on March 22, 2012. However, the Plaintiff transferred RMB11 million yuan to the Defendant to support the Defendant to deal with the cash-flow problem. On May 16, 2011, both sides signed *Written Agreement*. In this agreement, the amount of the ship price is RMB41 million yuan, and the Defendant still owed the outstanding ship price in sum of RMB5,440,000 yuan. In addition, the Defendant has paid RMB4,200,000 yuan, the Defendant still owed RMB1,240,000 yuan.

The court holds that this case is dispute over shipbuilding contract. Both sides signed the shipbuilding contract in good faith. Since it does not violate any mandatory provisions of regulation or law, it has the capacity to bind both parties. According to the shipbuilding contract, the Plaintiff built a ship for the Defendant. The ship after being inspected has been delivered, the Plaintiff completed the work as agreed. After the delivery of the ship, both sides reached an agreement on the amount of the balance to be paid, date of disbursement, method of payment, liquidated damages, etc. The terms thereof including the liquidated damages do not violate any provisions of regulation or law, and shall be valid and effective, and this agreement is a part of the shipbuilding contract. In addition, the Defendant shall fulfill the obligation for payment as agreed in the settlement agreement, and pay the full amount before October 20, 2011. The Defendant still owes RMB1,240,000 yuan so far. The Defendant claimed that it had paid the full amount of the ship price, but the evidence is insufficient, so the court does not support it. The last time the Defendant paid the ship price is March 22, 2012, after that, there is no further payment. According to that, the legitimate interests of the Plaintiff was infringed on March 23, the statute of limitation shall be counted therefrom. The Plaintiff claimed that it sent a letter to the Defendant on August 25, 2012 requesting the balance payment, and the Defendant replied on August 30, 2012, in this regard, the Plaintiff provided corresponding evidence, and held that it constituted a discontinuance of the statute of limitation. The Defendant argued it only received letters concerning the negotiation on the technology and quality of the ship rather than the letter the Plaintiff alleged demanding the balance payment, but the argument lacks evidence. Therefore, although the Defendant did not give a clear reply to the request for the arrears in the reply provided by the Plaintiff, but its reply corresponded to the letter on August 25, 2012 provided by the Plaintiff. Since the Defendant failed to prove the letter it received on the same day was another letter with other contents, the court holds that the Defendant received the letter of demand for balance payment from the Plaintiff on August 25, 2012, so the statute of limitation of the Plaintiff enforce the creditor's rights in this case should be discontinued. Moreover, the Plaintiff's filing the action on August 11, 2014 does not exceed the two-year statute of limitation. Therefore, the evidence for the claim that the litigation did not exceed its statute of limitation is insufficient, and the court does not accept that. It is well-founded in the perspective of law and shall be supported that the Plaintiff requested the Defendant to pay the balance payment of the ship price and the liquidated damages. The Defendant argued that the amount of liquidated damages was excessively high, and that the Plaintiff did not prove that it had suffered losses because of the violation of the contract. The court holds that the agreed amount of liquidated damages was not excessively high, the occurrence of losses is not a prerequisite for the payment of liquidated damages, and that the Defendant did not pay on time which led to the Plaintiff suffering losses. Therefore, there is no legal basis for the Defendant's allegation, and the court does not support it. The Defendant shall pay the outstanding ship price in sum of RMB1,240,000 yuan as well as corresponding liquidated damages according to the settlement agreement. According to the settlement agreement, the deadline for the final payment was October 20, 2011, therefore, the liquidated damages shall be counted from October 21, 2011 to July 20, 2014, which is based on the Plaintiff claim, amounting to RMB818,400 yuan (RMB1,240,000 yuan × 33 months × 2%).

Pulling the thread together, according to Article 109, Article 114 Paragraph 1 and Article 263 of the Contract Law of the People's Republic of China, the court hereby renders the judgment as follows:

The Defendant Yuehai Shipping Logistics Co., Ltd. shall, within ten days as of the effective day of this judgment, defray the Plaintiff Hainan Weilong Shipping Engineering Co., Ltd. ship price in sum of RMB1,240,000 yuan, and the liquidated damages in sum of RMB818,400 yuan, in aggregate amount of RMB2,058,400 yuan.

If the Defendant, Hainan Yuehai Shipping Logistics Co., Ltd. fails to fulfill its obligation to make the payments within the time limit provided by this judgment, the interest for the period of deferred payment thereon shall be double paid according to Article 253 of the Civil Procedure Law of the People's Republic of China.

Court acceptance fee in the amount of RMB23,267.20 yuan shall be assumed by the Defendant Hainan Yuehai Shipping Logistics Co., Ltd.

If not satisfy with this judgment, any party shall within fifteen days as of the service of this judgment, submit a statement of appeal to the court, with duplicates in the number of the opposing parties, so as to make an appeal before Hainan High People's Court.

Presiding Judge: CHEN Yinghong
Acting Judge: BAI Wenying
People's Juror: HUANG Xiaobo

November 10, 2014

Clerk: XIE Huijing

Hainan High People's Court
Civil Judgment

Hainan Weilong Shipping Engineering Co., Ltd.
v.
Hainan Yuehai Shipping Logistics Co., Ltd.

(2015) Qiong Min San Zhong Zi No.2

Related Case(s) This is the judgment of second instance, and the judgment of first instance is on page 407.

Cause(s) of Action 207. Dispute over shipbuilding contract.

Headnote Affirming lower court decision that the Plaintiff shipbuilder was entitled to recover unpaid balance for completion of construction of ship, affirming lower court decision that the Defendant's reply to the Plaintiff's request for payment was sufficient to interrupt the running of the two-year limitation period.

Summary The Plaintiff and the Defendant entered into a shipbuilding contract. The Plaintiff delivered the ship to the Defendant, however the Defendant still owed the Plaintiff a portion of the shipbuilding price. The Plaintiff sent a letter to the Defendant to request the unpaid amount, to which the Defendant replied that the Plaintiff's work was unacceptable. The Plaintiff then filed a suit for the payment. The court of first instance found for the Plaintiff, holding that the Defendant's response to the Plaintiff's letter of request was sufficient to interrupt the running of the limitation period. The Defendant appealed, and the appeal court recognized the trial court's decision, holding that the Defendant's reply to the Plaintiff's letter did constitute an interruption of the running of the limitation period.

Judgment

The Appellant (the Defendant of first instance): Hainan Yuehai Shipping Logistics Co., Ltd.
Domicile: Rm. 604, B Sanyou Department, No.35, Wuzhishan Road, Haikou City
Legal representative: TAN Xiaodan, general manager.
Agent *ad litem*: LI Ling, lawyer of Beijing Yingke Law Firm Fuzhou Office.
Agent *ad litem*: ZHUANG Juanjuan, lawyer of Beijing Yingke Law Firm Fuzhou Office.

The Respondent (the Plaintiff of first instance): Hainan Weilong Shipping Engineering Co., Ltd.
Domicile: Jinpaigang Development District, Lingao County, Hainan Province, China.
Legal representative: ZHENG Ligang, chairman.
Agent *ad litem*: LU Huimin, lawyer of Hainan Weidun Law Firm.
Agent *ad litem*: CHEN Shumei, lawyer of Hainan Weidun Law Firm.

Dissatisfied with (2014) Qiong Hai Fa Shang Chu Zi No.87 Civil Judgment rendered by Haikou Maritime Court with respect to the case arising from dispute over shipbuilding contract, the Appellant, Hainan Yuehai Shipping Logistics Co., Ltd. (hereinafter referred to as "Yuehai Company") filed an appeal against the Respondent, Hainan Weilong Shipping Engineering Co., Ltd. (hereinafter referred to as "Weilong Company") before the court on December 9, 2014. The court, after entertaining this case, organized the collegiate panel according to the law and held hearings in public respectively on February 3, 2015 and February 5, 2015. LI Ling and ZHUANG Juanjuan, agents *ad litem* of Yuehai Company, and LU Huimin and CHEN Shumei, agents *ad litem* of Weilong Company appeared in court to attend the trial. Now the case has been concluded.

Weilong Company alleged in the statement of claim that it concluded *Shipbuilding Contract for the Construction of a 13,800wt Bulk Carrier* (hereinafter referred to as the shipbuilding contract) with Yuehai Company on June 2, 2009, in which the name, amount, specifications, construction basis, cost and payment etc. of the vessel had been agreed, the predetermined ship price was RMB45 million. After signing the contract, Weilong Company built a 13800wt vessel (namely M.V. "HONG XIN 6") for Yuehai Company as agreed, which was qualified after being inspected. On May 16, 2011, Weilong Company delivered the ship to Yuehai Company and signed *Protocol of Delivery*. On the same day, both parties signed *Written Agreement*, which confirmed the ship price and the terms of payment. Up to this point Yuehai Company still owed a balance of payment amounting to RMB1,240,000. On August 25, 2012, Weilong Company sent a letter to Yuehai Company claiming the outstanding payment and liquidating damages, but Yuehai Company refused to pay due to quality problems. Weilong Company requested the court of first instance to order Yuehai Company: 1. pay the outstanding sum of the ship price namely RMB1,240,000; 2. pay liquidated damages in sum of RMB818,400; and 3. bear the court fees.

Yuehai Company failed to defend within the time limit for adducing, but it defended in the oral hearing:

1. Yuehai Company had fully paid the ship price involved. The ship concerned was constructed through the finance by International Far Eastern Leasing Co., Ltd., to achieve financing loans, both parties signed several agreements in the course of performing the contract. The last supplementary agreement was signed on June 16, 2011. According to this supplementary agreement, both parties agreed a total price of RMB44,056,185.28 yuan. Yuehai Company fully paid this amount on September 23, 2011, there was no payment in arrears.

2. By that date, the time limit for Weilong Company to file an action had already expired. Even if Yuehai Company defaulted the payment, there would have been no reasonable grounds for suspending or discontinuing the statute of limitations, (the time limit of July 30, 2014 for Weilong Company to file a litigation had already passed), whether based on Weilong Company's claim that the last payment was made on September 22, 2011, or according to the allegation of Yuehai Company that the last payment date was September 23, 2011. Weilong Company's claim that the statute of limitations of Yuehai Company was interrupted on August 25, 2012 could not be established, and Weilong Company should bear the corresponding legal consequences of the burden of proof.
3. The liquidated damages in this case agreed upon by both parties were too high, and Weilong Company did not prove liquidated damages. Therefore, Yuehai Company requested the courts to reject Weilong Company's claims.

The court of first instance found the facts of the subject case as follows:

On June 2, 2009, Weilong Company and Yuehai Company concluded *Shipbuilding Contract for the Construction of a 13,800wt Bulk Carrier*, in which the name, amount, specifications, construction basis, cost and payment etc. of the vessel had been agreed, the predetermined ship price was RMB45 million. On May 10, 2011, both parties sign *Supplementary Agreement*. After signing the contract, Weilong Company built a 13,800wt bulk carrier, of which the name was M.V. "HONG XIN 6" for Yuehai Company as agreed. The domestic ship inspection center of CCS Hainan after inspection issued an inspection certificate for the ship involved. On May 16, 2011, the two parties signed *Protocol of Delivery*, Weilong Company delivered the ship in port of Haikou. On the same day, both parties signed *Written Agreement*, which confirmed: 1. the ship price was RMB41 million yuan, Yuehai Company still owed RMB5,440,000; 2. the loan of RMB3 million Yuehai Company from Far Eastern should be paid to the account opened of Weilong Company; 3. Yuehai Company should pay RMB4 million to Weilong Company, if the sum was not paid as agreed, Weilong Company should pay an interest of 2% thereon. On August 25, 2012, Weilong Company sent a letter, referring M.V. "HONG XIN 6" has been delivered to your company on May 16, 2011, so far it has passed 15 months, but your company still owes our company the construction payment in sum of RMB1,240,000 (without interest), we hereby request your company to pay off the sum in arrears. On August 30, 2012, Yuehai Company replied as: "in view of the contents of the fax dated August 25, 2012, the requirements of your company are unreasonable and unprofessional." On August 11, 2014, Weilong Company filed an action before the court of first instance.

In September 2009, Yuehai Company signed No.IFELC09D011219-C-02 Agreement with Far Eastern. The main contents thereof were as follows: Yuehai Company, Far Eastern and Bank of Shanghai Co., Ltd. Pudong Branch signed *Bank of Shanghai RMB Unit Entrustment Loan Contract*, and Yuehai Company and Far Eastern agreed as supplement that: "(i) Yuehai Company shall pay RMB3 million yuan, as security for performance of the loan contract and the agreement by Yuehai

Company, to the designated account of Far Eastern by telegraphic transfer within three banking days prior to the date of drawdown as stipulated in the loan contract. (ii) Under the loan contract, in addition to conform to all the provisions concerned, the following conditions shall be satisfied so that Yuehai Company can withdraw RMB33 million yuan: …… Far Eastern has received a copy of the payment voucher which shows the sum paid by Yuehai Company to Weilong Company shall be no less than RMB15 million yuan This bulk carrier shall be insured against all risks and additional oil pollution risk upon confirmation of Far Eastern. The insurance amount under ship all risks shall be no less than RMB45 million yuan". Weilong Company issued a confirmation to Far Eastern, clarifying that after Yuehai Company paid the relevant sum to Weilong Company, there was no debtor-creditor relationship between Weilong Company and Yuehai Company. Therefore, *Protocol of Delivery* signed by Weilong Company and Yuehai Company emphasized as the following statement: "Weilong Company has paid the full amount of the ship price of the M.V "HONG XIN 6". After delivery, Yuehai Company obtained the ownership of M.V. "HONG XIN 6". The debt before the delivery of M.V. "HONG XIN 6" has nothing to do with Yuehai Company, and after being delivered, the loan thereon has nothing to do with Weilong Company".

From July 10 to September 8 in 2009, in order to assist Yuehai Company to finance and loan from Far Eastern and Bank of Shanghai Pudong Branch, Weilong Company transferred RMB8 million yuan to Yuehai Company in 7 times through online banking. Yuehai Company remitted RMB1 millionyuan to Weilong Company on July 10, RMB500,000 yuan on July 29, RMB1 millionyuan on July 31, RMB500,000 yuan on August 4, RMB15,00,000 yuan on the next day, RMB1 millionyuan on August 11, and RMB2,500,000 yuan on September 8. From June 18 to September 9, Yuehai Company remitted RMB13,556,185.28 yuan to Weilong Company in total. After deduction, Yuehai Company has virtually remitted RMB555,618.28 to Weilong Company. TAN Xiaodong, the legal representative of Yuehai Company signed on *YueHaiHang Statement of Account* on May 9, 2010 to confirm the statement of "the accounts have been confirmed correct". Weilong Company paid finance deposit in sum of RMB3 millionyuan again to Yuehai Company on September 22, 2011. From June 3, 2011 to March 22, 2012, Yuehai Company paid RMB37,200,000 yuan to Weilong Company in 9 times. From the day the two sides signed the contract to the day the subject action, Yuehai Company paid RMB50,756,185.28 yuan to Weilong Company, and the last payment was made on March 22, 2012. However, Weilong Company transferred RMB11 million yuan to Yuehai Company to support Yuehai Company to deal with the cash-flow problem. On May 16, 2011, both sides signed *Written Agreement*. In this agreement, the amount of the ship price is RMB41 million yuan, and Yuehai Company still owed the outstanding ship price in sum of RMB5,440,000 yuan. In addition, Yuehai Company has paid RMB4,200,000 yuan, Yuehai Company still owed RMB1,240,000 yuan.

The court of first instance held that this case was concerning dispute over shipbuilding contract. The parties signed the Shipbuilding Contract in good faith. Since it did not violate any mandatory provisions of regulation or law, it had the capacity to bind both parties. According to the Shipbuilding Contract, Weilong Company built a vessel for Yuehai Company. The vessel after being inspected has been delivered, Weilong Company completed the work as agreed. After the delivery of the vessel, both sides reached an agreement on the amount of the balance to be paid, date of disbursement, method of payment, liquidated damages, etc. The terms thereof including the liquidated damages did not violate any provisions of regulation or law, and should be valid and effective, and this agreement was a part of the Shipbuilding Contract. In addition, Yuehai Company should fulfill the obligation for payment as agreed in the settlement agreement, and pay the full amount before October 20, 2011. Yuehai Company still owed RMB1,240,000 yuan so far. Yuehai Company claimed that it had paid the full amount of the ship price, but the evidence was insufficient, so the court of first instance did not support it. The last time Yuehai Company paid the ship price was March 22, 2012, after that, there is no further payment. According to that, the legitimate interests of Weilong Company was infringed on March 23, the statute of limitations should be counted therefrom. Weilong Company claimed that it sent a letter to Yuehai Company on August 25, 2012 requesting the balance payment, and Yuehai Company replied on August 30, 2012, in this regard, Weilong Company provided corresponding evidence, and held that it constituted an interruption of the statute of limitations. Yuehai Company argued it only received letters concerning the negotiation on the technology and quality of the ship rather than the letter Weilong Company alleged demanding the balance payment, but the argument lacks evidence. Therefore, although Yuehai Company did not give a clear reply to the request for the arrears in the reply provided by Weilong Company, but its reply corresponded to the letter on August 25, 2012 provided by Weilong Company. Since Yuehai Company failed to prove the letter it received on the same day was another letter with other contents, the court of first instance held that Yuehai Company received the letter of demand for balance payment from Weilong Company on August 25, 2012, so the statute of limitations of Weilong Company to enforce the creditor's rights in this case should be interrupted. Moreover, Weilong Company's filing the action on August 11, 2014 did not exceed the two-year statute of limitations. Therefore, the evidence for the claim that the litigation did not exceed its statute of limitation was insufficient, and the court of first instance did not accept that. It was well-founded in the perspective of law and should be supported that Weilong Company requested Yuehai Company to pay the balance payment of the ship price and the liquidated damages. Yuehai Company argued that the amount of liquidated damages was excessively high, and that Weilong Company did not prove that it had suffered losses because of the violation of the contract. The court of first instance held that the agreed amount of liquidated damages was not excessively high, the occurrence of losses was not a prerequisite for the payment of liquidated damages, and that Yuehai Company did not pay on time which led to Weilong Company suffering losses. Therefore, there was no legal basis for Yuehai Company's allegation, and the court of first instance did not support it. Yuehai Company should pay the outstanding ship price in sum of RMB1,240,000 yuan as well as corresponding liquidated damages according to the settlement agreement. According to the settlement agreement, the deadline for the final payment was October 20, 2011, therefore, the liquidated damages should be counted from October 21, 2011 to July 20, 2014, which was based on Weilong Company claim, amounting to RMB818,400 yuan (RMB1,240,000 yuan × 33 months × 2%).

According to Article 109, Article 114 Paragraph 1 and Article 263 of the Contract Law of the People's Republic of China, the court of first instance rendered the judgment as follows: Yuehai Company should, within ten days as of the effective day of this judgment, defray Weilong Company the ship price in sum of RMB1,240,000 yuan, plus the liquidated damages in sum of RMB818,400 yuan, in aggregate amount of RMB2,058,400 yuan.

Yuehai Company dissatisfied with the judgment of first instance, and filed an appeal before the court, requested as follows: the judgment of first instance should be withdrawn and amended to reject4all the claims of Weilong Company according to the law; and Weilong Company should bear all the litigation fees. The grounds of appeal were as follows:

1. The authenticity and prohibitive force of part of evidence were incorrectly confirmed in the judgement of first instance.

   Yuehai Company did not deny that it received a fax from Weilong Company on August 25, 2012, but it argued the content was only concerning ship quality issues, and it was not a fax of which the content was about the demand for the balance payment of shipbuilding price of M.V. "Hongxin No.6" as alleged by Weilong Company. Yuehai Company adduced evidence for that. In the judgment of first instance, it was unreasonable that the court denied the probative force of the evidence adduced by Yuehai Company on grounds that the evidence submitted by Yuehai Company was neither a faxed copy nor the original, besides it bore no signature of Weilong Company, and based on a sentence in the reply of Yuehai Company on August 30, 2012 "the current request of your company in your fax sent on August 25, 2012 is unreasonable and unprofessional".

   1) There is partial understanding in the judgment of first instance on "what is the original fax". Under normal conditions, fax machines are divided into 2 kinds, namely thermal fax machine and plain A4 paper fax machine. When using a thermal paper fax machine, the original fax would form according to paper capacitor and paper mould; and when using a plain paper fax machine, the document directly from the recipient's fax machine was a copy of the document itself. Based on the characteristics of the technology, the fax machine Yuehai Company used was a plain paper fax machine, so the fax copy it received was a copy. Yuehai Company did not receive any other fax from Weilong Company on the very same day. If Weilong Company alleged it sent a number of faxes, the burden of evidence should lie on it. It is wrong that the judgment of first instance denied the probative force of the evidence of Yuehai Company under the condition that Weilong Company did not provide the evidence for its claim on the letter of the fax.

2) The authentication of the evidence in the judgment of first instance was against the law. Firstly, the letter dated August 25, 2012 Weilong Company provided was a statement of the parties. The law is clearly stipulated that the people's court shall, in combination with other evidence of this case, determine whether the party's statements could be admitted as basis to find the facts of the case, but the judgment of first instance denied the authenticity and the probative force of the evidence on ground that Yuehai Company failed to prove that it received any other letter from Weilong Company on the same day, it went against the law. Secondly, according to the new evidence to find Yuehai Company (namely *Yue Hai Hang Statement of Accounts* which was confirmed by TAN Xiaodan and JIANG Mou with signatures on May 9, 2010), the main difference between this evidence and *Yue Hai Hang Statement of Accounts* submitted by Weilong Company lied in that the three sums in total amount of RMB3,500,000 SU Weifeng and LIN Youyun remitted were excluded from the statement of accounts. There are two versions of the Yue Hai Hang Statement of Accounts, but the first version was canceled. So Yuehai Company actually did not receive transfer amount of RMB8,000,000. Thirdly, Weilong Company issued a value-added tax invoice with a face amount of RMB31,000,000, it could prove that Weilong Company issued the RMB31,000,000 value-added tax invoice according to Article 4 of *Supplementary Agreement of the Shipbuilding Contract for the Construction of a 13,800wt Bulk Carrier* (hereinafter referred to as the supplementary agreement) provided by Yuehai Company. Thus, it was wrong that the judgment of first instance refused to admit the evidence.

2. It was wrong finding of fact that the judgment of first instance held that Yuehai Company received a fax concerning demand for shipbuilding price from Weilong Company on August 25, 2012, and it constituted an interruption of statute of limitations.

1) One of the issues of this case is the existence of interruption of the statute of limitations. Article 140 of the General Principles of the Civil Law of the People's Republic of China stipulates that: a statute of limitation shall be discontinued if suit is brought or if one party makes a claim for or agrees to fulfillment of obligations. A new limitation shall be counted from the time of the discontinuance. Article 10 of the Provisions of the Supreme People's Court on Certain Issues concerning Application of the Statute of Limitations System in the Trial of Civil Cases stipulate that: " where one party delivers documents to the opposite party to claim his rights, and the opposite party affixes his signature or seal on the documents, or in the absence of signature or seal, it can be proven that such documents have been served; where a party concerned claims his rights by sending mail or electronic data, and the mail or electronic data arrive at or should have arrived at the opposite party, the statute of limitations shall be interrupted". In this case, except the letter dated August 25, 2012, Weilong Company had no other evidence to prove

Weilong Company had demanded for shipbuilding price against Yuehai Company, Weilong Company did not adduce any evidence that could prove it had faxed Yuehai Company. In both the fax and e-mail, Weilong Company did not mention the so-called "balance payment of shipbuilding price" issue, and Yuehai Company did not reply or confirm that payment. Thus, it is wrong that the judgment of first instance refused to admit the evidence.

2) In respect of burden of proof, Yuehai Company had proved the start and expiration of the statute of limitations, Weilong Company argued the statute of limitations was interrupted on the ground that it demanded Yuehai Company for the balance payment of ship price by fax on August 25, 2012, such fact was a rejoinder against the defense of Yuehai Company that the statute of limitations has expired, the fact on which such rejoinder was based should be proved by Weilong Company. Weilong Company had no evidence to prove that it had served any letter or notified Yuehai Company about the so-called "balance payment of shipbuilding price" issue, it should bear the legal consequence of failure of adducing evidence.

3. The liquidated damages ascertained by the judgment of first instance was too high.

According to Article 29 of the Interpretation of the Supreme People's Court on Several Issues concerning the Application of the Contract Law of the Peoples Republic of China (II): "where a party alleges that the agreed amount of liquidated damages is excessively high and requests an appropriate reduction thereof, the people's court shall adjust. According to the principles of fairness and good faith, take a measurement and render a decision on the basis of actual losses and by taking into consideration such comprehensive factors as the performance of contract, fault of the parties concerned and anticipated profits". This shows that the amount of liquidated damages refers to the actual loss, the purpose to adjust the amount of liquidated damages is to keep the loss caused by default basically equal to or roughly balance. Even if the fact that Yuehai Company occupied Weilong Company's funds established and Yuehai Company should pay the corresponding interest, Weilong Company should bear the burden of proof in terms of its actual losses. As Weilong Company failed to prove its losses, it was more reasonable to count the interest at the bank deposit rate over the capital occupation period as the loss.

In summary, the judgment of first instance unclearly found the facts and incorrectly applied the law. Request to amend the judgment according to the law.

Weilong Company contended as follows:

1. It was correct that the judgment of first instance admitted the authenticity and probative force of the fax dated August 25, 2012 and relative evidence submitted by Weilong Company. The fax Yuehai Company submitted was in suspicion of false. Firstly, the judgment of first instance held that Yuehai Company owed RMB1,240,000, the facts were clear and the evidence was sufficient. On August 25, 2012, Weilong Company faxed to Yuehai Company

requesting payment as soon as possible, it was quite a reasonable thing. The reason that Yuehai Company said the require of Weilong Company was unreasonable in the replying fax on August 30, 2012 lies in that Weilong Company refused to pay the ship collision repair costs in sum of RMB1,240,000 to Yuehai Company. Yuehai Company held that the outstanding sum should set off the repair costs, and the require of Weilong Company was unreasonable, so there were the words "the require is unreasonable". Secondly, Yuehai Company said the fax machine was a common one, the document came out the fax machine itself was a copy; since the fax was a copy, and the paper was common A4 paper, it could be maintained over a long period of time, and no seal could be seen from the evidence submitted by Yuehai Company. Thirdly, it was meaningless that Yuehai Company said it used a common fax machine.

2. In respect of *Yue Hai Hang Statement of Accounts*, in the second instance Yuehai Company submitted a piece of different *Yue Hai Hang Statement of Accounts* as new evidence, alleging that *Yue Hai Hang Statement of Accounts* Weilong Company submitted was an obsolete document, and the one Yuehai Company submitted was an effective document. First of all, *Yue Hai Hang Statement of Accounts* Yuehai Company submitted was not new evidence, the formation time thereof was as same as that submitted by Weilong Company, and Yuehai Company's adducing evidence had exceeded the time limit for burden of proof, so Weilong Company refused to examine it. Secondly, Yuehai Company confirmed the authenticity of *Yue Hai Hang Statement of Accounts* submitted by Weilong Company in the cross-examination of the first instance, but now it provided new evidence, it attempted to deny the evidence adduced in the original instance, Yuehai Company went back on its own words. It is not difficult to find that the evidence submitted by Yuehai Company have obvious mark of alteration. Also, Yuehai Company said it was RMB4,500,000 (RMB8,000,000-RMB3,500,000) rather than RMB8,000,000 that they received from Weilong Company. According to Yuehai Company's point of view, Yuehai Company owed a sum of RMB5,240,000 but not RMB1,240,000. Yuehai Company could not make out a good case. It was correct that the judgment of first instance did not admit the authenticity or the probative force of *Supplementary Agreement of the Shipbuilding Contract for the Construction of a 13,800wt Bulk Carrier*. Because the supplementary agreement is used for obtaining loans, but not the basis for the settlement between the two parties. Weilong Company issued a RMB31,000,000 value-added tax invoice and a receipt of RMB14,000,000 in order to assist Yuehai Company, Yuehai Company's arguments have no factual basis.

Weilong Company has never suspended dunning the arrears against Yuehai Company. Yuehai Company did not pay off the balance payment of shipbuilding price within the agreed period, it still owed RMB1,240,000. In addition to frequently calling and faxing the legal representative of Yuehai Company Tan Xiaodan and General Manager Zhang Weiguo, Weilong Company also sent staff to

Yuehai Company. Its dunning has never stopped, the allegation that Yuehai Company's claims exceed the statute of limitations never exists.

The calculation method of liquidated damages which is the declaration of true meaning of the two parties should valid and effective. Yuehai Company fails to pay within the agreed period, it shall be held liable for breach of contract. And the two parties agreed the liquidated damages as only two percent each month, which is not excessively high.

During the court of second instance, Yuehai Company submitted four pieces of new evidence:

1. *Yue Hai Hang Statement of Accounts* confirmed by TAB Xiaodan and JIANG Mou with signature on May 9, 2010, to prove *Yue Hai Hang Statement of Accounts* Weilong Company submitted in the first instance is a void document, the sums SU Huifeng remitted to LIN Youyun on July 31, JIANG Mou remitted to LIN Youyun on August 5 and JIANG Mou remitted to LIN Youyun on August 11 stated thereon are irrelevant to this case and should be deducted.
2. Two materials concerning the ship quality.
3. Ship inspection report.
4. The repairing project budget book.

Evidence 2 to evidence 4 is to prove the ship quality problems.

The cross-examination opinions of Weilong Company are as follows: evidence 1 had existed since 2010, it was not new evidence, so it refused to examine. The evidence was almost the same in form and signature as *Yue Hai Hang Statement of Accounts* submitted by Weilong Company in the first instance. A few words added in this evidence were different fonts and the handwriting is different from the previous, so there is an obvious suspect of fraud. Evidence 2 to 4 is not new evidence, it refused to examine.

As to evidence 1 submitted by Yuehai Company, the responsible person of Weilong Company at that moment, JIANG Mou, appeared in court as a witness, holding that *Yue Hai Hang Statement of Accounts* had two copies, one of which signed by TAN Xiaodan and preserved by Weilong Company, one signed by TAN Xiaodan and JIANG Mou and preserved by Yuehai Company. The contents of the two pieces of *Yue Hai Hang Statement of Accounts* are the same, where there was no question marks on the words of "except SU Weifeng and LIN Youyun" and three remittances and the aggregate sum actual remitted in account.

The authentication on the evidence of the court is as follows: in respect of evidence 1, as for whether it is new evidence, Yuehai Company argued it only found the evidence after filing the appeal, it belonged to new evidence. According to Article 41 of the Some Provisions of the Supreme People's Court on Evidence in Civil Procedures, new evidence in the second instance includes evidence found after the hearing of the first instance ends, so it can be admitted as new evidence; as for whether the evidence shall be admitted, except "SU Weifeng and LIN Youyun" written before TAN Xiaodan's writing "the accounts have been confirmed correct", JIANG Mou's signature and question mark behind three sums remitted to LIN

Youyun and the actual paid-in amount, the font, format and amount of *Yue Hai Hang Statement of Accounts* are basically the same with the one submitted by Weilong Company in the first instance. Yuehai Company argued the Yue Hai Hang Statement of Accounts submitted by Weilong Company had been set aside, but Weilong Company denied, the handler JIANG Mou appeared in court to testify that the contents of the two Yue Hai Hang Statements of Accounts had no difference, the Yue Hai Hang Statement of Accounts he signed was preserved by Yuehai Company.

The signing dates of two *Yue Hai Hang Statements of Accounts* are the same day, the time for each payment has been specified therein, the two parties would confirm with signature upon verification. If the previous statement of accounts having been confirmed with signature is void, the amount in dispute should be re-specified. However, *Yue Hai Hang Statement of Accounts* submitted by Yuehai Company only marks question mark on the three sums remitted to LIN Youyun and the actual paid-in amount, it does not conform to common sense that no recalculation of actual paid-in amount exists. The three sums amount to RMB3,500,000, in event of failure to transfer to the account, it is inconsistent with the facts that the two parties signed the Supplementary Agreement on May 16, 2011, confirming the outstanding shipbuilding price amounted to RMB5,440,000, and Yuehai Company paid RMB4,200,000 successively.

In summary, Yuehai Company confirmed the authenticity of *Yue Hai Hang Statement of Accounts* submitted by Weilong Company, the evidence submitted in the second instance is not sufficient to overturn the payable amount as confirmed in *Yue Hai Hang Statement of Accounts* submitted by Weilong Company, the evidence shall not be admissible.

As for evidence 2 to 4, during the first instance, Yuehai Company did not file a counterclaim or defense with regard to quality problems of the ship, so the judgment of first instance did not try the claim. Therefore, the quality of the ship does not fall into the scope of trial of the second instance, so the evidence shall not be reviewed.

During the second instance, Weilong Company applied for permitting witnesses JIANG Mou and LIN Mou to appear in court as witness, to prove that JIANG Mou had repeatedly called for the outstanding payment, and LIN Mou went to the office of Yuehai Company to dun the arrears with JIANG Mou in August 2013.

Yuehai Company's cross-examination opinion: JIANG Mou and LIN Mou are relatives of ZHAO Qingbo, chairman of Weilong Company, so the testimonies of witnesses thereof should not be admitted, no evidence can prove JIANG Mou and LIN Mou called and visited Weilong Company in terms of the arrears.

The ascertainment of the court on the testimonies of witnesses of JIANG Mou and LIN Mou is as follows: JIANG Mou and LIN Mou are employees of Weilong Company, they have a stake with Weilong Company. The fact that JIANG Mou and LIN Mou called and went to Yuehai Company for the dunning the arrears has no other corroborative evidence, therefore, the testimonies of witnesses of them shall not be adopted.

The facts found by the court are consistent with those identified by the first instance, the court hereby confirms.

The court holds that the issues in this case are: whether the action filed by Weilong Company exceeded the statute of limitations; and whether Yuehai Company should pay the construction price in sum of RMB1,240,000 and the liquidated damages in sum of and RMB818,400 to Weilong Company.

1. Whether the action filed by Weilong Company exceeded the statute of limitations.

   On June 2, 2009, Weilong Company signed *Shipbuilding Contract for the Construction of a 13,800wt Bulk Carrier* with Yuehai Company, Weilong Company has completed the work and delivered the ship. On May 16, 2011, the two parties signed a supplementary agreement to confirm the ship built by Yuehai Company was settle at RMB41,000,000, the remaining shipbuilding price amounted to RMB5,440,000, and the outstanding sum should be paid off before October 20, 2011. After the signing of the supplementary agreement, Yuehai Company paid Weilong Company RMB1,240,000, the time of the final payment is March 22, 2012. On August 25, 2012, Weilong Company sent a letter to Yuehai Company, claiming the ship was qualified, and the RMB1,240,000 in arrears should be paid off. Yuehai Company claimed that the fax they received was not that alleged by Weilong Company. The court holds that Yuehai Company submitted the letter dated August 25, 2012 does not show the faxing time, it cannot be seen as a fax copy, and the seal on the letter is absent of Weilong Company's seal, it only mentions M.V. "HONG XIN6" is qualified, the argument that Weilong Company raised the issue of poor quality and it demanded Weilong Company to undertake the responsibility is inadmissible. On August 30, 2012, Weilong Company sent a letter to Yuehai Company, saying "the current request of your company in your fax sent on August 25, 2012 is unreasonable and unprofessional". The statement can correspond to the letter of demand submitted by Weilong Company on August 25, 2012. In summary, it is not inappropriate that judgment of first instance held that Weilong Company's sending a letter to Yuehai Company on August 25, 2012 to demand the payment of shipbuilding price constituted an interruption of statute of limitations. The lawsuit brought by Weilong Company on August 11, 2014 did not exceed the two-year statute of limitations. The ground held by Yuehai Company that the action filed by Weilong Company had exceeded the statute of limitations cannot be established, the court does not support it.

2. Whether Yuehai Company should pay the construction price in sum of RMB1,240,000 and the liquidated damages in sum of and RMB818,400 to Weilong Company.

After Weilong Company signed the shipbuilding contract with Yuehai Company, Weilong Company has delivered the ship as agreed. The two parties signed a supplementary agreement on May 16, 2011, which confirmed the remaining shipbuilding price is RMB5,440,000, and Yuehai Company should pay off all the sum before October 20, 2011. After the signing of the supplementary agreement, Yuehai Company paid Weilong Company RMB4,200,000, and still left RMB1,240,000 in arrears, it already constituted a breach of contract. Yuehai Company shall pay the balance payment of the shipbuilding price in sum of RMB1,240,000 and the liquidated damages. Yuehai Company claimed the RMB31,000,000 value-added-tax invoice issued by Weilong Company could prove that Weilong Company issued invoice according to Article 4 of the supplementary agreement, Yuehai Company has performed the obligation for payment. The court holds that the supplementary agreement signed on June 16, 2011, the two parties shall on the spot settle the balance in sum of RMB14,056,185.28 according to the supplementary agreement, but after signing the supplementary agreement, Yuehai Company still made payments to Weilong Company until March 22, 2012, therefore, the contents of the supplementary agreement are inconsistent with the actual payment. Weilong Company argued that the supplementary agreement was signed in order to assist Yuehai Company to obtain loans, which can be proved by a series of supplementary agreements and running accounts between the two parties, the court shall admit. The allegation of Yuehai Company that the balance payment of the shipbuilding price should not be paid has no basis in fact, so the court shall not support. Article 107 of the Contract Law of the People's Republic of China provides, "if a party fails to perform its obligations under a contract, or its performance fails to satisfy the terms of the contract, it shall bear the liabilities for breach of contract such as to continue to perform its obligations, to take remedial measures, or to compensate for losses". The payment of liquidated damages is not based on whether or not loss is caused, the two parties agreed interest 2% per month, it does not fall into the circumstance of too much high interest. Yuehai Company claimed the liquidated damages was too high and shall be counted on the basis of the bank deposit rate over the same period, such claim cannot stand, the court does not support it.

To sum up, the facts were clearly ascertained and the laws were correctly applied in the judgment of first instance, so the judgment of first instance shall be affirmed. According to Article 170 Paragraph 1 Sub-paragraph 1 of the Civil Procedure Law of the People's Republic of China, the judgment is as follows:

Dismiss the appeal and affirm the original judgment; and

Court acceptance fee in amount of RMB23,267.2, shall be born by Hainan Yuehai Shipping Logistics Co., Ltd.

The judgment is final.

Presiding Judge: ZHAO Yinghua
Acting Judge: WANG Haijiao
Acting Judge: WANG Hao

March 17, 2015

Clerk: HUANG Jiachen

Appendix: Relevant Law

1. **Civil Procedure Law of the People's Republic of China**
   Article 170 After trying a case on appeal, the people's court of second instance shall, in the light of the following situations, dispose of it accordingly:
   (1) if the facts were clearly ascertained and the law was correctly applied in the first-instance judgment, the appeal shall be rejected in the form of a judgment and the first-instance judgment shall be recognized;
   (2) if the application of the law was incorrect in the first-instance judgment, the said judgment shall be amended according to the law;
   (3) if in the first-instance judgment the facts were incorrectly or not clearly ascertained and the evidence was insufficient, the people's court of second instance shall make a written order to set aside the judgment and remand to case to the first-instance people's court for retrial, or the people's court of second instance may amend the judgment after investigating and clarifying the facts; or
   (4) if there was violation of legal procedure in making the first-instance judgment, which may have affected correct adjudication, the judgment shall be set aside by a written order and the case remanded to the first-instance people's court for retrial.

   The parties concerned may appeal against the judgment or written order rendered in a retrial of their case.

Guangzhou Maritime Court
Civil Judgment

Hong Kong Everglory Shipping Co., Ltd. et al.
v.
TAN Dingzhao et al.

(2014) Guang Hai Fa Shang Chu Zi No. 340

Related Case(s) None.

Cause(s) of Action 193. Dispute over liability for ship collision damage.

Headnote Subrogated cargo insurer recovered damages from the shipowner in "both to blame" collision in proportion to their degrees of fault; owner of one ship held liable despite purported bareboat charter because charter had not been recorded.

Summary The Plaintiff, PICC Property and Casualty Company Limited Guangdong Branch, sued to recover damages from a collision between two vessels. M.V. "EVERGLORY", owned by Everglory, insured by Life Insurance Company, and M.V. "He Xing 888", owned by the Defendant TAN Dingzhao and TAN Dingcheng, which had been bareboat chartered to the Defendant Wei Gang Company. However, the bareboat charter party was never recorded, and the court found it to be invalid. The court found that the vessel M.V. "He Xing 888" was 60% at fault from various violations of navigation rules and that M.V. "EVERGLORY" was 40% at fault. The damages were thus calculated proportionately to the respective fault amounts.

Judgment

The Plaintiff: Hong Kong Everglory Shipping Co., Ltd.
Domicile: FZ2020, Room 2105, World Trade Center, 29–31 Chaiwanxiangli Street, Hong Kong Special Administration Region.
Legal representative: LIU Yongming, director.
Agent *ad litem*: HUANG Hui, lawyer of Guangdong Huang & Huang Co. Law Firm.
Agent *ad litem*: XIANG Wei, lawyer of Guangdong Huang & Huang Co. Law Firm.

© The Author(s), under exclusive license to Springer-Verlag GmbH, DE, part of Springer Nature 2021
M. Davies and J. Lin (eds.), *Chinese Maritime Cases*, Chinese Maritime Cases Series, https://doi.org/10.1007/978-3-662-63716-6_20

The Plaintiff: PICC Property and Casualty Company Limited Guangdong Branch.
Domicile: 3rd Floor, No.303 middle of Guangzhou Avenue, Guangzhou, Guangdong Province.
Legal representative: GUO Wenge, general manager.
Agent *ad litem*: HUANG Hui, lawyer of Guangdong Huang & Huang Co. Law Firm.
Agent *ad litem*: XIANG Wei, lawyer of Guangdong Huang & Huang Co. Law Firm.

The Defendant: TAN Dingzhao, male, Han, born on August 15, 1972.
Domicile: Room 201, Ladder Two of Yalinge, Qiaoya Garden, Tai Town Street Office, Taishan City, Guangdong Province.
Agent *ad litem*: CHEN Haojie, lawyer of Guangdong Everwin Law Office.
Agent *ad litem*: HU Xingjun, lawyer of Guangdong Everwin Law Office.

The Defendant: TAN Dingcheng, male, Han, born on January 20, 1977.
Domicile: Room 601, Line 60, Nan Chang Xin Cun, Tai Town Street Office, Taishan City, Guangdong Province.
Agent *ad litem*: CHEN Haojie, lawyer of Guangdong Everwin Law Office.
Agent *ad litem*: HU Xingjun, lawyer of Guangdong Everwin Law Office.

The Defendant: Zhuhai Weigang Tu Shi Fang Engineering Co., Ltd.
Domicile: Room 387, 3rd Floor, auxiliary building of the Guishan Town government's office building, Zhuhai, Guangdong Province.
Legal representative: XIA weizhong, manager.
Agent *ad litem*: CHEN Haojie, lawyer of Guangdong Everwin Law Office.
Agent *ad litem*: HU Xingjun, lawyer of Guangdong Everwin Law Office.

With respect to the dispute over the liability for ship collision damage, the Plaintiff Hong Kong Everglory Shipping Co., Ltd. (hereinafter referred to as Everglory), PICC Property and Casualty Company Limited Guangdong Branch (hereinafter referred to as Life Insurance Company) filed an action against the Defendants TAN Dingzhao, TAN Dingcheng and Zhuhai Weigang Tu Shi Fang Engineering Co., Ltd. (hereinafter referred to as Wei Gang Company)on December 13, 2013. After litigant materials being supplemented, the court accepted the case on April 22, 2014, and constituted the collegiate panel participated by Presiding Judge ZHANG Kexiong, Judge WU Guining and Acting Judge YIN Zhonglie according to the law. Clerk LI Chunyu took the charge of the recording of this case. On July 3, 2014, the court organized the evidence exchanges among the parties, and held hearings in public on January 7 and 8. HUANG Hui, XIANG Wei, agents *ad litem* jointly entrusted by the Plaintiffs Everglory and Life Insurance Company and CHENG Haojie, HU Xingjun, agents *ad litem* jointly entrusted by the Defendants TAN Dingzhao, TAN Dingcheng, appeared in court to attend the trial, the Defendant Wei Gang Company was summoned by the court and refused to attend without justified reasons. Now the case has been concluded after trial.

The Plaintiffs Everglory and Life Insurance Company jointly alleged that: on May 8, 2013, the collision between M.V. "EVERGOLRY" owned by Everglory, be insured by Life Insurance Company and M.V. "He Xing 888" owned by the Defendant TAN Dingzhao and Tan Ding Cheng, barely chartered by the Defendant Wei Gang Company happened in Ling Ding water channel, which led to the serious damage of M.V. "EVERGOLRY". There were six crew members of M.V."He Xing 888" fell into water, of whom three were rescued, two missing, one dead. After the collision, the Plaintiff Life Insurance Company paid fixing fee and other fees RMB3,635,601.18 to Everglory (hereinafter the currency not denied referred to as RMB) according to the insurance contract, and achieved the subrogation right according to the law. Additionally, the Plaintiff suffered the loss of fixing fee and so on RMB399,311.60 yuan, the Plaintiff Everglory compensated RMB1,200,000 yuan to the families of three missing and one dead crews according to fifty percent of the liability. The collision aforementioned was caused by the faulty of M.V. "He Xing 888" such as serious violation of voyage rules, mistake operation and so on, consequently, the three Defendant should bear 70% of the indemnity responsibility. The Plaintiff requested the court to order:

1. The three Defendants should bear joint and several compensation for personal injury RMB480,000 yuan to the Plaintiff Everglory and of which the interests should be counted according to the loan rate published by the People's Bank of China from October 10, 2013 to the actual pay off day.
2. The three Defendants should bear joint and several compensation for the loss of ship's fixing fees and other losses in sum of RMB279,518.12 yuan to the Plaintiff Everglory and of which the interests should be counted according to the loan rate published by the People's Bank of China from October 10, 2013 to the actual pay off day.
3. The three Defendants should bear joint and several compensation liability for the loss of ship's fixing fee and other losses RMB2,544,920.83 yuan to the Plaintiff Life Insurance Company and of which the interests should be counted according to the loan rate published by the People's Bank of China from October 16, 2013 to the actual pay off day.
4. The three Defendants should bear joint and several compensation for the loss of the application for property preservation RMB5,000 yuan to the Plaintiff Everglory.
5. The three Defendants should bear the legal costs of this case.

The Plaintiff Everglory submitted the following proof materials:

1. The registration certificate of M.V. "EVERGLORY".
2. The charter party and letter of commission of M.V. "He Xing 888".
3. Ship's certificate such as the class certificate and the name list of crews of M.V."EVERGLORY".
4. The report of the survey of the traffic accident on water.
5. The letter of guarantee and bank bills of paying the guaranty fund issued to Guangzhou Maritime Safety Administration.

6. The letter of guarantee issued separately to three wounded crews.
7. Three copies of settlement agreement and bank bills.
8. Three copies of receipts and the confirmation of releasing the liability.
9. The letter of confirmation.
10. The letter of guarantee of the salvage fee of M.V. "He Xing 888".

The Plaintiff Life Insurance Company submitted the following materials:

1. The policy of insurance of the ship insurance and the ship insurance clause of life insurance company (2009 edition).
2. The commission letter and the charter party of M.V. "He Xing 888".
3. Ship's certificates such as class certificate of M.V."EVERGLORY" and crew lists.
4. The report of the survey of the traffic accident on water.
5. The inspection report, license for business corporations, organization code certificate, license for insurance assessment business and personnel license for the practice of insurance assessment.
6. The bill for the ship repair, the bill of the repair projects, receipt and payment for water single.
7. Statement of the compensation of the premium concerning repairs charge and the electronic receipt of e-bank.
8. The voyage bill, invoice, receipt and email issued by Guangzhou China Shipping Agency Co., Ltd. (hereinafter referred as to China Shipping Agency), and the proof of payment of the Plaintiff Everglory.
9. The statement, invoice, receipt and the letter of presentation issued by Dongguan Hai Ming Shipping Agency Co., Ltd. (hereinafter referred as to Hai Ming Company), and the proof of payment of the Plaintiff Everglory.
10. The invoice and the receipt of inspection fee, issued by Classification Society and the payment instrument of the Plaintiff Everglory.
11. The statement of the premium of the ship concerning the cost such as the port charges and the electronic bill of Internet Bank.
12. Receipts and the letter of subrogation.
13. The credit certificate.

CHEN Feng, the examiner of Guangzhou Haizheng Insurance Adjustors & Surveyors Co., Ltd. (hereinafter referred as to Haizheng Company), entrusted by the Plaintiff Life Insurance Company appeared in court for being questioned.

The Defendant TAN Dingzhao, TAN Dingcheng jointly argued that:

1. The loss caused by the collision accident should be burdened by the Defendant Wei Gang Company, the charterer of M.V. "He Xing 888", and the Defendant TAN Dingzhao and TAN Dingcheng had no obligation to compensate. The Defendant TAN Dingzhao and TAN Dingcheng signed *Charter Party of M.V. "He Xing 888"* on October 10, 2011. The Defendant Wei Gang Company should be responsible for the safety accident happened during the ship leasing period, although this demise charter had not been registered. However, after the accident, the Defendants TAN Dingzhao and TAN Dingcheng

disclosed the charterer to the Plaintiff Everglory, and the Defendant Wei Gang Company held the meeting to consult with the Plaintiff as the charterer, which showed the Defendant Wei Gang Company would undertake the responsibility according to law, and compensated to the families of the casualty crews. M.V. He Xing 888 was operated by the Defendant Wei Gang Company, which also hired crews and paid the salary. According to Article 34 of the Tort Liability Law of the People's Republic of China, the loss caused by the collision accident in this case should be obliged to pay by the Defendant Wei Gang Company. According to the Article 6 of the Regulations of the People's Republic of China on Vessel Registration, as for the demise charter without being registered, the right claimed by the third party only had effect of the confrontation of registration when being related to the setup, transference, abolition. However, the loss caused by collision in this case had nothing to do with the setup, transference, elimination of the demise charter, therefore the Defendant Wei Gang Company should undertake the responsibility.
2. M.V. "EVERGLORY" had negligence out-look under the restricted visibility circumstances, neither sailing at a safe speed, nor releasing the sound signals ruled by regulations, which were also the important reasons causing the collision accident in this case. M.V "EVERGLORY" should bear important responsibility for the accident. There was no facts and legal basis for the Plaintiff requesting M.V. "He Xing 888" to burden 70% of the liability of collision.
3. The loss including ship's fixing charge claimed by both of the Plaintiffs was unreasonable.

The Defendant TAN Dingzhao and TAN Dingcheng submitted the following evidence materials:

1. The ownership registration certificate of M.V "He Xing 888".
2. The letter of authorization and the charter party of M.V. "He Xing888".
3. 3 copies of reconciliation agreement.
4. The protocol.

The Defendant Wei Gang Company had neither defensed nor submitted any evidence materials.

By the application of the Plaintiff Everglory, the court obtained the following evidence materials from Guangdong Maritime Safety Administration:

1. The discs and investigation report of the collision accident
2. The investigation materials of M.V. "He Xing 888": (1) 7 copies of the investigative records of crews and personnel concerned; (2) the policy of insurance; (3) the minutes of wreck salvage of M.V. "He Xing 888"; (4)the agreements of ship's registration and mandatory administration; (5) the assessment report of the loss caused by the sinking of M.V. "He Xing 888"; (6) the report of the accident on water; (7) ship's operation certificate for Hong Kong and Macao route, water transportation certificate, the business license and certificate of the entry of the Fidelity Fund for the third party's personal risk of

Taishan Hexing Shipping Co., Ltd. (hereinafter referred as to He Xing Company); (8) the business license, articles of association, receipts and measurement table of Wei Gang Company; (9) record of the accident scene and the weather forecast of coastal area; (10) AIS identification code certificate; (11) crew lists and the certificate of competency; (12) the ship's inspection certification; (13) the nationality papers of ship and the ownership registration certificate of the ship; (14) the rules for safety production of He Xing Company; (15) competency certificate of LI Dou, security chief of He Xing Company; (16) the quick reports of safety production accident of He Xing Company; (17) charter party, power of attorney, delivery receipts, bills of lading and payroll sheet; and (18) the organization chart of the safety production management stuffs in He Xing Company, weather forecast record, dynamic record of the ship, emergency address list, liability statement of contracting safety production, hidden trouble record and water transport permit
3. The investigation materials of M.V. "EVERGLORY": (1) the telegraph book of deck department, the telegraph book of the engine room department, log book and engine logbook; (2) assessment report; (3) insurance policy; (4) security report; (5) pilot card checking list; (6) weather forecast; (7) the damage inspection report issued by RINA; (8) crews' working and rest time recording chart and crew lists; (9) sailors certificate; (10) ship certificate; (11) agreement on managing the ship; (12) system documents of Fujian Hengfeng Shipping Co., Ltd. (hereinafter referred to as Hen Feng Company); (13) inspection records of the scene of the water accident; (14) inquiry record of personnel concerned; (15) the fact of collision given by the pilot ZHANG Yue; and (16) the sea protest given by the captain SHAO Ao.

Being summoned by the court, Wei Gang Company refused to attend this suit without justified reasons, which should be viewed as the abandon of the right to defend and question. The Plaintiff, Everglory, Life Insurance Company and the Defendants Tan Ding Zhao, Tan Ding Cheng had no objection to the following facts and evidence. The court confirms:

The owners of M.V. "He Xing 888" are the Defendants TAN Dingzhao and TAN Dingcheng, the manager is He Xing Company, the port of registry is Jiangmen port in Guangdong Province. The ship is the steel bulk cargo ship, the length overall is 63.98 m, the width is 13.20 m, the molded depth is 4.5 m, the gross weight is 1,288 tons, the net weight is 721 tons, the engine is an internal-combustion engine, the power is 402 Kw. The ship was built by Zhaoqing Shuishang District Changpai Ship Building & Repair Factory in December 2007. The inspection certificates of this ship were all complete and valid in the accident voyage, 6 crew members which met the lowest safety requirements, all of the crews held valid certificates. The ship broker and He Xing Company held business entity license and water transport license. This ship was demise chartered by the Defendant Wei Gang Company in the accident voyage, but the demise charter had not been registered in ship's registration authority. M.V. "EVERGLORY", of which the owner is the Plaintiff Everglory, the manager is Hen Feng Company, the port of registry is Panama. The ship is the steel bulk cargo ship, the length overall is 225 m, the width is 32.20 m, the molded depth is 18.30 m, the gross weight is 36,987 tons, the net weight is 22,691 tons, the engine is an internal-combustion engine, the power is 7,419 kw. The ship was built by TSUNEISHI SHIPBUILDING Co., Ltd. in May 1988. The inspection certificates of this ship were all complete and valid in the accident voyage. This ship had equipped with 26 crew members, which met the lowest safety requirements, all of the crews held valid certificates. The ship broker Hen Feng Company held the document of compliance issued by PMDS in Panama on August 9, 2012, which expired to July 6, 2016. M.V. "EVERGLORY" held the safety management certificate issued by PMDS in Panama on January 21, 2013, of which the period validity expired to July 20, 2013.

At around 1800 on July 5, 2013, M.V. "He Xing 888" left with no-load starting from Huangpu, Zhongshang to Nansha District, Guangzhou. Shortly after the voyage started, the ship received a phone call from the legal representative of Wei Gang Company, XIA Weizhong, demanding that the ship changed its destination to Hong Kong. At around 1800 on July 5, 2013, this ship left Changsha Bay Port, Hong Kong. When leaving the port, the draught of the nose was 3.6 m, the draught of stern was 3.8 m, intending to sail to the sea-fill area in Macao to unload. When setting off, this ship turned on the navigation lights, the radar operation in bridge and two VHF telephones. At that time, it was cloudy and a little bit rainy, the wind came from southeast was 2–3 level, visibility was good. At about 1850, this ship arrived in the water area near Hong Kong Qing Ma Bridge, of which the speed was approximately 7 knots, and the captain turned over his duty to the chief mate. At about 2030, this ship left Hong Kong water area and sailed at the direction of buoy light 5# and 6# of Ling Ding water avenue, intending to sail across the channel in the water area nearby 5# buoy light. At 2100, sailor ZHOU Zihua took over the bridge. At about 2115, the captain found that the rain became heavier and the visibility became worse, and then took the charge of the bridge. The captain found the echo of the 5# buoy light at Ling Ding avenue in the front and an imported vessel (M.V. "Xin Tai Cang") by looking radar, and adjusted the gain of radar to decrease the interference from rain. At that time, the course of the ship was about 330 degree, the speed was about 7 knots, 5# buoy light was in the left ahead of this ship, and the position of the ship was between the Tonggu Western Channel and 5# buoy light in Ling Ding Channel. Shortly after, when the portside of this ship was 100 m away from 5# buoy light in Ling Ding Channel, this ship turned left into the channel. Suddenly, the chief mate found there was a figure of a big vessel in the left ahead, without seeing the signal of the big vessel in front of this ship, telling the captain that "there is a big vessel". At this time, the captain saw the coming ship, and judged it was a huge imported vessel, saying that, "we may not cross it". Shortly after that, that ship turned on the searchlight irradiate to the nose of this ship, and turned its direction by using right rudder intending to across from the portside of the huge vessel. The chief master felt that the collision was inevitable, and immediately asked sailors to inform other crews to flee for their lives. After the sailor ran to the entrance to the stern's stair called the sailor LIN Pangming, who was off-duty finding that the vessel was coming speedily, and there was no time to inform another 2 crew members, so he returned the bridge. About 1 min after finding the vessel, during the course of the ship turned the direction to right, the area near crews' living area near the hold on ship's portside collided with the big vessel, and 3 crew members who were on duty in the bridge jumped to the water for escaping. After that, the big vessel continued to rush forward and roll the empennage of the portside of this ship, destroying crews' living area and part of the bridge. This ship sunk because of the water penetration of the hold and engine room, and being pressed of the empennage, and the location of it sinking was roughly at 22°20′ north latitude and 113°47′0.570 longitude. All of 6 crew members fell into the water, with 3 of them being rescued who were captain ZHOU Jinxiang, chief master LI Mingxiang and sailor ZHOU Zihua respectively, and 1 crew member was died, engine worker XU Jiankun, another 2 crew members were missing who were chief engineer FENG Jinru, sailor LIN Pangming respectively.

At 1725 on May 8, 2013, M.V. "EVERGLORY" left Mayong Haichang port in Dongwan without loading cargo, intending to sail to Adam Bay port in Indonesia, the draft of nose was 3.1 m and of stern was 7.6 m when leaving the port. When starting the voyage, the 2 radars, two VHF and AIS operations in bridge were all turned on, and the captain, pilot, chief master, and a sailor were on their duty in the bridge. The pilot gave the order for the engine bell rudder and directed the voyage, the captain supervise, kept a watch, the chief master handled the engine bell and supervised the sailor to operate the rudder, assisted watching out, and the sailor to handle the rudder. At that time, it was cloudy with raining slightly, the 2–3 level wind came from southeast, the visibility was good. After sunset, the ship turned on the navigation lights. This vessel navigated from the east Lotas east channel of Guangzhou port, the pilot worker gave the order to speed gradually to three forward. At about 2000, this ship arrived at 36# buoy light water area in Ling Ding channel in Guangzhou port, followed by M.V. "An Xu Shan" and M.V. "Zhong Ran Zhi Xing". The third mate and sailors went to the bridge to take their turn on duty from chief mate and another sailor. What remained unchanged was that the pilot worker took the charge of giving orders for engine bell, rudder and directed the navigation, the captain took the charge of supervision and watched out, the third mate took the charge of handling the engine bell, supervised sailors handling ruddle, assisted watching out, sailors handled rudder. At about 2120, this ship passed by 7#–8# buoy light on Ling Ding channel in Guangzhou port at the speed of 11.4 knots, the direction was roughly 163°, sky became darker, and rained suddenly, with the wind increased to 6 level southeast wind, the visibility declined sharply. The pilot worker gave the order to change the engine bell to 2 forward. After that, this ship voyaged along the right side of the channel, the direction was roughly 170°, the pilot worker found that, there was a ship echo (which is M.V. "He Xing 888") at about 30° at the left in front of the ship, more than 1 mile away, at the speed of 7.4 knots, the direction was 300°. Meanwhile, the pilot found that M.V. "Xin Tai Cang", an imported huge vessel passed by 3#–4# buoy light front just right now, sailing in the middle of the channel, which impeded this ship's navigation, so the pilot worker contacted M.V. "Xin Tai Cang" to require it to sail back to the right side of the channel through VHF. After contacting, pilot worker asked the third mate whether the small ship or the big one (which refers to M.V. "Xin Tai Cang") was closer, and the third mate answered that the small ship was closer. Then pilot worker gave the order to turn the direction to left by 2°–3°, and changed the direction to 167 degree. Since the rain became heavier, thickly dotted echo of rain spots made the echo of M.V. "He Xing 888" unrecognized. In order to draw the counter's ship's attention, the pilot worker ordered the third mate to turn on the search lights to shine this ship's nose direction to show the location of this ship. Shortly after that, the stuff on duty in the bridge saw the search lights of the counter ship, but it was held quickly since entering the fade zone. The pilot worker immediately gave the order to stop, and turned to right to maximum, while the collision happened not until the steerage reached, the nose of this ship collided with the counter's hold in front of the living area on portside, the time was approximately at 2124, the location was near the upstream of 6# buoy light, the speed of this ship when the collision happened was approximately 10 knots, the direction was about 167°, the intersection angle between 2 ships was approximately 30°.

The accident survey report concerning this collision in this case issued by Guangzhou Maritime Safety Administration had the same affirmation with the court, in the respect of accident reason and responsibility, held the opinion that M.V. "He Xing 888" had following faults: (1) under the circumstance of poor visibility, the vessel had entered the Ling Ding Channel. This vessel did not navigate with caution and sailed across the channel blindly, which interfered the safety of the ships sail along the channel without knowing whether there was a ship in the channel, and it was against the Article 8 of the Regulations for Safe Navigation in the Waters of the Pearl River Estuary and Article 2 Paragraph 1 of the International Regulations for Preventing Collisions at Sea, 1972, which was the main reason of the accident; (2) the captain, the pilot of this ship did not adjust the radar and range properly, did not turn on AIS, which led to not finding other ships early, and did not find the other ship until 1 min away from the collision happened, which existed ignorance and violated Article 5 of the International Regulations for Preventing Collisions at Sea, 1972, and that was one of the causes of the accident; (3) under the poor visibility, this ship did not release the signal according to the rules, which violated Article 35 Paragraph 1 of the International Regulations for Preventing Collisions at Sea,1972, and was one of the causes of the accident; (4) when finding M.V. "EVERGLORY", it was already in the right in front of this ship, two ships had come into the urgent dangerous situation, M.V. "He Xing 888" turned right blindly, sailed towards M.V. "EVERGLORY", which did not taken the proper measures of collision avoidance and there was not have the good seamanship. It violated Article 8 Paragraph 1 of the International Regulations for Preventing Collisions at Sea, 1972, and it was one of the causes of the accident; (5) under the poor visibility, the speed remained at approximately 7 knots, without taking measures to stop and slow down, without sailing at a safe speed, which violated Article 6 of the International Regulations for Preventing Collisions at Sea, 1972, and that was one of the causes of the accident. M.V. "EVERGLORY" had following faults: (1) M.V. "EVERGLORY" had not found the counter ship until 2120 approximately. It did not keep watching regularly in order to find other ships as early as possibly, which made it impossible to make a full assessment of the situation and the danger of collision, and it existed inorance and violated Article 5 of the International Regulations for Preventing Collisions at Sea, 1972, and it was one of the causes of the accident; (2) under the circumstance of poor visibility, the ship did not reduce the speed to the degree to maintain the effect of rudder, did not spare enough time to make an assessment to the dynamic of the counter ship when it found the disappearance and unknown dynamic condition of the radar echo of opposite ship, which violated Article 6 of the International Regulations for Preventing Collisions at Sea, 1972, and it was one of the causes of the accident; (3) rainstorm made the visibility poor, but this ship did not release the signals to show the exist of this ship and draw other ships' attention, which violated Article 35 Paragraph 1 of the International Regulations for Preventing Collisions at Sea, 1972, and it was one of the causes of the accident. To sum up, M.V. "He Xing 888" should undertake the main responsibility of the accident and M.V."EVERGLORY" should bear the secondary responsibility.

The Defendants TAN Dingzhao, TAN Dingcheng had objection to the affirmation concerning the captain and chief mate of M.V. "He Xing 888" adjusted radar gain or range improperly that led to not finding M.V. "EVERGLORY", and not turning on AIS in the accident survey report. The fact was that it was the bad weather that made radar unable to find M.V. "EVERGLORY", and AIS was not turned on since it was broken. According to the survey, when being examined by Guangzhou Maritime Safety Administration on May 9, 2013, ZHOU Jingxiang, the captain of M.V. "He Xing 888", claimed that: the AIS was not open since it was broken. There was nothing showed up in radar because it rained heavily at that time. I adjusted sleet and gain, but there seemed no effect, the echo of objection could not be recognized clearly. The chief mate LI Mingxiang of M.V. "He Xing 888" claimed that: in this voyage, the AIS had not been turned on when sailing from Hong Kong, it was light rain and radar could scan the sea surface, until the rain became heavier, it could scan nothing.

On May 13, 2013, M.V. "EVERGLORY" entered into Zhonghai Industry Co., Ltd. Pineapple Temple Ship Factory (hereinafter referred to as Pineapple Temple Factory), and the fix was finished on June 20.

On August 9, 2013, the Plaintiff Everglory, as the first party, the Defendants TAN Dingzhao, TAN Dingcheng and Wei Gang Company, as the second party, LI Xiuqun, the family member of XU Jiankun, as the third party, three parties signed the agreement for reconciling about the compensation of the death of XU Jiankun. Three parties agreed to compensating 800,000 yuan as the final solution for all of the lost caused by the death of XU Jiankun, and the first and the second party should prepay the compensation according to the responsibility pro-rata of 50% for each party, and the first and second party would refund any overpayment or a supplemental payment for any deficiency according to the final responsibility pro-rata. On September 4 and September 25, the Plaintiff Everglory, the Defendants TAN Dingzhao, TAN Dingcheng and Wei Gang Company signed the reconciliation agreement with the family members of FENG Jinru, FEN Xiyi and so forth, and the family members of LIN Bangming, LIN Jinwei and so on respectively, of which the content was the same as the agreement signed with the family members with XU Jiankun. The Plaintiff Everglory entrusted Huatai Insurance Agency & Consulant Service Limited to pay 400,000 yuan compensation to the family members of XU Jiankun, FEN Jinru and LIN Bangming on September 17, September 17, October 10 respectively.

The Plaintiff Everglory insured all risk insurance and so forth concerning M.V. "EVERGLORY" to the Plaintiff Life Insurance Company, the insurance money was 6 million dollars, the insurance period started from 0 o'clock on January 1, 2013 to 24 o'clock on December 31, 2013. With respect to the losses caused by this accident, the Plaintiff Life Insurance Company respectively paid compensation to the Plaintiff Everglory with 563,192.87 dollar on July 7, 2013 and 25,341.80 dollar on November 6, the insurance compensation including ship repairs was 588,534.67 dollar in total. On November 10, 2013, the Plaintiff Everglory issued receipts and letter of transfer right to the Plaintiff Life Insurance Company on November 10, 2013.

Additionally, by the application of Plaintiff Everglory, the court issued (2013) Guang Hai Fa Bao Zi No.181-2 Civil Ruling on November 13, 2013, ruling to freaze the shipping indemnity that the Defendants TAN Dingzhao and TAN Dingcheng possessed in PICC Property and Casualty Company Limited Huizhou Branch 1,200,000 yuan, sealed up the house property which located in No.1, Guishui West Bridge Industry Area, Guishui Village Community, Taichen Town in Guangdong Province, owned by the Defendant TAN Dingzhao and No.459 camper as well as Room 308, Block A, Building 4, Qifu Yuan, Liufu Mountain Villa, Tai Town, Tai Shan City in Guangdong Province. Therefore, the Plaintiff Everglory handed in the application fee 5,000 yuan for property preservation to the court.

With respect to other losses claimed by the two Plaintiff, the court recognizes as follows:

1. The loss of repairs to ship

The survey report issued by the Haizheng Company provided by the Plaintiff Life Insurance Company show that the repair bill issued by Pineapple Temple ShipFactory recorded 108 repair terms for M.V. "EVERGLORY", and the repair cost was 3,978,070.54 yuan in total. Haizheng Company was entrusted by Life Insurance Company to inspect the damage of M.V. "EVERGLORY" and assessed the repair terms and cost showed in the repair bill, holding the opinion that: the clearing fee, 5,766 yuan, for industrial rubbish in term 6 was unreasonable, and it shall be rejected; the ventilating time for forepeak, 28 days and the lighting time, 28 days in term 31 were overlong, instead, it should be calculated by the repair time of the part which was 14 days, the relative forepeak ventilating fee should be reduced to 10,080 yuan from 20,160 yuan, the lighting fee should be reduced by 12,740 yuan from 25,480 yuan; in term 51, the cost of pumping the water remained in the left and right double bases of No.3 and No.4 cabin were 3,072 yuan and 1,632 yuan respectively, and the pump task of the bottom of the 2 cabins on start-port should be owner's engineer, not belonged to the loss caused by the collision accident in this case, should deduct 1,536 yuan and 816 yuan respectively; the cost of removing the sludge in the double deck layer in term 52, the cost involved the starboard and middle double deck layer 75,040 yuan were owner's task and it should be deducted; in term 54, the cost of ironwork for the double deck layer in cabin 4, which was 748.46 yuan belonging to owner's project and it should be deducted; in term 55 the auxiliary hole cost of dismounting the baseboard on the right side was 2,020.80 yuan belonging to the owner's task and it should be deducted; in term 56, the renew cost of the structure of the double deck layer on the right side, 9,556.60 yuan, belonged to the owner's task and it should be deducted; in term 65, the cost of removing industrial rubbish was unreasonable and it should be deducted; in term 77, the foundry goods for screw propeller had been calculated 1 kg by mistake, so it should be deducted by 310 yuan; in term 92, the cost of removing the industrial rubbish, 1,116 yuan, was an unreasonable charge, and it should be deducted; in term 98, in the cost of changing 2 set of seabed plug, the cost which was 1,260 yuan belonging to owner's task, should be deducted; in term 99, the cost of cutting the old zinc spelter code pin, 1,880 yuan belonged to owner's task, and it should be deducted; in term 100, mounting zinc spelter for the ballast tank and forepeak belonged to owner's program, 5,820 yuan, the cost caused by it should be deducted; in term 103, to change new steel board, dealing with 2,000,000 tons of steel board in advance, in fact it was 18,000,000 tons approximately, so 1,000 yuan for the cost of 2 tons should be deducted, as aforementioned, 130,061.84 yuan in total should be deducted. The Plaintiff Everglory paid repair cost 624,160 dollars to Pineapple Temple Shipyard by 3 times, respectively on June 20, July 22, September 11, in 2013.

The Defendants TAN Dingzhao and TAN Dingcheng, on the base of the repair cost defined after being assessed by Haizheng Company, had obligation to the following cost: in term 6, the certifying cost, 1,200 yuan, for assisting dealing with the recycling of the rubbish, should be included in the rubbish charge in this term, which was repeating charge, should be deducted; in term 15, 18,600 yuan the cost for the supervision of costume and frontier inspection was administrated charge rather than shipyard charge item, should be deducted; in term 16, the cost of the hotel and the board and lodging of the owner's shipping stuff, 55,682 yuan, not in the scope of insurance indemnity, and it should be deducted; in term 31, the cost of setting ventilating plastic pipes, swing and dismounting electric cables, hauling and connecting lights, which were 450 yuan, 207 yuan, and 1,449 yuan respectively should be included in its charge for use, it should not be charged alone, and should be deducted; in term 33, the cost of hauling red strings, 600 yuan should be included in the charge for building framework, which was 1,152 yuan, and it should not be calculated alone again; in term 53, the cost of hauling and setting ventilating belts, swing draught fan, hauling and connecting electronic cables and lights, which was 1,050 yuan, 1,449 yuan and 1,656 yuan respectively should be included in the charge of ventilating in this term, which was 975,760 yuan, and it should not be calculated alone again; in term 57, the cost of hauling and setting ventilating belts, swing draught fans, and hauling and connecting electronic cables, 600 yuan and 414 yuan, should be included in the ventilating charge which was 14,400 yuan, and it should not be calculated alone again; in term 69, the cost of 2 days' inspection done by costume and frontier inspection, which was 1,200 yuan, administrative charge, and it should not be taken by the shipyard; In term 96th, the cost of 6 days' inspection done by costume and frontier inspection, which was 3,600 yuan, administrative charge, and it should not be taken by the shipyard; in term 98, the cost of hauling and setting ventilating belts, 300 yuan, should be included in the use charge rather than being calculated alone again; in term 14, the cost of keeping look at fire was calculated according to 2% of the total price, after adjusting accounts, the total price should be 367,7361.71 yuan, 2% of which was 73,547.23 yuan, so the charge for keeping look at fire should be reduced to 73,547.23 yuan from 75,000 yuan. In summary, the Defendants TAN Dingzhao and TAN Dingcheng held the opinion that 97,09.76 yuan should be deducted and the repair cost of M.V. "EVERGLORY" caused by this accident should be 3,750,908.94.

The court holds that Haizheng Company held the certificate for insurance assessment business, which included the inspection, test, assessment and accounting of the insurance object. The supervisor CHEN Haifeng had the insurance assessment occupation certificate, and he appeared in the court to receive request, the inspection report issued by him has already deducted unreasonable charge terms and the repair cost which was not caused by this accident, the repair cost of M.V. "EVERGLORY" which was defined to be caused by this accident was 3,848,008.70 yuan, the Plaintiff Everglory paid to Pineapple Temple Shipyard actually. The Defendants TAN Dingzhao and TAN Dingcheng although had obligation to the cost, which was 97,099.76 yuan, they did not submit counter evidence, the court does not support that. In summary, the court affirms that, the related loss such as repair cost of M.V. "EVERGLORY" caused by this collision is 3,848,008.70 yuan, the Plaintiff Everglory paid by dollar respectively on June 20, July 22, September 11, USD624,160 in total.

2. The cost paid in advance and taken by china shipping agency

The voyage reckoning provided by the Plaintiff Life Insurance Company showed that M.V "EVERGLORY", because of the collision accident, from May 13, 2013 to June 20, 2013, gave rise to the following cost: fees of berth in mount of 539.15 yuan, pilot charge in mount of 46,062.73 yuan, health inspection fee in mount of 336 yuan, escort fee in mount of RMB8,000 yuan, agency fee 30,000 yuan, land transportation fee RMB1,700 yuan, water transportation fee 1,000 yuan, incidental expenses 4,000 yuan, herein before are 91,637.88 totally, equivalent to 14,963.24 dollars. Life Insurance Company provided relevant invoices and receipts. The bank slips showed that Everglory paid 14,963.24 dollar for another to China Shipping Agency on July 26, 2013. The Defendants Tan Dingzhao and TAN Dingcheng held the opinion that Life Insurance Company did not provided evidence to prove the actual work, and China Shipping Agency's agency fee was issued by the form of formal invoice, which was not in accordance to legal regulations, and should not be recognized. The court holds that, in terms of fees of berth in mount of 539,15 yuan, Life Insurance Company submitted the invoice issued by Guangzhou Port Shipping Agency Co., Ltd. to China Shipping Agency; in terms of the pilot charge 46,062.73 yuan, Life Insurance Company submitted the counterfoil of pilot visa, receipts and advice of settlement of Guangzhou pilot station; in terms of sanitary inspection charge 336 yuan, the company provided the receipt issued by Huangpu Exit and Enter Inspection and Quarantine Bureau; in terms of escorting charge RMB8,000 yuan, which was provided with the invoice issued by Guangzhou Huangpu Suihai Service Center; in terms of agency fee RMB30,000 yuan, which was provided with formal invoice issued by China Shipping Agency; in terms of transportation fee on land 1,700 yuan and transportation fee on water RMB1,000 yuan, which were provided with informal invoice and relevant certificate for use; in terms of incidental fee RMB4,000 yuan, which was provided with formal invoice. Except for bank slips, in terms of the evidence herein before, Life Insurance Company provided relevant origin files for checking. The cost terms and the time when it caused matched the time when the collision in this case happened and the time of the repair followed up, China Shipping Agency only issued formal invoice in terms of some kind of cost but they were accepted by Everglory, and Everglory had paid actually as well. Although the Defendants TAN Dingzhao and TAN Dingcheng had obligations to it, they did not provide counter evidence. Therefore, the court affirms the aforementioned loss, and it is 14,963.24 dollars in total.

3. The cost advanced and paid by Hai Ming Company

The formal invoice issued by Hai Ming Company to Everglory provided by the two Plaintiffs showed that the towage fee was RMB8,160 yuan, joint inspection transportation fee was RMB11,628 yuan, the agency fee was RMB14,000 yuan, RMB33,788 yuan in total, converted into 5,539 dollars. Guangzhou Grain Coupon Car Renting Co., Ltd. issued a normal invoice of RMB8,100 yuan transportation fee to Everglory on May 20, 2013, Hai Ming Company issued a RMB14,000 yuan agency formal invoice to Everglory on May 7, 2013. Bank slips showed that the Plaintiff Everglory paid 5,539 dollar to Hai Ming Company on July 26, 2013 and marked out that it was port charge. The Defendant TAN Dingzhao and TAN Dingcheng had no obligation to the towage fee RMB8,160 yuan, but disagreed with the other two cost terms. The court holds that, for the towage fee RMB8,160 yuan, the Defendant TAN Dingzhao and TAN Dingcheng had no objection, the court affirms it. For the joint inspection charge RMB11,628 yuan, the Plaintiff only has provided transportation fee invoice of RMB8,100 yuan, which was not according to the amount of money written on the formal invoice issued by Hai Ming Company, furthermore, it could not prove whether it is relevant to the collision accident in this case, under the circumstance that the two Plaintiff had no further evidence to prove, the court does not affirm the joint inspection charge, RMB11,628 yuan issued by the two Plaintiffs. For the agency fee RMB14,000 yuan, since the time on the formal invoice issued by Hai Ming Company was earlier than the time when the collision happened, the two Plaintiffs had no evidence to prove the cost was relevant to the collision in this case, so the court does not affirm that. To sum up, the court affirms the loss above as 8,160 yuan.

4. Inspection fee of ship classification society

The bill issued by Italian Ship Classification Society (Hong Kong) provided by the two Plaintiffs showed that Italian Ship Classification Society (Hong Kong) carried out a temporary damage inspection to M.V. "EVERGLORY", in Nansha on May 30, 2013, of which the charge was 3,251.65 dollar; from May 18, 2013 to June 19, 2013, Pineapple Temple Shipyard carried out a temporary damage inspection to M. V. "EVERGLORY", of which the charge was RMB6,755.38 yuan, the charge herein before was 10,007.03 dollar. Bank slip showed that Everglory had paid 10,007.03 dollar to Italian Ship Classification Society (Hong Kong) on July 22, 2013. The Defendants TAN Dingzhao and TAN Dingcheng thought the evidence herein before formed abroad, the two Plaintiffs did not take relevant steps according to the regulation. Furthermore, the two Plaintiffs did not explain the cause of the charge, so the court refuses to affirm. The court holds that, the two Plaintiffs, as for the evidence materials herein before, did not take relevant steps such as notarization, attestation, but the time, terms shown in the herein before evidence coincide with the collision accident in this case, and can corroborate each other. Furthermore, the Plaintiff has paid actually, under the circumstances that the Defendants TAN Dingzhao and TAN Dingcheng do not provide counter evidence, the court affirms that the Ship Classification Society inspection charge caused from this collision accident is 10,007.03 dollar.

In summary, the loss that the collision accident brought to M.V "EVERGLORY" totally was 649,130.27 dollar and 8,160 yuan.

The court holds that, this case is dispute over damage liability of collision. According to Article 1 of the Some Provisions of the Supreme People's Court on the Scope of Cases to be Entertained by Maritime Courts, the dispute in this case is under special jurisdiction in maritime court. In this case, the place that the collision took place is the water area of Ling Ding Channel in Guangzhou port, the domicile of the three Defendants are all located in Guangdong Province, which are all in the scope of territory under the jurisdiction of the court. According to Article 30 of the Civil Procedure Law of People's Republic of China, the rule concerning the suit claiming for compensation caused by the loss caused by the collision or other maritime accidents is under the jurisdiction of the people's court of the place where the collision happened, the place where the collided ship reached at first, the place where the wrongdoing ship is arrested or the domicile of the Defendant, the court has jurisdiction. According to Article 269 of the Maritime Code of the People's Republic of China, the parties to the contract have no choice, the contract is applicable to the settlement of contract dispute, except as otherwise provided by law. If the parties to the contract have no choice, the contract is applicable to the law of the country that is most closely connected with the contract. Therefore, this case shall be applicable to the law of People's Republic of China.

The collision in this case happened in the water area in Ling Ding Channel of Guangzhou port, which shall be applicable to the Regulations for Safe Navigation in the Waters of the Pearl River Estuary and the International Regulations for Preventing Collisions at Sea, 1972, to divide the responsibility of the two parties to the collisions. Under the poor visibility, and the circumstances that in the exit of Ling Ding Channel, the big vessel was approaching, M.V. "He Xing 888" sailed through the channel without knowing whether there was a ship exiting the channel, which interfered the safety of the ship navigate alone the channel and violated

Article 8 of the Regulations for Safe Navigation in the Waters of the Pearl River Estuary and Article 2 Paragraph 1 of the International Regulations for Preventing Collisions at Sea, 1972; this ship did not find other ships until 1 min before the collision, which existed ignorance, and violated Article 5 of the International Regulations for Preventing Collisions at Sea, 1972; under the poor visibility, this ship did not release signals in accordance to regulations, which violated Article 35 Paragraph 1 of the International Regulations for Preventing Collisions at Sea, 1972; being faced with emergent danger, this ship turned its direction and sailed towards M.V. "EVERGLORY" blindly, which violated Article 8 Paragraph 1 of the International Regulations for Preventing Collisions at Sea, 1972; under the bad visibility, the ship remained sailing at the speed of 7 knots rather than safety speed, which was against Article 6 of the International Regulations for Preventing Collisions at Sea. M.V. "EVERGLORY" did not find the other ship as early as possible, therefore it could not make full assessment to the collision situation and the danger, which existed ignorance and was against Article 5 of the International Regulations for Preventing Collisions at Sea, 1972; under the circumstances that disappearance and unknown dynamic condition of the radar echo of the other ship, the ship did not reduce its speed to the degree that could merely hold the effect of the rudder. When the collision happened, the speed remained 10 knots rather than safety speed, which was against Article 6 of the International Regulations for Preventing Collisions at Sea, 1972; under the poor visibility this ship did not release the signals in accordance to the regulation, which was against Article 35 Paragraph 1 of the 1972 International Regulations for Preventing Collisions at Sea, 1972. Both M.V."He Xing 888" and M.V. "EVERGLORY" had fault to the collision in this case. Concerning M.V. "He Xing 888" sailed across the channel blindly under the poor visibility and without knowing the navigation situation of the ships sailing in the channel, not noticing M.V. "EVERGLORY" until 1 min before the collision, and then turned its direction towards M.V. "EVERGLORY", M.V "He Xing 888" should assume greater responsibility of negligence to the collision in this case. According the degree of the fault of M.V. "He Xing 888" and M.V. "EVERGLORY", the court holds that the two vessels shall assume 60% and 40% of the faulty responsibility of the collision respectively in this case.

The Plaintiff Everglory, as the owner of M.V. "EVERGLORY", the Defendants TAN Dingzhao and TAN Dingcheng, as the registered owners of M.V. "He Xing 888", according to Article 169 Paragraph 1 of the Maritime Code of the People's Republic of China, which is concerned with that if the colliding ships are all in fault, each ship shall be liable in proportion to the extent of its fault; if the respective faults are equal in proportion or it is impossible to determine the extent of the proportion of the respective faults, the liability of the colliding ships shall be apportioned equally and Article 4 of the Provisions of the Supreme People's Court on the Trial of Certain Issues in Cases of Disputes over Collision of Ships, concerning the compensation liability resulted from ship collision shall be born by the ship owners, or shall be born by the bareboat charterer if the ship collision occurs during the bareboat charter period and the bareboat charter is registered according to the law. The Plaintiff Everglory should assume the compensation liability caused by M.V. "EVERGLORY", the Defendants, TAN Dingzhao and TAN Dingcheng should assume the compensation liability caused by M.V. "He Xing 888". Although the collision in this case happened in the period when M.V. "He Xing 888" was demised by Wei Gang Company, after the accident Wei Gang Company also joined in handling and consulting the accident. Yet the bareboat charter was not registered according to law, it could not resist the third party. According to Article 4 of the Provisions of the Supreme People's Court on the Trial of Certain Issues in Cases of Disputes over Collision of Ships, Wei Gang Company did not assume the compensation liability of the collision in this case according to the law. The liability that the Defendants TAN Dingzhao, TAN Dingcheng assumed could be solved in another way through the charter between two parties. The Plaintiff, Everglory, Life Insurance Company and the Defendants TAN Dingzhao, TAN Dingcheng claimed that Wei Gang Company assumed the compensation liability directly, which had no legal basis. Therefore, the court does not support it.

According to Article 252 Paragraph 1 of the Maritime Code of the People's Republic of China, where the loss of or damage to the subject matter insured within the insurance coverage is caused by a third person, the right of the insured to demand compensation from the third person shall be subrogated to the insurer from the time the indemnity is paid and Article 93 of the Special Maritime Procedure Law of the People's Republic of China, concerning where the occurrence of an insured event is caused by a third party, after having paid insurance indemnity to the insured, the insurer may exercise by subrogation the right of the insured to demand indemnity against the third party up to the limit of insurance indemnity, the Plaintiff life insurance company, as the insurer of M.V."EVERGLORY", after paying the insurance compensation to the Plaintiff Everglory, the Plaintiff Life Insurance Company got subrogation of the damage of M.V. "EVERGLORY" in the scope of indemnity, and had the rights to claim compensation to the Defendants TAN Dingzhao, TAN Dingcheng.

The crews' personal compensation caused by the collision in this case is RMB2,400,000, the Plaintiff assumes 40% of the liability to pay the compensation, which means RMB960,000 yuan and the Defendants TAN Dingzhao and TAN Dingcheng assume 60% of the liability to pay the compensation, which means RMB1,440,000 yuan. The Plaintiff Everglory has compensated RMB1,200,000 yuan to the family members of the crews, the Defendant TAN Dingzhao and TAN Dingcheng shall compensate RMB240,000 yuan to the Plaintiff Everglory.

The Plaintiff Everglory claimed that the compensation of the loss of interest compensated by Defendants TAN Dingzhao and TAN Dingcheng should be counted according to corresponding bank rates published by the People's Bank of China from October 19, 2013, the last day of compensating for Everglory, which is reasonable. So the court supports it, and the loss of interest shall be counted to the date the judgment becomes final.

The collision in this case has brought to the Plaintiff Everglory the loss, 649,130.27 dollars and 8,160 yuan, the Defendants TAN Dingzhao and TAN Dingcheng shall assume 60% of the liability to pay the compensation, which means they shall compensate 649,130.27 dollars and 8,160 yuan. The Plaintiff Life

Insurance Company has paid indemnity 588,534,67 dollars to Everglory, the Defendants TAN Dingzhao and TAN Dingcheng assume 60% of the liability to pay the compensation, and shall compensate 353,120.80 dollars to Life Insurance Company. The Defendant Life Insurance Company claimed that the loss of interest compensated by the Defendants TAN Dingzhao and TAN Dingcheng shall be counted according to corresponding bank rates published by the People's Bank of China from November 6, 2016, which complies with the law. Therefore the court supports it. The Defendants TAN Dingzhao and TAN Dingcheng shall compensate for the loss 36,357.36 dollars and RMB4,896 yuan including the rest repair to the Plaintiff Everglory. The Plaintiff Everglory claimed that the loss of interest compensated by Defendants TAN Dingzhao and TAN Dingcheng shall be counted according to corresponding bank rates published by the People's Bank of China from October 10, 2013, which is supported by the court. The aforementioned loss of interests are all calculated until the day of judgment, the interests of dollars shall be calculated according to the mean price between RMB and dollars published by China's State Administration of Exchange Control on the date that the loss of interest begins to count.

The Plaintiff Everglory has handed in application fee 5,000 yuan to apply for property preservation, and the loss was caused because the Defendants TAN Dingzhao and TAN Dingcheng did not compensate to the Plaintiff Everglory. Therefore, the Defendants TAN Dingzhao and TAN Dingcheng shall compensate to the Plaintiff Everglory.

In summary, according to Article 169 Paragraph 1, Article 252 Paragraph 1 of the Maritime Code of the People's Republic of China, Article 4 of the Provisions of the Supreme People's Court on the Trial of Certain Issues in Cases of Disputes over Collision of Ships, Article 93 of the Special Maritime Procedure Law of the People's Republic of China, and Article 64 Paragraph 1 of the Civil Procedure Law of People's Republic of China, the court hereby renders the judgment as follows:

1. The Defendants TAN Dingzhao and TAN Dingcheng shall compensate the Plaintiff Hong Kong EVERGLORY Shipping Co., Ltd. for the personal injury compensation RMB240,000 yuan and the interests calculated according to the corresponding loan rate published by the People's Republic of China from October 10 to the day of judgment;
2. The Defendants TAN Dingzhao and TAN Dingcheng shall compensate the Plaintiff Hong Kong EVERGLORY Shipping Co., Ltd. for the loss such as repair cost USD36,357.36 and RMB4,896 yuan and the interests calculated according to the corresponding loan rate published by the People's Republic of China from October 10 to the day of judgment. (USD36,357.36 dollars shall be transferred to RMB according to the mean price between RMB and dollar published by China's State Administration of Exchange Control on October 10, 2013);
3. The Defendants TAN Dingzhao and TAN Dingcheng shall compensate the Plaintiff Hong Kong EVERGLORY Shipping Co., Ltd. for the loss of property preservation fee RMB5,000 yuan;

4. The Defendants TAN Dingzhao and TAN Dingcheng shall compensate the loss such as repair cost USD353,120.80 to the Plaintiff PICC Property and Casualty Company Limited Guangdong Branch and the interests, transferred into RMB according to the mean price between RMB and dollar published by China's State Administration of Exchange Control on November 6, 2013, and calculated according to the corresponding loan rate published by the People's Republic of China from then to the day of judgment;
5. Reject the claims of the Plaintiffs Hong Kong EVERGLORY Shipping Co., Ltd. and PICC Property and Casualty Company Limited Guangdong Branch against the Defendant Zhuhai Weigang Tu Shi Fang Engineering Co., Ltd.;
6. Reject other claims of the Plaintiffs Hong Kong EVERGLORY Shipping Co., Ltd. and PICC Property and Casualty Company Limited Guangdong Branch.

The obligation of payment above shall be completely fulfilled within 10 days as of the effective date of this judgment.

If the parties fail to fulfill the obligation of payment within the period provided in this judgment, the interest shall be double paid for the period of deferred payment according to Article 253 of the Civil Procedure Law of the People's Republic of China.

Court acceptance fee in amount of RMB52,231 yuan, reduced to RMB33,276 yuan since the two Plaintiffs reduced claims before the end of court investigation, the two Plaintiffs shall bear 6,640 yuan, and the Defendants TAN Dingzhao and TAN Dingcheng shall bear RMB26,636 yuan. Since the two Plaintiffs have paid the court acceptance fee RMB52,231 yuan in advance, agreed by the Plaintiff, the Defendants TAN Dingzhao and TAN Dingcheng shall pay RMB26,636 yuan which they shall bear directly to the Plaintiff, and the court shall separately return 18,955 yuan to the two Plaintiffs.

If not satisfy with this judgment, the Plaintiff Everglory may, within 30 days as of the service of this judgment, the Plaintiff Life Insurance Company and the Defendants TAN Dingzhao, TAN Dingcheng and Weigang Company may within 15 days as of the service of this judgment, submit a statement of appeal to the court, with duplicates in the number of the counter-parties, so as to make an appeal before the Guangdong High People's Court.

Presiding Judge: ZHANG Kexiong
Judge: WU Guining
Acting Judge: YIN Zhonglie

April 13, 2015

Clerk: LI Chunyu

Xiamen Maritime Court
Civil Judgment

Hongxin (HK) Container Development Limited
v.
Shanghai Hongsheng Gangtai Shipping Co., Ltd. et al.

(2015) Xia Hai Fa Shang Chu Zi No.378

Related Case(s) None.

Cause(s) of Action 219. Dispute over contract on lease of shipping container.

Headnote Container lessor obtained default judgment for return of containers and unpaid container hire, in the absence of appearance by container lessees and related Defendants.

Summary The Plaintiff, sued several Defendants for failure to pay the Plaintiff under the terms of a container leasing contract and supplemental agreement for the lease of 1,000 20-DC containers. The court heard this case in the absence of the listed Defendants both because their whereabouts were unknown and because they refused to attend trial without a justified reason, thereby forfeiting their litigation rights. After trial, the court ruled: (1) the container leasing contract and the supplemental agreement were terminated; (2) the Defendant Shanghai Gangtai must return the remaining 661 containers within 10 days or pay a penalty of USD2,000 per container; (3) the Defendant Shanghai Gangtai shall be liable for liquidated damages; (4) the Defendant Shanghai Gangtai shall be liable for all container hire unpaid since 1 March 2015; (5) the other Defendants are jointly and severally liable for the debt owed to the Plaintiff.

Judgment

The Plaintiff: Hongxin (HK) Container Development Limited
Domicile: Room 201-2, Floor 3, Hengsheng Wanzai Building, No.200 Wanzai Xuannishi Street, Hong Kong Special Administrative Region.
Domestic Contact Address: Floor 11, Yin Long Building, No.258 Dongdu Road, Xiamen City, Fujian.
Legal representative: YANG Zhenzhen, chairman of the board.

Agent *ad litem*: WU Zeliang, male, Han, born on June 12, 1976, staff of the Plaintiff's company.
Agent *ad litem*: WANG Wei, male, Han, born on April 29, 1989, staff of the Plaintiff's company.

The Defendant: Shanghai Hongsheng Gangtai Shipping Co., Ltd.
Domicile: Room 1001, No.53 Huangpu Road, Hongkou District, Shanghai.
Legal representative: ZHANG Lizhong.

The Defendant: Taizhou City Gangtai Shipping Co., Ltd.
Domicile: Room 604-606, No.A Dongfang Xingzuo Building, Tengda Road, Luqiao District, Taizhou City.
Legal representative: DING Genyou.

The Defendant: DING Genyou, male, Han, born on July 8, 1964
Domicile: No.83, Yinshui Road, Fengjiang Street, Luqiao District, Taizhou City, Zhejiang.
Regular domicile: Room 1001, Haiwan Building, No.53 Huangpu Road, Hongkou District, Shanghai.
Identity card number of citizen: 332603196407085411.

The Defendant: LI Xingling, female, Han, born on May 20, 1966, wife of the Defendant DING Genyou
Domicile: No.30, District 7, Fupai Village, Fengjiang Street, Luqiao District, Taizhou City, Zhejiang.
regular domicile: Room 1001, Haiwan Building, No.53 Huangpu Road, Hongkou District, Shanghai.
Identity card number of citizen: 332603196605205429.

The Defendant: DING Weimin, male, born on October 9, 1988, son of the Defendant DING Genyou
Domicile: No.83, Yinshui Road, Fengjiang Street, Luqiao District, Taizhou City, Zhejiang.
Regular domicile: Room 1001, Haiwan Building, No.53 Huangpu Road, Hongkou District, Shanghai.
Identity card number of citizen: 331004198810092218.

The Defendant: ZHANG Lizhong, male, Han, born on September 23, 1966
Domicile: No.30, District 7, Fupai Village, Fengjiang Street, Luqiao District, Taizhou City, Zhejiang.
Regular domicile: Room 1001, Haiwan Building, No.53 Huangpu Road, Hongkou District, Shanghai.
Identity card number of citizen: 332603196609235617.

The Defendant: HUANG Ping, female, Han, born on August 18, 1967, wife of the Defendant ZHANG Lizhong
Domicile: Room 401, the First Building, Da Caochang New Village, Luqiao Street, Luqiao District, Taizhou City, Zhejiang.

Regular domicile: Room 1001, Haiwan Building, No.53 Huangpu Road, Hongkou District, Shanghai.
Identity card number of citizen: 332603196708185520.

With respect to the case arising from dispute over container leasing contract filed by the Plaintiff, Hongxin (HK) Container Development Limited (hereinafter referred to as Hongxin Company) against the Defendants, Shanghai Hongsheng Gangtai Shipping Co., Ltd. (hereinafter referred to as Shanghai Gangtai), Taizhou City Gangtai Shipping Co., Ltd. (hereinafter referred to as Taizhou Gangtai), DING Genyou, LI Xingling, DING Weimin, ZHANG Lizhong and HUANG Ping to the court on May 12, 2015. The court, after entertaining the case, organized the collegiate panel according to the law. The court decided that the case should be heard with the absence of the Defendants, since the present whereabouts of the Defendants Shanghai Gangtai, Taizhou Gangtai, DING Genyou, HUANG Ping, DING Weimin, ZHANG Lizhong and LI Xingling were unknown and the above mentioned seven Defendants refused to attend the court without justified reasons, after service of the notice of responding to action and court summons by announcement on People's Court Daily by the court, the court held a hearing in public on October 9, 2015. WU Zeliang and WANG Wei, agents *ad litem* entrusted by the Plaintiff appeared in court to attend the trial. This case has been concluded now.

The Plaintiff Hongxin Company alleged that it, as the lessor, and the nine Defendants, including Shanghai Gangtai, Yingpeng Company, Taizhou Gangtai, DING Genyou, LI Xingling, DING Weimin, YING Hongjun, ZHANG Lizhong and HUANG Ping, as the lessees, signed the containers leasing contract and the supplemental agreement at Yin Long Building, Huli District, Xiamen City in 2013, which stipulated that the above mentioned Defendants jointly took lease on 1,000 20-DC containers from the Plaintiff. according to the general clause in Sub-paragraphs (b) of Paragraph and Paragraph 2 of Article 9 of the contract, if the lessee failed to pay the expenses in full and on time, and the sum of money unpaid was equal to one-month rent, the leaser should be entitled to request the lessee to pay the relevant expense immediately and claim for liquidated damages calculated on the basis of 0.1% of unpaid expense per day. At the same time, the contract clearly stipulated the other obligations and rights between two parties.

The Plaintiff had delivered 1,000 20-DC leasehold containers according to the contract, after the contract was signed. The Defendant Shanghai Gangtai issued the container receipt to the Plaintiff and confirmed that the Plaintiff had checked, accepted and used according to the agreement of the contract on May 2, 2013. However, the seven Defendants mentioned above did not pay for account payable such as rent according to contract. Although the Plaintiff asked for rent for several times, the seven Defendants did not take any actions to make payment.

In conclusion, the Defendants Shanghai Gangtai, Taizhou Gangtai, DING Genyou, LI Xingling, DING Weimin, and HUANG Ping did not perform the obligation of payment according to the contract and such behavior had already breached the contract. Therefore, the Defendants should be responsible for the liquidated damages for overdue payment. The Plaintiff requested the court to rule:

1. Pay total rent in amount of USD1,028,119.48 (RMB6,301,858.35 calculated at RMB exchange rate of 6.1295, similarly hereinafter) for container rent which was temporarily calculated by the time of February 2015 and the rent should be calculated by the agreed rent standard and be paid when all the containers are returned;
2. Pay the liquidated damages for overdue payment day, in amount of USD237,807.22 (RMB1,457,639.35), which was calculated on the basis of 0.1% of the outstanding sum per day from the overdue day to the actual payment temporarily calculated by the time of January 31, 2015;
3. Terminate the containers leasing contract numbered with Hongji (HK) (2013) (ZU) ZI No.23001 and pay liquidated damages in amount of USD340,447.80 (RMB2,086,774.79);
4. 661 20-DC containers shall be returned immediately (container number lists could be referred in attachment); otherwise, the Plaintiff should be entitled to compensation from the Defendants according to replacement value (22,000RMB/container) stipulated in as agreed in the containers leasing contract; and
5. Bear all the litigation charges, including court acceptance fee, charges of preservation and guarantee fee.

The agent *ad litem* of the Plaintiff alleged in the hearing that the contract was signed on February 20, 2013, Zhejiang Yingpeng Ship Equipment Manufacturing Co., Ltd. (hereinafter referred to as "Yingpeng Company") and YING Hongjun, the legal representative thereof were both parties to the contract, but Yingpeng Company actively cooperated with the Plaintiff so as to find out the whereabouts of containers during the process of taking containers back. Thereby, the Plaintiff agreed not to sue Yingpeng Company and its legal representative as well as not to charge the liquidated damages for contract termination listed in third litigation claim. The case did not involve performance bond or insurance bond. The current market replacement value for 20-DC container was about USD1,700. The Defendants' total account payable, account paid and the details of account unpaid as well as when would the Plaintiff send the reminder letter for account unpaid would be listed explicitly in a table after the court hearing.

After the court trial, the agent *ad litem* of the Plaintiff presented the introduction for account unpaid and subsequent account payable and the evidence of rent payment by the Defendants in which stated that the Defendants in the case accepted all together 1,000 20-DC containers and from March to May in 2015, before the litigation of this case, the Plaintiff had already taken 54 containers back voluntarily. And the Plaintiff took 285 containers back according to Litigation of Property Preservation No.182 Xia Hai Fa Shang Chu Zi (2015) after which the Plaintiff took no containers back. Therefore, when the judgments were taken into action, the Defendants should continuously pay monthly rent calculated by US dollars which had equal value with agreed daily rent RMB11.20/container based on the quantity of 661 containers [=1,000-(54-285), detailed container numbers could be referred in attachment], until all the containers were returned or the container's replacement value was paid. In this case, the claims of the Plaintiff can be further stated as follows: 1. the rent alleged by the Plaintiff in the first claim should be calculated from the overdue day, namely August in 2013, to February in 2015 and the total account unpaid was USD1,028,119.48; since March in 2015, the rent has been calculated on basis of 946 containers, for the reason that the Plaintiff took back 54 containers before the litigation of this case. The sentence "continue to calculate the charges according to the standard for container rent until all the containers are returned" referred to the charges calculated according to standard of rent rate for container, until the day that the Defendants actually return all containers or the Defendant paid the replacement value; 2. the second claim remains unchanged; 3. the third claim about the discharge of the containers leasing contract and the supplemental agreement involved remained unchanged; the Plaintiff gave up the liquidated damages for discharge of the contract; 4. the replacement price for container agreed in original contract should be adjusted, since the market replacement value for current 20-DC container was USD2,000 per container. Therefore, the total value would be 661 * 2000 = USD1,322,000 calculated by replacement value of new container. The Defendants thereby were requested to return 661 20-DC containers (detailed container numbers could be referred in attachment); otherwise, the Defendants were requested to pay compensation on the amount mentioned before in discount price; 5. the Defendants should bear all the litigation charges which included court acceptance fee, charges of preservation and guarantee fee.

In order to support its claims, the Plaintiff Hongxin Company presented the following evidential materials to the court:

1. Containers leasing contract numbered with (Hongji (HK) (2013) (ZU) ZI No.23001), to prove the container leasing fact and the obligations and rights between the Plaintiff and the Defendants Shanghai Gangtai and Taizhou Gangtai.
2. Supplemental agreement numbered with (Hongji (HK) (2013) (ZU) ZI No.23001-02), to prove the seven Defendants, as joint lessee, are entitled to enjoy the rights as well as be requested to perform the obligations under the contract.
3. Container receipt, to prove that the Plaintiff has delivered leasehold containers to the Defendants according to contract, and the Defendants has checked and accepted as well as used the containers.

The court held the hearing with the absence of the Defendants, after the notice of responding to action and court summons had been announced according to law and the Defendants Shanghai Gangtai, Taizhou Gangtai, DING Genyou, LI Xingling, DING Weimin, ZHANG Lizhong and HUANG Ping disappeared and thereby refused to attend the court without a warrant, which shall be regarded as the waiver of their litigation rights.

According to the materials of proof, objects of proof and hearing facts presented by the Plaintiff, the court hereby analyzes and affirms the facts as follows:

The containers leasing contract, the supplemental agreement and the container receipt presented by the Plaintiff are all written evidence and can be checked with their original documents. Both the Plaintiff and the Defendants has signed, sealed or put their fingerprint on the contract. According to Article 70 Subparagraph 1 of the Civil Procedure Law of the People's Republic of China, which stipulates that "the written evidence presented shall all be original documents" and Paragraph 1 of Article 91 of the Interpretation of the Supreme People's Court on the Application of the Civil Procedure Law of the People's Republic of China, which stipulates that parties that think law relationships are existed shall be responsible for proving such basic fact as the existence of law relationsHips and shall be able to prove that the two parties sign the containers leasing contract, define each party's obligations and rights as well as prove the fact that the Plaintiff has delivered the 1,000 20-DC containers involved to the Defendants according to the contract.

According to the analysis and confirmation of the evidence by the court and combining with the hearing, the court finds out the following facts:

The Plaintiff Hongxin Company, as the leaser, and the Defendants Shanghai Gangtai, Taizhou Gangtai, DING Genyou, LI Xingling, DING Weimin and the third party Yingpeng Company as well as Xiangxun Huili Investment Co., Ltd. (added by hand-written), as the lessees, signed the containers leasing contract numbered with Hongji (HK) (2013) (ZU) ZI No.23001 on February 20, 2013. The prelude of the contract stipulates that "according to the relevant law of the People's Republic of China and with the references of the international practices"; the parties signed this contract on the issues of shipping container lease. The contract is constituted by two parts: "business clause and general clause", in which the first part of business clause stipulates that the Plaintiff leases 1,000 20-DC containers to the Defendants with the tenancy term of 1,826 days. The detailed container numbers shall be referred in equipment interchange receipt (EIR), the container receipt and other valid documents of cargo's into or out of the scene. Paragraph 1 of Article 3, rent and payment in contract stipulates that rent for one day is US dollars that have equal value with RMB11.20 and the lessee shall pay the rent for the first month when the contract is signed (calculated from the first day of that month); and then the monthly rent after the first month shall be paid through the way of deferred payment according to the corresponding month of the day on which the contract is signed. The fifth item "the replacement value of leasehold objects" was defined as US dollars which is equal to RMB22,000. The Article 6 in the contract stipulates that the lessee shall pay for the liquidated damages for contract termination, which is equal to the amount of 25 months' rent, when the leaser executed the right to terminate the contract according to agreement in the contract or legal regulations. The Article 7 stipulates that all the lessees have jointly confirmed that the obligations and rights under this contract shall be entitled to all lessees, if any lessees shall execute the rights alone under this contract, it should be deemed that the rights are executed by all lessees; all lessees shall bear joint liability for the obligations under this contract and the leaser is entitled to request any lessee or all lessees to perform all the obligations and liabilities under this contract, and there would be no exemption or reduction of liability for other lessees, if the leaser does not claim or put off claiming its right to them. The second part of the contract general clause stipulates the other obligations and rights of two parties, in which the second item "lease term" shall include lease inception and the day that throw a lease. Unless there are other specified stipulations in the contract, the lessee shall not terminate or suspend the lease contract during the period of lease term. Paragraph1 of Article 9, "liability for breach of contract and legal remedy" stipulates that if the lessees shall at any time after the contract is signed have following actions: (1) do not accept or return leasehold objects on time or do not provide the Container Receipt of the leasehold objects on time; and (2) do not pay the expenses under this contract in full and on time and the amount paid has reached to the accumulated sum that is equal to one month's rent or other three conditions listed in the contract. Paragraph 2 clearly stipulates that the leaser is entitled to take one or more measures as follows, if conditions listed before happen. (1) Deduct the premium for lease, performance bond or deposit insurance. (2) Request the lessee to pay the liquidated damages for overdue payment which shall be calculated at the rate of 0.1% per day. (3) Request the lessee to pay the rent, three times higher than the standard rent, for these leasehold objects which have not been returned after the expiration of agreed term, except renewal agreement that the leaser and the lessee have both agreed. (4) Request that the contract shall be terminated partially or wholly and the leasehold objects shall be taken back; the leaser is entitled to charge the liquidated damages for contract termination from the lessee. If the liquidated damages, as the predetermined compensation, are unable to cover the loss suffered by the leaser, the lessee shall still compensate in full. Article 3 stipulates that if the leaser executes his right to terminate the contract according to legal provision or contract agreement, the lessee shall return all the leasehold objects within 10 days after receiving the notice of termination from the leaser; otherwise, the leasehold objects shall be deemed as having been lost, thereby, the lessee shall compensate the leaser according to the replacement value of the leasehold objects. The Plaintiff and the Defendant have signed, sealed or put their fingerprint on the contract. The title of lessee, "Xiangyun Huili Investment Co., Ltd." is hand-written at the end of the contract, and there is no company seal or signature of representatives.

Later, the Plaintiff Hongxin Company signed the supplemental agreement Hongji (HK) (2013) (ZU) ZI No.23001-02 with the Defendants Shanghai Gangtai, Taizhou Gangtai, DING Genyou, LI Xingling, DING Weimin, Ying Hongjun, ZHANG Lizhong, Huang Ling and the third party Yingpeng Company, which identified that the supplemental agreement should be the supplement of the containers leasing contract. The parties also jointly confirmed that YING Hongjun, ZHANG Lizhong and HUANG Ling should be added as the joint lessees and should be entitled to have the joint rights as well as bear joint obligations of the contract. Besides, the leaser was entitled to request any or all lessees to perform all obligations and rights under the supplemental agreement and the contract, and there would be no exemption or reduction of liability for other lessees, if the leaser did not claim or put off claiming his right to them.

The Plaintiff Hongxin Company presented the container receipt to the Defendant Shanghai Gangtai on May 2, 2013, which stipulated that 1,000 20-DC containers were accepted under the containers leasing contract (2013) (ZU) ZI No.23001 which was signed by two parties and Shanghai Gangtai was requested to check carefully and then stamp an official seal as well as page seal on the receipt, if everything was right. There was detailed information about container numbers of 1,000 containers, types of the container, delivery date, delivery place and numbers for placing the container on the container receipt. 198 containers were delivered on March 9; 386 containers were delivered on March 10; 166 containers were delivered on March 11; 50 containers were delivered on March 12; 100 containers were delivered on April 16; 100 containers were delivered on April 29. Shanghai Gangtai confirmed it by affixing a seal.

The stockholders of the company, DING Genyou, LI Xingling, DING Weimin, ZHANG Lizhong and HUANG Ping have collectively been out of touch, since February 2015; for the reason that the Defendants Shanghai Gangtai and Taizhou Gangtai got on badly with their business. Therefore, the Plaintiff Hongxin Company took legal action. According to the introduction for account unpaid and subsequent account payable and evidence of rent paid by the Defendant, which were presented by the Plaintiff; the Defendant Shanghai Gangtai owed the Plaintiff total rent USD1,028,119.48, calculated from August 2013 to the end of February 2015; the liquidated damages for overdue payment of rent were all together USD237,807.22 by January 31, 2015. The Plaintiff took 54 containers involved voluntarily during March to May in 2015. And the Plaintiff also took legal action to appeal for property preservation according to No.182 Xia Hai Shang Fa Chu Zi (2015) the dispute over contract on financing lease of containers. Besides, the Plaintiff took 285 containers back with the permission from the court; therefore, the Plaintiff of this case actually had 661containers that should be taken back, but had not for the time being.

The issues of this case are:

1. Whether it is clear and specific about what Plaintiff alleges that the rent unpaid by the Defendants and whether the lease contract could be terminated or not;
2. Whether the liquidated damages for overdue payment agreed in the contract is too high or whether it should be adjusted or not; and
3. Whether the replacement price of containers agreed in the contract is too high and whether it should be adjusted or not.

The court hereby considers this case as the dispute over containers leasing contract arising from not paying the rent. The applicable law for the judgment of this case should be firstly determined. Since the Plaintiff is the legal person of a legal person of Hong Kong Special Administrative Region, according to Article 19 of the Interpretation of the Supreme People's Court on Several Issues concerning the Application of the Law of the Application Law for Foreign-related Civil Relations of the People's Republic of China (I), the issues of the law application relevant to the civil relations in Hong Kong Special Administrative Region shall refer to the stipulations of the Law of the Application of Law for Foreign-related Civil Relations of the People's Republic of China. According to Article 41 of the

Law of the Application of Law for Foreign-related Civil Relations of the People's Republic of China, the parties concerned may choose the laws applicable to contracts by agreement. The laws of the People's Republic of China, thereby, could be applied to this case, since the Plaintiff and the Defendant have indicated that "according to relevant laws of the People's Republic of China and also refers to the international practice"; besides, the contract was signed in the territory of People's Republic of China as well as the delivery place of the subject matter, containers, involved, and the domicile of the Defendants. Therefore, this case shall apply with the laws of the People's Republic of China.

The containers leasing contract involved and its supplemental agreement shall be confirmed to be valid, since it contains legal contents and indicates the true meaning of two parties. The two parties shall be entitled to execute their rights as well as perform their obligations according to the contract. What the Plaintiff alleges that the seven Defendants, such as Shanghai Gangtai, shall bear joint liability for the debts under the contract are reasonable and should be supported according to Article 87 of the General Principles of Civil Law of People's Republic of China and Article 7, business clause in the containers leasing contract and its supplemental agreement, which stipulates that all the lessees shall have the obligations and rights under this contract and all the lessees shall bear joint liability for obligations under this contract. According to the Plaintiff's litigation claims and evidence as well as materials and after taking the focus of this case into consideration, the court hereby confirms as follows:

1. Issues about whether it is clear and specific about what Plaintiff alleges that the rent unpaid by the Defendants and whether the lease contract could be terminated or not; the Plaintiff alleged that the Defendants still owed the Plaintiff USD1,028,119.48 as the total rent for containers leasing contract involved by February, 2015; and the Plaintiff presented supplemental introduction for account unpaid and subsequent account payable as well as interpretations of documents for rent paid by the Defendants.

The court hereby considers that "the lessees should pay for the rent according to the agreed payment term. If the payment term is not agreed or ambiguously agreed, or could not be confirmed according to Article 61 in the contract, and if the lease term is less than one year, the payment should be made when it comes to the expiration of lease term; if the lease term is over one year, the payment should be made at the end of each year; for the rest of the lease term which is less than one year, the payment should be made at the expiration of the lease term". For the reason that all the Defendants did not appear in court, nor did they provide evidence to argue for themselves; therefore, it shall be deemed as waiver of their litigation rights. Besides, the Defendant Shanghai Gangtai and Taizhou Gangtai got on badly with their business, so the stockholder of the company were collectively out of touch on February 2015, leading to the suspension of the liner shipping and the vibration in domestic liner shipping industry for container transporting. The court has entertained cases on a series of disputes arising from the contract on relevant fuel supply of the vessel, the illegal lien ship transporting container and cargo, the leasing of the shipping container and the financing lease contract. According to Paragraph 1 of Article 93 of the Interpretation of the Supreme People's Court on the Application of the Civil Procedure Law of the People's Republic of China, which stipulates that "the party does not need to present evidence for the following facts", item 4 which stipulates that "the other fact can be presumed according to the known facts and rules of daily life experience" and Article 105 which stipulates that "the People's Court should examine the evidence comprehensively and objectively according to legal procedure; the People's Court should judge the power of evidence and the strength of such evidence power as well as publicly announce the reason and result of such judgment applying with rules of daily life experience and logical reasoning according to the legal provisions". Therefore, the introduction for account unpaid and subsequent account payable and documents for rent paid by the Defendants presented by the Plaintiff shall be admitted and the court presumes that it is true that the Defendants owed a large amount of rent to the Plaintiff. The total rent that Defendant owing to the Plaintiff shall be confirmed by the expiration term.

Paragraph 1 of Article 3, rent and payment in the first part of business clause of the contract involved explicitly stipulates that "rent for one day is US dollars that has equal value to RMB11.20 and the lessee shall pay the rent for the first month when the contract is signed (calculated from the first day of that month); and then the monthly rent after the first month shall be paid through the way of deferred payment according to the corresponding month of the day that contract is signed". Paragraph 2 of Article 7, obligations and rights of the lessee in the second part of general clause of the contract explicitly stipulates that "the lessee should pay rent in full and on time to the leaser according to the contract". Therefore, the rent payment appealed by the Plaintiff by February 2015 conforms to the legal provisions and has evidence, thereby, it shall be supported.

As for whether the containers leasing contract and the supplemental agreement could be terminated or not, the court considers that Article 9 Subparagraph 1(b) "liability for breach of contract and legal remedy" in the containers leasing contract stipulates that if, at any time after the contract is signed, the lessees do not pay the expenses under this contract in full and on time and the amount paid has reached to the accumulated sum that is equal to one month's rent or other three conditions listed in the contract. Paragraph 2 clearly stipulates that the leaser is entitled to take one or more measures as follows, if conditions listed before happen. (1) Deduct the premium for lease, performance bond or deposit insurance. (2) Request the lessee to pay the liquidated damages for overdue payment which shall be calculated at the rate of 0.1% per day. (3) Request the lessee to pay the rent, three times higher than the standard rent, for these leasehold objects which have not been returned after the expiration of the term, except renewal agreement that the leaser and the lessee have both agreed. (4) Request that the contract shall be terminated partially or wholly and the leasehold objects shall be taken back; the leaser is entitled to charge the liquidated damages for contract termination from the lessee. If the liquidated damages, as the predetermined compensation, are unable to cover the loss suffered by the leaser, the lessee shall still compensate in full. Article 3 stipulates that if the leaser executes its right to terminate the contract according to legal provision or contract agreement, the lessee shall return all the leasehold objects within 10 days after receiving the notice of termination from the leaser; otherwise, the leasehold objects shall be deemed as having been lost, thereby, the lessee shall compensate the leaser according to the replacement value of the leasehold objects. Based on the fact that the Defendant owes rent to the Plaintiff, the Plaintiff hereby alleged that the lease contract involved should be terminated. The condition for termination of the contract has been existed and the agreement is also reasonable. Therefore, according to Paragraph 2 of Article 93 of the Contract Law which stipulates that "the party shall reach an agreement on the conditions for the termination of the contract. When the conditions for termination of the contract exist, the party who has rights to terminate the contract shall terminate the contract" and Article 227 which stipulates that "if the lessee does not pay or delay paying for the rent without reasonable warrant, the leaser shall request the lessee to pay for the rent within the reasonable term. In case that the lessee shall not pay or delay paying for the rent, the leaser shall terminate the contract", this allegation of the Plaintiff shall be supported.

The Plaintiff Shanghai Gangtai insisted that the Defendants should pay for the rent according to rent standard stipulated in the containers leasing contract, which means that the rent for one day is US dollars that have equal value to RMB11.20, until all the containers have been returned. The court considers that the allegation of the Plaintiff shall be supported, since the Defendants breached the contract by terminating the containers leasing contract involved and its supplemental agreement. According to Article 97 of the Contract Law, "if the obligation has not been performed, such performance shall be terminated; if the obligation has been performed, the party could demand to make it return to the status quo or take other remedy measures and shall have rights to claim for the loss, after the termination of the contract". Therefore, after this judgment confirms that the termination of the contract has taken into effect, there will be no legal basis for the Plaintiff to claim rent again from the Defendants. Besides, the Plaintiff has already taken 54 containers back voluntarily from March to May in 2015, before the litigation of this case. And the Plaintiff took 285 containers back according to Litigation of Property Preservation No.182 Xia Hai Fa Shang Chu Zi (2015), after which the Plaintiff took no containers back. Therefore, the Defendants shall continuously pay monthly rent calculated by US dollars which has equal value to agreed daily rent RMB11.20/container based on the quantity of 661 containers [=1,000-(54-285), detailed container numbers could be referred in attachment], from March 1, 2015 to the day when the judgments are taken into action and the contract is terminated.

There are 661 containers that the Defendants have not returned to the Plaintiff, after the termination of the contract has been taken into effect by this judgment; therefore, the right should belong to the damage compensation right, after the Plaintiff terminates the contract and the performance of the obligation, rather than the request right for rent; and it is uncertain that how many containers could be actually taken back and it is lack of factual and legal basis, so the court does not support the Plaintiff's claim for rent calculated by the day that the containers are returned according to the judgment.

2. Issues about whether the liquidated damages for overdue payment agreed in the contract is too high or whether it should be adjusted or not. The Plaintiff alleged that the seven Defendants should jointly pay the liquidated damages for overdue payment until the day they actually pay. The Defendants owed liquidated damages for overdue payment to the Plaintiff totally up to USD237,807.22 calculated from August 2013 to January 31, 2015. The Plaintiff also presented the introduction for account unpaid and subsequent account payable and documents for rent paid by the Defendants.

The court considers that according to Paragraph 1 of Article 29 of the Interpretations of the Supreme People's Court on Several Issues concerning the Application of the Contract Law of the People's Republic of China (II), "if the party claims that the agreed liquidated damages are too high and requires that liquidated damages should be properly reduced, the People's Court should make judge based on the actual loss and take the performance of contract, fault degree of the party and expected benefits into consideration according to the principle of equity and good faith". Therefore, whether the agreed liquidated damages are too high and shall be procedurally determined by the claim of the party, rather than the court intervenes by itself on this point; in fact, it should be determined by actual loss suffered by the Plaintiff. Since the Defendants did not appear in court, which should be regarded as the waiver of litigation rights, the court does not adjust the sum of liquidated damages for overdue payment agreed in the contract.

According to the statements mentioned above, Paragraph 1 of Article 114 of the Contract Law stipulates that "two parties agree that if either party breach the contract, the party that breaches the contract shall pay certain sum of liquidated damages to the other party according to the circumstances of the breach or two parties could make an agreement on the calculating method for liquidated damages for breach of the contract", the court has confirmed the fact that the Defendant owed a large amount of rent to the Plaintiff; therefore, according to Article 9, "liability for breach of contract and legal remedy" and Sub-paragraph (b) of Paragraph 1 in the containers leasing contract involved stipulates that "do not pay the expenses under this contract in full and on time and the amount paid has reached to the accumulated sum that is equal to one month's rent". And Sub-paragraph (a) of Paragraph 2 stipulates that "request the lessee to pay the liquidated damages for overdue payment which shall be calculated at the rate of 0.1% per day". The Plaintiff now alleges that the liquidated damages for overdue payment should be calculated at the rate of 0.1% per day as agreed in the contract according to the rent that the Defendant owed. The court considers the allegation of the Plaintiff is true and has legal basis, therefore, it shall be supported.

The Plaintiff calculates the liquidated damages for overdue payment at agreed rate of 0.1% per day according to the sum of the rent that the Defendant owed, but the specific amount of overdue payment and the time of overdue payment were not provided and cannot be identified after the trial. Therefore, the court considers it as ambiguous litigation claims; and the Plaintiff admits that they have taken back through the other litigation case of property preservation measures in the court as well as taken back voluntarily 339 containers from February 2015 to the time before this litigation. Therefore, it is improper to take 1,000 containers as the cardinality to calculate the rent after February 2015. The Plaintiff claimed that the monthly rent for the liquidated damages for overdue payment that the Defendants owe should be calculated by taking the 661 containers that should be taken back while have not been taken back as the cardinality after February 2015, and then calculated with the standard of 0.1% per day.

3. Issues about whether the replacement price of containers agreed in the contract is too high and whether it should be adjusted or not.

The court considers that according to Article 97 of the Contract Law, "if the obligation has not been performed, such performance shall be terminated; if the obligation has been performed, the party could demand to make it return to the status quo or take other remedy measures and shall have rights to claim for the loss, after the termination of the contract", the Defendants breached the contract for the reason that the Defendants did not pay for the rent in full and on time as agreed in the contract. Therefore, the Plaintiff is entitled to terminate the contract and take back the leasehold objects according to the contract. It conforms to the legal provision that the Plaintiff requested the Defendants to return 661 containers, therefore, the court supports the Plaintiff's claim. The Defendants should return the containers that ought to be returned according to the requirements of the Plaintiff, if the Defendants failed to do so, the Defendants should compensate the damage according to the replacement value. But the replacement price of the container involved is obviously higher than that of market price, so it does not conform to the principle of returning to the status quo and completely compensating the actual loss according to the Contract Law. The Plaintiff now decreases the replacement price to USD2,000 per container from the original RMB22,000 per container, which is lower than the original replacement value agreed in the contract. Therefore, the Plaintiff exercised legal right of its own and did no harm to the Defendants. The Defendants shall calculate the compensation according to current market replacement value for container, which is USD2,000 per container.

In conclusion, according to Article 87 of the General Principles of the Civil Law of the People's Republic of China, Article 93, Paragraph 2 of Article 97, Paragraph 1 of Article 114, Article 226 and Article 227 of the Contract Law of People's Republic of China, paragraph 1 of Article 64 and Article 144 of the Civil Procedure Law of the People's Republic of China, the judgment is as follows:

1. The containers leasing contract numbered with Hongji (HK) (2013) (ZU) ZI No.23001 and the supplemental agreement numbered with Hongji (HK) (2013) (ZU) ZI No.23002 shall be terminated;
2. The Defendant Shanghai Gangtai shall return 661 containers (detailed container numbers referred to attachment) to the Plaintiff Hongxin Company within ten days after this judgment comes into effect; otherwise, the Defendant shall pay compensation according to the replacement value standard of USD2,000 per container;

3. The Defendant Shanghai Hongsheng Gangtai Shipping Co., Ltd. shall pay USD1,028,119.48 for the rent and the liquidated damages for overdue payment which is calculated at agreed standard of 0.1% per day from March 1, 2015 to the day of actual payment to the Plaintiff within ten days after this judgment comes into effect;
4. The Defendant Shanghai Hongsheng Gangtai Shipping Co., Ltd. shall pay the rent of 661 containers to the Plaintiff Hongxin Company. within ten days after this judgment comes into effect and the rent shall be calculated at the standard of USD which is equal to RMB11.20 per day from March 1, 2015 to the day that this judgment comes into effect;
5. The Defendants Taizhou Gangtai, DING Genyou, LI Xingling, DING Weimin, ZHANG Lizhong and HUANG Ping shall bear joint and several liability for the debt owing to the Plaintiff Hongxin Company; and
6. Reject the other claims of the Plaintiff Hongxin Company.

Court acceptance fee in amount of RMB80,724, the Plaintiff Hongxin Company. shall bear RMB10,724 and the Defendants Shanghai Hongsheng Gangtai Shipping Co., Ltd., TaizhouCity Gangtai Shipping Co., Ltd., DING Genyou, HUANG Ping, LI Xingling and ZHANG Lizhong shall jointly bear RMB70, 000.

In the event of dissatisfaction with this judgment, the Plaintiff Hongxin Company may within 30 days upon the service of this judgment and the Defendants Shanghai Hongsheng Gangtai Shipping Co., Ltd., Taizhou City Gangtai Shipping Co., Ltd., DING Genyou, LI Xingling, DING Weimin, ZHANG Lizhong and HUANG Ping may within 15 days upon the service of this judgment, submit a letter of appeal, together with duplicates in the number of the opposite party to the court, to lodge an appeal before Fujian High People's Court.

Presiding Judge: ZHOU Chengyou
Judge: DENG Jingang
Acting Judge: YOU Caimo

December 7, 2015

Acting Clerk: HONG Dewen

Appendix: Relevant Law

1. **General Principles of the Civil Law of the People's Republic of China**
   Article 87 When there are two or more creditors or debtors to a deal, each of the joint creditors shall be entitled to demand that the debtor fulfil his obligations, according to legal provisions or the agreement between the parties; each of the joint debtors shall be obliged to perform the entire debt, and the debtor who performs the entire debt shall be entitled to ask the other joint debtors to reimburse him for their shares of the debt.

2. **Contract Law of the People's Republic of China**

   Article 93 The parties may terminate a contract if they reach a consensus through consultation.

   The parties may agree upon conditions under which either party may terminate the contract. Upon satisfaction of the conditions, the party who has the right to terminate may terminate the contract.

   Article 97 After the termination of a contract, performance shall cease if the contract has not been performed; if the contract has been performed, a party may, according to the circumstances of performance or the nature of the contract, demand the other party to restore such party to its original state or adopt other remedial measures, and such party shall have the right to demand compensation for damages.

   Article 114 The parties may agree that if one party breaches the contract, it shall pay a certain sum of liquidated damages to the other party in light of the circumstances of the breach, and may also agree on a method for the calculation of the amount of compensation for the damages incurred as a result of the breach.

   Article 226 The lessee shall pay the rent at the agreed time. Where the time of payment is not agreed or the agreement is not clear, nor can it be determined according to Article 61 of this Law, the rent shall be paid at the end of the lease term if it is less than one year; if the lease term is one year or longer, the rent shall be paid at the end of each annual period, and where the remaining period is less than one year, the rent shall be paid at the end of the lease term.

   Article 227 Where the lessee fails to pay or delays in paying the rent without any reason, the lessor may require the lessee to pay the rent within a reasonable time limit. If the lessee fails to pay the rent at the end of such time limit, the lessor may terminate the contract.

3. **Civil Procedure Law of the People's Republic of China**

   Article 64 A party shall have the burden to provide evidence for its claims.

   Article 144 If the Defendant, having been served with a summons, refuses to appear in court without justified reasons, or if he withdraws during a court session without the permission of the court, the court may make a judgment by default.

   Prompt of Enforcement:

4. **Civil Procedure Law of the People's Republic of China**

   Article 239

(1) The time limit for the application for execution shall be two years. Suspension or interruption of the time limit for the application for execution shall apply to the provisions on suspension or interruption of the limitation period in the law.
(2) The above-mentioned time limit shall be calculated from the last day of the period of performance specified by the legal document. If the legal document specifies performance in stages, the time limit shall be calculated from the last day of the period of performance specified by the legal document. If the legal

document specifies performance in stages, the time limit shall be calculated from the last day of the period specified for each stage of performance. If the legal document fails to specify the period of performance, it shall be calculated from the date the legal document takes effect.

Ningbo Maritime Court
Civil Judgment

Huayu Electrical Appliance Group Co., Ltd.
v.
JC Logistics Service Co., Ltd. Ningbo Branch

(2013) Yong Hai Fa Shang Chu Zi No.579

Related Case(s) This is the judgment of first instance, and the judgment of second instance and the judgment of retrial are on page 476 and page 485 respectively.

Cause(s) of Action 223. Dispute over freight forwarding contract on the sea or sea-connected waters.

Headnote The Defendant freight forwarder held liable to the Plaintiff shipper for giving bill of lading for shipper's goods to the Plaintiff's buyer, so that buyer could take delivery of goods, even though buyer was named as shipper on the bill of lading, because the Plaintiff was actual shipper; however, the Plaintiff held 50% responsible for its own loss, because it had failed to inform the Defendant that it was the actual shipper.

Summary The Plaintiff-Shipper filed suit against the Defendant in a dispute over a freight forwarding contract. The Plaintiff agreed to sell refrigerators to a foreign buyer, who hired the Defendant to book space for the goods. A bill of lading naming the buyer as the shipper was issued to the Defendant, and the goods were loaded on to M.V. "YONGLIAN" in twelve containers. The Defendant gave the bill of lading to the foreign buyer instead of to the Plaintiff, and the Plaintiff was only able to collect USD30,508.50 of the total price of the goods (USD171,248.00) from the buyer. The remaining balance on the contract was USD140,739.50. The Plaintiff then filed an action requesting the court to order the Defendant to pay the remaining balance plus interest. The court first had to determine if there was a freight forwarding contract established between the two parties, and found that the relationship was established and unaffected by the buyer's status as the contractual shipper since the Plaintiff was the actual shipper. The Defendant was also obliged to affirm the Plaintiff's identity as the actual shipper. The court then determined that both parties were to be liable to bear half of the remaining balance on the contract. This was because the Plaintiff was entitled to receive the bill of lading from the

Defendant within the statute of limitations, giving it the legal basis to require the Defendant to compensate it for the unpaid balance. However, the Plaintiff failed to inform the Defendant that it was the actual shipper, so both parties shall bear the liability equally for the wrongful delivery of the bill of lading. Therefore, the Defendant was ordered to compensate the Plaintiff in the amount of USD70,369.75.

Judgment

The Plaintiff: Huayu Electrical Appliance Group Co., Ltd.
Domicile: No.168 North Ring Road, Zhouxiang County, Cixi City, Zhejiang Province.
Legal representative: XU Wanqun.
Agent *ad litem*: YE Yuanhua, lawyer of Beijing Dentons (Ningbo) Law Firm.

The Defendant: JC Logistics Service Co., Ltd. Ningbo Branch
Domicile: Rm 8-12, Yinyi Time Square, No.8 Lengjing Street, Haishu District, Ningbo City, Zhejiang Province.
Person in charge: Deng Zhishan, manager.
Agent *ad litem*: LIU Jihong, employee.
Agent *ad litem*: MA Yanqiong, employee.

With respect to the case arising from dispute over freight forwarding contract, the Plaintiff, Huayu Electrical Appliance Group Co., Ltd. (Huayu company) filed an action against the Defendant JC Logistics Service Co., Ltd. Ningbo Branch (Jincheng company) before the court on August 20, 2013. After entertaining this case on August 23, 2014, the court formed a collegiate panel and heard this case under summary procedure in public on October 12, 2013. However, due to the complexity of the details of this case, the procedure was transferred to ordinary procedure, another hearing was held in public on November 28, 2013. YE Yuanhua, agent *ad litem* of the Plaintiff, LIU Jihong and MA Yanqiong, agents *ad litem* of the Defendant appeared in court and participated in the action. Now the case has been concluded now.

The Plaintiff brought the lawsuit, alleging as follows: on October 24, 2012, the Plaintiff concluded the sales contract No.12HSN085 with an overseas buyer Homestar Electronic Industry Co., Ltd. (hereinafter referred to as Homestar), agreed the Plaintiff sold refrigerators to Homestar, of which the trade terms was FOB Ningbo. Afterwards, the Plaintiff entrusted the Defendant with the transport of the goods involved according to the requirement of Homestar. The Defendant accepted the entrustment, then delivered the goods to China Shipping Container Lines (Hong Kong) Co., Ltd. (hereinafter referred to as CSCL) for shipment from Ningbo in China to Tican in Negira. CSCL issued the seaway bill on December 24, 2012. There were 1,416 boxes loaded in 12 containers, the carrying vessel was M.V. "YONGLIAN", the voyage was Y052N. On the same day, the Plaintiff declared the export of the goods with the customs, it was stated on the customs declaration that the total price of the goods was USD171,248, the bill of lading was numbered with NGBTIN005310, vessel/voyage was M.V. "YONGLIAN"/Y052N. After the goods were shipped, the Plaintiff requested the Defendant to give the original B/Ls to it, but the Defendant gave the originals to Homestar rather than the Plaintiff, and Homestar had actually took delivery of the goods.

The Plaintiff held it was the actual shipper, it was entitled to obtaining of the original B/Ls, the Defendant's refusal to give the original B/Ls to it caused the loss of control of the goods, it thus sustained loss of price of goods. Therefore, the Plaintiff filed the action, requested the court to order the Defendant to compensate the Plaintiff the loss in sum of USD140,739.5 (the dollar currency converted the sum into RMB according to the central parity rate prevailing on August 12, 2013 published by the People's Bank of China was RMB867,870) and the interest thereon (the interest should be calculated from the February 1, 2013 to the day of payment designated by the judgment).

The Defendant defended as follows:

1. The Defendant accepted the entrustment of the foreign company Homestar, it had surrendered the B/Ls to Homestar. The evidence of the Plaintiff could neither prove it was the actual shipper of the goods involved, nor it entrusted the Defendant or others with the transport, thus they did not establish entrustment relation and the Plaintiff was not the actual shipper of this case.
2. In respect of the loss of the Plaintiff, the evidence of the Plaintiff could not prove the Plaintiff did not receive the price of the goods involved.
3. The Defendant had no fault in handling the goods involved, the declaration of customs and inland transport were carried out by the actual agent of the Defendant, the Defendant did not know and had no reason to know who was the declaration exporter.

In summary, the Defendant requested the court to dismiss the claims of the Plaintiff.

The Plaintiff in support of its claims submitted the following evidence with the period of adducing evidence:

1. Container equipment interchange receipt, packing list, receipt of container yard, responsibility agreement and B/Ls, to prove the Plaintiff entrusted the Defendant with the shipment of the goods and the Defendant accepted the entrustment of the Plaintiff.
2. Sales contract, commercial invoice, customs declaration and packing list, to prove the Plaintiff concluded a trade contract with a foreign company.
3. The dynamic conditions of the containers involved, to prove the goods involved had been taken delivery of.
4. The statement on the containerized goods under No.NGBTIN005310 bill of lading issued by Ningbo Baidu International Freight Forwarding Co., Ltd. (hereinafter referred to as Baidu Company), to prove Baidu Company delivered the goods to the Defendant.

Upon cross-examination, in terms of evidence 1, the Defendant held it had never seen the container equipment interchange receipt, the packing list or the receipt of container yard, and the Plaintiff did not submit the originals, it did not confirm the authenticity thereof; the responsibility agreement was blank, which was not in conformity with the situation it knew, it did not admit; it did not object the B/Ls.

The Defendant in support of its claims submitted the following evidence within the period of adducing evidence: 1. freight forwarding agreement; 2. entrusting order; 3. Ningbo valued-added invoice; and 4. B/Ls (same with those provided by the Plaintiff), to prove the shipper in this case was not the Plaintiff.

The Plaintiff after cross-examination held it had no objection to the freight forwarding agreement, and admitted Homestar was the contracting shipper; it did not confirm the authenticity of the entrusting order due to available verification; it had no objection to the valued-added invoice, but objected the relevancy thereof. The Plaintiff argued it was the foreign buyer who entrusted the Defendant with booking service, while it could not identify the internal arrangement with Ningbo Container Transport Co., Ltd. for the payment in terms of the goods involved due to its particular operation and the relation between the operator of the Defendant and other domestic companies. It did not object the B/Ls.

After trial, the court holds although the Plaintiff did not submit the originals of the container equipment interchange receipt, the packing list and the receipt of container yard in evidence 1, they can corroborate other evidence, the court hereby admits. As for evidence 2, the sales contract is a fax copy, which corroborates other evidence, the court hereby admits; the commercial invoice and packing list both are affixed with the bar seal of the Plaintiff, it conforms to the international practice, the court hereby admits. The customs declaration is original, the court hereby admits. As for evidence 3, it is not original, and it has not been notarized, the Defendant objected the authenticity thereof, therefore the court does not admit. As for evidence 4, it is original with the official seal of the issuer, it is a certificate rather than a statement of witness. It has no legal basis that the Defendant requested the legal representative of the issuer to appear in court as a witness, the court does not admit. The Defendant objected this evidence, but it failed to prove the official seal thereon was faked or there was other forgeries. The Plaintiff has performed its burden of proof, the court admits it. The pieces of evidence provided by the Defendant are originals, the court admits them.

Based on the statements in the hearing and the effective evidence having been identified above, the court ascertains the following facts:

Huayu Company signed a sales contract with a foreign buyer, Homestar on 24 October 2012, and the two parties agreed that Huayu Company sold refrigerators to Homestar, the trade terms was FOB Ningbo. Homestar authorized Jincheng Company to book space on December 11, 2012. Huayu Company delivered the goods to Jincheng Company as required by Homestar and entrusted Ningbo Baidu International Freight Forwarding Co., Ltd. (hereinafter referred to as Baidu Company) to undertake inland transportation and export declaration. The number of the B/L incorporated in the customs declaration was NGBTIN005310, there were 1,463 packages, 1,416 boxes in total, and the price of which amounted to USD171,248. Huayu Company was incorporated both as the export operator and the consignor. Baidu Company took delivery of the containers from the carrier on

December 20, 2012 and then had the goods loaded by Huayu Company, upon which it delivered the goods to China Shipping Container Lines (Hong Kong) Co., Ltd. (hereinafter referred to as CSCL) for shipment. CSCL issued a B/L numbered with NGBTIN00531. The shipper recorded on the B/L was Homestar, the goods were contained in 12 containers, there were 1416 boxes in total, the name of carrying vessel was M.V. "YONGLIAN", the voyage number was Y052N. Jincheng Company, after receiving the B/L issued by CSCL, delivered it to Homestar instead of Huayu Company. The goods were taken delivery of as soon as their arrival at the port of destination. Huayu Company had received payment for goods in sum of USD30,508.5, left USD140,739.5 unpaid. Huayu Company failed to collect the sum from Jincheng Company, filed an action to the court, requested the court to order Jincheng Company to compensate Huayu Company USD140,739.5 for the loss of payment for goods. (the dollar currency converted to currency according to the reference rate of dollars against Chinese yuan at 6.1665 published by the People's Bank of China prevailing on August 12, 2013 was RMB86,870) and the interest thereon which should be calculated from February 1, 2013 to the date of payment designated by the judgment according to the bank loan interest rate over the same time.

The court holds that: this case is arising from dispute over freight forwarding contract. The issues of this case are that whether a relationship of freight forwarding contract between the two parties was established and whether Jincheng Company should be responsible for the loss suffered by Huayu Company. Pursuant to the law, a contracting shipper refers to the person by whom or in whose name or on whose behalf a contract of carriage of goods by sea has been concluded with a carrier; an actual shipper refers to the person by whom or in whose name or on whose behalf the goods have been delivered to the carrier involved in the contract of carriage of goods by sea. In this case, Homestar entrusted Jincheng Company to book space, thus a relationship of freight forwarding contract between the two parties came into effect. In the present case, Homestar entrusted Jincheng Company to handle the booking service and set up the maritime freight forwarding contractual relationship with Jincheng Company. Homestar was the contractual shipper, but it did not affect the establishment of maritime freight forwarding contractual relationship between Huayu Company as the actual shipper and Jincheng Company. Huayu Company, as the seller of export goods under terms of FOB, entrusted Baidu Company to undertake the inland transport and custom clearance. The delivery of goods to the carrier by Baidu Company was in conformity with the traditional practice, Huayu Company was the actual shipper. Jincheng Company defended that it did not knew the existence or the identity of Huayu Company, it neither knew that Huayu Company was the owner of the goods, nor the goods involved were actually delivered by Huayu Company. The legal relationship of freight forwarding between the two parties and Huayu Company's identity of principal under the legal relationship of freight forwarding should be recognized based on the facts and applicable law, rather than on the condition whether the carrier was informed or not. As the freight forwarder, Jincheng Company was obliged to affirm the actual shipper of the goods via the receiver of the goods (inland carrier) or other means, so as to specify the receiver of the B/L. Jincheng Company also defended that although Baidu Company was on behalf of Homestar or any other third party to deliver the goods to it, but Jincheng Company did not provide any evidence, and this also went against the evidence provided by Baidu Company. Therefore, the defense of Jincheng Company, which was contrary to the legal provisions and facts, shall not be admitted. As for the issue whether Huayu Company requested Jincheng Company to deliver the B/L before the action, since there are no provisions on the time limit of delivery of B/L by Huayu Company to Jincheng Company, therefore, Huayu Company was entitled to deliver the B/L involved against Jincheng Company within the statute of limitations. But Jincheng Company sent the B/L involved to Homestar after the shipment of the goods, objectively, the possibility to send the B/L to Huayu Company, it confirmed to the facts of this case that Huayu Company directly required Jincheng Company to compensate for the loss. Accordingly, Huayu Company had legal basis to require Jincheng Company to compensate such loss, the loss of the title to the goods was directly caused by the wrongful act of Jincheng Company. In this case, Jincheng Company was the freight forwarder who undertook the booking space, Huayu Company entrusted another party to undertake inland transport and custom clearance, it failed to inform Jincheng Company of the fact that it was the actual shipper. It was another reason which caused the wrong operation of Jincheng Company, in addition, Huayu Company did not actively claim against Jincheng Company to recover the loss. Therefore, the two parties should be liable for the loss suffered caused by the wrongly delivery of B/L by Jincheng Company, they should bear the loss half and half. The amount of the loss had been proved by Huayu Company, namely it had already received USD30,508.5, with USD140,739.5 unpaid, Jincheng Company objected to that, but it failed to provide any rebuttal evidence, in that sense, the amount of the loss claimed by Huayu Company should be confirmed. Therefore, Jincheng Company should compensate Huayu Company the loss in sum of USD70,369.75 (USD140,739.5 × 50%). As for the interest claimed by Huayu Company should be counted from the date that the action was filed, since the loan interest rate was not specific, the court clearly decides that it shall be counted according to the loan interest rate stipulated by People's Bank of China. To sum up, the court supports the rational part of Huayu Company's claims. On March 3, 2013, according to the provisions of Article 406 Paragraph 1 of the Contract Law of the People's Republic of China and Articles 8 and 10 of the Provisions of the Supreme People's Court on Several Issues Concerning the Trial of Cases of Dispute over Maritime Freight Forwarding (the Maritime Freight Forwarding Provisions), the court renders the judgment as follows:

The Defendant JC Logistics Service Co., Ltd. Ningbo Branch shall compensate the Plaintiff Huayu Electrical Appliance Group Co., Ltd. USD3.5 million and the interest (the interest shall be calculated from May 19, 2011 to the day the Defendant actually pays the sum aforesaid) within ten days as of the effectiveness of this judgment.

Where the obliged party fails to perform the obligation of paying within the period prescribed herein, it shall, according to Article 253 of the Civil Procedure Law of the People's Republic of China, double pay the interest for the period of delayed performance.

Court acceptance fee in amount of RMB12,780 yuan, the Plaintiff Huayu Electrical Appliance Group Co., Ltd. shall bear RMB6,390 yuan and the Defendant JC Logistics Service Co., Ltd. Ningbo Branch shall bear RMB6,390 yuan.

In event of dissatisfaction with this judgment, a party may, within 15 days upon service of this judgment, submit a letter of appeal and six copies to the court, to lodge an appeal with the Zhejiang High People's Court. [The appeal entertainment fee is RMB12,780 yuan (the specific sum will be determined by Zhejiang High People's Court, more than one part is returned in advance), which shall be paid when the letter of appeal is submitted. If the sum has not been paid within seven days after the expiration of the appeal period, the appeal shall be automatically withdrawn. Account name: non-tax revenue settlement account of Zhejiang Province Finance Department; bank of deposit: Agricultural Bank West Lake Branch; account number: 398000101040006575, unit code: 515001].

> Presiding Judge: XIAO Zibo
> People's Juror: HU Xindi
> People's Juror: ZHOU Zhenyi
>
> March12, 2014
>
> Acting Clerk: ZHU Danying

Appendix: Relevant Law:

1. **Contract Law of the People's Republic of China**
   Article 406 Under a commission contract for value, if the principal sustains any loss due to the fault of the agent, the principal may claim damages. Under a gratuitous agency appointment contract, if the principal sustains any loss due to the agent's intentional misconduct or gross negligence, the principal may claim damages.
   Where the agent acts beyond the scope of authorization, thereby causing loss to the principal, it shall pay damages.
2. **Provisions of the Supreme People's Court on Several Issues concerning the Trial of Cases of Dispute over Freight Forwarding**
   Article 8 A freight forwarding enterprise accepts the entrustment of the contracting consignor with booking service, and accepts the entrustment of the actual consignor with delivery of goods, the actual shipper requests the freight forwarder to submit the bill of lading, sea waybill or other transport documents, the people's court shall support.
   Article 10 Where the principal claims for compensation against a freight forwarder on ground that the freight forwarder causes loss to the principal when handling maritime freight forwarding service, the people's courts shall support, unless the freight forwarder proves that it has no fault.

Zhejiang High People's Court
Civil Judgment

Huayu Electrical Appliance Group Co., Ltd.
v.
JC Logistics Service Co., Ltd. Ningbo Branch

(2014) Zhe Hai Zhong Zi No.72

Related Case(s) This is the judgment of second instance, and the judgment of first instance and the judgment of retrial are on page 469 and page 485 respectively.

Cause(s) of Action 223. Dispute over freight forwarding contract on the sea or sea-connected waters.

Headnote Affirming lower court's decision holding the Defendant freight forwarder and the Plaintiff shipper each 50% responsible for the Plaintiff's loss after the Defendant gave bill of lading to the Plaintiff's buyer; the Defendant should have given bill of lading to the Plaintiff as actual shipper but the Plaintiff failed to inform the Defendant in timely fashion that it was actual shipper; appeal and cross-appeal both dismissed.

Summary The Plaintiff-Shipper and the Defendant-Freight Forwarder both appealed the judgment of the Ningbo Maritime Court, which held both parties liable for half of the Plaintiff's losses in their dispute over freight forwarding contract. The Plaintiff agreed to sell refrigerators to a foreign buyer, who in turn hired the Defendant to book space aboard a vessel. The Defendant booked space for the goods on M.V. "YONGLIAN", and then gave the bill of lading to the foreign buyer instead of to the Plaintiff. The Plaintiff was only able to collect a portion of the payments due on the sales contract, leaving USD140,739.50 as the remaining unpaid balance. The Plaintiff filed action against the Defendant in order to collect the remaining balance. However, the Ningbo Maritime Court held that the Defendant was only liable for half of the remaining balance because, even though the Defendant failed to give the bill of lading to the Plaintiff, the Plaintiff failed to notify the Defendant that it was the actual shipper of the goods. Both parties appealed the lower court's judgment. The Plaintiff argued that the Defendant was obligated to deliver it the bill of lading and should be held liable for the full remaining balance on the grounds that the Defendant should have known that a domestic shipper was involved and should have inquired about its identity. The Plaintiff also asserted that it directly demanded the bill of lading from the Defendant via its inland transportation agent. The appeal court recognized the lower court's finding that there was a contractual relationship between the Plaintiff and the Defendant because the buyer, as the contracting shipper, entered into a contract with the Defendant to book space on a vessel for the carriage of goods of which the Plaintiff was the actual shipper. The appeal court also recognized the lower court's determination that the Defendant should be responsible for half of the remaining balance under the sales contract on the grounds that, even though the Defendant failed to seek out the identity of the actual shipper, the Plaintiff failed in its obligation to notify the Defendant of its identity as the actual shipper of the goods while also not requesting delivery of the bill of lading in a timely manner. Therefore, the appeal of both parties was dismissed and the original judgment was recognized.

Judgement

The Appellant (the Plaintiff of first instance): Huayu Electrical Appliance Group Co., Ltd.
Domicile: No. 168 North Ring Road, Zhouxiang County, Cixi City, Zhejiang Province.
Legal representative: XU Wanqun.
Agent *ad litem*: YE Yuanhua, Lawyer of Beijing Dentons (Ningbo) Law Firm.
Agent *ad litem*: PAN Anqi, Lawyer of Beijing Dentons (Ningbo) Law Firm.

The Appellant (the Defendant of first instance): JC Logistics Service Co., Ltd. Ningbo Branch
Domicile: Rooms 8-12, Yinyi Time Square, No.8 Lengging Street, Ningbo City, Zhejiang Province.
Person in charge: DENG Zhishan, Manager.
Agent *ad litem*: LIU Jihong, employee.
Agent *ad litem*: ZHENG Lianming.

The Appellants Huayu Electrical Appliance Group Co., Ltd. (hereinafter referred to as Huayu Company) and JC Logistics Service Co., Ltd. Ningbo Branch (hereinafter referred to as Jincheng Company) refused to accept the (2013) Yong Hai Fa Shang Chu Zi No.579 Civil Judgment made by Ningbo Maritime Court regarding the case arising from dispute over freight forwarding contract and lodged an appeal to the court. After entertaining this case on June 5, 2014, the court formed a collegiate panel and held a hearing in public on July 3 in the same year to try the case. YE Yuanhua, agent *ad litem* of the Appellant Huayu Company, LIU Jihong and ZHENG Lianming, agents *ad litem* of the Appellant Jincheng Company, appeared in court to attend the trial. Now the case has been concluded.

The court of first instance found the following facts: Huayu Company signed a sales contract with a foreign buyer, Homestar on October 24, 2012, and the two parties agreed that Huayu Company sold refrigerators to Homestar, the trade terms was FOB Ningbo. Homestar authorized Jincheng Company to book space on December 11, 2012. Huayu Company delivered the goods to Jincheng Company as required by Homestar and entrusted Ningbo Baidu International Freight Forwarding Co., Ltd. (hereinafter referred to as Baidu Company) to undertake inland transportation and export declaration. The number of the B/L incorporated in the customs declaration was NGBTIN005310, there were 1,463 packages, 1,416 boxes in total, and the price of which amounted to USD171,248. Huayu Company was incorporated both as the export operator and the consignor. Baidu Company took delivery of the containers from carrier on December 20, 2012 and then had the goods loaded in Huayu Company, upon which it delivered the goods to China Shipping Container Lines (Hong Kong) Co., Ltd. (hereinafter referred to as CSCL) for shipment. CSCL issued a B/L numbered with NGBTIN00531. The shipper recorded on the B/L was Homestar, the goods were contained in 12 containers, there were 1416 boxes in total, the name of carrying vessel was M.V. "YONGLIAN", the voyage number was Y052N. Jincheng Company, after receiving the B/L issued by CSCL, delivered it to Homestar instead of Huayu Company. The goods were taken delivery of as soon as their arrival at the port of destination. Huayu Company had received payment for goods in sum of USD30,508.5, left USD140,739.5 unpaid. Huayu Company failed to collect the sum from Jincheng Company, lodged an appeal to the court, requested the court to order Jincheng Company to compensate Huayu Company USD140,739.5 for the loss of payment for goods. (the dollar currency converted to currency according to the reference rate of dollars against Chinese yuan at 6.1665 published by the People's Bank of China prevailing on August 12, 2013 was RMB86,870) and the interest thereon which should be calculated from February 1, 2013 to the date of payment designated by the judgment according to the bank loan interest rate over the same time.

Jincheng Company defended in the first instance as follows:

1. Jincheng Company accepted the commission from an overseas company, Homestar, and delivered the B/L to Homestar after the shipment of the goods involved. The evidence of Huayu Company could not prove that Huayu Company itself was the actual shipper of the goods, and Huayu Company had no evidence to prove that it had ever entrusted Jincheng Company to undertake the shipment or it had entrusted any other company to perform the shipping service for Jincheng Company. Therefore, there was no commission relationship between them, Huayu Company was not the actual carrier in this case.
2. As for the loss claimed by Huayu Company, Huayu Company could not prove that it had not received the payment of the goods involved according to the evidence it provided.
3. Jincheng Company had no fault in the handling of the goods involved, the customs clearance and inland transport of goods involved were carried out by the actual shipper of Jincheng Company. Jincheng Company had no reason or access to know who was responsible for the customs clearance. To sum up, Jincheng Company requested the court to reject the claims of Huayu Company.

The court of first instance held that: this case was arising from dispute over freight forwarding contract. The issues of this case were that whether a relationship of freight forwarding contract between the two parties was established and whether Jincheng Company should be responsible for the loss suffered by Huayu Company. Pursuant to the law, a contracting shipper referred to the person by whom or in whose name or on whose behalf a contract of carriage of goods by sea has been concluded with a carrier; an actual shipper referred to the person by whom or in whose name or on whose behalf the goods have been delivered to the carrier involved in the contract of carriage of goods by sea. In this case, Homestar entrusted Jincheng Company to book space, thus a relationship of freight forwarding contract between the two parties came into effect. In the present case, Homestar entrusted Jincheng Company to handle the booking service and set up the maritime freight forwarding contractual relationship with Jincheng Company. Homestar was the contractual shipper, but it did not affect the establishment of maritime freight forwarding contractual relationship between Huayu Company as the actual shipper and Jincheng Company. Huayu Company, as the seller of export goods under terms of FOB, entrusted Baidu Company to undertake the inland transport and custom clearance. The delivery of goods to the carrier by Baidu Company was in conformity with the traditional practice, Huayu Company was the actual shipper. Jincheng Company defended that it did not knew the existence or the identity of Huayu Company, it neither knew that Huayu Company was the owner of the goods, nor the goods involved were actually delivered by Huayu Company. The legal relationship of freight forwarding between the two parties and Huayu Company's identity of principal under the legal relationship of freight forwarding should be recognized based on the facts and applicable law, rather than on the condition that whether the carrier was informed or not. As the freight forwarder, Jincheng Company was obliged to affirm the actual shipper of the goods via the receiver of the goods (inland carrier) or other means, so as to specify the receiver of the B/L. Jincheng Company also defended that although Baidu Company was on behalf of Homestar or any other third party to deliver the goods to it, but Jincheng Company did not provide any evidence, and this also went against the evidence provided by Baidu Company. Therefore, the defense of Jincheng Company, which was contrary to the legal provisions and facts, should not be admitted. As for the issue that whether Huayu Company requested Jincheng Company to deliver the B/L before the action, since there were no provisions on the time limit of delivery of B/L by Huayu Company to Jincheng Company, therefore, Huayu Company was entitled to delivery of the B/L involved against Jincheng Company within the statute of limitations. But Jincheng Company sent the B/L involved to Homestar after the shipment of the goods, objectively, the possibility to send the B/L to Huayu Company, it conformed to the facts of this case that Huayu Company directly required Jincheng Company to compensate for the loss. Accordingly, Huayu Company had legal basis to require Jincheng Company to compensate such loss, the loss of the title to the goods was directly caused by the wrongful act of Jincheng Company. In this case, Jincheng Company was the freight forwarder who undertook the booking space, Huayu Company entrusted another party to undertake inland transport and custom clearance, it failed to inform Jincheng Company of the fact that it was the actual shipper. It was another reason which caused the wrong operation of Jincheng Company, in addition, Huayu Company did not actively claim against Jincheng Company to recover the loss. Therefore, the two parties should be liable for the loss suffered caused by the wrongly delivery of B/L by Jincheng Company, they should bear the loss half and half. The amount of the loss had been proved by Huayu Company, namely it had already received USD30,508.5, with USD140,739.5 unpaid, Jincheng Company objected to that, but it failed to provide any rebuttal evidence, in that sense, the amount of the loss claimed by Huayu Company should be confirmed. Therefore, Jincheng Company should compensate Huayu Company the loss in sum of USD70,369.75 (USD140,739.5 × 50%). As for the interest claimed by Huayu Company should be counted from the date that the action was filed, since the loan interest rate was not specific, the original court clearly decided that it should be counted according to the loan interest rate stipulated by the People's Bank of China. To sum up, the court of first instance supported the rational part of Huayu Company's claims. On March 3, 2013, according to the provisions of Article 406 Paragraph 1 of the Contract Law of the People's Republic of China and Articles 8 and 10 of the Provisions of the Supreme People's Court on Several Issues Concerning the Trial of Cases of Dispute over Maritime Freight Forwarding (hereinafter referred to as the Maritime Freight Forwarding Provisions), the original court rendered the judgment as follows: Jincheng Company should compensate Huayu Company the loss of payment for goods in sum of USD70,369.75 and the interest thereon which should be calculated from August 20, 2013 to the day of payment designated by the judgment according to the loan interest rate promulgated by the People's Bank of China within ten days after the judgment entered into force. In the event of failure to fulfill the obligation for payment within the period designated by this judgment, the interest of the delayed period should be doubled according to the provisions of Article 253 of the Civil Procedure Law of the People's Republic of China. As for court acceptance fee of first instance in amount of RMB12,780, Huayu Company should bear RMB6,390 and Jincheng Company RMB6,390.

Both Huayu Company and Jincheng Company refused to accept the original judgment and lodged appeals with the court. Huayu Company alleged that there were some mistakes in terms of fact-finding and determination of liability in the original judgment, its reasons are listed below:

1. Huayu Company entrusted Baidu Company to undertake the inland transportation and the delivery of the goods involved.
2. According to Article 8 of the Maritime Freight Forwarding Provisions, as a freight forwarder, Jincheng Company was obliged to deliver B/L to the actual shipper, Jincheng Company should undertake sole liability for its wrongly delivery of B/L to the contracting shipper, Homestar, which caused Huayu Company's loss. The grounds are as follows: (1) now that Jincheng Company knew that it was a foreign company that entrusted it to book space, it should know that there was a domestic export enterprise (the actual shipper). Jincheng

Company should try to find out the identity of actual shipper through the inland transporter or other means, therefore Jincheng Company should bear the legal consequence caused by wrongful delivery of B/L; and (2) Huayu Company had contacted Jincheng Company directly and through Baidu Company and demanded the latter to deliver the B/L before the action. Besides, the law of China did not provide the time limit of claim of the delivery of B/L, thus, it was legal and reasonable for Huayu Company to demand Jincheng Company to deliver the B/L within the period of statute of limitations. To sum up, Huayu Company requested the court to revoke the original judgment and amend the judgment according to the law to that Jincheng Company should compensate Huayu Company the loss in amount of USD140,739.5 and the interest there on calculated from February 1, 2013 to the day of payment designated by the judgment according to the benchmark loan interest rate promulgated by the People's Bank of China,

Jincheng Company defended that its defense opinions were same as its grounds of appeal.

Jincheng appealed that:

1. Jincheng Company did have to deliver the B/L to Huayu Company since the latter was neither the contracting shipper recorded in the B/L nor the actual shipper. Although Baidu Company proved that it was an agent entrusted by Huayu Company to undertake the inland transport and custom clearance, it failed to explain that it delivered the goods as an agent. The yard receipt could not be deemed as the evidence of receipt of the goods, it was a mistake in common sense that the original court regarded the yard receipt as the receipt of goods, moreover, and the duplication of the yard receipt showed that Huayu Company was not the receiver of the goods. Therefore, Huayu Company could not be deemed as the actual shipper as provided by law. At the same time, Jincheng Company had never requested Huayu Company to deliver the original B/L, it was impossible for Jincheng Company to deliver the B/L to Huayu Company since it was unknown of the existence of Huayu Company before receiving the summons of the first instance.
2. It was not without time limit for Huayu Company to claim the delivery of B/L to Jincheng Company, the carrier was unable to deliver the goods to the goods receiver if the actual shipper did not claim for the delivery of B/L against the carrier, the goods would be under a state of non-taking delivery. According to the provisions of the Maritime Code of the People's Republic of China, the carrier can auction the goods within 60 days after the carrying vessel's arrival at the port of discharge.
3. Huayu Company had no evidence to prove the specific amount of the loss or to prove any faults of Jincheng Company. Huayu Company did not provide evidence of non-handling of tax rebate issued by Administration of Exchange Control and tax authority, which meant that Huayu Company had received the payment for goods.

To sum up, Jincheng Company requested the court to revoke the original judgment and reject all the claims of Huayu Company according to the law, and order Huayu Company to undertake all the court fees of the first and second instances of this case.

Huayu Company defended that:

1. The identity of Huayu Company as the actual shipper should be recognized by the fact ascertained by the court as well as applicable law, rather than Jincheng Company's awareness of the existence of the actual shipper.
2. Although the carrier took legal measures such as auction to deal with the non-taking delivery of the goods within 60 days after the arrival at the port, the holder of B/L or the shipper should undertake the legal liabilities, which had no connection to Jincheng Company as a freight forwarder. The non-taking delivery of the goods could not be deemed as the reason of Jincheng Company's wrongful delivery of the B/L, it would not affect Huayu Company to demand Jincheng Company to deliver the B/L.
3. Export tax rebate was irrelevant to the actual loss of the payment for goods. Under FOB terms, it was risk rather than title to goods transferred when the goods crossed the ship's rail. Whether the title to goods transferred depended on circulation of the corresponding trade contract and bills of lading. Jincheng Company shall undertake the whole liability for compensation for the loss was caused by its wrongful delivery of B/L to the overseas buyer Homestar. To sum up, Huayu Company requested the court to revoke the appeal lodged by Jincheng Company and revoke the original judgment. Besides, it insisted that Jincheng Company should compensate Huayu Company's loss in sum of USD140,739.5 and the interest which should be counted from February 1, 2013 to the date of payment designated by the judgment according to the benchmark loan interest rate promulgated by the People's Bank of China over the same period.

Huayu Company did not provide new evidential material in the second instance. Jincheng Company submitted the certificate issued by the overseas buyer Homestar, to prove that there were no direct legal relations of freight forwarding contract between it and Jincheng Company, the detailed contents of this certification are about: Homestar authorized Jincheng Company to deal with maritime freight forwarding, Homestar paid the costs arising therefrom. Jincheng Company informed Homestar of the detailed operation procedures first and the latter then informed Huayu Company. Huayu Company cross-examined the evidence and contended that this evidence is not new evidence in the second instance. Even though this is new evidence in the second instance, the validity of its content cannot be ascertained and it is irrelevant to this case. The existence of legal relationship of freight forwarding contact between Huayu Company and Jincheng Company could not be based on the statement of Homestar, the party who is not a party involved in this case. Upon examination, the court concludes that the legal relationship of freight forwarding contact between Huayu Company and Jincheng Company should be recognized according to the evidence of this case. The court does not admit the evidence provided by Homestar since it cannot prove the item that Jincheng Company purported to prove.

Upon hearing, the facts found in the original judgment can be ascertained.

The court holds that: based on the grounds of appeal and defenses of the two parties, the issues of this case are as follows: 1. whether the parties established a legal relationship of freight forwarding contract; 2. the affirmation of the amount of loss suffered by Huayu Company and whether Jincheng Company should be liable for such loss. The two parties raised no objection to the above-mentioned issues, the court analyzes as follows:

In respect of the first issues, according to the Maritime Freight Forwarding Provisions, a contracting shipper means the person by whom or in whose name or on whose behalf a contract of carriage of goods by sea has been concluded with a carrier; actual shipper means the person by whom or in whose name or on whose behalf the goods have been delivered to the carrier involved in the contract of carriage of goods by sea. In this case, Huayu Company signed a sales contract with Homestar on October 24, 2012, Huayu Company sold the goods involved to Homestar. On December 11, 2012, Homestar signed a freight forwarding agreement with Jincheng Company and entrusted the latter to book space, the relationship of maritime freight forwarding contract was established between the two parties. As the overseas buyer under the trade term of FOB, Homestar is the contracting shipper of the goods involved under the trade term of FOB Ningbo. Huayu Company was the domestic exporter who authorized Baidu Company to undertake the inland transport and custom clearance, Baidu Company then delivered the goods to the carrier CSCL. It is clearly incorporated in the statement issued by Baidu Company that "Baidu Company is authorized by Huayu Company to undertake the transport and custom clearance for the B/L numbered with NGBTIN005310. All the equipment interchange receipts, packing lists and yard receipt of CSCL were provided by Jincheng Company to Baidu Company." Therefore, Huayu Company is the actual shipper in this case and there exists a relationship of maritime freight forwarding contract between Huayu Company as the actual shipper and Jincheng Company.

In respect of the second issue: Huayu Company provided the sales contract and B/L involved as evidence to prove that the payment for the goods was USD171,248, and Huayu Company confessed it had received USD30,508.5, with the balance of USD140,739.5 unpaid. As Jincheng Company did not provide any rebuttal evidence, the amount of the loss USD140,739.5 determined by the original instance shall be deemed appropriate.

According to the Maritime Freight Forwarding Provisions, the freight forwarder shall deliver the B/L it acquires to the actual shipper. If the actual sipper is slack to request the freight forwarder to deliver the documentations, the freight forwarder should fulfill its obligations by timely inquire the actual shipper about the handling of the B/L and obtain a written confirmation from the actual shipper. In this case, Jincheng Company as the freight forwarder should at least find out the actual shipper through Baidu Company, however, Jincheng Company failed to prudently fulfill its obligation to ascertain the actual shipper of this goods, so as to affirm the receiver of the B/L. Jincheng Company delivered the B/L to the overseas buyer Homestar after the shipment of the goods involved, Huayu Company sustained loss of payment for goods, so Jincheng Company should undertake the liability for compensation. Jincheng Company only agented Homestar to book space in this case. Huayu Company authorized Baidu Company to carry out inland transport and customs clearance, but it failed to inform Jincheng Company of its own identity as domestic seller and actual shipper. Besides, Huayu Company did not timely request Jincheng Company to deliver the B/L, and it should undertake the corresponding civil liability for Jincheng Company's wrongly delivery of B/L. Therefore, it is appropriate that the original instance court identified that the two parties should be liable for the loss suffered by Huayu Company caused by Jincheng Company's wrongly delivery of B/L.

In summary, the court holds the grounds of appeal of Huayu Company and Jincheng Company cannot establish and the court does not admit. The facts were clearly, and the law was correctly applied, and the substance was handled properly in the first instance. According to Article 170 Paragraph 1 Sub-paragraph 1 of the Civil Procedure of the People's Republic of China, the judgment is as follows:

Dismiss the appeal and affirm the original judgment.

Court acceptance fee of second instance in amount of RMB12,780 yuan, the two Appellants Huayu Electrical Appliance Group Co., Ltd. and JC Logistics Service Co., Ltd. Ningbo Branch shall each bear RMB6,390 yuan.

The judgment is final.

Presiding Judge: HUANG Qing
Judge: ZHANG Shidong
Acting Judge: WU Yunhui

July 30, 2014

Clerk: DING Lin

The Supreme People's Court of the People's Republic of China Civil Judgment

Huayu Electrical Appliance Group Co., Ltd.
v.
JC Logistics Service Co., Ltd. Ningbo Branch

(2015) Min Ti Zi No.19

Related Case(s) This is the judgment of retrial, and the judgment of first instance and the judgment of second instance are on page 469 and page 476 respectively.

Cause(s) of Action 223. Dispute over freight forwarding contract on the sea or sea-connected waters.

Headnote Allowing appeal from decision of intermediate court of appeal holding the Defendant freight forwarder 50% responsible for giving bill of lading to the Plaintiff's buyer rather than to the Plaintiff, because evidence was not sufficient to establish that a freight forwarding contract existed between the Defendant and the Plaintiff, and so the Defendant could not be held liable for breach of contract.

Summary The Claimant/Defendant, JC Logistics, appealed judgment by the appeal court that it entered into a freight forwarding contract with the Respondent/Plaintiff, Huayu Company. The Supreme People's Court concluded that: (1) the evidence was insufficient to conclude whether the Claimant/Defendant accepted the Respondent/Plaintiff's entrustment to deliver the goods to the carrier and enter into a freight forwarding contract in relation with it; and (2) the decision of the first and second instance courts that the Claimant/Defendant wrongly delivered the bill of lading to the Respondent/Plaintiff's buyer were wrong in law, and should be reversed.

Judgment

The Claimant of Retrial (the Defendant of first instance, the Appellant of second instance): JC Logistics Service Co., Ltd. Ningbo Branch
Domicile: Rm 3-9, No.8, Calm Street, Haishu District, Ningbo City, Zhejiang Province.
Person in charge: DENG Zhishan, manager.

Agent *ad litem*: WANG Pengnan, lawyer of Liaoning WANG Pengnan & Co.
Agent *ad litem*: REN Tiejun, lawyer of Liaoning WANG Pengnan & Co.

The Respondent of Retrial (the Plaintiff of first instance, the Appellant of second instance): Huayu Electrical Appliance Group Co., Ltd.
Domicile: No.168, North Ring Road, Zhouxiang County, Cixi City, Zhejiang Province.
Legal representative: XU Wanqun, chairman of the board.
Agent *ad litem*: XU Lihua, lawyer of Beijing Dentons (Ningbo) Law Firm.
Agent *ad litem*: YE Yuanhua, lawyer of Beijing Dentons (Ningbo) Law Firm.

Dissatisfied with (2014) Zhe Hai Zhong Zi No.72 Civil Judgment rendered by the Zhejiang High People's Court with respect to the case airing from dispute over maritime freight forwarding contract, JC Logistics Service Co., Ltd. Ningbo Branch (hereinafter referred to as Jincheng Company), petitioned a retrial before the court against the Respondent Huayu Electrical Appliance Group Co., Ltd. (hereinafter referred to as Huayu Company). The court made a Civil Ruling (2014) Min Shen Zi No.2229, and decided to bring this case to trial. The court formed a collegiate panel to review this case, and held a hearing in public on March 31, 2015. WANG Pengnan, agent *ad litem* of Jincheng Company, YE Yuanhua, agent *ad litem* of Huayu Company appeared in court to attend the trial. Now the case has been concluded.

Jincheng Company refused to accept the judgment of second instance and petitioned for retrial with the court, alleging as follows:

1. There was no evidence supporting the ascertainment of the judgment of second instance that Jincheng Company and Huayu Company established relationship of freight forwarding contract.
2. There was no factual or legal basis for the ascertainment of the judgment of second instance that the freight forwarder was obliged to ascertain the actual shipper, and it was totally inconsistent with the practice of the freight forwarding.
3. Jincheng Company followed the instructions of the client Homestar, it had no fault, so it should not assume any external responsibility.
4. Even if the relationship of freight forwarding contract between Huayu Company and Jincheng Company was established, it fell into agent without payment. Jincheng Company had no fault, intention or gross negligence. Therefore, it had no liability against Huayu Company.
5. The conditions of application of Article 8 of the Provisions of the Supreme People's Court on Several Issues Concerning the Trial of Cases of Disputes over Maritime Freight Forwarding (hereinafter referred to as the Freight Forwarding Provisions) were as follows: firstly, the freight forwarder should accept the actual shipper's entrustment; secondly, the entrusted matter was to deliver goods to the carrier; thirdly, the actual shipper demanded the freight forwarder to the deliver the bill of lading. This article could only be applied if the three conditions were satisfied at the same time. In the subject case, none of the above

conditions was satisfied. It was wrong application of law that the court of second instance ordered that Jincheng Company was liable to Huayu Company.
6. In the case of both an actual shipper and a contracting shipper, the responsibility to deliver the bill of lading to which shipper lied in the carrier, which was irrelevant to the freight forwarder.
7. There was no causal relationship between Huayu Company's loss and the delivery of the bill of lading, Huayu Company had no right to claim for compensation against Jincheng Company. The sales contract between Huayu Company and Homestar did not stipulate L/C payment. Huayu Company had delivered the invoice, packing list and other documents to Homestar within 30 days after shipment. The failure to receive the payment was entirely a risk under the trade contract and had nothing to do with whether the bill of lading was delivered or not.

The basic facts found in the judgment of second instance lacked evidence to support, and the application of the law therein was clearly wrong, Jincheng Company requested the court to amend the judgment to reject all the claims of Huayu Company.

Huayu Company responded as follows:

1. The basic facts as determined by the judgment of second instance could be proved by container release order/equipment interchange receipt, packing list, copies of shipping order/station receipt, agreement on responsibility for self-transport and self-declaration, bill of lading, statement on the situation of containerized goods under No.NGBTIN005310 bill of lading, sales contracts, commercial invoices, customs declaration documents and other evidence it submitted and the power of attorney with regard to export goods provided by Jincheng Company.
2. With a comprehensive review of the evidence in this case, Jincheng Company and Huayu Company established a maritime freight forwarding contract. (1) Huayu Company entrusted Baidu Company to take container from Jincheng Company and deliver the goods to Jincheng Company after the container was packed. Jincheng Company also admitted that it received the goods from Baidu Company and issued the freight forwarding invoice to Baidu Company. (2) Baidu Company was entrusted by Huayu Company to deliver the goods to the container yard of CSCL according to the instructions of Jincheng Company. In the legal sense, Huayu Company should deliver the goods to Jincheng Company, there was no legal or contractual basis to deliver goods to CSCL.
3. Jincheng Company knew and should have known the existing and identification of Huayu Company, because Homestar was a foreign company, there ought to be a Chinese export company actually delivered goods.
4. Jincheng Company gave the bill of lading involved to the foreign buyer after the shipment of the goods, objectively, there was no possibility that Huayu Company could not deliver the bill of lading to Huayu Company, Huayu Company claimed for loss of goods price against Jincheng Company, it was in line with objective facts.

5. Jincheng Company, through invoicing to Baidu Company, collected agency fees, the relationship of freight forwarding contract was not free, it was onerous agent. Even if it was an agent without payment, Jincheng Company's wrong delivery of bill of lading constituted intention or gross negligence, and it should bear the liability for compensation.
6. Jincheng Company violated Article 8 of the Freight Forwarding Provisions, Jincheng Company delivered the wrong bill of lading to Homestar, resulting in that Huayu Company lost its title to the goods and suffered loss of payment. The settlement method agreed in the sales contract involved was "payment comes before delivery of original bill of lading", but not on the contrary. There was a legal causal relationship between the loss of Huayu Company and the wrong delivery of Jincheng Company.

Huayu Company submitted a copy of Ningbo value-added tax invoice numbered with No.004118843302124170 issued by Jincheng Company, and alleged Jincheng Company had collected freight forwarding agency fee through Baidu Company. Jincheng Company had no objection to the authenticity thereof but held this evidence had been existed in the files of the first instance, Huayu Company did not submit as evidence in the second instance, it was not new evidence at the stage of retail, and was irrelevant with this case.

Upon investigation, a copy of the invoice submitted by Huayu Company during the retrial had been referred to the court of first instance after the court hearing, together with this copy, a copy of cost confirmation was submitted. The court of first instance did not organize the parties to cross-examine due to the hearing had been closed. During the second instance, Huayu Company clearly expressed in court that the invoice and the cost confirmation form would not be submitted as evidence. The copy of the invoice is submitted again as new evidence during the retrial period, the court does not admit it.

Jincheng Company petitioned for retrial, and only objected to the fact concluded by the judgment of second instance that it had set up a freight forwarding contract with Huayu Company, and did not dispute the other facts ascertained in the judgment of second instance. The court confirms the facts the parties have no objection to.

It is otherwise found that Jincheng Company confessed in the court of first instance it issued invoices for the freight of the goods (RMB) to Baidu Company according to the instructions of Homestar. The copy of the cost confirmation submitted by Huayu Company after the hearing of the first instance shows, Homestar instructed Jincheng Company to write the title in invoice of the dollar part as "Ningbo Jiyuan Import and Export Co., Ltd." and the title in the invoice of dollar cost as Baidu Company. Huayu Company said in the second instance it would not submit the material as evidence.

The court holds that this case is arising from dispute over maritime freight forwarding contract. According to application for retrial of Jincheng Company and the defense of Huayu Company, the issues in the retrial of this case are: 1. whether Jincheng Company accepted Huayu Company's entrustment to deliver the goods to the carrier and set up freight forwarding contract relation with it; and 2. whether Jincheng Company shall be liable for compensation to Huayu Company.

1. Whether Jincheng Company accepted Huayu Company's entrustment to deliver the goods to the carrier and set up freight forwarding contract relation with it

   In the sales contract involved, it is agreed: the contract price is FOB Ningbo, Huayu Company is the seller under the sales contract and the actual shipper under the contract of carriage of goods by sea; Homestar is the buyer under the sales contract and contracting shipper under the contract of carriage of goods by sea. Jincheng Company and Homestar entered into a freight forwarding contract, Jincheng Company, as Homestar's freight forwarder, booked space. But it cannot be concluded that Jincheng Company established a freight forwarding contract with the actual shipper Huayu Company just because Jincheng Company handled the booking business of the subject transport. Huayu Company alleged the establishment of freight forwarding contractual relationship between it and Jincheng Company, Jincheng Company was its freight forwarder, it should prove they signed a freight forwarding contract or it entrusted Jincheng Company to actually engage in the freight forwarding business.

   Article 3 of the Freight Forwarding Provisions stipulates: "a people's court shall decide whether a marine freight forwarding contractual relationship is established according to the nature of the rights and obligations stipulated in the written contract, the name and manner in which the freight forwarding enterprise receives payment, the type of invoice issued, the fees charged, the trade usage between the two parties and other information on the actual performance of the contract". The courts of first and second instance identified Huayu Company entrusted Baidu Company with inland transport and cargo export declarations and other freight forwarding business, Baidu Company after taking empty containers and delivered the goods at Huayu Company to the maritime carrier China Shipping Container Lines Co., Ltd. The two parties have no objection thereto. There is no evidence that Huayu Company has entrusted or re-entrusted Jincheng Company through Baidu Company with freight forwarding services and deliver goods to the carrier.

   In the first instance, Jincheng Company admitted it issued an invoice with the title of Baidu Company, but it claimed that it wrote the title of the invoice of RMB part of the freight as Baidu Company according to the instruction of Homestar. This allegation can corroborate the original invoice of the part of US dollars of the freight and the confirmation of costs submitted by Jincheng Company in the first instance. Huayu Company did not submit any further evidence to prove that it had actually paid the agency fee through Baidu Company to Jincheng Company. In summary, the existing evidence cannot prove Huayu Company entrusted or re-entrusted Jincheng Company though Baidu Company with the freight forwarding business. First, the judgment of second instance identified the relationship of freight forwarding contract set up between the parties, the evidence is insufficient. The evidence provided by Huayu Company is insufficient to prove the facts it alleged, therefore it shall bear unfavorable consequences according to the provisions of Article 90 Paragraph 2 of the Interpretation of the Supreme People's Court on the Application of the Civil Procedure Law of the People's Republic of China.

2. Whether Jincheng Company shall be liable for compensation to Huayu Company

Article 8 Paragraph 1 of the Freight Forwarding Provisions provides "a freight forwarding enterprise accepts the entrustment of the contracting consignor with booking service, and accepts the entrustment of the actual consignor with delivery of goods, the actual shipper requests the freight forwarder to submit the bill of lading, sea waybill or other transport documents, the people's court shall support". This article applies to the circumstance where a freight forwarder accepts both the contracting shipper to book space and the actual consignor to deliver the goods to the carrier. According to the facts having been identified, Huayu Company is the actual shipper of the subject transport, but it entrusted Baidu Company to directly deliver the goods to the carrier, the existing evidence cannot prove that Huayu Company has entrusted Jincheng Company to deliver the goods to the carrier, so this case does not exist the circumstances as prescribed in Article 8 Paragraph 1 of the Freight Forwarding Provisions. So, Jincheng Company gave the bill of lading to Homestar, which booked space, there is no impropriety. The courts of first and second instance held that Jincheng Company wrongly delivered the bill of lading and ordered it to bear the liability for compensation, which constituted wrong application of law, and shall be corrected.

In summary, the facts were unclearly found and the application of law was wrong in the judgments of first and second instance, which shall be corrected according to the law. According to Article 170 Paragraph 1 Sub-paragraph 2 of the Civil Procedure Law of the People's Republic of China, Article 90 Paragraph 2 of the Interpretation of the Supreme People's Court on the Application of the Civil Procedure Law of the People's Republic of China, the judgment is as follows:

Revoke (2014) Zhe Hai Zhong Zi No.72 Civil Judgment rendered by Zhejiang High People's Court;

Revoke (2013) Yong Hai Fa Shang Chu Zi No.579 Civil Judgment rendered by Ningbo Maritime Court;

Reject the claims of Huayu Electrical Appliance Group Co., Ltd.

Court acceptance fee of first instance in amount of RMB12,780 and that of second instance in amount of RMB12,780, shall be born by Huayu Electrical Appliance Group Co., Ltd.

The judgment is final.

Presiding Judge: WANG Shumei
Acting Judge: FU Xiaoqiang
Acting Judge: HUANG Xiwu

April 30, 2015
Clerk: ZHAO Di

Shanghai Maritime Court
Civil Judgment

Hunan Zoomlion International Trade Co., Ltd. et al.
v.
Shanghai GCL International Co., Ltd. et al.

(2012) Hu Hai Fa Shang Chu Zi No.1208

Related Case(s) This is the judgment of first instance, and the judgment of second instance and the ruling of retrial are on page 552 and page 600 respectively.

Cause(s) of Action 202. Dispute over contract of carriage of goods by sea or sea-connected waters.

Headnote The carriers held to be entitled to rely on "perils of the sea" and "error of navigation" defenses in claim brought for damage to cargo of crawler cranes.

Summary The Plaintiff contracted with the first Defendant, a freight forwarder, for its crawler cranes to be carried from China to India. The first Defendant voyage-chartered the ship M.V. "Yuriy Arshenevskiy" from the second Defendant, which had chartered the ship from the third Defendant. The cargo was seriously damaged during the voyage. In an attempt to mitigate its losses, the Plaintiff requested the three Defendants to discharge the cargo at ports of refuge in China, but the three Defendants ignored this request and continued to instruct the vessel to proceed to India. As a result, a severe cargo loss incurred. The Plaintiff argued that the cargo damage happened during the period of the carrier's responsibility, and that the first Defendant was the contractual carrier and the second and third Defendants were the actual carriers.

The court held that the proximate cause of the cargo damage was the adverse weather conditions the ship encountered on the carrying voyage. As a result, the court held the carriers were not liable for the damage because of the "perils of the sea" defense under Chinese maritime law. The carriers were also entitled to rely on the defense of error in navigation because the ship's master had made a risky decision to change the route.

Judgment

The Plaintiff: Hunan Zoomlion International Trade Co., Ltd.
Domicile: No.307, Yinpen South Road, Changsha City, Hunan, the People's Republic of China.
Legal representative: CHEN Peiliang, general manager.

The Plaintiff: Zurich General Insurance Company (China) Limited.
Domicile: Room 603B, 605C, 606 and 607A, Floor 6, Office Building F, Phoenix Place, Tower 21, No.A5, Shuguangxili, Chaoyang District, Beijing, the People's Republic of China.
Legal representative: HU Xiaoqin, general manager.

The Plaintiff: Ping An Property & Casualty Insurance Company of China Ltd. Hunan Branch.
Domicile: Floor 1&3, New Age Business Plaza, No.161, Section 1, Furong Middle Road, Kaifu District, Changsha City, Hunan, the People's Republic of China.
Legal representative: CHENG Xiaozhong, general manager.

The Plaintiff: Sunshine Property & Casualty Insurance Co., Ltd. Hunan Branch.
Domicile: Floor 6, Xiangyu Zhongyang Office Building, Wuyi East Road, Furong District, Changsha City, Hunan Province, the People's Republic of China.
Legal representative: HU Xiangze, general manager.
Agent *ad litem* jointly entrusted by the four Plaintiffs: ZHAO Jinsong, lawyer of Shanghai All Bright (Shenzhen) Law Offices.
Agent *ad litem* jointly entrusted by the four Plaintiffs: QIU Biaoshan, lawyer of Shanghai All Bright (Shenzhen) Law Offices.

The Defendant: Shanghai GCL International Co., Ltd.
Domicile: Rm.2601, Baokuang International Building, No.218, Wusong Road, Shanghai City, the People's Republic of China.
Legal representative: MIAO Lufei, general manager.
Agent *ad litem*: LVHaiming, lawyer of Shanghai Zhendan Law Firm.

The Defendant: Shanghai Hengxin Shipping Co., Ltd.
Domicile: Room.131, No.69, Tongzhou Road, Shanghai, the People's Republic of China.
Legal representative: YUE Zhaofeng, general manager.
Agent *ad litem*: REN Yuwei, lawyer of Shanghai Rolmax Law Office.
Agent *ad litem*: HUA Lingling, lawyer of Shanghai Rolmax Law Office.

The Defendant: Murmansk Shipping Company.
Domicile: 15, Kominterna Street 183038, Murmansk, Russia.
Legal representative: A.M.Medvedev, chairman.
Agent *ad litem*: LI Rongcun, lawyer of Guangdong Wang Jing & Co. (Xiamen) Law Firm.

Agent *ad litem*: CHEN Yongcan, lawyer of Guangdong Wang Jing & Co. (Xiamen) Law Firm.

With respect to the case arising from dispute over contract of carriage of goods by sea, the Plaintiff Hunan Zoomlion International Trade Co., Ltd. (hereinafter referred to as "Hunan Zoomlion"), filed an action against the Defendants Shanghai GCL International Co., Ltd. (hereinafter referred to as "GCL"), Shanghai Hengxin Shipping Co., Ltd. (hereinafter referred to as "Shanghai Hengxin") and Murmansk Shipping Company (hereinafter referred to as "MSCO") before Xiamen Maritime Court and the case was accepted on December 22, 2011. GCL raised a challenge of jurisdiction during the period for submission of statement of defense, claiming that there was an agreement on jurisdiction between GCL and Hunan Zoomlion in*Annual Transportation Agreement on Indian Crawler Cranes* (hereinafter referred to as "annual transportation agreement"), so the case should be transferred to the court. Xiamen Maritime Court rendered the Civil Ruling (2012) Xia Hai Fa Shang Chu Zi No.7 that the dissension filed by GCL stood, and the case shall be handed over to the court for trial. Hunan Zoomlion, Shanghai Hengxin and MSCO were dissatisfied with the ruling and filed appeal. On June 19, 2012, Fujian High People's Court rendered a Civil Ruling (2012) Min Min Zhong Zi No.460 which dismissed the appeal and affirmed the original ruling. After the transfer of the case, the court accepted the case on August 29, 2012 and constituted the collegiate panel according to the law. On March 13, June 17 and July 25, 2013, the court organized three evidence exchanges among the parties respectively. On October 28, 2013, an experts hearing in respect of technical issues in this case was held. On December 12, 2013, the court held a hearing in public to try the case. Agent *ad litem* of the Plaintiff Hunan Zoomlion, QIU Biaoshan, agent *ad litem* of the Defendant GCL, LV Haiming, agents *ad litem* of the Defendant Shanghai Hengxin, REN Yuwei and HUA Lingling, and agent *ad litem* of the Defendant MSCO, CHEN Yongcan, appeared in court to attend the hearing. On December 30, 2013, Zurich General Insurance Company (China) Limited (hereinafter referred to as "Zurich China"), Ping An Property & Casualty Insurance Company of China Ltd. Hunan Branch (hereinafter referred to as "Ping An Hunan") and Sunshine Property & Casualty Insurance Co., Ltd. Hunan Branch (hereinafter referred to as "Sunshine Hunan") applied to join the proceeding as the co-Plaintiffs on the basis that they had obtained the right of subrogation. On January 3, 2014, the court allowed the application according to the law. On March 6, 2014, the court held a second hearing to try the case. Agent *ad litem* of the four Plaintiffs, QIU Biaoshan, agent *ad litem* of the Defendant GCL, LV Haiming, agents *ad litem* of the Defendant Shanghai Hengxin, REN Yuwei and HUA Lingling, and agents *ad litem* of the Defendant MSCO, LI Rongcun and CHEN Yongcan, appeared in court to attend the hearing. Now, the case has been concluded after trial.

The four Plaintiffs alleged in the statement of claim: On May 23, 2011, an annual transportation agreement was concluded by and between Hunan Zoomlion and GCL. Pursuant to the agreement, GCL shall carry Hunan Zoomlion's crawler cranes to India. During the period from June 22 to July 26, 2011, Hunan Zoomlion provided its own five Zoomlion crawler cranes (hereinafter referred to as "cargo concerned") to GCL for shipping. Pursuant to the voyage charter party it concluded with Shanghai Hengxin, GCL sub-entrusted Shanghai Hengxin to carry the cargo concerned via M.V. "Yuriy Arshenevskiy" chartered by Shanghai Hengxin. MSCO is the owner of M.V. "Yuriy Arshenevskiy". On August 2, 2011, after the loading of the cargo concerned, Union Ocean Shipping Co., Ltd. (hereinafter referred to as "Union Ocean"), as the agent authorized by Shanghai Hengxin, issued five sets of B/Ls No.SHM04, SHB11, SHB12A, SHB12B and SHB13 (hereinafter referred to as "House B/Ls") and surrendered them to Hunan Zoomlion through GCL. Later on, GCL got back the House B/Ls and provided Hunan Zoomlion with four sets of B/LsNo.SHM04, SHB11, SHB12 and SHB13 (hereinafter referred to as "Master B/Ls") issued by MSCO's agent Shanghai United International Ocean Shipping Agency Ltd. (hereinafter referred to as "Shanghai UNISCO"). The cargo concerned was seriously damaged during the voyage. In order to avoid the enlargement of losses, Hunan Zoomlion requested the three Defendants to discharge the cargo at such places nearby as Xiamen Port or Shanghai Port. However, the three Defendants ignored this request and continued to instruct the vessel to proceed to India, as a result of which tremendous enlarged losses were incurred to the cargo concerned. The four Plaintiffs held that, GCL was the contractual carrier in the carriage concerned, Shanghai Hengxin was sub-entrusted by GCL to carry the cargo concerned, and MSCO was the owner of the vessel and was in control over the manning and domination of the vessel, so both Shanghai Hengxin and MSCO were the actual carriers. The cargo damage happened during the period of the carrier's responsibility, and such damage was caused by improper lashing, negligence in care for cargo and the unseaworthiness of the vessel. Therefore, the three Defendants should bear joint and several liability for the cargo loss and relevant expenses. In addition, The Plaintiffs Zurich China, Ping An Hunan and Sunshine Hunan (hereinafter referred to as "co-insurers") alleged that they had indemnified the cargo losses according to relevant insurance contract and thus obtained the right of subrogation accordingly as per relevant laws.

And Hunan Zoomlion should be entitled to claim compensation for its losses which were not covered by the co-insurers. In this respect, the four Plaintiffs requested:

1. To order the three Defendants to jointly and severally compensate Hunan Zoomlion for the losses in sum of RMB2,619,148.53 and interests thereof (calculated from August 8, 2011 to the effective date of relevant judgment as per the loan interest rate published by the People's Bank of China during the corresponding period);
2. To order the three Defendants to jointly and severally compensate Zurich China for the losses in sum of RMB10,484,602 and interests thereof (calculated from February 1, 2013 to the effective date of relevant judgment as per the loan interest rate published by the People's Bank of China during the corresponding period);

3. To order the three Defendants to jointly and severally compensate Ping An Hunan for the losses in sum of RMB6,289,403.99 and interests thereof (calculated from February 1, 2013 to the effective date of relevant judgment as per the loan interest rate published by the People's Bank of China during the corresponding period);
4. To order the three Defendants to jointly and severally compensate Sunshine Hunan for the losses in sum of RMB4,190,468.40 and interests thereof (calculated from February 1, 2013 to the effective date of relevant judgment as per the loan interest rate published by the People's Bank of China during the corresponding period); and
5. To order the three Defendants to jointly and severally bear the court acceptance fees and the application fee for vessel arrest in (2011) Xia Hai Fa Bao Zi No.30 in sum of RMB5,000.

The Defendant GCL defended that:

1. Hunan Zoomlion was not a qualified Plaintiff. The trading party of the cargo concerned was not Hunan Zoomlion but Zoomlion International Trading (HK) Co., Limited (hereinafter referred to as "Zoomlion HK"). Hunan Zoomlion was not the owner of the cargo and it had no right to sue against GCL;
2. GCL was not a qualified Defendant. Although GCL concluded an annual transportation agreement with Hunan Zoomlion, this agreement had been unilaterally cancelled by Hunan Zoomlion. Therefore, there was only a relationship of shipping agency agreement between GCL and Hunan Zoomlion, and GCL had no fault during the agency;
3. The cargo damage concerned was caused by the vessel's encountering with extreme weather and adverse sea conditions, for which the carrier may be exempted from liability;
4. The losses claimed by the four Plaintiffs had no basis. There was a difference between the customs value and the invoice value of the cargo concerned, and Hunan Zoomlion had no basis to claim the cargo loss based on the invoice value; the condition of the cargo proved by the four Plaintiffs was the condition when the cargo had been shipped back to China. At that time, the cargo had temporarily stayed in Port of Xiamen, been carried to and long-term stockpiled in India, and had encountered adverse sea conditions again during its voyage back to China. The carrier should not be liable for the enlarged losses during that period. The four Plaintiffs failed to prove the actual condition of the damage efficiently; and
5. Zurich China, Ping An Hunan and Sunshine Hunan did not indemnify correctly, they cannot obtain the right of subrogation.

The Defendant Shanghai Hengxin defended that:

1. This case involved several contracts of carriage of goods by sea, and it was not clear which one was the basis of the claim raised by the four Plaintiffs in this proceeding. Hunan Zoomlion stated it was based on its transportation agreement with GCL, but essentially that agreement was a shipping agency agreement and

had been unilaterally cancelled by Hunan Zoomlion before the carriage of the cargo concerned. There was no basis for the four Plaintiffs to claim against Shanghai Hengxin and MSCO as actual carriers according to the shipping agency agreement between Hunan Zoomlion and GCL. As to the House B/Ls issued by Union Ocean, the four Plaintiffs failed to provide the originals. Under the situation when the Plaintiffs failed to prove that the B/Ls were authentic and legally possessed by Hunan Zoomlion, the rights of Hunan Zoomlion under the B/Ls should not be considered. As to the Master B/Ls, Hunan Zoomlion was neither the consignee nor the shipper described in the B/Ls. The four Plaintiffs were not qualified Plaintiffs if they claimed on basis of such B/Ls;
2. The concept of "actual carrier" in the Maritime Code of the People's Republic of China should only be used in B/L relationships, but Hunan Zoomlion was not the holder or consignee or shipper of the two B/Ls concerned. Therefore, the four Plaintiffs had no rights to claim against Shanghai Hengxin and MSCO as actual carrier;
3. MSCO was the owner of the vessel concerned who was in charge of the manning, supply and management of the vessel. On this account, it was MSCO, not Shanghai Hengxin, that actually performed the carriage;
4. The cargo damage was caused by force majeure, act of god and poor packing of the cargo. The carrier may be exempted from liability;
5. The amount of the losses claimed by the four Plaintiffs was unreasonable and untrue;
6. Hunan Zoomlion was not the owner of the cargo and had no actual loss in this case. It had no right to claim; and
7. It was stated in *Institute Cargo Clauses (A)* which was incorporated in the relevant insurance contracts that: "this insurance is subject to English law and practice". Under English law, the insurer should apply its right of subrogation in the name of the insured. If the insurer sued in its own name, the limitation period for litigation should be determined based on its date of litigation. Accordingly, the claim of co-insurers had exceeded the limitation period.

The Defendant MSCO defended that:

1. The four Plaintiffs were not qualified Plaintiffs. The seller stated in the sales contract and the invoice concerned was Zoomlion HK, and the expenses for back shipment to China were paid by Zoomlion HK or Zoomlion Heavy Industry Science & Technology Co. (hereafter referred to as "Zoomlion Heavy"). Therefore, Hunan Zoomlion was not a qualified Plaintiff. Since the rights of co-insurers derived from Hunan Zoomlion, they were not qualified Plaintiffs, either. In addition, the latest insurance policy issued in this case was signed by Zurich China solely, so accordingly Ping An Hunan and Sunshine Hunan were not qualified Plaintiffs;
2. MSCO was not the actual carrier. The Master B/Ls were straight B/Ls, Hunan Zoomlion was neither the shipper nor the consignee stated in these B/Ls and thus had no right under these B/Ls. The reason for MSCO to enter into this

transportation was the time charterparty they concluded with a Korean company Kings Ocean Shipping Company (hereinafter referred to as "Kings Ocean"). However, this time charterparty was a contract for property, not for transportation or shipping agency;
3. The cargo damage was due to poor packing and adverse sea conditions for which the carrier may be exempted from liability. Even though the carrier's decision to avoid typhoon was improper, it still was a matter of exemption;
4. Even if the four Plaintiffs were qualified, some of their claims were unreasonable and not claimable since the losses had been enlarged during the cargo's back shipment to China and the subsequent processes. The only reasonable claim left for Hunan Zoomlion was the arrest application fee after they had been indemnified by the insurers. The interests claimed by the co-insurers should be calculated from the date of litigation. There was no basis for the four Plaintiffs to claim in RMB uniformly since the loss for exchange rate was not claimable; and
5. Even if MSCO was deemed as actual carrier, MSCO was still entitled to enjoy the package limitation of liability and the limitation of liability for maritime claims. The accident concerned also caused other claims against MSCO, and the total claim amount was around USD4,800,000. In this case, the limit of liability for the carrier was around USD2,170,000 as per its proportion in the package limitation of liability.

Evidence adduced by all parties, their cross-examination opinions and determinations of the court are as follows:

1. Evidence adduced by four Plaintiffs, cross-examination opinions of three Defendants, and determinations of the court
(1) In order to prove the value of the cargo concerned, the four Plaintiffs submitted: evidence No.1 sale and purchase contracts, evidence No.2 commercial invoices, evidence No.3 packing lists and evidence No.4 lists of spare parts of crawler cranes.

GCL had no objection to the authenticity of the packing lists and the lists of spare parts of crawler crane. Shanghai Hengxin confirmed the authenticity of the sale and purchase contracts and the packing lists, but did not recognize the authenticity of the commercial invoices and the lists of spare parts of crawler cranes prepared by Zoomlion HK. MSCO confirmed the authenticity of the commercial invoices, packing lists and the lists of spare parts of crawler crane. All of the three Defendants held that the vendors under the sale and purchase contracts, commercial invoices and the packing lists was Zoomlion HK rather than Hunan Zoomlion, that the cargo prices indicated thereon was inconsistent with those on the customs declaration forms, that the two contracts were in fact purchase orders, and thus that this group of evidence could not prove the subject that the four Plaintiffs intended to prove. In addition, MSCO further contended that "as per the agreements of the contract, the conditions of receiving payment had been reached before the accident concerned; once the cargoes are lifting cross the ship board, risks thereof shall be transferred to the buyer; therefore, the substantial and procedural rights in respect of cargo losses shall be accordingly enjoyed by the buyer".

The court reckons that these evidence are originals, and the key information indicated therein can prove each other. As a relatively complete chain of evidence has been formed, the court approves the effectiveness and the probative force of them. As for the key disputes in the subject case whether Hunan Zoomlion is entitled to be the Plaintiff and the amount of cargo damage, the court's opinions will be elaborated below.

(2) In order to prove the contractual relationship of transportation between Hunan Zoomlion and the three Defendants, and GCL was the contractual carrier in the subject shipment, with Shanghai Hengxin and MSCO being the actual carriers and Hunan Zoomlion being the shipper, the four Plaintiffs submitted: evidence No.5 annual transportation agreement, evidence No.6 booking notes, evidence No.7 voyage charter party between GCL and Shanghai Hengxin, evidence No.8 mate's receipts, evidence No.9 House B/Ls, evidence No.10 Master B/Ls, evidence No.11 correspondences between Hunan Zoomlion, GCL and Shanghai Hengxin, evidence No.20 application for dissension on jurisdiction submitted by GCL to Xiamen Maritime Court, evidence No.21 Civil Ruling (2012) Xia Hai Fa Shang Chu Zi No.7, and evidence 22 Civil Ruling (2012) Min Min Zhong Zi No.460.

Except for the House B/Ls, GCL had no objection to the authenticity of this group of evidence, but held that the agreement had been cancelled before the cargo concerned was actually carried and provisions of the agreement in respect of port of destination, freight rate and quantity of shipment are widely divergent from the actual situation of the shipment, so the agreement could not prove that Hunan Zoomlion and GCL had the contractual relationship of transportation; that shipper indicated on the booking notes is Zoomlion HK and no descriptions referring to GCL are carried on the booking notes, so the booking notes could not prove Hunan Zoomlion as being the shipper or the contractual relationship of transportation; that the mate's receipts indicate the cargo concerned had defects in package; and that the correspondences prove that neither prior to or after the shipment of the cargo concerned, relevant parties had ever reached any agreement on the issuing form and content of the B/Ls. Except for the House B/Ls and the correspondences, Shanghai Hengxin had no objection to the authenticity of this group of evidence, but contended that shipper indicated on the booking notes is Zoomlion HK and the scheduled sailing dates indicated thereon are various, so the relevancy of the booking notes shall be doubted; that the notes on the mate's receipts and the Master B/Ls indicate the poor package of the cargo concerned; and that the correspondences indicate the real contractual intention between Hunan Zoomlion and GCL was GCL acted as the NVOCC to issue House B/Ls to Hunan Zoomlion and acted as the shipper to book shipment and obtain seaway bills issued by the actual carrier. MSCO had no objection to the authenticity of this group of evidence, but opined that this group of evidence demonstrates the cargo transportation concerned was carried out under the contract of transportation between Hunan Zoomlion and GCL; that GCL was the contractual carrier for the cargo concerned who entrusted the transportation to Shanghai Hengxin, and Shanghai Hengxin who issued the House B/Ls to Zoomlion HK was the actual carrier; and that from the beginning to the end, Hunan Zoomlion did not accept such Master B/Ls as indicating owners to be the carrier, and the Master B/Ls required should name Zoomlion HK as the shipper and Hanssy Shipping as the carrier. MSCO further contended the master only authorized Shanghai UNISCO to issue bills of lading in the name of the master, yet the latter issued such bills of lading as indicating the owners to be the carrier, which issuing act violates its power of agency, and that the shipper indicated on the booking notes is Zoomlion HK and the scheduled sailing dates are various, for which the relevancy of the booking notes was objected.

In consideration of the parties' accessibility to the evidence and their respective cross-examination opinions, the court confirms the authenticity and effectiveness of this group of evidence except for the House B/Ls. As for the authenticity of the House B/Ls, it is indicated in evidence No.11 submitted by the four Plaintiffs (email at 8:22PM on September 28, 2011) that "our company (Hunan Zoomlion) has returned the seven sets of house bills of lading to your company as requested by your company", and GCL also confirmed in the court hearing that they have surrendered a set of House B/Ls to Hunan Zoomlion and revoked them after the accident. Given so, it can be ascertained that there indeed existed a set of House B/Ls in the shipment concerned. In consideration that GCL should have had the ability to submit this set of House B/Ls or inform their source and location to the court but failed to do so, the court decides not to accept GCL's cross-examination opinion of objection to the authenticity of evidence No.9 House B/Ls. The evidence currently existing reveal that GCL had ever surrendered five sets of original bills of lading in the form of evidence No.9 to Hunan Zoomlion and revoked them after the accident, while as the carrier indicated on the House B/Ls Shanghai Hengxin denied they had authorized Union Ocean to issue such a set of B/Ls and no evidence can prove these B/Ls were issued under the authorization of Shanghai Hengxin, the House B/Ls could not prove Shanghai Hengxin as the carrier. The probative force of and the content to be proved by other evidence in this group will be considered by reference to all evidence having been submitted, and the disputed issues involved thereby will be elaborated in details below.

(3) In order to prove Hunan Zoomlion was entitled to the cargo concerned and was the holder of the B/Ls, the four Plaintiffs submitted: evidence No.14 statement, evidence No.15 customs declaration forms, evidence No.16 receipt issued by GCL for its revoking of the original B/Ls and the attachment thereof, evidence No.17 Master B/Ls reissued, and evidence No.18 B/Ls issued for the cargo back shipped to Shanghai China.

GCL and MSCO had no objection to the authenticity of this group of evidence. With no acknowledgement to the authenticity of the customs declaration forms due to lack of original, Shanghai Hengxin had no objection to the authenticity of the other evidence in this group. However, GCL held the legal position of Hunan Zoomlion could not be simply determined on the mere basis of the unilateral statement made by Hunan Zoomlion and Zoomlion HK. MSCO took the view that Hunan Zoomlion and Zoomlion HK had not held the House B/Ls when they were issuing the statement, and they were neither the shipper nor the consignee named by the Master B/Ls, thus such statement issued by them shall have no legal effectiveness. Shanghai Hengxin opined the statement was only a private agreement between Hunan Zoomlion and Zoomlion HK, and suspected in fact it was the relationship of sale and purchase contract that existed between the two parties. Meanwhile, all of the three Defendants contended the customs declaration price on the customs declaration form was different from the contract price, and this group of evidence could not reflect the ownership status of the cargo at the time of shipping or prove Hunan Zoomlion was entitled to the cargo and the legal holder of bills of lading.

By examining the form of the evidence and considering the cross-examination opinions of the three Defendants, the court confirms the authenticity and probative force of this group of evidence. With regard to key disputes such as the subject qualification of Hunan Zoomlion as being the Plaintiff and the amount of cargo damage, the court's detailed consideration will be elaborated below.

(4) In order to prove the cargo concerned had been damaged and the losses caused to Hunan Zoomlion thereby, the four Plaintiffs submitted: evidence No.12 *Loading Survey Report* No.110835MC issued by East China Adjusters & Surveyors Co., Ltd. (hereinafter referred to as the "loading survey report"), evidence No.13 sea protest, evidence No.19 correspondences between Hunan Zoomlion's agent and MSCO's agent, evidence No.23 and supplementary evidence No.10 business licenses of two translation companies, evidence No.24 *Survey Report* issued by Crawford China Limited (hereinafter referred to as "Crawford survey report"), supplementary evidence No.1 *Inspection & Appraisal Certificate* No.JD2012622 (B) issued by CCIC Hunan Co., Ltd. (hereinafter referred to as "CCIC inspection certificate"), supplementary evidence No.2 special payment certificate for import duties and VAT, supplementary evidence No.8 Chinese translation of attachment No.2 to evidence No.24 (export documents at Mumbai Port and Mundra Port, India), supplementary evidence No.9 invoices of port charges in Shanghai Port, supplementary evidence No.25 Civil Ruling (2011)Xia Hai Fa Bao Zi No.30, and supplementary evidence No.26 special receipt of court fees.

Having dissension to the authenticity of this group of evidence, GCL contended the sea protest could only reflect the fact that M.V. "Yuriy Arshenevskiy" had suffered severe sea conditions, but could not directly reflect the fact of cargo damage; the Crawford survey report failed to carry out proper survey and select materials impartially, which resulted in a wrong survey conclusion and thus could not be used a conclusive evidence for this case. Shanghai Hengxin viewed the authenticity of evidence No.19 correspondences could not be verified, but had no objection to the authenticity of this group of evidence apart from supplementary evidence No.1, 2 and 9. Shanghai Hengxin maintained that the loading survey report shew the cargo concerned was weakly packed before loaded; that the sea protest only proves M.V. "Yuriy Arshenevskiy" had sustained irresistible bad weather and sea conditions, but gives no detailed statement in respect of the damage to the cargo concerned; and that the surveyors issuing the crawford survey report were unilaterally entrusted by the cargo insurers, who not only surveyed the damage extent of the cargo, but also evaluated the amount of loss and contacted buyer to deal with the cargo residual value, and the report is not objectively impartial, with hasty and imprudent evaluation opinions, several mistakes in its content and evaluation conclusion conflicting with the disposal of residual value. Shanghai Hengxin further opined that the objectiveness, fairness and accuracy of the CCIC inspection certificate could not be ensured with no qualification certificates of the inspector and the inspector's institution submitted, inspection carried out 15 months later than the accident and unilaterally entrusted by Zoomlion Heavy, and no basis of the evaluation of residual value specified. Shanghai Hengxin also denied the relevancy with this case of import duties, value-added taxes and port charges at Shanghai Port. MSCO did not raise objection to the authenticity of this group of evidence, but held that the loading survey report demonstrates the cargo concerned was weakly packed before loading onboard; that the sea protest proves the crewmembers onboard had applied good seamanship and performed their obligation of due diligence to take care of cargo, yet the cargo losses could not be avoided; that the correspondences demonstrates given complicated problems in the back shipment of the cargo concerned, despite efforts, the vessel still had to proceed to India, and the suggestions given by Hunan Zoomlion was impractical as they did not extend their intention to discharge cargo until November 1; and that the fairness and neutrality of the Crawford survey report was doubtable, as its assessment on the cargo losses directly adopts the documents self-prepared by Hunan Zoomlion without any actual assessment and many mistakes exist in its content. In addition, all of the three Defendants held the payer indicated on supplementary evidence No.26 was Zoomlion Heavy instead of Hunan Zoomlion, so the application fee for vessel arrest shall not be supported.

In consideration that supplementary evidence No.1, 2 and 9 whose authenticity was doubted by Shanghai Hengxin and the invoices for transportation by land as attached to the Crawford survey report are originals, and the authenticity of evidence No.19 has been confirmed by MSCO, by examining the evidence and overall considering the cross-examination opinions put forward by three Defendants, the court confirms the authenticity and effectiveness of this group of evidence. The content of CCIC inspection certificate in regard to inspection could indicate the condition of the cargo concerned on November 1, 2012. Although the evaluation of residual value in the CCIC inspection certificate lacks necessary interpretation and explanation about its evaluation basis, and its probative force is not enough to reveal the fact independently, its content that corresponds to other evidence can be used to as a basis to ascertain the fact of the case. The probative force of and the subject to be proved by the other evidence in this group shall also be considered by reference to other evidence having been submitted to the court in the subject case.

(5) In order to prove the causes of accident and the carrier should not be exempted from liability, the four Plaintiffs submitted supplementary evidence No.3 meteorological certification issued by Shanghai Climate Center, supplementary evidence No.4 meteorological report issued by Shanghai Central Meteorological Station, supplementary evidence No.5 moving route of typhoon MUIFA, supplementary evidence No.6 news reports on typhoon MUIFA, supplementary evidence No.7 basic knowledge on vessel's avoidance of typhoon, supplementary evidence No.11 *Analysis Report on Causes of Cargo Damage Onboard M.V. "Yuriy Arshenevskiy" V.11125* (hereinafter referred to as "SMU report"), supplementary evidence No.12 *Survey Report on Cause of Damage to Zoomlion Cargoes Onboard M.V. "Yuriy Arshenevskiy" V.11125* (hereinafter referred to as "Crawford report on causes of cargo damage), supplementary evidence No.13 *Supplementary Opinions on Analysis Report on Causes of Cargo Damage Onboard M.V. "Yuriy Arshenevskiy" V.11125* (hereinafter referred to as the "supplementary opinions on SMU report"), and supplementary evidence No.14 *Analysis Report on Real-Time Wind Force and Wave Height* issued by East China Sea Forecast Center of State Oceanic Administration (hereinafter referred to as the "ECSFC report").

Except for supplementary evidence No.3, the three Defendants did not confirm the authenticity of supplementary evidence No.4 to No.7. Shanghai Hengxin opined the content of the above evidence are too broad without specific reference to the subject case and could not evidence the subject to be proved by them. MSCO considered seen from the source of evidence, the accuracy of these evidence could not be ensured. All of the three Defendants had no objection to the authenticity, legality and relevancy of the four reports as supplementary evidence No.11 to No.14. However, GCL held the records in deck log book and the statements of the Master and crewmembers in connection with the adverse sea conditions could not be overturned without direct contrary evidence; that the Crawford report on causes of cargo damage has no factual basis to make the deduction that the decision of M. V. "Yuriy Arshenevskiy" to sail to the south was for the purpose of reducing deviation, which neglects the records in the deck log book that M.V. "Yuriy Arshenevskiy" severally altered her course to reduce rolling and severally strengthened the cargo securing; that the SMU report overlooks the fact that the ballast water had changed the vertical distribution rate of cargo weight and wrongly deduces the so-called reasonable stowage and pre-stowage from the result of cargo damage; that the analyses in the supplementary opinions on SMU report are factually groundless, and its conclusion of non-seaworthiness drawn from improper stowage could not stand; and that the ECSFC report could not truthfully reflect the adverse sea conditions encountered by M.V. "Yuriy Arshenevskiy". Shanghai Hengxin considered that the SMU report and its supplementary opinions are both too theoretical and divergent from the practice, including the photos they are based on were taken in the course of lashing and securing at which time the lashing was not completed yet, and some were taken at the time of second lashing at Xiamen Port; that the ECSFC report is an evaluation report which can only serves an indirect evidence of the sea conditions, and its probative force is weaker than the direct evidence submitted by MSCO; and that the use of self-purchased equipment was allowed by the securing manual of M.V. "Yuriy Arshenevskiy", and what should the four Plaintiffs prove is the non-effectiveness of lashing and securing. MSCO refused to acknowledge the probative force of the four reports on the ground that they were all submitted beyond the time limitation for adducing evidence. MSCO further extended their opinion that the issuer of the Crawford report on causes of cargo damage had no qualification as adjusters, and the opinions extended were not justified; and although the SMU report and its supplementary opinions were issued in the name of Shanghai Maritime University, they were in fact issued by Professor WU Shangang personally. The analyses in the SMU report and its supplementary opinions deviate from the fact far away, and they adopt wrong analysis methods, unilaterally extract contents favorable to the principal, and lack scientific and reasonable demonstration. The standard used by the SMU report and its supplementary opinions to calculate the vessel's rolling amplitude that cargo securing is required to resist is wrong. Experts appointed by the parties have confirmed that the approval of its own class is not necessarily required for the securing equipment onboard, and some photos extracted by the report were taken in the course of loading, which cannot reflect the real condition of the cargo securing after its completion, especially after correction and reinforcement. MSCO further maintained that the ECSFC report relies on the data of typhoon wind circle published by the National Meteorological Center of CMA on the basis of typhoon structure of concentric circles, and neglects the relationship of mean wind and gust, so the conclusion of the ECSFC report should be wrong. Meanwhile, the ECSFC report demonstrates the fact that M.V. "Yuriy Arshenevskiy" suffered the largest wind and most adverse sea conditions at 0400hrs on August 7, and encountered mean wind of 8bft to 10bft at 1600hrs on August 6 to 0600hrs on August 7; in consideration of the relationship of mean wind and gust, it would be enough to prove the credibility of the records on the deck log book.

The court reckons that the authenticity and effectiveness of supplementary evidence No.4 may be confirmed as it is an original consistent with the document collected by the court from Shanghai Meteorological Bureau, while its probative force and the content to be proved by it shall be determined by reference to other submitted evidence. The authenticity of supplementary evidence No.5 to No.7 is confirmed via online searching, while they can only serve as the background information for the subject case, since their probative force is limited with no specific reference to the disputed fact of the subject case. As for the remaining four reports in this group of evidence, since the three Defendants had no objection to their authenticity, legality and relevancy and the dissensions on the subjects to be proved by them shall not prejudice their use in the subject case as evidence, the court approves their effectiveness as evidence, while their probative force and the subject to be proved by them shall be determined upon an overall consideration of all evidence submitted in the subject case.

(6) In order to prove that the co-insurers have obtained the subrogation right, the four Plaintiffs submitted: supplementary evidence No.15 co-insurance agreement, supplementary evidence No.16 goods in transit policy, supplementary evidence No.17 institute cargo clause (A), supplementary evidence No.18 application form of marine cargo Insurance, supplementary evidence No.19 payment vouchers from the bank, supplementary evidence No.20 reply on conversion of Zurich Insurance Company Limited Beijing Branch into Zurich General Insurance (China), supplementary evidence No.21 statement of facts, supplementary evidence No.22 receipt for indemnity paid in advance, supplementary evidence No.23 receipt of indemnity, and supplementary evidence No.24 letter of subrogation, all to prove the transportation insurance contract of the cargo concerned is legal and valid, and the fact that the insurers has made the insurance indemnification and obtained from the insured relevant rights and interests.

Both GCL and Shanghai Hengxin had no objection to the authenticity of this group of evidence. MSCO also had no objection to the authenticity of this group of evidence except for supplementary evidence No.19. The three Defendants acknowledged the fact that the co-insurers had paid insurance indemnity, but had dissension on the reasonableness of part of the indemnity, and contended that as Hunan Zoomlion confirms having transferred the full right of claim in respect of the cargo concerned to the insurers, Hunan Zoomlion shall have no right to claim for the cargo concerned any more. Shanghai Hengxin further opined that the carrier shall not bear the compensation liability for the 10% insurance bonus. MSCO also held that the policies submitted were in fact issued by Zurich China solely, and the co-insurance agreement and co-insurance policies provide the claim and recourse in connection with insurance shall be under the responsibility of Zurich China, so Ping An Hunan and Sunshine Hunan should have no right to sue in the subject case.

The court holds that as supplementary evidence No.19 whose authenticity was objected by MSCO is an original, and the cross-examination opinions of the three Defendants on the content to be proved by this group of evidence shall not prejudice their use as evidence in this case, by examination and verification, the court confirms the effectiveness and probative force of these evidence. And as for whether the claim of the co-insurers was time barred and whether the co-insurers have the right to claim, the court will elaborate the determinations in detail below.

2. Evidence adduced by the Defendant GCL, cross-examination opinions of four Plaintiffs and other Defendants, and determinations of the court
(1) In order to prove that the annual transportation agreement concluded by and between Hunan Zoomlion and GCL has been cancelled by Hunan Zoomlion, that between GCL and Hunan Zoomlion existed the agency relationship in connection with the cargo concerned, and that such relationship has been

disclosed by Hunan Zoomlion, GCL submitted evidence No.1-1 notarial certificate of Zoomlion's email dated on July 5 and November 1, 2011, evidence No.1-2 documents in respect of shipping consignment and customs declaration of cargo concerned, evidence No.1-3 freight of cargo concerned and vouchers for actual payment, evidence No.1-4 Hunan Zoomlion's letter of entrustment, evidence No.1-5 judicial appraisal opinions, and supplementary evidence No.1 long-term strategic cooperation transportation agreement.

Except for the authenticity of evidence No.1-4 letter of entrustment, the four Plaintiffs and MSCO had no objection to authenticity, legality and relevancy of this group of evidence. Meanwhile, the four Plaintiffs opined the content in connection with two QUY70 crawler cranes in evidence No.1-2 and the B/L No.SHB10 in evidence No.1-3 has no relevancy to the subject case, and held the authenticity and legality of the annual transportation agreement has been determined by the effective legal document of Xiamen Maritime Court and Fujian High People's Court, that GCL's position as the contractual carrier has been confirmed, that the annual transportation agreement was not formally cancelled but continued to be performed even seen from the situation of actual performance, that GCL was the carrier as having collected the ocean freight, and that the relationship between Hunan Zoomlion and GCL shall be determined on the basis of the annual transportation agreement instead of the framework agreement of long-term strategic transportation agreement. MSCO took the view that evidence No.1-1 and evidence No.1-5 demonstrate Hunan Zoomlion and GCL communicated with each other on the cancellation of the annual transportation agreement without official cancellation, which form the situation of actual performance, merely has the cargo quantity and the freight rate amended; that the commercial invoices in evidence No.1-2 were issued by Hunan Zoomlion to Zoomlion HK and are different from those issued to the Indian buyers, and the actual value of the cargo concerned shall be subject to the customs declaration form; that evidence No.1-3 proves that GCL who accepted the consignment of cargo and charged freight shall be the contractual carrier; and that evidence No.1-4 was issued after the accident which thus shall not prejudice GCL's legal status as a contractual carrier. Shanghai Hengxin did not acknowledge the authenticity of evidence No.1-1 as they considered the notary office only notarized the emails having been stored in the principal's computer, but had no objection to the authenticity, legality and relevancy of the other evidence in this group. Shanghai Hengxin further viewed that in evidence No.1-1 and evidence No.1-5, GCL did not consent to cancel the annual transportation agreement, and these two evidence are insufficient to prove GCL was engaged in the transportation concerned later as the forwarder; that in the commercial invoices in evidence No.1-2, the seller and buyer are indicated to be Hunan Zoomlion and Zoomlion HK respectively, that the allegation of agency relationship to sign the purchase and sale contract in evidence No.14 submitted by Hunan Zoomlion shall be fabrication; that evidence No.1-3 can prove GCL as the carrier who performed the annual transportation agreement signed with Hunan Zoomlion based on the freight rate re-agreed by both parties;

and that evidence No.1-4 could not prove the legal relationship between Hunan Zoomlion and GCL.

With respect to evidence No.1-4 letter of entrustment whose authenticity was challenged by the four Plaintiffs and MSCO, as the issuing date and its content corresponds to the three emails from September 19 to 20, 2011 submitted by the four Plaintiffs as evidence No.11, the court confirms the authenticity and effectiveness of this evidence. By comprehensively considering the cross-examination opinions of all parties, the court confirms the effectiveness and probative force of this group of evidence, while the content to be proved by them shall be finally determined by a comprehensive consideration of all evidence submitted.

(2) In order to prove that the cargo concerned was poorly packed, and that in spite of GCL's reminding, the cargo concerned was still shipped out with poor package, which shall have direct causal relationship with the cargo damage, GCL submitted evidence No.2-1 loading survey report and evidence No.2-2 cargo inspection report issued by GCL.

The four Plaintiffs acknowledged the authenticity, legality and relevancy of evidence No.2-1, but denied those of evidence No.2-2. The four Plaintiffs considered the loading survey report can evidence the cargo concerned were not correctly stowed and secured when loaded on board, and the cargo losses caused by improper stowage shall be born by the carrier; and according to the annual transportation agreement, GCL shall make necessary packing for the cargo concerned to avoid cargo damage. Shanghai Hengxin confirmed the authenticity, legality and relevancy of this group of evidence, and opined this group of evidence, together with the mate's receipt, would be able to prove that the cargo concerned was very weakly packed before loading onboard, which was the important cause of the cargo damage. MSCO recognized the authenticity of evidence No.2-1, believing such evidence can prove the poor package of the cargo concerned, but deemed the authenticity of evidence No.2-2 could not be verified.

The court reckons that evidence No.2-1 loading survey report is the same with the evidence No.12 submitted by the four Plaintiffs, thus the court confirms its effectiveness as an evidence, and its probative force and the content to be proved by it will be determined by the court upon a comprehensive consideration of all evidence submitted. Evidence No.2-2 is a document self-prepared by GCL and is an isolated evidence, so its authenticity and the relevancy with the cargo concerned could not be confirmed; and given neither the four Plaintiffs nor MSCO confirms its authenticity, and GCL had in the court hearing clearly denied the relationship between cargo package and cargo damage, the court does not confirm the effectiveness of this evidence No.2-2.

(3) In order to prove that the damage to the cargo concerned was caused by the sudden change of the route of typhoon MUIFA in the course of voyage which shall belong to force majeure, GCL submitted evidence No.3-1 sea protests, witness testimonies and extracted deck logbook and evidence No.3-2 typhoon route chart.

The four Plaintiffs did not recognize the authenticity of this group of evidence, and held these evidence proved the moving route of typhoon MUIFA was predictable, and the strongest wind suffered by M.V. "Yuriy Arshenevskiy" was 9bft, not exceeding the vessel's ability to resist wind. Both Shanghai Hengxin and MSCO acknowledged the authenticity, legality and relevancy of and the subject to be proved by evidence No.3-1, but had dissension on evidence No.3-2. Shanghai Hengxin also denied it had prepared and published such typhoon route chart. And MSCO contended the weather condition during the voyage shall be ascertained on the basis of the records on the deck log book.

As evidence No.3-1 comes from MSCO, by considering other parties' cross-examination opinions, the court confirms the effectiveness of this evidence, and its probative force will be determined upon comprehensive consideration of other evidence submitted in the subject case. And evidence No.3-2 was denied by the indicated issuer Shanghai Hengxin, and as an isolated evidence, its authenticity could not be reflected by other means, the court does not confirm the authenticity or effectiveness of this evidence.

(4) In order to prove that the damage to the cargo concerned was enlarged after back shipment to Shanghai Port and the possibility that the cargo was further damaged before or after the back shipment could not be excluded, GCL submitted: supplementary evidence No.2 *Survey Report (on-site inspection on the five shipments of crawler cranes exported to India when they were shipped back to Luojing Terminal in Shanghai due to the alleged damage during the carriage by sea)*issued by Q. Pro Surveyors & Loss Adjusters Co., Ltd. (hereinafter referred to as the "Q.Pro survey report").

The four Plaintiffs took the view that GCL failed to prove the survey contemplated in the Q.Pro survey report was carried out by qualified surveyors, so they did not recognize the legality and relevancy of this evidence. Both Shanghai Hengxin and GCL had no objection to the authenticity, legality and relevancy of supplementary evidence No.2.

As the survey report is an original and was issued by a qualified adjusters' company, the court holds the effectiveness of this evidence can be confirmed, and considers it, to a certain extent, can prove the objective condition of the cargo concerned when back shipped to Shanghai Port. However, the descriptions and the photos in the survey report in relation to the cargo damage could not prove the damage to the cargo concerned was obviously enlarged.

3. Evidence adduced by the Defendant Shanghai Hengxin, cross-examination opinions of the four Plaintiffs and other Defendants, and determinations of the court

(1) In order to prove Shanghai Hengxin was not the actual carrier of the cargo concerned, Shanghai Hengxin submitted: evidence No.1 Master B/Ls to prove MSCO was both the carrier and actual carrier under the involved contract of carriage of goods; supplementary evidence No.1 fixture note between GCL and Shanghai Hengxin to prove that between GCL and Shanghai Hengxin was the

relationship of voyage charter party, and no contractual relationship existed between Shanghai Hengxin and Hunan Zoomlion; supplementary evidence No.2 fixture note between Shanghai Hengxin and Hanssy Shipping (HK) Co., Ltd. (hereinafter referred to as "Hanssy HK") to prove that a voyage charter party was concluded by and between Shanghai Hengxin and the uninvolved party Hanssy HK; supplementary evidence No.3 Civil Judgment(2011) Min Ti Zi No.13 rendered by the Supreme People's Court to prove that the Supreme People's Court has specified "the actual carrier and its legal relationship shall be subject to the relationship under the bill of lading", and under the voyage charter party or other contracts, the alleged liability of the actual carrier shall not be pursued by breaking the privity of contract.

The four Plaintiffs confirmed the authenticity, legality and relevancy of evidence No.1 and supplementary evidence No.1, but did not recognize those of supplementary evidence No.2 by holding that page 1 of the supplementary evidence No.2 bears no stamp of Hanssy HK and the stamp on Page 1 was not Shanghai Hengxin's; the four Plaintiffs did not acknowledge the authenticity of supplementary evidence 3 as it is not an original and is irrelevant to the subject case. GCL confirmed the authenticity of the whole group of evidence, and recognized the contents to be proved by evidence No.1 and supplementary evidence No.1, but on the ground that the case described in supplementary evidence No.3 was diverted from the subject case, did not acknowledge the contents to be proved by it. MSCO confirmed the authenticity of both evidence No.1 and supplementary evidence No.1, but took the opinion that the Master only entrusted the agent to issue bills of lading in name of the Master, while the issuing act of Shanghai UNISCO exceeded its power of agency, so MSCO was neither the carrier no the actual carrier. MSCO further opined as Shanghai Hengxin delayed in submitting supplementary evidence No.2 without reasonable cause, the authenticity of this evidence could not be verified. And as for supplementary evidence No.3, MSCO considered the legal positions of the parties concerned shall be judged on basis of the evidence in the subject case according to law.

As the supplementary evidence No.2 is an original and as no strong basis was put forward by the four Plaintiffs or MSCO to support their challenge in its authenticity, the court does not accept their cross-examination opinions. Supplementary evidence No.3 is a judgment the Supreme People's Court rendered for other case which shall have no binding force over the subject case, so it may be deemed as the legal opinions of Shanghai Hengxin on this case; however, as it has no attesting effect for the subject case, the court does not confirm the effectiveness or probative force of this evidence. By comprehensively considering the cross-examination opinions extended by all parties, the court confirms the effectiveness of the other evidence in this group, and the legal positions of the involved parties to be proved by these evidence will be determined upon an overall consideration of all evidence submitted in the subject case.

(2) In order to prove that the lashing and securing at Shanghai Port in the voyage concerned had been approved by the shipowner, that the lashing and securing of the cargo concerned reached the requirements of *Securing Manual* and *CCS Code* of IMO, and that the accident concerned was caused by the force majeure of adverse sea conditions, Shanghai Hengxin submitted supplementary evidence No.4 receipt and supplementary evidence No.5 *Analysis and Appraisal Report on the Cargo Lashing/Securing on board M.V. "Yuriy Arshenevskiy"* issued by Mintaian Insurance Surveyors & Loss Adjusters Co., Ltd. (hereinafter referred to as "Mintaian report").

The four Plaintiffs viewed supplementary evidence No.4 was not original, and did not confirm its authenticity; they had no objection to the authenticity of the Mintaian report, but considered the analysis and conclusion in the report lacks evidence support, which is only made on the basis of the condition of re-lashing at Xiamen Port, so they did not acknowledge its legality or relevancy. GCL had no objection to this group of evidence. MSCO thought the supplementary evidence No.4 was actually provided by the lashing company, and the superintendent at that time was the charterer in fact, so this evidence can only indicate Shanghai Hengxin approved the lashing condition, but cannot demonstrate the shipowner's approval on the lashing/securing. MSCO had no objection to the authenticity of Mintaian report, but held the data used in the report could not be verified.

The court holds that as the head letters and the time of stowage operation indicated on the receipt correspond to other evidence of the subject case and it was consistent with the common practice for the Master or the C/O to check the lashing operation for and on behalf of the shipowner, given MSCO had no objection to its authenticity, the court confirms its effectiveness and probative force. According to the answer to the inquiry on LIN Wei, the issuer of Mintaian report in the expert hearing, the court holds the authenticity and evidence effectiveness of this report can be confirmed, but its probative force shall be determined upon comprehensive consideration of other evidence submitted.

4. Evidence submitted by the Defendant MSCO, cross-examination opinions of the four Plaintiffs and other Defendants, and determinations of the court

(1) In order to prove the seaworthiness of the vessel, MSCO submitted: evidence No.1 ship particulars to prove the basic information of M.V. "Yuriy Arshenevskiy" and Murmansk Shipping Company is the registered owner of the vessel; evidence No.2 certificate of the right to sail under the state flag of the Russian Federation, evidence No.3 minimum safe manning certificate, evidence No.4 international tonnage certificate, evidence No.5 international load line certificate, evidence 6 cargo ship safety construction certificate, evidence No.7 cargo ship safety equipment certificate, evidence No.8 cargo ship safety radio certificate, evidence No.9 classification certificate, evidence No.10 document of compliance, evidence No.11 safety management certificate, and evidence No.12 international ship security certificate, all to prove that both before and at the beginning of the voyage, the certificates onboard was in compliance with

relevant requirements, the ship construction, machines and equipment were in good condition, and the safety management system had obtained the recognition and approval of competent authorities, which was according to the requirements of the international conventions; evidence No.13 occasional survey report and evidence No.14 certificates of renewal allowance issued by RMRS to prove that after suffering from typhoon MUIFA, M.V. "Yuriy Arshenevskiy" called at Xiamen Port for inspection onto the vessel and the cargo onboard, the classification society RMRS issued an occasional survey report on the vessel, holding the vessel was able to safely continue her voyage to India and renewed part of the ship certificates; evidence No.15 crew list and evidence No.16 certificate of competency of crew to prove that M.V. "Yuriy Arshenevskiy" was sufficiently manned and all of the crew members held the certificate of competency issued by competent authority.

The four Plaintiffs opined that the crew list bears no marine endorsement and the certificates of competency of the C/O (which should be the S/O) and the motorman were not notarized/legalized, so they did not confirm its authenticity. The four Plaintiffs further held the voyage concerned did not satisfied with the requirement of minimum safe manning, so the vessel was unseaworthy. Except for the above mentioned, the four Plaintiffs confirmed the authenticity, legality and relevancy of this group of evidence, but held the completeness of ship certificates is a necessary condition rather than abundant condition for the vessel's seaworthiness, thus these evidence cannot demonstrate the legal or technical conditions of ship seaworthiness. Both GCL and Shanghai Hengxin had no objection to the authenticity, legality and relevancy of and the content to be proved by this group of evidence.

The court holds that although in terms of form, the crew list has not been approved by competent authority, and the certificates of competency of S/O Sergey Yu Nemchinov and the motorman Sergey L. Belyanka were not notarized/legalized, according to the notarial certificate (2011) Xia Lu Zheng Min Zi No.1314, when Xiamen Notary Office embarked onboard for evidence perseveration on September 2, 2011, the S/O had presented the original passport and signed on his testimony. Therefore, by comprehensive examination, the court holds this group of evidence is true and credible, and the effectiveness and probative force of them can be confirmed, which means this group of evidence may prove M.V. "Yuriy Arshenevskiy" in the voyage concerned was equipped with complete certificates and sufficient crew members.

(2) In order to prove that MSCO was not the actual carrier, MSCO submitted: evidence No.17 time charter party concluded by and between Kings Ocean and Hanssy HK and evidence No.18 time charter party concluded by and between the sihpowners and Kings Ocean, so as to prove that Hanssy HK was responsible for the loading, discharging, stowage, securing and lashing of the cargo, and actually performed the carriage, that although the Master was designated by the shipowners, the Master observed the instructions of Hanssy HK in respect of cargo transportation, and that with respect to the cargo

transportation, the authorization of the Master represented the authorization of Hanssy HK, including the authorization of issuance of B/Ls; evidence No.19 Civil Judgment rendered by Shanghai High People's Court (2002) Hu Gao Min Si (Hai) Zhong Zi No.11, evidence No.20 voyage instructions (emails on July 6 and July 27), and evidence No.21 notice of readiness, so as to prove that the time charter party provided the shipment booking and vessel operation were under the responsibility of the time charterer who engaged in transportation by using the chartered vessel was the actual carrier, that in the voyage concerned, Shanghai Hengxin acted for and on behalf of Hanssy HK to give voyage instructions, appoint the agent at the loading port and require M.V. "Yuriy Arshenevskiy" to receive weather forecasts and routing recommendations, and that the notice of readiness of M.V. "Yuriy Arshenevskiy" was issued to Shanghai Hengxin; evidence No.22 letter of authorization to sign B/L issued by the Master, to prove that according to the charter party, the Master of M.V. "Yuriy Arshenevskiy" for and on behalf of Hanssy HK authorized Shanghai UNISCO to issue the B/Ls; and evidence No.57 legal opinions of Professor SI Yuzhuo—*Identification of Actual Carrier and Its Liability Form under the Maritime Code of PRC* (hereinafter referred to as the "legal opinions") and its attachments, so as to prove MSCO was not the actual carrier of the carriage concerned and shall not be jointly liable for the cargo damage.

Both the four Plaintiffs and Shanghai Hengxin held no original of evidence No.17 was provided for check, and evidence No.19 is not a civil judgment and has different cause and background from the subject case, so they did not confirm the authenticity, legality or relevancy of evidence No.17 and evidence No.19. Except for these, the four Plaintiffs and Shanghai Hengxin had no objection to the authenticity of this ground of evidence, though opining this group of evidence could not achieve the their object of proof. The four Plaintiffs viewed that under time charter party, crew members are appointed by ship owners which means the ship owners actually control the vessel, so the shipowner shall be the actual carrier; and according to the privity of contract, the Defendants shall not refer to relevant terms in the time charter party to combat the Plaintiffs' claims; and as for the voyage instructions, Shanghai Hengxin instructed M.V. "Yuriy Arshenevskiy" to authorize the agent to issue B/Ls for and on behalf of the shipowner on basis of the mate's receipt, so the conclusion that the shipowner were not the actual carrier could not be drawn from the letter of authorization to sign B/L. GCL considered the authenticity of the two charter parties could not be judged, but had no objection to the authenticity and legality of the civil judgment and to the authenticity, legality and relevancy of the letter of authorization to sign B/L without confirmation on the subject to be proved by them. Except for the above mentioned, GCL had on objection to this group of evidence. Shanghai Hengxin held that the Master's right to issue original bills of lading was granted by the shipowner and under time charter party, it were the crew members employed by the shipowner who took possession of, cared for and transported the cargo concerned on behalf of the shipowners; that "voyage instructions" were only the communications between the Master onboard and Shanghai Hengxin who acted as the agent of Hanssy HK in respect of cargo loading of the voyage concerned and the port agent; that the notice of readiness could not represent any legal relationship; no words in the letter of authorization to sign B/L indicated such authorization came from Hanssy HK; and that according to clause 68 of the two time charter parties, even if the charterer issued the original B/Ls by itself, it was authorized by the shipowner, that is, the charterer issued such B/Ls on behalf of the shipowner, and the shipowner shall still bear corresponding legal consequence. As for evidence No.57 legal opinions, the four Plaintiffs held it was not a legal type of evidence, so they did not examine on it; and the conclusion of the legal opinions is neither consistent with the legislative purpose of the Maritime Code of the People's Republic of China nor the traditional theory, general saying or current trial practices. GCL confirmed its authenticity. Shanghai Hengxin confirmed the authenticity of the legal opinions, but held the opinions and legal theories therein are different from the judicial practice, and the attachments thereto are irrelevant with the subject case, which therefore, were deemed by Shanghai Hengxin should not be the evidence of this case.

The court holds the charter party in evidence No.18 is the original, and although evidence No.17 is a copy, from the voyage instructions, the email addresses of the senders and receivers indicated on the correspondences between M.V. "Yuriy Arshenevskiy" and the shipowner, and the background information indicated on the inspection and survey reports submitted to the court, the relationship of charter parties in chain as MSCO-Kings Ocean-Hanssy HK-Shanghai Hengxin-GCL in the voyage concerned shall be true and credible; and the key clauses in the two charter parties in respect of bills of lading are in accord and consistent with the voyage instructions, letter of authorization to sign B/L and the practical experiences. Therefore, the court confirms the effectiveness and probative force of these two charter parties. Judgment irrelevant with the subject case shall have no binding force over this case, while in nature, it can be considered as the legal opinions expressed by MSCO on the subject case. The judgment has no effect of evidence to the subject case, so the court does not confirm its effectiveness as evidence or its probative force; meanwhile, it should be noted that in the case of the judgment submitted as evidence, the time charterer's issuance of bills of lading in its own name is an important factor for it to be determined as the actual carrier, which is exactly different from the subject case. As for evidence No.57 legal opinions, given it is the original, the court confirms its authenticity. This legal opinions may be deemed as the theoretical support for MSCO's contentions, but not a legal type of civil evidence and cannot be used an evidence in this case or a basis to determine the fact of the case, so the court does not confirm its effectiveness as evidence. By examining the evidence and overall considering the cross-examination opinions of all parties, the court confirms the effectiveness and probative force of the other evidence in this group, while the contents to be proved by them shall be determined by comprehensive consideration of other evidence submitted to the court.

(3) In order to prove the vessel's encountering with the adverse sea conditions brought about by typhoon MUIFA is the direct cause of the damage to the cargo concerned and the poor package of the cargo concerned is an important cause of the cargo damage, MSCO submitted: evidence No.23 shipping order to prove the cargo concerned was poorly packed and the wooden frame was slacked; evidence No.24 typhoon forecasts and navigational warnings received via EGC, evidence No.25 AWT weather messages and routing recommendations and evidence No.26 online reports, all to prove that the typhoon forecast received by M.V. "Yuriy Arshenevskiy" before departing from Shanghai Port indicated typhoon MUIFA would make landfall in vicinity of Zhoushan Hangzhou on August 6 to 7, and would impact Shanghai in a close distance, so in consideration of the AWT routing recommendations and the actual conditions of the vessel and the cargo, M.V. "Yuriy Arshenevskiy" decided to proceed to Cheju Island for typhoon avoidance, while MUIFA seriously diverted from the forecast route on August 6 to 7, which resulted in M.V. "Yuriy Arshenevskiy" being impacted by the typhoon in a close distance and suffering from severe sea conditions, and the maneuvering onboard M.V. "Yuriy Arshenevskiy" accorded to the AWT recommendations; evidence No.27 deck log book, evidence No.28 sea protest and witness testimony, evidence No.29 correspondences between M.V. "Yuriy Arshenevskiy" and Shanghai Hengxin, evidence No.30 Correspondences between M.V. "Yuriy Arshenevskiy" and the shipowner, and evidence No.31 and No.32 videos (with translation of the Master's voiceover) and photos taken by crewmembers onboard M.V. "Yuriy Arshenevskiy" from August 5 to 7, all to prove that the vessel concerned suffered strong winds over 12bft (maximum 15bft), rolling up to 30~45 degrees (maximum 50 degrees), that before departing from Shanghai Port, the Master and the S/O of M.V. "Yuriy Arshenevskiy" had asked the sub-charterer to strengthen the lashing and securing of the cargo, and also instructed crewmembers to strengthen the lashing and securing of the cargo by using equipment onboard, and that the decision of typhoon avoidance of M.V. "Yuriy Arshenevskiy" has been approved by the sub-charterer, and after the accident, the vessel followed the instruction of Shanghai Hengxin to proceed to Xiamen Port.

The four Plaintiffs considered shipping order No.SHB10 has no relevancy to the subject case, and held the authenticity, legality and relevancy of evidence No.29 to 32 could not be confirmed. The Plaintiffs had no objection to the authenticity of the other evidence in this group, but viewed the wooden package of the cargo would not impair the cargo stowage or transportation safety, and the cause of cargo damage was the carrier's failure to stow and care of cargo properly; the EGC messages received by M.V. "Yuriy Arshenevskiy" had sufficiently reminded the feature of typhoon MUIFA that the moving route was uncertain and likely to change; both the AWT company and the Master thought it would be better to avoid typhoon at the anchorage; the online reports also gave sufficient forecasts to the uncertainty of typhoon MUIFA's moving route, and severally mentioned vessels should avoid typhoon at anchorage; records in the deck log book was exaggerated; and the witnesses who issued the testimony did not attend the court hearing. On the above grounds, the four Plaintiffs did not confirm the legality of this evidence. GCL had no objection to the authenticity and legality of the said evidence, and basically agreed on the subject to be proved by them. However, GCL objected the relevancy of the content of evidence No.31 and No.32 in respect of the deck cargo, and held evidence No.24 and No.25 cannot prove the lashing was slacked due to the poor package of deck cargo, and the requirement on lashing and securing put forward by the shipowner at the time of cargo loading has been properly satisfied with at Shanghai Port. Shanghai Hengxin had objection to the authenticity, legality and relevancy of evidence No.29, and held from the content, Shanghai Hengxin emphasized that "how to navigate depends on you, but safety firstly. PLS always keep safe distance to typhoon"; in fact, the Master as the superintendent had the first right of decision on navigational safety, and Shanghai Hengxin had no direct contractual relationship with MSCO and was neither the shipper nor the consignee who thus has no right under laws or contracts to give any voyage instruction to M.V. "Yuriy Arshenevskiy". Apart from the said, Shanghai Hengxin had no objection to the evidence in this group.

By examining the above evidence and sufficiently considering the cross-examination opinions, the court confirms the effectiveness and probative force of the above evidence, but the contents to be proved by them will be determined upon comprehensive consideration of other evidence submitted in this case.

MSCO also submitted evidence No.33 *Appraisal Opinions on Cause of Damage to Cargoes onboard M.V. "Yuriy Arshenevskiy" V.11125* issued by Dalian Maritime University Maritime Judicial Authentication Center (WANG Jianping, HONG Biguang and PU Renxiang) (hereinafter referred to as "DMU report"), to prove the vessel was seaworthy; the actual route of typhoon MUIFA differed significantly from the forecast route, as a result of which the vessel was impacted in a short distance and sustained wind up to 15bft and rolling up to 50 degrees, far beyond the extent of wind and wave that IMO requires vessels engaged in international service to resist; that the decision of M.V. "Yuriy Arshenevskiy" to sail to Cheju Island for typhoon avoidance was correct; the cargo stowage and securing in the voyage concerned basically was in compliance with the requirement of *Securing Manual* and *CSS Code* of IMO; in the course of voyage, in order to reduce the vessel's rolling, the Master onboard M.V. "Yuriy Arshenevskiy" had altered the course according to the actual sea conditions and the conditions of deck cargo, which was in compliance with good seamanship; the Master had performed the obligation of reasonable care for the cargo both at the port of loading and in the course of voyage; and the vessel's encounter with adverse sea conditions brought about by typhoon MUIFA was the direct cause of the cargo damage in the voyage concerned with the poor package of the cargo as an important cause.

The four Plaintiffs challenged the qualification of the three appraisers, and held the DMU report is based on exaggerated and one-sided weather information, jumps into conclusion partially, and lacks independency and preciseness. Both GCL and Shanghai Hengxin had no objection to the authenticity, legality and conclusion of the report, while Shanghai Hengxin contended the description that "Shanghai Hengxin canvassed the cargo and took the responsibility of loading, stowage, lashing, securing and other issues regarding transportation" was inconsistent with the fact.

Evidence No.55 *Analysis on Wind Force Suffered by M.V. "Yuriy Arshenevskiy" during Typhoon MUIFA in August 2011* issued by WU Liguang, the director of Pacific Typhoon Research Center, Nanjing University of Information Science & Technology (hereinafter referred to as "wind force analysis report"), to demonstrate the gusts suffered by M.V. "Yuriy Arshenevskiy" on August 6-7, and to prove the records in the deck log book regarding the sea conditions at the material time were true and credible while the forecasts of China Meteorological Administration on typhoon MUIFA had forecast error.

The four Plaintiffs had no objection to the authenticity of this analysis report, but considered no qualification certificate of the issuer was provided. Both GCL and Shanghai Hengxin had no objection to the authenticity, legality and relevancy of this analysis report. Moreover, the four Plaintiffs contended the data relied upon by the wind force analysis report was different from the data actually used by M.V. "Yuriy Arshenevskiy". It is groundless to deduce the typhoon forecast route was diverted to the east tremendously. Even if the gusts were over 10bft, due to the short-lasting time, the gusts would not influence the vessel's rolling. GCL held the report demonstrates the regional gale occurring in the area where typhoon passed by was a totally different concept of large gale circle.

The court holds that neither the DMU report nor the wind force analysis report were issued by appraisers determined by all parties through negotiation or appointed by the court, so neither belongs to the "appraisal opinions" stipulated in the Civil Procedure Law of PRC or other type of legal evidence. However, pursuant to the Civil Procedure Law of PRC, a party involved in the case may apply for the attending in court and provision of opinions of specialist(s) on professional issues. By examination, the issuers of the reports are equipped with relevant qualifications and certificates. The issuers of DMU report also have relevant professional knowledge, technology and experience, and two of the issuers attended the court hearing to accept inquiries from other relevant parties on the content of the report and confrontation with other expert witnesses appointed by other parties. Therefore, the content of the report and the opinions expressed by the issuers at court may support the defense opinions of MSCO, and be referred to by the court in judging the probative force of evidence and ascertaining facts.

(4) In order to prove the crewmembers onboard M.V. "Yuriy Arshenevskiy" had fulfilled their obligation of due diligence during the voyage concerned, MSCO submitted: evidence No.34 calculation of vessel's stability, evidence No.35 stowage plan, evidence No.36 correspondences between M.V. "Yuriy Arshenevskiy" and Shanghai Hengxin and evidence No.37 photographs of deck cargo Taken by crewmembers onboard M.V. "Yuriy Arshenevskiy" on August 5, so as to prove that M.V. "Yuriy Arshenevskiy" had relatively high stability and strength during the voyage concerned, that the cargo stowage met

the IMO requirements, that the Master and the S/O had twice asked the sub-charterer to strengthen the cargo lashing and securing before the vessel departure, and that the crewmembers onboard M.V. "Yuriy Arshenevskiy" had reinforced the lashing of deck cargo by using the steel chains on board; evidence No.38 statement of the Master, evidence No.39 statement of Chief Officer, evidence No.40 statement of Second Officer, evidence No.41 statement of Chief Engineer, evidence No.42 statement of Second Engineer and evidence No.43 statement of Duty Seaman, all to prove that in the course of the voyage concerned, the main engine and radio equipment onboard were all in normal and good condition, that M.V. "Yuriy Arshenevskiy" carried sea charts covering the sea areas of the voyage concerned and the guideline documents for typhoon avoidance, that the cargo securing and lashing in the voyage concerned was under the responsibility of the sub-charterer who at the requirement of the Master and the C/O, twice strengthened the lashing and securing before the vessel departure, that the crewmembers had twice used the steel chains onboard to reinforce the lashing when cargo on tween decks shake, that most deck cargo fell overboard when the vessel suffered hurricane in speed up to 50m/s and rolling up to 50 degrees on August 6-7, and that the maneuvering of M.V. "Yuriy Arshenevskiy" in the accident met good seamanship.

The four Plaintiffs had no objection to the authenticity, legality and relevancy of the calculation of vessel's stability and the stowage plan, but held that the weight distribution of stowage onboard met requirements did not mean the lashing and securing met requirements as well, let alone the carrier properly performed the obligation of care for cargo. In addition, the four Plaintiffs did not confirm the authenticity, legality and relevancy of evidence No.36 and No.37. GCL had no objection to the authenticity, legality and relevancy of the above evidence, basically agreed on the subject to be proved by them, but objected the relevancy of the part of evidence No.37 in connection with deck cargo. Shanghai Hengxin had no objection to the authenticity, legality and relevancy of evidence No.34, evidence No.35 and evidence No.37, but said the authenticity of evidence No.36 could not be confirmed. Shanghai Hengxin opined that the emails were sent to Hanssy HK rather than Shanghai Hengxin and the problems referred to in the email were all solved before the vessel departure. The four Plaintiffs had no objection to the authenticity of evidence No.38 to No.43, but did not confirm the relevancy of the content of these evidence regarding deck cargo. The four Plaintiffs also put forward as the witnesses did not attend at court which is inconsistent with the rule of evidence, they did not confirm the authenticity of partial statement in respect of the accident course. GCL had no objection to the authenticity and legality of the above evidence, but held evidence No.40 to No.43 could not reflect all the subjects that MSCO intended to prove, that the current evidence could not identify Shanghai Hengxin as the sub-charterer, and that the shift of deck cargo had no direct relationship with the cargo damage concerned. Although the relevant people indicated in evidence No.38 embarked onboard at Xiamen Port, they did not carry out joint inspection. Shanghai Hengxin had no objection to the authenticity, legality and relevancy of evidence

No.38, but considered Shanghai Hengxin had no direct contractual relationship with the shipowner and had no right to give voyage instructions to the shipowner. With respect to the saying of "sub-charterer" referred to in the statement of the Master, Shanghai Hengxin had objections. Shanghai Hengxin further acknowledged the authenticity, legality and relevancy of evidence No.39 to 43, and acknowledged they may evidence the facts of vessel navigation and management.

The court confirms the authenticity of the emails and photos submitted by MSCO as they have all notarized. Shanghai Hengxin had no objection to the narration that M.V. "Yuriy Arshenevskiy" received instructions directly from Shanghai Hengxin in the voyage concerned, and only defended them as being the agent of Hanssy HK contacting with M.V. "Yuriy Arshenevskiy". The court further confirms the effectiveness and probative force of evidence No.34 to No.37. By examining this group of evidence and comprehensively considering the cross-examination opinions of all parties, the court confirms the effectiveness and probative force of evidence No.38 to No.34, while the subjects to be proved by them will be finally determined upon comprehensive consideration of other evidence submitted to the court.

(5) In order to prove the shipowner of M.V. "Yuriy Arshenevskiy" had taken reasonable loss mitigation measures, MSCO submitted the following evidence: evidence No.44 application for discharge and cargo inspection onboard the vessel under arrest, evidence No.45 stevedore and extra labor working record, evidence No.46 daily report of the goods, evidence No.47 tally certificate and evidence No.48 on-the-spot record, all to prove M.V. "Yuriy Arshenevskiy" had reconditioned, re-lashed and re-secured the cargo at Xiamen Port; evidence No.49 application for discharge of M.V. "Yuriy Arshenevskiy", evidence No.50letter issued to Xiamen Terminals, evidence No.51 voyage instruction of Shanghai Hengxin, all to prove M.V. "Yuriy Arshenevskiy" had actively applied to the competent authority for discharge of the damaged cargo at Xiamen Port, while due to the objective limits, the discharge at Xiamen Port could not be achieved and M.V. "Yuriy Arshenevskiy" had to proceed to the port of destination in India for the cargo discharge; evidence No.54 statement of facts issued by LAI Shengfu and LI Yibin from Xiamen United International Ocean Shipping Agency Ltd. (hereinafter referred to as "Xiamen UNISCO"), to prove during the period when M.V. "Yuriy Arshenevskiy" berthed in Xiamen, MSCO entrusted Xiamen UNISCO, the superintendents and the lawyers to negotiate with various local terminals, customs and port management authorities in Xiamen in connection with discharge of the cargo; however, due to the cargo damage onboard and complicated customs procedures, after negotiations and communications by all parties for more than one month, M.V. "Yuriy Arshenevskiy" failed to obtain the approval from the customs on discharge of the cargo and had to leave for India according to the charterer's instructions.

The four Plaintiffs had objection to the authenticity, legality and relevancy of evidence No.44 to No.51 and held relevant applications was not intended to mitigate the cargo losses; they confirmed the authenticity of evidence No.54 statement of facts and the signature page (pages 623 and 626) of its attachment but could not ascertain the authenticity of other materials, holding that notwithstanding Hunan Zoomlion and GCL had found a suitable terminal to accept the cargo concerned if returned to Shanghai Port for discharge, MSCO kept ignoring the repeated requirement of Hunan Zoomlion. GCL held the authenticity of evidence No.51 needed to be confirmed by Shanghai Hengxin and had no objection to the authenticity and legality of other evidential materials, but argued evidence No.45 to No.48 merely reflected the discharge of deck cargoes, having no relevancy to the cargo concerned; GCL also asserted it was not clear whether evidence No.44 and No.49 had been actually submitted and entertained; evidence No.50 could not explain the reasons why the cargo concerned could not be discharged at Xiamen Port; evidence No.51 was only a bunking instruction and could not prove the subject it intended to prove; GCL's cross-examination opinions on evidence No.54 were basically the same with the four Plaintiffs. Shanghai Hengxin held evidence No.51 did not satisfy the requirements on email evidence in respect of the authenticity and the emails only contained such content as the contact methods of the bunkering agent in Hong Kong, and therefore, refused to recognize its authenticity, legality and relevancy; Shanghai Hengxin did not recognize the authenticity, legality or relevancy of evidence No.54 and deemed the witness issuing the testimonies shall attend in court and accept cross-examination; besides, not participating in the negotiations, Shanghai Hengxin could not confirm whether the facts stated by the evidence were true or not; Shanghai Hengxin had no objection to the authenticity and legality of other evidence of this set but could not confirm whether MSCO had actually filed the application as mentioned in evidence No.49 and No.50.

The court holds that more than one piece of evidence available prove M.V. "Yuriy Arshenevskiy" had ever retallied and retied the cargo concerned during her stay at Xiamen Port and all parties lodged no objection to this fact; evidence No.54 statement of facts was original and several evidence of this set could corroborate each other and prove MSCO had made attempts and efforts for obtaining approval on discharge at Xiamen Port and therefore, confirms the effect of evidence and probative force of evidence No.44 to No.51 and evidence No.54.

(6) In order to justify its objection to the loss, MSCO submitted the following evidence: evidence No.52 email exchanges between MSCO and the agent of Hunan Zoomlion, to prove Hunan Zoomlion shipped back the cargo concerned from India in May 2012 and required the parties concerned to participate in joint inspection at Zoomlion's factory in mid-December, but since the cargo was damaged during the loading operation for back shipment, Hunan Zoomlion asserted they would dispose of the cargo via auction to be held on January 28; evidence No.53 orange warning of typhoon, to prove the cargo concerned was influenced by typhoon "HAIKUI" during the voyage of back shipment;

evidence No.56 single price detail of crawler lifting box , to prove compared with the results of inspection in India and the cargo evaluation and residual value disposal upon back shipment, the losses of the cargo concerned had been further enlarged in the back shipment and subsequent disposal; evidence No.58 insurance certificates of cargo transportation (emails attached), to prove the insurance certificate concerned was issued by Zurich China, so Ping An Hunan and Sunshine Hunan had no right to file action.

The four Plaintiffs had no objection to the authenticity, legality and relevancy of evidence No.52 and No.53, but held the cargo damaged in the back shipment was in fact damaged during the loading operation and was not the cargo concerned, and the typhoon encountered on the way, except affecting the shipping date, did not actually influence the cargo onboard at all; the four Plaintiffs confirmed Hunan Zoomlion ever provided MSCO with a document used to give quotation for the buyer, which might be evidence No.56, but since the quotation was higher than the actual price as evidenced by the contract and commercial invoice, it could not be proved that losses had been enlarged; the four Plaintiffs did not confirm the authenticity of evidence No.58 due to lack of its original and held the insurance certificates as such had declared "this insurance certificate shall not come into effect until it is jointly signed by the insured or its agent", so the insurance certificates did not take effect and shall have no relevancy to the subject case. Both GCL and Shanghai Hengxin had no objection to the authenticity, legality, relevancy and the subject to be proved. However, Shanghai Hengxin further held evidence No.58 proved during the performance of the insurance contract concerned, it was modified that Zurich China was the sole insurer and issued the insurance policy, so Zurich China shall solely pay indemnities and then recover from the carrier.

The court, in consideration that the parties lodged no objection to evidence No.52 and evidence No.53, recognizes their effect of evidence and probative force, but holds the contents to be proved shall be further ascertained by extra reference to other evidence available; evidence No.56 single price detail of crawler lifting box was merely a "quotation" and could not represent the actual price of the cargo concerned, not to mention "the losses of the cargo concerned had been further enlarged in the back-shipment and subsequent disposal", and thus shall have no relevancy to the facts-in-dispute concerned and its effect of evidence and probative force shall not be recognized; in consideration that although the four Plaintiffs lodged objection to the authenticity of evidence No.58, the numbers of the five insurance certificates were utterly the same as those listed in page 52 of Crawford survey report submitted by the four Plaintiffs and other items of the same were also consistent with the cargo concerned, the court recognizes the effect of evidence of evidence No.58 and will ascertain its contents to be proved by extra reference to other evidence available. The "standing to sue" of Ping An Hunan and Sunshine Hunan will be detailed later.

5. Evidence collected by the court in light of laws

Upon application filed by the Defendant MSCO, the court issued an investigation letter to Shanghai Meteorological Bureau, making evidence investigation and collection with respect to the structure and position of the typhoon, and wind speed/scale that the vessel encountered at the material time of accident. On September 17, 2013, Shanghai Meteorological Bureau issued *Reply of Shanghai Meteorological Bureau to Investigation Letter of Shanghai Maritime Court* (Hu Qi Han (2013) No.117, hereinafter referred to as "SMB reply") and attached the real-time typhoon data and infrared images of geostationary satellite FY-2E corresponding to the positions of the vessel.

Since no objection was lodged by the parties concerned to the authenticity, legality and relevancy of the SMB reply, the SMB reply together with other effective evidence available can be used to prove the actual sea conditions encountered by M.V. "Yuriy Arshenevskiy".

On the basis of the said evidence recognized and the court hearing/investigation, the court ascertains the facts of the subject case as follows (remarks: refer to the standard times indicated by the evidential materials available. UTC was adopted by the messages received via EGC the emails from weather routing company while the GMT was adopted by the deck log book, both 8 hours later than Beijing time and of difference ignorable; part of the emails sent from M.V. "Yuriy Arshenevskiy" indicated Moscow time of daylight saving time which was 4 hours later than Beijing time):

1. Ship information and relationship under the charter party in connection with the voyage concerned

The vessel concerned M.V. "Yuriy Arshenevskiy" is a Russia-registered RoRo/break-bulk carrier, gross tonnage 18,574 tons, built in 1986 and registered in Russian Ship Classification Society. The owner of the vessel is MSCO.

On April 14, 2011, MSCO and Kings Ocean entered into a time charter party under which MSCO chartered M.V. "Yuriy Arshenevskiy" to Kings Oceans with a charter period of about 9 to 11 months starting from the date when the vessel was delivered. Earlier on April 7, 2011, Kings Ocean and Hanssy HK entered into a time charter party, according to which M.V. "Yuriy Arshenevskiy" was sub-chartered to Hanssy HK for a charter period of about 6 months starting from the date when the vessel was delivered. Clause 8 of the said two back-to-back charter parties prescribes, "the Captain (although appointed by the shipowner), shall be under the orders and directions of the Charterers as regards employment and agency; and charterers are to load, stow, trim, discharge, lash, unlash, dunnage, secure the cargo at their expense under the supervision of the Captain, who is to sign bills of lading for cargoes as presented, in strict conformity with mate's or tally clerk receipts." Both charter parties further agreed in "clause 41 bills of lading" of the additional clauses that "with reference to clause 8, it is understood that the Charterers and/or their agents may sign original bill(s) of lading, if required by charterers, on behalf of the Master strictly according to mate's receipts without prejudice to this charter party, through or in-transit bill(s) of lading not to be issued under this charter party."

With respect to the voyage concerned, namely M.V. "Yuriy Arshenevskiy" V.11125, Hanssy HK voyage chartered the vessel to Shanghai Hengxin and Shanghai Hengxin again voyage chartered the vessel to GCL. Both the said voyage charter parties agreed on the FLT freight clause.

During the voyage concerned, Shanghai Hengxin represented in their email exchanges with M.V. "Yuriy Arshenevskiy" that it as the sub-charterer gave instruction to the vessel "for and on behalf of Shanghai Hengxin Shipping Co., Ltd.".

2. Contents of contracts and B/Ls in connection with the relationship of carriage concerned

On March 25, 2011, GCL (Party A) and Hunan Zoomlion (Party B) concluded *Long-term Strategic Cooperation Transportation Agreement* with the validity term of one year, agreeing that "Party B entrusts Party A to act as its agent for cargo transportation business", and reaching agreements upon freight rate and operation manner. On May 23, 2011, GCL (Party A) and Hunan Zoomlion (Party B) concluded *Annual Transportation Agreement for Crawler Cranes to India*, agreeing: "Party B entrusts Party A to undertake the cargo transportation operation from Shanghai to Mumbai, India"; "freight rate: a) ocean freight for bulk cargo: USD45 per billable unit in average, on full-liner term, inclusive of other extra taxes of ocean transportation, stevedorage, stowage charge, trimming charge, tally fee and cargo securing fee. All cargoes will be stowed beneath the deck. b) Lump sum for port charges: RMB26.5 per billable unit, including all the fees and charges incurred for shipment booking and in the port zone, such as shipment booking fee, THC charge, customs declaration fee, documentary charge, unloading charge, shifting/movement charge, stowage and packing charges for the crawler cranes....", "operation manner: ...... j) Party A shall arrange specialists to supervise the whole process of cargo loading onto the carrying vessel and take photos for record for the purpose to ensure safe and proper vertical loading, stowage and securing of the cargo. k) After the cargo arrives at the destination port, Party B's engineers shall conduct initial inspection to the cargo. If damage or loss of cargo is found to be caused by Party A's faults during transportation, all the losses arising therefrom shall be undertaken by Party A. For serious losses, Party B shall be entitled to terminate this agreement".

On July 5, 2011, Hunan Zoomlion informed GCL via email that "as to the 'crawler cranes to India' project invited for bid by our company in May, for the customers' breach of contract, this project has been cancelled, so the annual transportation agreement for crawler cranes to India concluded by and between your company and our company could not be performed any more. It is now decided by our leadership after discussion that: this annual transportation agreement is cancelled....Upon receipt of your confirmation, we will formally send a notice to cancel the annual transportation agreement". On July 13, GCL replied that "as the transportation agreement is a tripartite cooperation agreement among the cargo owner, the forwarding agent and the shipowner, we had to notify such situation to the shipowner", and conveyed the reply of the shipowner Hengxin which was summarized as follows: 1. The unit price of USD48W/M for the 26 sets of crawler cranes firstly transported; 2. The ocean freight for the second shipment of 5 sets of crawler cranes ready to be transported to Mumbai shall be charged at USD50W/M. 3. The shipowner did not agree to cancel the original transportation agreement, but requested an additional transportation agreement to be concluded, under which it shall be agreed that the cargo quantity and ocean freight agreed under the previous agreement become invalid, but Zoomlion shall warrant that all their shipments of general cargo destined to Mumbai, India before March 2012 shall be carried by Hengxin. The next day, Hunan Zoomlion further replied via email, "first of all, we would like to declare that the subject agreement is not a tripartite agreement, and our company had neither signed nor stamped on the agreement concluded by and between your company and the shipowner, therefore, as for the requests put forward by the shipowner, please negotiate and handle the request by yourselves. We maintain our previous decision"; although agreeing to pay for the difference of ocean freight and port charges in connection with the said two shipments of cargo, Hunan Zoomlion insisted "the above is the final settlement of our company".

The cargo concerned was consigned by Hunan Zoomlion to GCL and delivered to the vessel by GCL in its own name. The mate's receipt concerned indicated the shipper was GCL and the shipping date was August 2, 2011, and bore the written remarks of "weak packing" or "wooden cases are weak packing, materials unknown, shipside shall not be responsible for damages during loading/ discharging" which was signed by the Master for confirmation. According to the bank slip, on September 8, 2011, Zoomlion Heavy paid USD201,179.31 to GCL and the charge item indicated by the special invoice for international freight agency was "ocean freight".

After the cargo concerned had been completely shipped onboard, GCL submitted the order B/Ls (namely House B/Ls) No.SHM04, SHB11, SHB12A and SHB13 to Hunan Zoomlion. However, after occurrence of the accident, these B/Ls were regained by GCL, with reason and whereabouts unknown. According to the copies of the B/Ls provided by Hunan Zoomlion now, the shipper indicated on this set of B/Ls was Zoomlion HK and Union Ocean alleged it issued these B/Ls on behalf of the carrier Shanghai Hengxin.

The voyage instruction sent by Shanghai Hengxin to the Master on July 6, 2011 expressly stated, "please authorize agent to sign the B/Ls in conformity with mate's receipt on your behalf". The Master ever issued the authorization document to UNISCO that "we hereby authorize you to issue the bill of lading with respect to the cargo shipped onboard for the subject voyage on behalf of me...." On September 19, 2011, Hunan Zoomlion confirmed their agreement to the vessel's issuance of the B/Ls in conformity with the mate's receipt and agreed GCL paid ocean freight to the shipowners in exchange for the B/Ls. On September 23, GCL surrendered to Hunan Zoomlion the four sets of straight B/Ls No. SHM04, SHB11,

SHB12 and SHB13 (namely Master B/Ls) issued by Shanghai UNISCO on behalf of MSCO as alleged, indicating the shipper was GCL, the consignee was an logistics company in India, the cargo concerned was 176 packages in quantity, gross weight totaled 855,780 kg and minor remarks were the same as the mate's receipt. Hunan Zoomlion, upon receipt of these B/Ls, immediately complained against GCL that without negotiation with and authorization from Hunan Zoomlion, GCL changed the carrier into MSCO, the shipper into GCL and the carrier into MSCO; it also held that since it was GCL who directly arranged the shipment and space booking with the shipowners in connection with the cargo concerned according to the annual transportation agreement for crawler cranes to India, the shipper under the B/Ls may be changed into GCL on the premise that GCL issued House B/Ls as carrier to Hunan Zoomlion, or GCL, after receipt of the order B/Ls issued by the Master, negotiated by endorsement the B/Ls to Hunan Zoomlion in exchange for the House B/Ls; in this regard, Hunan Zoomlion required GCL to immediately and unconditionally issue five sets of order B/Ls in the B/L format previously agreed, naming Hunan Zoomlion or Zoomlion HK as the shipper and "'Hanssy Shipping' as the carrier"; meanwhile, in order to resolve the problems as soon as possible, Hunan Zoomlion also indicated, "we would agree the Master to re-issue the straight B/Ls as an expedient, but the shipper and consignee must be Hunan Zoomlion." GCL then conveyed the requirement of Huanan Zoomlion to Shanghai Hengxin; Shanghai Hengxin insisted, "there is no agreement regarding the B/L alteration in the contract entered between GCL and our company. Our company issued the B/L according to the mate's receipt, which is not wrong at all, and the clients do not have the right to require our company to alter the B/Ls's content according to their requirement (especially under the condition that the shipowner firmly expressed their dissention)" and that the agreement between Zoomlion and GCL should have no relevancy to it.

After the cargo concerned arrived in India, Hunan Zoomlion surrendered the full set of Master B/Ls to GCL on March 1, 2012 in exchange for the 4 sets of straight B/Ls in the same number re-issued by Shanghai UNISCO on behalf of MSCO so as to facilitate the later receipt of cargo at Indian port. This set of B/Ls still names GCL as the shipper while changing the consignee into Zoomlion Trade (India) Private Limited.

3. Situation of typhoon MUIFA

From the evening of August 2 to the morning of August 4, typhoon MUIFA continuously and slowly moved westwards.

EGC's message at 19:56:06 on August 3 informed: wind gusts can be a further 40 percent stronger than the averages given here, and maximum waves may be up to twice the height. Message at 17:03:34 on August 6: frequent heavy squally (SQ) showers (SH) and thunderstorms (TS) within 300 nm from center of MUIFA. Message at 18:42:56 on August 6: radius of over 30 knot winds 300 miles east semicircle and 220 miles elsewhere. Radius of over 30 knot winds 300 miles east semicircle and 220 miles elsewhere. The first three messages on August 7 all stated radius of over 50 knot winds 120 miles east semicircle and radius of over 30 knot winds 325 miles east semicircle. All EGC messages, after forecasting the position of typhoon center, regarded there was 70% percent probability that the typhoon center would enter into probability circle.

According to the email sent from the weather routing company at 05:03:03 on August 4, 2011, "...Forecast confidence in the track of the typhoon remains moderate at this time. Captain, well noted vessel has sensitive deck cargo and has asked for permission to remain in port for the next several days. However, we note that the typhoon is currently heading for the Shanghai area for a direct hit. This would likely result in winds of 70 knots in the general vicinity of Shanghai with strong storm surge moving into the area as well. Considering this information, we do not know if the port of Shanghai will remain open and if it closes your vessel will likely have to seek shelter in open ocean. If the port of Shanghai does close and forces your vessel into the open ocean, then we suggest your vessel proceed along a best NE-ly heading to north of Cheju Island to gain some fetch limitation and clearance north and east of the typhoon. However, if your vessel is able to remain in port we suggest your vessel begin voyage around 08/12 to begin sailing outside the gale radius of the typhoon as it continues north. Please keep us closely advised to your intentions and the situation at the port of Shanghai so that we may keep you well advised". According to the email sent from the weather routing company at 15:03:26 on August 4, "the following update based on departure August 5,2011 in loading condition from Shanghai to Mumbai...3. Route recommendation: as conditions and safe navigation permit, best NE-ly heading to north/east of Cheju Island, to obtain clearance well north and east of typhoon MUIFA. Then best S-ly heading, adjusting course to ensure 300 nm clearance to its east. According to the email sent from the weather routing company at 22:53:50 on August 5, "...2. Route recommendation: direct north of Cheju Island remain valid; reason: avoid heavier adverse conditions associated with typhoon MUIFA."

As was reported by *Meteorological Message Certification Report* issued by Shanghai Central Meteorological Station, "based on the analysis of typhoon route and vessel position, it can be found that from August 6 to August 7, the vessel sailed within 7bft but never within 10bft gale wind circle on the right semi-circle of typhoon MUIFA."

The reply of Shanghai Meteorological Bureau dated September 17, 2013 asserted that, "according to the satellite images and other meteorological data, typhoon MUIFA was of an asymmetric structure and the vessel concerned was quite likely to at the edge of 10bft wind area, thus the possibility that 10bft winds might occur in the sailing area of the vessel concerned could not be ruled out". As was shown by the attachments thereto, due to the restricted temporal resolution of polar orbiting satellites, only two wind field retrieval images were obtained one day, from which it can be found at 2000 on August 6, 2011 and 0800 on August 7, 2011, the wind force at the vessel position was comparatively strong, about 28m/s (10-11bft).

According to the analysis on wind force suffered by M.V. "Yuriy Arshenevskiy" during typhoon MUIFA in August 2011 which was issued by WU Liguang, director of Pacific Typhoon Research Center, Nanjing University of Information Science & Technology, by comparison with the yearly average typhoon-forecast error of CMA in 2011, before and within a certain period after M.V. "Yuriy Arshenevskiy" departed from Shanghai Port, the forecasts of typhoon MUIFA's moving direction released by CMA were relatively reliable. However, after 0800 on August 6, the actual moving direction of typhoon MUIFA quite eastly deviated from the forecast track; after 0200 on August 6, the sea surface wind field showed significant asymmetry with gale zone to the east of typhoon center; at 0800 and 1400 on August 6, the mean wind speed at the position of M.V. "Yuriy Arshenevskiy" reached 7bft, and at 2000 on August 6 and 0800on August 7, in the 9bft wind circle; according to the satellite retrieved mean wind speeds at ship positions and in consideration of the linear relationship between mean wind and gust, gust scale that M.V. "Yuriy Arshenevskiy" confronted with at 0800 on August 6 might reach 9-11bft, 9-10bft at 1400 on August 6, 11-13bft at 2000 on August 6 and 11-13bft at 0800 on August 7. If taking into account the possible error in satellite retrieval, the vessel might suffer gusts of larger scale.

4. Course of the marine accident concerned

On the voyage concerned, 31 shipments of cargoes (inclusive of the 5 shipments concerned) were shipped onboard from Tianjin Port and Shanghai Port to India. After loading 5 shipments of cargo at Tianjin Port, M.V. "Yuriy Arshenevskiy" arrived at the second loading port Shanghai Port on July 30, 2011, berthed alongside Luojing Terminal at 1200UTC, began the loading operation at 1400UTC and at 0500UCT on August 3 completed the loading operation while the securing operation for the deck cargo continued. According to the accident analysis report issued by Mintaian Property Insurance Surveyors & Loss Adjusters Co., Limited and submitted by Shanghai Hengxin, cargo stevedore, lashing and securing were under the responsibility of Shanghai Hengxin who therefore, employed Shanghai Dongzhao Shipping Services Co., Ltd. to carry out the lashing operation.

East China Adjusters & Surveyors Co., Ltd. was entrusted by GCL to attend the site and supervise the whole loading operation. According to the loading survey report it then issued, the holds where the cargo concerned was loaded and stowed were in serviceable condition, and "all cargoes were in general good condition except scratched and rusted on surface. However, a few of steel jibs was packed weakly and loose wooden frames and most of steel jibs were no fitted wooden frames including important bottom for favorable stowage on board. And some light steel structures were lashed in the steel jibs in weak condition which is a risk at sea while the ship rowing and pitching during bad weather. So, parts of steel structure were secured with ropes and belts by cargo agent".

The five sets of crawler cranes concerned were loaded and stowed on tween deck No.2, 3 and 4. As was indicated on the deck log book, after completion of loading in each cargo hold, the vessel checked the securing and resolved outstanding issues. Under the voyage concerned, 3,021 tons of ballast water was loaded onboard, the GM of the vessel was 1.75m, and the angle of vanishing stability was larger than 60°.

Since August 2, the vessel began to receive forecast messages on typhoon MUIFA and route recommendation from the American weather routing company AWT ("Applied Weather Technology, Inc."), and the JMH meteorological facsimile chart and the navigation warning on weather conditions from JMA via EGC system. At 1347 (0547UTC) on August 3, the Master emailed Shanghai Hengxin, "stevedores make lashing beautifully but not accordance with good sea practice so for additional lashing according to our requirements take a more time", moreover the typhoon MUIFA was expected to arrive at NE of Taiwan Island on August 5, so if the vessel sailed on August 3, the vessel was expected to be at that area on August 5 also. In view of the above, the Master recommended the vessel stayed at Shanghai Port for two more days to avoid the typhoon. At 1458, Shanghai Hengxin replied: they agreed with the Master's recommendation, but since the port did not allow vessel's berthing, they instructed to shift M.V. "Yuriy Arshenevskiy" to anchorage for two days to avoid the typhoon and informed the lashing company to further lash and secure the deck cargo. At 1840UTC of August 3, M.V. "Yuriy Arshenevskiy" berthed at Wusong Anchorage No.5. At 2245UTC, 8 workers embarked onboard to continue the securing of the deck cargo. At 0300UTC of August 4, the C/O checked the securing conditions and resolved the outstanding issues; at 0700UTC, stevedores completed the cargo securing and left the vessel.

At 1216 (0416UTC) of August 4, the Master emailed Shanghai Hengxin, informing that the lashing operation had been completed at 0400UTC, requesting to further stay at Shanghai anchorage waiting for better weather, and seeking for the charterers' opinions on sailing. At 1432 of August 4 (0632UTC), the Master informed Shanghai Hengxin that according to the latest meteorological forecast, typhoon MUIFA would reach the area near Shanghai from August 6 to 7 and advised the charterers to require the agent at port to arrange pilotage service at night to proceed to the north of Cheju Island for typhoon avoidance. Shanghai Hengxin replied at 1711 of the same day that since the pilot schedule was very tight, it was finally fixed that the pilot would embark onboard the next day, stating "please make full arrangement for departure tomorrow morning", and asserting "heading to north of Cheju is Ok. It's a good plan" while pointing out "how to navigate depends on you. But safety firstly. Please always keep safe distance to the typhoon".

At 0722UTC of August 5, M.V. "Yuriy Arshenevskiy" heaved up the anchors. At 1300UTC, M.V. "Yuriy Arshenevskiy" adjusted her course to 61° and proceeded to Cheju Island. At 1610UTC of August 5, M.V. "Yuriy Arshenevskiy", sailing against northeast wind at the speed of 11m/s (6bft), rolled from side to side with the amplitude from 10°-12°. Under such circumstance, the coil pipes loaded in a steel packaging (crates) on top of the cover of hold No.2 were moving about (the whole pile) in line with the motion of the vessel and secured by the crew with the iron chains. To reduce rolling for better operation on deck, the course heading of 90° has been taken and was then adjusted to 75° at 2000UTC, proceeding to Cheju Island for avoiding typhoon.

From August 6 to 7, M.V. "Yuriy Arshenevskiy" met with typhoon MUIFAin a short distance. According to the deck log book, the videos taken onboard, and the real-time "report every four hours" made by M.V. "Yuriy Arshenevskiy" to the shipowner MSCO, at 0400UTC of August 6, "the chains installed by the crew gave given way and are ripped off", "to ensure the safety of the crew the load on cover No.2 has not been reinforced as the pile may fall apart"; at 0800UTC, "the load on cover No.2 has shifted as a result of rolling"; at 0900UTC, "the deck crew has proceeded to fasten the deck load on the cover of hold No.2 under the guidance of the first mate"; at 1600UTC, "the deck crew has completed fastening the deck load"; at 1620UTC, the load on hold cover No.2 has almost completely fallen down overboard and the vessel has sustained damage. At 1650UTC, the load from hold covers No.1 and 3 has fallen overboard and the load on hold cover No.5 has fallen apart. At 2120UTC, the hook attached to the deck got ripped off and the derrick of cargo crane 2A was swiveled toward the starboard together with the cabin. At 2400UTC, very frequent squalls during which it is not possible to measure the wind scale as the anemometer scale stopped at 36 m/s (12-13bft approximating to 13bft); the vessel speed periodically drops to 0 knots. At 0400UTC of August 7, squalls were occurring every 5-10 minutes and the vessel was rolling up to 40-45°, reducing the speed down to 0 knots; "during around 30 minutes, the vessel could not get out of that resonant rolling due to the great waves". At 0425UTC, the load from cover No.4 has fallen overboard almost entirely. The load on hold cover No.5 has completely fallen apart. The waves are up to 12 meters high. The wind is over 50 m/s (15-16bft approximating to 16bft). From afternoon of August 6 to noon of August 7, M.V. "Yuriy Arshenevskiy" adjusted the speed of her main engine and her course at times so as to avoid resonant rolling.

According to the deck log book, from August 6 to 7, 2011, the position of the vessel, her distance to the typhoon center (calculated on the basis of the actual position of typhoon center and the vessel position), the vessel's rolling amplitude and the cargo damage extent were as follows:

Time (GMT)	Distance to typhoon center (km)	Wind direction (°)/speed (m/s)/ scale (bft)	Rolling (°)	Remarks
061200	429	100/30/11	20	
061400	388	100/30/11		
061600	375	080/35/12	25	The deck cargo on the cover of hold No.2 shook.
061620	358	090/36/12	45-48	The deck cargo on the cover of hold No.2 fell overboard.
061650	362	080/36/12	45	The deck cargo on the cover of hold covers No.1 and 3 fell overboard and those on hold cover No.5 fell apart.
062000	322	090/38/13	30-35	One deck cargo on hold cover No.4 slid through the vessel.
062400	300	120/36/12	35	The vessel sailed at a standstill.
070400	262	160/40-50/15	40-45	The vessel sailed at a standstill.
070425	260	160/50/15	50	
070800	275	160/40/13	40	

(continued)

(continued)

Time (GMT)	Distance to typhoon center (km)	Wind direction (°)/speed (m/s)/ scale (bft)	Rolling (°)	Remarks
071200	374	190/20/8	35	
071600	438	180/18/8	10-15, 30 on resonant rolling	Passing the squally weather

5. Stay of M.V. "Yuriy Arshenevskiy" at Xiamen Port

At 0601 of August 7, the Master of M.V. "Yuriy Arshenevskiy" emailed to Kings Ocean, Shanghai Hengxin and MSCO, notifying that cargo on hatch covers No.1-4 fell overboard and got lost, and the cargo on hatch cover No.5 was partially damaged which also caused damage to the vessel. On August 9, M.V. "Yuriy Arshenevskiy" was instructed by "Shanghai Hengxin to "urgently sail to Xiamen Port. We will inform the agent arrange your vessel to berth and arrange lashing workers to do re-lashing for the cargo in holds". On August 10, the vessel arrived at Xiamen Port. On August 11, the Master submitted the sea protest to MSA Xiamen. From August 10 to14, M.V. "Yuriy Arshenevskiy" berthed alongside Modern Terminal of Xiamen Port to check the cargo damage and do the re-lashing work; since August 14, the vessel was anchored at Anchorage No.4 of Xiamen Port for matters subsequent to the accident.

During the period when M.V. "Yuriy Arshenevskiy" berthed at Xiamen Port, surveyors appointed by some of the cargo interests embarked onboard to carry out on-site inspection.

On August 24, Xiamen Maritime Court arrested M.V. "Yuriy Arshenevskiy" at the application of the outsider Sany Heavy Industry Co., Ltd. At the application of Hunan Zoomlion, continual arrest of M.V. "Yuriy Arshenevskiy" was granted on October 31, 2011. When the Plaintiff was negotiating with MSCO in respect of the LOU, the Plaintiff's agent *ad litem* repeatedly represented the requirement to redirect the vessel to Shanghai Port or Xiamen Port for discharge, inspection and disposal of the cargo concerned upon her release, and clearly advised "should the vessel proceed to Indian ports as the owners insist for the time being, a number of unforeseeable eventualities may readily occur to the catastrophic effect", "as the Indian consignee may refuse to take delivery of damaged cargo, and India has no technical conditions to repair the cargo and dispose of the residual value of the cargo. In order to make a more reasonable disposal of the cargo, our clients suggest the shipowner to direct the vessel back to the loading port for discharge of the damaged cargo."

During the vessel's stay at Xiamen Port, MSCO ever applied to competent department for cargo discharge and inspection, but due to failure to obtain approval from the local customs, the cargo concerned could not be discharged at Xiamen

Port. On the evening of November 1, 2011, the co-insurers' agent informed MSCO's agent by email, "Shanghai Customs had agreed re-import of the damaged cargo. In addition, Sany Heavy Industry Co., Ltd. (owner of the cargo not involved in the subject case) had found a suitable discharge terminal at Shanghai. Given the above two factors, it is reasonable and feasible for the vessel to proceed to Shanghai for cargo discharge after her release." The next day, M.V. "Yuriy Arshenevskiy" left Xiamen Port and continued to sail to India after her arrest was lifted.

6. Cargo losses, residual value disposal and other expenses

As was indicated on the Crawford survey report, on December 5, 2011, M.V. "Yuriy Arshenevskiy" berthed at Mundra Port "as the receiver refused to get the material unloaded at the port, vessels returned to sea." After the permission was granted, the vessel berthed alongside the terminal again on February 31, 2012. The cargo (including one set of QUY260 crawler crane concerned) was removed from the vessel to jetty from February 14, 2012 to February 20, 2012 and then shifted to storage yard at Mundra which was about 5 km from the port. On February 27, 2012, the vessel berthed at Mumbai Port and began the discharge operation in connection with the remaining 4 sets of crawler cranes (1 set of QUY260, 2 sets of QUY130 and 1 set of QUY80 crawler cranes), which was not completed until March 5. From the two inspections respectively at Mundra Port and Mumbai Port, it can be found the main machines of the five sets of crawler cranes concerned "almost become total loss", with the other parts such as jib sections damaged to varying extent and the 2 sets of QUY70 crawler cranes not involved in the subject case not obviously damaged.

From March 17 to 23, 2012, Hunan Zoomlion assigned personnel to India to evaluate the cargo losses together with the surveyors appointed by the co-insurers, and by comparison of the import customs clearance plus terminal charges and the freight for back shipment to China, and taking into consideration the limited conditions of India premise and inspection equipment, decided to carry the 5 sets of damaged crawler cranes to Chinese factories for comprehensive inspection and assessment.

From May 21 to 25, 2012, the 4 sets of damaged crawler cranes were loaded onboard M.V. "CARRARA CASTLE" at Mumbai Port. On June 9 of the same year, the other set of damaged crawler crane concerned was shipped onboard M.V. "CARRARA CASTLE" and shipped back to Shanghai. The parties concerned confirmed in the process of loading operation, damage to the QUY70 crawler crane not involved in the subject case happened while during the voyage for back shipment, it encountered the typhoons SAOLA and HAIKUI, causing the cargo concerned arrive at Luojing Terminal of Shanghai till August 9.

From August 9 to 13, 2012, the surveyors appointed by the co-insurers and the engineer of Zoomlion Heavy, after the cargo concerned was discharged at Shanghai Port, carried out a second cargo inspection through which it was concluded part of the jib sections did not have salvage value and was determined as constructive total loss. On November 15, 2012, China Certification & Inspection Group Hunan Co.,

Ltd. issued *Inspection Certificate*, indicating its surveyor attended Luojing Terminal and carried out on-site inspection into the 7 sets of crawler cranes (including the 2 sets of QUY70 crawler cranes not involved in the subject case) of Zoomlion Heavy back shipped, and found the main parts of the 7 sets of crawler cranes all seriously damaged, with the total residual value adjusted as RMB3,567,563. On November 6, the cargo was cleared by Shanghai Customs. On November 7, Hunan Zoomlion International Trade Co., Ltd. and Aspen International Logistics (Shanghai) Co., Ltd. signed the sale and purchase contract on aforementioned part of jib sections of damaged crawler cranes becoming constructive total loss and on November 10, further signed the document of "supplementary clause on weight", specifying the purchase price was RMB60,160. The remaining parts were carried to Zoomlion Heavy in Changsha City of Hunan for inspection and testing. Upon assessment, it was found that the repair costs of the remaining jib sections, main machines, counterweights, lifting hooks, toolkits of the 5 sets of damaged crawler cranes concerned were higher than the residual value, having constituted constructive total loss. After obtaining the co-insurers' approval, Hunan Zoomlion released the "notice on auction of 5 damaged crawler cranes from Zoomlion". On January 28, Hunan Zoomlion and Shenmu Nengwen Machinery Lifting Service Co., Ltd. signed *Purchase Confirmation on Goods Bid*, according to which Hunan Zoomlion shall sell the 5 sets of damaged crawler cranes at RMB5,000,000.00.

In March 2013, Shanghai Customs levied import duty in sum of RMB217,194.96 and import VAT in sum of RMB498,462.43 on the 5 sets of crawler cranes re-imported. In addition, in connection with the application to Xiamen Maritime Court for ship arrest, and the stay in India and back shipment of the cargo concerned, Hunan Zoomlion and its affiliated company also paid the application fee RMB5,000 for maritime preservation, ocean freight and costs for measurement survey and pre loading inspection in sum of USD306,400 incurred in India as well as costs in sum of USD240,025.78 incurred at Mumbai Port and Mundra Port, India, costs incurred at Shanghai Port totaling RMB403,606, and costs for carrying back to factory by land totaling RMB670,000.

7. Relationship between Hunan Zoomlion and the cargo concerned, and the cargo value

The 5 sets of crawler cranes are the cargo under three sales and purchase contracts, whose seller, according to the contracts, is all Zoomlion HK. Specifically, 2 sets of QUY260 crawler cranes are the cargo under the contract No.ZL-CR-EX-1105101 which specifies the buyer is Larsen & Toubro Limited and the contractual unit price USD1,128,710; 2 sets of QUY130 crawler cranes are the cargo under the contract No.ZL-CR-EX-1105102 which specifies the buyer is Ideal Movers (P) Ltd. and the contractual unit price USD532,000; 1 set of QUY80 crawler crane was the cargo under the contract No.ZL-CR-EX-1106177 and the contractual unit price USD315,120. Both of the latter two contracts define the word "affiliate" in their definition clause and specifies "for the purpose of this contract, when referred to one party, its affiliates are included"; moreover, under the appendix 1 to the two contracts, technical service is provided in the name of "ZOOMLION". Also, the seller under the appendix 2 to the contract No.ZL-CR-EX-1106177 is Hunan Zoomlion.

On July 28, 2011, the cargo concerned made export declaration to Wusong Customs of Shanghai Port, according to which, the export date is August 3, 2011, the operating unit and the shipping unit are both Hunan Zoomlion, the payment term is CIF, the cargo unit price was USD1,038,413.20, USD489,440 and USD289,910.40 respectively. The total value of the cargo concerned as declared to the customs was USD3,345,616.80.

On September 30, 2011, Hunan Zoomlion and Zoomlion HK jointly issued *Letter of Statement*, stating: I. Hunan Zoomlion is the owner of the cargo concerned as well as the contractual shipper and cargo-delivering shipper under the concluded contract of carriage of goods by sea, enjoying the full and sole entitlement to the cargo concerned. II. Zoomlion HK had acted as the contracting agent of Hunan Zoomlion to conclude the sale and purchase contracts with the cargo buyers and the final rights and interests under the contracts should be enjoyed by Hunan Zoomlion. III.Although in the B/Ls issued by Union Ocean for and on behalf of Shanghai Hengxin, Zoomlion HK. was indicated as the shipper therein, Hunan Zoomlion lawfully held these B/Ls and Zoomlion HK agreed to transfer all their rights and interests under the B/Ls (if any) to Hunan Zoomlion.

In connection with the back shipment of the cargo concerned to Shanghai, the straight B/L format of the outsider Navalmaer (UK) Ltd. was used under which the shipper is Zoomlion Trade (India) Private Limited and the consignee is Hunan Zoomlion.

8. Relationships under insurance contracts and payment of insurance indemnities

According to *Coinsurance Agreement* and *Supplementary Agreement on Coinsurance* signed by and among Zurich China, Ping An Hunan and Sunshine Hunan, and the goods in transit policy No.BJMC0710030041 (namely coinsurance policy) jointly issued by the said three parties on August 18, 2010, the said three parties were the co-insurers for the goods in transit of Zoomlion, amongst which Zurich China acted as the leading insurer, undertaking a coinsurance proportion of 50%, and was "entitled to take full responsibility to act for and on behalf of the three coinsurance parties to deal with daily businesses with the intermediary and the insured in light of this coinsurance agreement and the insurance policy"; Ping An Hunan and Sunshine Hunan undertook a coinsurance proportion of 30% and 20% respectively; the coinsured was Hunan Zoomlion, Mobile Crane Branch of Zoomlion Heavy and its subsidiary, associated and affiliated and interrelated companies, and joint ventures in which it now has or hereafter may have a direct or indirect insurable interest and other entities for whom they may have instructions to insure or deem themselves responsible to insure, as their respective interests may appear; the packing shall be "industry standard packing"; conditions of insurance includes institute cargo clauses A (1982) and prescribe "'English law and practice' in the law and practice clause shall be modified to be 'Chinese law and practice'";

under the "special conditions" clause, it is warranted by the insured that "...2.4 the subject matter insured is in perfect condition and is properly packed as from the time of attachment of this insurance". For the purpose of *Coinsurance Agreement*, the insurance period is from August 1, 2010 to July 31, 2011 which is further extended to December 31, 2011 by the *Supplementary Agreement on Coinsurance*.

As is shown by the evidence available, from July 2012 to August 2013, the co-insurers paid insurance indemnities totaling USD3,370,000 to the account of Hunan Zoomlion and Zoomlion Heavy in 11 instalments based on their respective coinsurance proportion. As was indicated by the claim computation form of marine transportation cargo insurance concerned, the aforementioned insurance indemnities includes the cargo insurance amount USD4,000,194, 90% of costs for measurement survey/pre loading inspection in amount of USD276,400, 90% of costs incurred at Mumbai Port and Mundra Port, India in sum of USD216,515, costs incurred at Shanghai Port in sum of USD63,561 (equal to RMB403,606), less the amount of cargo residual value USD812,225 (equal to RMB5,060,160) and the deductibles USD374,445 as re-negotiated between both parties. Hunan Zoomlion confirmed receipt of all of the said insurance indemnities and executed the subrogation receipt to the co-insurers.

The court holds, this case is a case regarding dispute over contract of carriage of goods by sea with foreign elements. As to the applicable law in this case, the four Plaintiffs, the Defendant GCL and the Defendant MSCO all agreed with application of the PRC law, but the Defendant Shanghai Hengxin held since the applicable insurance clauses in the insurance contracts chose English law, the English law should be referred to in respect of examination on the subrogation rights of the co-insurers, but agreed with the application of PRC law to other issues in this case. In this regard, the court holds, this case is not a case regarding dispute over insurance contract, so the agreement between the parties on the applicable law in the insurance contracts does not apply to this case, and according to the facts ascertained, it is expressed in the coinsurance agreement that "'English law and practice' in the law and practice clause shall be modified to be 'Chinese law and practice'", so Shanghai Hengxin's argument on law application lacks legal and factual basis and shall not be supported by the court. After comprehensive consideration of the situation of the parties concerned, the merits of the case and the arguments of the parties concerned on the law application, the court determines the PRC law which has closest connection with the dispute of this case as the applicable law.

Firstly, with respect to the causes of cargo damage, the biggest dispute between the Plaintiffs and the Defendants, the four Plaintiffs held the cargo damage should be attributed to seriously improper stowage, lashing and securing of the cargo concerned and the faults of the carrier and the actual carrier in custody of the cargo concerned; while the three Defendants held it was caused by M.V. "Yuriy Arshenevskiy"'s encountering adverse weather and severe sea conditions, and MSCO also held the packing of the cargo concerned was poor.

(1) Regrading to the loading and stowage

The experts appointed by the four Plaintiffs believed that, M.V. "Yuriy Arshenevskiy" sailed with partial load and large amount of deck cargoes in the voyage concerned, making the increase of transverse windage area and a relatively large dynamic heeling angle of the vessel when she sailed in winds and waves; the vertical distribution of cargo weights on decks, tween decks and holds was unreasonable in the voyage concerned (as far as general-cargo ships are concerned, the weight of cargo loaded in lower holds should be 65% of the total weight, and the weight of cargo loaded outside lower holds should be about 35%, in which the weight of cargo on deck should not exceed 10% of the total weight of cargo carried, while the weight ratios on the three positions in the voyage concerned were respectively 60.0%:25.5%:14.5%), failing to duly control the ship stability.

The court holds, in the shipping practice and experience, the vertical distribution of cargo weight is usually one of the stowage principles that needs to be considered for the purpose to control the ship stability under the situation of full load. The experts appointed by the four Plaintiffs also admitted in the experts hearing that the aforesaid ratios had not taken the weight of ballast water into consideration and the ballast water would influence the ratio of vertical weights, thus the said requirement on vertical distribution of cargo weight in stowage should not be absolutized. Especially in the event of partial load and good stability of the vessel, even if the vertical distribution of cargo weight does not fully meet the required ratio, it cannot be simply concluded that there are problems concerning the stowage plan and stowage of the vessel. In the subject case, no evidence could prove that the stability of the vessel at the time of departure involved problems; on the contrary, the voyage concerned was furnished with satisfactory stability calculation, and from the fact that M.V. "Yuriy Arshenevskiy" still could safely sail out after having been attacked by the typhoon at a close distance for a long time and had the cargo onboard seriously damaged, it can be inferred that the vessel actually kept a good stability during the voyage concerned. Therefore, the four Plaintiff's argument in this respect shall not be adopted by the court.

(2) Regarding to lashing and securing

The experts appointed by the four Plaintiffs opined, the cargo in holds and on decks in the voyage concerned was stowed over compactly, which was unfavorable for lashing operation and for the transverse lashing wires to obtain proper vertical securing angle; the lashing company used self-purchased equipment which were not indicated in *Cargo Securing Manual* of M.V. "Yuriy Arshenevskiy", rendering the lashing strength disqualified and the securing operation improper; the cargo in holds and on decks was unreasonably over-stowed; improper stowage and securing of adjacent cargo prejudiced the safety of the stowage and securing of the cargo concerned.

The court holds, the cargo concerned was all stowed in holds, and the cargo on decks outside the subject case whose lashing and securing did not affect the stability in the voyage concerned shall be irrelevant to this case. Judgment as to whether the lashing and securing were questionable or not shall refer to customary and reasonable practices and whether they can adapt to the common perils of sea that may be encountered by the planned cargo in the scheduled voyage, and should not be excessively required to realize the theoretical absolute safety of the cargo onboard totally regardless of the commercial efficiency and economic performance. The most essential and objective judgment on the lasing and securing of general-cargo vessels is the calculation or estimation of the overall securing force, but in the cross-examination of the experts hearing, no experts could obtain the basic data/materials necessary for calculation that can reflect the original securing method to make further effective calculation of the securing force, hence, none of the conclusion of the experts is sufficient to be solely accepted and adopted. Although the Defendants have provided prima facie evidence to prove that the lashing and securing of the cargo concerned conformed to usual requirements for the voyage, the evidence available indicates: 1.the lashing operation of the cargo concerned used self-purchased equipment. According to the shipping practice and experience, it is normal for multi-purpose ships to use lashing equipment not specified in the securing manual. Due to the diversity of cargo shipped, it is neither possible nor economical to require ship owner to equip onboard abundant quantity of various lashing equipment ready for use, particularly the kinds of steel wires which are usually disposable supplies and the accurate quantity needed could not be determined in advance. However, it is important that self-purchased equipment shall go through the authentication of competent classification society. Shanghai Hengxin alleged the securing equipment additionally purchased by the lashing company had passed the authentication of China Classification Society, while they failed to provide any effective evidence to make demonstration during the sufficient time for adducing evidence; therefore, a conclusion unfavorable to the carrier has to be drawn, namely, defects existed in the lashing and securing of the cargo concerned because lashing devices without effective authentication had been adopted; 2. the cargo concerned with irregular shapes was stowed relatively compactly, which was unfavorable to carry out the lashing operation, so relevant measures should have been taken to overcome the existing disadvantages so as to ensure effective lashing of the cargo concerned; 3. M.V. "Yuriy Arshenevskiy" had received the typhoon warning before departure, so she could have reasonably foreseen the poor sailing environment in the voyage concerned, and should have accordingly further increased the lashing standard for the cargo concerned in order to adapt herself to the special sea conditions in the voyage concerned. Nevertheless, no evidence was submitted to manifest that the carrier had taken reasonable measures to overcome or make up for the said defects in the lashing and securing. Therefore, it should be confirmed that the lashing and securing of the cargo concerned was defective for the subject cargo and voyage.

(3) Regarding to whether the carrier took good care of the cargo concerned

The four Plaintiffs took the view that, the stowage, lashing and securing of the cargo were seriously improper, and the carrier and the actual carrier did not care for the cargo with due diligence.

The court holds, the problems about stowage, lashing and securing have been elaborated above. As for whether the carrier had any other negligence in the custody of cargo, in light of the facts ascertained, the cargo concerned was loaded in holds asper the shipper's instructions; after the loading was completed in every shipping space, the vessel checked all and raised improvement requirements; before the vessel's departure at Shanghai Port, the Master of M.V. "Yuriy Arshenevskiy" demanded to postpone the sailing time to reinforce the cargo lashing and securing; and during the voyage, the crew members were twice ordered to strengthen the lashing of deck cargo. What needs to be specially mentioned is that, as recorded in the deck log book, under the circumstance of attack by typhoon MUIFA at a close distance, the crew still took risks to further reinforce the lashing under the order of the C/O at 0900UTC on August 6. Meanwhile M.V. "Yuriy Arshenevskiy" also exercised good seamanship to timely adjust her course and speed to mitigate rolling. Although the crew did not take special care for the cargo concerned during the voyage concerned, since the cargo concerned was stowed in holds, and on one hand, to strengthen lashing in holds under the rough sea condition would endanger the personal safety of the crewmembers, so it was improper to harshly require the crewmembers to care for the cargo regardless of their own safety; on the other hand, there is no proof that can evidence there existed effective measures that M.V. "Yuriy Arshenevskiy" should have taken but failed to reasonably take to avoid or mitigate the cargo damage. Therefore, based on existing evidence, it can be concluded that M.V. "Yuriy Arshenevskiy" had performed the obligation to properly and diligently take care of the cargo concerned in the voyage, and the four Plaintiffs' contention in this respect shall not be adopted by the court.

(4) Regarding to the sea conditions encountered by M.V. "Yuriy Arshenevskiy"

The four Plaintiffs deemed, the vessel did not enter the 10bft wind circle of the typhoon but was just close to the 10bft wind circle, so the largest wind force probably suffered by the vessel was merely 10bft. While the three Defendants contended, the deck log book should be relied upon to ascertain the real-time sea conditions encountered by the vessel, and the vessel had ever come across gust over 12bft and rolling beyond 30°.

The court holds, the deck log book and the videos taken by the crew are the original materials that reflect the sea conditions at the material time and also the prima facie evidence. Unless there is sufficient evidence to prove the contrary, records in the deck log book shall be fully respected. Firstly, the deck log book showed the wind force met by M.V. "Yuriy Arshenevskiy" at the material time already exceeded the highest scale of the wind gauge (36m/s), which means the gust force encountered by the vessel exceeded 12bft; this information itself already indicated the roughness of the sea conditions. Secondly, there was white foam on the sea that affected the visibility as observed from the videos taken by the crewmembers, which, according to the shipping practice and experience, indicated that the real-time wind force reached 11bft or more and the vessel rolled around 35°; further on the basis of the time when the videos were taken, the strength of typhoon was not the strongest at that time, so the video data and the deck log book can basically evidence each other. Thirdly, *Meteorological Message Certification Report* of Shanghai Central Meteorological Station provided by the four Plaintiffs asserted that, M.V. "Yuriy Arshenevskiy" was sailing within the 7bft wind circle on the right semi-circle of typhoon MUIFA but never entered into the 10bft gale wind circle. However, it shall be unscientific to thus deduce that the vessel did not encounter wind force of more than 10bft. The grounds are as below: 1. Typhoons are usually concentric circles of asymmetric structure, and as shown in the materials provided by Shanghai Meteorological Bureau, typhoon MUIFA was significantly asymmetric and the wind force in the right semi-circle where M.V. "Yuriy Arshenevskiy" lied was much greater than that in the left semi-circle. Therefore, it is unprofessional and inaccurate to judge the actual wind force suffered by M.V. "Yuriy Arshenevskiy" merely according to the gale wind circle. 2. It is the concept of mean wind that the forecasts of wind circle radius and wind scales released by the meteorological authority adopted, while in fact gust is usually stronger than mean wind by 1-2 scales or even more. As judged from the ship position, M. V."Yuriy Arshenevskiy" was at the edge of 10bft wind circle when closest to the typhoon center. The information from Shanghai Meteorological Bureau is basically identical to the wind field retrieval result in respect to 2000 on August 6, 2011 and 0800 on August 7, 2011 in the wind force analysis report provided by MSCO, namely, the wind suffered by M.V. "Yuriy Arshenevskiy" was around 11bft. Given the linear relationship between gust and mean wind and the unavailability of the wind field retrieval data under the most adverse sea condition due to technical restrictions, it can be conservatively estimated that the greatest wind force encountered by M.V. "Yuriy Arshenevskiy" reached over 12bft. To sum up, it can be ascertained that M.V. "Yuriy Arshenevskiy" had long suffered the rough sea of wind more than 12bft and rolling above 35° at the material time, so the four Plaintiff's argument in this regard shall not be adopted by the court.

(5) Regarding to poor package

MSCO viewed, according to the records in the loading survey report and the unclean remarks in the mate's receipt, wooden frameworks of the jib sections concerned were slacked, and such cargo was loaded onboard by means of "putting smaller into bigger" only tied by nylon belts, from which "poor package" should be recognized.

The court holds, the Defendants who contended the poor package of the cargo concerned shall adduce evidence to prove the package of the cargo concerned did not comply with the customary and reasonable requirements in the industry. For such heavy and large cargo of heavy machines in the subject case, traditional packing manners by using cartons and bags are improper due to their oversize and irregular shapes, but the method called "nude packing" of lashing, supporting and likewise is usually adopted. In the subject case, no qualified organizations or officers issued any special survey report over the packing problems to determine the poor package of the cargo concerned, while the Defendants also failed to prove the cargo concerned violated the reasonable packing requirements in respect of jib sections in the industry. Instead, as the long-term logistics cooperator of Hunan Zoomlion, GCL confirmed both the main machines and jib sections were packed in manners that were constantly used by the outstanding enterprises in the industry, and the subject cargo damage was irrelevant to the package. GCL also pointed out that, "industry standard packing" was required for the cargo in the goods in transit policy concerned and the insured had already warranted "the subject matter insured is in perfect condition and is properly packed", moreover the insurer after the occurrence of the accident did not raise any challenge to the package, so reasonable package of the cargo concerned could be decided. In addition, package mainly functions to protect the cargo during the loading/discharging, moving, storing and transportation rather than to be compatible with the lashing operation. Arranging proper place for cargo stowage, looking for appropriate securing positions and reinforcing the lashing should all belong to the obligations of the carrier to care for goods in due diligence. Especially in the subject case where Hunan Zoomlion was provided to pay freight by "liner terms", that is, the freight has included charges for stowing, trimming, tallying and lashing, it shall be the carrier's compelling obligation to strengthen the lashing of jib sections according to the foreseeable sea perils in the voyage concerned. Since the deck cargo over the hatch cover No.2 was not included in the cargo concerned and was not jib sections of the crawler cranes, even if any packing problems existed, it was irrelevant to the cargo concerned, it could neither thus deduct that the cargo concerned was poorly packed nor exempt or relieve the carrier's liability for the subject cargo damage. To conclude, no evidence proving there existed any packing problems to the cargo concerned and that the cargo damage was thus caused has been submitted, so the Defendant MSCO's defense in this respect shall not be adopted by the court.

In sum, the court holds the subject cargo damage was co-caused by the defects in the lashing and securing and the adverse sea conditions suffered by the vessel. As for which should be the leading reason, from the following shipment from Xiamen Port to Indian ports, it can be seen that the cargo concerned had been successfully carried to Indian ports after simple adjustment and reinforcement of lashing due to lack of the condition to discharge the cargo and rearrange, stow and lash after the serious damage accident, so it is reasonably inferable that the adverse sea conditions brought about by typhoon MUIFA shall be the uppermost and decisive reason for the cargo damage, though the defects in lashing and securing inevitably turned the lashing structure vulnerable or even prematurely collapsed in front of the adverse sea conditions, and aggravated the damage to the cargo. Through comprehensive consideration of the case, it is decided by the court that 80% of the cargo damage concerned shall be attributed to the adverse sea conditions while 20% to the defects in lashing and securing.

Besides, as for whether the carrier could be exempted from liabilities, the three Defendants contended, the cargo concerned was damaged due to typhoon MUIFA and the carrier could be entitled to exemptions of "acts of god" and "force majeure" in line with Article 51 Paragraph 1 Sub-paragraph 3 of the Maritime Code of the People's Republic of China and Article 311 of the Contract Law of the People's Republic of China; meanwhile, even if the typhoon avoidance measures were considered improper, Article 51 Paragraph 1 Sub-paragraph 1 of the Maritime Code of the People's Republic of China could also be invoked for exemption under the "fault in the navigation or management of the ship". The four Plaintiffs argued, typhoon MUIFA had been fully predicted by the carrier, and was avoidable and conquerable, constituting no acts of god or force majeure; and the Master and the crewmembers had no faults in the ship management inclusive of the decision on typhoon avoidance, thus shall not refer to corresponding exemptions.

The court holds, the Maritime Code of the People's Republic of China has clearly provided for the legal causes from which the loss of or damage to the goods happened during the period of carrier's responsibility shall not be assumed by the carrier; the subject case concerning the dispute over contract of carriage of goods by sea shall give priority to apply the special provision of Article 51 of the Maritime Code of the People's Republic of China on the principle of "applying maritime code to the most". As mentioned above, the court judges that the adverse sea conditions brought about by typhoon MUIFA shall be the main cause for the cargo damage. Typhoon scale forecast is a difficult problem commonly recognized all over the world, and there are many uncertain factors that will affect the typhoon movement, thus it is impossible to forecast typhoon very precisely on the basis of current technology. The wind and wave arising from the strong typhoon directly affecting the sea surface will constitute tremendous threat to the ship safety. Even those ships taking shelter in anchorages could not make sure everything will be sound under the attack of typhoon. Facing the threat of typhoon, ships could only take as reasonable typhoon avoidance as possible to avert or mitigate the damage to the most extent. As stated in the preceding, current evidence indicates that M.V. "Yuriy Arshenevskiy" had long encountered winds of over 12bft and rolling high than 35° at the material time, and the ECSFC report submitted by the four Plaintiffs also deemed M.V. "Yuriy Arshenevskiy" may suffer waves in height of 7-9m, while for most ships sailing at sea, waves in height over 6m can be a threat, and even for the large vessels on the ocean, 7-8m high waves and surges over 9m will also become disastrous. Therefore, the court holds, the adverse sea conditions to that extent suffered by M.V. "Yuriy Arshenevskiy" belongs to abnormal perils of sea and shall constitute such "perils of sea" in the nature of "acts of god" under the Maritime Code of the People's Republic of China, so the carrier may be legally exempted from the liability for the damage thus caused.

The court further holds, it is a common sense that errors would exist in typhoon forecast, and direction changes and speed increases are normal features of typhoons. The EGC used by M.V. "Yuriy Arshenevskiy" also gave reminders in this regard, so when choosing measures for typhoon avoidance, masters shall take reasonable consideration of such errors in typhoon forecast and make such a decision that could ensure the safety of the vessel, persons and the cargo to the largest extent rather than place the hopes on just passing by the typhoon. It is just because of this that masters usually take relatively conservative measures in avoiding typhoon which are even unreasonable or unnecessary in the opinions of non-professional persons. In the subject case, the Master's decision to reinforce the lashing while taking shelter at the anchorage after M.V. "Yuriy Arshenevskiy" completed loading at Shanghai Port is worth appreciation. But two days later when the typhoon was obviously turning its direction, the Master's choice to depart towards the northeast of Cheju Island for typhoon avoidance was not diligent but even a bit risky, which finally caused the vessel exactly entering the right semi-circle, namely the dangerous semi-circle of the typhoon center. At that time, it should be best to remain anchoring inside the port for sheltering typhoon, as a result of which the cargo damage concerned may be mitigated or even avoided. However, the Master has the "sole discretion" over the problems concerning the ship safety, that is, no matter the Master makes the decision as per whose instruction, to satisfy whose requirement, by adopting whose recommendation or upon the resolution of a meeting, once the Master determines, the decision will be deemed as the independent discretion of the Master himself. Although the Master had faults in deciding how to avoid the typhoon, such faults shall be deemed as the fault of the Master in navigation or management of the ship pursuant to the provision of Article 51 Paragraph 1 Sub-paragraph 1 of the Maritime Code of the People's Republic of China for which the carrier may be exempted from liability.

Besides, with respect to whether or not M.V. "Yuriy Arshenevskiy" was seaworthy during the voyage involved, which is relevant to the liability exemption issue, the four Plaintiffs held the cargo stowage, lashing and securing was seriously improper and that the carrier and actual carrier failed to duly care for the cargo concerned, which caused the vessel's unseaworthiness.

The court holds, according to Article 47 of the Maritime Code of the People's Republic of China which provides: "the carrier shall, before and at the beginning of the voyage, exercise due diligence to make the ship seaworthy, properly man, equip and supply the ship and to make the holds, refrigerating and cool chambers and all other parts of the ship in which goods are carrier, fit and safe for their reception, carriage and preservation", these are legal obligations upon the carrier (including the actual carrier) for ship seaworthiness and are also preconditions for the carrier to apply for liability exemption. When M.V. "Yuriy Arshenevskiy" departed from Shanghai performing the carriage involved, all the relevant ship certificates carried on board were in their validity period and in conformity with relevant requirements; meanwhile, by comparison with the certificate of minimum safety manning, the crew name list and the crew's competency certificates on board M.V. "Yuriy Arshenevskiy", the crew manning of the vessel was also in conformity with relevant requirements; the cargo concerned was stowed in the cargo holds as per the shipper's request, and according to the loading survey report, the holds where the cargo concerned was loaded and stowed were in serviceable condition; besides, as mentioned above, M.V. "Yuriy Arshenevskiy" was of good stability and the Defendants have fulfilled their obligation to submit prima facie evidence to prove the vessel's seaworthiness. To the contrary, the four Plaintiffs failed to provide comprehensive and effective contrary evidence, so the four Plaintiff's argument in this regard shall not be adopted by the court.

To conclude, as to the part of cargo losses caused by the vessel's encountering the typhoon MUIFA in near distance due to the Master's hasty decision to leave Shanghai Port, the carrier may also enjoy liability exemption according to the law. The three Defendants' defense in this part is partly adopted by the court.

Furthermore, regarding to whether or not the Defendants improperly enlarged the losses. The four Plaintiffs held that it was extremely unreasonable for M.V. "Yuriy Arshenevskiy" to sail to India after her stay in Xiamen Port. The carrier had a gross negligence for doing so and it should be liable for the enlarged losses caused hereby. GCL also considered M.V. "Yuriy Arshenevskiy"'s continuing the voyage caused a set of problems for the consequent handling of the accident, and immense obstacles for recognizing the losses. MSCO defended that during the period when M.V. "Yuriy Arshenevskiy" stayed in Xiamen Port, the shipowner had exerted its best efforts to strive for discharge of cargo at ports in China, but due to objective constraints, M.V. "Yuriy Arshenevskiy" had no choice but to continue her voyage to India. The shipowner had no fault in this respect.

The court holds that, the current evidence can prove that MSCO has endeavored to discharge cargo at Xiamen Port. It is due to the customs supervision and control that the damaged cargo cannot be discharged at Xiamen Port. This result is neither caused by any of the Defendants, nor any of their employees or agents, and it cannot be ascribed to any of the Defendants. In addition, the cargo concerned is just 5 out of 31 cargoes carried on M.V. "Yuriy Arshenevskiy". If the vessel sailed back to Shanghai Port, there would be also a lot of uncertainties. It would not only increase the carrier's legal risk for liability of breach of contract, but might further enlarge the losses of other cargo owners. Therefore, M.V. "Yuriy Arshenevskiy"'s continuing the voyage as per charterer's instruction does not have any significant fault. The subsequent logistic costs incurred to Hunan Zoomlion, namely the ocean freight, costs for measurement survey and pre loading inspection in sum of USD306,400 and the port ground fee in sum of USD240,025.78, all of which were incurred in India, are not enlarged losses caused by the three Defendants' misconducts, but losses which failed to be mitigated even though the carrier had exercised due diligence to assist Hunan Zoomlion in mitigation after the accident concerned caused by perils of sea. Therefore, Hunan Zoomlion cannot claim the carrier for compensation for such costs. For the same reason, the ground fee at Shanghai Port in sum of RMB403,606, the road freight for carriage of cargo back to factory in sum of RMB670,000, import duty in sum of RMB217,194.96 and the import VAT in sum of RMB498,462.43 due to expiration of one-year time limit for export rejects shall be also born by Hunan Zoomlion. Furthermore, the first two items of logistics costs would have incurred even if the cargo was transported back to discharge at Shanghai Port as per Hunan Zoomlion's instruction, and the last two items of duties have exceeded the scope of costs which can be reasonably foreseen according to Article 113 of the Contract Law of the People's Republic of China. Therefore, the court does not support the four Plaintiffs' claim in respect of these four items of losses.

Fourthly, as for whether or not Hunan Zoomlion is the qualified Plaintiff, GCL held that the owner of the cargo concerned is Zoomlion HK, so Hunan Zoomlion has no right to claim for cargo loss against the three Defendants in this case; Shanghai Hengxin considered that neither under the annual transportation agreement, nor under the House B/Ls or the Master B/Ls did the four Plaintiffs have a right to sue against Shanghai Hengxin; MSCO held that Hunan Zoomlion was neither the shipper nor the obligee of the cargo concerned, so it was not the qualified Plaintiff. The three Defendants also held that since Hunan Zoomlion had confirmed to transfer all their right to claim to the insurers, they had already lost the right to sue.

The court holds that, the transfer of cargo ownership is closely connected to the agreement in the sales contract between the parties. In order to prevent involvement of complicate disputes over sales contracts into carriage contract relationships, and also to increase the certainty of legal relationships in transportation, the litigious rights of the cargo interests in disputes arising from contracts of carriage of goods by sea does not need to be connected to their ownership of the cargo. The only thing Hunan Zoomlion needs to prove is that it legally has the right to control the cargo. According to the ascertained facts, Hunan Zoomlion signed a transportation agreement with GCL for the carriage of the cargo concerned, and in the light of the whole process of the carriage and the back shipment to China, Hunan Zoomlion is the party who delivers the cargo concerned to GCL, who is the business unit and consignor stated on customs declaration forms, and also the consignee stated on the B/L for the back shipment to China, and Hunan Zoomlion is the only party who sent instructions to the carrier in respect of the cargo concerned, and also the only party who claimed against the carrier in respect of the cargo concerned (the right of the co-insurers was subrogated from Hunan Zoomlion). Moreover, the seller defined in the sales contracts concluded Hunan Zoomlion's associated enterprises, and the named seller Zoomlion HK has also declared that Hunan Zoomlion has the full rights of the cargo. Therefore, Hunan Zoomlion has the right, as obligee of the cargo concerned, to raise a claim against the carrier on the basis of the contract of carriage of goods by sea. Although part of the costs in this case were paid by Hunan Zoomlion's associated enterprise, this internal relationship of payment and settlement between Hunan Zoomlion and their associated enterprise does not affect legal status and rights of Hunan Zoomlion in this case, and in the external relationship, these costs should be deemed to be paid by Hunan Zoomlion itself. Furthermore, although Hunan Zoomlion has obtained the indemnity from co-insurers, there is still a difference between the indemnity amount and their claim amount, and according to Article 95 of the Special Maritime Procedure Law of the People's Republic of China: "...where the losses of the insured caused by a third party cannot be fully covered by insurance indemnity, the insurer and the insured may act as co-Plaintiffs to claim compensation against the third party". As to whether these uncovered losses exist, or whether these losses should be supported is a question of another respect and has no relevancy with the litigious right of Hunan Zoomlion. Therefore, the court does not accept the three Defendants' defense in this respect.

Fifthly, as to whether or not the co-insurers are qualified Plaintiffs and whether or not their claims have exceeded the limitation of period for claims, the three Defendants held that, Hunan Zoomlion did not have any insurable interests in the cargo concerned, the indemnity made by co-insurers to Hunan Zoomlion was improper, there were defects in the source and basis of co-insurers' right of subrogation, so they cannot become qualified Plaintiffs according to the law. Shanghai Hengxin also held that the limitation period for claims by co-insurers had already exceeded. Furthermore, Shanghai Hengxin and MSCO held that the insurance policy concerned was issued by Zurich China independently, so Ping An Hunan and Sunshine Hunan had no right to sue.

The court holds that, it can be seen from the emails from the agent of co-insurers to the agent of MSCO after the accident concerned and the Crawford survey report submitted by the four Plaintiffs that, Zurich China has made the insurance adjustment and settlement towards the cargo damage to Hunan Zoomlion on the basis of five insurance certificates No.MIA0010018BG-0369/0375/0376/0370/0367. This procedure corresponds with the agreement in the co-insurance agreement that Zurich China has the full right to deal with daily businesses with the insured. However, this set of insurance certificates do not have the signature and stamp of the insured, and there is no evidence proving they have been accepted by Hunan Zoomlion. They cannot be deemed as "insurance certificates issued by the insurer separately" which is "at the request of the insured" as stipulated in Article 232 of the Maritime Code of the People's Republic of China. Therefore, this set of insurance certificates cannot deny the insurance contractual relationship proved by the goods in transit policy issued by co-insurers on August 18, 2010. According to the goods in transit policy, the insured is Hunan Zoomlion and other parties concerned such as the associated companies. Current evidence has proved that Zurich China, Ping An Hunan and Sunshine Hunan have paid the indemnity amounts to the insured as per their co-insurance proportions respectively, so they all have the right of subrogation against the responsible parties concerned in the limit of their indemnity amount according to the law. Moreover, it is stipulated in Article 14 of the Provisions of the Supreme People's Court on Several Issues about the Trial of Cases concerning Marine Insurance Disputes that: "the people's court that accepts a case involving any dispute over the insurer's exercise of the right of subrogation to claim for compensations shall only try the legal relationship between the third party that caused the insurance accident and the insured". Accordingly, there is no need to make a substantive judgment towards the insurance contractual relationship between co-insurers and the insured Hunan Zoomlion in this case. The three Defendants' defense, which alleged that the indemnities of co-insurers have exceeded their insurance responsibility and the insured has no right to accept the indemnity, does not affect co-insurers' right of subrogation. In addition, according to Article 15 of the Provisions of the Supreme People's Court on Several Issues about the Trial of Cases concerning Marine Insurance Disputes, in cases where the insurer, after obtaining the right of subrogation to claim for compensations, claims for the interruption of the limitation of actions for the reason that the insured filed a lawsuit, the people's court shall support the claim. In this case, the co-insurers joined the actions taken by the insured against a third party, the limitation period of actions had been interrupted, and had not been recalculated yet. Therefore, the claim of co-insurers does not exceed its limitation period of action. The court does not accept the three Defendants' defense in this respect.

Sixthly, regarding to whether or not GCL should be liable to compensate for the cargo damage, the four Plaintiffs alleged that GCL was the contractual carrier of the carriage concerned, but GCL held that the relationship between Hunan Zoomlion and GCL was a relationship of shipping agency agreement, and the annual transportation agreement had been unilaterally cancelled by Hunan Zoomlion before the carriage concerned. GCL was only a shipping agent of the transportation in this case.

The court holds that, this case is a dispute arising from contract of carriage of goods by sea, and the four Plaintiffs clearly stated to claim against GCL for the latter's liability as a carrier according to the annual transportation agreement. This agreement is between Hunan Zoomlion and GCL. Judging from the expressions used in this agreement such as "undertake (different from the words 'entrusts...to act as its agent' as used in long-term strategic cooperation transportation agreement) the cargo transportation operation from Shanghai to Mumbai, India", "after the cargo arrives at the destination port, ... If damage or loss of cargo is found to be caused by Party A's (GCL) faults during transportation, all the losses arising therefrom shall be undertaken by Party A", GCL has taken the exclusive right of management for Hunan Zoomlion's logistics to India, and taken the responsibilities as a carrier. Although there are some disputes between the two parties on whether the agreement should be cancelled or performed continuously, the current evidence has shown that the cargo concerned was delivered to GCL by Hunan Zoomlion according to the annual transportation agreement, and GCL never surrendered any acceptable transport documents to Hunan Zoomlion for Hunan Zoomlion to ensure their control over the goods. Therefore, no matter whether the annual transportation agreement had been effectively cancelled or not, the legal status, rights and obligations of both parties in the carriage concerned would be deemed according to the annual transportation agreement if no evidence can prove that GCL's legal status has been changed in this carriage through consensus of both Hunan Zoomlion and GCL. In this case, GCL accepted the cargo concerned, collected freight from Hunan Zoomlion, signed a voyage charterparty with Shanghai Hengxin in its own name and delivered the cargo concerned to the ocean carrier as the shipper. All these conducts correspond with the conduct of a "carrier" defined in the Maritime Code of the People's Republic of China. Therefore, GCL should be deemed as contractual carrier for the cargo concerned in this case, and responsible as a carrier towards Hunan Zoomlion for cargo concerned. It also should have the right to rely on the exemptions stipulated in the Maritime Code of the People's Republic of China, in other words, the liability for the aforesaid 20% cargo damage caused by defects in lashing and securing as determined by the court cannot be exempted by the carrier according to the law, so GCL shall be liable for such 20% loss.

Seventhly, as to whether or not Shanghai Hengxin should be liable to compensate for the cargo damage, the four Plaintiffs contended that Shanghai Hengxin was the actual carrier for the cargo concerned, while Shanghai Hengxin defended that the loading, lashing, securing and discharging of the cargo were just preparatory operations for carriage, so Shanghai Hengxin did not actually perform the carriage of the cargo concerned.

The court holds that, according to the definition of the "actual carrier" in Article 42 of the Maritime Code of the People's Republic of China, "performance of carriage of goods" is the essential requirement to determine an actual carrier, and the actual carrier's control over the cargo and the actual performance of carriage are the fundamental reasons for the law to break the privity of contract and specially stipulate the liability of actual carrier towards cargo owner. Therefore, "performance of carriage" should be explained as to control the vessel, manage the cargo, and personally perform the carriage. Although Shanghai Hengxin has performed cargo operations such as loading, discharging and lashing of the cargo concerned, and "load, handle, stow" is within the carrier's obligations to care for cargo as provided for in Article 48 of the Maritime Code of the People's Republic of China, it cannot be thus considered the one who has done those operations as the carrier or the actual carrier. As one link of the voyage charterparty chain, the loading, discharging and lashing performed by Shanghai Hengxin are not only the performance of their obligations agreed in FTL (abbreviation for "Full Liner Terms", which means the responsibility of loading and discharging is on shipowner's shoulder) in the voyage charterparty between them and GCL, but also the performance of the charterer's obligations on behalf of Hanssy HK in the time charter party between Hanssy HK and Kings Ocean. Since Shanghai Hengxin is neither the owner or bareboat charterer of the vessel, and there is no evidence which can prove their authorization on the issuance of the Master B/Ls, moreover they are not able to control over the vessel or manage the cargo during the actual carriage, as a result, Shanghai Hengxin is not the actual carrier for the cargo concerned. Although the court holds that there are defects in the cargo lashing and securing which is under Shanghai Hengxin's responsibilities, in light of the privity of contract and the legal provision that the carrier should be liable for the whole carriage, GCL as the carrier should compensate the cargo owner in advance, and then recover from Shanghai Hengxin in another claim. Therefore, Shanghai Hengxin shall not be liable for compensation in this case.

Eighthly, as to whether or not MSCO should be liable to compensate for the cargo damage, the four Plaintiffs held MSCO was the actual carrier for the cargo concerned, and that they had a gross negligence on care for cargo and thus should be liable to compensate for the cargo damage. Moreover, MSCO should be liable to compensate for the losses suffered by the legal holder of the B/Ls which was Hunan Zoomlion. However, MSCO defended that the shipowner was not the carrier or the actual carrier for the cargo concerned; and that even if the shipowner was deemed as the actual carrier, it should not be liable for compensation since the cargo damage was caused by perils of sea and poor packing.

The court holds that, MSCO never signed any carriage contract with Hunan Zoomlion, neither did Hunan Zoomlion book any shipping space with or deliver any cargo to MSCO. Although Hunan Zoomlion used to "hold" the Master B/Ls, but since it is not the shipper or consignee described in the B/Ls involved, and the straight B/Ls is non-transferable according to the law, Hunan Zoomlion is not the legal holder even if it possessed the B/Ls. In short, there is no evidence which can prove the existence of contract of carriage of goods by sea between Hunan Zoomlion and MSCO. Moreover, as mentioned above, the cargo damage was caused by adverse sea conditions and the defects of cargo lashing and securing. Although due to the Master's improper method to avoid typhoon, M.V. "Yuriy Arshenevskiy" was attacked by the typhoon in a close distance, MSCO has the right of exemption according to the law. Also, MSCO was not responsible for cargo lashing and securing, and there is also no problem in stowage/securing which would affect the stability and safety of the ship and thus have the shipowner blamed for ultimate responsibility. The current evidence also suggests that, after the completion of loading of each hold, the vessel had checked the condition of lashing and solved the problems founded. The vessel even particularly applied for anchoring in order to strengthen the lashing. Therefore, the ship owner had cautiously and appropriately fulfilled their obligations to care for cargo with due diligence, and should not be liable to compensate for the cargo damage caused by defects in lashing and securing. In addition, the court has determined that the shipowner had no obvious negligence in respect of finishing the planed voyage. Therefore, MSCO should not be liable for compensation in this case. Accordingly, the court does not support the claim in respect of the application fee for vessel arrest in sum of RMB5,000.

Ninthly, as to the amount of cargo losses, the three Defendants defended that, Hunan Zoomlion's carrying the cargo concerned back to China was unreasonable, which made the cargo losses enlarged during the period of its back shipment to China and the consequent processes; the amount of cargo losses should be determined on the basis of its condition in Xiamen Port. It was not objective for Hunan Zoomlion to determine the losses according to the final condition of the cargo when it arrived at Zoomlion Heavy's factory and to handle the salvage value of the cargo unilaterally. In addition, the cargo value should be subject to the value described in the customs declaration forms.

The court holds that, firstly, all the three Defendants failed to submit any explanation in respect of comparison of cargo condition before and after its back shipment to China even on the court's requirement, and there is no sufficient evidence proving the cargo damage has been enlarged substantially in this case. Secondly, it is incautious to determine a constructive total loss without using any relevant inspection equipment to conduct inspection. Hunan Zoomlion's decision to carry the cargo back to China had been confirmed and approved by the surveyor entrusted by insurers and the insurers themselves. In the absence of any sufficient contrary evidence to prove the feasibility and economic advantages of surveying the cargo and dealing with the salvage value in India, the three Defendants' doubts in respect of the back shipment of the cargo concerned to China cannot be supported. Thirdly, the comments from Puri Crawford & Associates India Pvt. Ltd. that the accessories of crawler cranes are repairable cannot deny the conclusion that the cargo concerned constituted conclusive total loss with no repair value after an overall inspection; the actual salvage value of the cargo is much higher that the value assessed in the CCIC inspection certificate, so the conclusion that the losses were enlarged on such basis can hardly be supported. Fourthly, Zoomlion Heavy, as the manufacturer of the crawler cranes concerned, has professional knowledge and relevant qualifications to determine the damage condition of the crawler cranes concerned. Although Zoomlion Heavy and Hunan Zoomlion are interested parties, since it is agreed by all parties in the court hearing that there are very limited numbers of units or institutions which are capable of doing the inspection for this special equipment concerned, the feasibility of letting an independent third party to inspect is objectively limited. Moreover, the surveyor entrusted by the insurers has fully involved in assessment on the cargo damage and the handling of salvage value. The conclusion of conclusive total loss also corresponded with the results of previous inspections. Therefore, the court finds the inspection result and handling of salvage value objective and reasonable. Accordingly, the court does not accept the three Defendants' defense that the back shipment of the cargo concerned to China had enlarged the cargo losses and the assessment amount of losses was not objective. However, the cargo price in sales contract and commercial invoice is different from the price described in the customs declaration forms. Although the four Plaintiffs explained that Hunan Zoomlion understated the cargo value because they could enjoy preferential tax policy for export, but they did not submit any relevant evidential documents. Therefore, this view shall not be supported. Customs declaration forms, as documentary evidence which is recognized and recorded by customs, has a higher probative force on the actual cargo value than the sales contract or commercial invoice which was self-issued. Therefore, the actual value of the cargo at the time of loading should be based on the amount described in the customs declaration forms. Since it is expressed in the customs declaration forms that the trading term is CIF, that is to say, the total price of the cargo described in the customs declaration forms contains the cargo value when loading, insurance fee and the freight. Therefore, the actual value of the cargo is USD3,345,616.80, and the compensation amount should be determined on the basis of such amount. The court accepts the three Defendants' defense on this respect.

Tenthly, with respect to limitation of liability, the three Defendants defended that, even if other defenses could not be supported, they still had the right to apply to the package limitation of liability and the limitation of liability for maritime claims as provided for in the Maritime Code of the People's Republic of China. They also held the limit for package liability should be USD2,584,455.60 (which was 1,711,560 Special Drawing Rights) according to the law. As for the limit of liability for maritime claims in this case, Shanghai Hengxin held it should be determined based on the percentage of the compensation amount as judged in this case in the amount of the total losses caused by the accident. MSCO considered it should be calculated according to the corresponding percentage in the limit of package liability for the cargo loss claim accepted by the courts of China, but in any event the compensation liability for the shipowner to bear would not exceed

USD2,190,390. For this, the four Plaintiffs alleged that, the cargo damage in this case resulted from acts of the carrier done recklessly and with knowledge that such damage would probably result. The carrier had no right to enjoy the limitation of liability.

The court holds that, according to Article 59 and Article 209 in the Maritime Code of the People's Republic of China, the carrier shall not be entitled to the benefit of the limitation of liability provided for in this law if it is proved that the damage of the goods and the loss which caused the claim resulted from an act or omission of the carrier done with the intent to cause such damage or recklessly and with knowledge that such damage would probably result. In this case, there is no evidence which can prove the cargo damage concerned arising from a marine accident is caused by an act or omission of the carrier done with the intent to cause such damage or recklessly and with knowledge that such damage would probably result, therefore, the carrier concerned should have the right to apply to package limitation of liability in respect of compensation for cargo damage. The number of package stated in B/Ls concerned is 176, and the gross weight is 855,780 kg. According to the calculation standard of "666.67 units of account per package, or 2 units of account per kilogram, whichever is the higher", the limit of package liability of the cargo loss in this case shall be 1,711,560 Special Drawing Rights (SDR). And about the limit of liability for maritime claims, since none of the three Defendants constituted a limitation fund for the liability for maritime claims, this question would only be considered on case-by-case basis. The gross tonnage of M.V. "Yuriy Arshenevskiy" is 18,574 tons, so according to the calculation method provided for in Article 210 of the Maritime Code of the People's Republic of China, the limit of liability for maritime claims in this case shall be 3,185,358 SDR.

In this case, since the cargo concerned has constituted a constructive total loss, the amount of cargo loss should be calculated after deducting the salvage value from the actual value of the cargo. The actual value described in the customs declaration forms is USD3,345,616.80. The court accepts the holding of the four Plaintiffs that the losses should be calculated in RMB per the exchange rate of 1:6.4305 between USD and RMB on the date of accident, namely, August 8, 2011, and the amount after exchange is RMB21,513,988.83. After taking off the salvage value of RMB5,060,160, the amount of cargo loss concerned is RMB16,453,828.83. In conclusion, GCL as the carrier should be responsible for 20% of the compensation, which is RMB3,290,765.77. Therefore, this case does not need to refer to limit of liability.

According to the claim computation form of marine transportation cargo insurance, Hunan Zoomlion has been fully indemnified in respect of the cargo loss concerned. Therefore, GCL should compensate the co-insurers in sum of RMB3,290,765.77. According to the respective proportions of their actual indemnity, namely, the coinsurance proportions, Zurich China should receive RMB1,645,382.89, Ping An Hunan RMB987,229.73, and Sunshine Hunan RMB658,153.15 for compensation.

In addition, as to the co-insurers' claim for loss of interests calculated from February 1, 2013 to the effective date of relevant judgment as per the loan interest rate published by the People's Bank of China during the corresponding period, the court holds that, the loss of interest claimed by the co-insurers is the fruits of the insurance indemnities they paid, so it should be calculated from the date of actual payment. Since the co-insurers made 11 separate payment from July 2012 to August 2013, the court considers that the contention of the co-insurers that the interest should be calculated from February 1, 2013 is reasonable and can be supported. And since the aforesaid three Plaintiffs are financial institutions, their request to calculate the interest as per the loan interest rate is reasonable and shall be supported.

According to Article 41, Article 42 Sub-paragraph 1, Article 46 Paragraph 1, Article 51 Paragraph 1 Sub-paragraph 1, Article 51 Paragraph 1 Sub-paragraph 3, Article 54, Article 55 Paragraph 1, Article 55 Paragraph 2 and Article 252 Paragraph 1 of the Maritime Code of the People's Republic of China, Article 64 Paragraph 1 of the Civil Procedure Law of the People's Republic of China, and Article 2 and Article 76 of the Some Provisions of the Supreme People's Court on Evidence in Civil Procedure, the court hereby renders the judgment as follows:

1. The Defendant Shanghai GCL International Co., Ltd. shall, within ten days as of the effective day of this judgment, compensate the Plaintiff Zurich General Insurance Company (China) Limited RMB1,645,382.89, plus the interest thereof (calculated from February 1, 2013 to the date when this judgment comes into effect according to loan interest rate of the same degree announced by the People's Bank of China during the corresponding period);
2. The Defendant Shanghai GCL International Co., Ltd. shall, within ten days as of the effective day of this judgment, compensate the Plaintiff Ping An Property & Casualty Insurance Company of China Ltd. Hunan Branch RMB987,229.73, plus the interest thereof (calculated from February 1, 2013 to the date when this judgment comes into effect according to loan interest rate of the same degree announced by the People's Bank of China during the corresponding period);
3. The Defendant Shanghai GCL International Co., Ltd. shall, within ten days as of the effective day of this judgment, compensate the Plaintiff Sunshine Property & Casualty Insurance Co., Ltd. Hunan Branch RMB658,153.15, plus the interests thereof (calculated from February 1, 2013 to the date when this judgment comes into effect according to loan interest rate of the same degree announced by the People's Bank of China during the corresponding period);
4. Not support the claims made by the Plaintiff Hunan Zoomlion International Trade Co., Ltd.; and
5. Not support the other claims made by the Plaintiffs Zurich General Insurance Company (China) Limited, Ping An Property & Casualty Insurance Company of China Ltd. Hunan Branch and Sunshine Property & Casualty Insurance Co., Ltd. Hunan Branch.

Court acceptance fee in amount of RMB159,743.11, the Plaintiffs Hunan Zoomlion International Trade Co., Ltd., Zurich General Insurance Company (China) Limited, Ping An Property & Casualty Insurance Company of China Ltd.

Hunan Branch and Sunshine Property & Casualty Insurance Co., Ltd. Hunan Branch shall jointly bear RMB126,616.98, and the Defendant Shanghai GCL International Co., Ltd. shall bear RMB33,126.13.

If the Defendant Shanghai GCL International Co., Ltd. fails to fulfill its obligation to make the said payments within the time limit provided by this judgment, the interest shall be double paid for the period of deferred payment according to Article 253 of the Civil Procedure Law of the People's Republic of China.

If not satisfy with this judgment, the Plaintiffs Hunan Zoomlion International Trade Co., Ltd., Zurich General Insurance Company (China) Limited, Ping An Property & Casualty Insurance Company of China Ltd. Hunan Branch and Sunshine Property & Casualty Insurance Co., Ltd. Hunan Branch, and the Defendants Shanghai GCL International Co., Ltd. and Shanghai Hengxin Shipping Co., Ltd. may within fifteen days as of the service of this judgment, and the Defendant Murmansk Shipping Company may within thirty days as of the service of this judgment, submit a statement of appeal to the court, with duplicates in the number of the counterparties, so as to make an appeal before Shanghai High People's Court.

Presiding Judge: QIAN Xu
Acting Judge: YANG Chan
Acting Judge: YANG Fan

May 28, 2014

Clerk: FEI Xiaojun

Appendix: Relevant Law

1. Maritime Code of the People's Republic of China

Article 41 A contract of carriage of goods by sea is a contract under which the carrier, against payment of freight, undertakes to carry by sea the goods contracted for shipment by the shipper from one port to another.

Article 42 For the purpose of this Chapter:

(1) "Carrier" means the person by whom or in whose name a contract of carriage of goods by sea has been concluded with a shipper;

...

Article 46 The responsibilities of the carrier with regard to the goods carried in containers covers the entire period during which the carrier is in charge of the goods, starting from the time the carrier has taken over the goods at the port of loading, until the goods have been delivered at the port of discharge. The responsibility of the carrier with respect to non-containerized goods covers the period during which the carrier is in charge of the goods, starting from the time of loading of the goods onto the ship until the time the goods are discharged therefrom. During the period the carrier is in charge of the goods, the carrier shall be liable for the loss of or damage to the goods, except as otherwise provided for in this Section.

...

Article 51 The carrier shall not be liable for the loss of or damage to the goods happened during the period of carrier's responsibility arising or resulting from any of the following causes:

(1) Fault of the Master, crew members, pilot or servant of the carrier in the navigation or management of the ship;

...

(3) Force majeure and perils, dangers and accidents of the sea or other navigable waters;

...

Article 54 When loss or damage or delay in delivery has happened from causes from which the carrier or his servant or agent is not entitled to exoneration from liability, together with another cause, the carrier shall be liable only to the extent that the loss, damage or delay in delivery is attributable to the causes from which the carrier is not entitled to exoneration from liability; however, the carrier shall bear the burden of proof with respect to the loss, damage or delay in delivery resulting from the other causes.

Article 55 The amount of indemnity for the loss of the goods shall be calculated on the basis of the actual value of the goods so lost, while that for the damage to the goods shall be calculated on the basis of the difference between the value of the goods before and after the damage, or on the basis of the expenses for the repair.

The actual value shall be the value of the goods at the time of shipment plus insurance and freight.

...

Article 252 When the loss of or damage to the subject matter insured within the insurance coverage is caused by a third person, the right of the insured to demand compensation from the third person shall be subrogated to the insured from the time the indemnity is paid.

...

2. Civil Procedure Law of the People's Republic China

Article 64 A party shall have the burden to provide evidence for its claims.

...

3. **Several Provisions of the Supreme People's Court on Evidence in Civil Procedures**

Article 2 The parties concerned shall be responsible for producing Evidence to prove the facts on which their own allegations are based or the facts on which the allegations of the other party are refuted.

Where any party cannot produce evidence or the Evidence produced cannot support the facts on which the allegations are based, the party concerned that bears the burden of proof shall undertake unfavorable consequences.

...

Article 76 Where a party makes statements for its allegations but fails to provide other relevant Evidence, the allegations thereof shall not be recognized, unless the other party so affirms.

Shanghai High People's Court
Civil Judgment

Hunan Zoomlion International Trade Co., Ltd. et al.
v.
Shanghai GCL International Co., Ltd. et al.

(2014) Hu Gao Min Si (Hai) Zhong Zi No.119

Related Case(s) This is the judgment of second instance, and the ruling of first instance and the ruling of retrial are on page 491 and page 600 respectively.

Cause(s) of Action 202. Dispute over contract of carriage of goods by sea or sea-connected waters.

Headnote Affirming lower court decision holding voyage charterer liable for cargo damage under long-term project cargo contracts.

Summary This is an appeal which arises from a dispute over contract of carriage of goods by sea. The Plaintiff Zoomlion and subrogated insurance companies allege that Shanghai GCL, the charterer and Defendant, Shanghai Hengxin and Murmansk should be held jointly liable to indemnify the Plaintiffs for the loss and damage of cargo and other related expenses. Shanghai GCL and Zoomlion had signed a "long-term strategic cooperation transport agreement". The loss happened during a passage under this agreement due to heavy weather. Nevertheless, the goods were brought to India and stored and shipped back to the port of origin later, resulting in more damage to the cargo. The identity of the carrier was disputed and the court held that Shanghai GCL is to be considered the carrier and therefore was the proper Defendant. The court based this on the transport agreement under which the cargo was shipped. The agreement identified Shanghai GCL as the carrier. Also, the court held that carrier Shanghai GCL is not liable for the loss by virtue of the ship's management and operation, as it was found to be adequate in light of the circumstances. However, the carrier Shanghai GCL is liable for the loss caused by the inadequate lashing/ binding of the cargo that happened prior to the storm. The court therefore affirms the original judgment, holding that Shanghai GCL is liable for compensation. Shanghai Hengxin and Murmansk are both held not liable.

Judgment

The Appellant (the Plaintiff of first instance): Zurich General Insurance Company (China) Limited.
Domicile: Room 603B, 605C, 606 and 607A, Floor 6, Office Building F, Phoenix Place, Tower 21, No.A5, Shuguangxili, Chaoyang District, Beijing, China.
Legal representative: HU Xiaoqin, general manager.
Agent *ad litem*: QIU Biaoshan, lawyer of Shanghai All Bright (Shenzhen) Law Offices.
Agent *ad litem*: WANG Yun, lawyer of Beijing Yingke (Shanghai) Law Firm.

The Appellant (the Plaintiff of first instance): Ping An Property & Casualty Insurance Company of China Ltd. Hunan Branch.
Domicile: Floor 1&3, New Age Business Plaza, No.161, Section 1, Furong Middle Road, Kaifu District, Changsha City, Hunan Province, China.
Legal representative: CHENG Xiaozhong, general manager.
Agent *ad litem*: QIU Biaoshan, lawyer of Shanghai All Bright (Shenzhen) Law Offices.
Agent *ad litem*: LI Min, lawyer of Beijing Yingke (Shanghai) Law Firm.

The Appellant (the Plaintiff of first instance): Sunshine Property & Casualty Insurance Co., Ltd. Hunan Branch.
Domicile: Floor 6, Xiangyu Zhongyang Office Building, Wuyi East Road, Furong District, Changsha City, Hunan Province, China.
Legal representative: HU Xiangze, general manager.
Agent *ad litem*: QIU Biaoshan, lawyer of Shanghai All Bright (Shenzhen) Law Offices.
Agent *ad litem*: LI Min, lawyer of Beijing Yingke (Shanghai) Law Firm.

The Appellant (the Defendant of first instance): Shanghai GCL International Co., Ltd.
Domicile: Rm.2601, Baokuang International Building, No.218, Wusong Road, Shanghai City, The People's Republic of China.
Legal representative: WEI Jiajuan, general manager.
Agent *ad litem*: WU Jianhong, lawyer of Shanghai Wintell & Co. Law Firm Ningbo Office.
Agent *ad litem*: CHEN Wei, lawyer of Shanghai Wintell & Co. Law Firm Ningbo Office.

The Respondent (the Defendant of first instance): Shanghai Hengxin Shipping Co., Ltd.
Domicile: Room.131, No.69, Tongzhou Road, Shanghai.
Legal representative: YUE Zhaofeng, general manager.
Agent *ad litem*: REN Yuwei, lawyer of Shanghai Rolmax Law Office.
Agent *ad litem*: HUA Lingling, lawyer of Shanghai Rolmax Law Office.

The Respondent (the Defendant of first instance): Murmansk Shipping Company.
Domicile: 15, Kominterna Street 183038, Murmansk, Russia.
Legal representative: A.M.Medvedev, chairman.
Agent *ad litem*: LI Rongcun, lawyer of Guangdong Wang Jing & Co. (Xiamen) Law Firm.
Agent *ad litem*: CHEN Yongcan, lawyer of Guangdong Wang Jing & Co. (Xiamen) Law Firm.

The Plaintiff of first instance: Hunan Zoomlion International Trade Co., Ltd.
Domicile: No.307, Yinpen South Road, Changsha City, Hunan Province, China.
Legal representative: CHEN Peiliang, general manager.
Agent *ad litem*: QIUBiaoshan, lawyer of Shanghai AllBright (Shenzhen) Law Offices.
Agent *ad litem*: ZHAO Jinsong, lawyer of Shanghai All Bright (Shenzhen) Law Offices.

Dissatisfied with the Civil Judgment (2012) Hu Hai Fa Shang Chu Zi No.1208 rendered by Shanghai Maritime Court in respect of the case of dispute over contract of carriage of goods by sea in which the Respondents Shanghai Hengxin Shipping Co., Ltd. (hereinafter referred to as "Shanghai Hengxin") and Murmansk Shipping Company (hereinafter referred to as "MSCO") and the Plaintiff of first instance Hunan Zoomlion International Trade Co., Ltd. (hereinafter referred to as "Hunan Zoomlion") were involved, the Appellants Zurich General Insurance Company (China) Limited (hereinafter referred to as "Zurich China"), Ping An Property & Casualty Insurance Company of China Ltd. Hunan Branch (hereinafter referred to as "Ping An Hunan"), Sunshine Property & Casualty Insurance Co., Ltd. Hunan Branch (hereinafter referred to as "Sunshine Hunan") and Shanghai GCL International Co., Ltd. (hereinafter referred to as "GCL") files an appeal before the court. After accepting the appeal on August 14, 2014, the court constituted a collegiate panel and held an hearing in public on December 2, 2014. QIU Biaoshan, agent *ad litem*jointly entrusted by Zurich China, Ping An Hunan, Sunshine Hunan (hereinafter referred to as "co-insurers") and Hunan Zoomlion, WU Jianhong, agent *ad litem* of GCL, REN Yuwei and HUA Lingling, agents *ad litem* of Shanghai Hengxin and LI Rongcun,agent *ad litem* of MSCO appeared in court to attend the hearing. Now, this case has been closed.

Hunan Zoomlion and the co-insurers alleged in the court of first instance: on May 23, 2011,*Annual Transportation Agreement on Indian Crawler Cranes* (hereinafter referred to as "annual transportation agreement") was concluded by and between Hunan Zoomlion and GCL. Pursuant to the agreement, GCL shall carry Hunan Zoomlion's crawler cranes to India. From June 22 to July 26, 2011, Hunan Zoomlion provided its own five Zoomlion crawler cranes (hereinafter referred to as "cargo concerned") to GCL for shipping. Pursuant to the voyage charter party it concluded with Shanghai Hengxin, GCL sub-entrusted Shanghai Hengxin to carry the cargo concerned via M.V. "Yuriy Arshenevskiy"chartered by Shanghai

Hengxin. MSCO is the owner of M.V. "Yuriy Arshenevskiy". On August 2, 2011, after the loading of the cargo concerned, Union Ocean Shipping Co., Ltd (hereinafter referred to as "Union Ocean"), as the agent authorized by Shanghai Hengxin, issued five sets of B/Ls No.SHM04, SHB11, SHB12A, SHB12B and SHB13 (hereinafter referred to as "House B/Ls") and surrendered them to Hunan Zoomlion through GCL. Later on, GCL got back the House B/Ls and provided Hunan Zoomlion with four sets of B/LsNo.SHM04, SHB11, SHB12 and SHB13 (hereinafter referred to as "Master B/Ls") issued by MSCO's agent Shanghai United International Ocean Shipping Agency Ltd. (hereinafter referred to as "Shanghai UNISCO"). The cargo concerned was seriously damaged during the voyage. In order to avoid the enlargement of losses, Hunan Zoomlion requested GCL, Shanghai Hengxin and MSCO to discharge the cargo at such places nearby as Xiamen Port or Shanghai Port. However, GCL, Shanghai Hengxin and MSCO ignored this request and continued to instruct the vessel to proceed to India, as a result of which tremendous enlarged losses were incurred to the cargo concerned. Hunan Zoomlion and the co-insurers held that, GCL was the contractual carrier in the carriage concerned, Shanghai Hengxin was sub-entrusted by GCL to carry the cargo concerned, and MSCO was the owner of the vessel and was in control over the manning and domination of the vessel, so both Shanghai Hengxin and MSCO were the actual carriers. The cargo damage happened during the period of responsibility due to GCL, Shanghai Hengxin and MSCO, and such damage was caused by improper lashing, negligence in care for cargo and the unseaworthiness of the vessel. Therefore, GCL, Shanghai Hengxin and MSCO should bear joint and several liability for the cargo loss and relevant expenses. In addition, the co-insurers alleged that they had indemnified the cargo losses according to relevant insurance contract and thus obtained the right of subrogation accordingly as per relevant laws. And Hunan Zoomlionshould be entitled to claim compensation for its losses which werenot covered by the co-insurers.

In this respect, Hunan Zoomlion and the co-insurers requested:

1. To order GCL, Shanghai Hengxin and MSCO to jointly and severally compensate Hunan Zoomlion for the losses in sum of RMB2,619,148.53 and interests thereof (calculated from August 8, 2011 to the effective date of judgment as per the loan interest rate published by the People's Bank of China during the corresponding period);
2. To order the CGL, Shanghai Hengxin and MSCO to jointly and severally compensate Zurich China for the losses in sum of RMB10,484,602 and interests thereof (calculated from February 1, 2013 to the effective date of judgment as per the loan interest rate published by the People's Bank of China during the corresponding period);
3. To order GCL, Shanghai Hengxin and MSCO to jointly and severally compensate Ping An Hunan for the losses in sum of RMB6,289,403.99 and interests thereof (calculated from February 1, 2013 to the effective date of judgment as per the loan interest rate published by the People's Bank of China during the corresponding period);

4. To order GCL, Shanghai Hengxin and MSCO to jointly and severally compensate Sunshine Hunan for the losses in sum of RMB4,190,468.40 and interests thereof (calculated from February 1, 2013 to the effective date of judgment as per the loan interest rate published by the People's Bank of China during the corresponding period); and
5. To order GCL, Shanghai Hengxin and MSCO to jointly and severally bear the court acceptance fees and the application fee for vessel arrest in Case (2011) Xia Hai Fa Bao Zi No.30 in sum of RMB5,000.

In the first instance, GCL defended:

1. Hunan Zoomlion was not a qualified Plaintiff. The trading party of the cargo concerned was not Hunan Zoomlion but Zoomlion International Trading (HK) Co., Limited (hereinafter referred to as "Zoomlion HK"). Hunan Zoomlion was not the owner of the cargo and it had no right to sue against GCL;
2. GCL was not a qualified Defendant. Although GCL concluded an annual transportation agreement with Hunan Zoomlion, this agreement had been unilaterally cancelled by Hunan Zoomlion. Therefore, there was only a relationship of shipping agency agreement between GCL and Hunan Zoomlion, and GCL had no fault during the agency;
3. The cargo damage concerned was caused by the vessel's encountering with extreme weather and adverse sea conditions, for which the carrier may be exempted from liability;
4. The losses claimed by Hunan Zoomlion and the co-insurers had no basis. There was a difference between the customs value and the invoice value of the cargo concerned, and Hunan Zoomlion had no basis to claim the cargo loss based on the invoice value; the condition of the cargo proved by Hunan Zoomlion and the co-insurers was the condition when the cargo had been shipped back to China. At that time, the cargo had temporarily stayed in Port of Xiamen, been carried to and long-term stockpiled in India, and had encountered adverse sea conditions again during its voyage back to China. The carrier should not be liable for the enlarged losses during that period. Hunan Zoomlion and the co-insurers failed to prove the actual condition of the damage efficiently; and
5. The co-insurers did not indemnify correctly, they cannot obtain the right of subrogation.

Shanghai Hengxin defended:

1. This case involved several contracts of carriage of goods by sea, and it was not clear which one was the basis of the claim raised by Hunan Zoomlion and the co-insurers in this proceeding. Hunan Zoomlion stated it was based on its transportation agreement with GCL, but essentially that agreement was a shipping agency agreement and had been unilaterally cancelled by Hunan Zoomlion before the carriage of the cargo concerned. There was no basis for Hunan Zoomlion and the co-insurers to claim against Shanghai Hengxin and MSCO as actual carriers according to the shipping agency agreement between Hunan Zoomlion and GCL. As to the House B/Ls issued by Union Ocean,

Hunan Zoomlion and the co-insurers failed to provide the originals. Under the situation where the B/Ls failed to be proved authentic and legally possessed by Hunan Zoomlion, the rights of Hunan Zoomlion under the B/Ls should not be considered. As to the Master B/Ls, Hunan Zoomlion was neither the consignee nor the shipper described in the B/Ls. Hunan Zoomlion and the co-insurers would not qualified Plaintiffs if they claimed on basis of such B/Ls;
2. The concept of "actual carrier" in the Maritime Code of the People's Republic of China should be effective only in B/L relationships, but Hunan Zoomlion was neither the holder of nor the consignee or shipper under the two B/Ls concerned. Therefore, Hunan Zoomlion and the co-insurers had no rights to claim against Shanghai Hengxin and MSCO as actual carrier;
3. MSCO was the owner of the vessel concerned who was in charge of the manning, supply and management of the vessel. On this account, it was MSCO, not Shanghai Hengxin, who actually performed the carriage;
4. The cargo damage was caused by force majeure, act of god and the shipper's poor packing of the cargo, so the carrier may be exempted from liability; and
5. The amount of the losses claimed by Hunan Zoomlion and the co-insurers was unreasonable and untrue; 6. Hunan Zoomlion who was not the owner of the cargo and had no actual loss in this case should have no right to claim; 7. It was stated in *Institute Cargo Clauses (A)* which was incorporated in relevant insurance contracts that: "this insurance is subject to English law and practice". Under English law, the insurer should exercise its right of subrogation in the name of the insured. If the insurer sued in its own name, the prescription should be counted based on the date of its suing. Given this, the claim of co-insurers had exceeded the limitation period.

MSCO defended:

1. Hunan Zoomlion and the co-insurers were not qualified Plaintiffs. The seller stated in the sales contract and the invoice concerned was Zoomlion HK, and the expenses for back shipment to China were paid by Zoomlion HK or Zoomlion Heavy Industry Science & Technology Co. (hereafter referred to as "Zoomlion Heavy"). Therefore, Hunan Zoomlion was not a qualified Plaintiff. Since the rights of co-insurers derived from Hunan Zoomlion, they were not qualified Appellants, either. In addition, the latest insurance policy issued in this case was signed by Zurich China solely, so accordingly Ping An Hunan and Sunshine Hunan were not eligible subjects;
2. MSCO was not the actual carrier. The Master B/Ls were straight B/Ls, Hunan Zoomlion was neither the shipper nor the consignee stated in these B/Ls and thus had no right under these B/Ls. The reason for MSCO to enter into this transportation was the time charterparty they concluded with a Korean company Kings Ocean Shipping Company (hereinafter referred to as "Kings Ocean"). However, this time charterparty was a contract for property, not for transportation or shipping agency;

3. The cargo damage was due to poor packing and adverse sea conditions for which the carrier may be exempted from liability. Even though the carrier's decision to avoid typhoon was improper, it still was a matter of exemption;
4. Even if Hunan Zoomlion and the co-insurers were eligible subjects, some of their claims were unreasonable and not claimable since the losses had been enlarged during the cargo's back shipment to China and the subsequent processes. The only reasonable claim of Hunan Zoomlion was the arrest application fee since they had been indemnified by the insurers. The interests claimed by the co-insurers should be calculated from the date of litigation. There was no basis for Hunan Zoomlion and the co-insurers to claim in RMB uniformly since the loss for exchange rate was not claimable; and
5. Even if MSCO was deemed as actual carrier, MSCO was still entitled to enjoy the package limitation of liability and the limitation of liability for maritime claims. The accident concerned also caused other claims against MSCO, and the total claim amount was around USD4,800,000. In this case, the limit of liability for the carrier was around USD2,170,000 as per its proportion in the package limitation of liability.

The court of first instance ascertained the facts of the subject case as follows (note: refer to the times indicated by the evidential materials.UTC was adopted by the messages received via EGC and the emails from weather routing company while the GMT was adopted by the deck log book, both 8 hours later than Beijing time—difference between the two is ignorable; part of the emails sent from M. V."Yuriy Arshenevskiy" indicated Moscowtime of daylight saving time which was 4 hours later than Beijing time):

1. Ship information and relationship under the charter party in connection with the voyage concerned

The vessel concerned M.V."Yuriy Arshenevskiy" is a Russia-registered RoRo/break-bulk carrier, gross tonnage 18,574 tons, built in 1986 and registered in Russian Ship Classification Society. The owner of the vessel is MSCO.

On April 14, 2011, MSCO and Kings Ocean entered into a time charter party under which MSCO chartered M.V."Yuriy Arshenevskiy" to Kings Oceans with a charter period of about 9 to 11 months starting from the date when the vessel was delivered. Earlier on April 7, 2011, Kings Ocean and HanssyHK entered into a time charter party, according to which M.V."Yuriy Arshenevskiy" was sub-chartered to Hanssy HK for a charter period of about 6 months starting from the date when the vessel was delivered. Clause 8 of the said two back-to-back charter parties prescribes, "the Captain (although appointed by the shipowner), shall be under the orders and directions of the Charterers as regards employment and agency; and charterers are to load, stow, trim, discharge, lash, unlash, dunnage, secure the cargo at their expense under the supervision of the Captain, who is to sign bills of lading for cargoes as presented, in strict conformity with mate's or tally clerk receipts."Both charter parties further agreed in "clause 41 bills of lading" of the additional clauses that "with reference to clause 8, it is understood that the

Charterers and/or their agents may sign original bill(s) of lading, if required by charterers, on behalf of the Master strictly according to mate's receipts without prejudice to this charter party, through or in-transit bill(s) of lading not to be issued under this charter party."

With respect to the voyage concerned, namely M.V. "Yuriy Arshenevskiy" V.11125, Hanssy HK voyage chartered the vessel to Shanghai Hengxin and Shanghai Hengxin again voyage chartered the vessel to GCL. Both the said voyage charter parties agreed on the FLT freight clause.

During the voyage concerned, Shanghai Hengxin represented in their email exchanges with M.V."Yuriy Arshenevskiy" that it as the sub-charterer gave instruction to the vessel "for and on behalf of Shanghai Hengxin Shipping Co., Ltd.".

2. Contracts and B/Ls in connection with the relationship of carriage concerned

On March 25, 2011, GCL (Party A) and Hunan Zoomlion (Party B) concluded *Long-term Strategic Cooperation Transportation Agreement* with a validity term of one year, agreeing that "Party B entrusts Party A to act as its agent for cargo transportation business", and reaching agreements upon freight rate and operation manner. On May 23, 2011, GCL (Party A) and Hunan Zoomlion (Party B) concluded *Annual Transportation Agreement for Crawler Cranes to India*, agreeing: "Party B entrusts Party A to undertake the cargo transportation operation from Shanghai to Mumbai, India"; "freight rate: a) ocean freight for bulk cargo: USD45 per billable unit in average, on full-liner term, inclusive of other extra taxes of ocean transportation, stevedorage, stowage charge, trimming charge, tally fee and cargo securing fee. All cargoes will be stowed beneath the deck. b) Lump sum for port charges: RMB26.5 per billable unit, including all the fees and charges incurred for shipment booking and in the port zone, such as shipment booking fee, THC charge, customs declaration fee, documentary charge, unloading charge, shifting/movement charge, stowage and packing charges for the crawler cranes....","operation manner: ......j) Party A shall arrange specialists to supervise the whole process of cargo loading onto the carrying vessel and take photos for record for the purpose to ensure safe and proper vertical loading, stowage and securing of the cargo. k)After the cargo arrives at the destination port, Party B's engineers shall conduct initial inspection to the cargo. If damage or loss of cargo is found to be caused by Party A's faults during transportation, all the losses arising therefrom shall be undertaken by Party A. For serious losses, Party B shall be entitled to terminate this agreement".

On July 5, 2011, Hunan Zoomlion informed GCL via email that "as to the 'crawler cranes to India' project invited for bid by our company in May, for the customers' breach of contract, this project has been cancelled, so the annual transportation agreement for crawler cranes to India concluded by and between your company and our company could not be performed any more. It is now decided by our leadership after discussion that: This annual transportation agreement is cancelled.... Upon receipt of your confirmation, we will formally send a notice to cancel the annual transportation agreement". On July 13, GCL replied that "as the transportation agreement is a tripartite cooperation agreement among the cargo owner, the forwarding agent and the shipowner, we had to notify such situation to the shipowner", and conveyed the reply of the shipowner Hengxin which was summarized as follows: 1. the unit price of USD48W/M for the 26 sets of crawler cranes firstly transported; 2. the ocean freight for the second shipment of 5 sets of crawler cranes ready to be transported to Mumbai shall be charged at USD50W/M.3.The shipowner did not agree to cancel the original transportation agreement, but requested an additional transportation agreement to be concluded, under which it shall be agreed that the cargo quantity and ocean freight agreed under the previous agreement become invalid, but Zoomlion shall warrant that all their shipments of general cargo destined to Mumbai, India before March 2012 shall be carried by Hengxin. The next day, Hunan Zoomlion further replied via email, "first of all, we would like to declare that the subject agreement is not a tripartite agreement, and our company had neither signed nor stamped on the agreement concluded by and between your company and the shipowner, therefore, as for the requests put forward by the shipowner, please negotiate and handle the request by yourselves. We maintain our previous decision"; although agreeing to pay for the difference of ocean freight and port charges in connection with the said two shipments of cargo, Hunan Zoomlion insisted "the above is the final settlement of our company".

The cargo concerned was consigned by Hunan Zoomlion to GCL and delivered to the vessel by GCL in its own name. The mate's receipt concerned indicated the shipper was GCL and the shipping date was August 2, 2011, and bore the written remarks of "weak packing" or "wooden cases are weak packing, materials unknown, shipside shall not be responsible for damages during loading/discharging" which was confirmed by the Master by signing. According to the bank slip, on September 8, 2011, Zoomlion Heavy paid USD201,179.31 to GCL and the charge item indicated by the special invoice for international freight agency was "ocean freight".

After the cargo concerned had been completely shipped onboard, GCL submitted the order B/Ls (namely House B/Ls) numbered SHM04, SHB11, SHB12A and SHB13 to Hunan Zoomlion. However, after occurrence of the accident, these B/Ls were regained by GCL, with reason and whereabouts unknown. According to the copies of the B/Ls provided by Hunan Zoomlion now, the shipper indicated on this set of B/Ls was Zoomlion HK and Union Ocean alleged it issued these B/Ls on behalf of the carrier Shanghai Hengxin.

The voyage instruction sent by Shanghai Hengxin to the Master on July 6, 2011 expressly stated, "please authorize agent to sign the B/Ls in conformity with mate's receipt on your behalf". The Master ever issued the authorization document to UNISCO that "we hereby authorize you to issue the bill of lading with respect to the cargo shipped onboard for the subject voyage on behalf of me...."On September 19, 2011, Hunan Zoomlion confirmed their consent to the vessel's issuance of the B/Ls in conformity with the mate's receipt and agreed GCL paid ocean freight to the shipowner in exchange for the B/Ls. On September 23, GCL surrendered to

Hunan Zoomlion the four sets of straight B/Ls No. SHM04, SHB11, SHB12 and SHB13 (namely Master B/Ls) issued by Shanghai UNISCO on behalf of MSCO as alleged, indicating the shipper was GCL, the consignee was an logistics company in India, the cargo concerned was 176 packages in quantity, gross weight totaled 855,780 kg and minor remarks were the same as the mate's receipt. Hunan Zoomlion, upon receipt of these B/Ls, immediately complained against GCL that without negotiation with and authorization from Hunan Zoomlion, GCL changed the consignee to order into a named consignee, the shipper into GCL and the carrier into MSCO; it also held that since it was GCL who directly arranged the shipment and space booking with the shipowners in connection with the cargo concerned according to the annual transportation agreement for crawler cranes to India, the shipper under the B/Ls may be changed into GCL on the premise that GCL issued House B/Ls as carrier to Hunan Zoomlion, or GCL, after receipt of the order B/Ls issued by the Master, negotiated by endorsement the B/Ls to Hunan Zoomlion in exchange for the House B/Ls; in this regard, Hunan Zoomlion required GCL to immediately and unconditionally issue five sets of order B/Ls in the B/L format previously agreed, naming Hunan Zoomlion or Zoomlion HK as the shipper and "'Hanssy Shipping' as the carrier"; meanwhile, in order to resolve the problems as soon as possible, Hunan Zoomlion also indicated, "we would agree the Master to re-issue the straight B/Ls as an expedient, but the shipper and consignee must be Hunan Zoomlion." GCL then conveyed the requirement of Huanan Zoomlion to Shanghai Hengxin; Shanghai Hengxin insisted, "there is no agreement regarding the B/L alteration in the contract entered between GCL and our company. Our company issued the B/L according to the mate's receipt, which is not wrong at all, and the clients do not have the right to require our company to alter the B/Ls's content according to their requirement (especially under the condition that the shipowner firmly expressed their dissention)" and that the agreement between Zoomlion and GCL should have no relevancy to it.

After the cargo concerned arrived in India, Hunan Zoomlion surrendered the full set of master B/Ls to GCL on March 1, 2012 in exchange for the 4 sets of straight B/Ls in the same number re-issued by Shanghai UNISCO on behalf of MSCO so as to facilitate the later receipt of cargo at Indian port. This set of B/Ls still names GCL as the shipper while changing the consignee into Zoomlion Trade (India) Private Limited.

3. Situation of typhoon MUIFA

From the evening of August 2 to the morning of August 4, typhoon MUIFA continuously and slowly moved westwards.

EGC's message at 19:56:06 on August 3 informed: wind gusts can be a further 40 percent stronger than the averages given here, and maximum waves may be up to twice the height. Message at 17:03:34 on August 6: frequent heavy squally (SQ) showers (SH) and thunderstorms (TS) within 300 nm from center of MUIFA. Message at 18:42:56 on August 6: radius of over 30 knot winds 300 miles east semicircle and 220 miles elsewhere. Radius of over 30 knot winds 300 miles east semicircle and 220 miles elsewhere. The first three messages on August 7 all stated radius of over 50 knot winds 120 miles east semicircle and radius of over 30 knot winds 325 miles east semicircle. All EGC messages, after forecasting the position of typhoon center, regarded there was 70% percent probability that the typhoon center would enter into probability circle.

According to the email sent from the weather routing company at 05:03:03 on August 4, 2011, "...Forecast confidence in the track of the typhoon remains moderate at this time. Captain, well noted vessel has sensitive deck cargo and has asked for permission to remain in port for the next several days. However, we note that the typhoon is currently heading for the Shanghai area for a direct hit. This would likely result in winds of 70 knots in the general vicinity of Shanghai with strong storm surge moving into the area as well. Considering this information, we do not know if the port of Shanghai will remain open and if it closes your vessel will likely have to seek shelter in open ocean. If the port of Shanghai does close and forces your vessel into the open ocean, then we suggest your vessel proceed along a best NE-ly heading to north of Cheju Island to gain some fetch limitation and clearance north and east of the typhoon. However, if your vessel is able to remain in port we suggest your vessel begin voyage around 08/12 to begin sailing outside the gale radius of the typhoon as it continues north. Please keep us closely advised to your intentions and the situation at the port of Shanghai so that we may keep you well advised". According to the email sent from the weather routing company at 15:03:26 on August 4, "the following update based on departure August 5, 2011 in loading condition from Shanghai to Mumbai...3. Route recommendation: as conditions and safe navigation permit, best NE-ly heading to north/east of Cheju Island, to obtain clearance well north and east of typhoon MUIFA. Then best S-ly heading, adjusting course to ensure 300 nm clearance to its east. According to the email sent from the weather routing company at 22:53:50on August 5, "...2.Route recommendation: direct north of Cheju Island remain valid; reason: avoid heavier adverse conditions associated with typhoon MUIFA."

As was reported by *Meteorological Message Certification Report* issued by Shanghai Central Meteorological Station, "based on the analysis of typhoon route and vessel position, it can be found that from August 6 to August 7, the vessel sailed within 7bft but never within 10bft gale wind circle on the right semi-circle of typhoon MUIFA."

The reply of Shanghai Meteorological Bureau dated September 17, 2013 asserted that, "according to the satellite images and other meteorological data, typhoon MUIFA was of an asymmetric structure and the vessel concerned was quite likely to at the edge of 10bft wind area, thus the possibility that 10bft winds might occur in the sailing area of the vessel concerned could not be ruled out". As was shown by the attachments thereto, due to the restricted temporal resolution of polar orbiting satellites, only two wind field retrieval images were obtained one day, from which it can be found at 2000 on August 6, 2011 and 0800 on August7, 2011, the wind force at the vessel position was comparatively strong, about 28m/s (10-11bft).

According to the analysis on wind force suffered by M.V. "Yuriy Arshenevskiy" during typhoon MUIFA in August 2011 which was issued by WU Liguang, director of Pacific Typhoon Research Center, Nanjing University of Information Science & Technology, by comparison with the yearly average typhoon-forecast error of CMA in 2011,before and within a certain period after M.V. "Yuriy Arshenevskiy" departed from Shanghai Port, the forecasts of typhoon MUIFA's moving direction released by CMA were relatively reliable. However, after 0800 on August 6, the actual moving direction of typhoon MUIFA quite eastly deviated from the forecast track; after 0200 on August 6, the sea surface wind field showed significant asymmetry with gale zone to the east of typhoon center; At 0800 and 1400 on August 6, the mean wind speed at the position of M.V. "Yuriy Arshenevskiy" reached 7bft, and at 2000on August 6 and 0800 on August 7, in the 9bft wind circle; according to the satellite retrieved mean wind speeds at ship positions and in consideration of the linear relationship between mean wind and gust, gust scale that M.V. "Yuriy Arshenevskiy" confronted with at 0800 on August 6 might reach 9-11bft, 9-10bft at 1400 on August 6, 11-13bft at 2000 on August 6 and 11-13bft at 0800 on August 7. If taking into account the possible error in satellite retrieval, the vessel might suffer gusts of larger scale.

According to the report issued by East China Sea Forecast Center of State Oceanic Administration, on the basis of the real-time data of buoys and other relevant data, the analysis on wind force and wave height suffered by M.V. "Yuriy Arshenevskiy" revealed that M.V. "Yuriy Arshenevskiy" might suffer winds in 10bft scale and waves in height of 7-9m during the period from 1600 on August 6 to 0200 on August 7.

4. Course of the marine accident concerned

On the voyage concerned, 31 shipments of cargoes (inclusive of the 5 shipments concerned) were shipped onboard from Tianjin Port and Shanghai Port to India. After loading 5 shipments of cargo at Tianjin Port, M.V."Yuriy Arshenevskiy" arrived at the second loading port Shanghai Port on July 30, 2011, berthed alongside Luojing Terminal at 1200UTC, began the loading operation at 1400UTC and at 0500UCT on August 3, completed the loading operation while the securing operation for the deck cargo continued. According to the accident analysis reportissued by Mintaian Property Insurance Surveyors & Loss Adjusters Co., Limited and submitted by Shanghai Hengxin, cargo stevedore, lashing and securing were under the responsibility of Shanghai Hengxin who therefore, employed Shanghai Dongzhao Shipping Services Co., Ltd. to carry out the lashing operation.

East China Adjusters & Surveyors Co., Ltd. was entrusted by GCL to attend the site and supervise the whole loading operation. According to the loading survey report it then issued, the holds where the cargo concerned was loaded and stowed were in serviceable condition, and "all cargoes were in general good condition except scratched and rusted on surface. However,a few of steel jibs was packed weakly and loose wooden frames and most of steel jibs were not fitted with wooden frames including important bottom for favorable stowage on board. And some light steel structures were lashed in the steel jibs in weak condition which is a risk at sea while the ship rowing and pitching during bad weather. So, parts of steel structure were secured with ropes and belts by cargo agent".

The five sets of crawler cranes concerned were loaded and stowed on tween deck No.2, 3 and 4.As was indicated on the deck log book, after completion of loading in each cargo hold, the vessel checked the securing and resolved outstanding issues. Under the voyage concerned, 3,021 tons of ballast water was loaded onboard, the GM of the vessel was 1.75m, and the angle of vanishing stability was larger than 60°.

Since August 2, the vessel began to receive forecast messages on typhoon MUIFA and route recommendation from the American weather routing company AWT ("Applied Weather Technology, Inc."), and the JMH meteorological facsimile chart and the navigation warning on weather conditions from JMA via EGC system. At 1347 (0547UTC) on August 3, the Master emailed Shanghai Hengxin, "stevedores make lashing beautifully but not accordance with good sea practice so for additional lashing according to our requirements take a more time", moreover the typhoon MUIFA was expected to arrive at NE Taiwan island on August 5, so if the vessel sailed on August 3, the vessel was expected to be at that area on August 5 also. In view of the above, the Master recommended the vessel stayed at Shanghai Port for two more days to avoid the typhoon. At 1458, Shanghai Hengxin replied: they agreed on the Master's recommendation, but since the port did not allow vessel's berthing, they instructed to shift M.V. "Yuriy Arshenevskiy" to anchorage for two days to avoid the typhoon and informed the lashing company to further lash and secure the deck cargo. At 1840UTC of August 3, M.V. "Yuriy Arshenevskiy" berthed at Wusong Anchorage No.5. At 2245UTC, 8 workers embarked onboard to continue the securing of the deck cargo. At 0300UTC of August 4, the C/O checked the securing conditions and resolved the outstanding issues; at 0700UTC, stevedores completed the cargo securing and left the vessel.

At 1216 (0416UTC) of August 4, the Master emailed Shanghai Hengxin, informing that the lashing operation had been completed at 0400UTC, requesting to further stay at Shanghai anchorage waiting for better weather, and seeking for the charterers' opinions on sailing. At 1432 (0632UTC) of August 4, the Master informed Shanghai Hengxin that according to the latest meteorological forecast, typhoon MUIFA would reach the area near Shanghai from August 6 to 7 and advised the charterers to require the agent at port to arrange pilotage service at night to proceed to the north of Cheju Island for typhoon avoidance. Shanghai Hengxin replied at 1711 of the same day that since the pilot schedule was very tight, it was finally fixed that the pilot would embark onboard the next day, stating "please make full arrangement for departure tomorrow morning", and asserting "heading to north of Cheju is Ok. It's a good plan" while pointing out "how to navigate depends on you. But safety firstly. Please always keep safe distance to the typhoon".

At 0722UTC of August 5, M.V. "Yuriy Arshenevskiy" heaved up the anchors. At 1300UTC, M.V. "Yuriy Arshenevskiy" adjusted her course to 61° and proceeded to Cheju Island. At 1610UTC of August 5, M.V. "Yuriy Arshenevskiy", sailing against northeast wind at the speed of 11m/s (6bft), rolled from side to side with the amplitude from 10°-12°. Under such circumstance, the coil pipes loaded in a steel packaging (crates) on top of the cover of hold No.2 were moving (the whole pile) in line with the motion of the vessel and secured by the crew with the iron chains. To reduce rolling for better operation on deck, the course heading of 90° has been taken and was then adjusted to 75° at 2000UTC, proceeding to Cheju Island for avoiding typhoon.

From August 6 to 7, M.V. "Yuriy Arshenevskiy" met with typhoon MUIFA in a short distance. According to the deck log book, the videos taken onboard, and the real-time "report every four hours" made by M.V."Yuriy Arshenevskiy" to the shipowner MSCO, at 0400UTC of August 6, "the chains installed by the crew gave given way and are ripped off", "to ensure the safety of the crew the load on cover No.2 has not been reinforced as the pile may fall apart"; at 0800UTC, "the load on cover No.2 has shifted as a result of rolling"; at 0900UTC, "the deck crew has proceeded to fasten the deck load on the cover of hold No.2 under the guidance of the first mate"; at 1600UTC, "the deck crew has completed fastening the deck load"; at 1620UTC, the load on hold cover No.2 has almost completely fallen down overboard and the vessel has sustained damage. At 1650UTC, the load from hold covers No.1 and 3 has fallen overboard and the load on hold cover No.5 has fallen apart. At 2120UTC, the hook attached to the deck got ripped off and the derrick of cargo crane 2A was swiveled toward the starboard together with the cabin. At 2400UTC, very frequent squalls during which it is not possible to measure the wind scale as the anemometer scale stopped at 36 m/s (12-13bft approximating to 13bft); the vessel speed periodically drops to 0 knots. At 0400UTC of August 7, squalls were occurring every 5-10 minutes and the vessel was rolling up to 40-45°, reducing the speed down to 0 knots; "during around 30 minutes, the vessel could not get out of that resonant rolling due to the great waves". At 0425UTC, the load from cover No.4 has fallen overboard almost entirely. The load on hold cover No.5 has completely fallen apart. The waves are up to 12 meters high. The wind is over 50m/s (15-16bft approximating to 16bft). From afternoon of August 6to noon of August 7, M.V."Yuriy Arshenevskiy" adjusted the speed of her main engine and her course at times so as to avoid resonant rolling.

According to the deck log book, from August 6 to 7, 2011, the position of the vessel concerned has her position, her distance to the typhoon center (calculated on the basis of the actual position of typhoon center and the vessel position), her rolling amplitude and the cargo damage extent shown in the below table:

Time (GMT)	Distance to typhoon center (km)	Wind Direction (°)/speed (m/s)/ scale (bft)	Rolling (°)	Remarks
061200	429	100/30/11	20	
061400	388	100/30/11		
061600	375	080/35/12	25	The deck cargo on the cover of hold No.2 shook.
061620	358	090/36/12	45-48	

(continued)

(continued)

Time (GMT)	Distance to typhoon center (km)	Wind Direction (°)/speed (m/s)/ scale (bft)	Rolling (°)	Remarks
				The deck cargo on the cover of hold No.2 fell overboard.
061650	362	080/36/12	45	The deck cargo on the cover of hold covers No.1 and 3 fell overboard and those on hold cover No.5 fell apart.
062000	322	090/38/13	30-35	One deck cargo on hold cover No.4 slid through the vessel.
062400	300	120/36/12	35	The vessel sailed at a standstill.
070400	262	160/40-50/15	40-45	The vessel sailed at a standstill.
070425	260	160/50/15	50	
070800	275	160/40/13	40	
071200	374	190/20/8	35	
071600	438	180/18/8	10-15, 30 on resonant rolling	Passing the squally weather

5. Stay of M.V."Yuriy Arshenevskiy" at Xiamen Port

At 0601 of August 7, the Master of M.V. "Yuriy Arshenevskiy"emailed to Kings Ocean, Shanghai Hengxinand MSCO, notifying that cargo on hatch coversNo.1-4 fell overboard and got lost, and the cargo on hatch cover No.5 was partially damaged which also caused damage to the vessel. On August 9, M.V. "Yuriy Arshenevskiy" was instructed by "Shanghai Hengxin to "urgently sail to Xiamen Port. We will inform the agent arrange your vessel to berth and arrange lashing workers to do re-lashing for the cargo in holds". On August 10, the vessel arrived at Xiamen Port. On August 11, the Master submitted the sea protest to MSA Xiamen. From August 10 to 14, M.V. "Yuriy Arshenevskiy" berthed alongside Modern Terminal of Xiamen Port to check the cargo damage and do the re-lashing work; since August 14, the vessel was anchored at Anchorage No.4 of Xiamen Port for matters subsequent to the accident.

During the period when M.V. "Yuriy Arshenevskiy" berthed at Xiamen Port, surveyors appointed by some of the cargo interests embarked onboard to carry out on-site inspection.

On August 24, Xiamen Maritime Court arrested M.V."Yuriy Arshenevskiy" at the application of the party not involved in the case, namelySany Heavy Industry Co., Ltd. At the application of Hunan Zoomlion, continual arrest of M.V."Yuriy Arshenevskiy" was granted on October 31, 2011. When the Plaintiff was negotiating with MSCO in respect of the LOU, the Plaintiff's agent ad litem repeatedly represented the requirement to redirect the vessel to Shanghai Port or Xiamen Port for discharge, inspection and disposal of the cargo concerned upon her release, and clearly advised "should the vessel proceed to Indian ports as the owners insist for the time being, a number of unforeseeable eventualities may readily occur to the catastrophic effect", "as the Indian consignee may refuse to take delivery of damaged cargo, and India has no technical conditions to repair the cargo and dispose of the residual value of the cargo. In order to make a more reasonable disposal of the cargo, our clients suggest the shipowner to direct the vessel back to the loading port for discharge of the damaged cargo."

During the vessel's stay at Xiamen Port, MSCO ever applied to competent department for cargo discharge and inspection, but due to failure to obtain approval from the local customs, the cargo concerned could not be discharged at Xiamen Port. On the evening of November 1, 2011, the co-insurers' agent informed MSCO's agent by email, "Shanghai Customs had agreed re-import of the damaged cargo. In addition, Sany Heavy Industry Co., Ltd. (owner of the cargo not involved in the subject case) had found a suitable discharge terminal at Shanghai. Given the above two factors, it is reasonable and feasible for the vessel to proceed to Shanghai for cargo discharge after her release." The next day, M.V."Yuriy Arshenevskiy" left Xiamen Port and continued to sail to India after her arrest was lifted.

6. Cargo losses, residual value disposal and other expenses

As was indicated on *Survey Report* issued by Crawford China Limited (hereinafter referred to as "Crawford survey report"), on December 5, 2011, M.V."Yuriy Arshenevskiy" berthed at Mundra Port "as the receiver refused to get the material unloaded at the port, vessels returned to sea." After the permission was granted, the vessel berthed alongside the terminal again on February 31, 2012. The cargo (including one set of QUY260 crawler crane concerned) was removed from the vessel to jetty from February 14, 2012 to February 20, 2012 and then shifted to storage yard at Mundra which was about 5 km from the port. On February 27, 2012, the vessel berthed at Mumbai Port and began the discharge operation in connection with the remaining 4 sets of crawler cranes (1 set of QUY260, 2 sets of QUY130 and 1 set of QUY80 crawler cranes), which was not completed until March 5. From the two inspections respectively at Mundra Port and Mumbai Port, it can be found the main machines of the five sets of crawler cranes concerned "almost become total loss", with the other parts such as jib sections damaged to varying extent and the 2 sets of QUY70 crawler cranes not involved in the subject case not obviously damaged.

From March 17 to 23, 2012, Hunan Zoomlion assigned personnel to India to evaluate the cargo losses together with the surveyors appointed by the co-insurers, and by comparison of the import customs clearance plus terminal charges and the freight for back shipment to China, and taking into consideration the limited conditions of India premise and inspection equipment, decided to carry the 5 sets of damaged crawler cranes to Chinese factories for comprehensive inspection and assessment.

From May 21 to 25, 2012, the 4 sets of damaged crawler cranes were loaded onboard M.V."CARRARA CASTLE" at Mumbai Port. On June 9 of the same year, the other set of damaged crawler crane concerned was shipped onboard M.V. "CARRARA CASTLE" and shipped back to Shanghai. The parties concerned confirmed in the process of loading operation, damage to the QUY70 crawler crane not involved in the subject case happened while during the voyage for back shipment, it encountered the typhoons SAOLA and HAIKUI, causing the cargo concerned arrive at Luojing Terminal of Shanghai till August 9.

From August 9 to 13, 2012, the surveyors appointed by the co-insurers and the engineer of Zoomlion Heavy, after the cargo concerned was discharged at Shanghai Port, carried out a second cargo inspection through which it was concluded part of the jib sections did not have salvage value and was determined as constructive total loss. On November 15, 2012, China Certification & Inspection Group Hunan Co., Ltd. issued *Inspection Certificate*, indicating its surveyor attended Luojing Terminal and carried out on-site inspection into the 7 sets of crawler cranes (including the 2 sets of QUY70 crawler cranes not involved in the subject case) of Zoomlion Heavy back shipped, and found the main parts of the 7 sets of crawler cranes all seriously damaged, with the total residual value adjusted as RMB3,567,563. On November 6, the cargo was cleared by Shanghai Customs. On 7 November, Hunan Zoomlion International Trade Co., Ltd. and Aspen International Logistics (Shanghai) Co., Ltd. signed the sale and purchase contract on aforementioned part of jib sections of damaged crawler cranes becoming constructive total loss and on November 10, further signed the document of "supplementary clause on weight", specifying the purchase price was RMB60,160. The remaining parts were carried to Zoomlion Heavy in Changsha City of Hunan for inspection and testing. Upon assessment, it was found that the repair costs of the remaining jib sections, main machines, counterweights, lifting hooks, toolkits of the 5 sets of damaged crawler cranes concerned were higher than the residual value, having constituted constructive total loss. After obtaining the co-insurers' approval, Hunan Zoomlion released the "notice on auction of 5 damaged crawler cranes from Zoomlion". On January 28, Hunan Zoomlion and Shenmu Nengwen Machinery Lifting Service Co., Ltd. signed *Purchase Confirmation on Goods Bid*, according to which Hunan Zoomlion shall sell the 5 sets of damaged crawler cranes at RMB5,000,000.00.

In March 2013, Shanghai Customs levied import duty in sum of RMB217,194.96 and import VAT in sum of RMB498,462.43 on the 5 sets of crawler cranes re-imported. In addition, in connection with the application to Xiamen Maritime Court for ship arrest, and the stay in India and back shipment of the cargo concerned, Hunan Zoomlion and its affiliated company also paid the application fee RMB5,000 for maritime preservation, ocean freight and costs for measurement survey and pre loading inspection in sum of USD306,400 incurred in India as well as costs in sum of USD240,025.78 incurred at Mumbai Port and Mundra Port, India, costs incurred at Shanghai Port totaling RMB403,606, and costs for carrying back to factory by land totaling RMB670,000.

7. Relationship between Hunan Zoomlion and the cargo concerned, and the cargo value

The 5 sets of crawler cranes are the cargo under three sales and purchase contracts, whose seller, according to the contracts, is all Zoomlion HK. Specifically, 2 sets of QUY260 crawler cranes are the cargo under the contract No.ZL-CR-EX-1105101 which specifies the buyer is Larsen & Toubro Limited and the contractual unit price USD1,128,710; 2 sets of QUY130 crawler cranes are the cargo under the contract No.ZL-CR-EX-1105102 which specifies the buyer is Ideal Movers (P) Ltd. and the contractual unit price USD532,000; 1 set of QUY80 crawler crane was the cargo under the contract No.ZL-CR-EX-1106177 and the contractual unit price USD315,120. Both of the latter two contracts define the word "affiliate" in their definition clause and specify "for the purpose of this contract, when referred to one party, its affiliates are included"; moreover, under the appendix 1 to the two contracts, technical service is provided in the name of "ZOOMLION". Also, the seller under the Appendix 2 to the contract No.ZL-CR-EX-1106177 is Hunan Zoomlion.

On July 28, 2011, the cargo concerned made export declaration to Wusong Customs of Shanghai Port, according to which, the export date is August 3, 2011, the operating unit and the shipping unit are both Hunan Zoomlion, the payment term is CIF, the cargo unit price is USD1,038,413.20, USD489,440 and USD289,910.40 respectively. The total value of the cargo concerned as declared to the customs is USD3,345,616.80.

On September 30, 2011, Hunan Zoomlion and Zoomlion HK jointly issued *Letter of Statement*, stating: I.Hunan Zoomlion is the owner of the cargo concerned as well as the contractual shipper and cargo-delivering shipper under the concluded contract of carriage of goods by sea, enjoying the full and sole entitlement to the cargo concerned. II.Zoomlion HK had acted as the contracting agent of Hunan Zoomlion to conclude the sale and purchase contracts with the cargo buyers and the final rights and interests under the contracts should be enjoyed by Hunan Zoomlion. III.Although in the B/Ls issued by Union Ocean for and on behalf of Shanghai Hengxin, Zoomlion HK was indicated as the shipper therein, Hunan Zoomlion lawfully held these B/Ls and Zoomlion HK agreed to transfer all their rights and interests under the B/Ls (if any) to Hunan Zoomlion.

In connection with the back shipment of the cargo concerned to Shanghai, the straight B/L format of Navalmaer (UK) Ltd. who is not involved in the subject case was used under which the shipper is Zoomlion Trade (India) Private Limited and the consignee is Hunan Zoomlion.

8. Relationships under insurance contracts and payment of insurance indemnities

According to *Coinsurance Agreement* and *Supplementary Agreement on Coinsurance* signed by and among Zurich China, Ping An Hunan and Sunshine Hunan, and the goods in transit policyNo.BJMC0710030041 (namely coinsurance policy) jointly issued by the said three parties on August 18, 2010, the said three parties were the co-insurers for the goods in transit of Zoomlion, amongst which Zurich China acted as the leading insurer, undertaking a coinsurance proportion of

50%, and was "entitled to take full responsibility to act for and on behalf of the three coinsurance parties to deal with daily businesses with the intermediary and the insured in light of this coinsurance agreement and the insurance policy"; Ping An Hunan and Sunshine Hunan undertook a coinsurance proportion of 30% and 20% respectively; the coinsured was Hunan Zoomlion, Mobile Crane Branch of Zoomlion Heavy and its subsidiary, associated and affiliated and interrelated companies, and joint ventures in which it now has or hereafter may have a direct or indirect insurable interest and other entities for whom they may have instructions to insure or deem themselves responsible to insure, as their respective interests may appear; the packing shall be "industry standard packing"; conditions of insurance includes institute cargo clauses A (1982) and prescribe "'English law and practice' in the law and practice clause shall be modified to be 'Chinese law and practice'"; under the "special conditions" clause, it is warranted by the insured that "…2.4 the subject matter insured is in perfect condition and is properly packed as from the time of attachment of this insurance". For the purpose of *Coinsurance Agreement*, the insurance period is from August 1, 2010 to July 31, 2011 which is further extended to December 31, 2011 by *Supplementary Agreement on Coinsurance*.

As is shown by the evidence available, from July 2012 to August 2013, the co-insurers paid insurance indemnities totaling USD3,370,000 to the account of Hunan Zoomlion and Zoomlion Heavy in 11 installments according to their respective coinsurance proportions. As was indicated by the claim computation form of marine transportation cargo insurance concerned, the aforementioned insurance indemnities includes the cargo insurance amount USD4,000,194, 90% of costs for measurement survey/pre-loading inspection in amount of USD276,400, 90% of costs incurred at Mumbai Port and Mundra Port, India in sum of USD216,515, costs incurred at Shanghai Port in sum ofUSD63,561 (equal to RMB403,606), less the amount of cargo residual value USD812,225 (equal to RMB5,060,160) and the deductibles USD374,445 as re-negotiated between both parties. Hunan Zoomlion confirmed receipt of full payment of the said insurance indemnities and executed the subrogation receipt to the co-insurers.

The court of first instance held that, this case is a case regarding dispute over contract of carriage of goods by sea with foreign elements involved. As to the applicable law in this case, Hunan Zoomlion, the co-insurers, the Defendant GCL and the Defendant MSCO all agreed with application of the PRC law, but the Defendant Shanghai Hengxin held since the applicable insurance clauses in the insurance contracts chose English law, the English law should be referred to in respect of examination on the subrogation rights of the co-insurers, but agreed with the application of PRC law to other issues in this case. In this regard, the court of first instance held this case is not a case regarding dispute over insurance contract, so the agreement between the parties on the applicable law in the insurance contracts shall not apply to this case, and according to the facts ascertained, it is expressed in the coinsurance agreement that "'English law and practice' in the law and practice clause shall be modified to be 'Chinese law and practice'", so Shanghai Hengxin's argument on law application lacked legal and factual basis and was not be supported by the court of first instance. After comprehensive consideration of the subject eligibilities of the parties concerned, the facts of the case and the arguments of the parties concerned on the law application, the court of first instance determined the PRC law which has closest connection with the dispute of this case as the applicable law.

Firstly, with respect to the cause of cargo damage, the major dispute among the parties concerned, Hunan Zoomlion and the co-insurers held the cargo damage should be attributed to the seriously improper stowage, lashing and securing of the cargo concerned and the faults of the carrier and the actual carrier in custody of the cargo concerned; while GCL, Shanghai Hengxin and MSCO held it was caused by the adverse weather and sea conditions encountered by M.V."Yuriy Arshenevskiy". MSCO also held the poor package of the cargo concerned was one of the causes.

(1) Regrading to the loading and stowage

The experts appointed by Hunan Zoomlion and the co-insurers believed that, M.V."Yuriy Arshenevskiy" who sailed with partial load and large amount of deck cargoes on the voyage concerned had a larger transverse windage area and a relatively large dynamic heeling angle when sailing in winds and waves; the vertical distribution of cargo weights on decks, tween decks and holds was unreasonable on the voyage concerned (as far as general-cargo ships are concerned, the weight of cargo loaded in lower holds should be 65% of the total weight, and the weight of cargo loaded outside lower holds should be about 35%, in which the weight of cargo on deck should not exceed 10% of the total weight of cargo carried, while the weight ratios on the three positions on the voyage concerned were respectively 60.0%:25.5%:14.5%), failing to duly control the ship stability.

The court of first instance held that: seen from shipping practices, the vertical distribution of cargo weight is usually one of the stowage principles that needs to be considered for the purpose to control the ship stability under the situation of full load. The experts appointed by Hunan Zoomlion and the co-insurers also admitted in the experts hearing that the aforesaid ratios had not taken the weight of ballast water into consideration and the ballast water would influence the ratio of vertical weights, thus the said requirement on vertical distribution of cargo weight in stowage should not be absolutized. Especially in the event that the vessel is partially loaded and has no wrong problem in stability, even if the vertical distribution of cargo weight does not fully meet the required ratio, it cannot be simply concluded that the stowage plan and stowage of the vessel is defective. In the subject case, no evidence could prove that the stability of the vessel at the time of departure involved problems; on the contrary, the voyage concerned was furnished with satisfactory stability calculation, and from the fact that M.V."Yuriy Arshenevskiy" still could safely sailed out after having been attacked by typhoon MUIFA at a close distance and for a long time and had the cargo onboard seriously damaged, it can be inferred that the vessel actually kept a good stability during the voyage concerned. Therefore, the argument of Hunan Zoomlion and the co-insurers in this respect was not supported by the court of first instance.

(2) Regarding to lashing and securing

The experts appointed by Hunan Zoomlion and the co-insurers opined: the cargo in holds and on decks on the voyage concerned was stowed over compactly, which was unfavorable for lashing operation and for the transverse lashing wires to obtain proper vertical securing angle; the lashing company used self-purchased equipment which were not indicated in *Cargo Securing Manual* of M.V."Yuriy Arshenevskiy", rendering the lashing strength disqualified and the securing operation improper; the cargo in holds and on decks was unreasonably stacked; improper stowage and securing of adjacent cargo impaired the safety of the stowage and securing of the cargo concerned.

The court of first instance held: the cargo concerned was all stowed in holds, and the cargo on deck was irrelevant to the subject case and their lashing and securing did not affect the stability on the voyage concerned. Judgment as to whether the lashing and securing were questionable or not shall refer to customary and reasonable practices and whether they can adapt to the common perils of sea that may be encountered by the planned cargo on the scheduled voyage, and should not be excessively required to realize the theoretical absolute safety of the cargo onboard, regardless of the commercial efficiency and economic performance. The most essential and objective method to judge the lasing and securing of general-cargo vessels is to calculate or estimate the overall securing force, but in the cross-examination of the experts hearing, no experts could obtain the necessary basic data/materials that can reflect the original securing method to make further effective calculation of the securing force, and hence, none of the conclusion of the experts is sufficient to be solely accepted and adopted. Although the Defendants had provided prima facie evidence to prove that the lashing and securing of the cargo concerned conformed to usual requirements for the voyage, the evidence available indicated: 1. The lashing operation of the cargo concerned used self-purchased equipment. Though it is normal in shipping practices for multi-purpose ships to use lashing equipment not specified in the securing manual, as due to the diversity of cargo shipped, it is neither possible nor economical to require ship owner to equip onboard abundant quantity of various lashing equipment ready for use, particularly the kinds of steel wires which are usually disposable supplies and the accurate quantity needed could not be determined in advance, what is important is that the self-purchased equipment shall go through the authentication of competent classification society. Shanghai Hengxin alleged the securing equipment additionally purchased by the lashing company had passed the authentication of China Classification Society, while they failed to provide any effective evidence to make demonstration during the sufficient time for adducing evidence; therefore, a conclusion unfavorable to the carrier had to be drawn, namely, defects existed in the lashing and securing of the cargo concerned because lashing devices without effective authentication had been adopted; 2. The cargo concerned with irregular shapes was stowed over compactly, which was unfavorable to carry out the lashing operation, so relevant measures should have been taken to eliminate the disadvantage and ensure effective lashing of the cargo concerned; 3. M.V."Yuriy

Arshenevskiy" had received the typhoon warning before departure, so she could have reasonably foreseen the poor sailing environment on the voyage concerned, and should have accordingly further increased the lashing standard for the cargo concerned so as to adapt herself to the special sea conditions on the voyage concerned. Nevertheless, no evidence was submitted to manifest that the carrier had taken reasonable measures to preclude or make up for the said defects in the lashing and securing. Therefore, it should be confirmed that the lashing and securing of the cargo concerned was defective for the subject cargo and voyage.

(3) Regarding to whether the carrier took good care of the cargo concerned

Hunan Zoomlion and the co-insurers took the view that the stowage, lashing and securing of the cargo were seriously improper, and the carrier and the actual carrier failed to care for the cargo with due diligence.

The court of first instance held: the defects in stowage, lashing and securing have been elaborated above. As for whether the carrier had any other negligence in the custody of cargo, in light of the facts ascertained, the cargo concerned was loaded in holds as per the shipper's instructions; after the loading was completed in every shipping space, the ship side checked the loading and raised improvement requirements; before the vessel's departure from Shanghai Port, the Master of M.V."Yuriy Arshenevskiy" required to postpone the sailing time to reinforce the cargo lashing and securing; and during the voyage, the crew members were twice ordered to strengthen the lashing of deck cargo. What needs to be specially mentioned is that, as recorded in the deck log book, under the circumstance of attack by typhoon MUIFA at a close distance, the crew still took risks to further reinforce the lashing under the order of the C/O at 0900UTC on August 6. Meanwhile M. V."Yuriy Arshenevskiy" also exercised good seamanship to timely adjust her course and speed to mitigate rolling. Although the crew did not take special care for the cargo concerned during the voyage concerned, since the cargo concerned was stowed in holds and on one hand, to strengthen lashing in holds under the rough sea condition would endanger the personal safety of the crewmembers, it was improper to harshly require the crewmembers to care for the cargo regardless of their own safety; and on the other hand, there is no proof that can evidence there existed effective measures that M.V."Yuriy Arshenevskiy" should have taken but failed to reasonably take to avoid or mitigate the cargo damage. Therefore, based on existing evidence, it can be concluded that M.V."Yuriy Arshenevskiy" had performed the obligation to properly and diligently take care of the cargo concerned on the voyage, and the contention of Hunan Zoomlion and the co-insurers in this respect was not adopted by the court of first instance.

(4) Regarding to the sea conditions encountered by M.V."Yuriy Arshenevskiy"

Hunan Zoomlion and the co-insurers considered the vessel did not enter the 10bft wind circle of the typhoon but just ever got close to the 10bft wind circle, so the largest wind force probably suffered by the vessel was merely 10bft. While GCL, Shanghai Hengxin and MSCO argued that the real-time sea conditions encountered by the vessel should be ascertained on the basis of the deck log book, and the vessel had ever come across gust over 12bft and rolling beyond 30°.

The court of first instance held: the deck log book and the videos taken by the crew were the original materials that could reflect the sea conditions at the material time and also the prima facie evidence. Unless there was sufficient evidence to prove the contrary, records in the deck log book shall be fully respected. Firstly, the deck log book showed the wind force met by M.V."Yuriy Arshenevskiy" at the material time already exceeded the highest scale of the wind gauge (36m/s), which meant the gust force encountered by the vessel exceeded 12bft; this information itself already indicated the roughness of the sea conditions. Secondly, from the videos taken by the crew members, white foam on the sea that affected the visibility could be observed, which, according to shipping practices, indicated that the real-time wind force reached 11bft or more and the vessel rolled around 35°; further on the basis of the time when the videos were taken, the strength of typhoon was not the strongest at that time, so the video data and the deck log book could basically evidence each other. Thirdly, *Meteorological Message Certification Report* of Shanghai Central Meteorological Station provided by Hunan Zoomlion and the co-insurers asserted that, M.V."Yuriy Arshenevskiy" was sailing within the 7bft wind circle on the right semi-circle of typhoon MUIFA but never entered into the 10bft gale wind circle. However, it shall be unscientific to thus deduce that the vessel did not encounter wind force of more than 10bft, for the following reasons: 1. Typhoons are usually concentric circles of asymmetric structure, and as shown in the materials provided by Shanghai Meteorological Bureau, typhoon MUIFA was significantly asymmetric and the wind force in the right semi-circle where M. V."Yuriy Arshenevskiy" lied was much greater than that in the left semi-circle. Therefore, it is unprofessional and inaccurate to judge the actual wind force suffered by M.V."Yuriy Arshenevskiy" merely according to the gale wind circle. 2. It is the concept of mean wind that the forecasts of wind circle radius and wind scales released by the meteorological authority adopted, while in fact gust is usually 1-2 scales or even more stronger than mean wind. As judged from the ship position, M. V."Yuriy Arshenevskiy" was at the edge of 10bft wind circle when closest to the typhoon center. The information from Shanghai Meteorological Bureau is basically identical to the wind field retrieval result in respect to 2000 on August 6, 2011 and 0800 on August 7, 2011 in the wind force analysis report provided by MSCO, namely, the wind suffered by M.V."Yuriy Arshenevskiy" was around 11bft. Given the linear relationship between gust and mean wind and the unavailability of the wind field retrieval data under the most adverse sea condition due to technical restrictions, it could be conservatively estimated that the greatest wind force encountered by M.V."Yuriy Arshenevskiy" reached over 12bft. To sum up, it could be ascertained that M.V."Yuriy Arshenevskiy" had long suffered the rough sea of wind more than 12bft and rolling above 35° at the material time, so the argument of Hunan Zoomlion and the co-insurers in this regard was not adopted by the court of first instance.

(5) Regarding to poor package

MSCO viewed, according to the records in the loading survey report and the unclean remarks in the mate's receipt, wooden frameworks of the jib sections concerned were slackened, and such cargo was loaded onboard by means of "putting smaller into bigger" only tied by nylon belts, which should be determined as "poor package".

The court of first instance held: MSCO who contended the cargo concerned were poorly packed shall adduce evidence to prove the package of the cargo concerned did not comply with the customary and reasonable requirements in the industry. For such heavy and large cargo of heavy machines in the subject case, traditional packing manners by using cartons and bags are improper due to their oversize and irregular shapes, but the method called "nude packing" of lashing, supporting and likewise is usually adopted. In the subject case, no qualified organizations or officers issued any special survey report over the package to determine the cargo concerned was poorly packed, while MSCO also failed to prove the cargo concerned violated the reasonable packing requirements in respect of jib sections in the industry. Instead, as the long-term logistics cooperator of Hunan Zoomlion, GCL confirmed both the main machines and jib sections were packed in manners that were constantly used by the outstanding enterprises in the industry, and the subject cargo damage was irrelevant to the package. GCL also pointed out that, "industry standard packing" was required for the cargo in the goods in transit policy concerned and the insured had already warranted "the subject matter insured is in perfect condition and is properly packed". Moreover, the insurer after the occurrence of the accident did not raise any challenge to the package, so package of the cargo concerned could be deemed reasonable. In addition, package mainly functions to protect the cargo during the loading/discharging, moving, storing and transportation rather than to be compatible with the lashing operation. Arranging proper place for cargo stowage, looking for appropriate securing positions and reinforcing the lashing should fall within the carrier's obligation to care for goods in due diligence. Especially in the subject case where Hunan Zoomlion was provided to pay freight by "liner terms", that is, the freight has included charges for stowing, trimming, tallying and lashing, it shall be the carrier's compelling obligation to strengthen the lashing of jib sections according to the foreseeable sea perils on the voyage concerned. Since the deck cargo over the hatch coverNo.2 was not included in the cargo concerned and was not jib sections of the crawler cranes, even if any packing problems existed, it was irrelevant to the cargo concerned, and it could neither thus deduce that the cargo concerned was poorly packed nor exempt or relieve the carrier's liability for the subject cargo damage. To conclude, no evidence proving there existed any packing problems in the cargo concerned and that the cargo damage was thus caused had been submitted, so MSCO's defense in this respect was adopted by the court of first instance.

In sum, the court of first instance held: the subject cargo damage was co-caused by the defects in the lashing and securing and the adverse sea conditions suffered by the vessel. As for which should be the leading reason, seen from the following shipment from Xiamen Port to Indian ports, it can be known that the cargo concerned had been successfully carried to Indian ports after simple adjustment and reinforcement of lashing due to lack of the condition to discharge the cargo for rearrangement, stowage and lashing after the serious damage accident, so it was reasonably inferable that the adverse sea conditions brought about by typhoon MUIFA shall be the uppermost and decisive reason for the cargo damage, though the defects in lashing and securing inevitably turned the lashing structure vulnerable or even prematurely collapsed in front of the adverse sea conditions, and aggravated the damage to the cargo. Through comprehensive consideration of the case, it was decided by the court of first instance that 80% of the cargo damage concerned shall be attributed to the adverse sea conditions while 20% to the defects in lashing and securing.

Besides, as for whether the carrier may be exempted from liabilities or not, GCL, Shanghai Hengxin and MSCO contended, the cargo concerned was damaged due to typhoon MUIFA and the carrier could be entitled to exemption from liability for "acts of god" and "force majeure" in line with Article 51 Paragraph 1 Sub-paragraph 3 of the Maritime Code of the People's Republic of China (hereinafter referred to as "Maritime Code") and Article 311 of the Contract Law of the People's Republic of China (hereinafter referred to as "Contract Law"); meanwhile, even if the typhoon avoidance measures were considered improper, liability exemption may also be claimed by invoking Article 51 Paragraph 1 Sub-paragraph 1 of the Maritime Code that provides "fault in the navigation or management of the ship" as one of the liability-exemptible event. Hunan Zoomlion and the co-insurers argued, typhoon MUIFA had been fully predicted by the carrier, and was avoidable and conquerable, constituting no acts of god or force majeure; and the Master and the crewmembers had no faults in the ship management inclusive of making decision on typhoon avoidance, thus shall not refer to corresponding exemptions.

The court of first instance opined: the Maritime Code clearly provides the legal events from which the loss of or damage to the goods arises during the period of carrier's responsibility shall not be under the carrier's liability. Given the subject case is a case concerning dispute over contract of carriage of goods by sea, in line with the principle of "applying maritime code to the most, the special provision of Article 51 of the Maritime Code shall preferentially apply to the case. As mentioned above, the court of first instance judged that the adverse sea conditions brought about by typhoon MUIFA shall be the main cause for the cargo damage. Typhoon scale forecast is a difficult problem commonly recognized all over the world, and there are many uncertain factors that affect the typhoon movement, thus it is impossible to forecast typhoon very precisely on the basis of current technology. The wind and wave arising from the strong typhoon directly affecting the sea surface constitute tremendous threat to the ship safety. Even those ships taking shelter in anchorages could not make sure everything will be sound under the attack of typhoon. Facing the threat of typhoon, ships could only take as reasonable typhoon avoidance measures as possible to avert or mitigate the damage to the most extent. As stated above, the then-current available evidence indicated that M. V."Yuriy Arshenevskiy" had long encountered winds of over 12bft and rolling high than 35° at the material time, and the ECSFC report submitted by Hunan Zoomlion and the co-insurers also considered M.V."Yuriy Arshenevskiy" might suffer waves in height of 7-9m, while for most ships sailing at sea, waves in height over 6m can be a threat, and even for the large vessels on the ocean, 7-8m high waves and surges over 9m will also become disastrous. Therefore, the court of first held the adverse sea conditions to that extent suffered by M.V."Yuriy Arshenevskiy" belongs to abnormal perils of sea and shall constitute such "perils of sea" in the nature of "acts of god" under the Maritime Code, so the carrier may be legally exempted from the liability for the damage thus caused.

The court of first instance further held that: it is a common sense that errors would exist in typhoon forecast, and direction changes and speed increases are normal features of typhoons. The EGC used by M.V."Yuriy Arshenevskiy" also gave reminders in this regard, so when choosing measures for typhoon avoidance, masters shall take reasonable consideration of such errors in typhoon forecast and make such a decision that could ensure the safety of the vessel, persons and the cargo to the largest extent rather than place the hopes on narrowly passing by the typhoon. It is just because of this that masters usually take relatively conservative measures in avoiding typhoon which seem to be unreasonable or unnecessary in the eyes of non-professional persons. In the subject case, the Master's decision to reinforce the lashing while taking shelter at the anchorage after M.V."Yuriy Arshenevskiy" completed loading at Shanghai Port was worth appreciation. However, two days later when the typhoon had obvious trend to turn its direction, the Master's choice to sail to the northeast of Cheju Island for typhoon avoidance was not diligent but even a bit risky, which finally caused the vessel exactly entering the right semi-circle, namely the dangerous semi-circle of the typhoon center. At that time, it should be best to remain anchoring inside the port for sheltering typhoon, which might be mitigated or even avoided the cargo damage concerned. However, the Master had the "sole discretion" over the problems concerning the ship safety, that is, no matter the Master made the decision as per whose instruction, to satisfy whose requirement, by adopting whose recommendation or upon the resolution of a meeting, once the Master determined, the decision should be deemed as the independent discretion of the Master himself. Although the Master had faults in deciding how to avoid the typhoon, such faults shall be deemed as the fault of the Master in navigation or management of the ship pursuant to the provision of Article 51 Paragraph 1 Sub-paragraph 1 of the Maritime Code, for which the carrier may be exempted from liability.

Besides, with respect to whether or not M.V. "Yuriy Arshenevskiy" was seaworthy during the voyage involved, which is relevant to the liability exemption issue, Hunan Zoomlion and the co-insurers held the cargo stowage, lashing and securing was seriously improper and that the carrier and actual carrier failed to duly care for the cargo concerned, which caused the vessel's un-seaworthiness.

The court of first instance held: according to Article 47 of the Maritime Code which provides "the carrier shall, before and at the beginning of the voyage, exercise due diligence to make the ship seaworthy, properly man, equip and supply the ship and to make the holds, refrigerating and cool chambers and all other parts of the ship in which goods are carrier, fit and safe for their reception, carriage and preservation", these are legal obligations upon the carrier (including the actual carrier) for ship seaworthiness and are also preconditions for the carrier to apply for liability exemption. When M.V. "Yuriy Arshenevskiy" departed from Shanghai to perform the carriage involved, all the relevant ship certificates carried onboard were in their validity period and in conformity with relevant requirements; meanwhile, by comparison with the certificate of minimum safety manning, the crew name list and the crew's competency certificates on board M.V. "Yuriy Arshenevskiy", the crew manning of the vessel was also in conformity with relevant requirements; the cargo concerned was stowed in the cargo holds as per the shipper's request, and according to the loading survey report, the holds where the cargo concerned was loaded and stowed were in serviceable condition; besides, as mentioned above, M.V. "Yuriy Arshenevskiy" was of good stability and the Defendants have fulfilled their obligation to submit prima facie evidence to prove the vessel's seaworthiness. To the contrary, Hunan Zoomlion and the co-insurers failed to provide comprehensive and effective contrary evidence, so the argument of Hunan Zoomlion and the co-insurers in this regard was not supported by the court of first instance.

To conclude, as to the part of cargo losses caused by the vessel's encountering the typhoon MUIFA in near distance due to the Master's hasty decision to leave Shanghai Port, the court of first instance held the carrier might also enjoy liability exemption according to the law. The defense of GCL, Shanghai Hengxin and MSCO in this part was partly adopted by the court of first instance.

Furthermore, regarding to whether or not the Defendants improperly enlarged the losses. Hunan Zoomlion and the co-insurers held that it was extremely unreasonable for M.V. "Yuriy Arshenevskiy" to sail to India after her stay in Xiamen Port. The carrier had a gross negligence in doing so and it should be liable for the enlarged losses caused hereby. GCL also considered the continued sailing of M.V. "Yuriy Arshenevskiy" caused a series of problems for the consequent handling of the accident, and immense obstacles to determine the losses. MSCO defended that during the period when M.V. "Yuriy Arshenevskiy" stayed in Xiamen Port, the shipowner had exerted its best efforts to strive for discharge of cargo at ports in China, but due to objective constraints, M.V. "Yuriy Arshenevskiy" had no choice but to continue her voyage to India. The shipowner had no fault in this respect.

The court of first instance held: the then-currently available evidence could prove that MSCO has endeavored to discharge cargo at Xiamen Port. It was due to the customs supervision and control that the damaged cargo could not be discharged at Xiamen Port. This result was neither caused by any of the Defendants, nor any of their employees or agents, and it could not be ascribed to any of the Defendants. In addition, the subject case only involved 5 out of 31 shipments of cargoes carried on M.V. "Yuriy Arshenevskiy". If the vessel sailed back to Shanghai Port, there would be also a lot of uncertainties. It would not only increase the carrier's legal risk for liability of breach of contract, but might further enlarge the losses of other cargo owners. Therefore, the continued sailing of M.V. "Yuriy Arshenevskiy" as per charterer's instruction did not have any significant fault. The subsequent logistics costs incurred to Hunan Zoomlion, namely the ocean freight, costs for measurement survey and pre loading inspection in sum of USD306,400 and the port ground fee in sum of USD240,025.78, all of which were incurred in India, were not enlarged losses caused by the three Defendants' misconducts, but losses which failed to be mitigated even though the carrier had exercised due diligence to assist Hunan Zoomlion in mitigation after the accident concerned caused by perils of sea. Therefore, Hunan Zoomlion had no right to claim compensation for such costs from the carriers. For the same reason, the ground fee at Shanghai Port in sum of RMB403,606, the road freight for carriage of cargo back to factory in sum of RMB670,000, import duty in sum of RMB217,194.96 and the import VAT in sum of RMB498,462.43 due to expiration of one-year time limit for export rejects shall be also born by Hunan Zoomlion. Furthermore, the first two items of logistics costs would have incurred as well even if the cargo was transported back to discharge at Shanghai Port as per Hunan Zoomlion's instruction, and the last two items of duties have exceeded the scope of costs which can be reasonably foreseen according to Article 113 of the Contract Law. Therefore, the court of first instance did not support the claim of Hunan Zoomlion and the co-insurers for these four items of losses.

Fourthly, as for whether or not Hunan Zoomlion was an eligible Plaintiff, GCL held that the owner of the cargo concerned was Zoomlion HK, so Hunan Zoomlion had no right to claim cargo loss against GCL, Shanghai Hengxin and MSCO in this case; Shanghai Hengxin considered that neither under the annual transportation agreement, nor under the House B/Ls or the Master B/Ls did Hunan Zoomlion and the co-insurers have a right to sue against Shanghai Hengxin; MSCO held that Hunan Zoomlion was neither the shipper nor the obligee of the cargo concerned, so it was not the qualified Plaintiff. GCL, Shanghai Hengxin and MSCO also held that since Hunan Zoomlion had confirmed to transfer all their right of recourse to the insurers, they had already lost the right to sue.

The court of first instance held that: the transfer of cargo ownership is closely connected to the agreement in the sales contract between the parties. In order to prevent involvement of complicate disputes over sales contracts into carriage contract relationships, and also to increase the certainty of legal relationships in transportation, the litigious rights of the cargo interests in disputes arising from contracts of carriage of goods by sea does not need to be connected to their ownership of the cargo. The only thing Hunan Zoomlion needed to prove was that it had the legal right to control the cargo. According to the ascertained facts, Hunan Zoomlion signed a transportation agreement with GCL for the carriage of the cargo concerned, and in the light of the whole process of the carriage and the back shipment to China, Hunan Zoomlion was the party who delivered the cargo concerned to GCL, who was the business unit and consignor stated on customs declaration forms, and also the consignee stated on the B/L for the back shipment to China, and Hunan Zoomlion was the only party who sent instructions to the carrier in respect of the cargo concerned, and also the only party who claimed against the carrier in respect of the cargo concerned (the right of the co-insurers was subrogated from Hunan Zoomlion). Moreover, the seller defined in the sales contracts included Hunan Zoomlion's associated enterprises, and the named seller Zoomlion HK had also declared that Hunan Zoomlion had the full rights of the cargo. Therefore, Hunan Zoomlion had the right, as obligee of the cargo concerned, to raise a claim against the carrier on the basis of the contract of carriage of goods by sea. Although part of the costs in this case were paid by Hunan Zoomlion's associated enterprise, this internal relationship of payment and settlement between Hunan Zoomlion and their associated enterprise did not affect legal position and rights of Hunan Zoomlion in this case, and in the external relationship, these costs should be deemed to be paid by Hunan Zoomlion itself. Furthermore, although Hunan Zoomlion had obtained the indemnity from co-insurers, there was still a difference between the indemnity amount and their claim amount, and according to Article 95 of Special Maritime Procedure Law of the People's Republic of China, where the losses of the insured caused by a third party cannot be fully covered by insurance indemnity, the insurer and the insured may act as co-Plaintiffs to claim compensation against the third party. The court of first instance held whether these uncovered losses existed, or whether these losses should be supported was a question in other respect and had no relevancy with the litigious right of Hunan Zoomlion. The defense of GCL, Shanghai Hengxin and MSCO in this part was not supported by the court of first instance.

Fifthly, as to whether or not the co-insurers were qualified Plaintiffs and whether or not the limitation of period for claims had expired when their claims were lodged, GCL, Shanghai Hengxin and MSCO held that, Hunan Zoomlion did not have any insurable interests in the cargo concerned, the indemnity made by co-insurers to Hunan Zoomlion was improper, there were defects in the source and basis of co-insurers' right of subrogation, so they cannot become qualified Plaintiffs according to the law. Shanghai Hengxin also held that the limitation period for claims by co-insurers had already exceeded. Furthermore, Shanghai Hengxin and MSCO held that the insurance policy concerned was issued by Zurich China independently, so Ping An Hunan and Sunshine Hunan had no right to sue.

The court of first instance held that: it could be seen from the emails from the agent of co-insurers to the agent of MSCO after the accident concerned and the Crawford survey report submitted by Hunan Zoomlion and the co-insurers that, Zurich China had made the insurance adjustment and settlement towards the cargo damage to Hunan Zoomlion on the basis of five insurance certificates No. MIA0010018BG-0369/0375/0376/0370/0367. This procedure corresponded with the agreement in the co-insurance agreement that Zurich China shall have the full right to deal with daily businesses with the insured. However, this set of insurance certificates bore no the signature and stamp of the insured, and there was no evidence to prove they had been accepted by Hunan Zoomlion. They could not be deemed as "insurance certificates issued by the insurer separately" which is "at the request of the insured" as stipulated in Article 232 of the Maritime Code. Therefore, this set of insurance certificates could not deny the insurance contractual relationship proved by the goods in transit policy issued by co-insurers on August 18, 2010. According to the goods in transit policy, the insured was Hunan Zoomlion and other parties concerned such as the associated companies. The then-currently available evidence proved that Zurich China, Ping An Hunan and Sunshine Hunan had paid the indemnity amounts to the insured as per their co-insurance proportions respectively, so they all had the right of subrogation against the responsible parties concerned in the limit of their indemnity amount according to the law. Moreover, it is stipulated in Article 14 of the Provisions of the Supreme People's Court on Several Issues about the Trial of Cases concerning Marine Insurance Disputes that the people's court that accepts a case involving any dispute over the insurer's exercise of the right of subrogation to claim for compensations shall only try the legal relationship between the third party that caused the insurance accident and the insured. Accordingly, there was no need to make a substantive judgment towards the insurance contractual relationship between co-insurers and the insured Hunan Zoomlion in this case. The defense of GCL, Shanghai Hengxin and MSCO, which alleged that the indemnities of co-insurers exceeded their insurance responsibility and the insured had no right to accept the indemnity shall not affect co-insurers' right of subrogation. In addition, according to Article 15 of Provisions of the Supreme People's Court on Several Issues about the Trial of Cases concerning Marine Insurance Disputes, in cases where the insurer, after obtaining the right of subrogation to claim for compensations, claims for the interruption of the limitation of actions for the reason that the insured filed an action, the people's court shall support the claim. In this case, the co-insurers joined the actions taken by the insured against a third party, the limitation period of actions had been interrupted, and had not been recalculated yet. Therefore, when the co-insurers made the claim, the limitation period of action had not yet expired. The defense of GCL, Shanghai Hengxin and MSCO was not supported by the court of first instance.

Sixthly, regarding to whether or not GCL should be liable to compensate for the cargo damage, Hunan Zoomlion and the co-insurers alleged that GCL was the contractual carrier of the carriage concerned. However, GCL held that the relationship between Hunan Zoomlion and GCL was a relationship of shipping agency agreement, the annual transportation agreement had been unilaterally cancelled by Hunan Zoomlion before the carriage concerned, and GCL was only a shipping agent of the transportation in this case.

The court of first instance held: this case is concerning a dispute arising from contract of carriage of goods by sea, and Hunan Zoomlion and the co-insurers clearly stated to claim against GCL for the latter's liability as a carrier according to the annual transportation agreement which was concluded between Hunan Zoomlion and GCL. Judging from the expressions used in the agreement such as "undertake (different from the words 'entrusts...to act as its agent' as used inlong-term strategic cooperation transportation agreement) the cargo transportation operation from Shanghai to Mumbai, India", "after the cargo arrives at the destination port, ... If damage or loss of cargo is found to be caused by Party A's (GCL) faults during transportation, all the losses arising therefrom shall be undertaken by Party A", it is the exclusive right of management for Hunan Zoomlion's logistics to India and the responsibilities as a carrier that was obtained and assumed by GCL under the agreement. Although disputes was aroused between the two parties in respect of whether the agreement should be cancelled or performed continuously, the then-current available evidence showed that the cargo concerned was delivered to GCL by Hunan Zoomlion according to the annual transportation agreement, and GCL never surrendered any acceptable transport documents to Hunan Zoomlion for Hunan Zoomlion to ensure their control over the goods. Therefore, no matter whether the annual transportation agreement had been effectively cancelled or not, the legal position, rights and obligations of both parties in the carriage concerned would be deemed according to the annual transportation agreement if no evidence could prove that GCL's legal position had been changed in this carriage through consensus of both Hunan Zoomlion and GCL. In this case, GCL accepted the cargo concerned, collected freight from Hunan Zoomlion, signed a voyage charterparty with Shanghai Hengxin in its own name and delivered the cargo concerned to the ocean carrier as the shipper. All these conducts correspond with the conduct of a "carrier" defined in the Maritime Code. Therefore, GCL should be deemed as contractual carrier for the cargo concerned in this case, and responsible as a carrier towards Hunan Zoomlion for cargo concerned. It also should have the right to rely on the exemptions stipulated in the Maritime Code, in other words, the liability for the aforesaid 20% cargo damage caused by defects in lashing and securing as determined by the court of first instance could not be exempted by the carrier according to the law, and the court of first instance held GCL liable for such 20% loss.

Seventhly, as to whether or not Shanghai Hengxin should be liable to compensate for the cargo damage, Hunan Zoomlion and the co-insurers contended that Shanghai Hengxin was the actual carrier for the cargo concerned, while Shanghai Hengxin defended that the loading, lashing, securing and discharging of the cargo were just preparatory operations for carriage, so Shanghai Hengxin did not actually perform the carriage of the cargo concerned.

The court of first instance held: according to the definition of the "actual carrier" in Article 42 of the Maritime Code, "performance of carriage of goods" is the essential requirement to determine an actual carrier, and the actual carrier's control over the cargo and the actual performance of carriage are the fundamental reasons for the law to break the privity of contract and specially stipulate the liability of actual carrier towards cargo owner. Therefore, "performance of carriage" should be explained as to control the vessel, manage the cargo, and personally perform the carriage. Although Shanghai Hengxin performed cargo operations such as loading, discharging and lashing of the cargo concerned, and "load, handle, stow" is within the carrier's obligations to care for cargo as provided for in Article 48 of the Maritime Code, it cannot be thus considered the one who did those operations as the carrier or the actual carrier. As one link of the voyage charterparty chain, the loading, discharging and lashing performed by Shanghai Hengxin were not only the performance of their obligations agreed in FTL (abbreviation for "Full Liner Terms", which means the responsibility of loading and discharging is on shipowner's shoulder) in the voyage charterparty between them and GCL, but also the performance of the charterer's obligations on behalf of Hanssy HK in the time charter party between Hanssy HK and Kings Ocean. Since Shanghai Hengxin was neither the owner nor bareboat charterer of the vessel, there was no evidence to prove their authorization on the issuance of the Master B/L, and they were not able to control over the vessel or manage the cargo during the actual carriage, Shanghai Hengxin was not the actual carrier for the cargo concerned. Although the court of first instance that there were defects in the cargo lashing and securing that was under Shanghai Hengxin's responsibilities, in light of the privity of contract and the legal provision that the carrier should be liable for the whole carriage, GCL as the carrier should compensate the cargo owner in advance, and then recover from Shanghai Hengxin in another claim. Therefore, the court of first instance held Shanghai Hengxin shall not be liable for compensation in this case.

Eighthly, as to whether or not MSCO should be liable to compensate for the cargo damage, Hunan Zoomlion and the co-insurers held MSCO was the actual carrier of the cargo concerned, had a gross negligence on care for cargo and thus should be liable to compensate for the cargo damage. Moreover, under the relationship of bill of lading, MSCO should also be liable to compensate for the losses suffered by Hunan Zoomlion who was the legal holder of the master bills of lading. However, MSCO defended that the shipowner was neither the carrier nor the actual carrier for the cargo concerned and even if the shipowner was deemed as the actual carrier, it should not be liable for compensation since the cargo damage was caused by perils of sea and poor packing.

The court of first instance held: MSCO never signed any carriage contract with Hunan Zoomlion, neither did Hunan Zoomlion book any shipping space with or deliver any cargo to MSCO. Although Hunan Zoomlion used to "hold" the Master B/Ls, but since it was not the shipper or consignee described in the B/Ls involved and the straight B/Ls is non-transferable according to the law, Hunan Zoomlion was not the legal holder even if it possessed the B/Ls. In short, there was no evidence which can prove the existence of contract of carriage of goods by sea between Hunan Zoomlion and MSCO. Moreover, as mentioned above, the cargo damage was caused by adverse sea conditions and the defects in cargo lashing and securing. Although M.V. "Yuriy Arshenevskiy" was attacked by the typhoon in a close distance due to the Master's improper method to avoid typhoon, MSCO shall have the right of exemption according to the law. Also, MSCO was not responsible for cargo lashing and securing, and there was also no problem in stowage/securing which would affect the stability and safety of the ship and thus have the shipowner blamed for ultimate responsibility. The then-currently available evidence also suggested that, after the completion of loading of each hold, the vessel had checked the condition of lashing and resolved the problems founded. The vessel even applied for anchoring particularly in order to strengthen the lashing. Therefore, the ship owner had cautiously and appropriately fulfilled their obligations to care for cargo with due diligence, and should not be liable to compensate for the cargo damage caused by defects in lashing and securing. In addition, the shipowner had no obvious negligence in respect of finishing the planed voyage. Therefore, MSCO should not be liable for compensation in this case. Accordingly, the claim in respect of the application fee for vessel arrest in sum of RMB5,000 was rejected by the court of first instance.

Ninthly, as to the amount of cargo losses, GCL, Shanghai Hengxin and MSCO defended that, Hunan Zoomlion's conduct of carrying the cargo concerned back to

China was unreasonable, which made the cargo losses enlarged during the period of its back shipment to China and the consequent processes; the amount of cargo losses should be determined on the basis of its condition in Xiamen Port. It was not objective for Hunan Zoomlion to determine the losses according to the final condition of the cargo when it arrived at Zoomlion Heavy's factory and to handle the salvage value of the cargo unilaterally. In addition, the cargo value should be subject to the value described in the customs declaration forms.

The court of first instance held: firstly, despite of the court's demand, none of GCL, Shanghai Hengxin and MSCO managed to submit any explanation in respect of comparison of cargo condition before and after its back shipment to China, and there was no sufficient evidence proving the cargo damage had been enlarged substantially by the back shipment. Secondly, it was incautious to determine a constructive total loss without using any relevant inspection equipment to conduct inspection. Hunan Zoomlion's decision to carry the cargo back to China had been confirmed and approved by the insurers and the surveyor entrusted by insurers. In the absence of any sufficient contrary evidence to prove the feasibility and economic advantages of surveying the cargo and dealing with the salvage value in India, the doubt of GCL, Shanghai Hengxin and MSCO in respect of the back shipment of the cargo concerned to China could hardly stand. Thirdly, the comments from Puri Crawford & Associates India Pvt. Ltd. that the accessories of crawler cranes were repairable could not deny the conclusion that the cargo concerned constituted conclusive total loss with no repair value after an overall inspection; the actual salvage value of the cargo was much higher than the value assessed in the CCIC inspection certificate, so the conclusion that the losses were enlarged on such basis can hardly be supported. Fourthly, Zoomlion Heavy, as the manufacturer of the crawler cranes concerned, had professional knowledge and relevant qualifications to determine the damage condition of the crawler cranes concerned. Although Zoomlion Heavy and Hunan Zoomlion were interested parties, since it was agreed by all parties in the court hearing that there were very limited numbers of units or institutions capable of doing the inspection for this special equipment concerned, the feasibility of letting an independent third party to inspect was objectively limited. Moreover, the surveyor entrusted by the insurers had been fully involved in assessment on the cargo damage and the handling of salvage value. The conclusion of constructive total loss also corresponded with the results of previous inspections. Therefore, the court of first instance held the inspection result and handling of salvage value objective and reasonable. Accordingly, the court of first instance did not accept the defense of GCL, Shanghai Hengxin and MSCO that the back shipment of the cargo concerned to China had enlarged the cargo losses and the assessment amount of losses was not objective. However, the cargo price in sales contract and commercial invoice was different from the price described in the customs declaration forms. Although Hunan Zoomlion and the co-insurers explained that Hunan Zoomlion understated the cargo value for the purpose to enjoy preferential tax policy for export, but they submitted no relevant evidential documents. Therefore, this contention could not stand. Customs declaration forms, as documentary evidence which is recognized and recorded by customs, has a higher probative force on the actual cargo value than the sales contract or commercial invoice which was self-issued. Therefore, the actual value of the cargo at the time of loading should be based on the amount described in the customs declaration forms. Since it was expressed in customs declaration forms that the trading term was CIF, that is to say, the total price of the cargo described in the customs declaration forms contained the cargo value when loading, insurance fee and the freight. Therefore, the actual value of the cargo was USD3,345,616.80, and the compensation amount should be determined on the basis of such amount. The defense of GCL, Shanghai Hengxin and MSCO in this respect was accepted by the court of first instance.

Tenthly, with respect to limitation of liability, GCL, Shanghai Hengxin and MSCO defended that, even if other defensescould not be supported, they still had the right to apply to the package limitation of liability and the limitation of liability for maritime claims as provided for in the Maritime Code. They also held the limit for package liability should be USD2,584,455.60 (which was 1,711,560 Special Drawing Rights) according to the law. As for the limit of liability for maritime claims in this case, Shanghai Hengxin held it should be determined based on the percentage of the compensation amount as judged in this case in the amount of the total losses caused by the accident. MSCO considered it should be calculated according to the corresponding percentage in the limit of package liability for the cargo loss claim accepted by the courts of China, but in any event the compensation liability for the shipowner to bear would not exceed USD2,190,390. For this, Hunan Zoomlion and the co-insurers alleged that, the cargo damage in this case resulted from acts of the carrier done recklessly and with knowledge that such damage would probably result. The carrier had no right to enjoy the limitation of liability.

The court of first instance held: according to Article 59 and Article 209 in the Maritime Code, the carrier shall not be entitled to the benefit of the limitation of liability provided for in this law if it is proved that the damage of the goods and the loss which caused the claim resulted from an act or omission of the carrier done with the intent to cause such damage or recklessly and with knowledge that such damage would probably result. In this case, there was no evidence which could prove the cargo damage concerned arising from a marine accident was caused by an act or omission of the carrier done with the intent to cause such damage or recklessly and with knowledge that such damage would probably result. Therefore, the carrier concerned should have the right to apply to package limitation of liability in respect of compensation for cargo damage. The number of package stated in B/Ls concerned was 176, and the gross weight was 855,780 kg. According to the calculation standard of "666.67 units of account per package, or 2 units of account per kilogram, whichever is the higher", the limit of package liability of the cargo loss in this case should be 1,711,560 Special Drawing Rights (SDR). And about the limit of liability for maritime claims, since none of GCL, Shanghai Hengxin and MSCO constituted a limitation fund for the liability for maritime claims, this question would only be considered on case-by-case basis. The gross tonnage of M.V. "Yuriy Arshenevskiy" is 18,574 tons, so according to the calculation method provided for in Article 210 of the Maritime Code, the limit of liability for maritime claims in this case should be 3,185,358 SDR.

In this case, since the cargo concerned had constituted a constructive total loss, the amount of cargo loss should be calculated after deducting the salvage value from the actual value of the cargo. The actual value described in the customs declaration forms was USD3,345,616.80. The court of first instance accepted the viewpoint of Hunan Zoomlion and the co-insurers that the losses should be calculated in RMB per the exchange rate of 1:6.4305 between USD and RMB on the date of accident, namely, August 8, 2011, which turned out to be RMB21,513,988.83. After taking off the salvage value of RMB5,060,160, the amount of cargo loss concerned was RMB16,453,828.83. In conclusion, GCL as the carrier should be responsible for 20% of the compensation, which was RMB3,290,765.77. Therefore, it was necessary for the case to refer to limit of liability.

According to the claim computation form of marine transportation cargo insurance, Hunan Zoomlion had been fully indemnified in respect of the cargo loss concerned. Therefore, GCL should compensate the co-insurers in sum of RMB3,290,765.77. According to the respective proportions of their actual indemnity, namely, the coinsurance proportions, Zurich China should be compensated of RMB1,645,382.89, Ping An Hunan RMB987,229.73, and Sunshine Hunan RMB658,153.15.

In addition, as to the co-insurers' claim for loss of interests calculated from February 1, 2013 to the effective date of relevant judgment as per the loan interest rate published by the People's Bank of China during the corresponding period, the court of first instance held that, the loss of interest claimed by the Co-insurance was the fruits of the insurance indemnities they paid, so it should be calculated from the date of actual payment. Since the co-insurers made 11 separate payments from July 2012 to August 2013, the court of first instance considered that the contention of the co-insurers that the interest should be calculated from February 1, 2013 is reasonable and can be supported. And since the co-insurers are financial institutions, their request to calculate the interest as per the loan interest rate was reasonable and was supported.

According to Article 41, Article 42 Sub-paragraph 1, Article 46 Paragraph 1, Article 51 Paragraph 1 Sub-paragraph 1, Article 51 Paragraph 1 Sub-paragraph 3, Article 54, Article 55 Paragraph 1, Article 55 Paragraph 2 and Article 252 Paragraph 1 of the Maritime Code of the People's Republic of China, Article 64 Paragraph 1 of the Civil Procedure Law of the People's Republic of China, and Article 2 and Article 76 of the Some Provisions of the Supreme People's Court on Evidence in Civil Procedure, the court of first instance rendered the judgment as follows: 1. GCL shall, within ten days as of the effective day of judgment of first instance, compensate Zurich China RMB1,645,382.89, plus the interest thereof (calculated from February 1, 2013 to the date when the judgment became effective at the same grade loan interest rate announced by the People's Bank of China during the corresponding period); 2. GCL shall, within ten days as of the effective day of judgment of first instance, compensate Ping An Hunan RMB987,229.73, plus the interest thereof (calculated from February 1, 2013 to the date when judgment of first instance became effective at the same grade loan interest rate announced by the People's Bank of China during the corresponding period); 3. GCL shall, within ten days as of the effective day of judgment of first instance, compensate Sunshine Hunan RMB658,153.15, plus the interests thereof (calculated from February 1, 2013 to the date when the judgment became effective at the same grade loan interest rate announced by the People's Bank of China during the corresponding period); 4. not support the claim made by Hunan Zoomlion; 5. not support the other claims made by the co-insurers.

Court acceptance fee in amount of RMB159,743.11, Hunan Zoomlion and the co-insurers shall jointly bear RMB126,616.98, and GCL shall bear RMB33,126.13.

The co-insurers was dissatisfied with the judgment of first instance, and filed appeal alleging:

1. As the shipowner of M.V. "Yuriy Arshenevskiy", MSCO managed the vessel, allocated crewmembers, actually used and controlled the vessel and accepted the sub-entrustment by the carrier to perform the transportation, which completely meet the definition of actual carrier under the Maritime Code, so MSCO should be the actual carrier of the cargo concerned.
2. Even though it was agreed upon in the time charter party concluded by MSCO and the carrier that the cargo stevedoring, lashing, stowage and securing shall be under the carrier's responsibility, MSCO should not be exempted from the liability for the cargo damage suffered by the shipper on the basis of the agreement of liability exemption in the time charter party concluded with the carrier.
3. Shanghai Hengxin accepted the sub-entrustment of the carrier GCL and entrusted a party not involved in the case to carry out the lashing and securing of the cargo concerned, so Shanghai Hengxin was also the actual carrier and should be jointly and severally liable with the carrier GCL for the damage to the cargo concerned.
4. The cargo stowage and lashing/securing were seriously improper and inconsistent with the requirements in *CSS Code* and *Cargo Securing Manual*, so the vessel was not seaworthy; as the cargo stowage was seriously improper, the space left in the cargo holds was insufficient for cargo securing operations and for the crewmembers to check the securing condition during sailing and conduct additional securing when necessary, and thus the carrier, neither before sailing nor during the voyage, performed or was able to perform its obligation of care for cargo.
5. The carrier failed to fulfill its obligation of care for cargo which resulted in the unseaworthiness of the vessel, so the carrier had lost the precondition and basis to invoke exemption. Even though the exemptible cause indeed existed in the subject case, the carrier should not refer to the exemption clause to be exempted from its liability for compensation.
6. It is factually and legally groundless for the court of first instance to hold that typhoon MUIFA and the adverse sea conditions caused thereby constituted

perils of sea in the nature of "act of god" under the Maritime Code and further determine that the carrier may be exempted from 80% of the liability.
7. The Master had no faults in making decision of typhoon avoidance, and the court of first instance failed to ascertain relevant facts properly. Therefore, Zurich China requested the appellate court to dismiss item 3 and item 5 of the judgment of first instance, and amend the judgment to that GCL, Shanghai Hengxin and MSCO shall bear the joint liability for compensation of RMB plus interests thereof calculated at the loan interest rate published by the People's Bank of China for the corresponding period from February 1, 2013 to the date when the judgment comes into force., Ping An Hunan requested the appellate court to dismiss item 3 and item 5 of the judgment of first instance, and amend the judgment to that the three Respondents shall bear the joint liability for compensation of RMB6,289,403.99 plus interests thereof calculated at the loan interest rate published by the People's Bank of China for the corresponding period from February 1, 2013 to the date when the judgment comes into force, and Sunshine Hunan requested the appellate court to dismiss item 3 and item 5 of the judgment of first instance, and amend the judgment to that the three Respondents shall bear the joint liability for compensation of RMB4,190,468.40 plus interests thereof calculated at the loan interest rate published by the People's Bank of China for the corresponding period from February 1, 2013 to the date when the judgment comes into force.

In response to the appeal of the co-insurers, GCL defended:

1. GCL was not the carrier of the cargo concerned, but the forwarding agent of Hunan Zoomlion, so GCL should not be held liable for the carriage of the cargo concerned.
2. It was correct for the court of first instance to hold that the direct cause of the damage to the cargo concerned was the force majeure caused by adverse sea conditions, and under such circumstance, the cargo lashing factor should be overwhelmed by the force majeure factor and shall not be held as a common cause of the damage to the cargo concerned, so GCL shall not be liable pro rata for the damage to the cargo concerned.

Shanghai Hengxin defended:

1. As for the causes of the damage to the cargo concerned in this case, comprehensive investigation and expert debates were conducted during the first instance procedures, and Shanghai Hengxin insisted that the force majeure should be the only and fundamental cause of the damage to the cargo concerned.
2. In this case, there existed two independent contractual relationships, namely, the contractual relationship between Shanghai GCL and Hunan Zoomlion, which was not under a contact of carriage of goods by sea as defined by the Maritime Code, and the relationship under a contract of carriage of goods by sea as evidenced by a bill of lading. The former legal relationship should only bind Shanghai GCL and Hunan Zoomlion, while in the latter relationship under a

contract of carriage of goods by sea as evidenced by a bill of lading, Hunan Zoomlion was neither the shipper nor could prove that it had other interests in the contract of carriage of goods by sea, so Hunan Zoomlion and the co-insurers should not have the title to claim. Seen from the B/Ls concerned, MSCO was the carrier, but neither GCL nor Shanghai Hengxin was a party to the legal relationship under a contract of carriage of goods by sea. 3. Whether from the current legislation or from the judicial practice, Shanghai Hengxin should not be deemed as the actual carrier, but only involved in a link of the whole charter party chain for signing the voyage charter party.

MSCO defended:

1. MSCO was neither the actual carrier nor the carrier of the cargo concerned, and should not be liable for the damage to the cargo concerned.
2. The stowage, lashing and securing of the cargo concerned satisfied the requirements of IMO and were not the cause of the damage to the cargo concerned.
3. Since M.V. "Yuriy Arshenevskiy" was seaworthy both before and at the beginning of the voyage concerned, and the crewmembers had taken reasonable care of the cargo, even if MSCO was determined as the carrier or the actual carrier, MSCO should in all events be entitled to liability exemption.
4. "Perils of the sea" was a concept completely different from "force majeure" and typhoon MUIFA encountered by M.V. "Yuriy Arshenevskiy" in this case constituted the "perils of the sea".

Hunan Zoomlion expressed its agreement with the appeal submissions made by the co-insurers and indicated that its submissions in this case would be subject to the submissions made by the co-insurers and that no independent submissions would be further made.

GCL was dissatisfied with the judgment of first instance, and filed appeal alleging:

1. GCL was not the carrier of the cargo concerned in this case, but only the forwarding agent of Hunan Zoomlion. Firstly, although *Long-term Strategic Cooperation Agreement on Transportation* between GCL and Hunan Zoomlion was named as "agreement on transportation", it had been clarified in its first clause that the relationship between two parties was forwarding agency relationship and the status of GCL was forwarding agent. Secondly, pursuant to the agreement under the annual transportation agreement for crawler cranes to India, Hunan Zoomlion had the right to unilaterally terminate the agreement and had in fact exercised such right. The annual transportation agreement for crawler cranes to India had already been terminated, so the legal relationship between GCL and Hunan Zoomlion should be considered on the basis of *Long-term Strategic Cooperation Agreement on Transportation*. Thirdly, in respect of the transportation of the cargo concerned, Hunan Zoomlion had issued separate booking notes to GCL, and the freight actually performed under the shipping agency

relationship was different from that specified in the annual transportation agreement for crawler cranes to India, which indicated that the performance of these two parties in the transportation of the cargo concerned was not based on the annual transportation agreement for crawler cranes to India. Lastly, although GCL had concluded a voyage charter party with Shanghai Hengxin in this case, for their long-term cooperation with GCL, both Hunan Zoomlion and Shanghai Hengxin had the knowledge that the status of GCL was forwarding agent, and Hunan Zoomlion even made a written confirmation in this regard. The fact that Hunan Zoomlion was dissatisfied with GCL being indicated as the shipper under the Master B/Ls could also prove that Hunan Zoomlion also deemed GCL as a forwarding agent at the time when the cargo concerned was shipped out.

2. The court of first instance made wrong determination on the liability for cargo lashing. The lashing standard of marine cargoes should be only required to meet the need of normal sailing at sea, and the cargo damage caused by the extreme weather on the voyage concerned should not be used to determine that the cargo lashing and securing was improper. Shanghai Hengxin had made clear instructions to M.V. "Yuriy Arshenevskiy" before she departed from Shanghai Port, after she encountered the typhoon MUIFA and before she departed from Xiamen Port. This sufficiently indicated the effective control of Shanghai Hengxin over the vessel, and their actual performance of loading, discharging and lashing further constituted their characters as actual carrier. Therefore, Shanghai Hengxin should be deemed as the actual carrier of the cargo concerned and should be liable for the cargo lashing and securing.
3. The decision of continuing the voyage to India made by MSCO hastily was cursory and irresponsible in which caused further enlargement of the cargo damage, and MSCO should bear liability accordingly for this.
4. It was legally groundless for the court of first instance to support the co-insurers' request for calculating the interest as per the loan interest rate on the ground that the co-insurers are financial institutions. Based on the above, GCL requested the appellate court to revoke the judgment of first instance and reject all the claimed filed by Hunan Zoomlion and co-insurers against GCL.

In response to GCL's appeal, the co-insurers defended:

1. The court of first instance had made correct determination on the legal position of GCL. After the occurrence of the accident concerned, GCL submitted to Xiamen Maritime Court the annual transportation agreement for crawler cranes to India as a significant basis to support its dissension on jurisdiction and now alleged that such agreement had been cancelled and terminated, which was groundless.
2. No evidence submitted could prove that any lashing equipment purchased for the cargo concerned had been recognized by China Classification Society.
3. Other defense submissions were the same with the appeal submissions.

Shanghai Hengxin defended: the legal relationship between GCL and Hunan Zoomlion was independent and the privity of contract should not be broken to pursue any other parties' legal responsibilities. The concept of actual carrier shall be limited to a bill of lading, because it is a legal system set up to protect the international trading order based a bill of lading and the basic business confidence of the consignee under the bill of lading and is a compulsory legislation. However, in this case, the contract between GCL and Hunan Zoomlion was obviously a private contract and thus had no binding effect upon any third party. The other submissions were the same with the submissions already made.

MSCO defended: the reason why M.V."Yuriy Arshenevskiy" continued the voyage to India was because only 2 of the 31 cargo owners requested to discharge the cargoes in Xiamen, but the other cargo owners did not raise such request. All the cargoes on board M.V."Yuriy Arshenevskiy" were exported to India. The export formalities for these cargoes had been completed and the export debate was even obtained for some of these cargoes, so numerous issues would be involved once the cargoes were returned. As a matter of fact, the reason why M.V."Yuriy Arshenevskiy" stayed in Xiamen for two months was because MSCO tried to satisfy Hunan Zoomlion's requirements to the maximum extent in the handling of the damaged cargo concerned, during which MSCO made its best endeavors to coordinate with the customs and other authorities. And it was under the circumstance that the coordination turned out to be fruitless that M.V."Yuriy Arshenevskiy", after obtaining the time charterer's consent, sailed to Hong Kong for bunkering and then proceeded to India. Therefore, GCL's blame was unreasonable.

During the second instance, GCL submitted the following new evidence: the letter of invitation to bid issued by Hunan Zoomlion and the reply of GCL, to prove that during the whole period of carriage, Hunan Zoomlion always regarded GCL as the forwarding agent and Shanghai Hengxin as the carrier.

To such new evidence, the co-insurers extended their cross-examination opinions as follows: these documents could not prove what GCL intended to prove. Other evidence should also be taken into consideration when the identity of GCL is determined. The content of the annual transportation agreement for crawler cranes to India clearly showed that GCL was the carrier of the cargo concerned.

Shanghai Hengxin released its cross-examination opinions as follows: the authenticity, legality and relevancy of such evidence could be confirmed, but the carrier discussed in this case should be the carrier under the contract of carriage of goods by sea as defined under the Maritime Code, who should have the rights and obligations as compulsorily provided for in the law, so the definition of the carrier should come from the legislation rather than a contract.

MSCO released its cross-examination opinions as follows: the authenticity of the evidence could be confirmed, but the evidence could not prove what GCL intended to prove, that is, the evidence could not prove that GCL was the forwarding agent of Hunan Zoomlion. However, the content of the evidence may corroborate that the real operating company of the cargo carriage concerned was in fact Hanssy HK.

As regards the said evidence, after verification, the court holds that, since the authenticity of the evidence has been confirmed by various parties, the court recognizes its authenticity, but seen from its content, such evidence can only prove that

Hunan Zoomlion invited its business partners, including GCL, to bid for its "annual transportation project on crawler cranes to India", and that GCL accepted the invitation and sent its price quotation to Hunan Zoomlion as required, rather than prove the legal position of GCL. Other evidence and facts of this case shall be considered to determine the legal position of GCL.

During the second instance, the co-insurers submitted the following new evidence:

1. Weather conditions posted by the media and corresponding typhoon avoidance measures, to prove that the typhoon was foreseeable, so the vessel should have been aware of the then-current weather and sea conditions before sailing and the influence of the typhoon on the vessel should have been avoided.
2. Meteorological message certification report, to prove the forecast message and real-time route of the typhoon.
3. *Regulations of Measures on Issuance and Dissemination of Meteorological Disaster Warning Signals*, to prove that according to the "orange alert" released on August 5, the date on which the vessel sailed, the vessel should return to the port for shelter, and the typhoon was apparently foreseeable, so the damage to the cargo concerned could have been avoided.
4. *Technical Operation Rules of Typhoon Avoidance of Ships promulgated by the Ministry of Transport*, which has specific and express provisions on the typhoon avoidance measures to be taken by ships, requesting the ships to sail into a refuge harbor before the serious threat of typhoon approaches.
5. A civil judgment rendered by Hainan High People's Court, to prove the ascertainments of fact and determinations of liability in cases involving similar typhoon condition in the judicial practices, which holds that typhoon could neither constitute force majeure nor "act of god" under the Maritime Code.

To such new evidence, GCL released its cross-examination opinions as follows: these documents were submitted beyond the time limit of adducing evidence granted by the appellate court and thus could not be accepted as new evidence; without prejudice to its submissions, GCL confirmed the authenticity of these documents, but did not confirm they could prove what the co-insurers intended to prove or they were relevant to this case, especially the civil judgment, as that case was different from this case.

Shanghai Hengxin cross-examined these documents and viewed that these documents should not be accepted as new evidence in the second instance and further released its opinions as follows:

1. As for evidence No.1 and evidence No.2, as a vessel would receive numerous meteorological and marine forecast messages during the voyage, in this case, the Master was so prudent to choose to follow the relatively more professional meteorological messages and guidelines and such a choice and judgment was reasonable. As to other alleged meteorological reports, as they were not submitted by the co-insurers until in the second instance, it could be shown that such reports were not easy to be available or they were not worthy to be noted.

The numerous professional discussions and experts' witness statements in hearing in this case could prove that the typhoon was unforeseeable and was strong enough to constitute act of god and force majeure for the vessel's navigation. Act of god is a unique liability exemption item under the Maritime Code, which gives more weight on the severity of the damage caused by a disaster other than the absolute unforeseeability.

2. As for evidence No.3 and evidence No.4, they were ministerial regulations and regulate administrative organs that issue meteorological disaster warning signals. The word "Guidelines" used in the guidelines attached to such regulations also showed that such guidelines aims to provide broad guidelines to avoid disasters or mitigate damage caused by disasters and had little significance in this case.
3. As for evidence No.5, it was a court judgment which is beyond the categories of evidence. Besides, the civil judgment submitted by the co-insurers was handed down a long time ago, many holdings in which were wrong and out-of-date. Meanwhile, according to the law, only the determination on the facts in an effective judgment may be referred to, while the determinations and discussions on the interpretation of legal provisions just inflect the collegiate panel's opinions at that time, so such civil judgment should have no referential value.

MSCO submitted its cross-examination opinions holding that these evidential documents should not be deemed as new evidence in the second instance:

1. Evidence No.1 was documents printed from websites and there existed the possibility that they had been revised, so their authenticity was not confirmed.
2. Evidence No.2 from the other perspective exactly proved that the actual moving route of the typhoon deviated from the forecasted route, which showed the typhoon was unforeseeable.
3. Evidence No.3 was not legal compulsory regulations but only industrial guidelines, which are not at the same level with the right of decision granted to the Master by the ISM Code and the SOLAS Convention and should not affect the Master's rights and powers under the international rules and regulations.
4. Evidence No.4 was also guidelines other than legal compulsory regulations.
5. Evidence No.5 was a judgment for an individual case, and the determination therein on the so-called force majeure was only the collegiate panel's personal opinions at that time and should not have any referential value.

After verification, the court holds that:

1. As to evidence No.1 and evidence No.2, as they may be validated from their source or the public information, the court confirms their authenticity. Evidence No.1 proves the information of typhoon MUIFA and the corresponding avoidance measures posted by various internet media and evidence No.2 shows the description of the real-time route of the typhoon MUIFA and the forecasts of its future route by the Meteorological Station.

2. As for evidence No.3, evidence No.4 and evidence No.5, as they are irrelevant to the facts of this case and do not conform to the definition of evidence for civil litigation as provided under the law, the court does not confirm their effect of evidenceiveness.

The other parties did not submit new evidence in the second instance.

As regards the facts the court of first instance ascertained, as the evidence submitted could support and prove these facts, the court confirms the facts the court of first instance ascertained.

The court holds:

This case is dispute over contract of carriage of goods by sea. As the destination port for the cargo concerned is outside the Chinese territory, this case is of foreign-related element. It is right for the court of first instance to determine that the laws of the People's Republic of China shall be the governing law to handle the disputes of this case according to the doctrine of the most real connection on the basis of comprehensive consideration of the parties concerned, the facts of the case and other factors, and the courts confirms such determination. According to the claim and defense submissions released and submitted by the parties during the second instance, the issues of this case during the second instance are: 1. the legal positions of GCL, Shanghai Hengxin and MSCO; 2. the causes of the damage to the cargo concerned; 3. the respective liability that GCL, Shanghai Hengxin and MSCO might bear; and 4. the amount of compensation the carrier shall undertake.

1. Regarding to legal position of GCL, Shanghai Hengxin and MSCO

As for the legal position of GCL, seen from the content of the annual transportation agreement for crawler cranes to India concluded between GCL and Hunan Zoomlion, the agreements that "Party B (Hunan Zoomlion) entrusts Party A (GCL) to undertake the cargo transportation operation from Shanghai to Mumbai, India", "freight rate", "if......postponement of shipping schedule or dead space was caused......, Party B(Hunan Zoomlion) shall indemnify Party A (GCL) the relevant costs caused by such postponement or dead space", "in the event of general average, YORK-ANTWERP RULES, 1974 shall apply", and so on are all beyond the general scope of a freight forwarding contract and meet the characteristics of a contract of carriage of goods by sea more. Seen from the acts conducted by GCL during the transportation concerned, it accepted the cargo concerned delivered by Hunan Zoomlion, collected ocean freight from Hunan Zoomlion, concluded with Shanghai Hengxin the voyage charter party in its own name, delivered the cargo concerned to the shipowner as the shipper and accepted the B/Ls issued by the shipowner's agent under which it was indicated as the shipper. All these acts are in conformity with the agreements between the two parties and are also in consistency with the normal operations of the contractual carrier in the shipping practice. Therefore, it is not improper for the first instance to determine that GCL was the carrier for the cargo concerned on such basis and the court confirms such determination. As GCL's appeal that it was the forwarding agent of Hunan Zoomlion other than the carrier for the cargo concerned was in lack of factual and legal basis, the court does not support such appeal.

As for the legal position of Shanghai Hengxin, according to the relevant provisions of the Maritime Code, the actual carrier means the person to whom the performance of carriage of goods, or part of the carriage, has been entrusted by the carrier, and includes any other person to whom such performance has been entrusted under a sub-contract. In this case, as Shanghai Hengxin was only responsible for the lashing and securing of the cargo concerned, but did not actually perform the carriage or part of the carriage of the cargo concerned, Shanghai Hengxin did not fall into the definition of the actual carrier under the law, and thus the court does not support the appeal of the co-insurers and GCL that Shanghai Hengxin shall be the actual carrier for the cargo concerned.

As for the legal position of MSCO, seen from the facts ascertained in this case, MSCO was the owner of the carrying vessel of the cargo concerned M.V. "Yuriy Arshenevskiy", accepted the entrustment of the carrier GCL, performed the carriage of the cargo concerned and issued the B/Ls which indicated that GCL was the shipper. All these acts enable MSCO to fall into the definition of the actual carrier under the law, so MSCO shall be determined as the actual carrier for the cargo concerned. It is improper for the court of first instance to determine that MSCO was not the actual carrier for the cargo concerned and the court corrects such determination. As the co-insurers' appeal that MSCO shall be determined as the actual carrier for the cargo concerned has factual and legal basis, the court accepts such appeal.

2. Regarding to causes of the damage to the cargo concerned

As for the causes of the damage to the cargo concerned, there exist disputes over the cargo stowage, the lashing and securing of the cargo, the carrier's custody of the cargo, the typhoon MUIFA and the typhoon avoidance measures.

With respect to the cargo stowage, as it was on the basis of photos that the experts made their deduction, but on one hand some photos did not reflect the whole situation and on the other hand some photos were taken at Xiamen Port when the cargoes were moved and could not reflect the condition before the occurrence of the accident, such photos cannot form a sufficient basis to determine relevant facts and the court does not accept the co-insurers' appeal in this regard.

With respect to the cargo lashing and securing issue, besides the various factors mentioned in the judgment of first instance, East China Adjusters & Surveyors Co., Ltd. unilaterally entrusted by GCL attended the site to supervise the whole loading operation and issued the loading survey report recording "……some light steel structures were lashed in the steel jibs in weak condition which is a risk at sea while the ship rowing and pitching during bad weather. So, parts of steel structure were secured with ropes and belts by cargo agent". Thereafter, the Master emailed to Shanghai Hengxin advising, "stevedores make lashing beautifully but not accordance with good sea practice so for additional lashing according to our requirements take a more time". After stevedores embarked onboard to continue the securing of the cargo, the C/O checked the securing conditions and found outstanding issues. Finally, it was not until0700UTCon August 4 that the stevedores completed the cargo securing and disembarked. It can be seen from the above facts that at least the cargo lashing and securing did not conform to the standard in the beginning. Though some issues found in the Master's and C/O's checking was solved, apparently the lashing and securing operations did not strictly conform to the standards, and it is hard to say whether some undiscovered issues still exist after the resolution. Therefore, in consideration of other facts the court of first instance ascertained, the court holds it is not improper to determine that the lashing and securing of the cargo concerned was related to the damage to the cargo concerned, and as GCL's appeal that the cargo lashing and securing did not constitute the cause of the damage to the cargo concerned is in lack of factual basis and the court does not accept it.

With respect to the relation between the damage to the cargo concerned and the typhoon MUIFA as well as the typhoon avoidance measures, the court holds, although the current technology cannot accurately foresee the moving route and strength of a typhoon, it is a matter of fact that encountering a typhoon might result in catastrophic consequences. Therefore, when a typhoon approaches, avoidance measures shall be taken with due diligence. Meanwhile, though a typhoon is hard to be accurately foreseen, the meteorological forecasts and historic data may provide a relatively sufficient basis for the decision-makers to make their judgment. Seen from the meteorological forecasts, it is possible that the typhoon MUIFA would land in Jiangsu Province or Zhejiang Province or go north along the coast. And seen from the historical data, most typhoons in this sea area went north along the coast. Therefore, when the typhoon was approaching and tended to change its direction, it is hard to consider it a prudent choice to depart from the anchorage good for typhoon avoidance and proceed to northeast in the direction of Cheju Island where the sea area is narrow and not good for typhoon avoidance, which is also inconsistent with AWT's recommendation that the vessel should sail on or around August 12 so as to avoid the typhoon's strong wind circle. Seen from the facts of this case, it was also because of the vessel's hasty sailing that the vessel encountered the typhoon MUIFA at a close distance and the damage to the cargo concerned was thus caused. Therefore, it is not improper for the court of first instance to determine that the Master of M.V."Yuriy Arshenevskiy" had faults in making decisions in typhoon avoidance and the court accepts and confirms such determination.

With respect to whether or not the carrier was improper in custody of the cargo concerned, the judgment of first instance has expounded this issue in details on the basis of the facts the court of first instance ascertained, and under the circumstance that the co-insurers did not submit any new evidence to prove new facts or raise their objection, the court will not repeat this issue or accept relevant appeals.

In conclusion, the damage to the cargo concerned was jointly caused by the defects in lashing and securing and the Master's faults in navigating the vessel when the typhoon MUIFA was approaching. Besides, it is not improper for the court of first instance to determine that 20% of the damage to the cargo concerned shall be attributed to the defects in lashing and securing after comprehensively considering the facts of this case, and the court confirms such determination.

3. Regarding to the respective liability that GCL, Shanghai Hengxin and MSCO might bear

According to the law, except otherwise provided for, the carrier shall be liable for the damage to or loss of the cargo occurring during its responsibility period. As the damage to the cargo concerned was jointly caused by the defects in lashing and securing and the Master's faults in navigating the vessel, while according to the law, the carrier shall not be liable for the damage to or loss of the cargo caused by the Master's faults in navigating the vessel, the carrier GCL thus shall be liable for the damage to the cargo concerned caused by the defects in lashing and securing and may be exempted from the liability for the damage to the cargo concerned caused by the Master's faults in navigating the vessel.

As regards the liability that the actual carrier MSCO might assume, though the cargo concerned was damaged during the carriage, as MSCO was not responsible for the lashing and securing of the cargo concerned, MSCO shall not be liable for the damage to the cargo concerned caused by defects in lashing and securing, and the liability for the damage to the cargo concerned caused by the Master's faults in navigating the vessel may be exempted according to the law, so MSCO shall not bear any liability in this case.

As to Shanghai Hengxin, as this case is dispute over contact of carriage of goods by sea, and Shanghai Hengxin was neither the carrier nor the actual carrier for the cargo concerned, there exists no legal basis to request Shanghai Hengxin to bear the compensation liability for the damage to the cargo concerned.

4. Regarding to amount of compensation the carrier shall undertake

With respect to the amount of the carrier's compensation liability, under the condition that the co-insurers and Hunan Zoomlion did not submit other sufficient evidence, it is not improper for the court of first instance to determine the actual value of the cargo concerned on the basis of the customs declaration recognized and recorded by the customs, and the court confirms such determination and dismisses the co-insurers' corresponding appeals. Though GCL alleged that the cargo loss was enlarged due to the vessel's continuing to proceed to India, it did not submit sufficient evidence to support its allegation, so the court does not accept its appeal in this regard. Besides, GCL also alleged that it was in lack of legal basis for the court of first instance to support the co-insurers' request that the interest of the compensation amount shall be calculated as per the loan interest rate, to which the court holds that financial institutions can generally achieve higher rate of return on capital and that it is not improper for the court of first instance to determine that the interest of the compensation amount shall be calculated as per the loan interest rate. As GCL did not submit contrary evidence either, the court thus confirms the determination of the court of first instance in this regard.

In conclusion, the damage of the cargo concerned was jointly caused by the defects in lashing and securing and the Master's faults in navigating the vessel. According to the law, the carrier GCL shall not be liable for the damage to the cargo concerned caused by the faults in navigating the vessel, but shall be liable to compensate for the damage to the cargo concerned caused by defects in lashing and securing. The court of first instance has made a correct judgment and the judgment of first instance may be maintained. The court dismisses all the appeals filed by the co-insurers and GCL. On such basis, according to the provisions of Article 170 Paragraph 1 Sub-Paragraph 1 and Article 175 of the Civil Procedure Law of the People's Republic of China, the court hereby renders the judgment as follows:

Dismiss the appeal and maintain the original judgment.

Court acceptance fee of first instance in amount of RMB159,743.11, shall be payable as per the judgment of first instance. Court acceptance fee of second instance in sum of RMB146,622.37,the Appellant Zurich General Insurance Company (China) Limited, the Appellant Ping An Property & Casualty Insurance Company of China Ltd. Hunan Branch and the Appellant Sunshine Property & Casualty Insurance Co., Ltd. Hunan Branch shall jointly bear RMB113,496.24; and the Appellant Shanghai GCL International Co., Ltd. shall bear RMB33,126.13.

The judgment is final.

Presiding Judge: DONG Min
Acting Judge: HU Hailong
Acting Judge: XVYijin

November 12, 2015

Clerk: CHEN Xi

Appendix: Relevant Law

Civil Procedure Law of the People's Republic China

Article 170 After trial, the people's court of second instance shall handle appeal cases according to the following different circumstances:

(1) Dismissing an appeal and sustaining the original judgment or ruling in the form of a judgment or ruling, if the original judgment or ruling is clear in fact finding and correct in application of law.
(2) Reversing, revoking or modifying the original judgment or ruling in accordance with law in the form of a judgment or ruling, if the original judgment or ruling is erroneous in fact finding or application of law.
(3) Issuing a ruling to revoke the original judgment and remand the case to the original trial people's court for retrial or reversing the original judgment after ascertaining facts, if the original judgment is unclear in finding the basic facts.

(4) Issuing a ruling to revoke the original judgment and remand the case to the original trial people's court, if the original judgment seriously violates statutory procedures, such as omitting a party or illegally entering a default judgment.

Where, after the original trial people's court enters a judgment for a case remanded for retrial, a party appeals the judgment, the people's court of second instance shall not remand the case again for retrial.

Article 175 The judgments and rulings of a people's court of second instance shall be final.

The Supreme People's Court of the People's Republic of China Civil Ruling

Hunan Zoomlion International Trade Co., Ltd. et al.
v.
Shanghai GCL International Co., Ltd. et al.

(2016) Zui Gao Fa Min Shen No.1602

Related Case(s) This is the ruling of retrial, and the judgment of first instance and the judgment of second instance are on page 491 and page 552 respectively.

Cause(s) of Action 202. Dispute over contract of carriage of goods by sea or sea-connected waters.

Headnote The Supreme People's Court refused retrial application and recognized lower court decisions about liability for cargo damage suffered during typhoon; freight forwarder held responsible for 20% of loss attributable to poor cargo lashing; shipowner held not liable for remaining 80% because of "perils of the sea" and "error in navigation" defenses.

Summary The Plaintiff contracted with the first Defendant, a freight forwarder, for its crawler cranes to be carried from China to India. The first Defendant voyage-chartered the ship M.V. "Yuriy Arshenevskiy" from the second Defendant, which had chartered the ship from the third Defendant. The cargo was seriously damaged during the voyage. In an attempt to mitigate its losses, the Plaintiff requested the three Defendants to discharge the cargo at ports of refuge in China, but the three Defendants ignored this request and continued to instruct the vessel to proceed to India. As a result, a severe cargo loss incurred. The Plaintiff argued that the cargo damage happened during the period of the carrier's responsibility, and that the first Defendant was the contractual carrier and the second and third Defendants were the actual carriers.

The court of first instance held that the proximate cause of the cargo damage was the adverse weather conditions the ship encountered on the carrying voyage. As a result, the carriers were held not liable for the damage because of the "perils of the sea" defense under Chinese maritime law. The carriers were also entitled to rely on the defense of error in navigation because the ship's master had made a risky decision to change the route. On appeal by the Plaintiff's cargo insurers, the appeal court upheld the judgment at first instance, holding that the first Defendant was liable for the cargo damage resulting from the defects in lashing and securing, which was 20% of the whole. The remaining 80% of the loss was caused by the Master's fault in navigating the vessel in a typhoon, for which the third Defendant as carrier was exempt. (The second Defendant was neither contracting carrier nor actual carrier, so it had no liability.)

The Plaintiff cargo insurers applied to the Supreme People's Court for a retrial. The court denied the retrial application and confirmed the findings of the court of first instance, which stated that the cause of the damage was due to the fault of the Master of the vessel.

Ruling

The Claimant of Retrial (the Plaintiff of first instance, the Appellant of second instance): Zurich General Insurance Company (China) Limited.
Domicile: 120 Floor 16, Shanghai World Financial Center, No.100 Century Avenue, China (Shanghai) Pilot Free Trade Zone, the People's Republic of China.
Legal representative: YU Luwei, general manager of the company.
Agent *ad litem*: LIU Lina, lawyer of Shanghai SG & CO PRC LAWYERS.
Agent *ad litem*: LI Rui, lawyer of Shanghai SG & CO PRC LAWYERS.

The Claimant of Retrial (the Plaintiff of first instance, the Appellant of second instance): Ping An Property & Casualty Insurance Company of China Ltd. Hunan Branch.
Domicile: Floor 1 & 3 New Age Business Plaza, No. 161, Section 1, Furong Middle Road, Kaifu District, Chargsha City Hunan Province, the People's Republic of China.
Person in charge: CHENG Xiaozhong, general manager.
Agent *ad litem*: LIU Lina, lawyer of Shanghai SG & CO PRC LAWYERS.
Agent *ad litem*: LI Rui, lawyer of Shanghai SG & CO PRC LAWYERS.

The Claimant of Retrial (the Plaintiff of first instance, the Appellant of second instance): Sunshine Property & Casualty Insurance Co., Ltd. Hunan Branch.
Domicile: Floor 6, Xiangiu Zhong yang Office Building, Wuyi East Road, Furong District, Changsha City, Hanan Province, the People's Republic of China.
Legal representative: HU Xiangze, general manager.
Agent *ad litem*: LIU Lina, lawyer of Shanghai SG & CO PRC LAWYERS.
Agent *ad litem*: LI Rui, lawyer of Shanghai SG & CO PRC LAWYERS.

The Respondent of Retrial (Defendant of first instance, the Appellant of second instance): Shanghai GCL International Co., Ltd.
Domicile: Room 2601, Baokuang International Building, No.218, Wusong Road, Shanghai, the People's Republic of China.
Legal representative: WEI Jiajuan, general manager.

The Respondent of Retrial (the Defendant of first instance, the Respondent of second instance): Shanghai Hengxin Shipping Co., Ltd.
Domicile: Room 131, No.69, Tongzhou Road, Shanghai, the People's Republic of China.
Legal representative: YUE Zhaofeng, general manager.

The Respondent of Retrial (the Defendant of first instance, the Respondent of second instance): Murmansk Shipping Company.
Domicile: 15, Kominterna Street, 183038 Murmansk, Russia.
Legal representative: A. M. Medvedev, chairman.
Agent *ad litem*: LI Rongcun, lawyer of Guangdong Wang Jing & Co. (Xiamen) Law Firm.
Agent *ad litem*: LI Lan, lawyer of Guangdong Wang Jing & Co. (Xiamen) Law Firm.

The Plaintiff of first instance: Hunan Zoomlion International Trade Co., Ltd.
Domicile: No.307, South Yinpen Road, Changsha, Hunan, the People's Republic of China.
Legal representative: CHEN Peiliang, general manager.

With respect to the case arising from dispute over contract of carriage of goods by sea between the Appellants of Retrial, Zurich General Insurance Company (China) Limited. (hereinafter referred to as Zurich China), Ping An Property & Casualty Insurance Company of China Ltd. Hunan Branch (hereinafter referred to as Ping An Hunan), Sunshine Property & Casualty Insurance Co., Ltd. Hunan Branch (hereinafter referred to as Sunshine Hunan), and the Respondents of Retrial, Shanghai GCL International Co., Ltd. (hereinafter referred to as Shanghai Jiexi), Shanghai Hengxin Shipping Co., Ltd. (hereinafter referred to as Shanghai Hengxin), Murmansk Shipping Company (hereinafter referred to as Murmansk), the Defendant of first instance, Hunan Zoomlion International Trade Co., Ltd. (hereinafter referred to as Zoomlion), the Appellants of Retrial disagreed the Shanghai High People's Court (hereinafter referred to as the court of second instance) (2014) Hu Gao Min Si (Hai) Zhong Zi No.119 Civil Judgment and applied for retrial. The court formed a collegiate panel to investigate the case, now the case has been concluded.

Zurich China, Ping An Hunan and Sunshine Hunan claimed that: firstly, the confirmation of legal status of Shanghai Hengxin made by the court of second instance was wrong. Shanghai Hengxin actually controlled the navigation of the ship, and its legal status in the cargo transportation involved should be recognized as the actual carrier, and jointly assume joint and several liability for cargo damage with Shanghai Jiexi and Murmansk. Secondly, the confirmation of damage to goods made by the court of second instance was wrong. The court of second instance had no factual or legal basis for the division of the causal force causing the cargo damage. The cause of the cargo damage in this case was improper lashing and securing, not the weather or the improper decision of the Master to avoid typhoon. In this case, there was no exemption from the fault of the Master of the ship, and the carrier could not claim exemption. Thirdly, the amount of loss confirmed by the court of second instance was wrong. Shanghai Jiexi, Shanghai Hengxin, and Murmansk should be liable for compensation for the part of the losses caused by the voyage of M.V. "Yuriy Arshenevskiy" ship to India. Fourthly, the court of second instance judged that Murmansk should not be liable for lashing and securing, which was wrong. The lashing and securing were an obligation that the carrier must perform. No matter whether any third party performed the specific lashing and securing operations, Murmansk as the actual carrier could not be exempted from liability. Moreover, Murmansk supervised, inspected and partially reinforced the lashing of the goods involved, and should be responsible for the improper lashing. In conclusion, they required the court to retry the case.

Murmansk argued that: firstly, the facts involved confirmed by the court of second instance were basically clear, and they were not inappropriate:

1. The confirmation of causes of the accident involved and division of causal force, the confirmation of the court of first instance had sufficient evidence, and the court of second instance did not deny the act of god. Zurich China, Ping An Hunan, and Sunshine Hunan did not submit any evidence to prove that Murmansk was at fault. The Master had absolute power over the safety of the ship, and the fault of decision-making for avoiding typhoon should belong to the fault of the Master in driving and managing the ship, which should be exempted from liability.
2. M.V. "Yuriy Arshenevskiy" sailed to India after the accident involved, which was not inappropriate. Zoomlion did not suggest to unload the goods at Shanghai Port until the day before M.V. "Yuriy Arshenevskiy" left Xiamen Port. The plan lacked feasibility and rationality. Moreover, Zoomlion's handling of the goods involved failed to fulfill its reasonable impairment obligations, resulting in an increase in the loss of goods involved. As a result, the Appellants had no right to require the compensation for the expansion of loss of the goods involved against Murmansk. Secondly, there was no wrong application of law by the court of second instance. Zurich China, Ping An Hunan and Sunshine Hunan meanwhile claimed that Shanghai Hengxin and Murmansk were the actual carriers, which was contradictory.

Shanghai Union International Ship Agency Co., Ltd. issued the B/L, which was beyond its right of agency, so the bill of lading should not be binding on Murmansk. The actual carrier was only responsible for the transportation that it actually performed. Article 61 of the Maritime Code of the People's Republic of China could not be understood as equal to the obligations of the actual carrier and all the obligations of the carrier. Murmansk was not engaged in lashing and securing operations, and should not be liable for compensation for the resulting cargo damage.

After investigation, the court holds that, the case is the dispute over contract of carriage of goods by sea. According to the application for retrial of Zurich China, Ping An Hunan and Sunshine Hunan, the issues of the case are that: firstly, cause of damage to goods; secondly, legal status of Shanghai Hengxin and the corresponding liability; thirdly, legal status of Murmansk and the corresponding liability; fourthly, liability for compensation for the voyage of M.V. "Yuriy Arshenevskiy" to India.

Firstly, cause of damage to goods.

1. According to the logbook, the video taken by the crew, and the relevant meteorological evidence and other materials, taking into account the asymmetric structure of the typhoon and the linear relationship between the average wind and the gust, the court of first instance determined that M.V. "Yuriy Arshenevskiy" encountered winds of level 12 or more for a long time, bad sea conditions where the ship rolled more than 35 degrees, which is not inappropriate.
2. When the typhoon was approaching and showing a turning trend, M.V. "Yuriy Arshenevskiy" hurriedly decided to leave the anchorage and drive to the narrow sea area that was not favorable for avoiding the typhoon, which lacked enough caution. The courts of first and second instances confirmed that the Master of M.V. "Yuriy Arshenevskiy" was at fault in the decision to avoid the platform and confirmed that the Master was at fault, which is not inappropriate. According to the Maritime Code of the People's Republic of China Article 51 Paragraph 1 Sub-paragraph 1 and Article 61, the carrier and the actual carrier are exempt from liability for cargo damage caused by the fault of the Master driving the ship. So, the court of second instance confirmed that the carrier and the actual carrier should not be liable for the losses caused thereby, which is not inappropriate.
3. According to the facts of the original review, the lashing and securing of the goods involved have defects, which are related to the occurrence of the damage of the goods involved. However, considering that after the accident, the goods involved were simply transported to Indian ports after simple sorting, reinforcement and lashing, the court of second instance reasonably concluded that the lashing of the goods involved was not the most important and decisive cause. Taking into account the aforementioned various reasons related to cargo damage, it was determined that improper lashing and securing would play a 20% role in the occurrence of cargo damage, which is not inappropriate. Zurich China and others claimed that the reason for the cargo damage involved was only lashing and securing, which lacks sufficient factual basis.

Secondly, legal status of Shanghai Hengxin and the corresponding liability

Though Shanghai Hengxin concluded back-to-back voyage charter parties with Shanghai Jiexi and Hanssy Shipping (HK) Co., Ltd., it has no direct carriage contract relationship with Zoomlion. Compared with Zoomlion, Shanghai Hengxin is not a carrier. Meanwhile, because Shanghai Hengxin was not the owner or bareboat charterer of the ship involved, it only lashed and secured the cargo involved, but did not actually engage in the transportation of the cargo involved, nor could it control the ship and control the cargo, and was not the actual carrier of the transportation involved. This case is the dispute over contract of carriage of goods by sea, because Shanghai Hengxin is not the carrier or actual carrier of the cargo involved, the court of second instance judged that it should not be liable for compensation for the damage to goods, which is not inappropriate.

Thirdly, legal status of Murmansk and the corresponding liability

Murmansk was the shipowner of M.V. "Yuriy Arshenevskiy" who transported the cargo involved and actually engaged in the transportation of the cargo involved. The Master also authorized Shanghai United International Ship Agency Co., Ltd. to issue the B/L that Shanghai Jiexi was the shipper on behalf of Murmansk, its behaviors are consistent with the provisions of actual carrier. The court of second instance held that Murmansk was the actual carrier of the carriage involved, which is not inappropriate. According to the facts of the original review, Shanghai Hengxin was responsible for the loading, unloading, lashing and securing of the cargo involved in the voyage, not Murmansk. The Master of M.V. "Yuriy Arshenevskiy" checked the lashing and securing situation and resolved the problems after loading, which proved that Murmansk, as the actual carrier, had properly and carefully performed the supervision duties, and the lashing and securing involved were not the issues related to the stability of the ship and endangering the safety of the ship, which should be the responsibility of the ship. The court of second instance judged that Murmansk should not be liable for 20% of losses caused by lashing, which is not inappropriate.

Fourthly, liability for compensation for the voyage of M.V. "Yuriy Arshenevskiy" to India

According to the facts found in the original review, Murmansk made attempts and efforts to unload the cargo at Xiamen Port, but the goods involved could not be unloaded at Xiamen Port due to customs supervision. The result cannot be blamed on Murmansk. In addition, the goods involved were only 5 of the 31 batches of goods carried by M.V. "Yuriy Arshenevskiy". If M.V. "Yuriy Arshenevskiy" returned to Shanghai Port, there were also many uncertainties, which not only increased the legal risk of the ship's external liability for breach of contract, but also resulted that other cargo owners suffered further losses. Accordingly, the court of second instance confirmed that subsequent logistics costs incurred by Zoomlion were not losses caused by the carrier's misconduct, but the carrier's reasonable and prudent but still unable to assist Zoomlion's reduced losses, so the carrier should not be liable for compensation, which is not inappropriate.

Pulling the threads together, the application for retrial of Zurich China, Ping An Hunan and Sunshine Hunan is not consistent with the Civil Procedure Law of the People's Republic of China Article 200. According to the Civil Procedure Law of the People's Republic of China Article 204 Paragraph 1, the Interpretation of the Supreme People's Court on the Application of the Civil Procedure Law of the People's Republic of China Article 395 Paragraph 2, the ruling is as follows:

Dismiss the application for retrial of Zurich General Insurance Company (China) Limited, Ping An Property & Casualty Insurance Company of China Ltd. Hunan Branch and Sunshine Property & Casualty Insurance Co., Ltd. Hunan Branch.

Presiding Judge: HU Fang
Judge: LI Guishun
Acting Judge: ZHANG Kexin
December 28, 2016
Clerk: LI Na

Shanghai Maritime Court
Civil Judgment

JIANG Haiping
v.
Shanghai New Qiao Insurance Brokers Ltd.

(2014) Hu Hai Fa Shang Chu Zi No.1410

Related Case(s) This is the judgment of first instance and the judgment of second instance is on page 615.

Cause(s) of Action 230. Dispute over marine insurance contract on the sea or sea-connected waters.

Headnote The Plaintiff shipowner unsuccessfully sued insurance broker for incorrectly stating trading limits on hull insurance policy after ship became a constructive total loss while trading beyond the declared limits; the Plaintiff had signed and accepted the policy without objection.

Summary The Plaintiff-Shipowner filed suit against the Defendant-Insurance Broker in a dispute over the trading limits within an insurance contract. The Plaintiff commissioned its agents to obtain insurance for its vessel. The agents got the Defendant to broker the insurance and submitted an Ocean Marine Insurance slip for the vessel to CCIC Shanghai through the services of the Defendant. An insurance policy with specific trading limits was created, and subsequently received by the Plaintiff, which did not object to any of the terms. The Plaintiff's vessel ran aground months later and was considered a constructive total loss. CCIC Shanghai sent a notice to the Plaintiff stating that the vessel had sailed outside of the trading limits when it ran aground, so the insurance policy and coverage was terminated. The Plaintiff filed suit against the Defendant alleging that the Defendant miswrote the trading limits, which caused the Plaintiff to unknowingly violate the policy and lose compensation equal to the value of its vessel. In dismissing the Plaintiff's claims, the court found that the Plaintiff's agents signed and sealed the insurance policy on the Plaintiff's behalf meaning that they confirmed the policy's terms, including the trading limits, without any objections. The court also determined that the Plaintiff was refused compensation because its vessel clearly went beyond the insured trading limits and would have violated the policy regardless of fault of the Defendant.

Judgment

The Plaintiff: JIANG Haiping, living in Zhoushan, Putuo District, Zhejiang.
Agent *ad litem*: ZHANG Jianxin, lawyer of Shanghai Hai Fu Law Firm.
Agent *ad litem*: YING Songbo, lawyer of Shanghai Hai Fu Law Firm.

The Defendant: Shanghai New Qiao Insurance Brokers Ltd.
Domicile: Pudong New Area, Shanghai City.
Legal representative: QIAO Gang, general manager.
Agent *ad litem*: HUA Lingling, lawyer of Shanghai Rolmax Law Office.

With respect to the case arising from dispute over marine insurance contract, the Plaintiff, JIANG Haiping, filed an action against the Defendant, Shanghai New Qiao Insurance Brokers Ltd., before the court on November 11, 2014. The court entertained the case on the same day, organized the collegiate panel according to the law, and held a hearing in public on January 19, 2015. The Plaintiff JIANG Haiping, ZHANG Jianxin and YING Songbo, agents *ad litem* of the Plaintiff, and HUA Lingling, agent *ad litem* of the Defendant appeared in court to attend the hearing. Now the case has been concluded.

The Plaintiff alleged that the Plaintiff was the shipowner of M.V. PING DA 7. In May 2013, the Plaintiff entrusted the Defendant as the insurance broker to deal with the ship insurance and protection and indemnity insurance (hereinafter referred to as P&I insurance) for M.V. PING DA 7. After the Defendant's agent, on May 21, 2013, China Continent Insurance Co., Ltd. Shanghai Branch (hereinafter referred to as "CCIC Shanghai") issued the ship insurance policy in terms of M.V. PING DA 7 according to the information and requirements given by the Defendant, underwriting all risks, before this, the policy of protection and indemnity insurance was also issued.

On December 11, 2013, M.V. PING DA 7happened stranding accident at the port of Pohnpei in the Federated States of Micronesia, and was considered as constructive total loss, the longitude of stranded location was 158°14.357' E. On December 25, 2013, CCIC Shanghai sent the notice concerning termination of ship insurance contract ofM.V. PING DA 7 to the Plaintiff, informing that the Plaintiff violated the trading limits warranty clause of the insurance contract, which requires the ship not to navigate beyond 150°E, therefore, they discharged the insurance contract. After verification, when the Defendant provided the information concerning ship insurance to CCIC Shanghai, miswrote the trading limits "not west of 60 degrees East and not East of 150 degrees East, not South of 20 degrees South and not North of 60 degrees North", the Defendant did not inform the Plaintiff the trading limits in the insurance policy was agreed as warranty clause and the corresponding legal consequences. The Defendant's fault in the course of undergoing insurance led to the Plaintiff's failure for gaining compensation from the insurer. Therefore, the Plaintiff requested the Defendant to compensate RMB10.8 million yuan and the corresponding interest (the interest should be calculated on the basis of the deposit interest rate over the same period RMB promulgated by of the People's

Bank of China from February 11, 2014 to the date of effectiveness of the judgment), and assume the case entertainment fee.

The Defendant defended that firstly, the Plaintiff had no capacity to initial legal procedures, under the insurance brokerage contract involved, Xin De Shipping Service Co., Ltd. (hereinafter referred to as "Xinde Company") entrusted the Defendant to purchase ship insurance and protection and indemnity insurance in terms of M.V. PING DA 7, there has no contractual relationship between the Plaintiff and the Defendant; secondly, the Defendant had no fault in fulfilling the insurance brokerage contract, Xinde Company entrusted the Defendant to purchase insurance for M.V. PING DA 7, the Defendant has informed all the progress and details to the Plaintiff in time, and asked for instructions and confirmation. The agreements on the trading limits in of all emails were all marked east longitude. the Defendant has informed the Plaintiff the fact that trading limits clause was the insurance clauses promptly. Later the Defendant made the slip and required the Plaintiff to confirm. After the Plaintiff signed and confirmed the slip, the insurance company made a policy, the Plaintiff raised no objections to the trading limits until the insurance accident happened. The Plaintiff now had no valid evidence to prove that it instructed the Defendant to undergo the insurance according to the trading limits alleged by it, the trading limits clause in the insurance clauses had been confirmed by the Plaintiff; thirdly, there was no causal and effect between the breach of contract of the Defendant claimed by the Plaintiff and the losses, the insurance company's rejecting to the claim of the Plaintiff was because the vessel involved sailed beyond the trading limits. Even if the Defendant miswrote the trading limits, as long as the Plaintiff's vessel sailed in the trading limits stated in the policy, it would not be rejected by the insurance company. Now the ship sailed beyond the trading limits, regardless of whether the trading limits clause was insurance clauses, the insurance company would refuse to compensate; fourthly, the Plaintiff did not suffer any loss, the Plaintiff has made a claim to the insurance company and has gotten compensation, regardless of the amount of compensation, it should be deemed that the Plaintiff had accepted full compensation. Therefore, the Defendant requested the court to reject the Plaintiff's claims.

The evidence presented by the Plaintiff to support its claims, the cross-examination opinions of the Defendant and the ascertainment opinions of the court are as follows:

Evidence 1, the ship ownership certificate of M.V. PING DA 7 to prove that the shipowner of M.V. PING DA 7 was the Plaintiff JIANG Haiping. The Defendant confirmed the evidence, so the court confirmed the validity and effectiveness of the evidence.

Evidence 2, the e-mails between Xinde Company and the Plaintiff and the Defendant to prove the Plaintiff commissioned the Defendant to handle marine insurance, the Defendant made an error in covering insurance operation. The Defendant confirmed the authenticity, legality and relevancy of the evidence, but it challenged the probative force of the evidence. It held that it had fulfilled the obligation for disclosure in the process of undergoing insurance, it committed no fault. The Defendant confirmed the authenticity of the evidence, so the court confirms the weight of the evidence, but holds that it cannot show that the Defendant has any fault in undergoing the insurance from the email, so the court does not admit the probative force of the evidence.

Evidence 3, ship insurance policy of M.V. QIAO TAI, to prove that the Plaintiff entrusted CHEN Lixin to communicate with the Defendant by phone about the insured coverage of M.V. PING DA 7 was same as that of M.V. QIAO TAI. Upon cross-examination, the Defendant held that the authenticity of the evidence could not be verified and had no relevancy with this case. the court holds that the evidence was a printed piece and no signature or seal of issuer, so the authenticity cannot be confirmed, and the contents of the evidence do not show that the coverage of M.V. PING DA 7 of coverage is as same as that of M.V. QIAO TAI, the relevancy with the case cannot be seen, so the court does not confirm the effect and probative force thereof.

Evidence 4, CHEN Lixin's question record of Xinde Company, to prove that the Defendant has fault in the trading limits when handling insurance. The Defendant's cross-examination opinion was that CHEN Lixin had an interest relationship with the Plaintiff, and the contents of the record and the contents of email was contradictory, it did not admit the authenticity of the evidence. the court holds that CHEN Lixin is the agent of the Plaintiff and has an interest relationship with the Plaintiff, there was no other evidence to prove the contents of evidence. In addition, CHEN Lixin in the record noted that he found the Defendant miswrote the trading limits as "not East of 60 degrees East" and asked the Defendant to change to "not East of 60 degrees West", but he also signed and confirmed the policy which noted the trading limits as "not East of 60 degrees East", so the statement and evidence submitted by the Plaintiff is contradictory, the court does not confirm the effect and probative force of evidence.

Evidence 5, the policy which was made by the Defendant for ship insurance for M.V. PING DA 7 to CCIC Shanghai, the policy eventually recorded trading limits as to "not East of 60 degrees East" and it was a warranty, to prove that the Defendant failed to arrange insurance as the request of the Plaintiff, so it was at fault. The Defendant confirmed the authenticity, legality and relevancy of evidence, but questioned the probative force thereof. The policy has the seal of Xinde Company and the signature of CHEN Lixin, it can prove the contents of the policy have been finally confirmed by the Xinde Company and CHEN Lixin. The court holds that the Defendant confirmed the authenticity of the evidence, so the court confirms the effect of evidence. Xinde Company and CHEN Lixin has confirmed the contents of policy, so the evidence cannot prove the Defendant has made a mistake in arranging insurance.

Evidence 6, the ocean shipping insurance policy issued by CCIC Shanghai, to prove that the Defendant did not insure according to the requirements of the Plaintiff, so the Defendant had fault. The court holds that the Defendant confirmed the authenticity of evidence, so the legality of the evidence shall be confirmed, but the evidence cannot prove the Defendant had fault in the process of arranging insurance, so the court does not confirm its probative force.

Evidence 7, the notice about discharge the ship insurance contract of M.V. PING DA 7 issued by CCIC Shanghai, to prove that the Defendant had fault in the process of arranging insurance. The Plaintiff cannot obtain insurance compensation for total loss of the ship. The Defendant confirmed the authenticity, legality and relevancy of the evidence, but the Defendant had objection to the probative force of the evidence, the Defendant thought that the evidence could not prove the Defendant had fault in the process of arranging insurance. The court holds that the Defendant confirmed the authenticity of the evidence as well as the effect of the evidence, but the evidence cannot prove that the Defendant had fault in the insurance process, so the court does not admit its probative force.

Evidence 8, the survey report issued by Shenzhen Wan Yi McLarens Insurance Survey Co., Ltd. Shanghai Branch (hereinafter referred to as McLarens Company), to prove that the grounding accident took place beyond the trading limits as prescribed in the insurance policy, the accident caused M.V. PING DA 7 total lost, and the grounding location was at 158 degrees east longitude. The Defendant confirmed the evidence, so the court confirms the effect and probative force of the evidence.

Evidence 9, preliminary design and quotation for refloating and towage of M.V. PING DA 7 made by Shanghai Darun Salvage Project Co., Ltd. (herein after Darun Company), to prove that the grounding accidents caused constructive total loss of M.V. PING DA 7. The Defendant confirmed the evidence, so the court confirms the effect and the probative force of the evidence.

Evidence 10, an email sent to CHEN Youmu, a lawyer not involved in this case, by the Defendant, to prove the Plaintiff's request for insurance, and the Defendant failed to find the error in the insurance policy. The Defendant cross-examined the evidence and held that the evidence had not been notarized, the authenticity could not be verified, and it did not affirm the legality thereof, and held even if the mail was true, the Defendant as an insurance broker, communicated with insurance company after the accident happened and consulted with a lawyer for the interests of the Plaintiff, the statement was not necessarily true and the contents showed that the Defendant arranged insurance according to the Plaintiff's requirements, the fault in trading limits was made by the insurance company, the Defendant did not have any fault. the court holds that the evidence is in the form of e-mail, without notarization and other evidence to corroborate, so the court does not confirm the probative force of the evidence, and the contents of the email do not show the Plaintiff's Insurance requirements.

Evidence 11, in May 2013, the emails between the Defendant and CCIC Shanghai in terms of the insurance for M.V. PING DA 7, to prove that the insurer had no special requirements on trading limits, the Defendant regarded the trading limits terms as a warranty, which limited the rights of the Plaintiff and increased the risk of the Plaintiff; The Defendant as an insurance broker who charged the insurer brokerage fees. The Defendant held that the evidence had not been notarized, the authenticity could not be verified, and it did not admit the legality, although the Defendant was the Plaintiff's agent, it was a practice that the Defendant charged the insurance company. The court holds that the evidence is an e-mail without being notarized, and there is no other evidence to confirm each other, so the court does not confirm the effect thereof, the contents of the consultation process between the Plaintiff and the Defendant for the insurance policy cannot be seen from the email.

Evidence submitted by the Defendant, the cross-examination of the Plaintiff and the ascertainment of the court are as follows:

The email sent to Xinde Company by the Defendant, which requires it to confirm the main clauses of the marine insurance and the information of the policy, is to prove that the Defendant has informed Xinde Company to confirm the main clauses of marine insurance, including the terms of the trading limits and sealed after the confirmation. The Plaintiff confirmed the authenticity, legality and relevancy of the evidence, but held that the Defendant did not insure according to his request and did not inform the impact of warranty clause on insurance claims. the court holds that the Plaintiff confirmed the authenticity of the evidence, so the probative force of evidence shall be confirmed. The insurance slip of M.V. PING DA 7 is affixed with the seal of Xinde Company and the signature of CHEN Lixin, it proves that Xinde Company and CHEN Lixin confirmed the contents of the insurance slip, so the court confirms the probative force thereof.

According to the above evidence identified and combined with the investigation in the trial, the court finds the following facts:

The Plaintiff was the shipowner of M.V. PING DA 7. In May 2013, the Plaintiff commissioned Xinde Company and CHEN Lixin to deal with ship insurance of M.V. PING DA 7. Xinde Company and CHEN Lixin immediately entrusted the Defendant as insurance broker for the insurance matters. On May 20, 2013, Xinde Company and CHEN Lixin submitted the ocean marine insurance slip of M.V. PING DA 7 to the CCIC Shanghai through the Defendant, and signed and sealed on the insurance slip. The next day, the CCIC Shanghai issued an ocean shipping insurance policy. The insured policy and the insurance policy both noted that the ship name was "Pinda 7", the insurer was the ship owner, the Plaintiff, Xinde Company, the operator of the vessel and Hong Kong Run Jiu Shipping Co., Ltd., the charterer of the vessel; the insured amount is RMB12,000,000; the trading limits are not west of 60 degrees East and not East of 150 degrees East, not South of 20 degrees South and not North of 60 degrees North; the term of coverage is from May 21, 2013 to May 20, 2014; the scope of liability and the applicable terms is subject to "86 terms against all risks"; and the deductible for each accident is RMB50,000 or 10% of the loss, and the deductible rate of total loss and constructive total loss is 10%. JIANG Haiping received the insurance policy and raised no objection.

On December 11, 2013, M.V. PING DA 7happened grounding accident in the port of Ponape in Western Pacific Micronesia, the longitude of the stranding location was 158°14.357' W. After that, McLarens Company was commissioned by the CCIC Shanghai and the Plaintiff to carry out a survey, it issued a survey report in terms of the grounding accident involved, the survey report stated that M.V.

PING DA 7 constituted a constructive total loss. Darun Company designed a plan for refloating and towage of M.V. PING DA 7, the quotation was RMB16.2 million yuan. On December 26 of the same year, CCIC Shanghai sent the notice on discharging the ship insurance contract of M.V. PING DA 7 to the Plaintiff, in which it was stated the location of the grounding accident was beyond the insured area listed on the policy, the Plaintiff violated the warranty of trading limits in the insurance contract, so it discharged the insurance contract because M.V. PING DA 7 sailed beyond trading limits.

The court holds that the case is arising from dispute over marine insurance contract. The Plaintiff is the owner of insured ship. When the Defendant accepted the commission of insurance, it should know the Plaintiff was actual insurer according to the ship certificates. The insurance contract eventually recorded the Plaintiff was the insurer, which indicated that the Defendant knew the Plaintiff was the actual counterparty to the insurance brokerage contract. Therefore, it shall be identified that the Plaintiff established insurance brokerage contract relationship with the Defendant in terms of ship insurance of M.V. PING DA 7 through the agent Xinde Company and CHEN Lixin. The capacity of the Plaintiff in the action is proper.

In respect of the losses suffered by the Plaintiff, according to the facts that have been identified, M.V. PING DA 7suffered a constructive total loss, the loss amount is RMB10.8 million yuan, namely the insurance amount, namely RMB1.2 million yuan deducting the deductible (10%). Although the Defendant argued that the Plaintiff had obtained the compensation from the insurer, the Defendant did not provide evidence to prove that the Plaintiff's loss has been made up or received compensation, so the court holds that the amount of losses suffered by the Plaintiff shall be RMB1.08 million yuan.

According to the provisions of Article 128 of the Insurance Law of the People's Republic of China, the insurance broker shall be liable for compensation according to the law for the loss of the insured and the insurer. Now the Plaintiff claimed that the Defendant miswrote the trading limits of the involved ship in the insured process, but the Plaintiff did not provide the evidence regarding insured requirement of the scope of voyage. On the contrary, the Plaintiff's agent Xinde Company and CHEN Lixin sealed and signed the policy to confirm the trading limits recorded on the policy. It showed that the Plaintiff and his agents had no objections to the trading limits insured by the insurance broker. The Plaintiff also has no evidence to prove that he has objections to the trading limits after signed the insurance contract, so the Plaintiff's existing evidence cannot prove the Defendant has fault. The Plaintiff was refused to be compensated by the insurer due to it beyond the agreement of the scope of navigation of insurance contract, the loss was caused by its own fault and has no relations with the Defendant. As for the Plaintiff claimed that the Defendant regard the trading limits as warranty clause without permission, because the Plaintiff's agent confirmed the contents of the insured policy, it cannot prove that the Plaintiff's claims is established, so the Plaintiff's claim against the Defendant to compensate for the loss shall not be supported.

To sum up, according to Article 402 of the Contract Law of the People's Republic of China, Article 128 of the Insurance Law of the People's Republic of China and Article 64 Paragraph 1 of the Civil Procedure Law of People's Republic of China, the judgment is as follows:

Not support the claims of the Plaintiff JIANG Haiping.

Court acceptance fee in amount of RMB86,600,shall be born by the Plaintiff.

If not satisfy with the judgment, the Plaintiff and the Defendant may submit a statement of appeal to the court within 15 days upon service of the judgment, and submit the copies according to the number of the opposite party and appeal to the Shanghai High People's Court.

Presiding Judge: JI Gang

Judge: ZHANG Jianchen

People's Juror: HUANG Wenya

March 19, 2015

Clerk: TANG Qin

Appendix: Relevant Law

1. Contract Law of the People's Republic of China

Article 402 Agent's Act Binding on Principal; Exceptions Where the agent, acting within the scope of authority granted by the principal, entered into a contract in its own name with a third person who was aware of the agency relationship between the principal and agent, the contract is directly binding upon the principal and such third person, except where there is conclusive evidence establishing that the contract is only binding upon the agent and such third person.

2. Insurance Law of the People's Republic of China

Article 128 An insurance broker shall be liable for damages or losses caused to the applicant or the insured due to the negligence of the insurance broker in the course of transacting insurance business.

3. Civil Procedure Law of the People's Republic of China

Article 64 A party shall have the responsibility to provide evidence in support of its own propositions.

......

Shanghai High People's Court
Civil Judgment

JIANG Haiping
v.
Shanghai New Qiao Insurance Brokers Ltd.

(2015) Hu Gao Min Si (Hai) Zhong Zi No.57

Related Case(s) This is the judgment of second instance, and the judgment of first instance is on page 607.

Cause(s) of Action 230. Dispute over marine insurance contract on the sea or sea-connected waters.

Headnote Affirming lower court decision holding that the Plaintiff shipowner was not entitled to recover damages from insurance broker for incorrectly stating trading limits on hull insurance policy after ship became a constructive total loss while trading beyond the declared limits; the Plaintiff had signed and accepted the policy without objection.

Summary The Plaintiff-Shipowner appealed from the lower court's rejection of its claims against the Defendant-Insurance Broker in a dispute over trading limits within an insurance contract. The Plaintiff's agents procured an insurance policy with specific trade limits for the Plaintiff's vessel from CCIC Shanghai through the Defendant. The agents signed and sealed the policy on behalf of the Plaintiff, meaning that none of them objected to the terms of the policy. Months later, the Plaintiff's vessel ran aground in a location beyond the policy's trading limits and was deemed a constructive total loss. This subsequently terminated the policy and its coverage since the Plaintiff sailed beyond the limits specified within the policy. The lower court rejected the Plaintiff's claims that the Defendant should be held liable for compensating the Plaintiff's losses since it miswrote the trade limits within the policy. On appeal, the Plaintiff argued that the lower court's rejection should be set aside because it found the facts and applied the law incorrectly. It also alleged that the Defendant had a duty as a professional in the insurance industry to check the correctness of the terms of the policy, and the Plaintiff's agents unwisely trusted the Defendant's discretion in not checking the trade limits. The present court recognized the lower court's rejection of the Plaintiff's claims on the grounds that the Plaintiff failed to submit the evidence necessary to show that the Defendant failed to incorporate the desired trade limits within the insurance policy. This was because the Plaintiff and their agents participated in the entire process whenever the limits were altered, and the Plaintiff's agents signed and sealed the policy, confirming all of its terms and the trade limits, on behalf of the Plaintiff.

Judgment

The Appellant (the Plaintiff of first instance): JIANG Haiping, living in Zhoushan, Putuo District, Zhejiang.
Agent *ad litem*: ZHANG Jianxin, lawyer of Shanghai Hai Fu Law Firm.
Agent *ad litem*: YING Songbo, lawyer of Shanghai Hai Fu Law Firm.

The Respondent (the Defendant of first instance): Shanghai New Qiao Insurance Brokers Co., Ltd.
Domiclie: Pudong New Area, Shanghai city.
Legal representative: QIAO Gang, general manager.
Agent *ad litem*: HUA Lingling, lawyer of Shanghai Rolmax Law Office.

Dissatisfied with (2014) Hu Hai Fa Shang Chu Zi No.1410 Civil Judgment with respect to the case arising from dispute over insurance broker contract, the Appellant, JIANG Haiping filed an appeal against the Respondent, Shanghai New Qiao Insurance Brokers Ltd. (hereinafter referred to as "New Qiao"), before the court. After entertaining this case on April 23, 2015, the court formed a collegiate panel according to law and held a hearing in public to try this case on May 15, 2015. JIANG Haiping and his agents *ad litem*, ZHANG Jianxin and YING Songbo, and HUA Lingling, agent *ad litem* of New Qiao, appeared in court to attend the hearing. Now the case has been concluded.

JIANG Haiping alleged in the first instance that JIANG Haiping was the shipowner of M.V. PING DA 7. In May 2013, JIANG Haiping entrusted New Qiao as the insurance broker to deal with the hull insurance and P&I insurance (hereinafter referred to as P&I insurance) for M.V. PING DA 7. After New Qiao's agent, on May 23, 2013, China Continent Insurance Co., Ltd. Shanghai Branch (hereinafter referred to as "CCIC Shanghai") issued the hull insurance policy in terms of M.V. PING DA 7 according to the information and requirements given by New Qiao, underwriting all risks, before this, the policy of P&I insurance was also issued.

On December 11, 2013, M.V. PING DA 7happened stranding accident at the port of Pohnpei in the Federated States of Micronesia, and was considered as a constructive total loss, the longitude of stranded location was 158°14.357' E. On December 26, 2013, CCIC Shanghai sent the notice concerning termination of hull insurance contract of M.V. PING DA 7 to JIANG Haiping, informing that JIANG Haiping violated the trading limits warranty clause of the insurance contract, which requires the ship not to navigate beyond 150°E, therefore, they discharged the insurance contract. After verification, when New Qiao provided the information concerning hull insurance to CCIC Shanghai, miswrote the trading limits "not west of 60 degrees East and not East of 150 degrees East, not South of 20 degrees South and not North of 60 degrees North", New Qiao did not inform JIANG Haiping the trading limits in the insurance policy was agreed as warranty clause and the corresponding legal consequences. New Qiao's fault in the course of undergoing insurance led to JIANG Haiping's failure for gaining compensation from the insurer. Therefore, JIANG Haiping requested New Qiao to compensate RMB10.8 million yuan and the corresponding interest (the interest should be calculated on the basis of the deposit interest rate over the same period RMB promulgated by of the People's Bank of China from February 11, 2014 to the date of effectiveness of the judgment), and assume the case entertainment fee.

New Qiao defended that firstly, JIANG Haiping had no capacity to initial legal procedures, under the insurance brokerage contract involved, Xinde Shipping Service Co., Ltd. (hereinafter referred to as "Xinde Company") entrusted New Qiao to purchase hull insurance and P&I insurance in terms of M.V. PING DA 7, there has no contractual relationship between JIANG Haiping and New Qiao; secondly, New Qiao had no fault in fulfilling the insurance brokerage contract, Xinde Company entrusted New Qiao to purchase insurance for M.V. PING DA 7, New Qiao has informed all the progress and details to JIANG Haiping in time, and asked for instructions and confirmation. The agreements on the trading limits in of all emails were all marked east longitude. New Qiao has informed JIANG Haiping the fact that trading limits clause was the insurance clauses promptly. Later New Qiao made the slip and required JIANG Haiping to confirm. After JIANG Haiping signed and confirmed the slip, the insurance company made a policy, JIANG Haiping raised no objections to the trading limits until the insurance accident happened. JIANG Haiping now had no valid evidence to prove that it instructed New Qiao to undergo the insurance according to the trading limits alleged by it, the trading limits clause in the insurance clauses had been confirmed by JIANG Haiping; thirdly, there was no causal and effect between the breach of contract of New Qiao claimed by JIANG Haiping and the losses, the insurance company's rejecting to the claim of JIANG Haiping was because the vessel involved sailed beyond the trading limits. Even if New Qiao miswrote the trading limits, as long as JIANG Haiping's vessel sailed in the trading limits stated in the policy, it would not be rejected by the insurance company. Now the ship sailed beyond the trading limits, regardless of whether the trading limits clause was insurance clauses, the insurance company would refuse to compensate; fourthly, JIANG Haiping did not suffer any loss, JIANG Haiping has made a claim to the insurance company and has gotten compensation, regardless of the amount of compensation, it should be deemed that JIANG Haiping had accepted full compensation. Therefore, New Qiao requested the court to reject JIANG Haiping's claim.

The court of first instance found the following facts: JIANG Haiping was the shipowner of M.V. PING DA 7. In May 2013, JIANG Haiping commissioned Xinde Company and CHEN Lixin to deal with hull insurance of M.V. PING DA 7. Xinde Company and CHEN Lixin immediately entrusted New Qiao as insurance broker for the insurance matters. On May 20, 2013, Xinde Company and CHEN Lixin submitted the ocean marine insurance slip of M.V. PING DA 7 to CCIC Shanghai through New Qiao, and signed and sealed on the insurance slip. The next day, CCIC Shanghai issued an ocean shipping insurance policy. The insured policy and the insurance policy both noted that the ship name was M.V. PING DA 7, the insurer was the ship owner, JIANG Haiping, the operator of the vessel Xinde Company, and the charterer of the vessel was Hong Kong Run Jiu Shipping Co., Ltd.; the insured amount was RMB12,000,000; the trading limits are "not west of 60 degrees East and not East of 150 degrees East, not South of 20 degrees South and not North of 60 degrees North"; the term of coverage was from May 21, 2013 to May 20, 2014; the scope of liability and the applicable terms were subject to 86 terms against all risks; and the deductible for each accident was RMB50,000 or 10% of the loss, and the deductible rate of total loss and constructive total loss was 10%. JIANG Haiping received the insurance policy and raised no objection.

On December 11, 2013, M.V. PING DA 7happened grounding accident in the port of Ponape in Western Pacific Micronesia, the longitude of the stranding location was 158°14.357' W. After that, McLarens Shanghai was commissioned by the CCIC Shanghai and JIANG Haiping to carry out a survey, it issued a survey report in terms of the grounding accident involved, the survey report stated that M. V. PING DA 7 constituted a constructive total loss. Darun Company designed a plan for refloating and towage of M.V. PING DA 7, the quotation was RMB16.2 million yuan. On December 26 of the same year, CCIC Shanghai sent the notice on discharging the hull insurance contract of M.V. PING DA 7 to JIANG Haiping, in which it was stated the location of the grounding accident was beyond the insured area listed on the policy, JIANG Haiping violated the warranty of trading limits in the insurance contract, so it discharged the insurance contract because M.V. PING DA 7 sailed beyond trading limits.

The court of first instance held that the case was arising from dispute over insurance brokerage contract. JIANG Haiping was the owner of insured ship. When New Qiao accepted the commission of insurance, it should know JIANG Haiping was actual insurer according to the ship certificates. The insurance contract eventually recorded JIANG Haiping was the insurer, which indicated that New Qiao knew JIANG Haiping was the actual counterparty to the insurance brokerage contract. Therefore, it should be identified that JIANG Haiping established insurance brokerage contract relationship with New Qiao in terms of hull insurance of M.V. PING DA 7 through the agent Xinde Company and CHEN Lixin. The capacity of JIANG Haiping in the action was proper.

In respect of the losses suffered by JIANG Haiping, according to the facts having been identified, M.V. PING DA 7 was deemed as a constructive total loss, the loss amount was RMB10.8 million yuan, namely the insurance amount, namely RMB1.2 million yuan deducting the deductible (10%). Although New Qiao argued that JIANG Haiping had obtained the compensation from the insurer, New Qiao did not provide evidence to prove that JIANG Haiping's loss has been made up or received compensation, so the court of first instance held that the amount of losses suffered by JIANG Haiping should be RMB1.08 million yuan.

According to the provisions of Article 128 of the Insurance Law of the People's Republic of China, the insurance broker should be liable for compensation according to the law for the loss of the insured and the insurer. JIANG Haiping claimed that New Qiao miswrote the trading limits of the involved ship in the insured process, but JIANG Haiping did not provide the evidence regarding insured requirement of the scope of voyage. On the contrary, JIANG Haiping's agent Xinde Company and CHEN Lixin sealed and signed the policy to confirm the trading limits recorded on the policy. It showed that JIANG Haiping and his agents had no objection to the trading limits insured by the insurance broker. JIANG Haiping also had no evidence to prove that he had objections to the trading limits after signed the insurance contract, so JIANG Haiping's existing evidence could not prove New Qiao has fault. JIANG Haiping was refused to be compensated due to it beyond the agreement of the scope of navigation of insurance contract, the loss was caused by its own fault and has no relations with New Qiao. As for JIANG Haiping claimed that New Qiao regarded the trading limits as a warranty clause without permission, while JIANG Haiping's agent confirmed the contents of the insured policy, his claims could not stand, so the claim of JIANG Haiping against New Qiao for compensation for the loss should not be supported.

To sum up, according to Article 402 of the Contract Law of the People's Republic of China, Article 128 of the Insurance Law of the People's Republic of China and Article 64 Paragraph 1 of the Civil Procedure Law of People's Republic of China, the court of first instance rejected the claims of JIANG Haiping and judged JIANG Haiping should bear the court acceptance fee in amount of RMB86,600.

JIANG Haiping disagreed with judgment of first instance and appealed. He claimed that the court of first instance found facts unclearly and applied the law incorrectly. Firstly, in the original instance, JIANG Haiping provided evidence 10, namely the email from New Qiao to Lawyer CHEN Mouyi, a party not involved in this case on January 1, 2014 to prove that the trading limit requested by JIANG Haiping was "not East of 150 Degrees West". New Qiao made an error when issuing or checking the insurance slip, which caused the trading limit as stated in the insurance policy was "not East of 150 Degrees East". The court of the original instance did not admit the probative force of the evidence as it was an email without notarization and there was no other evidence to corroborate, it lacked legal basis. Secondly, New Qiao, as an insurance broker which provided professional services, should bear obligations with more due diligence and attention to ensure the correctness of the print and check of the insurance policy. CHEN Lixin did not check carefully when signing and sealing the insurance slip, since it trusted New Qiao, but New Qiao committed fault in the trading limits at first. Thirdly, New Qiao copied words concerning the trading limits in the P&I policy mechanically, as a result, the error continued. New Qiao took the trading limits as a warranty unreasonably, while it would not be requested by domestic ship insurance brokers, it went against domestic insurance practice. Therefore, JIANG Haiping requested the court to set aside the judgment of the first instance and amend the judgment to support his claims filed in the first instance according to the law.

New Qiao did not submit written defense during the defense period. It defensed in the second instance that the judgment of the original instance found facts clearly and applied law correctly. Firstly, evidence 10, which was provided by JIANG Haiping in the original instance, the evidence form thereof was illegal. It is correct that the original court did not admit the evidence as JIANG Haiping did not fulfill his obligation for burden of proof appropriately. Secondly, this case was arising from dispute over hull insurance, during the process of procuring the ship insurance, New Qiao insured under the request of JIANG Haiping absolutely. The trading limits on the insurance slip, which JIANG Haiping had confirmed by seal, were same with the trading limits on the final insurance policy. Thirdly, both the agreement on trading limits during the process of procuring the P&I insurance and the trading limit on the insurance slip of the P&I insurance was "not East of 150 Degrees East". There was no fault for insurer of P&I insurance in the issue of the insurance policy according to the insurance slip. Therefore, New Qiao requested the court to dismiss the appeal and affirm the original judgment.

JIANG Haiping submitted a new set of evidence in the second instance: New Qiao sent two emails to ZHANG Jianxin, agent *ad litem* entrusted by JIANG Haiping with counsel of the insurance terms of M.V. PING DA 7 on January 8, 2014. These two emails can prove the authenticity of evidence 10 submitted in the first instance, namely there was a default in the making of the P&I policy. JIANG Haiping handled notarization of the two emails and evidence 10 submitted in the first instance.

In terms of the evidence submitted by JIANG Haiping, New Qiao after cross-examining confirmed the formal authenticity of the two emails, but did not recognize the contents of emails and the relevancy with this case. New Qiao held the emails were produced during the negotiation in terms of P&I insurance, New Qiao as the insurance broker of JIANG Haiping strove for compensation towards the P&I insurer after the subject accident happened. The contents thereof these emails are not authentic and they could not be evidence to prove that New Qiao had a fault when making the policy.

The court admits the formal authenticity of the two emails since they have gone through notarization and New Qiao confirmed the formal authenticity thereof. Evidence 10 JIANG Haiping submitted in the first instance was emails New Qiao sent to Lawyer CHEN Mouyi. The court of first instance did not admit the formal authenticity, because JIANG Haiping did not handle notarization in the first instance, the court did not admit its probative force. Since JIANG Haiping handled notarization for the emails, therefore the court admits the formal authenticity thereof. The two emails JIANG Haiping submitted in the second instance reflect the contents of the email QIAO Mou, the legal representative of New Qiao, which forwarded the hull insurance insurer's e-mail, to Lawyer ZHANG Jianxin, JIANG Haiping's agent *ad litem*, and the email JIANG Haiping submitted in the first instance which New Qiao sent to Lawyer CHEN Mouyi is also concerning whether the insurer had a fault in the process of making the P&I policy. So, these three emails cannot be taken as evidence to prove New Qiao had fault during the procuring of insurance. The court does not admit the relevancy of the three emails with this case.

New Qiao also submitted a new set of evidence: the copies of the confirmation of P&I insurance quotation for M.V. PING DA 7, which was signed and sealed by JIANG Haiping and Xinde Company, to prove the trading limits in the P&I

insurance requested by JIANG Haiping are also "not West of 60 degrees East and not East of 150 degrees East not South of 20 degrees South and not North of 60 degrees North". So the P&I insurer had no fault in making policy.

In terms of the evidence submitted by New Qiao, JIANG Haiping after cross-examining confirmed the formal authenticity of this set of evidence, but held the confirmation of quotation was formed after the wrong information passed between New Qiao and the P&I insurer, in addition, a common shipowner cannot know the contents or words, New Qiao did not give any specialized guidance to JIANG Haiping. In a word, the evidence could not prove that New Qiao had no fault in procuring P&I insurance and hull insurance, the probative force should not be admitted.

The court confirms the authenticity of this evidence, although it is a copy the confirmation of the quotation of P&I insurance of M.V. PING DA 7, JIANG Haiping had no objection to its form. The emails suggest that the trading limits in the confirmation of quotation are "not West of 60 degrees East and not East of 150 degrees East, not South of 20 degrees South and not North of 60 degrees North", which have no difference with those stated in the policy issued by CCIC Shanghai. New Qiao used the copies to prove it had no fault when P&I insurer made the policy, but in this case, JIANG Haiping claimed New Qiao had fault in undertaking the hull insurance rather than P&I insurance, so the court holds the copies of confirmation have no relevancy with this case.

The facts found by the court of first instance can be proved by relevant evidence. Although JIANG Haiping objected those facts, but he did not provide sufficient evidence, so the court admits these facts.

The court finds out some other facts: according to evidence 2 submitted by JIANG Haiping in the first instance, namely the emails between CHEN Lixin (Xinde Company) and JIANG Haiping, at 1521 on May 8, 2013, CHEN Lixin sent an email to JIANG Haiping about the quotation of hull insurance of M.V. PING DA 7, the email New Qiao sent to Chen Lixin was attached thereto. The trading area in the email was "Southeast Asia and the Pacific, Indian Ocean Routing Area"; at 2000 on May 14, 2013, CHEN Lixin sent an email to JIANG Haiping about the quotation after negotiation, the email New Qiao sent to CHEN Lixin was also attached thereto. The trading area is "not allowed to sail between America and Atlantic and/or Pacific Routing Area, the trading limits are not West of 90 degrees East and not East of 180 degrees East, not South of 15 degrees South and not North of 60 degrees North"; at 0901 on May 15, 2013, CHEN Lixin sent an email to JIANG Haiping, with the email New Qiao sent to CHEN Lixin being attached to, saying that the insurer had agreed with extension of the trading limits, but the premium should be increased. In this email, the trading limits are expressed as "not West of 60 Degrees East and not East of 150 Degrees East, not South of 29 Degrees South and not North of 60 degrees North", which were cited from the reply of the insurer; in the email sent at 1042 on May 15, 2013, the trading area was "not allowed to sail between America and Atlantic and/or Pacific Routing Area, the trading limits are not West of 60 degrees East and not East of 150 degrees East, not South of 20 degrees South and not North of 60 degrees North". The trading limits in the email sent at 1111on May 15, 2013 are same with those in the email sent at 1042 on May 15, 2013.

The court holds that the case is dispute over insurance brokerage contract. JIANG Haiping is the shipowner of M.V. PING DA 7. He authorized Xinde Company and CHEN Lixin to procure insurance for M.V. PING DA 7. Xinde Company (insurance broker) procured hull insurance with CCIC Shanghai. The court of first instance held that there was an insurance brokerage contract between JIANG Haiping and New Qiao. It shall be recognized.

JIANG Haiping argued that he entrusted New Qiao with the hull insurance of M.V. PING DA 7, the trading limits should be "not West of 60 degrees East and not East of 150 degrees West, not South of 20 degrees South and not North of 60 degrees North". But New Qiao had got it wrong when it procured hull insurance with CCIC Shanghai. The trading limits were expressed as "not West of 60 degrees East and not East of 150 degrees East, not South of 20 degrees South and not North of 60 degrees North". New Qiao came to an agreement that the trading limits should be a warranty without authorization of JIANG Haiping.

Then, M.V. PING DA 7 ran aground at 158°14.357′E (158 degrees 14.357 min east longitude), and it was deemed as a constructive total loss. CCIC Shanghai terminated the contract because JIANG Haiping breached the warranty on trading limits (of the insurance contract), and it caused the loss in an amount of RMB10,800,000 to JIANG Haiping, together with the interest thereon, and New Qiao should pay for his claims. New Qiao argued that it strictly followed JIANG Haiping's instructions on trading limits when procured insurance with CCIC Shanghai, which was "not West of 60 degrees East and not East of 150 degrees East, not South of 20 degrees South and not North of 60 degrees North". CHEN Lixin and New Qiao confirmed that through signature and seal on behalf of JIANG Haiping. Therefore, New Qiao did not breach the insurance brokerage contract and had no causal relationship with the losses JIANG Haiping claimed.

The court holds that firstly, JIANG Haiping did not submit evidence that can prove the trading limits are "not West of 60 degrees East and not East of 150 degrees West, not South of 20 degrees South and not North of 60 degrees North" when he authorized New Qiao to cover hull insurance for M.V. PING DA 7; secondly, it can be known from emails sent between CHEN Lixin (Xinde Company) and New Qiao during May 8, 2013 and May 15, 2013 that at first, the trading area was "Southeast Asia and the Pacific, Indian Ocean Routing Area", then it was altered to "not allowed to sail between America to Atlantic and/or Pacific Routing Area, the trading limits are not West of 90 degrees East and not East of 180 degrees East, not South of 15 degrees South and not North of 60 degrees North", and then the insured requested to make a change, which finally was "not West of 60 degrees East and not East of 150 degrees East, not South of 20 degrees South and not North of 60 degrees North", JIANG Haiping and CHEN Lixin (Xinde Company) participated in the whole process; thirdly, the trading limits in the final policy which CHEN Lixin and Xinde Company signed and sealed on behalf of JIANG Haiping are also "not West of 60 degrees East and not East of 150 degrees East, not South of 20 degrees South and not North of 60 degrees North", the same with the record of the original policy; finally, there is no material difference whether the trading limits should been recorded on the right side of the policy or on the "special agreement" column of special agreement listing page. In view of the above, the grounds of appeal held by JIANG Haiping that New Qiao gave wrong information about trading limits to insurer when procured hull insurance for M.V. PING DA 7 lack factual basis, which shall not be adopted by the court.

To sum up, under the hull insurance brokerage contract, the grounds of appeal held by JIANG Haiping that New Qiao, the insurance broker, had default and such default existed causal relationship with the losses of JIANG Haiping incurred by the stranding of M.V. PING DA 7 lack evidence and cannot stand, the court shall not support. The decision of the original judgment is correct, and shall be sustained. According to Article 170 Paragraph 1 and Article 175 of the Civil Procedure Law of the People's Republic of China, the judgment is as follows:

Dismiss the appeal and affirm the original judgment.

Court acceptance fee of first instance in amount of RMB86,600, shall be undertaken as decided in the original judgment and that ofsecond instancein amount of RMB86,600, shall be born by the Appellant JIANG Haiping.

The judgment is final.

Presiding Judge: DONG Min
Acting Judge: XV Yijin
Acting Judge: HU Hailong

July 22, 2015

Clerk: CHEN Xi

Appendix: Relevant Law

1. Civil Procedure Law of the People's Republic of China

Article 170 After trying a case on appeal, the people's court of second instance shall, in the light of the following situations, dispose of it accordingly:

(1) If the facts were clearly ascertained and the law was correctly applied in the original judgment, the appeal shall be rejected in the form of judgment and the original judgment shall be recognized;
(2) If the facts were wrongly ascertained or the application of law was incorrect in the original judgment, the said judgment shall be amended according to the law;
(3) If the basic facts were not clearly ascertained in the original judgment, the people's court of second instance shall make a written order to set aside the original judgment and remand the case to the original people's court for retrial, or the people's court of Second instance may affect the judgment after investigating and clarifying the facts; or

(4) If there was a serious violation of legal procedures such as omitting any party or making an illegal absentee judgment in the original judgment, the said judgment shall be set aside by a written order and the case remanded to the original people's court for retrial.

If the party files an appeal against the judgment made in the retrial by the court originally tried the case, the people's court of second instance shall make a judgment according to the law.

Article 175 The judgment and written order of the people's court of second instance shall be final.

Tianjin Maritime Court
Civil Judgment

Jiangsu Eastern Heavy Industry Co., Ltd.

v.

Nanjing Twin Rivers Shipping Co., Ltd.

(2012) Jin Hai Fa Shang Chu Zi No.784

Related Case(s) None.

Cause(s) of Action 207. Dispute over shipbuilding contract.

Headnote The purchaser of a newly-built ship held to be entitled to refuse delivery because of shipbuilder's lateness; the Third Party funding the purchase held to be entitled to withhold payment installments because of shipbuilder's delays.

Summary The Plaintiff-Seller contracted with the Defendant-Buyer for the construction of two ships. The Plaintiff-Seller, the Defendant-Buyer and the Defendant-Third Party formed a tripartite agreement whereby the Defendant-Third Party would assume some of the Defendant-Buyer's rights and obligations arising from the original shipbuilding contract.

Among other things, the tripartite agreement stipulated that the Defendant-Third Party would pay the Plaintiff-Seller for the ship construction. However, a series of conditions in the tripartite agreement were required on the part of the Plaintiff-Seller before the Defendant-Third Party was required to pay.

The Defendant-Buyer refused to take delivery of one of the vessels because the Plaintiff-Seller was late in beginning its construction. Additionally, the Defendant-Third Party refused to pay for the vessel because several provisions in the parties' tripartite agreement had not been satisfied. As a result, the Plaintiff-Seller sued the Defendant-Buyer for wrongful termination of contract and the Defendant-Third Party for delayed installment payments.

The issues before the court were 1) whether the Defendant-Buyer could reject the disputed vessel; 2) whether the Defendants-Third Party's installment payments were late; and 3) whether the Defendant-Buyer had a right to terminate the underlying shipbuilding contract.

Here, the court held the underlying contract was a contract for hired work (ship construction), not a sales contract. In doing so, the court reasoned it was a contract for hired work because, among other reasons, it was signed before the actual ship construction began, and the Defendant-Buyer was involved with the construction process. Because this was a contract for hired work, it was a contract for specific, irreplaceable subject matter, a vessel. Since the Plaintiff-Seller did not satisfy the conditions as provided in the tripartite agreement and underlying agreement regarding the construction of the vessel, the court held the Defendant-Buyer had a right to refuse delivery of the vessel. Moreover, the Plaintiff-Seller breached the underlying agreement by not satisfying the above-referenced conditions.

The court also held that, because the Plaintiff-Seller failed to satisfy conditions in the parties' tripartite agreement, the Defendant-Third Party were not late in providing installment payments. Further, the court held the Defendant had a right to terminate the agreements because the Plaintiff-Seller did not begin the vessel construction pursuant to the time provided in the underlying agreements.

Judgment

The Plaintiff: Jiangsu Eastern Heavy Industry Co., Ltd.
Domicile: Port of Shi Wei, Jingjiang City, Jiangsu Province.
Legal representative: JIN Xin, chairman of the company.
Agent *ad litem*: ZHAO Jinsong, lawyer of Shanghai All Bright Law Offices.
Agent *ad litem*: DUANQingxi, lawyer of Shanghai All Bright Law Offices.

The Defendant: Nanjing Twin Rivers Shipping Co., Ltd.
Domicile: Floor 19, Building 5, Nanjing Zhongtai International Plaza, Middle Jiangdong Road, Jianye District, Nanjing City, Jiangsu Province.
Legal representative: MOU Ling, chairman of the company.
Agent *ad litem*: ZHANG Chuanping, female, legal director of the company.
Domicile: Room 205, No.37, Ertiao Lane, Baixia District, Nanjing City, Jiangsu Province.
Agent *ad litem*: HU Zhengliang, lawyer of Shanghai Wintell & Co. Law Firm.

The Third Party: Minsheng Financial Leasing Co., Ltd.
Legal representative: KONG Linshan, chairman of the company.
Agent *ad litem*: YAN Shaofang, lawyer of Beijing Baoying Law Firm.

With respect to the case arising from dispute over shipbuilding contract, the Plaintiff, Jiangsu Eastern Heavy Industry Co., Ltd., filed an action against the Defendants, Nanjing Twin Rivers Shipping Co., Ltd. and Minsheng Financial Leasing Co., Ltd. (hereinafter referred to as Minsheng Company) before Tianjin Maritime Court and the case was accepted on October 15, 2012. After the entertainment, a collegial penal composed of Presiding Judge CHEN Jianpeng, Acting Judges CAO Ke and ZHANG Junbo was formed by the court according to the law to try the case. During the trial, the Plaintiff applied to the court for withdrawing the action against the Defendant and it had been granted by the court. In view of

Minsheng Company had legal interest with the handling of the case, the court informed the above-mentioned company as the Third Party to participate in the proceedings. The court held hearings in public on January 15, 2013 and on February 26, 2013 respectively for the trial of the case. Agent *ad litem* of the Plaintiff, DUAN Qingxi, original agent *ad litem*, ZHU Lianhai, agents *ad litem* of the Defendant, HU Zhengliang and ZHANG Chuanping, agent *ad litem* of the Third Party, YAN Shaofang, attended the first hearing. Agents *ad litem* of the Plaintiff, DUAN Qingxi and ZHAO Jinsong, agents *ad litem* of the Defendant, HU Zhengliang and ZHANG Chuanping, agent *ad litem* of the Third Party, YAN Shaofang, attended the second hearing. Now the case has been concluded.

The Plaintiff alleged: on October 22, 2010, the Defendant agreed to conclude the No.JEHIC10-No.811 *Shipbuilding and Sale Contract* with the Plaintiff (hereinafter referred to as "shipbuilding contract") and agreed that the Plaintiff built a 47,500-ton bulk cargo ship No.JEHIC10-No.811 (hereinafter referred to as "No.811 ship") for the Defendant and the contract price was RMB175 million. On October 27, 2010, the Defendant, the Third Party entered into *Triple Agreement of the Shipbuilding and Sale Contract No.JEHIC10-No.811* with the Plaintiff (hereinafter referred to as "tripartite agreement") and agreed that the shipbuilding amount shall be paid by the Third Party. As a guarantee for the shipbuilding amount, the Plaintiff applied to China Construction Bank Corp Jingjiang Branch (hereinafter referred to as the "Jingjiang Construction Bank") to issue three copies letter of guarantee to the Third Party. Currently, the Defendant and the Third Party paid to the Plaintiff three advance payment in sum of RMB96,250,000. Therein, the second instalment of the advanced payment delayed in payments, the fourth and the fifth instalment of advanced payment has not been paid.

On September 20, 2010, the Defendant issued *Notice on the Termination of the Contract* (hereinafter referred to as notice on termination) to the Plaintiff, and the contract was wrongfully terminated, and the Defendant requested the Plaintiff to refund RMB96,250,000 and compensation for other loss. The Plaintiff held that the aforesaid actions of the Defendant belonged to fundamental breach of the contract which had caused heavy economic loss to the Plaintiff. The Plaintiff hence requested the court to order the Defendant to bear the fee arose from ship-building in the amount of RMB8,750,000 and the interest of RMB3,173,150 and compensate the loss caused to the Plaintiff by the refusal to accept ship of the Defendant, and the litigation costs of this case jointly.

The Defendant defended: firstly, there was no basis in law for the Plaintiff to allege the wrongfully act of releasing shipbuilding contract of the Defendant; secondly, the Plaintiff's claim cannot be established that the Plaintiff alleged the breach of contract of the Defendant by failing to pay off the second, fourth and fifth advance payment, because: 1. Minsheng Company paid off the second advance payment according to the shipbuilding contract and the tripartite agreement; and 2. the Plaintiff failed to meet payment terms of the fourth and fifth advance payment; thirdly, the loss claimed by the Plaintiff cannot be supported, the reasons were as follows: 1. the Plaintiff had no right to claim that the Defendant owed the fee of shipbuilding in the amount of RMB8,750,000, as the act of the Defendant to wrongfully release contract did not exist; 2. the Defendant did not break the contract for failure to pay the second, fourth and fifth advancement, hence, the Plaintiff's claim cannot be established that the Plaintiff suffered interest loss in the amount of RMB3,173,150; and 3. the Plaintiff's claim cannot be established that the Plaintiff suffered economy loss in amount of RMB1,896,000 from the refusal to accept the ship by the Defendant, because the Defendant did not have the act of wrongfully releasing the contract and refusing to accept the ship.

The Third Party stated: the Plaintiff, Defendant enter into tripartite agreement with the Third Party. As the letter of guarantee of payment in advance of the Third Party, the Plaintiff applied to Jingjiang Construction Bank to issue three copies of the letter of guarantee and then the Defendant and Third Party had paid some payment to the Plaintiff. According to the agreement, the dispute arose between the Plaintiff and the Defendant shall not be participated by the Third Party and any liability shall not be born by him.

The issues of the case are as follows:

1. Whether the Defendant breached the contract or not during executing of the contract; and.
2. Whether the claimed amount was real and rational or not.

The Plaintiff submitted the following evidence:

1. Shipbuilding contract, to prove the contractual relationship about ship building between the Plaintiff and the Defendant;
2. The tripartite agreement, to prove that the Plaintiff, the Defendant and the Third Party entered into the tripartite agreement and the Third Party replaced the Defendant to pay the Plaintiff the payment after the second installment of advance payment;
3. The No.1136913007letter of advance payment guarantee, keel-laying proof issued by CCS, payment notice, EMS mailing list, electronic remittance and bank receipt, to prove that the Defendant delayed 84 days in paying keel-laying schedule payment;
4. Notice of termination sent by the Defendant on September 20, 2010, three copies issued by Jingjiang Construction Bank, to prove that the Defendant had no right to claim to terminate the contract involved and the condition of the refund under three copies of the letter of guarantee had not yet been available;
5. Proof of launching stage issued by CCS (safety operation report), to prove that the Defendant delayed 179 days in paying launching progress payment;
6. Sea trial and ship delivery notice, to prove that the Defendant delayed 87 days in paying ship-delivery progress payment;
7. No.811 ship sea trail report and the cover of test of trial trip report, to prove that the Plaintiff finished the sea trial of No.811 ship on September 28, 2012;
8. EMS express delivery inquiry sheet and express waybill, to prove that the Plaintiff sent the Third Party the second instalment of payment document of No.811 ship, which received hereby at 10:45 am on November 21, 2011. The aforesaid documents were also sent to the Defendant;

9. Catalogue of the No.811 ship building drawings, to prove that YU Shufeng representing the Defendant had signed in relevant drawings of involved ship sent by the Plaintiff in January 2011;
10. The card of YU Shufeng, sending and receiving record form of documents and e-mail, to prove that YU Shufeng was the Defendant's staff;
11. No.JEHIC10-810 *Shipbuilding and Sale Contract* (hereinafter referred to as "No.811 ship shipbuilding contract"), to prove that the agreement concerned specific account in the contract involved;
12. Payment notice and bank's receipt vouchers (account No.32001766236052 506270), to prove that the Defendant had no objection to regarding the account as the Plaintiff's specific account for shipbuilding;
13. The Defendant issued notice of termination to the Plaintiff on November 16, 2011, to prove that the true reason why the Defendant did not sign and seal on the keel-laying proof was preparing to abandon ship rather than No.811 ship did not satisfy the keel-laying conditions;
14. The letter sent to the Defendant by the Plaintiff on November 19, 2011, to prove that the Plaintiff did not agree with termination of the contact proposed by the Defendant on November 17, 2011, and the Plaintiff had started to build No.811 ship on November 17, 2011;
15. The launching notice of No.811 ship was sent to the Defendant by the Plaintiff on June 26, 2011 and the Defendant replied to the Plaintiff on the second day, to prove that the Plaintiff had informed the Defendant of launching time of No.811 ship and even though the Defendant received, the Defendant refused to cooperate;
16. The letter sent to the Defendant by the Plaintiff on August 21, 2012, to prove that the Defendant had received the sea trial notice of No.811 ship but refused to cooperate;
17. Sea trial certificate, to prove that the ship trial voyage certificate had been awarded to No.811 ship on August 22, 2012 and the ship intended to proceed trial voyage on August 26, 2012;
18. Ship minimum safety manning certificate, to prove that the Plaintiff got temporary certificate for the purpose of trial voyage;
19. Certificate of ship's nationality, to prove that the Plaintiff got temporary nationality certificate for the purpose of trial voyage;
20. The reply issued by Jiangsu Maritime Safety Administration, to prove that the Defendant made malicious report in order to achieve goal of abandonment of ship;
21. Resale contract of No.811 ship, to prove that the ship involved was equipped with another four cranes and the resale price was USD14,580,000;
22. The contract of the Plaintiff purchasing four cranes, to prove that four cranes cost USD1,080,000;
23. Notice of ship presale, express waybill and network inquiry, to prove that the Plaintiff had sent preemptive buying notice to the Defendant according to the contract;

24. China Classification Society inspection notice (signed by the ship surveyor HENG Lin), to prove that the certificate of No.811 ship issued by China Classification Society was valid;
25. The ship inspection sheet, to prove that the former subsection inspection of No.811 ship was qualified;
26. Visa application form of ship in voyage, to prove that No.811 ship departed from the port and started to trial voyage within 24 h after the visa on September 24, 2012; and
27. The trial report of No.811 ship, to prove that the trial time was from September 25 to 28, 2012;
28. Pier lease agreement, to prove that the No.811 ship's daily berth fee was RMB1800.

The cross-examinations of the Defendant on the Plaintiff's evidence are as follows: having no objection to authenticity of evidence 1, evidence 2, but holding that the Plaintiff's claim in proof purpose was not accurate that the Third Party paid off the payment instead of the Defendant, actually the Defendant transferred part rights and duties under the agreement to the Third Party; having no objection to the authenticity of evidence 3 but objected to the purpose of proof of the evidence, the keel-laying proof lacked the signature of the Defendant and did not meet the conditions for payment of the second installment; having no objection to authenticity of evidence 4 but objected to the purpose of proof of the evidence, three copies of letter of guarantee could not prove that the Defendant had no right to cancellation and refund conditions were not yet available; having no objection to authenticity of evidence 6 but objected to the purpose of proof of the evidence, the Defendants had no obligation to pay for the fifth installment, and the trial ship notice had no relationship with whether schedule payment be paid or not; having no objection to authenticity of evidence 8 but the content recorded on the query form was not according to real situation, payment notice needed the Defendant to confirm, the keel-laying proof was incomplete, and there was no signature of the Defendant, which was inconsistent with the shipbuilding contract and tripartite agreement; having no objection to authenticity of evidence 9 but objected to the purpose of proof of the evidence, the evidence was the sketch requiring to submit for censorship rather than returned drawings(construction drawings) approved by Classification Society; having no objection to authenticity of evidence 10, evidence 11, evidence 12 but objected to relevancy, the evidence involved was documents of No.811 ship and had no relationship with the case; having no objection to authenticity of evidence 13 but objected to the purpose of proof of the evidence, considering the Plaintiff did not prepare to lay keel, the Defendant did not sign on keel-laying proof; having no objection to authenticity of evidence 14 but objected to the purpose of proof of the evidence, the evidence was a letter made by the Plaintiff himself and there was no other evidence to prove that the Plaintiff started to build No.811 ship on November 17, 2011; having no objection to authenticity of evidence 15, evidence 16, evidence 23 and evidence 26 but objected to the purpose of proof of the evidence, the aforesaid evidence was concerned with No.810 ship rather than No.811 ship; having no objection to authenticity of evidence 17 to evidence 19, evidence 25 but objected to the purpose of proof of the evidence, the aforesaid evidence indicated the identification number was No.810 ship rather than No.811 ship concerned in this case; having no objection to authenticity of evidence 20 but objected to the purpose of proof of the evidence, complaint letter was sent by the Defendant to ship management department under the situation that the Plaintiff refused to rebuild the involved ship; having objection to evidence 5, evidence 7, evidence 21, evidence 22, evidence 22, evidence 24, evidence 27 and evidence 28.

The cross-examinations of the Third Party on the Plaintiff's evidence were as follows: having no objection to evidence 1, evidence 2, prepayment guarantee in evidence 3, evidence 4 to evidence 6 and evidence 8; but objected to authenticity of keel-laying proof and payment notice in evidence 3 and to the relevancy of evidence 7 and evidence 9 to evidence 28, holding that the aforesaid evidence had no relationship with him.

The Defendant submitted evidence materials as follows:

1. Shipbuilding contract, to prove that the Defendant had concluded ship-building contract with the Plaintiff under which both parties agreed the payment conditions of shipbuilding prepayment and the delivery time was June 5, 2012, and the cumulative time allowed to postpone or not was 90 days;
2. Tripartite agreement, to prove that the Plaintiff, the Defendant and the Third Party has concluded tripartite agreement and agreed that the Defendant assigned the ship-building contract to the Third Party. The ship price shall be paid by the Defendant to the Plaintiff about unpaid part under the contract. The Plaintiff agreed to hereof. The other rights and duties of the Defendant under the contract were still exercised by the Defendant, except for the agreement concerned shipbuilding payment, ownership or partial ownership of the ship, beneficiary under letter of guarantee of prepayment and ship ownership registration;
3. Notice of rescission, to prove that the Defendant gave notice to the Plaintiff on September 20, 2012;
4. Keel-laying proof, to prove that the Defendant, the Plaintiff and China Classification Society signed a keel-laying proof on January 18, 2012;
5. Prepayment notice and domestic express mail list, to prove that the Defendant received the notice of second instalment of prepayment on February 2, 2012 mailed by the Plaintiff on January 30;
6. Mail of payment notice concerned No.JEHIC10-No.811 contract, to prove that the Defendant sent email to the Plaintiff on February 6, 2012 in order to inform the Plaintiff that the notice of second prepayment instalment sent on January 30 had been received but the Third Party did not receive and requested the Plaintiff to send one payment notice to the Third Party to improve the procedure of payment;
7. Electronic receipt of China Minsheng Bank, to prove that the Third Party paid the second installment of advance payment to the Plaintiff on February 20, 2012;

8. Certificate of notification and mailing, to prove that the Defendant informed the Plaintiff that it would come to know about the fund usage condition of shipbuilding specific account on November 25, 2011;
9. Certificate of informing letter and mailing, to prove that the Defendant requested the Plaintiff to set up immediately an independent specific account for shipbuilding prepayment of the involved ship;
10. Letter on the item of the 47500 ton bulk cargo ship, to prove that the Defendant received the letter from the Plaintiff on December 16, 2011, the Plaintiff informed the Defendant to set up a specific account of ship involved in this case;
11. Email concerned setting up payment notice, to prove that the Defendant sent email to the Plaintiff requesting the Plaintiff set up the second installment of prepayment notice of ship involved in this case according to the specific account set by the Defendant;
12. The letter sent by the Defendant to the Plaintiff on December 13, 2011, to prove that the Defendant requested the Plaintiff according to the spirit of coordinate to immediately send the Defendant the keel-laying preparation and relevant documents in order to prove whether the ship satisfied the keel-laying condition or not;
13. The drawings of 47500 ton of bulk cargo ship returned by China Classification Society, to prove that the Plaintiff delivered returned trial drawings of No.810 ship and No.811 ship to the Defendant's supervision and inspection team on January 16 and 17, 2012;
14. Mail and attachments sent by the Plaintiff to the Defendant on January 16, 2012, to prove that the Plaintiff sent the Defendant the subsection outfitting and painting plan summary list in second week in 2012, subsection construction or subsection outfitting and painting plan summary list and cargo ship No.7#47500BN project management network diagram in January 2012;
15. Mail sent by the Plaintiff to the Defendant on March 4, 2011, to prove that the overall plan for No.811 ship, but the Plaintiff did not follow the plan to build the ship;
16. Keel laying certificate, to prove that No.811 ship laid keel on June 12, 2012, which was more than 7 months later than the overall production plan of the Plaintiff;
17. Notice sent by the Plaintiff to the Defendant on June 15, 2012, the reply sent by the Defendant to the Plaintiff on June 18, 2012, to prove that the Plaintiff informed the Defendant of the decision that the subsection and equipment of No.810 ship would change into No.811 ship and the shipowner changed into the Defendant, the semi-products and ancillary equipment of No.811 ship changed into No.812 ship and the shipowner changed into Zhoushan Zhongchang Shipping Co. Ltd.; the Defendant informed the Plaintiff of the Plaintiff's serious breach of contract, the Defendant would not agree;
18. The letter sent by the Plaintiff's quality control department to the Defendant's supervision and inspection team on July 12, 2012 and the reply sent by the Defendant's supervision and inspection team to the Plaintiff's quality control

department on the next day, to prove that the Plaintiff's quality control department informed the Defendant's supervision and inspection team that No.811 ship's subsection examined by the Plaintiff's application was in line with the subsection of No.810 ship, and requested the Defendant to examined; the reply sent by the Defendant's supervision and inspection team requested the Plaintiff to strictly follow the No.811 ship to construct and to conscientiously execute the contract;

19. The letter sent by the Defendant to the Plaintiff on July 30, 2012, to prove that the Defendant asked the Plaintiff to resume construction of No.811 vessel as soon as possible;
20. The notices of the International Maritime Organization number (hereinafter referred to as "IMO number") of No.810 vessel and No.811 vessel and the Chinese versions thereof, to prove that the IMO number of the No.810 vessel was 9618628 and the No.811 was 9618630, therefore the Plaintiff should not use the No.811's IMO number on other vessel;
21. The letter sent by the Defendant on August 16, 2012 to ask the Plaintiff to stop the disinformation conduct, to prove that the Defendant asked the Plaintiff to correct the error immediately and restore the construction of the No.811 vessel;
22. Notarial paper made by the Notarial Office of Zhongshan Nanjing Jiangsu, to prove that the notary saw the segmentations of No.811 vessel at the Plaintiff's place, and the logo and the IMO number of the No.810 vessel had changed into No.811 vessel;
23. The reply sent by the Defendant to the Plaintiff on August 21, 2012 about the seaworthiness notice, to prove that the Defendant asked the Plaintiff to stop the disinformation conduct and restore the construction of the No.811 vessel abide by the convention and contract;
24. The inquiry & request about the Plaintiff changing the vessel logo sent by the Defendant to the China Classification Society Jiangsu Branch and the reply thereof, to prove that the China Classification Society Jiangsu Branch notified that the inspection documents about the No.810 vessel were still valid and the Plaintiff should not change the vessel number in these documents, the new documents after July 16, 2012 should indicate that the No.811 vessel was the No.810 vessel;
25. The re-inquiry & request about the Plaintiff changing the vessel logo sent by the Defendant to the China Classification Society Jiangsu Branch and the re-reply thereof, to prove that the China Classification Society Jiangsu Branch recognized that the vessel number in the draft report was wrong and it should be No.810 vessel; that the signed report should be a copy of the draft data, the project team has recovered the original of the draft;
26. Payment order to be confirmed on November 17, 2011, to prove that the payment notice proposed by the Plaintiff that it was already served on November 21, 2011 was not qualified;
27. E-mails sent by the Plaintiff to the Defendant on July 1, 2012 and November 1, 2012 and the certificate of commencement of No.810 vessel, to prove that the

No.810 vessel hold the ceremony marking the start of construction work on July 15 but had the condition to start building the vessel until November 5;
28. Minutes of coordination meeting, to prove that the Plaintiff took the form of commencement and received money in the course of building the ship so that the shipowner got angry with it. After the coordination by the Third Party, the Plaintiff was requested to give detailed construction plan, ensure construction according to the schedule, not delay anymore and provide the preparing materials of No.811 vessel before construction according to the requirements of the Defendant to mention;
29. The tip-off letter, to prove that the Defendant complained to the vessel management department after the Plaintiff breached the contract and did not concern about the Defendant's warning and suggestion; and
30. E-mail sent by the Plaintiff on May 23, 2012 and keel laying certificate of No.810 vessel and relevant photos, to prove that the logo written on the certificate of sea trial belonged to No.810 and the Plaintiff had the default conduct that they used the segmentations of No.810 vessel to hold the ceremony of keel laying for other shipowner while the Plaintiff built the series of 47500 ton vessel.

The cross-examinations of the Plaintiff on the Defendant's evidence are as follows: having no objection to evidence 1-3, evidence 7, evidence 8, evidence 11-21, evidence 23-27; having no objection to the authenticity of evidence 4 but having objection to the purpose of proof of the evidence, the involved vessel had the condition to be built on November 17, 2011, because the Plaintiff and the China Classification Society had signed on the commencement certificate of ship but the Defendant did not sign on it, the Plaintiff held that the signing date of the commencement certificate was November 17, 2011 rather than January 18, 2012; having no objection to the authenticity of evidence 5 but having objection to the purpose of proof of the evidence, the Defendant had received the second installment of payment notice on November 21, 2011, the aforementioned two evidence did not affirm that the original payment notice was invalid; having no objection to the authenticity of evidence 6 but having objection to the purpose of proof of the evidence, the document sent by the Plaintiff to the Third Party was not defective; having no objection to the authenticity of evidence 9 but having objection to the purpose of proof of the evidence, the demand of the Defendant was not in line with the contract; having no objection to the authenticity of evidence 10 but having objection to the purpose of proof of the evidence, the exclusive bank account was set by the Plaintiff to maintain cooperative linkages; having objection to the authenticity of evidence 22, evidence 29; having objection to the authenticity of the minutes of meeting on December 1, 2011 under evidence 28 but having no objection to the authenticity of the minutes of meeting on August 26, 2011; having no objection to the authenticity of the e-mail, the first photo and keel laying certificate under evidence 30 but having objection to the authenticity of the other three photos.

The cross-examinations of the Third Party on the Defendant's evidence are as follows: having no objection to the authenticity of evidence 1-3, 7, the minutes of meeting on December 1, 2011 under evidence 28; having objection to the relevancy of evidence 4-6, 8-27, the minutes of meeting on August 26, 2011 under evidence 28, evidence 29, evidence 30, holding that the aforementioned evidence had nothing with him.

The Third Party submitted the following evidence:

1. The electric remittance receipt of China Minsheng Bank, to prove the time of payment;
2. The electric payment receipt of the Third Party, to prove that the Third Party had received the second prepayment in sum of RMB8,750,000 on February 16, 2012; and
3. The copy of payment notice of the Plaintiff, to prove that the Third Party received the payment notice sent by the Plaintiff at the beginning of February 2012.

The Plaintiff had no objection to the evidence of the Third Party.

The Defendant had no objection to the evidence of the Third Party.

The determinations of the court about the evidence submitted by the Plaintiff were as follows: the court recognizes the authenticity and confirms the probative force of evidence 1; affirming the authenticity of evidence 2, to prove that the Plaintiff had signed a tripartite agreement with the Defendant and the Third Party and agreed that the Defendant transferred the obligation to pay after the second installment of the advance payment to the Third Party; affirming the authenticity of evidence 3 but it shall not prove that the Defendant delayed to pay the keel-laying schedule payment because the date that the Plaintiff started to build the vessel was January 18, 2012; affirming the authenticity of evidence 4 but the evidence could not illustrate whether the Defendant had the right to terminate the contract and whether the condition to refund the payment under the letter of indemnity was satisfied; affirming the authenticity of evidence 6, but it shall not prove that the Defendant was delayed by 87 days in terms of payment of delivery schedule payment because the contract did not stipulate that the Defendant shall pay the delivery schedule payment when the vessel was in the trial; affirming the authenticity of evidence 8, to prove that the paying vouchers of 2nd installment payment of No.811 vessel sent by the Plaintiff on November 19, 2011 was signed by the Third Party at 10:45 am on November 21, 2011, but the paying vouchers and the ship building permission were not according to the condition stipulated in the contract; affirming the authenticity of evidence 9, to prove that the submitting plans of the relevant vessel sent by the Plaintiff in January 2011 was signed by the representative of the Defendant YU Shufeng; affirming the authenticity of evidence 10, to prove that YU Shufeng was the Defendant's staff; affirming the authenticity of evidence 11, evidence 12, to prove the content and the performance of the contract of No.811 vessel; affirming the authenticity of evidence 13, to prove that the Defendant asked the Plaintiff to terminate the building contract of No.810 and

No.811 ship on the grounds of the Plaintiff's delay in building the vessel; affirming the authenticity of evidence 14, to prove that the Plaintiff did not agree to terminate the contract but cannot prove that the Plaintiff started building the No.811 vessel on November 17, 2011; affirming the authenticity of evidence 15, to prove that the Plaintiff informed the Defendant of the changed time when the No.811 vessel would launched from a shipyard, but the Defendant thought the vessel was the No.810 vessel and refused to take part in the launching ceremony; affirming the authenticity of evidence 16, to prove that the Defendant received the trial notice but the Defendant believed that the vessel was not the No.811 vessel but the No.810 vessel so that the Defendant refused to take part in the trial; affirming the authenticity of evidence 17-19, to prove that the Plaintiff draw the certificate of seaworthiness, minimum safe manning and certificate of registry for the changed No.811 vessel; affirming the authenticity of evidence 20, to prove that the Defendant reported the Plaintiff on the ground that the Plaintiff used the No.810 vessel to replace the No.811 vessel and changed the vessel name and the IMO number to Jiangsu Maritime Safety Administration; affirming the authenticity of evidence 21, to prove that the changed vessel was sold at the price of 14,850,000 dollar after increasing equipment such as four cranes and so on; affirming the authenticity of evidence 23, to prove that the Plaintiff had sent the notice of preferential purchase to the Defendant; affirming the authenticity of evidence 24, evidence 25, to prove that the segmentation and equipment of the No.810 vessel was qualified; affirming the authenticity of evidence 26, to prove that the Plaintiff applied for a voyage visa for the changed No.811 vessel on September 24, 2012; evidence 5, evidence 7, evidence 22, evidence 27 lacked original ones and evidence 28 lacked relevant supporting materials such as invoice and payment voucher, and the Defendant had objection to these evidence, thus the court does not affirm these evidence.

The determinations of the court about the evidence submitted by the Defendant are as follows: the court confirms the probative force of evidence 1-3, evidence 7, evidence 8, evidence 11-21, evidence 23-27, minutes of meeting on August 26, 2011 under the evidence 28, the e-mail, the first photo and birth certificate under evidence 30; affirming the authenticity of evidence 4-6, evidence 9, evidence 10, evidence 4 proved that the Defendant believed that the No.811 vessel approximately qualified the building condition on January 18, 2012 and singed the ship building permission on the same day; evidence 5 proved that on February 2, 2012 the Defendant received the notice of the second installment of advance payment sent by the Plaintiff on January 30; evidence 6 proved that the Plaintiff sent an e-mail to tell the Plaintiff that they received the second prepayment notice on December 6, 2012, but the Third Party did not receive it and asked the Plaintiff to send another notice to them; evidence 9 proved that the Defendant asked the Plaintiff to set an exclusive bank account for the relevant vessel on November 30, 2011; evidence 10 proved that the Plaintiff informed the Defendant on December 6, 2011 that he had set an exclusive bank account for the prepayment of building of the ship; affirming the authenticity of evidence 22 because it was issued by the notary organs and evidence 22 proved that the Plaintiff changed the logo and IMO number of No.810 vessel into No.811 vessel; affirming the authenticity of the minutes of meeting on December 1, 2011 under evidence 28 for the Third Party who took part in the meeting had no objection to it, it proved that the Plaintiff agreed to provide the building materials of No.811 vessel to the Plaintiff; evidence 29 and evidence 20 submitted by the Plaintiff can support each other, thus the probative force of evidence 29 can be confirmed by the court to prove that the Defendant reported the Plaintiff on the ground that the Plaintiff used the No.810 vessel to replace the No.811 vessel and changed the vessel name and the IMO number to Jiangsu Maritime Safety Administration; not affirming the authenticity of the last three photos under evidence 30.

The court confirms the probative force of evidence submitted by the Third Party.

According to the evidence with the probative force ascertained by the court and the circumstances of the hearings, the court finds out that: the Plaintiff and the Defendant signed the ship building contract on October 22, 2010. The contract stipulated that the Plaintiff built the No.JEHIC10-81 bulk-cargo vessel whose deadweight was 47500 tons for the Defendant and the contract price was RMB175,000,000 yuan and the contract price shall be paid by the buyer to the seller in five installments as follows: (1) the 1st installment: the sum of RMB8,750,000 yuan, representing 5 percent (5%) of the contract price, shall become due and payable and be paid by the buyer concurrently with this contract being singed; (2) the 2nd installment: the sum of RMB52,500,000 yuan, representing 30 percent (30%) of the contract price, shall become due and payable and be paid after cutting steel of the vessel; (3) the 3rd installment: the sum of RMB35,000,000 yuan, representing 20 percent (20%) of the contract price, shall become due and payable and be paid after keel-laying of the vessel; (4) the 4th installment: the sum of RMB35,000,000 yuan, representing 20 percent (20%) of the contract price, shall become due and payable and be paid after launching of the vessel; (5) the 5th installment: the sum of RMB43750000 yuan, representing 25 percent (25%) of the contract price, shall become due and payable and be paid when the vessel was delivered.

In the contract, the Plaintiff was called "seller" and the Defendant was called "buyer". The chapter 1 article 5 stipulated that the seller may, at its sole discretion and responsibility, subcontract any portion of the construction work of the vessel to experienced subcontractors, but delivery and final assembly into the vessel of any such work subcontracted shall be at the seller's shipyard. The seller shall remain responsible for such subcontracted work, meanwhile the Plaintiff may not subcontract the entire building construction to a third party. The Plaintiff shall bear unlimited joint and several liabilities; the chapter 2 article 3(b) stipulated the condition to pay the second instalment was: (1) the Defendant received the original advance prepayment guarantee of the 2nd installment; (2) the Defendant received the original payment order; and (3) the Defendant received the original ship building permission with signature of the Plaintiff, the China Classification Society and the representative of the Defendant. The Defendant shall pay the second installment within 5 workdays thereafter; the chapter 2 article 5 stipulated that all payments made by the buyer prior to delivery of the vessel shall be in the nature of advance to the seller; the chapter 3 article 2-6 stipulated the vessel's speed, excessive fuel consumption, deadweight, hold capacity, ballast water discharge time and if the built vessel do not satisfy these demand to some level, the contract price shall be reduced correspondingly; the chapter 4 article 1 stipulated that it is the Plaintiff's responsibility to submit the drawings & technical documents of the vessel for approval. The Plaintiff shall submit four copies of each drawings & technical documents and other reasonable technical information to the Defendant or their representative. All the drawings & technical documents shall be submitted before cutting steel of the vessel; otherwise, article 4 also stipulated that the supervisor shall have the right to inspect the No.811 vessel's building at the seller's vessel yard; the chapter 7 article 1 stipulated that the vessel shall be delivered to the Defendant in safe mooring condition at the Plaintiff's shipyard before or on June 5, 2012; article 4 stipulated that the risks and the possession attached to the vessel transfer to the Defendant when the vessel is delivered; article 8 stipulated the conditions that the delivery has been prolonged automatically are as follows: (1) for revision, correction and supplement to the contract; (2) for the representative of the Defendant absenting from the trial; and (3) for the Defendant not paying the undue receivables in time. Except the conditions above, the delay of the delivery shall not exceed 90 days, otherwise the Plaintiff shall refund to the Defendant the full amount of all sums already paid by the Defendant under this contract, together with interest on such installment at the rate of 8 percent (8%) per annum; chapter 18 stipulated that the Plaintiff shall set a specified account in the bank accepted by the Defendant. The Plaintiff undertakes to use the prepayment in contractual purpose and authorizes the Defendant to supervise the funds using situation at any time.

On October 27, 2010, the Plaintiff, the Defendant and the Third Party signed the tripartite agreement, stipulating that part of the rights and obligations under the contract shall be transferred to the Third Party, the Third Party paid the installment except the 1st and the 2nd installment (For the 2nd installment the Defendant already paid RMB8,750,000 yuan to the Third Party.) and took the possession of the No.811 ship then provided the vessel as the lease item to the Defendant for its use. The Defendant was still be liable for the other responsibility under the ship building contract.

On December 14, 2010, the Defendant remitted the 1st installment in sum of RMB8,750,000 yuan to the account whose account number was320017662360 52506270 (hereinafter referred to as 6270 account) at Jingjiang Construction Bank as the Plaintiff required. The Plaintiff sent the drawings & technical documents of No.811 vessel to the Defendant in January 2011. The Plaintiff sent the general master schedule of No.811 vessel to the Defendant on March 4, 2011: the vessel cut steel on September 16, 2011; the vessel laid keel on November 1, 2011; the vessel launched on January 30, 2012; the vessel was delivered on April 30, 2012; the Plaintiff applied the IMO number for the No.811 vessel, the IMO number was 9618630.

On August 26, 2011, the Third Party organized the Plaintiff, the Defendant and the China Classification Society to hold a meeting about the building program of 47,500 ton vessel, the Plaintiff gave the new master schedule and was going to start building the ship on October 5, 2011; the Defendant requested the Plaintiff to strictly carry out the shipbuilding plan according to the master schedule, and the Plaintiff was no longer allowed to adjust the schedule. The Plaintiff said it would speed up production, strictly implement the production schedule and ensure the planned delivery of the vessel. But the Plaintiff failed to start the construction of No.811 vessel on October 5, 2011 and on October 22, 2011 the Plaintiff gave a new schedule to delay the starting date to November 30, 2011.

On November 16, 2011, the Defendant sent the letter to the Plaintiff to terminate the contract on the ground that the Defendant lost confidence in the completion of the construction of the vessel after the Plaintiff repeatedly delayed the staring date. On November 19, 2011, The Plaintiff replied to the Defendant that they disagreed to terminate the contract because the No.811 vessel had started to be built on November 17, 2011. At the same day, the Plaintiff sent the documents such as building certification issued by China Classification Society, advance prepayment guarantee of the 2nd installment, ship building permission signed by the Plaintiff and the China Classification Society, payment notice required to be confirmed by the Defendant. Among them, the documents sent to the Third Party were the original ones, the payment notice required the Third Party to remit the second installment of prepayment to the 6270 account before November 24, 2011. The first two documents sent to the Defendant were the copied ones, building permission and payment notice were the original ones and the Defendant was required to stamp on them. The Defendant and the Third Party both received these documents on November 21, 2011, but the Defendant hold that the No.811 vessel did not meet the requirement to start building so that the Defendant did not stamp on it. The Third Party hold that the above documents do not meet the contract terms of payment and did not pay it.

On November 28, 2011, the Defendant asked the Plaintiff for the use of funds in shipbuilding special account and found that 6270 account was a joint account of a series of 47500 ton vessels rather than a special account for the Defendant. Thus, on November 30, the Defendant requested the Plaintiff for the establishment of an independent special account. On December 6, 2011, the Plaintiff set a special account 32001766236052509 020 (hereinafter referred to as the 9020 account) for the Defendant in Jingjiang Construction Bank, and notified the Defendant.

On December 1, 2011, the Third Party organized the Plaintiff and the Defendant to have a second production coordination meeting. The Defendant held that the Plaintiff did not construct in the series of 47500 ton vessel construction process and the plans had been changed for several times. Thus, it required the Plaintiff to submit the related starting preparatory work and production planning and materials of the construction of No.811 vessel to the Defendant for verification in order to confirm that whether the ship met the conditions for the construction; the Plaintiff agreed to submit the above-described materials to the Defendant before December 9, 2011. It was not until January 16 and 7, 2012 that the Plaintiff submitted China Classification Society vessel back trial plan of No.811 vessel, painting plan summary list in second week in 2012, subsection construction or subsection outfitting and painting plan summary list and cargo ship project management network diagram in January 2012 to the Defendant, the Defendant alleged that No.811 vessel, on January 18, 2012, basically met the starting conditions and signed the construction certificate. On the same day, the Defendant asked the Plaintiff to reissue the second installment notice according to the 9020 account. On January 30, 2012, the Plaintiff mailed the newly issued payment notice to the Plaintiff. The Defendant received it on February 2, 2012, and informed the Plaintiff and the Third Party on the 6 of this month that it had not yet received newly issued payment notice. The Defendant required the Plaintiff to send another piece to the third person to improve the payment procedures. On February 7, 2012, the Plaintiff sent the payment notice to the Third Party.

On February 16, 2012, the Defendant, according to the tripartite agreement, paid RMB875 million to the Third Party. The Third Party paid RMB52.5 million to the Plaintiff on February 20, 2012 upon receipt of the aforesaid payment. On June 12, 2012, vessel No.811 was connected in the dock, and the Plaintiff, the Defendant and the China Classification Society signed the birth certificate. The Third Party on July 11, 2012 paid the third installment in sum of RMB35 million to the Plaintiff.

It is also found that the Plaintiff and the Defendant on October 22, 2010, also signed a No.JEHIC10-810 shipbuilding contract in which the Plaintiff agreed for the Defendant to build vessel No.810 with delivery date of March 5, 2012, and other terms and conditions of which were the same as the that of vessel No.811 shipbuilding contract. The IMO number of this vessel which the Plaintiff applied for was 9618628. Vessel No.810 on July 15, 2011 kicked off, on November 5, 2011 began to cut steel plate and on December 19, 2011, the vessel was put up on the slipway and the Defendant and the Third Party paid the above three installments to the Plaintiff's 6270 account. On June 9, 2012, the Defendant asked to terminate the contract, and the Plaintiff agreed with the advance payment returned in full amount on July 15, 2012.

On June 15, 2012, the Plaintiff informed the Defendant of its decision of changing the number of vessel No.810 into JEHIC10-811 (hereinafter referred to as the disputed vessel), the number of vessel No.811 into JEHIC10-812 and the shipowner into Zhoushan Zhongchang Shipping Co., Ltd. The Defendant did not agree and asked the Plaintiff, according to the shipbuilding contract, to continue to build vessel No.811, but the Plaintiff held that the disputed vessel was vessel No.811, therefore the two sides had disputes. The Plaintiff continued to build the disputed ship, while the Defendant refused to supervision and inspection.

On June 28, 2012, the disputed ship was launched. Since August 11, 2012, the Plaintiff had change the IMO number on the hull of the ship from 9618628 to 9618630, the vessel name from the "Chang Fa Door" to "Chang Gui Door". On September 20, 2012, the Defendant informed the Plaintiff to cancel the shipbuilding contract and the tripartite agreement on the ground that the Plaintiff failed to build the vessel No.811 in the final delivery period stipulated in the contract, and demanded the refund of the advance payment in sum of RMB96.25 million, interest and compensation of other losses, but the Plaintiff did not agree. On September 25, 2012, the disputed ship began sea trial. On January 9, 2013, the Plaintiff prepared to sell the disputed vessel, and sent a priority purchase notice to the Defendant, but the

Defendant did not respond. On January 23, 2012, the Plaintiff resold the disputed vessel at the price of 14.85 million US dollars. The contract stipulated that the Plaintiff was responsible for the installation of four cranes and other equipment in this vessel.

The court holds that: The case is dispute over shipbuilding contract. The Plaintiff and the Defendant had dispute on the nature of the contract. The Plaintiff held that the shipbuilding contract was a contract of sale while the Defendant alleged that this contract was a contract of hired works. The court holds that this vessel construction contract in the present case was consisted of the shipbuilding contract and the tripartite agreement. Owing to the fact that the tripartite agreement only stipulated that the Defendant transferred some of the rights and obligations under the shipbuilding contract to the Third Party and did not change the main contents of the shipbuilding contract, the shipbuilding contract should be used to determine the nature of the contract.

In the shipbuilding contract, the Plaintiff was called the "seller", the Defendant was called the "buyer" and the payment of contract was called the "advance payment". But exploring the true intention of the parties should adhere to the principle of purpose of interpretation and overall interpretation, and the title and related terms could not determine the nature of the shipbuilding contract:

Firstly, from the perspective of the purpose of the contract, the purpose of the contract of sale is to transfer the ownership of the subject-matter while the purpose of a contract of hired works is to deliver the work product. In this case, when the Plaintiff and the Defendant signed the contract, the vessel had not yet been built. The true intention of the Defendant was the construction of vessel rather than the sale of vessel. In addition, the chapter 3 of the contract had a clear agreement for the ship speed, fuel consumption, deadweight, tank capacity and other parameters, if the relevant parameters of the built vessel are below that of the stipulated, the price should be reduced. The above-mentioned contract embodied that the purpose of the contract in this case was to focus on the accomplishment of the work product rather than the transfer of the ownership.

Secondly, from the perspective of the degree of involvement of the party who undertakes the obligation of the payment during manufacturing process, the involvement of the hirer in the contract will be deeper, and the supervision and inspection of the whole process of the manufacture of the subject-matter will generally be carried out. While in the contract of sale, generally the buyer will not be involved in the manufacturing process of the subject-matter, and only inspects its quality on the delivery of the subject-matter. In this case, chapter 4 of the shipbuilding contract made clear agreement on the Defendant's approval of the ship's construction plan, drawings and the inspection of the vessel's construction processed by the appointed representative, which embodied the Defendant's involvement in the whole construction process.

Thirdly, from the perspective of the performance requirements of the contract, the contract of hired works requires the hiree to complete the main work in person, while the contract of sale does not require the seller to manufacture the subject-matter in person. Article 5 of chapter 1 of the shipbuilding contract stipulated that the Plaintiff may subcontract the segmentation of the vessel construction to a qualified and experienced subcontractor, but the submission of the subcontracting and the final on-board installation shall be completed at the Plaintiff's place, and the construction of the entire vessel cannot be outsourced. The above-mentioned agreement stated that the Plaintiff should personally complete the main work of the vessel construction. In summary, from the perspective of the purpose and main contents of the contract, the nature of this shipbuilding contract was a contract of hired works.

As to the nature of the contract, the Plaintiff claimed that pursuant to the Article 264 of the Contract Law, the hiree is entitled to a possessory lien on the completed work product. Owing to the fact that the possessory lien is jus in re aliena, before delivery, the ownership of the subject-matter in the contract of hired works belongs to the hirer. Article 4 of chapter 7 of the contract stipulated that ownership and risk of the vessel should be transferred from the Plaintiff to the Defendant at the time of delivery, indicating that the ownership of the subject-matter belongs to the Plaintiff before delivery. This was different from the stipulations of the contact of hired works, therefore, the shipbuilding contract shall not be deemed as the contract of hired works. In this regard, the court holds that the Article 264 of the Contract Law, via the establishment of the promissory lien, aimed at guaranteeing the realization of the hiree's claims, but this article shall be arbitrary and allow the parties to "agree otherwise". The shipbuilding contract in this case protected the claims of the Plaintiff by means of not transferring the ownership before the delivery of the subject-matter, and this shipbuilding contract belonged to the "agree otherwise" in the Article 264 from the perspective of the content and was consistent with that article from the perspective of the purpose. Therefore, the case will be in the framework of the contract of hired works to determine the parties' rights and obligations and examine their performance.

According to the contract of shipbuilding and tripartite agreement, the hiree's rights and obligations belonged to the Plaintiff and the rights and obligations of the hirer belonged to the Defendant and the Third Party. Among all, the Third Party's rights were to obtain the ownership after delivery of the vessel and the obligations were to pay the amount after the second installment of advance payment (RMB8.75 million of the second installment was paid by the Defendant to a Third Party in advance); hirer's other rights and obligations belonged to the Defendant. During the process of the performance of the contract, the parties had disputes on the issue of whether the Defendant had breached the contract, which included the following three issues: 1. whether the Defendant had the right to reject the Plaintiff's substituting No.810 vessel for vessel No.811; 2. whether the Defendant had delayed the payment of the second, fourth and fifth installment; and 3. whether the Defendant had the right to terminate the contract on September 20, 2012. In this regard, the court holds that:

1. Whether the Defendant had the right to reject the Plaintiff's substituting No.810 vessel for vessel No.811

Owing to the fact that this shipbuilding contract was a contract of hired works, and an important feature of the contract of hired works is the specificity of the subject-matter, therefore the subject-matter of the contract in the present case was irreplaceable. In addition, in terms of this case, the shipbuilding contract expressly stated that the subject-matter vessel No.811 was a specific object, and that the ship had been specified at the time of the connection in the dock, namely on June 12, 2012, which was irreplaceable. The Plaintiff changed the number of vessel No.810 into JEHIC10-811, the IMO number on the hull from 9618628 to 9618630, vessel name from the "Chang Fa Door" to "Chang Gui Door". In fact, the Plaintiff substituted vessel No.810 for vessel No.811. This behavior, which did not meet the demand of the specificity of the subject-matter, was a breach of the contract.

In addition, although the vessel No.810 and vessel No.811 were constructed according to the same drawings, the construction crew, construction time and construction schedule were not identical. More importantly, vessel No.810 was an uncompleted vessel during contract period (the vessel should be delivered on June 4, 2012 at the latest but at this time the ship had not been launched into the water), thus, the fact that the Plaintiff substituted vessel No.810 for vessel No.810 was also contrary to the principle of good faith.

In summary, the Defendant had the right to reject the Plaintiff's substituting No.810 vessel for No.811 vessel.

2. Whether the Defendant had delayed payment of the second, fourth and fifth installments

For the second installment, pursuant to the tripartite agreement, the payment should be paid by the Third Party, but the Defendant should pay the Third Party RMB875 million in advance. It should be investigated whether the Defendant's payment time was before the expiration of the second period of payment of the Third Party.

Pursuant to article 3 (b) of chapter 2 of the shipbuilding contract, the payment of the Third Party shall be subject to the following conditions: (1) receipt of the original guarantee for the second installment of advance payment made by the Plaintiff's bank; (2) receipt of the original certificate of construction signed by the Plaintiff, classification society and the representative of the Defendant; and (3) receive the Plaintiff's original payment notice. On November 21, 2011, the Third Party received a letter of guarantee sent by the Plaintiff, the commencement certificate signed by the Plaintiff and classification societies on November 17, 2011, the original payment notice needed the Defendant to confirm, the parties had no disputes on the bond, but had dispute on whether the commencement of the certificate and payment notice were in line with the contract agreement.

For the commencement certificate, the court held that the contract was signed by the Plaintiff, classification societies and the Defendant, obviously, the certificate of commencement lacking signature of the Defendant was not consistent with the agreement in form. In essence, pursuant to clause 1 of chapter 4 of the contract, the Plaintiff is responsible for submitting drawings. All plans and drawings shall be submitted prior to the commencement of construction. As the drawing before the drawing was only design drawings, only approved by the classification society can the drawings be retired as the basis for the construction of the ship, so the agreement should be understood that the Plaintiff should submit the returned drawings to the Defendant before the construction of the ship. The Defendant had the right to sign the certificate of commencement upon receipt of the drawing of withdrawal. In fact, because during the construction process of the vessel No.810, the Plaintiff started the construction first in form, and then started the actual construction (on July 15, 2011 the Plaintiff held a groundbreaking ceremony, on November 5, 2011 the Plaintiff began cutting steel), in the tripartite coordination meeting held on December 1, 2011 the Defendant required the Plaintiff to report the relevant preparatory work and production plans, the information about the construction of the vessel No.811 to the Defendant to verify whether the ship met the start conditions, the Plaintiff agreed and submitted the 811 vessel's retired drawings and related documents to the Defendant on January 16 and 17, 2012, the Defendant on January 18, 2012 signed a commencement certificate. The above facts showed that the commencement certificate met the contract requirements until January 18, 2012.

As to the payment notice, the Plaintiff and Defendant had disputes mainly on whether the account 6270 listed in the notice was a special account in the contractor not. The court holds that, pursuant to agreement in chapter 18 of the shipbuilding contract, the special account should be earmarked, the Defendant had the right to verify funds paid situation of the special account. As can be seen from the above agreement, the purpose of establishing a special account was to facilitate the hirer to supervise the funds and protect their interests. The 6270 account was the common account for the Plaintiff to build a series of 47500 ton ships, not only payments of vessel No.811 were paid to this account, other shipbuilding payments of shipowner were also paid to the account. Obviously, the account was not conducive to the regulation of the hirer, was not conducive to protect their interests, which did not belong to the special account of the contract. Therefore, the payment notice received by the Third Party on December 21, 2011 was not consistent with the contract. At the request of the Defendant, the Plaintiff set up the special account on December 6, 2011, and on February 7, 2012 sent the Third Party a modified payment notice, the notice was recognized by the Defendant and a third person. As the parties cannot prove the time that the Third Party received the notice, the court confirms that, pursuant to fact that the Third Party on November 21, 2011 received the materials sent by Plaintiff on November 19, 2011, the Third Party's receiving time shall be February 9, 2012.

Pursuant to article 3 of chapter 2 of the shipbuilding contract, the second payment shall be paid within 5 working days after the receipt of the letter of guarantee. However, the guarantee was only one of the above three payment documents, the court holds that the true means of clause was that after the payment conditions were fulfilled, the payment preparation period of 5 working days was given to the payer. As a result, the Third Party shall pay within 5 working days after the last document (payment notice), namely before February 16, 2012. And the Defendant's time to pay RMB8.75 million yuan was February 16, which did not violate the shipbuilding contract and tripartite agreement.

As for the fourth and fifth instalments, pursuant to the agreement of the tripartite agreement, the payment shall be paid by the Third Party, so the Defendant does not have the problem of deferring payment. In addition, pursuant to the contract, the terms of fourth and fifth payment was launching and delivery of the vessel No.811, but the Plaintiff replaced vessel No.810 with vessel No.810 on June 15, 2012, which showed that it no longer fulfilled the obligation to build vessel No.811, and at this time the work of the ship closing in the dock had been carried out only for three days, far from the standard of launch. Accordingly, the Third Party did not have the obligation to pay the above two payments.

3. Whether the Defendant had the right to terminate the contract on September 20, 2012.

As mentioned above, the Third Party paid the second installment of payment at the latest on February 16, 2012, but the actual payment date was February 20, 2012, delayed four days. Pursuant to chapter 8 of the shipbuilding contract, the Plaintiff's delivery date automatically extended 4 days, namely extended to June 9, 2012. Chapter 8 of the shipbuilding contract also stipulated that, except for automatic extension, the delay of the date of delivery due to other reasons shall not exceed 90 days. Therefore, the Plaintiff's latest delivery date was September 7, 2012. Obviously, the Plaintiff did not complete the vessel No.811 construction work at this time. Therefore, the Defendant had the right to cancel the shipbuilding contract within 14 days after the expiry of the delivery period, namely September 21, 2012, pursuant to the contract.

In summary, the Defendant in the performance of shipbuilding contracts and tripartite agreement process did not breach the contract.

As for whether the loss claimed by the Plaintiff was true and reasonable, the court holds that the Plaintiff's claim was based on the existence of the breach of contract and the wrong termination of the contract, but in fact the Defendant did not breach the contract, whereas the Plaintiff did not complete the construction work of the ship within the contract period. The Defendant terminated the shipbuilding contract and tripartite agreement pursuant to the agreement. Therefore, the court does not support the claim of the Plaintiff.

In summary, according to Paragraph 2 of Article 56 of the Civil Procedure Law of the People's Republic of China, Article 6, Paragraph 2 of Article 93, Article 251, Article 253, Article 260, Article 264 of the Contract Law of the People's Republic of China, the court renders the judgment as follows:

Reject the claims of the Plaintiff Jiangsu Eastern Heavy Industries Co., Ltd.

Court acceptance fee in amount of RMB104,718.5, shall be born by the Plaintiff Jiangsu Eastern Heavy Industries Co., Ltd.

If not satisfy with this judgment, within fifteen days from the date of service of the judgment, a petition for appeal and six copies may be submitted to the court. The appeal shall be filed to the Tianjin High People's Court and, within seven days from the date of submitting the statement of appeal, the appeal fee shall be paid according to the unaccepted amount of the judgment of first instance (bank of account: Tiancheng Branch of Agricultural Bank of China, No.02-200501012001686; account name: Tianjin High People's Court Organ Financial Department). Once Overdue, it shall be disposed as the automatic withdrawal of the appeal.

Presiding Judge: CHEN Jianpeng
Acting Judge: CAO Ke
Acting Judge: ZHANG Junbo
May 17, 2012

Clerk: ZHANG Guojun

(Editor's Note: There was an appeal, where the appeal court, Tianjin High People's Court, affirmed this judgment of Tianjin Maritime Court. The citation of the appeal judgment is (2013) Jin Gao Min Si Zhong Zi No. 58. The appeal judgment was not released to public domain. This case was selected as a model case in Volumn 22 of Year 2015 of the People's Justice Precedent – an official journal published by the People's Supreme Court of the People's Republic of China.)

Tianjin Maritime Court
Civil Judgment

Jianxin Finance Leasing Co., Ltd.
v.
Wenzhou Changjiang Energy Shipping Co., Ltd.

(2015) Jin Hai Fa Shang Chu Zi No.663

Related Case(s) None.

Cause(s) of Action 214. Dispute over ship financial leasing contract.

Headnote Default judgment for Plaintiff finance company for non-payment of rent and for reimbursement of expenses advanced on behalf of Defendants, which did not appear to defend.

Summary The Plaintiff Jianxin Finance Leasing Company sued Defendant Wenzhou Changjiang Energy Shipping Company for breach of a ship financing contract, and three other Defendants as guarantors of the first Defendant's debt. Plaintiff alleged that Defendant had not paid overdue rent, and that it was entitled to liquidated damages for the nonpayment of rent, and for the Plaintiff's expenses in advancing ship use fees, the crew's wages, and redundancy fees to the according to their crew's employment agreements. None of the Defendants appeared in court, and none submitted any evidence. The court found for the Plaintiff on all aspects of its claim.

Judgment

The Plaintiff: Jianxin Finance Leasing Co., Ltd.
Domicile: Floor 6, Building 4, No 1. Yard, Changan Xinrong Center, Nao Shi Kou Street, Xicheng District, Beijing.
Legal representative: GU Jingpu, chairman.
Agent *ad litem*: WANG Dong, lawyer of Beijing Tianda Gonghe Law Firm.
Agent *ad litem*: GUO Limei, lawyer of Beijing Tianda Gonghe Law Firm.

The Defendant: Wenzhou Changjiang Energy Shipping Co., Ltd.
Domicile: No.500 Coast Airport Avenue, Wenzhou, Zhejiang.
Legal representative: YANG Xuanjian, executive director and general manager of the company.

The Defendant: Zhejiang Changjiang Energy Development Co., Ltd.
Domicile: Coast Lantian Industrial Park, Longwan District, Wenzhou, Zhejiang.
Legal representative: WAN Fangrong, executive director and general manager of the company.

The Defendant: WAN Fangrong, Male, Han, born on July 3, 1994, living in Wuchang District, Wuhan, Hubei.

The Defendant: YANG Xuanjian, Male, Han, born on March 5, 1964, living in Bajia Village, Shacheng Town, Longwan District, Wenzhou, Zhejiang.

With respect to the case arising from dispute over ship finance leasing contract the Plaintiff, Jianxin Finance Leasing Co., Ltd. filed an action against the Defendants, Wenzhou Changjiang Energy Shipping Co., Ltd. (hereinafter referred to as Shipping Company), Zhejiang Changjiang Energy Development Co., Ltd. (hereinafter referred to as Energy Company), WAN Fangrong and YANG Xuanjian before the court. The court entertained the case on August 24, 2015 and organized the collegiate panel consisting of Acting Judge CAO Ke as Presiding Judge and Acting Judges WU Wenzhe as well as ZHANG Jie according to the law. The court held the public trial on October 26 and November 27, 2015. WANG Dong, agent *ad litem* of Plaintiff, attended the hearing; the four Defendants did not appear in the hearing after being summoned by the court according to law, the court thereby tried this case by default. Now the case has been concluded.

The Plaintiff alleged that the Plaintiff signed Finance Leasing agreement on M. V. CHANG NENG 19, a LPG vessel, with Shipping Company on June 14, 2010, and Energy Company, WAN Fangrong and YANG Xuanjian respectively signed the Letter of Guarantee on the same day so as to bear the responsibility for whole joint liability about the debt of Shipping Company under the leasing contract. Since the business of Shipping Company did not go well, the company was unable to pay the principal and interest of the rent during the performance of the lease contract. The two parties thereby signed two Supplementary Agreements which adjusted the amount of rent on January 12 and April 11, 2012, whereas Shipping Company did not perform its obligation of payment. The Plaintiff signed the *Agreement of Contract Termination and Redelivery of Ship* with Shipping Company on November 13, 2014. The two parties agreed to terminate the contract ahead of schedule and Shipping Company should return the ship involved and pay the overdue rent as well as overdue liquidated damages to the Plaintiff. The Plaintiff made the payment of crew's wage, redundancy pay, fuel pump fee and tax for Shipping Company after the above agreements were signed. Shipping Company returned the ship involved to the Plaintiff on November 19, 2014, but the company did not pay the overdue rent, overdue liquidated damages and advance payment to the Plaintiff. Therefore, the Plaintiff requested court's judgments: 1. Shipping Company should pay all together RMB51,302,395 for overdue rent and overdue liquidated damages; 2. Shipping Company should pay all together RMB744,271.78 for advance payment of crew's wage, fuel pump fee and tax to the Plaintiff; 3. Shipping Company should pay the overdue liquidated damages for above sum (apart from advance payment for tax) calculated from the payment day to the actual payment day. according to what announced by People's Bank of China, RMB benchmark interest rate for 3-5 years' loan increases by 50% and the daily interest rate are calculated by 360 days in one year; 4. Energy Company, WAN Fangrong and YANG Xuanjian should be responsible for the joint and several liability for the above payment; 5. the four Defendants should bear the litigation fee in amount of RMB318,513.

The four Defendants neither appeared in court, nor did they submit written defence.

The court ascertains that:

The Plaintiff signed the *Transfer Contract* and No. 001-000034-001 *Leasing Agreement* (here in after referred to as leasing contract) with Shipping Company. The two parties agreed that the type of transaction belongs to the way of Finance leasing leaseback. The Plaintiff should get the ownership of the vessel, after all of the payment was made for purchase of M.V. CHANG NENG 19 to Shipping Company. And Shipping Company should bear all taxes arising from the transfer of ship; the Plaintiff chartered the bareboat to Shipping Company with the leasing term of 60 months calculated from the lease inception (the day that the Plaintiff paid the sum for the transfer of the ship), after the Plaintiff has been transferred M.V. CHANG NENG 19; Shipping Company should pay the sum including the rent, service charge (calculated by 1.5% of the ship transfer fund) to the leaser according to amount, payment time and the way of payment listed on the attached list of leasing contract. The payment period for the rent is after the quarter, totally 20 phases, which was from October 14, 2010 to July 14, 2015; rent was calculated on the base of leasing cost and leasing interest, the calculating method of leasing rate is as follows: RMB benchmark interest rate (herein after referred to as BIR) for 3-5 years' loan announced by People's Bank of China on the day of lease inception increases by 5%, the Plaintiff should send the rent payment sheet which lists the actual amount of rent and rent payment date to Shipping Company within ten working days after lease inception, if there were any inconsistence between rent payment sheet and the agreement attached table, the rent payment sheet shall prevail. From the next year of the year which the lease inception belongs to, the leasing rent should be adjusted according to BIR used on the first day (1 January) of the year and next several years; the fund which is due should be paid according to sequence of the fund such as rent, service charge, other fund (if any) and overdue liquidated damages, except that there are other agreements in the leasing contract. Shipping Company should bear all fees related with ship maintenance and repair as well as the associated obligations, including but not limited to operating costs, navigation fees, fuel supply costs, towage fees, salvage fees and remuneration, during the occupation and utilization of the ship; after the Plaintiff confirmed that Shipping Company had performed all duties and obligations under the leasing contract at the expiration of the lease, the ownership of ship should be transferred to Shipping Company automatically. The Plaintiff should have right of recourse for all unpaid overdue rent, undue rent, overdue liquidated damages and other payables under the leasing contract, in case that Shipping Company failed to make it. The

Plaintiff also has right to charge the overdue liquidated damages calculated from the expiring date to the actual payment day toward Shipping Company for all overdue unpaid fund according to attached table and the overdue liquidated damages is BIR increasing by 50% and should be calculated with daily interest rate which is one year (365 days), and calculated by days. The day for rent payment is the day for the expiration day. The day for other fund payment is actually the expiring date for other payables.

Energy Company, WAN Fangrong and YANG Xuanjian respectively presented the Letter of Guarantee to the Plaintiff on the same day. It was jointly agreed in three Letters of Guarantee that Energy Company, WAN Fangrong and YANG Xuanjian acted as warrantors and Shipping Company should bear the joint guarantee liability for its debt toward the Plaintiff according to above leasing contracts. The guarantee should cover the sum that Shipping Company should pay to the Plaintiff such as due rent, all undue rent, over liquidated damages, service fees and other payables or other obligations that has not been performed under the leasing contract; the guarantee period starts from the day that the leasing contract come into effect to the next two years after expiration of Shipping Company's performance for all debts under the leasing contract; if warrantor fails to perform the obligations, warrantors should pay overdue liquidated damages to the Plaintiff, such overdue liquidated damages is actually BIR which has been increased by 50%, and daily interest rate is calculated by 365 days which is one year, in other words, charge fees according to the number of days; if there are any amendments, complement or change(includes but not limits to change the amount of rent payment, the way of payment, the payment account number, lease inception, the day of payment and so on), and no matter whether such changes would bring more responsibilities to warrantor or not, the warrantor should confirms that permission would be made in advance and promise to bear joint guarantee liability of all debts for Shipping Company according to the agreement of the guarantee under the changed leasing contract.

The Plaintiff paid all money for purchasing the ship involved which was all together RMB70,400,000 on July 14, 2010. The Plaintiff performed its obligations for the payment of ship; the leasing contract involved should thereby be performed.

The leasing contract involved was performed normally from the lease inception to October 2011. Since Shipping Company was unable to pay for rent according to the lease contract, the Plaintiff signed a Supplementary Agreement (here in after referred to as Supplementary Agreement One) which adjusted the amount of rent payable with Shipping Company on January 12, 2012. The two parties agreed that Shipping Company should only pay the due rent interests on January 14, 2012, the principal of rent which was RMB3,520,000 could be paid later by dividing it into rent amount of each phases through paying average capital after each quarter. At the mean time, Shipping Company should pay for prepaid rent which was RMB528,000 before January 14, 2012. But Shipping Company still failed to perform its obligation of payment according to contract after the adjustment was made. The Plaintiff again signed the Supplementary Agreement (here in after referred to as Supplementary Agreement Two), which agreed to adjust the amount of rent payable again with Shipping Company on April 11, 2012. The two parties agreed that Shipping Company should only pay the due rent interests on April 14, 2012, the principal of rent which was RMB3,771,429 could be paid later by dividing it into rent amount of each phases through paying average capital after each quarter. At the mean time, Shipping Company should pay for proportional prepaid rent. The new rent payment table (see Table 1 Rent payment Table) was formed after adjusting; the rent payment table agreed in the lease contract and *Supplementary Agreement One* become invalid. The two parties also signed the *Agreement of Contract Termination* which stipulated that if Shipping Company failed to pay rent or any other fund payable according to the *Supplementary Agreement Two*, and still could not make it after the Plaintiff urged the company to pay fund, then the leasing contract and the *Supplementary Agreement* should be terminated immediately. Shipping Company should return the ship involved to the Plaintiff within 10 days after the contract was terminated and managed to cancel the bareboat charter. After Agreement of Contract Termination was signed, the agreement did not be performed in real, lease contract involved and Supplementary Agreement did not be terminated and ship involved was still rented by Shipping Company. Shipping Company respectively paid the agreed monthly rent interests from 14 January 2012 to July 14, 2012, and the company also prepaid the rent RMB1,056,000 in twice and offset the rent interests and partial rent cost which should be paid on 14 October 2012. In addition, the company also paid RMB329,406 on August 14, 2012, offset the partial rent cost which should be paid on July 14, 2012; paid RMB200,000 on April 15, 2013, offset the partial rent cost which should be paid on April 14, 2012; paid RMB200,000 on August 19, 2013, offset the partial rent cost which should be paid on July 14, 2012; the company did not pay the rest of due rent and interest according to the *Supplementary Agreement Two*. The Plaintiff signed the *Agreement of Contract Termination* and *Redelivery of Ship* jointly with Shipping Company, warrantor Energy Company, WAN Fangrong and YANG Xuanjian. The agreement stipulates that: the lease contract and relative Supplementary Agreement should be terminated ahead of schedule. Shipping Company should return M.V. CHANG NENG 19 to the Plaintiff and bear the fees when ship was returned so as to guarantee that ship was in seaworthiness as well as to bear the crew's wage and redundancy payment arising before and when returning the ship; Shipping Company should pay all matured rent unpaid and overdue liquidated damages up to the day of sign which is agreed amount of money (see Table 2 Matured Rent Unpaid and Overdue Liquidated Damages) according to attachment of the agreement within 20 work days after the agreement was signed; Shipping Company should pay rent and overdue liquidated damages calculated from the next day of agreement was signed to the complete of the ship returning (calculated by lease contract and relative Supplementary Agreement) to the Plaintiff within 20 work days after returning the ship. In addition to the above amounts, Shipping Company should pay other payables of lease contract and Supplementary Agreement according to amounts and dates which was stated in a written notice from the Plaintiff; if the company fail to pay any above mentioned amount, it should calculates the overdue liquidated damages according to BIR which has been increased by 50%, and daily interest rate is calculated by 360 days which is one year; Shipping Company promised not to claim for compensation, payment or payment of price difference on the value of ship or equipment on ship or the value of accessory from the Plaintiff; Shipping Company should fully prepare and maintain the ship so as to make the ship transportation can be performed at any time and the company should also bear the resulting cost, when the company returned the ship to the Plaintiff; the company should also bear all fees such as crew's wages, bonuses, redundancy payment and port fees related to ship arising before or when returning the ship; each guarantors should respectively and simultaneously bear joint liability of all obligations and responsibilities under this agreement toward Shipping Company, and the guarantee period was for two years calculated from the day that the company breached the contract.

After the agreement was signed, Shipping Company returned M.V. CHANG NENG 19 to the Plaintiff on November 19, 2014. On October 31, 2014, the Plaintiff paid RMB222,000 to an outsider for surcharge of ship fuel for Shipping Company. The Plaintiff paid RMB93,000 for crew's wage and redundancy payment which was calculated from October 21, 2014 to the day of returning the ship for Shipping Company on November 28, 2014. The Plaintiff sent Advanced Warning Letter and Claim Notice to four Defendants on April 9, 2015. The four Defendants were required to pay matured rent unpaid, overdue liquidated damages and disbursement within 20 work days after receiving the above mentioned documents. The four Defendants all received the above mentioned documents on April 10, 2015, but did not make the payment. The Plaintiff paid the tax all together RMB429,271.78 for Shipping Company at company's application on May 25, 2015.

It is also ascertained that YANG Xuanjian was the legal representative of Shipping Company, WAN Fangrong was the legal representative of Energy Company and Shipping Company was wholly-owned subsidiary of Energy Company.

The above mentioned facts can be proved by these documents presented by the Plaintiff which include No. 001-0000034-001 Leasing Agreement and Attached Table, Assignment Agreement, three Letters of Guarantee, two Supplementary Agreements, Agreement of Contract Termination, Agreement of Contract Termination and Redelivery of Ship, Power of Attorney, Payment Notice, crew's wage and fees confirmation table, Purchases and Sales Contract and invoices, the document of receiving the ship, Advanced Warning Letter and Claim Notice, Application Letter and Tax Payment Letter, the referring information in national enterprises' credit information announcement net, payment vouchers of ship price, crew's wage and redundancy payment, and ship fuel and industrial and commercial registration information of Shipping Company and Energy Company collected by the court ex officio. The court affirms the authenticity and probative effect of the above mentioned evidence.

Four Defendants failed to appear in court, it thereby was considered as a waiver of the rights to make cross-examination toward the Plaintiff's evidence, and the four Defendants did not provide evidence either.

Table 1 Rent payment table

phase	Rent payment day	Amount of rent	Prepaid rent	Service charge	Totally payment of each phases	Returned leasing cost	Repayment interest	Leasing cost balance
0	2010/07/14		0	1,056,000	1,056,000			70,400,000
1	2010/10/14	4,608,102	0	0	4,608,102	3,520,000	1,088,102	66,880,000
2	2011/01/14	4,565,362	0	0	4,565,362	3,520,000	1,045,362	63,360,000
3	2011/04/14	4,554,510	0	0	4,554,510	3,520,000	1,034,510	59,840,000
4	2011/07/14	4,507,894	0	0	4,507,894	3,520,000	987,894	56,320,000
5	2011/10/14	4,460,000	0	0	4,460,000	3,520,000	940,000	52,800,000
6	2012/01/14	894,863	528,000	0	894,863	0	894,863	52,800,000
7	2012/02/14	329,406	0	0	329,406	0	329,406	52,800,000
8	2012/03/14	308,154	0	0	308,154	0	308,154	52,800,000
9	2012/04/14	329,406	528,000	0	329,406	0	329,406	52,800,000
10	2012/05/14	318,780	0	0	318,780	0	318,780	52,800,000
11	2012/06/14	329,406	0	0	329,406	0	329,406	52,800,000
12	2012/07/14	4,380,318	0	0	4,380,318	4,061,538	318,780	48,738,462
13	2012/10/14	4,963,931	0	0	4,963,931	4,061,538	902,393	44,676,924
14	2013/01/14	4,888,731	0	0	4,888,731	4,061,538	827,193	40,615,386
15	2013/04/14	4,797,184	0	0	4,797,184	4,061,538	735,646	36,553,848
16	2013/07/14	4,730,976	0	0	4,730,976	4,061,538	669,438	32,492,310
17	2013/10/14	4,663,133	0	0	4,663,133	4,061,538	601,595	28,430,772
18	2014/01/14	4,587,934	0	0	4,587,934	4,061,538	526,396	24,369,234
19	2014/04/14	4,502,926	0	0	4,502,926	4,061,538	441,388	20,307,696
20	2014/07/14	4,433,448	0	0	4,433,448	4,061,538	371,910	16,246,158
21	2014/10/14	4,362,336	0	0	4,362,336	4,061,538	300,798	12,184,620
22	2015/01/14	4,287,136	0	0	4,287,136	4,061,538	225,598	8,123,082
23	2015/04/14	4,208,667	0	0	4,208,667	4,061,538	147,129	4,061,544
24	2015/07/14	4,135,926	1,056,000	0	3,079,926	4,061,544	74,382	0

Table 2 Matured Rent Unpaid and Overdue Liquidated Damages

Lessee: Wenzhou City Changjiang Energy Shipping Co., Ltd.
Monetary Unit: RMB Yuan

No	Date	Matured rent unpaid	Overdue liquidated damages	Total
1	2014/09/24	39,844,395	5,142,957	44,987,352
2	2014/09/25	39,844,395	5,154,985	44,999,380
3	2014/09/26	39,844,395	5,167,013	45,011,408
4	2014/09/27	39,844,395	5,179,041	45,023,436
5	2014/09/28	39,844,395	5,191,069	45,035,464
6	2014/09/29	39,844,395	5,203,097	45,047,492
7	2014/09/30	39,844,395	5,215,125	45,059,520
8	2014/10/01	39,844,395	5,227,153	45,071,548
9	2014/10/02	39,844,395	5,239,181	45,083,576
10	2014/10/03	39,844,395	5,251,209	45,095,604
11	2014/10/04	39,844,395	5,263,237	45,107,632
12	2014/10/05	39,844,395	5,275,266	45,119,661
13	2014/10/06	39,844,395	5,287,294	45,131,689
14	2014/10/07	39,844,395	5,299,322	45,143,717
15	2014/10/08	39,844,395	5,311,350	45,155,745
16	2014/10/09	39,844,395	5,323,378	45,167,773
17	2014/10/10	39,844,395	5,335,406	45,179,801
18	2014/10/11	39,844,395	5,347,434	45,191,829
19	2014/10/12	39,844,395	5,359,462	45,203,857
20	2014/10/13	39,844,395	5,371,490	45,215,885

The court considers that the outstanding issues in this case are as follows: 1. the legal relationships between the Plaintiff and the four Defendants, and whether the four Defendants should be responsible for paying debt to the Plaintiff; 2. the specific amount and the basis filed by the Plaintiff. It is now recognized as follows:

1. The legal relationships between the Plaintiff and the four Defendants and whether the four Defendants should be responsible for paying debt to the Plaintiff.

   This case is arising from disputes over ship finance leasing contract. The *Assignment Agreement*, the *Leasing Agreement*, the two *Supplementary Agreements*, the *Agreement of Contract Termination* and *Redelivery of Ship*, the *Contract Termination Agreement* were signed by the Plaintiff and Shipping Company under true intention, they do not violate mandatory provisions of law and all should be established and come into effect according to law. The Plaintiff is the lessor, Shipping Company is both the seller and the lessee and both sides should perform the rights and obligations according to law under the relationship of Finance Leasing Contract formed by series of agreements. The Plaintiff accordingly paid money for ship purchase to Shipping Company and thereby obtained the ownership of the ship involved. The Plaintiff also delivered the ship in the way of bareboat charter, while Shipping Company failed to pay the rent on time and in full amount, therefore the company should bear the liability for breach of contract.

The *Letter of Guarantee* and *Agreement of Contract Termination* and *Redelivery of Ship* were signed by the Plaintiff and Energy Company, WAN Fangrong and YANG Xuanjian under true intention, therefore, it did not violate mandatory provisions of national law and all should go into effect according to law. Energy Company, WAN Fangrong and YANG Xuanjian are all warrantors in the relationship of guarantee contract formed by the above mentioned agreements. They bear joint guarantee liability for the debt toward Shipping Company under the Contract on Finance Lease involved. In case that Shipping Company breaches the contract, the Plaintiff are required to be responsible for guarantee liability during the guarantee period, and Energy Company, WAN Fangrong and YANG Xuanjian should all bear joint compensation liability for the debt of Shipping Company toward the Plaintiff.

2. The specific amount and the basis filed by the Plaintiff.
1) Matured rent unpaid and overdue liquidated damages

The Plaintiff and the four Defendants agreed in Agreement of Contract Termination and Redelivery of Ship that the amount of matured rent unpaid and overdue liquidated damages which were calculated until to October 13, 2014, should be determined by the agreement attachment (see the Table 2 of this judgments). Attachment 1, as the component of the agreement between the Defendants and the Plaintiff shall be binding upon both parties. The court affirms that the contents recorded in the attachment 1 should be the calculation basis. according to attachment 1, the matured rent unpaid up to July 14, 2014 and overdue liquidated damages up to October 13, 2014 are all together RMB45,215,885. The payment day for rent which calculates from July 14, 2014 to October 13, 2014 is October 14, 2014 according to agreement in the *Contract on Ship Finance Lease* involved, therefore, the rent calculated from July 14, 2014 to October 13, 2014 has not been included in attachment 1. Since the Plaintiff and Shipping Company have replaced the previous agreement of lease and Supplementary Agreement with new rent payment sheet (see Table 1 in this judgment) and the attachment 1 of the *Agreement of Contract Termination* and *Redelivery of Ship* applies the rent calculating methods stated in the *Supplementary Agreement Two*, therefore, the rent calculating methods agreed in the *Supplementary Agreement Two* are the final calculating methods recognized by the Plaintiff and the Defendants which can be applied to the Contract on Finance Lease involved. The amount of rent which is from July 14, 2014 to October 13, 2014 is RMB4,362,336 according to the *Supplementary Agreement Two*. Therefore, the total amount of overdue liquidated damages and matured rent unpaid up to October 13, 2014 is RMB49,578,221.

According to the *Agreement of Contract Termination* and *Redelivery of S*hip, Shipping Company should pay the above mentioned fund within 20 work days after October 13, 2014, in other words, before November 11, 2014, otherwise, the overdue liquidated damages should be calculated by BIR increasing by 50% and should be calculated by days which are one year (360 days). Since Shipping Company failed to pay the above mentioned sum on time, the overdue liquidated damages should be calculated by BIR which increases by 50% from the day of November 11, 2014; and the overdue liquidated damages which should be paid to the Plaintiff is all together RMB49,578,221 up to the day that the payment is actually made.

2) Fees for ship using and overdue liquidated damages

The *Contract on Ship Finance Lease* involved has been terminated since October 13, 2014 according to the *Agreement of Contract Termination and Redelivery of Ship*. Shipping Company does not need to pay for rent after the termination of the contract. But Shipping Company should pay fees related to ship using to the Plaintiff, since during the period of October 14, 2014 to November 19, 2014 (the day of actual returning), Changjiang Shipping Company kept and used the ship involved. In fact, the agreement in the *Agreement of Contract Termination and Redelivery of Shi*p which stipulates that Shipping Company should pay the Plaintiff the above mentioned rent according to the *Lease Contract* and *Supplementary Agreement Two* is actually the agreement of both sides on calculating methods of fees for ship using. The fees for ship using are all together RMB1,724,174 calculated from October 14, 2014 to November 19, 2014 according to the *Supplementary Agreement Two*. It is agreed in the *Agreement of Contract Termination and Redelivery of Ship* that Shipping Company should pay the above mentioned fund within 20 work days after November 19, 2014, in other words, before December 18, 2014. Otherwise, the overdue liquidated damages should be calculated by BIR increasing by 50% and should be calculated by days which are one year (360 days). Since Shipping Company failed to pay the above mentioned sum on time, the overdue liquidated damages should be calculated by BIR which increases by 50% from the day of December 18, 2014; and the overdue liquidated damages which should be paid to the Plaintiff is all together RMB1,724,174 up to the day that the payment is actually made.

3) Disbursement and overdue liquidated damages

As agreed in the lease contract between the Plaintiff and Shipping Company, Shipping Company should bear the obligations of ship's maintenance and all related fees including but not limited to the ship's operation fees, fuel supply costs and remuneration and so on during its occupation of ship involved. The two parties also agreed in the *Agreement of Contract Termination and Redelivery of Ship*, Shipping Company should bear the maintenance fees when returning the ship so as to make sure that the ship was in seaworthiness; the company should also bear the crew's wage and redundancy payment related to the ship happening before and while returning the ship and should also pay other payables agreed in lease contract and Supplementary Agreement according to amount and date which were stipulated on written notice sent by the Plaintiff.

During the period of returning the ship involved, in order to ensure the security and normal operation of the ship, the Plaintiff paid the crew's wage and redundancy payment in advance for Shipping Company which was all together RMB93,000 and surcharge of ship fuel which all together RMB222,000. Shipping Company should repay all together RMB315,000 to the Plaintiff for such advance.

The Plaintiff sent Claim Notice for above mentioned fees to the four Defendants on April 9, 2015, which required the four Defendants to pay fees to the Plaintiff for advance within 20 work days after receiving the notice. The four Defendants all received the above documents on April 10, 2014, but did not make the payment. Therefore, the overdue liquidated damages paid by the Plaintiff for the company should be calculated by BIR increasing by 50% from May 12, 2015 to the day that payment was actually made.

4) Advance tax payment

Shipping Company should bear all taxes arising from ship transfer as agreed in lease contract. Finance Leasing Contract involved adopted the way of finance leasing leaseback. Shipping Company failed to pay the rent which leaded to the termination of the contract, withdrawal of the ship involved by the Plaintiff and the ownership of the ship failed to be transferred. Therefore, it should be deemed as buying and selling behavior between the two parties to withdraw the ship from Shipping Company. according to relative stipulations of national tax law, Shipping Company should pay for value-added tax and relative taxes and should also issue the valued-added tax invoice to the Plaintiff. Shipping Company apply to the Plaintiff and the Plaintiff paid the tax in advance for the company all together RMB429,271.78 according to application and the Plaintiff had rights to require Shipping Company to pay for the fund.

In conclusion, Shipping Company should pay the Plaintiff overdue liquidated damages and matured rent unpaid up to October 13, 2014 which is all together RMB49,578,221 and the overdue liquidated damages for the above mentioned fund which is calculated by RMB benchmark interest rate for 3-5 years' loan increases by 50% from November 11, 2014 to the actual payment day; fees for ship using from October 14, 2014 to November 19, 2014 which is all together RMB1,724,174 and the overdue liquidated damages for the above mentioned fund which is calculated by RMB benchmark interest rate of People's Bank of China for 3-5 years' loan increases by 50% from December 18, 2014 to the actual payment day; advance payment is RMB315,000 and the overdue liquidated damages for the above mentioned fund which is calculated by RMB benchmark interest rate of People's Bank of China for 3-5 years' loan increases by 50% from May 12, 2015 to the actual payment day; advance payment is RMB429,271.78. Energy Company, WAN Fangrong and YANG Xuanjian, as warrantors, shall bear joint and several liability for payment toward the Plaintiff. The court thereby supports the claims of the Plaintiff.

According to stipulations in the Articles 93, 97, 107 and 248 of the Contract Law of People's Republic of China, Articles 18 and 31 of the Guaranty Law of People's Republic of China, Article 64 Paragraph 1 and Article 144 of the Civil Procedure Law of People's Republic of China, the judgment is as follows:

1. The Defendant Wenzhou Changjiang Energy Shipping Co., Ltd. shall pay overdue liquidated damages and matured rent unpaid up to October 13, 2014 to the Plaintiff Jianxin Finance Leasing Co., Ltd., in a total amount of RMB49,578,221, within 10 days after the judgment comes into effect;
2. The Defendant Wenzhou Changjiang Energy Shipping Co., Ltd. shall pay overdue liquidated damages of above fund (calculated by 150% of RMB benchmark interest rate of People's Bank of China for 3-5 years' loan from November 11, 2014 to the actual performance day which is within the payment period decided by the judgment) to the Plaintiff Jianxin Finance Leasing Co., Ltd.;
3. The Defendant Wenzhou Changjiang Energy Shipping Co., Ltd. shall pay fees for ship using from October 14, 2014 to November 19, 2014 which is all together RMB1,724,174 to the Plaintiff Jianxin Finance Leasing Co., Ltd. within 10 days after the judgment comes into effect;
4. The Defendant Wenzhou Changjiang Energy Shipping Co., Ltd. shall pay overdue liquidated damages of above fund (calculated by 150% of RMB benchmark interest rate of People's Bank of China for 3-5 years' loan from December 18, 2014 to the actual performance day which is within the payment period decided by this judgment) to the Plaintiff Jianxin Finance Leasing Co., Ltd.;
5. The Defendant Wenzhou Changjiang Energy Shipping Co., Ltd. shall pay crew's wage, redundancy payment and surcharge of ship fuel which are all together RMB315,000 to the to the Plaintiff Jianxin Finance Leasing Co., Ltd. within 10 days after the judgment comes into effect;
6. The Defendant Wenzhou Changjiang Energy Shipping Co., Ltd. shall pay overdue liquidated damages of above fund (calculated by 150% of RMB benchmark interest rate of People's Bank of China for 3-5 years' loan from May 12, 2015 to the actual performance day which is within the payment period decided by this judgment) to the Plaintiff Jianxin Finance Leasing Co., Ltd.;
7. The Defendant Wenzhou Changjiang Energy Shipping Co., Ltd. shall pay the tax advanced by Jianxin Finance Leasing Co., Ltd. to the Plaintiff which is all together RMB429,271.78 within 10 days after the judgment comes into effect;
8. The Defendants Zhejiang Changjiang Energy Development Co., Ltd., WAN Fangrong, YANG Xuanjian, shall bear joint and several liability for compensation of the above unpaid debt; the Defendants Zhejiang Changjiang Energy Development Co., Ltd., WAN Fangrong and YANG Xuanjian shall be entitled to claim compensation from the Defendant Wenzhou Changjiang Energy Shipping Co., Ltd. after they bear the guarantee liability.

If the Defendants fail to perform its payment obligations during the designated period of this judgment, the Defendants shall double pay the interest for the period of delayed performance according to stipulation in Article 253 of the Civil Procedure Law of People's Republic of China.

Court acceptance fee in amount of RMB318,513, shall be born by the Defendants Wenzhou Changjiang Energy Shipping Co., Ltd., Zhejiang Changjiang Energy Development Co., Ltd., WAN Fangrong and YANG Xuanjian.

In the event of any dissatisfaction with this judgment, a party may submit letter of appeal together with duplicates in the number of the opposing party within 15 days of the service of this judgment to make an appeal before Tianjin High People's Court. Court acceptance fee of appeal should be paid according to the dissatisfied amount against the judgment of first instance within 7 days after presenting the letter of appeal, otherwise, the appeal will be deemed to be withdrawn automatically. (Bank of Deposit: Agricultural Bank of China Tianjin Tiancheng Branch, account name: Finance Department of Tianjin High People's Court. Number of account: 02200501040006269).

Presiding Judge: CAO Ke
Acting Judge: WU Wenzhe
Acting Judge: ZHANG Jie

December 30, 2015

Acting Clerk: MA Sai

Tianjin Maritime Court
Civil Judgment

LI Chunjiang et al.
v.
Tanggu Water Conservancy Project Company et al.

(2013) Jin Hai Fa Shang Chu Zi No.521

Related Case(s) None.

Cause(s) of Action 243. Dispute over marine development and utilization of sea

Headnote Maritime court held to have jurisdiction over claims under sales contract, despite the fact that the claims would not normally fall within its jurisdiction, because Defendants had not objected to lack of jurisdiction and because contracts concerned marine development and utilization.

Summary The Plaintiffs filed suit against three Defendants: WANG Ziliang ("Ziliang"), Tanggu Water Conservancy Project Company ("Tanggu"), and Yangtze River Nanjing Waterway Engineering Bureau ("Yangtze"). Plaintiffs sought compensation for unpaid work pursuant to their contract to construct embankment cofferdams. Tanggu and Yangtze argued that they had no relationship with Plaintiff and, therefore, no obligation to render payment. Further, Ziliang and the other Defendants argued that this was a sales contract and, therefore, outside the jurisdiction of the court of exclusive jurisdiction.

The court held that: (1) the contract was not a contract in construction but one in sales; (2) though a sales contract, the failure of the Defendants to object to jurisdiction as well as the fact that the contracts concerned marine development and utilization projects effectively established the court's jurisdiction; (3) Ziliang and Tanggu were liable to Plaintiffs because they had given agency authority to Ziliang; (4) Yangtze shall not bear liability to Plaintiffs since the contract was not a construction contract; and (5) liable Defendants should pay interest under the benchmark loan interest rate of the People's Bank of China starting from the day after the account was settled (24 September, 2011). All other claims dismissed.

© The Author(s), under exclusive license to Springer-Verlag GmbH, DE, part of Springer Nature 2021
M. Davies and J. Lin (eds.), *Chinese Maritime Cases*, Chinese Maritime Cases Series, https://doi.org/10.1007/978-3-662-63716-6_27

Judgment

The Plaintiff: LI Chunjiang, male, born on 11 April 1963, Han, living in No.62 Tanggu Yongshan Street, Binhai New District, Tianjin.

The Plaintiff: ZHANG Shimeng, male, born on 4 June 1974, Han, living in No.103, Door 1, Building 5, Fujian Tanggu West Road, Tanggu Binhai New District, Tianjin.
Agent *ad litem* of the two Plaintiffs: WANG Hong, lawyer of Beijing Dentons (Tianjin) Law Firm.
Agent *ad litem* of the two Plaintiffs: LIU Jing, lawyer of Beijing Dentons (Tianjin) Law Firm.

The Defendant: Tanggu Water Conservancy Project Company.
Domicile: No.55, Tanggu Fuzhou Road, Binhai New Districta, Tianjin.
Legal representative: SONG Jinli, general manager.
Agent *ad litem*: LI Dongfeng, lawyer of Tianjin Jin Huada Law Firm.

The Defendant: Yangtze River Nanjing Waterway Engineering Bureau.
Domicile: No.9, Jiangbian Road, Xiaguan District, Nanjing, Jiangsu.
Legal representative: YANG Ruiqing, director of the bureau.
Agent *ad litem*: CHANG Baoyu, staff of the bureau.

The Defendant: WANG Ziliang, male, born on August 5, 1953, Han, living in Lubei Town, Zhalute Flag, Tongliao, Inner Mongolia.
With respect to the case arising from dispute over marine development and utilization, the Plaintiff LI Chunjiang filed a litigation against the Defendant Tanggu Water Conservancy Project Company (hereinafter referred to as "Tanggu Water Conservancy Company") and the Defendant Yangtze River Nanjing Waterway Engineering Bureau (hereinafter referred to as "Nanjing Waterway Bureau") before the court. The court entertained the case on August 12, 2013, applied ordinary procedure, and constituted the collegiate panel consisted of Acting Judge CHEN Jianpeng as Presiding Judge, Acting Judges ZHANG Junbo and CAO Ke according to the law. The court held a hearing in public on September 26, 2013. The Plaintiff LI Chunjiang and his agents *ad litem*, WANG Hong and LIU Jing, LI Baoguo, agent *ad litem* of the Defendant Tanggu Water Conservancy Company and CHANG Baoyu, LIU Yiguo, agents *ad litem* of the Defendant of Nanjing Waterway Bureau, appeared in court and participated in the action. After the trial, ZHANG Shimeng applied to join the proceeding as co-Plaintiff on October 10, 2013 because of his partnership with LI Chunjiang, and the court permitted the application. The two Plaintiffs applied to make WANG Ziliang join the proceeding as the co-Defendant on May 28, 2014, and the court permitted the application. Because the case was involved in criminal offense, the court ruled to suspend the trial on June 16, 2014. And then the court restored the hearing, the Defendant Tanggu Water Conservancy Company revoked the authorization of LI Baoguo, and

the company entrusted LI Dongfeng as the agent *ad litem* in this case. The Defendant Nanjing Waterway Bureau revoked the authorization of LIU Yiguo. Due to the work, members of the collegiate panel were changed that Acting Judge LIU Shuli, FU Xiaoke and ZHANG Junbo, and LIU Shuli was as Presiding Judge. The court held two hearings in public on April 10 and May 11, 2015. In the first hearing, the Plaintiff LI Chunjiang and WANG Hong and LIU Jing, agents *ad litem*, CHANG Baoyu, agent *ad litem* of the Defendant Nanjing Waterway Bureau, and LI Dongfeng, agent *ad litem* of the Defendant Tanggu Water Conservancy Company, the Defendant WANG Ziliang appeared in the court and participated in the action. In the second hearing, the Plaintiff LI Chunjiang and LIU Jing, agent *ad litem*, CHANG Baoyu, agent *ad litem* of the Defendant Nanjing Waterway Bureau, and LI Dongfeng, agent *ad litem* of the Defendant Tanggu Water Conservancy Company and the Defendant WANG Ziliang, appeared in the court and participated in the action. This case has now been concluded.

The Plaintiff alleged that in February 2010, the Defendant Tanggu Water Conservancy Company and the Defendant Nanjing Waterway Bureau signed "Tianjin Nangang Industrial Zone B03 embankment cofferdams (M-S), A04 embankment cofferdams (L-M) and A03 embankment cofferdams (P-Q) engineering subcontract. They made an arrangement that Tanggu Water Conservancy Company built Tianjin Nangang Industrial Zone B03, A04, A03 embankment cofferdams project. In terms of the above involved project contracted by the Defendant Tanggu Water Conservancy Company, the Plaintiff provided riprap cofferdam construction according to the specified dimensions and specifications of the Defendant Tanggu Water Conservancy Company and project payment was totally RMB6,052,150 (the following payment currency are RMB). After the Defendant Tanggu Water Conservancy Company paid the project payment of RMB3,252,150 to the Plaintiff. the Defendant Tanggu Water Conservancy Company, he no longer fulfilled the payment obligation. Until now, the Defendant Tanggu Water Conservancy Company owed the Plaintiff the project payment of RMB2,800,000. The Plaintiff held that the Defendant Tanggu Water Conservancy Company entrusted the Defendant WANG Ziliang to be responsible for the related business of involved project, the Defendant Nanjing Waterway Bureau was the developer of the involved project. Three Defendants all had obligation to pay the project payment to the Plaintiff. So the Plaintiff requested the court to order: 1. Three Defendants shall pay the project payment of RMB2,800,000, afterwards, the Plaintiff reduced the litigation request to 2,100,000 and requested to pay the interest of the above payments. 2. The court fees of this case shall be born by the three Defendants.

The Defendant Tanggu Water Conservancy Company defended that Plaintiff's statements was not consistent with the fact, Tanggu Water Conservancy Company did not undertake the corresponding reclamation project and Tanggu Water Conservancy Company had no legal relationship with the two Plaintiffs, therefore there did not exist the fact that Tanggu Water Conservancy Company ordered the Plaintiff to complete the corresponding project. In fact, the Defendant WANG Ziliang and the Plaintiff were buyer-seller relationship because WANG Ziliang bought some building stones from the Plaintiff. The involved dispute shall belong to dispute over sales contracts, not belong to the scope of maritime court. According to the relevant provisions of the civil procedure law, the case should be transferred to a court with jurisdiction. To sum up, all the claims of the Plaintiff shall be rejected.

The Defendant Nanjing Waterway Bureau defended that the relationship between the Plaintiff and the Defendant WANG Ziliang was the relationship of sales contract. Nanjing Waterway Bureau and the two parties of the contract did not have any legal relationship and did not assume any legal obligations. It was absolutely groundless that the Plaintiff requested Nanjing Waterway Bureau to pay payment. Nanjing Waterway Bureau was not the developer but the contractor of the project.

The Defendant WANG Ziliang defended that he and the Plaintiff was just buyer-seller relationship.

According to the Plaintiff's claims and three Defendants' defense, the issues of this case are as follows:

1. Legal relationship between two parties.
2. Whether the three Defendants assumed the payment obligation and the manner and amount of obligation.

The Plaintiffs provided the following evidence to prove his claims:

Evidence 1, the copy of reports on the implementation procedures of financial information, to prove that construction contractual relationship existed between Tanggu Water Conservancy Company and Nanjing Waterway Bureau. Tanggu Water Conservancy Company were responsible for the involved project of Nanjing Waterway Bureau, and entrusted WANG Ziliang to be responsible for specific agreements of the involved project. The purpose of proof No.2, as the son of WANG Ziliang, WANG Yefeng participated in the related matters of the involved project.

Evidence 2, IOU and delivery orders, and copies, to prove that regarding to the involved project, the Plaintiff provided riprap cofferdam construction according to specified dimensions and specifications designated by WANG Ziliang, the agent of Tanggu Water Conservancy Company, and thus producing project payment RMB6,052,150.

Evidence 3, the detailed list of WANG Ziliang's project debt.

Evidence 4, phone records and written records between the Plaintiff and SUN Zhiqiang.

Evidence 5, IOU signed by WANG Yefeng. Evidence 3-5, to prove that Tanggu Water Conservancy Company still owed RMB2,100,000.

Evidence 6, instruction of IOU of RMB3,200,000 issued by WANG Yewei, copies, to prove that regarding to the involved project, WANG Yefeng confirmed he owed the Plaintiff RMB3,200,000.

Evidence 7, the transport list of Kuaijie Stone Transport Company in Binhai New District, the copies, to prove that the Plaintiff provided specific circumstance of quantities of the involved project.

Evidence 8, the report of the implementation and negotiation procedures on financial information, the purpose of proof was the same as Evidence 1.

Evidence 9, all evidence in (2013) Jin Hai Fa Shang Chu Zi No.27 case provided by Nanjing Waterway Bureau, to prove that Tanggu Water Conservancy Company entrusted WANG Ziliang as their agent to be responsible for relevant matters of the involved project. WANG Ziliang was the agent of Tanggu Water Conservancy Company.

Evidence 10, inquiry records of SUN Zhiqiang(the Eighth Criminal Investigation Brigade Public Security Bureau, Dagang Branch, in Binhai New District, Tianjin, on 10 June 2013),the first purpose of proof was that SUN Zhiqiang was responsible for financial supervision of the involved project. The second purpose of proof was that WANG Yefeng assisted WANG Ziliang to handle the related matters of the involved project. The third purpose of poof was that SUN Zhiqiang paid the Plaintiff RMB450,000 as the project payment according to WANG Yefeng's instructions.

Evidence 11, inquiry records of WANG Ziliang (Detention Center of Public Security Bureau, Tanggu Branch, in Binhai New District, Tianjin, on 4 July 2013), to prove that WANG Yefeng was the son of WANG Ziliang, who was responsible for contacting with engineering suppliers and other related issues in the involved project.

Evidence 12, the inquiry records of WANG Yefeng (Detention Center of Public Security Bureau, Dagang Branch, in Binhai New District, Tianjin, on March 2, 2015), the first purpose of proof, to prove that WANG Yefeng was responsible for the field management of the involved project. The second purpose was to confirm the authenticity of evidence 2 provided by the Plaintiff, to confirm the quantities of the involved project provided by the Plaintiff and confirm that the Plaintiff provided over the involved project payment of RMB6,000,00 as for the quantities of the involved project. The third purpose was to confirm the authenticity of evidence 5 provided the Plaintiff, the project payment of 3,200,000 owning the Plaintiff from September 20, 2011 (evidence 8-12 taken according the application of the Plaintiff).

The Defendant Tanggu Water Conservancy Company cross-examined the evidence submitted by the Plaintiff: evidence 1 and 8 could not prove that the Plaintiff and the Defendant Tanggu Water Conservancy Company had a legal relationship. In evidence 2, there was objection to the authenticity of delivery note, contents of which were uncertain and added later. The unit price and the amount of delivery note were added later, and the delivery note could prove that WANG Ziliang and the Plaintiff had an sales or purchase contract relationship; there were no cross-examination opinions on evidence 3-6; evidence 7 was summarized by the Plaintiff himself according to evidence 2, its authenticity could not be confirmed. The sub-contract of evidence 9 was confirmed, and Tanggu Water Conservancy Company did issue the letter of authorization. Tanggu Water Conservancy Company issued the authorization letter aiming at Nanjing Waterway Bureau instead of the Plaintiff; the authenticity of the form of evidence 10 was confirmed but the authenticity of the contents was not confirmed; There were no cross-examination opinions to evidence 11; the authenticity of evidence 12 could not be confirmed, and the purpose of proof of the Plaintiff could not be recognized. It was illogical that the Plaintiff proved the construction contract relationship according to the words of the construction project payment, and the evidence could only be used to prove the buyer and seller contractual relationship.

The Defendant Nanjing Waterway Bureau cross-examined the evidence submitted by the Plaintiff: there was no objection to the authenticity and legality of evidence 1 and 8, but the relevancy. It could not prove the Plaintiff's purpose of proof. Matters emphasized in evidence 8 had a reference value but did not have a certainty. The authenticity of evidence 2 was not recognized, the evidence could be confirm with evidence 12, and could prove the relationship between the Plaintiff and the Defendant was a seller-buyer relationship. Evidence 3 was the arrangement of the account, and did not have any relevancy. Evidence 4 did not have relevancy. Evidence 5 and Evidence 6 did not have any relevancy. Evidence 6 was just a personal statement and did not have an probative effect. Evidence 7 was the summary of the Plaintiff according to evidence 2 and did not have probative effect. Evidence 9 was recognized; The authenticity of the forms of evidence 10 and 11 were recognized but the authenticity of the contents were not recognized. Evidence 12 could be clearly seen that it was a dispute over sales contract.

The Defendant WANG Ziliang cross-examined the evidence submitted by the Plaintiff: evidence 1 and 8 were not recognized; evidence 2 could not be verified because of DU Yinli's absence. As for IOU signed by WANG Yefeng, if he recognized it, WANG Ziliang would recognize it too. Evidence 3 was just the arrangement of account and did not have relevancy with this case. Evidence 4 was not recognized because it did not have any have relevancy with this case. The IOU of evidence 5 was recognized, but the sum needed to be verified. Evidence 6 was not recognized. Evidence 7 was not recognized because it was not signed. Evidence 9 was recognized, and the authenticity of evidence 10 was recognized. Evidence 11 did not have any relevancy with this case. There was no objection to evidence 12.

The Defendant Tanggu Water Conservancy Company submitted an evidence to the court: payment certificate, to prove the fact that WANG Ziliang and the Plaintiff settled the project payment of RMB250,000 on March 2, 2012, and to prove that the item of payment was the payment of goods.

The Plaintiff cross-examined the evidence submitted by the Defendant Tanggu Water Conservancy Company: the evidence could prove the contractual relationship between Tanggu Water Conservancy Company and the Plaintiff, its authenticity could be recognized. In addition, after getting the check from Tanggu Water Conservancy Company the Plaintiff returned the check back to the Defendant WANG Ziliang, so the Plaintiff did not get the money.

The Defendant Nanjing Waterway Bureau cross-examined the evidence submitted by Tanggu Water Conservancy Company: The evidence proved that the contract between the Plaintiff and WANG Ziliang was sales contract.

The Defendant WANG Ziliang cross-examined the evidence submitted by Tanggu Water Conservancy Company: there were sales contractual relationship between the Plaintiff and him.

The Defendant Nanjing Waterway Bureau submitted 2 pieces of evidence to the court: evidence 1 Tianjin Nangang Industrial Zone B03 embankment cofferdams (M-S), A04 embankment cofferdams (L-M) and A03 embankment cofferdams (P-Q) construction agreement, to prove that Nanjing Waterway Bureau sub-contracted parts of contracts to the Defendant Tanggu Water Conservancy Company.

The Plaintiffs cross-examined the evidence of the Defendant Nanjing Waterway Bureau: they had no objection to the authenticity and it could prove that Nanjing Waterway Bureau was the developer and Tanggu Water Conservancy Company was the subcontractor of the whole contract.

The Defendant Tanggu Water Conservancy Company and WANG Ziliang had no objection to the two pieces of evidence provided by Nanjing Waterway Bureau.

The court ascertains the Plaintiff's evidence: evidence 1 and 8 were the same evidence, evidence 8 was taken from the involved criminal case files of WANG Yefeng from Tianjin Binhai New District People's Court, its authenticity can be confirmed, but it is an negotiation report, the audit unit emphasized in the report, "As the payment data provided by WANG Ziliang was out of order, some evidence cannot be used as the basis for payment, the above implemented negotiation procedures did not constitute an audit or review, so we did not make an audit or review to the above results of implementation procedures. Therefore, this audit was for reference only." Based on the view of audit unit, the court considered that the evidence in this case only can be applied as a reference. In evidence 2, because the signature of delivery note was WANG Yefeng and DU Yinli, the court verified the authenticity of the delivery note (see evidence 12). WANG Yefeng claimed that our staff had an on-site confirmation of the volume and issued the delivery notes to them, the money was not confirmed but the unit price was agreed before, we hired DU Yinli to take over the goods at the site. There was no objection to the delivery note the court showed on the spot. Combined with evidence 12, the court confirms the authenticity of delivery note, but the sum of money was added afterwards, the Plaintiff failed to provide effective evidence concerning the unit price of the material, so the court did not confirm the sum of the bill of payment added afterwards. Evidence 3 did not have any signature of the issuing unit, the sources cannot be identified, so the court shall not confirm. Evidence 4 was a piece of sound recording, due to the authenticity of recording cannot be verified, and the amount of debt that the Plaintiff claimed did not be confirmed in recording, the court believed that the evidence cannot achieve the purpose of the Plaintiff's proof. Evidence 5 was an IOU to ZHANG Shimeng issued by WANG Yefeng on 24 September 2011, which wrote the amount of debt about RMB3,200,000. The court verified the evidence to WANG Yefeng (see Evidence 12), WANG Yefeng confirmed the IOU was true, the court confirmed the evidence. Evidence 6 was the unilateral statement of the Plaintiff, but WANG Yefeng had confirmed the authenticity of IOU. The court considers that the evidence can confirm the amount of debt that confirmed by the two parties on September 24, 2011 was about RMB3,200,000. Evidence 7 was not stamped with the seal of any unit, the source was unknown, authenticity cannot be confirmed. Evidence 9 was confirmed by WANG Ziliang and the Defendant

Nanjing Waterway Bureau, so the court adopts evidence 9. Evidence 10 the inquiry records of SUN Zhiqiang and evidence 11 the inquiry records of WANG Ziliang. The records above was transferred according to the Plaintiff's application from the involved criminal case files of WANG Yefeng in Tianjin Binhai New District People's Court, the above inquiry records both can prove that WANG Yefeng was the son of the Defendant WANG Ziliang, WANG Yefeng assisted WANG Ziliang to handle the relevant matters of the involved project. SUN Zhiqiang's record could prove that he was responsible for the supervision of funds of involved project. SUN Zhiqiang paid RMB4,500,000 to LI Chunjiang according to WANG Yefeng's request on March 1, 2013. Evidence 12 was the inquiry records the court made to WANG Yefeng. The court believed it could prove that the Plaintiff provided materials and supplies to the involved project, WANG Yefeng was in charge of field management in involved project. The IOU of RMB3,200,000 was confirmed after the Plaintiff checked the account with WANG Yefeng on September 24, 2011.

The court ascertains the Defendant Tanggu Water Conservancy Company's evidence: the payment certificate stated that LI Chunjiang received RMB250,000 paid by WANG Ziliang, and SUN Zhiqiang, and the person to handle the matter was WANG Yefeng. Combing with evidence 8, the court confirms the authenticity of the evidence. The Plaintiff cross-examined the money was paid by cheque, after getting the check, the Plaintiff took it to WANG Yefeng. In regard of this, the Defendant WANG Ziliang claimed in the court: "the Plaintiff received money from the Defendant, Tanggu Water Conservancy Company, but he gave it back to his son." So the court holds that the evidence cannot prove that the Plaintiff had actually received the payment of RMB250,000.

The court ascertains the evidence of the Defendant Nanjing Waterway Bureau: because the Plaintiff, the Defendant Tanggu Water Conservancy Company and WANG Ziliang all confirmed the authenticity of evidence, the court confirms the authenticity of the evidence.

The court finds that as the contractor, the Defendant Nanjing Waterway Bureau signed Tianjin Nangang Industrial Zone B03 dam embankment (M-S), A04 dam embankment dam (L-M) and A03 embankment dam (P-Q) project construction agreement with the developer Tianjin Nangang Industrial Zone Development Co. Ltd. on February 26, 2010. They agreed Nanjing Waterway Bureau contracted B03 dam embankment (M-S), A04 dam embankment dam (L-M) and A03 dam embankment (P-Q) project construction.

Nanjing Waterway Bureau and Tanggu Water Conservancy Company signed Tianjin Nangang Industrial Zone B03 dam embankment (M-S), A04 dam embankment (L-M) and A03 dam embankment (P-Q) project sub-contracting contract, they agreed that Tanggu Water Conservancy Company contracted the part work of the above project, the subcontract construction segment included S-Q (B03 North), 100 meters south of Q, 100 meters of A03 east of Q, a total length was about 1,931 meters. WANG Ziliang, the representative of Tanggu Water Conservancy Company signed on the subcontract agreement. Tanggu Water Conservancy Company issued authorization letter to WANG Ziliang.

The authorization letter stated: the client is Tianjin Tanggu Water Conservancy Company, the legal representative is SONG Jinli, the bailee is WANG Ziliang. The letter claimed that "I am SONG Jinli, the legal representative of Tianjin Tanggu Water Conservancy Company, now entrust WANG Ziliang as my agent, be responsible for the relevant affairs like the signing, construction and settlement of A04 embankment dam engineering contract in Tianjin Nangang Industrial Zone in the name of me. The relevant documents, which are signed by the bailee, shall be recognized by me. I hereby declared. Under the authority of the client, the client does not have the authority to transfer." The authorization letter was stamped with the seal of Tanggu Water Conservancy Company and the personal seal of the legal representative SONG Jinli.

In the subcontracted project of Tanggu Water Conservancy Company, the Plaintiff LI Chunjiang and ZHANG Shimeng provided building materials, such as stone, crushed stone, mountain skin, etc. WANG Ziliang's son, WANG Yefeng was in charge of the site management of the involved project. DU Yinli, who was employed by WANG Yefeng and WANG Ziliang mainly was responsible for receiving material at construction site, confirming volume and issuing the delivery note to the two Plaintiffs. The Plaintiff ZHANG Shimeng and WANG Yefeng checked the debts of both parties on September 24, 2011. WANG Yefeng issued an IOU to ZHANG Shimeng, which stated: "I owe ZHANG Shimeng RMB3,200,000 today." WANG Yefeng paid RMB450,000 through the outsider SUN Zhiqiang on March 1, 2013, and the Plaintiff LI Chunjiang recognized to have paid RMB70,000 to WANG Yefeng in 2012 in the court.

Another investigation, the original name of the Defendant Tanggu Water Conservancy Engineering Company was Tianjin Tanggu District Water Conservancy Engineering Company, and it changed into the current name afterwards.

The court holds that the case is a dispute over building materials trading in the development and utilization of the sea between the Plaintiff ZHANG Shimeng, LI Chunjiang and the Defendant. The relationship between the Plaintiff and the three Defendants was not construction contract relationship. The legal relationship between the Plaintiff and the Defendant shall be determined by the concrete behavior of the Plaintiff and the Defendant in the sub contract works. The transaction was the behavior that the seller transfers the ownership of subject matter to the buyer and the buyer pays money for it. Construction, usually refers to the project is built on schedule. The purpose of transaction is to transfer the ownership of the subject matter, while the purpose of construction is to carry out the project on schedule. When WANG Yefeng was asked whether LI Chunjiang and ZHANG Shimeng participated in the involved project as well as the way of participation in the court, they replied that "they were involved in it, they mainly were responsible for providing materials; Providing block stone, crushed stone and mountain skin. They transferred them by ship or by motor and dropped them into construction site directly, then unloaded mainly mountain skin at the designated place." Combined with the name of the delivery note submitted by the Plaintiff, as well as the statement of delivery note, such as evidence 2-4 delivery notes stated: "44880 building stone sent by LI Chunjiang has been received today". The could held that the act of the Plaintiff and the Defendant in the involved project is more consistent with the characteristic of act of sales. The Plaintiff transferred the ownership of building materials to the Defendant, and dealed with them according to the Defendant's request, only the place of delivery and method of it were special. The place of delivery was construction site and method of delivery was jettisonin.

Whether the court has jurisdiction over the case. The Defendant Tanggu Water Conservancy Company believed that the case belonged to dispute over sale contract, so it should be accepted by the common court. As the specialized court, the court violated the provisions of the exclusive jurisdiction for accepting the case. The case shall be transferred to the common court. The court holds that the Defendant Tanggu Water Conservancy Company's claims cannot be established. Firstly, the involved construction materials happened under the marine development and utilization projects, disputes over marine development and utilization are the exclusive jurisdiction of the maritime court. A number of parties were involved in the dispute in this case, which needed to find out the legal relationship between the parties under the ocean development and utilization project, and then determined the main persons responsible for the payment. Therefore, the court accepting the case did not violate the provisions of the exclusive jurisdiction. Secondly, the provisions of the civil procedure law, the objection should be raised during the period of defense if the party has any objection, but the party has not raised jurisdiction objection, and promises to reply the defense, it can be regard as the People's Court has jurisdiction, (except the violation of the level of jurisdiction and exclusive jurisdiction). The case was accepted on 14 August 2013, and the first hearing was on 26 September 2015, the Defendant Tanggu Water Conservancy Company did not raise jurisdiction objection during the period of defense before the hearing, and replied the defense. According to the provisions of the civil procedure law, the court believed there was no legal basis that the Defendant Tanggu Water Conservancy Company raised jurisdiction objection to the court on 23 March 2015. To sum up, the court has jurisdiction over the case.

Regarding the legal relationship between the Defendant Tanggu Water Conservancy Company and WANG Ziliang, and who should pay the payment of the involved case. Both Tanggu Water Conservancy Company and WANG Ziliang claimed that WANG Ziliang signed subcontract through borrowing the qualification of Tanggu Water Conservancy Company, and engaged in concrete construction and settlement of the involved project, so the corresponding obligation should be taken by WANG Ziliang. The court believed that the two Defendants' claims were untenable. The reasons included two aspects: the first reason was the two Defendants did not provide definite evidence to prove that the existence of the behavior of borrowing qualification; the second reason was that Tanggu Water Conservancy Company had issued an authorization letter to WANG Ziliang, which indicated clearly WANG Ziliang was the representative of the legal representative, and also authorized WANG Ziliang to handle the signature, construction and settlement of the sub contract in the name of legal representative. The authorization letter was stamped with the seal of Tanggu water Conservancy Company and the legal representative, which reflected the true intention of Tanggu Water Conservancy Company. Based on this, it can be determined that the Tanggu Water Conservancy Company and WANG Ziliang formed a principal-agent relationship, Tanggu Water Conservancy Company was the principal and WANG Ziliang was the agent, and the consequences of the agent's actions shall be born by the principal. To sum up, the court holds that the Defendant, Tanggu Water Conservancy Company should bear the liability for payment to the two Plaintiffs.

Whether Nanjing Waterway Bureau shall bear joint and several liability. The court had identified that the relationship between the Plaintiff and the Defendant Tanggu Water Conservancy Company was not a construction contract relationship, so the Plaintiff's claim that as the developer of the project, Nanjing Waterway Bureau undertook joint and several liability within the scope of owing Tanggu Water Conservancy Company project payment had no legal basis, therefore, the court does not support.

The amount of debt. A key evidence of the involved case was IOU WANG Ziliang, son of WANG Yefeng issued to ZHANG Shimeng on September 24, 2011, and IOU sated that the amount of debt was RMB3,200,000. As for the formation background of involved IOU, WANG Yefeng stated to the court that "at the beginning, our debt was more than RMB6,000,000, and paid back several times. After that ZHANG Shimeng asked me to settle the account, when we finished it, we made a final IOU." The court held WANG Yefeng was responsible for the site management of the project involved, in view of WANG Yefeng's role in the project involved, WANG Yefeng's confirmation of debt was true and should be adopted. Regarding "About RMB3,200,000" specified in the IOU, the Plaintiff's explanation was that normal debt was more than RMB3,250,000, RMB50,000 and fraction were erased. The Defendant Tanggu Water Conservancy Company and WANG Ziliang believed the word "about" in IOU indicated the amount was uncertain. According to the common sense the court believed "About RMB3,200,000" specified in the IOU indicated that the actual amount may be slightly more than the amount and may be slightly less than the amount. In view of the two parties failed to provide effective evidence to prove the amount of the specific amount of arrears. The court confirmed that the amount of arrears was RMB3,200,000 on September 24, 2011. The Defendant Tanggu Water Conservancy Company claimed to pay RMB250,000 to LI Chunjiang on March 2, 2012. Regarding this, the Plaintiff's explanation was: "When I got the check, WANG Yefeng said that the project was short of money, and let me give it to him to firstly pay the other persons' money, so I gave the check back to him." The Defendant Tanggu Water Conservancy Company argued that Li Chunjing had actually obtained RMB250,000. LI Chunjiang then gave it back to WANG Yefeng, which reflected that the two sides formed a loan relationship. The court holds that the claim of the Defendant Tanggu Water Conservancy Company was untenable. First of all, the money was paid by check (reflected in the annex of Evidence 8). The Defendant Tanggu Water Conservancy Company did not provide evidence to prove that the Plaintiff had extracted money under the check in the payment bank stated in the check. Secondly, the Defendant WANG Ziliang stated in the trial that LI Chunjiang had given the money back to WANG Yefeng. Finally, the payment certificate of disputed RMB250,000 provided by Tanggu Water Conservancy Company stated that WANG Yefeng was the handler. Therefore the court believed that after getting the check LI Chunjiang gave it back to the payment handler, this situation cannot confirm that the Defendant Tanggu Water Conservancy Company had paid RMB250,000. Based on the fact the court also found that after WANG Yefeng issued IOU of RMB3,200,000 on September 24, 2011, the Plaintiff received material fees of RMB700,000 in 2012, and received material fees of RMB450,000 in 2013. To sum up, the court recognized that the Defendant Tanggu Water Conservancy Company owed the two Plaintiffs total amount of construction material fees of RMB2,050,000 (3,200,000 − 700,000 − 450,000 = 2,050,000). In addition, the Plaintiff asked the Defendant to pay the interests of the debt, from the last batch of delivery date of March 27, 2011 to the day of actual performance, the interest rate shall refer to the benchmark loan interest rate of the People's Bank of China. The court held that the Plaintiff's claim that the interest rate shall refer to the benchmark loan interest rate of the People's Bank of China had a legal basis, which should be supported. But the Plaintiff claimed that the date should be calculated from the last batch of supply on March 27, 2011, which was groundless, because the account was settled down on September 24, 2011, therefore the court believed it was more reasonable to calculate the interests from September 25, 2011.

To sum up, in accordance with Article 63 Paragraph 2 of the General Principles of Civil Law of the People's Republic of China, Article 107 of the Contract Law of the People's Republic of China, Article 64 Paragraph 1 of the Civil Procedure Law of the People's Republic of China, the judgment is as follows:

1. The Defendant Tanggu Water Conservancy Engineering Company shall, within ten days as of the effective day of this judgment, pay the debt of RMB2,050,00 and the above interest to the Plaintiff LI Chunjiang and ZHANG Shimeng (calculated from 25 September 2011 to the date when this judgment becomes effective at the same grade loan interest rate announced by People's Bank of China during the corresponding period);

2. Reject the Plaintiff ZHANG Shimeng and LI Chunjiang's claims to the Defendant Yangtse River Nanjing Waterway Engineering Bureau;

3. Reject the Plaintiff ZHANG Shimeng and LI Chunjiang's claims to the Defendant WANG Ziliang.

4. Reject other claims of the Plaintiffs ZHANG Shimeng and LI Chunjiang.

If the Defendant Tanggu Water Conservancy Engineering Company fails to fulfill its obligation to make the said payments within the time limit provided by this judgment, the interest shall be double paid for the period of deferred payment according to Article 253 of the Civil Procedure Law of the People's Republic of China.

Court acceptance fee in amount of RMB29,200, RMB22,892 shall be born by the Defendant Tanggu Water Conservancy Engineering Company, and RMB6,308 shall be born by the Plaintiffs LI Chunjiang and ZHANG Shimeng.

If dissatisfied with this judgment, the Plaintiffs and the three Defendants shall within fifteen days as of the service of this judgment, submit a Statement of Appeal to the court, with 5 duplicates before the Tianjin High People's Court. If the fee is not paid within seven days after the period of appeal expires, the appeal will be deemed automatically withdrawn. [Deposit bank: Tianjin, Agricultural Bank of China, Tiancheng Branch 02200501040006269; Name of account: Tianjin High People's Court].

Presiding Judge: LIU Shuli
Acting Judge: ZHANG Junbo
Acting Judge: FU Xiaoke

May 19, 2015

Clerk: SONG Wenjie

Guangzhou Maritime Court
Civil Judgment

LI Xuelan et al.
v.
Ningbo Jialili Shipping Co., Ltd.

(2015) Guang Hai Fa Chu Zi No.397

Related Case(s) None.

Cause(s) of Action 193. Dispute over liability for ship collision damage.

Headnote Rejecting plaintiffs' claims for damages in relation to wrongful death action, holding that Defendant had already paid Plaintiffs more than was actually owing as a matter of law.

Summary The Plaintiffs filed suit against Defendant after a ship collision that caused the deaths of two crew members. The Plaintiffs were related to those who died, and sued for funeral expenses, death compensation, medical expenses, cost of lost labor, cost of dependents' living, mental damage compensation, transportation fees, accommodation fees, funeral expenses, and all the other rights and costs associated with the deaths. Ningbo Jialili Company paid a lump-sum compensation of RMB850,000 after the accident; however, the Plaintiffs alleged that this did not adequately provide for all the costs for which the Defendant was liable.

The court held that the Defendant, in fact, paid more than it was liable for to the Plaintiffs and, accordingly, dismissed the suit of the Plaintiffs, holding them liable for the litigation fee in this case.

Judgment

The Plaintiff: LI Xuelan, female, Han, born on June 18, 1971, living in Xiang Qi Town, Teng County, Guangxi Zhuang Autonomous Region, wife of LU Yuansheng and mother of LU Yingjun.

The Plaintiff: LU Yuxiang, male, Han, born on December 2, 1938, living in Teng County, Guangxi Zhuang Autonomous Region, father of Lu Yuansheng.

The Plaintiff: CHEN Xiuying, female, Han, born on December 15, 1940, living in Teng County, Guangxi Zhuang Autonomous Region, mother of LU Yuansheng.

The Plaintiff: LU Yixiu, female, Han, born on July 15, 1994, living in Teng County, Guangxi Zhuang Autonomous Region, daughter of LU Yuansheng and the Plaintiff LI Xuelan.

The Plaintiff: LU Yihong, female, Han, born on September 25, 1998, living in Teng County, Guangxi Zhuang Autonomous Region, daughter of LU Yuansheng and the Plaintiff LI Xuelan.

The Plaintiff: LU Yiyu, female, Han, born on January 20, 2000, living in Teng County, Guangxi Zhuang Autonomous Region, daughter of LU Yuansheng and the Plaintiff LI Xuelan.

The Plaintiff: LU Yiquan, female, Han, born on May 10, 2001, living in Teng County, Guangxi Zhuang Autonomous Region, daughter of LU Yuansheng and the Plaintiff LI Xuelan.

The Plaintiff: LU Huayue, female, Han, born on December 6, 2003, living in Teng County, Guangxi Zhuang Autonomous Region, daughter of LU Yuansheng and the Plaintiff LI Xuelan.

The Plaintiff: LU Yian, male, Han, born on June 15, 2006, living in Teng County, Guangxi Zhuang Autonomous Region, son of LU Yuansheng and the Plaintiff LI Xuelan.

Legal agent: LI Xuelan, female, Han, born on June 18, 1971, living in Xiang Qi Town, Teng County, Guangxi Zhuang Autonomous Region, mother of the Plaintiffs LU Yihong, LU Yiyu, LU Yiquan, LU Huayue and LU Yian.

Agent *ad litem* of the nine Plaintiffs: WANG Guoan, lawyer of Guangdong Guangxin Junda Law Firm.

Agent *ad litem* of LI Xuelan, LU Yihong, LU Yiyu, LU Yiquan, LU Huayue and LU Yian: ZHENG Xiaozhe, lawyer of Guangdong Guangxin Junda Law Firm.

Agent *ad litem* of LU Yuxiang, CHEN Xiuying and LU Yixiu: ZHANG Zhongbo, lawyer of Guangdong Guangxin Junda Law Firm.

The Defendant: Ningbo Jialili Shipping Co., Ltd.
Domicile: No.208 Gu Lin Section, Yin Xian Avenue, Yin Zhou District, Ningbo City, Zhejiang.
Legal representative: LI Ailiang, general manager.
Agent *ad litem*: CHANG Wen, lawyer of Jiangsu Tianmao Law Firm.
Agent *ad litem*: ZHANG Lu, lawyer of Jiangsu Tianmao Law Firm.

With respect to the dispute over the liability for vessel collision damage and for the harm of personal injury, the Plaintiffs LI Xuelan, LU Yuxiang, CHEN Xiuying,

LU Yixiu, LU Yihong, LU Yiyu, LU Yiquan, LU Huayue and LU Yian, filed litigation against the Defendant Ningbo Jialili Shipping Co., Ltd. to the court on December 24, 2014, then supplemented and corrected materials on April 22, 2015. After accepting this case, the court constituted the collegiate panel according to the law. On June 15, 2015, the court organized the evidence exchange among the parties respectively before trial and held a hearing in public to try this case. The Plaintiff LI Xuelan, agents *ad litem* of the Plaintiffs WANG Guoan, ZHENG Xiaozhe, ZHANG Zhongbo, agents *ad litem* of the Defendant CHANG Wen and ZHANG Lu, participated in the hearing. Now the case has been concluded.

The nine Plaintiffs jointly alleged that on May 17, 2013, the Plaintiff LI Xuelan and her husband LU Yuansheng navigated M.V. "Yue Zhao Qing Huo 3846" near 500 meters north of the buoy "Guangzhou Port 74" and the vessel collided with high-speed sailing M.V. "Jialili 22" and sank. LU Yuansheng and LU Yingjun died, and Lu Xuelan was rescued after falling into the water. M.V. "Yue Zhao Qing Huo 3846" sank on the spot. M.V. "Jialili 22" ran away after causing the accident on the spot, and neither saved lives nor called the police. After the accident, the Plaintiff LI Xuelan signed the *Agreement on Compensation for Marine Accident* with the Defendant. The Defendant paid lump-sum compensation RMB850,000 to the Plaintiff LI Xuelan, including the total loss cost of M.V. "Yue Zhao Qing Huo 3846", funeral expenses, death compensation, medical expenses, cost of lost labor, cost of dependents' living, mental damage solatium, transportation fee, accommodation fee and all the other rights and cost the Plaintiff LI Xuelan claimed; The wreck of M.V. "Yue Zhao Qing Huo 3846" was salvaged and disposed by the Defendant, and the Defendant had the rights of ownership and domination of the wreck. The Agreement on Compensation for Marine Accident was unfair, unreasonable and unacceptable for the nine Plaintiffs. Though M.V. "Yue Zhao Qing Huo 3846" shall take the main liability, the Defendant did not take the legal salvage obligation after Lu Xuelan, LU Yuansheng and LU Yingjun fell into the water, which led to the death of LU Yuansheng and LU Yingjun. Therefore the Defendant shall take full responsibility for the compensation. The compensation RMB850,000 the Defendant paid couldnot make up for the physical and mental damage of the nine Plaintiffs. The nine Plaintiffs had the rights to claim the Defendant for all the losses in property and human lives. Pursuant to the provisions of the Tort Liability Law of the People's Republic of China, the Interpretation on Certain Issues concerning the Determination of Compensation Liability for Mental Damage in Civil Torts of the Supreme People's Court, the Interpretation on Certain Issues concerning the Application of Law in the Trial of Cases Involving Compensation for Personal injury of the Supreme People's Court and other regulations, the Defendant should compensate all the losses the nine Plaintiffs suffered. Deducting RMB850,000 the Defendant paid to the nine Plaintiffs, the Plaintiffs requested the court to order the Defendant to compensate the nine Plaintiffs the losses in property and human lives in the sum of RMB1,296,401.60. The Defendant should bear the litigation fee of this case.

The Plaintiffs submitted the following evidential documents in the time limit for adducing evidence: 1. copies of identification card of LI Xuelan, LU Yuxiang,

CHEN Xiuying, LU Yixiu, etc., the copies of household registration book of the nine Plaintiffs, the notarization provided by the Notarial Office of Teng County, Guangxi Zhuang Autonomous Region to prove the family relation between LU Yuansheng and LI Xuelan, etc.; 2. copy of marriage certificate of LI Xuelan and LU Yuansheng; 3. medical certificate of the death of LU Yuansheng and LU Yingjun; 4. social assistance certificate of the Plaintiff LU Yixiu, the certificate of Community Committee of Chengnan Community, Teng Zhou Town, Teng County, Guangxi Zhuang Autonomous Region; 5. Conclusive Documents of Waterway Traffic Accident Investigation; the *Agreement on Compensation for Marine Accident*; 6. (2014) Guang Hai Fa Xing Chu Zi No.7 administrative judgment of the court; 7. basis and method calculation of the compensation claims of the nine Plaintiffs.

According to the application of the nine Plaintiffs, the court obtained the relevant materials of the collision of M.V. "Yue Zhao Qing Huo 3846" and M.V. "Jialili 22" from Guangzhou Maritime Safety Administration.

The Defendant rebutted that:

1. The collision accident of the vessels the Plaintiffs alleged was true, but the Defendant raised an objection to the amount of compensation. The loss in human lives shall be about RMB1,499,914, and the loss of wreck shall be RMB400,000.
2. After the accident, the Defendant performed the salvage obligation. Pursuant to Article 169 of the Maritime Code of the People's Republic of China, each ship shall be liable in proportion to the extent of its fault. According to the responsibility confirmation provided by the Maritime Safety Administration, the Defendant should take the secondary responsibility. It was comparatively reasonable to undertake 30%-40% responsibility.
3. The Defendant had paid the nine Plaintiffs RMB850,000 and undertaken the wreck salvaging cost RMB420,000. If calculated according to the proportion of the loss and the responsibility, the amount paid by the Defendant had exceeded the amount the Defendant should pay. The claims of the nine Plaintiffs lacked factual and legal basis, therefore the Defendant requested the court to reject the claims of the Plaintiffs.

The Defendant submitted the following evidence materials in the time limit for adducing evidence:

1. Conclusive Documents of Waterway Traffic Accident Investigation, the Agreement on Compensation for Marine Accident;
2. Receipt;
3. Contract of the wreck salvage and the remittance receipt of Agricultural Bank of China;
4. Agreement on the sale of the vessel and certificate.

The nine Plaintiffs had no objection to the authenticity of the evidence materials from the Defendant and the relevant materials of the collision of M.V. "Yue Zhao

Qing Huo 3846" and M.V. "Jialili 22" from Guangzhou Maritime Safety Administration from the court, but they claimed that the *Agreement on Compensation for Marine Accident* signed by both sides was illegal and unfair. The Defendant should take full compensation responsibility for the death of LU Yuansheng and LU Yingjun. The Defendant had no objection to the authenticity of the evidence materials from the nine Plaintiffs and the relevant materials of the collision of M.V. "Yue Zhao Qing Huo 3846" and M.V. "Jialili 22" from Guangzhou Maritime Safety Administration from the court. The court holds that the evidence submitted by the Plaintiffs and the Defendant can be recognized as the basis of the fact of this case.

After adducing evidence and cross-examination during the court hearing, combining with the evidence and statements provided by all parties, the court ascertains the following facts through investigation:

The registered shipowner of M.V. "Jialili 22" was the Defendant. The shipowner of M.V. "Yue Zhao Qing Huo 3846" was LU Yuansheng.

At 1957 on May 17, 2013, M.V. "Jialili 22" was in the process sailing in the west channel entrance of Lian Hua Shan, and it collided with M.V. "Yue Zhao Qing Huo 3846" which was crossing ahead the exit of the channel near 500 meters north of buoy Guangzhou Port 74#. This accident caused the sinking of M.V. "Yue Zhao Qing Huo 3846" on the spot. Persons on board LU Yuansheng, LI Xuelan and LU Yingjun all fell into the water. LU Yuansheng and LU Yingjun drowned. LU Yuansheng is the husband of LI Xuelan. LU Yingjun was the daughter of LU Yuansheng and LI Xuelan.

On October 15, 2013, Guangzhou Maritime Safety Administration made the maritime conclusive document, the [2013] No.01, the Conclusive Documents of Waterway Traffic Accident Investigation. It ascertained that in this accident, during M.V. "Yue Zhao Qing Huo 3846" crossed ahead the channel, it did not take the obligation of giving way ship, neglected to keep lookout, lacked sufficient estimate of the emergency situation, crossed ahead the channel, caused the emergency collision situation and led to the accident, which were the main causes of the accident; M.V. "Jialili 22" did not sail at a safe speed, and it did not take the right avoidance measures when met with the emergency situation, which were the secondary causes of the accident. Therefore M.V. "Yue Zhao Qing Huo 3846" shall take the main responsibility and M.V. "Jialili 22" should take the secondary responsibility.

The Plaintiffs and the Defendant had no objection to the conclusion ascertained in the Conclusive Documents of Waterway Traffic Accident Investigation by Guangzhou Maritime Safety Administration that M.V. "Yue Zhao Qing Huo 3846" shall take the main responsibility and M.V. "Jialili 22" shall take the secondary responsibility. The nine Plaintiffs claimed that although M.V. "Yue Zhao Qing Huo 3846" shall take the main responsibility, the drowning of LU Yuansheng and LU Yingjun was caused by the legal salvage obligation that the Defendant shall take. Therefore, the Defendant should take full compensation responsibility.

On May 24, 2013, with the witness of the director of Guangzhou Xingang Marine Departure Chen Zhigang, the brothers of the Plaintiff's husband Lu

Yuanqiang and Lu Yuandong, the Plaintiff LI Xuelan, as the second party, and the Defendant, as the first party, signed the Agreement on Compensation for Marine Accident after negotiating the matters concerned with the compensation of the collision accident of M.V. "Yue Zhao Qing Huo 3846" and M.V. "Jialili 22". The main contents of this agreement included: 1. the first party should pay lump-sum compensation RMB850,000 to the second party. The compensation included the total loss cost of M.V. "Yue Zhao Qing Huo 3846", funeral expenses, death compensation, medical expenses, cost of lost labor, cost of dependents' living, mental damage solatium, transportation fee, accommodation fee and all the other rights and cost the Plaintiff LI Xuelan claimed; 2. because the second party was incapable to salvage M.V. "Yue Zhao Qing Huo 3846", the second party agreed the first party to be in charge of the salvage of the wreck, and the first party shall take the salvage cost. The Defendant had the rights of the ownership and domination of the wreck; 3. the amount should be paid in full by three installments. The first installment RMB100,000 had been paid on May 20, 2013. The second installment RMB350,000 should be paid in full within 2 weekdays after signing this agreement. The third installment RMB400,000 should be paid in full within 7 weekdays after ascertaining LU Yuansheng owned the full property right of M.V. "Yue Zhao Qing Huo 3846"; 4. after paying the amount above, both the first and the second party couldnot regret. The signature of the second party equaled the abandonment of all the rights claimed. The nine Plaintiffs ascertained LI Xuelan had received the compensation RMB850,000 paid by the Defendant.

Concerning the salvage of the sunken ship M.V. "Yue Zhao Qing Huo 3846", the Defendant signed the wreck salvage contract with Dongguan Jianhua dredging and salvage navigational engineering Co. Ltd. on May 24, 2013. The Defendant consigned Dongguan Jianhua dredging and salvage navigational engineering Co. Ltd. to salvage M.V. "Yue Zhao Qing Huo 3846". The salvage cost included RMB420,000, adding the wreck of M.V. "Yue Zhao Qing Huo 3846". The Defendant separately paid Dongguan Jianhua dredging and salvage navigational engineering Co. Ltd. RMB220,000 and RMB200,000 on May 27 and May 31.

Concerning the value of M.V. "Yue Zhao Qing Huo 3846", in the process the nine Plaintiffs signing the *Agreement on Compensation for Marine Accident* with the Defendant, the nine Plaintiffs submitted the Defendant an agreement on the sale of the vessel and a certificate to prove that LU Yuansheng bought M.V. "Yue Zhao Qing Huo 3846" from LI Lan on November 24, 2011, and LU Yuansheng paid the purchase price of the ship RMB400,000. Therefore LU Yuansheng was the shipowner.

Concerning the situation of rescuing the persons fell into the water, after the accident, the Defendant immediately reported to Vessel Traffic Service Center of Guangzhou Maritime Safety Administration. The Defendant took the measures of throwing lifebuoy and lifeboat to salvage at the same time. After receiving the report, Guangzhou Maritime Safety Administration immediately dispatched ships to the scene of the accident to salvage. The Plaintiff LI Xuelan was rescued by M.V. "Hai Xun 1511". The Plaintiffs alleged that the left side of the stem of M.V. "Yue Zhao Qing Huo 3846" collided with the bulbous bow of M.V. "Jialili 22". The crews of M.V. "Jialili 22" did not throw the lifeboat to salvage at the first time. The captain commanded the crews to throw the right lifebuoy and the right lifeboat, but these measures were entirely ineffective. The Defendant was indolent in performing its legal salvage obligation and took the undue measures. The Defendant should take full responsibility for the death of LU Yuansheng and LU Yingjun.

It is otherwise found that according to the 2014 Calculation Standard for Personal Injury Compensation of Guangdong, the 2013 per capita disposable income of urban residents in the province was RMB32,598.70 per year, the per capita consumption expenditure of urban residents in the province was 24,105.60 per year, the average annual salary of the workers in state owned units in general area of Guangdong Province was RMB59,345, the accommodation fee was RMB340 per day and the food allowance was RMB100 per day.

This case is the dispute over property losses and personal injury liability caused by ship collision. For all the cost of losses the nine Plaintiffs claimed, according to the evidence submitted by the Plaintiffs and the Defendant, the Tort Liability Law of the People's Republic of China, Interpretation on Certain Issues concerning the Application of Law in Trial of Cases Involving Compensation for Personal Damage of the Supreme People's Court and relevant provisions of other laws and regulations, the court ascertains the following facts:

1. The death compensation of LU Yuansheng and LU Yingjun.

    Pursuant to Article 29 of the Interpretation on Certain Issues concerning the Application of Law in Trail of Cases Involving Compensation for Personal Damage of the Supreme People's Court, "the compensation for death shall be calculated for a period of 20 years based on the per capita disposable income of the urban residents or the per capita net income of the rural residents at the place where the court accepting the case was located during the previous year. However, if the victim is of or above the age of 60, one year shall be deducted from the period for each year of increase in age. If the victim is of the age of 75 or above, the period shall be calculated for a period of five years". This case was accepted in 2015. The death compensation of LU Yuansheng and LU Yingjun shall be calculated according to 2014 Calculation Standard for Personal Injury Compensation of Guangdong Province. LU Yuansheng was born on December 28, 1962. LU Yingjun was born on September 9, 2012. Their household registration was non-agricultural household registration. Therefore is should be calculated according to the 2013 per capita disposable income of urban residents in the province which was RMB32,598.70 per year, the death compensation of LU Yuansheng and LU Yingjun summed up to RMB1,303,948, that is RMB32,598.70×20 years×2 = RMB1,303,948.

2. The funeral expenses of LU Yuansheng and LU Yingjun.

    Pursuant to Article 27 of the Interpretation on the Supreme People's Court on Certain Issues concerning the Application of Law in the Trial of Cases Involving Compensation for Personal Injury, "the funeral expenses shall be calculated based on the monthly average wage of the workers at the place where the court accepting the case was located during the previous year, and shall be the total amount of such wages for six months". According to the standard of the 2013 average annual salary of the workers in state-owned units in general area of Guangdong Province which was RMB59,345. The funeral expenses shall be calculated by the total amount of six months. The funeral expenses of LU Yuansheng and LU Yingjun summed up to RMB59,345.

3. The living expenses for a person receiving maintenance and support.

Pursuant to Article 28 of the Interpretation of the Supreme People's Court on Certain Issues concerning the Application of Law in the Trial of Cases Involving Compensation for Personal Injury, "the living expenses for a person receiving maintenance and support shall be calculated based on the degree of the loss of ability to work on the part of the person providing the maintenance and support and according to the per capita consumption-type expenditures of the urban residents and the per capita annual living expenditures of the rural residents at the place where the court accepting the case was located during the previous year. If the person receiving maintenance and support is a minor, such living expenses shall be calculated for a period up to the age of 18. If the person receiving maintenance and support has neither the ability to work nor other source of income, the period shall be 20 years. However, if the person receiving maintenance and support is of or above the age of 60, one year shall be deducted from the period for each year of increase in age. If the person receiving maintenance and support is of the age of 75 or above, the period shall be calculated for a period of five years" and "a person receiving maintenance and support means a minor for whom the victim is obliged to maintenance and support according to the law, or a victim's adult close relative who has lost the ability to work and has no other source of income. If the victim shares the maintenance and support with any other person, the person obligated to compensate shall only compensate the portion for which the victim is liable according to the law. In the event of multiple persons receiving maintenance and support, the cumulative amount of annual compensation in total shall not exceed the amount of per capita consumption-type expenditures of urban residents or the amount of per capita annual living expenditures of rural residents for the previous year". When LU Yuansheng died in 2013, the situation of the persons who need to receive maintenance and support from LU Yuansheng was: his father LU Yuxiang, who was born in December, 1938, 74 years old, needs to be paid the living expenses for a person receiving maintenance and support of 6 years; his mother CHEN Xiuying, who was born in December, 1940, 72 years old, needs to be paid the living expenses for a person receiving maintenance and support of 8 years; his second daughter LU Yihong, who was born in September, 1998, 14 years old, needs to be paid the living expenses for a person receiving maintenance and support of 4 years; his third daughter LU Yiyu, who was born in January, 2000, 13 years old, needs to be paid the living expenses for a person receiving maintenance and support of 5 years; his forth daughter LU Yiquan, who was born in May, 2001, 12 years old, needs to be paid the living expenses for a person receiving maintenance and support of 6 years; his fifth daughter LU Huayue, who was born in December, 2003, 9 years old, needs to be paid the living expenses for a person receiving maintenance and support of 9 years; his son LU Yian, who was born in June, 2006, 6 years old, needs to be paid the living expenses for a person receiving maintenance and support of 12 years.

According to the provisions above and the age of persons receiving maintenance and support, the living expenses for persons receiving maintenance and support which LU Yuansheng should undertake was ascertained as follow: from 2013 to 2016, the persons receiving maintenance and support are the Plaintiffs LU Yuxiang, CHEN Xiuying, LU Yihong, LU Yiyu, LU Yiquan, LU Huayue and LU Yian, so the living expenses from 2013 to 2016 are RMB24,105.60 × 4 = RMB96,422.40; LU Yihong will be 18 years old in 2017 and the persons receiving maintenance and support are the Plaintiffs LU Yuxiang, CHEN Xiuying, LU Yiyu, LU Yiquan, LU Huayue and LU Yian, so the living expenses in 2017 will be RMB24,105.60; LU Yiyu will be 18 years old in 2018 and the persons receiving maintenance and support are the Plaintiffs LU Yuxiang, CHEN Xiuying, LU Yiquan, LU Huayue and LU Yian, so the living expenses in 2018 will be RMB24,105.60; from 2019 to 2020, the six-year period of maintaining and supporting of LU Yuxiang will expire and LU Yiquan will be 18 years old, therefore the persons receiving maintenance and support are the Plaintiffs CHEN Xiuying, LU Huayue and LU Yian and the living expenses from 2019 to 2020 will be RMB24,105.60 × 2 = RMB48,211.20; in 2021, the eight-year period of maintaining and supporting of CHEN Xiuying will expire and the persons receiving maintenance and support are the Plaintiffs LU Huayue and LU Yian and the living expenses in 2021 will be RMB24,105.60; from 2022 to 2024, the person receiving maintenance and support is the Plaintiff LU Yian. His mother is the Plaintiff LI Xuelan and LI Xuelan should take half support obligation, so the living expenses of the Plaintiff LU Yian from 2022 to 2024 is RMB105.60 ÷ 2 × 3 = RMB36,158.40. To conclude, the living expenses for persons receiving maintenance and support which LU Yuansheng should undertake are RMB253,108.80.

4. The reasonable funeral expenses paid by the nine Plaintiffs.

For this claim, the nine Plaintiffs did not submit evidence to prove. But the court considers that after this accident, it must generate the cost of lost labor, transportation fee, accommodation fee and other reasonable expenses for the nine Plaintiffs to handle funeral arrangement. Refer to "Yue Cai Ting [2014] No.67 Provision" by Finance Department of Guangdong Province, according to the standard of accommodation fee RMB340 per day and the food allowance RMB100 per day. The court discretionarily ascertains that the cost of lost labor, transportation fee, accommodation fee and other reasonable expenses caused by the arrangement of the funeral is RMB10,000.

5. The mental damage solatium.

Pursuant to Article 18 of the Interpretation the Supreme People's Court on Certain Issues concerning the Application of Law in the Trial of Cases

Involving Compensation for Personal Injury, "where a victim or a close relative of the deceased suffers mental damage, and the compensation appellant files an action with a people's court claiming solatium for mental damage, such solatium shall be determined by applying the Interpretation on Certain Issues Concerning the Determination of Compensation Liability for Mental Damage in Civil Torts of the Supreme People's Court" and the provisions of Article 8 Paragraph 2 of the Interpretation on Certain Issues concerning the Determination of Compensation Liability for Mental Damage in Civil Torts of the Supreme People's Court, "when infringement causes mental damage to another person with serious consequences, a people's court may, in addition to ordering the infringer to bear civil liability of cessation of infringement, rehabilitation of reputation, elimination of impact, and/or offer an apology, etc., also order the infringer to make appropriate compensation for mental Damage based on the claim of the victim", considering that LU Yuansheng and LU Yingjun died in this accident and the nine Plaintiffs got both the physical and mental damage, so the court ascertains that the Defendant shall pay the nine Plaintiffs the mental damage solatium RMB50,000 for the death of LU Yuansheng and LU Yingjun, according to the Article 10 of the Interpretation on Certain Issues concerning the Determination of Compensation Liability for Mental Damage in Civil Torts of the Supreme People's Court about the factors to ascertain the amount of the mental damage compensation.
6. The losses of M.V. "Yue Zhao Qing Huo 3846" and materials on the ship.
Concerning the value of M.V. "Yue Zhao Qing Huo 3846", when the nine Plaintiffs negotiated with the Defendant, they had provided the vessel purchase agreement and confirmed that the purchase price of this ship was RMB400,000. So the court ascertains that the price of M.V. "Yue Zhao Qing Huo 3846" is RMB400,000. In addition, the Plaintiffs claimed that the losses of materials on the ship caused by this accident is RMB50,000, but the nine Plaintiffs did not submit the relevant evidence of the goods on board or the materials equipped. Therefore the Plaintiffs should take the adverse consequence of failure on the burden of proof. Considered that M.V. "Yue Zhao Qing Huo 3846" was sunk and the nine Plaintiffs had objective difficulties in adducing evidence, the court discretionarily ascertains that the losses of materials on the ship is RMB20,000.

The court holds that:
This case is a dispute over the damage responsibility of ship collision and the damage responsibility of personal injury. After this accident, as the maritime safety administration, Guangzhou Maritime Safety Administration made the Conclusive Documents of Waterway Traffic Accident Investigation after investigating. It ascertained that, when M.V. "Yue Zhao Qing Huo 3846" crossed ahead the channel, it did not take the obligation of a giving way ship, neglected to keep lookout, lacked sufficient estimate of the emergency situation, crossing ahead the channel caused the emergency collision situation and led to the accident, which were the main causes of the accident. M.V. "Jialili 22" did not sail at a safe speed and take the right avoidance measures when it met with the emergency situation,

which were the secondary causes of the accident. Therefore M.V. "Yue Zhao Qing Huo 3846" shall take the main responsibility and M.V. "Jialili 22" shall take the secondary responsibility. The Plaintiffs and the Defendant both had no objection to the responsibility undertook by all parties. The court admits the *Conclusive Documents of Waterway Traffic Accident Investigation*. Combined with the degree of default of the ship collision accident, the court ascertains that M.V. "Yue Zhao Qing Huo 3846" shall take 60% fault liability of the ship collision accident and M. V. "Jialili 22" shall take 40% fault liability of the ship collision accident.

The Plaintiff LI Xuelan is the wife of LU Yuansheng and mother of LU Yingjun; The Plaintiffs LU Yuxiang and CHEN Xiuying are parents of LU Yuansheng; The Plaintiffs LU Yixiu, LU Yihong, LU Yiyu, LU Yiquan, LU Huayue and LU Yian are LU Yuansheng's children and LU Yingjun's brothers and sisters. LU Yuansheng and LU Yingjun died in the ship collision accident. The nine Plaintiffs have the right to file claims with the Defendant according to the provisions of Article 18 Paragraph 2 of the Tort Liability Law of the People's Republic of China, "if the infringee dies, his close family members shall have the right to request the infringer to assume tort liability".

Article 16 of the Tort Liability Law of the People's Republic of China provides that, "any person who harms other people and causes personal injury shall be subject to compensation for medical expenses, nursing expenses, traveling expenses and other reasonable expenses paid for the purpose of treatment and recovery, as well as income reduced due to the loss of labor hours; in case of causing disability, payment shall be made for disability appliance expenses and disability compensation; in case of causing death, payment shall be made for funeral expenses and death compensation". Article 17 Paragraph 3 of the Interpretation of the Supreme People's Court on Certain Issues concerning the Application of Law in the Trial of Cases Involving Compensation for Personal Injury provides that, "in the event of the death of the victim, the person obligated to compensate shall, in addition to making compensation for the relevant expenses specified in Paragraph 1 of this Article according to the facts of rescue and treatment, make compensation for funeral expenses, living expenses of any dependents, death compensation expenses, the traveling expenses and accommodation expenses paid and the loss of income due to absence from work incurred by the victim's relatives for funeral arrangements as well as other reasonable expenses". The death compensation expenses, funeral expenses and living expenses of any dependents and other expenses claimed by the nine Plaintiffs are in the compensation coverage provided above. The Defendant shall take the relevant compensation liability.

According to the laws, judicial interpretations and the evidence adducing by the interested parties, the losses of the nine Plaintiffs caused by this accident include: the death compensation of LU Yuansheng and LU Yingjun RMB1,303,948, the funeral expenses of LU Yuansheng and LU Yingjun RMB59,345, the living expenses for persons receiving maintenance and support RMB253,108.80, the reasonable funeral expenses paid by the nine Plaintiffs RMB10,000, the mental damage solatium RMB500,000, the losses of M.V. "Yue Zhao Qing Huo 3846" and materials on the ship RMB420,000, totally RMB2,096,401.80. According to Article

169 of the Maritime Code of the People's Republic of China, "if the colliding ships are all in fault, each ship shall be liable in proportion to the extent of its fault; if the respective faults are equal in proportion or it is impossible to determine the extent of the proportion of the respective faults, the liability of the colliding ships shall be apportioned equally. The ships in fault shall be liable for the damage to the ship, the goods and other property on board pursuant to the proportions prescribed in the preceding paragraph. Where damage is caused to the property of a third party, the liability for compensation of any of the colliding ships shall not exceed the proportion it shall bear. If the ships in fault have caused loss of life or personal injury to a third party, they shall be jointly and severally liable therefor. If a ship has paid an amount of compensation in excess of the proportion prescribed in paragraph 1 of this Article, it shall have the right of recourse against the other ship(s) in fault", apart from the mental damage compensation RMB500,000 undertook by the Defendant, for other losses of the nine Plaintiffs RMB2,046,401.80, calculating in the 40% rate of compensation liability, the Defendant should compensate the nine Plaintiffs RMB818,560.72. The Defendant paid salvage cost RMB420,000 for salvaging M.V. "Yue Zhao Qing Huo 3846", calculating according to the 60% rate of compensation liability of M.V. "Yue Zhao Qing Huo 3846", the nine Plaintiffs should take salvage cost RMB252,000. To sum up, after the accident in this case, the Defendant paid the nine Plaintiffs RMB850,000 which had exceeded the amount the Defendant should take. That the nine Plaintiffs' claimed that the Defendant shall compensate RMB1,296,401.40 more lacks factual and legal basis and shall be dismissed. After the accident, the Defendant immediately reported to Vessel Traffic Service Center of Guangzhou Maritime Safety Administration and took the measures of throwing lifebuoy and lifeboat to salvage the persons fell into the water at the same time. It conformed with the provisions of Article 166 of the Maritime Code of the People's Republic of China. The Defendant performed the legal salvage obligation. Because the salvage on the sea existed the factor of uncertain risks, it made the salvage far more difficult than rescued on land. Therefore, it was difficult to ascertain if the Defendant performed legal salvage obligation according to the place throwing the lifebuoy and lifeboat which was accurate and effective or not and the time spent. After this accident of this case happened, the Conclusive Documents of Waterway Traffic Accident Investigation made by Guangzhou Maritime Safety Administration did not have the ascertainment that "the Defendant ran away after the accident and the Defendant did not perform legal salvage obligation". Therefore, the nine Plaintiffs' claim that after LU Yuansheng and LU Yingjun fell into water, the Defendant did not perform legal salvage obligation immediately and it led to the death, so the Defendant shall take full responsibility. The claim lacks reasons and basis. Therefore the court will not support. Pursuant to Article 169 of the Maritime Code of the People's Republic of China and Article 64 Paragraph 1 of the Civil Procedure Law of the People's Republic of China, the judgment is as follows:

Reject all the claims filed by the Plaintiffs LI Xuelan, LU Yuxiang, CHEN Xiuying, LU Yixiu, LU Yihong, LU Yiyu, LU Yiquan, LU Huayue and LU Yian.

The nine Plaintiffs claimed to reduce the amount of litigation request before the court investigation ended. Court acceptance fee of this case in amount of RMB16,468, the Plaintiffs shall bear court acceptance fee.

If dissatisfy with this judgment, within 15 days as of the service of this judgment, the Plaintiffs and the Defendant can submit a Statement of Appeal to the court, with duplicates in the number of the counterparties, so as to make an appeal before the Guangdong High People's Court.

Presiding Judge: XIONG Shaohui
Judge: ZHANG Kexiong
Acting Judge: YANG Yaxiao

August 25, 2015

Clerk: LU Shiying

Guangzhou Maritime Court
Civil Judgment

LIN Guihe
v.
PICC Property and Casualty Company Limited Shunde Branch

(2008) Guang Hai Fa Chu Zi No.259

Related Case(s) This is the judgment of first instance, and the judgment of second instance and the ruling of retrial are on page 701 and page 727 respectively.

Cause(s) of Action 230. Dispute over marine insurance contract on the sea or sea-connected waters.

Headnote Hull insurer required to indemnify assured for cost of raising sunken vessel.

Summary The Plaintiff, LIN Guihe, the insured, brought suit against Defendant, PICC Property and Casualty Company Limited Shunde Branch, for failure to indemnify him for the loss of the vessel, "Nangui machine 035". The vessel was insured up to RMB4,500,000 from the period of April 13, 2007 to April 12, 2008. However, on June 15, 2007, M.V. NAN GUI JI 035 sank after it collided with the national line G325 Jiujiang bridge. On January 18, 2008, M.V. NAN GUI JI 035 was cut and dredged, and the dredging charges arising from this were about RMB8,370,000. On January 31, 2008, the Plaintiff submitted the insurance indemnity application and corresponding claim materials and requested the Defendant to pay the insurance indemnity in the amount of RMB4,500,000, but the Defendant did not indemnify. The court found that the collision within the scope of the Defendant insurer's liability and ordered it to indemnify the Plaintiff in the amount of RMB3,499,500, which after deducting the deductible of RMB349,950, shall be RMB3,149,550.

Judgment

The Plaintiff: LIN Guihe, male, Han, born on October 23, 1966, living in Shunde District, Foshan City, Guangdong.
Agent *ad litem*: XU Guangyu, lawyer of Guangdong Haijian Law Firm.
Agent *ad litem*: LI Zhenhai, lawyer of Guangdong Haijian Law Firm.

The Defendant: PICC Property and Casualty Company Limited Shunde Branch.
Domicile: No.346 Jianhai North Road, Shunde District, Foshan City, Guangdong.
Person in charge: XIE Zewei, general manager of the branch.
Agent *ad litem*: HUANG Zhuo, lawyer of Guangdong Zhengda United Law Firm.
Agent *ad litem*: YANG Meihua, lawyer of Guangdong Zhengda United Law Firm.

With respect to the case arising from dispute over vessel insurance contract filed by the Plaintiff LIN Guihe against the Defendant PICC Property and Casualty Company Limited Shunde Branch on May 6, 2008, the court, after accepting the case, according to law formed a collegiate panel consisted of Judge XIONG Shaohui as Presiding Judge, Judge ZHANG Kexiong and Acting Judge GU Enzhen to hear the case, the Clerk LIANG Xiaolei recorded this case. For the related function departments had not made maritime survey report to the accident involved with this case, and because this report could have a directly influence on the ascertainment of the case's fact, the trial was vindicated to pause on May 26, 2008. After the reason of suspension eliminated, the trial was recovered on September 17, 2013. Because of the alteration of staff, collegiate panel of this case had an alteration that Judge HUANG Weiqing acted as Presiding JudgeCHENG Shengxiang and WU Guining acted as Judge, Clerk CHEN Di and LI Chunyu recorded in this case. The parties were convened to exchange evidence before trial on October 16, 2013. The case was heard in public on November 20, 2013. XU Guangyu and LI Zhenhai as agents *ad litem* of the Plaintiff, and HUANG Zhuo and YANG Meihua as agents *ad litem* of the Defendant appeared in the court to attend the hearing. The PlaintiffLIN Guihe, and YANG Xiong, who was not involved in the case, appeared in court to be questioned on December 11, 2013. The two sides were convened to court for additional cross-examination on April 2, 2014. LI Zhenhai as agent *ad litem* of the Plaintiff, and HUANG Zhuo and YANG Meihua as agents *ad litem* of the Defendant, appeared in court to attend the hearing. Now the case has been concluded.

The Plaintiff argued that on April 12, 2007, the Plaintiff covered M.V. NAN GUI JI 035 with the Defendant against all risks of coastal and inland river vessel, added one fourth additional insurance and propeller's particular loss insurance, and so on. After underwriting, the Defendant issued the vessel insurance policy, the number of which is PCBA20074471021000001. Both the insured value and insured amount were RMB4,500,000. The insurance term was from April 13, 2007 to April 12, 2008. The Plaintiff had paid total insurance amount to Defendant as agreed. On

June 15, 2007, M.V. NAN GUI JI 035 had sank after it collided with the national line G325 Jiujiang bridge. On December 27, 2007, the Plaintiff submitted the Notice of Abandonment to the Defendant and required to abandon M.V. NAN GUI JI 035, but the Defendant had not responded all the time. On January 18, 2008, M.V. NAN GUI JI 035 had been cut and drudged, the drudging charges arising from this is about RMB8,370,000. On January 31, 2008, the Plaintiff submitted the insurance indemnity application and corresponding claim materials and requested the Defendant to pay the insurance indemnity in amount of RMB4,500,000. But the Defendant had not indemnified them. Because the drudging charges of M.V. NAN GUI JI 035 was far beyond its hull value and the hull had been cut into two parts, M.V. NAN GUI JI 035 shall be ratified the constructive total loss. According to the insurance contract signed by two parties, M.V. NAN GUI JI 035 suffered total loss for collision, which should be in the scope of the Defendant's liability, the Defendant should pay the Plaintiff insurance indemnity in amount of RMB4,500,00 immediately. Therefore, the Plaintiff requested that the Defendant should be judged to pay them insurance indemnity in amount of RMB4,500,000 of M.V. NAN GUI JI 035 and the bank business loan interest over the same period from May 6, 2008 to date of the judgment, and bear the litigation fee for the subject case.

The Plaintiff submitted the following evidence materials:

1. Insurance policy, to prove that there was an insurance contract relationship between the Plaintiff and the Defendant and the content of the insurance clauses.
2. Invoice of the premium, to prove that the Plaintiff had paid the insurance premium as agreed.
3. Ship's ownership, to prove YANG Xiong was the owner of M.V. NAN GUI JI 035.
4. Ship's management Agreements, to prove Plaintiff had lent RMB5,000,000 to YANG Xiong, the Plaintiff had right to join the management of the ship and deduct RMB50,000 from benefits from the employment of ship to offset the loan. YANG Xiong mortgaged the ship to the Plaintiff and agreed to underwrite ship insurance in the name of the Plaintiff, the Plaintiff had the priority right to get compensation from insurance indemnity in order to offset the loan.
5. Ship's lease contract, to prove that YANG Xiong rent out his ship to CHEN Weihong who employed crew and operated the ship.
6. Certificate of ship's nationality, to prove that the ship operator was Nanhai Yuhang Shipping CO. LTD of Foshan City.
7. Inspection Certificate of inland river ships, certificate of inland river ships' seaworthiness, Ship Minimum Safety Manning Certificate, Crew List, seafarer's certificate of competency, to prove that the vessel "Nangui machine035" was seaworthy.
8. Investigation report of the accident of Guangdong "6•15" ship's colliding with Jiujiang bridge, to prove that M.V. NAN GUI JI 035 collided with the Jiujiang bridge.

9. Notice of Abandonment, to prove that the Plaintiff sent the *Notice of Abandonment* to the Defendant on December 28, 2007.
10. General dredging amount of the sank vessel, to prove the dredging fee of "Nangui machine 035" was RMB8,373,645.
11. Lawyer's letter, to prove that the Plaintiff had sent the amount of dredging fee to the Defendant, and required the Defendant to give definite answer about whether accepting the *Notice of Abandonment* before January 1, 2008.
12. News report, to prove that M.V. NAN GUI JI 035 had been cut and dredged out on January 18, 2008.
13. Insurance indemnity application, to prove that the Plaintiff had lodged a claim to the Defendant on January 31, 2008.
14. Contract of transfer of the self-unloading ship, to prove that the value of M.V. NAN GUI JI 035 was RMB7,280,000.

The Defendant defended that: (1) the Plaintiff was neither the "Nangui machine 035"ship's owner nor the ship's operator, so had no property right for this ship; the ship's operating risk should be undertaken by CHEN Weihong, the Plaintiff had no legal responsibility for the operation; the Plaintiff did not have contract right for the ship. So, the Plaintiff did not have insurable interest in the vessel. (2) Shipmaster and some crew of M.V. NAN GUI JI 035 obtained the crew certificate in an abnormal manner, the seafarers were not qualified for the requirements, the ship was unseaworthy; and the shipmaster had violated criminal laws and committed criminal offences in this accident, and had been investigated for criminal responsibility. Pursuant to the stipulations of Sub-paragraph 1 and Sub-paragraph 4 of Article 3 Exclusion liability of the insurance contract, the insurer should not be liable for this. (3) According to the particular agreements of the insurance policy, when indemnify the total loss of the insured vessel, the rate of the deductible should be 20 percent, after deducting the deductibles, the total amount of indemnity should be RMB3,600,000. (4) According to the particular agreements of the insurance policy, the highest indemnity of the drudge is RMB200,000 in each accident, therefore, after deducting RMB200,000, the insurer should not pay the insurance indemnity.

The Defendant submitted (2012) Hui Zhong Fa Xing Yi Zhong Zi No.111 Criminal Ruling as an evidence.

According to the Defendant's application, the court entrusted Guangdong Mingjianwenshu Judicial Appraisal Center to authenticate the time of handwriting and printing and the manufacturing years of paper of the vessel management agreement, after receiving the entrustment, Guangdong Mingjianwenshu Judicial Appraisal Center gave the authentication report.

After the trial cross-examination, (2012) Hui Zhong Fa Xing Yi Zhong Zi No.111 Criminal Ruling submitted by the Defendant was judged to be an effective legal document and was admissible. Evidence 1, 2, 3, 4, 5, 10, 11, 13 and 14 submitted by the Defendant, had the originals to check, and also were related to this case, which shall be admissible. The other evidence submitted by the Plaintiff were mutual corroborative with the above admissible evidence and shall also be admissible.

According to the admissible evidence and opinions on cross-examination submitted by parties to the case and statement of accounts, the facts through investigation were as follows:

M.V. NAN GUI JI 035 was a self- discharging large junk and registered as a inland river vessel, length overall was 75.18 M, breadth was 15.20 M, depth was 4.5 M, gross tonnage was 1,599 tons, net tonnage was 895 tons; the kind of main engine was internal-combustion engine; the navigational area was class A; the Port of Registry was Foshan; YANG Xiong was the shipowner and obtained the ownership on August 2, 2005; Foshan Nanhai Yuhang Shipping Co. Ltd. was the operator of the ship.

On August 1, 2005, YANG Xiong and LI Xingyi signed the contract of transferring the self-discharging ship, and they had an appointment that LI Xingyi will transfer M.V. NAN GUI JI 035 to YANG Xiong at RMB7,280,000, and it was LI Xingyi who should be responsible for managing the transferring procedures.

On September 20, 2006, YANG Xiong signed the ship's charter party with CHEN Weihong, and made an appointment that YANG Xiong would rent M.V. NAN GUI JI 035 to CHEN Weihong, the charter term started from October 1, 2006 to September 30, 2007, the monthly rent was RMB100,000, CHEN Weihong should be responsible for employing or firing captain or other seamen and the vessel's maintenance.

On November 10, 2006, the Plaintiff as Party A and the Defendant as Party B concluded the vessel's management agreement, and made an appointment that Party A had the right to join "Nangui machine 035"ship's management, and the thing such as contacting with the ship's renting, for the reason that the Party B had borrowed RMB5,000,000 to buy M.V. NAN GUI JI 035; Party B paid the loan RMB50,000 to the Party A monthly, Party A had right to deduct directly from the "Nangui machine 035"ship's operating income; Party B mortgaged M.V. NAN GUI JI 035 to Party A for securing Part A's claims; Party B agreed to underwrite the insurance in the name of Party A, if the total loss insurance accident occurs to "Nangui machine 035", Party A has the priority right to be repaid from the insurance indemnity so as to offset the Party B's loan, the balance shall fall to Party A's share. After court trial, The Plaintiff and YANG Xiong recognized to the court that the appointment "the balance shall fall to Party A's share" in the Agreement was a clerical error, the true expressed meaning of two parties was that the balance shall fall to Party B's share. The two Parties had not handled mortgage registration formalities of M.V. NAN GUI JI 035.

As to the facts stated above recorded in ship's management Agreement that YANG Xiong borrowed RMB5,000,000 from Plaintiff. The Plaintiff stated that he lent RMB5,000,000 to YANG Xiong, both of them did not sign the loan contract, and he failed to require YANG Xiong to present the debt evidence, and failed to stipulate the loan interest, the above stated loan in amount of RMB5,000,000 was paid by stages but incapable of providing payment voucher. YANG Xiong stated that he indeed borrowed RMB5,000,000 from the Plaintiff, but both the thing borrowing and repaying the loan were managed by his father. He was not clear about the details of the loan and repayment. It was confirmed that the Defendant owed the Plaintiff RMB3,680,000 after the accident. The Plaintiff confirmed that YANG Xiong had repaid the loan of RMB1,320,000 and was still owed RMB3,680,000.

During hearing of this case, the Defendant thought that there exists doubt about the formed time of the above mentioned ship's management Agreement so as to apply to identify the formed time of handwriting and printing and the manufacturing years of the paper. The court entrusted Guangdong Mingjianwenshu judicial expertise center to made an identification. After testing, Guangdong Mingjianwenshu judicial expertise center made the appraisal opinions that the formed time of the handwriting and printing cannot be ascertained. The Defendant should pay appraisal fee RMB1,100 to Guangdong Mingjianwenshu judicial appraisal center.

On April 12, 2007, the Defendant procured a hull insurance from the Plaintiff, he issued a policy with the number PCBA20074471021000001, it stated that the insured was the Plaintiff, the insured vessel was M.V. NAN GUI JI 035, the insurance was the coastal and inland river vessel's all risk, plus one forth additional coverage and the propeller's single loss insurance, both the insurance value and amount were RMB4,500,000, and the premium was RMB54,000, the insurance period lasted from April 13, 2007 to April 12, 2008, the attached sheet of the policy especially stated that RMB10,000 or 10 percent of loss sum was deductible in each accident, whichever was higher; when indemnified the total loss of the insured vessel (or constructive total loss), the deductible rate was 20 percent; the highest limit of salvage charges in each accident should be RMB200,000; the limit of the individual value compensation should be the insurance sum as clearly indicated in the policy; the policy assume all risks insurance according to the coastal and inland river vessel insurance Clause. The first article total damage insurance of the coastal and inland river vessel insurance Clause regulates that this insurance will indemnify total loss of the insured vessel resulted from the following reasons: a. the gale of magnitude 8 or higher, flood, earthquake, tsunami, thunderstruck, mountain's fall, landslip, debris flow, ice; b. fire or explosion; c. collision, striking; d. being stranded, striking a reef; e. being capsized or sunk arising from the above item 1 to 4 disaster or accident; f. ship's missing. The second all risks insurance Clause agrees that this insurance will assume the following responsibilities and charges of the insured vessel's total damage or partial damage resulted from the first listed six reasons: first, collision and striking liability, namely that the insured vessel collides with other vessels or dock, harbor facilities or navigation mark at navigable waters so as to cause immediate damage or fees to the above objects, including the direct loss of the carried cargo, the insurer should bear the indemnity liability by the law. For each collision, striking liability, the insurer just indemnify three fourths of the amount of indemnity, but during insurance, the highest indemnity should not exceed the amount of vessel's insurance at once or accumulated times. Second, general average, salvage and sue and labor, including that when the insurance accident occurs to the insured vessel, the necessary and reasonable fees or salvage charges paid by the insured in taking salvage actions for preventing or reducing the damage. The third Clause that Exclusions liability agrees that the insured vessel's damage, liability and expenses caused by the following cases, the indemnity should not be born by this insurance, including the Clause 1 that the vessel' being unseaworthy and unsuitable for towing (including the vessel technical conditions, manning, embarkation and so on, the tugged vessel's damage, liability and expenses arising from tugging action, all damage, liability and expenses arising from tugging action of non tugboat) and the Clause 4 the intentional action and criminal activity of the insured and its represent (the captain is included).

At around 4 in the morning on June 15, 2007, the captain SHI Guide drove M.V. NAN GUI JI 035 loaded with river sand, on the way from Gaoming of Foshan to Shunde, when sailing, the surface of river had light fog. When about 5 in the morning, Haishou Xinsha Weideng vessel passed through starboard of the vessel, the surface of river was covered by thick fog, the visibility declined dramatically, however, SHI Guide did not take actions as required to maintain proper lookout, choose a safe place to drop anchor and sail in a safe navigational speed, and still took risk to run without confirming whether the front visible white light was the light of the main channel or not. When this vessel was approaching to the Jiujiang bridge, the captain SHI Guide realized that M.V. NAN GUI JI 035 had deviated the main course severely for the vessel colliding the navigation mark about 80 m faraway, even though SHI Guide did not take suspension action, instead, he tried to turn around the bow to place between pier and to sail, and was credulous that the vessel could avoid the collision with the Bridge pier. About 10 past 5 in the morning, M.V. NAN GUI JI 035 collided with the bridge pier 23 for its deviation from the navigation course and the captain SHI Guide's severely misjudgment, which also led to the collapse of the bridge pier 23, 24, 25 with the carried bridge floor. The bow of M.V. NAN GUI JI 035 was plunged into water for being smashed by the collapsed bridge's body, and the stern broke the surface of the water. After the accident, the transport Agency transport safety committee set up the accident investigation group, to carry out the investigation to the reason of the accident, and made out the *Guangdong "6•15" Vessel Colliding with Jiujiang bridge Pier Accident Investigation Report in September of 2008*, the result indicated that M.V. NAN GUI JI 035 did not overload, the seaman equipment met the requirement of the Vessel's Minimum Safety Manning Regulation; it was recognized that the direct reason of the accident was that the captain SHI Guide did not take actions such as keeping normal lookout, driving in a safe speed or stopping sailing when he drove in the restricted visible water area, and sailed in full speed to the bridge blindly, and did not take an appropriate emergency measure when finding the urgent danger, so, it was judged as a single responsible accident that vessel colliding with bridge, M. V. NAN GUI JI 035 shall take full responsibility for this. Guangdong People's Government established "6•15" vessel colliding with Jiujiang bridge pier accident provincial government investigation group, Guangdong Bureau of Safe Production Supervision and Administration was responsible for making out Jiujiang bridge "6•15" Vessel Colliding with Bridge Pier Accident Investigation Report, it turned out that captain SHI Guide held the inland river vessel second-class captain competency certificate issued by Liuzhou marine board, but SHI Guide stated that he cheated on two subjects in the test of the second-class captain upgrading and then passed the test; it was confirmed that the accident was a vessel colliding with bridge pier single liability accident, the direct reason was that captain SHI Guide did not keep normal lookout, drive in a safe speed or take any actions like stop driving and misjudged the navigation mark, took risk to drive in full speed to the bridge when in the bad vision water area. Besides, SHI Guide took wrong actions after finding urgent danger, the indirect reason included something like captain SHI Guide was not qualified for the second-captain requirements and so on. On December 15, 2001, Guangzhou City Haizhu District People Court made out (2010) Hai Xing Chu Zi No.661 judicial verdict over the case, the people's procurator of Guangzhou Zhuhai accused SHI Guide of traffic offending in this case, the verdict was as following: SHI Guide violated the marine traffic transportation regulation, which led to major traffic accident, SHI Guide was judged to commit traffic offences and was sentenced to six years in prison. SHI Guide appealed against the decision. On September 13, 2013, Guangzhou City Intermediate People's Court made (2012) Hui Zhong Fa Xing Yi Zhong Zi No.111 Criminal Ruling and the verdict was as follows: SHI Guide violated marine traffic transportation regulation, led to the major traffic accident, which constituted the crime of causing traffic casualties, he shall be legally punished, the appeal was dismissed, the original judgment should be maintained.

On December 27, 2007, the Plaintiff sent the *Notice of Abandonment* to the Defendant, claimed that due to the special location of the sank M.V. NAN GUI JI 035, the salvage charges were far beyond the value of M.V. NAN GUI JI 035, so M.V. NAN GUI JI 035 should be constructive total loss and gave an abandonment to the Defendant, the Defendant was required to give a definite respond that if he will accept the abandonment before December 31, 2007.

On January 7, 2008, the Plaintiff sent the Defendant an email, claimed that according to the Sank Vessel Salvage Construction Organization Design and Sank Vessel Salvage General Count provided by Jiujiang bridge repaired engineering general contract program and Foshan City Shunde District Rongqi Water Transport Co. LTD, because the bow of M.V. NAN GUI JI 035 was held down by the collapsed bridge pier, it was very likely needed to be cut and drudged out under water, the vessel had been damaged beyond repair, besides, the salvage budgets of M.V. NAN GUI JI 035 was RMB8,373,645, which was far beyond the vessel value and should be constructive total loss, the Defendant was required to give a clear respond about whether accepted abandonment before January 11, 2008.

On January 18, 2008, M.V. NAN GUI JI 035 was cut and dredged out, some parts of salvaged vessel's body was deposited in the Dandansha island in downstream of Jiujiang bridge. On January 31, 2008, the Plaintiff claimed insurance indemnity from the Defendant.

On January 31, 2008, the court made a Civil Ruling of (2007) Guang Hai Fa Chu Zi No.332-3, and gave an auction to the dredged M.V. NAN GUI JI 035. On March

28, 2008, M.V. NAN GUI JI 035 had been auctioned by the court by the law, the transaction price was RMB1,080,000, the fee arising from this auction was RMB79,500.

The court holds that this case is the dispute over vessel insurance contract.

After accepting the insurance against hull from the Plaintiff, the Defendant issued the policy on April 12, 2007, the Plaintiff was the insured, the insurance contract between the Plaintiff and the Defendant was established on April 12, 2007.

Concerning the controversial issue that if the Plaintiff shared the insurable interest of M.V. NAN GUI JI 035, according to the vessel management agreement signed by the Plaintiff and the ship-owner YANG Xiong of M.V. NAN GUI JI 035 on November 10, 2006, YANG Xiong mortgaged the vessel to the Plaintiff, the vessel mortgage contract was established between the Plaintiff and YANG Xiong, but two sides did not underwrite the vessel mortgage registration. Because M.V. NAN GUI JI 035 was registered as the inland river vessel, the voyage of the accident was from Foshan Gaoming to Foshan Shunde's inland lane, therefore, M. V. NAN GUI JI 035 was not belong to the stipulated vessel in Article 3 of the Maritime Code of the People's Republic of China, the related regulations about vessel mortgage in the Maritime Code of the People' Republic of China cannot apply to this case. When the vessel mortgage contract was signed and the accident happened, the Property Law of the People's Republic of China did not carry out, according to the principle of non-retroactivity of law and exception retroactivity, the related regulations of vessel mortgage in Property Law of the People's Republic of China was not applicable. The Vessel Regulations of the People's Republic of China Governing the Registration of Ships and the Guaranty Law of the People's Republic of China effective at that time made related regulations to the vessel mortgage separately. According to the principle that upper laws are superior to lower laws, the related regulations about vessel mortgage of the Guaranty Law of the People's Republic of China shall apply to this case. According to Article 41 of the Guaranty Law of the People's Republic of China that if the litigant mortgage the properties as regulated in Article 42 in this Law should underwrite the mortgage properties' registration, the mortgage contract shall take effect from the day of registration and the regulations about handling the mortgage properties' registration in Article 42 Sub-paragraph 4 that mortgage properties like aircraft, vessel and vehicle should be governed by the transportation facility registration department. The vessel in this case was not handled the mortgage registration, the vessel mortgage contract between the Plaintiff and YANG Xiong did not take effect, therefore, the Plaintiff did not have the mortgage right to M.V. NAN GUI JI 035. Though the Plaintiff did not have the mortgage right to M.V. NAN GUI JI 035, it could be seen from the content of vessel management Agreement that the Plaintiff's lending money was agreed to give YANG Xiong to buy M.V. NAN GUI JI 035, and the Plaintiff was agreed to share part right to manage M.V. NAN GUI JI 035 and could also deduct parts from operating income of each month to refund the money lent by YANG Xiong, the Plaintiff had been also entitled to buy the insurance in the name of himself. It could be seen that the Plaintiff had a strong legally economic interest relationship with M.V. NAN GUI JI 035, the Plaintiff had the demand for transferring risk, it should be confirmed that the Plaintiff had a legally economic interest relationship with M.V. NAN GUI JI 035. According to the regulation of Insurance Law of People's Republic of China rectified in the 30th meeting of the ninth National People's Congress Executive Committee held on October 28, 2002 (thereafter the Insurance Law of the People's Republic of China 2002), the insurance interest refers to the insured share the legally acknowledged interest to the object of insurance. Only if the insured and the object of the insurance constitute the legally economic interest relationship, the insured was judged to have the insurance interest. Therefore, when the insurance contract of this case was established and the accident happened, the Plaintiff had the insurance interest in M.V. NAN GUI JI 035. The Defendant's defense about the Plaintiff did not have the insurance interest in M.V. NAN GUI JI 035 lacked facts and legal basis, shall not be sustained.

When it comes to the controversial issue that if there existed insurance exclusion liability, the Defendant held that the captain and some seamen of M.V. NAN GUI JI 035 obtained the sailor's certificate in an abnormal manner, the seamen were not qualified for the requirements, the vessel was unseaworthy, and the captain of M.V. NAN GUI JI 035 had criminal illegal and criminal act, according to the regulation of Paragraphs 1 and 4 of the insurance contract's third Clause Exclusions' liability, the insurer did not bear the indemnity liability. Concerning the issue of vessel's unseaworthiness, according to the ascertained fact, the Plaintiff had right to manage vessel's operation, but was failed to provide evidence to prove he had employed seamen, and he was not obligated to investigate whether seamen obtained the seafarer's certificate of competency in an illegal manner or not. Although the effective criminal ruling made by Guangzhou Intermediate People's Court confirmed that the captain passed the test of obtaining the certificate by cheating, when vessel's operator employed seamen, he judged seamen's qualification for the position only by their competency certificate. It was impossible for them to investigate if the captain take the illegal action when obtaining captain's certificate. Only vessel's operator took the Duty of Prudence, employed the seamen holding the competency certificate, would they finish the examination duty. The Defendant proposed to be free of liability for vessel's unseaworthiness, which lacked the facts, shall not be sustained.

When it comes to the issue of criminal activities, the paragraph 4 of insurance's exclusions liability's Clause 3 in this case stated as following: intentional act or illegal act of the insured and its represent (including captain). Clause 3 of Reply of the China Insurance Regulatory Commission on the Definition of Illegal Acts as Excluded Liabilities in Insurance Clauses made by China's insurance supervision committee on September 6, 1999 regulated that in the insurance clause, if regard the general illegal acts as exclusion liability, it should be taken the enumeration method, such as drunk driving, driving without license and so on; if state like illegal acts, it only refers to the intentional illegal acts. The insurance clause of this case is standard term, which took the description of violating the law, therefore, shall be understood as an intentional illegal act. The captain SHI Guide of this case was condemned committing traffic offence, which belonged to a criminal negligence, the

Defendant proposed to be free of liability for the captain's illegal act, the reason lacked legal basis, shall not be sustained.

The insurance contract of this case was the consensus agreement of two party's litigants, without violating the mandatory provisions of the current laws and administrative laws, should be legal and effective. The Plaintiff was the insured, the Defendant was the insurer. The accident of this case happened on June 15, 2007, was a single liability that the vessel colliding with bridge. This accident should be the insurance accident as agreed in the insurance contract that the Defendant should be responsible for indemnity. According to Article 24 Paragraph 1 of the Insurance Law of People's Republic of China (2002), an insurer shall, after receiving a claim for indemnity or payment of insurance from an insured or a beneficiary, make an examination and decision in time, and then inform the Insured of the result of the ascertainment; if the insurance liability is included, the insurer shall make compensation or payment within ten days after reaching the agreement of compensation or payment of premium with the insured or the beneficiary. And the insurer shall make compensation or payment according to the insured amount and according to the time limit for compensation or payment as agreed in the insurance contract. If there was no insurance exclusions, the insurer shall perform the duty of compensation.

The vessel of this case had been actually dredged and auctioned by the court, after deducting the auction fee, the residual value of the vessel was RMB1,000,500. Because the vessel had residual value and there was no evidence to indicate that the Plaintiff had paid the fee of dredge and salvage, the Plaintiff's claim that the fee of dredge and salvage exceeded the residual value and the vessel constituted the total loss could not set up, this case was not the total loss accident. The agreed insurance value of the insurance in this case was RMB4,500,000, the vessel's residual value was RMB1,000,500, the Plaintiff's suffered loss was RMB3,499,500, according to the special regulation of the insurance contract, in each accident, the deductible was RMB10,000 or 10 percent of the damaged amount, whichever was higher, the deductible of the Defendant in this case was RMB349,950. The agreed insurance value in this case was RMB4,500,000, which shall be the full insurance contract, the Defendant should pay insurance indemnity in amount of RMB3,499,500, after deducting the deductible RMB349,950, it should be RMB3,149,550. The Plaintiff lodged claim to the Defendant on January 31, 2008, the Defendant should inspect and settle in time, the Defendant did not settle the claim and thereby caused interest's loss of the Plaintiff, the interest thereof should be calculated as requested by the Plaintiff from 6th May 2008, and based on the interest rate for liquid capital load in RMB over the corresponding period as promulgated by the People's Bank of China, to the date of payment set by this judgment. The Plaintiff's request was sustained.

To sum up, according to Article 24 Paragraph 1 and Article 40 of the Insurance Law of the People's Republic of China 2002, and Article 64 Paragraph 1 of the Civil Procedure Law of the People's Republic of China, the judgment is as follows:

1. The Defendant PICC Property and Casualty Company Limited Shunde Branch shall indemnify the Plaintiff LIN Guihe insurance indemnity in amount of RMB3,149,550 and the interest thereof (calculated from May 6, 2008, and based on the interest rate for liquid capital load in RMB over the corresponding period as promulgated by the People's Bank of China, to the date of payment set by this judgment);
2. Reject the claims filed by the PlaintiffLIN Guihe.
The above obligation of payment shall be fulfilled within 10 days after this judgment enters into effect. For failure to fulfill the obligation of payment within the period designated by this judgment, interest on the debt for the delayed period shall be doubled, pursuant to Article 253 of the Civil Procedure Law of the People's Republic of China.

Court acceptance fee in amount of RMB42,800, the Defendant shall bear RMB29,956, and the Plaintiff shall bear RMB12,844. The appraisal fee in amount ofRMB1,100, shall be born by the Defendant.

In case of dissatisfaction with this judgment, the Plaintiff and the Defendant may within 15 days upon the service of this judgment, submit a statement of appeal to the court, together with copies according to the number of the opposite parties, and appealed to the Guangdong High People's Court.

Presiding Judge: HUANG Weiqing
Judge: CHENG Shengxiang.
Judge: WU Guining.

May 15, 2014

Clerk: CHEN Di
Clerk: LI Chunyu

Guangdong High People's Court
Civil Judgment

LIN Guihe
v.
PICC Property and Casualty Company Limited Shunde Branch

(2014) Yue Gao Min Si Zhong Zi No.112

Related Case(s) This is the judgment of second instance, and the judgment of first instance and the ruling of retrial are on page 689 and page 727 respectively.

Cause(s) of Action 230. Dispute over marine insurance contract on the sea or sea-connected waters.

Headnote Denying claim for an indemnity under a hull insurance policy for a ship that sank, on the ground that the Plaintiff had not adequately proved that he had an insurable interest, as he had merely loaned money to the owner of the ship under an informal loan agreement; reversing lower court decision.

Summary M.V. NAN GUI JI 035 sank due to an allision with a bridge and was declared a constructive total loss. The Plaintiff sued for an indemnity under the hull insurance policy after the Defendant insurer refused to pay. The Defendant argued that the ship was not a constructive total loss because it had residual value, and that the Plaintiff did not have an insurable interest, as he had merely loaned money to the owner under an informal loan and ship management agreement. The court of first instance held that the ship was not a constructive total loss but held that the Plaintiff did have an insurable interest. The court of first instance awarded the Plaintiff damages for the value of the ship, minus its residual value and a 20% deductible in the hull policy. Both parties appealed. The appeal court reversed the lower court's decision, holding that the Plaintiff did not have an insurable interest, as he had not provided adequate evidence that he was in effect, a mortgage lender.

Judgment

The Appellant (the Plaintiff of first instance): LIN Guihe, male, born on 23 October 1966, Han, living in Shunde District, Foshan, Guangdong.
Agent *ad litem*: XU Guangyu, lawyer of Guangdong Haijian Law Firm.
Agent *ad litem*: LI Zhenhai, lawyer of Guangdong Haijian Law Firm.

The Appellant (the Defendant of first instance): PICC Property and Casualty Company Limited Shunde Branch.
Domicile: No.346 Jianhai North Road, Shunde District, Foshan City, Guangdong.
Person in charge: XIE Zewei, general manager of the branch.
Agent *ad litem*: HUANG Zhuo, lawyer of Guangdong Zhengda United Law Firm.
Agent *ad litem*: YANG Meihua, lawyer of Guangdong Zhengda United Law Firm.

Dissatisfied with the Civil Judgment (2008) Guang Hai Fa Chu Zi No.259 rendered by Guangzhou Maritime Court in respect of the case of dispute over ship insurance contract between which the Appellant LIN Guihe and the Respondent PICC Property and Casualty Company Limited Shunde Branch (hereinafter referred to as "PICC Shunde") were involved, they separately filed an appeal before the court. After accepting the case, the Court constituted a collegiate panel. On July 16, 2014, the Court investigated the case, Appellant LIN Guihe and XU Guangyu and LI Zhenhai as his agents *ad litem* and HUANG Zhuo as agent *ad litem* of PICC Shunde attended the court investigation; on July 17, 2014, the court investigated the outsiders YANG Xiong and YANG Sanzhu regarding the situation involved; on October 14, 2014, the court made a supplementary court investigation, LIN Guihe and LI Zhenhai as his agent *ad litem*, and YANG Meihua as agent *ad litem* of PICC Shunde attended the court investigation; on July 22, August 18, September 15 and November 26, 2014, the court inquired the parties regarding identification of matters, LIN Guihe and LI Zhenhai as his agent *ad litem*, and HUANG Zhuo as agent *ad litem* of PICC Shunde attended the Courtroom Inquiry. On April 10, 2015, the court organized the cross-examination regarding the judicial appraisal conclusion, LIN Guihe and LI Zhenhai as his agent *ad litem*, and HUANG Zhuo as agent *ad litem* of PICC Shunde, and LI Xianqian, GUAN Yanjun and others as the appraisers of Guangdong Nantian Judicial Expertise Institute attended the cross-examination; on July 23, 2015, the court re-investigated the case, LI Zhenhai as LIN Guihe's agent *ad litem* and HUANG Zhuo as agent *ad litem* of PICC Shunde attended the court investigation. Now this case has been concluded.

LIN Guihe refused to accept the judgment of first instance, filed an appeal to the court and requested that the judgment of first instance should be amended that in the first term of judgment, PICC Shunde should pay insurance compensation RMB4,500,000 to LIN Guihe which the interest calculated since 6 May 2008 to the payment date of verdict decision according to People's Bank of China lending rates over the same period interest; and the second term of judgment should be revoked and PICC Shunde born all the fees of litigation in the case of first instance and the second instance. The reasons are that: 1. The involved allision accident caused the total loss of M.V. NAN GUI JI 035. In the accident, M.V. NAN GUI JI 035 was hitted by the collapsed parts of the Jiujiang bridge, and lead to the bow failed in the river. In December 2007, due to the budget of salvage fees RMB8,373,645 far more exceeded the value of the ship RMB7,280,000, it should be recognized to be constructive total loss. LIN Guihe issued a notice of abandonment to PICC Shunde, but he did not receive any reply. In January 2008, the ship was cut to be salvaged.

In addition to the bow, the rest parts of the ship was salvaged out of the water and auctioned, but the bow was still sinking under the river. Whether the vessel should be recognized to be a constructive total loss should be judged not whether the insurer did the actual payment of salvage and rescue fees but according Article 246 of the Maritime Code of the People's Republic of China: "where a ship's total loss is considered to be unavoidable after the occurrence of a peril insured against or the expenses necessary for avoiding the occurrence of an actual total loss would exceed the insured value, it should constitute a constructive total loss." As for whether the insurer actually paid the fees, or related parties claimed to the shipowner, which had nothing to do with the identification of constructive total loss. According to Article 249 of the Maritime Code of the People's Republic of China: "where the subject matter insured has become a constructive total loss and the insured demands indemnification from the insurer on the basis of a total loss, the subject matter insured should be abandoned to the insurer. The insurer may accept the abandonment or choose not to, but should inform the insured of his decision whether to accept the abandonment within a reasonable time." PICC Shunde did not reply within the reasonable period on whether accept the abandonment, which could presume the ship constituted a total loss. The first instance identified that M.V. NAN GUI JI 035 did not constitute a total loss only on the grounds of LIN Guihe's non-payment of salvage and rescue fees, which did not comply with the above provisions and also did not comply with the objective conditions that the ship was severely damaged and completely lost the original form and utility; what's more, after the accident, the ship was facing a huge amount of claim from the bridge owner and its insurer, although parts of the ship salvaged out of the water were auctioned, the ship owner could not finally obtain the proceeds from the auction. 2. PICC Shunde had no right to deduct 20 percent of deductibles. Firstly, from perspective of effectiveness of the special agreement and hull insurance clauses, whether the special agreement stated by the deductibles for the total loss (or constructive total loss) of insured ship was 20%, or hull insurance clause stated by the insurer deducted deductibles for each compensation according to the stipulations in the insurance policy (except for total loss, collision, allision) was by unilaterally provided by PICC Shunde. LIN Guihe confirmed this. Under the condition that PICC Shunde could not prove that the foregoing provisions had not been discussed with LIN Guihe, the foregoing hull insurance clause did not belong to the standard terms stipulated in the Contract Law of the People's Republic of China: "the parties for repeated use and pre-prepared, and in the time of the conclusion of the contract not negotiated with the other party", but was specially agreed as non-standard terms, hence, this case did not apply Article 41 of the Contract Law of the People's Republic of China: "provisions of the format clause and non format inconsistent of, non format terms provisions should be used". Secondly, according to the law applicable principles of the general law and special law, general provisions and special provisions, Article 41 of the Contract Law of the People's Republic of China was the general provisions of the contract, and the Insurance Law of the People's Republic of China (2002) was as a special law of insurance contract, Article 31 thereof, "for insurance the terms of the contract, the insurer and the insured, the insured or the beneficiary of a dispute, the people's court or an arbitration organ should be favorable to the insured and the beneficiary explanation" was the special regulation of the insurance contract. When both had conflict, Article 31 of the Insurance Law of the People's Republic of China (2002) should be applied to make a favorable interpretation to the insured, LIN Guihe, which was that according to Article 11 of involved hull insurance clause, deductible should not be deduct. Other effect judgment when dealing with the similar case, made the explanation against the insurer. 3. The insurance indemnity should not deduct the residual value of M.V. NAN GUI JI 035. That PICC Shunde did not reply within a reasonable time whether to accept the abandonment should be deemed not to accept the abandonment and give up the right to the ship. According to Article 255 of the Maritime Code of the People's Republic of China: "after the occurrence of a peril insured against, the insurer is entitled to waive his right to the subject matter insured and pay the insured the amount in full to relieve himself of the obligations under the contract", it had no right for PICC Shunde to deduct the rest value of the ship in the insurance indemnity. The law applied in the first instance is improper, resulting the wrong identify of the amount of compensation, so the court was requested to correct.

According to LIN Guihe's appeal, PICC Shunde in the second instance defended that:

1. M.V. NAN GUI JI 035 did not constitute a total loss. The ship was auctioned by the court of first instance after salvage part of which, left residual value of RMB1,000,500 yuan after deducting related expenses. There was no evidence in this case to prove that LIN Guihe paid actually salvage and rescue fees. The claim of LIN Guihe on "salvage and rescue fees was more than the residual value" was lack of factual basis, and his abandonment was not satisfied with the formal elements stipulated in the law and was also not accepted by PICC Shunde. Hence, it was untenable that the ship constituted a total loss.
2. It was reasonable and legitimate to deduct the residual value. Under situation that the ship did not constitute a total loss, according to the agreement in the Insurance Contract between the two parties and the related legal stipulations, even if the insurer was required to make compensation, he also had right to deduct the mentioned residual value from the insurance indemnity. That LIN Guihe's loss was identified as RMB3,499,500 in the first instance was confirmed to the objective facts.
3. It was legal and valid to deduct deductible Special agreements in the attached list of involved insurance policy explicitly recorded that "deductible in each accident is RMB10,000 yuan or 10% of the loss, whichever is higher." Hence, although the insurer should take the responsibility of the insurance indemnity, he also had reasonable reasons to deduct relevant deductible during calculating the amount of compensation.

PICC Shunde refused to accept the judgment of first instance and appealed to out court, requested the Court to revoke the first term of judgment of first instance and rejected all claims by LIN Guihe, and it also requested that legal expenses shall be born by LIN Guihe. The reasons were that:

1. There was no insurance interest for LIN Guihe to the involved ship. Firstly, it was unable for LIN Guihe to reasonably explain the financing source of so-called loan. He neither provided certificate of indebtedness or the loan contract, nor showed the payment voucher to YANG Xiong, and that the IOU of RMB5,000,000 was paid in cash did not conform with the usual trading habits. LIN Guihe claimed that he gave interest-free loan to YANG Xiong, and YANG Xiong each month only repaid RMB50,000 to Lin Guihe. However, during periods of several years, Lin Guihe and Yang Xiong had never done reconciliation, and Lin Guihe also failed to provide the appropriate evidence on the so-called fact that YANG Xiong had repaid RMB1.32 million—above mentioned aspects were all obviously went against common sense, which could be enough to show that there was no real loan contractual relationship between Lin and Yang. Even if there was loan contractual relationship between Lin Guihe and Yang Xiong, it did not mean LIN Guihe had insurance interest to the ship owned by YANG Xiong. Secondly, there was no close and legal stake between LIN Guihe and M.V. NAN GUI JI 035. The effect of criminal adjudication in (2012) Sui Zhong Fa Xing Yi Zhong Zi No.111 stated that LIN Guihe testified as a witness that YANG Xiong owned the ship and in August 2004 LIN Guihe served as a clerk of the ship. He was responsible for maintenance, loading and unloading, recruiting the crew, dealing with certificates, handing fees and so on. Thus, there was not existence of some legal relationship between LIN Guihe and the ship owner YANG Xiong on operation of the ship. LIN Guihe's so-called "matters that managing and contacting with the charters" were limited to performing his duties as a clerk. He had no right to operate or manage the ship in his own name, and to possess, use, profit or dispose the ship. LIN Guihe did not rely on the ship as material basis of profits, so he did not need to take the risk of ship damage or operation.

2. The loss caused by the involved accident belonged to the exclusions agreed in insurance contract. In this case, the captain SHI Guide, the duty sailor Huang Yuyou, and other sailors LI Yizhuan, LIN Shixin, LI Huiqiang, LUO Zhichao, etc. by improper means obtained the relevant certificates, or did not hold any certificates, resulting in M.V. NAN GUI JI 035 in fact failed to meet the requirement of safe manning, which became the main reason of accident of the ship crashing the bridge. Aforementioned effective criminal judgment had been identified that LIN Guihe existed the action of dealing with certificates for some crew through illegal means. And LIN Guihe as the person in charge of recruiting the crew, he should have known some of the crew without certificate of competency or through illegal means to obtain a certificate, but he still employed them to work on aboard, which was malicious. It was improper in first instance decision that the ship operator judged whether he was competent only according to the certificate when hiring the crew and unable to examine the irregularities when obtaining the certificate. And there was no evidence to prove that it was

improper to identify that LIN Guihe recruited the crew, or he had no obligation to review the crew whether to obtain illegal certificate. According to Article 3 of the Coastal and Inland Waterway Hull Insurance Clause: "the insurer does not take responsibilities for loss, damage caused by unseaworthiness (including being properly mannered, equipped or loaded, etc.) or intentional or illegal act of the Insured and his representative (including the captain)." PICC Shunde was unnecessary to perform insurance indemnity obligation to LIN Guihe.

Regarding the appeal of PICC Shunde, LIN Guihe defended in second instance:

1. Regarding whether LIN Guihe had insurance interest of M.V. NAN GUI JI 035. Because LIN Guihe and YANG Xiong were friends and had weak legal consciousness, both parties did not sign a loan contract, nor agreed interest, only agreed monthly repayment amount; As a guarantee, Yang agreed to insure in the name of LIN Guihe, so LIN Guihe had the priority of compensate when the loss happened; the ship was demise chartered, LIN Guihe only charged for hire, with no need to manage the ship, and still able to be engaged in other business and get the profit—the situation was not unusual. LIN Guihe had the insurance interest of M.V. NAN GUI JI 035 based on the relationship of loan. If PICC Shunde doubted the loan and repayment facts between Lin Guihe and Yang Xiong, then it shall provide appropriate evidence to prove. PICC Shunde had known the ship was owned by YANG Xiong when the it accepted the insurance, but it did not mention the problem of insurance interest during charging premiums. China People's Property Insurance Co., Ltd. Guangdong Branch (hereinafter referred to as PICC Guangdong)—the level of which is higher than that of PICC Shunde, recognized the facts that in the other subrogation case caused by the allision accident involved, LIN Guihe lent money to YANG Xiong for purchasing M.V. NAN GUI JI 035, and he was the inventor of the ship. While, PICC Shunde in the face of the insurance indemnity submitted the defense of insurance interest, which obviously breached good faith.
2. Regarding whether belonged to exclusion. M.V. NAN GUI JI 035 at the time of the accident was demise chartered, the crew including the captain all hired by demise charterer CHEN Weihong, so it had no relation to LIN Guihe. According to the relevant provisions, the sailors and the mechanics of inland ships had no need to pass the exam, just only filling in forms of the maritime department, handing over photos and paying fees, and then the certificate could be obtained, so there was not existence of situation that "through improper means to obtain a certificate". The report of the Department of Transportation Safety Board related to the accident involved and the effect criminal adjudication all confirmed the crew of M.V. NAN GUI JI 035 to be competent and seaworthy. That PICC Shunde Appellant that the incompetence of the crew and unseaworthiness of the ship lacked factual basis. The grounds of appeal of PICC Shunde were untenable, and should be rebut.

During the hearing of second instance, LIN Guihe provided evidence as followed: 1. The complaint filed by PICC Guangdong on (2008) Guang Hai Fa Zhong

Zi No.44 Civil Judgment; 2. the defense filed by LIN Guihe on (2008) Guang Hai Fa Zhong Zi No.44 Civil Judgment; 3. (2008) Guang Hai Fa Zhong Zi No.44 Civil Judgment; 4. (2008) Yue Gao Fa Shen Jian Zai Zi No.90 Civil Judgment; 5. inland ship crew competency examination and Certification Rules of the people's Republic of China (printed materials); 6. Code of Inland Waterway Grading Regulation (1986) of Register of Shipping of PRC (copy materials). Among them, evidence 1, 2 and 3 was to prove the fact that the PICC Shunde Filiale knew the facts of LIN Guihe lent money to YANG Xiong for purchasing ship and LIN Guihe had insurance interest of M.V. NAN GUI JI 035; evidence 4 was to prove when there was conflict between the content in the insurance policy and the insurance clauses, the explanation shall be unfavorable to the insurer; evidence 5 was to prove that there was no need to pass any competency examinations to access Inland Ship Mechanic and Sailors Certificate; evidence 6 was to prove the navigation limits of M.V. NAN GUI JI 035 belonged to grade A, so the ship was "seagoing vessel" stipulated by the Maritime Code of the People's Republic of China. PICC Shunde thought: the above-mentioned evidence 1, 2, 3, 4 were not the new evidence stipulated by law. It had no objection to the authenticity and legality of the evidence above mentioned, but had objections to relevancy of the evidence. PICC Shunde was not one of the parties of (2008) Guang Hai Fa Zhong Zi No.44 case, thus, evidence 1, 3 could not prove that it had known the debt matters so called by LIN Guihe when it issued the insurance policies involved in the case; evidence 2 was only stated by LIN Guihe, there was no evidence to prove it; That case involved in evidence 4 had nothing to do with this case, the condition of that case was different from that of this case, and it was not comparable. In addition, only based on the relevant provisions of crew competency exam certification, it was not enough to deny the fact was identified by effective criminal judgment, and the relevant provisions of the division of Inland River shipping district was also not enough to prove that M.V. NAN GUI JI 035 was a seagoing vessel. The court holds that: evidence 5, 6 mentioned above all were normative documents, which could not reflect the relevant facts in this case, so they were not the evidence of the case. PICC Shunde issued the insurance policies involved in the case in April 2007 before the allision accident. (2008) Guang Hai Fa Zhong Zi No.44 case was filed by PICC Guangdong in March 2008 after the allision accident. And as the branch of business entity who separately obtains a business license, PICC Shunde was not the party of (2008) Guang Hai Fa Zhong Zi No.44 case, while PICC Guangdong Branch was not the party of this case. There was no evidence to show the connection between the two parties on hull insurance business involved in the case, or to prove that the related statement made by PICC Guangdong in another case had been recognized by PICC Shunde, so the statement in evidence 1 and 3 made by PICC Guangdong in another case was not enough to prove the related conditions of involved insurance; The content of evidence 2 was only stated by LIN Guihe unilaterally and there was no effective evidence to prove it, so it was insufficient to prove the content real and objective; (2008) Yue Gao Fa Shen Jian Zai Zi No.90 Civil Judgment had nothing to do with this case, so evidence 4 could not prove the related facts in this case. The relevancy of the above-mentioned evidence 1, 2, 3, 4 and the case could not be identified, or the evidence 5, 6 was the normative documents that was unable to reflect the objective facts, so the court did not confirm its probative force.

Although LIN Guihe submitted the evidence in the second instance, but its probative force could not be confirmed. The relevant evidence could prove the facts found out in the first instance, after fact-finding, which was proper, so the court shall confirm the facts recognized in first instance.

According to the (2014) Wen Jian Zi No.3 judicial authentication opinions in first instance issued by Guangdong Mingjian Manuscript Judicial Appraisal Center, the supplementary identification as follows:

Guangdong Mingjian Manuscript Judicial Appraisal Center tested the ship management agreement through multiple determination methods—through the dissolution method on the same condition of two handwritten signature to conduct oxidation treatment and measure the time of dissolution; Through fading technique method on the same condition of printed strokes to conduct oxidation treatment and measure value of the image color gamut. As the ability to melt resistance and antioxidant of the strokes in checked materials for more than thirty days was not clearly improved, according to the experimental data and the preservation conditions during experiment to analysis synthetically, it was unable to determine the formation time of the handwritten strokes and printed strokes in the agreement.

According to the enterprise machine-readable files modification registration data provided by PICC Shunde in second instance and issued by the Market Safety Supervision Bureau in the Shunde District, Foshan City, the court made an supplemental judgment as follows:

PICC Shunde, formerly known as PICC Property and Casualty Company Limited. Shunde Company, was approved to rename as the PICC Property and Casualty Company Limited. Shunde Branch on October 13, 2014.

In the course of investigation in the second instance, LIN Guihe and PICC Shunde both confirmed that: LIN Guihe was the applicant and the insured in the involved ship insurance contract.

In the course of hearing in the second instance, in order to find out the relationship between LIN Guihe and M.V. NAN GUI JI 035 and the conditions that the amount of loan, payment and being not yet paid referred by LIN Guihe between YANG Xiong. Besides inquiry to the party of this case LIN Guihe in the court investigation, the court also separately invested and made a written record to the third party YANG Xiong and YANG Sanzhu, according to Article 67 Paragraph 1 of the Civil Procedure Law of the People's Republic of China. LIN Guihe and PICC Shunde had no objection to the authenticity, legality and relevancy of the two records of the court investigation. According to the court investigation on July 16, 2014 and the above-mentioned 2 investigation records, the relevant circumstances were found out as follows:

LIN Guihe alleged in the statement of claim that: he was employed in 1993 by YANG Xiong's father, YANG Sanzhu, and he was friend with YANG Sanzhu. For purchasing of M.V. NAN GUI JI 035, YANG Sanzhu and YANG Xiong proposed borrowing money requirement to Lin Guihe. They did not sign a written contract nor other written form of confirmation. They did not agree interest and repayment period, only a verbal agreement that YANG Xiong monthly repaid RMB50,000 and YANG Sanzhu undertook the repayment guarantee liability. Around August 2005, the total loan amount was RMB5,000,000, about 70% of which transferred to YANG Sanzhu's bank account. About 30% of the loan was delivered to YANG Sanzhu in cash. The cumulative total amount of the repayment was RMB1,320,000 from YANG Xiong. From November 2006 to May 2007, YANG Xiong monthly repaid RMB50,000 in cash directly or sometimes by deduction of ship hire; The other repayment was transferred by YANG Xiong through bank in multiple times to return. YANG Sanzhu never repaid to him, the money transferred between them was without written records, and both parties did not issue a receipt, even nor reconciliation. After YANG Xiong in August 2005 bought M.V. NAN GUI JI 035, he firstly operated by himself and collected hire, then in November 2006, the ship was demise chartered to CHEN Weihong for operating. During the demise charter, he was commissioned by YANG Xiong for collecting the hire; and he was commissioned by CHEN Weihong for dealing with agent certificates, inspection issues and participation in hiring some of the crew, but he was not onboard. YANG Xiong and he signed a involved ship management agreement on 10 November 2006, whose purpose was to provide protection for their own interests.

YANG Xiong defended that: LIN Guihe was his father YANG Sanzhu's friend. From August 2005 to June 2007, he was a student at Industry and Trade Career Academy in Guangdong. He was to buy a ship for starting a business, so he through his father YANG Sanzhu borrowing RMB5,000,000 from LIN Guihe. Until June 2007, the occurrence of allision accident related to the case, he still owed LIN Guihe about RMB3,000,000. About whether the loan agreed interest and repayment period, whether signing a written loan contract, and the specific times and amount of the payment by LIN Guihe, whether the financial sources of repayment and the repayment amount as well as the way to repay to LIN Guihe, whether having vouchers or written records of repayment and loan, whether he managed and operated M.V. NAN GUI JI 035, whether LIN Guihe participated in the operation and management of the ship, after bareboat charter whether he charged hire from CHEN Weihong and way of charging hire and so on, he could not recall anything mentioned above. His had ever participated in signing the Ship Management Agreement involved in the case with LIN Guihe, but he did not remember the time and the purpose of the agreement.

YANG Sanzhu defended that: from August 2005 to June 2007, his son YANG Xiong was in school. As a friend of LIN Guihe, he lent LIN Guihe RMB5,000,000 for YANG Xiong buying M.V. NAN GUI JI 035. The two parties did not sign a written contract or agreement on interest and repayment period. LIN Guihe delivered the loan to him by installments partly in cash or partly by way of transfer, and the amount of each delivery was different, of which was mostly by bank transfers. After the purchase of M.V. NAN GUI JI 035, due to YANG Xiong still in school, then he authorized LIN Guihe to assist management. The ship from September 2006 was demise chartered to CHEN Weihong to operate, but it was without registration procedures. He knew nothing about how CHEN Weihong managed it and whether LIN Guihe participated in the management or were engaged in the relevant work and so on. CHEN Weihong paid hire to him monthly in cash, the amount was generally RMB100,000, and the monthly payment time was unfixed. He and LIN Guihe did not make a formal negotiation on repayment, and only agreed verbally that after receiving hire, he repaid RMB50,000. After receiving the hire paid by CHEN Weihong, of which RMB50,000 was paid to LIN Guihe, but the duration of the way of repayment was not clear; In addition, other income had also been used to repay the loan; The repayment to LIN Guihe was partly in cash and partly by the way of bank transfer, but bank transfer was the majority. YANG Xiong had no ability to repay, or actual repaid. YANG Xiong and LIN Guihe had ever reconciled and confirmed in written the amount of arrears. Until the occurrence of allision accident involved in case, he still owed money about RMB3,000,000 to LIN Guihe. It was not clear for him whether LIN Guihe and YANG Xiong signed the involved ship management agreement.

The court requested LIN Guihe, YANG Xiong and YANG Sanzhu to provide bank vouchers, other written documents or other evidence related to the loan, repayments, reconciliation involved in the case, but none of them submitted.

During the second instance, PICC Shunde submitted a decommissioned authentication application to the court. As evidence itself had doubts, the organization commissioned by the first instance lacked corresponding authentication ability and was unable to make authentication conclusions, it requested to retest the formation time of two strokes of "YANG Xiong" and "LIN Guihe" handwritten signatures and the printed handwriting in LIN Guihe's first instance evidence, ship management agreement. The court held that: The evidence had important influence to ascertain the facts of the case. PICC Shunde in first instance had applied for authentication and obtained the permission. Owe to commissioned organization, it failed to make a clear conclusion. PICC Shunde's aforesaid application was reasonable and necessary, so it shall be permitted. PICC Shunde and LIN Guihe did not reach an agreement on the choice of specific Judicial Appraisal Center, but they agreed to select Judicial Appraisal Center decided by the court; PICC Shunde requested Judicial Appraisal Center with appropriate authentication capability, while LIN Guihe required to choose Judicial Appraisal Center from the Court Judicial Commissioned Professional and Technical Institutions Register. Listed in the Court Judicial Commissioned Professional and Technical Institutions Register and Judicial Appraisal Center on Physical Evidence related to manuscripts included Guangdong Tianzheng Judicial Appraisal Center, (manuscripts, audio and video materials authentication), Guangdong Nantian Judicial Appraisal Center, (manuscripts, strokes authentication). After consultation, Guangdong Tianzheng Judicial Appraisal Center, clearly replied that it did not have the qualification of authenticating formation time of files, and did not to accept the commission. The court next according to the relevant provisions and procedures, commissioned Guangdong Nantian Judicial Appraisal Center to authenticate the application matters mentioned by PICC Shunde. PICC Shunde and LIN Guihe had no objection to this. After Guangdong Nantian Judicial Appraisal Center, accepted commission, determined the notice of abandonment and (2008) Guang Hai Fa Chu Zi No.234-3 as samples and disputed evidence of ship management agreement as test materials from materials provided by both parties and without objection, to carry out authentication work. After the completion of the authentication work, Guangdong Nantian Judicial Appraisal Center issued Yue Nan (2014) Wen Jian Zi No.666 judicial authentication opinions on March 6, 2015. On April 10, the court organized the two parties and appraisers participated in the forensic appraisal activities LI Xiaoqian, GUAN Yanjun etc. to cross examine on the judicial authentication opinions. Regarding to LIN Guihe's proposed objection, Guangdong Nantian Judicial Appraisal Center on April 8 issued the *Reply of Objection of Judicial Authentication Opinions on Manuscripts* and its annex, on April 21, issued the Instructions on Time Identification Equipment and the Relevant Work. For the authentication, PICC Shunde paid appraisal fee of RMB50,728 to Guangdong Nantian Judicial Appraisal Center, paid court fees of appraisers in sum of RMB3,000 to the Court; the court paid fees of appraisers in sum of RMB3,000 to the Guangdong Nantian Judicial Appraisal Center.

PICC Shunde had no objection to the judicial authentication opinions and conclusions mentioned above, and thought that the judicial results showed that LIN Guihe colluded with the third party YANG Xiong to forge ship management agreement. According to the civil procedural principles of fairness and honesty, LIN Guihe should burden the corresponding appraisal fees and the court fees of appraisers. LIN Guihe had objection to the above-mentioned judicial authentication opinions and conclusions, the main reasons were that: The authoritative and effective national technical specification was not adopted in the authentication; The authentication results impacted by the paper, ink, printing ink, preservation environment and other factors did not have been taken into consideration, and the collected samples were too little; the conclusion was contradict with the conclusion that was authenticated in the first instance on the same matter. LIN Guihe provided the following evidence for that: 1. (2014) Wen Jian Zi No.3 judicial authentication opinions (copies) issued by Guangdong Mingjianwenshu Judicial Appraisal Center; 2. notice on the relevant matters concerning the formation time of the entrusted documents issued by the Supreme People's Court Judicial Administration Equipment Authority [Fa Si (2008) No.12] (printouts); 3. Authentication Opinions on the Formation Time of Documents (website printouts) issued by Zhejiang High People's Court; and 4. (2014) Mao Zhong Fa Shen Jian Min Zai Zi No.6 Civil Judgment (printouts). PICC Shunde did not recognize the above-mentioned evidence, thinking that it was not sufficient to overturn the authentication conclusions in the second instance. The court held that: although the above-mentioned evidence 1 was the authentication opinion made by other Judicial Appraisal Centers on the same matter, but it had no direct relationship with the authentication, and it could not prove the relevant circumstances of the authentication. Evidence 2 was the Supreme People's Court's file. Its contents mainly was samples provided by the inspection units to authenticate the formation time of documents. While, the materials of the authentication with no objection were used as samples, which were consistent with the notification requirements; Evidence 3 was a document of Zhejiang High People's Court from the website, contents in which showed that the subjects of the documents were all classes of courts in Zhejiang and it was inner guidance document in Court in Zhejiang and without the validity of legal norms; The authenticity of the evidence 4 could not be confirmed, and the cases related to it had nothing to do with this case. Above-mentioned evidence 2, 3, 4 could not prove that the relevant circumstances of this authentication, so the court did not recognize its probative force. In addition, before the cross examination was organized by the court to all parties on the aforesaid judicial authentication opinions, LIN Guihe applied that ZHANG Ning from Guangdong Watson Judicial Appraisal Center as the expert with specialized knowledge to appear in court cross examination, which shall be permitted by the court. But ZHANG Ning did not appear in the court cross examination, and LIN Guihe interpreted it as "family affairs and personal reasons". Through review, Yue Nan (2014) Wen Jian Zi No.666 judicial authentication opinions issued by Guangdong Nantian Judicial Appraisal Center explicitly recorded the contents and materials commissioned to authenticate, the basis and technical methods of authentication, so demonstrated the authentication process, with clear authentication conclusions and attached with Judicial Appraisal Center and qualification certificates of Judicial Appraisal Center and appraisers. And the appraisers according to the court notice to appear in court to testify, accept inquiry and replied the doubt of the parties in written, which complied with Article 78 of the Civil Procedure Law of the People's Republic of China, Article 29 of the Some Provisions of Supreme People's Court on Evidence in Civil Procedures, so the court confirms the probative force on the aforesaid judicial authentication opinions and related information.

According to (2014) Wen Jian Zi No.3 judicial authentication opinions (copies) issued by Guangdong Mingjianwenshu Judicial Appraisal Center, the Reply of Objection of Judicial Authentication Opinions on Manuscripts, and its annex, the Instructions on Time Identification Equipment and the Relevant Work, the notice of adducing evidence and the proof of service of (2008) Guang Hai Fa Chu Zi No.234-3 in court of first instance, notice of abandonment, in first instance, the court investigation, questioning and cross examination related to authentication of the second instance, the court ascertained the following facts:

Guangdong Nantian Judicial Appraisal Center held judicial authentication licenses issued by the justice department of Guangdong province, and its business scope included document authentication and trace authentication etc.; Appraisers involved in the appraisal LI Xiaoqian, GUAN Yanjun and YANG Zeli all had judicial appraiser certificates, categories were all "document authentication (full-time)". Guangdong Justice Department on June 23, 2010 issued the Reply to confirm the methods of testing formation time of documents by computer, and its contents were: "Guangdong Nantian Judicial Appraisal Center invented Nantian Mingjian System of Inspecting Formation Time of Documents, which had been granted the national patent by a method and computer system of testing formation time of documents by the computer", and was authenticated by the experts from Shenzhen Science and Technology Industry and Information Committee, got scientific and technological achievements registration certificates, and accordingly made the ink color gamut inspection work instructions for the practice of document authentication. According to the implementation the notice of accreditation criteria of identifying the qualification of Judicial Appraisal Center, to further promote the Qualification Identification of Judicial Appraisal Center [Si Jian (2009) No.10], confirmation procedures with non-standard methods and inspection methods of testing formation time of documents by computer were confirmed and put on records. On June 25, 2012, Guangdong Provincial Department of Justice issued Yue Si Ban (2012) No.128 the Reply to agree the non-standard methods of seven categories including document authentication used by Guangdong Tiannan Judicial Appraisal Center, and put on records, and the authentication of formation time of documents used in authentication business of this Center NJD/ZD-D-10-2007, ink color gradation test NJD/ZD-D-13-2009 and VSC6000 function test method NJD/ZD-D-14-2012 were put on records.

During the cross examination process, LIN Guihe and appraisers from Guangdong Nantian Judicial Appraisal Center all confirmed: On the aspects of authentication of formation time of documents, at present there were no relevant national standards, or industry standards or technical standards and technical specifications approved by most experts in this field.

PICC Shunde and LIN Guihe had no objection to the authenticity of testing materials involved and samples. The two samples were respectively notice of abandonment and the notice of adducing evidence of (2008) Guang Hai Fa Chu Zi No.234-3. Sample, notice of abandonment, was LIN Guihe's first instance evidence and its original copy was submitted by the PICC Shunde in the second instance. The printed time of the document was December 27, 2007, in which there was LIN Guihe's handwritten signatures–LIN Guihe confirmed, and the document was printed on December 27, 2007. On the same day, he signed by himself on the document, and he submitted the original copy to PICC Shunde; PICC Shunde had no objection to LIN Guihe's aforesaid statements. Another sample, the notice of adducing evidence of (2008) Guang Hai Fa Chu Zi No.234-3, was the legal document in first instance printed and sealed by court of first instance, and the original copy of it was submitted by LIN Guihe in the second instance. The court of first instance accepted the case on May 7, 2008 and the date recorded in the notice and the date of the notice signed by LIN Guihe's lawyer, LI Zhenhai were all on May 9, 2008 – both parties all confirmed that the actual printed time of court document were consistent with the recorded time of that,

Yue Nan (2014) Wen Jian Zi No.666 judicial authentication opinion recorded:

1. Basic situation: the commissioner was the Guangdong High People's court; the commissioned authentication matter was the printed characters on the ship management agreement whose nominal time was on 10 November, 2006, and authentication of formation time of "LIN Guihe" and "YANG Xiong" handwritten signatures; inspection materials were the original copy of ship management agreement, sample was whose nominal time was on May 9, 2008, and the content was the printed text of the original notice of adducing evidence and whose nominal time was on December 27, 2007, and original notice of abandonment with "LIN Guihe's handwritten signature".

2. Inspection Case Abstract: parties was doubted the formation time of printed text and handwritten signature.
3. The inspection process: authentication methods was based on the Instruction of Authenticating the Formation Time of Documents NJD/ZD-D-10-2007, the Instruction of Ink Color Gradation Test NJD/ZD-D-13-2009; The used instruments were VSC600 document authentication instrument and Nantian Mingjian document formation time inspection system. Through review and inspection, inspected materials and sample materials were basically in good condition, the printed text on the inspected materials was accumulated by black toner, showing was output by laser printer, and the text strokes were clear; LIN Guihe, YANG Xiong handwritten signatures were dark green ink, hard pen writing. The carriers of inspected materials and samples were A4 printing paper, and paper was with different color. (a) Regarding the test for formation time of printed text of inspected materials. Through the inspection of VSC6000 document inspection instrument, the ink marks of printed text in inspected materials were the same as those of notice of adducing evidence in samples, it had condition of authenticate the formation time of printed text in inspected materials by the method of ink color gradation, but it needed to adjust the paper color. Conducting ink collection and inspection of the two ink marks of printed text in inspected materials and the two ink marks of printed text in samples, and adjusting the paper color, it found out that the two ink color gradation values of inspected materials were 13763, 13759. There was 4 between them, and daily variation value was 7, so the two ink marks were formed at the same time and average value was 13761; the two ink color gradation values in samples were 12608, 12604. The difference between them was 4, and daily variation value was 8, so the two ink marks were formed at the same time and average value was 12606. The average value of ink color gradation in inspected materials was 1155 greater than that of notice of adducing evidence in samples. (b) Regarding the inspection of the formation time of the handwritten signature of inspected materials. Through the inspection of VSC6000 document inspection instrument, the ink marks of two "LIN Guihe" and "YANG Xiong" handwritten signatures in inspected materials were the same as those of "LIN Guihe" handwritten signatures in notice of abandonment of samples, it had condition of authenticating the formation time of ink marks of handwritten signatures in inspected materials by the method of ink color gradation, but it needed to adjust the paper color. Conducting ink collection and inspection of the two ink marks of handwritten signatures in inspected materials and the two ink marks of handwritten signatures in samples, and adjusting the paper color, it found out that the two ink color gradation values of handwritten signatures in inspected materials were 17090, 17088. The difference between them was 2, and daily variation value was 7, so the two ink marks were formed at the same time and average value was 17089; the ink color gradation value of handwritten signatures in samples was 17007, and daily variation value was 7, so the average value of ink color gradation of two handwritten signatures in inspected materials was 82 greater than that of notice of abandonment in samples.

4. Analysis and explanation: the change rule of ink color gradation value was gradation value is greater, it is further than now, whereas the recenter; similar color gradation value is formed at the same time, whereas not formed at the same time. (a) As the average value of ink color gradation of printed text in inspected materials was greater than that of notice of adducing evidence in samples, so inspected materials were formed earlier than samples. According that the daily variation average value of ink marks of printed text both in inspected materials and samples were 7.5, the printed text in inspected materials was formed about 5 months earlier than that of notice of adducing evidence in samples. (on May 9, 2008). (b) As the average value of ink color gradation of two handwritten signatures in inspected materials was greater than that of handwritten signature of notice of abandonment in samples, so inspected materials were formed earlier than samples. According that there was difference of 82 between the average value of ink color gradation of two handwritten signatures in inspected materials and that of handwritten signature in samples, and the both daily variation value of ink marks were 7.5, the two handwritten signatures in inspected materials were formed about 12 days earlier than handwritten signature of notice of abandonment in samples (on December 27, 2007) 0.5.The authentication opinions: the formation time of the printed text in ship management agreement was not its nominal time "On November 10, 2006", but it was formed around in December 2007. The formation time of "LIN Guihe" and "YANG Xiong" handwritten signatures of the inspected material, ship management agreement, was not its nominal "On November 10, 2006", but was formed in around December 2007.

In addition, after receiving Yue Nan (2014) Wen Jian Zi No.666 judicial authentication opinion, LIN Guihe, on March 16, 2015, applied to the court for commissioning other qualified Judicial Appraisal Center to authenticate printed text in ship management agreement and formation time of "LIN Guihe" and "YANG Xiong" handwritten signatures again, on the grounds that he had objection to authentication opinion, and aforesaid authentication conclusion lacked the basis. The court ascertained that the judicial authentication opinion had recorded clearly the inspection process and the used instruments and methods, and made specific analysis to the data, which indicated that the authentication conclusion had sufficient basis. Although LIN Guihe had objection, but he did not submit evidence to prove the existence of re-authenticated conditions listed in Article 27 Paragraph 1 of the Some Provisions of Supreme People's Court on Evidence in Civil Procedures. Therefore, the aforesaid re-authenticated application did not comply with the law, and the court shall not permit it.

In addition, after receiving Yue Nan (2014) Wen Jian Zi No.666 judicial authentication opinion, LIN Guihe, on 16 March, 2015, applied to the court for commissioning other qualified Judicial Appraisal Center to authenticate printed text in ship management agreement and formation time of "LIN Guihe" and "YANG Xiong" handwritten signatures again, on the grounds that he had objection to authentication opinion, and aforesaid authentication conclusion lacked the basis.

The court ascertains that the judicial authentication opinion had recorded clearly the inspection process and the used instruments and methods, and made specific analysis to the data, which indicated that the authentication conclusion had sufficient basis. Although LIN Guihe had objection, but he did not submit evidence to prove the existence of re-authenticated conditions listed in Article 27 Paragraph 1 of the Some Provisions of Supreme People's Court on Evidence in Civil Procedures. Therefore, the aforesaid re-authenticated application did not comply with the law, and the court shall not permit it.

After the court organized both parties and judicial appraisers to cross examine on Yue Nan (2014) Wen Jian Zi No.666 judicial authentication opinion, LIN Guihe, on April 17, 2015, applied to the court for entrusting other qualified institution to authenticate whether the types and components of ink marks of printed text in the ship management agreement as inspected materials and notice of adducing evidence as samples were the same, and whether the types and components of ink marks of two handwritten signatures in the ship management agreement as inspected materials and handwritten signature in notice of abandonment as samples were the same, whose reason was that the VSC6000 document inspection instrument could not authenticate the types and components of ink marks, whether the ink marks were the same in inspected materials and samples could not be confirmed, so it had no condition of authenticating the formation time of handwritten signatures and printed text by the method of ink color gradation. The court ascertained that the choice of samples, judging whether the types of ink marks in inspected materials and samples were the same, and whether samples could be used in this case were all authentication methods and inspection process. Appraisers when appearing in court to Reply questions had explained related questions, made it clear that in the use of ink color gradation test method, judging whether they were the same ink marks was only physically inspected by the instruments, and did not need to conduct chemical composition analysis. LIN Guihe did not provide sufficient evidence to prove the necessity of aforesaid authentication application, and it was meaningless to prove the related facts in this case. According to Article 121 Paragraph 1 of the Interpretation of the Supreme People's Court on the Application of the Civil Procedure Law of the People's Republic of China, the court shall not permit it.

After the court replied two LIN Guihe's aforesaid authentication application, LIN Guihe, on July 29, 2015, submitted authentication application to the court again, in addition to the authentication requests listed in two aforementioned application, he also increased one: if the court did not commission others to authenticate, he would request to submit the original inspected materials and samples involved in previous authentication to LIN Guihe, and LIN Guihe would himself commissioned Guangdong Tianzheng Judicial Appraisal Center to authenticate, in order to ascertain the facts of the case. His reasons and the reasons of two aforesaid authentication application were basically the same. The court ascertains that: as previously mentioned, under the condition that Yue Nan (2014) Wen Jian Zi No.666 judicial authentication opinion could be confirmed and the authentication conclusion could be admissible, LIN Guihe failed to provide evidence to prove the existence of the legal situation to re-authenticate or the necessity of the authentication, his authentication application made no sense to prove the relevant facts in this case. Guangdong Tianzheng Judicial Appraisal Center made a clear reply previously that it had no ability to authenticate the formation time of documents, did not accept such authentication commissions. That LIN Guihe commissioned the center lacked feasibility. According to Article 121 Paragraph 1 of the Interpretation of the Supreme People's Court on the Application of the Civil Procedure Law of the people's Republic of China, Article 27 Paragraph 1 of the Some Provisions of Supreme People's Court on Evidence in Civil Procedures and so on, the court did not permit matters of LIN Guihe's this authentication application.

The court holds that:

This case is the dispute over ship insurance contract. The two parties had no objection to the fact that M.V. NAN GUI JI 035 sank due to allision with the national highway G325 Jiujiang bridge, and LIN Guihe was as the applicant and the insured of the involved ship insurance contract, which was confirmed by the Court. According to the appeal, the defense and the court investigation, the court determined that the dispute in the second instance was mainly whether PICC Shunde shall bear the responsibility for insurance compensation to LIN Guihe. To solve the problem, we must first determine whether LIN Guihe had insurance interest to M.V. NAN GUI JI 035.

The main evidence that LIN Guihe had insurance interest to M.V. NAN GUI JI 035 was ship management agreement. Because the both parties had dispute over the formation time of evidence, Guangdong Mingjian Document Judicial Appraisal Center entrusted by the court of first instance could not make a clear authentication conclusion, in order to find out the relevant facts, Guangdong Nantian Judicial Appraisal Center entrusted by the court of second instance, authenticated the formation time of printed text and handwritten signatures. Guangdong Nantian Judicial Appraisal Center was the legal Judicial Appraisal Center, which had document identification ability. LIN Guihe had no objection to the qualification of the center and the court commissioning it to authenticate. Appraisers participated in the appraisal also had corresponding appraisal practice certificate, therefore, the qualification of Judicial Appraisal Center and appraisers was in conformity with the relevant provisions of the law. Both parties had no objection to the authenticity of two materials in this authentication and confirmed the fact that handwritten signature of notice of abandonment was formed on December 27, 2007, printed text of notice of adducing evidence was formed during the period from May 7, 2008 to May 9, 2008. And through the inspection of Guangdong Nantian Judicial Appraisal Center, the types of 2 materials and ink marks in inspected materials were the same, and which were in line with the required conditions of Judicial Appraisal Center, so the two copies of materials could as the samples of authentication. LIN Guihe had objection on grounds of "the amount of samples was too small", but did not provide enough evidence or provisions to prove that the samples needed in authentication had the requirement of the amount, and only one copy of sample could not be authenticated, so the aforesaid objection lacked basis, which could not be established. Article 22 of the General Rules of the Judicial Appraisal Procedure of the Ministry of Justice: "judicial appraiser shall be according to the following sequence of compliance and the adoption of the technical standards and technical specifications in this field: (1) national standards and technical specifications; (2) competent authority for judicial authentication, judicial authentication industry organization or relevant departments in charge of industry to develop industry standards and technical norms; and (3) recognized by most experts in the field of professional technical standards and technical specifications. Without the technical standards and technical specifications prescribed in the preceding paragraph, the relevant technical specifications that may be formulated by the judicial authentication institutions shall be adopted." Accordingly, even if authenticating the formation time of documents lacked corresponding national standards and technical standards industry standards and technical specifications, technical standards and technical specifications recognized by most experts in the professional fields. Judicial Appraisal Centers could still apply themselves to carry out appraisal work. Although Guangdong Nantian Judicial Appraisal Center used irrelevant technical specifications made by itself in this authentication, but they belonged to the scopes of the General Rules of the Judicial Appraisal Procedure of the Ministry of justice, won the national patents and was confirmed and put on records by the competent administrative authorities, so they could be applied to the appraisal work. LIN Guihe had objection to methods of this authentication on the grounds of "not authoritative, effective national technical norms", his reasons were not sufficient, so they could not be established. Authentication opinions illustrated the questions of adjusting paper colors and authenticating types of ink marks regarding on the contents authentication process and Replies when appraisers appearing in court to Reply questions, and this belonged to the scopes of authentication methods and operations. Although LIN Guihe held that paper, ink, oil ink, preservation environment and so on could affect the authentication results, but he failed to clear specific degrees that the aforesaid factors impacted the authentication conclusion. He also failed to provide evidence to prove the situation that the improper above factors leaded to wrong authentication conclusions is correct, therefore, his claim lacked factual basis and could not be established. As for authentication of the same issues, Guangdong Mingjian Documents Judicial Appraisal Center commissioned by the court of first instance adopted the dissolution method, fading method and so on, which could not make a clear conclusion on the formation time of documents. Because of the different authentication methods and equipments used by different authentication, institutions, which may directly affect the authentication results, so there was no contradictory between the two aforesaid authentication results. To sum up, Yue Nan (2014) Wen Jian Zi No.666 judicial authentication opinion issued by Guangdong Nantian Judicial Appraisal Center was in line with the requirements of the relevant laws in contents and forms, the case also had no evidence showed that the used samples, methods and the corresponding operation processes in this authentication were improper and influenced the accuracy. Although LIN Guihe had objection, but he did not provide sufficient reasons and corresponding evidence to support his claim, according to Article 71 of Some Provisions of Supreme

People's Court on Evidence in Civil Procedures Entrusted by the People's Court identification department to make appraisal conclusion, "if the parties do not enough to refute evidence to the contrary and the reasons can be identified by the proof force", the court confirms the probative force of the authentication opinion and admitted its conclusion. Accordingly, it could be confirmed that the ship management agreement was actually formed around in December 2007. LIN Guihe's claim the agreement signed on November 10, 2006 did not confirm to the objective facts.

After PICC Shunde accepted LIN Guihe's buying insurance, issued the insurance policy on April 12, 2007, so the involved ship insurance contract was established on 12 April 2007. At that time, Article 12 of the Insurance Law of the People's Republic of China (2002) stated: "the insured shall have the insurable interest in the subject matter of the insurance. The applicant had no insurable interest in the subject matter of the insurance contract, and the insurance contract is invalid. Insurable interest refers to the legal recognition of the insured to the subject matter of the insurance. The object of insurance refers to the property as an object of insurance and the life and body of the person concerned." The object to involved ship insurance contract was M.V. NAN GUI JI 035, LIN Guihe as the applicant, shall have insurance interest to the ship, which was that he shall have practical and legal interest association with the ship. It needed to be judged by the relevant facts. LIN Guihe himself claimed that he had insurance interest to the ship, because the ship owner Yang for purchasing the ship lent RMB5,000,000 from him. mortgaged the ship to him, repaid the loan by parts of the operating incomes, and agreed that he had right to participate in the management of the ship and purchased insurance in his own name. The corresponding evidence was ship management agreement, LIN Guihe's statements and investigation records of the third parties, YANG Xiong and YANG Sanzhu. according to the authentication results on formation time of documents, the ship management agreement was actually formed later than the establishment of the involved ship insurance contract, but also later than the occurrence that allision of the ship with the bridge, so the agreement was not enough to prove that when the involved ship insurance contract established or involved allision accidents happened, situations recorded in the agreement and claimed by LIN Guihe had objectively existed. According to the investigations to LIN Guihe and related third parties YANG Xiong and YANG Sanzhu in the first and second instance, as for loan matters, three persons all confirmed that loan payments were conducted between the LIN Guihe and YANG Xiong's father YANG Sanzhu; LIN Guihe and YANG Sanzhu all confirmed most loan was paid by bank transfer and a small part of the loan was in cash. As for payment and repayment, YANG Xiong said they were dealt with by his father, and he had nothing about related situations. LIN Guihe stated that he received repayment in sum of RMB1.32 million, parts of them were directly deducted from the ship hire, parts of them were repaid by YANG Xiong by bank transfer or in cash, and YANG Sanzhu never repaid to him; YANG Sanzhu stated that ship hires were charged by him, he repaid the parts of loan by the ship hires and other incomes, partly by the bank transfer and partly in cash payment to LIN Guihe. But because YANG Xiong had no ability to repay, so he never repaid to LIN Guihe. Thus, the above three persons as the direct loan parties, had apparent contradictions to the statements regarding on matters related to money, and PICC Shunde did not confirm them. Through the requests of the court, three persons also failed to provide any bank transfer vouchers and other written documents or other effective evidence to prove situations claimed by them, so the above litigant's statements and the witnesses testimony were not sufficient to prove objective existence of the fact that LIN Guihe lent money to YANG Xiong. Accordingly, under the situation that the fact that YANG Xiong had claims to LIN Guihe could not be confirmed, YANG Xiong mortgaged M.V. NAN GUI JI 035 to LIN Guihe, which lacked objective rationality, and at that time, it shall be according to the regulations of the Guaranty Law of the People's Republic of China and the Regulations of the People's Republic of China Governing the Registration of Ships regarding on that the ship mortgage shall be handled to the registration organ in mortgage registration and mortgage contract came into effect since the day of registration. M.V. NAN GUI JI 035 did not apply for mortgage registration and had no publicity, so LIN Guihe's claim that he enjoyed a mortgage to the ship lacked factual basis, and could not be established. In addition, according to the LIN Guihe's statements, he engaged in the work related to M.V. NAN GUI JI 035, which limited to Charging hires commissioned by ship owner YANG Xiong, handling documents, inspection and participating in hiring crews commissioned by the charterer CHEN Weihong, not participating in the ship operation and management and obtaining economic benefits; and LIN Guihe, YANG Xiong, YANG Sanzhu had obvious different opinions in statements about operation and management, charging hires, repayment operation of M.V. " Nanguiji 035". The case had nor other valid evidence to prove LIN Guihe indeed obtained repayment from the ship's operating incomes. In summary, Although LIN Guihe claimed he enjoyed mortgage of M.V. NAN GUI JI 035, had right to participate in the management of the ship, and obtained repayment from the ship's operating incomes on the basis that he loaned to YANG Xiong, he did not provide sufficient and effective evidence to prove that, according to the Article 64 Paragraph 1 of the Civil Procedure Law of the People's Republic of China: "parties to put forward their own ideas, have the responsibility to provide evidence" and Article 90 of Interpretation of the Supreme People's Court on the Application of the Civil Procedure Law of the People's Republic of China "parties to put forward their own litigation request according to the facts or rebuts the facts, shall provide evidence to prove that, except as otherwise stipulated by law. Before making a decision, the parties failed to provide evidence or the evidence is not sufficient to prove the allegation of fact, by bears the burden of proof to prove that the responsibility of the parties bear the provisions of the negative consequences". LIN Guihe shall bear the negative consequences of failing to bear the burden of proof, and the above claims lacked factual basis, and were not tenable. Accordingly, LIN Guihe could not prove he had practical and legal interest association with M.V. NAN GUI JI 035, so his claim that he had insurance interest to the ship lacked factual and legal basis, and the court did not support him. according to Article 12 Paragraph 1 of the Insurance Law of the People's Republic of China (2002), LIN

Guihe as the applicant and the insured had no insurance interest to the insurance object, M.V. NAN GUI JI 035., the involved ship insurance contract was invalid. According to Article 56 of the Contract Law of the People's Republic of China, "invalid or revoked contract ever from the very beginning legally binding", PICC Shunde as the insurer did not have to bear the responsibility of the insurance compensation. The judgment of the first instance on the claim that LIN Guihe had insurance interest to M.V. NAN GUI JI 035, PICC Shunde shall pay the insurance compensation to him was improper, the court shall correct it.

As for the fact whether M.V. NAN GUI JI 035 in the allision accident was a total loss, the loss and damage caused by allision was excluding insurance liability and concrete calculation of insurance compensation amount, due to no relation to the results of the case, so they shall not be reviewed in this case.

As for the burden of appraisal fees, Chap. 2 Measures on the Payment of Litigation Costs, was "scopes of paying litigation expenses", including contents of Article 6 to Article 12 of it; Chap. 5 was "the burden of litigation expenses", including the content of Article 29 to Article 43 of it. Article 6 stimulates: "the parties shall pay to the people's court litigation costs include: (1) the case acceptance fee; (2) application fee; (3) the witnesses and expert witnesses, interpreters, adjustment of personnel in the people's court for the date of the transportation fees, accommodation, living expenses and lost income subsidy." Article 12 stimulates "litigation process for identification, announcement, inspection and translation, evaluation, auction, sale, storage, transportation, ship supervision happened shall be born by the party's expenses, the people's court according to the who advocates, who the burden of principle, determined by the parties paid directly to the relevant institutions or units, people the court shall not withhold and pay", because the provisions of Chap. 2 was about the requirements of paying litigation costs in advance, from the above law, appraiser fees belong to the costs parties shall pay to the court. Appraisal fees in the litigation belong to costs the parties directly pay to the relevant institutions and the people's court shall not collect. Both of them belong to the scope of litigation expenses. The authentication results in second instance showed that the actual formation time of ship management agreement provided by the LIN Guihe and as one of the important evidence in this case, did not confirm to the time it recorded ostensibly. LIN Guihe in the lawsuit of the case made statements which was inconsistent with the facts. It directly impacted finding out the facts of the case and trial results, and led to the occurrence of twice authentication in first instance, second instance and corresponding appraisal fees, expert costs. Lin's act violated Article 13 Paragraph 1 of the Civil Procedure Law of the People's Republic of China: "civil litigation should follow the honest credit principle", and his litigation request shall not be supported. PICC Shunde also failed show clearly that it did not agree to accept related appraisal fees, so according to Article 29 Paragraph 1 of the Mesures on the Payment of Litigation Costs "litigation costs shall be born by the losing party burden, undertaken voluntarily by the parties except the provisions of the prevailing", appraisal fees in sum of RMB1,100 for the first instance, appraisal fees in sum of RMB50,728, appraisal fees in sum of RMB3,000 for the second instance all shall be born by LIN Guihe.

To sum up, the court of first instance is wrong in identifying the facts, the application of law, and handling the results, the court shall correct them. The appeal by PICC Shunde is reasonable, the court shall approve it; LIN Guihe's appeal lacks sufficient evidence, the court shall not support it. According to Article 12 Paragraph 1 Paragraph 2 of the Insurance Law of the People's Republic of China (2002), Article 56 of the Contract law of the People's Republic of China, Article 64 Paragraph 1, Article 170 Paragraph 1 Sub-paragraph 2 of the Civil Procedure Law of the People's Republic of China, Article 90 of the Interpretation of the Supreme People's Court on the Application of the Civil Procedure Law of the People's Republic of China, the judgment is as follows:

1. Revoke the Civil Judgment (2008) Guang Hai Fa Chu Zi No.234 by Guangzhou Maritime Court;
2. Reject all the claims of LIN Guihe against PICC Shunde.

Court acceptance fee of first instance in amount of RMB42,800, and the appraisal fees in amount of RMB1,100, all shall be born by LIN Guihe. As the appraisal fees of first instance have been paid by PICC Shunde, LIN Guihe shall pay it within 10 days as of the service of this judgment to PICC Shunde.

Court acceptance fee of second instance of the appeal filed by LIN Guihe in amount of RMB16,954, shall be born by LIN Guihe himself; court acceptance fee of second instance of the appeal filed by PICC Shunde in sum of RMB31,996 shall also be born by LIN Guihe. The court will return the entertainment fee for the second instance prepaid by PICC Shunde in amount of RMB31,996. LIN Guihe shall within 10 days as of the service of this judgment pay court acceptance fee of second instance in sum of RMB31,996 to the court. The appraisal fees of second instance in amount of RMB50,728 and the appraiser fees in amount of 3,000, shall all be born by LIN Guihe. As the above two fees had been paid by PICC Shunde, LIN Guihe shall pay the sum within 10 days as of the effective of this judgment to PICC Shunde.

The judgment is final.

Presiding Judge: DU Yiliang
Acting Judge: LI Mintao
Acting Judge: MO Fei

October 23, 2015

Clerk: PAN Wanqin
Clerk: LI Junsong

Appendix: Relevant Law

1. **Insurance Law of the People's Republic of China (2002)**
   Article 12 An applicant shall have an insurable interest in the subject matter of the insurance. The applicant has no insurable interest in the subject matter of the insurance contract, and the insurance contract is invalid. Insurable interest refers to the legal recognition of the insured to the subject matter of the insurance. The object of insurance refers to the property as an object of insurance and the life and body of the person concerned.
2. **The Contract Law of the People's Republic of China**
   Article 56 Invalid contracts or the revocation of the contract has no legal binding. Part of the contract is invalid, does not affect the effectiveness of other parts, the other part is still effective.
3. **The Civil Procedure Law of the People's Republic of China**
   Article 13 Civil action should follow the principle of good faith. The parties shall have the right to dispose of their own civil rights and litigation rights within the limits prescribed by law.

   Article 64 Parties to their own claims, have the responsibility to provide evidence. If the parties and their agents are unable to collect the evidence themselves due to objective reasons, or if the people's court considers the evidence needed to hear the case, the people's court shall investigate and collect. The people's court shall, according to the legal procedures, examine and verify the evidence comprehensively and objectively.

   Article 67 The people's court shall have the right to investigate and collect evidence from the relevant units and individuals, and the relevant units and individuals shall not refuse to do so. The people's Court of the relevant units and individuals put forward the certificate documents, should identify the authenticity, review to determine its effectiveness.

   Article 78 Parties to the opinion of the identification of the objection or the people's court that the identification of the person is necessary to appear in court, the identification of people shall appear in court to testify. By the people's court, the identification of the person who refused to testify in court, the opinion might not be identified as a basis for the identification of the facts; the parties to pay the fees may be required to return the cost of identification.

   Article 170 After trial, the people's court of second instance shall handle appeal cases according to the following different circumstances:

   (1) Dismissing an appeal and sustaining the original judgment or ruling in the form of a judgment or ruling, if the original judgment or ruling is clear in fact finding and correct in application of law;
   (2) Reversing, revoking or modifying the original judgment or ruling according to law in the form of a judgment or ruling, if the original judgment or ruling is erroneous in fact finding or application of law;

(3) Issuing a ruling to revoke the original judgment and remand the case to the original trial people's court for retrial or reversing the original judgment after ascertaining facts, if the original judgment is unclear in finding the basic facts; and
(4) Issuing a ruling to revoke the original judgment and remand the case to the original trial people's court, if the original judgment seriously violates statutory procedures, such as omitting a party or illegally entering a default judgment.

Where, after the original trial people's court enters a judgment for a case remanded for retrial, a party appeals the judgment, the people's court of second instance shall not remand the case again for retrial.

4. **Measures for the Payment of Litigation Fees under the State Council**
Article 6 Parties to the people's court shall pay the litigation costs include:

(a) The case acceptance fee;
(b) Application fee; and
(c) Witnesses, appraisers, translators, adjustment in the people's court for the designation of appearing in court on the date the transportation fee, accommodation, living expenses, and delays subsidies.

Article 12 In the process of litigation for identification, announcement, reconnaissance, translation, assessment, auction, sale, storage, storage, transportation, ship supervision according to law shall be by the cost burden on the parties, the people's court according to the who advocates, who will bear the burden of principle, decided by when things people paid directly to the relevant agencies or units, the people's court shall not be collected on behalf of.

Article 29 Litigation costs shall be born by the losing party unless the prevailing party is willing to bear the burden of the lawsuit. Part of the winning, some of the lost, the people's court according to the specific circumstances of the case of the parties to determine the amount of litigation costs born by the parties. Where the parties lose the lawsuit, the people's court decides the amount of the cost of litigation costs born by the parties according to the interests of the subject matter of the litigation. The people's court shall, according to the provisions of the third paragraph of the eleventh paragraph of the civil procedure law, provide for the translation of local ethnic languages and languages.

5. **General Rules of the Judicial Expertise Procedure of the Justice Department**
Article 22 The identification of a judicial expert shall comply with and adopt the technical standards and technical specifications of the professional field in the following order:

(a) National standards and technical specifications;
(b) The industry standards and technical specifications formulated by the competent department of judicial expertise, the judicial expertise organization or the relevant industry authorities; and

(c) The technical standards and technical specifications of the majority of experts in the field of professional.

Without the technical standards and technical specifications prescribed in the preceding paragraph, the relevant technical specifications that may be formulated by the judicial authentication institutions shall be adopted.

6. **Interpretation of the Supreme People's Court on the Application of the Civil Procedure Law of the People's Republic of China**

   Article 90 Parties shall provide evidence to prove that their claim is based on the facts or the basis of the claim against the other party's claims, except as otherwise provided by law. Before making a decision, the parties fail to provide evidence or evidence is not sufficient to prove the facts of the claim, the parties bear the burden of proof to bear the adverse consequences of the parties.

   Article 121 Parties to apply for identification can be put forward before the expiration of the time limit for evidence. The matters to which the application is identified are not related to the facts to be proved or to be of no significance to prove the facts to be proved, and the people's court shall not permit. If the people's court approves the application for identification of the parties concerned, it shall, in consultation with the parties concerned, determine the qualified person. If a party fails to negotiate, the people's court shall appoint. according to the investigation and collection of evidence according to the conditions of the collection of evidence, the people's court shall, according to the terms of reference for the identification, in the opinion of the parties, the designated qualified person.

7. **Some Provisions of Supreme People's Court on Evidence in Civil Procedures**

   Article 27 The parties can Challege the people's Court's instructed institution to make the identification with evidence to prove the existence of one of the following circumstances, and the people's court shall permit for re-identification:

   (a) Institution or experts of institution do not have the qualifications to identify;
   (b) The identification procedures are in serious violation of the law;
   (c) The basis of identification conclusion is obviously insufficient; and
   (d) Other circumstances that identification conclusion cannot be used as evidence.

   Article 29 The judges shall examine whether the identification conclusion issued by the institution contains the following contents:

   (a) The name or the name of the principal, and the contents of the identification;
   (b) Materials entrusted to the commission;
   (c) The basis for the identification and the use of scientific and technological means;
   (d) Description of the identification process;

(e) A clear conclusion of the appraisal;
(f) Description of the qualification of the institution of the expert; and
(g) The signature and seal institutions.

Article 71 Towards the conclusion of the identification institution instructed by People's court, if the parties do not have enough evidence to refute, the court can admit its power of proof.

The Supreme People's Court of the People's Republic of China Civil Ruling

LIN Guihe
v.
PICC Property and Casualty Company Limited Shunde Branch

(2016) Zui Gao Fa Min Shen No.1452

Related Case(s) This is the ruling of retrial, and the judgment of first instance and the judgment of second instance are on page 689 and page 701 respectively.

Cause(s) of Action 230. Dispute over marine insurance contract on the sea or sea-connected waters.

Headnote The Supreme People's Court recognized lower court decision denying Plaintiff's claim for an indemnity under a hull insurance policy for a ship that sank, on the ground that the Plaintiff had not adequately proved that he had an insurable interest, as he had merely loaned money to the owner of the ship under an informal loan agreement.

Summary M.V. NAN GUI JI 035 sank due to an allision with a bridge and was declared a constructive total loss. The Plaintiff sued for an indemnity under the hull insurance policy after the Defendant insurer refused to pay. The Defendant argued that the ship was not a constructive total loss because it had residual value, and that the Plaintiff did not have an insurable interest, as he had merely loaned money to the owner under an informal loan and ship management agreement.

The court of first instance held that the ship was not a constructive total loss but held that the Plaintiff did have an insurable interest. The court of first instance awarded the Plaintiff damages for the value of the ship, minus its residual value and a 20% deductible in the hull policy. Both parties appealed. The appeal court reversed the lower court's decision, holding that the Plaintiff did not have an insurable interest, as he had not provided adequate evidence that he was in effect, a mortgage lender.

The Plaintiff appealed to the Supreme People's Court, which dismissed the case since the Plaintiff had provided insufficient evidence to refute the lower courts' findings under de novo review.

Ruling

The Claimant of Retrial (the Defendant of first instance, the Appellant of second instance): LIN Guihe, Male, Han, born on October 23, 1966, living in Shunde District, Foshan City, Guang dong.
Agent *ad litem*: XU Guangyu, lawyer of Guangdong Haijian Law Firm.
Agent *ad litem*: LI Zhenhai, lawyer of Guangdong Haijian Law Firm.

The Respondent of Retrial (the Defendant of first instance, the Appellant of second instance): PICC Property and Casualty Company Limited Shunde Branch
Domicile: No.346 Jianhai North Road, Shunde District, Foshan, Guangdong.
Legal representative: XIE Zewei, general manager of the branch.
Agent *ad litem*: HUANG Zhuo, lawyer of Guangdong Zhengda United Law Firm.
Agent *ad litem*: YANG Meihua, lawyer of Guangdong Zhengda United Law Firm.

With respect to the case arising from dispute over ship insurance contract between the Claimant of Retrial, LIN Guihe, and the Respondent of Retrial, PICC Property and Casualty Company Limited. Shunde Branch (hereinafter referred to as PICC Shunde), the Claimant of Retrial disagreed with the Guangdong High People's Court (2014) Yue Gao Fa Min Si Zhong Zi No.112 Civil Judgment, and applied for retrial to the court. The court formed a collegiate panel to investigate the case, now the case has been concluded.

LIN Guihe claimed that: the judgment of second instance confirmed that LIN Guihe had no insurance benefits to M.V. NAN GUI JI 035, which lacked evidence to prove, the confirmation of facts and application of law were wrong. The accident involved caused the total loss of M.V. NAN GUI JI 035. PICC Shunde should pay 3.6 million yuan of insurance compensation according to the insurance value and insurance amount agreed by both parties. Firstly, PICC Shunde's superior company, China People's Property & Casualty Co., Ltd. Guangdong Branch, admitted that LIN Guihe had an insurance interest in the round in a separate suit. Secondly, the investigation records of the shipowner YANG Xiong and his father YANG Sanzhu of M.V. NAN GUI JI 035 were consistent with the contents of the Ship Management Agreement submitted by LIN Guihe. Thirdly, the Judicial Appraisal Opinion issued by Guangdong Nantian Judicial Appraisal Institute had unlawful appraisal procedures, unscientific appraisal methods, and evidently insufficient evidence conclusion, so it was wrong that the court of second instance accepted it. Fourthly, the court of second instance disapproved LIN Guihe's application for reassessment, depriving him of the right to submit rebuttal evidence. So he required to retry the case.

PICC Shunde argued that: firstly, the appraisal made by Guangdong Nantian Judicial Appraisal Institute was lawful and valid, LIN Guihe could not prove that he had insurance benefits to the ship involved. Secondly, the issue of the case was the exemption liability in the insurance contract, so PICC Shunde had right to be exempted.

The court holds that, the case is the dispute over ship insurance contract, according to the application of retrial of LIN Guihe, the issue of review is whether LIN Guihe has insurance benefits to M.V. NAN GUI JI 035.

The court of second instance found out that, after accepting LIN Guihe's insurance, PICC Shunde issued the insurance policy on April 12, 2007. According to the Insurance Law of the People's Republic of China (2002) Article 12, as the policy holder, LIN Guihe should have an insurance interest in M.V. NAN GUI JI 035, the subject of the insurance contract. LIN Guihe submitted the Ship Management Agreement to the court of second instance, advocating that he borrowed 5 million yuan from the shipowner YANG Xiong. YANG Xiong mortgaged the ship and repaid the loan with part of the operating income of the ship, and agreed that he had the right to participate in the management of the ship and apply for insurance in his own name, so he had an insurance interest in the ship.

Because the parties in this case disputed the formation time of the *Ship Management Agreement*, the court of second instance entrusted Guangdong Nantian Judicial Appraisal Institute to appraise the formation time of the printed text and handwritten signature in the agreement. The Institute issued Yue Nan [2014] Wen Jian Zi No.666 Judicial Appraisal Opinion, which stated that: the formation time of the printed text on the Ship Management Agreement and the signature texts of "LIN Guihe" and "YANG Xiong" were not the nominal time, but were formed around December 2007. Guangdong Nantian Judicial Appraisal Institute was an appraisal institute with judicial appraisal permission including document appraisal and trace appraisal. The personnel involved in the appraisal of the involved documents possess the corresponding judicial appraisal practice certificate. The procedure was legal. The parties of the case recognized that, there was no relevant national standard, industry standard or technical standard or technical standard recognized by most experts in the field in terms of the time of document preparation. According to the General Rules of Judicial Appraisal Procedure of the Ministry of Justice Article 22, in the absence of corresponding national standards and technical specifications, industry standards and technical specifications, and technical standards and technical specifications recognized by most experts in the professional field, the appraisal agency could apply the relevant technical specifications formulated by itself to carry out appraisal work. Guangdong Nantian Judicial Appraisal Institute used the self-developed technical specifications in this appraisal. The technology obtained national patents and was confirmed and filed by the competent judicial administrative agency. LIN Guihe disputed the appraisal on the grounds that the appraisal method was not recognized by the relevant state authorities and recognized in the industry, which lacked legal basis. LIN Guihe did not provide sufficient evidence to prove that the technical specifications adopted in this appraisal were inappropriate and affected the accuracy of the results. According to the Some Provisions of the Supreme People's Court on Evidence in Civil Procedures Article 71, the court of second instance confirmed the probative force of the appraisal opinion, the confirmation of the conclusion was not inappropriate. LIN Guihe applied for reassessment, but did not provide evidence to prove that there were situations that should be reassessed as stipulated in the Some Provisions of the

Supreme People's Court on Evidence in Civil Procedures Article 27 Paragraph 1, the court of second instance disapproval the application for reassessment, which is not inappropriate. According to the conclusion of the Judicial Appraisal Opinion, the Ship Management Agreement submitted by LIN Guihe was actually formed around December 2007, later than the establishment time of the ship insurance contract involved, and later than the time when the ship touched the bridge accident. LIN Guihe had an insurance interest in the ship involved at the time of establishment or when the touch accident involved happened. In order to confirm the relationship between LIN Guihe and M.V. NAN GUI JI 035, the amount of loans, repayments and outstanding amounts between him and YANG Xiong claimed by LIN Guihe, the court of second instance conducted inquiry surveys to the outsiders YANG Xiong and YANG Sanzhu. YANG Xiong, YANG Sanzhu, LIN Guihe's statements on the specific matters of loans and repayments had obvious contradictions, and none of them could provide bank vouchers, written vouchers, or other evidence related to the loans, repayments, and reconciliations involved. The court of second instance confirmed that the statements and investigation records of the above parties were insufficient to prove the objective existence of the fact that LIN Guihe borrowed money from YANG Xiong, which is not inappropriate. LIN Guihe's statement that he was engaged in rent collection, annual inspections and crew participation in connection with M.V. NAN GUI JI 035 is not sufficient to prove that LIN Guihe had an insurance interest in the ship involved. The Plaintiff in other case submitted by LIN Guihe is China People's Property & Casualty Co., Ltd. Guangdong Branch, it is not the party, PICC Shunde, of this case, and the time of compliant is March 24, 2008, which is before the issuance of the Judicial Appraisal Opinion, so LIN Guihe claimed that PICC Shunde recognized that he had insurance benefits to the ship involved, which lacks basis.

Pulling the threads together, the court of second instance confirmed that LIN Guihe had no insurance benefits to the ship involved, which is not inappropriate. The application of retrial of LIN Guihe is not according to the Civil Procedure Law of the People's Republic of China Article 200. According to the Civil Procedure Law of the People's Republic of China Article 204 Paragraph 1, the ruling is as follows:

Dismiss the application of retrial of LIN Guihe.

Presiding Judge: HU Fang
Judge: LI Guishun
Acting Judge: HOU Wei

September 2, 2016

Clerk: LI Na

Wuhan Maritime Court
Civil Judgment

LIU Fengxi
v.
Ningbo Junsheng Yuanda Shipping Co., Ltd. et al.

(2015) Wu Hai Fa Shang Zi No.00599

Related Case(s) None.

Cause(s) of Action 226. Dispute over contract for employment of seaman.

Headnote The Plaintiff seafarer held to be entitled to recover underpaid wages from contractual employer and owner of vessel on which he had worked; the Defendants were jointly and severally liable, and the Plaintiff was held to be entitled to a maritime lien over the vessel.

Summary The Plaintiff LIU Fengxi, upon arrangement with the Defendant Shanglun, boarded M.V. YUAN SHENG 18 at Changzhou Port in Jiangsu and worked as the fourth engineer. Due to a downturn in the shipping market, Plaintiff was to disembark the ship at Zhoushan Port in Zhejiang. On the day of his disembarkation, Defendant Shanglun paid the Plaintiff repatriation expenses in the sum of RMB800. The next day, Plaintiff and Defendant Shanglun settled wages in which the wage confirmation form recorded LIU Fengxi as having served as the fourth engineer of M.V. YUAN SHENG 18 but wages for four months totaling RMB16,900 were deducted. Plaintiff filed a lawsuit, claiming payment of his wages, repatriation expenses, lawyer's fees and other fees against the Defendants, and requested the court to confirm he should be entitled to a maritime lien over M. V. YUAN SHENG 18.

The court confirmed that a contract existed between Plaintiff and Defendant Junsheng, which was the owner of M.V. YUAN SHENG 18, and that Defendant Junsheng was the actual employer of Plaintiff. Plaintiff had provided labor services, so Defendant Shanglun should pay wages accordingly. The Plaintiff's actual workplace was M.V. YUAN SHENG 18 owned by Defendant Junsheng, which had used and controlled Plaintiff's labor. Accordingly the court held the two Defendants were jointly and severally liable for the Plaintiff's wages. Plaintiff was entitled to a maritime lien over M.V. YUAN SHENG 18.

Judgment

The Plaintiff: LIU Fengxi, male, Han, born on December 31, 1970, living in Hai'an Jiangsu
Agent *ad litem*: XIA Bing, lawyer of Beijing Zhonglun W&D (Wuhan) Law Firm.

The Defendant: Ningbo Junsheng Yuanda Shipping Co., Ltd.
Domicile: 15/F, Block B, Pacific Place, No.565, Jingjia Road, Jiangdong District, Ningbo City, Zhejiang.
Legal representative: SUN Hecheng, chairman.

The Defendant: Ningbo Shanglun Co., Ltd.
Domicile: Fl.15, Block B, Pacific Place, No.565 Jingjia Road, Jiangdong District, Ningbo City, Zhejiang.
Legal representative: CHEN Shide, general manager.

With respect to the case arising from a seafarer labor contract dispute, the Plaintiff LIU Fengxi filed an action against the Defendants Ningbo Junsheng Yuanda Shipping Co., Ltd. (hereinafter referred to as Junsheng Company), and Ningbo Shanglun Co., Ltd. (hereinafter referred to as Shanglun Company), since the registry port of the Plaintiff's ship is Jiangsu Province Changzhou City, which is under the jurisdiction of the court, according to Article 6 Paragraph 2 Sub-paragraph 5 of the Special Maritime Procedure Law of the People's Republic of China, the court shall have jurisdiction. After entertaining this case on April 22, 2015, the court applied to summary procedure and appointed Judge CHEN Rong as sole judge. On May 25, the court held a hearing in public, XIA Bing, agent *ad litem* of the Plaintiff LIU Fengxi, appeared in court and participated in the hearing. The Defendants Junsheng Company and Shanglun Company did not appear in court to participate in the hearing without proper reason after being summoned by the court, the court tried the case by default. Now the case has been concluded.

The Plaintiff LIU Fengxi alleged as follows: on January 18, 2015, the Defendant Shanglun Company arranged him to work on board M.V. YUAN SHENG 18 which was owned by the Defendant Junsheng Company, the boarding port was Changzhou Port in Jiangsu. On April 17, 2015, the Plaintiff left from the ship at Zhoushan Port in Ningbo. Upon the confirmation of the Plaintiff and Shanglun Company, during the period the Plaintiff worked on M.V. YUAN SHENG 18, the Plaintiff still had not received four months of wages in sum of RMB16,900 yuan. According to the Maritime Code of the People's Republic of China, the seafarer's claim for wages fell into maritime lien. The actual employing unit Junsheng Company and the employer Shanglun Company were obliged to pay the wages jointly and severally. The Plaintiff filed an action to protect his legal interests, and requested the court to judge: 1. the two Defendants should pay the wages in sum of RMB16,900 yuan; 2. the two Defendants should pay the repatriation costs in sum of RMB2,000 yuan; 3. the two Defendants should compensate for the lawyer's fee of the Plaintiff in sum of RMB850 yuan; 4. the Plaintiff should shall be entitled to payment in priority from the proceeds of the auction price of M.V. YUAN SHENG 18; 5. the two Defendants should bear the litigation fees of this case.

The Defendant Junsheng Company did not appear in court to participate in the hearing, it submitted an oral defense before the hearing, alleging: it confirmed the Plaintiff's claim for the wages. The Plaintiff has received the repatriation expenses in sum of RMB800 yuan, the registration form signed by the Plaintiff could prove. The Plaintiff's attorney's fee had no merits, it did not confirm.

The Defendant Shanglun Company did not appear in court to participate in the procedures, it submitted an oral defense before the hearing, alleging: it confirmed the Plaintiff's claim for the wages. It did not recognized the repatriation expenses, and argued that it paid the disembarkation travel expenses to the Plaintiff on the day of repatriation, namely April 16, 2015, the registration form signed by the Plaintiff could prove that.

In order to support his claims, LIU Fengxi submitted the following evidence to the court within the time limit of adducing evidence:

1. A copy of the Nationality Certificate of M.V. YUAN SHENG 18, to prove the registered owner of the ship on which the Plaintiff worked namely M.V. YUAN SHENG 18 was the Defendant Junsheng Company, and the operator was the Defendant Shanglun Company.
2. Salary confirmation form, to prove that on April 17, 2015, the Defendant Shanglun Company confirmed it owed the Plaintiff LIU Fengxi the wages in amount of RMB16,900 yuan.
3. Seafarer's Competency Certificate of the Plaintiff, to prove the proper capacity of the Plaintiff.
4. The seafarer's service book of the Plaintiff, to prove the Plaintiff boarded on M.V. YUAN SHENG 18, as well as the time and place of boarding and disembarkation.
5. Civil Commission Contract, invoice of lawyer's fee and receipts, to prove that the Plaintiff has actually paid lawyer's fee.

The court holds that evidence 1-5 submitted by the Plaintiff have the authenticity, and the evidence can corroborate. The two Defendants, without proper reason, did not appear in court to participate in the procedures, its shall deem as waiver of the right of cross-examination. At the same time, the two Defendants confirmed the amount of the wages they owed to the Plaintiff in the defense. Therefore, the court admits the evidence mentioned above. The evidence can be admitted as the basis for the finding of facts.

The Defendant Junsheng Company did not submit evidence during the time limit of adducing evidence.

In support of its defense, the Defendant Shanglun Company submitted the following evidence to the court during the time limit of adducing evidence: the registration form of seafarers' disembarkation travel fee on M.V. YUAN SHENG 18, to prove that the Defendant had paid the Plaintiff LIU Fengxi the repatriation expenses in sum of RMB800 yuan.

The Plaintiff LIU Fengxi raised no objection to the authenticity of the evidence.

The court holds that the registration form of travel expenses submitted by the Defendant Shanglun Company, the Plaintiff had no objection to the authenticity thereof, it can be admitted as evidence to identify the facts of this case.

After adducing evidence and authentication in court, combined with the statements of the parties, the court finds the following facts:

On January 18, 2015, the Plaintiff LIU Fengxi, upon arrangement by the Defendant Shanglun Company, boarded on M.V. YUAN SHENG 18 at in Changzhou Port in Jiangsu Province and work as the fourth engineer. Due to the downturn in shipping market, on April 16 in the same year, the Plaintiff was to disembark the ship at Zhoushan Port in Zhejiang. On that day, the Defendant Shanglun Company paid the Plaintiff repatriation expenses in sum of RMB800 yuan. On April 17, the Plaintiff and the Defendant Shanglun Company settled wages, the wage confirmation form recorded LIU Fengxi served as the fourth engineer of M.V. YUAN SHENG 18, wages of four months in total amount of RMB16,900 yuan were defaulted, the Plaintiff confirmed with signature, and Shanglun Company confirmed with seal. On April 20, the Plaintiff signed a Civil Commission Contract with XIA Bing, an attorney of Beijing Zhonglun W&D (Wuhan) to commission XIA Bing as his attorney. On April 21, the Plaintiff paid XIA Bing the attorney fee in sum of RMB850 yuan. On the same day, the Plaintiff filed a lawsuit, claiming for payment of his wages, repatriation expenses, lawyer's fee and other fees against the Defendants, and requesting the court to confirm he should be entitled to maritime lien in terms of the above-mentioned fees on M.V. YUAN SHENG 18.

It is also found that the Defendant Junsheng Company is the registered owner of M.V. YUAN SHENG 18, and the Defendant Shanglun Company is the registered operator. On May 4, 2015, the Plaintiff LIU Fengxi filed an application for property preservation to the court, he requested the court to seal M.V. YUAN SHENG 18, the ship owned by the Defendant Junsheng Company, the court made a ruling to permit such application.

The court holds that this case is concerning dispute over the seafarer labor contract. The Plaintiff LIU Fengxi was arranged by the Defendant Junsheng Company to work on M.V. YUAN SHENG 18 which was owned by the Defendant Shanglun Company, the court, on the basis of the facts that the Defendant Shanglun Company arranged the Plaintiff to work on board the ship, settled unpaid wages with the Plaintiff, and paid repatriation expenses, etc., ascertains the contractual relationship between the Plaintiff and the Defendant was established, and the Defendant Shanglun Company is the actual employing unit of the Plaintiff. The Plaintiff has provided labor services, the Defendant Shanglun Company should pay the corresponding wages. The Plaintiff's actual workplace is M.V. YUAN SHENG 18 owned by the Defendant Junsheng Company, the Defendant Junsheng Company is the user and dominator of the Plaintiff's labor force, it should be the actual employment unit of the Plaintiff. Both the Defendants Shanglun Company and Junsheng Company are counterparties of the Plaintiff in the labor relationship, they benefited from the Plaintiff's labor. Article 66 of the Labor Contract Law of the

PRC stipulates that labor dispatch is generally carried out on temporary, supplementary or alternative jobs. The Defendant Junsheng Company arranged the Plaintiff who has a seafarer's certificate of competency of to work on the ship involved in a certain position, which was not temporary or auxiliary position, and it does not conform to the provisions.

In this case, the two Defendants did not appear before court and participate in the procedures without proper reason, nor submitted to the court between the two Defendants to send the labor contract, it can be regarded as unclear agreement on the obligations such as payment of wages. In summary, the act of the two Defendants damages the Plaintiff's economic interests, they shall be jointly and severally liable for the wages of the Plaintiff. Since the Plaintiff has received disembarkation travel expense in sum of RMB800 yuan from the Defendant Shanglun Company, he did not submit any evidence to prove that the travel expenses actually generated. Therefore, the court does not support the claim of the Plaintiff the Defendant should pay the repatriation expense in sum of RMB2,000 yuan. The Plaintiff requested that the two Defendants to pay the attorney' fees, the court does not support. According to Article 22 Paragraph 1 of the Maritime Code of the People's Republic of China, seafarers' wages falls into scope of the maritime claims which shall be entitled to maritime liens. The court affirms that the Plaintiff enjoys maritime lien in respect of his wages during M.V. YUAN SHENG 18.

In summary, according to Article 30 Paragraph 1 and Article 92 of the Labor Contract Law of the People's Republic of China, Article 21 and Article 22 Paragraph 1 of the Maritime Code of the People's Republic of China, Article 144 of the Civil Procedure Law of the People's Republic of China, the judgment is as follows:

1. The Defendant Ningbo Shanglun Co., Ltd. shall pay the Plaintiff LIU Fengxi the wage in sum of RMB16,900 yuan one time within 10 days after the effective date of this judgment;
2. The Defendant Ningbo Junsheng Yuanda Shipping Co., Ltd. shall bear joint and several liability for the aforementioned payment;
3. Confirm the Plaintiff LIU Fengxi shall enjoy maritime lien in terms of the wages in sum of RMB16,900 yuan against M.V. YUAN SHENG 18 which is owned by the Defendant Ningbo Junsheng Yuanda Shipping Co., Ltd.;
4. Reject other claims of the Plaintiff LIU Fengxi.

If the Defendants fail to fulfill its obligation to make the said payments within the time limit provided by this judgment, the interest shall be double paid for the period of deferred payment according to Article 253 of the Civil Procedure Law of the People's Republic of China.

Court acceptance fee shall be reduced by half to RMB5 yuan due to the application of summary procedures, and litigation preservation fee is RMB189 yuan, the total sum is RMB194 yuan, shall be born by the Defendants Ningbo Junsheng Yuanda Shipping Co., Ltd. and the Defendant Ningbo Shanglun Co., Ltd. The two Defendants shall pay the court acceptance fee together with the sum designated by the first and two items of this judgment to the Plaintiff LIU Fengxi.

If dissatisfy with this judgment, the parties may, within fifteen days as of the service of this judgment, submit a Statement of Appeal to the court, with duplicates in the number of the opposing parties, so as to make an appeal before the Hubei High People's Court.

The Appellant shall prepay the case entertainment fee in terms of the dissatisfied sum as determined in this judgment according to Article 13 Paragraph 1 of the Measures on the Payment of Litigation Costs, and remit to the Hubei Province Prime People's Court. Bank of Deposit: Agricultural Bank of China Wuhan City East Lake Branch; Account Name: Hubei Province Department of Finance Non-tax Revenue Fiscal Account; Account Number: 052101040000369. The bank voucher shall indicate Hubei High People's Court or the unit code "103001" of Hubei High People's Court. If the Appellant fails to prepay the appeal fee within seven days after the expiration of the appeal period, the appeal shall be automatically withdrawn.

Acting Judge: CHEN Rong

May 30, 2015

Clerk: WANG Peilin

Wuhan Maritime Court
Civil Judgment

MAO Chuanwu
v.
Fengdu County Fengping Shipping Investment Co., Ltd.

(2015) Wu Hai Fa Shang Zi No.00134

Related Case(s) None.

Cause(s) of Action 207. Dispute over shipbuilding contract.

Headnote Purchaser of newly-built ship held to be entitled to withhold from payment to shipbuilder sums that purchaser had paid to workers injured during shipbuilding process, as the shipbuilding contract provided that any injuries were to be solely the responsibility of the shipbuilder and not the purchaser.

Summary The Plaintiff MAO Chuanwu was hired to build six vessels for Defendant, Fengdu County Fengping Shipping Investment Co., Ltd. The Defendant paid an advance to the Plaintiff, which included a portion of the price of the ships and other expenses. Defendant refused to pay the full amount of the balance of the purchase price, and Plaintiff sued to collect the withheld amount. The contract between the parties included a provision stating that MAO Chuanwu should strictly implement operational procedures and should prohibit operations that were against safety rules, and that liability for any occurrence of injury, disability and death should be solely born by MAO Chuanwu without any liability of Fengping Company. Three workers hired by MAO Chuanwu were injured during the construction of one of the six vessels. Fengping paid for all of the medical expenses and costs associated with the accident. The Court held that MAO Chuanwu was liable for the medical costs and that Fengping's was entitled to deduct its contribution from the remaining payment due for the six vessels.

Judgment

The Plaintiff: MAO Chuanwu, male, born on December 4, 1949, living in Fengdu County, Chongqing City.
Agent *ad litem*: ZHANG Kun, lawyer of Chongqing Xinkai Law Firm.

The Defendant: Fengdu County Fengping Shipping Investment Co., Ltd.
Domicile: Group 6, Dingzhuang Village, Sanhe Street, Fengdu County, Chongqing City.
Organization Code: 68149449-8.
Agent *ad litem*: QIN Guo, lawyer of Chongqing Tianyu Sanxing Law Firm.

With respect of the case arising from dispute over shipbuilding contract, the Plaintiff MAO Chuanwu filed an action against the Defendant Fengdu County Fengping Shipping Investment Co., Ltd. (hereinafter referred as "Fengping Company") before the court on January 8, 2015, this case was concerning dispute over a maritime contract, and the domicile of Fengping Company was Fengdu County, Chongqing, which was under the case entertainment scope and jurisdiction area of the court. The court had jurisdiction over the case according to law. After docketing the case on January 13, 2015, Judge GONG Wenjing was designated to be sole judge to try this case under summary procedure. Then, because of the complexity of this case, the court legitimately tried the case according to the general procedure. The collegiate panel was consisted of Presiding Judge LIU Dong, Judge KONG Linggang and Acting Judge JIANG Zhangpeng. This case was tried in public on April 27, 2015 and June 30, 2015. The Plaintiff MAO Chuanwu, ZHANG Kun, agent *ad litem* of the Plaintiff and QIN Guo, agent *ad litem* of the Defendant Fengping Company, appeared in court and participated in the action. This case has now been concluded.

The Plaintiff MAO Chuanwu alleged that he had altogether constructed 6 hulls and pontoons for Fengping Company during February 2010 and September 2011. The ship prices due was RMB2,168,205. Fengping Company actually paid RMB2,012,205. Deducting the ship prices in sum of RMB13,795, which Fengping Company should pay to it, ruled by Wuhan Maritime Court in another case, Fengping Company still defaulted MAO Chuanwu the ship prices in sum of RMB142,205. After several unsuccessful collections, MAO Chuanwu sued and requested the court to order the Fengping Company to pay the outstanding ship prices in sum of RMB142,205 together with the interest thereon and liquidated damages in sum of RMB60,000, and to bear the litigation fee of this case.

The Defendant contended that: 1. upon verification, the fact that MAO Chuanwu built the above-mentioned ships for Fengping Company was true and Fengping Company had actually paid RMB2,012,205 to MAO Chuanwu; 2. the agreed ship prices of M.V. "Jiang Ji Yun 1219" should be RMB68,000 rather than RMB76,000 alleged by MAO Chuanwu; in addition to the money paid to MAO Chuanwu, Fengping Company also advanced compensation for industrial injuries, living expenses and insurance premiums for MAO Chuanwu. After the relevant fees were settled, Fengping Company no longer defaulted MAO Chuanwu any money. What MAO Chuanwu alleged was untrue; and 3. the disputes of this case had been tried by another court, thus, MAO Chuanwu loaged two suits in terms of the same case. In conclusion, Fengping Company requested the court to reject the claims of MAO Chuanwu.

To support his claims, the Plaintiff MAO Chuanwu submitted the following evidence to the court:

Evidence 1: the 48m Floating Crane pontoon Hull Construction Contract, to prove MAO Chuanwu built the 48m floating crane pontoon hull for the Fengping Company and the ship price was RMB68,000.

Evidence 2: the Hull Construction Contract for M.V. "Jiang Ji Yun 1209", to prove the total ship price of the ship was RMB510,000.

Evidence 3: a material issued by Fengping Company, to prove the subsequent construction and management fees for M.V. "Jiang Ji Yun 1207" and M.V. "Jiang Ji Yun 1208" and added processing fee for M.V. "Jiang Ji Yun 1210" were altogether RMB43,000.

Evidence 4: Hull Construction Contract, to prove the ship price of M.V. "Jiang Ji Yun 1231" was RMB760,000.

Evidence 5: a copy of the starting meeting for the ship M.V. "Jiang Ji Yun 1219" and the related list of participants, to prove the ship was built by MAO Chuanwu.

Evidence 6: a book of account, to prove the total ship prices MAO Chuanwu received was RMB2,012,205. Deducting the RMB13,795 confirmed by Wuhan Maritime Court, Fengping Company shall still pay RMB142,205.

Evidence 7: partial payee checks and banking statements issued by MAO Chuanwu copied from Fengping Company, to prove the ship prices that Fengping Company had paid was RMB2,012,205.

Evidence 8: written testimonies of Witness ZHANG Gan, CHEN Gang and LI Yanhua and the notarial deed thereof, to prove M.V. "Jiang Ji Yun 1219" was built by MAO Chuanwu and the ship prices was RMB760,000.

Evidence 9: Inland Ship Inspection Certificates of M.V. "Jiang Ji Yun 1219", M.V. "Jiang Ji Yun 1231", M.V. "Jiang Ji Yun 1208", M.V. "Jiang Ji Yun 1207", M.V. "Jiang Ji Yun 1210" and the pontoon "Yuantong Floating Crane 6", to prove the ships built by MAO Chuanwu all passed through the inspection.

Evidence 10: 5 copies of Shipbuilding Inspection Application, to prove that MAO Chuanwu applied for the ship inspection.

Evidence 11: (2013) Wu Hai Fa Shang Zi No.00264 Civil Judgment and (2014) E Min Si Zhong Zi No.00264 Civil Judgment, to prove the court only confirmed that Fengping Company defaulted RMB13,795 ship prices for M.V. "Jiang Ji Yun 1231".

Evidence 12: excerpt records of Fengping Company's VAT and turnover provided by MAO Chuanwu through Fengdu Administration of Taxation, to prove the ship prices involved in the 6 payment receipts issued by MAO Chuanwu which were not provided to the court by Fengping Company, could be referred to the excerpt records.

Evidence 13: CD and evidence of identity of Witness Mao Chuanrong and LI Yanhua, to prove M.V. "Jiang Ji Yun 1231" was built by MAO Chuanwu.

After the first evidence exchange, MAO Chuanwu applied to the court for ordering the Expenses Claim Sheet of the 6 case-involved ships and the Receipt issued by MAO Chuanwu from Fengping Company. He also applied to the court for ordering the trial records of the (2013) Wu Hai Fa Shang Chu Zi No.00264 Civil Judgment, to prove the ship prices Fengping Company has paid to the MAO Chuanwu. And before the second trial, MAO Chuanwu applied for Witness CHEN Gang, LI Yanhua and Qin Dayun to testify in court, to prove the construction situation of M.V. "Jiang Ji Yun 1219". Since Fengping Company recognized MAO Chuanwu built M.V. "Jiang Ji Yun 1219" and confirmed the actual ship prices it paid to MAO Chuanwu in the second trial, MAO Chuanwu withdrew the application for ordering evidence and witness's testifying in court in the second trial. And after the first evidence exchange, MAO Chuanwu applied to the court for conducting survey of the starting situation of the ship M.V. "Jiang Ji Yun 1219" from Chongqing Peiling Port and Shipping Authority, to prove MAO Chuanwu actually built the ship for Fengping Company. Since Fengping Company recognized this fact in the second hearing, MAO Chuanwu expressed that he would not submit the investigative records made by the court at Chongqing Peiling Port and Shipping Authority as evidence, the court permits that.

As regard to the evidence submitted by MAO Chuanwu, the cross-examination of Fengping Company argued that: 1. it had no objection to the authenticity of evidence 1, 2, 3 and 4, but the involved dispute had been tried in another case; 2. evidence 5 was a copy, it questioned the authenticity of evidence 5 and the purpose MAO Chuanwu wanted to prove; 3. evidence 6 was made unilaterally by MAO Chuanwu and had no probative force; 4. evidence 7 was a copy and its authenticity should not be confirmed; 5. as for evidence 8, all the witnesses did not appear in court, thus the authenticity of their testimonies could not be confirmed; 6. it had no objection to the authenticity of evidence 9, but this evidence could not prove MAO Chuanwu was the shipbuilder; 7. it had no objection to the authenticity of Evidence 10, but this evidence had no relations with this case; 8. it had no objection to the authenticity, legality or relevancy of evidence 11, this evidence proved that the dispute involved had been tried; 9. it had no objection to the authenticity of evidence 12, but this evidence had no relations with this case; 10. the witnesses mentioned in evidence 13 did not appear in court, thus the authenticity of their testimonies shall not be confirmed.

The court holds that: since Fengping Company has no objection to the authenticity of evidence 1, 2, 3, 4, 9, 10, 11 and 12, the court affirms the evidence according to the law. As evidence to identify relevant facts of this case, evidence 5 provided by MAO Chuanwu conforms to the facts identified by the trial, so the court affirms it according to the law; although evidence 6 is an unilateral document made by MAO Chuanwu, Fengping Company admits its actual payment to MAO Chuanwu, so the court affirms this partial fact; evidence 7 can corroborate with evidence 4 submitted by Fengping Company, so the court affirms it according to the law; although the witnesses mentioned in evidence 8 and evidence 13 could not appear in court, Fengping Company admitted the fact that MAO Chuanwu actually built M.V. "Jiang Ji Yun 1219", so the court affirms this fact. But the above testimonies cannot prove the ship prices of M.V. "Jiang Ji Yun 1219" is RMB760,000.

To support its allegations, Fengping Company provided the following evidence to the court within the time limit:

Evidence 1: (2013) Wu Hai Fa Shang Zi No.00264 Civil Judgment and (2014) E Min Si Zhong Zi No.00264 Civil Judgment, to prove the case-involved dispute has been tried, relevant legal documents have come into effect and this case shall not be tried again.

Evidence 2: the 48m Floating Crane pontoon Hull Construction Contract, the Construction Project Contract for M.V. "Jiang Ji Yun 1209" and the Hull Construction Contract, to prove the rights and obligations of both parties during the construction of the ship.

Evidence 3: [2012] Feng Ren She Shang Xian Ren Jue Zi No.68 Determination of Work Injury, [2012] Feng Ren Jian (Chu) Zi No.103 Conclusion, a copy of Expenses Claim Sheet, a copy of Receipt, a copy of Chongqing Fengdu Special Hospital Medical Expenses Receipt, 3 copies of People's Liberation Army Health Care Special Medical Expenses Receipt, a copy of Special Compensation Note of Chongqing Medical Use of Blood and the Chongqing Work Injury Insurance Medical (Rehabilitation) Expenses Audit Statement, to prove that Fengping Company advanced the RMB173,645 work injury compensation expenses for MAO Jiayan, one of MAO Chuanwu's workers; 2. a copy of Expenses Claim Sheet and 1 copy of Receipt, the [2013] Feng Lao Ren Zhong An Zi No.115 Arbitral Meditation, the [2013] Feng Ren Jian (Chu) Zi No.70 Disability Certificate and the [2012] Feng Ren She Shang Xian Ren Jue Zi No.51 Conclusion, to prove Fengping Company advanced the RMB55,000 work injury compensation expenses for QIN Dayuan, one of MAO Chuanwu's workers; 3. a copy of Expenses Claim Sheet and 1 copy of Receipt, the [2012] Feng Lao Ren Zhong An Zi No.153 Written Arbitral Meditation, the [2012] Feng Ren She Shang Xian Ren Jue Zi No.53 Disability Certificate and the [2012] Feng Ren Jian (Chu) Zi No.106 Conclusion, to prove Fengping Company advanced the RMB40,000 worker injury compensation for LI Yongde, one of MAO Chuanwu's workers;

Evidence 4: 1. 2 copies of Living Expenses Sheets of All Vonstruction Teams in Fengping Company, the Attendance Sheet and the Staff Meal Table of Fengping Shipyard from October 2011 to July 2012, to prove that meal expenses of MAO Chuanwu's workers in Fengping Company was RMB21,430; 2. 3 copies of Premium Tables of All Construction Teams in Fengping Company, to prove that Fengping Company advanced the RMB9,274.5 premium for MAO Chuanwu's workers, which is part of the cost born by MAO Chuanwu according to the contract.

Evidence 5: 26 Receipts, to prove that the actual ship prices and other expenses Fengping Company paid to MAO Chuanwu was RMB2,012,205.

Through cross-examination, MAO Chuanwu held that: 1. he had no objection to the authenticity of evidence 1, but (2013) Wu Hai Fa Shang Zi No.00264 was an lawsuit for M.V. "Jiang Ji Yun 1231" and the current lawsuit was for 6 ships; he had no objection to the authenticity and relevancy of evidence 2; 3. he had no objection to the authenticity of evidence 3 and confirmed MAO Jiayan, QIN

Dayuan, LI Yongde were MAO Chuanwu's workers, but the worker injury compensation shall be born by Fengping Company; 4. he questioned the authenticity of evidence 4 regarding meal expenses and held that during the construction of M.V. "Jiang Ji Yun 1231", the workers actually had meals in Fengping Company, but the amount of the expenses was not clear; as for the premiums, Fengping Company indeed bought premiums for his workers, but the premium amount and the insured were not clear without specific lists; and 5. he had no objection to evidence 5.

The court holds that: since MAO Chuanwu has no objection to the authenticity of evidence 1, 2, 3 and 5 submitted by Fengping Company, the court affirms the evidence according to the law and adopts the evidence as basis to identify relevant facts of this case; Evidence 4 is a document unilaterally made by Fengping Company, but MAO Chuanwu admitted his workers actually had meals in Fengping Company during the construction of M.V. "Jiang Ji Yun 1231", so the court affirms the authenticity of this partial facts; as for the premiums, the court holds that Fengping Company did not provide enough evidence to prove that it had bought insurance for MAO Chuanwu's workers and did not provide relevant premium receipts, so the court does not ascertain this part of expenses.

The court finds the following facts:

On February 20, 2010, MAO Chuanwu signed the *48m Floating Crane Pontoon Hull Construction Contract* with Fengping Company, agreeing that MAO Chuanwu built a pontoon for Fengping Company and the total project ship price was RMB68,000. On March 11, the two parties signed the Hull Construction Contract for M.V. "Jiang Ji Yun 1209", agreeing that MAO Chuanwu would construct the 91.8m hull and the total project ship price was RMB510,000.

On July 3, Fengping Company adjusted the total ship price to RMB515,000. Article 5 of the above-mentioned two contracts stipulate:

1. MAO Chuanwu shall strictly implement the operation procedures and prohibit operations against rules to avoid accidents. Any occurrence of large and small injury, disability and death accident shall be solely born by MAO Chuanwu, and has no relations with Fengping Company. The costs have been included in the ship price.
2. MAO Chuanwu shall buy accident insurances for construction workers. The beneficiary was MAO Chuanwu. On September 20, 2011, MAO Chuanwu signed the Hull Construction Contract with Fengping Company, agreeing that MAO Chuanwu built a ship (M.V. "Jiang Ji Yun 1231"), which is 107.8m in length, 17.2m in breadth and 5.6m in depth, for Fengping Company and the ship price was RMB760,000; MAO Chuanwu shall strictly implement the operation procedures and prohibit operations against rules to avoid accidents. Any occurrence of large and small injury, disability and death accident shall be solely born by MAO Chuanwu and with no relations with Fengping Company; MAO Chuanwu shall buy accident insurances for construction workers. The beneficiary was MAO Chuanwu. Fengping Company shall bear physical examination fee of 40 or less people and other fees shall be born by the MAO Chuanwu. In addition to the above-mentioned three ships, MAO Chuanwu had an oral

agreement with Fengping Company in 2010, agreeing that MAO Chuanwu would build a ship (M.V. "Jiang Ji Yun 1219") with the same specifications of M.V. "Jiang Ji Yun 1231". In addition, MAO Chuanwu had an oral agreement with Fengping Company in March 2010, agreeing that MAO Chuanwu would in charge of the subsequent construction and management of M.V. "Jiang Ji Yun 1207" and M.V. "Jiang Ji Yun 1208". The living expenses of workers which ought to be paid by Fengping Company was RMB68,000. During the performance of the above-mentioned contract, Fengping Company had paid 26 sums to MAO Chuanwu, altogether amounting to RMB2,012,205.

During the performance of the above-mentioned shipbuilding contract, MAO Chuanwu hired workers to be responsible for the construction of specific projects according to the agreement. Among these workers, LI Yongde, MAO Jiayann and QIN Dayuan respectively were injured in December 2011, April 2012 and May 2012. Fengping Company paid worker injury compensation in amount of RMB40,000 to LI Yongde. Fengping Company paid worker injury compensation in amount of RMB60,000 to MAO Jiayan and advanced medical expenses in amount of RMB113,645 for him. And Fengping Company paid worker injury compensation in amount of RMB55,000 to QIN Dayuan. The above payments were altogether RMB268,645.

Since the beginning of the construction of M.V. "Jiang Ji Yun 1231", workers employed by MAO Chuanwu had been having meals in Fengping Company. From September 2011 to July 2012, the meal expenses were RMB21,430.

It is also found that on January 14, 2013, MAO Chuanwu filed a lawsuit before the court as Fengping Company defaulted the ship price of M.V. "Jiang Ji Yun 1231" in amount of RMB134,570. After the first trial, the final judgment of Hubei High People's Court recognized that Fengping Company defaulted in the payment of RMB13,795 ship prices of M.V. "Jiang Ji Yun 1231" for MAO Chuanwu.

The court holds that this case is concerning dispute over ship construction contract. The written contracts and oral agreements are both the real intentions of MAO Chuanwu and Fengping Company, shall lawfully establish and be legitimate and effective. Both parties shall exercise their rights and fully perform their obligations according to the contracts. Any breaching of the agreements shall bear corresponding civil liabilities. Although MAO Chuanwu filed a lawsuit in terms of Fengping Company's default of the ship price of M.V. "Jiang Ji Yun 1231" in (2013) Wu Hai Fa Shang Zi No.00264 Case, he claimed for settlement of the ship prices of six ships altogether in this case. The claims, supporting facts and reasons of the two cases are different, so they are not repeated cases. The claim that this case violating "the ne bis in idem principle" raised by Fengping Company lacks factual and legal basis, so the court does not support it.

In view that both parties made settlements of the ship prices of the six ships altogether in the lawsuit, so the court will verify the costs occurred during the construction of the six ships, and determine the final settlement amount. According to the trial, the outstanding issues of this case are as follows: 1. What is the specific ship price of the ship M.V. "Jiang Ji Yun 1219" agreed orally by the two parties? 2.

Who shall bear the compensation for worker injury of MAO Jiayan, QIN Dayuan and LI Yongde advanced by Fengping Company? 3. Whether the living expense and premiums advanced by Fengping Company are true and who shall bear them?

As to the first issue, the court holds that both parties signed no written contract for the construction of M.V. "Jiang Ji Yun 1219". MAO Chuanwu held that the construction costs were RMB760,000, on the ground that the specifications of M.V. "Jiang Ji Yun 1219" were the same as those of M.V. "Jiang Ji Yun 1231", the ship prices should be naturally identical; Fengping Company held that the ship price of M.V. "Jiang Ji Yun 1219" was RMB680,000 according to oral agreement, on the ground that the specifications of M.V. "Jiang Ji Yun 1231" were the same as those of M.V. "Jiang Ji Yun 1219", but their construction time had a one-year gap. Because of the rising prices and rising labor costs, the ship prices of M.V. "Jiang Ji Yun 1231" was raised from RMB68,0000 to RMB760,000. The court holds that, due to MAO Chuanwu and Fengping Company did not provide evidence to prove the both agreed ship prices of M.V. "Jiang Ji Yun 1219" and did not provide evidence to prove that the market price during the construction of the ship, so the court, from a point of fairness, takes the respective amounts claimed by both parties as the basis and adopts the weighted average amount as the ship prices of M.V. "Jiang Ji Yun 1219", namely RMB720,000.

As to the second issue, MAO Chuanwu holds that Fengping Company should be responsible for the worker injury compensation and he should not bear the corresponding liabilities. The court holds that, according to the contract, during the construction of the ship, any occurrence of large and small injury, disability and death accident shall be solely born by MAO Chuanwu and with no relations with Fengping Company. The relevant fees have been listed in the ship prices. And according to the provisions of Article 3 Paragraph 1 Sub-paragraph 4 and Article 3 Paragraph 2 of the Provisions of the Supreme People's Court on Several Issues concerning the Trial of Injury Insurance Administrative Cases, Fengping Company subcontracted its contracting business in violation of regulations to MAO Chuanwu, a natural person without subject qualifications for employing workers. Since workers employed by MAO Chuanwu suffered injuries and deaths in line of duty during the construction of the ships involved, so Fengping Company, as the company responsible for worker injury insurance, has the right of recourse against MAO Chuanwu after bearing the compensation liabilities for the casualties. Therefore, the total worker injury compensation and medical expenses in amount of RMB268,645 paid by Fengping Company for LI Yongde, MAO Jiayan, and QIN Dayuan shall be ultimately born by MAO Chuanwu. When settling the payment, this part shall be deducted from the ship prices paid by Fengping Company.

As to the third issue, the court holds that: in the trial, MAO Chuanwu has recognized that since the start of construction of M.V. "Jiang Ji Yun 1231", his workers had lunches in Fengping Company, but the specific amount is not clear. According to the Staff Meal Table from October 2011 to July 2012 submitted by Fengping Company, most of MAO Chuanwu's workers had lunches in Fengping Company, which conforms to the statement of MAO Chuanwu, so the court affirms the meal fees is RMB21,430. This part of fees shall not be born by Fengping Company and shall be deducted from the ship price settlements; as for the premiums, since Fengping Company did not provide a specific list of the insured and the premium invoices, whether Fengping Company bought insurance for MAO Chuanwu's workers could not be recognized, the specific amount of the premiums can neither be recognized, so the court does not affirm the premiums advanced by Fengping Company.

In conclusion, the court holds that according to the agreement, Fengping Company shall altogether pay ship prices and other fees in amount of RMB2,131,000 (68,000 + 515,000 + 72,000 + 76,000 + 68,000 = 2,131,000) to MAO Chuanwu. Fengping Company has paid RMB2,012,205 to MAO Chuanwu. And Fengping Company advanced industrial injury compensation in amount of RMB268,645 to the workers for MAO Chuanwu. MAO Chuanwu shall pay worker meal fees of RMB21,430 to Fengping Company. These 3 payments are altogether RMB2,302,280. After offsetting the RMB2,131,000 Fengping Company shall pay, Fengping Company has not defaulted MAO Chuanwu any ship prices. Fengping Company shall not pay any other payments. The claim raised by MAO Chuanwu that Fengping Company defaulted his ship prices and constitutes a breach of contract, lacks factual basis, the court does not support. According to Article 60 of the Contract Law of the People's Republic of China and Article 64, Article 142 of the Civil Procedure Law of the People's Republic of China, the judgment is as follows:

Reject the claims of the Plaintiff MAO Chuanwu against the Defendant Fengdu County Fengping Ship Investment Co., Ltd.

Court acceptance fee in amount of RMB4,333, shall be born by the Plaintiff MAO Chuanwu.

In case of dissatisfaction with this judgment, the Plaintiff and the Defendant may within 15 day upon the service of this judgment submit a statement of appeal to the court, together with copies according to the number of the opposite parties, the appellate court shall be Hubei High People's Court. The appeal court entertainment fee shall be prepaid by the Appellant upon submission of the statement of appeal according to the unsatisfied appeal amount and provisions regarding Paragraph 1 of Article 13 of the Measures on Payment of Litigation Costs. The remittance shall be paid to Hubei High People's Court. The opening bank is Agricultural Bank of China Wuhan City Donghu Branch. The account name is Non-tax Revenue Settlement Account of Hubei Province Finance Department. And the number of account is 052101040000369-1. The purpose column of banking credentials shall be marked with "Hubei High People's Court" or the unit code "103001" of Hubei High People's Court. If the fee not be paid within seven days after the time limit of appeal expires, the appeal shall be deemed as automatic withdrawal.

Presiding Judge: LIU Dong
Judge: KONG Linggang
Acting Judge: JIANG Zhangpeng

July 3, 2015

Clerk: YANG Hongbo

Guangzhou Maritime Court
Civil Judgment

Mitsui O.S.K. Lines, Ltd.
v.
Guangdong Shunde Local Product Import and Export Co., Ltd. et al.

(2014) Guang Hai Fa Chu Zi No.339

Related Case(s) None.

Cause(s) of Action 202. Dispute over contract of carriage of goods by sea or sea-connected waters.

Headnote Ocean carrier held to be entitled to recover container demurrage fees and costs from importer and freight forwarder who failed to collect container upon delivery.

Summary The Plaintiff Mitsui O.S.K. Lines, Ltd., filed this complaint pursuant to a dispute over a contract of carriage of goods against the Defendants Guangdong Shunde Local Product Import and Export Co., Ltd. and Shenzhen Rundakang Trade Co., Ltd. Plaintiff claimed that Defendants contracted to ship a 20ft cargo container from Malaysia to China via Hong Kong port, but that the Defendants have not yet collected the container. Plaintiff requested that the court order the Defendants to retrieve their cargo, and sued for demurrage and storage fees. The court held that Plaintiff was the carrier of the goods and the Defendant Run Da Kang Co. was the consignee, so Defendant was obligated to pay all fees related to the failure to collect the cargo. The court ordered the Defendant Shenzhen Rundakang Trade Co., Ltd to compensate the Plaintiff for container demurrage totalling RMB12,400 and storage fees totaling HKD10,986.

Judgment

The Plaintiff: Mitsui O.S.K. Lines, Ltd.
Domicile: 1-1, Toranomon, 2-Chome, Minato-Ku, Tokyo, Japan.
Legal representative: Koichi Muto, chairman of the board and representative director of Mitsui O.S.K. Lines, Ltd.
Agent *ad litem*: CHEN Paiqing, lawyer of Shanghai Fulandelin Law Firm.

The Defendant: Guangdong Shunde Local Product Import and Export Co., Ltd.
Domicile: 12, 14, 16, 18, North Ronggui Avenue, Shunde District, Foshan City, Guangdong, the People's Republic of China.
Legal representative: HE Tianwen.
Agent *ad litem*: SUN Zhenlin, lawyer of Guangdong Juli Law Firm.
Agent *ad litem*: LIANG Minyu, trainee lawyer of Guangdong Juli Law Firm.

The Defendant: Shenzhen Rundakang Trade Co., Ltd.
Domicile: 26C, Yonghui Building, Guoqi mansion, Shangbunan Road, Nanyuan Street, Futian District, Shenzhen City, Guangdong, the People's Republic of China.

With respect to the case arising from dispute over contract of carriage of goods by sea between the Plaintiff Mitsui O.S.K. Lines, Ltd. and the Defendants Guangdong Shunde Local Product Import and Export Co., Ltd. (hereinafter referred to as Shunde Local Product Company) and Shenzhen Rundakang Trade Co., Ltd. (hereinafter referred to as Rundakang Company), the Plaintiff filed it to the court on March 10, 2014. After accepting this case, the court organized a collegiate panel, and gathered all parties to disclosure evidence on September 10, 2014. The trial of judges conducted a hearing in public. CHEN Paiqing, agent *ad litem* of the Plaintiff, and SUN Zhenlin and LIANG Minyu, agents *ad litem* of the Defendant Shunde Local Product Company, attended the trial. Via being serviced summons to appear in court by the announcement, the Defendant Rundakang Company refused to attend the trial without cogent reason, therefore a trial by default was conducted according to the law. The Plaintiff listed Shenzhen Hongli International Freight Forwarding Co., Ltd. (hereinafter referred to as Hongli Company) as the Defendant when it filed the case, and Hongli Company attended the trial on September 10, 2014. The Plaintiff drew back its file against Hongli Company after the court hearing, and the court permitted it by making a ruling. Now the case has been concluded.

The Plaintiff alleged that: in May 2012, the Plaintiff accepted a booking from oversea shipper to carry a series cargo loaded by a 20ft container, which number was GLDU3548513 from Port Klang, Malaysia to Port Yantian, and Shenzhen via Hong Kong. This container cargo was shipped on May 26, 2012, and carried by M.V. MOL Empire's 55183 voyage to Hong Kong. The agent of the Plaintiff in the departure port issued the original bill of lading No.MOLU15320933655 to the shipper, which indicated the consignee was Shunde Local Product Company, port of loading was Port Klang, Malaysia, port of discharge was Hong Kong, and the delivery place was Port Shunde Rongqi. Later the shipper required to change the delivery place from Port Shunde Rongqi to Port Shenzhen Yantian, and instructed the Plaintiff to deliver the goods involved to Shunde Local Product Company and Rundakang Company in the new delivery place without bill of lading after returning the original bill of lading to the agent of the Plaintiff in the departure port. After the goods involved had been transmitted in Hong Kong, they were carried by the feeder vessel to Port Shenzhen Yantian and discharged on June 29, 2012.

Shunde Local Product Company and Rundakang Company entrusted Hongli Company to get the Delivery Order in return with a copy of the bill of lading, guarantee and letter of delegation from the feeder shipowner after the goods involved entered the port. However, the two Defendants had not taken delivery of the goods so far, which resulted in the goods involved keeping piling up at the port of destination and the Plaintiff's containers had been kept occupied. According to the charging standard, the Plaintiff executed at the port of destination, container demurrage caused by the goods involved had reached RMB276425 by February 12, 2014. Meanwhile, the goods involved caused storage fee HKD85486 that shall be paid to Port Yantian. The Plaintiff had carried the goods to the destination port and fulfilled its responsibilities as a carrier according to the shipper's entrustment. Shunde Local Product Company and Rundakang Company picked up the goods with the copy of bill of lading they signed and letter of guarantee. They should be bound by the bill of lading, fulfill their responsibilities as shippers, timely take delivery of the goods, unbox and return the containers to the carrier. The Plaintiff requested the court to judge: 1. Shunde Local Product Company and Rundakang Company should jointly and severally pay container demurrage RMB12,400 to the Plaintiff; 2. Shunde Local Product Company and Rundakang Company should jointly and severally pay terminal storage fee HKD85,486 to the Plaintiff; 3. Shunde Local Product Company and Rundakang Company should jointly and severally bear the litigation costs in this case.

The Plaintiff submitted the following evidence within time limit for adducing evidence: 1. copy of the bill of lading with the Defendant Rundakang Company and Hongli Company's seals in its reverse side, to prove the contract relationship of carriage of goods by sea involved; 2. letter of guarantee, letter of delegation and *Delivery Order*, to prove that the Defendant Shunde Local Product Company and Rundakang Company had gained the title to the goods; 3. proof of the presence of the container, to prove No.GLDU3548513 container was detained at the Port Shenzhen Yantian; 4. charging standard of the storage fee, to prove that No. GLDU3548513 container had caused storage fee; 5. charging standard of container demurrage published on the Plaintiff's website, to prove the loss of the container demurrage of No.GLDU3548513. The Plaintiff submitted the following evidence after trial; 6. original bill of lading endorsed by the shipper and returned to the Plaintiff, to prove that the shipper involved had endorsed the original bill of lading and returned it to the Plaintiff and the Defendant Shunde Local Product Company was the consignee of the goods carriage involved; 7. email of the notice of the return of the original bill of lading, to prove that the agent of the Plaintiff at the port of loading instructed the agent of the Plaintiff at the port of discharge to deliver the goods involved to Shunde Local Product Company without the bill of lading after receiving the original bill of lading from the shipper; 8. receipts of storage fee issued by Yantian International Container Wharf Co., Ltd., to prove the amount of storage fee caused by container No.GLDU3548513; 10. bills and expenses invoices, to prove handling expenses caused by container No.GLDU3548513; 11. payment details and payment reports, to prove the handling expenses of container No.GLDU3548513 that had been paid by Plaintiff.

The Defendant Shunde Local Product Company defended that:

1. Shunde Local Product Company did not qualify to be a Defendant. Firstly, Shunde Local Product Company had neither any contract of carriage of goods by sea nor any other debtor-creditor relationships with the Plaintiff, and it also did not have any debtor-creditor relationships or guarantee relationships related to the Plaintiff with Shunde Local Product Company and Hongli Company. Secondly, Shunde Local Product Company never issued any letter of guarantee to the Plaintiff, therefore the letter of guarantee submitted by the Plaintiff was suspected of forgery. Thirdly, the shipper recorded in the bill of lading involved was the one that established the relationship of the contract of carriage of goods by sea with the Plaintiff, not Shunde Local Product Company. The bill of lading involved was issued under shipper's order, and Shunde Local Product Company did not hold the bill of lading involved and never sealed or ascertained it. Fourthly, according to the evidence submitted by the Plaintiff, actual consignee of the goods involved was Rundakang Company, not Shunde Local Product Company. What's more, the import duties and import VAT of the goods involved were all paid by Rundakang Company. Hence the goods involved were actually bought by Rundakang Company, not Shunde Local Product Company.
2. The loss claimed by the Plaintiff lacked the evidence, and did not actually happen. The Plaintiff failed to submit evidence to prove that the parties of the contract of carriage of goods by sea had agreed on container demurrage and storage fee caused by delaying taking delivery of goods, Therefore the claim of the Plaintiff lacked the basis of the contract; charging standards of container demurrage and storage fee submitted by Plaintiff were both unilateral evidence without confirmation of the other party and review and record by the authority of commodity prices, which could not be deemed as the basis of the facts; the Plaintiff also did not submit the evidence to prove the storage fee of the port it claimed had paid to related terminal units, therefore the loss did not actually happen.
3. The claim of the Plaintiff to ask indemnity for the loss of container demurrage and storage fee from Shunde Local Product Company had no basis of contract or law. Even the agent import of the goods involved was Shunde Local Product Company, the liabilities and consequences caused by which shall be taken by consignor of the import business; Shunde Local Product Company was neither the other party of the contract of carriage of goods by sea nor the guarantee, therefore the liabilities resulted from the contract involved shall be born by responsible subjects of the contract and had no relationship with Shunde Local Product Company's business; the extended use and stockpiling at the port of destination of the Plaintiff's container were because the actual consignee of the goods involved Rundakang Company and its authorized consignee delayed or refused to deliver the goods, so the actual consignee shall be liable for the resulting damages; Even though the letter of guarantee involved was issued by Shunde Local Product Company, according to the content of guarantee, the scale of liability of Shunde Local Product Company was limited to indemnity

for cargo loss caused by wrong delivery, not included the liability caused by delay or refusal of taking delivery of goods by actual consignee. The claim of the Plaintiff was beyond the scale of the letter of guarantee involved but in the liability scale agreed in the contract of carriage of goods by sea. The Defendant requested the court to dismiss the claim of the Plaintiff against Shunde Local Product Company.

The Defendant Shunde Local Product Company submitted the following evidence within the time limit for adducing evidence: 1. the special payment book of customs import duty and import value-added tax was to prove that import duties and import value-added tax of the goods involved had been paid by Rundakang Company and Rundakang Company was the involved buyer of this case and the actual consignee of the goods; 2. the seal record proof was to prove that Shunde Local Product Company did not use the seal in the letter of guarantee involved and the letter of guarantee was suspected of being forged.

The Defendant Rundakang Company neither defensed nor submitted any evidence materials.

Hongli Company defensed when attended the trial: 1. Hongli Company was authorized by Rundakang Company to exchange for the Delivery Order from Shenzhen Ya Lian Li Cheng Fu Port and Shipping Service Co., Ltd. with the letter of guarantee jointly issued by Shunde Local Product Company and Rundakang Company in July 2012 to apply for handling import customs formalities in Dapeng Customs for the goods involved. After receiving tax form, Hongli Company delivered it to a representative of Rundakang Company Yangfan, and Rundakang Company paid import customs duties on its own. The customs cleared the goods on September 4, Rundakang Company notified Yangfan to receive materials and handle delivery formalities by his own, but he did not come to receive. Hongli Company was not the party to the contract of carriage of goods by sea involved, it only provided authorized clearance service of goods involved to customs and had no business with the Plaintiff. Hongli Company requested the court to reject the claims against it.

Hongli Company submitted the following evidence during the trial: goods declaration for importation of goods involved and special payment book of customs overdue fine were to prove that Hongli Company accepted Rundakang Company's entrustment to handle import clearance formalities of the goods involved and had no relationship with the sale of goods and contract of carriage of goods by sea.

For the purpose of ascertaining the fact of the case, the court collect No.531620121161029613 Customs declaration for import of the goods involved, special payment book for import tariff, special payment book for import VAT, special payment book for customs detention fees and other materials such as relevant declaration entrustment agreements, formal invoice, Packing List, sales or purchase contract, bill of lading, the switched bills of lading and delivery order.

The Defendant Rundakang Company refused to attend the trial although the court had used subpoena of declared from serviced, so it shall be deemed as waiving the right to cross-examine evidence submitted by other parties. Hongli

Company published its cross-examine opinions and submitted evidence materials, but the court had allowed the Plaintiff to withdraw the file against Hongli Company by a ruling, Hongli Company had quit this case and was not a party in this case, therefore the court refuses to accept cross-examine opinions published in trial and cross-examine evidence materials submitted in trial by Hongli Company.

Through cross-examine in the trial, the Defendant Shunde Local Product Company both ascertained the authenticity of proof of the presence of the container submitted by the Plaintiff and the Plaintiff ascertained the authenticity of seal record certificate submitted by the Defendant Shunde Local Product Company. The court ascertains the probative force of aforementioned evidence.

The Defendant Shunde Local Product Company filed objection to the authenticity, legality and relevancy of the copy of the original bill of lading, letter of guarantee, letter of delegation and delivery order with the seal on it submitted by the Plaintiff. The court held that there are originals for verification of aforementioned evidence, the recorded contents are also related to the dispute of this case, under the situation of no sufficient contrary evidence, ascertains its probative force.

The Defendant Shunde Local Product Company filed an objection to the authenticity, legality and relevancy of the storage fee charges and container demurrage charges submitted by the Plaintiff. The court held that aforementioned evidence is information that can be openly queried, its authenticity can be ascertained. As to whether it's sufficient to prove the Plaintiff's claim, other facts and evidence shall be comprehensively combined to decide.

The Defendant Shunde Local Product Company filed objection to the relevancy of the original bill of lading endorsed by the shipper submitted by the Plaintiff. The company thought it had nothing to do with itself. The court holds that the evidence can be verified by the original, therefore its authenticity can be ascertained. Its content has a relationship with this case, so its probative force can be ascertained.

The Defendant Shunde Local Product Company filed objection to the relevancy of the email of the notice of the return of the original bill of lading submitted by the Plaintiff. The company thought it had nothing to do with itself. The court holds that the content of email can be verified with other evidence which probative force has been ascertained so its probative force shall be ascertained.

The Defendant Shunde Local Product Company filed objection to the relevancy of invoice of No.GLDU3548513 container storage fees, bill of handling fees and expense invoice, bank account notice and payment report of the storage fees, payment details and payment reports of handling fees submitted by the Plaintiff. The company considered that they had not relevant with the Defendant Shunde Local Product Company. Therefore they could not be deemed as the basis of the fact of this case. The court holds that the invoice of storage fees submitted by the Plaintiff is original and its content has relationship with the disputes of this case, so under the situation of no sufficient contrary evidence, the probative force of them shall be ascertained; the bank account notice and payment report of the storage fees can be verified with the content of the invoice of storage fees, so its probative force shall also be ascertained. As to bill, invoice, payment details and payment reports of container handling fees submitted by the Plaintiff, their contents have no relationship with the Plaintiff's claims and the disputes of this case, so their probative force shall not be ascertained.

The Plaintiff filed objection to the authenticity of customs import duty and import value-added tax special payment book submitted by the Defendant Shunde Local Product Company. The court holds that although the Plaintiff Shunde Local Product Company did not submit the original evidence to verify, this evidence is the same as the one collected by the court from Dapeng Customs. Therefore their probative force shall be ascertained.

According to the aforementioned evidence that has been ascertained the probative force and trial statement of parties and Hongli Company, the court concludes:

In May 2012, Alfred minerals & Commodity Procurement (hereinafter referred to as Alfred Company) in Malaysia and Alfred Mineral booked space from the Plaintiff and entrusted the Plaintiff to carry Zeolite of one 20ft container from Port Kelang in Malaysia to Port Shenzhen Yantian in China. The Plaintiff accepted the entrustment to carry the goods involved and issued the original bill of lading No. MOLU15320933655 on May 27. The heading of the bill of lading was the Plaintiff's name, shipper was loaded as Alfred Company, the consignee and notify party were both the Defendant Shunde Local Product Company, the ship name was "Mitsui Empire", the voyage was 55183, the receiving place and port of loading were both Port Kelang in Malaysia, the port of discharge was Hong Kong, China, the delivery place was China, goods were 500 pieces of Zeolite packing in a 20ft container No.GLDU3548513. After the shipment of the goods involved, Alfred Company stamped its seal in the reverse side of the original bill of lading and delivered it to the Plaintiff in Kuala Lumpur, Malaysia. The agent of the Plaintiff in Malaysia notified by email that full set of original bill of lading No. MOLU15320933655 had been withdrawn in Kuala Lumpur. On July 6, the delivery of goods could be conducted under the situation without the original bill of lading. The shipper was Alfred Company, consignee and notify party was the Defendant Shunde Local Product Company, the goods were loaded in a 20ft container No. GLDU3548513. After the goods transferred in Hong Kong, they were carried by M. V. Kam Wui No.2637 voyage to Port Shenzhen Yantian, China on June 29, 2012, and were storaged in Yantian International Container Port Co., Ltd (hereinafter referred to as Yantian Port Company), the number of bill of lading of relevant two voyage was LG1204676.

During the transportation period of the goods involved, the Defendant entrusted Hongli Company in its own name as its agent to handle import declaration business, and provided the copy of the bill of lading No.MOLU15320933655, letter of delegation and letter of guarantee to Hongli Company. The reverse of the copy of the bill of lading had the Defendant Rundakang Company's official seal. Letter of delegation was issued to Shenzhen Ya Lian Li Cheng Fu Shipping Service Co. Ltd. (hereinafter referred to as Ya Lian Company), the shipping agent of Plaintiff in Shenzhen, the commissioning party was the Defendant Rundakang Company, the commissioned party was Hongli Company, and affixed the Defendant Rundakang Company's official seal. It recorded that the Defendant Rundakang Company entrusted Hongli Company to handle procedures of changing documents and delivering goods, the 20ft container No.GLDU3548513's zeolite, which carried by M.V. "Kam Wui" No.2637 voyage to Port Yantian from Ya Lian Company. The letter of guarantee indicated that it was issued by the Defendant Shunde Local Product Company as the name of the consignee to the Plaintiff, and had its oval seal in the Chinese and English name. The Defendant Shunde Local Product Company entered the guarantee as joint and several liability guarantor, and affixed its official seal as the identity of ultimate consignee. The letter of guarantee showed that in consideration of the Plaintiff agreed the following goods (ship name "Mitsui Empire", voyage No.55183, bill of lading No.MOLU15320933655) could be delivered to the receiver with the bill of lading that had been endorsed by the receiver. The Defendant Shunde Local Product Company recognized the delivery act of the Plaintiff was according to the requirements of this letter of guarantee, and declared and guaranteed at the same time that only receiver rather than any other persons, units or companies had the right to take delivery of goods. Since the Defendant Shunde Local Product Company did not endorse in the bill of lading, it especially authorized receivers representing the Defendant Shunde Local Product Company to add a suitable endorsement in the bill of lading. Simultaneously, the Defendant Shunde Local Product Company guaranteed that the Plaintiff would not suffer any claim indemnity or rights argument because of delivery of the goods, and any consequence the Plaintiff suffered from the delivery act, the Defendant Shunde Local Product Company shall be responsible for the compensation. Hongli Company accepted the Defendant Shunde Local Product Company's entrustment, the two parties signed delegation agreement of declaration of customs on June 27, which recorded that the Defendant Shunde Local Product Company entrusted Hongli Company to handle import customs clearance of a set of zeolite origin of Malaysia. This set of goods was imported on June 29, 2012, the total value of goods was USD3000, the relevant number of bill of lading was LG1204676, and the number of Customs Declaration Form was 161029613.

Hongli Company then began to handle import customs clearance affairs of the goods involved, after affixed its official seal on the aforesaid copy of the bill of lading with the Defendant Shunde Local Product Company's official seal, the company turned to Ya Lian Company to exchange the delivery order. On July 11, 2012, Ya Lian Company issued the delivery order, which recorded consignee/notify party was the Defendant Shunde Local Product Company, and announced that the procedures of 500 pieces, 25000 kg zeolite carried in 20ft container No. GLDU3548513 by M.V. "Kam Wui" voyage No.2637 from Hong Kong to Shenzhen Yantian had finished. Hongli Company represented the Defendant Shunde Local Product Company for signing the delivery order.

Hongli Company declared import goods for the goods involved to Dapeng Customs on July 2, 2012, the number of relevant Declaration of imported goods was 531620121161029613, and the recorded operating unit was the Defendant Rundakang Company, consignee unit was Shenzhen Li Yuan Kang Trade Co., Ltd. (hereinafter referred to as Li Yuan Kang Company), transporting way was waterway transport, the number of bill of lading was LG1204676, country of shipment was Malaysia, port of loading was Hong Kong, the domestic destination was Shenzhen, goods were 500 pieces of zeolite carried by container No. GLDU3548513, gross weight was 25000 kilograms and the total value was USD3,000. On August 4, Dapeng Customs filled in and issued import customs special payment book and import VAT special payment book, and the recorded payment unit was the Defendant Rundakang Company (Li Yuan Kang Company). It asked for paying import duties RMB8,215.09 and import VAT RMB22,882.19 of 25000 kilograms zeolite under No.531620121161029613 customs declaration before August 20. Since the payment unit did not pay aforesaid import duties and import VAT, on September 14, Dapeng Customs filled in and issued customs overdue fine special payment book, and the recorded payment unit was the Defendant Rundakang Company. It asked for paying import duty overdue fine RMB98.58 and import VAT overdue fine RMB274.58 before September 29. After the Defendant Rundakang Company paid aforesaid import duties, import VAT and their overdue fine, customs clearance procedures of goods involved were finished, Hongli Company got customs clearance document on September 14 and informed the Defendant Rundakang Company to receive customs clearance document and pick up the goods, but the Defendant Rundakang Company replied that it need not pick up the goods, neither received customs clearance document. the goods involved were stockpiled in Yantian Port Company all the time because no one picked them up.

On September 17, October 16 and November 13, Yantian Port Company issued the Plaintiff's Hong Kong agent three invoices successively, asking the Plaintiff to pay storage fees of container No.GLDU3548513 HKD1, 897 from July 11 to July 31 (HKD61 per day from July 11 to July 24, HKD149 per day from July 25 to July 31), HKD4,619 from August 1 to August 31(HKD149 per day), HKD4,470 from September 1 to September 30 (HKD149 per day). The Plaintiff paid Yantian Port Company aforesaid storage fees through its Hong Kong agent on November 6 2013, November 13, 2012, and June 18, 2013 successively. It was further ascertained that the charging standard of storage fees published on Internet by Yantian Port Company was free for import container goods for 10 days since the second day after discharging. A 20ft container would be charged HKD61 per day from the 1st day to the 14th day after the charging time began, and HKD149 per day from the 15th day.

On March 10, Yantian Port Company issued a proof of the presence of the container to argue that container No.GLDU3548513 was discharged on June 29, 2012 and was had been stored in Yantian Port Company over 600 days.

The standard of the container demurrage published in the Plaintiff's website for a 20ft container imported from Port Shenzhen Yantian was free for three days, RMB175 per day per container from the first day to the tenth day after the charging time began, RMB215 per day per container from the 11th day to the 30th day, and RMB270 per day per container hereinafter.

It was also indicated by relevant evidence the court collected from Dapeng Customs that contract for the sale of goods handed over to Dapeng Customs to put on records when the goods involved were imported and applied to the customs. The contract recorded that the buyer of goods was Defendant Rundakang Company, the seller of goods was Chit Shing Marble Co. Ltd. in Hong Kong, and relevant form invoices also recorded they were issued to the Defendant Rundakang Company.

It was further ascertained that the Defendant Shunde Local Product Company registered and recorded its company official seal and financial special seal in public security organization of Shunde District, Foshan, and the aforesaid oval seal affixed in guarantee did not exist.

The Plaintiff proposed that both Defendants were consignees of the goods involved. The Defendant Shunde Local Product Company was the pointed consignee of shipper Alfred Company but it assigned the consign rights to the Defendant Rundakang Company through the letter of guarantee. The Defendant Shunde Local Product Company regarded itself never took part in any transportation or trade of goods involved, it was involved in dispute of this case only because there was a seal of its name affixed to the letter of guarantee, and the seal was not its officially used seal, so could not rule out the possibility of forgery. At the same time, president evidence was sufficient to prove that consignee of goods involved was the Defendant Rundakang Company and had no relevancy with the Defendant Shunde Local Product Company. The court considers although the original bill of lading issued by the Plaintiff for transporting the goods involved listed the Defendant Shunde Local Product Company as the consignee, the bill of lading has been returned to the Plaintiff by shipper Alfred Company and never delivered to the Defendant Shunde Local Product Company or the Defendant Rundakang Company. Therefore, the transportation of the goods involved is not the bill of lading transportation mode, we need to ascertain according to actual procedure of handling consign rather than deem the Defendant Shunde Local Product Company as the consignee only according to the records in the bill of lading. This case has ascertained the Defendant Rundakang Company entrusted Hongli Company to handle import customs clearance affairs for it. The Defendant Rundakang Company as the import operating company of goods involved paid import duties, import VAT and its overdue fine of goods involved. The delivery order issued by the Plaintiff's shipping agent Ya Lian Company also indicated the consignee or notify party was the Defendant Rundakang Company. After finished import customs clearance affairs, Hongli Company also notified the Defendant Rundakang Company to pick up the goods involved. After the Defendant Rundakang Company said that it refused to pick up the goods involved, there were no others claims that it had the right to pick up the goods involved so far. As for position of the Defendant Shunde Local Product Company in the transportation of goods, except its seal of its name is affixed to the letter of guarantee issued to the Plaintiff, there is no other evidence to show that the Defendant Shunde Local Product Company once takes part in the delivery work of the goods involved. Moreover, if the recorded content is true, the letter of guarantee shows the Defendant Shunde Local Product Company has transferred its right of picking up the goods involved to the Defendant Rundakang Company, the Defendant Shunde Local Product Company no longer needs to act as the consignee of the goods involved. In conclusion, it shall be deemed that the consignee of the goods involved is the Defendant Rundakang Company.

According to the apply for property preservation of the Plaintiff, the court made (2014) Guang Hai Fa Chu Zi No.339-14 Civil Ruling to preserve the same value as RMB97,886 property of the Defendant Shunde Local Product Company, the Defendant Rundakang Company and Hongli Company. The Plaintiff paid application fee for property preservation RMB998.86 to the court.

The court recognized that this case is a dispute over the contract of carriage of goods by sea. The Plaintiff is a legal person setting up outside the People's Republic of China, the goods involved were carried from Port Klang, Malaysia to Port Shenzhen Yantian by sea, so this case is a dispute over the contract of carriage of goods by sea concerning foreign affairs because it has foreign factors.

All parties did not reach agreement on an applicable law to solve this case's dispute, according to Article 269 of the Maritime Code of the People's Republic of China, this case shall apply the law of the state in which the contract is most closely connected. The destination of transporting the goods involved and two Defendants' domiciles are all within the territory of the People's Republic of China, so the law of the People's Republic of China has closely connected with the contract involved. Therefore it shall apply the law of the People's Republic of China to solve substantive dispute of this case.

The Plaintiff is the carrier of transporting goods involved, and the Defendant Rundakang Company is the consignee of the aforesaid goods. The Defendant Rundakang Company, as the consignee of the transporting goods involved, refused to pick up the goods under the situation that the goods had arrived at the port of discharge, import customs clearance affairs had been finished and the condition of picking up the goods had been possessed. According to the Article 86 of the Maritime Code of the People's Republic of China, If the goods were not taken delivery of at the port of discharge or if the consignee has delayed or refused the taking delivery of the goods, the Master may discharge the goods into warehouses or other appropriate places, and any expenses or risks arising therefrom shall be born by the consignee., the Defendant Rundakang Company shall bear the expenses of not taking delivery of the goods.

The Plaintiff requested demurrage charge for container demurrage No. GLDU3548513 RMB12,400. The court has ascertained the goods involved were transported to Port Shenzhen Yantian on June 29, 2012. Because the Defendant Rundakang Company refused to take delivery of the goods, the goods involved and the container No.GLDU3548513 had stayed at Port Shenzhen Yantian for a long time, therefore, the container could not transfer into business, and the Plaintiff had the right to ask for demurrage charge for container demurrage. According to the charging standard of container demurrage published on the website of the Plaintiff, the fees of extended use of a 20ft container imported from Port Shenzhen Yantian for 54 days are RMB12,400, but the actual detaining time of container No. GLDU3548513 at Port Shenzhen Yantian is far from this. Simultaneously, RMB12,400 does not exceed the demand fees for resetting the same type of container, so the Plaintiff's request has its basis, and shall be supported.

The Plaintiff requested for port's storage fees HKD85,486 of container No. GLDU3548513 at Port Shenzhen Yantian. After the goods involved arrived at Port

Shenzhen Yantian on June 29, 2012, the Plaintiff had paid storage fees HKD10,986 to Yantian Port Company because the Defendant Rundakang Company refused to take delivery of the goods and the goods had been stayed for a long time and storaged in Yantian Port Company. The aforesaid fees shall be paid by the Defendant Rundakang Company. However the evidence submitted by the Plaintiff could only prove that the Plaintiff had paid storage fees HKD85,486, the Plaintiff failed to submit evidence to prove the rest storage fees of its request had actually happened. Because of lack of factual basis, this request could not be supported. Therefore, the Defendant Rundakang Company shall compensate the Plaintiff storage fees HKD10,986.

The Plaintiff claimed the Defendant Shunde Local Product Company and Rundakang Company jointly shall bear the responsible of compensation. The Defendant Shunde Local Product Company regarded itself had never made such letter of guarantee, the seal of its name affixed to the letter of guarantee was not the one it registered and recorded in the public security organization, so there was a possibility of forgery. At the same time, according to the content of guarantee, the Plaintiff's request was beyond the scope of the guarantee involved. The oval seal with the Defendant Shunde Local Product Company's name both in Chinese and English affixed to the guarantee involved was not the one it registered and recorded in the public security organization, but the Defendant Shunde Local Product Company did not provide evidence to prove the seal it registered and recorded in the public security organization was the only one it used, so it could not deny the effect of letter of guarantee only because the seal affixed in guarantee was not the one it registered and recorded in the public security organization. But for the content of guarantee, the letter of guarantee warranted that "the Plaintiff would not suffer any claim indemnity or rights argument because of the delivery of the goods, the Defendant Shunde Local Product Company was responsible for the compensation for any consequence the Plaintiff suffered from the delivery act." In this case, the goods involved were detained at Port Shenzhen Yantian before delivery and were not actually delivered, so the request of the Plaintiff for the loss of demurrage charge for the container demurrage and storage fees was not caused by the delivery action and beyond the scope of the letter of guarantee. Therefore, the Defendant Shunde Local Product Company's defense shall stand. The Plaintiff's claim lacks of factual basis and shall not be supported.

According to Article 86 of the Maritime Code of the People's Republic of China and Article 144 of the Civil Procedure Law of the People's Republic of China, the judgment is as follows:

1. The Defendant Shenzhen Rundakang Trade Co., Ltd. shall compensate the Plaintiff Mitsui O.S.K. Lines, Ltd. container demurrage RMB12,400.
2. The Defendant Shenzhen Rundakang Trade Co., Ltd. shall compensate the Plaintiff Mitsui O.S.K. Lines, Ltd. storage fees HKD10,986.
3. Reject other claims of the Plaintiff Mitsui O.S.K. Lines, Ltd.

The aforesaid obligations of money payment shall be fulfilled in 10 days after this judgment comes into effect.

If obligations of money payment shall not be fulfilled in pointed period, payment of interests on debt during the period of delay in performance shall be double according to Article 253 of the Civil Procedure Law of the People's Republic of China.

Court acceptance fee in amount of RMB1,798 and application fee of property preservation in amount of RMB998.86, shall be born separately by the Plaintiff Mitsui O.S.K. Lines, Ltd. for RMB2,059.32 and the Defendant Shenzhen Rundakang Trade Co., Ltd. for RMB737.54.

If dissatisfy with this judgment, the Plaintiff Mitsui O.S.K. Lines, Ltd. Shall within 30 days as of the service of this judgment, and the Defendant Guangdong Shunde Local Product Import and Export Co., Ltd. and Shenzhen Rundakang Trade Co., Ltd. shall within 15 days as of the service of this judgment, submit a Statement of Appeal to the court, with duplicates in the number of the counterparties or representatives, so as to make an appeal before the Guangdong High People's Court.

Presiding Judge: SONG Ruiqiu
Judge: PINGYANG Danke
Acting Judge: WANG Xin

July 16, 2015

Clerk: SHUJian

9783662637159VOL01